CONTENTS

LIST OF ILLUSTRATIONS	7
LIST OF RECIPIENTS	9
INTRODUCTION	11
PART ONE: 1887—1891	23
PART TWO: 1892—1896	193
PART THREE: 1897—1908	271
PART FOUR: 1909—1917	517
PART FIVE: 1918—1928	639
PART SIX: 1929—1939	753
EPILOGUE	923
INDEX	925

THE LETTERS OF
W. B. YEATS

W. B. YEATS *circa* 1935

THE LETTERS
OF
W. B. YEATS

EDITED BY

ALLAN WADE

OCTAGON BOOKS

A DIVISION OF FARRAR, STRAUS AND GIROUX
New York   1980

Copyright 1953, 1954, by Anne Butler Yeats

All rights reserved—no part of this book may be reproduced in any form without permission in writing from the publisher, except by a reviewer who wishes to quote brief passages in connection with a review written for inclusion in magazine or newspaper.

*Reprinted 1980
by special arrangement with Macmillan Publishing Co., Inc.*

OCTAGON BOOKS
A DIVISION OF FARRAR, STRAUS & GIROUX, INC.
19 Union Square West
New York, N.Y. 10003

Library of Congress Cataloging in Publication Data

Yeats, William Butler, 1865-1939.
   The letters of W. B. Yeats.

   Reprint of the 1955 ed. published by Macmillan, New York.
   Includes bibliographical references and index.
   1. Yeats, William Butler, 1865-1939—
Correspondence. 2. Authors, Irish—20th century
—Correspondence. I. Wade, Allan, 1881-1955.

[PR5906.A4 1980]   821'.8 [B]   79-28701
ISBN 0-374-98833-1

Manufactured by Braun-Brumfield, Inc.
Ann Arbor, Michigan
Printed in the United States of America

ILLUSTRATIONS

W. B. YEATS *circa* 1935   *Frontispiece*
   from a photograph by Howard Coster

KATHARINE TYNAN, 1887   *facing page* 52
   from a painting by John Butler Yeats in the Gallery of Municipal Art, Dublin. By permission of the Dublin Corporation

W. B. YEATS BEFORE AUTUMN, 1889   146
   from a photograph by M. Glover, Dublin

W. B. YEATS IN THE 'NINETIES   146
   from a photograph by Lafayette, Dublin

LADY GREGORY   288
   from a painting by Antonio Mancini in the gallery of Municipal Art, Dublin. By permission of the Dublin Corporation

FLORENCE FARR   400

JOHN QUINN AND W. B. YEATS, 1904   412
   from a photograph by Arnold Genthe, New York

LETTER TO EDMUND GOSSE   596
   from the original in the Brotherton Library, Leeds

LETTER TO HENRY JAMES   600
   from the original in the Houghton Library, Harvard

OLIVIA SHAKESPEAR   722

W. B. YEATS IN OLD AGE   830

LIST OF RECIPIENTS

Academy, The Editor of the, 206, 373
Allingham, Mrs. William, 446
Archer, William, 530

Barnes, George, 878, 879
Barry, Dr. William, 316
Bodkin, Thomas, 749
Bookman, The Editor of the, 218
Boyd, Ernest, 591, 592, 601
Bridges, Robert, 268, 278, 281, 286, 353, 580, 593, 596, 598, 599, 614, 695
Bridges, Mrs. Robert, 774
Brown, Martin E., 908
Bullen, A. H., 376, 411, 456, 457, 464, 469, 478, 483, 484, 485, 486, 487, 488, 489, 491, 497, 503, 504, 550, 575, 578, 659

Campbell, Mrs. Patrick, 360
Campbell, Stella (Mrs. Mervyn Beech), 531
Clinton-Baddeley, V. C., 919
Cockerell, Sir Sydney, 381, 397, 404, 467, 472, 550, 556
Cronan, Mary, 30

Daily Chronicle, The Editor of the, 308
Daily Express (Dublin), The Editor of the, 246, 338
Davies, Mrs. Llewelyn, 885
Davray, Henry D., 265
De Valera, Eamonn, 877
Dolmetsch, Arnold, 372
Duffy, Sir Charles Gavan, 151, 152, 212
Dulac, Edmund, 661, 693, 699, 702, 830, 890, 892, 893

Farr, Florence (Mrs. Edward Emery), 259, 401, 450, 453, 454, 455, 457, 462, 467, 468, 471, 479, 481, 490, 492, 498, 507, 508, 511, 525, 569
Fay, Frank, 355, 371, 377, 409, 424, 439, 443, 465
Field, Michael, 407
Francis, René, 562
Fredman, Miss, 664
Freeman's Journal, The Editor of the, 335, 356

Gael, The Editor of the (Dublin), 55

Gael, The Editor of the (New York), 328
Gardner, Frederick Leigh, 282, 283
Garnett, Edward, 207, 214, 215, 222, 223, 225, 227, 432
Gogarty, Oliver St. John, 891
Gosse, Edmund, 258, 549, 550, 556, 557, 563, 565, 572, 596, 597, 600, 701
Gregg, Frederick J., 31
Gregory, Lady, 287, 288, 289, 290, 291, 292, 298, 299, 300, 302, 303, 305, 311, 312, 314, 317, 318, 328, 329, 331, 333, 334, 335, 337, 338, 339, 341, 342, 344, 345, 346, 349, 351, 355, 359, 361, 362, 363, 364, 367, 370, 375, 376, 379, 380, 382, 385, 387, 389, 390, 391, 393, 395, 396, 398, 399, 400, 412, 414, 419, 422, 426, 428, 429, 430, 432, 435, 437, 442, 444, 445, 449, 523, 525, 527, 529, 530, 538, 541, 542, 544, 545, 546, 547, 552, 553, 554, 564, 573, 575, 577, 581, 609, 611, 612, 615, 626, 628, 629, 630, 631, 632, 633, 634, 643, 644, 645, 646, 647, 668, 669, 701, 737, 738, 744, 759, 761, 763, 767, 769, 770, 773, 777
Grierson, H. J. C., 536, 570, 686, 690, 693, 709, 796, 837
Griffith, Arthur, 352
Gwynn, Stephen, 410, 473, 653

Heald, Edith Shackleton, 887, 888, 894, 895, 896, 898, 900, 901, 905, 906, 907, 911, 912, 913, 915, 918, 919, 921, 922
Healy, James A., 898
Henley, W. E., 158, 178
Hone, Joseph M., 593, 605, 728, 779, 786, 790, 791, 792
Horniman, Miss A. E. F., 500
Horton, W. T., 260, 261, 262, 263, 325
Hunter, Dorothea, 264, 293

Irish Press, The Editor of the, 882
Irish Times, The Editor of the, 579, 888

James, Henry, 599
Johnson, Lionel, 228
Joyce, James, 800

Kennedy, W. S., 654
King, Richard Ashe, 707

9

Lane, Sir Hugh, 573
Lewis, P. Wyndham, 762, 776
Lister, Miss E. M., 491, 493, 505, 506, 561

MacBride, Maud Gonne, 909
Macleod, Fiona, 279, 301, 357
Macnamara, Brinsley, 656, 657
Mannin, Ethel, 831, 833, 835, 844, 846, 850, 863, 864, 867, 869, 872, 881, 884, 885, 889, 899, 902, 904, 914, 916, 917, 920
Martyn, Edward, 315
Mathews, Elkin, 378
Moore, George, 347
Morning Leader, The Editor of the, 319
Morris, May, 724

Nation, The Editor of the (London), 527
Newbolt, Henry, 366, 369
Noyes, Alfred, 412

Observer, The Editor of the, 616
O'Casey, Sean, 740
O'Donoghue, D. J., 73
O'Faolain, Sean, 766, 822
O'Grady, Standish, 307
O'Leary, Ellen, 69, 109
O'Leary, John, 37, 45, 47, 56, 81, 91, 94, 107, 108, 124, 127, 134, 141, 146, 159, 162, 167, 168, 177, 180, 184, 185, 198, 199, 200, 202, 208, 210, 212, 213, 216, 220, 226, 228, 229, 230, 231, 235, 237, 251, 263, 264, 267, 282, 284, 285, 411
Outlook, The Editor of the, 297

Palmer, Herbert E., 688
Palmstierna, Baron Eric, 811
Pelham, Lady Elizabeth, 922
Phelps, W. Lyon, 660
Poetry, The Editor of, 584, 585
Purser, Sarah, 235

Quinn, John, 402, 406, 446, 451, 461, 495, 502, 509, 512, 594, 610, 614, 645, 651, 658, 663, 673, 682, 703

Rhys, Ernest, 90, 137, 821
Ricketts, Charles, 436, 587, 691
Rossi, Mario M., 783, 784, 796, 818
Rothenstein, William, 501, 569, 834
Royal Irish Academy, The President of the, 716
Royal Irish Academy, The Secretary of the, 732
Royal Literary Fund, The Secretary of the, 598
Russell, George (AE), 111, 182, 183, 294, 296, 315, 324, 327, 342, 381, 402, 415, 433, 466, 655, 665, 666, 670, 774
Russell, Father Matthew, 61, 78, 104, 128, 130, 136, 142, 180

Sassoon, Siegfried, 707
Saturday Review, The Editor of the, 348, 365

Shakespear, Olivia, 233, 240, 255, 256, 436, 439, 615, 625, 627, 661, 667, 669, 671, 675, 677, 678, 679, 680, 681, 684, 687, 689, 694, 696, 697, 698, 704, 705, 707, 708, 711, 712, 713, 714, 716, 718, 719, 721, 722, 723, 725, 726, 728, 730, 732, 733, 734, 736, 742, 743, 744, 745, 746, 747, 748, 758, 760, 763, 764, 765, 766, 767, 768, 770, 771, 772, 775, 776, 779, 780, 781, 782, 783, 785, 788, 789, 793, 794, 795, 797, 798, 799, 802, 803, 804, 805, 806, 808, 809, 810, 811, 812, 813, 814, 815, 816, 818, 819, 820, 822, 823, 825, 826, 827, 829, 830, 832, 835, 851, 854, 856, 860, 861, 866
Sharp, William, 266
Shorter, Clement, 320, 334, 348, 648, 652
Shorter, Mrs. Clement (Dora Sigerson), 321
Speaker, The Editor of the, 285
Spectator, The Editor of the, 132
Starkey, James S. (Seumas O'Sullivan), 792
Strong, L. A. G., 708, 787, 877
Symons, Arthur, 458, 459

Tynan, Katharine, 33, 34, 35, 39, 40, 43, 45, 48, 51, 52, 53, 54, 57, 60, 62, 65, 66, 68, 70, 72, 74, 76, 77, 80, 81, 82, 83, 84, 92, 95, 96, 100, 102, 105, 111, 112, 113, 115, 116, 120, 121, 126, 129, 131, 132, 135, 137, 139, 140, 142, 144, 147, 149, 152, 153, 155, 157, 161, 164, 166, 169, 172, 174, 175, 176, 178, 186, 188, 203, 207, 252, 253, 254, 257, 476, 482, 581, 585

United Ireland, The Editor of, 213, 238, 241
United Irishman, The Editor of the, 333, 408
Unnamed Correspondents, 32, 103
Unwin, T. Fisher, 221, 258

Verschoyle, Derek, 809

Wade, Allan, 523, 671, 674, 676
Walkley, A. B., 405
Watkins, Vernon, 907
Wellesley, Dorothy, 836, 838, 839, 841, 842, 843, 844, 845, 847, 848, 852, 854, 857, 858, 859, 860, 862, 864, 865, 868, 870, 871, 873, 875, 880, 883, 886, 897, 899, 900, 902, 903, 908, 910, 912, 913, 916, 918
White, Elizabeth, 103
Wollman, Maurice, 840

Yeats, Elizabeth C., 662, 673
Yeats, John Butler, 236, 474, 513, 524, 528, 532, 533, 535, 539, 547, 548, 554, 558, 559, 567, 571, 583, 586, 588, 589, 590, 602, 605, 606, 608, 624, 626, 649, 650, 652, 655
Yeats, Lily, 179, 239, 242, 243, 244, 252, 260, 301, 306, 323, 326, 416, 418, 551, 603, 676

INTRODUCTION

I

In making this selection of the letters of W. B. Yeats from the very large number which I have seen, I have chosen those which can, in the widest sense, be considered autobiographical. Fortunately Yeats is among the most communicative of letter-writers; whatever happened to him, whatever he did or wrote, what opinions he formed —all must be told to somebody. It seems probable that if all his correspondence had survived it might form an almost complete autobiography, except for his childhood and youth, his memories of which are preserved in his book *Reveries*. If we may take him at his word when, in one of the earliest surviving letters, he declares that he usually wrote not more than two letters in six months, it is not likely that many written in boyhood or early youth still await discovery. But from the time he left Ireland for London in 1887 he became a diligent letter-writer, and this is surprising when one remembers that his eyesight was poor and his health, even in early manhood, rarely good. Constantly he writes that he is suffering from a cold or has had an attack of influenza. At first he found life in London detestable, and it was, no doubt, a consolation to him to send long letters to his friends in Ireland, recounting the details of his life, the work he was doing, his failures and his few successes, his opinions of the people he met, and so on. Throughout his life he seems to have felt the need of some sympathetic woman-friend as the recipient of his confidences; Katharine Tynan is the earliest of them, followed later by Florence Farr, by Olivia Shakespear, and by Lady Gregory. During the last few years of his life he formed several new friendships, and to these we owe the published correspondence with Dorothy Wellesley and his letters to Ethel Mannin and Edith Shackleton Heald.

II

The majority of the letters printed here have been transcribed from the originals or from photostats and microfilms, with the following exceptions. Where I have been unable to trace the originals a small number have been taken from copies, or from drafts found among Yeats's papers, and an even smaller number from the texts already printed in volumes of reminiscences or biographies. Letters to the Press are reprinted from the files of the papers in which they appeared or from cuttings in scrap-books preserved by Mrs. Yeats or myself. Yeats occasionally took part in newspaper controversies, but I have included here no letters which need to be read in connection with other correspondents' letters if their bearing is to be appreciated, nor any letters which merely correct some factual error. The letters to Katharine Tynan, now in the Huntington Library, San Marino, California, have been transcribed, arranged and edited, with copious informative notes, by Dr. Roger McHugh of University College, Dublin, and I have been able to make grateful use of his labours in the first section of this book. Another group of letters, those addressed to John Quinn, fall into a special category; they are taken from a selection made by Lennox Robinson, from the typescripts now in the New York Public Library, of letters to Quinn from those writers and artists whose work he collected. It had been intended to issue these in a volume, and the selection was submitted, in each case, to the various writers. Yeats went carefully over his own letters, suggested certain omissions, and even revised the text here and there; these letters, therefore, appear as he would have liked posterity to see them. The projected volume was not published, and Lennox Robinson kindly gave me the use of his typescripts.

Mrs. Yeats made it possible for me to examine many of the surviving letters which Yeats wrote to his father and his sisters, a very large number addressed to Lady Gregory, and those written to his old friend Mrs. Shakespear. It will be found that there is a considerable gap in this last series, between the years 1904 and 1917. After Mrs. Shakespear's death in October 1938, her son-in-law, Ezra Pound, sent back to Yeats all the letters from him which she had kept, and these unfortunately reached him while he was staying away from home, and some of them he destroyed, apparently at random. Had they been sent to him in Dublin Mrs. Yeats would have ensured their preservation. By this accident we have probably lost much valuable information; to Mrs. Shakespear he was able to write of all his interests without restraint; details about his work, his reading, his health, his family, his other friends, his political ideas, his occult experiences and beliefs, small domestic happenings, jokes and gossip all find their place in the later letters addressed to her, letters which are perhaps the most vivid and varied in the whole collection. 'I write to you,' he says, 'as to my own past.'

The letters to Florence Farr and those to AE, previously published by the Cuala Press and the *Dublin Magazine* respectively, have been newly transcribed from the original manuscripts; those addressed to Dorothy Wellesley are only a selection made with her consent from the very much larger number included in *Letters on Poetry from W. B. Yeats to Dorothy Wellesley* (Oxford, 1940). Certain of the letters to John O'Leary and his sister, which are now in the Berg Collection in the New York Public Library, have appeared in the Library's *Bulletin* before being printed here. Some of the other letters to O'Leary I have taken from copies in the Central Library, Belfast; Mr. John Bebbington, the Librarian there, believes them to be in the handwriting of D. J. O'Donoghue. Except for these, all the earlier letters are in Yeats's handwriting, and to the end of his life he preferred to write to his more intimate friends in this way whenever possible. In London he sometimes allowed his correspondence to accumulate and then dictated a number of letters at Miss Jacobs' typewriting office opposite the British Museum. When his eyesight was particularly bad, Miss A. E. F. Horniman acted from time to time as his amanuensis. During his long visits to Coole Park Lady Gregory often typed letters for him, and after his marriage Mrs. Yeats did the same.

'My handwriting is a dreadful thing to inflict upon anyone,' Yeats said once, in apology for sending Edmund Dulac a dictated letter; and to Sir Sydney Cockerell he confessed that he found his own manuscripts quite illegible after a fortnight. The earlier letters are the easiest to decipher, though even in them one is occasionally baffled; as he grew older, and especially during periods of ill health, his handwriting became worse and worse. I cannot claim to have solved every problem successfully; some words remain completely illegible and of others I have had to guess the meaning from the context; such guesses I have marked with a query.

III

Although I have cast my nets in many directions and as widely as possible, there is much that is missing from this collection. Madame Maud Gonne told me that all her papers, including many letters from Yeats, were destroyed during the Irish Civil War; I am able to give only one late letter to her, which appeared in Joseph Hone's Life of Yeats. Other letters perished during the bombing of London in the second world war: these included many to W. T. Horton, some to Dr. Edith Sitwell and some to Sir Alec Martin, while others to Edmund Dulac were rendered illegible by water. Some correspondents have not preserved their letters, some have lost them. I have been unable to trace any letters to 'Macgregor' Mathers or to his wife, to Miss Horniman, or to Mrs. Patrick Campbell, who may, her daughter thinks, have disposed of any she had kept during her stay in America. There are none to George Moore; Joseph Hone, who had access to Moore's papers while writing his Life of Moore, believes that he had destroyed everything of the sort; I am able to print only one uncompleted draft found among Yeats's papers.

No doubt there were many more letters to George Russell than I print here; Mr. Diarmuid Russell says that his father was a most inveterate tearer-up; fortunately AE gave Dr. J. S. Starkey (Seumas O'Sullivan) a small packet of letters from Yeats to himself, and these were kindly put at my disposal.

The late Mrs. William Sharp left two boxes of papers to her executor with instructions that the contents were to be destroyed unexamined, and her wishes were obeyed; it is likely that Yeats's letters to Sharp and to 'Fiona Macleod' thus perished. Those given here are taken from Mrs. Sharp's biography of her husband.

Not many letters to J. M. Synge exist, and the few which remain, now in the possession of Mr. Edward M. Stephens, Synge's nephew, deal only with Abbey Theatre affairs, mostly advice or instructions to Synge during a short tour made by the company in the Irish provinces. If the two friends corresponded on literary matters no trace of the correspondence has survived.

It is certain that Yeats wrote to Bernard Shaw from time to time. Shaw left letters and documents in the hands of the Public Trustee with instructions that they should be given to the British Museum or, failing acceptance, to any other suitable collection. At my last enquiry I learnt that the sorting of these had not yet been begun; I cannot therefore be sure that any letters from Yeats are among them. Certain letters to James Joyce were in the possession of Mr. J. J. Slocum; it is understood that they will be acquired by Yale University, but while negotiations are still in progress, neither Mr. Slocum nor the Yale Librarian, though both expressed willingness, felt able to allow me to reproduce them. Any letters to Ezra Pound are believed to be under seal in his flat at Rapallo, and unavailable. Mr. Gordon Craig wrote to me that he preferred to keep his letters from Yeats for use in his own memoirs. Some letters to Lionel Johnson were lent by Miss Johnson to a gentleman who was writing a book on that poet, and have not been heard of since. A very few American collectors have not cared to reply to my enquiries, even to the extent of disclosing what letters they possess.

The correspondence between Yeats and his friend Sturge Moore has recently been published under the careful editorship of Ursula Bridge. Very much of this is devoted to long philosophical discussions between the two poets in which it is essential to read both writers; to have included Yeats's letters alone in the present collection, had that been possible, would have been, in Henry James's phrase, like trying to cut with one blade of a pair of scissors.

At her desire I have included no letters to Mrs. Yeats.

IV

Certain omissions, indicated by dots, have been made from the text of some of the letters. Generally speaking these are of three kinds: first, I have omitted some names and passages which might give displeasure to people still living; secondly, when Yeats repeats an anecdote or some piece of amusing news in more than one letter, sometimes using almost the same words, I have retained only the fullest version; and thirdly I have omitted, particularly from the letters to Lady Gregory, a mass of business detail connected with the Abbey Theatre, discussions of the frequent squabbles and jealousies among the company, or of the merits of plays in manuscript of which the title is often not given, and of the legal and other negotiations which took place when Miss Horniman severed her connection with the theatre and allowed herself to be bought out. When Yeats was, at various times, in charge of the theatre and Lady Gregory at Coole, he sent her long dictated letters, sometimes more than one a day, full of information which may possibly, at some distant date, interest the historian of the Abbey Theatre's earlier days, but which would, I felt, destroy the balance of this collection, overwhelming the reader with accounts of those vexations which caused the poet to put his

> curse on plays
> Which have to be set up in fifty ways,
> On the day's war with every knave and dolt,
> Theatre business, management of men.

V

Yeats was an uncertain and erratic speller, as he was always ready to admit. In his earlier letters spelling mistakes are, on the whole, infrequent, but as he grew older his spelling deteriorated. Mrs. Yeats says that it was always at its worst when he was overtired, ill or worried. It was not necessarily difficult words over which he came to grief; so simple a word as 'indeed' will sometimes be written 'endeed,' and he was capable of spelling his daughter's name 'Ann' and 'Anne' in the same letter. I have not thought it necessary to perpetuate these mistakes; to do so would, I believe, in the long run appear merely tediously pedantic; but I have allowed an occasional mistake to remain where Yeats has himself expressed his uncertainty. The spelling of proper names has been corrected except in the case of the old Irish names, about which there seems to have been little agreement in the earlier days of the Gaelic revival. Thus Oisin becomes for a time Usheen and then reverts to Oisin again; Cuchullin, Cuchoollin, Cuhoolin and Cuchulain are all spellings which may be found in Yeats's various editions; it has seemed best to allow him to spell these and other Gaelic names according to his conviction at the time of writing. I have not felt obliged to print the sign ampersand to represent the little jig which Yeats, like so many others, employs for 'and,' nor to reproduce the little cross which generally does duty for the word 'to.'

The punctuation of the letters is often chaotic. Yeats writes to Robert Bridges in 1915: 'I do not understand stops. I write my work so completely for the ear that I feel helpless when I have to measure pauses by stops and commas.' On at least one occasion he invoked Ezra Pound's help in the punctuation of a book of his verse; and his works owe much to the care given them, in this respect, by his publishers. In his letters his use of commas is infrequent; he often opens a paragraph or sentence with quotation marks or a bracket and forgets to close it; the possessive case is sometimes indicated by a separate 's' following the word without apostrophe, but often the 's' is left out altogether; even a full stop at the end of a sentence is sometimes missing. These obvious faults I have silently corrected, and I have not hesitated to introduce commas into sentences which, without them, are either ambiguous or almost meaningless.

It will be observed that Yeats almost invariably signed his name in full, 'W B Yeats,' even in letters to his father, his sisters, or his most intimate friends; the signature was always run together without stops after the initial letters, and I have tried to suggest this by omitting them in print. He sometimes signed 'yrs siny' or 'affecly,' and these abbreviated words I print in full. Many of the letters to comparative strangers are signed 'yours' followed by a quite illegible scrawl running diagonally up the sheet from left to right; this, I believe, was an intentional vagueness which he left his correspondent to interpret as best pleased him; such letters here are signed simply 'yours.'

The dating of the letters has not been easy. Yeats rarely mentioned the year in which he wrote, sometimes merely gave the month or the day of the week, sometimes no date whatever. Luckily some of his correspondents preserved the envelopes, and so the postmarks, if legible, have provided dates, though these could not always be relied on because various biographers and students who have had access to some of the letters were not always careful to replace a letter in its right envelope, thus making confusion worse confounded.

Most of the dating has been done from internal evidence. Yeats provided many clues by referring to some publication or the production of some play; and often a letter to one correspondent which can thus be definitely dated will help towards the dating of another. When I have felt certain of a correct date I give it in square brackets; when I feel morally certain but am unable to give definite proof I have marked a query; when the date is merely a reasonable guess I have used the words 'probably' or 'possibly.' Some few letters I cannot date; these I have placed in positions which seem to me at least not definitely wrong.

Each address from which Yeats wrote is given in full the first time it occurs, but abbreviated to the essential thereafter. As a matter of convenience the address is printed on the right side of the page, the date on the left. The beginnings and endings of letters have, in every case, been run together in a single line. It has seemed best to adopt a uniform method of printing titles: accordingly, names of poems, stories and articles are given in roman type and between quotation marks; names of books, plays, periodicals and ships in italics.

A certain amount of annotation of the letters seemed to be necessary to explain or elaborate references which might otherwise be obscure. I have made the notes as brief as possible, and have not given many cross-references, trusting that the index will give sufficient help when necessary.

VI

Besides those already mentioned, Mrs. W. B. Yeats, Mr. Lennox Robinson and Dr. Roger McHugh, I wish to express my grateful thanks for allowing me to transcribe letters in their possession or, in some few cases, for sending me careful copies or for notifying me of the whereabouts of certain letters, to Colonel Russell K. Alspach, Mr. Clifford Bax, Mrs. Mervyn Beech, Sir Edward Bridges, Professor Van Wyck Brooks, Sir Sydney Cockerell, Mr. Carl Dolmetsch, the late Edmund Dulac, Mr. Richard Ellmann, Mr. Gerard Fay, Mr. J. E. Geohegan, Mr. David Garnett, Dr. Oliver Gogarty, Sir Herbert Grierson, Father Aubrey Gwynn, S.J., Mr. Rupert Hart-Davis, Miss Edith Shackleton Heald, Mr. James A. Healy, Mr. Joseph Hone, Mrs. Dorothea Hunter, Miss Ethel Mannin, Mr. A. Miller (of Frank Hollings), Mr. Alfred Noyes, Mr. Sean O'Faolain, Mrs. Sturge Moore, Mr. P. S. O'Hegarty, Mr. Herbert Palmer, Mr. Ivor L. Poole, the Rev. Raymond Roseliep, Professor Mario M. Rossi, Dr. J. S. Starkey, Miss Meum Stewart, Mr. L. A. G. Strong, Professor H. O. White, Mr. Maurice Wollman and Mr. Gerald J. Yorke; also, for permission to use letters now in their keeping, to the Keeper of Manuscripts at the British Museum, the Keeper of Western Manuscripts at the Bodleian Library, Oxford, Dr. R. J. Hayes, Librarian of the National Library of Ireland, Mr. John Bebbington of the Central Library, Belfast, the Librarian of the Brotherton Library, Leeds, the Trustees of the Huntington Library, San Marino, California, Professor William A. Jackson of Harvard University Library, Mr. James T. Babb of the Yale University Library, the Librarian of the New York Public Library and the Librarian of the H. W. and A. A. Berg Collection therein, the Librarians of the University of Buffalo, of the University of Illinois, of Wellesley College, Massachusetts, of the British Drama League, and the Committee and Secretary of the Royal Literary Fund.

I owe especial thanks to Mrs. W. B. Yeats for much help in compiling my notes, and to Mr. P. S. O'Hegarty who supplied me with invaluable information about political history in Ireland and about some of the lesser-known Irish personalities mentioned in the letters. I would also like to acknowledge the help I have received from Mr. Donald Boyd and Mr. Maurice Farquharson of the B.B.C., Mr. V. C. Clinton Baddeley, Sir Edward Bridges, Mr. Guy Chapman, Sir Sydney Cockerell, Mr. Earl Daniels, Mr. Walter de la Mare, Mr. J. E. Geohegan, Mr. C. R. Groves of the Theosophical Society, Mr. Joseph Hone, the Office of the Lord Chamberlain, Mr. Lennox Robinson as Secretary of the Irish Academy of Letters, the Secretary of the Royal Society of Literature, Mr. Noel F. Sharp, Dr. Martin Shaw, Mrs. Ruth Simon, Dr. James S. Starkey, Mr. Edward M. Stephens, Mr. John L. Sweeney, Mr. Vernon Watkins, Miss Marion Witt and Mr. Gerald J. Yorke.

ALLAN WADE

May, 1954

PART ONE
1887—1891

INTRODUCTION TO PART ONE

IN September of the year 1863 John Butler Yeats, a young law student of twenty-four, with a small property in County Kildare, married Susan, sister of a school friend and daughter of William Pollexfen, a prosperous ship-owner and merchant of Sligo.

In Dublin, where J. B. Yeats was keeping his terms with the intention of becoming a barrister, the young couple took possession of a newly built house then called No. 3 Sandymount Avenue, later known as 1 George's Ville, and now 5 Sandymount Avenue. Here, on June 13, 1865, nearly two years after their marriage, was born their first child, the future poet. He was christened William Butler, William being the name of both his Yeats and Pollexfen grandfathers, Butler a family name, his great-great-grandfather having married a Mary Butler. Next year Mrs. Yeats paid a visit to her parents, presumably taking her small son with her, and in Sligo, in August 1866, a daughter was born, who was christened Susan Mary, though in later life she was always known to her family as Lily.

J. B. Yeats was called to the bar in 1866, and it seems that he might have done well in the law—he was a man of alert and original mind and had devilled for the famous advocate Isaac Butt, who had promised to advance his interests. But he had always wished to become a painter, and in 1867 he decided to abandon the law for the profession of art. Feeling that he could follow this better in England, he moved with his family to London, settling first at 23 Fitzroy Road, Regent's Park, and entered Heatherley's Art School in Newman Street. In London three more children were born: in 1868 another daughter, christened Elizabeth Corbet (who became 'Lolly' to her family), Corbet being the family name of J. B. Yeats's mother; another son, Robert, in 1870; and finally, in 1871, the youngest son, Jack Butler, who was to become the great Irish painter.

All W. B. Yeats's earliest memories, of his childhood and boyhood, are concerned with Sligo. Dublin left no impressions at all, and it seems that he can have been little in Fitzroy Road, for he could only remember looking out of a window there and seeing some boys playing in the street. With the family constantly increasing, the elder Yeats children were naturally sent as much as possible to the Pollexfens in Sligo in the care of their grandmother and aunts; there were also Yeats relations still living in the neighbourhood, descendants of W. B. Yeats's great-grandfather John Yeats, who had been Rector of Drumcliffe. In his *Reveries over Childhood and Youth* Yeats writes almost entirely of Sligo; in 1873 the whole family was there on a visit, for at the death of Robert, in March, 'just three years old' as his sister Lily recorded, he remembers sitting happily with her, both drawing ships with their flags at half-mast, in imitation of the Pollexfen ships in Sligo harbour. In Sligo he learned to ride and to swim, and as he grew older went further afield, exploring the countryside and climbing the mountains. In a letter of 1888 to Ernest Rhys he even speaks of Sligo as his native place.

After Heatherley's, J. B. Yeats attended the Academy School and presently began to exhibit his paintings. In 1874 the family moved to Edith Villas, West Kensington, and in the following year, when he was ten, Willie was sent to the Godolphin School in Hammersmith. Here he remained for about five years, not very happy and not learning very much; feeling himself an Irish boy among foreigners and barbarians. He went twice a year for his holidays to Ireland, the journeys being made in one or other of the Pollexfen ships plying between Liverpool and Sligo. Natural history was his chief interest.

In 1876 the Yeats family moved yet again, taking a house at 8 Woodstock Road in the newly built village of Bedford Park, Chiswick. They stayed there for about four years, until, owing to the difficulties which arose in connection with his County Kildare property because of the Land war, J. B. Yeats found it necessary to return with his family to Ireland. In the early eighties they lived at Howth, J. B. Yeats having a studio in Dublin, and Willie was able once more to explore rocks and caves and thickets.

Presently his father told him to go and put himself to school at the Erasmus High School in Harcourt Street, Dublin, and there he remained for three years, learning more than he had done in London. When he left school in 1883 J. B. Yeats wished him to go on to Trinity College, Dublin, where he himself had been, as well as his father, grandfather and great-grandfather; but Willie resisted and said he would prefer to study art. The household had now removed to a red-brick villa at Terenure, which none of them liked, and Willie became a student first at the Metropolitan School of Art and later at the Royal Hibernian Academy School. Among his fellow students at the Metropolitan was George Russell, already painting the visions his mysticism induced him to see, and with him Yeats formed a friendship which lasted, with occasional disagreements, until Russell's death in 1935.

Before he left the High School Yeats had already begun to write poetry. In a letter to Lady Gregory many years later he said that since he was seventeen he had never failed to finish any poem or story he had written, and he was seventeen in 1882. Much of his early work was in dramatic form, and several notebooks still exist bearing various dates in 1884, each containing a dramatic poem of some length. In that same year he fell in love with a distant cousin, Laura Armstrong, and wrote her, he says, a number of bad poems. A letter from her which has survived calls him 'the Poet.' But it was not until 1886 or thereabouts that he finally decided to give up his art studies and become a writer; he told R. Farquharson Sharp, who had asked him for some details for a biographical dictionary, that there was a period of indecision. Meanwhile some of his early work had been printed in the recently founded *Dublin University Review*; two of his lyrics appeared there in March 1885, to be followed by other lyrics and by three of his dramatic poems, 'The Island of Statues,' 'The Seeker,' and 'Mosada.' Presently he began to send work to a couple of small Catholic periodicals, the *Irish Monthly* and the *Irish Fireside*, but it is unlikely that these contributions earned him any money. His father had been painting many portraits of Dublin celebrities, and now decided that he would perhaps do better if he settled once more in London. So in the spring of 1887 a house was found at 58 Eardley Crescent, Earl's Court, and while it was being made ready Willie stayed by himself in lodgings in Berkley Road, off Regent's Park Road. After rather less than a year in the Earl's Court district the family moved once more to what Yeats describes as 'a fine roomy house,' 3 Blenheim Terrace, Bedford Park, and this was to remain their home for many years. J. B. Yeats began to supplement his painting by drawing illustrations for the magazines; the family property in County Kildare had been sold, and life was far from prosperous.

Meanwhile Yeats did not find it easy to get a hearing in London, and in his first year there only one poem, 'King Goll,' was printed in an English periodical, the *Leisure Hour*; articles and poems still went to Ireland, to appear in the *Gael* and the *Irish Monthly*. But he soon began to contribute to two American papers, the *Providence Sunday Journal*, and later, with an introduction from John O'Leary, to the *Boston Pilot*, and for these contributions he was paid. The summer and autumn of 1887 he spent in Sligo, first at Rosses Point, where his uncle George Pollexfen had a small summer cottage, and then at his grandfather's house in Sligo town. Here he finished his long narrative poem 'The Wanderings of Oisin,' which had been begun the year before. Plans were made, possibly at John O'Leary's instigation, to publish this, with a selection of his lyrical poems, by subscription.

In London, acquaintance with Ernest Rhys, a Welsh mining engineer who had taken to literature as a profession, led to a commission in 1888 to compile a small book of *Irish Fairy and Folk Tales* for a series of shilling volumes called the Camelot Classics, of which Rhys was editor. The work was poorly paid; in his letters Yeats says he was to get £7, in his *Autobiographies* he says he received £12; possibly, as the book sold well, he received a second payment. This was followed by a selection of stories from William Carleton, hurriedly put together and published in 1889 in the same series; and then by two little volumes of *Representative Irish Tales*, compiled for the American publishers, Putnam's; this brought him £20. But the small sums he earned mostly went to help defray the family expenses, and it is evident from his letters that he was almost always desperately short of money. Nobody seemed to bother about his health and he was probably continuously underfed; his letters frequently report 'collapses.' He would have liked to find some regular employment but this idea was opposed by his father, who wished him to remain a writer and to keep his independence. York Powell, a friend of the family, secured him two small commissions from the publisher David Nutt, to copy rare books in the Bodleian Library, and these took him to Oxford for several short periods, each a respite from the London he still hated. He seems not to have visited Ireland either in 1888 or 1889.

In his *Autobiographies* Yeats says he cannot recall who introduced him to William Morris; the letters suggest it may have been H. H. Sparling, Morris's future son-in-law. Soon he began to attend the Socialist debates and to stay on afterwards for supper at Kelmscott House, Hammersmith, on Sunday evenings. The Socialism interested him only faintly, but for Morris personally he felt a deep admiration which remained with him always. At these suppers he first met Bernard Shaw, Walter Crane, Emery Walker and Sydney Cockerell; in the *Autobiographies* Shaw appears under the initial D. Towards the end of 1888 Lily Yeats began work as assistant to May Morris with her embroideries, at first for a very small salary.

Later in the year W. E. Henley's name begins to appear; he lived not far from Bedford Park and entertained his little following of clever young writers at Sunday suppers. Next year he began to accept contributions from Yeats to the *Scots Observer*, essays on folk-lore and reviews at first, and presently poems and stories; at last Yeats had found an opening for his work. At Henley's he met Oscar Wilde, who showed his young compatriot much kindness, reviewing his folklore book, and in due course his first book of poems, and taking him home to meet his wife and children.

The early weeks of 1889 were marked by four events, each of them important in Yeats's development. After long delays his first book of verse, *The Wanderings of Oisin and other Poems*, had appeared, and his letters are full of excitement as he enumerates the favourable reviews and quotes the opinions and preferences of his different friends; at last he could feel established as a poet. Almost immediately afterwards an introduction from John O'Leary brought Maud Gonne to the house in Bedford Park, and Yeats succumbed instantly to her enthusiasm and beauty; the devotion which was to bring him much unhappiness and much fine poetry began forthwith. Maud Gonne praised his poems and urged him to write a play which might be performed in Dublin. With herself in his mind as the heroine he began work on *The Countess Kathleen*, founding it on a story from his own collection of folk tales; here was the idea which led, by slow degrees, to his long campaign that was to give Ireland a dramatic literature and a national theatre. Yet one more activity was added:

at the invitation of Edwin Ellis, an old associate of his father's, he began an intensive study of the work of Blake and an interpretation of the Prophetic Books. Four years were to be spent on this exhausting task, which resulted in the three-volume edition of the *Works of William Blake*, issued by Quaritch in 1893. Although now superseded by more modern and more accurately printed editions, this was, in its day, an important contribution to Blake study.

This work tied him to London, and it was only in the summer of 1891 that he was able to visit Ireland, spending some time with his school friend Charles Johnston in County Down and paying brief visits to the Tynan family at their farm Whitehall, near Clondalkin, County Dublin. He was in Dublin in August, and again in October, at the time of Parnell's funeral, returning to London very soon afterwards.

The Blavatsky Lodge had been founded in 1887, and soon after he arrived in London Yeats had joined the Theosophical Society, remaining a member until, apparently as the result of some criticisms he had published, he was asked to resign his membership in 1890. Meanwhile he had made the acquaintance at the British Museum of Liddell Mathers, and early in 1890 had undergone initiation into the Hermetic Order of the Golden Dawn, a society founded by Mathers and others for the study and practice of ceremonial magic.

To all these activities and interests Yeats was presently to add two more, the founding in London of the Rhymers' Club early in 1891, and of an Irish Literary Society in the winter of that year. At about the same time Fisher Unwin published *John Sherman*, the short novel of life in Sligo and London on which Yeats had worked for several years. It had a moderate success and soon went into a second impression, bringing in what then seemed to its writer a decent sum in royalties, for *The Wanderings of Oisin* can have brought him only reviews and some small measure of fame; at the end of 1891 money seemed somehow still to be owing to the publisher; Yeats had to borrow £2 10*s*. from John O'Leary to buy up the remaining copies of the book for transfer to Fisher Unwin.

This first section of letters begins almost simultaneously with Yeats's removal to London, and covers the section of his autobiography called *Four Years*. In Katharine Tynan he found the earliest of that series of women confidantes to whom he could express himself fully and freely. She was four years older than he was, and success had come to her early and easily; her first book appeared in 1885, and she could always find a ready market for her poems, articles and reviews. All this must have seemed miraculous to Yeats with his boxes of unaccepted manuscripts; but he delighted in her success, only urging her to write on Irish themes and to avoid all colouring but that of her own countryside. The long series of letters to her, supplemented by those to John O'Leary and his sister Ellen, and to Father Matthew Russell, editor of the *Irish Monthly*, gives a very detailed picture of Yeats's early life in London and an almost complete history of his literary fortunes from the time the Yeats family left Dublin for London till the end of the year 1891. He had begun to establish his name as a poet; Henley was ready to print his contributions in the *National Observer*; his play *The Countess Kathleen* was finished, though not yet published. The years of apprenticeship were over.

1887-1891

TO MARY CRONAN[1]

My dear Mary Cronan, I send you the verses you asked for I have very few poems under a great many hundred lines but of those I have this is the shortest and most intelligible its subject was suggested by my last two visits to Kilrock. I am afraid you will not much care for it—not being used to my peculiaritys which will never be done justice to until they have become classics and are set for examinations. Yours truly   W B YEATS

PS As you will see my great aim is directness and extreme simplicity.

> A flower has blossomed, the world heart core
> The petal and leves were a moon white flame
>   colour
> U gathered the flower, the ~~soul~~less lore
>   measure
> The aboundant ~~meadow~~ of youth and fame
> Many men gather and few may use
> T[he] sacret oil and the sacret cruse

[1] This, the earliest letter written by Yeats which has so far come to light, is taken from a pencil draft made on a sheet of paper torn from an exercise book, and is in the possession of Mrs. Yeats. Mary Cronan cannot now be identified, and the only clue to the date of the letter is the reference to Kilrock, which suggests that it was written while the Yeats family were living at Howth; it is probably not later than 1884, and may be earlier.

On the reverse of the sheet the poem is written; it is not necessarily certain that this is the poem which Yeats sent, but it seems likely that it may be.

This is the only place where I have given Yeats's spelling, both in letter and poem, without correction.

TO FREDERICK GREGG[1]

[*Possibly early* 1887]

Rosses Point
Sligo

My dear Gregg, I have only read four books of George Eliot's—*Silas Marner*—*Romola*—*Spanish Gypsy*—and a volume of selections. I don't mean to read a fifth.

Reasons why:

Firstly. Tito, her most famous character, is as interesting as a cat on the vivisection table. In him there is none of that beauty that Hugo gave to everything he touched, not only to Esmeralda but to the hunchback. In literature nothing that is not beautiful has any right to exist. Tito is created out of anger, not love.

Secondly. She understands only the conscious nature of man. His intellect, his morals,—she knows nothing of the dim unconscious nature, the world of instinct, which (if there is any truth in Darwin) is the accumulated wisdom of all living things from the monera to man, while the other is at the very most the wisdom gathered during four score years and ten.

Thirdly. Her beloved analysis is a scrofula of literature. All the greatest books of the world are synthetic, homeric.

Fourthly. She has morals but no religion. If she had more religion she would have less morals. The moral impulse and the religious destroy each other in most cases.

Fifthly. I never met a George Eliotite who had either imagination or spirit enough for a good lie.

Sixthly. In the *Spanish Gypsy* there are seven arguments of about fifty pages each. This is the way she describes passion.

Seventhly. She is too reasonable. I hate reasonable people, the activity of their brains sucks up all the blood out of their hearts.

I was once afraid of turning out reasonable myself. The only business of the head in the world is to bow a ceaseless obeisance to the heart. Yours sincerely   W B YEATS

P.S. I am coming home next week.

[1] Frederick J. Gregg, who had been at the High School with Yeats, was a young Irish writer who contributed to the *Irish Monthly*. In 1888 two poems by him were included in *Poems and Ballads of Young Ireland*. Later he emigrated to America where he worked as a journalist.

TO AN UNNAMED CORRESPONDENT

March 11th [1887]   10 *Ashfield Terrace*
Harolds Cross

Dear Sir, Excuse me not having answered your letter before. At first I was of opinion that you were decidedly right; on second thoughts I was not sure; third thoughts that I was decidedly right. I meant by the two lines

> 'From the hills of earth have pealed
> Murmurs of her children talking' [1]

that loud continuous confluence of murmurs that I have heard going up from a wooded mountain at dawn.

As to the lion and whether a roar may be musical or not, I think all uncivilized beast sounds have a certain cadence in them; prose and discord are in the main modern brain-products, not of the primeval world which had only a heart and no brain.

However I will keep your letter by me and consider these things when I reprint the two poems.

Have we not a common friend in T. Lyster? He tells me—if I am not mistaken in your identity—that you are an admirer of Walt Whitman. To me also Whitman is the greatest teacher of these decades. So we have also a common enthusiasm.

If I can lay hands on a copy I will send you my poem *Mosada*, either in *University Review* or the reprint, if you have not seen it. Yours very sincerely   W B YEATS

P.S. Please excuse this somewhat rudderless scrawl. I write not

---

[1] These lines occur in the first verse of a poem, 'A Dawn-Song,' which had appeared in the *Irish Fireside* on February 5, 1887. The verse ran:

> From the waves the sun hath reeled,
>   Proudly in his saffron walking;
> Sleep in some far other field
>   Goes his poppies now a-hawking;
> From the hills of earth have pealed
>   Murmurs of her children talking—
> My companions, two and two,
>   Gathering mushrooms in the dew.

The poem was never reprinted.

The allusion to the lion's musical roar occurs in the poem 'On Mr. Nettleship's Picture at the Royal Hibernian Academy,' first published in the *Dublin University Review*, April 1886, and included in *The Wanderings of Oisin*, 1889, though afterwards discarded.

more than one or two letters in six months, and so to compose a more elaborate affair would be a sort of alpine journey.

TO KATHARINE TYNAN [1]

Wed 27 [*April* 1887]   6 *Berkley Road*
                                     Regent's Park Road

My dear Miss Tynan, I hear Bale [?] was much pleased with your article. I suppose you have heard from him.

I saw Todhunter.[2] He is busy writing a book of Irish poems on something the same plan as de Vere's *Innisfail*.

I feel more and more that we shall have a school of Irish poetry—founded on Irish myth and history—a neo-romantic movement.

I shall commence tomorrow or the next day my review of your book for the *Gael*.[3] Have you seen the cover yet or will you see it

[1] Katharine Tynan (1861–1931) was the daughter of Andrew Tynan, a prosperous farmer living at Whitehall, Clondalkin, Co. Dublin. Yeats had met her about 1885 and was often entertained at Whitehall. From 1887, when the Yeats family moved to London, he took great comfort in writing to her frequently, finding in her a sympathetic correspondent and a link with Ireland and his friends in Dublin. Katharine Tynan seems to have had much journalistic talent and in her volumes of reminiscences gives frequent lists of the magazines and periodicals, in England, Ireland and America, to which she contributed. In 1893 she married Henry A. Hinkson, a barrister and novelist, who became a resident magistrate in Co. Mayo. After his death in 1919 she made her home in England, producing novels in great profusion. She wrote reminiscences of Yeats in *Twenty-Five Years* (1913) and *The Middle Years* (1916) where she printed, in a rather haphazard way, extracts from his letters to her.

[2] Dr. John Todhunter (1839–1916), an Irishman of Quaker stock, was educated at Trinity College, Dublin, and, after studying at Vienna, achieved some success in medicine. He held the chair of English Literature at Alexandra College, Dublin, where he lectured for four years. Later he migrated to London where he became a neighbour and friend to the Yeats family in Bedford Park, and devoted himself to writing poetry and plays. Yeats contributed a short biographical note on him to the *Magazine of Poetry*, Buffalo, New York, in April 1889. This has been reprinted by Dr. Roger McHugh in his edition of the *Letters to Katharine Tynan*, 1953.

[3] The *Gael*, the official organ of the Gaelic Athletic Association, was a penny weekly paper, first issued in the Spring of 1887, and edited by P. T. Hoctor. It paid much attention to national pastimes but also devoted a certain amount of space to literature, this department being apparently under the control of John O'Leary, a patron of the Association. Here were published his own lectures, serials and verse by his sister Ellen, and contributions from his disciples, Yeats, T. W. Rolleston, Douglas Hyde and Katharine Tynan.

At present no file of the *Gael* is known to have survived. The information here given is derived from some notes by the late Dr. J. S. Crone, Deputy Coroner of Middlesex, who was compiling an (unfinished) 'Handlist of Dublin before publication? I have written a couple of ballads which will probably appear in the *Gael*. Did you care for my Finn article, or has it appeared?—for I have not heard.

London is just as dull and dirty as my memory of it. I do not like it one whit better. You will see by the heading of this letter that I am in lodgings by myself, our house being still in disorder. I like being by myself greatly. Solitude, having no tongue in her head, is never a bore. She never demands of us sympathies we have not; she never makes the near war on the distant.

Downey, the publisher and author of *The House of Tears*, has seen and much admired one of your poems.

My sisters are still in Liverpool and Jack is still stopping with my uncle Varley and my Father is painting at Oxford. So you see we are a divided family at present and Rose is sullen and homesick —this latter we are all a little, I think. My Father has a large water-colour in the Academy, that grey thing he did in Dublin of the Girl with the Basket.

Remembrances to everybody, Your friend ever,   W B YEATS

TO KATHARINE TYNAN

8th May [1887]   58 *Eardley Crescent*
     South Kensington

My dear Miss Tynan, I received the [*Irish*] *Firesides* this morning. Your article on O'Shaughnessy is admirable and well-written in every way.

Indeed you are right, I ought to have crossed the line with you at Blackrock; I do not know why I did not. I was blaming myself for it afterwards. I am very sorry. I wrote two letters, one to you and one to Miss O'Leary, and then threw them aside, meaning to re-write them, I think, but someone found Miss O'Leary's note and

---

Periodical Publications before 1909.' Unfortunately his maid, by accident, put most of his notes and extracts into the dustbin and they were destroyed at the refuse depot.

Part of a single page of the *Gael* for April 16, 1887, exists among Yeats's papers. In it a note headed 'To our Readers' regretted that pressure of athletic news had crowded out Mr. Yeate's [*sic*] Fin MacCumhaill, but hoped that it would be published next week. Presumably therefore it appeared in the issue of April 23. From the same page a part headed 'Original Poetry' has been cut out; this may indicate that a poem by Yeats had been printed on April 16.

posted it or else I did myself in sheer absence of mind, unless an eastern Mahatma carried it through the air, travelling 'on the pure cold wind and on the waters wan.' I have written to Miss O'Leary to find out whether he put a stamp on.

I am no more at Berkley Road by myself but here at Eardley Crescent.

A few more paragraphs will finish the article on your book, which may be out any day now, I suppose. Rolleston,[1] acting on my suggestion, prompted in my turn by Lester, has sent a review of your book to the *Academy* but, since I hear he does not like the religious poems and thinks 'Diarmuid and Grainne' not like Ferguson, which is true, and that therefore it is not as good as it might be, which is not true, for all imitation is barren, I am sorry I made any suggestion in the matter. However, he thinks 'Aibhric' very good indeed and altogether the best thing you have ever done.

I was in the House of Commons last Friday night. Healy made a rugged, passionate speech, the most human thing I heard. I missed Dillon, however. Altogether I was delighted with Healy; the others on both sides were sophisticated and cultivated. In him there was a good earth power.

I would be very glad to meet Mr. Ranking.[2] I hear that Burne-Jones is a furious Home Ruler, says he would be a Dynamiter if an Irishman. Your friend ever, W B YEATS

TO KATHARINE TYNAN

May 18th '87   *58 Eardley Crescent*

My dear Miss Tynan, I hoped to have heard from you but suppose you are busy. You do not know what a satisfaction a letter is. Any breath from Ireland blows pleasurably in this hateful London where you cannot go five paces without seeing some wretched object broken either by wealth or poverty.

[1] Thomas William Rolleston (1857–1920), one of O'Leary's most devoted disciples, was a scholar in Greek, Gaelic and German literature. From August 1885 he was editor of the *Dublin University Review*. He was a close friend of Yeats and helped to found the Rhymers' Club in 1891. He published a translation of Epictetus (1888) and Selections from Plato (1892), as well as a Life of Lessing (1889) and a volume of verse, *Sea Spray* (1909).
[2] Montgomery Ranking, a friend of Katharine Tynan's, was a poet and a reviewer on the London *Graphic*.

I have finished and sent off my review for the *Gael* and sent off likewise the proofs to Mr. Legge—I mean, took them to him and, finding him out, thrust them through his letter-box and heard them spreading out on the floor like a pack of cards.

I am horribly irritable and out of sorts. Living over at Berkley Road by myself, I tried experiments in cheap dining—for a man, if he does not mean to bow the knee to Baal, must know all such things —making my dinner off vegetables and so forth. After some time I was gaunt and nervous and able to do little work and since then have had a variable assortment of coughs, colds and headaches. All this I write, not to weary you with any of my personal grievances against the Universe, but because I fear it has wrought ill for the review. You would be astonished at the number of petulant pages against this man or that other I have chopped out of it. Though now, as it stands, it is a calm though not very brilliant exposition of your book.

I have met some literary men over here with the usual number of *bons mots* and absence of convictions that characterises their type. One, however, has no *bons mots* and several convictions—a Welshman, Ernest Rhys, editor of the *Camelot Classics*. I rather like him. I recommended your poems to him strongly. He knew your name but not your work. He tells me a friend of his is editing for the 'Canterbury poets' a book of Irish songs. Knowing that the *Irish Monthly* had published at various times articles on Irish poets, some little known of, I ventured to suggest that he should write to Father Russell and knew not in what numbers these articles or Miss Kavanagh's little poems appeared.

I wish I could get a copy of Sir Charles Gavan Duffy's article on Miss O'Leary's songs. I will get one somewhere and let him see it. Your poems Ernest Rhys will make sure are known to his friend.

I have sent two ballads to the *Gael*; one I expect O'Leary will like, one not. You, I think, will like the one O'Leary will not and care less for the other, and I will agree with you.

I have been to several studios; amongst others, Smaltz'ses—a good-hearted, vain, empty man. What a very small soul goes to a great piece of prosperity!

Todhunter has gone down to Oxford to see the performance of the *Alcestis*. When he comes back, he is to read me a long Irish legendary poem he has done. Those were fine 'Shan Van Vocht' verses of his in *North and South*. We may have them for the ballad book if we wish.[1] I suppose naught has changed with you except outer nature. The wild briar roses must be holding their festival through all your lanes.

There! I have sent you a short letter and a longer one; now in your turn post me a good many pages. Yours forever W B YEATS

TO JOHN O'LEARY [2]

Monday [*Probably late May* 1887] *58 Eardley Crescent*

My dear Mr. O'Leary,[3] Thank you very much for the cheque. What you say about the style of the article is I think true. And one of the ballads is certainly morbid (the woman about whom it is, is now in the Sligo madhouse or was there some while since). However I do not think the Howth one morbid, though now in thinking it over

---

[1] Plans were being made to produce a small anthology of verse by modern Irish poets, and it is evident from the letters which follow that the choice of its contents was in the hands of John O'Leary and his sister. Yeats sent poems and suggestions from London, and the work of dealing with the publishers, M. H. Gill & Co., was undertaken by Katharine Tynan. *Poems and Ballads of Young Ireland* appeared in May 1888. The several references to 'our ballad book' that follow in the correspondence are all to this.

[2] From a copy thought to have been made by D. J. O'Donoghue.

[3] John O'Leary (1830–1907) was born at Tipperary. He entered Trinity College, Dublin, and had intended to become a barrister, but finding that this would necessitate an oath of allegiance to the English Crown, he turned to the study of medicine. Becoming a leading member of the Fenian organization, he was arrested in 1865, chiefly on account of his writings in the *Irish People*, tried, condemned and sentenced to twenty years' imprisonment. After serving five years of his sentence, mostly in Portland prison, he was released on condition that he did not return to Ireland for fifteen years. These years he spent in Paris, where he is said at one time to have shared lodgings with Whistler and George du Maurier; in 1885, as soon as he was free to do so, he returned to Ireland. His sister, Ellen O'Leary, his junior by one year, had also contributed to the *Irish People* but had escaped arrest and continued to live at Tipperary awaiting her brother's return. Together they set up house in Dublin, where O'Leary lived quietly, surrounding himself with many books and giving his support to the Nationalist movements of the time. Yeats met him first at the Contemporary Club and soon became one of his most devoted disciples. In his *Autobiographies* Yeats recounts how he attended meetings and debates at a Young Ireland Society and learned to overcome his shyness by speaking in public. 'From these debates,' he writes, 'from O'Leary's conversation, and from the Irish books he lent or gave me has come all I have set my hand to since.'

In this letter Yeats is evidently discussing his review of Katharine Tynan's *Shamrocks* which he told her in his letter of May 18 that he had posted. It was probably published in the *Gael* on May 28. See letter to Katharine Tynan of May 31.

I quite agree with you that neither are suitable for a newspaper. I enclose a ballad on another Sligo story something like Douglas Hyde[1] though not suggested by him for I have long had it in my mind.

I think you mistake me about 'the probably highest judge' (Miss Christina Rossetti). I did not quote her as an ally but as an opponent for the religious poems *she* likes—the ' Sanctuary ' and its tribe—I do not so much care for. The religious poems *I* like being 'St. Francis,' 'Heart of a mother' and their tribe. In these poems more than in any of the others the form and matter seem to me in perfect unison and the simplicity greatest.

If you cannot use the two ballads I would be glad if you would send them [back] as I think I would like to send them to Father Russell, at least one of them—though probably they will not suit him either. Is there any news from John Boyle O'Reilly? [2] I hope the poems did not go astray, as I have only a rough copy and have made more important and radical changes—however I daresay I can partially remember them. I hope you are all well. I will write soon to Miss O'Leary. Yours very sincerely   W B YEATS

P.S.1. On second thoughts the Sligo ballad of the mad woman was, I fear, not only morbid in subject but a little so in treatment. It was a mere experiment.

P.S.2. The ballad I enclose I believe to be good. The copy I send you has many corrections my own has not, so please return it if you cannot make use of it. I wrote this letter yesterday morning but kept it back to finish the ballad.

Todhunter has a new poem that will suit our ballad book. Miss Tynan tells me she has done a new legendary poem. I wonder would it suit also. It is on an incident in the 'Voyage of Maeldun.' If

---

[1] Douglas Hyde (1860–1949) was educated at Trinity College, Dublin. He published many translations from the Irish and was one of the founders of the Gaelic League in 1893 and its first president. Several plays which he wrote in Gaelic are translated by Lady Gregory in *Poets and Dreamers*, 1903. He was President of Eire from 1938 to 1945.

[2] John Boyle O'Reilly (1844–1890) had been arrested in 1860 and transported to Australia. He escaped to the United States and became a naturalized American citizen. Devoting himself to journalism, he eventually became editor and part proprietor of the *Boston Pilot*, and was one of the leaders of the cause of Irish Nationalism in America. O'Leary had evidently written to enlist his interest in Yeats's work. Some time later Yeats contributed a series of news letters under the title 'A Celt in London' to the *Pilot*, and these, together with some articles from the *Providence Sunday Journal*, were collected and reprinted by Mr. Horace Reynolds in *Letters to the New Island*, Harvard University Press, 1934.

enclosed ballad is suitable I will add a short note giving the story and saying when it took place. In one point you will see it differs from Hyde's—in mine the rebel goes over the cliff. When you are sending the next *Gael* would you kindly send me one or two more copies of my article.

TO KATHARINE TYNAN

31 *May* [1887]   58 *Eardley Crescent*

My dear Miss Tynan, *Shamrocks* arrived all right this morning; the binding is very pretty. Miss O'Leary tells me you are pleased with my review. I must now do one for the *Fireside*. I want you to send me, if you can, some of the reviews in the Irish papers; *Freeman*, *United Ireland*, etc. I feel almost as anxious about it as if it were my own book. And tell me of any English notices and I will get the papers.

I saw your friend, Mr. Legge; breakfasted with him.[1] He seems eager about literature and spent much time painting a French phrase on his mantelpiece. Ernest Rhys, of the Camelot Classics, I have seen also; a not brilliant but very earnest Welshman.

I am about to write some articles on Irish literature for the *Leisure Hour*. I have no news—one day here is much like another day. I read every morning from 11 to 1.30 at the Art Library, South Kensington Museum, where I am now writing, a very pleasant place, the air blowing through the open windows from the chestnut trees, the most tolerable spot London has yet revealed to me. I then dine and through the afternoon write or try to write, as fate and langour, the destroyer, will have it, and in the evening read out to my father, who is afraid to task his eyes. Mitchel's *Jail Journal* has sufficed us for many days now.

I sent two ballads to O'Leary for the *Gael*. He does not like them and he will not use them and, if you care for them, would you kindly send them to Father Russell for the *Irish Monthly*?

There is a society at whose meetings Michael Field (Miss Bradley) is to be seen sometimes. It is called the 'Society of the New Life' and seeks to carry out some of the ideas of Thoreau and

[1] Dr. Roger McHugh identifies him as James Legge (1815–1897), Professor of Chinese at Oxford.

Whitman. They live together in a Surrey village. Ernest Rhys is to bring me to a meeting. Michael Field is a bird of another feather from these London litterateurs, whom I cannot but rather despise.

Now write to me a letter much longer than this one I send you, and tell me much about everybody and everything and still more about yourself. Your Friend,   W B YEATS

I have not got Russell's address [1] but will write to Johnston for it.[2] Have forgotten to do so hitherto—but will write at once.

TO KATHARINE TYNAN

June 25, 1887   58 *Eardley Crescent*

My dear Miss Tynan, I saw Mr. Ranking on Thursday. He is decidedly interesting, seems much disappointed and pathetically angry against everybody and everything modern and yet is withal, I think, kindly. He looks older than in your photograph and in his long dressing-gown was not unlike a retired and somewhat sentimental old cavalry officer spending his latter days between a laugh and a tear. I fear despondence and indifferent health have left him little energy for any good purpose. I asked him did he know Watson's work and recited—

> 'In mid whirl of the dance of Time ye start,
>   Start at the cold touch of Eternity,
> And cast your cloaks about you and depart.—
>   The minstrels pause not in their minstrelsy' [3]

When I came to the third line, he gave the queerest little shudder

---

[1] George William Russell (1867–1935), a fellow-student with Yeats at the School of Art in Dublin, later to become famous as AE, poet, painter, editor and mystic.

[2] Charles Johnston, a schoolfellow and early friend of Yeats, was the son of William Johnston of Ballykilbeg, Co. Down, the leader of the Orangemen. He became a theosophist and founded the Hermetic Society in Dublin; it was with an introduction from him that Yeats met Madame Blavatsky and became for a time a member of the Theosophical Society in London. Charles Johnston joined the Indian Civil Service, but the later part of his life was spent in New York. In a note in *Early Poems and Stories* (1925) Yeats says that he only retained some of his earliest poems in his later collections because they had pleased Johnston.

[3] From William Watson's second book of verse, *Epigrams of Art, Life and Nature*, 1884.

and looked down at his dressing-gown, and I changed the subject. He has written, he says, a lengthy review of your book for the *Graphic*.

I met, some while since, Sparling, editor of *Commonweal*, and Miss Morris's intended.[1] He it is who is bringing out that Irish poem-book I told you of. A friend of yours, he says, a Mr. McCall, I think, is also a friend of his. On the whole, I hated Sparling at first sight;

> 'None ever hate aright
> Who hate not at first sight'

but begin rather to like him now. London literary folk seem to divide into two classes; the stupid men with brains and the clever ones without any. Sparling, I fear, belongs to the latter; Ernest Rhys and possibly Mr. Ranking, to the first. The latter is the most numerous—young men possessing only an indolent and restless talent that warms nothing and lights nothing.

Indeed I find little good, with scarcely an exception, in any of these young literary men—feel malignant on the whole subject and made myself uncivil, I fear, to young Sparling; however, he seems to bear no malice and I begin to like him in a moderate sort of way. He lectured on Irish Rebel songs last Sunday sympathetically and well. I was introduced to Miss Morris afterwards. She is decidedly beautiful and seems very intelligent. Sparling knows and much admires your 'Flight of the Wild Geese,' from which I conclude it will figure in his poem-book. Concerning our own ballad book, would not your legend poem of the saint on his island be perhaps suitable after its appearance in *Blackwood*? Todhunter has done two more ballads for us, or rather a ballad and a story poem, somewhat long but very vigorous, dealing with Martial Law times in Ireland. He will send them to me shortly to be sent on. Did I tell you that he read out a very fine 'Children of Lir' the other night? His high-water mark so far, I think.

Some few days later I read my 'Oisin,' which was very well

[1] Herbert Halliday Sparling was a disciple of William Morris, whose daughter May he married. He edited an anthology *Irish Minstrelsy* in 1887 in the Canterbury Poets series, and when an enlarged edition was published in the following year he included Yeats's ballad 'The Priest of Coloony,' now called 'The Ballad of Father O'Hart.' Since Yeats refers to this poem, in his letter of February 12, 1888, as one which Katharine Tynan already knew, it may have been first printed in the *Gael*.

received, especially the second part. The third remains still little more than commenced. When you see the O'Learys, would you ask them to show you those ballads they have of mine, more especially 'Lug na Gall,' and tell me how you like them.

Now I want you to write and tell me about all that you are writing and doing. Did that poem get into *Blackwood's?* Is your novelette finished? Have you done anything for the ballad book? How are your dogs? Do you see Miss O'Leary often? Is your book selling well? Do you see Miss Kavanagh [1] and the Sigersons? [2] Is your 'Children of Lir' commenced? Is it very hot in Ireland? Being quite out of breath, I bring my letter and my questions to an end. Yours very affectionately   W B YEATS

On looking over what I wrote about Mr. Ranking, it seems all premature and little to the point. I shall perhaps reverse it next time.

July 1

I had thrown this letter aside and forgotten it, except that occasionally I remembered, just as the postman came, that as I still owed you a letter I had no chance of one from you.

Last Sunday evening I had supper at Morris's—pictures by Rossetti all round the room and in the middle much Socialistic conversation. Morris kindly asked me to write for the *Commonweal* somewhat on the Irish question. However, though I think Socialism good work, I am not sure that it is my work.

Have there been any more reviews of *Shamrocks*, Gregg's or anyone else's? Did Miss Kavanagh tell you I sent one to the *Fireside?* I will send today 'King Goll' to Miss O'Leary and go and hurry up Dr. Todhunter so that there need be no further delay.

I find this hot weather very trying and go about like a sick wasp, feeling a sort of dull resentment against I know not what. I was

[1] Rose Kavanagh (1861-1891) was a poet and friend of the O'Learys. She wrote for the *Irish Fireside* and conducted the Juvenile Section under the pseudonym 'Uncle Remus.' Yeats wrote of her death and of her work in the *Boston Pilot*, April 11, 1891.

[2] Dr. George Sigerson (1838-1925) was Professor of Botany and Zoology at University College, Dublin, but his main literary interest was in Gaelic poetry, of which he made many translations. He published *Bards of the Gael and Gall* in 1897. Both he and his wife, Hester, a sister of Ralph Varian, an Irish poet and anthologist, contributed to *Poems and Ballads of Young Ireland*. Their two daughters, Dora and Hester, both wrote poetry; Dora became the wife of Clement Shorter, the journalist and editor.

introduced to Sharp of the *Sonnets of this Century* and hated his red British face of flaccid contentment.[1] However, it seems just possible that I may be able to get away to Sligo this summer, going by Liverpool and on from there in a relation's steamship for cheapness.

I do not think I shall ever find London very tolerable. It can give me nothing; I am not fond of the theatre, literary society bores me, I loathe crowds and was very content with Dublin, though even that was a little too populous, but I suppose—

> 'Wherever in the wastes of wrinkling sand
> Worn by the fan of ever flaming time,
> Longing for human converse, we have pitched
> A camp for musing in some seldom spot
> Of not unkindly nurture, and let loose,
> To roam and ponder, those sad dromedaries
> Our dreams, the master of the pilgrimage
> Cries, "Nay, the caravan goes ever on,
> The goal lies further than the morning star".'

I am writing on Irish poets for *Leisure Hour*, also on Irish Fairies.

TO KATHARINE TYNAN

Monday [after July 9, 1887]   *58 Eardley Crescent*

My dear Miss Tynan, I enclose your copy of the *Register* which I had forgotten before, also 'Baron of Bray' with a few suggested emendations in the rhythm.

I want you to find out would Mrs. Sigerson mind these being made, if you think them needful. I send them to you, hearing the materials for the ballad book are now with you. My emendations are hurriedly made. Perhaps you or Mrs. Sigerson herself could improve on them but, as it stood, the rhythm seemed to halt. Perhaps you had better not show the ballads to Gill until you have the whole of Todhunter's contribution, namely—

The Martial Law story in blank verse,

---

[1] William Sharp (1855–1905) afterwards became a close friend of Yeats. In later years, writing as 'Fiona Macleod,' he was associated with the Celtic movement. See note 1, p. 266.

43

    The Shan Van Vocht,
    The Coffin Ship—and two songs and a short ballad, the name of which I forget.

These I sent a week ago to Miss O'Leary but they do not seem to have arrived.

I believe my *Fireside* review of your book has come out but I have not seen a copy. Could you kindly send me one? I hope you did not mind my fault-finding. I was only allowed very little space and that made it very difficult to say all that should have been said. Many things I would have liked to praise I could not even mention. I saw no 'proof' and so must have been sadly misprinted, I fear. I saw Mr. Ranking's review in the *Graphic* and liked it and liked him also when I met him. Do not mind what I said in that letter. I see everything through the coloured glasses of my own moods, not being, I suppose, very sympathetic.

I was at Morris's again since I wrote and like Morris greatly, though I find much in his philosophy of life altogether alien. He talks freely about everything; called the English 'The Jews of the North,' and seems greatly worshipped by those about him; by young Sparling especially, who carries it so far that, when he was telling Rhys about his engagement to Miss Morris, [he] said, 'She is very beautiful. Morris, you know, says so,' taking Morris's opinion as final in all matters—as, indeed, the only opinion. Meanwhile Morris denounces hero-worship, praising the northern gods at the expense of the Greek, because they were so friendly, feasting and warring with man and so little above him. Your friend,   W B YEATS

P.S.1. 'King Goll' will not appear for a month yet, I hear now.
P.S.2. I find Todhunter will not be able to let us have the 'Banshee,' wishing to print it in his own book this autumn.
P.S.3. When you ask Gill about the expense of the book, ask also how much a cheap paper-covered edition would cost.

I have just read Rolleston's review of *Shamrocks*, agreeing not at all.

TO JOHN O'LEARY

Tuesday, July [1887]   *58 Eardley Crescent*

My dear Mr. O'Leary, Have Dr. Todhunter's MSS turned up as yet, I posted them a week ago. You have not said whether you care for 'Lug Na Gall,' I hope you will let me see a proof especially as I have a rather important note to add. Miss O'Leary speaks of it as from the other side than Hyde's. Of course that is not so, the Cromwellian being used dramatically alone. My note will state the old legend and point out the place of its happening. Would you kindly let me have the two poems you did not care for back as *I did not keep a copy of either.*

I have just heard that 'King Goll' will not appear until September, being crowded out of the August *Leisure Hour*. I have seen no copy as yet of the *Fireside*. I hope Miss Tynan will like my review therein, and am glad to hear that her book is selling steadily; have you heard any particulars?

I have just seen Rolleston's review in the *Academy*, seems not much to the point though some of it is good—much too like the average *Academy* manner. I may be wrong though.

I have been asked to edit an Irish or other volume in the *Camelot Classics* and have thought of Croker's *Irish Fairy Tales* but fear the copyright has not lapsed—could you suggest me some book? I am working hard at my articles for the *Leisure Hour*.

Dr. Todhunter tells me that he wishes to reserve the 'Banshee' for a new book of his own this autumn—so we will have to content us with the poem of his I sent. Yours sincerely   W B YEATS

TO KATHARINE TYNAN

Monday [*Summer* 1887]   *58 Eardley Crescent*

My dear Miss Tynan, I enclose the review you asked for, I hope it does not come too late. I take up your letter and see I should have sent it some days ago and also that ten lines was the needed length. But, if necessary, you or Ashe King[1] might shorten it. I waited on,

---

[1] Richard Ashe King (1839–1932), born in County Clare, was for some years a clergyman. He wrote a number of novels under the pseudonym 'Basil,' and contributed a small book on Swift in Ireland to the *New Irish Library*. He was literary editor of *Truth* for thirty-eight years.

hoping to get some more subtle or suitable words but they would not come.

I have been thinking about the women of the poets but have not read the modern men for so long a time that I really cannot help you at all, I fear. Swinburne's chief women creations are, I suppose, Queen Mary [in] 'Chastelard' and Iseult in 'Tristram of Lyonesse,' which I have read lately, both resembling each other much, both passionate and gorgeous animals, one innocent, the other malignant. Morris's chief woman, I imagine, is Gudrun but it is some years since I read the poem. I only dimly remember her. Morris has, however, I believe, a greater range of characterisation than Swinburne, though he has done nothing perhaps as powerful as Queen Mary in 'Chastelard.' Do you not think there is considerable resemblance between the heroines of all the neo-romantic London poets; namely, Swinburne, Morris, Rossetti and their satellites? For one thing, they are essentially men's heroines, with no separate life of their own; in this, different from Browning's. Tennyson's are, I believe, less heroic than any of the others and less passionate and splendid but realised, as far as they go, more completely, much more like actual, everyday people. Witness *Mary Tudor* [1] and the aristocratic young ladies in the *Idylls of the King*.

I have a notion, but am not sure, that Rossetti's are a more spiritual version of the same type as Swinburne's and Morris's. These are only apologies for ideas on the subject and will help you little, I fear.

I was quite pleased with a little poem called 'Outlaws' in the *Gael* by Hyde. I hope he is putting it in our ballad book. I was at Morris's last night. He says he makes only a hundred a year by his books, all told, and denounces the British public because, he says, it only reads scandal and the newspaper. Your friend ever,

W B YEATS

I have not been reading Browning this long while, but I imagine his heroines are actualized like Tennyson's but are not so much types as his and much more of the brain than his and less of the heart.

The heroines of the neo-romantic school are powerful in

[1] Presumably Tennyson's play *Queen Mary*.

conception, shadowy and unreal in execution; Browning['s] and Tennyson['s] poor in conception, perfectly realised in execution.

I send you Morris's Socialist poems in case you have not seen them.[1]

TO JOHN O'LEARY [2]

Friday, August 4[5] [1887]   58 *Eardley Crescent*

My dear Mr. O'Leary, I heard from Miss Kavanagh this morning and return John Boyle O'Reilly's letter. I have I find a copy though an imperfect one of my poem. Will I, as Miss Kavanagh suggests, write it up and send it to you? Or will we wait to see if the old copy turns up? I enclose a poem from the Gaelic made from a prose version given by Walsh in the introduction to his book of poems.[3] It might be suitable for the *Gael*, if so might I see a proof, as a misprint in a short lyric is quite ruinous and as I am always especially unfortunate in that way. Douglas Hyde's two poems are

---

[1] *Chants for Socialists* by William Morris, published in 1885.
[2] From a copy thought to have been made by D. J. O'Donoghue.
[3] *Irish Popular Songs* by Edward Walsh, Dublin, James M'Glashan, 1847. In his introduction Walsh gives the following translation of a Gaelic song:

> My hope, my love, we will proceed
> Into the woods, scattering the dews,
> Where we will behold the salmon, and the ousel in its nest,
> The deer and the roe-buck calling,
> The sweetest bird on the branches warbling,
> The cuckoo on the summit of the green hill;
> And death shall never approach us
> In the bosom of the fragrant wood!

This Yeats transformed into a lilting poem:

> LOVE SONG
> From the Gaelic.
>
> My love, we will go, we will go, I and you,
> And away in the woods we will scatter the dew;
> And the salmon behold, and the ousel too,
> My love we will hear, I and you, we will hear,
> The calling afar of the doe and the deer,
> And the bird in the branches will cry for us clear,
> And the cuckoo unseen in his festival mood;
> And death, oh my fair one, will never come near
> In the bosom afar of the fragrant wood.

As this poem appeared in *Poems and Ballads of Young Ireland*, it seems not unlikely that O'Leary had previously found room for it in the *Gael*. Yeats did not reprint it in any of his books.

47

very good indeed. My father was greatly delighted with 'Outlaws.' I hope it is for our ballad book, which same book need surely be delayed no longer. Miss O'Leary I find by her letter thinks 'King Goll' put off indefinitely—that is not so, for I hear it will be out in a fortnight.

My article on Irish Ballads for *Leisure Hour* is now ready to be copied out.[1] It has been a long job. I have seen the *Union*, sent by a conservative relative, and read in it much about the *Gael* and the athletic &c. I have been a great many times at William Morris's lately. Tell Miss O'Leary that he thinks Moore much underrated nowadays—tell her also that the editor of the Irish poem book about to appear in 'Canterbury Poets' will include one or two of hers quoted in *Dublin University Review*. He suggests by the way that we should allude to each other's ballad books in our prefaces (are we to have a preface?) which I fear is 'log-rolling.' However if his book is a good book I see no objection. The next time you hear from me I will be at Sligo I hope, for I start possibly next Tuesday. I shall be there some few weeks and return possibly by Dublin. I have an article in the stocks for the *Gael* but have laid it aside for the present. Yours sincerely　　　　　　　　　　　　　　　　　W B YEATS

Miss Tynan tells me she has not shown poems to Gill yet, but waits for Todhunter.

TO KATHARINE TYNAN

Saturday [Probably August 13, 1887]　　　　*Rosses Point*
　　　　　　　　　　　　　　　　　　　　　　　　Sligo

My dear Miss Tynan, You will see by the top of this letter that I am down at Sligo. I reached here Thursday morning about 2 o'c., having come by Liverpool, but will return by Dublin perhaps.

Have been making search for people to tell me fairy stories and found one or two. I hope to get matter enough for an article or so. Have you heard about your story yet? I too am resolved to try story-writing but so far have not made a start. I will send my first

---

[1] Yeats's essay 'Popular Ballad Poetry of Ireland' was not printed in the *Leisure Hour* until more than two years later, in November 1889.

to the *Gael*. I got the last number with Todhunter's 'Lament of Ailinn,' which seems to me no good and possibly should not be included in our ballad book, especially as we will have three or four from him without it. In so small a book everything should be good. My 'King Goll' ought to be out in a day or two, a week at most.

I fear the few rambling thoughts on poetic women I sent will not have helped you, or the review scrap. I hope you did not feel bound to this last but if it was not suitable got someone else to touch it up or re-write it.

I saw Mr. Ranking just before I left London and found him very friendly and pleasant. He was much irritated by Rolleston's review in the *Athenaeum* [*Academy*]. I had almost forgotten what I should have said at the beginning; that Aubrey de Vere sent me his last book. I have been busy reading it and find it wonderfully pleasant and kindly and beautiful. Have you seen it? It came through Father Russell.

It is a wonderfully beautiful day. The air is full of trembling light. The very feel of the familiar Sligo earth puts me in good spirits. I should like to live here always, not so much out of liking for the people as for the earth and the sky here, though I like the people too. I went to see yesterday a certain cobbler of my acquaintance and he discoursed over his cat as though he had walked out of one of Kickham's novels. 'Cats are not to be depinded on,' he said; and then told me how a neighbour's cat had gone up, the evening before, to the top of a tree, where a blackbird used to sing every night, 'and pulled him down;' and then he finished sadly with, 'Cats are not to be depinded upon.'

I have been reading Philip Bourke Marston's stories.[1] Some of them are good, very good, but the most [are] indifferent and all a little feverish. You'll remember, won't you, your promise to send me the reviews of *Shamrocks* to read as soon as you have them all stuck in a book? Your friend,   W B YEATS

Write soon and more than one sheet if possible.

P.S. Monday. I enclose these trivial verses, the first fruit of my fairy-hunting.

[1] Philip Bourke Marston's *For a Song's Sake and other stories*, with a Memoir by William Sharp, was published by Walter Scott in 1887.

The Fairy Doctor.[1]

The fairy doctor comes our way
Over the sorrel-coloured wold;
Now sadly, now unearthly gay!
A little withered man, and old.

He knows by signs of secret wit
A man whose hour of death draws nigh
And who will moan in the under-pit
And who foregather in the sky.

He sees the fairy hosting move
By heath or hollow or rushy mere,
And then his heart is full of love,
And full his eyes of fairy cheer.

Cures he hath for cow or goat,
With fairy-smitten udders dry;
Cures for calf with plaining throat,
Staggering with languid eye,

Many herbs and many a spell
For hurts and ails and lovers' moan—
For all save he who pining fell
Glamoured by fairies for their own.

Greet him courteous, greet him kind,
Lest some glamour he may fold
Closely round us body and mind,
The little withered man and old.

W B YEATS

You must tell me whether you like it. I will maybe have the editing of Croker's *Fairy Tales* for the Camelot Classics but have been this long time waiting for Rhys to decide.

How does your article go on? I wish it were an Irish article, though at the commencement one, I suppose, cannot chose one's

---

[1] 'The Fairy Doctor' was published in the *Irish Fireside*, September 10, 1887. Yeats reprinted it in *The Wanderings of Oisin*, 1889, but excluded it from *Poems*, 1895, and all collections after that.

own subjects always; but remember, by being Irish as you can, you will be more original and true to yourself and in the long run more interesting, even to English readers.

I am going now to a farmhouse where they have promised me fairy tales, so I can write no more.

TO KATHARINE TYNAN

Saturday [*Autumn* 1887]   *Rosses Point*

My dear Miss Tynan, I was very glad to get the Liverpool review of *Shamrocks*, it ought to greatly help. I see the reviewer picks out my own favourite 'The Heart of a Mother.' I will keep the paper safely for you but wish to keep it by me for a few days yet.

My plans are very hazy just now, depending on the weather. Miss O'Leary has asked me to stop at Rathgar Road for a few days, if I reach Dublin before Mr. O'Leary's return. But I hardly know when I leave, as I wish greatly to finish 'Oisin' first; but the weather breaking might send me off any time, as my uncle stops here only so long as it is fine. 'Oisin' goes ahead famously, the country helps one to think.

I went last Wednesday up Benbulben to see the place where Dermot died, a dark pool, fabulously deep and still haunted and 1732 feet above the sea line, open to all winds. Tracks of sheep and deer and smaller tracks of hares converging from all sides, made as they go to drink. All peasants at the foot of the mountain know the legend, and know that Dermot still haunts the pool, and fear it. Every hill and stream is someway or other connected with the story.

Have you heard about your story yet? The one you sent to *Household Words*, I think.

I lived some days in a haunted house a little while ago, heard nothing but strange knockings on the walls and on the glass of an old mirror. The servant, one evening before I heard anything, heard the stamping of heavy feet, the house being empty.

Jack has gone home a few days now but I sent on the *Ally Sloper*. I think I have no other news. Am as usual fighting that old snake, reverie, to get from him a few hours each day for my writing. Your friend,   W B YEATS

TO KATHARINE TYNAN

25th of October [1887] *Charlemont*
Sligo

My dear Miss Tynan, Don't be angry with me for not having written—I will like better to stop at Whitehall than anywhere else. Strewn about my desk are the first pages of at least three different letters started on various dates to you, and all left only started, on various excuses; firstly, because—and this is something more than an excuse—I wanted to be able to tell you when I would start from this, and my start has depended on two things. First, I want to finish 'Oisin' before I leave, and he has been very obdurate, had to be all re-written once—the third part, I mean—but has gone very well today. I may finish this week. And also I did not fix a day until I heard from home, and now I hear they wish me not to come home just yet. Lilly, you see, is not well yet of her bad suppressed rheumatism attack and Mamma is not well either. However, I dare say a week longer here is all I shall stay. But it is very hard for me to fix a day for certain, 'Oisin' being unfinished. I suddenly remember that perhaps my putting off longer my visit to Dublin may inconvenience you, as you may wish to go to England; you had some such plan. If so, tell me and I will start in a few days. But if not, I will wait till 'Oisin' is finished and one or two other odds and ends.

I had thought to have left when my uncle left Rosses Point but I am now with my grandfather, so my address is—

C/o William Pollexfen, Esq.,
Charlemont, Sligo.

Write and tell me what you are doing and what you have done of late. I am as hungry for news as Robinson Crusoe.

I must go now for my walk, having but an hour till tea-time. Your friend, always,   W B YEATS

I enclose an advertisement of Sparling's book, which he sent me.

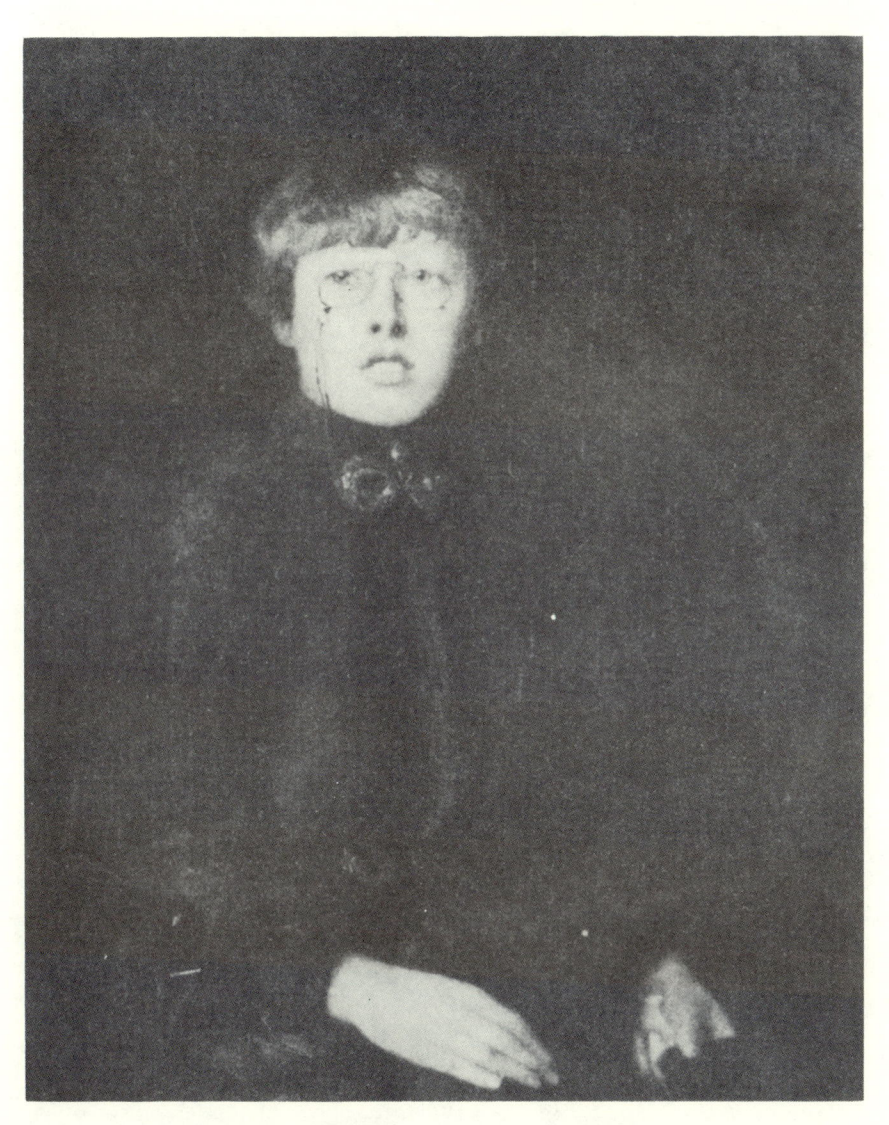

KATHARINE TYNAN, 1887

TO KATHARINE TYNAN

Sunday [Autumn 1887]   *Charlemont*

My dear Miss Tynan, As to the place of my birth—I was born in Dublin, at Sandymount, and as to that sonnet, here it is.

        She who dwelt among the Sycamores.[1]

A little boy outside the sycamore wood
Saw on the wood's edge gleam an ash-grey feather;
A kid, held by one soft white ear for tether,
Trotted beside him in a playful mood.

A little boy inside the sycamore wood
Followed a ringdove's ash-grey gleam of feather;
Noon wrapt the trees in veils of violet weather,
And on tiptoe the winds a-whispering stood.

Deep in the woodland paused they, the six feet
Lapped in the lemon daffodils; a bee
In the long grass—four eyes droop low—a seat
Of moss, a maiden weaving. Singeth she,
'I am lone Lady Quietness, my sweet,
And on this loom I weave thy destiny.'

But would not 'Stolen Child' or 'Meditation of Old Fisherman' be much more understandable? Or, if you wish him to quote—for in this matter I leave myself wholly in your hands—from my more *literary* work, that song commencing:

        Oh wanderer in the southern weather,
        Our isle awaits us; on each lea
        The pea-hens dance, in crimson feather
        A parrot swaying on a tree
        Rages at his own image in the enamelled sea.

---

[1] 'She who dwelt among the Sycamores' had appeared in the *Irish Monthly* in September 1887. Yeats reprinted it in *The Wanderings of Oisin*, and gives an explanation of its meaning in a letter to Ellen O'Leary on Feb 3, 1889 (p. 109). Later he excluded it from his books and was annoyed when George Russell (AE) reprinted it in *A Celtic Christmas*, December 1902, professing to have disliked it always. See letter to Lady Gregory, pp. 389–90.

    The other lines quoted are from 'An Indian Song'. in the *Dublin University Review*, December 1887; the poem, finally called 'The Indian to his love,' underwent many revisions, but was never discarded by Yeats, appearing to the end in his various *Collected Poems*.

Rather a favourite of my own. You will remember it in one of the final *Dublin University Reviews*. I cannot recall the whole correctly. Enough of this, however!

Lately, between a severe cold and cough and that savage greybeard, Oisin, I have had a bad time of it. Between them very sleepless! But now am much as usual.

The dog-cart you speak of will do beautifully for my townward excursions. I will shortly let you know when I start but still have no exact date—dates are the first-born of Satan, mainly. 'Old Chaos' was the only person, old or young, ever extant, who understood freedom properly.

Lilly, I believe, spells her name with a y and two l's; and is better—quite well now, almost.

Will you thank Mr. Piatt [1] for intending to mention my work, though, I dare say, I ought to thank you, rather, but you know I am not unthankful. I must finish to catch the post. Your Friend,
W B YEATS

TO KATHARINE TYNAN

Friday [Autumn 1887]　　　　　　　　　　　　　　　　*Charlemont*

My dear Miss Tynan, 'Oisin' having come to an end, nothing now remaining but the copying out, if quite convenient to you I will be with you Tuesday next by the train that reaches the Broadstone at 4.15 in the afternoon. This finishing off of 'Oisin' is a great relief; never has any poem given me such a trouble. Making me sleepless a good deal, it has kept me out of spirits and nervous—the thing always on my mind—these several weeks back. It seems better now than when I was working it out. I suppose my thinking so badly of it was mainly because of colds and headaches mixing themselves up, with the depression that comes when one idea has been long in the mind, for now it seems one of my successes. Two days ago it seemed the worst thing I ever wrote. A long poem is like a fever —especially when I am by myself, as I am down here. This to me is the loneliest place in the world. Going for a walk is a continual meeting with ghosts. For Sligo for me has no flesh and blood

[1] John James Piatt was American consul at Queenstown.

attractions—only memories and sentimentalities accumulated here as a child, making it more dear than any other place.

I was going along the side of the river a few days ago, when a man stopped me and said, 'I think I should know you, sir.' I found out he knew me well as a child. He asked me to go for a row with him, saying, 'Come, we will tell old yarns,' and with old yarns, mainly fairy yarns collected round about here, I have filled two note-books—you shall hear the best when we meet.

Did I tell you Lolly is writing a story?—a good one, Papa says. I wish Lilly had some such thing on hands, especially now that she may not go out. She will find things very dull this winter with that desponding temperament of hers. My mother is somewhat better, is to come down here, if well enough to travel, which I fear is doubtful. Jack is going to South Kensington School of Art and sent me a good drawing the other day, which I enclose. I had spelt 'metre' wrongly, hence the drawing, which is a recognisable likeness enough.

You have not told me this long while what you are writing, so, when I see you, you may expect many questions on that head. I myself have nothing to read you but 'Oisin', 'Dhoya' [1] and some few scraps, but have much to tell of. You have many poems to read, I hope. Your friend, W B YEATS

Say if Tuesday is convenient.

TO THE EDITOR OF THE *GAEL* [2]

23rd November, 1887

Dear Sir, I write to correct a mistake. The curious poem in your issue of the 19th inst. was not by me, but by the compositor, who is evidently an imitator of Browning. I congratulate him on the

[1] This is the earliest mention of the short story 'Dhoya' which Yeats sent to John O'Leary for the *Gael* (see letter to him of December 13, 1887) where it may or may not have appeared, since the *Gael* was suspended in January 1888. The story was printed with 'John Sherman' in Fisher Unwin's Pseudonym Library in 1891.
[2] This letter to the *Gael* was reprinted in the *Irish Monthly* of July 1891, from which the text is now taken. Yeats's earlier published work suffered much from misprints, some of which, no doubt, were due to his difficult handwriting.

exquisite tact with which he has caught some of the confusion of his master. I take an interest in the matter, having myself a poem of the same name as yet unpublished. Yours faithfully W B YEATS

TO JOHN O'LEARY

Dec 13 [1887]   *Whitehall*
                  Clondalkin

My dear Mr. O'Leary, I see by the paper the *Gael* will come out as a Xmas number. I repent me of the idea of sending 'Dhoya' elsewhere and send it to you hoping it may suit for the Xmas number, for some number anyway.

Miss Tynan's cold is much better, otherwise no news to speak of. Yours sincerely   W B YEATS

TO JOHN O'LEARY[1]

Saturday [? *December* 1887   58 *Eardley Crescent*
or January 1888]

Dear Mr. O'Leary, I don't remember about the other post card. I have been looking for it, but I suppose I must have got it and forgotten.

I got one from Miss O'Leary and will write soon. I have just heard from Sparling who asks me to make suggestions about improving his book as an edition de luxe is coming out. I fear it wants so much that it is not improvable. Have you or Douglas Hyde or anybody noticed any little points that will help him? The book has been a wonderful success.

I was at Madame Blavatsky's.[2] She abused me over the spiritual-

---

[1] From a copy thought to have been made by D. J. O'Donoghue.

[2] Helena Petrovna Blavatsky (1831–1891) was born in South Russia, the daughter of Colonel Peter Hahn. After a stormy youth she married General Nikifor Vasilevich Blavatsky, a man many years her senior, but soon left him and spent many years wandering in Europe and India. An interest in spiritualism caused her to found the Theosophical Society in New York with the help of Colonel H. S. Olcott in 1875; three years later a branch was formed in London. Madame Blavatsky came to London in 1884, accompanied by Olcott

istic affair. A second-sighted person there, who is rather a fool otherwise, told me true things about myself—such as that I had had rheumatism in the arms and shoulders lately, and tried to mesmerise me, but Madame Blavatsky stopped him. Anyway he was having no effect. They all look to Ireland to produce some great spiritual teaching. The Ark of the Covenant is at Tara, says the second-sighted person, but he's a fool.

Things seem better here—my father's drawings a little more in request. I am busy at an article of folklore and have almost finished it.

I have sent no forms [1] to Rolleston. Could he get me any filled up do you think, if so let him have those I sent you, or some of them, if not send them back as I have only a few. I send a few old book catalogues. I hope they are [the] sort of things you want. Will send many more in time. My sister Lolly has written a really good little story—she will do well in time, lives on the right mental plane for that sort of work. Yours very sincerely, W B YEATS

TO KATHARINE TYNAN

Feb. 12th [1888]   *58 Eardley Crescent*

My dear Miss Tynan, I have not written for some time now for I have been very busy—have written a long article, nearly 50 MS pages long of Folklore, and copied out most of my poems for the book—and so often, when I wished to write in the evening, was somewhat too tired. Rhys has written from America asking me to bring out in the Camelot series a book of selected Folklore.

I am trying to get some sort of regular work to do, however; it is necessary, and better anyway than writing articles about things that do not interest one—are not in one's line of development—not that I am not very glad to do the Folklore book or anything that

---

and an Indian sage Mohini J. Chatterji; the latter visited Dublin, probably in 1885 or 1886, when Yeats met him and was inspired to write his Indian poems, two of which were printed in the *Dublin University Review* in 1886. The Blavatsky Lodge was opened in London in 1887. Madame Blavatsky was the author of *Isis Unveiled* and many other books on theosophy.

[1] The allusion to 'forms' indicates that the plan to publish a volume of Yeats's poems by subscription had by now taken shape. The forms were printed by Sealy, Bryers & Walker of Dublin and were sent out to possible subscribers, apparently before a publisher for the book, *The Wanderings of Oisin and other poems*, had been found. It seems very likely that O'Leary had first suggested the scheme.

comes to my hand. The hope of regular work may come to nothing. As soon as the copying out of 'Oisin' is over, I set to work at a short romance. To me the hope of regular work is a great thing, for it would mean more peace of mind than I have had lately, but Papa sees all kinds of injury to me in it. It makes him quite sad. Perhaps the loss of mental liberty entailed in routine is always harmful. On the other hand, it would save me from the insincerity of writing on all kinds of subjects, of writing on other men's truth. And I am anxious to look about me and become passive for a while too. I have woven about me a web of thoughts. I wish to break through it, to see the world again.

Yesterday I went to see, in a city hotel, an acquaintance who has had sudden and great misfortunes, come in these last few days to a crisis. I knew this but was not able to let him know that I did. I was sent by his family, who were anxious about him. We talked of all manner of things; of the theatres, of politics, of ghosts; meanwhile I saw his hands and eyes moving restlessly and that his face was more shrunken than when I saw him some months before. Of course all this pained me at the time but I know (now that he is out of my sight) that if I heard that he was dead I would not think twice about it. So thick has the web got. An accident to one of my MSS or a poem turning out badly would seem of more importance. Yet I do not think I am an egotist. There are a few whose welfare, I think, is more to me than my own. It is all the web. If I had routine work for a time, I could break it. The web has grown closer lately, perhaps because I have not had as good health as usual.

I must often have seemed dreadful to you as I sometimes did to myself. You used to say I had no heart—that is all the web.

Lilly writes often from Yorkshire, most delightful letters, full of humour. She has developed quite a talent that way. Lolly works industriously at her stories. Jack draws as usual. Mamma is much better. We are still looking for a new house at Bedford Park. We must leave this at the end of March.

Rhys mentions in his letter that Whitman is a great admirer of Samuel Ferguson. The little deformed lady at *Atalanta* talked with enthusiasm of your poetry, and praised the poem you sent them. Sparling is going to put 'Father John O'Hart' in the 'Edition de Luxe' of his book.

I went to see Madame Blavatsky on Wednesday but found she

had gone away for her health but sent the Countess Wachtmeister [1] to look after her study, with orders to sleep there even, so close must she watch over the sacred MSS. When she heard I had been to a spiritualistic seance, she told me she had gone to many till Madame Blavatsky told her it was wrong. So you need not fear for a spiritualistic influence coming to me from that quarter.

She told me of horrible things she has seen or believes she has seen at seances. She has seen the medium thrown down by a spirit and half-stifled, the marks of fingers coming on his throat and, finally, his clothes set on fire. She declares she has seen distant places in mirrors and crystals. Being rich, it seems, she has travelled much in search of magic in its many forms. Is a clairvoyant, likewise has seen many visions, some beautiful. Has more titles than talent but is interesting, on the whole.

A sad accident happened at Madame Blavatsky's lately, I hear. A big materialist sat on the astral double of a poor young Indian. It was sitting on the sofa and he was too material to be able to see it. Certainly a sad accident!

I saw Todhunter yesterday (Sunday, for I am finishing this letter on Monday). He has finished 'Deirdre' and begins soon the 'Children of Turann.'

Last night at Morris's I met Bernard Shaw, who is certainly very witty. But, like most people who have wit rather than humour, his mind is maybe somewhat wanting in depth. However, his stories are good, they say.

Both Papa and Edwin Ellis [2]—the only people who have seen it

[1] The Countess Wachtmeister was assistant secretary of the Theosophical Society.
[2] Edwin John Ellis (1848–1918), poet and painter, was a friend of J. B. Yeats and had at one time shared a studio with him. These two, with the painters J. T. Nettleship and George Wilson, sometimes called themselves 'The Brotherhood.' Ellis lived for many years in Italy, where he farmed, and some unsigned paragraphs dealing with his life and the nature of his work, in which it is tempting to suspect the hand of Yeats, appeared in the *Bookman*, February 1893. The final paragraph reads, 'Mr. Ellis has now deserted Perugia, and is married and settled in London, pulling his old manuscripts from their corners, and shaking the dust from his old poems, and getting new ones written.' In his collected *Poems* of 1895 Yeats dedicated 'The Wanderings of Oisin' to Ellis. Besides his collaboration with Yeats in the three-volume *Works of William Blake*, Ellis published some volumes of poetry, *Fate in Arcadia*, 1892, and *Seen in Three Days*, 1893, both illustrated by himself and both reviewed by Yeats in the *Bookman*; a drama in verse, *Sancan the Bard*, 1895, from which Yeats took the plot of his play *The King's Threshold*; and a small number of novels. He also edited a two-volume *Poetical Works of William Blake* in 1906 and wrote *The Real Blake* in 1907.

—say that the last part of 'Oisin' is much the best. Edwin Ellis praises the whole poem much.

Lolly has the clasp you gave her on, it looks very well indeed, quite beautiful. Jack has gone to the meeting in Hyde Park for the reception of the Irish Members.[1]

It is quite a pleasure to write to you, therefore I have prolonged this letter beyond my news. But you must write me a good long letter and tell me what you are doing and so forth. I feel like Robinson Crusoe in this dreadful London.

I am very anxious about this search for regular work. Neither I nor Papa know well how to set about it. But I imagine Mr. Bale will help us. Papa spoke to him. I am hurrying on with the copying out for the book. As, judging by something Mr. Traill said, that might help in the matter, and if the immediate hope of something breaks down, Papa wants me to write a romance; all, I suppose, in the vain hope that in the eleventh hour this regular employment he thinks such an evil might be unnecessary.

United Ireland has not yet paid me, bad luck to it. When it does I mean to pay my debts. They must wait until then.

I have sent two poems to Boyle O'Reilly. By the way, did Father Russell like the poem I sent him? Has Mr. Griffin come to town yet? I have a book of his to send him, when I hear where he is. Your friend, W B YEATS

You would be quite pleased with me if you knew how industrious I have been lately.

Don't say anything to anyone about my hope of getting some employment. It may come to nothing.

TO KATHARINE TYNAN

Monday [? February 1888] 58 *Eardley Crescent*

Dear Miss Tynan, I write again without waiting for your letter because I heard at the Bales' the other day that they will want a third

[1] The meeting in Hyde Park was organized to welcome T. D. Sullivan and other Irish Members of Parliament who had been imprisoned under the Crimes Act. It was held on February 13, 1888.

and last article on Irish peasant life from you, and fear they may not have told you, remembering they did not do so before.

Mr. O'Leary sent me a lot of filled up forms the other day. I have 90 copies promised for, at least, now. And so hope to publish this spring season. I will be ready as far as copying out goes before the end of the month, easily.

When I last wrote I was out of spirits, what with fatigue and being somewhat unwell. Whenever I write you a letter so full of myself and my sensations, you may know that I am tired or unwell. Then one is either like a sick wasp or a cat going about looking for someone to rub itself against.

It is pleasant to think that this letter will go away out of this horrid London and get to the fields and rattle along in the basket with the letters from Clondalkin to Whitehall. I wish I could fold myself up and go in it. A good ghost they say, you know, can hide in a diamond or any such small thing.

I suppose the buds are all coming out with you. Here there is snow on the ground.

Any news of our ballad book? Will it be soon out? Did I tell you that Rhys says Whitman is a great admirer of Ferguson? By the way, I read Ferguson almost every evening for a short while. Are there any other of his books out since the *Lays of the Western Gael* at a 1/–?
Your friend   W B YEATS

TO FATHER MATTHEW RUSSELL[1]

March 6 [1888]   58 *Eardley Crescent*

My dear Father Russell, Many thanks—a great many—for your list of names. Getting my MSS in order has taken all my time and thought—hence all my letters have remained unanswered. Under the circumstances I hope you will forgive this long delay. I have been much hurried over the MSS, fearing to miss the spring season. The book will make, I imagine, about 140 pages. Todhunter, who is himself printing a volume of Irish poems on Deirdre, the Children of Lir, and such, will speak to Kegan Paul today for me. I have about

[1] Father Matthew Russell, S.J., a brother of Lord Russell of Killowen, was editor of the *Irish Monthly* for nearly forty years. He had published there some of Yeats's earliest poems in 1886 and 1887.

110 names so far and will want a hundred and fifty or more but they will come in time.

I sent, some while since, a long article on Fairies to a London magazine but have not heard as yet. Fairies are not popular this side of the water, are considered unscientific. There will be half a dozen poems about them in my book.

What a horrid place this London is! I wonder at that water for overflowing and drowning all those poor Chinamen busy with their opium dreams, and leaving this horrid black place alone.

Dr. Todhunter's book will be out about the same time as my own and will be called, he thinks, *The Banshee* or *The Three Sorrows of Story-telling*, the whole in long unrhyming lines—alexandrines I think you call them. Yours sincerely   W B YEATS

March 13

Correcting MSS has so filled my mind I find I forgot to post this. Yesterday I brought my MSS to Kegan Paul who says I will need about 200 subscribers or 180 anyway. I have about 130 or so but will get the others without doubt. Everyone is so kind in the matter. O'Leary has just sent me a lot of names including Justin McCarthy, Stopford Brooke, Gavan Duffy. He has worked wonderfully for me; indeed I could not have managed without him.

TO KATHARINE TYNAN

March 14th [1888]   *58 Eardley Crescent*

Dear Miss Tynan, My poems have at last gone in to Kegan Paul.[1] He says I will want about 150 or two hundred subscribers (I have 130 or thereabouts), also that I should publish at 3/6, not 5/-, as a 3/6 book is cheaper to get up; but as this matter is not yet settled—he putting the decision off—we must, I suppose, get names on the old understanding. Of course, a given number of names go for less, if 3/6 is the price that will have to be weighed against the cheaper estimate. Which can only be done when I hear from him.

[1] *The Wanderings of Oisin and other poems* was published by Kegan Paul, Trench & Co. but owing to unexpected delays did not appear until January 1889. The book was published at 5/-.

I don't much take to him. Coffey [1] and Todhunter had spoken of me, so he professed much interest in all my doings. I gave, I fear, very monosyllabic answers, not much liking his particular compound of the superciliousness of the man of letters with the oiliness of a tradesman.

That was on Monday. Yesterday I spent answering letters, for they had all been neglected while working at the MSS. Pat Gogarty [2] sent me, by the way, a really fine story—But I put off writing to you till today, that I might write at leisure. I have much improved 'Mosada' by polishing the verse here and there. I have noticed some things about my poetry I did not know before, in this process of correction; for instance, that it is almost all a flight into fairyland from the real world, and a summons to that flight. The Chorus to the 'Stolen Child' sums it up—that it is not the poetry of insight and knowledge, but of longing and complaint—the cry of the heart against necessity. I hope some day to alter that and write poetry of insight and knowledge.

Todhunter's book has gone or is about to go to Kegan Paul. It will contain 'Children of Lir,' 'Children of Turann' and some shorter Irish poems. His 'Deirdre' will not be ready in time. The books may help each other by drawing attention to the subject of old Celtic Romance, which Kegan Paul assures me is not popular. And by drawing attention to it, draw attention to each other.

I have a couple of poems that may suit the *Providence Journal*, one being the 'Phantom Ship.' Would you kindly send me the Editor's address? I suppose there is plenty of time for them to appear before the book comes out. I sent two to the *Pilot* but have not heard. I wrote, by the way, to *United Ireland*, some ten days or a week ago, but have not been paid yet. . . .

Mr. Montgomery Ranking has changed his lodgings some time, the landlady says, and she does not know where he is. Do you? I suppose a note addressed to the *Graphic* office would find him out.

I was at a sort of Socialist tea meeting at Kelmscott House of

---

[1] George Coffey (1857–1916) was an archaeologist and was Keeper of Antiquities in the Irish National Museum. He published a guide to the Antiquities, and numerous papers in the *Transactions of the Royal Irish Academy* and the *Journal of the Society of Antiquaries*. He became paralysed and the last years of his life were spent in bed.

[2] Pat Gogarty was a shoemaker of Clondalkin. Yeats refers several times in his letters to stories received from him and mentions him, though not by name, in his introduction to *Representative Irish Tales*, Putnams', 1891.

late and talked a long time to Mrs. Cunninghame Graham, a little bright American.

Fahy [1] I saw one day in the British Museum reading room (Sparling introduced us), a very brisk, neat, little man. Asked me down to his Irish Literary Club. Seems a king among his own people and what more does any man want? I hear they—that is, the members of the Club—sing his songs and have quite a Fahy cult. Wish we had him in our ballad book, which comes out when? Gill seems slow about it.

We go to our new house, 3 Blenheim Road, Bedford Park, on the 25th of this month; a fine roomy house, which by good luck we have got very cheap. Bedford Park is the least Londonish place hereabouts, a silent tree-filled place where everything is a little idyllic, except the cockroaches that abound there. The quantity of new wood brings them, and the old wood brings a stray nightingale now and again, says rumour, and certainly thrushes and blackbirds in almost country plenty. I will have a study to myself with one of those white wooden balconies native to that part of the world. Your Friend always   W B YEATS

P.S. Mamma and Lilly do not come home till after the move.

P.S. 15th of March. No news yet about any regular work. Todhunter says my bad writing and worse spelling will be much against me but thinks I may get something to do in the way of an assistant librarianship. Meanwhile he says my book is likely to succeed, says good Irish reviews, in the present state of English opinion, may do much, and a successful book may help me in the other matter. Writing articles seems not very satisfactory, I have two long ones still waiting the decision of Editors. One has been a month waiting, the other nine months. Besides a few odd poems waiting here and there. Sorry I did not begin besieging Editors a year or two ago, but it has been my misfortune never to have faith in success or the future. I have a few more things to do for the book, a few lines to add. Then I begin an Irish story; I do not believe in it, but it may do for some Irish paper, and give me

[1] Francis A. Fahy (1854–1935), born near Kinvara, was the founder in 1883 of the Southwark Irish Literary Club, at which Yeats lectured. He wrote a number of popular songs and ballads, the best of which have recently been republished with an introduction by P. S. O'Hegarty, *The Ould Plaid Shawl*, Dublin, 1949.

practice. Todhunter found Kegan Paul, on Tuesday, reading my poems, but no verdict of course yet from that quarter.

There is a robin singing the dirge of yesterday's rain outside my window, the most cheerful creature I have seen these many days, and I see only the rain that is coming.

TO KATHARINE TYNAN

22nd March [1888]   *58 Eardley Crescent*

Dear Miss Tynan, I send you the only forms I can find.

Mr. O'Leary told Sealy, Bryers and Walker to send on 50 to me but they never came.

I dare say you would get some from Mr. O'Leary. I will write to him about it tonight. I cannot write much now to you—as I am writing in Horne's office (Horne of the *Hobby Horse*).[1] He may be here any time.

I have been busy these last two days making up material in the British Museum reading room for a story about Father John O'Hart.

Horne has just come in and tells me that your poem will be in next *Hobby Horse*.

I was at the Southwark Literary Club last night. Crilly lectured on Miss Fanny Parnell.

I must finish now as I want to talk to Horne. Your Friend,

W B YEATS

I got £2 from *United Ireland*; as soon as I get it changed I will send your father the 5/- I borrowed.

---

[1] Herbert Percy Horne (1864-1916), architect and writer on art, was editor of the *Century Guild Hobby Horse* and its successor the *Hobby Horse*, a quarterly magazine. He shared a house in Charlotte Street, Bloomsbury, with Selwyn Image (1849-1930), a designer and worker in stained glass, and with the poet Lionel Johnson (1867-1902), and it was perhaps through him that Yeats first met Johnson. Horne was a member of the Rhymers' Club, and published a volume of verse, *Diversi Colores*, in 1891. He spent much of his later life in Italy and became a great authority on Botticelli.

TO KATHARINE TYNAN

April 11, 1888   3 *Blenheim Road*
Bedford Park

My dear Miss Tynan, I send the 5/- I owe your father. I was about to send it some time ago when paid by *United Ireland* but there was a sudden call for money—we were changing houses—and so I have had to wait till now. Give him my apologies.

Last night Todhunter read out the latter part of his 'Deirdre.' It will not be in his coming book, being too long, he says. Which book will be out before mine. I go again to Kegan Paul this week; he is away at present. My difficulty is the need of some 80 more subscribers—3/6 being the price per copy unless I take Todhunter's suggestion of sending my subscribers 2 copies for their 5/- instead of one. In that way turning 200 copies at 5/- into 400 at 2/6, 2/6 being about the ordinary price of a 3/6 book, when you take the discount off. Not quite the price, but 3d. under. Mrs. Mead of *Atalanta* once did much the same, she says, which comforts me, for I feared it somewhat ceremonious as well as a losing arrangement, exhausting my whole edition but 100. I may manage otherwise. Kegan Paul seems to think June time enough to be out. So can wait a bit. Perhaps I will reduce the size of the book. At any rate 3/6 is likely to be the price. A 5/- book should be over 200 pages. I will decide this week and write after seeing Kegan Paul. Whatever be decided on I will submit to O'Leary for his opinion, he having got so many names for me. If it comes to lightening the ship I will hardly know what to throw overboard—the 'Seeker' for one thing, I fear, and 'Ferencz Renyi.' The Irish poems must all be kept, making the personality of the book—or as few thrown over as may be.

I am reading up for my romance—eighteenth century [1]—all day long. I should dream of it, only I do not dream much. I am very cheerful over it. Making my romance, I have so much affirmative in me that even that little wretch Sparling, with his atheisms and negations, does not make me melancholy or irritable when I meet him in the British Museum.

I have gone there every day for some time. Today I did not go, feeling tired after Todhunter. After breakfast I got out on the roof

[1] No eighteenth-century romance by Yeats is known to exist. He was soon to begin his short novel of contemporary Irish and London life, *John Sherman*.

under the balcony and arranged a creeper that climbs over it. Everything seemed so delighted at the going of the East wind—so peaceful and delighted. It almost seemed that if you listened you could hear the sap rising in the branches—bubble, bubble. Later on I read Mitchel. I must have my mind full of that century. Tomorrow I read old magazines of the period. I have a long list of them.

Jack had his first printed drawing the other day in the *Vegetarian*, a drawing of Fairies. There will be another this week. I will try and get you a copy. He has also a gossipy paper sent him to illustrate —on a country house.

I send you a copy of Morris's play;¹ it is a little soiled as it is one of the copies used by the actors, no other being to be had. He is writing another—of the middle ages this time. Horne of the *Hobby Horse* tells me that Christina Rossetti has a wonderfully high opinion of your poetry, and also says your poem will come out [in the] next *Hobby Horse*.

As to the matter of the copy of the picture. I will try—or get my father to make a sketch of me. But wait till this reading is over.

On Thursday Mamma and Lilly come home.

I met John Burns and his wife at Morris's, Sunday evening—a fine black-bearded man, full of zeal. A sailor once. Denounced Leighton's pictures. The reason came out after a bit. The paddle of the boat in the 'Arts of Peace' at South Kensington was much too large.

I will write no more now as I mean to let you know when I have seen Kegan Paul. Yours affectionately,   W B YEATS

P.S. Todhunter's 'Deirdre' is fine in everything but Deirdre herself. He has made her too querulous and complaining and modern. —No ancient placidity of nerves about her at all.

¹ William Morris's play was *The Tables Turned; or Nupkins Awakened*. It was published at the office of the *Commonweal*. The first performance was given in the Hall of the Socialist League on October 15, 1887. An account of this, on 'the long top floor of that warehouse in the Farringdon Road,' was given by Bernard Shaw in an essay 'William Morris as actor and dramatist' in the *Saturday Review*, October 10, 1896, reprinted in *Our Theatres in the Nineties*, Volume II. Yeats appears to have seen a revival of the play in June 1888.

TO KATHARINE TYNAN

20th April 1888   *3 Blenheim Road*

My dear Miss Tynan, I saw Kegan Paul on Monday. 3/6 as the price seems decided on. However, nothing is decided on, until I get his final estimate, which he promises in a few days. Also he has to read through the poems, which it seems he has not yet done. If I act on that suggestion of giving three copies to the two-copy people for their 10/- and so on with the four-copy people, etc. I have close on sufficient copies subscribed for. If Kegan Paul and I do not come to terms, I may miss the season, though I should be printed cheaper elsewhere, I am told.

Last night I went with Mrs. Todhunter to a meeting of a woman's political association, an invitation I accepted in sheer absence of mind, having no knowledge of the fact till Mrs. Todhunter told me of it. However, I then heard your friend Tom Gill making a speech. He is not much used to speaking, I imagine, his sentences come out rustily. I talked for a few minutes to another friend of yours—Miss Mabel Robinson.[1] But too short a time to learn anything of herself or her opinions. I hear a novel of hers called *Disillusion* much and often praised by Mrs. Todhunter. I have not so far been able to get you any of Jack's drawings in the *Vegetarian* but will order them today at the railway bookstall. He has a great many taken; only three have yet come out.

Tuesday I had one of my collapses, having done over-much walking and over-much reading lately, I suppose—I walk much of the way to the British Museum. I stopped therefore at home that day and, being under orders to do little reading, planted seeds in pots all round the balcony, sweet-peas, convolvulus, nasturtium and such like—and in the garden a great many sunflowers, to the indignation of Lilly and Jack, who have no love for that modest and retiring plant.

Do you remember how they used to mock at me because years ago, when we were here before, I said I would have a forest of sun-

[1] Frances Mabel Robinson was a daughter of G. T. Robinson, F.S.A., and sister of Mary Robinson (Madame Darmesteter). Mabel Robinson, besides writing a number of novels, of which *Disenchantment* (which Yeats here calls *Disillusion*) was published in 1886, was the author of an *Irish History for English Readers*, 1886. George Moore, who was a friend of the sisters, writes in *Avowals* of his meetings, at their house, with Walter Pater and Henry James.

flowers and an underwood of love-lies-bleeding and there were only three sunflowers after all? Well, I am having my revenge. I planted the forest and am trying to get the love-lies-bleeding and they say they don't like love-lies-bleeding a bit.

I thought I was in for a considerable collapse but it wore off. I could only speak with difficulty at first. I was the same way, only worse, when finishing 'Oisin.'

How the robins and sparrows in the virginia creeper are singing away! When you read this—if you read it in your study—your robins will be singing away likewise, maybe, and the sparrows chirping. Mine are all busy making their nests, carrying away small things from off the balcony and sometimes tugging at a grass blade in the garden underneath. I wonder what religion they have. When I was a child and used to watch the ants running about in Burnham Beeches, I used often to say, 'What religion do the ants have?' They must have one, you know. Yet perhaps not. Perhaps like the Arabs they have not time. Well, they must have some notion of the making of the world.

I must now go to work. Write me a long letter as much about yourself and your thoughts and your work as you can. Your friend,

W B YEATS

Many thanks for the forms.

TO ELLEN O'LEARY

1st of May [1888]   3 *Blenheim Road*

Dear Miss O'Leary, When your letter came I had just been considering the question whether I had, or not, acknowledged the latest batch of forms. I could not for the life of me remember nor can I now. I have—if I adopt the suggested arrangement with the 2 and 3 copy people—close on a sufficiency but cannot say for certain until I get Kegan Paul's final estimate. He is very dilatory about it.

The *English Illustrated* has refused my Fairy article, bad luck to them. I shall try elsewhere, where I do not yet know.

I read the 'proofs' of Todhunter's book yesterday—the 'Children of Lir' and 'Sons of Turann' are quite wonderful, almost like Ferguson. They will become Irish classics I believe. Our ballad book should be ready by this surely. Will they send me my six copies—six is it not?—or must I write for them? I am very anxious to see it. Have been watching the post, therefore, these last days.

I was at a big 'Home Rule' party at a Mrs. Hancock's Saturday. Mrs. Gladstone was there and made a speech, a very short one, likewise Stransfield, Justin McCarthy, and Lord Aberdeen made speeches long or short. All these good English Home Rule people, how they do patronise Ireland and the Irish. As if we were some new sort of deserving poor for whom bazaars and such like should be got up. Yet they are really in earnest on this Home Rule question I think.

I have been twice at the French class at Morris's. A queer jumble it is of all sorts of scholars, from Sparling who doesn't know a word of French to one or two quite instructed. William Morris himself has not joined us yet but may be expected next time or next after. It is rather amusing, everyone tries to talk French whether they know any or not. Yours affectionately   W B YEATS

TO KATHARINE TYNAN

May 1888   3 *Blenheim Road*

My dear Miss Tynan, I enclose list of *errata* in Todhunter's poems.[1] He wishes if possible to have it printed on a slip of paper and gummed in the books. I have added one mistake in 'King Goll.' It is a pity to give you so much trouble but I do not know who it should be sent to else. I offered to send it, as I was writing.

Everybody praises the book. Todhunter, Edwin Ellis, York Powell, the historian,[2] Stevens of the *Leisure Hour* are the most notable I have heard speak of it. York Powell when I saw him, the day after (I think) he had been given his copy by Todhunter, had read it all and had written the names of the contributors after the names of poems in the 'Contents,' which shows interest. You and Douglas Hyde seem to have interested him more especially. Your

---

[1] The errata slip was intended for the little anthology *Poems and Ballads of Young Ireland* which had just been published. It appears in all later copies.
[2] Frederick York Powell (1850–1904) was a very unconventional don of Christ Church, Oxford, and Regius Professor of History. He had a London house in Bedford Park to which he went for week-ends, and was a great friend of J. B. Yeats and all his family. Yeats included two of his translations from the French of Paul Fort in *The Oxford Book of Modern Verse*.

'Shamus Dhu' pleased him much. He also praised 'The Story of Clessamnore' as did Todhunter, who is greatly pleased with the book. 'St. Michan's Churchyard' Todhunter praised also. Of course the dedicatory poem is liked by everyone. I read out Rolleston's 'Dead at Clonmacnoise' to Edwin Ellis, who said it was like Victor Hugo.

Poor Dr. Sigerson's 'Exile's Return' is least cared for, perhaps, yet there are one or two good lines, only it is a little confused. The book is certainly interesting. My remaining copy has been much read. It is continually in some one's hands, my father's more especially. He praises your landscape bits in 'Michael Dwyer.' He says you describe beautifully rich arable land such as lies about your own house. He objected a little to the word 'amethyst' which you use; thinking, I suppose, that it spoilt the simplicity.

I need not say I admire the book and your choice in binding. If there is anything I object to, it's the conventional and badly drawn little harp in the corner, and I do not object much to that. Will you let me see the reviews? I will show them to Todhunter. How many copies do we get? Miss O'Leary said six. I only got three, as did Todhunter.

I have not seen the *Irish Monthly*, nor have I since leaving Dublin. I would much like to see it, for your poem's sake, and also because it always interests me in itself. I hope you will give or lend me a copy. Your recent poems have been beautiful, any you send me, so full of calm and temperance as well as the old qualities of energy and beauty. I think you will be right to make your ballad Irish, you will be so much more original—one should have a speciality.

You have yours in Ireland and your Religion. I cannot now think of a subject but will be on the look out—perhaps in the Sarsfield age there was something. There are many in Hugo's ballads—which you will remember are printed according to the dates of their events. You might rehandle one of them.

'Evelyn Pyne' [1] has turned up as a writer of poems in *Lucifer*; they think no end of 'Mr. Pyne' as they call her. One man on the staff is quite enthusiastic; has bought both her books and compares her metre to Swinburne. Has had quite considerable correspondence with her, never dreaming she was not 'Evelyn Pyne, Esq.' He is the editor of the new Wagner journal, the *Meister*.[2]

[1] The pseudonym of a Miss Noble.
[2] W. Ashton Ellis.

I also am writing a short story [1]—it goes on fairly well, the style quite sane and the theme modern, more character than plot in it. Because of this I have not been going into the museum of late but will do so shortly—tomorrow most likely. So absorbed have I been, I really forgot about Miss Probyn till this moment.

The little poem—I should have come to it before—is beautiful. My father is also delighted with it. I think you have made a new start forward lately, as for me I am stationary or advancing only on the side of prose.

I hope all your people are well. What fine weather this is—all green leaves coming out. Yours ever   W B YEATS

TO KATHARINE TYNAN

May 19 [1888]   3 *Blenheim Road*

Dear Miss Tynan, I send at last Miss Probyn's publishers' names. I could not send it before as my father was very anxious for me to go on with my story, so I was not in town at all.

This is the list:

> *A Ballad of the Road and other Poems*, 1883
>   (W. Satchell & Co., London)
> *Who Killed Cock Robin* (*a tale*), 1880
>   (Literary Production Committee, London)
> *Robert Treselian*, (a story), 1880
>   (*The Sea Side Annual*)
> *Once! Twice! Thrice! and Away*, (a novel), 1878
>   (Remington & Co., London).

I saw Mr. Ranking at last. He wished to be remembered to you. I showed him the ballad book. He will review it but has not yet got it. I suppose it will be sent.

By the way, a few people like Aubrey de Vere, Gavan Duffy, etc., might perhaps be sent copies from the common stock. Do you not think so? As we have each so few.

'St. Francis and the Wolf' is beautiful—most beautiful—it is one of your very best, it has all the beauties of your new manner, like

---

[1] Probably the beginning of 'John Sherman.'

'St. Francis to the Birds.' My Father, and indeed we all are, is delighted with it. It is so temperate and *naive* and simple. Like 'St. Francis to the Birds' and 'Fionnula,' it has a peculiar kind of tenderness which I think you only among contemporaries understand. It comes from your religion, I suppose, yet I do not find it in other Catholic poetry. Even in your poetry, I think, it has only come this last year or so.

My story goes well, the plot is laid mainly in Sligo. It deals more with character than incidents. Sparling praised it much, thinks my skill lies more in character drawing than incident.

I have been asked to lecture on Irish Folklore at the Southwark Literary Club in June.

I had almost forgot to tell you that, through a mistake of Kegan Paul's, my book will have to wait till autumn, worse luck.

I sent a short while ago an article on Allingham to *Providence Journal*. I hope they will return it if not suitable. I think it is moderately good.

I read your little eighteenth-century poem to Mr. Ranking. He likes it, I think, as did my father. Did I speak of it in my last letter? It is a very pretty little song.

Good wishes to all, yours ever,   W B YEATS

Sparling reviews ballad book in *Commonweal*.

TO [? D. J.] O'DONOGHUE[1]

May 19 [1888]   3 *Blenheim Road*

Dear Mr. O'Donoghue, I shall be very glad to lecture. I have a never-delivered lecture on the 'Folk lore of the West of Ireland' already written, so I am ready for any date you name.

My book, owing to a mistake of Kegan Paul's, has been delayed too long for this spring season; it will not come out till early autumn.

The little ballad book you mention is a joint matter got up by a dozen or so of us: Rolleston, Douglas Hyde ('An Craoibhin

---

[1] D. J. O'Donoghue (1866–1917) wrote Lives of William Carleton and of James Clarence Mangan, and compiled a very useful biographical dictionary of Irish poets. He was Librarian of University College, Dublin, from 1909 till his death.

Aoibhin'), Miss Tynan, Dr. Sigerson ('Patrick Henry') and a few more. Dr. Todhunter also contributes some good poems. By the way I should bring him down to one of your meetings I think. He is very Irish and interests himself much in the early romances, is bringing out a volume with poems on 'Children of Lir' etc.

I saw Sparling last night; he has not yet heard from you, but I mentioned to him your intention to ask him to lecture. He will do so gladly.

I shall be down at meeting you mention most likely. Yours
W B YEATS

P.S. Sparling is, I believe, to edit Mangan. I have some intention of doing 'Folk Lore' book as you say. But the editor of series is in America and I wait his return to decide some matters about it. He asked me some while since but I am waiting to talk over details.

TO KATHARINE TYNAN

June [1888]   *3 Blenheim Road*

My dear Miss Tynan, I have got that book of selected fairy tales to do for the Camelot Classics. It must be done by the end of July. The time is too short to make a really good book, I fear. I hope to get Davis to edit in Canterbury Poets.[1] I have not yet asked but will if this fairy book looks well when done. All this—the fairy book and plans for Davis book—is not much liked by my father, who does not wish me to do critical work. He wants me to write stories. I am working at one, as you know. It is almost done now. There is some good character drawing, I think, but the construction is patchy and incoherent. I have not much hope of it. It will join, I fear, my ever-multiplying boxes of unsaleable MSS—work too strange one moment and too incoherent the next for any first-class magazine and too ambitious for local papers. Yet I don't know that it is ambition, for I have no wish but to write a saleable story.

Ambitious, no—I am as easily pleased as a mouse in the wainscot,

---

[1] Thomas Davis (1814–1845) was in 1842 a founder, with Charles Gavan Duffy and John Dillon, of the *Nation* newspaper to which he contributed largely both verse and prose. His early death at the age of 31 was a severe blow to the Young Ireland party, of which he was the leader and main inspiration.

and am only anxious to get along without being false to my literary notions of what is good. I shall only get seven guineas for this fairy book, but it is very pleasant working for a certainty. Can you send me any suggestions? I am at present extracting tales from Croker, Carleton and Kennedy. Do, like a good Katharine, search up suggestions for me. I have written to Rolleston for Lady Wilde's book. Do you know any others or of any odd tales anywhere? There was a book of Irish fairy tales announced about a month ago in the *Pall Mall*. Do you remember its name, etc?

My lecture on Sligo fairies at the Southwark Irish Literary Club went off merrily. Todhunter took the chair. Lady Wilde, not being able to come herself, sent a folklore specialist, a big placid clergyman called Ponsonby Lyon. I must write in this letter no more bookish news as I know you think me too little interested in other things. The real fact of the matter is that the other things at present for many reasons make me anxious and I bury my head in books as the ostrich does in the sand. I am a much more human person than you think. I cannot help being inhuman, as you call it, these times. On the rare occasions when I go to see anyone, I am not quite easy in my mind, for I keep thinking that I ought to be at home trying to solve my problems—I feel as if I had run away from school.

So you see my life is altogether ink and paper. But it is hard to go on industriously writing for the MSS boxes. It tends to bring about a state of things when one is too idle to be industrious and too industrious to be idle. However, I am exemplary at present. I really do at most times a fair amount of work, I think, and have written lately everything with a practical intention, nothing for the mere pleasure of writing, not a single scrap of a poem all these months.

We have a little cousin staying with us, Geraldine by name. She and Jack keep up a continuous joking together. At dinner they have to be kept quiet, almost by force. At the end of our garden is a pleasant shady place between a beech-tree and a chestnut. Jack has put up a hammock there.

He has another batch of drawings in the *Vegetarian* and is going next Saturday to a picnic given by the Vegetarian Society, I think, to make sketches for the paper.

I have nothing new about Miss Noble (is she married yet?) not having seen my informant of *Lucifer*, except that the first of two articles on her poetry came out in a late number. I don't know whether I told you that the very simple-minded musician who reviews and is so enthusiastic about her blushed when he was told 'Mr. Pyne' was a lady. Her poems in *Lucifer* are quite long. I have not read them.

Father Fitzpatrick has not yet turned up; I shall be delighted if he does.

In looking over your letter I see you are in hot water with Miss Johnston; you should remind her that George Eliot liked nothing so much as a talk about dress.

I am delighted about your *Good Words* poem.

Send me all news about Ballad book, and *Irish Monthly* when it reviews us.

By the bye, Russell [1] is not so much a theosophist, as you call him, as a mystic of mediaeval type. You must not blame him for that; it gives originality to his pictures and his thoughts.

What are you writing now? How goes your story? Yours always,
                                            W B YEATS

TO KATHARINE TYNAN

June [circa *June* 20, 1888]   *3 Blenheim Road*

My dear Miss Tynan, My father wants me to get him a copy or two of ballad book. How much are they? And would it do for you to get me, next time you are at Gill's, three copies, and get them to add the price to my share in the expenses of book? Or must I send the money?

Did you see the attack in *United Ireland* on Taylor [2] last week? My father is anxious to see it and tried to get a copy yesterday in the Strand without success. If any day you are in town you could get me a copy, I would be glad. I am afraid you will not thank me for these two requests. I do not want you to go out of your way for them, merely if you are in town and near Gill's and Abbey Street.

---

[1] George Russell (AE), not Father Matthew Russell of the *Irish Monthly*.

[2] John F. Taylor, an able advocate who was called to both the English and Irish Bars. He was a follower of O'Leary's but was inclined to be unfriendly to Yeats, with whom he had many controversies. Yeats gives a vivid portrait of the 'red-headed orator' in his *Autobiographies*.

We heard about Taylor from Miss Purser,[1] who is sketching Lilly in the next room at this moment.

She went yesterday to *Good Words* with the drawing for your poem. They have not yet decided but seem to think her 'Mermaid' would shock their readers. They had a mermaid once before and got letters about it.

I was at the east end of London on Sunday to see Morris act in his Socialist play. He really acts very well. Miss Morris does not act at all but remains herself most charmingly throughout her part. She acts Mary Pinch.

Morris tells me he is writing a romance about the ancient Romans. He is going to abuse them, he says.

Do you know who Miss Maclintock is or was—who wrote articles in the old *Dublin University Mag.* about 1875 on 'Folklore in Ulster'? I want to quote from her articles and must first get her leave, I suppose. I suppose Dr. Sigerson could tell me.

When I wrote last I was in bad spirits and tired and talked about myself, of course, and talked gloomily.

My story is going well, another chapter will finish it. It is rather a curious production for me—full of observation and worldly wisdom or what pretends to be such. Yours ever,   W B YEATS

Now you must send me a long letter about your doings and your thoughts.

TO KATHARINE TYNAN[2]

[*Summer* 1888]   [3 *Blenheim Road*]

I cannot write much of a letter this time, for we have run short of candles and I have only a little piece, now about coming to an

[1] Sarah Purser (1848–1943) was a distinguished Irish portrait painter. In her younger days she lived in Paris where she studied art at Julien's atelier in the late '70's and again about 1880, and became a friend of many of the great French artists of the time. Specimens of her work are in many Irish and Continental galleries; her portrait in oils of Maud Gonne hangs in the Dublin Municipal Gallery, as do also pastels of Yeats and Maud Gonne, companion pieces. She was the first woman member of the Royal Hibernian Academy, and organized the 'Tower of Glass,' stained-glass works co-operatively run, which sent work to many countries, and from which came the plain-glazed windows in the foyer of the Abbey Theatre. She was considered, with some justice, to be 'the wittiest woman in Ireland.'

[2] Text from Katharine Tynan's *The Middle Years*, 1916.

end. It will only last about five minutes at most, and you know what a slow writer I am.

Do you like Todhunter's *Children of Lir?* Dowden does not like the metre. Gladstone, in acknowledging a copy that was sent him, said he had read it all through and praised the metre especially.

It has been raining all day. I could not get in to the Museum and so lost my day. When I wrote you that despondent letter I had one of my dreadful despondent moods on; partially fatigue. To keep happy seems like walking on stilts. When one is tired one falls off and comes down to the clay.

The wick of the candle has tilted over on its side and will be out in a moment. Your friend W B YEATS

P.S. I light a match to address the envelope.

TO FATHER MATTHEW RUSSELL

July 5 [1888]   3 *Blenheim Road*

Dear Father Russell, D. R. McNally's book is not in the Museum catalogue.[1] Do you know when it came out? Is it an original collection or a compilation? Do you know anyone who has a copy they could lend for a week or two? I have many stories about the fairies but am hard up for Banshee and Pooka stories and also for stories of the 'headless coach' type. I would add a section about Giants but only know by way of material Carleton's 'Legend of Knockmany.' I am anxious to have a section on Irish Saint stories and wish to give the prophecies of St. Columkille. The peasantry know them well. There was a book published some years ago in Dublin I am told containing them. Do you know anything about it? I have only to do with Irish tales. The books and articles I shall use are these

    Kennedy's books
    Croker's *Legends of the South of Ireland*

[1] Yeats in this letter is seen to be busy with the preparation of his *Fairy and Folk Tales of the Irish Peasantry*, which was published in the autumn of this year. The book he enquires about was *Irish Wonders* by D. R. McAnally, Jr., published in Boston, 1888. Apparently he did not find the book until the following year; he reviewed it in the *Providence Sunday Journal*, July 7, 1889. Here he constantly spells the author's name McNally.

Lady Wilde's *Ancient Legends of Ireland*
Various articles in *Dublin University Review*
Mrs. Crowe's *Ghost stories etc.* From this I take the story of Castlereagh and the 'Radiant Boy'
Carleton's *Traits and Stories*
Lover's *Legends and Stories of Ireland*
The *Folklore Journal* and *Folklore Record*
Hibernian Tales
Mrs. S. C. Hall's *Ireland*

I shall make extracts from all the above.

I have yet to look through the Dublin *Penny Journal* and other Dublin magazines and Barrington's *Recollections* for Banshee tales.

The book must be finished by the end of month.

Many thanks for your suggestions. Yours very sincerely

W B YEATS

I am most anxious about stories of the Croker type, that is to say stories about Fairies, Ghosts, Banshees &c. I hardly know if I will have space to include any of what they call 'Household Tales', that is to say stories of the Cinderella kind. I will include some if possible but fear want of space.

This letter is very badly written but I have to hurry away to the Museum.

I wonder how I could find out McNally['s] London publisher. Though likely enough the book would be expensive.

P.S.2. I have just got your note with Count Plunkett's most valuable suggestions for which thanks to him and you. I shall look up the books he speaks of to-day.

Do you know the date of D. R. McNally's book? I could find out the London publisher if I had that.

In my search for matter I have come on much strange literature —notably a Dublin magazine of 1809 devoted to ghost stories and such like. I have looked through several histories of magic. In the various lists of folklore books given at the end of English and foreign folklore authorities there is hardly any mention of Irish books unhappily.

I looked up the Columkille prophecies but did not find the picturesque ones I heard down in the country. Must look again.

I am afraid I have bothered you with a great many questions. I fear you are busy and these questions are a trouble. If so do not mind about them. I can get along with present material.

TO KATHARINE TYNAN

25 July [1888]   *3 Blenheim Road*

My dear Miss Tynan, A great many thanks for the introduction. I am going to Lady Wilde's reception this afternoon. She was not visible—being not yet up, needing, as the servant put it, 'a great deal of rest,' when I called last Sunday afternoon. I wonder if I shall find her as delightful as her book—as delightful as she is certainly unconventional.

My folklore matters wind up next Monday or Tuesday for the present. My introduction and most likely the last few sections of book not going in till later.

In the meanwhile I shall go for a few days to Oxford perhaps, to copy an MS or some such thing in the Bodleian for a friend of York Powell's—a very pleasant little job, if it comes to anything.

Are you ever going to write to me? Do you know it is two months, all but two days, since you wrote? And I, generous minded person, am writing to you now to heap coals of fire—your letter when it comes will have to be very long or—

I am writing in the British Museum and the man has just brought me Sir William Wilde's *Irish Popular Superstitions* from which I have to make an extract, so this note must wind up presently.

Walter Scott is going to print my Fairy Book at once, so it will be out in a month or two—it has been a very laborious business but well worth doing, for all the material for poetry, if for nothing else.

You and I will have to turn some of the stories into poems. Russell copied out some folk tales not to be got at this side of the channel in the National Library. It was very good of him as he has not much time these days. You see him sometimes, I suppose.

Jack is drawing 'Menu' cards and 'Race' cards. Miss Purser has sold a good many for him. They are very witty little cards, some of them.

What is Miss Kavanagh doing? And what is the ballad book

doing in the way of sale? About yourself: have you any new ventures in hands? My story waits for its last chapter and will have to wait till immediate work concludes. Your friend always,

W B YEATS

When you write remember I want to hear much about yourself.

TO JOHN O'LEARY

27 July [1888]   *3 Blenheim Road*

Dear Mr. O'Leary, I am so busy over Folk lore I have no time to write a letter, merely this note. The story I spoke of would I find come in useful, it is in the same volume as the Ossianic Tales of Kennedy, it [is] a witch tale about the origin of some lake or other, a very wild American Indianish tale. I have to get my book into Walter Scott and Co's hands by Monday or Tuesday.

I have some more old book lists for you, will send them in a day or two.

I have been unable to find time to write to Miss O'Leary lately but will do so first thing when this book is off my hands. Yours always   W B YEATS

The magazine is not in British Museum.

TO KATHARINE TYNAN

August 25th [1888]   *3 Blenheim Road*

My dear Miss Tynan, I have at last found time to write. Such work as I have had lately! These last two days I have had to take a rest, quite worn out. There are still a hundred pages of Aesop [1]—when they are done I shall get back to my story, in which I pour out all my grievances against this melancholy London—I sometimes imagine that the souls of the lost are compelled to walk through its streets

---

[1] The book which Yeats copied on this occasion was published by David Nutt in 1889: *The Fables of Aesop* as first printed by William Caxton in 1484 with those of Avian, Alfonso and Poggio, now again edited and induced by Joseph Jacobs. 2 pts. Bibliothèque de Carabas Series. Vol. 4, 5.

perpetually. One feels them passing like a whiff of air. I have had three months of incessant work without a moment to read or think and am feeling like a burnt-out taper. Will you write me a long letter all about yourself and your thoughts? When one is tired, the tendril in one's nature asserts itself and one wants to hear about one's friends.

Did I ever tell you that a clairvoyant, who had never seen me before, told me months ago that I had made too many thoughts and that for a long time I should have to become passive? He told me besides in proof many things he had no way of hearing of. Most passive I have been this long while, feeling as though my brain had been rolled about for centuries in the sea, and, as I look on my piles of MSS, as though I had built a useless city in my sleep. Indeed, all this last six months I have grown more and more passive, ever since I finished 'Oisin', and what an eater-up of ideals is passivity, for everything seems a vision and nothing worth seeking after.

I was at Oxford but was all day busy with Aesop. I dined two or three times with the Fellows and did not take much to anyone except Churton Collins, who, as you remember, attacked Gosse so fiercely—he was there for a few days like myself—a most cheerful, mild, pink and white little man, full of the freshest, the most unreasonablest enthusiasms.

I wonder anybody does anything at Oxford but dream and remember, the place is so beautiful. One almost expects the people to sing instead of speaking. It is all—the colleges I mean—like an opera.

I will write again before long and give you some news. I merely write to you now because I want a letter, and because I am sad. My fairy book proofs are waiting correction. Yours always,   W B YEATS

P.S. I saw Kegan Paul lately, he will go on with my book now.

TO KATHARINE TYNAN

Enclosed letter has lain on my table this long while.

August 30th [1888]

My dear Miss Tynan, I have just heard from the Sigersons, who were here last night, that 'Fluffy' is dead and that you have written a beautiful elegy thereon. I am really sorry about Fluffy and look forward to reading the poem in the *Irish Monthly*. The younger Miss Sigerson thought it a very good poem indeed, in your later style, and tells me of some other on the stocks.

She is greatly enthusiastic about Henley's little book [1] which would be really a wonderful affair if it was not so cobwebby. I have not read the Hospital part yet. He had his leg cut off there. Should like him greatly but for the journalists who flock about him. I hate journalists. There is nothing in them but tittering, jeering emptiness. They have all made what Dante calls the Great Refusal. That is, they have ceased to be self-centred, have given up their individuality. I do not, of course, mean people like O'Brien [2] who have a message to deliver but the general run, especially the successful ones. The other night I sat there without a word out of me, trying to pluck up resolution to go, but Henley wanted to see me about something and so I waited. The shallowest people on the ridge of the earth!

Please do not mind my writing these opinions to you. I like to write to you as if talking to myself. [*Unsigned.*]

TO KATHARINE TYNAN

Sept. 6th [1888]   *3 Blenheim Road*

Dear Miss Tynan, You told me some time ago that some of your subscribers for my book were 3/6. Could you remember who? As the price will have to be 5/-. However, 3/6 will be all asked in cases where that is the arrangement and where one does not like to ask the people to become 5/- folk. Anybody you do not think would mind, would you ask? Only at 5/- can I get sufficient, I fear. The difference in case of the 3/6 I will pay myself by getting more names. I have several sure.

I got the first 'proof' today, so you see there is no time to lose. So would you kindly let me know. Do you think this will cause much confusion? Fortunately almost all the names were got under the old arrangement.

[1] *A Book of Verses* by W. E. Henley, published by David Nutt, 1888.
[2] This allusion is probably to William O'Brien (1852–1928), journalist and Nationalist Member of Parliament. He founded the weekly paper *United Ireland*, was prosecuted nine times for political offences and spent more than two years in prison. He was one of Parnell's chief lieutenants but joined his opponents Dillon and Davitt after the split. He wrote a good patriotic autobiographical novel, *When we were Boys*, 1890.

I am not very hopeful about the book. Somewhat inarticulate have I been, I fear. Something I had to say. Don't know that I have said it. All seems confused, incoherent, inarticulate. Yet this I know, I am no idle poetaster. My life has been in my poems. To make them I have broken my life in a mortar, as it were. I have brayed in it youth and fellowship, peace and worldly hopes. I have seen others enjoying, while I stood alone with myself—commenting, commenting—a mere dead mirror on which things reflect themselves. I have buried my youth and raised over it a cairn—of clouds. Some day I shall be articulate, perhaps. But this book I have no great hopes of—it is all sluggish, incoherent. It may make a few friends, perhaps, among people of my own sort—that is the most. Do what you can for it.

As to what you say of 'a third manner,' a return to early colouring. Certainly your colouring is a great power but you should be careful to make it embody itself, I think, in easily recognizable natural landscapes, as in your 'Children of Lir,' and keep it always secondary to the theme, never being a colourist for the mere sake of colour. Average, little-read people will say the reverse perhaps to you, but do you not think I am right? The poem you send has that naivety you know how to use so well. The earliest verses are very good; indeed it is all a good little poem, not so good, though, as the 'St. Francis' one in a late *Irish Monthly*.

Coffey sent me a postcard quoting *Ireland under Coercion* [1] about the 'Stolen Child.' Very favourable; something about 'the spirit of Heinrich Heine singing by moonlight on a sylvan lake.' To which spirit the author compared. To what or whom he compared the rest of us I know not, as I did not see the rest. He appears to have written on the ballad book politically likewise. Your friend ever   W B YEATS

TO KATHARINE TYNAN

[*After September* 6, 1888]   3 *Blenheim Road*

Dear Miss Tynan, Last time I wrote, if I remember correctly, I left many things unanswered. I wrote, I think, in much hurry about

[1] A book by an American author, William Henry Hurlbert, published in 1888.

'forms' for *Oisin*. (By the way I imagine Kegan Paul will charge full 5/-.)

I will go and see Ranking as soon as ever I have a day; at present the folklore still is not quite off my hands—the folklore and Aesop. Ranking lives now at the very other side of London.

You ask about Aesop. Nutt, the publisher, is bringing out a reprint of a very scarce copy of Aesop published by Caxton. And I am making a copy for the printers. York Powell, who got me the job, made a mistake and thought the only copy was at Oxford in the Bodleian. And so I had a very pleasant week in his rooms down there. I am now—when folklore gives me time—finishing it in the British Museum. Where, by the way, I saw Renan wandering about yesterday looking very like an old fat priest.

I have not done very badly these last few months. And it has been lucky, as my father's finishing the story in *Atalanta* has left him once more dependent on stray drawings. Not that I have done well exactly. However, I have had as much work as I could do—only badly paid. Did you read my article in *Providence Journal*?[1] I got £5 for Aesop only but will get about another £1. I do not yet know what fairy book will bring. I have had £5 as an instalment. I forgot to ask you if you read the 'Phantom Ship' in *Providence Journal*. I mean to review Todhunter there. The worst of me is that if my work is good it is done very very slowly—the notes to folklore book were done quickly and they are bad or at any rate not good. Introduction is better. Douglas Hyde gave me much help with footnotes, etc.

I had almost forgotten to say how gladly I will do some sort of a sketch of you and your doings for the American friend. But please tell me some more about it. Am I to describe your house and surroundings and yourself just, or do a general sketch of your literary life? Will you not tell me, in any case, some of the things you want said and should I do it at once? I shall have more time shortly. Could you tell me of any article of the kind you wish? Or shall I go my own road? I would sooner go yours. There must be several things you wish said. And have you any dates that are landmarks in your literary life and development? How long should it be?

The other day I met a most curious and interesting man—I do

[1] Yeats's article in the *Providence Journal* was on William Allingham, 'The Poet of Ballyshannon,' and appeared on September 2, 1888. It is reprinted in *Letters to the New Island*, 1934. The poem 'The Legend of the Phantom Ship' had appeared in the same paper on May 27.

not wish to say yet whether he be of interest in himself, but his opinions are—at Madame Blavatsky's, where I go about once every six weeks. Do you remember an interview in the *Pall Mall* with a man called Russell, an American, who came over to England with his wife to teach gesture according to the system of some French philosopher? That was the man. We left Madame's at 11 and walked up and down Notting Hill till 1 o'c in the morning, talking philosophy. He was going to stop with the Shellys for a while; on his return I shall see more of him. The interesting thing about him is that he is a dandy as well as a philosopher.[1] A perpetual paradox. He is naturally insignificant in looks, but by dint of elaborate training in gesture has turned himself into quite a striking looking person. There was a sketch of him in the *Pall Mall*. He is the most interesting person I have met at Madame's lately; as a rule one meets the penitent frivolous there. Still frivolous, only dull as well. She devours them, as she herself says, like the locust in the Apocalypse.

Lately I have read much of George Meredith's poems. They are certainly very beautiful, and have far more suavity and serenity than I had expected. Henley is very cobwebby after them and not very spontaneous. To me Henley's great fault is his form. It is never accidental but always preconceived. His poems are forced into a mould. I dislike the school to which he belongs. A poem should be a law to itself as plants and beasts are. It may be ever so much finished, but all finish should merely make plain that law. Read Meredith's *Love in the Valley*. It is full of a curious intricate richness.

I enclose a couple of lyrics of my own for your opinion. One is made out of three lines of verse I picked up in Sligo—Old Irish verse.[2]

I have had a great deal of trouble over the folklore, the publishers first making me strike out 100 pages, on the ground that the book was too long and then, when two thirds was in print, add as many pages of fresh matter—because they had made a wrong calculation, and I had to set to work copying out and looking over material

---

[1] Dr. Roger McHugh has identified this Russell as Theodore Russell, an American exponent of the Delsarte theories of gesture, who frequented Madame Blavatsky's house for a time at this period. In her diary Elizabeth Yeats wrote: 'Jan 14, 89. Lily and I went with Willie to the beautiful Theodore's, as his friends call him, otherwise Mr. Russell, an American and a Delcartanist (don't know how it is spelt,) but anyway it appears Delcartus was a teacher of gesture.'

[2] The two lyrics enclosed with the letter were, Katharine Tynan says, 'Down by the Salley Gardens' and 'To an Isle in the Water.'

again, as the pages struck out had to do with the section already in type. It is, however, at last off my hands, almost.

Hear the ballad book has been reviewed in the *Saturday* but whether favourably or Saturdayishly I know not.

You would have been much amused to have seen my departure from Oxford. All the while I was there, one thing only troubled my peace of mind—the politeness of the manservant. It was perpetually 'Wine, sir? Coffee, sir? Anything, sir?' At every 'sir,' I said to myself, 'That means an extra shilling, in *his* mind, at least.' When I was going I did not know what to give him, but gave him five shillings. Then suddenly thought I had given him too little. I tried a joke. My jokes had been all failures so far with him. It went explosively and I departed sadly knowing I had given too much.

I have corrected the two first parts of 'Oisin.' The second part is much more coherent than I had hoped. You did not hear the second part. It is the most inspired but the least artistic of the three. The last has most art. Because I was in complete solitude—no one near me but old and reticent people—when I wrote it. It was the greatest effort of all my things. When I had finished it I brought it round to read to my Uncle George Pollexfen and could hardly read, so collapsed I was. My voice quite broken. It really was a kind of vision. It beset me day and night. Not that I ever wrote more than a few lines in a day. But those few lines took me hours. All the rest of the time I walked about the roads thinking of it. I wait impatiently the proofs of it. With the other parts I am disappointed —they seem only shadows of what I saw. But the third must have got itself expressed—it kept me from my sleep too long. Yet the second part is more deep and poetic. It is not inspiration that exhausts one, but art. The first parts I felt. I saw the second. Yet there too, perhaps, only shadows have got themselves on to paper. And I am like the people who dream some wonderful thing and get up in the middle of the night and write it and find next day only scribbling on the paper.

I have added to the book the last scene of 'The Island of Statues' with a short argument to make all plain.[1] I am sure the 'Island' is good of its kind.

[1] In *The Wanderings of Oisin* Yeats included only the third scene of Act II of 'The Island of Statues,' preceded by a 'Summary of Previous Scenes' in prose.

I was then living a quite harmonious poetic life. Never thinking out of my depth. Always harmonious, narrow, calm. Taking small interest in people but most ardently moved by the more minute kinds of natural beauty. 'Mosada' was then written and a poem called 'Time and Vivien' which you have not seen. It is second in my book. Everything done then was quite passionless. The 'Island' was the last. Since I have left the 'Island,' I have been going about on shoreless seas. Nothing anywhere has clear outline. Everything is cloud and foam. 'Oisin' and the 'Seeker' are the only readable result. In the second part of 'Oisin' under disguise of symbolism I have said several things to which I only have the key. The romance is for my readers. They must not even know there is a symbol anywhere. They will not find out. If they did, it would spoil the art. Yet the whole poem is full of symbols—if it be full of aught but clouds. The early poems I know to be quite coherent, and at no time are there clouds in my details, for I hate the soft modern manner. The clouds began about four years ago. I was finishing the 'Island.' They came and robbed Naschina of her shadow. As you will see, the rest is cloudless, narrow and calm.

I meant to wind up this so long letter before this, but in order to propitiate you for all this literariness must add a more human sheet or half-sheet.

Charley Johnston was at Madame Blavatsky's the other day with that air of clever insolence and elaborate efficiency he has ripened to such perfection. The before mentioned penitent frivolous delight in him.

If you only saw him talking French and smoking cigarettes with Madame's niece. He looked a veritable peacock. Such an air too of the world-worn man of society about him, as if he also were one of the penitent frivolous instead of a crusading undergraduate.

You will have to read straight through my book of folklore. It was meant for Irish poets. They should draw on it for plots and atmosphere. You will find plenty of workable subjects. I will expect to hear, as soon as you get the book, your opinion of my introduction —a very few pages it is, too.

Hyde is the best of all the Irish folklorists. His style is perfect —so sincere and simple—so little literary.

I have been looking out in vain for the longer review of Todhunter in the *Irish Monthly*. Has the *Freeman* reviewed him yet, or the *Nation*? What of the Pan Celtic?[1] They sent me a prospectus. Should I join? Would it help my book or could I be of any use as a member living over here?

When I see *Atalanta* with your poem, you will hear from me again. Your friend always, W B YEATS

The *Saturday has* reviewed us Saturdayishly. Henley says he has nothing to do with it. Have not seen review yet. Went to Henley's (where Heaven knows there is little inducement to go) to find out for Miss O'Leary, and heard the interesting question of the thickness of steaks in different parts of the world discussed at great length.

Everyone is very kind there—but, the Lord deliver us from journalists! I met Sladen, the Australian poet, and liked him. He much admires your poems. Henley praises 'St. Francis,' thinks it the best of yours he has seen. His book has been a great success. The expenses were very heavy, as a large number of copies were printed expensively on Japanese paper. At midsummer he had made twopence profit. There has been a good sale since.

This very long letter has grown bit by bit. Several times I thought it had come to an end, but there being no stamps in the near neighbourhood, each time adding a bit. When my story, which I am once more at work on, came to a check at any time, I took up this letter and added a bit.

Outside my window the balcony is covered with a whirl of fire-red leaves from the virginia creeper. Today it is raining and blowing and they are flying hither and thither or gathered in corners, sodden with wet. How saddening is this old age of the year. All summer the wooden pilasters of the balcony have been covered with greenest leaves and pinkest sweet-pie flower. Now even the horse-chestnut has begun to wither. The chestnuts fall every now and then with quite a loud rustle and thud and the whole house at the garden side is covered with a crimson ruin of creeper and the sunflowers are all leaning down weighted by their heavy seeds.

Has Ashe King reviewed the ballad book? A review in *Truth* would help it. Has it sold at all well? I see it for sale at Irish Exhibition.

[1] A Dublin Literary Society founded in 1888.

A copy should be sent to British Museum. Irish publishers are careless about this as I found in folklore hunts.

P.S. (2) Just got your letter. Could you send me the sketch of you in *Nation*? The description of your own which you refer to would much help.

Certainly I will try and get to see Mr. Ranking as soon as I can.

Proofs I will send one of these days with pleasure; just now I am going through them with Todhunter. Tomorrow or next day I will send them or the first batches, the rest after.

I have an amusing piece of news you may not have heard. Charles Johnston has followed Madame Blavatsky's niece to Moscow and will there be married to her. He will be back in London with his wife on October the 8th. They told nobody about it. The girl's mother—says Madame—cries unceasingly and Madame herself says they are 'Flap Doodles.' Johnston *was* in the running for Mahatmaship and now how are the mighty fallen! Theosophy despairs, only the young wife of the dandy philosopher of gesture throws up her eyes and says 'Oh, that beautiful young man and how wicked of Theosophy to try and prevent people from falling in love!' Madame covers them with her lambent raillery.

The future Mrs. Johnston is very nice, decidedly pretty, with a laugh like bells of silver, and speaks several languages and is not older than Johnston. If you only heard Madame Blavatsky trying to pronounce Ballykilbeg!

Your poem on Fluffy is very good, full of unstrained naivety, but will write about it when I see the 'Children of Lir.' Want to catch post now and get some afternoon tea, which I hear clattering below.

This letter is none of your 'cock-boats' but a regular 'three-decker' of a letter.

TO ERNEST RHYS[1]

[*September–October* 1888]   *3 Blenheim Road*

My dear Rhys, I see by the paper of the day before yesterday that Folk Lore book is out. . . . The book is full—at least my part of it

[1] Text from *Letters from Limbo* by Ernest Rhys, London, 1936.

is—with yarns about Sligo: in addition Sligo is my native place—considering which they will probably blow trumpets to some small extent and sell some copies as well as helping the sale down there of my poems now being printed. . . . I had almost forgotten to say that if they send a copy to *Lucifer* Madame Blavatsky will review it. . . . Make plain to the mind of Scott that I have taken much trouble and that there is *original matter of value which no one else could have got*, that is to say Douglas Hyde's stories—one of them the finest thing in the book. . . . Yours very sincerely

W B YEATS

TO JOHN O'LEARY

[*September or October* 1888] *3 Blenheim Road*

Dear Mr. O'Leary, The enclosed order form is not very legible, Kegan Paul cannot make it out. The trouble is in the name I imagine.

One of the Sligo papers has given two columns of quotations from Folk Lore book. They quoted all the parts about Sligo including my two poems. This is the first review yet.

What Irish American papers should I tell Walter Scott to send to besides *Boston Pilot*?

I have had a letter from Russell lamenting over what he calls 'that detestable rumour' about C. Johnston. He is very amusing on the subject. Never will he make any one his ideal again etc. Miss Tynan, he says, will crow over him. Yours very sincerely

W B YEATS

TO JOHN O'LEARY

Oct 8 [1888][1] *3 Blenheim Road*

My dear Mr. O'Leary, I quite let the acknowledgement of those forms and cheques slip out of my mind. Your letter to-day for the first time brought them to memory. I suppose they were crowded

[1] This letter was printed in the *Irish Book Lover*, November 1940, but was there wrongly dated 1890; all the references in it show that it belongs to 1888. In the magazine it was given a second and longer postscript which can, from internal evidence, be dated 1889.

into forgetfulness by the telegrams wherewith Walter Scott's printer was pelting me at the time—however, that matter is over and the book out. I send this post or next a copy to Miss O'Leary. I brought 'forms' to Kegan Paul and one of the cheques—the one pound cheque I had to borrow for a few days but will send amount to Kegan Paul tomorrow or next day when paid for Folk Tales book. Rhys (editor of Camelot Classics) is much delighted with Folk Tale book: says it is one of the half dozen books of his series he is proud of.

The article on Allingham is all you say most likely as well as much misprinted. I find it hard not to think of somebody like Sparling when writing prose and writing at them. I have some notion of doing Todhunter for *Providence Journal*,[1] also Professor Rhys'[2] (not Camelot Rhys) book on ancient Celtic religion. My novel or novelette draws to a close.[3] The first draft is complete. It is all about a curate and a young man from the country. The difficulty is to keep the characters from turning into eastern symbolic monsters of some sort, which would be a curious thing to happen to a curate and a young man from the country. . . .

We are all well. I am writing to Miss O'Leary. Yours very sincerely   W B YEATS

Kegan Paul cannot make out enclosed three forms, no more can I. I send them in hopes you will remember the names.

TO KATHARINE TYNAN

Nov. 14 [1888]   *3 Blenheim Road*

Dear Miss Tynan, I send you remainder of the proofs. They came this morning.

[1] This intention was carried out somewhat later. A review, 'Dr. Todhunter's Latest Volume of Poems,' appeared in the *Providence Sunday Journal*, February 10, 1889.
[2] Professor John Rhys (1840–1915), a famous Celtic scholar, Principal of Jesus College, Oxford. His lectures 'On the Origin and Growth of Religion, as illustrated by Celtic Heathendom' were published in 1888. I have not discovered any review of the book by Yeats.
[3] This refers to the short novel *John Sherman* which was published in Fisher Unwin's Pseudonym Library in November 1891. Yeats adopted the pseudonym Ganconagh (love-talker), 'a diminutive being of the same tribe as the Leprecaun, who personated love and idleness.'

I will at once now—this week at any rate—start that sketch of you and your surroundings. My father will help me at it. I would have done it before this but on reading my story to Edwin Ellis, Saturday week, he suggested alterations of much importance on which I am still at work and it is quite needful for me to get this story in some editor's hands at once, as we have not been doing very well lately. I think however three days will quite finish it and I will be able to do that sketch of you on Saturday or at least Sunday. I hope you will forgive this great delay. Please tell me one or two dates—they may be useful. Though indeed I think I will want little in the way of dates—but when did you first write, when first publish? Where? Any others that may occur to you would be guides. I think I can do a good little article on you.

Please tell me what pleases you best and least in those proofs I send. What of the lyrics? York Powell curiously likes 'Moll Magee' best so far as he has read, that is to about page 90. Tell me also, taking the book as a whole, what seems best.

I am trying to get work on the *Dictionary of National Biography*. Henley recommended me to Sealy. He tried to get me the writing of a life of Mitchel in the Great Writers series of Scott's but the editor Marzials (a very poor writer and shallow man judging by his life of Hugo) thought nothing of Mitchel and only knew him as the author of the *History of Ireland*, the worst of his books. I shall edit another Camelot but am waiting to see Rhys on the matter—selected translations of old Irish epics—Deirdre, etc., occurs to me. By the way, have you read the Fairy Tales yet? There are some would do for ballads, I think. I shall some day try my hand at 'Countess Kathleen O'Shea' and the 'Devil and the Hearth-money Man,' the first in some more elaborate way than a ballad, perhaps. It is a subject that would suit you, I think. Do you feel inclined to try it? I wait impatiently the Xmas paper with your 'Kinsale' ballad. You will send it me when it appears, will you not? Also your story or tell me where I can get it.

I am reading Tolstoi—great and joyless. The only joyless man in literature, so different from Turgenev. He seems to describe all things, whether beautiful or ugly, painful or pleasant, with the same impartial, indifferent joylessness.

Also I have just read Meredith's *Diana*. He makes the mistake of making the reader think too much. One is continually laying the book down to think. He is so suggestive, one's mind wanders. The really great writers of fiction make their readers' minds like sponges.

How I long for your opinion on this little story of mine, a very quiet, plotless little story.

But all this is too bookish—but really I have no news except that 'Daniel O'Connell,' our black kitten, having eaten too much melon, is sleeping it off at my feet. Yours always, W B YEATS

P.S. What of poor Ranking? Did you write?

TO JOHN O'LEARY

Nov [19, 1888] *3 Blenheim Road*

Dear Mr. O'Leary, Walter Scott has written asking me to advise him as to the best Irish newspapers to advertise the *Fairy and Folk Tales* in. Could you give me some suggestions? What Cork papers for instance? which of the Dublin papers? I suppose *Irish Times, Freeman, Express*. I am thinking of writing to Miss Kavanagh for some particulars of Northern papers.

Todhunter is giving a lecture at a school near this next Friday on Irish Fairy Tales and will use my book largely I think.

The poems should be out in a month at most. I have sent off some days the last 'proofs.'

Things are much as usual with me. My Father sent his story to *Harper's* and has begun another short one. These stories of his are quite poetical affairs. The new one deals with the West of Ireland. My own tale is at present being rewritten in the latter parts.

I am expecting Crook here this evening. You will remember Crook. He is settled at Clapham now.

What is Douglas Hyde doing? I wrote to Frenchpark twice and have not heard—the last letter only five days since however—so suppose he must be in Dublin or some other where out of Roscommon and busy. William Morris praises much Hyde's stories in Folklore book.

I have to get to work at my story—the *motif* of which is hatred of

London—so please forgive this lean and short letter and forgive my troubling you about the newspapers. Yours very sincerely

W B YEATS

I hope Miss O'Leary is keeping better.

TO KATHARINE TYNAN

Dec. 4th [1888]   *3 Blenheim Road*

Dear Miss Tynan, I send you at last that sketch of you and your surroundings. If you can think of anything further you would like me to say, send it back to me with your notes for alterations. I wrote it yesterday, the first clear day I had. I would have done it long ago but thought it would be a work of several days. However my practice over *Sherman* has made my prose come much more easily.

I am now setting to work on an article on Todhunter's book.

I hope this sketch of you will please you. As your friend wants to use it with something of her own, if I remember rightly, I was afraid to make it longer. Was it Curran or another who lived once at Whitehall? Do not forget to correct it if I have put the name wrong. Indeed make any alterations you like.

Do you know about the best Irish papers for literary advertisements? Walter Scott wrote to me some time since to ask where they should advertise folklore book. I wrote and asked O'Leary and Miss Kavanagh (she being the only journalist of my acquaintance) but have not heard.

There is little news to tell—the best is that Lilly is working at embroidery with Miss Morris every day. She is to be a kind of assistant of hers. She has for a fellow-worker a Miss Mason, daughter of the celebrated painter of the 'Harvest Moon.' She likes it greatly; they make cushion covers and mantelpiece covers without end. She dines at the Morris's every day.

Morris is greatly disturbed by little boys who insist on playing under his study windows. He rushes out every now and then and drives them off. There is a parrot in the house that keeps up a great noise whistling and sneezing and holding conversations with itself. He is used to the parrot and does not mind it. The parrot's favourite is one of the servants. It likes her because she makes so much noise and hops all over the house after her, copying every noise she makes.

This letter is very short but do not be led astray by it; send me a very long one in answer. Yours always, W B YEATS

I saw your article on William O'Brien, it was copied in Sligo paper. Very good in many ways. More about it next letter.

TO KATHARINE TYNAN

Dec. 21 [1888] *3 Blenheim Road*

My dear Miss Tynan, Would you kindly send on the enclosed letter to Prof. Joyce. I cannot recall his address. You should read it, as it is about the old song 'Shule Aroon' and may interest you.[1] Prof. Joyce is, as you know, the great authority on Irish songs. Do you often see him?

I am writing an article on an old blind Gaelic poet of the last century called Hefernan for the *Dictionary of National Biography*. He wrote the original of Mangan's 'Kathleen Ny-Houlahan.' If this article does, I shall most likely do other Irish writers for them.[2] Henley has also recommended me to *Chambers' Encyclopaedia* for Irish subjects. I should rather like such work for the present, my great wish being to do no work in which I should have to make a compromise with my artistic conscience. When I cannot write my own thoughts—wishing never to write other people's for money— I want to get mechanical work to do. Otherwise one goes down into the whirlpool of insincerity from which no man returns. I am to write a series of articles on the difference between Scotch and Irish fairies for some new paper. These articles are to be done on approval, but Henley feels small doubt of placing them. All will go well if I can keep my own unpopular thoughts out of them. To be mechanical and workmanlike is at present my deepest ambition. I must be

---

[1] Yeats published a note on R. L. Stevenson's use, in *The Master of Ballantrae*, of the song 'Shule Aroon' in the *Boston Pilot*, December 28, 1889. (See *Letters to the New Island*, pp. 91–92.)

[2] No notice of the poet Heffernan (or O'Heffernan) appears in the *Dictionary of National Biography*, and Yeats's name does not figure in the list of contributors.

careful in no way to suggest that fairies, or something like them, do veritably exist, some flux and flow of spirits between man and the unresolvable mystery. Do you know that passage in de Vere's 'Legends of the Saints' on the hierarchy of the angels? It is the most Miltonic passage written this long while. Not that fairies are angels.

I am going to tell you a spiritualistic story. Do not be angry! I tell it because it is pretty. It is about Mrs. Anna Kingsford.[1] After her death, Maitland went down to her tomb and entreated her for days in his mind to make some sign that all was well with her. No sign came. The other day he handed a letter to a friend of mine who knew Mrs. Kingsford, and asked whose writing it was. My friend at once recognised Mrs. Kingsford's writing. He asked her to look at the date. It was dated some time in November last, long after Mrs. Kingsford's death. This was the letter:

> 'My dear Caro, (or some such name)—You are losing your faculties. You could not hear my voice. I cannot speak to you through mediums.'

The letter came from a young Scotch girl who had known Mrs. Kingsford so slightly that it is thought she had not even seen her writing. One night in the dark she had felt impelled to get writing materials, and under some influence wrote this letter. She was then living in the Highlands. Her family said she was possessed by devils, and have sent her to very strict relations in Ireland. I met Maitland at Lady Wilde's last week. He talked much of Mrs. Kingsford. I could hear her name in every conversation held. He is an old man with a shrunken chest. He praised her continually.

Madame Blavatsky says there were two Mrs. Kingsfords, 'a good woman and a woman of the world who dyed her hair.' 'She was good,' she added, 'but her progress came more from intelligence.' It was quite pathetic to watch Maitland that day at Lady Wilde's. For the first time Mrs. Kingsford interested me. She must have been good to have inspired so many people with affection.

I have one of my 'collapses' on. I have had it these last three or four days. It is a very uncalled for 'collapse,' as I have given up going out in the evenings to see anyone, so as not to get tired out. I

---

[1] Anna Kingsford, M.D. (1846–1888), was a very successful doctor, a pioneer in the cause of the higher education of women, a vegetarian and a theosophist. She was president of the Theosophical Society in 1883, and founded the Hermetic Society in 1884. Her life was written by Edward Maitland.

find a single vigorous conversation, especially if any philosophic matter comes up, leaves me next day dry as a sucked orange.

Today, Tuesday, I take up this letter to finish it—the collapse is done, thank goodness. I got the Xmas *Weekly Freeman* with your long ballad (Miss Kavanagh sent it to me) and read it to Papa. He objects to your describing the whole of England as in grief because of this French Knight. It would only have affected the nobility. He also objects to the Queen and her ladies going down the Thames from Windsor to bring from the Tower the Lord of Kinsale. The line he likes best is 'Her grave would call me from all lands.' I like the ballad myself in all the latter parts best and think there is a deal of fine romantic energy about it, but do not think it one of your very best. I mean it is not as good as 'Heart of a Mother' and 'St. Francis to the Birds' or 'Children of Lir.' I am not very fond of retrospective art. I do not think that pleasure we get from old methods of looking at things—methods we have long given up ourselves—belongs to the best literature. Your 'St. Francis' was not retrospective, the St. Francis within you spoke. Neither was the 'Heart of a Mother' retrospective.

I do not mean that we should not go to old ballads and poems for inspiration, but we should search them for new methods of expressing ourselves. I think your work has gained much from study of old ballads, but this time you have tried to express feelings quite different from those habitual with you, and have as a result described things from without—more picturesquely than poetically. Your old knight, however, I think is very fine—but as to the rest, you have sacrificed all things to colour. In the last ballad before this, 'The Children of Lir,' the colour is most rich but it is not put in for its own sake—the rich greys and glimmerings of sunset round the four swans seeming in some mysterious way full of affection and spiritual meaning. Your love of colour too was made to serve a real vision of a scene such as we have all known; the same was true though in a less degree of 'Aibhric.' Your best work—and no woman poet of the time has done better—is always where you express your own affectionate nature or your religious feeling, either directly or indirectly in some legend; your worst, that which stands in your way with the best readers, where you allow your sense of colour to run away with you and make you merely a poet of the picturesque.

I am afraid you will be angry with me, first because I told you a spiritualistic story, secondly because I criticise in this way your last ballad. The latest—the youngest—is I know always the best loved. The want of your poetry is, I think, the want also of my own. We both of us need to substitute more and more the landscapes of nature for the landscapes of art. I myself have another and kindred need— to substitute the feelings and longings of nature for those of art. The other change—a less important one—you perhaps need most. It is curious—do forgive me all this—that your other fault, that of sometimes a little overstating the emotion, is only present when your landscapes are those of art. We should make poems on the familiar landscapes we love, not the strange and rare and glittering scenes we wonder at; these latter are the landscapes of art, [? not] the range of nature.

Maybe I should not say these things, as all poets get plenty of hostile criticism without getting it from their friends but then, I think, I know your work better than any newspaper man. Now, no more bookishness. I had long arrears of criticism to make up for.

Lilly—as you know—goes every day to William Morris's to embroider. So far she gets about thirteen shillings a week but will get more as she learns. She dines there every day and likes going very much.

Did I tell you about the parrot who loves one of the servants because she makes so much noise? . . . Sweeps it has a deadly fear of. If one appears at the end of the road, it trembles; when one is in the house, it almost dies.

Lolly had a story taken by the *Vegetarian*. They gave it to Jack to illustrate. I send you a number with drawings of Jack's to a poem of mine.[1] Do not forget to send me the *Nation* with the article about you. . . .

Here are two verses I made the other day: There is a beautiful Island of Innisfree in Lough Gill, Sligo. A little rocky Island with a legended past. In my story I make one of the characters whenever he is in trouble long to go away and live alone on that Island—an

---

[1] The poem published in the *Vegetarian*, December 22, 1888, was 'A Legend'; it was there written out and illustrated by Jack B. Yeats, occupying two full pages. Yeats included the poem in *The Wanderings of Oisin*, but did not reprint it in later collections.

old daydream of my own. Thinking over his feelings I made these verses about them—

I will arise and go now and go to the island of Innisfree
And live in a dwelling of wattles, of woven wattles and woodwork made.
Nine bean-rows will I have there, a yellow hive for the honey-bee
And this old care shall fade.

There from the dawn above me peace will come down dropping slow,
Dropping from the veils of the morning to where the household cricket sings;
And noontide there be all a glimmer, and midnight be a purple glow,
And evening full of the linnets' wings.[1]

I write this letter today hoping it will be in time for Xmas and close it with many good wishes. Yours always   W B YEATS

TO KATHARINE TYNAN

Jan. 13 [1889]   *3 Blenheim Road*

Dear Miss Tynan, I found enclosed letter to Professor Joyce on my desk today so, unless I posted a copy, must have forgotten to enclose it in my last letter to you. Please send it to him. Read it first; the version of 'Shule Aroon' may interest you.

You will have got the book by this. Were you a subscriber or was it your father? If you were not, or even if you were, I will send you a copy from myself. Just this moment I have not one by me, except those which have to be posted to one or two people who paid me instead of Kegan Paul. And I know that either you or your father have a copy. I shall be slightly uneasy until the 3/6 people have all paid up their 5/-. However there were but few such and O'Leary thinks none of them will mind.

[1] This is the earliest known version of the famous 'Lake Isle of Innisfree.' Comparison with the later version, first printed in the *National Observer*, September 12, 1891, and included in *The Countess Kathleen* volume of 1892, shows Yeats's skill in revision at its best.

I am anxious to hear what you think of the third part of 'Oisin' and of the rest of the book. What you like best therein. Does 'Mosada' or 'Oisin' please you most? etc.

I have not yet decided as to what papers it had best be sent to. I want information especially about American ones and have applied to O'Leary. Could you also give some suggestions thereon?

I sent a long article on Todhunter's book to the *Providence Journal* and a shorter one to the *Nation*. About this last I have not yet heard. If you happen to be in town would you ask about it, as I forgot to tell them to return it if not suitable. There was an article on my fairy book, I am told, in the *Nation* some while since. Could you get me a copy? I am also anxious to see that article about yourself you spoke of.

Todhunter is trying to get the reviewing of me for the *Academy*. It will be good luck if he does get it.

Have you heard of the new American serial the *Review of Poetry*, a Mr. Moulton edits it? I am to do a sketch of Todhunter's life for it. Dr. Todhunter wrote to the editor giving names of Irish poets, yourself, myself, etc. He sent [a] copy of my book.

My prose is coming much more easily. I have finished this week a long article on McNally's *Irish Wonders*, a somewhat unfavourable review for *Providence Journal*, and am looking about for some other paper that I can review same book in now that my mind is full of the subject. Do you think the *Catholic World* would take an article from me?

Did I tell you that Henley praised your 'St. Francis to the Birds'? He had seen it quoted, I think, as he did not know the book. Yours always   W B YEATS

Lilly likes going greatly to the Morris's. Morris—Miss Morris says—once tried to do embroidery himself. He was going away somewhere and made Miss Morris thread him several hundred needles as that was, he said, the hardest part of the work. He gave it up, however. The other day he said there would soon be nobody in the world but Jews and Irish. Lilly asked him which would he be. He said certainly not a Jew. Every day he has some little joke. The other day he said, 'All hands talk French' and then he began the most comic mixture of French and English.

TO KATHARINE TYNAN

Jan. 24th [1889]   3 *Blenheim Road*

My dear Miss Tynan, I think I must have sent a letter about Father Fitzpatrick and other matters to O'Leary by mistake instead of you, as he writes to say Father Fitzpatrick was not one of the names he got me, and as you have not written. The letter also enclosed a note to Prof. Joyce. I have asked O'Leary did I send it to him. Only thus can I explain his allusion to Father Fitzpatrick.—Father Fitzpatrick has gone to the Orange States for his health and Kegan Paul asks me should they cancel the order or send the book to the Orange States. Which do you think?

William Morris is greatly pleased with *Oisin* and is going to review it for *Commonweal*. I met him yesterday in Holborn and he walked some way with me and talked of it. Rhys promises a review, also an article entitled 'New Celtic Poetry' thereon. I do not see why, when he does it, he should not say a good word for the rest. So could you get me a copy of ballad book? I have not one—gave only copy to Sigersons for some problematical French journalist. Rhys is an ardent Welshman and might be persuaded to consider us all as a school of 'New Celtic' poets. Especially as his mind runs in the direction of schools. The book would have to be got at once, I think. I wonder how ballad book has sold.

Would you ask Collis to review my poems off his own copy for *Express* and whatever other paper he writes for? Unless someone else offers. I have not given names of *Express* and *Irish Times* to Kegan Paul, as you suggested Collis. Did I tell you that Todhunter has done me for *Academy*?

Not a soul have I yet heard from about the book. Even you have only written—and that an age since—when all was in proof about first two parts of 'Oisin.' Rolleston sent merely a short note to say he would review in *Pilot* and that he could have spared some of 'Oisin' for the sake of 'Island of Statues.' I was getting quite out of conceit with 'Oisin' until I met Morris.

Fairy book is reviewed in February *Woman's World* by Oscar Wilde, who promises to try and get reviewing of poems for *Pall Mall*.[1]

---

[1] Wilde's review of *Fairy and Folk Tales* appeared in *Woman's World*, February 1889. He reviewed *The Wanderings of Oisin* twice: in *Woman's World*, March 1889, and in the *Pall Mall Gazette*, July 12, 1889. All these were reprinted in *Reviews*, 1908, a volume of his Collected Works.

I have not yet seen *Woman's World*. The fairy book has been a great success Rhys tells me. Yours always,   W B YEATS

TO AN UNNAMED CORRESPONDENT

Jan 30 [1889]   *3 Blenheim Road*

Dear Sir, I have long had it on my mind to answer your note. Please excuse delay. Your liking for 'Time and Vivien' pleases me, the substance of it was written before anything else in book, and like most things old has pleasant associations gathered about it. 'Oisin' seems to divide my readers more than anything else. Prof Dowden likes it best, so does William Morris (who intends some sort of review I believe), the rest for the most part do not take to it, finding it I imagine uncouth. No reviews that matter as yet, review copies being but just gone out. Two friendly ones that do not matter there have been—one likes 'Oisin' best, other does not. Yours very truly
                                                              W B YEATS

TO MISS L. WHITE[1]

Jan 30 [*Postmark Jan* 31, 1889]   *3 Blenheim Road*

Dear Miss White, I have in the first place to apologize for slight damage to your MS. My study window was open and the wind blew your MS into the fender where a red hot coal somewhat charred one corner.

The poems seem to me musical and pleasant. There are some really poetic phrases such as 'breathing light' in the blank verse lines, and what the 'Merrow' says about 'The landfields, dark and still,' and that other line about the sea lying dim ('dim' and 'hill', by the way, are too nearly rhymes without being so, to come so close together as they do in this verse). I very much like the verse on the trees that saw naught beyond autumn 'and breathed half timidly soft love songs through their crimson-stained leaves.' It is the most poetic of

[1] Miss Elizabeth White (known as Lily) was a sister of Professor H. O. White of Trinity College, Dublin. She died young. References to her poems appear in the letters to Father Russell and Katharine Tynan which follow.

your details perhaps, but I like the 'Merrow's Lament' best as a whole. Blank verse is the most difficult of all measures to write well. A blank verse line should always end with a slight pause in the sound. Words like 'for' at the end of the eighth line of 'A Mother's Dream' and 'who' at the end of second line on the next page are not good final words. Such words have no natural pause after them. They belong really to the next line. There are not however more than two or three such lines in the poem.

You should send these poems to the *Irish Monthly*, the editor is the Rev Matthew Russell, St. Francis Xavier's, Upper Gardener Street, Dublin. The *Monthly* is the only literary magazine in Ireland and there is quite a bevy of poets gathered about it. The editor is a Catholic priest of a most courteous kindly and liberal mind. I should think 'Slumber Song' would suit him admirably and also the 'Merrow's Lament' if he has not lately risen in arms against the fairies. I always have suspected him of thinking them unchristian creatures. He has himself published some little books of verse. Of course the *Monthly* does not pay for its verse. How few magazines do. But if you send these you will be in good company—all Irish writers of poetry, no matter of what persuasion, sooner or later seem to find their way thither.

You will find it a good thing to make verses on Irish legends and places and so forth. It helps originality and makes one's verses sincere, and gives one less numerous competitors. Besides one should love best what is nearest and most interwoven with one's life. Yours very truly   W B YEATS

P.S. I see that your letter dates from near Banbridge. My grandfather was rector there years ago.

[*on envelope*] My grandfather was rector of *Tullylish* near Banbridge. W B Y

TO FATHER MATTHEW RUSSELL

Jan 31 [1889]   3 *Blenheim Road*

My dear Father Russell, A great many thanks for your kind review of poems. Curious[ly] enough for a long time I got no criticisms at all on book and then on the same day came the first reviews, *Irish*

Monthly, *Manchester Guardian*, *Manchester Chronicle* and letters from Dowden and yourself.

Manchester Guardian very favourable, likewise *Manchester Chronicle* though this last too short for any purpose. Dr. Todhunter has written review in *Academy*. It has not yet appeared. I was greatly pleased with Montague Griffin's criticism. Dr. Todhunter praised it much, thought it the most thoughtful yet. I do not expect any very immediate popularity for any of my poems. They are too remote from common life. 'Oisin' is more liked than I expected. Dowden thinks it, as do I, the best poem in book by a great deal, but I expect people generally will think it a little mad. By the way I got a lot of verses from a stranger, sent me for an opinion the other day, a Miss L. White who lives in Co. Down. The verses were somewhat artless but musical and sincere and having often really pretty phrases. She asked me could I tell her of any paper or magazine to send them to. I recommended yours. So I dare say you will hear from her. I dare say you will not thank me for sending another writer of verse to knock at your gate. But then, you know, you keep a kind of college of the bards. By the by I found a wonderful account of the old bardic colleges in a life of Clanricarde published in 1722, how the building was commonly in a garden remote from the world and without windows, and how the bardic pupils composed, on set themes, in perfect darkness that nothing might distract their minds.

Have you given me the whole of Father Dillon's address? I[t] seemed meagre for so great a distance. Yours very sincerely

W B YEATS

TO KATHARINE TYNAN

Jan 31 [1889]　　　　　　　　　　　*3 Blenheim Road*

Dear Miss Tynan, I got the first criticisms of my book all on the same day. On Tuesday came Dowden's letter, Father Russell's, quoting a capital criticism of Montague Griffin's, the *Manchester Guardian's* and *Manchester Chronicle's* notices, and also, I forgot to say, the *Irish Monthly* notice enclosed in Father Russell's letter. So far all favourable. *Guardian* finds me rough but praiseworthy and likes me better than any other writer on Irish Myth, except Tennyson in 'Voyage of Maeldune,' but at the same time seems to know nothing of Irish writers on Irish myth, as Aubrey de Vere is taken as typical of the tribe. On the whole I should say *Guardian* does not like me much. *Chronicle* favourable but too short for any purpose. Dowden very favourable, likes '*Oisin*' very much the best; wants me to set to work on a poetic drama for Ellen Terry. I will enclose Father Russell's note for the sake of Griffin's criticism, if I can find it. Miss Gonne [1] (you have heard of her, no doubt) was here yesterday with introduction from the O'Learys; she says she cried over 'Island of Statues' fragment, but altogether favoured the Enchantress and hated Na[s]china. Did I tell you that William Morris likes the book greatly and intends, if he has time, to review me in the *Commonweal*. Such are all criticisms so far. Todhunter's article is not yet out. . . .

My ideas of a poem have greatly changed since I wrote the 'Island.' 'Oisin' is an incident or series of incidents; the 'Island of Statues' a region. There is a thicket between three roads, some distance from any of them, in the midst of Howth. I used to spend a great deal of time in that small thicket when at Howth. The other day I turned up a poem in broken metre, written long ago about it. The thicket gave me my first thought of what a long poem should be. I thought of it as a region into which one should wander from the cares of life. The characters were to be no more real than the shadows that people the Howth thicket. Their mission was to lessen the solitude without destroying its peace.

The other day Edwin Ellis read me an Arcadian play he has written. In it everything is careworn, made sick by weariness. I told him it was the Garden of Eden, but the Garden when Adam and Eve have been permitted to return to it in their old age. 'Yes,' he said, 'and they have found the serpent there grown old too and regretting their absence and nibbling their initials on a tree,' which was quaint. He is the most enthusiastic reader of my poems and takes greatly to 'Oisin.' I wish you could see some of his own

[1] This was Yeats's first meeting with Maud Gonne. In her diary Elizabeth Yeats, his younger sister, wrote: 'Jan 30. Miss Gonne, the Dublin beauty (who is marching on to glory over the hearts of the Dublin youths), called today on Willie, of course, but also apparently on Papa . . . Jan 31. Willie dined at Miss Gonne's tonight.' It was with an introduction from John O'Leary that Maud Gonne called at the house in Bedford Park, and it was, it seems, O'Leary who had first inspired her with Nationalist enthusiasm.

poems; his Arcadian play contains this beautiful line describing the heroine—

'Seven silences like candles round her face,'

meaning she was so calm and stately and awe-inspiring. But on the whole his verses lack emotional weight. Still he will have, I believe, a small niche some day.

I got, did I tell you, a bundle of verses for an opinion on them from a stranger the other day. Some lady in Co. Down. I spent a long time trying to say something pleasant about them without saying too much. They were not very good, though sincere and musical. You I suppose often get such letters. It was my first. How this letter rambles on in a rudderless way. In the old letter I mentioned of yours there is a little poem. I forgot, I think, to tell you at the time that it is very pretty. I envy your power of writing stray snatches of verse. I cannot do it at all. With me everything is premeditated for a long time. When I am away in the country and easy in my mind I have much inspiration of the moment—never here. I have written no verse for a long time.

In the same old letter I see you ask about my mother. She is as usual, that is to say feeble and unable to go out of doors or move about much. Our little black cat, Daniel O'Connell, ate some mice that had been poisoned and he died last Sunday.

On second thoughts I enclose Dowden's letter and the *Manchester Guardian* review. Ellis says my poems are not rough but the style is one people will have to get used to. Montague Griffin says much the same and contrasts with Irving's acting. Please return D's letter and review. Yours always,   W B YEATS

In *Woman's World* for Feb. is long and friendly notice of Fairy book.

TO JOHN O'LEARY [1]

Feb 1 [1889]   3 *Blenheim Road*

Dear Mr. O'Leary, Kegan Paul writes to me that the copies for J. R. Eyre and J. A. Fox were wrongly addressed—I dare say some one at the Contemporary will trace where Eyre is. Did I get Fox's name from you? I do not know him, I think. If I did not get his

[1] From a copy thought to have been made by D. J. O'Donoghue.

name from you, I must, I suppose, hunt round until I find out where I got it. I will ask Miss Tynan this post.

Miss Gonne came to see us the day before yesterday. I dined with her and her sister and cousin last night. She is not only very handsome but very clever. Though her politics in European matters be a little sensational—she was fully persuaded that Bismarck had poisoned or got murdered the Austrian King or prince or what was it? who died the other day. It was pleasant, however, to hear her attacking a young military man from India who was there, on English rule in India.. She is very Irish, a kind of 'Diana of the Crossways.' Her pet monkey was making, much of the time, little melancholy cries on the hearthrug—the monkeys are degenerate men, not man's ancestors, hence their sadness and look of boredom and old age— there were also two young pigeons in a cage, whom I mistook for sparrows—it was you, was it not, who converted Miss Gonne to her Irish opinions? She herself will make many converts.

Dowden wrote me about my book the other day and urged me to write a poetic drama with a view to the stage. I have long been intending to write one founded on the tale of 'Countess Kathleen O'Shea' in the folk lore book. I will probably begin one of these days. No review except *Manchester Guardian* and *Irish Monthly* thus far. Both good. *Monthly* of course so. William Morris will I hope review in *Commonweal*.

I hope Miss O'Leary and yourself are keeping well. I enclose a receipt for your £2.10.0 sent me this morning by Kegan Paul. I explained to them the mistake about the 20/- and the 10/- as far as I knew it. Yours always sincerely W B YEATS

TO JOHN O'LEARY

Feb 3 [1889] *3 Blenheim Road*

My dear Mr. O'Leary, 'Tincture' and 'Cincture' are used by me quite correctly.[1] See Webster's Dictionary, it says tincture primarily is 'a

[1] O'Leary seems to have been critical of this couplet which appeared in the first published version of *The Wanderings of Oisin*:
> Her hair was of a citron tincture
> And gathered in a silver cincture.

In spite of his defence Yeats removed the lines in later versions, and replaced them by the single line
> A citron colour gloomed in her hair.

tinge or shade of colour; as a *tincture* of red' and cincture is 'that which encompasses or encloses.' The *Freeman* reviewer is wrong about peahens, they dance throughout the whole of Indian poetry. If I had *Kalidasa* by me I could find many such dancings. As to the poultry yards, with them I have no concern. The wild peahen dances or all Indian poets lie.

About the cheques! The only one that now perplexes me is one for 10/– paid about a month after the first. It is credited to you in Kegan Paul's book. I have no remembrance of any sum of 10/–.

I am very sorry to have given so much trouble. The mistake about Dr. Fitzgerald's cheque was wholly my fault.

About the American papers! Your letter from Tipperary I received all right of course and acted on it and sent also to all American papers mentioned in the list you sent Dr. Todhunter, so you need not trouble about them any more. I do not remember the letter 'a couple of months since,' about American papers, though I do remember one about that date, which you very kindly sent me, on the subject of Irish provincial papers for Walter Scott to advertise the folklore book in. I am very sorry indeed for giving you all this trouble.

That *Freeman* review will do no harm. It is the kind of criticism every new poetic style has received for the last hundred years. If my style is new it will get plenty more such for many a long day. Even Tennyson was charged with obscurity, and as to charges of word torturing etc, the first thing one notices in a new country is its outlandishness, after a time its dress and custom seem as natural as any others. I sent no copy to *Irish Times* or *Mail* as I wait to see if anyone, Collis or another, will come forward. I asked Miss Tynan to hunt up Collis (she suggested him for *Irish Times* and *Mail*). I am very sorry indeed to have given you so much trouble. Yours always sincerely   W B YEATS

TO ELLEN O'LEARY

Feb 3rd [1889]   *3 Blenheim Road*

My dear Miss O'Leary, You will see by my letter to Mr. O'Leary that I still hold to 'cincture' and 'tincture' and have enrolled Webster on my side. Words are always getting conventionalized to some secondary meaning. It is one of the works of poetry to take the truants in custody and bring them back to their right senses. Poets are the policemen of language; they are always arresting those old reprobates the words. 'Tincture' is such an old fellow he ought to know better than to have hidden in a medicine bottle for so long.

You ask me what is the meaning of 'She who dwelt among the Sycamores.' She is the spirit of quiet. The poem means that those who in youth and childhood wander alone in woods and in wild places, ever after carry in their hearts a secret well of quietness and that they always long for rest and to get away from the noise and rumour of the world.

Here is a little poem written last night with something of the same feeling. It is not very good but then you know the youngest is always the best loved—hence I quote it:

> Come and dream of kings and kingdoms,
> Cooking chestnuts on the bars;
> Round us the white roads are endless,
> Mournful under mournful stars.
>
> Whisper or we too may sadden—
> Round us herds of shadows steal;
> Care not if beyond the shadows
> Passes Fortune's flying wheel.
>
> Kingdoms falling, kingdoms rising,
> Bowing servants, pluméd wars,
> Weigh them in an hour of dreaming,
> Cooking chestnuts on the bars.[1]

Did I tell you how much I admire Miss Gonne? She will make many converts to her political belief. If she said the world was flat or the moon an old caubeen [2] tossed up into the sky I would be proud to be of her party.

I am very sorry to hear how ill you have been lately. You need not trouble to answer this. I will write shortly at greater length. Yours always

W B YEATS

[1] This poem was published, with some revision, under the title 'In the Firelight' in the *Leisure Hour*, February 1891, but was never reprinted by Yeats.
[2] The Oxford English Dictionary defines 'caubeen' as 'an Irish hat.'

TO KATHARINE TYNAN

Feb. 6th [1889]   *3 Blenheim Road*

Dear Miss Tynan, I have just heard from Kegan Paul. The copy was sent some little while since to *United Ireland*. Would you ask them again? A great many thanks for your good offices in that direction. I have both written and sent a copy to Miss Whiting. The *Freeman* review of my book must have been done by some person of old-fashioned tastes. He seemed to have suspected me of Aestheticism. Peahens do dance. At least they dance throughout the whole of Indian poetry. The reviewer was evidently friendly but disgusted. 'Oisin' will rouse much opposition because it has more imaginative energy than any other poem in the book. To many people nothing seems sincere but the commonplace. The *Monthly* speaks of another review of *Oisin*. I hope Father Russell will have one—'Oisin' needs an interpreter. There are three incompatible things which man is always seeking—infinite feeling, infinite battle, infinite repose—hence the three islands. If I can sell the 200 copies or so that remain of my book in anything like decent time, I shall care little about reviewers' likings or dislikings. I would then have made things simple for my second book.

Griffin writes me that his father, who knows well the old legends, says my 'Oisin' gave him a better idea of the mingled nobility and savagery of the ancient heroes than MacPherson's 'Ossian.' Yours alway,   W B YEATS

Almost every poem in book has been liked better than the rest by somebody—a good sign. . . .

TO GEORGE RUSSELL (AE)

Feb 8th [1889]   *3 Blenheim Road*

My dear Russell, I got the paper you sent me with the *Oisin* review. Very many thanks. Do you know who wrote it? . . .

Write and tell me what you like best and what worst, and what the other students who got copies think. The people of my own age are in the long run the most important. They are the future. I am starting a new drama founded on an Irish folk-tale. The best plot I ever worked on. So much about myself. What are you doing? You have not written lately. Where is Hughes? Is he your companion in that projected American trip? Is it still projected? I have heard many regret your coming departure and one names Hughes as your probable fellow traveller. Are any dates or other matters decided on?

I am sorry that the whole of 'The Island of Statues' is not in my book. It would have increased the book in size too much. It will be printed later on in some future volume.¹

Do you see Miss Tynan often? She has several times mentioned your name. Yours very sincerely   W B YEATS

TO KATHARINE TYNAN

Feb. [after 21st, 1889]   *3 Blenheim Road*

Dear Miss Tynan, I enclose another letter to Prof. Joyce. I sent his letter to me to Henley so have not got his address. Forgive my bothering you. It is another question about a song.

Enclosed are two reviews of no particular interest but please return them with the others some day, in case I want to advertize at any time they would be needful. The *St. James's Budget* one is good, considering source. Todhunter's *Academy* notice has not yet appeared, though it has been some time in print. The book is having some sale, how much I do not know,—little, I expect.

You will be surprised to hear what I am at besides the new play; a commentary on the mystical writing of Blake. A friend is helping me or perhaps I should say I am helping him as he knows Blake much better than I do, or anyone else perhaps. It should draw notice—be a sort of red flag above the waters of oblivion—for there is no clue printed anywhere to the mysterious 'Prophetic Books'— Swinburne and Gilchrist found them unintelligible.

Poor Pigott! ² One really got to like him, there was something so

---

¹ The whole of 'The Island of Statues' was never included in a future volume, and the scene printed in *The Wanderings of Oisin* was not again reprinted. For the whole poem it is still necessary to consult the *Dublin University Review*, April to July 1885.

² In 1887 *The Times* published a series of articles 'Parnellism and Crime,' and on April 18 printed a facsimile letter, purporting to bear Parnell's signature, condoning the Phoenix Park murders of 1882. The publication caused con-

frank about his lies. They were so completely matters of business, not of malice. There was something pathetic too in the hopeless way the squalid latter-day Erinyes ran him down. The poor domestic-minded swindler!

Write, you have been silent a long time—your last letter was on the 26th of January. Yours always, W B YEATS

P.S. Henley liked my article and asks for others. O'Donoghue (a little clerk of much literary ardour) is to read a paper on *Oisin* at the Southwark Literary Club. That wretched not ill-meant *Freeman* notice is only unfavourable review yet. On 15th *Lucifer* will have very favourable review from Dr. Carter Blake. It will be thoughtful certainly, old-fashioned probably, eccentric perhaps.

TO KATHARINE TYNAN

[End of] Feb.–March 8 [1889]   3 *Blenheim Road*

My dear Miss Tynan, I got the first substantial gain from my book yesterday. The editor of *Leisure Hour* sent five pounds as an instalment for an article of mine which he has been trying to make his mind up about for a year, at the same time writing to me about *Oisin*, 'every line, almost every word is alive.'

I do not believe he would ever have taken the article but for *Oisin*. I got my proof-sheets of an article on the difference between Scotch and Irish Fairies from Henley's new paper, the *Scots Observer*, the day before yesterday. I am to do other papers on same subject for him. I also have two articles with editor of *Providence Journal*. So you see I am doing better than usual and feeling sounder financially. That miserable *Nation* however has never acknowledged an article—almost the best I have done—on Todhunter's book.

---

sternation in the Liberal Party and was thought to have damaged the cause of Home Rule irretrievably. In the House of Commons Parnell denied all knowledge of the letter and declared the signature a forgery. In 1888 a Special Commission of three judges was appointed to investigate the charges made in *The Times*. Richard Pigott, a journalist of dubious reputation, who had forged this and other letters, had sold them, through an intermediary, to *The Times*. Called as a witness before the Commission, he broke down under cross-examination by Sir Charles Russell, Parnell's counsel, and the next day fled the country. A warrant was issued for his arrest on a charge of perjury, but when the police tracked him to a hotel in Madrid he committed suicide.

What I want to tell you about is my new poem. A Drama founded on the Countess Kathleen O'Shea in Folklore book. (Did you see the long and naively scientific review of Fairy Book in *Athenaeum*? Oscar Wilde says I should have replied. But I was too lazy—there was 3¼ columns—delighted Rhys by being so much longer and more serious than Camelots get mostly.) This new poem of mine promises to be my most interesting poem and in all ways quite dramatic, I think. I shall try and get it acted by amateurs (if possible in Dublin) and afterwards try it perhaps on some stage manager or actor. It is in five scenes and full of action and very Irish.

Did you read that delightful saint story in *Irish Monthly* called the 'Rapt Culdee'?—if not do, and write a poem about it.[1] He lived in your own neighbourhood at Tallaght. A great many poems should be written on him. I may do a drama about him some day. Do not forget him. He is charming.

All this note is without news or thought but I have to get in to British Museum.

I write mainly to persuade you to write to me. Do you know, wretch, that your letters grow few and fewer or else I think they do. Yours always,   W B YEATS

Cannot find *Evening Mail*, will send it again.

I read your poem on the wood-carver in an old *Hobby Horse* and think it most beautiful—have things to say about it but no time now.

P.S. I wrote enclosed letter four days ago and forgot to post it. What I wished to say about your *Hobby Horse* poem is that it is one of your very best. Your great gift of colour never in this poem overloads and smothers the feeling. Everything is harmonious and tender. It is full too of beautiful single lines. But it seemed to me the moment I read it that it had been better perhaps without the last two verses. I read it to my father without comment; he made the same criticism. It is not that the idea of these two verses is not pleasant. To me it is an especially pleasant one, but without them I think there had been more unity and a better climax. Neither are the two verses so condensed and magical in expression as the others.

I brought your book to Rhys the other day that he might include

---

[1] 'The Rapt Culdee' was a story of St. Aengus. Katharine Tynan wrote a poem called 'The Hiding-away of Blessed Aengus.'

you in his article on New Celtic poetry. He is anxious for the Ballad Book. Did you tell Gill to send one?

Lolly is doing embroidery now as well as Lilly. She works at home in spare moments. She cannot go with Lilly because of the housekeeping which is all on her hands, as my mother has a long time been unable for it.

My father has done a large portrait of Lilly that he probably will send to the Academy.

We have seen Legge once or twice. One evening he and Crook were here. Last night I met him at Horne's (*Hobby Horse* Horne). He had been in the Commission Court when Pigott's escape was announced, and describes it as a great scene. Poor Pigott!

Do not forget to consider the 'Rapt Culdee.' You could make a poem out of him quite as charming as your St. Francis poems. Indeed, considering that he lived so near you, a poem upon him is clearly your duty.

Where is that story of the Lord of Kinsale to be found?

The Pigott affair must have been a blow to our Dublin Unionist friends. I wish I were back amongst them to see what change is in their opinions or what loophole they have found—

But here I am stranded for I know not how long, in the London desert. As soon as ever I find my work beginning to sell somewhat, I shall be away out of this, to where there is something of green to look at. Yours always, W B YEATS

Did I tell you I dined at the National Liberal Club with T. P. Gill, M.P.? Coffey introduced me. I like him greatly.

I found this P.S. and letter stamped and addressed (and unposted) in my pocket today (March 8th).

TO KATHARINE TYNAN

March 9th [1889]   *3 Blenheim Road*

Dear Miss Tynan, You know how to praise. What a good untiring friend you are! I got the article today and write at once to thank you. It is a most generous article. By the same post came the *Scots Observer* with a splendid article by Henley headed 'A New Irish Poet.'

Strange that the best articles yet should come by the same post. Henley after 'Oisin' praises 'King Goll,' 'Song of the last Arcadian' and 'Old Fisherman' and 'Island of Statues.' 'Last Arcadian' is, he says, more subtle than any other poem in book. 'Kanva on God' he also praises. He is most enthusiastic throughout. I have just heard by this post that there is a capital review in *Saturday* of this week, but have not seen it, of course. I will send you *Scots Observer* shortly.

What a jumble of letters I sent you yesterday. I was taking the letter to the post when I found in my pocket a letter stamped and all, which I thought had gone to you long ago. I opened the letter I had just written and added the other without having time even to read it. I fear the two letters between them contain too much mere personal news, the fortunes of articles, the book, etc. But then you know I have little more to write about, especially when as at present I am deep in lengthy MSS.—the portcullis is down. I am looking for dramatic thoughts. I do not know what is going on in the house, and what is the good of writing gossip of the people one meets one moment and forgets the next?

Hey ho, I wish I was out of London in order that I might see the world. Here one gets into one's minority among the people who are like one's self—mystical literary folk, and such like. Down at Sligo one sees the whole world in a day's walk, every man is a class. It is too small there for minorities. All this bloodless philosophical chatter is poor substitute for news, but then I have none. 'You must not go to the pear-trees for apples,' as our Allingham said, or me for news. Again a great many thank-yous for your generous article. Yours always, W B YEATS

TO KATHARINE TYNAN

March 21 [1889]   3 *Blenheim Road*

Dear Miss Tynan, I send you the *Saturday* and *Scots Observer* reviews, also the numbers of the *Hobby Horse* you asked for. I wonder would Father Russell draw attention to *Saturday* notice in *Monthly*. I believe that notice will help me a great deal.

Who told you that I am 'taken up with Miss Gonne'? I think she is very good-looking and that is all I think about her. What you say of her fondness for sensation is probably true. I sympathise with her love of the national idea rather than any secondary land movement, but care not much for the kind of Red Indian feathers in which she has trapped out that idea. We had some talk as to the possibility of getting my 'Countess O'Shea' acted by amateurs in Dublin and she felt inclined to help, indeed suggested the attempt herself if I remember rightly. I hardly expect it will ever get outside the world of plans. As for the rest, she had a borrowed interest, reminding me of Laura Armstrong without Laura's wild dash of half-insane genius. Laura is to me always a pleasant memory. She woke me from the metallic sleep of science and set me writing my first play.[1]

Do not mistake me, she is only as a myth and a symbol. Will you forgive me for having talked of her? She interests me far more than

---

[1] Laura Armstrong was a very distant cousin of Yeats's (through the Corbet family) and was one of his early loves. He first saw her driving in a dog-cart at Howth, her lovely red hair blowing in the wind. One single letter of hers to Yeats has been preserved:

10.8.84.
60 *Stephen's Green*
Dublin.

My dear Clarin, What can I say to you for having been so rude to you—in not being at home when you called and I had asked you? I am really very sorry about it. I hope you will forgive me. It so happened that I was positively obliged to go out at the hour I had appointed for you to come but it was only to a house quite close here—and I had told our maid to send me over word when you *came*—she did so (but I find since it was just before you *went*!) and I was rising to leave the room—I looked out of the window and to my great disappointment saw my Clarin leaving No. 60. It was too bad—and I am indeed sorry I missed you.—I like your poems more than I can say—but I should like to hear you read them. I have not nearly finished them. Could you come some afternoon—and read a little to me—I shall be in all Tuesday afternoon. *I promise!* so can you come? I should have written to you sooner but I have been away from home. Pray excuse my silence. Trusting to see 'the poet'—! and with kind regards. Believe me Ever yours 'Vivien.'

An unpublished lyric of this period was almost certainly written with Laura Armstrong in mind:

> A double moon or more ago
>   I writ you a long letter, lady,
>   It went astray or vexed you, maybe,
> And I would know now yes or no.
>
> Then dying summer on his throne
>   Faded in hushed and quiet singing;
>   Now winter's arrow's winging, winging,
> And autumn's yellow leaves are flown.
>
> Ah we poor poets in our pride
>   Tread the bare song road all our summer,

Miss Gonne does and yet is only as a myth and a symbol. I heard from her about two years ago and am trying to find out where she is now in order to send her *Oisin*. 'Time and the Witch Vivien' was written for her to act. The 'Island of Statues' was begun with the same notion, though it soon grew beyond the scope of drawing-room acting. The part of the enchantress in both poems was written for her. She used to sign her letters Vivien.

What a neat letter you write and what a ragged affair is this of mine.

Do you ever see Lippman [1] now? Do any of the old set speak to him, Mrs. Coffey, etc? I saw his book for sale the other day—a new edition apparently.

Did you ask Gill to send me a copy of the ballad book for Rhys? I am afraid of his doing the article without it. I gave him your book. He has written something on my book which I have not seen.

Lolly is teaching at a Kindergarten School in Bedford Park but will get no payment for a year, which seems hard—however she is learning the system, which is something. She has not been well lately but seems better now. Lilly enjoys the embroidering much. These last few days she has had the teaching of two new assistants of Miss Morris's. Miss Morris was not there yesterday (they have moved to a house a little way from the Morris's) as Sparling is ill, somewhat seriously I am afraid. At present I know no more than the fact of his illness.

I notice by your letter that you see Russell now and then. Tell him to write to me. Tell him myself and a friend are writing a book on Blake and perhaps he will send me a letter with some Blake criticisms.

    To wake on lips of some newcomer
    'A poor man lived here once and died.'

    How could we trudge on mile by mile
      If from red lips like quicken berry,
      At some odd times to make us merry,
    Came nowise half of half a smile?

    And surely therefore would I know
      What manner fared my letter, lady,
      It went astray or vexed you, maybe,
    A double moon or more ago.

[1] Lippman, a Russian and possibly a refugee nihilist, frequented the Morris circle for a time. He borrowed money and went to America where he posed as a Count Zubof. On the verge of marriage to a millionairess, he was exposed and committed suicide.

Do you ever see Allen? *Lucifer* folk sent him my fairy tale book for review and he makes no sign. Finds I suppose unpaid *Lucifer* articles thankless jobs.

What have [you] written lately? What poetry? What prose? I always like details on these matters.

You have never sent me the *Nation* article on yourself you promised.

I must wind up this letter presently and get to work on the 'Countess O'Shea' that my mind may be full of it when I go for my walk an hour hence. It is a wild windy night, the sky full of ravelled clouds and [?] greeny blue—the sort of night that stimulates thought and I must out. Yours always, W B YEATS

Do not forget to send me all news of your prose and poetry.

Saturday.

P.S. [1] I got your note just now. Will send on 9/1, if possible, next week. 275 was a very fair sale considering all things. Has the sale ceased and if so how many of the remaining copies are bound? Dr. Todhunter agrees with me that as soon as the sale of the 1/6 copies *is at an end*, the rest should be bound in some cheap way (brown paper he suggests as cheap and curious) and sold for a few pence each. I suggested 6d., he says that is too much and that 3d. would be enough. In this way the book would get distributed. Of course it would not be well to do so until the 1/6 sale ends certainly. What do you think of this scheme? We would reach a class quite out of reach of the 1/6 book and might sell among the ballad books in small country towns. The brown paper covers might be labelled 'Second Edition' (I suppose it would be fairly enough second edition) or 'Cheap Edition.' A few 1/6 copies should be kept—as many as are now bound. This would be better than letting the books go to loss. You will remember that at the very beginning I proposed this cheap edition. I do not think any copies bound as at present should be cheapened.

I do not send *Saturday* notice of *Oisin* as you have seen it—but enclose *Scots Observer* one. *Atalanta* promises review in May number. No American reviews as yet. I have stuck all yet received into a book

---

[1] The postscript refers to the first issue of *Poems and Ballads of Young Ireland* in 1888. A re-issue in paper covers, using the unsold sheets, appeared in 1890, price 6d.; and there was a further re-issue in 1903.

which I will let you see when they wind up, 22 thus far. Mostly all praise my dramatic sketches most after 'Oisin.' 'Time and Vivien' seems liked.

I am delighted to hear about the 'Culdee.' How do you treat it? Will you bring in local scenery? I hope you will do that. It would be a fine thing to write a poem that always would be connected with Tallaght in people's minds. All poetry should have a local habitation when at all possible. Some day we shall have to publish another ballad book containing the best of our national and local songs and ballads. By 'our' I mean yours and mine. You were not quite at your best in *Ballads of Young Ireland*, 1888—at least not always at your best. Though York Powell greatly likes your 'Michael Dwyer.' Did I ever tell you that?

Have heard from Father Russell he will quote *Saturday* notice—would you kindly let him see *Scots Observer* one.

[*On envelope*] I see in Father Russell's letter about Miss Wynne's good fortune. How did Andrew Lang come across her poems? This letter has been unposted some days (March 25th).

Would you kindly let Miss O'Leary see *Scots Observer* notice, she would perhaps send it on to Father Russell. In a letter just arrived she asks to see it (March 26th).

TO KATHARINE TYNAN

April 10 [1889]   *3 Blenheim Road*

Dear Miss Tynan, Lolly has gone to Dublin to stay with the Wellington Road people. She started this morning. I gave her a book of Montague Griffin's to give you for him. She has not been very well; combined housekeeping and kindergarten anxieties have been too much for her, perhaps.

I enclose Dr. Todhunter's *Academy* review, which please return as I have no other copy.

I cannot just now send you the money for Gill. I thought to send it last week but the money I was expecting—£3.10. from *Scots Observer*—was all absorbed by pressing house expenses. Which I fear will be the same with a small amount I expect tomorrow from *Leisure Hour*. However, I will have it soon. I must break off this letter—only written to tell you about Lolly—very presently, to write an article on Village Ghosts for *Scots Observer* that will bring in a couple of pounds. I have also some notes to do for *Manchester Courier*. A man came yesterday morning and asked me to do literary gossip for it, so please send me any news about literary persons and books you may hear and that is fresh. Any Dublin doings of the kind you may know of. What books is Miss Mulholland busy about and what do you yourself intend? I can trumpet such things now and then perhaps.

Walter Paget and my Father are using me as a model and are doing two portraits in competition against each other—Paget is Cassell's chief illustrator. So far my father's portrait is beyond all comparison the best.[1] Yours always W B YEATS

I enclose a letter from Nettleship which please keep safe, as I value it much.

TO KATHARINE TYNAN

April 21 [1889] *3 Blenheim Road*

Dear Miss Tynan, Have you any novels of Carleton's besides the short stories? I have them but am trying to borrow somewhere one or two of his longer tales such as *Willy Reilly* or *Valentine McClutchy* or, indeed, any of them. The *Scots Observer* people have asked me to write an article on him apropos of the *Red Haired Man's Wife*, the posthumous tale of his discovered somewhere and printed the other day by Sealy, Bryers & Walker. Could you beg borrow or steal any Carletons for me? I am afraid I shall have to buy them if you have none, and my finances are low these times. Tract Society are full up with drawings and, as a result, my father has sold but little lately. Accordingly the family 'swalley hole,' to use a Sligo term, is unusually greedy. I have been doing rather well fortunately.

[1] It is not known if the portrait by J. B. Yeats still exists. If it does, it would show the young bearded Yeats. A portrait by Walter Paget's brother, H. M. Paget, the brother-in-law of Florence Farr, is in the Belfast Municipal Art Gallery; it is dated April 6th 1889 and depicts Yeats wearing a small chin beard. It is reproduced as frontispiece to *Letters to the New Island*. It is probable that Yeats confused the brothers' names and wrote 'Walter' for 'Henry.' H. M. Paget lived for a time in Bedford Park and often invited J. B. Yeats to share his studio and his models for the pleasure of his conversation.

I told you about the man who came and asked me to do literary notes for the *Manchester Courier*. They give me very little trouble and are fairly profitable. I got £7 for an article in *Leisure Hour* and have had two in *Scots Observer* and I sent off another. The *Scots Observer* pays well, about £1 a column. These matters have made the *Countess* fare but badly. Fortunately my constitutional indolence brings my thoughts swinging perpetually back to it by their own weight. I am not half industrious enough to drive my thoughts. They go their own road and that is to imaginative work. I shall have a day at the *Countess* tomorrow. To me the dramatic is far the pleasantest poetic form. By the way, I have written two sets of verses to illustrations sent to me by the Tract Society. I quote one to show you how orthodox I can be—the illustration was a wretched thing of a girl in church—

>She prays for father, mother dear,
> To Him with thunder shod,
>She prays for every falling tear
> In the Holy Church of God.

(The spiritual church, of course)

>For all good men now fallen ill,
> For merry men that weep,
>For Holiest teachers of His will,
> And common men that sleep.

>The sunlight flickering on the pews,
> The sunlight in the air,
>The flies that dance in threes and twos,
> They seem to join her prayer.

>Her prayer for father, mother dear,
> To Him with thunder shod,
>A prayer for every falling tear
> In the Holy Church of God.[1]

You see how proud of myself I have been for being so businesslike. I have been making amends to myself by doing little else than plant sunflowers and marigolds all afternoon.

[1] This poem was printed, under the title 'In Church,' with an illustration, in the *Girl's Own Paper*, June 8, 1889. The other poem mentioned, 'A Summer Evening,' was published in the same paper on July 6, 1889. Yeats never reprinted them.

I saw Coffey and Mrs. Coffey last week. I dined at Mrs. Lawrence's—that Miss Ramsey (now Mrs. Butler) who was senior wrangler the other year—the papers talked a lot about her—sat next. Do you know it is possible to be a senior wrangler and yet have only the most commonplace ideas?

What poor delusiveness is all this 'higher education of women.' Men have set up a great mill called examinations, to destroy the imagination. Why should women go through it, circumstance does not drive *them*? They come out with no repose, no peacefulness, their minds no longer quiet gardens full of secluded paths and umbrage-circled nooks, but loud as chaffering market places. Mrs. Todhunter is a great trouble mostly. She has been through the mill and has got the noisiest mind I know. She is always denying something. To return to Miss Ramsey (Mrs. Butler). She is about 23 and is married to a man of 60, he being the only senior wrangler attainable. He is Master of Trinity [1] and very chatty and pleasant and quite human. He seemed enormously interested in Mrs. Coffey's baby. Talked much too about Ireland.

Lady Wilde spoke the other day of some prose of yours (she said you sent it her I think). She said 'every sentence was so beautifully poised.' She thinks you should write a good deal of prose. I hope, rather, you are doing plenty of poetry. How goes the 'Rapt Culdee'? —though indeed it were a good thing if your prose stories do well. They help the imagination, I think. You have told me nothing lately about that story you had taken—Has it come out?

I know I gained greatly from my experiment in novel writing. The hero turned out a bad character and so I did not try to sell the story anywhere. I am in hopes he may reform.

You will have seen Lolly by this and heard all news.

There has been a great row in the Theosophical Society. Madame Blavatsky expelled Mrs. Cook (Miss Mabel Collins) [2] and the President of the Lodge for flirtation (Mrs. Cook has a husband living), and Mrs. Alicia Cremers, an American, for gossiping about it. As a result, Madame Blavatsky is in high spirits. The society is like the 'happy family' that used to be exhibited round Charing Cross Station

[1] Rev. H. Montague Butler (1833–1918), Headmaster of Harrow, 1859–1885, and Master of Trinity College, Cambridge, from 1886.
[2] Mabel Collins (Mrs. Keningale Cook) was the daughter of Mortimer Collins, a popular novelist and verse-writer. Besides her writings on theosophy Mabel Collins produced a number of novels.

—a cat in a cage full of canaries. The Russian cat is beginning to purr now and smoothen its fur again—the canary birds are less by three—the faithful will be more obedient than ever.

Jack has just arrived from his volunteering at Brighton. He has made many sketches—and gives an amusing account of everything. He enjoyed himself much. Your friend, W B YEATS

Do not be disgusted at these trite verses for the Tract Society. I shall never do any more, I think.

Have you heard anything of this new novel of Carleton's? Do you know if it has been touched up by anyone (as I rather fear from the preface)?

[*On envelope*] I have the *Traits and Stories of Irish Peasantry* of course.

TO JOHN O'LEARY

May 7 [1889] *3 Blenheim Road*

Dear Mr. O'Leary, I should have thanked you before for the Carletons, but the day I got them I started for Oxford and only returned the day before yesterday. Down there I had no time to write letters at all, what with copying out in the Bodleian all day and dining with dull college dons—friends of York Powell with whom I stopped, or regular dinners at Commons—in the evening. Met one or two people of interest, however—a student on the ground floor had got my book—he was of interest of course—they have it too in the Oxford Union.

I have started reading Carleton's *Miser*,[1] and will write to the Coffeys about what Carletons they have as soon as I hear of their return to Dublin. My father will ask the Butts[2] about him. They, or their father, knew him well, of course.

[1] Yeats was now busy reading for the volume *Stories from Carleton* which appeared in August 1889. The full title of the *Miser* is *Fardorougha the Miser; or, The Convicts of Lisnamona*; it was published in Dublin in 1839.

[2] Presumably the children of Isaac Butt, Q.C., a celebrated Irish advocate and the leader of the Irish Parliamentary party before Parnell. He had been a friend of Yeats's grandfather, the Rev. John Yeats, and would have helped J. B. Yeats in his legal career had he not abandoned the Bar to become an artist. In his *Early Memories* (1923) J. B. Yeats calls him 'that man of genius engulfed and lost in law and politics.' A portrait of him is reproduced in *Letters of J. B. Yeats*, London, 1944; New York, 1946.

I have been busy with Blake. You complain about the mysticism. It has enabled me to make out Blake's prophetic books at any rate. My book on him will I believe clear up that riddle for ever. No one will call him mad again. I have evidence, by the way, to show that he was of Irish extraction—his grandfather was an O'Neal who changed his name for political reasons. Ireland takes a most important place in his mystical system.

You need not be afraid of my going in for mesmerism. It interests me but slightly. No fear of Madame Blavatsky drawing me into such matters—she is very much against them and hates spiritualism vehemently—says mediumship and insanity are the same thing.

By the way there has been a stir lately among the faithful. Madame Blavatsky expelled Mrs. Cook (Mabel Collins) a most prominent theosophist writer and daughter of Mortimer Collins, and expelled also the president of the lodge for flirtation; and expelled an American lady for gossiping about them. Madame Blavatsky is in great spirits, she is purring and hiding her claws as though she never clawed anybody. She is always happy when she has found a Theosophist out and clawed him. She thinks she is the most long suffering person. One day she said 'Forty thousand theosophists are gushing away, I try to stop them, then they scratch.' According to her there are about half-a-dozen real theosophists in the world and one of these is stupid (Olcott, I imagine).[1] The rest she classifies under the head 'flap doodles.' Come to see her when you are in London. She is the most human person alive, is like an old peasant woman, and is wholly devoted, all her life is but sitting in a great chair with a pen in her hand. For years she has written twelve hours a day.

I have no theories about her. She is simply a note of interrogation. 'Olcott is much honester than I am,' she said to me one day, 'he explains things. I am an old Russian savage,' that is the deepest I ever got into her riddle.

I read a scene of my new play to an actress yesterday, she seemed to think it suitable in all ways for the stage. I think you will like it. It is in all things Celtic and Irish. The style is perfectly simple and I have taken great care with the construction, made two complete prose versions before writing a line of verse.

[1] Colonel Henry Steel Olcott (1832–1907) was born at Orange, N.J. He was a President Founder of the Theosophical Society, and an editor, after Madame Blavatsky, of the *Theosophist*. A notice of his life appears in the *Dictionary of American Biography*, Vol. XIV.

Miss O'Leary wished to keep the reviews of my book she had. I return those of which I have duplicates.

My father is delighted with Miss O'Leary's poem in the *Irish Monthly* and so am I.[1] It is most simple, delicate, and tender. I shall write to her very presently. I have to go out now—have been unwell these last two days (through want of exercise I suspect) but am nearly all right again now, still do not care to write much.

Forgive me all this chatter about Madame Blavatsky. Yours very sincerely
W B YEATS

I hope Miss O'Leary's health will feel the benefit of this good spring weather.

TO KATHARINE TYNAN

May 9th [1889]   *3 Blenheim Road*

Dear Miss Tynan, That you are coming to London is the best news I have heard this long time. I shall work hard at the *Countess* that it may be finished when you come. The Meynells are not so very far from us by good luck. An easy tram ride away. You will see Bedford Park at its best, all the trees and flowers in their full dress. There will be quite a number of people to bring you to see. Todhunter and York Powell, who both admire your work, are near at hand.

Jack and myself begin painting a design on my study ceiling today. We have had it long in our minds to do it. We have been putting it off. Now we set to work to have it done when you arrive.

I wrote last night to Henley and asked him to send me the *Scots Observer* with your poem when it comes out. I do not see the paper except when it contains some contribution of my own.

Lolly is home again of course and working very well. She tells me odd scraps of news about you all. Jack says she is on her good behaviour but that she will get 'a fling in her tail' soon.

About Carleton. John O'Leary has sent me some novels of his. I have not yet done much work on the subject, for I am only just

[1] Miss O'Leary's poem in the *Irish Monthly* of May 1889 was called 'My Own Galtees.' The Galtees are a range of hills in Co. Tipperary.

home from Oxford, in addition to which I have not been well the first days of this week but am all right again. Had a pleasant time at Oxford. Dined a good deal with the Fellows and did not enjoy that much but found the evening at York Powell's with an occasional friend of his very pleasant. I found a student there who had bought my book. They have got it at the Oxford Union. Your friend always,
                                                              W B YEATS

TO JOHN O'LEARY

July 10th [1889]   *3 Blenheim Road*

My dear Mr. O'Leary, I send herewith the catalogues—I papered them up for posting a week ago. Had a kind of notion I might get more. I have sent all from the shops I pass going to the Museum. I daresay however they will have new ones out by this—I will try anyway. I am very seldom in town these days however. I will be one day this week I think.

Miss O'Leary tells me that Carleton's best are *The Nolans* and *Father Connell*.[1] Do you know any one who could lend them me? If not perhaps you might chance on copies at some old book stall. I would send you the amount. I am also in need of a novel or two of Banim's—his best. Carleton I shall read all through probably, the others only in their best work. Yet I don't know that I shall read all Carleton, that depends on my getting or not getting books, and so forth. I must read one or two of his period of decadence however. My introduction, though mainly of course busy with Carleton, will touch on all the chief Irish novelists of peasant life I hope. Banim and Kickham in chief.

I am delighted to hear you will be in London soon. There are several people in Bedford Park anxious to meet you—notably York Powell the translator of sagas, historian.

[1] Either Miss O'Leary or more probably Yeats himself was mistaken in attributing *The Nolans* and *Father Connell* to William Carleton. They were written by the Banim brothers, Michael (1796–1874) and John (1798–1842). The brothers collaborated, but John was the more professional and prolific of the two. In *Representative Irish Tales* Yeats tentatively gives the authorship of *The Nolans* to John and of *Father Connell* to Michael, but each contributed chapters to the other's book. Yeats says 'The genius of John Banim was certainly the more vehement and passionate.'

Coffey's notice of my book was very good barring that he slighted my demon in the second part—a great favourite of mine. Miss Mulholland's notice in *Irish Monthly* also very good—I mean that I am pleased with her liking for the little Indian scene.

Miss Tynan was with us for a short time: she has got stouter and looks very well, looks indeed in every way better than when I saw her in Dublin.

After I have finished the Carleton book I may possibly, or probably rather, do a volume of old Celtic romances for the series—reprints of various translations. This will take me to Dublin I imagine.

I will write to Miss O'Leary soon again. Yours very sincerely

W B YEATS

TO FATHER MATTHEW RUSSELL

July 13 [1889]   *3 Blenheim Road*

My dear Father Russell, A very great many thanks for printing Miss Mulholland's very kind notice of my book. I left the copy of the *Monthly* with that little poem about my book at Oxford so did not know the name of the author, or I would have written to thank him.[1] If you happen to be writing to him at any time you might say I mentioned it to you. Quite apart from my natural liking for the subject I think it was a very pretty little poem.

I enclose a poem by a friend which I hope you may find suited to your magazine. Miss Tynan and I both think it a beautiful sonnet. Edwin Ellis the author is not a young man but a kind of a genius who has kept himself buried away for years in Italy, painting and reading Dante.

I am writing an introduction to Carleton's *Traits and Stories* for the Camelot Series and intend contrasting him with Kickham and Banim. Miss Tynan says you could perhaps lend me Kickham's *Knocknagow*. I know his other novels. It is laborious doing all the reading needful. What a voluminous creature Carleton was! I have still close on 15 novels to get through—leaving Banim out of count.

---

[1] The poem which Yeats here mentions was 'To William B. Yeats' by Robert Reilly, published in the *Irish Monthly* of May 1889.

What do you think is Banim's best? I must take merely a few specimen nibbles at him.

In all ways I am a deal busier than I care to be—am reviewing Carleton's *Red Haired Man's Wife* for *Scots Observer* by the way. Do you know from what source it came and whether anybody has added to or altered it?

I have a play on the old Irish folk tale, 'The Countess Kathleen O'Shee', half written. It is wholly my best poem I imagine and is meant for the stage if possible.

I have been trying to persuade Miss Tynan to write a Miracle play. It would be a new poetic form for her and a new form often means a new inspiration.

It is very good of you to send the *Irish Monthly*. I enjoy it always greatly—that article on the 'Rapt Culdee' in a recent number was one of the most charming articles I know. Miss Tynan has written a poem on this Culdee and I shall probably do another. Yours very sincerely   W B YEATS

Miss Tynan was staying with us lately for a week but she has now gone to another friend's. She is greatly in request.

If this little poem of Edwin Ellis's happens to suit you I could bring him the proof sheet, if you would send it to me, or you could send direct to Edwin J. Ellis Esq. 40 Milson Road. Addison Road. Kensington. London.

TO KATHARINE TYNAN

July 16 [1889]   *3 Blenheim Road*

Dear Miss Tynan, Where were you on Sunday, you sinner? I went to Miss Hickey's,[1] giving up another engagement and one I was anxious to keep, for the purpose. Miss Little was there to meet you.

I want you to come here next Saturday to meet Nettleship.[2] I saw him today and he can come. If you cannot, let me know in time to put him off. He will be with us at 8 o'c. Come you, for tea at

---

[1] Emily Hickey (1845–1924), born in Co. Wexford, was a poet and lecturer on English Language and Literature. With Dr. F. J. Furnivall she founded the Browning Society in 1881.

[2] J. T. Nettleship (1841–1902), the painter, a friend of J. B. Yeats.

6.30 and as much earlier as you like. Stay the night if you can. As to Mrs. Pritchard! Do as you like about her. We shall be of course glad to see her.

I have got *Fairy and Folk Tales* for you. I am busy with Carleton; have got to have 'copy' for book ready in three days and introduction in ten.

I just remember that you wish to show Mrs. Pritchard Bedford Park. Do not forget to come early so as to have daylight. Would Mrs. Pritchard's coming necessitate your going home very early? If that is so, you had better arrange to bring her another day and stay the night on Saturday. I will try to get York Powell and it is no easy job to get him at any early hour and I somewhat misdoubt the punctuality of Mr. Nettleship.

Papa and Lilly have gone to Burnham Beeches for today and tomorrow. Yours always, W B YEATS

TO FATHER MATTHEW RUSSELL

[circa *July* 1889] *3 Blenheim Road*

My dear Father Russell, A great many thanks for the book which I will return as soon as I have read it. Many thanks also for the promise of the poem book. Anything that anybody may be doing in the way of Irish poetry interests me greatly. The Young Ireland impulse seems to have died out and one is always on the watch for any sign of a new start. I imagine it will be something much more complex than anything we have had in Ireland heretofore and that it will appeal to, and draw its material from, more numerous classes than Young Ireland did. These are the bubbles I blow about it anyway.

I have to finish Carleton in a hurry to try and get the editor of the series out of a scrape and may after all be unable to discuss Kickham as much as I had wished, but shall take the matter up in articles.

By the way I think you are unjust to Carleton; he has drawn beautifully many entirely Catholic forms of life and virtue, and whatever he has said against the priests is mild indeed in comparison to his ferocious attacks on the clergy of the Protestant church in say

Valentine McClutchy. He has drawn the characters of several Catholic clergymen most sympathetically and beautifully. His heart always remained Catholic, it seems to me. I may be wrong for there are still a good number of his novels I have had no time to read, but what anti-Catholic feeling he ever had seems to have died out after the first few years. Unhappily the *Traits and Stories* were written in those years. *Fardorougha the Miser* seems his best novel. I wish it were reprinted. *McClutchy* contains the best scenes almost of any, but as a whole it seems less artistic—too much caricature and so forth.

I must finish this now as I have to write my introduction to-day. Yours very sincerely   W B YEATS

TO KATHARINE TYNAN

July 25th [1889]   *3 Blenheim Road*

Dear Miss Tynan, We shall all be delighted to have you with us. I shall be at Paddington at 5.25 on Monday.

I have not yet written about Ibsen. The article still waits for the duello, to get done.

I have seen a good deal of Mrs. Alexander Sullivan. She is looking much better than when I wrote last and seems to have quite recovered her spirits. She is coming this evening to meet York Powell, Sydney Hall and Miss Purser. I wrote an article for her a day or two ago—something about Dr. Cronin. She is not yet sure that he is dead at all. He seems to have been a great rascal. It was really a very becoming thing to remove him—if he be dead and the man found at Chicago be not someone else. A Spy has no rights.[1]

There! You will be angry with me for all these dreadful sentiments. I may think the other way tomorrow.

Do you know who I heard from? Miss Little (you remember her?) sent me Mrs. Bryant's address, who wishes me to call on her, also her own. Yours always,   W B YEATS

[1] In May 1889 a certain Dr. Cronin was murdered in Chicago. Suspicion fell on members of one of the Irish-American Fenian Societies there, and Alexander Sullivan, a rich lawyer, was arrested, but afterwards released. Cronin was thought to have been a spy, though this was never established. His death was probably due to some internal stress or quarrel in the Clan na Gael. Yeats's article has not been traced.

TO THE EDITOR OF THE *SPECTATOR*

July 29, 1889 *3 Blenheim Road*

Sir, In a kindly notice of my volume of poems, your reviewer asks where I got the materials for 'The Wanderings of Oisin.' The first few pages are developed from a most beautiful old poem by one of the numerous half-forgotten Gaelic poets who lived in Ireland in the last century. In the quarrels between the saint and the blind warrior, I have used suggestions from various ballad Dialogues of Oisin and Patrick, published by the Ossianic Society. The pages dealing with the three islands, including your reviewer's second quotation, are wholly my own, having no further root in tradition than the Irish peasant's notion that Tir-n-an-oge (the Country of the Young) is made up of three phantom islands. I am, Sir, etc.   W B YEATS

TO KATHARINE TYNAN

[*August* 1889] *2 St. John's Villas*
St. John's Road
Oxford

Dear Miss Tynan, I am down here at Oxford and shall be, until the end of next week at earliest, copying a thing in the Bodleian.[1]

I copy six and a half hours each day, then go for a walk until tea time making up lines for 'the Countess' the while. After tea I read Kickham (for a couple of volumes of selections from the Irish novelists I shall probably be doing for Putnam, the Boston publisher),[2] but on the whole am too tired after tea to do much good at anything. So you see the poem for *East and West* will have to elbow out 'the Countess.' I will begin thinking on the matter tomorrow and probably may get started on Sunday.

I am in lodgings here and do not know a soul (the Hunts have left for a month). I lodge in the same rooms Vigfusson (the Icelander who died the other day—a friend of York Powell's) lived in. The landlady is a good woman with a pale ungenial English face, and

---

[1] The book Yeats was copying for David Nutt was *Hypnerotomachia, The Strife of Love in a Dreame*, a translation of the first book of *Hypnerotomachia Poliphili* by Francesco Colonna. The reprint was edited by Andrew Lang and published by Nutt in 1890 as Volume III of the Tudor Library.

[2] *Representative Irish Tales* appeared in the Knickerbocker Nuggets series published by G. P. Putnam's Sons in March 1891.

there is a big engraving on the wall called 'The Soldier's Dream,' and two more (the Bartolozzi school) of children being led through the sky by a couple of guardian angels with pointed noses.

I am always glad to get away by myself for a time and should be contented enough here but for the miserable allegory I copy out for Nutt. I am sorry to have had to come thither the very day John O'Leary started for London (he stays a month however) and sorry too to have missed Pat Gogarty, who by strange ill-luck called the very day I left. He has been a month in Paris and is now on his way homeward.

Of course we shall be delighted to have you with us, any time you come. I hope you will stay a good while. You can, if you like, always have my study or the drawing-room to work in. And have them to yourself if you like.

Apropos of which, Mrs. Stannard said she cannot work unless all her family are in the room with her. She once tried to work alone but cried from sheer loneliness.

I cannot well send a copy of my poems to the French lady, I fear, until I get home. I shall have to go to Kegan Paul for a copy.

I have a good deal of work to do at present, more than I can manage, all at Irish literary subjects—which is as it should be. I wish you had made up the Irish novelists and folklorists. You with your ready pen would find plenty to say about them. There is a want for a short book (about 150 pages or 200) on Irish literature. Lives and criticism of all the writers since Moore. It would sell largely, I hope, and do good work I am sure. Some day you or I must take it in hand. There is a great want for a just verdict on these men and their use for Ireland. I have often thought of setting about such a book and may when I have got on more with the novel-writers. The worst would be one's necessity of blaming so many whose use is not yet exhausted.

Blake is likely to be, I dare say, the one big prose matter I shall try just yet, however. By big I mean not articles, merely. Though [the] Blake book will be truly a biggish book.

What a downpour it has been this afternoon. I have written this letter instead of going for a walk. Now it is clearing up, and a sparrow is beginning to chirp. Yours always, W B YEATS

Write again soon and let me know about your plans.

Lilly and Jack are in Ireland (I suppose you know) at least Jack is and Lilly has either started or is about to do so. Lolly is housekeeping or will when she comes back from Haslemere, where she is staying for a few days with the Nashes. She will be home in a day or two now.

I must go for my walk now.

TO JOHN O'LEARY [1]

Thursday [August 1889]   2 *St. John's Villas*
                                                         Oxford

Dear Mr. O'Leary, Two days ago I heard from Miss O'Leary that you were on your way to London. Here I am down in Oxford, by evil fortune, and will be for the next nine days I foresee. I am copying out for Nutt the publisher, who like all his race is in a hurry, a dull old allegory about love written by an Italian, who deserved to be forgotten long ago, and translated into fairly good English and published in a book full of misprints by an Elizabethan who wrote well enough to have known better. However the thing may be good enough, but then I copy $6\frac{1}{2}$ hours a day at it, never taking pen from paper except for a dip of ink. Covering so much paper gives one a fellow-feeling for the wandering Jew. Certainly he covered miles and years and I but foolscap, but then he walked fast and the years did not matter to him.

Papa writes to me that there is an M.P., one Atherley Jones—a Bedford Parkite and tepid Whig or some such thing—very anxious to meet you. Indeed there are many most anxious, notably York Powell, who is away now for a week or two.

Pat Gogarty, the Clondalkin shoemaker, called to see me I am told the very day I came down here—he is over for a few days. He has really sent one or two capital studies of peasant life as far as substance and sincerity go but written in an old fashioned clumsy way.

I am reading *Knocknagow* here in the evening and have Banim's *Croppy* to begin next. However, I am rather too tired at night—I take a longish walk when the library closes—to read much. When

[1] From a copy thought to have been made by D. J. O'Donoghue.

walking I go on with my Irish play *The Countess Kathleen*. I always find it pleasant being alive and would be quite happy but for the Italian and his allegory. Yours very sincerely, W B YEATS

TO KATHARINE TYNAN

Wednesday [circa *August* 14, 1889]   *St. John's Villas*
                                                            Oxford

Dear Miss Tynan, I find I shall be able to leave this on Friday afternoon. My work will then be finished. Are you coming to us this week; if so, when, and would you like me to meet you at any railway station and help with the luggage if it be after Friday afternoon?

This is a most beautiful country about here—I walked sixteen miles on Sunday—going to the places in Matthew Arnold's poems —the ford in the 'Scholar Gipsy' being the furthest away and most interesting.

How very unlike Ireland this whole place is—like a foreign land (as it is). One underftands (a long f, I notice, has got in here out of the book I am copying) English poetry more from seeing a place like this. I only felt at home once—when I came to a steep lane with a stream in the middle. The rest one noticed with a foreign eye, picking out the stranger and not as in one's own country the familar things for interest—The fault, by the way, of all poetry about countries not the writer's own.

The people, I notice, do not give you 'a fine day' or answer yours as in Ireland. The children seem more civil, I think (perhaps, however, generations of undergraduates have scared them into good behaviour).

It is just possible but unlikely (very) that I shall not get away from this until Saturday morning.

O'Leary was at Blenheim Road I hear on Sunday.

You will have plenty of time to write when you come, as everyone has left town by this. Let me know your intentions in matter of arrival.

Have started poem for you but made little progress. Yours always,   W B YEATS

TO FATHER MATTHEW RUSSELL

[*Probably September* 1889] 3 *Blenheim Road*

Dear Father Russell, I shall at once send *Irish Monthly* to Edwin Ellis [1] who by the by is writing together with me a book on William Blake's hitherto never made out 'Prophetic Books.' Blake's grandfather I have found out by chance was a Cornelius O'Neal who took the name of Blake to dodge his creditors, so we may almost claim Blake for an Irish poet.

You ask in your book notes for some one to translate Hyde's Folklore book. He is going to do so himself. Only to-day I sent on a note from a publisher over here offering to take a book from him. The publisher (Nutt) had read his stories in my fairy book. It will be a great event I believe. He is the best of all Irish folklorists and may do for us what Campbell did for Scotland. I wonder when he will give us a volume of ballads by the by.

I am up to the ears in Irish novelists, making up the subject with view of a probable two volume selection of short stories of Irish peasant life for Putnam's *Knickerbocker Nugget* series. Do you know of any off the general track of Carleton, Banims, Griffin, Lover, etc? Any whose copyrights have lapsed or who would give leave to reprint (in America where leave is hardly needed)? It would be somewhat of an advertisement. The thing may not come off, however I am daily expecting a final clinching of the matter. The stories I am giving range from 20 to 80 pages (in a few cases of important people).

You will have got my *Carleton* by this. The introduction was done very hastily to get Rhys out of a difficulty made by some one or other not being up to date.

Miss Tynan is in London once more and staying with the Meynells. She goes about everywhere and seems much in request. She has got a monthly letter to do for *East and West*.

Do not forget that you promised me a copy of 'Alice Esmonde's' poems—I saw advertised in the *Monthly* a while since a book called *Lays of South Sligo*. Was there any good in the book? or any legend even? All things about Sligo interest me and if you have a copy by you (you noticed it I believe) I should like to see it.

[1] Edwin Ellis's sonnet 'The Chosen,' which Yeats had sent in, was printed in the *Irish Monthly* of September 1889.

Miss A. I. Johnston['s] verses in last *Monthly* are very pretty.
Yours very sincerely   W B YEATS

TO ERNEST RHYS[1]

[Probably September 1889]   [3 *Blenheim Road*]

... I am busy just now in starting a London branch of the Young Ireland League, and expecting a batch of young Irishmen here this evening, but am going on with things rather mechanically, feeling bored to death with most things in life and out of it. These fits from the old serpent come often but we live through them anyhow. You have not told me what you are writing....

... Mrs. Besant, you may not have heard, has turned theosophist and is now staying with Madame Blavatsky. She is a very courteous and charming woman. John O'Leary is now in London and I can write no more now as I am due at his lodgings in an hour's time and they are some distance off.

TO KATHARINE TYNAN

[circa *October* 10, 1889]   3 *Blenheim Road*

My dear Miss Tynan (I wonder if it would matter if I put your Christian name, by the bye), I enclose order for 10/- as what is due from me for Ballad book. I have not your letters by me but think 9/8 was the amount and I owe you 3 or 4 pence besides—if it was more—if either debt was more—let me know. Could you get Gills to send me three copies of the book (one for Lilly)—I can get them I suppose now that all is paid—I have not a single copy. Do you remember O'Leary's suggestion (he thought I should remind you) that the book be now published in paper at 6d. and in cloth of some cheap kind at 1/- (I mean the 1/- copies were O'Leary's suggestion) say 100 1/- copies.

Enough of mere mercantile matters. I am in the *Magazine of*

[1] Text from *Letters from Limbo* by Ernest Rhys. London, 1936.

Poetry but have not seen it [1]—have been waiting for funds to write for a copy—will tomorrow.

I have not with my whole heart forgiven that subediting *Tablet* man for going off to the train with you in the remaining cab seat and he with so many sins already on his soul—those *Pall Mall* verses in chief and the way he got them published.

Your letter to my father was very interesting and all that about your dog, in chief, so. With us there is nothing to tell other than that Jack has come home with a number of sketches of Sligo. I have got one framed for my room. He keeps shouting, mostly Sligo nonsense rhymes (he always comes home full of them) such as

> 'You take the needle and I'll take the thread
> And we'll sew the dog's tail to the Orangeman's head.'

You must be settling down by this, though indeed you seem at home and comfortable at all times (unlike me, the sole of whose foot is uneasy). You must be settling down—writing, and that kind of thing—not minding this dripping autumn. Do not forget that I am expecting a letter, and do not make it short merely because there is no news in this of mine—I have none but Blake news, for that matter goes on well. The book may be done by January if this Putnam affair does not take all my time.

I have just—this moment—got a letter from Le Gallienne's publisher,[2] asking for an experimental dozen of *Oisin*, sale or return of course, and promising to advertise me—with Press opinions—in his catalogue. Which reminds me that I want to advertise—as will Todhunter, Miss O'Leary, Douglas Hyde—at the end of the 6d. and 1/- ballad books. When Gill is ready, let me know and we will send in.

Le Gallienne's publisher's reader seems confident that publisher will sell *Oisin*. I have no faith that way nor have had, I shall sell but not yet. Many things, my own and others, have to grow first.

When you write, always tell me what you are writing, especially what poems, the journalism interests me more dimly of course, being good work for many people, but no way, unless on Irish matters,

---

[1] An article on Yeats by Katharine Tynan was published in the *Magazine of Poetry* (Buffalo, New York) in October 1889. It was followed by a liberal selection of his poems from *The Wanderings of Oisin*.

[2] Elkin Mathews, who combined the professions of publisher and bookseller at his little shop in Vigo Street, off Regent Street.

good work for you or me, unless so far as it be really forced on us by crazy circumstance. At least I think this way about it, not with any notion of poet's dignity, of course, but because so much in the way of writing is needed for Irish purposes. You know all this as well as I do however. Much may depend in the future on Ireland now developing writers who know how to formulate in clear expressions the vague feelings now abroad—to formulate them for Ireland's, not for England's, use. Well! One could run on endlessly in this kind of way and you who love men and women more than thoughts would always grow indignant. Yours always,

W B YEATS

TO KATHARINE TYNAN

October 23 [1889]   *3 Blenheim Road*

My dear Miss Tynan, I want you to tell me anything you know about poor Miss O'Leary's death.[1] When did she die and so forth? I know nothing but the vaguest rumours. Last week O'Leary wrote to me from Paris saying 'a horrible calamity has come and the light of my life has gone out.' He said nothing more definite. On Sunday and yesterday I saw him (he came Saturday from Paris). He gave me Miss O'Leary's proof-sheets, saying that she had wished me to correct them. He is evidently grieving very much. He makes constant indirect allusions to his trouble but says nothing definite. I would not be certain of her death at all only that on Monday I heard by chance that Miss Gonne was in London and rushed off at once and saw her for about five minutes or less. She was just starting for Paris. She knew no more than that Miss O'Leary died at Cork some few days ago. Do you know whether there was any kind of a public funeral? Were there any notices in any papers?

By the bye, did you get my last letter enclosing 10/- for Gill in payment of my share of ballad book expenses? I corrected proofs of *East and West* ballad so I dare say next number will contain it.

You will probably see me in Dublin next spring or before. O'Leary asks me to stay with him for a while if I pass through on my way to Sligo. Yours always,   W B YEATS

[1] Ellen O'Leary had died suddenly on October 16 during a visit to Cork while her brother was in Paris.

TO KATHARINE TYNAN

Oct. 6th [for Nov. 6th 1889]   *3 Blenheim Road*

My dear Katey, I send you a *Leisure Hour* with an article on Irish ballad writers, written more than two years ago. It is very incomplete—you are not mentioned at all—The reason is that when I wrote I intended to deal with contemporary writers in a separate article. The *Leisure Hour* people, however, having an Irish story and other Irish things running, were afraid of so much Ireland. My ballad is in *East and West*.[1] I was almost forgetting the thing I am writing about—I knew there was something and could not think what.

A great many thanks for your pleasant little notice of me in the *Magazine of Poetry*. It is [as] good as possible. There are just one or two little matters you were in error about. It is quite true that I used constantly when a very small child to be at Sandymount Castle but it was not my birthplace. I was born at a house in Sandymount Avenue. A little house, which my old Uncle looked on with some scorn, and called even on the outside of his letters 'the Quarry Hole,' because he remembered there being, when he was a young man, a quarry hole where it was afterwards built.

The place that has really influenced my life the most is Sligo —There used to be two dogs there, one smooth-haired, one curly-haired—I used to follow them all day long. I knew all their occupations, when they hunted for rats and when they went to the rabbit warren. They taught me to dream, maybe. Since then I follow my thoughts as I then followed the two dogs—the smooth and the curly—wherever they lead me.

Our little black cat caught a mouse the other day; since then she is not half so amusing—Lolly says she feels the responsibility of life and is always thinking. She has suddenly grown up.

There is really nothing to record in the way of news other than this mouse. I have one of the drawings Jack made in Sligo framed and hung up in my study.

I will write about Miss O'Leary in the *Providence Journal* but perhaps I should wait until her poems are out. They cannot be long now.

I have just seen—Lady Wilde sent it me—your article on the

[1] 'The Ballad of the old Foxhunter' appeared in *East and West*, November.

Cardinal. A very good article it is. Am very glad to hear of 'The Culdee' coming out in Xmas *East and West*. My little 'Fox-hunter' ballad seems liked—Jack with his horse-loving tendency likes it best of my short poems. A friend of Ellis's meditates a picture on the subject to be called 'The March Past.' Hounds and horse being led past their dying owner.

I have met lately an amusing musical and literary family. The Miss Keelings. One sings, one writes novels, some of which have been most successful. The novel-maker has just published a clever sentimental book called *In Thoughtland and Dreamland*.[1] I had tea with them yesterday and they told me a good story of their childhood. One day they went into the store-room to see what they could see. There was a box full of apples. They knew it would be very wicked to take one, so instead they bit a piece out of each one and then turned the good sides up. Their mother knew which had bitten each apple because one had lost one tooth, one another. They used to live in the same house we lived in at Earl's Court when we came to London two and a half years ago. Mrs. Wheeler was full of tales of them. The novel-maker has described the Earl's Court house in her last book. Yours always, W B YEATS

TO JOHN O'LEARY

Dec 9th [1889]   *3 Blenheim Road*

Dear Mr. O'Leary, A great many thanks for the two *Pilots*. The reason I said so little about Miss O'Leary was not at all that I did not wish to say a great deal but that Miss Tynan wrote to me and said that she was writing a notice for the *Pilot* and asking me if I were writing anything to let it be for the *Providence Journal* (an article I have put off until I come to do the poems) and so I felt bound not in any way to forestall her, but in my next *Pilot* letter (one that has not yet been printed) I wrote a long paragraph which I hope you will like and wrote to Boyle O'Reilly at the same time asking leave to review the poems for him, as soon as they are published. When I saw how meagre the notice in the *Pilot* letters you saw was (I

[1] Elsa D'Esterre-Keeling, the novelist, was born in Dublin. She was a high-school mistress from 1884 to 1890 at Oxford and in Kensington. She wrote a number of novels and became a member of the London Irish Literary Society. Yeats wrote of *In Thoughtland and Dreamland* in the *Boston Pilot*, November 23, 1889.

happened to see another copy) I felt sorry, very sorry, that I had taken care not to forestall Miss Tynan. (The *Pilot* assuredly would not have minded two notices.) Will the book be soon out? I hope to write all I can about it.

By the by I have found those *Christian Examiner* stories of Carleton's I had mislaid. I am working away at this American book of Irish stories and intend writing one for it myself, if I can get up the needful resolution and dialect. Yours very sincerely

W B YEATS

Did you lose a sleeve link (or part of one) when here one evening? We have found one.

TO KATHARINE TYNAN

Tuesday [*mid-December* 1889]   *3 Blenheim Road*

My dear Katey, Please remember you owe me a letter. I am not going to confirm you in your sins by writing one until I get it. This is merely a note to tell you that I am reading for that book of Irish Tales and that you promised me a story of Miss Mulholland's and one or two others.

Do not let Gill bring out the cheap edition of *Young Ireland* ballad book before getting from me and Hyde advertisements of our books.

I have a lot of things to say but will say nothing

> *Write to me*
> *Write to me*
> *Write to me*

Till then I am dumb. It is about six week s since your letter was due. Yours,

W B YEATS

TO FATHER MATTHEW RUSSELL

December [1889]   *3 Blenheim Road*

My dear Father Russell, A great many thanks for the two *Monthlys* with Miss Mulholland's [1] stories, they are very pleasant and pretty.

---

[1] Rosa Mulholland, daughter of J. S. Mulholland, M.D., of Belfast, married Sir John T. Gilbert, LL.D., in 1891. She wrote numerous stories and novels. Yeats

I think I will use 'Bet's Matchmaking' but will not decide yet. It is not quite in my scheme, I am trying to make all the stories illustrations of some phase of Irish life, meaning the collection to be a kind of social history. I begin with *Castle Rackrent* [1] and give mainly tales that contain some special kind of Irish humour or tragedy. 'Molly the Tramp' is a very good tale but then it is above all things a tale and not also a little loophole for looking at Irish life through. Molly is just a pathetic heroine of romance. She might have strayed over the sea from an English city. The heroines of Carleton or Banim could only have been raised under Irish thatch. One might say the same in less degree of Griffin [2] and Kickham [3] but Kickham is at times, once or twice only, (and merely in his peasant heroines I think) marred by having read Dickens; and Griffin, most facile of all, one feels is Irish on purpose rather than out [of] the necessity of his blood. He could have written like an Englishman had he chosen. But all these writers had a square-built power no later Irishman has approached. Above all Carleton and Banim had it. They saw the whole of everything they looked at, (Carleton and Banim I mean) the brutal with the tender, the coarse with the refined. In Griffin and Kickham the tide began to ebb. Kickham had other things to do and is not to be blamed in this matter. It has quite gone out now—our little tide. The writers who make Irish stories sail the sea of common English fiction. It pleases them to hoist Irish colours—and that is well. The Irish manner has gone out of them though. Like common English fiction they want too much to make pleasant tales—and that's not at all well. The old men tried to make one see life plainly but all written down in a kind of fiery shorthand that it might never be forgotten.

---

did not include either of the stories here mentioned in *Representative Irish Tales* but chose instead a tragic story 'The Hungry Death.'

[1] *Castle Rackrent* (1800) by Maria Edgworth (1769–1849), one of her best books, was first published anonymously.

[2] Gerald Griffin (1803–1840) was born in Limerick. He wrote a number of plays and novels of which the most famous is *The Collegians* (1829). Yeats describes it as 'the most finished and artistic of all Irish stories.' It was dramatized freely, and from it Dion Boucicault took the materials of his celebrated drama *The Colleen Bawn*.

[3] Charles Kickham (1825–1882), novelist and poet, joined the Fenian movement and was, with T. C. Luby and John O'Leary, one of the triumvirate who controlled its action in Ireland. Arrested in 1865 he was sentenced to fourteen years' penal servitude but was released after four years on account of ill health. He wrote three novels, *Sally Kavanagh*, *Knocknagow* and *For the Old Land*, besides poems and ballads. *Knocknagow* has been the most popular and best loved of Irish novels since its publication.

Miss Mulholland's little stories are very charming indeed (and one should not fight with cherry trees for not growing acorns); a pleasant fireside feeling and a murmur of the kettle goes through them—a domesticity that is not especially Irish however. Certainly if I get her leave I will use one of her short tales, and may quite reverse my feeling about her not giving us Irish life and Irish manner, like Carleton and Banim, when I have read one of the long novels which I shall do before criticising her in the Irish story book. I was not so much thinking of her as of one or two others in what is here said of later Irish novels in general. Probably I shall use 'Bet's Matchmaking,' it is a charming story but then it is generalized life—such feeling, such incidents, might have cropped up anywhere. Generalizing in all things, that is our big sin now—and virtue.

Did Scott send you my *Carleton*? If not let me know please.

I have yet to thank you for the book of poems *Remembrance*.[1] I wrote about them a short paragraph in my last *Boston Pilot* letter. There are lines and stanzas of a good deal of charm but all is too subjective and sad. She is so subjective that reading her poems is like looking through a window pane on which one has breathed. She also too seldom develops a single idea but instead stitches a number of different ones together. I have been looking for her book to pick out the pages I like especially but have mislaid it or lent it.

It is very good of you to keep sending me the *Monthly*, it constantly is full of most interesting things. Yours very truly

W B YEATS

TO KATHARINE TYNAN

Thursday [*December* 26, 1889]   *3 Blenheim Road*

My dear Katey, Could you get me the story or two you mentioned soon now, as I promised to give the publisher a list of contents by the 5th of January?

Father Russell sent me Miss Mulholland's 'Molly the Tramp' and 'Bet's Matchmaking.' I will try and use the last, though neither comes exactly within the definition of my book, being in no way distinctively Irish life, though happening in Ireland. However, 'Bet's Matchmaking' is a very pretty tale.

[1] *Songs of Remembrance* by Margaret Ryan is mentioned by Yeats in his *Boston Pilot* letter of November 23.

Did I tell you we have found a new long poem of Blake's? Rossetti mentioned its name, no more. We are the only people who ever read it. It is two thousand lines long or so and belongs to three old men and their sisters [1] who live away at Redhill in Surrey. Ellis and myself go from time to time and do a day's copying out at it. The old men are very hospitable and bring out 30-years old port-wine for us, and, when I am copying, the oldest of the old men sits beside me with a penknife in his hand to point my pencil when it blunts. Their house is a great typical bare country house. It is full of Blake matters. The old men and their sisters are like 'a family of pew-openers' Ellis says. Blake is their Church; at the same time they are no little troubled at the thought that maybe he was heretical. I tried to convince them of his orthodoxy and found it hard to get the great mystic into their little thimble.

Yes, my beard is off! and whether for good I don't know. Some like it, some not. Madame Blavatsky promised me a bad illness in three months through the loss of all the mesmeric force that collects in a beard—one has gone by. When she sees me she professes to wonder at my being still on my legs. It makes a great change. I felt quite bewildered for a time at losing the symbol I knew myself by—I mean changing it so. I still feel somewhat like the sweep in the story whose face was washed in the night, so that when he saw himself in the glass in the morning he said they had woke[n] the wrong man.

Do not leave me so long without a letter next time.

The Coffeys are over here. I am going to breakfast with them tomorrow.

So Rolleston is trying to get a professorship in Australia. He will be a loss in many ways. I was always hoping he would drift into things—do something for nationalism, political or literary, though indeed I fear the scholastic brand was too deep in his heart. He is a loss anyway, however.

Lilly has not been well just lately, she is taking a holiday for a few days now—going to stay with friends, the Gambles, until Monday and then perhaps, if not better, on, she and Lolly, to Brighton. Today she is at the Morris's spending the day.

[1] The three old men and their sisters were the Linnell family, children of Blake's patron John Linnell. The poem was *Vala*, also known as *The Four Zoas*; it was first printed in the three-volume *Works of William Blake*, edited by Ellis and Yeats and published by Bernard Quaritch in 1893.

Lilly and Lolly have had a lot of presents and cards—more than usual, a good deal, I think.

Jack is at Portsmouth. He and a friend walked there. It took them three days. They come back tomorrow; they are staying with some relations of the friend's.

Oscar Wilde mentioned his hearing from you about *East and West* and asked if it was a paper meant to improve people. I said not, so he will probably write for it.

There is a tintinnabulation of tea things outside, bringing this to an end, but indeed I have written a good long letter, longer than yours, worse luck. Yours,

                                                    W B YEATS

[*On envelope*] I hear that a painter, Montefiore, is making the subject of my *East and West* poem the subject of his Academy picture. He says it is the best subject he ever had.

TO JOHN O'LEARY [1]

[*December 26, 1889*]   3 *Blenheim Road*

Dear Mr. O'Leary, Do you remember if *Father Connell* was among the Banims I returned? You have, I think you said, Kickham's *Sally Kavanagh*. Could you lend it me to extract the 'School Master's Story' or some such thing for the Putnam book? It is getting on now to the time of winding up the matter. I promised them a list of contents by the 5th of Jan but will not get preface done yet a bit. Please send me a postcard if you have *Father Connell*.

You mentioned some early works of Lefanu's about Ireland. One you said was called the *Cock and Anchor* I think. I do not find it in the Museum's catalogue. However plenty of Irish books are not in it. . . .

Sir Charles Gavan Duffy [2] has not sent me those letters of Keegan's he promised. I am thinking of writing about them and also about Mangan and I have a notion of beginning, as soon as the stories are arranged for Putnams', the little history of 'Irish Literature of this Century.' Rhys doubts not that Scott would publish it. I shall be systematically political or national anyway through-

[1] From a typescript in the National Library of Ireland.
[2] See letters to Sir Charles Gavan Duffy of March 17 and April 15, 1890 (pp. 151–152).

W. B. YEATS BEFORE 1889

W. B. YEATS IN THE NINETIES

out the thing. Mangan will make a lecture to begin with. What is Sir Charles Gavan Duffy's address? . . . Yours very sincerely

W B YEATS

TO KATHARINE TYNAN

13 Jan. [1890]   *3 Blenheim Road*

My dear Katey, A great many thanks for the *Hibernian Magazine*. I have not read more than the one story 'A Tepid Bath' but, as I have a few days longer than I thought to get ready the book, will read further. 'A Tepid Bath' is amusing but forgive me for not including it for it is not in any way illustrative of Irish life. Besides, too, I have plenty of humorous tales. Tragic matter foils me much more. 'Hungry Death,' which Father Russell sent me, will surely go in and it is very fine. 'How I became a Zouave' will do also, I think. Who is 'Bridget'? I will have to write for leave to use it of course. 'Tepid Bath' has a touch of the old *Handy Andy* stage Irishman—a creature half schemer half dunce, with little truth to nature about him and what truth there is true only of the dependent class that grew up round a contemptuous and alien gentry.

By the bye have you seen my letter in the *Nation* of last week on Carleton in reply to a review of *Stories from Carleton* that brought up his Protestant period against him? At the foot of my letter they protest that they did not say anything against him as a whole but only against the anti-Catholic that was in him for a time. It is amusing to find printed after my letter a note from a Tipperary priest thanking them for their timely protest against this republication of Carleton's stories and wondering that I would edit such a book. He at any rate read them, as I did—O these Bigots—fortunately their zeal is not equalled by their knowledge. I dare say I surprised some folk by reminding them of the numberless books full of the most ardent defence of the Catholic priesthood written by Carleton and by showing how very little there is of his anti-Catholic work and how early it was. I dare say, though, they are no bigots—people have so long passed on the calumny that unenquiring people might well come to believe that all he wrote was bitterly sectarian.

Here is a little song written lately—one thing written this long while bar prose. It is supposed to be sung by a mother to her child—

> The Angels are sending
>   A smile to your bed,
> They weary of tending
>   The souls of the dead.
>
> Of tending the seven—
>   The planets' old brood:
> And God smiles in heaven
>   To see you so good.
>
> My darling I kiss you
>   With arms round my own,
> Ah how shall I miss you
>   When heavy and grown.[1]

The last two lines are suggested by a Gaelic song quoted in Griffin's *Collegians*.

I can write no more now. I have just had Russian influenza and it leaves one curiously weak for a day or two and I can by no means fix my mind farther on this letter. Yours always,   W B YEATS

[*On envelope*] Could you get me a *Nation* for last week and current week; there may be a letter I should answer? I can send you the money if you send them. I do not know if my letter came out last week or the week before—last week, I think. If you find it was last week you need not get me that number. I hope this is not too much trouble but you will be in town, I dare say, and can so get it.

[2] I did not post the enclosed as I wanted to put in a new version of the small song and the influenza came on again at once after my making it, or rather influenza plus cold came. I am now much as I was when writing enclosed. Song in new version goes (I write it over the page, on second thoughts):—

> A Cradle Song.
> The angels are bending
> Above your white bed,

---

[1] This poem, of which two versions are given in this letter, was printed as 'A Cradle Song' in the *Scots Observer*, April 19, 1890, and included in *The Countess Kathleen* volume of 1892. Yeats revised it many times in later collections of his poetry.

[2] Text of the remainder of this letter taken from Katharine Tynan's *The Middle Years*, 1916.

> They weary of tending
> The souls of the dead;
>
> And God smiles in heaven
> To see you so good,
> And the old planets seven
> Grow sweet with His mood.
>
> I kiss you and kiss you,
> With arms round my own,
> Ah how shall I miss you
> My darling when grown.

Is not this better than the other? I write no more—writing this much with trouble.

TO KATHARINE TYNAN

Feb. 27 [1890]   *3 Blenheim Road*

My dear Katey, I have been a long while without writing I fear. The Putnam book and some Blake copying has kept my thoughts busy and away from letter writing. When I let so long go by, do be forgiving and write as I do when you are silent. But ah, you are too law-abiding and keep to the letter of the law and wait my answer.

Lilly is staying for a week at the Morris's but is here tonight as we expect Edith Wyse that was and her husband that is. They are passing through London on their honeymoon.

Lilly tells me that Lippman forged letters from Morris to himself and has been using them in New York. The *New York World* telegraphed to Morris to know if they were genuine. I don't understand that poor wretch Lippman, there was little real bad at the heart of him in the days we knew him—It must be a kind of mania—some queer thing awry in his imagination.

Rolleston writes to me from Germany, saying that he will settle in London in a month or so and asking who it was reviewed him in the *Freeman*. He thought I had done it. Do you know? No review pleased him so well.

Feb. 28th

I had to break off last night on the arrival of Edith Wyse that was, now Mrs. Meredith. The husband seems a good fellow. He is not handsome but is very pleasant looking.

To return to Rolleston. If you have the *Freeman* review by you, I would like to see it, as I have to review him for the *Scots Observer*.[1]

O'Leary writes that he also has some notion of coming to London. This Tipperary business seems to have crippled his income or else threatens to do so.

My father is painting a large portrait of me for the Academy and using all my available time for sittings. He constantly reminds himself to do the sketch of me you asked for but finds himself—Academy time drawing near—too anxious I imagine to work—all sittings on the portrait.

Lolly has passed her kindergarten examination all right, the first one, the next comes on in early summer.

There, I have given all the news. As for myself I am deep in Putnam's job, finishing the last two or three days' work. Then comes an article on Nettleship's designs for the *Art Review*—great designs never published before—and later an article on Blake and his anti-materialist Art, for somewhere, describing experiments lately made by me, Ellis, Mrs. Besant, etc., in clairvoyance, I being the mesmerist; and experiments in which a needle suspended from a silk thread under a glass case has moved to and fro and round in answer to my will, and the will of one or two others who have tried, no one touching the glass; some experiments too of still stranger nature.

Probably if I decide to publish these things I shall get called all sorts of names—impostor, liar and the rest—for in this way does official science carry on its trade. But you do not care for magic and its fortunes and yet your Church's enemy is also materialism. To prove the action of man's will, man's soul, outside his body would bring down the whole thing—crash—at least for all who believed one; but, then, who would believe? Maybe my witnesses, more prudent than I, shall bid me remain silent.

What are you writing? I was greatly pleased to hear of you doing a life of someone; your prose is often so very good that it may be a quite notable book. Lady Wilde praised your prose style again to me yesterday.

[1] I have not been able to trace this review.

Have you heard Oscar's last good thing? He says that Sharp's motto should be

Acutis decensus averni

(Sharp is the descent into Hell). The phrase as you know begins in the orthodox way *Facilis* (easy) . . . By the bye, have you gone on at all with your Greek?

March 4th

The Putnam book goes off, for certain tomorrow, thank goodness. The general introduction still remains, however. Is the story true that we have just heard that Miss Johnston is going to be married to Wright? We heard it was all settled.

Lilly is home again from the Morris's. She came last night.

Todhunter has written a charming little Arcadian play to be acted in Bedford Park. He read it out on Sunday evening. Mrs. Emery and Paget take chief parts.[1]

Last time I wrote I sent you some little verses and you never said anything about them. Did you like them? Yours always,

W B YEATS

TO SIR CHARLES GAVAN DUFFY[2]

March 17 [1890]   *3 Blenheim Road*

My dear Sir Gavan Duffy, When I met you with Mr. O'Leary last year you very kindly offered me the use of some unpublished letters of Mangan's, also of the peasant poet Keegan's. I am now thinking out a lecture on Mangan as a preliminary to writing a study of him for a projected little book that has been long in my mind. I write to

[1] John Todhunter's play *A Sicilian Idyll* was first played at 'the little club theatre' in Bedford Park on May 5, 1890. It was revived in the same year at St. George's Hall on July 1 (see letter to Katharine Tynan of that date, p. 154), and again at the Vaudeville Theatre on June 15, 1891 (see letter to John O'Leary, June 1891, p. 168). The play was published by Elkin Mathews.

[2] Sir Charles Gavan Duffy (1816–1903) was a journalist, editor and statesman. With Davis and Dillon he founded the famous Dublin newspaper the *Nation* in 1842 from which sprang the Young Ireland movement. In 1848 he was arrested for treason but not convicted. In 1855 he emigrated to Australia and remained there till 1880, becoming Speaker of the Australian House of Assembly. The latter part of his life was spent mainly in the South of France, at Nice.

remind you of your kind promise in this matter of both men—Mangan and Keegan. I should have written before but up to this have had no time to turn to anything so unbusinesslike as lectures or essays on Irish poets. I am however free now for a bit. I sent off yesterday the MSS for a book of selected Irish Fiction that has filled up all my days, this good while. Yours very truly   W B YEATS

TO SIR CHARLES GAVAN DUFFY

April 15th [1890]   *3 Blenheim Road*

My dear Sir Charles Gavan Duffy, Thank you very much for the Keegan letters.[1] I will take great care of them and return them as soon as possible. I shall try and find out who these Irish Exhibition Committee men are and write to them on the matter of Mangan's letters, unless you think Father Mehan's friends are more likely to succeed than I. I do not know anyone connected with the Exhibition. I have not done more yet than glance at the Keegan papers but what I have seen promises well for their genuine interest. Yours very sincerely   W B YEATS

P.S. I have stamped this letter sufficiently at any rate and please forgive my forgetfulness about the last.

TO KATHARINE TYNAN[2]

May [? 1890]   [*3 Blenheim Road*]

... If I was over in Ireland, I would ask you to collaborate with me on that little miracle play I suggested to you on the Adoration of the Magi. I have written so much in dramatic form that I could perhaps help by working a little prose sketch in dialogue to be turned into verse by you. Would collaboration make it hard for you to work or easy?

You will like Blake's system of thought. It is profoundly Chris-

---

[1] Yeats wrote a few paragraphs on the letters of John Keegan, author of 'Caoch O'Leary,' in an article in the *Boston Pilot*, dated April 21 and published May 17, 1890. He contributed an article 'Clarence Mangan's Love Affair' to *United Ireland*, August 22, 1891.

[2] Text from Katharine Tynan's *The Middle Years*, 1916.

tian—though wrapped up in a queer dress—and certainly amazingly poetical. It has done my own mind a great deal of good in liberating me from formulas and theories of several kinds. You will find it a difficult book, this Blake interpretation, but one that will open up for you, as it has for me, new kinds of poetic feeling and thought...

TO KATHARINE TYNAN

May 30th [1890]   *3 Blenheim Road*

Dear Katey, I see by the *Irish Monthly* that the 6d. *Poems and Ballads of Young Ireland* is out in brown paper and gilt (silver would surely have been the orthodox marking for brown paper covers?). Could you get Gill to send me a copy or two—say three—? I will try and get it noticed. I may get some sort of review in *Pall Mall* and *Scots Observer* as well as mention it myself in the *Boston Pilot*. But please get me these review copies at once or I may be forestalled by some unfriendly or less friendly notice than I hope to secure.

By the by, I thought you were to let us know so that Todhunter and myself might put advertisements of our books at the end. I thought indeed that we were all to do so, dividing the extra expense. Perhaps it is not yet too late to slip them in at the back of the cover; if so I will tell Todhunter and get him, I doubt not, to print a notice of his *Banshee*—with press opinions—at some local printers and send it. I will try and do the same. You have such things, I dare say, already. They would help the sale of the Ballad Book itself—as people would see by them when they turned over the leaves that we are folk who have 'been praised by a heavy review,' to quote a ballade by a neighbour of ours—it would influence reviewers likewise.

I have to go to work at Blake over at the Linnells' at Chelsea. They have a deal of Blake MS.—and so wind up this note. Write soon to me. Yours always,   W B YEATS

TO KATHARINE TYNAN

July 1 [1890]   *3 Blenheim Road*

My dear Katey, I have been so long in writing because I hoped to send you some notes or perhaps an abstract of the little 'Mystery

Play' on the Adoration of the Magi that I propose. I found however that I could not get on without knowing the Catholic tradition on the subject and so far I have not had time to look it up in some dictionary of legend at the Museum.

I am working at Blake and such things. The *Art Review* has come to an end and so unhappily my article on Nettleship's designs is useless. I shall get the editing of a book of reprints of lives of one or two such men as Fighting Fitzgerald I think. These books do not really pay as well as articles, but they help one to make up subjects that are afterwards of great use. I shall be writing some Blake articles at once now. We—Ellis and myself—intend posting one or two to *Scribner's*.

I have seen Miss Imogen Guiney several times.[1] She was out here one Sunday. We all like her greatly. Someone here said she is just like one of the heroines in Howells's novels.

I have gone to see her once or twice when going in to the Museum, but have not seen her just lately, for I have been doubly a prisoner through some work on Irish Novelists for Putnam and a cough now taking its departure.

Lolly is getting ready for her kindergarten exam now almost at hand. Lilly goes to Sligo in August and Jack also. My mother is as usual, that is, better in actual health than she used to be but feeble as to nervous power and memory.

I don't know that there is much more news. Oh yes, there is. Todhunter has written a new play—a prose and verse play on a subject mixed up with the discovery of the printing press. His *Sicilian Idyll* is being acted again tonight at St. George's Hall, Holborn, for the benefit of some charity. Mrs. Andrew Hart bears all expenses. It will be published in an *edition de luxe* in autumn, with frontispiece by Walter Crane.

July 5th

I have been in the Museum much lately reading up the duellists and outlaws for this Unwin book [2]—going through contemporary

[1] Louise Imogen Guiney (1861–1920), born in Boston, Mass., was author of several volumes of poetry, and of books on Robert Emmet, Hurrell Froude and Edmund Campion. She was postmistress of Ashburnham, Mass., 1894–1897, and later worked in the Boston Public Library. From 1901 till the end of her life she made her home in England.

[2] Yeats had undertaken to compile a volume dealing with Irish Adventurers for Fisher Unwin's 'Adventure Series.' It is evident from letters to Edward

154

and chap-book records. Whether the book comes off or no, they will serve me for articles at any rate.

Are you well on with the life of the nun you are doing? I hope they give you a fairly free hand in the matter and allow you to make her human. Not too much of the white light of piety. Remember it is the stains of earth colour that make man differ from man and give interest to biography.

July 15*th*

When I finished the above I had no stamp and then forgot it, a financial crisis of a moderately severe kind driving things out of my head.

The little poem you so much liked was in the *Scots Observer* a couple of weeks ago. York Powell liked it greatly.

I shall get to Ireland some time this year but when I do not know.

The book of duellists, etc., and the Blake must first be finished. Yours at all times, W B YEATS

Can you tell me what the *Pilot* gives you for a column or for an article of average length? They give me one pound for my 'Celt in London' letter. I am thinking of asking for more—I fixed a pound myself, I think, in the beginning. I don't want to write to *Pilot* on the matter until I know what their usual pay is.

TO KATHARINE TYNAN

Sunday September [7, 1890]   3 *Blenheim Road*

My dear Katey, I have again delayed long in answering your letter. Blake and other matters have kept me busy and I put off writing from day to day. But do not think it is any forgetfulness brought on, as you put it, by 'frivolous London life.' London life, for one thing, has taken its 'frivolity' to Brighton and elsewhere this time of year, and all times I see but little of it. Nor if I did could it put you or

---

Garnett which follow that he assembled the greater part of the material, and wrote and sent in his introduction. But the volume never appeared and all trace of his work for it has vanished. He did, however, publish an article 'A Reckless Century. Irish Rakes and Duellists' in *United Ireland*, September 12, 1891, and this perhaps represents an offshoot of his work on the book.

Ireland or aught else much out of thought, for I set small store by it and would gladly never look upon it again. I will, if any chance makes it possible, find my way to Dublin before the year's end and avail myself of your invitation (it ought to have a quicker response from me), but some time now I am a prisoner.

Blake keeps me to my desk. Quaritch has finally agreed to publish the book, giving us by way of payment 13 large paper copies each—they will be worth at the smallest £3 apiece, I suppose. We are to have reproductions of all the illustrations to the prophetic books—about 160 drawings in all—and charts and maps as many as we need. There will be two volumes, one containing the mystical poems—one of these, *Vala*, a poem of great length and beauty, never having been printed or even read before—the other volume will contain our commentary. The whole book will be in printer's hands before winter, I hope, and will be, as far as illustrations and general size and get-up are concerned, the most important thing done as yet upon Blake. Our part will, I believe, give to the world a great religious visionary who has been hidden.

I am also editing, or trying to edit, a book of Irish Adventures for Unwin. If my introduction pleases him I am to get twenty pounds; if not five pounds. Whether it will please I do not know. I am to give in it 'A vivid view of Irish Life in the eighteenth century' and am quite new to historical writing as well as up to my ears in Blakean Mysticism, with scarcely a moment for anything else. If all goes well, I shall have this twenty pounds and another from Putnam for the book of Irish Novelists, some time this winter, and so may manage to get something out of it to take me to Ireland and on to Sligo for a while. I wish very much to finish somewhere in peace verse enough for another book and perhaps start a romance.

I think now I have said all I need say of my own matters. I hope yours go on well—the 'Nun' and the rest. Always tell me of any poems you are doing. Our work, after all, is our true soul, and to know how that goes is the great thing.

Lilly and Lolly are back now—Lilly from Sligo—she stayed but a day in Dublin, else she had gone to see you—and Lolly from her seaside month's tuition. Jack is still in Sligo, he had some drawings in the *Daily Graphic* last Friday week but I have not seen them yet. He has been offered the illustrating of a book and will, I conclude, accept.

Please forgive me if I write no more. I am tired for some reason or other and therefore dispirited and have the wish to keep such ever away from what I write and so end this. Do not revenge my double delay by keeping me long out of an answer to this, but write within a week or so. Yours always, W B YEATS

TO KATHARINE TYNAN

Oct. 6 [1890]   *3 Blenheim Road*

My dear Katey, I got a list from Kegan Paul a little while ago of people who by oversight had not paid their subscriptions for *Oisin*. I find A. Tynan, C/o Miss K. Tynan, Whitehall, etc., is set down for 5/3. Forgive me bothering you but Kegan Paul is dunning for the amount due. O'Leary has written to some and I to the others. Please let the 5/3 be sent by your brother—your brother is it not?—to Kegan Paul, Trench, Trübner & Co., Paternoster Square, London, E.C., and not to me.

I have been photographed by Hollyer as Henley wanted me for some collection of his contributors' photos he is making. The proofs are, except in one case—he gives four positions—not very good. I will send you one as soon as I get any.

I suppose you have heard that Ernest Rhys is engaged to Miss Little—the pretty one—Miss Grace Little.

I have retouched my story 'John Sherman' and I am trying to get it published. Edward Garnett, author of *The Paradox Club*, is going to read it and see if it will suit the publisher he reads for, i.e. Fisher Unwin.[1]

Mr. O'Leary showed me a letter in which you speak of publishing a new book next year and of selecting the contents when I am with you. How glad I shall be to see you and go through the poems with you! I hope to get away in six weeks or so but am now a prisoner with perpetual Blake—Blake—Blake.

Ellis, I hear, made a very brilliant speech on the subject at the 'Odd Volumes' dinner last Friday. Quaritch, our publisher, brought him down and fired him off, as it were. It was intended for an

[1] Edward Garnett (1868–1937) was at this time reader for Fisher Unwin. A man of acute literary taste and judgement, he was responsible for the discovery and publication of very many books of lasting value. It was doubtless at his instigation that Unwin became the publisher of several of Yeats's earlier books.

advertisement, I suppose. He exhibited a huge chart of mine representing Blake's symbolic scheme in a kind of genealogical tree.

O'Leary has been staying with us for a few days. He left yesterday however. How I envy him going over to Ireland.

London is always horrible to me. The fact that I can study some things I like here better than elsewhere is the only redeeming fact. The mere presence of more cultivated people, too, is a gain, of course, but nothing in the world can make amends for the loss of green field and mountain slope and for the tranquil hours of one's own countryside.

When one gets tired and so into bad spirits it seems a special misfortune to live here—it is like having so many years blotted out of life.

Write soon. You see I have not waited for your letter and so have especial claims in the matter of a speedy reply. When you write, always tell me about yourself and what you are doing or thinking about. It is not so much news I want as to feel your personality through the ink and paper. Think of me in this matter as most exacting—you cannot tell me enough about yourself. Yours always, W B YEATS

P.S. When I get over to Ireland I also will try and get a new book of poetry into shape, that is to say I will finish up the play I showed you and write some more ballads and so forth.[1] I shall also have to do, then or a little later, this Unwin Essay on Ireland in the last century for the book of adventure.

[On envelope] There was a well intentioned but absurdly patronizing review of *Oisin* in the *Weekly Register* a week ago.

TO W. E. HENLEY

[*Very early*] Nov [1890] 3 *Blenheim Road*

Dear Mr. Henley, I enclose two short poems [2] for *Scots Observer* if suitable. 'The Old Pensioner' is an almost verbatim record of words by an old Irishman.

[1] Yeats's second collection of poetry which was eventually published by T. Fisher Unwin in his 'Cameo Series' in September 1892, under the title *The Countess Kathleen and Various Legends and Lyrics*.
[2] 'The Old Pensioner' was printed in the *Scots Observer*, November 15. The

I will send the photograph you asked for a while since in a few days. I had one taken for the purpose about a month ago but for some reason or other the copies have not turned up yet. Cloudy weather may explain it perhaps. Yours very truly W B YEATS

TO JOHN O'LEARY

[*Very early*] Nov [1890] *3 Blenheim Road*

Dear Mr. O'Leary, I put off writing to you day after day in hope that the photographs would turn up and I could send you one. They came last night. The delay was caused by the cloudy weather in all likelihood. Another reason why I did not write was that I hoped to be able to get near enough to a wind up of this Blake job to say when I could get to Dublin. However the *Weekly Review* [1] has come to take three days out of every week and so prolong indefinitely the length of the Blake writing, especially as a bad influenza cold has lost me some time. Ellis is away too. I could I dare say go over now and finish the book in Dublin but then I should have to return presently, to go through it all with Ellis. I may however at a later stage of the work go over. I am working at the paraphrases and chapters on the separate books and when they are done may not wait here to do the general account but go to Dublin for the purpose. I can not say definitely until I see Ellis. Meanwhile I am a prisoner.

Your letter has come since I wrote the foregoing sentences. Many thanks for enclosure which I will send on at once to Kegan Paul, Trench & Co. I have been unable to send you the money you lent, for things have been a little unfavourable to us lately. I have

---

other poem Yeats sent was probably 'The Lake Isle of Innisfree,' the next to be published, on December 13, in Henley's periodical which had by that time changed its name to the *National Observer*.

[1] At present it has not been possible to identify this publication. The British Museum authorities have made an intensive search and can find no paper of this title at the appropriate date, nor is it mentioned in *The Times Handlist* of English Periodicals. Enquiry at the Library of the London Theosophical Society yielded no result. A letter from J. B. Yeats to O'Leary, in the National Library of Ireland, dated November 18, 1890, says: 'The weekly review from what I learn means to be very energetic. I fancy C. Johnston, half literary man, half man of action, will make a good journalist.' The mention of Johnston suggests that the paper had a theosophical content.

got at last the first proof sheets of that book for Putnam's and so may have some soon but when I do not know.

Ellis's father old Alexander Ellis F.R.S.[1] died a few days ago, suddenly while Ellis was at Brighton. I do not know if it makes any change in Ellis's affairs. I have not seen him.

The papers you sent us about Swift McNeil and Balfour were amusing and not cheerful in some ways. Firstly McNeil talked possible sense ridiculously in the wrong place and secondly that other nationalist McSweeny (or some such name) who opposed him was, when he half apologised for having been in jail saying he *'probably deserved it for breaking the law,'* something worse than ridiculous. However all roads lead to Rome I suppose, even those of McNeil and McSweeny. I mean that they are nationalists of a kind and intend right things.

I was at the Littles' last night with Rhys. He and Miss Grace Little will be married in January. He has taken a cottage in South Wales.

So I hear that Miss Johnston has started or has something to do with a vegetarian restaurant in Dublin. Do you know where it is? I hear also that she has broken off her engagement to Wright. Some Theosophical dispute, or such thing, at bottom of it.

By the by I have had to resign from inner section of Theosophical Society because of my first article on *Lucifer* [2] in *Weekly Review*. They wanted me to promise to criticise them never again in same fashion. I refused because I looked upon request as undue claim to control right of individual to think as best pleased him. I may join them again later on. We are of course good friends and allies—except in this matter and except that I told them they were turning a good philosophy into a bad religion. This latter remark has not been well taken by some of the fiercer sort. Relations have been getting strained for about a year—on these points.

How does the biography go on? I am very glad to hear about the poems. Yours very truly   W B YEATS

[1] Alexander John Ellis, F.R.S. (1814–1890), a famous philologist and mathematician, had died on October 28.

[2] *Lucifer* was the organ of the London Theosophical Society. Yeats had contributed an article 'Irish Fairies, Ghosts, Witches, etc.' to its pages on January 15, 1889.

TO KATHARINE TYNAN

Nov. [1890]   *3 Blenheim Road*

My dear Katey, I have put off writing to you day after day in hope of being able to come to some decision as to when I would be able to leave here for Dublin. I find however that I cannot yet say. Blake work still keeps me. I must leave a great portion of the book in a complete state even if I do some of it in Dublin. I must get over to Dublin or Sligo or somewhere soon however, for I am struggling with the difficulties of semi-collapse. I have something wrong with my heart but not of an important nature. The doctor says that I have been wearing myself out and has directed me to live more deliberately and leisurely. By no means an easy thing for anyone of my temperament. There is nothing serious wrong with me, I believe, so be not alarmed. I am somewhat better than I was a few days ago as it is.

Ellis is working away at the reproductions of Blake drawings. The book will contain a great number. It will be a very big book in two volumes—the second containing the reproductions of the 'prophetic books' with their illustrations, the first our accounts of the philosophy.

What are you doing in the matter of verse? I had a little poem in the *Scots Observer* the other day and they have another coming shortly. I have also done one that I mean to send to the *English Illustrated*. All three are Irish and I think fairly good. How does the life of the Nun go on?

I expect it will be a very picturesque little book. I am sure you will make it so unless you are specially unfortunate in the life it describes.

This is a miserably short and empty letter but I must go to work at Blake. Send me a good long letter though I do not deserve it for letting so long go by without answering your last. Yours always,

                                                 W B YEATS

TO KATHARINE TYNAN

Dec. 4th, 1890   *3 Blenheim Road*

My dear Katey, I send you that long-promised photograph. I shall expect your opinion of it quite soon. It is, I think, good.

My health is rather better but the doctor has told my father to bid me take great care, from which I judge that I shall be a trifle invalided these coming weeks at least. I find myself soon tired and otherwise lacking my old initiative.

I see much of Johnston and his wife. He has been in all ways greatly improved by his Indian work. He lives close to Madame Blavatsky with whom he is on as good terms as he is on bad with her followers, who say he is conceited beyond endurance, etc. I too have had a quarrel with the followers and [have] withdrawn from all active work in the society. I wrote some articles they objected to about *Lucifer*. Madame Blavatsky told me some months ago that the taking off of my beard would bring me disaster in matter of health through loss of 'magnetism' or for some other eccentric reason of the same kind. So see now what you and my other friends have got upon your souls. Yours very truly, W B YEATS

TO JOHN O'LEARY [1]

Jan. 21 [1891] *3 Blenheim Road*

My dear Mr. O'Leary, My only excuse for not having written before is that I have been deeply entangled in Blake and so kept putting off. I had finished about ten days ago almost the whole of the general account when I discovered a mistake, unimportant in itself but deeply woven into the method of expression, and had to start several chapters afresh. I have until this week not been in town for a long time, hence I have not yet sold your books but will do so in the next few days. I have been working on in a kind of desperation, putting off everything, not even writing a single verse or article of any kind. I have Miss O'Leary's book, Todhunter's *Sicilian Idyll*, a book for *National Observer* (late *Scots*), a volume of verse by Miss Wynne, a play of Ibsen's and O'Donnell's poems all waiting leisure for treatment. The first mentioned will come first. The reason why I am afraid of leaving Blake for a time is that Ellis is in a hurry and if I leave it may do some of my chapters himself and do them awry. Providence has stopped off his terrible activity for the present with twelve lectures for the University Extension. He may awake at any moment however and attack my province with horse, foot and

---

[1] From a copy thought to have been made by D. J. O'Donoghue.

artillery. The boundary mark between his and mine being a not over well defined bourne. I had to put up a notice against trespassers a couple of weeks ago. Ellis is magnificent within his limits but threatens to overthrow them, and beyond them he is useless through lack of mystical knowledge. It is just as well that he does perhaps, as I am always tending to stop and consider and reconsider when I should be going ahead. I give up all hope of fixing a date for my Dublin visit until the printer has got the first half of this book. But for the mistake I spoke of I should have fixed one perhaps. Enough of Blake and more than enough.

Todhunter, I think, will review Miss O'Leary's poems. A copy should be sent to the *Academy* and one to him (for which he will send subscription). I fear I cannot do anything with *National Observer* in the matter, as Henley, I think, looks after all the verse himself. If you send him a copy I will write to him about it but cannot foretell result. He is an unpersuadable [?] kind of man. Have all the subscribers got their copies? A week or so ago Mrs. Hancock of 125 Queen's Gate, Kensington, had not. I sent her 2/6 and address to Oldham (I believe) a long while ago.

Jan 22nd

In the last *Spectator* you sent you ask me to forward it to Miss Tullock but forgot to give her address. You ask me also to send her your 'Byron.' Do you mean the *Academy* article or the life of him by Roden Noel? I will send the Irish books tomorrow. It seems as though Parnell's chances had greatly improved these latter weeks. His last two speeches were wonderfully good. I wish I was over in Ireland to see and hear how things are going. The Hartlepool victory should help him by showing that his action has not injured the cause over here as much as people say.[1] My father is bitterly opposed to Parnell on the ground chiefly, now, of his attacks on his followers. To me, if all other reasons were absent, it would seem plain that a combination of priests with the 'Sullivan gang'[2] is not

[1] At the Hartlepool election on January 22, 1891, C. Furness, a Liberal, beat the Conservative candidate, Sir W. Gray, by 298 votes. This was expected to further the cause of Home Rule.
[2] The 'Sullivan gang' consisted of the Sullivans and the Healys. A. M. Sullivan had secured control of the *Nation*, a very influential nationalist weekly, after Gavan Duffy left Ireland, and he and his brother, T. D. Sullivan, were both M.P.s. The Healys were Tim and Maurice, both M.P.s, and connected with the Sullivans by marriage. All were very bitter against Parnell.

likely to have on its side in political matters divine justice. The whole business will do this good anyway. The Liberals will have now to pass a good measure if any measure at all—at least so I read the matter. *Daily News* this morning has a long article on Hyde's book which I have not yet seen. I shall ask *Scots Observer* for it.[1]
Yours very sincerely   W B YEATS

Am in much better health than I was—fortunately for Blake's book. My heart troubles me now but seldom. . . .

TO KATHARINE TYNAN

March 5 [1891]   *3 Blenheim Road*

My dear Katey, I am again greatly behind hand in this matter of letter writing. But do not think that you are out of my thoughts because I let the weeks go by without a letter. I am one of those unhappy people for whom between act and deed lies ever the terrible gulf of dreams. I sit down to write and go off into a brown study instead. At least, if circumstances offer me the slightest excuse.

My excuse these times has been that Blake still hangs in the balance—it always seems possible that a month, say, might finish it and yet now one thing, now another, brings delay. When I begin writing to you—I have so started several times—I stop and say, 'What shall I say about times and dates? When may I hope to be in Ireland?' and thereon I am down into the gulf and the letter is put off until I have more exact information.

Probably your London visit will come before my Irish one. One thing that delays us is that I no longer go to Edwin Ellis's house to work through the MSS. with him but have to wait until we can meet here, or in the Museum, or at the publisher's. Mrs. Ellis got the curious delusion that I had some mesmeric power over her that made her ill. The sight of me made her grow white with terror. She has now got over the delusion and wants me to go there again but I am afraid of its returning and so stay away. She is so horribly

[1] Yeats reviewed Douglas Hyde's *Beside the Fire* in the *National Observer*, February 28. The review was reprinted, under the title 'The Four Winds of Desire,' in the first edition of *The Celtic Twilight*, 1893.

hysterical and has had her head turned by a too constant and wholly unthinking sense of the unseen universe and of its unknown powers.

Yesterday I got a paper with Miss Kavanagh's death announced in it. It was a great shock to us all. Lolly had some knowledge of how very ill she was but I had none. The last I heard was that she was better. I had no expectation whatever that we would lose her so soon. Only the other day I re-read 'St. Michan's Churchyard' and thought how charming it was. Everything she did was so like herself—it had the same quiet and gentle sincerity. It was so entirely untouched by the restless ambition that makes writers untrue to themselves. She was essentially, it seems to me, what people mean by the phrase 'a beautiful soul.' To you and me and all of us she is in every way a loss. Some of the pleasure of writing is gone in that we cannot send her any more anything that we write. How our old circle is broken up—first Miss O'Leary and now Miss Kavanagh. I think of sending some notice of her to the *Pilot*, unless you wish to do so.[1] I will write one tomorrow and send it unless you tell me that you have intentions of so doing, in which case my account can go elsewhere. So please let me know at once.

Miss Kavanagh's death is in itself much sadder than Miss O'Leary's. Miss O'Leary had had a full and not wholly short life while Miss Kavanagh dies with all her plans and projects uncompleted, all her promise unfulfilled. I feel sure that we take up our half-done labours in other lives and carry them to conclusion. If it were not so, the best of lives were not worth living and the universe would have no order and purpose. I think you have some such thought in one of your poems.

I think I shall be able to get *John Sherman* published. I am going next week to offer it to Heinemann and if he does not take it I can, I think, get it taken by Fisher Unwin for his Pseudonym Library. Edward Garnett, Unwin's reader, is quite enthusiastic about it. If I can get *Sherman* and my play, *The Countess Kathleen*, together with 'Blake' published this year I should be well in evidence. The two volumes of collected Irish Stories I edited for Putnam are printed and may be published any day now. If *Sherman* gets printed I shall be greatly pleased. There is more of myself in it than in anything I have done. I don't imagine it will please many people but some few

---

[1] Yeats wrote an article on Rose Kavanagh in the *Boston Pilot*, April 11, 1891.

it may please with some kind of permanent pleasure. Except for the wish to make a little money, I have no desire to get that kind of fussing regard a book wins from the many. To please the folk of few books is one's great aim. By being Irish, I think, one has a better chance of it.

Over here there is so much to read and think about that the most a writer can usually hope for is that kind of unprosperous prosperity that comes from writing books that lie amid a half dozen others on a drawing-room table for a week.

You have not told me anything about your life of a nun for a long time—or indeed, for that matter, anything about anything. You have the bad habit of keeping to the letter of the law in the matter of correspondence. Once when you did not write to me for a great while, I wrote without waiting for your letter. You, however, have a most un-Irish love for law and order in this matter.

Rhys is up in London again with his wife. We got to the Littles' tonight to meet them. He seems much rejoiced at the change in his prospects and grown eloquent in person, as before by letter, over the general delightfulness of his life in Wales.

I hear Miss Mulholland is in London. I called on her last week but she was out. The Meynells has [have] expressed a wish to have her portrait in *Merry England* and my father will make a sketch if we can get her to sit.

When do you come to London? My own dislike for the place is certainly not on the decrease. When Blake is done I shall go to Ireland and find my way down to the West and stay there as long as possible. I have much to write and much to think of—I can do it best down there. Yours very truly,   W B YEATS

TO KATHARINE TYNAN

[*March* 1891]   3 *Blenheim Road*

My dear Katey, I enclose this with *Irish Tales*. Please tell me what you think of the dedicatory lines to the Irish abroad.

I was very—very—sorry to hear that you were ill but hope that you are well now, as I judge you to be from a review of Hyde's book by you that O'Leary sent me. A very good review, better in some ways than my *National Review* one, and done, I feel sure, with much more ease and speed.¹ But please tell me whether you were seriously ill. This is but poor sympathy coming so late in the day but I kept waiting on for this book of Irish tales—due three weeks ago.

My *John Sherman* has at last been taken by Fisher Unwin for his Pseudonym Library. I am to get a royalty but not until it gets into its second thousand if it ever does so.

Blake 'proofs' are coming in—2nd vol. proofs—the MS. for the 1st vol. is not quite finished. Printers will probably start at it next week—start at 1st pages—before last are finished in MS. The illustrations look well in the proofs.

Did O'Leary show you a poem of mine in *National Observer* called 'A Man who dreamed of Fairy Land'? Henley liked it very much and some friends here say it is my best; that is to say, Arthur Symons ² and Edward Garnett do. Yours as ever,   W B YEATS

Your Cruikshank *Sketchbook*, if a genuine 1st edition—there was a reprint ten years ago—is worth about 30/-. I thought to see Quaritch about it months ago but have never done so—not having spoken to him since I lunched with him at the start of the bargain. Nothing has turned up to bring me to him and when something or other has sent me into his shop he was not there.

TO JOHN O'LEARY

[? *April* 1891]   3 *Blenheim Road*

Dear Mr. O'Leary, The 'proofs' of the Blake book are coming in slowly, we are printing bit by bit—writing and printing going on at once. The illustrations look right well. I have reviewed the *Lays of Country, Home and Friends* for the *Pilot* and will try and do so for *National Observer* next week.³ I am just now writing the preliminary memoir for the first volume of Blake—Ellis wants that at once.

¹ Yeats evidently writes *National Review* in mistake for *National Observer*. For his review of Douglas Hyde's book see note 1, p. 164.
² This is the first mention of Arthur Symons (1865–1945), who became a great friend. It was about this date that the Rhymers' Club was founded, Symons being one of the members.
³ Yeats wrote of Ellen O'Leary's *Lays of Country, Home and Friends* in the *Boston Pilot*, April 18, but does not seem to have reviewed it in the *National Observer*.

Could you send me a card with Ashe King's address that I may get Putnam to send him a review copy of *Irish Tales*, also please tell me if Miss Gonne has returned to Dublin? I did not write to her because I wanted to get *Irish Tales* to give her a copy and do not like to chance sending it to that French address, which by the by I could not read with any certainty. Did you like the introduction to *Irish Tales*?

Putnam seems inclined to act on my suggestions as to Irish papers and Irish reviewers. Is Coffey noticing books anywhere? The book ought to make a good text for anybody who wants to do an article on Irish things in general—and King's articles in *Freeman* are general enough God knows. I shall have prospectuses of the Blake in a day or so and shall send you one or two. They give a specimen illustration that may interest you. My story *John Sherman* has been taken by Unwin for the Pseudonym Series but don't tell any one the name of it as Unwin I believe makes rather a point of the Pseudonymous nature of the books.

How are you getting on with the Memoir? Yours very sincerely
W B YEATS

TO JOHN O'LEARY [1]

[*June* 1891] *3 Blenheim Road*

Dear Mr. O'Leary, I did not answer before because I knew I should have to write almost at once again if I took your hint about the postcard, as I want you to address the enclosed to Rolleston whose Irish address I have mislaid. I could not, however, write before to-day as I have been very busy. Todhunter has had a play on and I have had to review it twice and write only on chance of reviews being printed too; to see it twice and lose time helping to hunt up people to fill empty places as well as writing hard at Blake. This last because I want to be in Ireland by the middle of July and must see a lot for the printers done before then. I am going to stay with Charles Johnston who will have Ballykilbeg to himself for a couple of weeks and shall then endeavour to spend a week in Dublin if the Tynans will take me in. I can only get away for a very short time

[1] From a typewritten copy.

pending the completion of Blake and am afraid of facing Dublin distractions before I give a little while to country placidity. I see by your note that you hope to be in London. I hope your visit here will not coincide by any ill chance with mine to Dublin. I am rather in a difficulty about Miss O'Leary's poems. I find it almost impossible to review it for so ultra-Tory a paper as the *National Observer*; when I do an article I intend for *Providence Journal* I shall try again. In any case I shall again remind Todhunter about *Academy* (I did so remind him once but he has been busy with his plays); if he is not going to do it I can try and get it from Cotton and can write review either before leaving this three weeks hence or when in Ballykilbeg. . . . When I consented to Henley's suggestion that I should review it for him I had no idea how difficult it would be. If I were a Tory it would be easy enough, or if I could descend to writing as a Tory who did not let his politics quite kill literary sympathies. A few saving clauses would make all well, but they are just what I cannot put in.

The article on Blake you sent me has proved most useful. When did it appear? . . . I cannot find where I put P.B. notice [1] but will ransack my pockets and table for it, in a day or two. *I promise*.

My novel has gone to press but does not come out until September. I have sent in with it, to be put in the same volume, a short tale of ancient Irish legendary days and called the book *John Sherman and The Midnight Ride*.[2] The second part of the title refers to second story. My pseudonym is Ganconagh, the name of an Irish spirit. I am very glad to hear news about the progress of your book and the course of events in Tipperary. Yours very sincerely   W B YEATS

TO KATHARINE TYNAN

[*In week ending June* 27, 1891]   *3 Blenheim Road*

My dear Katey, I send you the Henley notes. I tell about all that I know but fear that but little of it will do for your purpose. Some of it would hardly do for the public press. I trust your discretion in the matter. The wild and reckless early life of the Stevenson

[1] Probably a slip for B.P. (*Boston Pilot*).
[2] *The Midnight Ride* or *Rider* were evidently alternative titles which Yeats was considering for the story *Dhoya*. He eventually reverted to the original title when the story appeared, with *John Sherman*, in the Pseudonym Library.

Henley circle, for instance, would hardly do for public press. I forgot, I see, to mention that Henley is a burly man with a beard and a restless way of sitting and moving—somewhat like W. Morris in this—and that one of his good points is his sympathy with young writers.

Last week Todhunter's play was acted.[1] I saw it twice, helped hunt up people to fill vacant seats and reviewed it twice. I also wrote a very important essay called 'The necessity of symbolism' for the book on Blake [2] and went through it with Ellis and made suggested alterations. The visit to Ireland makes some hurry needed in order to leave the printers enough to go on with. This was the reason of my delay about the Henley notes. Take Oscar Wilde for another of your subjects. He is *actual* now because of his just published *Intentions* (a wonderful book) and his enlarged edition of *Dorian Gray*. Describe the serious literary side of his life—his fairy tale book *The Happy Prince* and these last books and mention his poems slightly but not slightingly. Let Nettleship stand over until autumn, when the book of designs will be out or until I can let you see 'proofs' if such things come my way. It is not decided quite who will edit it but I may do so in all likelihood. His book on Browning should be known to you also. 'The Rhymers' Club' will publish a book of verse almost at once. You might take it as a subject of one article. It will give you a chance of saying much about the younger writers—Le Gallienne, A. Symons and so forth. I think Blake should justify you in giving me a notice—if it comes in time. In any case, *John Sherman and The Midnight Rider* by 'Ganconagh' will serve if you care for it. It comes out in September. The incognito will be pretty transparent because of a poem which is in both my book and in *The Midnight Rider*.

You have not told me what you think of the introduction to *Irish Tales*. Please do so. Favourable or the reverse, I want your opinion.

Have you seen a pretty little book called *A Light Load* by Dollie

---

[1] At the Vaudeville Theatre Dr. Todhunter had revived *A Sicilian Idyll* together with a new play *The Poison Flower*, founded on Hawthorne's story 'Rappacini's Daughter,' with Florence Farr in the leading part. Yeats reviewed the production in the *Providence Sunday Journal*, July 13, and in the *Boston Pilot* August 1. The venture was not a success and Yeats refers to it, without mentioning Todhunter by name, in the opening of his essay 'The Theatre' in *Ideas of Good and Evil*, 1903.

[2] This formed the first chapter of the section 'The Symbolic System' in *The Works of William Blake*, Vol. I.

Radford? It seems to me pleasant and is the work of the wife of one of our 'Rhymers.' I have heard several people praise *Whisper!* [1] by the bye—*A Light Load* and *Whisper!* have the same kind of charm and I hear them mentioned together. Mrs. Radford gave me her book yesterday; here is a stanza

> 'The love within my heart for thee
> Before the world was had its birth,
> It is the part God gives to me
> Of the great wisdom of the earth.'

Are they not fine? They have a largeness of thought and feeling above mere prettiness. It is the best stanza in the book, I think, but still there are other good things. All trifling, more or less like *Whisper!*, but equally genuine and more thoughtful.

When does your new poem-book come? May I see the selection you have made for it when I get to Dublin? I hope you will be able to put me up for a few days on my way back from Johnston's. I am taking this chance of a short holiday as Blake seems stretching out beyond all belief and so making all waiting to get off after it is done useless. I am feeling the want of new scenes and old faces. I have not been out of London for longer than a few days at Oxford and two days with Edward Garnett in Surrey since I came last from Ireland, and feel my imagination rather overpowered by continual London din. When Blake is done I shall get clean away, however, for a longer stay, I hope. I must write more poetry and cannot do it here, where everything puts one's nerves on edge.

Perhaps my Ballykilbeg visit may help my imagination to work again. I want to get to Dublin not merely to see you and other good friends but to have some talk with knowledgeable folk about my essay on Ireland in the eighteenth century for Unwin's Adventure Series.

When will I get a copy of your life of the Nun? Please send me as soon as possible the full title for mention in the *Pilot*. They paid me for last two articles so I want to write for them again.

You talk of *trying* to get me a copy. Now do manage it. I have surely earned it by never failing to let you have copies of my books and may beside be useful to you in the matter of reviews.

[1] Yeats had already made brief mention of *Whisper!* by Frances Wynne in his article in the *Boston Pilot*, April 18. 'Miss Wynne is but a writer of pretty skilful and rather trivial verses.'

I like your Lynch man pretty well and my sisters like him very well.[1] He has a vile philosophy and an unelastic though clever mind like Elton, whom you met here.[2] He seems full of projects and has the advantage of being the first Irishman I have met who *has* a philosophy to be detested.

I have done my duty by him and introduced him to some literary folk he wanted to meet and shall try and see more of him, but find I judge people to a great extent by their attitude on certain great questions, and that he is, so far as I now see, committed though less hopelessly than his prototype, Elton, to the side which is not mine. I shall however know when his book on the philosophy of criticism comes out. Yours always, W B YEATS

TO KATHARINE TYNAN

[*July* 1891] *3 Blenheim Road*

My dear Katey, I see by *Irish Monthly* that your *A Nun—her Friends and her Order* is out. If you have not been able to keep me a copy, get me a review copy at any rate. I can review it in the *Pilot* certainly and elsewhere probably. I can also if I care for it, and I feel sure I will, get it reviewed probably in some of the papers over here—the *Anti-Jacobin* and the *Star* I think very likely and perhaps also in the *Pall Mall* and one or two others. To do so, however, I should have a copy as soon as you possibly can, as I shall leave for Ireland in about ten days, I expect, and may have some difficulty in getting it read and in looking up friends about it if it comes late in the ten days.

Owing to the Rhymers' Club I have a certain amount of influence with reviewers. I can probably besides before-mentioned papers get you a note in the *Speaker* at least and certainly can help you with the *Queen*. The *Speaker* reviews are unfortunately very few and far between. The notes however are very much in the friendly hand of

---

[1] Probably Arthur Lynch (1861–1934) who wrote books of criticism and philosophy. He lived much in Paris where he worked as a journalist. See also letter to John O'Leary, November 1891 (p. 191).

[2] Almost certainly Oliver Elton (1861–1945), an old friend of the Yeats family. He was Professor of English Literature at the University of Liverpool from 1900 to 1925. Author of many books including a Life of York Powell, 1906. He contributed a memoir of John Butler Yeats to the edition of his *Letters* published in 1944.

John Davidson. The *Academy* must also be looked up. If you like I can myself ask for it there. I must however read it first as it may be a very good book and yet a difficult one—if you have made it very Catholic—to review for a Churchless mystic like me. I mean that an ardent believer *might* be better for you as far as *Academy* is concerned. I think, however, that it is important that someone should ask for it or they may bunch it up with a lot of other books.

I gather from the *Irish Monthly* that you have done your work in the very best spirit and look forward to reading it with excited expectation. Your first prose book is a momentous matter and may be the beginning of a new literary life for you. I am myself busy with new work. Fisher Unwin are going to reprint my articles on folklore etc. from the *National Observer* with what additional articles on Irish subjects I can get together this summer and Jack is to make twenty illustrations.[1] This is just the kind of thing I have been looking for, as it will enable me to write articles, putting my best work into them without feeling that they will be lost in mere ephemeral journalism. I have also expectations of getting *The Countess Kathleen* and some ballads and lyrics taken for the Cameo Series. The reader says he will take them if he likes 'The Countess' as well as he does the rest of my poems. Dr. Todhunter says 'The Countess' is my best work so far and I dare say the reader will think the same. I shall submit to him the 3 Acts I have finished and do the rest in Ireland.

I am also to edit a volume of Irish Fairy Tales [2] for children and in all likelihood a book of Irish Poems, which will enable me to include you, Rolleston and the rest of our little school of modern Irish poets. I have likewise the Introduction to those wretched 'Irish Adventures' waiting writing. *The Countess* however will be the first venture I think and may follow *John Sherman* almost immediately.

So you see I shall be well represented this year even without the Magnum Opus which grows more and more intricate and I hope more and more profound every day. The mystics all over the world will have to acknowledge Ellis and myself among their authorities.

[1] Fisher Unwin did not reprint Yeats's articles on folklore. But the book appeared in 1893 as *The Celtic Twilight*, published by Lawrence & Bullen. It had however only a frontispiece by J. B. Yeats instead of the twenty illustrations by Jack B. Yeats.
[2] *Irish Fairy Tales*, edited by Yeats, appeared in Fisher Unwin's 'Children's Library' in 1892. It contained two illustrations by Jack B. Yeats.

We shall help good people 'to make their souls' quite as much as any of your *Irish Monthly* writers who seem, by the by, to be discovering, in the very kindest way, however, the cloven hoof in my *Irish Tales*. They kept dead silence over the Carleton and now awake to murmur—and yet I gave nothing but stories admitted by all men to be masterpieces of literature, and literature alone was in my bond. The book has been very well received on the whole—much better received than anything of mine except the poems. The reviews have been longer than were given to the *Fairy Tales*—a much more elaborate and useful book—or, as far as Ireland was concerned, to *Oisin*. There are still a number—the *Star*, the *Pall Mall* and the *Academy*—which are a-writing in friendly hands. The *Saturday Review* is the only hostile paper yet. I am rather anxious about *Sherman*. It is good, I believe, but it will be a toss-up how the reviewers take it—for if they look for the ordinary stuff of novels they will find nothing.

Do what you can for it—for a success with stories would solve many problems for me and I write them easily.

I saw Miss Frances Wynne on Wednesday and asked her and her young man for Sunday evening. Will get some people who know her book to meet her. Yours, W B YEATS

This is a horribly bookish letter but I began it with your 'Nun' and one book led to another.

Who wrote the charming article on Miss Kavanagh in current *Irish Monthly*? It is signed 'O.K.' Write as soon as possible in the matter of the Nun.

TO KATHARINE TYNAN

[*July* 16, 1891]   3 *Blenheim Road*

My dear Katey, A great many thanks for your letters and for the book which has just reached me. (It came yesterday. O'Leary has it until tonight.)

I am to do you for Miles at once, as the next volume [1] is the volume of Ladies Poets.

[1] Of *The Poets and the Poetry of the Century*: an anthology in 8 volumes, 1892, edited by Alfred H. Miles.

After my wish to see you, this is the cause of my going to Whitehall on my way north. He [Miles] told me the memoirs would be too late in a month or three weeks hence.

If you intend to have any people at your place on Sunday afternoon, would you be so kind as to ask Russell. I want to see him and talk of several matters. Yours always affectionately,   W B YEATS

I have only been able to read one chapter of your book but will get further with it before I see you.

TO KATHARINE TYNAN

[*July* 24, 1891] *Ballykilbeg*
  C. Down

My dear Katey, I arrived here yesterday and spent the evening letting up fire balloons and hunting them across country and am today writing the notice of Miss O'Leary for Miles. I asked Charles Johnston did he remember a boy at Harcourt St. called Hinkson.[1] He said he did and that he was a very nice fellow and had 'the true instincts of the scholar.' It is about the first instance in which I have heard him praise any Harcourt St. boy.

Please tell me the date of your first book and also of *Shamrocks*. I did not bring either over with me, unfortunately. Could you post me a copy of *Shamrocks*? I would return it and I fear I need it for this notice. Please tell me also the date of your first printed poem and where it appeared. Please say the nature of your first work; was it Catholic or Irish or what? What writer first woke up your imagination? Was it Rossetti?

It would be a great convenience if you could post me both *Shamrocks* and *Louise de [la] Vallière*. It is a troublesome thing to ask but I need them and I would send them back the day after I sent the notice.

I left my razor strop behind me—also my brush and comb and am rather astray for lack of them. Could Dan find them and send them to me?

[1] Probably Henry A. Hinkson who married Katharine Tynan in 1893. See note to letter of April 27, 1887 (p. 33).

Charles Johnston sends you his kind remembrances. Yours always,
　　　　　　　　　　　　　　　　　　　　　　　　W B YEATS

I saw the *National Press* review of the *Nun* in the train yesterday—most unjust and I suspect Taylor of being the author by the style.[1] It touches a defect but only a superficial one, and makes it appear typical of the whole. It will stir up your friends, however. The poem he quotes with disapproval seemed to me particularly good. The *National Press* was probably glad enough to have an article attacking you, in revenge for your father's and your own Parnellism. The papers on your own side will be made all the more favourable by this attack.

TO KATHARINE TYNAN

[*late July* 1891]　　　　　　　　　　　　　　　　　　*Ballykilbeg*

My dear Katey, The poems arrived this morning and I have just finished the critical notice.[2] *Shamrocks* has not, however, turned up yet and I cannot let Miles go to press with what you have sent, without 'St. Francis and the Birds,' so I shall only send him the critical notices this time and let the selection follow. I think you will like my notice of you; it is a success, I think.

Could you send me that account the peasant gave of her vision of St. Joseph? The 'never starched in this world' thing, if you can give it me, will make the fortune of my introduction to the *Fairy Tales*. I would like to get it at once because I shall be paid the moment the introduction is done and my sister wants some money.

The thing I asked you for was not a razor but a razor-strop—that is, a thing for sharpening a razor on. Mine is a thing like a strap with a ring at each end and like this. [*Here he gives a rough sketch*.] Dan will be able to find it.

I am doing a certain amount of writing—the notices of Miss O'Leary and Miss Wynne have gone in—but much of my time is

[1] Probably John F. Taylor, for whom see note on p. 76.
[2] Although Yeats evidently wrote a short essay on Katharine Tynan's work to appear in the series *The Poets and the Poetry of the Century*, to be followed by a selection from her poetry, it was apparently not used; the essay which was printed is signed by A. H. Miles himself. Yeats contributed essays on William Allingham to the fifth volume and on Ellen O'Leary to the seventh volume of the series, but Frances Wynne received no notice at all.

spent in helping to make fire balloons and in letting them off, and in exploring old castles and in such-like country pursuits. I have found no folklore nor hear of any to speak of, and am in all ways living a good out-o'-door life with little of the mind in it.

I went into *United Ireland* offices, by the by, before leaving Dublin, and found them anxious for literary articles. Why don't you contribute? Yours always, W B YEATS

TO JOHN O'LEARY

Tuesday [? August 1891]   54 *Lower Mount St.*
Dublin

My dear Mr. O'Leary, Before I left London you were so good as to say that if I was in a fix for a pound or two when in Dublin you would lend it me. I am rather in a fix just this moment. I have enough for my own expenses but have just heard from my sister that she is going to Sligo a week earlier than I had thought and that she wants £2 I was to give her for her expenses. I had intended to send it out of some money I am to get from Fisher Unwin for my new book of Irish Fairy Story but the MS lies waiting for some stories that Douglas Hyde promises me and I fear will not reach Unwin in time for the money to serve my sister's need. I can return the £2 next week together with what I already owe you. Could you send it me in time for me to send it to my sister this week as she starts for Sligo next Monday?

My father is doing well or about to do well. He has got a portrait of Mrs. Conolly to do for which he will get £50 and after that another in Yorkshire for £40 and probably one of Miss Conolly.

I had a good time in Co. Down with Johnston and shall return there again next week in all likelihood. I came yesterday for a week.

I have been down to *United Ireland* and was well received and find them ready for articles. I have not yet seen Leamy but shall try to do so to-day.[1] I saw the sub-editor. Yours very sincerely

W B YEATS

[1] Edmund Leamy (1848–1904), the editor of *United Ireland*, was a solicitor and B.L. but did very little law practice. He was elected M.P. for Waterford in 1880, for N.E. Cork in 1885, for South Sligo in 1887, and for Kildare in 1900, was a supporter of Parnell and stood by him at the split. He published a book of original *Irish Fairy Tales*, and wrote verse, but his poems have never been collected.

Please excuse the soiled paper—it is *studio* paper and as such has a time honoured right to be soiled.

On second thoughts would you be so very good as to send the £2 direct to Lilly.

TO KATHARINE TYNAN

[*Late August* 1891] *54 Lower Mount St.*

My dear Katey, I enclose £1 in extinction of my debt and also 2/6 which please give to the servant. It suddenly occurs to me by the by that I owe you 1/- or so besides the £1 but as I have no postal order for this amount will have to let it wait until we meet. The *Providence Journal* money came today. I do believe that I left that miserable strap for sharpening my razor on at your house again; if so, please send it. I wrote you a post card to this effect yesterday but do not think I posted it. Please send me also the MS. of *The Countess Kathleen* as I have some notion of going on with it. I tried the experiments the Sigersons [1] wanted on Monday evening with much success. They will tell you about it if you care to ask.

Please send me a postcard to say when you get this as I have lost money in the post before now—Yours always,   W B YEATS

'Mangan' out in *United Ireland* and vilely misprinted.[2]
Jack comes to Dublin on Saturday.

TO W. E. HENLEY

Sept 4th [1891] *3 Upper Ely Place*
Dublin

Dear Mr. Henley, I send you a book of sonnets by Rhys with drawings by my brother who is about 19 years old and means to take to illustrating. The drawings seem to me to have a very genuine tragic intensity that makes them something much more than caricatures—

---

[1] For the Sigerson family see note on letter of June 25, 1887 (p. 42).
[2] Yeats contributed an essay 'Clarence Mangan's Love Affair' to *United Ireland*, August 22.

Perhaps you might, if you care for them, get some one to say a good word for them of some kind in the *National Observer*.

Unwin will send you in a day or two a story of mine called *John Sherman*. There is a little thing bound up with it called *Dhoya* that may please you. There is a poem of mine that was in my book embedded in *Dhoya*, so the pseudonymity—this thing comes out in the Pseudonym Library—is not very profoundly kept.

I send you by the same post with this an article on a curious Dublin visionary and a little poem.[1]

My visionary by the by showed me your 'God in the Garden' poem and called it one of your best things. He is a reader of your verse and in all ways one of the few true students of poetry I know. I think with him about your 'God in a Garden.' Its verse has a fine ringing sound. Yours very sincerely W B YEATS

Please send proofs—if enclosed poem etc. suit you—to 3, Upper Ely Place, Dublin.

TO LILY YEATS

Sunday [in pencil 11 October 1891]   3 *Upper Ely Place*

My dear Lilly, Please send me as soon as possible Allingham's *Poems*. I want it to make selection from for Miles' *Poets and Poetry*.

I shall turn up in London in about ten days but may return here for a while after three weeks or so though this is not at all likely.

I send you a copy of *United Ireland* with a poem of mine on Parnell [2] written the day he died to be in time for the press that evening. It has been a success.

The Funeral is just over. The people are breathing fire and slaughter. The wreaths have such inscriptions as 'Murdered by the Priests' and a number of Wexford men were heard by [a] man I know promising to remove a Bishop and seven priests before next Sunday. Tomorrow will bring them cooler heads I doubt not.

[1] The article, 'An Irish Visionary,' an early study of AE, was printed in the *National Observer* of October 3. The poem sent with it may have been the dirge from *The Countess Kathleen*, which was printed in the issue of October 31 under the title 'Kathleen.'

[2] 'Mourn—and then Onward,' printed in *United Ireland*, October 10. Yeats never reprinted it.

Meanwhile Healy is in Paris and the people hunt for his gore in vain. Dillon and he are at feud and the feud is being fought out by the *Freeman* and *National Press* in diverse indirect fashions.

Tell Jack I have no more fairy articles at present but will get some done soon.

I have finished *The Countess Kathleen* and am doing stray lyrics and things. Yours   W B YEATS

TO FATHER MATTHEW RUSSELL

[October or November 1891]   *3 Blenheim Road*

My dear Father Russell, I send you a copy of my novel *John Sherman*.[1] If you will kindly review it and say that it is mine I shall be well pleased. People are given to thinking I can only write of the fantastic and wild, and this book has to do, so far as the long story is concerned, with very ordinary persons and events. This is why I want it to be known as mine—the poem at page 187 is in my book of poems so the disguise is not very deep. I shall probably write other stories but of a more dramatic and stirring kind if this goes at all well. Dowden quotes *Sherman* in the *Fortnightly* by the by. He told me he likes the story, that 'it is full of beautiful things' and 'very interesting' though not a strong and dramatic story in any way, nor of course was it [so] intended. The American edition has been sold and success seems likely.

Miss Tynan has just sent me the proofs of her new book. It will be a charming volume—and much the most artistic she has yet done. Yours very truly   W B YEATS

TO JOHN O'LEARY

Monday [? November 1891]   *3 Blenheim Road*

Dear Mr. O'Leary, A great many thanks for your postcard. Mrs. Miles has already sent me the book. It would not have mattered but

---

[1] *John Sherman and Dhoya* by Ganconagh was published in Fisher Unwin's Pseudonym Library in November 1891, but it is possible that Yeats may have had some advance copies to send out for review.

for a notion I have of doing a poem on one of the stories to put into the book with *The Countess Kathleen*. *John Sherman* comes out this week. I hear I am likely after all to get something for it. Garnett says £30 probably, which will be very good indeed for a first story. Blake goes slowly ahead. Ellis took off a bundle of MSS for the printer last Friday. I am only too anxious to get it done that I may be back in Ireland. What did you decide—if anything—at the Committee meeting? I want to know about this and about the political situation. A copy of *United Ireland* will serve as an answer to the second question and a post-card for the first whenever you feel inclined to send one.

Lionel Johnson who is an Irishman talks of being in Ireland next Spring and of lecturing if we like to the Young Ireland League or to our Dublin Social and Literary Club. Rhys also has intentions of turning up and would lecture, but would sooner, I imagine, find some audiences that would pay like the English and American audiences he is used to. He has a kind of Pan-Celtic enthusiasm which will spur him on to lecture under either condition however, I think. He seems well content with his Welsh life and has a son. He was up here for a few days interviewing publishers etc. He is writing stories and is trying to get one of them taken with illustrations by my brother. Rolleston I have not yet seen but expect him this evening—this being our monthly 'at home.' Lynch declares that 'the Rhymers' are his 'enemies.' They have probably been reviewing him. I expect him also to-night and one or two of his 'enemies.' We had a 'Rhymers' [1] meeting at Ellis's for Miss Gonne who has now departed for Paris where she stays for a week or ten days more, probably, and then returns here for a few days and so back to Dublin. Help her to help on the Young Ireland League, for what she needs is some work of that kind in which she could lose herself, and she is, so far, enthusiastic about the League. Oldham who does not

[1] The Rhymers' Club had been founded, probably some time early in 1891, by Yeats, Ernest Rhys and T. W. Rolleston. The other members of the club were John Davidson, Ernest Dowson, E. J. Ellis, G. A. Greene, A. C. Hillier, Herbert P. Horne, Selwyn Image, Lionel Johnson, Richard Le Gallienne, Victor Plarr, Ernest Radford, Arthur Symons and John Todhunter. In his *Autobiographies* Yeats says that William Watson was also a member but never came to the meetings, while Francis Thompson came but was not a member. Meetings were usually held in an upper room at the Cheshire Cheese in Fleet Street, though occasionally elsewhere as this letter shows. The first *Book of the Rhymers' Club* was published by Elkin Mathews in February 1892, the *Second Book of the Rhymers' Club* by Elkin Mathews and John Lane in June 1894.

believe in it will probably try to damp her ardour. She could help by getting people together at her rooms and persuading them to lecture. She could also help the Dublin Social and Literary Club greatly by the same kind of method.

 I have sent copies of *Sherman* for review to *United Ireland* and *Irish Monthly* and told them that they may say who wrote it if they like. I shall send a copy as soon as I get one to O'Donovan of the *National Press* and ask him for a notice. If Ashe King has not sent you his copy yet I will get you one. Please let me know by postcard. Yours always sincerely   W B YEATS

 Ellis is getting a volume of his poems with twenty or thirty drawings through the press.

TO GEORGE RUSSELL (AE)

Sunday [*Nov* 15, 1891]   3 *Blenheim Road*
[*Postmark Nov* 20, 1891]

My dear Russell, I forgot *Tired*, I wish you would send it me—also my *Fairy and Folk Tales of the Irish Peasantry* and Rousseau's *Confessions* whenever you have read it. There is no hurry about Rousseau but *Tired* and the other send soon. I am very sorry to have to bother you about them.

 I had a wonderfully smooth passage—the smoothest I ever remember—and arrived without any general fatigue but with no end of a bad cold. I am now getting on with Blake and hope to see the book done before long and myself back in Ireland. I have seen Miss Gonne several times and have I think found an ally in the cousin with whom she is staying. An accidental word of the cousin showed me they had been discussing me together and reading my poems in the vellum book,[1] and yesterday the cousin gave me a hint to go to Paris next Spring when Miss Gonne did—so you see I am pretty cheerful for the time until the next regiment of black devils come. Tomorrow Miss Gonne is to be initiated into [the] G[olden] D[awn] [2]

---

 [1] A manuscript book, bound in vellum, in which Yeats copied some of his love poems. It still exists, and is in the possession of Mr. Sean MacBride.
 [2] The Order of the Golden Dawn was a Secret Society founded in 1887 in London by three men, a Dr. Woodman, Dr. Wynn Westcott, Coroner for North

—the next day she goes to Paris but I shall see her on her way through London a couple of weeks later. She promises to work at the Young Ireland League for me this winter. Go and see her when she gets to Dublin and keep her from forgetting me and occultism.

Your vision about her has been curiously corroborated in all the main points by the Kaballistic seership of Mrs. Mathers,[1] helped out by Miss Gonne's own clairvoyance. The story was worked out in great detail.

Thursday

Since writing the above the initiation has taken place and Miss Gonne has started for Paris. I have been writing Blake all day, or trying to do so which is quite as laborious, and shall send off a good bulk of MSS to the printer this week. I am sending you a couple of books of Blake [2] of which I have other copies now—you have seen them but may like to own them.

Give my remembrances to Dick and Mrs. Dick. Yours very truly

W B YEATS

I will write to Dick.

TO GEORGE RUSSELL (AE)

[? *November* 1891]   3 *Blenheim Road*

My dear Russell, Tell me about Miss Johnston's Restaurant. Some one told me it had come to an end. I want to know as soon as possible, otherwise I should have one or two letters to write in

London, and S. Liddell Mathers, for the study and practice of ceremonial magic. Yeats had met Mathers at the British Museum, where he worked much in 1888 and 1889, and became a member in March 1890. Members of the Order could pass through three degrees and each member took a new motto (by the initial letters of which he was known) with each degree attained. Those who reached the inner order were known either by their main motto in the outer order or by their motto in the inner order according to whom they were writing. Yeats's usual signature was D[aemon] E[st] D[eus] I[nversus]; an article by him signed thus appeared in the *Irish Theosophist*, October 1892.

[1] Mrs. Mathers was a sister of the French philosopher Henri Bergson. Mathers (for whom see note 3, p. 208) had made her acquaintance when she was a student at the Slade School.

[2] These 'books of Blake' were facsimiles of two of the Prophetic Books and formed part of Volume III of Ellis's and Yeats's *Works of William Blake*. They are now in the possession of Dr. James S. Starkey (Seumas O'Sullivan) of Dublin.

connection with our attempt at a social and literary club—letters to Ashe King and Miss Johnston. I fear, however, that my news is correct. Tell me what you know of Miss Johnston's plans, if she has any. I heard about the Veg. from Ernest Rhys who heard of it from Miss Little.

I am getting on with Blake. The Memoir, about 60 pages, is being printed and there is about as much more of the explanatory part to follow up with. *The Countess Kathleen* has not gone to Unwin yet for I am slowly correcting it and getting other verses ready to go with it. Henley has written to me about *Sherman and Dhoya*. He likes them very much but likes 'Dhoya' best. I hope he will review them. So much for my literary affairs.

I will write again more at length about the past incarnation story, for now I write in haste merely seeking information about Miss Johnston and the Veg. Mrs. Mathers, who was the seer, had not heard of your vision. Hers was not absolutely identical in its details but curiously alike in total effect. She had made Miss G—— a priestess of a temple in Tyre and connected her with someone who, she said afterwards, resembled me, though she was not quite certain. This man lived in the desert and had much the same story as yours except there was an episode apparently later than anything you had arrived at in which he helped me to escape from the Temple. She afterwards went away by herself into the desert and died there. This was corroborated by a dream continually recurring with Miss G—— of journeying on and on in a desert. Yours very sincerely

W B YEATS

TO JOHN O'LEARY

Wednesday [? November 25, 1891] *3 Blenheim Road*

Dear Mr. O'Leary, Could you lend me £1? I will return it to you as soon as anybody pays me anything. I am owed various amounts by various people but my only regular and certain paymaster, the *Providence Journal*, has either not taken or has postponed my article sent last month. The late editor Williams is now doing most of the literary work himself. Hence the rest of us are elbowed out to some extent. I can't trouble the *National Observer* until their proper pay day comes round as they rather resent one's doing so I think. They have asked me, by the by, for stories like 'Dhoya' if I can make them short enough to fit their pages. I doubt if it can be done but mean to try.

You need not return the copy of *John Sherman* which you have, as I have got a few more copies. Did Ashe King like it? Henley praises it and it seems generally to be liked. If you meet Taylor ask him what he thought of it.

Blake goes on slowly—a good big bundle of MSS has gone to the printers. I am bringing the MS of my new book of poems to Fisher Unwin to-day but do not think they will be out until next April as the man who is publishing *The Book of the Rhymers' Club* wants to keep the copyright of the poems it contains until the end of March. Some of my best lyrics are to be in it, so I must wait until April to reprint them. What of The Young Ireland League? I wrote to Lavelle for information and got no answer. If you meet him please stir him up. Miss Gonne will be in Dublin in 10 days or less. She returns to London from Paris in two or three days. The main reason why I ask you for the loan of this £1 is that I do not want to be without the price of cabs etc while she is here and I have promised to take her to one or two plays. Sometimes post me a *United Ireland* as I never see an Irish paper here by any chance. Yours always

W B YEATS

I have just heard from Lavelle about the League. They were waiting until things had settled down after Parnell's death.

TO JOHN O'LEARY

[*December* 1891]   *3 Blenheim Road*

Dear Mr. O'Leary, The day your postal order came a sum of £10 reached me as a first instalment for *John Sherman*. I was not able to cash the cheque until Monday and so used a fraction of your £1 for some short railway journeys I had to make upon Sunday. I had intended to return the £1 at once after Monday and so did not send acknowledgement and then I found so many small bills—house bills —crying out for payment that I was afraid I might not be able to manage it. Some days passed by in the same doubt—the order which I enclose being all the time on my table awaiting posting. Only to-day I found it was all right about the bills and that I will have plenty out of my £10 for all immediate need. I therefore send back the £1 with a very great many thanks. Miss Gonne is still in Paris. She wrote to me last week to say she was coming at once and would let me know when to expect her but as yet I have not heard anything definite. You misunderstood me about the cabs. She does not let me pay the whole fare but stipulated a good while ago that she should pay her own share. When I wrote to you I had however if I remember rightly just three halfpence and no hope of more for a month and had she come at once as I expected I should have been in a fix. Fisher Unwin has taken *The Countess Kathleen* and will publish it as the April volume of his *Cameo Series*. I am to add lyrics and ballads at the end of the book. I have a vague chance of getting it acted but will write again when there is something definite. The *United Irelands* etc. were very welcome. Again thanks and apologies. Yours ever   W B YEATS

Have you heard what Taylor thought of *Sherman*?

TO KATHARINE TYNAN

[circa *December 2nd*, 1891]   *3 Blenheim Road*

My [dear] Katey, The books I left with Dr. Sigerson for you were Hyde's *Beside the Fire*, the *Kilkenny Journal* and one or two more whose names I do not remember. Of course I had nothing to do with the Manzoni and Bret Harte things. Did I tell you how fine I think the poems in your new book are? They are quite your best work. The 'Apologia' is exquisite. Rolleston likes it best of all your work.

There is a man here—a well-known journalist, Fox-Bourne by name—who has been wholly captivated by your *Nun*. I am glad to hear that the book has sold so well. My own *Sherman* is doing well—I got my first £10 for it last Saturday and shall, I hear, get about £30 at any rate. Unwin is to bring out *The Countess Kathleen*. The Blake too is going ahead. But I am not very well these days and so take little joy out of this glimmering of ampler life and success. Never did the mountain of deeds seem so steep and my feet so poor at climbing. I have one of my fits of depression. It will go by after a week or two. I imagine I have already written to you in the past from the deeps of more than one, but as life goes on they blacken. One knows at the worst of them, however, that the sun and the wind will together make the path merry again. I say all this to explain why I have not written before. I keep my black moods out of my letters by keeping my letters out of my black moods. I write now because I have your questions about the books to answer.

Did you get a post-card I sent you asking for Miss Fagan's address? I met her in an omnibus and asked her to come and see us and then, finding we would not be in that day, wrote to you for her address that I might ask her for some other day. You did not send it and she came and found only my mother, I believe. I am going to write and ask her for next Monday however. Her address being, I think, 'Alexandra Mansions;' my mother thinks it was that; if it was not would you let me know?

The Book of the Rhymers' Club has been taken by Elkin Mathews and will appear about Xmas. It is a very fine work and will give you material for an article or two.

I enclose a page from the 'proof' of Edwin Ellis's book of poems *Fate in Arcadia*. I think it is very pretty. 'For N——' is not his best for it rather lacks music, of which he has plenty at most times, but is good, I think. I have a fancy for the last verse but one.

Henley has asked me for things like 'Dhoya' for the *National Observer* and writes praises of *John Sherman*. When you review it you might perhaps, if you think it is so, say that Sherman is an Irish type. I have an ambition to be taken as an Irish Novelist, not as an English or cosmopolitan one choosing Ireland as a background. I studied my characters in Ireland and described a typical Irish feeling in Sherman's devotion to Ballah. A West of Ireland feeling, I might almost say, for, like that of Allingham for Ballyshannon, it is West rather than National. Sherman belonged like Allingham to the small gentry who, in the West at any rate, love their native places without perhaps loving Ireland. They do not travel and are shut off from England by the whole breadth of Ireland, with the result that they are forced to make their native town their world. I remember when we were children how intense our devotion was to all things in Sligo and still see in my mother the old feeling. I claim for this and other reasons that *Sherman* is as much an Irish novel as anything by Banim or Griffin. Lady Wilde has written me an absurd and enthusiastic letter about it. She is queer enough to prefer it to my poems. The reviews are nearly all good so far. Yours very sincerely,

W B YEATS

TO KATHARINE TYNAN

[*Late December* 1891]　　　　　　　　　　*3 Blenheim Road*

My dear Katey, I have sent a long review of your book to the *Evening Herald*.¹ I sent it on Monday and am very sorry I was not able to send it before. I have been rather unwell this last fortnight and quite without the initiative needed for a start at anything but my daily round of Blake chapters. The printer has about 170 pages in his hands now and the rest will follow as fast as he can print it.

All Xmas week I have been wretchedly headachy and that kind of thing, and hope my headache has not got into the review. It is enthusiastic at any rate. I will review you again for the *Pilot*, perhaps somewhere else, so I think I deserve a copy even if 'old acquaintance sake' were not enough. I am too hard up at present to buy a copy.

I am busy getting up a London Irish Literary Society—to be a branch ultimately of Young Ireland League. We are asking Gavan Duffy to be President and are hoping to get Stopford Brooke for one of the vice-presidents, and Rolleston promises to be another. I have put your book down to be got for the library. I want you to review Dr. Todhunter's *Banshee* for the *Evening Herald*. He has published a 1/- edition, rather a 1/- rebinding of his 'remainders' with Sealy, Bryers & Co., and we must do all we can to sell it off. I will do it for *United Ireland*.² The Rhymers' Book is in proof so you will soon be able to say a good word for us there, I hope.

Ernest Rhys is in Dublin. Do you know him? I am writing to give him a note of introduction to you. His address is c/o Miss Little, 6 Lower Fitzwilliam Street, Dublin. He and his wife are both over.

¹ Dr. Roger McHugh discovered this review of Katharine Tynan's *Ballads and Lyrics* in the (Dublin) *Evening Herald*, January 2, 1892, and reprinted most of it in his edition of the *Letters to Katharine Tynan*, 1953.
² Yeats's review, headed 'Dr. Todhunter's Irish Poems,' appeared in *United Ireland*, January 23, 1892.

Did I tell you that my *Countess Kathleen* comes out in April and that the book of Fairy Tales I edited for Unwin is to appear soon —what a terribly bookish letter this is! But then the four walls of my study are my world just now. Do you see the *National Observer?* If you do, please tell me what you thought of my 'Epitaph' and what you think, when you see it, of my next poem 'Rosa Mundi.' But I must wind up this now, for when one is unwell there is only ink in one's veins and ink when one expects human nature is deadly dull and I must bore you with no more of it. Yours always,

W B YEATS

PART TWO

1892—1896

INTRODUCTION TO PART TWO

'IT was the death of. Parnell,' Yeats wrote in *Four Years*, 'that convinced me that the moment had come for work in Ireland, for I knew that for a time the imagination of young men would turn from politics.' And he went on to describe his founding of the London Irish Literary Society with T. W. Rolleston's help, and said that after a few months he went to Dublin and founded there a similar society.

This was apparently in the early summer of 1892. He stayed at 53 Mountjoy Square and spent some six weeks interviewing likely supporters and lecturing in provincial towns. Maud Gonne was giving him her help, and he writes cheerfully to O'Leary of his progress.

There was a scheme on foot for a National Publishing Company, to bring out a cheap series of good books for Irish readers, and a further scheme to establish libraries in country districts. Old Sir Charles Gavan Duffy, lately returned from half a lifetime in Australia, was to direct the company. Yeats had already proposed a similar series of books to his London publisher, through his friend Edward Garnett, Unwin's reader. It seemed probable that there might be an amalgamation of the publishing schemes, the books to appear with a London and a Dublin imprint. Yeats had gone to Sligo to stay with George Pollexfen, and presently he heard with dismay that Gavan Duffy was proposing to Unwin that he should issue a series of shilling books, 'The New Irish Library,' with himself and possibly Rolleston as editors. This was Yeats's own scheme, communicated to Duffy by him. He wrote frantically to Garnett and to O'Leary on the subject but without avail. He had been squeezed out.

In Sligo he had been at work compiling for Unwin a book

dealing with Irish Adventurers which, however, was never published. *The Countess Kathleen and Various Legends and Lyrics* came out in September and was well received; and the editor of the newly founded literary monthly the *Bookman* had begun to give him a fair amount of reviewing, so that his own affairs were a little more prosperous. He stayed on in Sligo well into late autumn; his grandmother Pollexfen had died and his grandfather did not long survive her. When eventually he got away he returned to Dublin, taking rooms in the same house as John O'Leary in Clontarf, and here began to write some short stories for Henley's *National Observer*. At the end of the year he went back to London, 'in despondency,' as he recalled in May 1935 when writing a preface for his *Early Poems and Stories*. He felt that his attempt to work for Ireland had failed.

By February or March 1893 he was again in Sligo. The edition of Blake on which he and Edwin Ellis had worked for four years had at last appeared; his remuneration for this consisted of a number of copies of the large paper edition. In May he seems to have lectured in Dublin to the National Literary Society.

There are no letters for the latter part of 1893. It seems likely that Yeats divided his time between London and Sligo; he was writing more stories, reviewing for the *Bookman* and the *Speaker*, and preparing for the press a small book of his articles and stories about folklore, *The Celtic Twilight,* for which he had found a new publisher, the firm of Lawrence and Bullen, the active partner in which was A. H. Bullen, a very distinguished scholar and an authority on Elizabethan literature. The book appeared in December. Bullen had also commissioned from him a volume of selections from Blake, and this too appeared in 1893. In the late autumn he was probably in Sligo.

Bedford Park possessed a small club theatre, for which John Todhunter had written a pastoral play, produced there in 1890, the chief woman's part being taken by a professional actress, Florence Farr. She was a Mrs. Emery but was separated from her husband who had gone to America. She spoke verse well and in a manner of which Yeats approved, and he wrote enthusiastically of her performance. They became friends, and discovered that they shared an interest in the occult; Florence Farr was a member of the Golden

Dawn; she was the elder by five years. Presently she made a small success in Ibsen's *Rosmersholm*, and by 1893 she was preparing to go into theatre management. She asked Yeats to write a one-act play which would serve as a curtain-raiser and contain a part for her little niece Dorothy Paget. Yeats worked hard, and more quickly than was usual with him, and by February 1894 had completed *The Land of Heart's Desire*. The effort had exhausted him and he went over to Paris to spend a short holiday with Mathers and his wife, and to see Maud Gonne. This was the first of many visits; Mathers urged him to write his impressions of Paris, saying he would never see it again with the same eyes, but apparently he did not do so. He attended, however, a performance of Villiers de l'Isle Adam's *Axel*, of which he sent an account to the *Bookman*.

In March came the performance, at the Avenue Theatre, of Todhunter's *A Comedy of Sighs*, preceded by *The Land of Heart's Desire*. The little fairy play was liked well enough, but Todhunter's play was given a hostile reception, nobody quite knew why. It ran for a fortnight only and then was replaced by Shaw's *Arms and the Man*, Yeats's play remaining in the bill for a few weeks longer. He was constantly at the theatre, losing no opportunity of seeing his work in performance so that he might learn to make it more dramatically effective. Fisher Unwin published the text in a paper-covered volume with a design by Aubrey Beardsley and the edition was speedily exhausted. *The Second Book of the Rhymers' Club* came out soon afterwards and this, too, probably helped to strengthen Yeats's reputation.

About this time Lionel Johnson introduced him to a cousin, Mrs. Olivia Shakespear, a beautiful and talented woman, the wife of a solicitor much older than herself, and this was the beginning of a close friendship which endured for the remainder of her life. She was of about Yeats's age and lived almost as long as he, dying in October 1938.

The autumn of 1894 found Yeats in Sligo again. Fisher Unwin had agreed to bring out a collected volume of his plays and poems, and he was busily at work revising and rewriting *The Wanderings of Oisin*, *The Countess Cathleen*, and many of his lyrics. He had also begun work on a new play, *The Shadowy Waters*, the theme of which he had worked over in boyhood. In Sligo he made the acquaintance of the Gore-Booth family of Lissadell; the two daughters of the house, Constance and Eva, he was to celebrate years afterwards in a well-known poem,

> Two girls in silk kimonos, both
> Beautiful, one a gazelle.

He was again very hard up; he had edited an anthology for Methuen, *A Book of Irish Verse*, and until it was published, in 1895, he was tied to Sligo. In the hard winter which lasted many months at the beginning of that year there was skating on the lake and the Gore-Booth sisters made coffee for the skaters.

In the summer he was back at Bedford Park, and probably soon afterwards he made his first move towards an independent life, going to share a set of chambers in Fountain Court, Temple, with his friend Arthur Symons, occupying the rooms belonging to Havelock Ellis who was away from London at the time. Yeats says that the arrangement lasted some twelve months, but actually it can hardly have been more than eight at the most. At the end of July 1895 he is still writing from Bedford Park; on New Year's Day 1896 he tells his sister Lily that he likes his rooms in the Temple and is likely to stay there until March.

March 25 would be an appropriate date for him to begin his tenancy of the rooms at 18 Woburn Buildings, near St. Pancras Church, which were to remain his London headquarters for over twenty years. The year 1896 brought him a little more prosperity. After Aubrey Beardsley had been unceremoniously dismissed from *The Yellow Book*, the publisher Leonard Smithers had asked Arthur Symons to be editor of a new literary and artistic periodical *The Savoy*, with Beardsley as Art Editor. The magazine appeared in January, at first quarterly, and then, from July onwards, monthly; but it did not outlast the year. Yeats contributed to six of the eight numbers published—poems, stories and essays, including three important articles on Blake—and, as he told O'Leary, he had been able to raise his prices a little.

In August he took Arthur Symons on a small tour to the West of Ireland. They stayed with Edward Martyn at Tillyra Castle in Galway, and from there made an expedition to the Aran Islands. Yeats had agreed with Bullen to write a novel, and was visiting the islands partly with the intention of finding local colour for his book. In September they went on to Rosses Point and to Sligo; Symons recorded his impressions in three essays which he published in the *Savoy*.

In December Yeats was again in Paris, this time staying at the Hôtel Corneille in the Rue Corneille; it seems probable that Symons was with him, for both men attended the performance of Alfred Jarry's *Ubu Roi*, given by the Théâtre de l'Œuvre. It was during this visit and in this hotel, Yeats notes specifically, that he first met J. M. Synge.

1892-1896

TO JOHN O'LEARY

[*Late* 1891 *or early* 1892] 3 *Blenheim Road*

Dear Mr. O'Leary, Will you be so good as to help me out of a difficulty? There is still £2-3-10 owing to Kegan Paul on *Oisin* and they threaten me with lawyers. I want to take the remaining 100 copies out of their hands and get Fisher Unwin to sell them which he will do with ease. There is, as it is, some slight sale and a steadily increasing one. The new book will sell the rest of the copies. I want you to lend me £2-10-0 so that I can make the transfer at once.

Rolleston has told you, I hear, about our Literary Club. I am chiefly anxious about it because I have a plan for a new 'Library of Ireland' which I have talked over with Garnett. He believes that if we could get 500 subscribers for books at 2/- to be published every two months or so, through the Young Ireland League and its branches—of which the Irish Literary Club, London, will be one—that Unwin would take up such a library, giving me a free hand and letting us couple an Irish publisher with him. He would trust to English sale to make it pay. We ought to get 500 subscribers with ease. If we got 800 hundred [*sic*] or so, we could do without Unwin at all. Each branch of the Young Ireland League might take so many copies, and we could publish the library under its auspices. Of course we cannot count on Unwin but there is a good chance.

I will get you some occult catalogues as soon as I get to town. I have not been very well lately and have been a little stay at home. The Blake is to be done by March at latest or by the end of February if possible and my poems will be out by April. Thank you very much for *United Ireland*, I am always very glad to get it.

I was very sorry to hear that you have had the influenza. Yours always   W B YEATS

TO JOHN O'LEARY

[*Late 1891 or early 1892*]   3 *Blenheim Road*

Dear Mr. O'Leary, Thank you very much for sending the money. I would have acknowledge[d] it yesterday but I was away in town all day long and did not get home until late.

I will copy out the article you want the next time I am in the Museum which will be this week I think. There has turned up a new Blake MS which will keep me out of town to-day and perhaps to-morrow.

Our Irish Literary Society, London, promises well in all ways. We have an opening meeting very soon now and it has done one good deed anyway. It has stirred up Rolleston's Irish ardour again. I hear from Garnett that O'Grady is to do a book of Fin McCool stories for their *Children's Library*. All such books seem to me to be clear gain for Irish feeling. My own *Irish Fairy Stories* will be out very soon now with two drawings by Jack.

I am correcting the new book of poems for the press. The *Countess Kathleen* takes 100 pages and there will be 30 or 40 pages of lyrics and ballads. It comes out early in April, about the same time as the Blake probably. Fisher Unwin talks of reprinting Wolfe Tone's Memoirs with an introduction by Rolleston and notes by Barry O'Brien.[1] He first thought of Barry O'Brien doing the whole thing but I got him to change his mind by talking it over with Garnett. He is going to bring out a series of Memoirs in which Rolleston could I dare say get the doing of Wolfe Tone. He is friendly to Irish matters of all kinds. Yours always   W B YEATS

[1] Richard Barry O'Brien (1847–1918), Irish writer and journalist, lived in London and was Chairman and eventually President of the Irish Literary Society which Yeats helped to found in this year. His best known works are his Life of Charles Stewart Parnell (1898) and his Life of Lord Russell of Killowen (1901). He was at one time editor of the *Speaker*, a Liberal weekly paper, to which Yeats occasionally contributed.

TO JOHN O'LEARY

[? circa *January* 1892] 3 *Blenheim Road*

Dear Mr. O'Leary, Miss Gonne returned to Paris last week. She was here for about ten days and then went back to deliver a series of lectures which she prepared over here. She will be in London again in March on her way to Ireland where she hopes to be able to help in the work of the Young Ireland League. You will remember the plan for the starting of village libraries which was put forward at the convention. She will be able she thinks to get money in Paris to help on such a project as soon as it is properly under way.

Our 'Irish Literary Society' [1] goes on well and promises to be larger than we expected. Our men are eager over the publication project.[2] What I suggest to do in the matter is this. Our London society will guarantee a sale of (say) 200 copies at a 1/- each. 10 or 20 members or more can easily subscribe that amount amongst them. Miss Gonne will get her French organization to take a certain number on the same understanding. There are now I think five literary societies in Dublin counting the new one at which Coffey spoke the other day. They might surely be got to take 40 or 50 copies apiece or (say) 300 amongst them. Cork and Belfast and wherever else there are Young Ireland Societies or branches of the Young Ireland League can be appealed to by circular and otherwise to take part.

[1] A preliminary meeting at the Yeats house in Bedford Park to discuss plans for an Irish Literary Society in London was held on December 28, 1891, and was attended by Yeats, Dr. Todhunter, T. W. Rolleston, J. G. O'Keefe and W. P. Ryan. (See *The Irish Literary Revival*, by W. P. Ryan, 1894.) The Society was actually founded on May 12, 1892, at the Caledonian Hotel in the Adelphi, London, and on Saturday, July 23, in the same year a garden party was held at Oak Tree House, Hampstead, at the invitation of the English artist Henry Holiday and his wife, enthusiastic supporters of Home Rule, at which Sir Charles Gavan Duffy, the President, delivered an inaugural speech. About three hundred people were present. After this the Society seems not to have made much progress until March 1893, when Stopford Brooke delivered the inaugural lecture at the Society's newly acquired premises in Bloomsbury Mansions.

[2] This scheme ultimately became *The New Irish Library*, a series of shilling volumes published by Fisher Unwin. Although apparently planned by Yeats, the scheme was taken out of his hands and the series was edited by Sir Charles Gavan Duffy with assistance from T. W. Rolleston and Douglas Hyde. No book by Yeats appeared in it, nor those suggested by York Powell and Lionel Johnson. Standish O'Grady (1846-1928), the author of a *History of Ireland, Heroic Period*, and of many books and stories on Irish subjects, contributed *The Bog of Stars and other stories of Elizabethan Ireland*.

If we can get 800 or 900 copies subscribed we can start without chance of a loss. Once under way with a couple of volumes or so the series would sell itself I believe. Rolleston promises to do for the first volume a history of Fenianism of a popular nature and to fill it with sound national doctrine. I would myself do 'a ballad chronicle of Ireland'—a Davis idea—selected from all the ballad writers and piece the poems together with short historical notes.

For later volumes I have been offered 'the Ossianic Stories' by York Powell and Education in Ireland by Lionel Johnson. O'Grady would probably do a book also and I myself have a wish to write a manual of Irish literature in the present century. Such a series should have I think three directors who could show the various parties that it was national and not party—you and Sigerson might make two of them. I should myself be editor and should have no Barry O'Brien or anyone else except the directors associated with me to hamper my action. (I am told that if Unwin took this series he would make this a condition for he knows me and not the others.)

Apropos of Barry O'Brien and the Wolfe Tone. I did not recommend Rolleston until I had found out from him that he knew the subject thoroughly. He told me he had worked at it exhaustively and knew it quite as well as O'Brien. Irish literature has been far too much in the hands of the men of learning who cannot write. This is I think one of the reasons why so few people read Irish books. I wish you however would do the preface to the Wolfe Tone instead of either Rolleston or O'Brien.[1] By the by I helped to stop off another man of learning the other day who came trying to get a book from Unwin to do. The man of learning who has no literature is my natural enemy. I sometimes think he is the enemy of the human race. Did I tell you about the 'Irish Saga Series' that Unwin is thinking of? Douglas Hyde who is now in London came with me to see Garnett the other day who thinks Unwin will take it up. It is to give standard translations by Hyde of the old Epic Tales and will consist of 8 or 9 volumes. Hyde is to send in a scheme for the first three or four in a couple of weeks. It will make the old stories accessible for the first time to everybody. It will I fear however make Unwin less inclined to start another Irish series at present. We can however surely get on without him. I do not think any

[1] *The Autobiography of Wolfe Tone*, edited by R. Barry O'Brien, was republished by Fisher Unwin in 1893.

more than you do that we can work 'The Young Ireland League Library' by subscription in the ordinary sense, but surely it can be done in the way I suggest and by the Irish Societies of all kinds guaranteeing a sale of so many copies among their members. 10 members if they subscribe 5/- apiece can guarantee 100 copies which should be sold by the sec of their society. As soon as I get to Dublin, or before, I propose to have printed a circular explaining the scheme. Our men here say that we should also have a pamphlet series giving reprints to some extent of famous speeches and selections from the works of forgotten or little read poets.

If we do such a series Hyde would give us his translations from Gaelic ballad writers to make one pamphlet of (say) 24 pages and would publish under our auspices *at his own expense* a pamphlet of his original ballads and Todhunter would do the same with his Irish poems—those already published and his unpublished *Deirdre*—if we would take them for the larger series. I mean he would pay all expenses. I am not quite sure of the advisability of this however. If you meet any of the Young Ireland League men I wish you would tell them of this project of publication. You might also I think try —if you approve of it—to enlist Coffey's good will and get him to talk over the others.

Fisher Unwin is taking over the 80 or 90 copies I have left of *Oisin* and is putting them into a handsome binding with a frontispiece by Ellis.[1] The Blake book is getting near the finish, so you see my literary affairs are going not ill. I hardly think I shall get to Ireland until end of March. Yours   W B YEATS

TO JOHN O'LEARY

[*February* 1892]   *3 Blenheim Road*

Dear Mr. O'Leary, Have you by any chance a copy of Mitchel's *Apology for the British Government in Ireland*? I particularly want to refer to it just at present. Could you lend it me if you have it? I would send it back all safe.

There is a certain Mrs. Rowley, who is a friend of Miss Gonne's and I think I may say of mine for I saw her several times when Miss

---

[1] This re-issue of *The Wanderings of Oisin* appeared in May 1892. The frontispiece by Edwin Ellis could well have been spared.

Gonne was in London and liked her very much. She is Irish and anxious to help in any way she can in Ireland. Miss Gonne has filled her with an idea of trying to keep a kind of 'salon' where conservatives and nationalists might meet and she has gone to Dublin and is now staying at 44 Stephen's Green. If you come across her—she is anxious to see you and I promised to write to you about her—you might talk this matter over with her. She is kindly and well meaning, and ardently Irish but has not a big intellect or anything of that kind. She knows the Coffeys but does not seem, I think, to have quite hit it off with Mrs. Coffey whom she met in the old days before or just after her marriage. She knows the Parnells slightly.

About Rolleston's proposed *History of Fenianism*—to which you object. The way it presents [itself] to me is this. He can write better than most people and has an enthusiasm for the subject and could by going back to the newspapers of the time (as he is willing to do) and to the published books on the subject get easily enough information to make an inspiring book of 200 pages. If he does not do it now while there are people living who can correct his mistakes, it will be done far more inaccurately by the historians of the future. It would be better for it to be done by a man who can write so as to inspire people, than by one who had perhaps more information but not his writing power. This is my feeling on the whole question of the projected series. Let them be done by good Irishmen who can write and then they will be read. Rolleston is not the ideal historian of this subject but he has the right feeling and seems the best man we could get so far as I can see. He at any rate is trained in the art of making up a subject.

I hope to get to Dublin next month myself.

I have a copy of *The Book of the Rhymers' Club* for you and will send it tomorrow. Yours   W B YEATS

My poems are going to press first thing next week.

TO KATHARINE TYNAN

March 2nd, 1892   *3 Blenheim Road*

My dear Katey, First to answer your questions about the collection of 'Irish Love Songs' of which, by the by, I heard from Unwin's reader with great satisfaction, for no one could do it so well as you. You should, I think, include a fair number from Davis. He is very Irish, and I find he grows upon me, partly because of his sincerity. His 'Plea for Love' is, I think, the best of all. You might also use 'The Marriage,' 'Love's Longings,' 'The Boatman of Kinsale' and 'Maire Bhan a Stor.' You should, I think, get Sigerson or someone of that kind to give you phonetic equivalents; the Gaelic spelling he adopts is his own. 'Eoghan' for instance should be written as it is pronounced, 'Owen.' Do not forget to include 'Kathleen O'More' a marvellous lyric attributed to Reynolds. I think that 'The Girl with the Fine Flowing Hair' in Walsh's *Irish [Popular] Songs* is good, too.

There was a little thing by Hyde in our Ballad Book, 'Have you been on the Mountains and seen there my Love?' which might go in. You might perhaps give from *Oisin* 'To an Isle in the Water' and an 'Old Song Resung,' for they are more obviously Irish than my recent attempts at love-poetry, of which I enclose one or two things. I would have been of much greater help to you a while ago but I have not been reading the Irish Ballads very recently and so cannot advise you so well thus. By the by, would not 'The Fairy Song' in the *Rhymers' Book* do for your purpose? It is extremely Irish and has been greatly liked. It is a love-poem of a kind. You will be able to choose at any rate what you want of mine from *Oisin*, the *R. Book* and the MSS. I send.

But enough of this matter. Blake is getting through the press—about two thirds, and that the most troublesome part, is gone to press and most of it is already in proof. I am also correcting *The Countess Kathleen* for the press and getting ready a quantity of lyrics and ballads to go with it. It will be infinitely my best book. I have had rather a bad autumn with poor health and poorer spirits or I had made it better than it is. Health and spirits are I suppose mixed up in some queer way—not quite as the materialists say, but in some fashion. I shall be back in Dublin again very soon now and look forward much to seeing you. I am always more at home in Dublin than any other where. My sisters send you greetings and ask when you will be in London as they enjoy your visits so greatly. Yours always,   W B YEATS

The following lyrics may perhaps help you to select something for your book. The first was written some months ago, the second the other day.

When you are old.

When you are old and grey and full of sleep
    And nodding by the fire, take down this book,
    And slowly read and dream of the soft look
Your eyes had once and of their shadows deep;

How many loved your moments of glad grace
    And loved your beauty with love false or true,
    But one man loved the pilgrim soul in you,
And loved the sorrows of your changing face;

And bending down beside the glowing bars
    Murmur, a little sad, 'From us fled Love;
    He paced upon the mountains far above
And hid his face amid a crowd of stars.'[1]

When you are Sad.

When you are sad
    The mother of the stars weeps too,
And all her starlight is with sorrow mad
    And tears of fire fall gently in the dew.

When you are sad
    The mother of the wind mourns too,
    And her old wind that no mirth ever had
Wanders and wails before my heart most true.

When you are sad
    The mother of the wave sighs too,
    And her dim wave bids man be no more glad,
And then the whole world's trouble weeps with you.[2]

I don't know whether these poems are not too literary for your purpose. A book such as you are doing should be Irish before all

---

[1] This poem appeared in *The Countess Kathleen and Various Legends and Lyrics*, 1892 and was reprinted in *Poems*, 1895. A revised version appeared in the 1899 edition of *Poems* and in all later collected editions.

[2] This poem appeared in *The Countess Kathleen and Various Legends and Lyrics*, 1892, but in no later collections.

else. People will go to English poetry for 'literary poetry' but will look to a book like your collection for a new flavour as of fresh-turned mould. Davis, Ferguson, Allingham, Mangan, and Moore should be your mainstay, and every poem that shows English influence in any marked way should be rejected.

No poetry has a right to live merely because it is good. It must be The Best of Its Kind. The best Irish poets are this, and every writer of imagination who is true to himself absolutely may be so. I forgot to say in my letter that I would, if I were you, include Lover's 'Whistling Thief' and Walsh's 'Mo Crao[i]bhin Cno' and 'Mairgread ne Chealleadh' (quite love poem enough), also 'A Love Ballad' by Mangan (it is in Gill's third collection and is from the Irish).

TO THE EDITOR OF THE *ACADEMY*

March 16, 1892 *London*

I thank your anonymous correspondent for giving me this opportunity of explaining that Tristram St. Martin's ballad and my own have a common origin, although I never saw 'He sent his angel' until some time after writing 'Father Gilligan.' The author of *Christ in London* himself told me the story on which both poems are founded as a curious piece of folk-lore given him by a friend. I wrote 'Father Gilligan' at once; but knowing that Tristram St. Martin himself intended a ballad on the subject, kept it back for some time in order to give him the advantage of prior publication. When I did at last publish it, about two years ago, in the *National Observer*, I told him that I had done so and gave him the date of the paper; and from that day to this he has never told me or any one else, so far as I know, that he considered himself ill-treated. I have never claimed the story as mine, but both in the *National Observer* and in *The Book of the Rhymers' Club* have given full credit where it is due, namely, to its inventors, the peasantry of Castleisland, Kerry. The passages quoted by your correspondent are almost word for word from the folk-tale as I heard it.

It may comfort your correspondent, however, to know that even if I had seen Tristram St. Martin's ballad before writing mine, and had never heard the story apart from the ballad, I should none the less have considered myself perfectly justified in taking a legend that belonged to neither of us, but to the Irish people. Tristram St. Martin has done one interesting ballad, but I do not think he is so triumphantly successful in the present instance as to have made the story his until time shall end. I am even inclined to say that he is but 'illy blest' in having so ardent a champion, ready to come forth with quotations that certainly do not show a very subtle sense of the peculiarities of Irish folk-lore. On other subjects he is more at home and more worthy of quotation.[1]   W B YEATS

TO KATHARINE TYNAN

[Postcard, Postmark Chiswick April 12, 1892]

United Ireland has asked me to fix the price of a long narrative poem—'The Death of Cuchullin'—about a column long, which I have sent them. They feel they say 'a timidity' in doing so. You have done verse for them and can tell me what I should ask. Let me know as soon as possible. Yours ever,   W B YEATS

Unwin praises your reviews of books in the *Independent* much.

TO EDWARD GARNETT

[? *June or July* 1892] [2]   53 *Mountjoy Square*
Dublin

My dear Garnett, I am more busy than ever over this 'National Literary Society.' It is growing under our hands into what promises to be a work of very great importance. We are endeavouring to found reading rooms in connection with federated societies through the country and propose to supply them with small selections of books—worth not more than £5 or £6 pounds [*sic*]—as nucleus of

[1] *The Christ in London and other Poems* by Tristram St. Martin, London: Authors' Co-operative Publishing Co. Ltd., a small paper-covered volume of not very distinguished poetry, was issued in 1890. The poem which Yeats had been accused of plagiarising was called 'He sent his Angel' and contained the line 'Ah, who would choose a life so illy blessed.' I have been unable to discover the identity of Tristram St. Martin.
[2] On the back of the sheet on which this letter is written are some memoranda dated June 8, 1892, but the reference to Duffy's speech suggests that it may have been written after July 23.

lending libraries and to send them lecturers from time to time. This is Miss Gonne's special part of the work and she proposes to lecture through the country in its aid. I send you Duffy's speech which will explain the other part of the work—the book production—which we expect to help considerably by turning these reading rooms into centres of distribution. We are having two meetings in the next two weeks—the first a small gathering of representative people to launch this publishing company, the second a large public one to open in due order our session of lectures etc.

When will *The Countess Kathleen* be out? It would be an advantage if it came soon as the reviews here in Ireland would help the society, and the sale would in its turn be helped probably by the coming meetings at which my name will of necessity be rather prominent. They are dreadfully dilatory it seems to me over it. Even if the publication is delayed for any reason surely it is bound by this and I could have some advance copies for friends.[1]

Ellis has just published his book of poems *Fate in Arcadia*.[2] It seems to me a very marvellous book. If you come across it read 'The Hermit Answered,' 'The Outcast,' 'The Maid's Confession' and 'Himself', though all indeed have I think some beauty of their own. They seem to me too to have much that is profound in them and in their strange mysticism. Yours always W B YEATS

I wonder will destiny drive you in the direction of Dublin.

TO JOHN O'LEARY

[? *July* 1892] 53 *Mountjoy Square*

Dear Mr. O'Leary, I wrote to Mathers [3] but found that he is as I feared in Paris. He has written me a long letter going into the

---

[1] This is not merely an author's impatience. The book had certainly been set up in type since April. A licence for performance of *The Countess Kathleen* was issued by the Lord Chamberlain to the Athenaeum Theatre, Shepherd's Bush, on May 5, and a copyright performance was given there on the following day. The copy in the Lord Chamberlain's department is made up of page-proofs, with pencilled corrections and alterations in Yeats's hand. But the book was not published until September.

[2] Yeats reviewed Edwin J. Ellis's *Fate in Arcadia*, under the title 'A New Poet,' in the *Bookman* in September 1892.

[3] Samuel Liddell Mathers (1854–1918) was born in Hackney, London, son of William M. Mathers, a commercial clerk. His early life was spent with his widowed mother at Bournemouth. After her death in 1885 he moved to London

question of organization. I would send it on to you but he has mixed up with it some occult matters which are of course private. He would be glad to meet any one who came from us, and would go carefully into the whole question. If you know any one in Paris or going to Paris they might see him. His address is S. L. MacGregor Mathers, 121 Boulevard St. Michel, Paris. He will hardly be in London for some time. He is strong for an immediate commencement on the ground of the length of time such things take. I am writing to him an explanation of my own position in the matter and the reasons I see for some delay. My own occult art (though I cannot expect you to accept the evidences) has again and again for a longish time now been telling me of many curious coming events and as some have come true (all that have had time) I rather expect the others to follow suit and the time for his plan among the rest.

The Literary Society goes on well. We have got leave to hold our committee meetings in the 'Mansion House.' Miss Gonne who is back here since Sunday has secured Ludwig [1] to sing at her concert. He is coming over on purpose. She did not speak for Morton. She offered to go down for two days and he said she should go for ten days and that two would be worse than useless and that his whole chance of election depended on her. She replied that she had work to do in Dublin and could not. He then wrote that if he was not returned he hoped he might never see her again. He must have quite lost his head over this election.

When am I to do that 'Causerie' for the *Speaker*? [2] I have waited to hear from Barry O'Brien but have not done so.

Ellis is out of town in a House Boat at Henley-on-Thames. Yours very sincerely
W B YEATS

---

and through Freemasonry and Rosicrucianism became acquainted with Dr. Woodman and Dr. Wynn Westcott, under whose tuition he studied magic and made a translation of Rosenroth's *Kabalah Denudata*. In 1890 he was appointed Curator of the Horniman Museum at Forest Hill, founded by F. J. Horniman, M.P., and now national property. He lost this post in 1891, as the result of a quarrel, and went with his wife to Paris where he lived for the rest of his life, and where Yeats often visited him. He took the additional name MacGregor and declared his succession to the Jacobite title of 'Count of Glenstrae,' often appearing in full Highland costume, as did his associate Aleister Crowley.

[1] Ludwig was the professional name of an Irish singer, William Ledwidge. He had a fine voice but refused, on patriotic grounds, to accept engagements abroad, preferring to sing rebel ballads at concerts and between the acts of opera at home.

[2] The 'causerie' for the *Speaker* was not published until August 1893. Its title was 'The Message of the Folk-lorist.'

TO JOHN O'LEARY

[*During the week ending July* 23, 1892]   *53 Mountjoy Square*

Dear Mr. O'Leary, We have postponed our concert until after the inaugural meeting which will, I believe, take place in the second week in August at the Antient Concert Rooms.¹ We hope by that time to have the program of our autumn session arranged so that we can distribute it at the meeting. The concert, which will probably take place in Horse Show week, will be an item. We will have our permanent reading room taken too, I hope, by the opening of our session. We have had to postpone the concert through delays about Ludwig and other things of the kind. Next Monday—the 25—we have a general meeting of *the members* to adopt rules and nominate the officers. We intend to start a 'Contemporary' of our own as soon as we have our reading room. This is, I believe, all the news concerning [the] society.

As to my suggestion about Mathers. In suggesting to you that if any advanced Nationalist was going to Paris he should see Mathers, I was acting to some extent on the advice of Quinn,² to whom I showed Mathers's letter—he gave me leave to show it. Quinn held the matter of some possible importance. Mathers is a specialist and might have given useful advice to anyone who thinks as you do. 'He might be useful' was your own phrase. Now as to Magic. It is surely absurd to hold me 'weak' or otherwise because I chose to persist in a study which I decided deliberately four or five years ago to make, next to my poetry, the most important pursuit of my life. Whether it be, or be not, bad for my health can only be decided by one who knows what magic is and not at all by any amateur. The probable explanation however of your somewhat testy postcard is that you were out at Bedford Park and heard my father discoursing about my magical pursuits out of the immense depths of his ignorance as to everything that I am doing and think-

---

[1] The Antient Concert Rooms, situated in Brunswick (now Pearse) Street, Dublin, could seat about 800 people. The hall, which still exists, though now used as a cinema, was the scene of the first production of the Irish Literary Theatre in May 1899, when *The Countess Cathleen* by W. B. Yeats and *The Heather Field* by Edward Martyn inaugurated the movement which led, five years later, to the establishment of the Abbey Theatre.

[2] Possibly Dr. J. P. Quinn, a member of the National Literary Society, and certainly not John Quinn, Yeats's friend the Irish-American lawyer, whom at this time he had not met.

ing. If I had not made magic my constant study I could not have written a single word of my Blake book, nor would *The Countess Kathleen* have ever come to exist. The mystical life is the centre of all that I do and all that I think and all that I write. It holds to my work the same relation that the philosophy of Godwin held to the work of Shelley and I have always considered myself a voice of what I believe to be a greater renaissance—the revolt of the soul against the intellect—now beginning in the world. By all this I have, however, probably called down upon myself another reproving post card which shall be like to the other in all things. It is my own fault I daresay, for I sometimes forget that the word 'magic' which sounds so familiar to my ears has a very outlandish sound to other ears.

Miss Gonne has given up her rooms in Paris—which means, I imagine, that she intends to live more constantly in Ireland and devote herself to the work *here*. She is now with her sister, 25 Hans Place, but returns next week, I believe. When do you return? Duffy comes over, I believe, in a week or two.

I have Armstrong's [1] collected works—nine volumes—to review for *Bookman*, and have given them a preliminary notice, mainly hostile, in this week's *United Ireland*, also like treatment to Larminie.[2]

Does Barry O'Brien want that 'causerie'? He was to write to me and has not.

Hyde has settled with Unwin about his translations of Gaelic sagas, and got very good terms.[3] I am writing this post to Duffy. Yours very sincerely   W B YEATS

[1] George Francis Savage-Armstrong (1845–1906) was Professor of History and English Literature at Queen's College, Cork. Yeats's review of his collected verse appeared, under the title 'Noetry and Poetry,' in the *Bookman*, September 1892.

[2] William Lariemin was the author of *Glanlua and other Poems*, London, 1889, *Fand and other Poems*, Dublin, 1892, and collected and translated a volume of *West Irish Folk Tales and Romances*, London, 1893. He contributed one essay, 'Legends as Material for Literature,' to the discussion in the Dublin *Daily Express* which was republished as *Literary Ideals in Ireland*, London and Dublin, 1899. Yeats's reviews in *United Ireland*, July 23, 1892, were included, with others, not, I think, by him, under the heading 'Some New Irish Books,' and were unsigned.

[3] In spite of this statement by Yeats, Douglas Hyde's proposed translations of Gaelic Sagas were not then published by Fisher Unwin. In 1895, however, he issued a small volume by Hyde containing 'The Three Sorrows of Story-Telling' and 'Ballads of St. Columkille.'

TO SIR CHARLES GAVAN DUFFY [1]

[? During week ending July 23, 1892]   *[? 53 Mountjoy Square]*

... our Dublin society. About a fortnight or three weeks later we hope to be ready for our inaugural meeting. Perhaps you will be in Dublin then and will be so kind as to take the chair. The young men wish greatly that you would.

J. T. Kelly will I believe also write to you. Yours very truly

W B YEATS

P.S. It seems to Mr. O'Leary and myself that it would be a good step towards ensuring circulation to fix as soon as possible upon the first 3 volumes of the proposed library. Mr. O'Leary and myself think that a good first volume would be a life of Wolfe Tone by T. W. Rolleston who has long wished to do such a book and would, I doubt not, do it gladly for the library. Mr. O'Leary has written to him on the subject but has not yet heard. Mr. O'Leary thinks that my 'Ballad Chronicle' would make a good second volume. For the third volume he suggests that Lady Wilde be asked to take up again the book on Sarsfield that had been projected for her. We of course wish to know if you think this a good selection or if you have anything to say in opposition or in modification.

TO JOHN O'LEARY

[During week ending July 23, 1892]   53 Mountjoy Square

Dear Mr. O'Leary, The meeting on Monday is not our inaugural meeting but the general meeting of members to nominate President, Vice President, Committee etc and to adopt the rules. You will I believe be elected President while Father Finlay, Dr. Sigerson, Count Plunkett, Ashe King, Father Dennis Murphy, Douglas Hyde and Gavan Duffy will be put forward for election as Vice Presidents. There is I admit a certain difficulty in putting up Gavan Duffy as one of several Vice Presidents but it is inevitable. He is coming over in his own words 'to consult with our committee' and he can only

---

[1] Fragment, being pages 9, 10 and 11 of a letter of which the remainder is missing.

do this properly by being on that committee. We could hardly put him on in any other way than as a Vice President. Finlay and Donovan are afraid of your Presidency and so we put on, as you see, a fair number of Federationists.

The Inaugural meeting will be in the second week in August probably at the Antient Concert Rooms. Sigerson agrees to give the address.

I think this is all the news I have. Let me know if you know what Rolleston's views are as to the book scheme. I have not heard from him. Yours   W B YEATS

TO THE EDITOR OF *UNITED IRELAND*

[Published September 10, 1892]

Dear Sir, Two or three of the reviews of my *Countess Kathleen* have misread my rhyming claim to be considered 'one with Davis, Mangan, Ferguson,' and one of them has based on this misconception a reproof for my supposed lack of modesty. I did not in the least intend the lines to claim equality of eminence, nor does the context bear out such a reading, but only community in the treatment of Irish subjects after an Irish fashion. I send this letter to you as the matter concerns my Nationalist readers, if it concerns anybody at all, and but little the readers of the papers that made the comment. Yours very truly   W B YEATS

TO JOHN O'LEARY

Sunday [October 16, 1892]   c/o *George Pollexfen*
                          Thornhill, Sligo

Dear Mr. O'Leary, Thank you very much for Miss Gonne's note which I return. I had however heard from herself. She has indeed been better in the matter of letters and written at greater length and in a more cordial spirit than she has done for a long time. I had a long letter yesterday and another the day before. She is to be in Dublin on the 1st of November and was to leave Royat for Paris yesterday (15th). She is very eager about the work and asked many questions. I have heard from Quinn about the society.

I have almost finished my introduction to the volume of 'Irish Adventurers.' I really think this is well nigh all the news I have barring various incantations and invocations of the fairies at their secret spots, but these things are hardly in your line.

I think that Leamy ought to be asked for a lecture by our Society. The thing of his in the *Independent* seems very right in spirit though somewhat flimsy in substance so far as report goes.

You will have heard of my grandmother's death—I send paper with funeral in it. My grandfather is dying too. Yours sincerely

W B YEATS

TO EDWARD GARNETT

[? *late October* 1892]   *Thornhill*

My dear Garnett, I shall finish my introduction to the 'Irish Adventurers' tomorrow and post it to you. I hope the thing will do. It is I think fresh and has a little novel information in it. I want you to let me know whether I can include 'Freeney the Robber' or does Whibley still intend to use him?

Why have you not sung out? I was very triumphantly successful in an invocation of the Fairies at a noted locality of theirs two days ago.[1] My uncle and cousin both got into the trances, the first very slightly and the second very deeply and all kinds of strange music and voices were heard and all sorts of queer figures seen. You I think have seen the symbols worked and so may understand the methods.

Please let me know about the 'adventurer' introduction as soon as possible as I shall be in suspense until I hear.

How does the *Imaged World* thrive? Please let me know before any work of yours comes out as I am now reviewing on the *Bookman* and may be able to be of use. Yours truly   W B YEATS

[1] An account of this invocation of the fairies appeared under the title 'Regina, Regina Pigmeorum, Veni' in *The Celtic Twilight*, published in December 1893. Edward Garnett's book *An Imaged World* was published in 1894.

TO EDWARD GARNETT

[? *Autumn*, 1892]   *Thornhill*

My dear Garnett, I hear that Rolleston and Duffy have been trying to negociate with Unwin for a series of national books. A difficulty arose some time ago between Duffy and all the most important members of the committee of the National Literary Society, Dublin, who consider themselves unfairly treated by Duffy. In any case it is rather unfair of him—if the rumour be true—to try to continue negociations which you will remember I began last spring, without consulting me, as he only heard of these negociations and of Unwin's views on the subject of Irish books from me. I wrote him a letter upon the whole matter when I began my work in Ireland. The same holds good for Rolleston. Can you let me know what has really occurred? We have had for some time an offer from an Irish publisher who is ready to publish a series of books for us—for the National Literary Society, Dublin—on condition that we guarantee a sale of 1000 copies. Perhaps Unwin would make ultimately some arrangement whereby the Dublin publisher and himself could work together, as an Irish name upon the books is important. Do not make any arrangement for giving the editorship to Duffy, for there is the strongest possible feeling here against the series being edited from Nice. Duffy is also much too old and much too long out of touch to be a good editor. Count Plunkett, Douglas Hyde or myself would be the right people to choose from. At any rate as I practically planned and started this whole Irish literary movement I do not think that anything should be done behind my back. The National Literary Society here promises to be quite strong enough to make the success of a series of books but it certainly will not put its shoulder to the wheel to back up a series of Duffy's for he has enraged our members by such a complex series of false moves. If I can make arrangements such as will be required for the circulation of books among the literary societies and Young Ireland societies in the country I think that I should be consulted about the editorship. It is a question that needs very careful consideration. I hope you will let me know about the whole matter for I am quite in the dark about it.

I should also say that many of the books proposed by Duffy for his Irish series were books which I got promised for the series I explained to you. I was quite ready to let the 'Company' have them but now the 'Company' appears to be abandoned I do not think that I should let Duffy and Rolleston—who is entirely under the influence of D at present—go with my scheme to Unwin as if it all came out of Duffy's head, or rather with my scheme mingled with his own ever changing plans, and not consult me about the proceeding to the very slightest extent.

Do what you can to help me in this matter and believe me that I see in it no personal issue but one important for the literary movement here in Ireland. Remember that Duffy is so unpopular here in Ireland—for old reasons which I need not go into—that we were only able to partially suppress a disturbance got up against him at our inaugural meeting, and that we have more than once kept the papers from attacking him. Yours W B YEATS

O'Leary feels even more than I do on these points and has been urging me for some time to write a protest to Rolleston against his general conduct in connection with the company. He has to-day forwarded me a letter from a well-known Irishman in London saying, among much else, 'the real truth is if Rolleston is not careful in working with Mr. Duffy we shall be all at cross purposes' and complaining of Duffy's attempts to 'boss,' as he puts it, the whole scheme. It is this letter which now induces me to write to you.

TO JOHN O'LEARY [1]

[*? late October* 1892] *Thornhill*

Dear Mr. O'Leary, I have written a letter to Garnett asking for information about Duffy and Rolleston's negociations and putting our case in such a way as will I think stop all such treacherous dealing. Duffy and Rolleston only knew of Unwin's views on the question of a national series from me and knew quite well that it was I who had interested him in the matter; it was therefore treacherous to go and try to continue negociations which I had begun without consulting me. I cannot understand why Rolleston cannot see this. I will not I think write to Rolleston until I have Garnett's reply. I suggest to Garnett that Bryers and Unwin might perhaps share the

[1] On black-edged paper.

risk between them. I have however put the case very strongly against any dealing whatever with Duffy. This last action of his and R's simply means war and I think now that they have chosen Unwin's house for a battle-ground we rout them with ease, especially as Unwin makes all depend on the Irish organization. I am inclined to think that I should go to London in December or January and try to arrange the matter. Bryers (supposing Unwin does not join in) asks to have 1000 copies sale guaranteed. Barry O'Brien and myself could get the Council of the London Society—(no matter what Rolleston did)—to guarantee about 300 I believe. The Dublin Society could do at least as well. The other four hundred should be easily managed among some of the other societies. As soon as I return to Dublin I shall draw up a definite proposal for series of books, submit this to you and to Count Plunkett, and after modification send it to Unwin and ask him to agree, upon certain guarantees, to publish such a series uniting his name with Bryers' and appointing myself, Plunkett or Hyde editors. One advantage such a series will have over a series published by a *definitely national* publishing company is that O'Grady will write for us without fear of the *Express* in his heart. Yours always W B YEATS

PTO. I am for some reason or other not over well—the doctor says that I should rest from thought to some extent and that is not over easy as I have rather too much time for it down here. I am however getting plenty of writing done and setting my purse in order I hope, though payment will not come in just yet. And I am doing this without I think writing too much. I am a deal better than I was.

[*Continued in purple pencil*] Are you sure I did not return you Miss Gonne's letter? I seem to remember doing so. The more I think over that Duffy and R. business the worse it looks. When I hear from Garnett I shall probably write to Unwin himself. Our point of view is clear—all depends on our organization and we will not work for a series ruled by Duffy. I think we had better try how the ground lies with Unwin, before putting R. on his guard by remonstrating with him.

TO THE EDITOR OF THE *BOOKMAN*[1]

[*Published November* 1892]

The one great difficulty that besets all speculation as to who should be Laureate is that for one cause or another the only men who have clear right to the position are the last to whom it is likely to be offered, or by whom it would be accepted if it were. Mr. Swinburne has hardly so entirely thrust underground his old convictions, or so utterly forgotten his lines about 'a linnet chirping on the wrist of kings' to take an office directly from the Court; nor would Mr. William Morris be ready to exchange lectures at Kelmscott House for songs about royal marriages, no matter how large a hogshead of sherry were made over to him in the bargain. When the conditions attaching to a post intended for the chief poet of an age are such as to render it impossible to the only two men fitted for it alike by genius and the acclaim of the best public of their day, surely the time has come when these conditions should be mended. If they be not mended, for the ending of any so venerable and honourable a thing as the Laureateship should be out of all question, we shall see the supreme artist who is gone succeeded by some unreadable mediocrity or fluent monger of platitudes, his throat still hoarse from self-advertisement. All the public officers, from the Prime Minister downwards, were once Court officials, but now they are responsible to the nation and to the nation alone. Surely it is time to transform the Laureateship also, and to expect no Laureate in return for his pension and his sherry to do other than celebrate, if he be so minded, for the muses make but indifferent drudges, matters of national importance, great battles if he hold them to be waged in a just cause, the deaths of famous men of thought and action, and the ever-coming never-come light of that ideal peace and freedom whereto all nations are stumbling in the darkness. In the

---

[1] Lord Tennyson, the Poet Laureate, had died on October 6th. In the November issue of the *Bookman* were published four letters, under the general heading 'The Question of the Laureateship,' the third being signed R. B., the others unsigned. 'We wrote,' said the Editor, 'to four distinguished poets asking whether, in their opinion, the laureateship should be continued, and if so, on whom it should be conferred.' Yeats's authorship of the second letter is established by his letter to John O'Leary which here follows; it is to the editor's credit that he already considered Yeats 'a distinguished poet' though at that date he had only produced two small volumes of verse, the second published in that very year.

old days the imagination of the world would have fared but ill without its kings and nobles, for in those times, when few could read and pictures were many a mile between, they kept before men's minds a more refined and ample ideal of life than was possible to the small chief in his rush-strewn tower or to the carle in his poor cottage. By a phantasmagoria of royalties and nobilities the soul of the world displayed itself, and whatever there was in the matter of court poet or court pageantry helped it to draw them away from their narrow circle of eating and sleeping, and getting and begetting. It showed them life under the best conditions, and king or queen, baron or duke, became to them a type of the glory of the world. Thus at any rate do I, with my perhaps too literary eyes, read history, and turn all into a kind of theatre where the proud walk clad in cloth of gold, and display their passionate hearts, that the groundlings may feel their souls wax the greater. But now no man can say that life displays itself under the best conditions in royalties and nobilities, for refinement and ample life have gone out into the highways and byways, and the Laureate should go after them, and be their master of the revels.

Surely most of us, whatever be our politics, feel that *The Idylls of the King* are marred a little by the dedications to the Prince Consort and to the Queen, and not necessarily because either was unworthy of exceeding praise, but because neither represents to us a fuller and more beautiful kind of life than is possible to any mere subject, and because the attempt to make them do so, even though so mighty a poet made it, has a little lessened the significance of the great imaginative types of Arthur and Guinevere, and cast round the greatest romantic poem of the century a ring of absurdity. We can only just tolerate Spenser's comparison of the Queen of the Fairies to Queen Elizabeth, for even then all such comparisons were growing obsolete, whereas we can hardly forgive at all this injury which the Court poet of our day has done to the laurelled poet of the people. Were not this alone sufficient reason, even if all others were lacking, for nationalizing the Laureateship? Once do this in some conspicuous fashion, and the post will become the greatest honour any country could confer upon a man of letters, and neither Mr. Swinburne or Mr. Morris will find reasons to refuse it. Either would make a worthy successor to Wordsworth and Tennyson, Morris the worthier of the two, perhaps, for he is still producing work scarce a whit less moving than were the songs and stories of his youth, while Mr. Swinburne has been these many days, if we consider his verse alone, too careful of the sound, too careless of the sense.

This letter of mine has gone into matters far removed from literary criticism and is more than a little discursive, but I know not when a man has so good a right to be discursive and have his say according to his whim as when he is suggesting something which has not the slightest chance of being done. Besides, if I had not talked somewhat of things in general I should have had to discuss the claims of all kinds of perfectly absurd people, and even to take seriously him of whom it has been said that he calls himself 'of Penbryn,' [1] to be distinguished from his namesake of Parnassus.

TO JOHN O'LEARY

[Nov 1892]   Thornhill

Dear Mr. O'Leary, Miss Gonne has returned to Paris to carry out her 'Tweed' scheme and to give a few lectures. She promises to return by the 12th or 14th and says she has got a great many books for the libraries. I have remained here not because I heard this but because my grandfather had a sudden change for the worse yesterday week and was not expected to live more than a few days. My uncle did not wish me to return just then. I had meant to go on Monday morning but have stayed on. Quinn promised me news of the literary society but has not written so that I know not what is being done but expect that it must be time to begin the lecture session in due course so that I should not remain much longer. I am anxious however to get a story written and another article done so as to get a certain amount of money due to me. I will telegraph when I am starting. Unwin writes to say that *Countess Kathleen* is selling 'very fairly well' but gives no particulars. 'It is always difficult' he writes 'to sell a book of poems' but mine is having 'a very friendly reception.' I imagine that there will be a steady sale right on.

You did not see last *Bookman* did you? the second of the four

[1] Lewis Morris (1833–1907), author of *The Epic of Hades* and numerous other volumes of verse, lived at Penbryn House, Carmarthen, Wales. He did not become Laureate, but was knighted in 1895.

letters on the Laureateship was mine. I review Tennyson's *Death of Œnone*[1] for next number. Also I hope O'Grady['s] *Finn and his Companions*.[2] I have done a couple of poems and a story for the *National Observer*,[3] also articles for *United Ireland*[4] and for *Chicago Citizen*.[5]

The 'Adventures volume' will I fear be delayed for a short time as they are going to bring out a re-issue of the series. I am writing to Garnett to let me know the date of publication. Yours always

W B YEATS

A postcard about Literary Society would be a godsend.

TO T. FISHER UNWIN[6]

[? *November* 1892]   [*Thornhill*]

Dear Mr. Unwin, Mr. John O'Leary has sent me a letter written to him by a prominent member of the Irish Literary Society, London, from which I learn that Mr. Rolleston has opened negotiations with you for the publication of a series of Irish books. I do not know how you look upon this matter but I firmly believe that such a series will be a great success if backed up by the enthusiasm of the young men over here and by the help of our Irish writers. I think however that it is only fair for me to tell you that I think Mr. Rolleston has been a little hasty in submitting to you a scheme the details of which are quite unknown to us here. We hold strong views about the question of the proposed books and their writers and naturally

---

[1] Yeats reviewed *The Death of Œnone* in the *Bookman*, December 1892.

[2] I can find no review of Standish O'Grady's *Finn and his Companions* in the *Bookman*, but Yeats gave it a brief mention in his letter to the *Boston Pilot* of November 19, 1892.

[3] Only one poem appeared in the *National Observer* about this date, namely 'The Rose in my Heart,' published on November 12. The story was 'The Devil's Book,' the first of what afterwards became the Red Hanrahan series, published on November 26.

[4] The article for *United Ireland* may have been 'Hopes and Fears for Irish Literature' already published on October 15, or possibly 'The De-Anglicising of Ireland' which appeared in the form of a letter on December 17, 1892.

[5] Search by myself in the file of the *Chicago Citizen* in the British Museum, and another search kindly undertaken by Miss Elizabeth Baughman, Reference Librarian of the Chicago Historical Society, have failed to discover any contribution to the paper by Yeats.

[6] From a typewritten copy.

would like to have a voice in drawing up whatever scheme be submitted to you for acceptance, rejection or modification. I am writing all this to Mr. Rolleston and suggest to you in the meanwhile that you delay finally settling the matter until I have had time to submit Mr. Rolleston's proposal—which I have asked him for—to a committee of our best men here—Count Plunkett, Douglas Hyde, John O'Leary, etc. I propose then, if it be necessary, to cross to London and see the best men of the Irish Literary Society, London, with the same view. There has been considerable friction between Sir Charles Gavan Duffy and our men, and I am afraid that if something such as I propose is not done Count Plunkett will conclude negociations which he opened months ago with his Irish publisher and our movement may split up on lines which the press will soon turn into a dispute of Parnellite Dublin and the Parnellite young men in the country parts, against what they will call 'West British' and 'Whiggish' Duffy and Rolleston. All the most ardent of the young men are Parnellites and would be only too ready to raise such a cry against Duffy, who is unpopular for Michellite [?] reasons. It should be perfectly easy to get the series accepted as a great national work, but such it can only be, I believe, if backed by our organization and our lectures and by the press over here. I propose to return to Dublin on Saturday or Sunday and will at once summon a committee. Yours sincerely W B YEATS

TO EDWARD GARNETT

[? *November* 1892] *Thornhill*

My dear Garnett, I have written to Unwin on the matter—do not be alarmed for I wrote in quite dispassionate mood and curse no man. I have also written to Rolleston and cursed him and Gavan Duffy as curtly [?] but as vigorously (can you understand the combination?) as I can. I have asked that his proposal to Unwin be submitted to a special committee in Dublin and then with its modifications be submitted to a special committee in London and that the two organizations abide by the result. I have merely written to Unwin to tell him that some consideration of Rolleston's proposal is necessary on our part if we are to throw ourselves into the thing with vigour and stave off a rival library to yours which an Irish publisher offered to bring out two months ago. O'Leary and others are ready to push on this Dublin library and write to me about it. I asked Unwin not to sign the agreement until he has heard from us. I have not done this because I doubt that your good offices are all sufficient but because I want Duffy and Rolleston to feel my hand in the matter in as direct a way as possible and so stave off further trouble. They have so far ignored us here in every way in their power—making use of us however as a springboard when needful.

Please send me any news of Rolleston's proposal. Yours sincerely   W B YEATS

I go to Dublin on Sunday, will then consult a committee and if need[ed] can cross over to London as soon as I have its recommendations. Thank you for good offices in the matter of *Adventure* volume. Ellis writes to me that Blake will hardly be out of the binders' hands much before Xmas. It has gone to 3 vols.

TO EDWARD GARNETT

Private   Lonsdale House
[? *November* 1892]   St. Lawrence Road
                                                    Clontarf
                                                    Dublin

My dear Garnett, I write partly on my own motion and partly on the motion of Mr. John O'Leary. I think we ought to try and come to some arrangement about the book scheme. I am satisfied that it is a matter of vital importance to secure the help of the National Literary Society. If this society could establish libraries and educate branches throughout Ireland the scheme would be made a success. The books could be taken round by our lecturers—Ashe King who is just about to start to lecture at Loughrea, or Hyde who will go to Westport in a few weeks, could do much in this way—and sold at the lectures as the Fabian Society people do. We could get our agents in provincial towns to push them also. In fact there are many ways in which the Society could help this project. But the Irish Society must be considered and consulted if it is to help. To put the matter into practical form I would suggest that an agreement between Fisher Unwin on the one hand and Sir Gavan Duffy and Douglas Hyde (who is to be sub-editor) on the other should be prepared and that the agreement should contain a clause binding Sir Charles Duffy and Douglas Hyde to secure the co-operation of the Irish and London Society in promoting the sale of the books. A clause of this kind will bring Duffy and the two societies into line. I would further suggest that a draft of the proposed agreement be sent to John O'Leary for his perusal. It is not merely a question of getting the societies to do nothing against the scheme but of getting their *active* and enthusiastic support and of keeping it when got. Yours very sincerely W B YEATS

P.S. Mr. O'Leary asks me to say that the need for this arrangement comes largely from the fact that Rolleston—perhaps against his will—will otherwise be completely ruled by Duffy. Duffy, though very ready to bow to force, will bow to no advice not backed by force. Such is at any rate Mr. O'Leary's belief and he should know him. Of course there will be no opposition to the series. We all want books. But the lack of enthusiasm for this series may prevent its being properly pushed here. Mr. O'Leary has immense influence and it were well to get his support and not merely his tolerance. I thought the proposed committee might serve all purposes but have been met by this statement that it has no means of enforcing its decisions. The result here is that Mr. O'Leary's supporters here do not take enough interest in the proposed arrangement to come down and vote for it. Hence though the society *nominally* is quite content with Hyde's editorship it is *really* quite the other way. Whatever be the result of this letter or of arrangements generally I shall do all I can to push the series but should feel more certain of success if we had positive influence.

This is of course private but if you want any definite expression of opinion, either for Unwin or for the Committee of Irish Literary Society, you can get it by writing to Mr. John O'Leary. He is at Lonsdale House, St. Lawrence Road, Clontarf, Dublin. Though this is private I leave you to act upon your own judgement as to the use you make of its contents.

TO EDWARD GARNETT

Private   *Lonsdale House*
Thursday [? November 1892]

My dear Garnett, I telegraphed to you to-day because I heard from London that Unwin was getting alarmed about the book project. Under these circumstances we must be very cautious. We want books—books under good conditions if possible—but books at any rate. My own pathway in the matter is particularly difficult. If in trying to carry out the proposed compromise I had been too Duffyite I could not have got the section who have opposed him to have anything to do with the arrangement. I have therefore emphasized the influence the society will have through Hyde as much as possible and thereby drawn down the thunders of Duffy's two supporters and I fear that some rumour of said thunders may have got to Unwin.

I believe that if Unwin were to put the clause which I suggest into the agreement it would bring us all into line. The section here who have opposed the absolute predominance of Sir Gavan Duffy would become enthusiastic or sufficiently so to carry everything we want and to work up a public, while the thick and thin supporters of Duffy would have to come into line with us. Mr. O'Leary would have a real influence over the scheme then and his name would balance the 'federationist' name of Duffy and all would become smooth.

At the same time do as you think fit about letter. Find out Unwin's state of mind before using it. It might be the way out of the difficulty. Duffy could guarantee the support of the London Society, Hyde of the Irish. In this way Unwin's interests would be safe-guarded.

Please send me a word as to Unwin's point of view and as to what he has heard from Dublin. I may be able to give some information of a useful kind. Yours ever   W B YEATS

If it be needful to say who the suggestion about the 'clause' comes from, Mr. O'Leary says that his name may be mentioned. My name must on no account be mentioned to anyone.

TO JOHN O'LEARY

[*? late autumn*, 1892]   *3 Blenheim Road*

Dear Mr. O'Leary, Could you not get the Committee elected next Thursday? Make plain to Sigerson or to anyone who opposes from his side that Rolleston does not oppose this scheme at all, and that it will make peace and that Unwin refuses to go on with the project unless we support him, and support means influence over the series or must be made to mean this. The London Society has chosen a committee of six or seven. This I think is too large. The committee should be elected next Thursday so that both committees can get to work at once. Douglas Hyde consents to be assistant editor. I would not have taken the post as people would have been liable to accuse me of having fought for my own hand.

The Company is definitely dead. They found that a capital of 3000 shares would not be enough to keep the necessary staff of manager, clerks etc going. They then started the project of a general publishing company with 10,000 shares and were getting support when Duffy withdrew because it suddenly struck him that he could only control the Irish series and not the whole publishing work. 'He would not be responsible for what he could not control' etc. The old cry in a more absurd form!

I have written to Plunkett about the proposed committee and told him that all here are anxious to have the committee in working order by next Saturday. Yours very truly   W B YEATS

TO JOHN O'LEARY

[*? early* 1893]   *3 Blenheim Road*

Dear Mr. O'Leary, I did not write before for there was nothing definite to say. Barry O'Brien at first was strong for the proposal which he told you of. It was however obvious that Gavan Duffy would refuse it, at the same time our position is strong, for Unwin refuses to go into the scheme at all unless we are all agreed. At the Committee last Saturday the following proposal was agreed to by those present, though a vote was not taken, that Sir Gavan Duffy be editor in chief with two sub-editors—T. W. Rolleston and Douglas Hyde (to represent us and have his name on all books) and, and this the most important point, that the London Society elect a committee of three to draw up list of books, the Dublin Society to do the same. Then lists to be thrown into one, each perhaps giving way in smaller matters, so that the final list represent both and yet be not too long. This final list to be sent to Gavan Duffy for his approval. If he agree to it or to the greater portion all will be well. If not we should have to do without him.

Duffy has accepted the Hyde proposal but has not yet been informed about the second one nor perhaps need be until the list is made. We should I think merely formally agree to the list of books I brought over (to the bulk of which Rolleston says Duffy makes no objection), the Society should approach you, Plunkett, and myself as committee. This will bring us all into harmony and establish our right to a voice in the matter. The London Society will circularize all its members in the matter of the review and believes that it can sell 200 at least.

I am editing a volume of Blake lyrics for *The Muses' Library* and shall get £25 for it.

The Blake book will be ready some time next week I believe.

Yours ever   W B YEATS

TO EDWARD GARNETT

[1893]   *Thornhill*

My dear Garnett, I sent you from Dublin part of the contents of 'The Adventurer volume.' You have somewhere a list of the total [?] contents. It was somewhat as follows

        Introduction
        1 Fighting Fitzgerald
        2 Tiger Roche
        3 —— Maguire (British Museum)
        4 Freeney the Robber
        5 Rogues and Rapparees
        6 Michael Dwyer
        Notes

I have sent you no 1, no 2, no 4, no 5—3 and 6 will have to be got at Unwin's expense—at least 3 will. 6 I could get probably.

How do you prosper with Blake, for I hear the *Speaker* has sent it to you? Yours   W B YEATS

TO LIONEL JOHNSON [1]

[February or March 1893]   *Thornhill*

My dear Johnson, Some friends and myself are interested in [a] projected Irish Magazine which is intended to be the organ of our literary movement.[2] It is to cost 6d a month and the first number is to appear if possible on May 21st (June number). Will you give us some contribution, verse or prose? You need not do so at once but let us have your name to put in our list of contributions. We want to get a strong list as it is the only way of getting advertisements.

Thank you very much for your review of Blake in *Westminster*[3] (my sister says it was yours) it was the best yet in every way. The mention of occult societies and the like came very much from our resolve not to hide our debt to the men who have been fighting the battle. It is so easy to earn a little credit for a kind of academical mysticism which ignores or even sneers at the true students. It was for this reason and from no wish to claim secret knowledge that we put in the book the hints you objected to. My own position is that an idealism or spiritualism which denies magic, and evil spirits even, and sneers at magicians and even mediums, (the few honest ones) is an academical imposture. Your Church has in this matter been far more thorough than the Protestant. It has never denied *Ars Magica* though it has denounced it. Yours ever   W B YEATS

TO JOHN O'LEARY

Jan 5th [1894]   *3 Blenheim Road*

Dear Mr. O'Leary, The cause of the delay about the money is this. I owed last summer about £14 but while over here had as much

---

[1] From a typewritten copy.
[2] This projected Irish Magazine does not seem to have appeared.
[3] The review here mentioned, 'A Guide to Blake,' was printed, unsigned, in the *Westminster Gazette*, February 16, 1893; it may well have been written by Johnson. He reviewed the book also in the *Academy*, August 26, 1893; this review was reprinted in *Post Liminium: Essays and Critical Papers*, London, 1912.

money as I required for my expenses and some pounds over with which I paid a portion of my debts—a number of small sums which I was afraid of forgetting—and set aside £4 or £5 as well to lessen the remainder. The day before I started for Ireland there was a sudden crisis here at home, which swept away £4. When I got back to Ireland my income went down at once for various reasons. I had not expected this and I never have had more than a few shillings over my expenses, which few shillings went in small driblets but my only extravagance, a few picture frames and the like. But including this I do not think I have ever spent more than 25/- a week. Now that I am back here I shall have money again but at the present moment have little more than my fare to Paris where I am to stay with some friends for ten days or so. I do not look upon this as an extravagance however as I must live somewhere. I always contribute here of course. I have for about two months now done work which cannot bring in a penny for a month or two. I have been writing a play ever since I came over, for instance, which is to be produced in March,[1] and am now merely going to Paris, until the time comes for the rehearsals. I thought to pay you something at Xmas when I got £10 as the second instalment for *The Celtic Twilight* but found that my landlady absorbed too much of it and with the exception of a couple of pounds from the *Bookman* I have had nothing since.

Meanwhile I have plenty of commissions for work if I can only do it and can I think promise the £7–10/- or the bulk of it before the end of March—or at any rate the bulk of it.

Please burn this letter. . . . Yours truly   W B YEATS

I thought I had given you *The Celtic Twilight* but finding I had not went to Lawrence & Bullen to get one and found both out of town. You shall have one immediately.

TO JOHN O'LEARY

Feb 7th [1894]   *3 Blenheim Road*

Dear Mr. O'Leary, An egg I had thought the reverse of ripe hatched last night unexpectedly, hence I send £1 to the lessening of the debt.

---

[1] *The Land of Heart's Desire.* See note 2, p. 230.

If the hatching of the next were a little more certain I would send a few shillings more but cannot as things are. The effort to get my play finished has tired me out and now that it is done and gone to the typewriter for the actors I shall rest till rehearsals begin. I am going to Paris tonight to stay with the Mathers at 1 Avenue Duquesne and am taking introductions to Verlaine and Mallarmé,[1] other introductions I have refused, for just now I want a quiet dream with the holy Kabala for bible and naught else, for I am tired—tired.

I send you a *Celtic Twilight*. Yours ever   W B YEATS

TO JOHN O'LEARY

[*April* 15, 1894]   3 *Blenheim Road*

Dear Mr. O'Leary, I have been unable to write for the last three weeks as I have been in the hands of the oculist and without glasses—or I should have written before this. For a couple of years it has been getting more and more difficult for me to do any steady reading as my eyes begin to get uncomfortable in a few minutes. I find now that I am never to read more than a quarter of an hour at a time. I have then to stop and rest for a few minutes—this same in a less degree applies to writing. I have 'conical cornea' in the left eye and 'stigmatism' in the right. The left eye is now practically useless. At the same time I should get on all right with care. I suppose I shall have to very much drop reviewing and take to stories entirely which will be better artistically at any rate. The immediate result of all this on top of my work at the theatre has meant very little money. I had hoped to send you some before this. I got last night a bill from Mrs. Carew the existence of which I had absolutely forgotten. I shall however I think be able to pay it this week as the *Speaker* owes me some pounds. Enough however of such mere bothers.

Todhunter's play *The Comedy of Sighs* was taken off last night.[2]

[1] It is probable that these introductions were given Yeats by Arthur Symons. Symons had entertained Verlaine during his visit to London in 1893, had translated some of his poems, and was to translate some by Mallarmé. It is, however, possible that the introduction to Mallarmé came from York Powell who, later, arranged for him to lecture at Oxford.

[2] Florence Farr had taken the Avenue Theatre in Northumberland Avenue for a season of plays, with backing from Miss A. E. F. Horniman. *A Comedy*

My little play *The Land of Heart's Desire* is however considered a fair success and is to be put on again with the play by Shaw which goes on next week. It is being printed by Unwin and will be sold in the theatre with the programmes. The whole venture has had to face the most amazing denunciations from the old type of critics. They have however been so abusive that a reaction has set in which has brought a rather artistic [?] public to the theatre. The takings at the door rose steadily but not rapidly enough to make it safe to hold on with Todhunter's play which was really a brilliant piece of work. If Shaw's play does well a new play of mine will be put on— a much more ambitious play than anything I have yet done. It will give you some notion of the row that is going on when I tell you 'chuckers out' have been hired for the first night of Shaw. They are to be distributed over the theatre and are to put out all people who make a row. The whole venture will be history anyway for it is the first contest between the old commercial school of theatrical folk and the new artistic school. Yours   W B YEATS

TO JOHN O'LEARY

June 26th [1894]   3 *Blenheim Road*

Dear Mr. O'Leary, I fear I never sent you a copy of my play.[1] I now do so. The edition is quite exhausted. An edition has been arranged for in America, and Unwin is considering the wisdom of a new edition here.

George Russell has, as I dare say you know, published a little book of verse,[2] which is exceedingly wonderful. I think we will be able to organize a reception for it. It is about the best piece of

---

of Sighs by John Todhunter, with Yeats's *The Land of Heart's Desire* as a curtain raiser, had its first performance on March 29, 1894. It was badly received and remained in the bill only until April 14. The theatre was then closed for a week's rehearsals, and *Arms and the Man* by Bernard Shaw produced on April 21, Yeats's play being retained as curtain raiser until May 12, after which a new one-act play was substituted, a not unusual device of the time, as the critics were then asked to pay the theatre a second visit.

[1] *The Land of Heart's Desire* had been published by Fisher Unwin in April; the American edition, issued by Stone & Kimball, Chicago, appeared in the following autumn.

[2] *Homeward: Songs by the Way*, the first book of poems by George Russell (AE), was published by Whaley, Dublin, 1894.

poetical work done by any Irishman this good while back. It is the kind of book which inevitably lives down big histories and long novels and the like. It is full of sweetness and subtlety and may well prove to have three or four immortal pages.

I send you *The Second Book of the Rhymers' Club* in which everybody is tolerably good except the Trinity College men, Rolleston, Hillier,[1] Todhunter and Greene,[2] who are intolerably bad as was to be expected—Todhunter is of course skilful enough with more matter of fact themes and quite admits the dreadful burden of the T.C.D. tradition—and some are exceedingly good, notably Plarr,[3] Dowson, Johnson and Le Gallienne.

I should have gone to Dublin before this, even though it were but to return in the autumn for the performance of my new play but for sheer impecuniousity which I am about to clear off to some extent by an Irish Anthology [4] which is nearly finished. Do you remember getting from me a little green paper-covered book called I think, *Irish Ballad Poetry* [5] and containing work by Kickham and De Vere's *Bard Ethell*? [6]

If you have it by you I wish you could send it me as it would save me a very great deal of trouble. I have tried to buy a copy but

[1] Arthur Cecil Hillier published no volume of his own verse, but was translator, with Ernest Dowson and G. A. Greene, of Richard Muther's *History of Modern Painting*.

[2] George Arthur Greene published *Italian Lyrists of To-Day*, Translations from Contemporary Italian Poetry, London, 1893; *Dantesques*: a Sonnet companion to the Inferno, London, 1903; and *Songs of the Open Air*, London, 1912.

[3] Victor Gustave Plarr published two small volumes of verse, *In the Dorian Mood*, London, 1896, and *The Tragedy of Asgard*, London, 1901, as well as a volume of reminiscences of Ernest Dowson in 1914. He was for many years Librarian of the Royal College of Surgeons.

[4] *A Book of Irish Verse*, selected from Modern Writers with an introduction and notes by W. B. Yeats, was published by Methuen & Co., London, in March 1895.

[5] The book Yeats was asking for was *Ballads, Popular Poetry and Household Songs*, collected and arranged by Duncathail [Ralph Varian]. It was published in 1865 by McGlashan & Gill, Dublin, both in cloth and paper covers, and was freely reprinted in the following years. It contains *The Bard Ethell*, a long poem by Aubrey de Vere, which Yeats included in his *Book of Irish Verse*.

[6] Aubrey Thomas de Vere (1814–1902) was born in Co. Limerick and educated at Trinity College, Dublin. He spent most of his long life in Ireland and published many books, in verse and prose, now almost forgotten. Yeats wrote of him: 'His few but ever memorable successes are enchanted islands in grey seas of stately impersonal reverie and description, which drift by and leave no definite recollection.' A Selection from the Poems of Aubrey de Vere and Sir Samuel Ferguson (1810–1886) chosen by W. B. Yeats was announced in 1908 by the Cuala Press as ready early in 1909, but it was not issued.

neither Gill's or Duffy's agent here know anything of it. It cost 6d when I bought it.

I have written a severe article on 'The New Irish Library' which will appear in the August *Bookman*.[1] An inevitable re-organization of the scheme is at hand, and therefore it seems better to speak out. I believe that my article will only make patent the latent convictions of all the people here. Surely this world has not seen a more absurd 'popular series' than this one, and the sale has very properly fallen steadily.

I have no information about the Library Committee or the Nat. Lit. Society itself, though I have written twice for it—the last time to Kelly.

Dora Sigerson is here and she and Miss Piatt [2] came with me to see Bernard Shaw's play at the Avenue and were, I think, well pleased.

Any news of your book? I saw a passing allusion to its approaching publication in the *Pall Mall* or *Westminster*. Yours ever

W B YEATS

TO OLIVIA SHAKESPEAR [3]

August 6/94   *3 Blenheim Road*

My dear Mrs. Shakespear, I have been wanting to make another suggestion about *Beauty's Hour*; [4] and, as you are getting near the end, make it now instead of waiting until I see you in September. I think Gerald wants a slight touch more of definition. A few lines

[1] Yeats's review in the *Bookman*, August 1894, is headed 'Some Irish National Books' and reviews *The New Spirit of the Nation*, edited by Martin MacDermott, and *A Parish Providence* by E. M. Lynch, an adaptation of Balzac's *Médecin de Campagne*. In his review Yeats seems to suppose that 'E. M. Lynch' was a pseudonym of Gavan Duffy's, but in this he was mistaken.

[2] Miss Piatt, either sister or daughter of John James Piatt. Yeats had written an unsigned review of *An Enchanted Castle* by Sarah Piatt in the *Speaker*, July 22, 1893.

[3] It is probable that Yeats first made the acquaintance of Olivia Shakespear in May 1894.

[4] Mrs. Shakespear published some half-dozen novels between 1894 and 1910, the earliest being *Love on a Mortal Lease*. The short novel which Yeats discusses here, *Beauty's Hour*, was published in the *Savoy*, August and September 1896, but was not issued in book form. *The Journey of High Honour* mentioned in the postscript was her second novel and was published in 1895, so Yeats had evidently read it in manuscript.

early in the book would do all needed. You find he develops into rather a plastic person; and this is the best thing for the plot, but you should show that this is characterization and not a limitation of knowledge. Might he not be one of those vigorous fair-haired, boating, or cricket-playing young men, who are very positive, and what is called manly, in external activities and energies and wholly passive and plastic in emotions and intellectual things? I met just such a man last winter. I had suspected before that those robust masks had often and often a great emotional passivity and plasticity but this man startled me. He was of the type of those who face the cannon's mouth without a tremor, but kill themselves rather than face life without some girl with pink cheeks, whose character they have never understood, whose soul they have never perceived and whom they would have forgotten in a couple of months. Such people are very lovable, for both their weakness and their strength appear pathetic; and your clever heroine might well love him. She could see how strong and courageous he was in the external things, where a woman was weak, and could feel instinctively how much in need of protection and care in those deeper things where she was strong. This criticism occurred to me soon after I left you and I longed to ask you to read me all the Gerald bits again before you started but did not do so because I knew you would be busy your last afternoons in London. I only bother you with it now that you may have it with you while you are writing, instead of its pursuing you through I know not what traveller's vicissitude.

I think you have chosen wisely in making Dr. Trefusis read the mystics rather than the purely magical books I suggested. *The Morning Redness* by Jacob Boehme is a great book beautifully named, which might do, and *The Obscure Night of the Soul* by St. John of the Cross is among the most perfectly named things in the world.

I will perhaps write to you again about your kind letter, for I have much to say and I want this to reach you this evening and so must end now. I saw Mrs. Emery yesterday and found that she had been very delighted with you.

That you like my stories is a very great pleasure and the best of pleasures. Yours always sincerely and gratefully   W B YEATS

The books have just come: many thanks. I am sorry you took so much trouble.

P.S. I have just found your letter. I think Lionel's book [1] very wonderful and agree with you about caring more for his theories about literature in general than those about Hardy in particular. However his summing up of the scenic qualities of Hardy in the chapter 'Wessex' and elsewhere is very stately. I feel however that there is something wrong about praising Hardy in a style so much better than his own. I wish he had written instead of Dante or Milton.

I hope you have not been seriously ill and will soon be able to work again as vigorously as of old. I am glad that not writing makes you miserable—heartless though the remark be—but this ensures me the pleasure of many another *Journey of High Honour*.

TO JOHN O'LEARY

[? autumn 1894]   *3 Blenheim Road*

Dear Mr. O'Leary, Please send on 'proofs.' You said you were sending them so I did not write about them.

I fear there is but little news of any kind—unless one talks about the weather which is horrible like a furnace.

My 'Sullivan the Red' stories have roused York Powell into great enthusiasm.

I am going to Elkin Mathews one of these days to arrange for a volume of Irish essays, chiefly of fierce mockery of most Irish men and things except the men and things who are simple, poor of imagination, and not I fear too many. Yours ever   W B YEATS

TO SARAH PURSER

Sept 1st [? 1894]   *3 Blenheim Road*

My dear Miss Purser, I have been an unconscionable time about writing to thank you for your charming embroidered book cover and can only ask you to excuse me because—well, on general principles.

[1] *The Art of Thomas Hardy* by Lionel Johnson was published in 1894.

The book cover is at this moment helping to civilize a novel all about North of Ireland presbyterians and succeeding as well as could be expected under the circumstances. It shall have a better and easier task presently.

I have heard of you in the letters of that imp out of *The Land of Heart's Desire* (letters Mrs. Paget has shown me), and which are so very lifelike, that I am almost convinced of the real existence of the imp.[1] This is a sign of the return of the age of faith. Yours sincerely

W B YEATS

TO J. B. YEATS

Nov 5th [1894] *Thornhill*

My dear Papa, I am doing nothing except the play *The Shadowy Waters* which will I think be good. It is however giving me a devil of a job. More than anything I have done for years. In my struggle to keep it concrete I fear I shall so overload it with legendary detail that it will be unfit for any theatrical purposes—at least as such are carried out at present.

George has been away at Leopardstown where Dunmorgan ran second, and is in good spirits. He has just come back with a racing man with him, under whose technical conversation I groan.

Many thanks for the *Westminster*. I am in many ways glad the Judge row has broken out, as I have disliked and suspected the man for years.[2] I am writing for the papers containing the other articles—I have known the facts for twelve months or so. The

---

[1] This may possibly be a playful reference to Dorothy Paget, Florence Farr's niece, a girl of about ten, who had made her first appearance on the stage as the fairy child in *The Land of Heart's Desire* earlier in the year.

[2] William Q. Judge, a lawyer's clerk in Col. Olcott's brother's office in America, was a prominent member of the Theosophical Society there. After the death of Madame Blavatsky in 1891 the London Theosophical Society was led by Mrs. Annie Besant. Judge came to England and endeavoured to assume the leadership there, producing messages supposedly deposited in sealed envelopes by occult influences. The *Westminster Gazette* published a series of articles between October 29 and November 8, 1894, written by F. Edmund Garrett, under the heading *Isis Very Much Unveiled. The Truth about the Great Mahatma Hoax*, accusing Judge of trickery. Much correspondence followed and the articles and letters were republished by the paper as a shilling pamphlet. Judge replied, with a denial of the charges, in the *Westminster* of December 8 and 9.

paper seems to have got them pretty correctly—at least as Judge's opponents hold them to be.

I want you to send me a copy of the *Fortnightly* which is lying about somewhere with Johnson's article on Pater;[1] also Miss Vynne's book *Honey of Aloes* [2] which I forgot. Yours affectionately

W B YEATS

Unwin has accepted my terms finally and will bring out *Countess Kathleen, Land of Heart's Desire* and the lyrics which he has as soon as I find time to correct them.

TO JOHN O'LEARY [3]

Nov 10 [1894] *Thornhill*

Dear Mr. O'Leary, A great many thanks for the newspapers (where by the way did you clip the little fragment of Lang's article from?) I am working at my new poem *The Shadowy Waters* [4] and when this is done and dispatched to Elkin Mathews, begin correcting my other poems for a collected edition with Unwin. I was very glad to get out of Dublin, for Dublin and London between them tired me out, or I should have run down to see you one morning before leaving. I however made my stay as short as I was able and every house

---

[1] Lionel Johnson's article, 'The Work of Mr. Pater,' appeared in the *Fortnightly Review*, September 1894.

[2] *Honey of Aloes and other Stories* by Nora Vynne. London: Ward Lock & Bowden, 1894.

[3] From a copy thought to have been made by D. J. O'Donoghue.

[4] *The Shadowy Waters*, on which Yeats had worked since he was a boy, seems to have been near enough completion to be sent to Elkin Mathews for publication, but it is evident from later letters that Yeats could not finish it then to his satisfaction. Late in 1896 he sent either a version or a synopsis of the play to Leonard Smithers, who intended to publish it with illustrations by Aubrey Beardsley. Beardsley hoped to make six pictures for it, but Yeats has stated that he only finished one and died before he could do the rest. Eventually a version of the play appeared in the *North American Review*, May 1900, and it was published in book form by Hodder & Stoughton, London, at the end of that year. It was first played by the Irish National Theatre Society at the Molesworth Hall, Dublin, on January 14, 1904. Florence Farr gave a performance of it for a Theosophical Convention at the Court Theatre, London, on July 8, 1905. Yeats then rewrote the play completely and the new version appeared in *Poems, 1899–1905*, 1906; this was followed by an acting version, played at the Abbey Theatre on December 8, 1906, and published separately in 1907.

was full—a great many of them with running the erratic O'm [*word indecipherable*].

I have just sent off a letter arguing with McGrath for his remarks apropos of M'Call about the iniquity of writing for an English audience—the upshot of it is that as long as the Irish public knows nothing of literature Irish writers must be content to write for countries that know nothing of Ireland. I wonder will McGrath publish my letter.[1] I have got some more folklore but have no time to use it yet and have got some books to review but no time to review them till this play is done. O'Grady's *Cuchullin* is a wonderful thing —the best thing he has done.

Miss Lawless's last book should be good by *Independent* review. I hear that Hinkson is editing for Mathews a book of verse by T.C.D. men.

I heard from Hyde who was much pleased with the result of the meeting at the Irish Lit. in London. Talks of running down here. Yours sincerely   W B YEATS

TO THE EDITOR OF *UNITED IRELAND*

Nov. 10 [1894]   *Sligo*
[*Published November* 24, 1894]

Dear Sir, In a notice of Mr. M'Call's wholly interesting and partly charming little book, you mention 'that Americans did not mind the London critics,' and point the moral with the statement that 'an adamantine indifference to the judgment' of every public but the public of Ireland is 'the only honourable position for an Irish book to take up.' I am afraid that the history of America is hardly upon your side, for Walt Whitman, the most National of her poets, was so neglected and persecuted that he had, perhaps, fallen silent but for the admiration and help of a little group of Irish and English artists and men of letters; while countless feeble persons reproduced in crude verse amid wild American applause the fashions of other countries and the sentimentalities of their own. The truth is that the

[1] John McGrath, who succeeded Edmund Leamy as editor of *United Ireland*, in reviewing a book of poems, *Irish Nóiníns* [Daisies] by P. J. M'Call (Cavallus), had suggested that Irish writers should ignore the opinions of any critics outside Ireland.

public of America was, and the public of Ireland is, uneducated and idle, and it was often necessary for an original American writer, and it is often necessary for an original Irish writer, to appeal first, not to his countrymen, but to that small group of men of imagination and scholarship which is scattered through many lands and many cities, and to trust to his own influence and the influence of his fellow-workers to build up in the fullness of time a cultivated public in the land where he lives and works. The true ambition is to make criticism as international, and literature as National, as possible. A contrary ambition would, in Ireland, be peculiarly evil, for it could but set the opinions of our daily papers above the opinions of great scholars, and make a vacant and uninstructed public the masters of the men of intellect.

I write this letter because your notes seem to me to represent a common opinion and one which can only postpone the day when writers, whom you admire not less than I—Miss Barlow, Miss Lawless, Dr. Hyde and Mr. O'Grady—whose memorable *Coming of Cuchullin* lies upon my table—and others, shall have as much influence in purely intellectual matters as, say, members of Parliament, Town Councillors, and other illustrious but not very literary personages. Yours sincerely   'A Student of Irish Literature'

TO LILY YEATS

Nov 23rd [Postmark 1894]   *Thornhill*

My dear Lily, Unwin wants to put a photo of me in some sort of annual he is getting out and writes to me for one. I have none by me and so must ask you to send him that Hollyer one at once—I asked him to return it.

I have been staying at Lissadell for a couple of days and have enjoyed myself greatly. They are delightful people. I am to lecture to the parishioners of their clergyman, a Rev Mr. Lefanu—some relation of the great man of that name—on Irish fairy lore. All the while I was at Lissadell I was busy telling stories—old Irish stories —first to one then another and then telling them over again to the sick Miss Gore upstairs. Miss Eva Gore-Booth shows some promise as a writer of verse. Her work is very formless as yet but it is full of telling little phrases. Lissadell is an exceedingly impressive house inside with a great sitting room as high as a church and all things in good taste—much more pleasant than the Connellys' which was full of eighteenth century curiosities and otherwise uncomfortable to the mind and memory. But outside it is grey, square and bare yet set amid delightful grounds. They talk of my going there again to interview some old man who is believed to have much folklore.

The new play has had [? to wait] for several things this week but to-day I take it up again. It will be my best I think.

Uncle George has made about £60 by a bet on Dunmorgan who won at Newmarket yesterday. It does not seem to have greatly raised his spirits however, as his rheumatism is still rather bad and Kate threatening—as she does periodically—to leave him. She is divided between apparent desire to go and intense jealousy of the woman she quite erroneously believes selected to succeed her. Yours affectionately

W B YEATS

TO OLIVIA SHAKESPEAR

Nov 28th 94 *Thornhill*

My dear Mrs. Shakespear, Your little novel [1] is delightful. It does not try so difficult a thing, it is not so complex and subtle as *Love on a Mortal Lease* but within its narrower limits it is both wise and moving. Your heroine—your Mrs. Brandon—is a delightful person and Felicia only less so. My uncle has also read the book with great satisfaction. What fault I would find I have already found with *Love on a Mortal Lease*. First of all you do not know mankind anything like as well as womankind. I wonder how you would fare were you to pick out some eccentric man, either from among those you know, or from literary history, from the Villiers De Lisle Adams and Verlaines, and set him to make love to your next heroine? If you could make your men salient, marked, dominant, you would at once treble the solidity of your work. As yet your heroes are not only a little shadowy in characterization, but too passive, too much driven hither and thither by destiny. They are refined, distinguished, sym-

[1] *The Journey of High Honour.*

pathetic, not because you have given them this for their character but because your own character and ideals are mirrored in them. And even in quite obvious things—things which you have certainly imagined for them—you leave them too indefinite. I had a clear unchangeable vision of your heroine at once, but I found that both the men kept taking the appearance of various pictures, friends and the like. After a bit Brandon settled down despite my best endeavour into the likeness—the perfectly irrelevant likeness—of a distracted husband in one of Orchardson's pictures; while Christopher, as soon as I had discovered his approximate age, put on the form of a certain ungainly, long-suffering and freckled publisher's reader.[1] You will remember that this is an old complaint of mine. You *think* the events sometimes when you should *see* them and make your

[*The remainder of this letter is missing.*]

TO THE EDITOR OF *UNITED IRELAND*[2]

[*Published December* 1, 1894]

Dear Sir, I know perfectly well what Emerson wrote about the 'wit and wisdom' of the *Leaves of Grass*, but cannot see how his praise alters the fact that while Mr. W. M. Rossetti was bringing out an English selection from Whitman's poems, and Mr. Ruskin and George Eliot celebrating their power and beauty, the American public was hounding their author from a Government post because of their supposed immorality, or that when in his old age all Europe had learned to honour his name the leading magazines of his country were still not ashamed to refuse his contributions. Whitman appealed, like every great and earnest mind, not to the ignorant many, either English or American, but to that audience, 'fit though few,' which is greater than any nation, for it is made up of chosen persons from all, and through the mouths of George Eliot, Ruskin and Emerson it did him honour and crowned him among the immortals.

However, I expect that we are merely quarrelling about words,

[1] Possibly his friend Edward Garnett.
[2] The Editor, in a friendly rejoinder to Yeats's previous letter, remarked that it might well have been signed 'A Maker of Irish Literature,' and quoted Emerson's approval of Walt Whitman's poetry.

for I agree with you that if we are ever to have an Irish reading public we must have an Irish criticism to tell it what to read and what to avoid. I do not, however, think that it is brought any nearer by bidding Irish writers develop 'an adamantine indifference to the judgment of every public but the public of Ireland' as 'the only honourable position' to take up. It is not a matter in any sense for the authors, but for the journalists, editors, and newspaper owners of Ireland. If good criticism be written in Irish newspapers it will carry its due weight with authors and public alike; but so long as Irish critics are forced to criticise Irish books in English papers you will have no criticism in Ireland that any man will listen to. One or two of our papers are doing a little, a very little, but in the main the amateur is supreme, and the few articles that show knowledge and that far rarer thing judgment, are lost and unnoticed amid an empty ritual of convention and prejudice. Yours sincerely
'A Student of Irish Literature'

TO LILY YEATS

Dec 16th [in pencil 1894]   *Thornhill*

My dear Lilly, I have just returned from Lissadell where I have been staying first with the Gore-Booths and afterwards at the Parsonage. I lectured in the school house on Fairy lore chiefly to an audience of Orangemen. It was a novel experience. I found that the comic tales delighted them but that the poetry of fairy lore was quite lost on them. They held it Catholic superstition I suppose. However I had fortunately chosen nothing but humorous tales. The children were I believe greatly excited. Mr. Jones of Roughley said afterwards that now there should be another lecture to put my lecture 'on a sound religious basis' for he feared it may have sent away many of the audience with the idea that the fairies really existed. Mr. Jones was christened by our great-grandfather. I got a good bit of folklore at Lissadell, for the Gore-Booths brought me to see an old tenant who poured out quantities of tales.

Folk lore was a new experience to them. They had not thought it existed. They have now got all my books—including a large-paper copy of *The Countess Kathleen*. They are a very pleasant, kindly, inflammable family. Ever ready to take up new ideas and new things. The eldest son is 'theoretically' a home ruler and practically some kind of a humanitarian, much troubled by the responsibility of his wealth and almost painfully conscientious. He and the clergyman—Lefanu—are full of schemes. He is not however particularly clever and has not, I imagine, much will. He was on a ranch in America and picked up his ideas there. The strongest willed of them is I think old Miss Gore who is an invalid and is mostly invisible but is always more or less behind the scenes like an iron claw.

She is very much of a Tory and cares for nothing but horses. Sir Henry Gore-Booth thinks of nothing but the north pole, where his first officer to his great satisfaction has recently lost himself and thereby made an expedition to rescue him desirable.

You ask about *Under the Moon*.[1] I have got fairly good terms. A royalty from the first copy and recovery of the copyright after a term of years, also the right to decide all questions of binding, printing etc. I am correcting *Oisin* and find it a job. I intend to make additions to *The Countess Kathleen*.

Your horoscopes struck me as very good—yours less so than the others. Lolly's was particularly good. Jack's was good too. Yours affectionately W B YEATS

[*On envelope*] I am always glad to see papers.

TO LILY YEATS

Dec 26th [1894] *Thornhill*

My dear Lilly, A great many thanks for the handkerchief and please convey my thanks to Lolly for the others. I am sorry to have sent

[1] *Under the Moon* was the title first considered for the collection of poems and plays which Fisher Unwin was preparing to publish. The issue for 1894–95 of *Good Writing about many books mostly by their Authors*, an annual publication to announce books in preparation, contained the following notice: 'Old writers were of opinion that the moon governed by her influence peasants, sailors, fishermen and all obscure persons, and as the symbols of Mr. Yeats's poetry are taken almost wholly from the traditions and manners of the Connaught peasantry, he has selected the title *Under the Moon* for his forthcoming book.... Mr. Yeats has written of the beautiful and singular legends of Ireland, not from any archaeological or provincial ambition, but with the desire of moulding the universal substance of poetry into new shapes, and of interpreting, to the best of his power, the spirit of Ireland to itself.' This does not, as do most of the contributions, bear the author's signature in facsimile at the end, so it cannot

you nothing, but I possess nothing but a 2/- piece and a halfpenny —borrowed—and will be no wealthier until Methuen chooses to publish *A Book of Irish Verse*. I have been doing next to no articles for all my time has been taken up with the new poems and the revision of the old ones. I am half through the revision of *The Wanderings of Oisin*, now *The Wanderings of Usheen*. I do the new poems always before dinner and work at the old one[s] after, and am getting on very slowly.

Mathews has sent me proofs of Johnson's book of verse.[1] It is exceedingly stately and impressive and will make a stir. It is however monotonous and will scarce be very popular. He has sent me also proofs of a charming little book by Selwyn Image.[1] I have just finished reading *The Prisoner of Zenda*. It is a book certainly not to be laid down till one has got through it; but infinitely below Stevenson, from whom Hope has evidently learned all he knows—at least in romance. The characters are puppets—very witty and gallant puppets, but puppets all the same.

I am very bookish at present, being busy, so you must excuse no better letter than this.

Mrs. Shakespear—Johnson's cousin—has sent me her last novel, a most subtle delicate kind of book.

Is there a book called *The Heroick Enthusiasts* lying about belonging to York Powell? I cannot remember if I took it to Dublin. If I did not you might send it to me. Yours affectionately

W B YEATS

TO LILY YEATS

Jan 20th [1895]   *Thornhill*

My dear Lilly, I have read Miss Hopper [2] and like her. I wrote to Mrs. Hinkson for the book. The only inexplicable plagiarism is I

---

with certainty be ascribed to Yeats, but it was doubtless inspired by him. The volume was eventually given the simple title *Poems*. For many years it was the book by which he was most widely known.

[1] Lionel Johnson's *Poems*, 1895, and Selwyn Image's *Poems and Carols*, 1894, were both published by Elkin Mathews.

[2] Nora Hopper (1871–1906) was the author of *Ballads in Prose*, 1894, *Under Quicken Boughs*, 1896, and other books. She was of Irish descent but had never lived in Ireland. She married W. H. Chesson. Yeats wrote of her work in *A Treasury of Irish Poetry*, 1900.

think 'The lay brother' which she should have seen is lifted body and bones from Mrs. Hinkson. The rest are the plagiarisms of inexperienced enthusiasm I think. She has take[n] us as documents, just as if we had written hundreds of years ago. There is an amusing note in which she takes a wholly fanciful line out of 'A man who dreamed of faery land' as a mythological authority. She has great artistic gifts, great gift for style, but is as yet lacking in solidity and clearness. I like best 'Daluan', 'The Gift of Aodh and Una' and 'The Four Kings' which are wonderful. I am looking out for a place to review her in. 'The Irish Literary Movement' is flourishing. A lecture on Sir Samuel Ferguson, which was read at the Irish Lit Society London by Roden Noel, was read in Dublin the other day by Miss Hickey, with the Archbishop in the chair and Dowden, Sir William Stokes, Prof Mahaffy, Judge Fitzgibbon, the Master of the Rolls and Prof Ingram all to make speeches about it; and the best of the joke is that it was described by one of the speakers as a lecture written for, and delivered to, an English audience—not one word was said about the Irish Lit Society and Prof Dowden expressed scorn for the Irish Lit movement and Irish Lit generally, for which he has been catching it from all the Dublin papers—even the *Irish Times* which had a leader on him. He has written a rather feeble protest.

Uncle George has had an astrological triumph. Some friend sent him a birth date of a child and asked him for a horoscope. He made one but wrote—he did not even know the child's name or whether it was a boy or a girl—that it was no use judging it, as the child, if it had not died at birth, could not out live infancy, and that death would probably be caused by fits.

He showed me the answer the other day. The friend had sent the birth date as a test. The child had died of fits ten or eleven days after birth. He showed me the figure before sending it, and I remarked that the mental planets were so afflicted, that if it lived it would have something wrong with its brain. Unfortunately he did not put this in the judgement. The doctor said had the child lived it would have been an idiot. He has done one or two others and they have all been excellent.

I have had to put *The Shadowy Waters* aside for the present and the poem for the *Saturday Review* and am trying to get the revision of *The Countess Kathleen* done and some more stories.

I have been to the Cockrams to lunch but otherwise have been only out of the house for my constitutional with Uncle George. I am reading French and getting on with my work fairly well. Yours affectionately W B YEATS

TO THE EDITOR OF THE *DAILY EXPRESS* (DUBLIN)
[*Published February* 27, 1895]

Sir—During our recent controversy with Professor Dowden certain of my neighbours here in the West of Ireland asked me what Irish books they should read. As I have no doubt others elsewhere have asked a like question, I send you a list of thirty books, hoping Mr. O'Grady, Mr. Rolleston, Mr. Ashe King, or some other Irish literary man will fill up the gaps. I have excluded every book in which there is strong political feeling, that I may displease no man needlessly, and included only books of imagination or books that seem to me necessary to the understanding of the imagination of Ireland, that may please myself and the general reader. By this means I may have got nearer to what the next century will care for than had I enumerated substantial volumes 'that no gentleman's library should be without.' For it is possible that people, both in and out of Ireland, will be singing

> 'Tis my grief that Patrick Loughlin is not Earl of Irrul still,
> And that Brian Duff no longer rules as lord upon the hill;
> And that Colonel Hugh O'Grady should be lying cold and low,
> And I sailing, sailing swiftly from the county of Mayo.[1]

when the excellent books of criticism, scholarship and history that we teach in our schools and colleges, and celebrate in our daily papers, shall have gone to Fiddler's green. For the best argumentative and learned book is like a mechanical invention and when it ceases to contain the newest improvements becomes, like most things, not worth an old song. Here then is my list, and I will promise you that there is no book in it 'that raves of Brian Boru' half as much as Burns did of Bruce and Wallace, or has an 'intellectual brogue' more 'accentuated' than the Scottish characteristics in Scott and Stevenson.

[1] From 'The County of Mayo,' a translation from the Irish of Thomas Lavelle, by George Fox (? 1809–after 1848). Yeats included this poem in *A Book of Irish Verse*, 1895.

NOVELS AND ROMANCES

1. *Castle Rackrent* by Miss Edgeworth.
2. 'Father Tom and the Pope' by Sir Samuel Ferguson (in *Tales from Blackwood*).
3. *Fardorougha the Miser* by William Carleton (out of print).
4. *The Black Prophet* by William Carleton (out of print).
5. *Traits and Stories of the Irish Peasantry* by William Carleton.
6. *The Nolans* by John Banim (out of print).
7. *John Doe* by John Banim (bound up with *Crohore*).
8. *The Collegians* by Gerald Griffin.
9. 'Barney O'Reirdan' by Samuel Lover (in *Legends and Stories of the Irish Peasantry*).
10. *Essex in Ireland* by Miss Lawless.
11. *Charles O'Malley* by Charles Lever.
12. *The Bog of Stars* by Standish O'Grady (New Irish Library).
13. *Ballads in Prose* by Miss Hopper.

FOLK LORE AND BARDIC TALES

14. *History of Ireland—Heroic Period* by Standish O'Grady (out of print).
15. *The Coming of Cuchullin* by Standish O'Grady.
16. *Fin and his Companions* by Standish O'Grady.
17. *Old Celtic Romances* by P. W. Joyce.
18. *Silva Gadelica* by Standish Hayes O'Grady.
19. *Beside the Fire* by Douglas Hyde.
20. 'Teig O'Kane' by Douglas Hyde (in *Fairy and Folk Tales of the Irish Peasantry*).
21. *History of Early Gaelic Literature* by Douglas Hyde (New Irish Library).
22. *Mythologie Irlandaise* by D'Arbois Joubainville.

HISTORY

23. *The Story of Ireland* by Standish O'Grady.
24. *Red Hugh's Captivity* by Standish O'Grady (out of print).
25. *A Short History of Ireland* by P. W. Joyce.

POETRY

26. *Irish Poems* by William Allingham.
27. 'Conary' by Sir Samuel Ferguson (in *Poems*).

28. *Lays of the Western Gael* by Sir Samuel Ferguson.
29. *Love Songs of Connacht* by Douglas Hyde (second edition in the press).
30. *Ballads and Lyrics* by Mrs. Hinkson.

The Nolans and *Fardorougha the Miser* and *The Bog of Stars* are probably the most memorable among the tragic, *Castle Rackrent* among the half tragic half humorous, and the *Traits and Stories*, *Charles O'Malley*, 'Father Tom and the Pope,' and 'Barney O'Reirdan' among the humorous tales. I do not think modern fiction has any more strange, passionate and melancholy creation than the old miser Fardorougha, or anything more haunting than the description of the household of the spendthrift squireen in the opening chapters of *The Nolans*, or the account a little further on of the 'spoiled priest' taking the door from its hinges to lay upon it the body of his mistress, and of the old men bringing him their charity. These books can only have been prevented from taking their place as great literature because the literary tradition of Ireland was, when Carleton and Banim wrote, so undeveloped that a novelist, no matter how great his genius, found no fit convention ready to his hands, and no exacting public to forbid him to commingle noisy melodrama with his revelations. England can afford to forget these books, but we cannot, for with all their imperfections they contain the most memorable records yet made of Irish habits and passions. *Charles O'Malley*, 'Father Tom and the Pope,' 'Barney O'Reirdan' and the *Traits and Stories* are also in a sense true records, but need no recommendation, for the public has always given a gracious welcome to every book which amuses it and does not bid it take Ireland seriously, while *Castle Rackrent*, which it has begun to forget, is still, and will be for generations to come, a classic among the wise. I have included, though with much doubt, *Essex in Ireland*, because, despite its lack of intensity, it helps one, when read together with the passionate and dramatic *Bog of Stars*, to imagine Elizabethan Ireland, and certainly does contain one memorable scene in which the multitudes slain in the Irish war rise up complaining; and I have regretfully excluded Miss Barlow's *Irish Idylls* because, despite her genius for recording the externals of Irish peasant life, I do not feel that she has got deep into the heart of things. I, indeed, feel always that both Miss Lawless and Miss Barlow differ as yet from the greater Irish novelists in being only able to observe Irish character from without and not to create it from within. They have, perhaps, bowed to the fallacy of our time, which says that the fountain of art is observation, whereas it is almost wholly experience. The creations of a great writer are little more than the moods and passions of his own heart, given surnames and Christian names, and sent to walk the earth. *Ballads in Prose* is, on the other hand, an absolute creation, an enchanting tender little book full of style and wild melancholy. It contains also many simple and artful verses about gods and fairies, which will probably outlive estimable histories and copious criticisms that the proud may be humbled.

The most memorable books in the section Folk Lore and Bardic Tales are Mr. O'Grady's *History of Ireland: Heroic Period*, and his *Coming of Cuchullin*, and his *Fin and his Companions*. But as he, like the men who cast into their present shape the Icelandic Sagas, retells the old tales in his own way, he should be read together with *The History of Early Gaelic Literature*, and if possible with the *Silva Gadelica*. However, it will not be to these indispensable and learned books that the imagination will return again and again, but to his description in *The Coming of Cuchullin* of Cuchullin hunting the iron-horned enchanted deer in his battle fury, or to that chapter in the *History* where he stands dying against the pillar stone, the others drinking his blood at his feet; or to the account in *Fin and his Companions* of the seven old men receiving Fin upon the mountain top and putting the seven pieces of the lark upon his platter, and saying one to another, when he weeps because of their poverty, 'The young have sorrows that the old know nothing of.' Lady Wilde's *Ancient Legends* is the most imaginative collection of Irish folk-lore, but should be read with Dr. Hyde's more accurate and scholarly *Beside the Fire*. Lady Wilde tells her stories in the ordinary language of literature, but Dr. Hyde, with a truer instinct, is so careful to catch the manner of the peasant story-tellers that, on the rare occasions when he fails to take down the exact words, he writes out the story in Gaelic, and then translates it into English. If the reader have a special liking for folk-lore, he can pass on to Mr. Larminie's copious collection or to Mr. Curtin's two books, or to the various books and articles of the late Patrick Kennedy. I have added one book of a foreign writer, *Mythologie Irlandaise*, for it is scarcely possible to understand Irish bardic and folk lore at all without its vivid and precise account of the ancient Pagan mythology of Ireland and of the descent of the mischievous fairies and spirits from the ancient gods of darkness and decay, and of the descent of the beautiful and kindly people of the raths and thorn trees from the gods of light and life.

Mr. O'Grady's *Story of Ireland* and his *Red Hugh* are the only purely artistic and unforensic Irish histories we have, but as they are limited, like every work of art, by the temperament of their writer, and show all events in a kind of blazing torchlight, they should be read with Dr. Joyce's careful and impartial and colourless volumes.

A reader new to Irish poetry had best begin with Allingham's *Irish Poems* and Dr. Hyde's *Love Songs of Connacht* for in them is the blossom of all that is most winning in Irish character; and pass on to the epic measures of 'Conary' and *The Lays of the Western Gael*; nor should he neglect *Ballads and Legends*, for Mrs. Hinkson has given a distinguished expression to much that is most characteristic in Irish Catholicism. The greater portion of Irish poetry is, however, made up of stray ballads and lyrics by Mangan, Davis, Doheny, Casey, Callanan, Walsh, Reynolds, Moore, Fox, and others among the dead, and by Mr. Aubrey De Vere, Mr. Johnson, Mr. Rolleston, Dr. Todhunter, and 'AE,' among the living; and of these there is no excellent anthology. Unless the reader will accept a forthcoming anthology of my own, he must in most cases search for the best Irish verse through old ballad books, and be content to find one or two good poems to a volume. There are, however, a few books other than ballad books, such as Mangan's *Poems* (the little threepenny edition), De Vere's *Innisfail*, and 'AE's' *Songs by the Way*—this a very notable book, but not specially Irish in subject—and two ballad books, Sir Gavan Duffy's *National Poetry* and Mrs. Hinkson's *Irish Love Songs*, which do not lose the needle in the haystack. *The Irish Song Book* (New Irish Library) also contains some good verses, but, as it was compiled more for the music than for the verse, it excludes much of the best and includes much which, though very singable, has little of the rapture and precision of good poetry.

Many of the best books in my list can only be got at the second-hand book shops, while in some cases poorer books by the same writers are constantly reprinted. The truth is that chance has hitherto decided the success or failure of Irish books; for one half Ireland has received everything Irish with undiscriminating praise, and the other half with undiscriminating indifference. We have founded the National Literary Society and the Irish Literary Society, London, to check the one and the other vice and to find an audience for whatever is excellent in the new or the old literature of Ireland. Political passion has made literary opinion in Ireland artificial, and, despite one of your correspondents, we are not to blame if our remedy seem artificial also. Our justification is the steadily increasing sale of Irish books and the steadily increasing intelligence of Irish criticism. Yours truly W B YEATS

TO JOHN O'LEARY

Feb 30th [1895] *Thornhill*

My dear Mr. O'Leary, I enclose a cutting from *New Ireland Review* which quotes a passage evidently about the Contemporary Club, yourself, and a somebody made up of Taylor and Oldham. I send also a copy of Wednesday's *Express* [1] with letters by myself and a Mr. Hanniman on 'The Best Thirty Irish Books.' I wish you would write. It seems to me an excellent opportunity for getting a little information about Irish books into the heads of Dublin Unionists. The good effects of the Dowden controversy is shown by the debate and vote at a College Historical. I have written to a long list of persons, even to Stopford Brooke among the rest, asking them to contribute, in the hope of a long discussion like that in the *Freeman* on the best hundred. I have asked Barry O'Brien to slang my frivolity.

I have had the influenza but am better and almost think [? through] the rewriting of my things for the collected edition. *A Book of Irish Verse* will be out in a few days.

Many thanks for papers. Yours ever W B YEATS

I sent Mrs. Carew a small instalment of my debt.

[1] The *Daily Express*, a Dublin newspaper, was founded in 1851 and should not be confused with the London daily paper of the same name. It appears now as the *Daily Express and Irish Daily Mail.*

TO LILY YEATS

March 3rd [*Postmark* 1895]   *Thornhill*

My dear Lilly, I am always [? almost] through with the correction of my things for Unwin's republication of them. Tell papa that *The Countess Kathleen* is radically different at the end and *The Wanderings of Usheen* at the beginning and middle. I am beginning to think of getting on at Roscommon to Douglas Hyde but may think and no more for a bit. I shall go from that to Dublin and be there a few days then go to London. I started a new controversy in the *Express* last Wednesday with a long letter—a column and a half—on 'the best thirty Irish books' and would send you a copy but I have none, all having gone to various people I want to contribute. The Dowden controversy has had for one of its results a well attended debate in College Historical Society which passed almost unanimously the resolution 'that the Irish Literary revival is worthy of support.' Dowden was in the chair and had some more dabs at us.

George has got the influenza, is in bed very bad with it at present. I had it lightly last week—was in bed a part of two or three days with it.

We had great skating here—the river up to the lake being frozen as far as the windmill. The Miss Gore-Booths were there and made coffee on the shore. Yours affectionately   W B YEATS

Am beginning to think about writing to Jack as I hear he said something in a letter to George about joining the Irish Lit Society.

TO KATHARINE TYNAN [1]

[circa *March* 12, 1895]   [*Thornhill*]

I included no verse of my own in this book, because I have left out or criticised unfavourably in the introduction so many well known Irish poets. I did not want to appear to prefer my own work. I hope you were not displeased with my slight mention of you in the *Express* letter, but I was afraid of the charge of 'log-rolling' which would have taken the significance away from my placing you among the few poets in my high list. Your poems in *A Book of Irish Verse*

[1] Text from the *Yale Review*, Winter 1940.

seem to me by far the finest things in all the latter part of the book. I wish I were as certain of the immortalities of anything I have written or will write as I am of the immortality of 'Sheep and Lambs.' Now that Christina Rossetti is dead, you have no woman rival. You, Ferguson and Allingham are, I think, the Irish poets who have done the largest quantity of fine work. Mangan and de Vere have each done three or four wonderful things, but have in them no copious streams of beauty. The others . . . are merely men who prolong delightfully the inspiration of the Gaelic poets, they have no fountain of song in themselves, no streaming beauty.

I have been busy correcting my own things, getting ready a collected edition, containing all I like in the *Oisin* and *Kathleen* volumes and putting them together with *The Land of Heart's Desire*. I have rewritten almost everything from the *Oisin* book and large quantities of the play of *The Countess Kathleen*. It has been a frightful business but is now practically finished.

P.S. I hope you will not think my introduction to *A Book of Irish Verse* unpleasantly fault-finding, but I felt my criticism would carry no weight unless I separated myself from the old gush and folly. I want people to accept my praise of Irish books as something better than mere national vanity.

TO KATHARINE TYNAN [1]

[*March* 25, 1895] [*Thornhill*]

I should have written before to thank you for your review—a most admirable one—of *A Book of Irish Verse* had I not been busy getting the last touches put to my collected volume of verse. I have just tied up the packet and am free again for the moment. You should be rather glad than otherwise at attacks like the *Figaro* one. They always mark the period when a reputation is becoming fixed and admitted. At first a writer is the enthusiasm of a few. He is not yet important enough to be attacked. Then comes the day when the pioneer spirits think his fame assured and perhaps a little slacken in his advocacy, and the yet unconvinced may begin to carp and abuse. Do you remember how Kipling got at that stage and stayed in it

[1] Text from the *Yale Review*, Winter 1940.

for a few months some years ago? Your next book of verse will probably reach the general public—the public who are not professed readers of verse—and after that you will be abused no more for the journalist must respect his paymasters . . .

I believe that in about a year or perhaps two years you will find that the Irish Unionists will begin to read Irish things greedily. I have been amazed at the interest the people here have taken in anything I have told them and in the *Express* controversy . . . I wrote that introduction to *A Book of Irish Verse* partly with a view to this type of reader. The great thing I thought was to convince them that we were critics and writers before all else and not heady and undiscriminating enthusiasts . . .

Every new Irish writer will increase the public for every other Irish writer. Your copy of Miss Hopper is at this moment crusading at Lady Gore-Booth's and the whole family have taken to Irish things. They are now busy with O'Grady, and were a little while ago on the hunt for folklore among their tenants. *Maelcho*,[1] despite my promise to return it at once, has only just returned from another Unionist household where it has carried on a not less efficacious evangel. They have got from me *The Wanderings of Cuchulain*.[2] A copy of Russell is also on the wander and one of the Gore-Booths has taken to your section of *A Book of Irish Verse* and has asked many questions about you. These people are much better educated than our own people, and have a better instinct for excellence. It is very curious how the dying out of party feeling has nationalized the more thoughtful Unionists. Parnellism has helped also and the expectation of Balfour's immense local government scheme. How ever this is too big a subject to get on to at the end of my second sheet.

TO KATHARINE TYNAN[3]

[*April* 7, 1895]   [*Thornhill*]

My new book is in the press—all the old things are rewritten. I wonder how they will receive it in Ireland. Patronize it, I expect,

[1] *Maelcho*, a historical novel, by Emily Lawless, London: Smith Elder & Co., October 1894.
[2] Probably *The Coming of Cuchulain* by Standish O'Grady, which Yeats had reviewed in the *Bookman*, February 1895, under the title 'Battles Long Ago.'
[3] Text from the *Yale Review*, Winter 1940.

and give it faint praise, and yet I feel it is good, that whether the coming generations in England accept me or reject me, the coming generations in Ireland cannot but value what I have done. I am writing at the end of the day, and when I am tired, this endless war with Irish stupidity gets on my nerves. Either you or I could have had more prosperous lives probably, if we left Ireland alone and went our way on the high seas—certainly we could have had more peaceable lives. However if the sun shines in the morning I shall be full of delight and of battle and ready to draw my bow against the dragon.

TO OLIVIA SHAKESPEAR

April 7th [1895] *Thornhill*

My dear Mrs. Shakespear, Alas I am still here in the West and cannot get away for the next three weeks or so. I had to lay the play aside and revise my already published poems for a one-volume re-issue and after three months' work completed the revision last week. The earlier things and much of *The Countess Kathleen* are completely rewritten. I am now trying to do some wild Irish stories which shall not be mere phantasies but the signatures—I use a medium's term—of things invisible and ideas. I should greatly like to have a talk with you about Maeterlinck. His play about the blind people and the dead priest in the snow is delightful.[1] I feel about his things generally however that they differ from really great work in lacking that ceaseless revery about life which we call wisdom. In all the old dramatists, Greek and English, one feels that they are all the time thinking wonderful, and rather mournful, things about their puppets, and every now and then they utter their thoughts in a sudden line or embody them in some unforeseen action. I said to Verlaine, when I saw him last year, 'Does not Maeterlinck touch the nerves sometimes when he should touch the heart?' 'Ah yes,' said Verlaine, 'he is a dear good fellow and my very good friend, but a little bit of a mountebank.' This touching the nerves alone, seems to me to come from the lack of revery. He is however of immense value as a force helping people to understand a more ideal drama.

[1] *Les Aveugles*, published in 1890. An English translation by Laurence Alma Tadema, *The Sightless*, was included in a volume of the Scott Library in 1892.

What have you found beyond the monk? You might possibly find a sepulchre but as you have begun with a religious porter at the gate have more probably kept to religious symbols. The symbol is a complex one so that I cannot define its influence shortly. Yours sincerely W B YEATS

Lionel's poems are delightful and curiously distinguished but they would need a letter to themselves and I want you to get this by Friday and so must to the post.

TO OLIVIA SHAKESPEAR

April 12th [Postmark Apr 13, 1895]   *Thornhill*

My dear Mrs. Shakespear, The vision is correct in one thing and the rest is merely the opening of a vision. I do not tell you what is right, or the exact nature of the symbol you have used, because I will make the vision complete itself when I see you, and it is best that it do all the explaining. You had better not try and go on with the vision yourself. You are probably very sensitive to these 'astral forces'—to give them the old name—and once one gets to heterogeneous symbols—the ploughed field, the smoke, the little figures etc—one gets into dangerous ground. Every influence has a shadow, as it were, an unbalanced—the unbalanced is the Kabalistic definition of evil—duplicate of itself. There are means of driving away an influence the moment one finds it to be unbalanced, or unpleasant in any way, but I cannot give you these means. You may be seeing these things very faintly—merely as phantasies—but you can never tell when they may become vivid and masterful, so had best try and see no more for the present.

I am delighted at your liking 'The Two Trees.' It is a favourite of mine, and you and one other person are the only people who have said they like it. The other person, by the by, is a Miss Eva Gore-Booth, daughter of Lady Gore-Booth of Lisadell, Sligo. She has some literary talent, and much literary ambition and has met no literary people. I have told her about you and, if the chance arise, would like you to meet her. I am always ransacking Ireland for people to set writing at Irish things. She does not know that she is the last victim—but is deep in some books of Irish legends I sent her—and may take fire. She needs however, like all Irish literary people, a proper respect for craftsmanship and that she must get in England.

I shall look forward to your new novel with great curiosity and interest. I think you have done exactly right in taking a salient character. You have an inalienable delicacy and subtlety of treatment. You need never seek for the half-tints, but must strive for the black and white. I wish you would do the same with your men. In a letter some time ago you said I complained that you wrote too exclusively of love. I did not mean to. I meant that the parts of your books which were not about love were not carefully studied enough, were not salient enough. I no more complain of your writing of love, than I would complain of a portrait painter keeping to portraits. I would complain however if his backgrounds were too slightly imagined for the scheme of his art. I have never come upon any new work so full of a kind of tremulous delicacy, so full of a kind of fragile beauty, as these books of yours however.

I have not re-written 'Innisfree' or 'The Two Trees.' The things I have re-written are *The Wanderings of Oisin* and all the lyrics practically which I care to preserve out of the same volume; and the end and beginning of *The Countess Cathleen.*

Lionel scoffs at the monk and his like, because, in his heart of hearts, he believes in them and holds them to be powers of the air and of darkness. Yours sincerely W B YEATS

TO KATHARINE TYNAN

July 31 [1895]   3 *Blenheim Road*

My dear Mrs. Hinkson, I have asked the *Bookman* people to send you the August number which contains my article on contemporary Irish prose writers; I enclose herewith a copy from *United Ireland* of my first article, the one on the writers of the past. The next will be on contemporary Irish poetry and deal with your work very largely, perhaps mainly (this depends whether I decide to re-do de Vere, or, as is more likely, content myself with the mention I have given him in the first article. Only the accident of his long life makes him a contemporary and I should not think of doing him again, were not my first mention of him so slight).

I should be glad of some notice in the *Independent* and it had best come before my criticism of your work. These *Bookman* articles are my only way of getting at the Irish public. The first was copied by the *Express* as well as by *United Ireland*.

The cover of my book with Unwin has caused quite a flutter of approval among his clerks but I have not yet seen it. Fell's design I have seen and that is very admirable. I have chosen for the substance a curious dove-grey. I wonder when your miracle plays come out? Yours truly W B YEATS

TO T. FISHER UNWIN

Nov 3rd [? 1895] *c/o Arthur Symons*
Fountain Court
Temple

Dear Mr. Unwin, I have been so busy that I have only just found time to find and tear out the articles on Irish Literature [1] which I want you to publish in a pamphlet under the title *What to read in Irish Literature*. When I have restored certain quotations cut out by the *Bookman* people for lack of space, and written half a dozen pages or so of introduction on the relation of such literature to general literature and culture and to contemporary movements, there should be material enough for a decent shilling's worth. Yours sincerely W B YEATS

TO EDMUND GOSSE

Saturday [Nov. 23, 1895] *Fountain Court*
[Endorsed in pencil 25.11.95]

Dear Mr. Gosse, I have been so busy of late working against time at a wretched story which has in the end refused to achieve itself that

[1] Yeats contributed a series of four articles on 'Irish National Literature' to the *Bookman*, July to October 1895. The project of republishing these in volume form seems to have gone no further.

I have postponed everything including my answer to your kind letter about my book. Besides I have had a better reason: Mr. Heinemann's reissue of *King Erik*[1] has been looking at me from the bookshelf opposite my seat, for the last few weeks, and I have waited for the leisure to discover if some bits that fascinated me when a boy would or would not have faded by this. The scene that gave me the most pleasure was Scene ii of Act IV and I find the old charm there and elsewhere. For quite a time the learned princess sitting among the tropical flowers haunted me; and one line used constantly to run in my head

> The knowledge of strange worlds has been a thirst
> Unslaked

as the centre of the scene. I remember even, in a way I then had, trying to symbolise the impression of the scene, and writing some lines of bad verse about a dead lizard covered with the pollen of flowers.

Thanking you again for your kind letter I remain Yours sincerely

W B YEATS

TO FLORENCE FARR

[*December* 1895] *Fountain Court*

My dear S S D D,[2] Has the magical armageddon begun at last? I notice that the *Freeman's Journal*, the only Irish paper I have seen, has an article from its London correspondent announcing inevitable war and backing it up with excellent argument from the character of Cleveland.[3] The war would fulfil the prophets and especially a prophetic vision I had long ago with the Mathers's, and so far be for the glory of God, but what a dusk of the nations it would be!

---

[1] First published in 1876 by Chatto and Windus. Reissued by William Heinemann in a new binding in 1893.

[2] In this letter Yeats uses the initials of Florence Farr's name in the Order of the Golden Dawn, Sapientia Sapienti Dona Data. As Mathers's representative in the London 'Temple' of the Order she was superior in standing to Yeats.

[3] The reference to President Cleveland suggests the Venezuelan Crisis and his message to Congress on December 17, 1895. Mrs. Yeats has, moreover, traced an article on the subject in the *Freeman's Journal*, December 19. The letter is therefore written on or about that date. [Note in the Cuala Press edition of the Letters to Florence Farr, edited by Clifford Bax.]

for surely it would drag in half the world. What have your divinations said or have they said anything? When will you be in town next? Could you come and see me on Monday and have tea and perhaps divine for armageddon? Yours ever W B YEATS

TO LILY YEATS [1]

Wednesday [in pencil 1 Jan 1896] *Fountain Court*

My dear Lilly, I send you a new year's book which had gone some days ago but for an unusually violent attack of procrastination. Thank you very much for the manuscript band. Symons admires it so much that he has asked me to ask you whether you could get others and if so at how much as he would like to get a half dozen or a dozen.

I am very content in my rooms here in the Temple and am likely to stay where I am until March.

My book has been selling well and my new book *The Secret Rose* is nearly finished and will be out about June I imagine or perhaps earlier. Yours affectionately W B YEATS

TO W. T. HORTON [2]

April 13th, 1896 18 *Woburn Buildings*

My dear Horton,[3] I received the enclosed from 'A.P.S.'[4] to-day. You should apply to him for MSS which is I believe the rule. I would have told you this but it is so long since I was a neophyte

---

[1] Lily Yeats was at this time staying at Hyères in the South of France.
[2] From a typewritten copy.
[3] William Thomas Horton (1864–1919) was a black-and-white artist of a strongly mystical nature. He contributed to the *Savoy* in 1896 and it is probable that he first met Yeats in that year. In 1898 Yeats wrote an introduction to Horton's first published book of drawings, *A Book of Images*, London: Unicorn Press. Although Horton seems to have decided not to become a member of the Golden Dawn he remained on very friendly terms with Yeats for many years. Yeats wrote of him in his poem 'All Souls' Night,' written at Oxford in 1920.
[4] Alfred Percy Sinnett (1840–1921), a journalist and Editor of the *Pioneer* of India. He became interested in theosophy and wrote *The Occult World*, 1881, and many other books on occultism. He was a member of the Golden Dawn.

that I have forgotten the details; and supposed as you do that the instruction came from the Order.

Egyptian faces may very well come to you after your initiation, as the Order is greatly under Egyptian influence; but one can never say whether a specified vision is or is not authentic without submitting it to an actual occult examination. The great matter is to remain positive to all apparitions and to work on in the G[olden] D[awn] as far as the 5–6 grade before attempting much or any practical occult work such as invocation. You should get A.P.S. to send you with your material for examination 'The Banishing Lesser Ritual of the Pentegram' as you are entitled to it and may find it of importance. It is a great help against all obsession.

I am greatly pleased that you are pleased with my verses, particularly that you like 'Red Rose.'[1] Yours sincerely   W B YEATS

TO W. T. HORTON[2]

April 30th, 1896   18 *Woburn Buildings*

My dear Horton, I am very sorry to hear your decision about G.D. If I thought it were any use I would urge you to get permission from the G.D. to delay for a time and so be sure of not acting upon a sudden impulse. Even a month, which you could quite well take without any explanation to the Order, would make your decision safer. People with your ascendant are almost always dangerously impulsive and should guard themselves against their own defects. Our Order is not, as you seem to think, 'spiritist' in any sense but wholly opposed to spiritism. (I should have thought the Harris sentences referred rather to the Red Hill and the like experiences.) Nor is our Order anti-Christian. That very pentagram which I suggested your using is itself, as you would presently have learned, a symbol of Christ. I am convinced however that for you progress lies not in dependence upon a Christ outside yourself but upon the Christ in your own breast, in the power of your own divine will and divine imagination, and not in some external will or imagination however divine. We certainly do teach this dependence only on the

---

[1] 'Red Rose' probably refers to the poem 'To the Rose upon the Rood of Time.'

[2] From a typewritten copy.

inner divinity, but this is Christianity. The uttermost danger lies for you in emotional religion, which will sap your will and wreck your self control. I do not mean that you cannot progress outside the G.D. but that you should read or study in some unemotional and difficult school. Jacob Boehme is certainly the greatest of the Christian mystics since the middle ages and none but an athletic student can get to the heart of his mystery. You would I think find him consonant with your temperament. But no matter what school you study in you must expect to find progress beset by false intuition and the persecution of phantoms. Our past and its elementals, masked often as angels of light, rise up always against our future. Of course my friendship has nothing to do with your going on or not going on in the G.D. Yours ever W B YEATS

I shall look out for you on Friday.

TO W. T. HORTON [1]

May 5th, 1896   18 *Woburn Buildings*

My dear Horton, A friend who is only in London for a day has summoned me to him for Friday afternoon. I shall therefore be out from 2 o'clock. Could you come at 11.30 instead and breakfast with me (you will have breakfasted so long before that it will nearly serve for lunch). I do not agree with your letter but we can talk of other things. I hold as Blake would have held also, that the intellect must do its utmost 'before inspiration is possible.' It clears the rubbish from the mouth of the sybil's cave but it is not the sybil. Even Miss Horniman [2] is not so purely intellective as you think. She has (for

[1] From a typewritten copy.
[2] Annie E. F. Horniman (1861–1937) was the daughter of F. J. Horniman, M.P. who was chairman of the firm of W. H. and J. Horniman and Co. Ltd., well-known tea merchants. He was a great collector of curios and founder of the Horniman Museum at Forest Hill. At the Slade School Miss Horniman had been a friend of Mlle Bergson, who became Mrs. Mathers, and was a member of the Golden Dawn. She was a friend and admirer of Yeats for many years, financed the season of plays at the Avenue Theatre for Florence Farr in 1894, and acted as amanuensis for Yeats from time to time when his sight was especially bad. She bought and restored the Abbey Theatre, Dublin, and gave the Irish National Theatre Society the free use of it, with an additional annual subsidy, from 1904 till 1910, when she withdrew. In 1907 she founded the Manchester Repertory Theatre.

months) given away thousands to help certain artistic purposes which she loves most passionately. She is merely one end of the beam, you and I are the other. Yours ever   W B YEATS

TO W. T. HORTON [1]

[*Undated*]   18 *Woburn Buildings*

My dear Horton, Remember what Blake has said of the accuser of sin. In my own belief the Divine Humanity cannot enter the heart till the heart ceases from indignation. The Christ who has moved the world was half Indian half Greek in temper. He saw the world as a fire of love, but from this fire fell not Hebraic heat, the moral self-indulgence of a sensual race—but a pure Greek light. Yours ever   W B YEATS

TO JOHN O'LEARY

May 26th [? 1896]   18 *Woburn Buildings*

Dear Mr. O'Leary: Please send me your address as I am anxious to send you the money I have owed you for so long. £6 is if I remember rightly the amount. I do not care to trust money to the hazard of Sigersonian untidiness. I vividly remember some old pamphlets or the like that got swallowed in that volcano and were heard of no more. I sent them there, I think, to be returned to you when we were all living out Rathgar way. At least there is some such cloud floating about my mind and as it is late and I am too sleepy to be selective I mention it here.

Are you likely to be in London this year? Yours ever
                                                        W B YEATS

I hear that there is a rumour in Dublin that I have recently married a widow. I am charmed and longing for particulars.

[1] From a typewritten copy.

TO JOHN O'LEARY

[? *June–July* 1896]   18 *Woburn Buildings*

My dear Mr. O'Leary: I did not send you the money before because Smithers, the publisher of the *Savoy*,[1] was short of funds and asked me to wait; and I send only £3.5.0 now because I am short in my turn. I could have sent you the whole sum when I wrote first but now I must wait a little before sending the remainder. You shall have it almost at once however. I have I believe definitely turned the corner thanks partly to the *Savoy* which came in the nick of time to let me raise my prices and to keep me going until I got the new prices generally accepted. *Rosa Alchemica*, the thing McGrath likes so much, is about to be translated into French and has drawn a wild eulogy from George Moore. I am now writing a rather elaborate series of essays on Blake for the *Savoy* but find my critical style much more intractable than my style to narratives. They are good in thought but scarcely good in form, except here and there.

I shall pass through Dublin some time in August I believe on my way to Tory Island where I go for local colour for a new story. Yours ever   W B YEATS

TO DOROTHEA HUNTER[2]

Tuesday [1896 *or later*]   18 *Woburn Buildings*

My dear Mrs. Hunter, I am very anxious to consult with you and Mr. Hunter about the Divine World in our little scheme, but next Sunday is unfortunately out of the question, as I have to speak at a meeting on that day. Could I go down to you on (say) Friday morning and work on the gods during the afternoon and evening

---

[1] Leonard Charles Smithers (1861–1907) was a native of Sheffield, and practised there for some time as a solicitor. He came to London and was partner in a printing business with H. S. Nichols, a bookseller and publisher, and eventually established a publishing firm of his own. Besides the *Savoy* of 1896 he produced a number of finely illustrated books, notably two collections of Aubrey Beardsley's drawings and Max Beerbohm's first book of caricatures.

[2] Yeats made the acquaintance of Mrs. Hunter at the Theosophical Society about 1889 or 1890. He considered that she had a faculty of clearly discerning in symbolic picture the essence of a myth or legend, and conducted experiments with her, Mr. Hunter making drawings of the gods as described by the 'seers.' She was a member of the Golden Dawn, as was Miss Briggs.

and stay with you until Saturday on which day I have to speak at a meeting at the Irish Lit. Society? Perhaps however Mr. Hunter cannot spare any time except on Sunday.

I told Miss Briggs our plan as she is certainly one of the best of our seers, and she said she would like to go out to you, if you would let her, in the evening, and work at some visions of the Divine World. She thought perhaps I would be with you on Saturday, and at the time I had forgotten the Irish Lit. meeting, she may not therefore be free on Friday.

The really important thing is to get the talismatic shape of the Gods done. We might work at them for a short time on Friday afternoon, and perhaps again on Saturday morning. Yours sincerely
W B YEATS

If Friday does please let me know tomorrow. Do as you think about Miss Briggs.

TO HENRY D. DAVRAY[1]

August 12*th* [1896]   18 *Woburn Buildings*

Dear M. Davray: A very great many thanks for your charming notice of my poems in the *Mercure de France*. It is a most delicate criticism, and I think it is not merely the natural partiality of the writer praised in it that makes me think it a most delicate example of the difficult art of praise. I shall look forward to your essay in *L'Ermitage* with expectant pleasure.

I do not know whether I mentioned in my last letter, apropos of your and M. Merrill's [2] interest in Ellis's and my book on Blake, that I am now doing some articles on Blake in the *Savoy* which, if M. Stuart Merrill has not seen it, I would gladly send to you for

[1] French man of letters and journalist. For many years he contributed regularly to the *Mercure de France* reviews of current English literature. He published French versions of many of the earlier books of H. G. Wells and other English writers, and translated Yeats's 'The Sad Shepherd,' 'The Untiring Ones' (from *The Celtic Twilight*), and 'Rosa Alchemica.'

[2] Stuart Merrill (1868–1915) was born on Long Island but educated at the Lycée Condorcet in Paris. After studying law in New York he returned to France and became one of the symbolist poets who derived from Mallarmé. His translation of some poems by Yeats appeared in Paul Fort's magazine *Vers et Prose* in 1905.

him. You yourself see the *Savoy*, I believe, regularly. Very many thanks for your thought of translating *The Celtic Twilight*. I shall publish this autumn a book of phantastic stories called *The Secret Rose* which will interest you I think; *Rosa Alchemica* is one of the stories and the rest are something after the same fashion.

Hoping to meet you soon I remain, Yours sincerely

W B YEATS

TO WILLIAM SHARP

[*August* 1896] *Tillyra Castle*
 Co. Galway

My dear Sharp, Many thanks for your letter. You must have written it the very morning I was writing to Miss Macleod.[1] I have just returned from the Aran Islands where I had gone on a fishing boat, and where I go again at the end of this week. I am studying on the islands for the opening chapter of a story I am about to set out upon. I met two days ago an old man who hears the fairies, he says, every night and complains much that their singing keeps him awake. He showed me a flute which he had got, thinking that if he played it they might be pleased and so cease teasing him. I have met much curious lore here and in Aran.

I have had some singular experiences myself. I invoked one night the spirits of the moon and saw between sleep and waking a beautiful woman firing an arrow among the stars. That night she appeared to Symons who is staying here, and so impressed him that he wrote a poem on her, the only one he ever wrote to a dream, calling her the fountain of all song or some such phrase. She was the symbolic Diana. I invoked a different spirit another night and

---

[1] Fiona Macleod was William Sharp himself. An early acquaintance of Yeats (see note 1 on p. 43), Sharp was a busy literary journalist whose work included lives of Rossetti, Shelley, Heine and Browning, a number of volumes of verse and several novels. From 1894 onwards he established a second reputation as Fiona Macleod with novels and short stories such as *Pharais, The Sin-Eater, The Washer of the Ford*, and was considered the leading representative of the Scottish branch of what was then called 'The Celtic Renaissance.' The identity of Fiona Macleod was very carefully concealed, and the question whether Fiona represented an alternative personality or was merely a literary device has never been satisfactorily resolved. Yeats seems to have believed in the separate existence of Fiona Macleod for a long time and may not have known the truth until after Sharp's death.

it appeared in dreams to an old French Count, who was staying here, and was like Symons ignorant of my invocations. He locked his door to try to keep it out. Please give my greeting to Miss Macleod. Yours sincerely W B YEATS

TO JOHN O'LEARY[1]

Friday [? December 1896]   *Hôtel Corneille*
                                               5 Rue Corneille
                                                        Paris

Dear Mr. O'Leary, My father has sent on to me your letter to him. I have written to the *Bookman* for leave to review your book [2] and to my father for the book, and begun an article, based on my memory, of what I read of it and on my knowledge of your movements, that I may not be late for the January number. I am sorry you think I avoided you when I was passing through Dublin. The fact is, I was in Dublin the first time only one day, and as I had Arthur Symons with me had to spend that day, first in a hunt for Dowden's address and then in an expedition out to Dalkey where he lives. We got to Dublin on Saturday and left for Co. Galway on Monday morning. We hurried on so as to catch Paul Bourget who was staying there but about to leave. On my way back I stayed a longer time in Dublin but thought you were in London, which you were until a few days before I left Dublin. A day or two after I got to London I called at Dr. Ryan's and asked for you thinking you were there.

I have come here to study some local things and people for a novel which I have contracted with Lawrence and Bullen to write.[3]

---

[1] From a copy thought to have been made by D. J. O'Donoghue.

[2] *Recollections of Fenians and Fenianism*, a book which had been long in preparation, was published in 1896. It proved somewhat disappointing, and when Yeats reviewed it in the *Bookman*, February 1897, he devoted most of his space to an account of O'Leary and his influence on the younger generation of Irishmen.

[3] The title of the novel on which Yeats worked for many years was *The Speckled Bird*. He never decided to publish it, and indeed the manuscript which exists is not entirely finished. Part of a chapter, edited by Joseph Hone, appeared in the *Bell*, Dublin, March 1941. The £50 advance which Yeats received from Lawrence & Bullen was later deducted from his royalties on his book of essays, *Ideas of Good and Evil*, 1903. See letter to Lady Gregory, ? December 22, 1901 (p. 361).

They are to pay me £2 a week for six months while I write it. The scene is laid first in the Aran Isles and then in Paris. I have already been to the Aran Islands to study them and am going again. The book is to be among other things my first study of the Irish Fairy Kingdom and the mystical faith of that time, before I return to more earthly things. There are certain preliminary studies in my new book *The Secret Rose* which will be out very soon. I am also printing a play on like terms with a different publisher.[1] Next week the novel begins. These arrangements are my attempt to escape from journalism. Yours ever W B YEATS

I shall be in Dublin in March on my way to Aran.

TO ROBERT BRIDGES

Monday Dec 7th [1896]   *Hôtel Corneille*

Dear Sir: When you wrote to me your kind letter about my verses, I postponed writing an answer out of sheer procrastination until I was ashamed to write without sending you the poor amends of a book of my verses or stories. A book of stories was on the point of coming out and I waited for it. It was however delayed and is now again delayed so that I must trust to no better help than my apologies. Your praise of my work gave me great pleasure as your work is to me the most convincing poetry done by any man among us just now. I said this to Brandes, the Norwegian, the other day when he was praising all manner of noisy persons. Your work alone has the quietude of wisdom and I do most firmly believe that all art is dedicated to wisdom and not because it teaches anything but because it reveals divine substances. Your *Achilles in Scyros* and your *Prometheus* have been to me a delight over a fair number of years now and only need a stage dedicated to wisdom, such as has been in many ages, to justify their form.   [*Unsigned*]

[1] No doubt this refers to *The Shadowy Waters*, which was to have been published by Leonard Smithers. See note 4, p. 237.

PART THREE

1897—1908

INTRODUCTION TO PART THREE

'IN 1897,' Yeats wrote to Olivia Shakespear many years later, 'a new scene was set, new actors appeared.' Chief of these were J. M. Synge, recently met in Paris, George Moore, and Lady Gregory. Synge for a time did not come into the dramatic movement; he was presently to visit the Aran Islands, encouraged doubtless by Yeats's account of them. Moore Yeats already knew; both writers describe a meeting in the Cheshire Cheese tavern at some earlier date, Moore's account in *Hail and Farewell* being dramatized in his usual fashion, but it seems that they had not hitherto been closely acquainted. In *Ave* Moore gives a slightly burlesque description of the call made upon him by Yeats and Edward Martyn, but this may well have had some foundation in fact. What he contrives to minimize is the wild enthusiasm he then felt for Yeats and his work; he accepted some help from him in the writing of his novel *Evelyn Innes*, in the earlier versions of which Yeats figures, thinly disguised as the musician Ulick Dean, and declared *The Countess Cathleen* to be the finest verse play written since Shakespeare.

Lady Gregory also Yeats had met the previous summer when staying with Edward Martyn at Tillyra Castle, her own home at Coole Park being not far distant, and he had been her guest there for a few days. Now she had taken a flat in London, and there Yeats discussed with her his old wish to found an Irish theatre. She undertook to collect a guarantee fund for the production in Dublin of *The Countess Cathleen* and a prose play by Edward Martyn, *The Heather Field*, in the construction of which Moore had had a hand.

Another new friend Yeats made at this time was Robert Bridges, who presently invited him to stay at Yattendon. The friendship, founded on mutual respect, continued until Bridges's death.

In April 1897 Bullen published *The Secret Rose*, a collection of the stories Yeats had written during the previous five years, illustrated with drawings by his father.

The summer was spent at Coole Park, and from this time onward he was to make Lady Gregory's house his home during the summer months. His health was not good, and his nervous system badly shaken by years of unrequited love for Maud Gonne; to distract his thoughts and to keep him much in the open air Lady Gregory took him with her to visit the peasants' cottages in the neighbourhood and he began to make a large collection of folklore and stories, part of which he used in a series of articles in English reviews, and from which Lady Gregory eventually compiled two volumes, published many years later.

Yeats was full of plans. Besides those for the Irish Literary Theatre he was involved in arrangements for a memorial to Wolfe Tone and celebrations of the rising in 1798, and became chairman of the London committee; that autumn, with Maud Gonne, he visited various towns in England, holding meetings and making speeches. With her also, and with help from Mathers, he evolved a scheme for an Order of Celtic Mysteries, the headquarters of which should be a Temple of the Heroes at Castle Rock on Lough Key. The rituals which he worked out for this Order still exist, but the Order itself was never founded.

Next year he paid another visit to Paris for consultation with Mathers, and in April presided at the Inaugural Banquet of the '98 Celebrations Committee in London. In June he was in Dublin as representative of the London Committee to attend demonstrations in connection with '98, and then went on to Coole to work at his novel. In August there was another banquet and a demonstration in London, followed immediately by the celebrations in Dublin. The autumn he spent with his uncle in Sligo, coming up to Dublin at the end of the year. *Tableaux vivants* of scenes from *The Countess Cathleen* were being arranged at the Chief Secretary's Lodge in Phoenix Park; Yeats would not be present but gave some advice about the costumes.

Early in 1899 he went again to Paris to see Maud Gonne, and then returned to London for rehearsals of the plays for the Irish Literary Theatre performances. These took place, after many difficulties had been overcome, at the Antient Concert Rooms, Dublin, in May. At almost the same time *The Wind Among the Reeds* was published, a slim volume containing all the lyrics he had written since 1892. This added greatly to his reputation, and was 'crowned' by the literary weekly the *Academy* as the best book of poetry published in the year, the author being awarded a prize of twenty-five guineas.

In the summer he was still working on *The Shadowy Waters* at Coole, and then moved over to Tillyra Castle for collaboration with George Moore. Together they were planning a play on the story of Diarmuid and Grania; Moore had also undertaken to rewrite a play of Martyn's, *The Tale of a Town,* for the second year's performances of the Irish Literary Theatre, and in this also Yeats took some part. The collaborators returned to London and continued their work there. By the end of the year Yeats managed at last to finish *The Shadowy Waters.*

Soon after the second year's performances were over he was faced with trouble about the Golden Dawn. Mathers's behaviour had become outrageous and Yeats headed a revolt against him. There were violent scenes with Mathers's envoy, Aleister Crowley, whose antics, as Yeats described them to Lady Gregory, now appear sufficiently ridiculous but were, no doubt, alarming to the somewhat unworldly members of the Order. After the difficulties had been surmounted Yeats seems, for a time, to have become head of the Order's London branch or 'Temple.'

Diarmuid and Grania, by Yeats and Moore, was produced in October 1901 by F. R. Benson's Shakespeare Company at the Gaiety Theatre, Dublin, and the Irish Literary Theatre brought its proposed three years' experiment to an end. Its place was soon taken by a little company of Irish amateur players organized and directed by the enthusiastic brothers Willie and Frank Fay. At Coole Yeats began, with Lady Gregory's help, to write a number of one-act plays in prose, and in the following year the Fays produced the first of these, *Cathleen ni Hoolihan,* and a play on the Deirdre story by AE. The company adopted the name of the Irish National Theatre Society, with Yeats as President, and Maud Gonne, Douglas Hyde and George Russell as Vice-Presidents.

Yeats was now beginning to find in lecturing a fairly profitable means of supplementing his income; he had given up any regular journalism, and the returns from his books were small. With Florence Farr and Arnold Dolmetsch, the discoverer and player of ancient music, he had worked out a system for the recitation of poetry to musical notes which he named 'Speaking to the Psaltery,' and gave a lecture, with demonstration of the method by Florence Farr and others, at Clifford's Inn Hall, Fleet Street, in June 1902.

That autumn Yeats first met John Quinn, a successful Irish-American lawyer, who came to Coole while on a visit to the West of Ireland. Quinn was a great collector and patron of Irish art and literature, and was to prove himself a very staunch friend and helper in years to come. He promised to look into the possibilities of a lecture tour in America.

Yeats had suggested to George Moore a further collaboration on a plot of his own devising, but the matter had not gone far before he felt he could write the play he had in mind better without Moore's help. Moore, however, was unwilling to fall out of the scheme and declared he was writing a novel on the theme and would injunct Yeats if he used it in a play. Yeats hurriedly wrote *Where there is Nothing*, a prose play in five acts, Lady Gregory and Douglas Hyde giving him some help since time was pressing, and arranged to have it published as a supplement to the Nationalist weekly paper the *United Irishman*. Nothing more was heard of Moore's novel; for some time the two men were not on speaking terms, and the breach between them was never entirely closed.

In February 1903 Maud Gonne became the wife of Major John MacBride, in Paris. The news came as a great shock to Yeats and he suffered keenly; it is said that the letter reached him as he was about to deliver a lecture, and though he went through the task successfully he could not afterwards remember a word he had spoken.

Mrs. J. B. Yeats had died in 1900 after a long illness which had incapacitated her for any active life, and in 1902 the family came back to Ireland, taking a house named Gurteen Dhas at Churchtown, Dundrum, a little way outside Dublin. Here Elizabeth Yeats, the younger sister, decided to establish a small printing press. This, the Dun Emer Press as it was first called, was to publish all Yeats's new work in small limited editions on hand-made paper, as well as other books by living Irish writers, and small selections from the work of their predecessors. A start was made in August 1903 with *In the Seven Woods*, a collection of new lyrical and narrative poems and a new play, *On Baile's Strand*, which Yeats intended to form part of a cycle of plays on the life of Cuchulain, the Irish Achilles.

Earlier in the year the Irish Players paid a flying visit to London at a week-end, and made a very favourable impression by their simplicity and naturalness. Their programme included Yeats's two plays *Cathleen ni Hoolihan* and *A Pot of Broth*. His book of essays, *Ideas of Good and Evil*, came out almost at the same moment, and his play *Where there is Nothing*, the first volume of 'Plays for an Irish Theatre,' a little later. A. H. Bullen had now become his publisher in chief so far as England was concerned, and the Macmillan Company of New York were bringing out his books in America.

Summer was spent as usual at Coole, and by August he had finished a new verse play *The King's Threshold*; it was produced that autumn in a programme which contained also Synge's first work for the theatre, *In the Shadow of the Glen*. Immediately afterwards Yeats sailed for America on his first lecture tour there, which John Quinn had arranged for him. The tour was a great success; he delivered more than forty lectures, travelling as far west as California, which delighted him. He stayed over into the New Year, delivering a speech on Robert Emmet to an immense audience in New York on February 28, 1904, and then sailed for Europe, having for the first time in his life earned a substantial sum of money. After a stay in Dublin he went over to London for rehearsals of the Stage Society's production of *Where there is Nothing*. Most of the summer and autumn he spent at Coole, writing a new play, *Deirdre*; he had to come up to Dublin in August for the hearing of the application for a patent for the Abbey Theatre, which his friend Miss Horniman had bought and reconstructed, and was giving for the free use of the National Theatre Society. In spite of some opposition a restricted patent was granted.

The Abbey opened on December 27, 1904, and from now Yeats's winters had to be divided between Dublin and London. The company still consisted largely of unpaid amateurs, and the theatre was at first run on a democratic basis, plays, dates and casting being decided by vote. This soon proved completely impracticable, and in October 1906 Yeats, Lady Gregory and Synge were appointed Directors.

To mark Yeats's fortieth birthday, in June 1905, a number of his friends, at Lady Gregory's suggestion, subscribed to present him with a copy of the Kelmscott Chaucer. In July Florence Farr arranged a performance of *The Shadowy Waters* for a theosophical convention in London, and immediately afterwards Yeats retired to Coole to rewrite the play entirely.

Next summer he was still at work on *Deirdre*, and in the autumn Bullen published *Poems, 1899–1905*, containing *In the Seven Woods*, all the lyric poetry he had written since 1899, and revised versions of *The Shadowy Waters, On Baile's Strand* and *The King's Threshold*. In his preface Yeats wrote rather ruefully that 'it seems to me very little to have been so long about . . . I am a little disappointed at the upshot of so many years.' His responsibilities at the Abbey were proving a great hindrance to his own work and meant a sacrifice of income; he managed, however, to deliver some lectures with Florence Farr in the English provinces from time to time.

In January 1907 there was a riot at the Abbey over Synge's *The Playboy of the Western World*. Yeats was lecturing in Aberdeen, the guest of Professor Grierson, and received a telegram about it late at night. He hurried back to Dublin, convened a debate on the play at the theatre, and, facing a partly hostile audience, made a fine speech in defence of the artist's freedom.

That spring, a manager having been found for the Abbey, he joined Lady Gregory and her son Robert in Venice, and made a short tour among the North Italian cities, a tour which made a lasting impression reflected often in his future work.

Bullen now proposed, with financial assistance from Miss Horniman, to bring out a Collected Edition of Yeats's writings, and the summer and autumn at Coole were spent in careful revision of his earlier work. He was anxious that this edition should establish a definitive text for many years, and his letters to Bullen show his determination to have the work carried out exactly as he wished. He had taken a dislike to *Where there is Nothing* and was allowing Lady Gregory to refashion the theme entirely to an eighteenth-century fantasy called *The Unicorn from the Stars*. There were to be portraits of the author in the edition and Augustus John came to stay at Coole to make drawings for an etching, though this work was not used until a much later date.

That autumn the Abbey continued to be troublesome, and as the result of internal dissensions the brothers Frank and Willie Fay, who had been the mainstay of the company, resigned.

In London, in the spring of 1908, Yeats sat to Charles Shannon for a portrait, a commission from John Quinn, and at the same time

Kathleen Bruce, the sculptress, designed the mask now in the National Portrait Gallery; soon afterwards John Sargent made the fine charcoal drawing which formed the frontispiece to the first volume of the Collected Edition and has figured so often in later books by and about Yeats.

In September at Coole he began work on the scenario of a new play, *The Player Queen*, which had been verbally commissioned by Mrs. Patrick Campbell, who had promised to come to Dublin to play Deirdre with the Abbey Theatre company. This she did in November, her visit adding greatly to the prestige both of the theatre and of Yeats as a playwright.

The Collected Edition began to appear in the autumn, eight finely printed volumes, half-bound in vellum with grey linen sides. In sales it proved only a moderate success and not more than two-thirds of the thousand copies were disposed of. Yeats's public was not yet a large one, and it was thought in some quarters almost a mark of presumption that a writer still in his early forties should have aspired to the dignity of a collected edition. There were even rumours, which may have been in part malicious, that he intended to write no more.

He spent the month of December in Paris, taking lessons to improve his French, and seeing Maud Gonne, who had now been separated from her husband for some years.

1897-1908

TO ROBERT BRIDGES

Jan 10*th* [1897]   203 *Boulevard Raspail*
Paris

Dear Sir: A great many thanks for your letter. It is curious my leaving mine unsigned. Your surmise, however, was right; I was and indeed am sunk in work, about which I am very much in earnest. When I wrote I was more or less desperate about a dramatic poem which refused to go faster than my average of some eight or nine lines a day, despite material necessities that it should, and am still in a tempered desperation. I am trying for a more remote wisdom, or peace, for they are much the same, and find it hard not to lose grip on the necessary harvest of mere exterior beauty, in seeking for this visionary harvest. I am doing my best work or my worst and do not well know which.

A thousand thanks for your invitation to pay you a visit in Spring. It will be a great pleasure to do so. You are fortunate in being able to live in the country where our moods have a proper living ritual to honour them. My work continually brings me to cities. You wonder why I am in Paris and I can allege no better reason than a novel, which I have undertaken to write, and which brings its central personages from the Aran Islands to Paris.

I too would much like to discuss with you questions of rhythm, for though I work very hard at my rhythm, I have but little science on the matter and as a result probably offend often. Without a consistent science it is difficult to distinguish between licence and freedom. You are probably right about the word 'bag.'[1] I changed

[1] In his poem 'Fergus and the Druid' the Druid gives Fergus 'a little bag of dreams,' and in the version published in the *Countess Kathleen* volume of 1892

it because of the urgency of someone or other who thought the word ugly for a close. Yours   W B YEATS

I return to London next week and after then will be at 18 Woburn Buildings, Euston Road.

TO FIONA MACLEOD [1]

[? *Early January* 1897]   [*Paris*]

My dear Miss Macleod, I owe you a letter for a long time, and can only promise to amend and be more prompt in future. I have had a busy autumn, always trying to make myself do more work than my disposition will permit, and at such times I am the worst of correspondents. I have just finished a certain speech in *The Shadowy Waters*, my new poem, and have gone to the Café du Musée de Cluny to smoke and read the Irish news in *The Times*. I should say I wrote about your book of poems as you will have seen in the *Bookman*.[2] I have just now a plan I want to ask you about. Our Irish Literary and Political literary organizations are pretty complete (I am trying to start a Young Ireland Society, among the Irish here in Paris at the moment) and I think it would be very possible to get up Celtic plays through these Societies. They would be far more effective than lectures and might do more than anything else we can do to make the Irish, Scotch and other Celts recognise their solidarity. My own plays are too elaborate, I think, for a start, and have also the disadvantage that I cannot urge my own work in committee. If we have one or two short direct prose plays, of (say) a mythological and folklore kind, by you and by some writer (I may be able to move O'Grady, I have already spoken to him about it urgently) I feel sure we could get the Irish Literary Society to make a start.

---

the last two lines read:
>   'Ah! Druid, Druid, how great webs of sorrow
>   Lay hidden in that small slate-coloured bag!'

In *Poems*, 1895, Yeats changed the final word from 'bag' to 'thing,' and so it has remained; Robert Bridges had urged him to retain 'bag.'

[1] Text from *William Sharp* (*Fiona Macleod*) by Elizabeth A. Sharp. London, 1910. See footnote no. 1, p. 266.

[2] Yeats reviewed Fiona Macleod's *From the Hills of Dream* in the *Bookman*, December 1896.

They have indeed for some time talked of doing my *Land of Heart's Desire*.

My own theory of poetical or legendary drama is that it should have no realistic, or elaborate, but only a symbolic and decorative setting. A forest, for instance, should be represented by a forest pattern and not by a forest painting. One should design a scene which would be an accompaniment not a reflection of the text. This method would have the further advantage of being fairly cheap, and altogether novel. The acting should have an equivalent distance to that of the play from common realities. The plays might be almost, in some cases, modern mystery plays. Your *Last Supper*, for instance, would make such a play, while your story in the *Savoy* would arrange as a strong play of merely human tragedy. I shall try my own hand possibly at some short prose plays also, but not yet. I merely suggest these things because they are a good deal on my mind, and not that I wish to burden your already full hands. My *Shadowy Waters* is magical and mystical beyond anything I have done. It goes but slowly however, and I have had to recast all I did in Ireland some years ago. Mr. Sharp heard some of it in London in its first very monotonous form. I wish to make it a kind of grave ecstasy.

I am also at the start of a novel which moves between the Islands of Aran and Paris, and shall have to go again to Aran about it. After these books I start a long-cherished project—a poetical version of the great Celtic epic tale, Deirdre, Cuchullin at the Ford, and Cuchullin's death, and Dermot and Grainne. I have some hopes that Mr. Sharp will come to Paris on his way back to England. I have much to talk over with him. I am feeling more and more every day that our Celtic movement is approaching a new phase. Our instrument is sufficiently prepared as far as Ireland is concerned, but the people are less so, and they can only be stirred by the imagination of a very few acting on all.

My book *The Secret Rose* was to have been out in December but it has been postponed till February.[1] If I have any earlier copies you shall have one. I am specially curious to know what you think of a story called 'The Adoration of the Magi' which is half prophecy of a very veiled kind. Yours truly   W B YEATS

[1] *The Secret Rose* was not in fact published until April. Nor did it contain the story 'The Adoration of the Magi,' Bullen having suddenly taken fright about including it. But he issued it privately in an edition of one hundred and ten copies in company with another story, 'The Tables of the Law,' in June.

TO ROBERT BRIDGES

March 16th [1897]　　　　　　　　　　18 *Woburn Buildings*

Dear Mr. Bridges: I have just got back from Ireland and found your letter waiting for me. A very great many thanks. May I come down on next Saturday week? I do not say next Saturday because I am just renewing my recollection of your plays, as a prelude to an article, which the *Bookman* asked me to do some time ago, but which has got postponed through my dislike of reading in the British Museum. I have now however got the books I wanted and will be through in about a week and will be able to talk of them. Your lyrics and one or two of the plays are too vivid to me to need a new memory; but some I read long ago; and *Nero* I am reading for the first time. My first reading of your work was in a book lent me by Prof. Dowden a great many years ago. *Prometheus the Firegiver* it was. I remember talking about it with your friend Father Hopkins, and discussing your metrical theories.

I have been on an absurd crusade among absurd people and it will be a pleasure of the best to talk of poetry in the country. The roof at the garden end sounds charming. Yours　　W B YEATS

TO ROBERT BRIDGES

March 24th [1897]　　　　　　　　　　18 *Woburn Buildings*

Dear Mr. Bridges: I will [come] by the 1.55 from Paddington on Saturday next.

I have now read all the plays except *The Christian Captives* which I shall probably read before Saturday unless an unfortunate ballad of my own [1] which has got to get done stop me. The second part of *Nero*, and my old favourite *Achilles in Scyros* and *The Return of Ulysses* delight me most I think. I read the end of the *Ulysses* with the utmost excitement. You have held a clear mirror to the magnificent rush of the greatest of all poetry, the end of the Odyssey. It would be a fine thing on the stage and should get there in time.[2] Yours ever　　　　　　　　　　　　　　　W B YEATS

[1] Probably 'The Blessed,' published in the *Yellow Book* in April.
[2] Yeats's essay was published in the *Bookman*, June 1897, where it was simply headed 'Mr. Robert Bridges.' He included the essay in *Ideas of Good and Evil* under the title *The Return of Ulysses*.

TO JOHN O'LEARY

March 31st [1897]   18 *Woburn Buildings*

Dear Mr. O'Leary: Miss Gonne has sent me a letter of the Comte De Crémont's telling how Macarthy Tealing has gone to Paris and [is] representing himself in her presence and in the presence of another member of the committee of the Association of St. Patrick as deputed to denounce Miss Gonne as an English and German spy. Tealing is at present a candidate for the post of Honorary Correspondent for Ireland in the Society. The Comte De Crémont is anxious to prevent his election and asks that so[me] representative Irishmen write and tell him of Mr. Tealing's right to represent Ireland, to denounce Miss Gonne etc. I wish you would write, as your word would of course carry more weight than anybody else's. The Comte De Crémont is Hon Sec of the Society and his address is 33 rue d'Amsterdam. I have written telling of Tealing's expulsion from the Young Ireland Society some years ago for insolence to yourself. Tealing has for years been slandering Miss Gonne in the most ignoble and infamous way. Pat O'Brien has been urging me to write a letter to one of the Dublin papers about him, but I do not care to make a matter of this kind public, if it can be dealt with otherwise. The less said about it to people whom it does not concern the better.

I shall be here another month and then go to my uncle.

I send a copy of *The Secret Rose*. Yours ever   W B YEATS

TO F. L. GARDNER [1]

Die ♂ [? *Spring*, 1897] [2]

V H et Care Frater, I herewith enclose 2 forms of Petition [3] signed as requested.

---

[1] Frederick Leigh Gardner, a member of the Golden Dawn, was on the Stock Exchange but also dealt privately in occult literature. He financed the publication of Mathers's translation of *The Book of the Sacred Magic of Abra-Melin the Mage*, 1898, and was the compiler of *A Catalogue Raisonné of works on the Occult Sciences*, privately printed, 1903. He died about 1925.

[2] The date of this letter is uncertain, but as it refers to the expulsion of Miss A. E. F. Horniman from the Order of the Golden Dawn by MacGregor Mathers, which took place about December 1896, and seems to have been written from Sligo, it may perhaps belong to the spring of 1897.

[3] The form of Petition referred to ran as follows:

Private and Confidential

I the undersigned having heard with the profoundest regret and sorrow, that you

I don't quite like its wording in some points.

As however there is apparently an object in *not delaying* I am sending it on as it is to you, but with *the express stipulation* that you consult with V H Fra[ter] L[evav]i O[culos. i.e. P. W. Bulloch] and V H Sapientia [Sapienti Dono Data i.e. Mrs. Emery—Florence Farr] before sending it, and being guided by their opinion as to whether it is judicious to *send it* and *on its form.*

You will understand that I am most anxious to help in any way I can, and would go a long way to do anything for our V H S[oror] F[ortiter Et Recte i.e. Miss Horniman] but before sending forward such a petition would consult the other experienced F[ratres] and S[orores] as to the advisability of doing so and its form. I know nothing of the facts, and they may. And I would be slow in putting it in any form that would not meet with our V H Soror F......'s own approval, or at which she might feel affronted, when she came to know of it.

And if I can be of any further use, command me, Fraternally yours   F. L.[1]

V H Fra De Profundis ad Lucem
Please note My address is simply Sligo and *not* Rosses Point.

TO F. L. GARDNER

Die ☉ [*Probably* 1896 *or* 1897][2]

Care V H Frater, It is proposed to undertake in vision an Analysis of the Paths of the Tree of Life.

[S. L. MacGregor Mathers, S Rioghail Mo Dhream ⑤ = ⑥, Deo Duce Comite Ferro ⑦ = ④] as a representative of the Second Order [the Rosae Rubeae et Aureae Crucis] have thought it necessary to remove our V H Soror F[ortiter] et R[ecte, Miss Horniman] from the Roll of the Order: Do hereby most respectfully *Petition* for the reconsideration of this decision on the ground that she has for so long been so earnest a student and so energetic and self sacrificing a teacher to those junior to her. For a Member who has proved herself so devoted to the Order I would ask for a Merciful Judgement of her failings, whatever they may have been, and hope that you may be able to obtain a reversal of the Judgement pronounced against her. Believe me, Your earnest and devoted pupil.

[1] Mrs. Yeats says that F. L. stood for Festina Lente, presumably Yeats's motto in the outer Order.

[2] This letter is placed here merely for convenience; I have no means of dating it. It may be earlier than the letter which precedes it; it is not likely to be later as Yeats spent his summers at Coole rather than in Sligo after 1897.

Each Fra[ter] or Soror to explore one or more paths and report result to me (as representing the Order in this matter).

If you desire to take part, please send me before 12th inst name of Sign Rising—or of Sign Rising *and* principal Influences in your Horoscope; this will show which of the Paths (on the Tree of Life) you are most in affinity with.

The Paths will be allotted as far as possible among the Fra[tres] and Sorores according to their Astrological affinities.

I write this letter by direction of the Higher Members of the Second Order. Fraternally Yours   D E D I

Enclose reply in an envelope a/d to W B YEATS
c/o Geo Pollexfen
Sligo

TO JOHN O'LEARY

[*? May* 1897]

P.S.[1] My eyes have been rather bad of late. I have to be very careful and find any steady reading almost impossible. It has been difficult to me for some years, difficult when ever the book needed close and [*illegible*] attention. My eyes seem very much dependent on my general health and I have had a lot of colds and the like small ailments lately. When I get rid of them this will improve.

A great many thanks for the *Secret Rose* reviews which are almost the only ones I have seen. The book was certainly well received, much better than I expected. I am going to Tillyra Castle on the 16 or 17 of this month and am hoping against hope that the London committee will not want me to go to the Dublin convention on the 20th or that I shall discover a good excuse for not going. I want simply to think and write and forget these brawls. I shall probably be at Tillyra for a month and then go to Lady Gregory of Coombe [*sic*], Galway, and then back here.

My novel is going on slowly and I am writing my usual reviews. I am to do Sigerson [2] but have not yet seen the book. Yours
W B YEATS

[1] Only the postscript of this letter has survived.
[2] An unsigned review of George Sigerson's *Bards of the Gael and Gall* appeared in the *Bookman* of October 1897, but I do not think it was written by Yeats.

TO THE EDITOR OF THE *SPEAKER*

May 18th, 1897   *Sligo*

Dear Sir, Owing to the fact that I have been travelling about, I have only just got the *Speaker* of May the 8th with your review of *The Secret Rose*. I hope your reviewer will not think me ungrateful for his generous praise if I reply to one or two of his criticisms of fact. He objects to my descriptions of the Irish monks in 'The Crucifixion of the Outcast,' and says 'the old Irish monks stood for gentleness and peace in a cruel and savage age.' 'The Crucifixion of the Outcast' is founded upon an eleventh century Irish romance,[1] and follows the original very closely; nor is the old romance the only witness upon my side, for Giraldus Cambrensis speaks of the fierceness of our very saints, and explains it by the great difficulty they had in preserving their property in so violent a land. Nor is your reviewer more correct in saying that when I make 'the Prior look for judgement to a saint instead of to the King of Saints' I commit 'the error of an Irish Protestant.' I am far away from books, and so cannot quote my authorities; but it is certainly true that Irish Christianity fell from its first simplicity in the century before the coming of the Danes and that many of the religious communities looked to be judged by their founders, who had, perhaps, in some places but stepped into the shoes of local gods. 'The Crucifixion of the Outcast' is, I claim, a fairly true picture, though history was no part of my purpose, of certain things and emotions in that time of decadence. It is one of several stories in my book about Irish saints and monks, and it is the only one in which my story, and the symbolism which is the heart of my story, compelled me to emphasise their fierceness rather than their ecstasy and piety. Yours very sincerely

                                                           W B YEATS

TO JOHN O'LEARY

May 30th [1897]   *c/o George Pollexfen Esq.*
                                                                  Sligo

Dear Mr. O'Leary ... I would have written before, but my eyes have been bad, so that I have had to keep my writing down to a

[1] *The Vision of MacConglinne.* An edition of this, edited by Kuno Meyer and published by David Nutt, was reviewed by Yeats in the *Bookman*, February 1893.

minimum. A great many thanks for the *Librarian* which I should not otherwise have seen as I do not subscribe to an agency. The book (*The Secret Rose*) has on the whole been very well reviewed and there is talk of its being translated into French. It is at any rate an honest attempt towards that aristocratic esoteric Irish literature, which has been my chief ambition. We have a literature for the people but nothing yet for the few. My long novel goes ahead slowly but promises well I think. Yours ever   W B YEATS

The Feis was by all accounts a great affair.[1]

TO ROBERT BRIDGES

Sunday [*June* 1897]   *Rosses Point*
                                                    Sligo

My dear Mr. Bridges: You will have enough knowledge of my delays in answering letters to understand that when I did not write in answer to your last letter and ask you to tell me what you thought of *The Secret Rose*, it was from no lack of desire for your opinion but sheer procrastination as usual. I am now in Sligo with an uncle who reduces my habits into order as a mangle does clothes. He is the genius of regularity and the result is that whenever I get here I begin to think of my sins and to answer letters steadily. Did you get *The Celtic Twilight* which I asked Bullen to send you? Could you without too much trouble tell me what you think of it and of *The Secret Rose*? If you tell me the parts you like best and the parts you like worst, it will not be much trouble, and will be useful to me.

My article on your work is in the *Bookman* this month, and I have asked them to send you a copy: You must not judge it as you would judge an essay meant to be permanent. It is merely [*word illegible*] journalism like all my criticism so far, and done more quickly than I would like. One has to give something of one's self to the devil that one may live. I have given my criticisms. Yours ever
                                                    W B YEATS

[1] Feis Ceoil, Festival of Music.

TO LADY GREGORY [1]

Saturday [*Postmark July* 24, 1897]　　　　　　*Rosses Point*

My dear Lady Gregory: George Russell and myself will reach Gort by the train that gets there at 1.27 on Monday. He has made drawings since he came here of quite a number of supernatural beings. The resemblance between the things seen by him at certain places and the things seen there at different times by a cousin of mine have been very curious. They have met however and so as we say 'may have got the things out of each other's sphere' although they did not talk about them. Yours　　　　　　W B YEATS

TO LADY GREGORY

[*Postmark Oct* 3, 1897]　　　　　　*Manchester*

My dear Lady Gregory: I find that Miss Gonne has to return to London for a few hours before going to Dublin. She goes first to a meeting at Hanley (wherever that is). I shall go with her. We had a long and exhausting political meeting this morning and will have another to-night.[2] After the meeting this morning Miss Gonne and myself went to the picture gallery to see a Rossetti that is there. She is very kind and friendly, but whether more than that I cannot tell. I have been explaining the Celtic movement and she is enthusiastic over it in its more mystical development, and tells me that her cousin Miss May Gonne, who is clever I think, will be anxious to

---

[1] Lady Gregory (1852–1932) was the youngest daughter of Dudley Persse of Roxborough, Co. Galway. She had married, as his second wife, Sir Robert Gregory of Coole Park, Gort, who had died in 1892 leaving her with one son, Robert. She first met Yeats in August 1896 when he was staying with Edward Martyn at Tillyra Castle, Galway, and invited him to spend a few days at Coole. She was then aged 44, Yeats 31. Next year she took a flat in Queen Anne's Mansions, Westminster, where Yeats called on her and discussed his plans for starting an Irish Theatre. Realizing that he was very unhappy and that he was neglecting his health, Lady Gregory took him under her care, and did what she could to make his life more comfortable. From 1897 until he acquired his Tower at Ballylee some twenty years later, Yeats spent almost every summer at Coole Park, at first collecting folklore with Lady Gregory's help from the cottages of the near-by peasantry, and later encouraging her in her writing of plays for the Abbey Theatre. They remained friends until her death.

[2] These meetings were held in connection with preparations for the 1798 Celebrations. The evening meeting took place at the Manchester Free Trade Hall; there appear to have been no disturbances.

help to act or whatever we like. She will, Miss Gonne thinks, go to Dublin to work on committee etc if we like. She and Miss Gonne are going to some place in the West, if Miss Gonne can make time, to see visions. I told Miss Gonne what Lady Mayo said about her losing a lot of money at Aix les Bains (I spell that word obscurely to hide my ignorance) and she says it is quite accurate except that she won £100 instead of losing. This is a very feeble letter, the sort of thing one writes when one is ten years old. 'It is a fine day. How are you? A tree has fallen into the pond. I have a new canary' etc. You know the style, but I have been chairman of a noisy meeting for three hours and am very done up. I have a speech to prepare for to-night. Everything went smoothly this morning in spite of anonymous letters warning us to keep a bodyguard at the door. Perhaps the disturbance waits for to-night. I find the infinite triviality of politics more trying than ever. We tear each other's character in pieces for things that don't matter to anybody. Yours
                                                             W B YEATS

TO LADY GREGORY

Monday   27 *South Great Frederick St*
[*Postmark Nov* 1, 1897]   *Dublin*

My dear Lady Gregory: I find our prospects good in Dublin.[1] The Contemporary Club was enthusiastic, and there are I hear two possible small theatres that have or will have licences. We have also, thanks to the good will of T. P. Gill, some new guarantors. I enclose list with Gill's name to it, and G. Barton promised but left town without saying the amount.

How extraordinarily good you are—wine and all manner of biscuits and bottled fruit have just come. Nobody has ever shown me such kindness. Everybody tells me how well I am looking, and I am better than I have been for years in truth. The days at Coole passed like a dream, a dream of peace.

There was a man at the Contemporary whose uncle was Biddy Early's landlord. He evicted her and she cursed him and presently a

[1] Yeats is evidently now beginning to be busy with plans for the first performances of the Irish Literary Theatre.

LADY GREGORY

house he was in caught fire and fell on him and burnt him. I also got a curious story from another man there about a way of cursing by making a fire of stones and bidding the curse stay until the stones were burned.

I saw Russell on Sunday for a bit, but had to spend much of my time looking for rooms. I have got very suitable ones and shall now get all the committees etc here.

I am afraid Miss Gonne will have a bad time in America. O'Leary has heard from there that the Irish parties, opposed to hers, have been busy circulating the spy story. They have made it most detailed, including machinations against Ireland by an imaginary brother. Yours   W B YEATS

TO LADY GREGORY

Saturday   27 *South Great Frederick St.*
[*Postmark* Nov 6, 1897]

My dear Lady Gregory: I send the article.[1] I send the whole that you may see how it looks, and where the interpolated bits come in. You will see I have not got very far, so great is the material. Our prospects about the play are good. We will know all we want to know in a day or two, perhaps to-night, as some one is going to see Gunn of the Gaiety Theatre on whose good will depends the freedom we will have when we come to arrange our performances in a hall. If he is favourable and will not interfere, and we have reason to believe he will not, we will engage the hall at once. John Redmond has given his name, but has not specified the amount. I have not sent off those prospectuses to the people you mention because I found that I wanted two of them for Redmond and Dowden and may want the other two. So soon as the hall is taken I can write with more effect. Magee (John Eglinton), who has given his name, has written to Dowden, and Dowden has already committed himself more or less favourably to him. Everybody here is enthusiastic. The press will give us a great backing. Plunkett in his speech at the Agricultural dinner made a slight allusion to the project, and

[1] Probably 'The Prisoner of the Gods,' the second of a series of essays on folklore which Yeats wrote with help from Lady Gregory. It was printed in the *Nineteenth Century*, January 1898.

talked a good deal about our intellectual movement. He called upon me to speak immediately after him. My speech was very well received. I will send you the *Homestead* with a report as soon as I get it.

A man told me yesterday that the people of Muagh say that their late Bishop Ryan was greatly learned in fairy things, he used to tell them that the fairies were the dead.

The hamper came on Thursday. How can I thank you?

Russell is to come here on Monday to make a sketch of me for you, he says. Yours sincerely W B YEATS

The new bits of folklore are of great value. I have kept back the May Day battle, as I shall want to write at some length about it and we may learn more.

TO LADY GREGORY

Nov 17th [1897]   27 *South Frederick Street*

My dear Lady Gregory: I have had rather a blow about the 'Tribes of Danu' article.[1] The enclosed letter will explain what has happened. The *New Review* has I imagine changed hands. I will write a new first article as soon as possible and put the two in the hands of an agent. It may be for the best in the end. I send you also a letter from Ford Madox Hueffer which will interest you. I replied of course that I should greatly like to get the old woman stories. Please keep the letter for me. Our work here is still in the balance. Horace Plunkett is pressing our case on the authorities to see if we can get a special permission to perform in a non-patent hall. 'The Gaiety' is full at the season we want it, even if it were not much too large. We can do no more until we hear the result of Plunkett's effort. Of enthusiasm for our plan there is no limit if the law will but make it possible.

Martyn[2] returns to London to-morrow (Thursday) and I will

[1] 'The Tribes of Danu,' the first of the folklore essays, had been published in the *New Review*, November 1897.
[2] Edward Martyn (1859–1923), a wealthy landowner of Tillyra (or Tulira) Castle, Galway, was one of the founders of the Irish Literary Theatre and generously financed the performances given during the three years it existed. His own plays show the influence of Ibsen, whose work he admired greatly. After 1901 he ceased to work with Yeats, though they remained on friendly

return on Monday next. I am but waiting to get some pictures and books I left here long ago packed up to go to London with me.

There is a possibility of George Russell becoming of all things in the world one of Plunkett's organizers. They want a man to organize agricultural banks and I suggested him. He seems to combine the three needful things—business knowledge, power to make a speech, enthusiasm. He is at this moment asking his flock if they can get along without him for most of the month and on their answer depends his decision. I would not have urged him to give up a certainty like Pim's for an uncertainty like Plunkett's did I not know that he was going to leave Pim's in any case. The American Theosophists have been asking him to give up Pim's and write for them and have promised him a small income. This would, as I think, be much greater uncertainty than Plunkett's and I am afraid that his conscience would compel him to write too much and not perhaps always in his best way. He would feel bound to be very propagandist. T. P. Gill backs up Russell strongly so that I think he will get it if he will take it. It would give him a great knowledge of Ireland and take him out of the narrow groove of theosophical opinion.

Young Grace[1] the theatrical person has been in. He is an amusing contrast to Russell. All his people are rich and he is rich, but the one thing he asks about anybody is 'does he make money?'. Altogether a lamentable but harmless person. We have set him to read Ibsen, whom he will hate, in spite of the fact that we have assured him that Ibsen makes money. Yours W B YEATS

TO LADY GREGORY

Saturday [*Postmark Nov* 20, 1897]   27 *South Frederick St.*

My dear Lady Gregory: I shall cross over on Monday night as I have some things to do here on Monday. I have arranged with

---

terms till the end of his life. George Moore, who had known him from boyhood, in *Hail and Farewell* draws a half mocking, half affectionate portrait of him as 'dear Edward.' Martyn founded 'The Irish Theatre' in Dublin in 1914 for the production of non-peasant plays and translations of foreign masterpieces. He was President of Sinn Fein, 1904 to 1908.

[1] Valentine Grace took the part of Shemus Rua in the production of *The Countess Cathleen* when it was performed by the Irish Literary Theatre in May 1899. He also appeared in the same part in the *tableaux vivants* at the Chief Secretary's Lodge in January 1899. See note on p. 306.

Martyn to meet him and Miss Farr at my place on Tuesday, if she can come. I have telegraphed to her and had meant on getting her answer to ask you to join us. Martyn has not more than a few days in London so I pitched on Tuesday as the first possible day. If Miss Farr is engaged that evening I will go to you with pleasure. I will write as soon as I hear and tell you how to find Woburn Buildings. I am quite free Thursday evening.

I think Russell is going to take Plunkett's offer. At first he refused on the ground of its being impossible for him to leave the little Dublin group of mystics for so long at a time. I brought some of the mystics to him and they all promised to hold together and work on while he was away, and now I think it is all right. Plunkett saw Pim yesterday and Pim gave Russell a very high character. Russell sees Anderson, Plunkett's chief organizer, on Monday and will then decide finally. He saw Plunkett yesterday. His work will be organizing co-operative banks in the congested districts of the West. Did you like his sketch of me in the *Homestead*? He is sending you the original which is in chalk on brown paper.

I am glad you like my brother's drawings. If his exhibition does well or fairly well he intends to go to the West of Ireland next year.
Yours   W B YEATS

O'Grady is writing a little book on the Fenian movement. It will be wild and stirring enough in all conscience, if it carries out his intentions. He is the first Fenian Unionist on record.

TO LADY GREGORY

Dec 24th [1897]   18 *Woburn Buildings*

My dear Lady Gregory: I should have written to thank you for the things which came all safely, the pen and the rest. A very great many thanks. I feel provisioned for a voyage and a shipwreck on a desert island.

I am trying to arrange terms with *Cosmopolis* for the 'Celtic Movement' and will begin my second article for Knowles at once after Xmas.

I have not yet seen Barry O'Brien. I was to have seen him last

Wednesday but he did not come because of the phantom sore throat. I see him in his own house on Tuesday night, to discuss '98 matters with him, Davitt and others. I will either discuss the Celtic Theatre with him then, or arrange a date for doing so.

I will send the proofs back in a few days and write to you about them. They are very interesting. I am just going out to get some presents for my sisters and then go home until Monday. Yours

W B YEATS

TO DOROTHEA HUNTER

Sat Jan 1st 1898 18 *Woburn Buildings*
  Upper Woburn Place
  (5 minutes from Gower St. station. Ring top bell left-hand side)

Dear Mrs. Hunter, I wish you and your husband would come to my at home on Monday next. I expect Osman Edwards, a rather well known critic of French literature, Sarojini Chattopâdhyây, a charming princess of Hyderabad who will come in Eastern costume, Mrs. Emery, Miss Alma Tadema and Arthur Symons—all people interested in mysticism. If you can come I want you to come a little before the others who come a little after eight. Come about 7.30 and don't dress of course. I want to talk to you and your husband about a certain part of our Celtic project in which you can be a great help. I am following out a plan laid down long ago, and after consultation with our chiefs. It is going to be a great movement in the end. I do not want you to mention this among the other members for the present as I want us all to do a little irresponsible experimentation for a while. I have had a number of visions on the way home, greatly extending the symbolism we got tonight. The souls of ordinary people remain after death in the waters[1] and these waters become an organized world if you gather up the flames that come from the waters of the well when the berries fall upon it, and

[1] The magic well of Connla lies at the foot of a mountain ash. Those who gaze therein may, if they can find a guide, be led to the Fount of Perpetual Youth. The ash berries fall into the waters and turn them to fire. Connla, the Druid, is the Guardian of the Well. [Note by Mrs. Hunter.]

make them into a flaming heart, and explore the waters with this as a lamp. They are the waters of emotion and passion, in which all but purified souls are entangled, and have the same relation to our plane of fixed material form as the Divine World of fluid fire has to the heroic world of fixed intellectual form. I have been shown also that beside Fergus, the dark being, who carried the child, there are two very old shadows, who flit about in the Woods, strange half-naked beings who are shadows even to the heroes and are the oldest of the heroic race and represent Kether and Chochmar.

As I saw them they were withered and little with age. Yours sincerely   W B YEATS

TO GEORGE RUSSELL (AE)

Saturday 22 Jan [1898]   18 *Woburn Buildings*

My dear Russell, I feel certain that things will greatly improve with you in a month or so. I do entreat you to give this work a fair trial. It is so unlike all you have done that it was certain to trouble you and absorb your thoughts at first. Every change of life, everything that takes one out of old habits, even a change for the better troubles one at first. But remember always that now you are face to face with Ireland, its tragedy and its poverty, and if we would express Ireland we must know her to the heart and in all her moods. You will be a far more powerful mystic and poet and teacher because of this knowledge. This change of life will test you as a man and a thinker and if you can gradually build up a strong life out of it you will be a bigger soul in all things. You are face to face with the heterogeneous, and the test of one's harmony is our power to absorb it and make it harmonious. Gradually these bars, hotels and cottages and strange faces will become familiar, gradually you will come to see them through a mist of half humorous, half comical, half poetical, half affectionate memories and hopes. The arguments you use, and the methods you adopt, will become familiar too and then your mind will be free again.

When I began speaking on politics first my mind used to be absorbed for days before and very anxious, and now I hardly think of what I am going to say until I get to the meeting, and when it is over it goes straight out of my mind. Do not be troubled because you cannot write. I confess I did not expect you would be able to write just at first.

Do you know I now think *The Earth Breath* quite your best work. There are great poems in it. It is an enormous advance in art too. 'Janus' cannot help being immortal and 'Dream love' is fine in style as a Jacobean lyric and has a far finer style than many Jacobean writers ever had. I think you will yet out-sing us all and sing in the ears of many generations to come. Absorb Ireland and her tragedy and you will be the poet of a people, perhaps the poet of a new insurrection.

I am deep in 'Celtic Mysticism,' the whole thing is forming an elaborate vision. Maud Gonne and myself are going for a week or two perhaps to some country place in Ireland to get as you do the forms of gods and spirits and to get sacred earth for our evocation. Perhaps we can arrange to go somewhere where you are, so that we can all work together. Maud Gonne has seen vision of a little temple of the heroes which she proposes to build somewhere in Ireland when '98 is over and to make the centre of our mystical and literary movement.

I shall be in Ireland about the 20 or 23 of Feb. and will be in Dublin for a week or two arranging '98 work.[1] If you like I think I could arrange, though I am not altogether sure, to join you wherever you are then and we could make time to work at the Celtic mysticism together. I feel pretty sure I could arrange this.

I have just finished my review of you for the *Sketch*.[2] Yours
W B YEATS

PS. How much a week could I live for in the country if I stayed a couple of weeks or so? Could I do it for 30/–? Please let me know about this soon. I have a lot to say about the mysticism but will write later on.

[1] The '98 Celebrations were organized to commemorate Wolfe Tone and the insurrection of 1798. They were many and various, and extended more or less through the year; they included torchlight processions, speeches, resolutions by various local bodies such as Corporations, of loyalty to the ideal, pilgrimages to battlefields and graves, and the erection of monuments. Yeats was chiefly concerned with the celebrations in London and in Dublin. See note on pp. 302–3.

[2] A review by Yeats of AE's second book of verse *The Earth Breath* appeared in the *Sketch*, April 6, 1898.

TO GEORGE RUSSELL (AE)

[? *February* 1898]   18 *Woburn Buildings*

My dear Russell, This is merely a word to say that I will write next week: and to answer your question about Symons' and Johnson's opinion of *The Earth Breath*. Johnson I have not seen except for a few minutes, except in general society; and though he spoke of your work as a whole I cannot remember what he said of *The Earth Breath*. Symons on the other hand is full of admiration. He tried to get it for review from the *Athenaeum* but failed. In a review of Stephen Phillips' book (the book that got the £100 prize) he wrote that 'a perfectly achieved poem like AE's "Janus" outweighs a whole volume like Phillips''; but the *Athenaeum* cut out the reference. Edmund Gosse, who did not like your work at first, is now enthusiastic but I do not think he has seen *The Earth Breath*. I mean to get him to read it. I feel absolutely confident of the book now. I know everything almost by heart. I do not agree with you altogether about the two poems in the letter. The second interests me less than the first but mainly I think because of one or two harsh lines. The first goes to pieces at the end but has the making of a good poem. I will venture to send you a suggested correction of it. I chiefly dislike the repetition of Carrowmore. The faults are very slight. I am very glad you have got that bit of folk lore. It has been recorded but by no trustworthy person and without authority. Please let me have it sometime with the name of the village and story teller. I shall be very grateful for any folk lore you get me. I go to Dublin next week, I believe, but return by the 20th. I go over again later on. Maud Gonne has changed the date for me as we have '98 work to do. I am busy with an essay 'The Celtic Movement.' Yours sincerely

W B YEATS

TO GEORGE RUSSELL (AE)

March 27 [? 1898]   18 *Woburn Buildings*

My dear Russell: When do you come to London? Lady Gregory wants to know for one thing.

I have bought O'Curry's *Manuscript Materials* and his *Manners and Customs* and also *The Migration of Symbol* to help us over the Celtic order. By the by when Miss Gonne and myself were seeing visions in Dublin we got a message for you which was 'number the people of God.' Does it mean anything to you? Is it an appeal to you to help in that systematization which you so dislike? Miss Gonne and myself both got a message for you, which seemed to be the same thing, but in different words. These messages at the worst are messages from one's deeper self. Systematization can however wait till your feet have got firm in the new stirrups. I go to Paris on the 14th of April, I believe, to see the Mathers on Celtic things. I have just heard, curiously enough, that Mrs. Mathers has been seeing Conla and without knowing that we have been invoking him constantly.

I wish you would send me a couple of copies of the new *Internationalist*. I will send the money afterwards. I do not know where to get it here. Yours W B YEATS

TO THE EDITOR OF THE *OUTLOOK*

[*Published April* 23, 1898]

A friendly paragraphist in the *Outlook* for April 16 regrets that when I sit 'down to write for a prosaic world' I am unable 'always to separate the dreams and poetic fancies from the realities' I have 'witnessed'; and wishes that I would be 'sure of my facts.' He says that when I wrote, in the *Fortnightly Review*, 'The most of the Irish country people believe that only people who die of old age go straight to some distant Hell or Heaven or Purgatory. All who are young enough for any use ... are taken ... by the fairies; and live, until they die a second time, in the green "forts,"' I wrote what is nearly altogether 'the dream of a poetical folk-lorist.'

If your paragraphist will consult my article in the January number of the *Nineteenth Century*, of which these sentences are the summary, he will find that I have been very careful about my facts and have quoted witness after witness. And if your paragraphist, who is, perhaps, a Catholic, will wait until I have completed the series of essays, of which the essay in the *Fortnightly* is but the third, he will find that the Irish peasant has invented, or that somebody has invented for him, a vague, though not altogether unphilosophical, reconciliation between his Paganism and his Christianity.

W B YEATS

TO LADY GREGORY

25 *April* [1898]   *Aux soins de Monsieur Mathers MacGregor*
87 Rue Mozart
Auteuil, Paris

My dear Lady Gregory: I enclose a cutting from the *Outlook* which may interest you. It is my reply to the first Catholic objection to the folk lore articles. The little rejoinder at the end is too general to matter.

I have been here in Paris for a couple of days. It is wonderful weather. The trees out everywhere. I have been out on a bicycle in the Bois de Bologne and it was like a summer ride. I am buried in Celtic mythology and shall be for a couple of weeks or so. Miss Gonne has been ill with bronchitis. One of her lungs is affected a little so that she has to rest. She is unable to do any politics for the time and looks ill and tired. She comes here to-morrow to see visions. Fiona Macleod (this is private as she is curiously secret about her movements) talks of coming here too, so we will have a great Celtic gathering.

I shall go from this almost direct to Ireland—spending about a week in London on the way.

I got a letter from Russell a little before I left London. He has a mild fit of his old gloom through having to dine with parish priests every night. He was going to dine the day he wrote with a bishop and was hoping to have a theological argument. 'That is a bright spot in my fortune' he said.

Symons seems on the verge of falling in love with a serpent charmer and is writing better than ever. His Aubrey Beardsley essay is a masterpiece. Yours always   W B YEATS

My host is a Celtic enthusiast who spends most of his day in highland costume to the wonder of the neighbours.

TO LADY GREGORY

[*June* 14, 1898]

c/o George Russell
10 *Grove Terrace*
Grove Park
Rathmines
Dublin

My dear Lady Gregory, Miss Gonne was thrown from a car yesterday by a horse falling. Her arm is broken and her face scratched and bruised. I have not seen her. I was not with her at the demonstrations when the accident happened. I was to have gone, but was sitting to my father for the new sketch instead. I did not know until a few minutes to nine to-day when a messenger came to tell me. We were to have travelled as far as Athenry together. I have just seen the doctor and on his advice have taken the responsibility of writing to her sister. She is so self-reliant that she would probably ask no one to nurse her, if she could get on at all without—I cannot leave now. I am taking a room at the same lodging with Russell. The doctor tells me that the break is not a bad one. It is what they call the ulna which soon mends. I am most anxious about the shock for she has been very ill this spring with her old trouble in her lungs, and was looking pale and ill as it was.

I will write again very soon, about this and about other things. I am very sorry about all these delays but I must stay here for a little, a few days at any rate.

My dear Lady Gregory, I have seen Miss Gonne since I wrote the enclosed letter. She is much better than I feared. She is quite cheerful and talkative. The first accounts were really alarming. I will stay however for two or three days to see if I can be of any use about political correspondence and the like. She is going to stay at the Pursers', (Sarah Purser the artist) so soon as her arm is in a cast.

Now about other matters. I have just heard a piece of information at which I am not very pleased though I have half expected it. Russell has married Miss North. An aerial Theosophic marriage. It came off a day or two ago and the bride is off to Mullingar by herself. Mrs. Russell is a person who sees visions and is well-bred and pleasant enough; but I suppose I would never think anybody quite good enough for Russell. She has, as I have noticed, been in love with him for years. He has got into the habit of looking after her. She is consumptive and has some literary power. I imagine you will like her. Yours always   W B YEATS

My father's new sketch is good I think.

TO LADY GREGORY

Wednesday [*June* 29. *Postmark July* 1, 1898]   18 *Woburn Buildings*

My dear Lady Gregory: I have not yet heard from Russell. I am lingering on here because I have been expecting Miss Gonne every day and I have some talismans to give her. I will not however delay much longer—I thought she would have been here last week. I wrote to Healy and Dillon and Redmond about the theatrical licensing clause and got a promise from Healy and Dillon to support it and a letter, which I think means support but I am not sure, from Redmond. As Clancy, follower of Redmond, has taken it up Redmond is safe I conclude. I have asked Martyn to send the letters on to you. The clause comes on after the Whitsuntide holidays.

I had a great battle with George Armstrong at the Irish Lit Society last Friday. He lectured on 'The Two Irelands in literature' and his whole lecture was an attack on 'the Celtic movement' and was full of insinuations about conspiracies to prevent his success as a poet and to keep him out of anthologies etc. He spoke for two hours. I replied with a good deal of fierceness and described the barrenness of the so called educated intellect of Ireland and traced it to the negations of Armstrong's 'Ireland' and told how all the cleverer of the young men were leaving him and his and coming to us. I then attacked Armstrong's scholarship and showed that his knowledge of Irish things was of the most obsolete kind. I believe I was unanswerable, at any rate Armstrong made no attempt to answer but excused himself because of the lateness of the hour, which was weak as he had sought the contest himself and made the hour late by speaking for two hours. Father Barry, who was in the chair, said to me afterwards 'thank you for your speech. I agreed with almost every word of it.' I was glad of this as it was probably the fiercest speech the society has heard and I was afraid my hearers may not have understood that conspiracy insinuation enough to understand why. The whole thing delighted me as it shows how angry we are making our enemies, how seriously they are feeling our attack. Armstrong has lectured a number of times before like this I believe.

Get Moore's *Evelyn Innes* from the library. I am 'Ulick Dean' the musician. Yours   W B YEATS

TO FIONA MACLEOD [1]

[After June 1898]

... I have read *Green Fire* since I saw you. I do not think it is one of your well-built stories, and I am certain that the writing is constantly too self-consciously picturesque; but the atmosphere, the romance of much of it, of 'The Herdsman' part in particular, haunts me ever since I laid it down.

'Fiona Macleod' has certainly discovered the romance of the remote Gaelic places as no one else has done. She has made the earth by so much the more beautiful ...

TO LILY YEATS

July 11*th* [*Postmark* 1898]   c/o *Lady Gregory*
                                              Coole Park
                                              Gort
                                              Co. Galway

My dear Lilly: I have been here some time, writing my novel which goes well but slowly. I work from 11 to 2 and read and walk and write other things the rest of my time. My eyes have been rather bad again but not bad enough to stop work. I must rest a minute or two every 20 minutes or so. I have no news, for Galway [is] not the place for it, at least no news of this world—I have plenty of the other. For instance—a woman who came here to mend chairs

---

[1] Fragment. Text from *William Sharp* (*Fiona Macleod*) by Elizabeth A. Sharp. London, 1910.

went a walk down the avenue with the housemaid last week and presently both came in in a fainting state. They had seen the fairies —tall figures with black tall hats ('steeple hats') and ruffs. Evident Elizabethans (I saw an Elizabethan woman here a year ago). That night, later on, one of them was going upstairs to bed and saw a portrait of Mary Queen of Scots that is here, and fainted because she recognized the ruff.

The way I saw my Elizabethan was I seemed to wake up in the middle of the night—not exactly to wake but to see the room and the bed and everything quite clearly—and I saw her pass through the room. I do not believe it was a dream.—This is all the news from here. Papa seemed well when I saw him in Dublin. He has done a new sketch of me for Lady Gregory, with which she is greatly pleased. It is certainly the best he has done of me. She is going to keep it, and the Hyde and the Russell, in London so somebody may see them there and want a portrait of themselves. I had almost forgotten, by the by, that I have begun Irish and am getting on fairly well with it.

Remember me to Jack and Cottie. Yours affectionately

W B YEATS

I open this letter again to say that I hope Jack will accept Lady Gregory's invitation. She wants him to come this month (as her house is full of children in August). They will find it very quiet and pleasant here. No guests to speak of at first and a little later probably Hyde and Lord Castletown. Jack will find plenty to sketch round about. I hope their coming will not upset your plans but it would be a pity for them not to come.

TO LADY GREGORY

Thursday   18 *Woburn Buildings*
[*August* 11. *Postmark Aug* 12, 1898]

My dear Lady Gregory: I hope to get back to Coole early next week. I have had a rather troublesome time here. The Banquet[1]

---

[1] An inaugural Banquet of the '98 Centennial Association of Great Britain and France was given in London on April 13 at the Holborn Restaurant. Yeats took the chair and delivered a speech on 'The Union of the Gael.' The celebra-

went well, but the public demonstration has been mismanaged in the most amazing way by our tom fools. A principal speaker was the Vicar of Plumpton who recommended everybody to buy a breech-loader and prepare for the day of battle and wound up by singing a patriotic song apparently of his own making. He described himself as being at war with all his neighbourhood about the Irish question. I don't wonder. He hopped about too in a most surprising way. The papers have made game of me rather less than I expected in spite of the fact that I was in such a rage I forgot to put one of the resolutions. The one fine thing was old Cipriani who spoke in French with the air of a man on a battlefield—he has been on forty and refused the Legion of Honour after one of them. He got a tremendous reception. Our Dublin demonstration is on Monday. I may get to Galway on Wednesday. We go to Dublin Saturday morning. Yours   W B YEATS

P.S. I wrote the enclosed yesterday morning and then finding that I had forgot the really important thing, my eyes, and kept it back to add to it. Your letter came last night and I am ashamed of myself for not having written long ago.

Dr. Lang says that the eye which has been so bad for years that it has been useless is worse, but that the other is exactly as it was. His words were 'the eye is going on very well.' The weakness lately seems to be a matter of general health. I must not try them too much, and I am to wash them in some borax mixture. He asked me what use I was making of them. Was I reading too much MS etc. He tried me with all kinds of glasses and said that my glasses were all right.

TO LADY GREGORY

Nov 6 [1898]   *Thornhill*

My dear Lady Gregory: The port came a couple of days ago and I thank you very much. It has already saved me from threatenings of

---

tion to which this letter refers began with a Banquet at Frascati's Restaurant on August 9, which was followed by the London Commemoration Meeting at St. Martin's Hall on August 10 with Yeats in the chair and Maud Gonne as the principal speaker. The Dublin Commemoration was held on Monday, August 15, and was a great success, with Dillon and Redmond on the platform.

toothache. I do not think that the cold will have done me any harm however. My uncle by the by has improved a good deal—I don't know whether it is visions or something else but he is really pleasant and companionable. He is just at this moment in one of his bad fits—but it is nothing to his old ones—owing to the fact that I am in general hot water and the inhabitants attack him as they can't get at me. He brought me to a Masonic concert on Thursday and somebody sang a stage Irishman song—the usual whiskey shallelagh kind of thing—and I hissed him and lest my hiss might be lost in the general applause waited till the applause was done and hissed again. This gave somebody else courage and we both hissed. My uncle defends me, but admits that he makes but a poor hand of it and gets beaten, as I can well believe. I do not send you the *Express* with my 'Eglinton' controversy as I think you said that the *Express* is sent to you. I write again next week and Russell joins in.[1] I am going to try and widen the controversy if I can into a discussion of the spiritual origin of the arts. In this way we will keep people awake until we announce 'The Irish Literary Theatre' in December and discuss that. I want Martyn's book to come out with Moore's preface just before the announcement is made. I hear that the preface is done.[2] There have been some very good articles in the *Express* on the point of view that Ireland being poor must preserve the virtues of the poor, spirituality, ideality. Have you read them? One last week called 'Celtic Ideals' or some such thing was particularly good. I am trying to appeal to the writers of these articles in my controversy with 'Eglinton' in hopes of gradually building up a school of spiritual thought in Ireland.

No, I do not think the *Fortnightly* putting off my article will matter as I conclude it will be in next time, and Miss Gonne does

---

[1] 'John Eglinton' is the pseudonym of W. K. Magee, Irish essayist. In the autumn of 1898 an article of his, 'What should be the subjects of National Drama?' in the *Daily Express*, Dublin, provoked a discussion in which Yeats, AE, and William Larminie took part. Their articles were reprinted in 1899 as a small pamphlet, *Literary Ideals in Ireland*. 'John Eglinton' was for many years Assistant Librarian of the National Library of Ireland, and as a friend of George Moore's he figures in the trilogy *Hail and Farewell*. Yeats wrote an appreciation of his earlier work in the *United Irishman*, November 9, 1901, but did not reprint it. His later writings include *Anglo-Irish Essays*, 1917, *Irish Literary Portraits*, 1935, and a *Memoir of AE*, 1937.

[2] *The Heather Field* and *Maeve* by Edward Martyn, with an introduction by George Moore, was published in 1899 by Duckworth & Co., London. The plays are dedicated to George Moore, W. B. Yeats and Arthur Symons.

not seem anxious to go to Dublin or to make any plans just now. I shall therefore not leave this until I go to London early in December. My uncle has been busy since I began this letter in developing the most wonderful series of symptoms of ill health and his depression grows. He is just my father's age and looks fifteen or twenty years younger, so well does he watch over himself. There is no doubt however that he is much more tolerable than I have ever known him. He has a wonderful old servant who is a mine of fairy lore. I have taken down quantities. She is really a kind of saint and is supremely happy. She sees fairies and angels continually. She foretold I was to get a present. She said 'there is a drop of drink for you' some days before the port came. She saw it in a tea cup. Yours W B YEATS

TO LADY GREGORY

Dec 22 [*Postmark* 1898]   6 *Castlewood Avenue*
Rathmines

My dear Lady Gregory: I forgot to ask you something which I have long meant to ask you. Would you agree to collaborate with me in the big book of folk lore?[1] One hand should do the actual shaping and writing—apart from peasant talk—and I would wish to do this. In some cases my opinions may be too directly mystical for you to accept. In such cases I can either initial the chapters containing them or make a general statement about them in the preface. If you agree to this, all future essays can either appear over our two signatures or I can add a footnote saying that a friend, whose name I do not give, because it is easier to collect if one is not known to be writing, is helping me throughout. Please agree to this arrangement as I dislike taking credit for what is not mine and it will be a great pleasure to do this work with you.

    I go to Sligo to-morrow so write c/o George Pollexfen, Thornhill, Sligo as before.

    I am going to see Lady Fingal this afternoon about Lady Betty

[1] The 'big book of folk lore' of which Yeats writes here did not appear until 1920 when it was published as *Visions and Beliefs in the West of Ireland* by Lady Gregory, with terminal essays and notes by Yeats.

Balfour's 'living pictures' from *The Countess Kathleen*.[1] I find it was she started the idea. Lady Fingal told Russell that she hoped Miss Gonne would take the principal part. Imagine Miss Gonne at the Chief Secretary's Lodge! Yours ever   W B YEATS

TO LILY YEATS

Dec 25 [*Postmark* 1898]   *Thornhill*

My dear Lilly: I sent you and Lolly a blotter and card case, or whatever you call it, respectively; and hope they got safe. I wrote your address down for the people in the shop; and afterwards it occurred to me that my writing was so bad that the things may have gone to 'the street that is called straight' in Jericho or whatever other town of the Bible it is in. I must thank both you and Lolly for the cigarette case which is charming and useful.

I expect now to be in London about the second week in January. All my Irish plans are going well. We have taken the hall for our plays for the week following May 8th. Meanwhile they are getting up at the Chief Sec Lodge 'living pictures' from *The Countess Kathleen*. As I have explained that I cannot possibly go near the Chief Sec Lodge, or take any part in the performance, Lady Fingal is trying to arrange for me to meet Lady Betty Balfour at her house (Lady Fingal's) that I may advise about costumes etc. This may keep me a little while in Dublin but I won't wait if it means delaying more than a week or so. We are [to] carry on all manner of propaganda in Dublin so as to prepare the people for the plays and expect a great success. Dublin is waking up in a number of ways and about a number of things. Russell is doing a good part in the awakening. He is a most amazing person. He is at the moment busy over a scheme to settle the congested districts on a plan of his own invention. Gerald Balfour has described it as the only practical scheme yet thought of, and is going to introduce a bill—which

---

[1] This entertainment took place at the Chief Secretary's Lodge, Phoenix Park, Dublin, in January 1899. Nine *tableaux vivants* were staged, each illustrating an episode in the play; the Countess of Fingal represented the Countess Cathleen; Valentine Grace, Shemus Rua; Miss Penn and Miss Ruth Balfour, Maire and Teig; Miss Harriet Stokes, Oona; and Mr. Rolleston and Mr. Coffey, the Two Demons. The full cast is given by Mr. P. S. O'Hegarty, who possesses a programme, in the *Dublin Magazine*, January–March 1940.

Russell and certain solicitors and others are now consulting over—to make it possible. He is also making up his case for an attack on T.C.D. and is working with Osbourne and Miss Purser and a lot of others to get up a loan exhibition of pictures which he suggested. He also sees the gods as of old and preaches of them to a group of young persons. He has begun to write very fine prose. Yours affectionately

                                                                               W B YEATS

TO STANDISH O'GRADY[1]

[*Published Christmas*, 1898]

Dear Mr. O'Grady, You ask me to explain how I came to write anything so unlike the rest of my writings as this little bit of fooling. You know that a whole cycle of stories and poems were written about Reynard the Fox in the Middle Ages, and how the tricks Reynard played upon the wolf and the lion and other beasts was a cover for much fantastical satire of the lords and priests. When I was about eighteen I came upon a Connaught folk tale of a tinker and Death and the Devil; and a little later on I found that it existed in Russia, where it had gathered unto itself the man who crowed to shame St. Peter, and some other old tales. I began what was to be a long poem in octosyllabic verse, the verse of the Reynard poems, meaning to make the tinker a type of that kind of jeering, cheating Irishman called 'a melodious lying Irishman' in another folk tale; and to bring him through many typical places and adventures. I remember planning out a long conversation between him and a certain portentous professor of Trinity whom I changed into a lap dog, and set to guard the gates of Hell, and I intended to have written many conversations with many portentous persons. Gradually the thought of the enemies I should make if I succeeded, and of the number of verses I should have to write even if I did not, damped my courage, and I gave up my epic and wrote this little tale instead. I do not think much of it, but it has amused people who do not care for my poems or my romantic stories, and it is all

---

[1] *Michael Clancy, the Great Dhoul, and Death* was first published in *The Old Country*, a Christmas Annual, in 1893. When Standish O'Grady republished it in the *Kilkenny Moderator* five years later Yeats prefaced it with the following letter. The story has not been included in any of his books.

I have left of a good intention. I commend it to your tolerance—I wrote it long ago, and it does not mean anything in particular; but had that first book, of which it is in part the shrivelled remnant, brought on the other works, Death and Devil would probably have become fantastic images of the sterility and the fruitfulness of the world. There is humour and fantasy as well as miraculous poetry in our old legends, and one can find in them all kinds of meanings. They will some day be the themes of poets and painters in many countries, and the substance of a new romantic movement, which will have found its beginning in your own beautiful and paramount books. They are the greatest treasure the Past has handed down to us Irish people, and the most plentiful treasure of legends in Europe; and I have always considered that you yourself have done more than all others to dig away the earth that has so long lain upon their beauty. Yours sincerely   W B YEATS

TO THE EDITOR OF THE *DAILY CHRONICLE*[1]

Jan. 27, 1899

Sir, Mr. William Archer said of my play, *The Countess Kathleen*, 'To do the poem justice the whole mounting should be ... elaborate and rich,' and then spoke of the great expense this would be, and of the bankruptcy such great expense in the service of a play, which could never be popular, might bring upon a theatre. Mr. Moore replied that he hoped 'Mr. Yeats would have the play performed without scenery and without costumes' when it is performed in Dublin next May, and told how he takes much greater pleasure in rehearsals than in any elaborately and richly mounted performance. I think I am more in agreement with Mr. Moore than with Mr. Archer, but I am not altogether in agreement with him, for I see in my imagination a stage where there shall be both scenery and costumes, but scenery and costumes which will draw little attention to themselves and cost little money. I have noticed at a rehearsal how the modern coats and the litter on the stage draw one's attention, and baffle the evocation, which needs all one's

[1] A review of Edward Martyn's play *The Heather Field* in the *Daily Chronicle* by William Archer led to a controversy between him and George Moore in that paper in January 1899.

thought that it may call before one's eyes lovers escaping through a forest, or men in armour upon a mountain side. I have noticed, too, how elaborate costumes and scenery silence the evocation completely, and substitute the cheap effects of a dressmaker and of a meretricious painter for an imaginative glory. I would have such costumes as would not disturb my imagination by staring anachronism or irrelevant splendour, and such scenery as would be forgotten the moment a good actor had said, 'The dew is falling,' or 'I can hear the wind among the leaves.' Sometimes a shadowy background, a pattern of vague forms upon a dim backcloth, would be enough, for the more the poet describes the less should the painter paint; and at the worst one but needs, as I think, enough of scenery to make it unnecessary to look at the programme to find out whether the persons on the stage have met indoors or out of doors, in a cottage or in a palace. Mr. Moore thinks it is better to find this out from the programme, but I want to be able to forget everything in the real world, in watching an imaginative glory. Such scenery might come, when its makers had mastered its mysteries, to have a severe beauty, such as one finds in Egyptian wall paintings, and it would be more beautiful, even at the beginning, than the expensive scenery of the modern theatre, even when Mr. Tree has put into the boughs in the forest those memorable birds that sing by machinery.

We have forgotten that the Drama began in the chanted ode, and that whenever it has been great it has been written certainly to delight our eyes, but to delight our ears more than our eyes. Greek actors with masks upon their faces, and their stature increased by artifice, must have been content to delight the eyes with but an austere and monotonous beauty, and Elizabethan actors who had to speak so much that would seem irrelevant poetry to modern audiences must have thought oratory a principal part of acting. I believe that the reason why the men of letters of this century have failed to master the technique of the modern theatre, while the men of letters of past times mastered the technique of the theatre of their times without difficulty, is that the modern theatre has discovered that you can move many thousands, who have no imagination for beautiful words to awaken, by filling the stage with landscapes, which are at the best like the landscapes of Mr. Leader, and with handsome men and women in expensive dresses, who pose when happily inspired like persons in popular German pictures. The accepted theory is that men of letters have suddenly lost the dramatic faculty, but it is easier to believe that times and seasons change than that imagination and intellect change; for imagination and intellect are that which is eternal in man crying out against that which is temporal and perishing. The literature and painting of our time, when they come out of a deep life, are labouring to awaken again our interests in the moral and spiritual realities which were once the foundation of the arts; and the theatre, if it would cease to be but the amusement of idleness, must cast off that interest in external and accidental things which has marred all modern arts, and dramatic art more than any. To dream of this is not, as I understand Mr. Archer to say, 'to dream of a theatre where there shall be no actors, no scenery, no public,' but of a theatre which is a part of the intellectual life. It cannot, however, become a part of the intellectual life until it escapes from that general public whose slave it has become, for you cannot make the general public care for anything more like literature than those plays which Mr. Archer calls good plays because they are as good as a good ephemeral novel. The general public reads ephemeral novels, and goes to the theatre that it may be entertained and soothed; and it will always hate literature and the arts because it will always shrink from the laborious or exhausting ecstasy in which literature and the arts are understood. The theatre can only escape by working for that small public which cares for literature and the arts without losing all hope of the theatre; and how small it is is shown by the impossibility of making a play of Ibsen's run for more than a few afternoons. If we are to have an endowed theatre, it should work for this public, which will grow a little larger in time; for compromise is as impossible in literature as in matters of faith. We will work for it in Dublin, producing our plays at the same time every year, that persons who have ceased to read theatrical news may come to know about us; and we will produce them inexpensively and for but a few days, that we may be independent of popular taste, and, as I hope, with austere and grave costumes and scenery, that we may appeal to the imagination alone.

The lull in the political life of Ireland has been followed, among the few, by an intellectual excitement so remarkable that a learned German is writing a book about it; and among the many, by that strange sense of something going to happen which has always in all countries given the few their opportunity. The best among the leisured class have begun to read Irish books and Irish history with a curious passionate interest, and the unleisured class has always had its ballads and legends, which are the beginnings of literature and the arts. We will have difficulty at first, for some who do not dislike the modern theatre, or who dislike it for wrong reasons, will come to see our plays out of patriotism, and miss that appeal to the senses which they have mistaken for drama; but even they will not hate us as London playgoers hated the founders of the Independent Theatre. We will, however, gradually draw to us no great audience indeed, but one drawn from different classes, which will add to a true understanding of drama an interest in the life and in the legends on which our plays are founded so deep that it will give us that freedom to experiment, that freedom to search for the laws of what is perhaps a lost art, which even the most cultured London audience, with its half-conscious disbelief in the theatre, would not be able to give us. I know these people upon whom I rely, for I have worked with them and lived with them, and though I have heard them discuss what would seem to most Englishmen hopes and beliefs too wild even for laughter, I have not heard them exalt material above immaterial things, or claim any foundations for the arts but in moral and spiritual truths. The contemplation of great sacrifices for great causes, the memory of rebellions and executions, the reveries of a religious faith, founded in visions and ecstasies, and uncountable old tales told over the fire, have given them imaginative passions and simple and sincere thoughts. W B YEATS

TO LADY GREGORY

Saturday [*February* 4, 1899]   203 *Boulevard Raspail*
                                    Paris

My dear Lady Gregory, I send you a *Chronicle*, which you may not have seen. Martyn is sure to have shown you the others with Moore's letters. I mislaid my copies and could not find them in the hurry of leaving London on Tuesday. I don't know whether things are well or ill with me, in some ways ill, for she has been almost cold with me, though she has made it easy for me to see her.[1] If you knew

[1] The allusion is evidently to Maud Gonne, at this time living in Paris.

all, and of course I have not been able to tell you all, as you know, you would understand why this love has been so bitter a thing to me, and why things I have known lately have made it, in a certain sense, the bitterer, and the harder. It may be that Russell is right. I have little to set against what he says except a few omens. I would not so much lament, but I am sure that if things remain as they are she will never leave this life of hatred which a vision I made her see years ago told her was her deepest hell, and contrasted with the life of labour from the divine love, which was her highest heaven. Write and tell me what you are doing—whenever things are going ill I find myself thinking of my peaceful months at Coole—and when you will be in London. You need not allude in your letter to what I have written about my own matters unless you want to, but write about other things.

I have not sent your article to the *Express* yet, but I want Martyn to try and get the other literary theatre articles together. Mrs. Emery and George Moore met last Saturday. I brought Mrs. Emery to see him. It was very amusing. Moore began with hostility but softened so remarkably that he kept urging her to come and dine with him to discuss the thing, and she kept suggesting that Martyn might be asked too—not thinking a dinner alone with Moore desirable—and he kept saying 'I tell you he knows no more about managing a theatre than a turbot from the North Pole.' That dinner will not come off. Moore used to be always abusing Mrs. Emery and her acting. He called her 'the woman with the big nose' she says; but he was full of compliments on Saturday. She was very amusing about it in the train.

My brother is coming to London and I will see him there in a week or so. His plan is to take the hall for my father's work for the week after his own exhibition, as he says the hall is too small for both. He and my sister Lolly will pay for it between them. Yours sincerely
W B YEATS

TO LADY GREGORY

Thursday [*Postmark Feb* 10, 1899] *203 Boulevard Raspail*

My dear Lady Gregory: I think I shall be in London Wednesday or Thursday. M[aud] G[onne] talks of crossing over on Tuesday but she seldom gets away the day she expects. We shall cross over together. I have had rather a depressing time here. During the last months, and most of all while I have been here, she has told the story of her life, telling gradually, in more detail, all except a few things which I can see are too painful for her to talk of and about which I do not ask her. I do not wonder that she shrinks from life. Hers has been in part the war of phantasy and of a blinded idealism against eternal law.

I am probably more depressed than I should be as I am emerging, with a headache, out of a cold of an astonishing violence that kept me in bed without eating anything for a day and then went completely. M G is quite convinced that it is the work of a certain rival mystic, or of one of his attendant spirits. She points out that I went to see him without it and came back with it, which is circumstantial evidence at any rate. I am trying to get the 'copy' of a new edition of my book of poems with Unwin ready for the Press. Unwin is in a hurry to get it out in time to benefit by the Irish Literary Theatre as an advertisement. I am abolishing the old cover which tries me by its facile meaninglessness and trying to get one of Althea Gyles's [1] put in its place. The delay in the publication of *The Wind Among the Reeds* has been caused by the delay of the American printers. They have been expecting the printed sheets for some time. It might be out almost any time now for the sheets have probably arrived by this. They were expecting them the week I left, last week, and it should take a couple of weeks to bind and dry—however they have expected them often when they did not come.

I will let you know, as soon as I know definitely, when I return.
Yours ever   W B YEATS

M G is going to Ireland to the evicted tenants.

[1] A young Irish artist and poet of whose work Yeats thought well. She had made the elaborate cover design for *The Secret Rose*, 1897, and those for the new edition of *Poems* in 1899 and for *The Wind Among the Reeds* in the same year. Yeats wrote an essay on her work, 'A Symbolic Artist and the Coming of Symbolic Art,' in the *Dome*, December 1898, but never reprinted it. It was accompanied by reproductions of her drawings. He also wrote a short note on her verse in *A Treasury of Irish Poetry*, 1900.

TO LADY GREGORY

Tuesday   *203 Boulevard Raspail*
[*Feb.* 14. *Postmark Feb* 15, 1899]

My dear Lady Gregory: I shall return Thursday night unless some unexpected thing happens. Maud Gonne has been delayed in Paris for another week and I do not like to stay so long as I imagine Martyn is getting impatient. Things have not gone so well, not that anything very ill has happened, that I should want to linger on.

    I unfortunately left your article in London but I will send it to the *Express* as soon as I get back. I will also do my article immediately so as to keep things going. Everybody here has the influenza including myself. Yesterday a French writer, Davray, saw my face through the window of the café on the ground floor of the hotel where I stay and came in to see me. I asked him why he looked so depressed. He answered 'I have the influenza and I am divorcing my wife.' I do not wonder at the last. I remember telling you about her. He is the only French writer I have seen. I have seen Synge. He is really a most excellent man. He lives in a little room, which he has furnished himself. He is his own servant. He works very hard and is learning Breton. He will be a very useful scholar. I hear that there is an article, very friendly to me, about Irish literature in the *Débats*. It is by a French journalist who was at my second '98 dinner in London. I saw the *Express* with Synge and read Martyn's article—good enough in thought but curiously clumsy as writing. Much worse than his little Galway Feis article which was lifted by enthusiasm. Moore's preface [1] is translated in the February *Mercure de France* (translated by the unhappy Davray). Ireland must be growing famous in the Latin Quarter where Symons and Moore are almost the only English writers they know of. Meanwhile I still continue to get letters of the usual kind from Rolleston complaining of Moore. Rolleston, like his only teacher the *Spectator*, is always like an old lady with a lot of parcels in the middle of a crowded crossing. Yours ever   W B YEATS

---

    [1] The preface to Edward Martyn's volume of plays *The Heather Field and Maeve*, London, 1899.

TO GEORGE RUSSELL (AE)

Monday [*Postmark Mar 6, 1899*]　　　　　18 *Woburn Buildings*

My dear Russell, I congratulate you on the birth of your son of which I have heard from Lady Gregory. I think that a poet, or even a mystic, becomes a greater power from understanding all the great primary emotions and these one only gets out of going through the common experiences and duties of life.

I have just written an attack on Trinity College under the heading 'The Academic Class and the Agrarian Revolution.' It is apropos of Atkinson and I am sending it to Gill.[1] Moore is delighted with the bits I quoted. I dined with Lady Gregory last night. He was there, looking, as some friend of Miss Farr's said, like a 'boiled ghost.' He was most enthusiastic about your little sketch in chalk of Coole garden and asked me to tell you that he liked it. He does not think the figure subjects so good. He says however that you should exhibit your landscapes. He is quite the most exacting critic I know. He is also enthusiastic about your prose.

We have had to make a change in our plans about the theatre. We use professional actors altogether—except for some of my crowds—and have to rehearse this side of the water. I am therefore only going to Dublin with Miss Farr for a short time at the end of March to complete the arrangements in Dublin. We then return here and go over with our company a few days before the performances begin in Dublin.

Please remember me to Mrs. Russell. I have been long meaning to write to her and thank her for sending the cape. Yours
　　　　　　　　　　　　　　　　　　　　　　W B YEATS

TO EDWARD MARTYN[2]

March 22 [1899]　　　　　　　　　　18 *Woburn Buildings*

My dear Martyn: You are wrong about the facts to begin with.[3] Coffey told Gill that he supposed Dr. Molloy would omit what

---

[1] This article was published in the *Daily Express* (Dublin) on March 11.

[2] From a draft written by Yeats, in the possession of Mrs. Yeats.

[3] Accounts of Martyn's indecision about the orthodoxy of *The Countess Cathleen* and his frequent threats to withdraw his backing from the Irish Literary Theatre appear in George Moore's *Hail and Farewell: Ave*, and in Yeats's *Dramatis Personae*.

Coffey thought to be heterodox passages. Gill, whom I have just seen, heard Dr. Molloy and listened very carefully because of what Coffey had said and assures me that he omitted nothing from the pages selected for him.

Now I am ready to omit or change any passages which you may think objectionable. Taking into consideration the extreme difficulties in which your backing out at this stage will involve Lady Gregory, George Moore, Gill, the National Literary Society, yourself and myself, and the miserable scandal it will make, I think I have the right to ask you to do this. I am entirely convinced that the play contains no passages which can give offence to any Catholic. If you cannot and do not wish to point out these passages, remembering your guarantee and the scandal your withdrawal of it would make, the suspicion this would throw upon the literary movement in Ireland and even upon people like Horace Plunkett who have supported that movement, I am bound to ask you to take the only other course—to submit the matter to an arbitrator, Dr. Barry, Dr. Delaney, Dr. Vaughan, Father Finlay or any other competent and cultured theologian. I will take out or change any passage objected to by the arbitrator.

Of course I need not remind you that we have very little time to lose. Yours sincerely   W B YEATS

TO DR. WILLIAM BARRY [1]

March 24th [1899]   18 *Woburn Buildings*

Dear Dr. Barry: I don't know if you have heard of our project of a literary theatre in Dublin, at which two plays already published were to be performed—the *Heather Field* by Mr. Martyn and *The Countess Cathleen* by myself. I enclose the list of guarantors that you may see how much interest the project has awakened. It has now been suggested that there are some passages in the latter play which might be objected to by a Catholic audience as not being in harmony with Catholic theology. I do not myself see anything in the play that could give offence, but as the last thing I desire is to give legitimate offence to any of my countrymen I have proposed that your opinion

[1] From a draft written by Yeats, in the possession of Mrs. Yeats.

should be asked on the play, in case you would be kind enough to take the trouble of looking through it. The representation of the play has been fixed for the 8th of May and as it would be too late for us to find another to put in its place I have offered to alter or omit any passages that a theologian of so much literary culture as yourself may object to. It never occurred to me that a work of imagination could be expected to have a definite theological basis. One has of necessity to leave out, in a work of imagination, the reservations and saving clauses which one puts into a scientific treatise. I send you a copy of the book by this post and as we have so little time to lose I will ask leave to call on you on Monday to talk over the matter if you can spare me the time. I would not venture to ask this if it was a personal matter but the withdrawal of the play at this late moment would need public explanations that might cause a good deal of ill feeling.[1] Yours very sincerely

W B YEATS

TO LADY GREGORY

Sunday [April 9, 1899]   18 *Woburn Buildings*

My dear Lady Gregory: I got back last Friday after a very busy week in Dublin. The last time we saw Martyn and [he] was in excellent spirits but said that if any person 'in authority' was to speak he would withdraw again. Last night I saw Moore. He lamented his lost row. He had hoped to write an article called 'Edward Martyn and his soul.' He said 'It was the best opportunity I ever had. What a sensation it would have made. Nobody has ever written that way about his most intimate friend. What a chance! It would have been heard of everywhere.'

You will be interested to hear that Miss Gonne is probably coming with me to see Plunkett about a project to settle the evicted tenant question. Russell has been acting as an intermediary between

[1] In his reply to this letter, Father William Barry, the author of *The New Antigone* and several other novels, wrote: 'From the literal point of view theologians, Catholic or other, could object that no one is free to sell his soul in order to buy bread for the starving, but Saint Paul says: "I wish to be anathema for my people," which is another way for expressing what you have put into the story. I would give the play and the explanation afterwards.'

them. The scheme is his. To-night she and Russell have another talk and then she sees Gill. She is anxious to prevent the MPs exploiting the tenants for the benefit of the parliamentary fund. The thing is private as yet.

Mrs. Emery asks me to ask you to suggest to Edward Martyn that he give me my expenses. She said something about it, and he said 'pay anything of that kind you think fit' or some such phrase. She however does not like to do so from her own initiative.

I think our plays will do well for they have undoubtedly roused a great deal of interest in Dublin. The *Express* interview was almost wholly with me. Mrs. Emery gave a few biographical facts and then handed the reporter over to me. The *Independent* one was almost equally with her, Martyn and myself. Yours ever   W B YEATS

TO LADY GREGORY

April 27 [*Postmark Ap* 29, 1899]   18 *Woburn Buildings*

My dear Lady Gregory: I send you O'Donnell's latest. I hardly think it will do us much harm. Everybody tells us we are going to have good audiences. My play too is acting wonderfully well. Several people have said that it acts better, instead of worse, than it reads. The actors all pretty good. The first demon is a little over violent and restless but he will improve.

Lionel Johnson has done a prologue which I enclose. Who do you think can be got to read it? Martyn wants Lecky and thinks he might do it for you, but I expect he is too timid. Of course we could get an actress to speak it but some person of note would be best, I suppose. What do you think? [1]

I cross over—with Mrs. Emery—on Wednesday night. The rest come over the next [day] after a last rehearsal of *The Heather Field* in London.

I have been commissioned to do an article—5000 words or so—on The Intellectual Movement in Ireland for the *North American Review* and I am to get £30 for it. This will be my first work when

[1] Lionel Johnson's prologue for the opening performance of the Irish Literary Theatre on May 8 was printed in the first number of *Beltaine*, a little magazine which served also as a programme. The prologue was eventually spoken by Florence Farr's niece, Dorothy Paget.

I get out of the hurry scurry of daily rehearsal. When do you get to Dublin and where do you stay? Yours ever W B YEATS

TO THE EDITOR OF THE *MORNING LEADER*

[*Published May* 13, 1899]

Cardinal Logue has condemned *The Countess Cathleen* without having read it, and with a singular naiveté has said in his very letter of condemnation that he has not read it. His reckless indignation is a part of that carelessness and indifference which the older generation in Ireland has too often shown in the discussion of intellectual issues. He represents in no way the opinion of the younger and more intellectual Catholics, who have read his letter with astonishment.

The charges which seem to have moved the Cardinal are that the writer has blasphemed because he has made devils and lost souls blaspheme, and that he has slandered Ireland because he has made certain peasants sell their souls to the Devil for money and made two peasants thieves and a peasant woman an adultress. 'Mr. Yeats has made two of his peasants thieves—is this Celtic? He has made a peasant woman false to her husband—is this Celtic?' asks a pamphlet which has been sent all over Ireland. The first argument would prove that *Paradise Lost* and *Faust* and the Book of Job are blasphemous, and the second argument is irrelevant even if it were not absurd.

The play is symbolic: the two demons who go hither and thither buying souls are the world, and their gold is the pride of the eye. The Countess herself is a soul which is always, in all laborious and self-denying persons, selling itself into captivity and unrest that it may redeem 'God's children,' and finding the peace it has not sought because all high motives are of the substance of peace. The symbols have other meanings, but they have this principal meaning.

The Countess Cathleen is a spiritual drama, and the blind bigots of journalism, who have made no protest against the musical burlesques full of immoral suggestion which have of late possessed the Dublin theatres, have called it a blasphemy and a slander. These attacks are welcome, for there is no discussion so fruitful as the discussion of intellectual things, and no discussion so needed in Ireland. The applause in the theatre has shown what party has the victory.

W B YEATS

TO CLEMENT SHORTER[1]

May 27 [in pencil 1899]   *Coole Park*

My dear Shorter: You were so good as to offer to advise me about my next agreement with a publisher. The other day I was looking over some old papers and found to my surprise that my agreement with Unwin for my collected volume of poems, of which a new edition has just been published, lapses in October of this year. I thought it did not lapse for two years yet. I wrote to Unwin giving notice that I should ask for a better royalty and a different agreement. I enclose his answer which is all right so far as it goes. I want you to suggest what I should ask. The book is published at 7/6 nett and I get at present $12\frac{1}{2}$ per cent on the published price in England which is I should think too small on a nett book; and half the proceeds of sale of 'advance rights' etc to America. I don't want you to take much trouble but I want you to advise me as to what would be a fair royalty. As Unwin has just published a new edition I cannot very well take it out of his hands.

As a result of the success of 'The Irish Literary Theatre' I have a chance of getting *The Shadowy Waters* done in London in autumn and am therefore setting to work to finish it. I told you about it I think. It is rather a wild little play about the length of *The Land of Heart's Desire*, which acted rather less than 25 minutes, and probably the best verse I have written. Do you think a play of this length is too long for a magazine, American or English? I should want to get it published before it was acted if possible.

I am afraid I am asking you a number of troublesome things.

Tell Mrs. Shorter that I think one result of 'The Irish Literary Theatre' is that we are going to get considerable influence in Trinity

[1] Clement Shorter (1857–1926) began life as a civil servant but soon turned to journalism and became editor of the *Illustrated London News* and the *Sketch*. He married Dora Sigerson, daughter of George Sigerson (see note 2 on p. 42). In 1916 and 1918 he printed privately small limited editions of Yeats's *Easter 1916* and *Nine Poems*.

College—a thing most of us had despaired of. Tyrrell has declared himself converted to our movement. I go up to Dublin next Wednesday—at least I have been asked and think I will go—to preside at a debate on 'The Irish Literary Theatre' at the College Historical Society.

I see that Mrs. Shorter's book is out but I have not yet seen it.

We are thinking out a plan for publishing translations of stories by O'Grady, Fiona Macleod and the rest of us in Gaelic at a very low price for the use of the peasantry. Yours sincerely   W B YEATS

TO MRS. CLEMENT SHORTER (DORA SIGERSON)

June 21 [*in pencil* 1899]   *Coole Park*

My dear Mrs. Shorter: I have been a long time about writing to thank you for your book,[1] but a rheumatic attack is in part to blame. I like best among the ballads I think 'The White Witch,' 'The Banshee,' and 'The Wind on the Hills'. They have most, as I think, of the atmosphere of Ireland, and are least in the general old ballad manner and most in the Irish ballad manner; and are therefore the more original. 'The White Witch' is the most perfect; really concentrated very Irish stories with nothing to amend; but 'The Banshee' is nearly as fine. There is one line however that you should mend—the line 'Half maddened by her kiss.' Both Lady Gregory, who knows the people well, and myself felt at once that this was wrong. It is in the wrong key. It has association from a different world. 'Enchanted' yes, 'half maddened' no. I cannot analyse my instinct about it, but I know it is wrong, and wrong enough to spoil the poem. Perhaps its association with novels and poems about a different world is a chief part of its wrongness.

I think you should work on these concentrated little ballads in this metre. You have a most real gift for them. 'The White Witch,' and 'The Banshee' and 'I have been to Hy Brasail' are all perfectly in the atmosphere of Irish Folk Lore. I do not think 'The Fairies' is quite as true. I myself try to avoid the word 'fairy' because it has associations of prettiness. *Sidhe* or 'gentry' or 'the others' is better. The Irish peasant never thinks of the fairies as pretty. He thinks of them as terrible, or beautiful, or as just like mortals. A line like 'The

[1] *Ballads and Poems*, London, Bowden, 1899.

fairies, the fairies, the mischief loving fairies' suggests prettiness at once. Nor would an Irish peasant 'love' the fairies. She would fear them or honour them but not 'love' them.

I like 'Ireland' best among the lyrics. 'A brown tumult of wings' is a most beautiful line. I do not quite understand the grammatical structure of the first stanza, but if you could clear this up it would be a really lovely little song.

'False Deirbhorgil' is the best of the longer ballads. I do not like 'the lash of tempest.' The phrase is too modern and is a little conventional. The *caesura* is wrong on line 5 of page 45. The word 'come' is too strong a syllable. It takes the accent and so moves the *caesura* too far forward. 'Upon' instead of 'come on' would be all right. I don't like the row of dots you put at the end of the first verse. They are a bad modern device and quite needless. I think a kind of half ballad, half lyric, is your best manner, though I may only like this best because I think it is the kind of poem I like myself —a ballad that gradually lifts, as 'The Wind on the Hills' lifts, from circumstantial to purely lyrical writing. If you work on you are quite sure to do finer and finer work just because you write in such a simple and circumstantial way. You build up from the ground instead of starting like most writers of verse with an insincere literary language which they can apply to anything. Try however, I think, to build about a lyric emotion. I only learnt that slowly and used to be content to tell stories. 'The Little Brother' lacks I think its lyrical emotion, and remains a mere painful little story. One must always have lyric emotion or some revelation of beauty.

I am working at my *Shadowy Waters* and it is getting on far better than when I left it aside a couple of years ago. Since then I have worked at Irish mythology and filled a great many pages of notes with a certain arrangement of it for my own purposes; and now I find I have a rich background for whatever I want to do and endless symbols to my hands. I am trying to get into this play a kind of grave ecstasy.

Please thank Mr. Shorter for all his kindness about my poems. Dr. Nicoll will have told him that we are in correspondence about my book.[1] Yours sincerely W B YEATS

[1] William Robertson Nicoll (1851–1923), a Free Church minister, was editor of the *British Weekly*, the *Bookman* and other periodicals, and also literary adviser to the firm of Hodder & Stoughton which published Yeats's play *The Shadowy Waters* in December 1900.

You must not mind my having found so many little faults but I always myself think criticism is helpful just in so far as it is minute and technical. I have marked some other things which we can discuss when I see you.

TO LILY YEATS

July 12 [*Postmark* 1899]   *Coole Park*

My dear Lilly: I should have written long ago; but have really been very busy. Most times it is procrastination, but this time it has been regular hours which seem to have left me no time for anything. No, I have nothing to do with that Polytechnic so please tell Susan Mitchell. I have a namesake who gets married and votes and does all kinds of embarrassing things. I forget how many letters of congratulation I had when the unnecessary man got married.

I am not now at Coole Park but shall be there again after a couple of days. Lady Gregory and her niece and myself are in a little shooting lodge in the hills. It is on a hill surrounded on every side by a great wood full of deer. Deer heads look down at me from the walls while I write and there is a gentle hum, from where a swarm of wild bees have made a nest in the wainscot under one of the windows. They come in and out through the open window and being wild bees are gentle and do not sting anybody. They are not used enough to people to be afraid and angry. There is a faint smell of their honey everywhere.

The Shadowy Waters is not finished, but is going on well. I am very impecunious but fortunately it does not matter just now. The *Fortnightly* and the *Contemporary* which have had articles of mine for months still do not publish them. I have just sent off an article to the *North American Review* for which I am to get £30 some day; it is on the intellectual movement in Ireland; and I am making notes for an article on the philosophical ideas in Shelley's poetry. I have made up my mind to review no more books because, though it brings in money more quickly, it gets me into all kinds of difficulties and quarrels and wastes my time.

Remember me to Uncle George. Yours sincerely
                                                               W B YEATS

TO GEORGE RUSSELL (AE)

August 27 [Possibly 1899]   *Coole Park*

My dear Russell: When you write to me about the symbol please tell me the figures you saw as well as the conclusions you come to. I saw the white door to-day and the white fool; he was followed out of the door by a marriage procession who had flowers and green boughs. Last night I had a dream of two lovers, who were being watched over by a blackbird, or raven, who warned them against the malice and the slander of the world. Was this bird a transformation of Aengus or one of his birds?

You are perhaps right about the symbol, it may be merely a symbol of ideal human marriage. The slight separation of the sun and moon permits the polarity which we call sex, while it allows of the creation of an emotional unity, represented by the oval and the light it contains. I am very curious to see your symbol. I may be getting the whole story of the relation of man and woman in symbol—all that makes the subject of *The Shadowy Waters*. If you can call up the white fool and have the time I wish you could make a sketch of him, for Dalua seems to be becoming important among us. Aengus is the most curious of all the gods. He seems both Hermes and Dionysus. He has some part perhaps in all enthusiasm. I think his white fool is going to give me a couple of lines in *The Shadowy Waters*.[1]

I am more inclined to interpret Mrs. O'Grady's 'false virgin' as a metaphor for nature, for the external, fixed, opaque world, for what Blake calls *Vala* and which he identifies with the Virgin Mary in one of her aspects. Blake calls her both sin and 'the law'—I found once some traditional authority for this idea. Christ himself must himself have been one of the followers of Aengus. Has not somebody identified him with Hermes?

---

[1] The first published version of *The Shadowy Waters* (1900) opens with the lines

> 'His face has never gladdened since he came
> Out of that island where the fool of the wood
> Played on his harp.'

Yeats evidently refers to AE in his essay 'The Queen and the Fool' in the enlarged edition of *The Celtic Twilight*, 1902: 'a truly great seer who saw a white fool in a visionary garden.'

I have been trying to see things in your way in the woods and with some success. I think I shall go on trying. Yours ever

W B YEATS

You are very much missed here by everybody. Everybody is singing your praises.

TO W. T. HORTON[1]

Sept. 3rd, 1899   *Coole Park*

My dear Horton, I have been a long time without writing to thank you for your Poe.[2] I like the Raven on the head of Pallas about best. I like next the drawing on page 18—a really admirable grotesque. I do not know why you or indeed anybody should want to illustrate Poe however. His fame always puzzles me. I have to acknowledge that even after one allows for the difficulties of a critic who speaks a foreign language, a writer who has had so much influence on Baudelaire and Villiers de L'Isle Adam has some great merit. I admire a few lyrics of his extremely and a few pages of his prose, chiefly in his critical essays, which are sometimes profound. The rest of him seems to me vulgar and commonplace and the Pit and the Pendulum and the Raven do not seem to me to have permanent literary value of any kind. Analyse the Raven and you find that its subject is a commonplace and its execution a rhythmical trick. Its rhythm never lives for a moment, never once moves with an emotional life. The whole thing seems to me insincere and vulgar. Analyse the Pit and the Pendulum and you find an appeal to the nerves by tawdry physical affrightments, at least so it seems to me who am yet puzzled at the fame of such things. No, your book is the *Pilgrim's Progress*. You could do that in a fine ancient spirit, full of a sincere naivety.

The night you saw me I was conscious of seeing you but I had been trying to get away on a different business for a week and one's spirit goes to many places one knows nothing of. Your inner life

[1] From a typewritten copy.
[2] *The Raven* and *The Pit and the Pendulum*. By E. A. Poe. Edition de luxe with Seven Fine Chalk Drawings by W. T. Horton reproduced in Photogravure by Lemercier & Co. of Paris. London: Leonard Smithers, 1899.

may however have merely projected before you some image of me, raked up out of your memory, for some purpose of its own, some message but half remembered perhaps on waking, of which my image seemed a fitting signature. Yours ever   W B YEATS

I shall be in Ireland until late autumn.

TO LILY YEATS

Nov 1 [Postmark 1899]   *Coole Park*

My dear Lilly: No, I had not seen any of the papers you sent and I was very glad to get them. Also I have looked in the glass and my eyes have not grown blue. That was a false dream. Cast it out—and go on sending the papers, any papers except the *Spectator* which I see and detest.

I have been at Tillyra, where Moore has been staying and have started a play with him for the Irish Literary Theatre on Dermot and Grania.[1] We have made the first draft and have got, as I think, a very powerful plot and arrangement of scenes. It will be a wonderful part for a great actress if she can be found. Moore is in boundless enthusiasm. The play will be in prose. We made the first draft while I was at Tillyra—the 'scenario,' that is a very full and rather lengthy account of all the scenes written like a story—and Moore is now writing the play out fully. He will then give it to me and I will go over it all putting it into my own language so as to keep the same key throughout and making any other changes I think fit and send it back to Moore. The passage in Rolleston's letter to the *Echo*, which was marked, does mean 'a wobble' of course. He grows more and more a country clergyman's daughter's dream of a perfect gentleman every day. He is the flawless blossom of Irish gentility.

I was going on to George from Tillyra when I heard that the October-November stars had laid him out. He is getting better now

[1] The earliest mention of *Diarmuid and Grania*, the play which Yeats and George Moore collaborated in writing for the third and final year of the Irish Literary Theatre. A text of the play, which remained unpublished for many years, was edited by William Becker and printed in the *Dublin Magazine*, April–June 1951. It is evident from this letter that the scenario was not written, as Becker supposed, by Lady Gregory but by the collaborators themselves. Lady Gregory, however, wrote the story of the play for publication in *Samhain*, 1901.

and must rejoice as an astrologer as much as he sorrows as a man. I may go on to him in a couple of weeks but am more likely to go to London. You must be much cheered by the war news to-day. The spectacle of John Bull amassing 70 or 100 thousand men to fight 20 thousand and slapping his chest the while and calling on the heavens to witness his heroism has not been exhilarating. Ireland seems to be really excited and I am not at all sure that Maud Gonne may not be able to seriously check enlisting. She is working with extraordinary energy. Yours affectionately   W B YEATS

TO GEORGE RUSSELL (AE)

Nov [1899]   *Coole Park*

My dear Russell . . . I think you are wrong about *The Shadowy Waters*. The picture was more impressive in its old form and I regret the loss of the Fomor, but the poetry is richer and more various in the new and it is getting written more easily. The new form will act much better. Moore does not much like my idea of the proper way of speaking verse; but he is wrong. I want to do a little play which can be acted and half chanted and so help the return of bigger poetical plays to the stage. This is really a magical revolution, for the magical word is the chanted word. The new *Shadowy Waters* could be acted on two big tables in a drawing room; not that this will please you who don't much like acting at all I think. Moore told me he was going to tell you about *The Tale of a Town*—a great secret—and our changes in it.[1] Moore has written a tremendous scene in the third act and I have worked at it here and there throughout. If Martyn will only consent, it will make an immense sensation and our theatre a national power.

Did Moore show you the scenario of *Grania* for our third year, or tell you of the proposed one act play on 'The Play-hunters?'[2]

I am very sorry you are not coming here and I have plenty to talk

[1] *The Tale of a Town* by Edward Martyn had been proposed for production by the Irish Literary Theatre in its second year. Both Yeats and George Moore considered it hopelessly undramatic and it was rewritten by Moore, with some help from Yeats, and produced as *The Bending of the Bough* at the Gaiety Theatre, Dublin, on February 19, 1900, Moore's name appearing alone as author.

[2] This probably refers to *The Place-hunters*, a political comedy in one act by Edward Martyn. It was published in the *Leader*, July 26, 1902.

over. If you come into the neighbourhood by a change of plan Lady Gregory asks me to say this. I am glad to hear about the evicted tenants. Yours ever W B YEATS

TO THE EDITOR OF THE *GAEL* (NEW YORK)

[Published December 1899] *[Coole Park]*

A thousand thanks for the article in the *Gael*.[1] I am all the better pleased because many people whom I respect do not recognize that I have always written as an Irish writer and with Ireland in my mind. I have taken up Gaelic again, and though I shall never have entire mastery of it, I hope to be able to get some of the feeling of the language . . . I shall stay on in Ireland until I have finished a longish poem . . . I shall be in Dublin in February for the performance of the Irish Literary Theatre. W B YEATS

TO LADY GREGORY

Monday [Postmark Nov 20, 1899] 18 *Woburn Buildings*

My dear Lady Gregory: I stayed two days in Dublin and crossed over on Friday night. I have seen nobody as yet except Symons, Althea Gyles and my people. Yesterday morning Althea Gyles appeared. The brokers were going to be put in at her rooms on Monday and she arrived with a bundle of books, which she wanted to put in safety. She took the brokers quite cheerfully and seemed to rather enjoy the sensation. She has been tried in her absence and ordered to pay the whole sum, instead of instalments, owing to the fact that she had forgotten all about it and about the trial.

The editor of the *Dome*,[2] who is as you know a nonconformist

---

[1] The article to which Yeats refers was written by Stephen MacKenna and was published in the August issue. This letter was evidently written soon afterwards, while Yeats was still at Coole.

[2] The *Dome* appeared first as a quarterly magazine from March 1897 to May 1898 and afterwards monthly from October 1898 to July 1900. It was edited by E. J. Oldmeadow, who was also managing director of the Unicorn Press. He was a novelist and a writer on music, and in later life, having become a Roman Catholic, he edited the *Tablet*.

minister, is at once embarrassed and flattered by a very mad young person, who has written him a series of love letters beginning 'adored Arthur' under the belief that he is Symons disguised. He has met her once or twice in the park to do her good and remonstrate and try and convince her that he is not Symons. She was not convinced however until the real Symons went. He did not like her a bit. She thought that the whole *Dome* was written by Symons under various names. I saw Gill in Dublin. The *Express* is still waiting a purchaser. Dalziel has made a bid and they are now waiting to see if anybody will make a better. Gill says he has no responsibility for the paper at present.

I saw Russell in Dublin. He has abandoned all his faith in Mrs. Tingley, who has done some outrageous things, and he is accordingly going to start his own little mystical group. He asked for one of my pastels and I said he might have whichever he liked and to my surprise he picked the one we both thought a failure. He said it was the most original. Miss Gonne was full of her enlistment crusade. She came over with me but went on to Paris at once. I think this is about all my news and I have not put it well because I am at Bedford Park and trying to talk to my sisters while I write. My father likes the pastels and thinks the wood and the sunset the best. Yours always   W B YEATS

Get last Saturday's *Irish People* and read a letter of Russell's—a very fine impassioned letter. O'Brien is quite civil.

TO LADY GREGORY

Tuesday Nov. 28 [*Postmark* 1899]   18 *Woburn Buildings*

My dear Lady Gregory: Moore has really very much improved the play. He has now rewritten again the third and fourth act[s] and has almost abolished Foley. He no longer comes into the third act at all. I am sure he has done everything with a bad grace, but he has really made a new thing of the play even since you saw it. There was no use keeping fragments of Martyn's work merely because they were his. Of course one cannot help being sorry for Martyn and I wish very much you could get him to agree to put his name together with Moore's to the play. I have already urged this on Moore, who makes the lame excuse that it would make the play too important. The fact is that both he and Martyn are very cross with each other. I think Moore will not really however object to sign with Martyn. It is foolish of Martyn to call the play 'ugly,' for ugly as it is from my point of view and yours, it is beauty itself beside what it was; and as for 'commonness' in the writing, neither of them know what style is, but Moore can at least be coherent and sensible.

Moore asked me to go there to-night to meet Ben Webster 'to decide on a final text' but I had promised to dine with Mrs. Kate Lee the singer. I need hardly say that I am sorry for Edward, but whatever may be said of the personal rights and wrongs, the artistic rights are with Moore. I wish it was the other way.

A very unpleasant thing has happened but it is so notorious that there is no use in hiding it. Althea Gyles, after despising Symons and Moore for years because of their morals, has ostentatiously taken up with Smithers, a person of so immoral a life that people like Symons and Moore despise him. She gave an at home the other day and poured out tea with his arm round her waist and even kissed him at intervals. I told her that she might come to my 'at homes' as much as she liked but that I absolutely forbade her to bring Smithers (who lives by publishing books which cannot be openly published for fear of the law). Last night she came, and afterwards Smithers, and now I am writing to repeat more emphatically my refusal to have Smithers come. This may, and probably will, make her quarrel with me, for which I shall be sorry as I imagine I am about the only person who belongs to the orderly world she is likely to meet from this out. She seems to be perfectly mad, but is doing beautiful work. I did my best last week to make her see the necessity for some kind of disguise, but it seems to be a point of pride with her to observe none. It is all made the more amazing because she knows all about Smithers's past. She is in love, and because she has some genius to make her thirst for realities and not enough of intellect to see the temporal use of unreal things she is throwing off every remnant of respectability with an almost religious enthusiasm. Certainly the spirit 'blows where it listeth,' and the best one can give its victims is charity. Yours always W B YEATS

P.S. I have not yet sent those pictures to be framed. A great many thanks for what you say about them and also for that parcel.

P.S.2. Wednesday. I saw Moore last night after all. He wrote while I was there to suggest to Martyn that they should both sign the play. I saw the letter and it was everything that could be desired. There is almost nothing left of Martyn in the play except the foundation of plot—dialogue and characterizations are now all new. Moore sent Martyn Ben Webster's letters. Ben Webster says the play is now quite right. He has accepted the part of the hero and a very excellent actor called Fulton has agreed to play Kerwin. Moore is very emphatic about Martyn being given no further advice as he is so afraid of what he may do but you will of course use your own discretion about this. He says that Martyn has left the matter now in his hands and the thing to do is to push on our arrangement. He denies ever having threatened to stop the performances. He says he merely said that the committee would not he was sure agree to substitute a play of Ibsen's for *The Tale of a Town*. I found him very irritated with Martyn but I think I moderated him. He says his brother calls Martyn 'an old woman who ought to be given a parrot in a cage.'

TO LADY GREGORY

Thursday [December 21, 1899]   18 *Woburn Buildings*

My dear Lady Gregory: I have been long about writing but I have had a rather distracting time with one thing and another and have been trying to get my poem finished for next Saturday and will almost succeed. I am about twenty or thirty lines from the end. The thing grows wilder and finer as it goes on I think. I have thought out the staging carefully and will get a strange grey dreamlike effect.

Friday

I was interrupted yesterday. This morning some port wine came for which I know I have to thank you. Nothing could be more welcome. It is one in the morning and I am not sleepy and have lit my fire and shall have some with hot water to make me sleepy. A great many thanks. I have not yet read the Raftery with enough of thought to make my criticism; but I see it is full of beautiful things. I will take it to Bedford Park, when I go on Sunday until after Friday as I rather think Mrs. Old wants a. holiday. I shall be less disturbed now for I have just got to the end of *The Shadowy Waters* and two days' revision here and there will leave it ready for the *North American Review*. To-morrow evening I read it to Moore and Gosse and Barry (the novelist). The *North American Review* for December has got my article—I think it reads well.

I am afraid it will be some time before Althea Gyles does that bookplate. I have heard or seen nothing of her since I wrote her that letter, and expect, or rather Symons suspects, that Smithers has forbid[den] her to come near me. In which case I shall hardly see her until Smithers is a lost illusion. I wish I could have postponed the quarrel until the plate was done but it was not possible, for I could not have permitted my guests to meet Smithers, who would have come drunk as likely as not. Althea Gyles hardly means a final quarrel as she has left a number of her books with me including some in a loose brown paper which she asked me not to look at— I conclude they have affectionate inscriptions. I keep all these to evade the bailiffs but refused some improper Japanese ivories which are probably loans from the admirable Smithers.

Moore has worked a lot on *The Tale of a Town*; and I have a little, since you saw it, and it is now extraordinarily fine and he has done a fine preface too. It is now a splendid and intricate gospel of nationality and may be almost epoch-making in Ireland. A chief part of what I have done in it is that I have rewritten Dean's speech in the first act. My anxiety at the moment is how to get at the Dublin press as I shall not be there some weeks beforehand as I was last year; and I am afraid Martyn has been abusing Moore's play to people there. Mrs. Coffey told Mrs. Emery a week ago 'that Martyn said it was not good and she thought he might be right, for "you see Moore can't construct."' She 'would feel more easy if Martyn's version had been taken' etc., or 'if it were by Martyn' or something to that effect. I am afraid of this depressing her energy and others through her, and it shows me that we must not ask Martyn to work up the press.

The other things have come from the stores and I thank you a thousand times. Yours ever   **W B YEATS**

TO THE EDITOR OF THE *UNITED IRISHMAN*

[Published January 20, 1900]

Dear Sir, I am told that Mr. Redmond has now sufficient money to make the final arrangements for the statue of Mr. Parnell. I hope I am not too late in pointing out that the disgraceful statues erected to the memory of distinguished Irishmen in recent years show that the usual Dublin method for choosing a sculptor must be changed. I remember reading some months ago that the Lord Mayor of Dublin was visiting the studios of sculptors in America that he might choose one. I hope this is not true, for it is obvious that the matter should be in the hands of an expert Committee. I have no doubt that Sir Walter Armstrong, the Director of our National Gallery, would not only serve on such a Committee but would give advice about its constitution. The Committee might be asked to choose three or four Sculptors among whom Mr. Redmond and his committee could pick out a man to their mind should they not care to leave the matter wholly to the experts. The man once found, he might be asked to submit designs, though he would probably do better if he did not. Experience has shown that this method, which has been adopted in India lately, produces better work than any competition of designs; for few men do their best when their getting work at all is dependent on their pleasing anybody but themselves. The good sculptor, poet, painter or musician pleases other men in the long run because he has first pleased himself, the only person whose taste he really understands. Work done to please others is conventional or flashy and, as time passes, becomes a weariness or a disgust. Yours truly   W B YEATS

TO LADY GREGORY

Wednesday [January 31, 1900]   18 *Woburn Buildings*

My dear Lady Gregory: I will dine with you to-morrow (Thursday) as you suggest. I want the statement at the earliest possible moment. *Beltaine* [1] should be done to-morrow by rights but one thing or another has kept me back. Martyn has done an excellent article.

[1] *Beltaine* (The Irish Spring Festival) was an occasional publication, edited by Yeats, and was the organ of the Irish Literary Theatre. Three numbers were published in 1899 and 1900 after which it was succeeded by *Samhain* (The Irish Festival of Harvest).

I am sorry the Irish party has had the inconsiderateness to unite before *The Bending of the Bough* came out. The third act goes perfectly now and Martyn has had another row but I cannot judge of its intensity from Moore's vehement account. Moore promises to raise a certain amount of money if Martyn goes out, and I think I can count on Miss [*name obliterated*] (one must not of course mention her name in the matter) for more, but at any rate I shall do all I can to keep Martyn, but make plain that what is indispensible is the good work we may yet do and not the money which another may give as well as he, and that if he goes nothing is changed except that his place is empty. Yours ever W B YEATS

TO CLEMENT SHORTER

Wednesday [? Feb. 14, 1900]   18 *Woburn Buildings*

My dear Shorter: Most unhappily I will be in Ireland for The Irish Literary Theatre by Sunday. We cross on Saturday. I was very sorry not to have got to you that Sunday but I was quite incapable of moving with influenza—I disregarded it until Sunday but collapsed then. I am all right now.

I shall be glad when the theatre week is over—there is the usual promise of disturbance—this time over Moore's play which is quite falsely supposed to be satire on everybody and everything. Somebody is certain to find his face in the mirror and to try if he can break the glass. Yours sincerely W B YEATS

TO LADY GREGORY

Thursday [Postmark Mar 1, 1900]   18 *Woburn Buildings*

My dear Lady Gregory: The *Dome* people want to issue both numbers of *Beltaine* together in stiff boards, and they want an account of this year's plays such as you did of last year's to bind up with the numbers. Could you do this?[1] The extracts from the Dublin papers

[1] Eventually Yeats himself wrote an account of the performances of the Irish Literary Theatre in 1900, and this appeared as the third number of *Beltaine* in April.

and from the *Observer* and *Chronicle* and *The Times* perhaps would be what one wants. The little book should be useful to us in many ways.

I have got £6–6 from Elkin Mathews so I can last out till the American pays.

Poor Dowson is dead. Since that girl in the restaurant married the waiter he has drunk hard and so gradually sank into consumption. It is a most pitiful and strange story. Yours ever

W B YEATS

TO LADY GREGORY

Monday [*Postmark Mar* 12, 1900]   18 *Woburn Buildings*

My dear Lady Gregory: I have measured the breadth of the wire mattress part of the bed—it is 41½ inches.

I send all the cuttings about the theatre including some reviews not worthy of presentation [? preservation].

I saw Shaw to-day. He talks of a play on the contrast between Irish and English character which sounds amusing. He came to the 'Three Kings' on Saturday. I replied to a speech of his and pleased the Fellowship very much by proving that Shaw's point of view belonged to a bygone generation—to the scientific epoch—and was now 'reactionary.' He had never been called reactionary before. I think I beat him. He was not in very good form however.

I shall drop in to-morrow afternoon about tea time (five o'clock) on the chance of seeing you—Moore was round with a project yesterday—but don't stay in for me. I have a friend coming here in the evening. Yours   W B YEATS

Moore has sent a letter to all the Dublin papers about the Queen's visit which will amuse you.

TO THE EDITOR OF THE *FREEMAN'S JOURNAL*

[*Published March* 20, 1900]

Dear Sir, Let any Irishman, who believes the Queen's visit to Ireland to be non-political, buy the current number of *Punch*. He will there find a cartoon representing the Irish members gazing, in various attitudes of terror, at a proclamation announcing this visit, while a picture of President Kruger, who is made to look as much like a chimpanzee as possible, lies at their feet, having fallen from the shaking hands of one of them. The Irish members are made as hideous as President Kruger is made and the whole is inspired by national hatred. The advisers of the Queen have not sent into Ireland this woman of eighty-one, to whom all labours must be weariness, without good reason, and the reason is national hatred—hatred of our individual national life, and, as Mr. Moore has said, 'to do the work her recruiting-sergeants have failed to do,' 'with a shilling between her finger and thumb and a bag of shillings at her girdle'; and it is the duty of Irishmen, who believe that Ireland has an individual national life, to protest with as much courtesy as is compatible with vigour.

Mr. Moore has said that he leaves others to suggest a form of protest. I suggest a form. It has been announced that the Queen will leave Windsor for Ireland on April 2nd. That is a remarkable day, for on that day a hundred years ago the Act of Union, having been pushed through the Irish Parliament by bribery, was introduced into the English Parliament. 'The Articles of Union,' writes John Mitchel, 'were now brought forward as terms proposed by the Lords and Commons of Ireland in the form of resolutions; and on April 2, 1800, the Duke of Portland communicated to the House of Lords a message from the King, and at the same time presented to them, as documents, a copy of the Irish address with the resolution.'

I propose that a great meeting be summoned in the Rotunda on that date to protest against the Union and to dissociate Ireland from any welcome that the Unionist or the time-server may offer to the official head of that Empire in whose name liberty is being suppressed in South Africa, as it was suppressed in Ireland a hundred years ago. I propose that Mr. John O'Leary be the chairman, and that all Irish members be upon the platform. If the people are left to organise their own protest, as they did on Jubilee night, there will be broken glass and batoned crowds. The people will ask themselves, as they did on Jubilee night—'Is it worth troubling about leaders who are afraid to lead?' And let no Irishman suppose that this is not his business. Mr. Redmond, when he spoke in the House of Commons, spoke in the name of Ireland; and every Irishman who would not sell his country for an Imperialism that is but materialism, more painted and flaunting than of old, should speak his mind. Yours, etc.

W B YEATS

TO LADY GREGORY

March 29 [1900]   18 *Woburn Buildings*

My dear Lady Gregory: I sent you an *Express* with Martyn's letter about [*illegible*] and a letter from Trotter. The *Express* has had some letters since about it and the *Independent* has had a good deal of comment, including a leader in which they speak of its having made a sensation, or some such phrase. I have just heard that the Irish party has accepted a proposition of a meeting of protest against the Act of Union but whether they mean to make it in Dublin or at a mere meeting of the party, where it will be useless, I don't know. Maud Gonne is seriously ill with *enteritis* and will hardly be well in time to do anything with the crowds. O'Brien, as well as Dillon, has now stolen Moore's thunder, and made a speech about 'Chamberlain's recruiting sergeant,' and Moore's 'smart' friends are cutting him. He is in fine spirits as a result.

My essay on Symbolism [1] has grown to be a rather elaborate thing—about four times as long as I expected. It is in four parts of which I have one still to write. It is I think good. And I have just heard from Moore that Fitts is delighted with *Shadowy Waters*, but does not know when the war will let him publish it. That he likes it is really a relief as I was getting anxious—one never knows how people will take a half mystical poem.

Now that I have had to read Symons's book [2] very carefully I have found it curiously vague in its philosophy. He has not really thought about it and contradicts himself sometimes in the same sentence, but there is a great deal of really very fine criticism.

I must end this very scrappy note, and having some bovril out of one of the big bottles, get on with that essay. Yours ever

W B YEATS

[*On envelope*] Have finished essay since writing but have still to copy and revise.

[1] Yeats's essay 'The Symbolism of Poetry' was published in the *Dome*, April 1900, and reprinted in *Ideas of Good and Evil*, 1903.
[2] *The Symbolist Movement in Literature* by Arthur Symons, London: Heinemann, 1899, contained a long dedication to Yeats.

TO THE EDITOR OF THE *DAILY EXPRESS* (DUBLIN)

April 3rd, 1900   London

Sir, Whoever is urged to pay honour to Queen Victoria tomorrow morning should remember this sentence of Mirabeau's—'The silence of the people is the lesson of kings.' She is the official head and symbol of an empire that is robbing the South African Republics of their liberty, as it robbed Ireland of theirs. Whoever stands by the roadway cheering for Queen Victoria cheers for that Empire, dishonours Ireland, and condones a crime.

But whoever goes to-morrow night to the meeting of the people and protests within the law against the welcome that Unionists and time-servers will have given to this English Queen, honours Ireland and condemns a crime. Yours sincerely   W B YEATS

TO LADY GREGORY

Tuesday   18 *Woburn Buildings*
[*April* 10. *Postmark Apr* 12, 1900]

My dear Lady Gregory: I should have written before but I have been busy and not over well. I had an influenza cold last week, from which I was rescued by the champagne, only to find influenza change to indigestion. However I am well again. You will have seen about Lecky by that paper I sent you. I hear it is quite true but have hardly made up my mind to take the version of an *Express* press cutting having just reached me to write to the *Express* pointing out that it can't be true because he had nothing to resign as his guarantee had not been renewed. I think this will greatly irritate him and, may be, lead to a controversy about the Queen in the *Express* which would make both Moore and myself quite happy. I did another 'Queen letter,' by the by, which I will send you if I can find a copy and Moore is at the moment doing another. I wrote that resolution, which the Irish party proposed at their party meeting on April 2nd, and tried in vain to get Harrington to resign in favour of MacBride of the Irish Brigade.

Maud Gonne has just passed through London (I saw her yesterday) on her way to Dublin, where a number of her newspapers has been suppressed to her great joy, as it will give a lift to the circulation, and where, not at all to her joy, the editor has been imprisoned for a month for horsewhipping the editor of the *Dublin Figaro*, who wrote something against her, but what she does not know. The *Figaro* is a kind of society paper and very loyal as you may imagine. It thought Moore's play very unjust to that 'great country' England. I have had a long letter from Rolleston in which he speaks of the Queen's personal opinions on the evidence of what he calls 'circles to which I have access.' I met an Irish member the other day, who was quite seriously convinced that Rolleston had got a place. He even thought he knew what place it was and all about it.

I forgot to tell you that the big bottle of champagne blew up, and Mrs. Old, who was quite close to it at the time, said 'I could have better spared St. Pancras Church.' (She does not approve of the Church of England.)

My father has amazed us all by going to Paris to see the Louvre. He is there now staying in some hotel York Powell recommended. He has paid all his debts, and must feel very unlike his old self. I never knew him beforehand so anxious to see anything.

I don't think we need be anxious about next year's theatre. Moore talks confidently of finding the money, and I feel sure that our present politics will have done more good than harm. Clever Unionists will take us on our merits and the rest would never like us at any time. I have found a greatly increased friendliness on the part of some of the young men here. In a battle, like Ireland's, which is one of poverty against wealth, one must prove one's sincerity, by making oneself unpopular to wealth. One must accept the baptism of the gutter. Have not all teachers done the like?

Symons says that essay of mine is among the best things I have done. I will send it you when it comes out. Yours always

W B YEATS

TO LADY GREGORY

April 25th [*Postmark* 1900]   18 *Woburn Buildings*

My dear Lady Gregory ... I have had a bad time of it lately. I told you that I was putting MacGregor out of the Kabbala.[1] Well last

[1] The affairs of the Isis-Urania Temple of the Golden Dawn in London had reached a climax. Mathers, who had become increasingly autocratic, wrote to

week he sent a mad person—whom we had refused to initiate—to take possession of the rooms and papers of the Society. This person seized the rooms and on being ejected attempted to retake possession wearing a black mask and in full highland costume and with a gilt dagger by his side. Having failed in this he has taken out a summons on the ground that he is Mathers' 'envoy,' and that there is nothing in the constitution of the Society to enable us to depose Mathers. Charles Russell, the son of the Lord Chief Justice, is acting for us, and is trying to keep my name out of the business. The case comes on next Saturday and for a week I have been worried to death with meetings, law and watching to prevent a sudden attack on the rooms. For three nights I did not get more than $4\frac{1}{2}$ hours sleep any night. The trouble is that my Kabbalists are hopelessly unbusinesslike and thus minutes and the like are in complete confusion. I have had to take the whole responsibility for everything, to decide on every step. I am hopeful of the result. Fortunately the wretched envoy has any number of false names and has signed the summons in one of them. He is also wanted for debt and a trade union representative is to attend court on Saturday. The envoy is really one Crowley, a quite unspeakable person. He is I believe seeking vengeance for our refusal to initiate him. We did not admit him because we did not think a mystical society was intended to be a reformatory.

I arraigned Mathers on Saturday last before a chapter of the Order. I was carefully polite and I am particularly pleased at the fact that in our correspondence and meetings not one word has been written or said which forgot the past and the honour that one owes even to a fallen idol. Whatever happens the archives of the Society will have nothing unworthy to pass down to posterity. We have barbed our arrows with compliments and regrets and to do him justice he has done little less. The 'envoy' alone has been bitter and violent and absurd. Mathers like all despots must have a favourite and this is the lad.

Florence Farr accusing Dr. Wynn Westcott of having forged documents on which the Order had been founded. A Committee of members of the second order (R.R. & A.C.) consisting of Florence Farr, Yeats, Mrs. A. E. Hunter, P. W. Bullock and two others was formed to investigate these charges. This incensed Mathers, who then deputed Aleister Crowley, a member of the Ahathoor Temple in Paris, to take possession of the Society's premises and documents. On April 19 the Committee passed a resolution suspending Mathers and others from membership of the Second Order.

I sent you my last thing on the Queen.[1] Graves has resigned his secretaryship of the Irish Lit Society on the ostensible ground of health but really I am told because the fact that I have come out second on the list of those elected for the Committee—with the largest number of votes I have ever got—shows, he considers, that the Society is 'disloyal.' His brother Charles Graves has been bothering him. Yours ever   W B YEATS

TO LADY GREGORY

Saturday [*Postmark Apr* 28, 1900]   18 *Woburn Buildings*

My dear Lady Gregory: If Synge is in Paris, and is in his old rooms his address is

> John M Synge
> 90 Rue d'Assas
> Paris

If you see him please give him my apologies for not having written to him and say that I have meant to do so month by month. You might suggest too that he send some essay or the like to

> The Editor of the *Dome*
> Unicorn Press
> 7 Cecil Court
> St Martin's Lane

and say that I suggested it.

There is nothing at the Irish Lit on Saturday. Certainly I shall keep Thursday free. I shall be very glad when you are back.

I am expecting every moment a telegram to say how the case goes at the Courthouse. I have had to go through this worry for the sake of old friends, and perhaps above all for my uncle['s] sake. If I had not the whole system of teaching would have gone to wrack and this would have been a great grief to him and others, whose whole religious life depends on it. I do not think I shall have any more bother for we have got things into shape and got a proper executive now and even if we lose the case it will not cause any confusion

---

[1] Presumably a short article 'Noble and Ignoble Loyalties' which was published in the *United Irishman*, April 21.

though it will give one Crowley, a person of unspeakable life, the means to carry on a mystical society which will give him control of the conscience of many.

I hope to be deep in my novel by Monday. Yours always

W B YEATS

[*On back of envelope*] Just got telegram about law case. We have won. Other side fined £5.¹

TO LADY GREGORY

May 1*st* [*Postmark* 1900]   18 *Woburn Buildings*

My dear Lady Gregory: I shall be delighted to give you dinner on Thursday I need hardly say; and shall keep the other evening free. If you like we can drop in at the 'Three Kings' on Saturday evening for I ought to make a speech there, and Saturday afternoon might we not go to a matinée of *Richard II* which is on again (I am trying to pluck up my courage enough to get passes from Benson on the strength of the Irish Lit Theatre).

The Macmillans are wavering over the idea of making me a very good offer for all my books. I doubt if they will really come to the point, for they have asked to see *Shadowy Waters* and that they will dislike as their rather conventional adviser does not like my later work. He is a man of the Lockhart type—an objective person. Yours always

W B YEATS

TO GEORGE RUSSELL (AE)

[circa *May* 1900]   18 *Woburn Buildings*

My dear Russell, I do not agree with you about the ancient 'planets.' The word 'seven' throws the imaginative strength back to the time when the planets were gods. The planets of science are round

¹ The case did not actually come into court, Crowley's solicitor signing an undertaking by which the summons was withdrawn and £5 costs were to be paid within seven days. Yeats probably misunderstood a vaguely-worded telegram.

objects, flattened a little top and bottom and quite without feet. To write of a material object being 'fiery footed' is almost always to write from the phantasy rather than the imagination. The imaginative deals with spiritual things symbolized by natural things —with gods and not with matter. The phantasy has its place in poetry but it has a subordinate place.

Let 'Dana' go in by all means, though I am a little doubtful if it is quite desirable to speak of the form of a goddess as 'vague.' The conception seems a little modern. It seems an application to a form, of a word which gets its appropriateness, such as it is, from being used about a doctrine. It is not however incorrect. I think I would myself avoid it in poetry for the same reason that I would avoid 'haunted' and because vague forms, pictures, scenes etc. are rather a modern idea of the poetic and I would not want to call up a modern kind of picture. I avoid every kind of word that seems to me either 'poetical' or 'modern' and above all I avoid suggesting the ghostly (the vague) idea about a god, for it is a modern conception. All ancient vision was definite and precise. I admit however that I am not certain that I would have objected to the word if Rolleston had not drawn attention to it.

I do not understand what you mean when you distinguish between the word that gives your idea and the more beautiful word. Unless you merely mean that beauty of detail must be subordinate to general effect, it seems to me just as if one should say 'I don't mind whether my sonata is musical or not so long as it conveys my idea.' Beauty is the end and law of poetry. It exists to find the beauty in all things, philosophy, nature, passion,—in what you will, and in so far as it rejects beauty it destroys its own right to exist. If you want to give ideas for their own sake write prose. In verse they are subordinate to beauty which is their soul. Isn't this obvious?

Private. Our recent quarrel with MacGregor has been a small triumph for our clairvoyants and thaumaturgists. Once all legal and practical argument urged us to immediate action; and our clairvoyants held us back on the ground that if we waited he would 'do something so outrageous' that our waverers would waver no more but that if we didn't wait we would have disaster. We waited and he behaved in several amazing ways and sent over a certain unspeakable mad person to represent him. We found out that his unspeakable mad person had a victim, a lady who was his mistress and from whom he extorted large sums of money. Two or three of our thaumaturgists after, I think, consulting their master, called her up astrally, and told her to leave him. Two days ago (and about two days after the evocation) she came to one of our members (she did not know he was a member) and told a tale of perfectly mediaeval iniquity—of positive torture, and agreed to go to Scotland Yard and there have her evidence taken down. Our thaumaturgist had never seen her, nor had she any link with us of any kind. It and much else that has happened later is a clear proof of the value of systematic training even in these subtle things.

The unspeakable mad person is a much worse —— —— and has gone into this dispute with us in part because of our refusal to teach him and in part to earn knowledge from MacGregor. MacGregor apart from certain definite ill doings and absurdities, on which we had to act, has behaved with dignity and even courtesy. A fine nature gone to wrack. At last we have got a perfectly honest order, with no false mystery and no mystagogues of any kind. Everybody is working, as I have never seen them work, and we have fought out our fight without one discourteous phrase or irrelevant issue. Yours sincerely W B YEATS

TO LADY GREGORY

Saturday   18 *Woburn Buildings*
[*June* 2. *Postmark June* 5, 1900]

My dear Lady Gregory . . . I shall certainly not go to America with Moore. The reason you gave was quite final. Russell's reasons do not influence me. Russell has the defects of his qualities and where a moral dislike or disapproval of anybody comes in, his judgement ceases to be dispassionate. His letter irritated me a little. He has bemoralized me as long as I can remember, and nobody likes, or, as I agree with Goethe in thinking, is benefited by being bemoralized. The attitude of bemoralization is not the attitude of understanding. There is of course a good deal of truth in what he says about my indolence, there is also a characteristic exaggeration; and there was no truth at all about what he said to you some time ago about its being better for me morally to finish the novel or something of that kind. He himself has again and again begun things and never finished them, while I, since I was seventeen, have never begun a story or poem or essay of any kind that I have not finished.

He and I are the opposite of one another. I think I understand people easily and easily sympathize with all kinds of characters and easily forgive all kinds of defects and vices. I have the defect of this quality. Apart from opinions, which I judge too sternly, I scarcely judge people at all and am altogether too lax in my attitude towards conduct. He understands nobody but himself and so must always be either condemning or worshipping. He is a good judge of right and wrong so long as they can be judged apart from people, so long as they are merely actions to be weighed by the moral sense. He took the wrong side in the theosophical dispute some years ago because his hero-worship of Judge blinded him to Judge's actions, and when he speaks of any action connected with a man like either Moore or Symons he is liable to be equally wrong because of his condemnation of the man. His moral enthusiasm is with him an active inspiration but it makes him understand ideas and not human nature. One pays a price for everything.

I must end now or I shall miss the post. Yours always

W B YEATS

[*On back of envelope*] There is a deal about Raftery in the novel.

TO LADY GREGORY

Wednesday   18 *Woburn Buildings*
[*June 6. Postmark June 7, 1900*]

My dear Lady Gregory: No certainly I was not cross with you but I daresay I was a little cross with myself. I did not really know that I had left you longer than usual without a letter but I can certainly remember not writing once or twice because I wanted to wait till I had done some more work. I have not in my memory had such a number of little distractions. I have however done well what work I have done. The new bits of the novel are really good and for the first time it is real novel writing and not essay writing or lyrical prose or speculative thought merely. It is now characterization and conversation. I got *John Sherman*, I remember, written in much the same way, little bits at a time, only in *John Sherman* I started right. I have written out in prose the substance of some lyrics. But judged by bulk I have really done very little work.

I have found by the by the French source of the *Countess Cathleen* story. I send you the opening and end of the story as the French book gives it. The middle is the same as in my *Fairy and Folk Tales* except for the names. You will see he speaks of it as Irish. Please keep the extract for me, as I shall want to make a note for my next edition. I copied it at the British Museum.

I wish very much I was at Coole for I am tired of this noisy town, which grows more noisy every day. On all hands rejoicing of the most ecstatic kinds. It is hard enough to sympathize with other people's pleasures at the best of times but this kind of pleasure can only make one think of the country. Even the fact that MacGregor's masked man Crowley has been making wax images of us all, and putting pins in them, has not made life interesting. Yours always

W B YEATS

I have done nothing about Courtney since I sent the new essay[1] and that letter, which I did about eight days later than the time I wrote the letter—if I remember rightly. I don't think I can do more just now. If it is not in the July number I can attack again. I got a mere formal acknowledgement.

[*On envelope*] I have got Deeney's book to review for the *Speaker*. It is a good little book.[2]

TO LADY GREGORY

Wed [*Dec.* 12. *Postmark Dec* 13, 1900]   18 *Woburn Buildings*

My dear Lady Gregory... Yesterday I spent going through heaps of letters and arranging papers—play was finished Monday—and to-day I start essay, and, you will be sorry to hear, some slight

---

[1] 'Irish Witch Doctors,' published in the September *Fortnightly Review* of which W. L. Courtney was editor.
[2] *Peasant Lore from Gaelic Ireland* by Daniel Deeney, reviewed by Yeats in the *Speaker*, July 14.

revision of *Countess Cathleen*. To-night Russell,[1] Robert's Oxford friend, comes to see me and to-morrow afternoon Cyril French comes to talk over Althea Gyles's money affairs. She has made up her quarrel with me and I have been three times to see her. The first time she cried over Wilde's death. She said 'He was so kind, nobody ever lived who was so kind.' As she said it I thought of Homer's description of the captive women weeping in seeming for Patroclus yet each weeping for her own sorrow because he was ever kind. I told her you had thought of going to see her. She was evidently very pleased and said "That was very good of her, and I would have very much liked to have seen her'. . . . Yours always

W B YEATS

TO GEORGE MOORE[2]

[*? January* 1901]　　　　　　　　　　　18 *Woburn Buildings*

My dear Moore: You say both should make concessions. I think so too, but so far I have made them. I have recognized that you have a knowledge of the stage, a power of construction, a power of inventing a dramatic climax far beyond me, and I have given way again and again. I have continually given up motives and ideas that I preferred to yours, because I admitted your authority to be greater than mine. On the question of style however I will make no concessions. Here you need give way to me. Remember that our original compact was that the final words were to be mine. I would never have begun the play at all, but for this compact. It is no use going on with the work at all if we are not clear on this point. I send you what seems to me a sufficient version of Act 1. I will listen to any suggestions you make, or consider any emendations of language as I have always done, but the final version must be in my words or in such words of yours as I may accept. Remember that this is the original compact. If I hear that you have accepted this Act 1. I will go on to Act 2. It will be a pity if we fall out over a few phrases after so much planned work together.

[1] A. G. B. Russell, editor of *The Letters of William Blake*, London: Methuen, 1906. He is now Lancaster Herald.
[2] From an unfinished draft in the possession of Mrs. W. B. Yeats. This letter evidently refers to the play *Diarmuid and Grania* on which Yeats and Moore were at work.

There is only one alternative and this is the alternative I offered you weeks ago. I will accept any form of words of yours that Symons approves of. I have perfect trust in his judgement and so should you as you have got him to revise a novel. This was no part of our compact but it seems to me reasonable.

You will have been amused at Symons' marriage.[1] It explains his neglect of his [*word illegible*]

TO THE EDITOR OF THE *SATURDAY REVIEW*

[*Published March* 16, 1901]

Sir, Two or three weeks ago Mr. Runciman [2] said that I called a method of speaking verse, of which I approve, 'Cantilation.' Now that a morning paper has announced that an 'epidemic of Cantilation' has reached New York and that a New York clergyman has lectured about the 'glorious future' that lies before America in 'developing Cantilation,' you will perhaps permit me to say that Mr. Runciman invented the word. I never used it, and I don't mean to, and I don't like it, and I don't think it means anything. Yours sincerely

W B YEATS

TO CLEMENT SHORTER

Friday [? *March* 1901]　　　　　　　　18 *Woburn Buildings*

My dear Shorter: Moore has just embarrassed me very much. He asked me what I was doing Sunday evening. I said dining with you and he said 'Well I'll go with you. Ask Shorter if I may. I want to meet Mrs. Shorter before I go to Ireland.' He has taken a Dublin house as you know and goes there in a couple of weeks.[3] Now what am I to do? I am afraid you don't care about Moore but embarrassed as I am I shall be four times as embarrassed if I may not bring him. Send me a note tomorrow and tell me what to do. Yours

W B YEATS

[1] Arthur Symons married Rhoda Bowser on January 19, 1901.
[2] J. F. Runciman was at this time the music critic of the *Saturday Review*.
[3] George Moore moved into his house in Ely Place, Dublin, some time in April 1901.

TO LADY GREGORY

Thursday [*Postmark Apr* 25, 1901] *Shakespeare Hotel*
Stratford on Avon

My dear Lady Gregory... This is a beautiful place. I am working very hard, reading all the chief criticisms of the plays and I think my essay will be one of the best things I have done. The more I read the worse does the Shakespeare criticism become and Dowden is about the climax of it. I[t] came out [of] the middle class movement and I feel it my legitimate enemy.

The Benson company are playing wonderfully and really speaking their verse finely. Mrs. Benson was a really admirable 'Doll Tearsheet' last night in *Henry IV*. It is delightful seeing the plays in an atmosphere of enthusiasm and in this beautiful place. The theatre is a charming gothic red brick building in a garden with a river flowing by its walls. It is thronged every night—indeed they had to get me a kitchen chair to sit on the night I came. I see a good deal of the Company and would see more but that I am very busy. One young man keeps coming to me here to invite [me] up the river in a boat—but I am too busy. I am working in the library of the Shakespeare institute which is attached to the theatre and the librarian has given up to me his private room. But for a half hour or so for lunch I am here all day, from 10 to six when I dine and dress for the theatre. I feel that I am getting deeper into Shakespeare['s] mystery than ever before and shall be perfectly happy until I have to begin to write and that will be, as always, misery. The boy has just brought me in a translation of Gervinus' Commentaries and I must to work again. I do not even stop for afternoon tea. Yours

W B YEATS

TO LADY GREGORY

Tuesday [*Postmark May* 21, 1901] *c/o George Pollexfen*
Sligo

My dear Lady Gregory: I got here last night.

I had written this sentence when your letter came. I will send off the card. I was indeed this moment looking in vain for copies which I thought I had brought to shew you. The essay runs to two numbers [1] and has delighted Moore. I think I really tell for the first time the truth about the school of Shakespeare critics of whom Dowden is much the best.

Last Saturday and to my great surprise I met Bullen in Dublin. He has not as I had hoped handed my works over to Hodder and Stoughton—the negociation may however come off—and has been trying to sell copies in Dublin. He told me that he was amazed to find the hostility to me of the booksellers. ——, he declared, seemed to hardly like to speak my name. I am looked upon as heterodox it seems. *The Secret Rose* was strange to say particularly disapproved of, but they spoke with hostility of even *The Shadowy Waters*. Russell told me before I saw Bullen that clerical influence was he believed working against me because of my mysticism. He accuses Father Finlay and his Jesuits of working behind Moran. Memory of the *Countess Cathleen* dispute accounts for a good deal. Bullen found the Protestant booksellers little better and asked me if T.C.D. disliked me. Magee, the College publisher, said 'What is he doing here? Why doesn't he go away and leave us in peace?' He seems to have suspected me of some deep revolutionary designs. As Bullen was rather drunk when he told me these things, I asked his traveller, whom I saw on Monday, and got the same account. He has tried to sell a book of Carleton's too, and said that Carleton and myself were received with the same suspicion. This was of course because of his early stories.

I imagine that as I withdraw from politics my friends among the nationalists will grow less, at first at any rate, and my foes more numerous. What I hear from Bullen only confirms the idea that I had at the time of *The Countess Cathleen* row that it would make a very serious difference in my position outside the small cultured class. Which reminds me that I met Grace in Dublin. He had it seems written to me asking permission to play *The Countess Cathleen* at Burr wherever that is, but the letter had gone astray. It was very daring of him and I would rather like to have seen him try the experiment.

Beltaine ought to come out quite early this year—Moore and Oldmeadow both think it should. I am very much inclined to ask

---

[1] The essay 'At Stratford-on-Avon,' appeared in the *Speaker*, May 11 and 18, and was reprinted in *Ideas of Good and Evil*, 1903.

A. P. Watt[1] to try and arrange for it somewhere on a royalty basis. This partly for the pleasure of referring Oldmeadow to Watt—I have handed all my books to Watt except the book Unwin has. I think I should hand this over too although he can do nothing for me there at present, and will of course take ten per cent. It seems to me that it will be better worth his while to look after my affairs if he has all, and that I should be able to say 'He does everything' and so not have to make an invidious selection. What do you think? I feel I ought to hand it over before arranging about *Beltaine*. I have as you know given Watt complete discretion about the other books. *Beltaine* should be a Gaelic propaganda paper this time and might really sell very well.

I brought a man to Moore to propose a Gaelic dramatic touring company. Moore is excited about the scheme, and will try to get money for it. It was in part a scheme of poor Rooney's, whose death has plunged everybody into gloom.[2] Griffith has had to go to hospital for a week, so much did it affect him.

My uncle, who is High Sheriff this year, has had a hint from people here, that I must not go near the Constitutional Club, where I have no desire to go. This because of my letter about the late Queen. Between my politics and my mysticism I shall hardly have my head turned with popularity.

Moore dismissed his sixth cook the day I left—six in three weeks. One brought in a policeman, Moore made so much noise. Moore brought the policeman into the dining room and said 'Is there a law in this country to compel me to eat that abominable omelette?'
Yours always   W B YEATS

TO LADY GREGORY

Saturday [*Postmark May* 25, 1901]   *Thornhill*

My dear Lady Gregory: Yes, we should offer *Beltaine* to Dublin publishers, but insist on its being done as well as possible—I certainly

[1] A well-known literary agent who presently handled all Yeats's publishing arrangements.
[2] William Rooney (1873–1901) was chief assistant to Arthur Griffith on the *United Irishman*. He was considered another Thomas Davis and stood in relation to the Sinn Fein movement as Davis did to 'Young Ireland.' He died in his 28th year. His *Poems and Ballads* were published posthumously in 1902 and his *Prose Writings* in 1909. Yeats dedicated the first edition of *Cathleen ni Hoolihan* (1902) to his memory.

like the woodcut idea—and then if the publishers refuse send it to Watt and write a note in *Beltaine* on those publishers. I don't know which would do the most good, publication in Dublin or the note on publishers. I certainly agree to give profits to the Gaelic League. The only thing I really care about is the get up of the thing. I have always felt that my mission in Ireland is to serve taste rather than any definite propaganda.

It is of course possible that Bullen and his traveller may have had too great expectation of the success they would have with my books and so have exaggerated the significance of the opposition. —— was I understand especially emphatic. It is of course impossible to know to what extent the feeling against me is more than a vague distrust, a vague feeling that I am heterodox.

My father is delighted with my second article on Shakespeare. He has just written to say that it is 'the best article he ever read.' He has sent off four copies. The truth is that Dowden has always been one of his 'intimate enemies' and chiefly because of Dowden's Shakespeare opinions.

I am in a hurry to catch the post. Yours sincerely

W B YEATS

P.S. I fear I wrote in rather a depressed state of mind the other day, but the truth is I have been in rather low spirits about my Irish work lately and quite apart from anything Bullen said. I am in an ebb tide and must wait the flow.

TO ARTHUR GRIFFITH[1]

July 16 [1901]   *Coole Park*

My dear Griffith: My little play *The Land of Heart's Desire* has had so far as I can make out a great success in America. Lady Gregory a few days ago got the idea that you might perhaps write a paragraph on it if she sent you material. She has copied out as you will see by the enclosed a great many press notices, in which you may find

[1] Arthur Griffith (1872–1922) had, in his early days, some experience of journalism in Johannesburg. Returning to Ireland in 1899, he founded the weekly paper the *United Irishman* which he edited until 1906, after which date it became *Sinn Fein*. He was arrested in 1916 but was released with the other leaders, including Mr. De Valera, in June 1917. He was Vice-President of the Dail in 1918 and secured the Treaty of 1921. He died, probably from exhaustion, in 1922.

something to quote. She thinks it will help our Theatre as it will make people take me more seriously as a dramatist. However that may be, I would like some little record in some Irish paper and in your paper by preference. I always write for my own people though I am content perforce to let my work come to them slowly.

I am just starting a little play about Cuchullin and Concobar [1] partly I dare say encouraged by this American success. The seeming impossibility of getting my work sufficiently well performed to escape mere absurdity had rather discouraged me.

I thought your comment on Moore's letter entirely admirable. It was vigorous, just and courteous. I hear he has just finished his attack on Mahaffy which is certain to be amusing, and by no means courteous. I hope he does not make a martyr of Mahaffy though. Yours sincerely W B YEATS

TO ROBERT BRIDGES

July 20 [1901] *Coole Park*

My dear Mr. Bridges: Certainly Mrs. Waterhouse [2] may include 'The Lake Isle of Innisfree' and 'The Sorrow of Love' in her book. I confess I grow not a little jealous of 'The Lake Isle' which has put the noses of all my other children out of joint; and I am not very proud of 'The Sorrow of Love'—I wonder does she know my book *The Wind Among the Reeds*—but as she will.

I shall be away all summer for I shall not leave Ireland until after the performances by 'The Irish Literary Theatre' which begin on Oct 21. I shall hardly be back until early November. Might I not run down to you for a winter day or two? The country is always beautiful whatever the season.

I take up your letter again and notice to my distress that it is dated June 18 but the reason of the delay is that I have been moving about and so have only just opened the box of books and letters, which my housekeeper in London sent on to me here.

I am writing a half lyrical half narrative poem on two old Irish lovers, Baile Honey-Mouth, and one Alyinn—to write the names as they are spoken. I then go on to other stories of the same epoch. I have in fact begun what I have always meant to be the chief work of my life—the giving life not to a single story but to a whole world of

[1] *On Baile's Strand.*   [2] Robert Bridges's mother-in-law.

little stories, some not indeed very little, to a romantic region, a sort of enchanted wood. The old Irish poets wove life into life, thereby giving to the wildest and strangest romance the solidity and vitality [of] the *Comédie Humaine*, and all this romance was knitted into the scenery of the country. 'Here at this very spot the fairy woman gave so and so the cup of magic mead. Not there by the hillock but here by the rock' and so on. This work has not been possible to me hitherto, partly because my verse was not plastic enough and partly for lack of a good translation. But now my friend Lady Gregory has made the most lovely translation, putting the old prose and verse not into the pedantic 'hedge schoolmaster' style of her predecessors, but into a musical caressing English, which never goes very far from the idioms of the country people she knows so well. Her book, which she is about two thirds through, will I think take its place between the *Morte d'Arthur* and the *Mabinogion*.

I have a notion of getting one of these stories, in which there are dialogues in verse, spoken by a reciter who will chant the dialogues in verse to a psaltery. Dolmetsch has interested himself in the chanting—about which you ask me—and has made a psaltery for Miss Farr. It has 12 strings, one for each note in her voice. She will speak to it, speaking an octave lower than she sings. In our experiments in London we found your verse the most suited of all verse to this method. She recited your 'Nightingales,' your 'Muse and Poet' and a third poem of yours whose name I forget. You should hear but had better wait until she has got used to the psaltery and has perfected the method with Dolmetsch a little more. We found that the moment a poem was chanted one saw it in a quite new light—so much verse that read well spoke very ill. Miss Farr has found your verse and mine [? and] a little modern lyric verse to be vocal, but that when one gets back a few generations lyric verse ceases to be vocal until it gets vocal as song not as speech is, as one approaches the Elizabethans. We had great difficulty even with Keats and though we got a passage which is splendidly vocal we had to transpose a line because of a construction, which could only be clear to the eye which can see several words at once.

I shall be altogether content if we can perfect this art for I have never felt that reading was better than an error, a part of the fall into the flesh, a mouthful of the apple. Yours sincerely

W B YEATS

TO FRANK FAY[1]

August 1 [1901] *Coole Park*.

Dear Mr. Fay: I was altogether pleased with your article on *The Land of Heart's Desire* in the *U.I.* I am very glad too that you are going to say something about the Gaiety Theatre's dread of naming either Moore or myself. I am more surprised at Hyland's stupidity than at his fear, for he can hardly expect us not to say what 'the play by an Irish author' is. He has been very nervous from the start and even feared that doing a play by us might keep people away from Benson's Shakespeare performances. The ordinary theatre-going person in Dublin, of the wealthier classes, dislikes our movement so much that Hyland has something to say for himself. An esteemed relative of my own told me, a while back, that Douglas Hyde had said 'in a speech that he hoped to wade through Protestant blood,' and would hardly believe me when I denied it. They look on us all in much the same way—'Literary Theatre' 'Gaelic League' are all one to them. . . .

I wish very much that my work were for the Irish language for many reasons. I hope to collaborate with Hyde in a little play in it shortly.

I shall be in Dublin for your performances in 'The Antient Concert Rooms.' I see by the paper that they begin on the 26th. Yours sincerely W B YEATS

FRAGMENT: PROBABLY FROM A LETTER TO LADY GREGORY

[? *October* 1901] [*Dublin*]

Yesterday we were rehearsing at the Gaiety.[2] The kid Benson is to carry in his arms was wandering in and out among the artificial ivy. I was saying to myself 'Here are we a lot of intelligent people, who might have been doing some sort of work that leads to some

[1] Frank Fay was at this time writing dramatic criticism in the *United Irishman.* It seems probable that Arthur Griffith had passed on to him the American criticisms which Yeats had sent him with his letter of July 16.
[2] The rehearsals were for *Diarmuid and Grania* by George Moore and W. B. Yeats, produced on October 21.

fun. Yet here we are going through all sorts of trouble and annoyance for a mob that knows neither literature nor art. I might have been away in the country, in Italy, perhaps writing poems for my equals and my betters. That kid is the only sensible creature on the stage. He knows his business and keeps to it.' At that very moment one of the actors called out 'Look at the goat eating the property ivy.'

TO THE EDITOR OF THE *FREEMAN'S JOURNAL*

November 14, 1901

Dear Sir, A phrase in a letter which you publish to-day makes it desirable that I should define the attitude of the Irish Literary Theatre and my own attitude towards the proposed censorship. Mr. Moore makes his proposal on his own authority. The Irish Literary Theatre gives no opinion. When Mr. Moore told me his plan I said that I had no belief in its practicability, but would gladly see it discussed. We cannot have too much discussion about ideas in Ireland. The discussion over the theology of *The Countess Cathleen*, and over the politics of *The Bending of the Bough*, and over the morality of *Diarmuid and Grania* set the public mind thinking of matters it seldom thinks of in Ireland, and I hope the Irish Literary Theatre will remain a wise disturber of the peace. But if any literary association I belong to asked for a clerical censorship I would certainly cease to belong to it. I believe that literature is the principal voice of the conscience, and it is its duty age after age to affirm its morality against the special moralities of clergymen and churches, and of kings and parliaments and peoples. But I do not expect this opinion to be the opinion of the majority of any country for generations, and it may always be the opinion of a very small minority. If Mr. Moore should establish a national theatre with an ecclesiastic for a censor, and ask me to join the management I shall refuse, but I shall watch the adventure with the most friendly eyes. I have no doubt that a wise ecclesiastic, if his courage equalled his wisdom, would be a better censor than the mob, but I think it better to fight the mob alone than to seek for a support one could only get by what seems to me a compromise of principle.

A word now upon another matter. You suggest in your review

of Mr. Martyn's plays that certain changes made by Mr. George Moore in his adaptation of *The Tale of a Town* for the Irish Literary Theatre were made for political reasons. This was not the case. Every change was made for literary and dramatic reasons alone.

W B YEATS

TO FIONA MACLEOD [1]

Saturday [? November 1901]   18 *Woburn Buildings*

My dear Miss Macleod, I have been a long while about thanking you for your book of poems,[2] but I have been shifting from Dublin to London and very busy about various things—too busy for any quiet reading. I have been running hither and thither seeing people about one thing and another. But now I am back in my rooms and have got things straight enough to settle down at last to my usual routine. Yesterday I began arranging under their various heads some hitherto unsorted folk-stories on which I am about to work, and to-day I have been busy over your book. I never like your poetry as well as your prose, but here and always you are a wonderful writer of myths. They seem your natural method of expression. They are to you what mere words are to others. I think this is partly why I like you better in your prose, though now and then a bit of verse comes well, rising up out of the prose, in your simplest prose the most, the myths stand out clearly, as something objective, as something well born and independent. In your more elaborate prose they seem subjective, an inner way of looking at things assumed by a single mind. They have little independent life and seem unique; your words bind them to you. If Balzac had written with a very personal, very highly coloured style, he would have always drowned his inventions with himself. You seem to feel this, for when you use elaborate words you invent with less conviction, with less precision, with less delicacy than when you forget everything but the myth. I will take as example a prose tale.

That beautiful story in which the child finds the Twelve Apostles eating porridge in a cottage, is quite perfect in all the first part, for

---

[1] Text from *William Sharp (Fiona Macleod)* by Elizabeth A. Sharp. London, 1910.
[2] *From the Hills of Dream.*

then you think of nothing but the myth, but it seems to me to fade to nothing in the latter part. For in the latter part the words rise up between you and the myth. You yourself begin to speak and we forget the apostles, and the child and the plate and the porridge. Or rather the more mortal part of you begins to speak, the mere person, not the god. You, as I think, should seek the delights of style in utter simplicity, in a self-effacing rhythm and language; in an expression that is like a tumbler of water rather than like a cup of wine. I think that the power of your work in the future will depend on your choosing this destiny. Certainly I am looking forward to 'The Laughter of the Queen.'[1] I thought your last prose, that pilgrimage of the soul and mind and body to the Hills of Dream, promised this simple style. It had it indeed more than anything else you have done.

To some extent I have an advantage over you in having a very fierce nation to write for. I have to make everything very hard and clear, as it were. It is like riding a wild horse. If one's hands fumble or one's knees loosen one is thrown. You have in the proper sense far more imagination than I have and that makes your work correspondingly more difficult. It is fairly easy for me, who do so much of my work by the critical, rather than the imaginative faculty, to be precise and simple, but it is hard for you in whose mind images form themselves without ceasing, and are gone as quickly perhaps.

But I am sure I am right. When you speak with the obvious personal voice in your verse, or in your essays, you are not that Fiona who has invented a new thing, a new literary method. You are that Fiona when the great myths speak through you. . . . Yours

W B YEATS

I like your verses on Murias and like them the better perhaps because of the curious coincidence that I did in summer verses about lovers wandering 'in long forgotten Murias.'

[1] Possibly a reference to "The Laughter of Scathach the Queen', a short story about Cuchulain now included in the section *Seanachas* in Vol. II of 'The Works of Fiona Macleod,' London: Heinemann, 1910.

TO LADY GREGORY

Tuesday   18 *Woburn Buildings*
[*Nov.* 19. *Postmark Nov* 20, 1901]

My dear Lady Gregory: That is good news about my father. I should think that he had better get some kind of agent—there must be such people—to arrange the matter in America, if he knows nothing of Quinn. There must be some way of doing this sort of thing—Osbourne should know. I need hardly say that he is quite welcome to sell the portrait I have.

How Moore lives in the present! If the National Theatre is ever started, what he is and what I am will be weighed and very little what we have said or done. A phrase more or less matters little. When he has got more experience of public life he will know how little these things matter—yet I suppose we would both be more popular if I could keep from saying what I think and he from saying what he does not think. You may tell him that the wisest of men does not know what is expedient, but that we can all get a very good idea as to what is our own particular truth. The more we keep to that the better. Cajolery never lighted the fire. If he knows Harold Large's address get him to send it to me—if you meet him. I shall write to him myself as I have to ask him about other things.

I have a book of highland Fianna material, which I can let you have when you like—*The Feans* by J. G. Campbell. Grania in this book is the wife of Finn before she runs away with Diarmuid and is described as not very particular in the choice of her lovers. Finn in one version has her buried alive. I am half inclined to write for the printed text of the play a preface describing the various versions of the tale—and so dispose of Irish criticism once for all. . . .

I have not yet been to see A. P. Watt but may go to-morrow. I have written to Dolmetsch to talk about the chanting with him; and have proposed a lecture with illustrations to pay him for the psaltery. I saw Mrs. Emery last night. She had arranged to give Dolmetsch £4 for psaltery, but he forgot all about this and spent £10 on it. I shall do an article and get it into one of the Reviews and then give the lecture, and so get Mrs. Emery out of the difficulty. She paid part of the money by performances of a very amateurish Egyptian play rather nicely on Saturday. Yours sincerely   W B YEATS

TO MRS. PATRICK CAMPBELL [1]

[*November* 1901]   18 *Woburn Buildings*

Dear Mrs. Patrick Campbell . . . Will you permit me to thank you by letter for the performance? [2] Your acting seemed to me to have the perfect precision and delicacy and simplicity of every art at its best. It made me feel the unity of the arts in a new way. I said to myself, this is exactly what I am trying to do in writing, to express myself without waste, without emphasis. To be impassioned and yet to have a perfect self-possession, to have a precision so absolute that the slightest inflection of voice, the slightest rhythm of sound or emotion plucks the heart-strings. But do you know that you acted too well; you made me understand a defect in Björnson's play which I had felt but had not understood when I read it. Björnson's hero could only have done those seen or real miracles by having a religious genius. Now the very essence of genius, of whatever kind, is precision, and that hero of his has no precision. He is a mere zealous man with a vague sentimental mind—the kind of man who is anxious about the Housing of the Working Classes, but not the kind of man who sees what Blake called 'The Divine Vision and Fruition.' I happened to have in my pocket *The Revelation of Divine Love*, by the Lady Julian, an old mystical book; my hand strayed to it all unconsciously. There was no essential difference between that work and your acting; both were full of fine distinction, of delicate logic, of that life where passion and thought are one. Both were utterly unlike Björnson's hero.

The actor played him to the life; but I was miserable until he was off the stage. He was an unbeliever's dream of a believer, an Atheist's Christian. . . .   W B YEATS

TO MRS. PATRICK CAMPBELL [3]

November 1901   18 *Woburn Buildings*

. . . Yes, I agree with you that Björnson's play is a fine thing—living, passionate, touching issues of life and death. In London the

---

[1] Text from *My Life and some Letters* by Mrs. Patrick Campbell. London, 1922.

[2] Mrs. Campbell had produced Björnson's *Beyond Human Power* at the Royalty Theatre, London, for a short series of matinée performances, on November 7, 1901.

[3] Fragment. Text from *My Life and some Letters* by Mrs. Patrick Campbell. London, 1922.

subjects which people think suitable for drama get fewer every day. Shelley said that when a social order was in decay, the arts attached themselves to the last things people were interested in—imaginatively interested in. Here people look on the world with more and more prosaic eyes, as Shelley said they did in dying Greece. There, as here, nothing kept its beauty but irregular love-making. He called the poetry that had irregular love for subject and was called immoral, 'The Footsteps of Astrea departing from the world.'

W B YEATS

TO LADY GREGORY

Sunday night   18 *Woburn Buildings*
[*? Dec 22. Postmark ? Dec* 23 1901]

My dear Lady Gregory . . . I have written a new lyric—quite a good one—and also a little essay about old Farrell and the woods of Coole which is less good, and some *Celtic Twilight* odds and ends. Bullen comes in to-morrow night. A. P. Watt has strongly advised my accepting Bullen's offer to take the book of essays instead of the novel, as £50 on account is more than one can ordinarily get for essays. Bullen was to have seen A. P. Watt on Friday about it. He was to arrange terms for new *Celtic Twilight* also, also I think for new edition of *Secret Rose* (this in two volumes, one to contain 'Hanrahan' re-written as we planned, and the other the other stories —3/6 a volume).

I told A. P. Watt and Bullen both that I would do just as A. P. Watt advised. If Bullen gets these books I have all but persuaded him to turn Irish publisher (he is Irish), that is to say to have a Dublin office and to think seriously about Irish writers and printers—and have also got him greatly excited about the idea of publishing a series of Irish Catholic religious pictures by Jack and other people. He has been greatly tickled by the idea of Jack's crucifixion with the impenitent thief as principal character—he kept chuckling over it for a long time. When A. P. Watt rather advised Bullen, and not only for the *Celtic Twilight* stories but for the new books, I told him that Bullen was anything but steady. A. P. Watt merely muttered something like 'the better they are the more they drink' or 'the better the man the more he drinks' or something equally surprising coming from such a whitehaired Father Xmas.

You will remember *Mosada,* a bad early play of mine—which is in the Usheen book—and which was printed in a shilling pamphlet long ago in Dublin. Well a shabby relation of mine (father of the 'bold bad one') has prosecuted a borrower of books and got £5 instead of *Mosada* which the borrower had lost. I wrote a letter for the prosecuted man, who called on me, saying it was worth, so far as I knew, nothing (I said I thought there was no demand). However my miserable relation got Elkin Mathews to swear it was worth £10. I heard nothing of the case until the borrower came to me on the morning of the trial. Yours always   W B YEATS

I suppose you will be here in January some time—before I do my preface at any rate.

Dolmetsch says 'the chanting' is now quite perfect in theory and only requires a little practice. He says it is 'a new art.' We can now make a perfect record of everything.

TO LADY GREGORY

Jan. [1902]   18 *Woburn Buildings*

Dear Lady Gregory... I do not know what length my preface to your book [1] will be. It may be quite short. I shall have to read the proofs before I know what length. It may be fairly long. I am as you can imagine short enough of money. I have just scraped on by various expedients. *The Celtic Twilight* new chapters are coming [out] in the *Speaker,* at a low price though, and I have got a friend to advance me the price of them as I have written each one, but for this I should have collapsed. In a few days I hope the agreement for *The Celtic Twilight* new edition will be signed and then I shall get a few pounds in advance and that will keep me going till I am paid for some of the things A. P. Watt has placed. I may wire to you for £3 or £4 for preface but I shall wait until I see if the agreement gets signed all right. I dine with Bullen to-morrow. If I am absolutely

[1] *Cuchulain of Muirthemne:* the story of the Men of the Red Branch of Ulster, arranged and put into English by Lady Gregory, with a Preface by W. B. Yeats, was published in London by John Murray in April 1902.

on my beam ends I shall simply wire the words 'Shall I do preface now' and you will understand. I will probably not finish the preface anyway until you are over, if that will do. It will hardly be wanted just yet as it will be the last thing printed. After a rather gloomy time I seem to have emerged into fairly good spirits—the best for a very long time. Masefield has got a post in the country whither he goes in about 8 days. When he is gone I shall I expect be gloomy enough until you are over but just now I am so well content, and I cannot tell why, that I feel as if I had no nerves, as if I were a mere wooden image, a philistine that is. I 'evoked' myself into this state on New Year night.

I met Mr. and Mrs. Strong yesterday. They asked about you and are going to ask me to dinner for Mr. Strong wants to talk about 'my wonderful essay on magic.'[1] He thinks he has identified the magician and doctor in the vision but is not sure. He says it was a wonderful historical picture and must be a picture of some definite man. Yours always   W B YEATS

TO LADY GREGORY

Monday night   18 *Woburn Buildings*
[*Jan.* 13. *Postmark Jan.* 14, 1902]

My dear Lady Gregory, That £10 is very much too much. I really do not know what I can find to say which will be worth that but I will do my best. Let me have a copy of the complete proofs and I may do something not as inadequate as I fear. I am still enveloped in the new edition of *The Celtic Twilight*—the mere writing out of what I have already done takes a surprising time, but the book will be much better than it was. I am using a good deal of my Sligo information. I should be done this week of a certainty and then I shall get back to Cuchullain and I hope finish him out of hand, finish him enough at any rate for Martyn to judge of it. I have my 'chanting' essay to do also—it will be a considerable addition to the book of essays but is in any case a necessity that I may launch Mrs. Emery.

[1] Yeats's essay 'Magic' had appeared in the *Monthly Review*, September 1901. It was reprinted in *Ideas of Good and Evil*, 1903.

I have done a great deal of work at my Magical Rites, sketched them all out in their entirety. I have gone through some black spots too but have emerged at last into a cheerful mood, which really seems as if it were going to last for a while. Yours always

W B YEATS

TO LADY GREGORY

Jan. 20th [1902]   18 *Woburn Buildings*

My dear Lady Gregory, I have just received through A. P. Watt an account of the sales of *Samhain*. They printed 2000 and have sold 1628 and sent about 100 out to review so they have only about 300 (rather less) unsold. Royalties amount to £5-14-3, which I shall ask A. P. Watt to send (minus his 10 per cent) to the Sec. of Gaelic League, Dublin. Do you think I should specify the purpose? Say an Oireachtas prize. I merely said in *Samhain* that the proceeds should be given to the Gaelic League. If we asked them to give (say) £5-5 (A. P. Watt's royalties will swallow 10/-) for the best Irish song to an Irish air and did it in the name of 'the Irish Literary Theatre' that song would advertise us for ever. Is not that a subtle device? Will you ask Martyn if he approves? Is it necessary to ask Hyde? The money is my own and so I need not drag in the Theatre and can give it from the editor of *Samhain* if I like, but the theatre would get an advertisement.

Edward Martyn is being called a pagan at last. I send you the *Catholic Register* with the only letter in the controversy that I have seen. I shall get the other copies. I am afraid the bad reception that Edward's plays seem to be getting won't improve the hopes of the Literary Theatre. To-night before I go to bed I shall take out my MS of Cuchullain and do a few lines—for I have just finished *Celtic Twilight*.[1] It is nearly twice as big as it was and will have, besides my father's drawing of 'The Last Gleeman,' Jack's 'Memory Harbour' in colour and perhaps Russell's drawing of 'Knocknarea.' It will be the same size as *The Secret Rose* but be plainly got up but for some little emblem in the corner. My other books will be issued

[1] The enlarged edition of *The Celtic Twilight*, 1902, appeared without illustrations except for a frontispiece portrait of the author by J. B. Yeats. 'Memory Harbour' by Jack B. Yeats was used, many years later, as an illustration to *Reveries Over Childhood and Youth*, 1915.

in the same form so as to make a uniform edition. I have had a letter from an Edinburgh publisher asking me to edit a book of selections from Spenser for £35. It is good pay and I am writing to ask when it will be wanted. I may do it if I have not to do it at once.[1] I have a good deal to say about Spenser but tremble at the thought of reading his six books.

12.30. Masefield—who is off to the country to be sec. to a picture gallery—has been in, so I shall not begin Cuchullain to-night. The little bit about Maeve that you sent me has come very well into *The Celtic Twilight*. Russell's *Deirdre* rather embarrasses me. I do not believe in it at all. If it is offered to us I shall have to vote against it and if I do I shall seem to be doing so in the interest of my own 'Cuchullain.' Maud Gonne saw two acts of it played at the Coffeys' and I must say liked them very much. She is anxious by the by to play Kathleen ny Hoolihan for us. She will certainly be a draw if she does. Fay could easily find all the rest of the company. It will be a great pity if Martyn withdraws. Hyde's new play with Hyde in it and Maud Gonne in my play would really draw a fine house—and Cuchullain will really be very good too.

When do you come over? Soon now I suppose.

Let me know at once what you think about the proposed Gaelic League prize. Yours always   W B YEATS

My alchemist [2] is very anxious to have a look at that magic book of Robert's. He says it is really valuable. Could you bring it when you come? He has just made what he hopes is the Elixir of Life. If the rabbits on whom he is trying it survive we are all to drink a noggin full—at least all of us whose longevity he feels he could honestly encourage.

TO THE EDITOR OF THE *SATURDAY REVIEW*

5 March 1902   *London, N.W.*

Sir, J. F. R. in last week's *Saturday Review* condemned the Purcell Society and practically told his readers that the performances, which

[1] *Poems of Spenser* selected and with an introduction by W. B. Yeats. Edinburgh: T. C. & E. C. Jack. The book was not published till October 1906.
[2] Probably the Rev. W. A. Aytoun, an Oxfordshire clergyman, who was a member of the Golden Dawn. Yeats wrote of him in *The Trembling of the Veil*.

are to be given in Great Queen Street next week, will not be worth going to. I know nothing of music. I do not even know one note from another. I am afraid I even dislike music and yet I venture to contradict him. Last year I saw *Dido and Aeneas* and *The Masque of Love*, which is to be given again this year, and they gave me more perfect pleasure than I have met with in any theatre this ten years. I saw the only admirable stage scenery of our time, for Mr. Gordon Craig has discovered how to decorate a play with severe, beautiful, simple, effects of colour, that leave the imagination free to follow all the suggestions of the play. Realistic scenery takes the imagination captive and is at best but bad landscape painting, but Mr. Gordon Craig's scenery is a new and distinct art. It is something that can only exist in the theatre. It cannot even be separated from the figures that move before it. The staging of *Dido and Aeneas* and of *The Masque of Love* will some day, I am persuaded, be remembered among the important events of our time. Yours truly

W B YEATS

TO HENRY NEWBOLT [1]

[*March*] 1902   *Shakespeare Festival Club*
                                            Stratford-on-Avon

Dear Mr. Newbolt, Can you come and see me on Monday evening? I shall be back at 18 Woburn Buildings, Upper Woburn Place. I am asking Sturge Moore.

I have come here for the Shakespeare Cycle. I have brought your book [2] with me, and read it at intervals in my work. You have set many wise and true and beautiful things to rhyme. Yours is patriotism of the fine sort—patriotism that lays burdens upon a man, and not the patriotism that takes burdens off. The British Press just now, as I think, only understands the other sort, the sort that makes a man say 'I need not trouble to get wisdom, for I am English and my vices have made me great.'

Any time Monday after 8. Your sincerely   W B YEATS

[1] Text from *The Later Life and Letters of Sir Henry Newbolt*. London, 1942.
[2] *The Sailing of the Long-Ships*. London: Murray, 1902.

TO LADY GREGORY

Saturday [*March* 22, 1902]   18 *Woburn Buildings*

Dear Lady Gregory... I am going to surprise you by an idea that has been in my head lately. I never until yesterday spoke of it to anybody. I have an idea of going on the stage in small parts next autumn for a few months that I may master the stage for purposes of poetical drama. I find I could get on quite easily, and that with the exception of rehearsal times it would only take my evenings. Does the idea seem to you very wild? I should make about £2 a week, and learn my business, or at any rate never have to blame myself for not having tried to learn it. I would not of course go on in my own name and I would tell people exactly why I did the thing at all. I believe that I construct all right—but I have very little sense of acting. I don't see my people as actors though I see them very clearly as men. Moore sees them always as actors.

Moore writes to me, by the by, that 'the acting of Russell's play is the silliest he ever saw'—Miss Quinn I suppose is the sinner. He wants Kathleen ny Hoolihan not to sit down by the fire and croon but to walk up and down in front of the stage, so as to dominate the stage. He thinks she should be excited as the French are going to land. I have replied that she looks far ahead and far backward and cannot be excited in that sense, or rather she will be a less poetical personage if she is. However I have told Miss Gonne, to whom I have sent Moore's letter, to do as she likes. One must judge of these things on the stage. I shall go over and see for myself on Wednesday or Thursday. I shall stay at 8 Cavendish Row. Yours ever

W B YEATS

TO LADY GREGORY

April 3rd [1902]   8 *Cavendish Row*
Dublin

My dear Lady Gregory... The plays came off last night and both really very great successes.[1] They took to *Deirdre* from the first.

[1] The plays were *Deirdre* by AE and Yeats's *Kathleen ni Hoolihan*. They were given by W. G. Fay's Irish National Dramatic Company at St. Teresa's Hall, Clarendon Street, Dublin, on April 2, 3 and 4. Maud Gonne took the part of the Old Woman in *Kathleen ni Hoolihan*.

The hall was crowded and great numbers could not get in. I hated *Deirdre*, in fact I did not remain in the theatre because I was so nervous about it. I still hate it, but I suppose Moore is the only person who shares my opinion. When I saw it in rehearsal I thought it superficial and sentimental, as I thought it when it came out in the *New Ireland Review*. *Kathleen ni Hoolihan* was also most enthusiastically received. Its one defect was that the mild humour of the part before Kathleen came in kept the house in such delighted laughter, that it took them some little while to realize the tragic meaning of Kathleen's part, though Maude Gonne played it magnificently, and with weird power. I expect that I should have struck a tragic note at the start—I have an idea of revising it before I put it in a book and of making Kathleen pass the door at the start. They can call her over and ask her some question and she can say she is going to old 'so and so's' and pass on (they might ask her to come in and she might not have time). When she came in the second time she might say that old so and so was shearing his sheep or the like and would not attend to her. You will be sorry to hear that I have just dictated a rough draft of a new *Grania* second act to Moore's typewriter. He is to work on it in Paris. He gave me a few ideas and I worked over them and I think got the most poetical and beautiful material that we have put into the play as yet. He is delighted and will write the act and then send it to me for revision.

April 5

The plays are over. Crowds have been turned away from the doors every night, and last night was the most successful of all the performances. The audience now understands *Kathleen ni Hoolihan* and there is no difficulty in getting from humour to tragedy. There is continual applause. And strange to say I like *Deirdre*. It is thin and faint but it has its effect of wall decoration. The absence of character is like the absence of individual expression in wall decoration. It was acted with great simplicity. The actors kept very quiet, often merely posing and speaking. The result was curiously dreamlike and gentle. Russell is planning a play on the children of Turann and will I imagine do quite a number of plays. The costumes and scenery designed by him were really beautiful—there was a gauze veil in front. It was really a wonderful sight to see crowds of people standing up at the back of the hall where they could hardly ever see because of the people in front—I heard this from one of them—and yet patient and enthusiastic.

I imagine that the De Freyne estate agitation is breaking down.[1] Miss Gonne has had a number of letters from the tenants this week begging her to go down and arrange a settlement. All the tenants they say would agree to take quite a small concession. She won't interfere however as the United Land League is in possession.

I met O'Grady this morning and found him groaning under the weight of his commercial responsibility.

Cuchullain,[2] which I have gone over with Moore, is still in want of a little simplification which I am trying to get into it. I think I shall get it simple enough for Fay in the end. Yours ever

W B YEATS

TO HENRY NEWBOLT[3]

April 5, 1902   8 *Cavendish Row, Dublin*
(*after Wednesday next*, 18 *Woburn Buildings Euston Road*)

Dear Newbolt, I enclose the article on 'Speaking to the Psaltery' (or 'to musical notes' if you prefer that) and I would be greatly obliged if you put it in the May number.[4] If it is not out then I shall not be able to give my lecture until autumn.

Our plays have been a great success—both AE's *Deirdre* and my *Kathleen ny Hoolihan*. Crowds have been turned away at the doors and great numbers stood about the walls with patient enthusiasm. They had to stand through all the intervals too, for they were packed too close to move. It was only a hall, not a theatre, but we could have filled quite a big place, I think. Our actors were amateurs—

---

[1] The Defreyne Estate in Roscommon was one of the very disturbed estates from the eighties down to 1902–3. On this estate the thatched roofs of the cabins were set on fire by the bailiffs and police so that they could not be lived in after evictions. Maud Gonne spoke on platforms in Roscommon about this, and gave the whole situation publicity. The tenants then refused to pay rent, and a very menacing situation led to the Land Conference and the Wyndham Land Act of 1903.

[2] Evidently the play eventually called *On Baile's Strand*.

[3] Text from *The Later Life and Letters of Sir Henry Newbolt*. London, 1942.

[4] 'Speaking to the Psaltery' appeared in the *Monthly Review* (of which Newbolt was editor) for May, and was reprinted in *Ideas of Good and Evil*, 1903.

but amateurs who are trying to act with wonderful simplicity and naivety. Their method is better than their performance, but their method is the first right one I have seen. In *Deirdre*, a dim dreamlike play, they acted without 'business' of any kind. They simply stood still in decorative attitudes and spoke. AE had designed all the scenes and costumes and they were excellent. The night before last one of the actors, who a little while ago was an agricultural labourer, came round to read me a play which he has written about the United Irish League in the style of the only dramatist he has ever read—Ibsen. It had real substance, but little execution. Something, I think, must come out of all this energy and delight in high things. Yours sincerely

W B YEATS

TO LADY GREGORY

[*Postmark April* 10, 1902]   18 *Woburn Buildings*

My dear Lady Gregory . . . Martyn has rather irritated me. I got him to write to U[*nited*] I[*rishman*] about the plays and he has written rather abusing the actors, whom one wants to encourage. He is going to bring English actors over for his play and is 'laying pipe.' I forgot this. And poor Fay and his company did wonders. There is an announcement in this week's *U.I.* of the autumn 'Samhain' dramatic festival they are preparing.

I have a plan for a little religious play in one act with quite as striking a plot as *Kathleen*—it cannot offend anybody and may propitiate Holy Church. I have also a plot for a little comedy in one act. Cousins, Fay says, has sent him the best one act play he has seen for years.[1] So all is going well. I am working at my novel—dictating to a typewriter. I dictated 2000 words in an hour and ten minutes yesterday—and go on again tomorrow. This dictation is really a discovery.

Certainly I shall keep the 25th free. I take chair at Irish Lit on the 26th. The *Quarterly* has an essay on 'Gaelic Revival' quoting your translation from Hyde and praising and quoting verses of mine. It is clearly Gwynn's work. Yours ever

W B YEATS

[1] James H. Cousins, an Ulster poet, published several volumes of verse between 1894 and 1908. His play *The Racing Lug* was produced by the Irish National Dramatic Company at the Antient Concert Rooms, Dublin, on October 31, 1902.

TO FRANK FAY[1]

April 21st, 1902   18 *Woburn Buildings*

Dear Mr. Fay, I have written a long reply to Edward Martyn in which I have renewed my praise of your and your brother's company.[2] I want to make people understand the importance of the St. Teresa's Hall experiment, and to prepare them for future work. You might join in if you see a chance. When Edward Martyn said to me that your brother over-acted his part I was not quite sure at first that there was not some truth in it. I was trying to find out the cause of the laughter, and as you know was planning alterations in the play, blaming myself in chief. Friday night convinced me, however, that none of the blame was your brother's and very little of it mine. I did not criticise the acting in my letter to you, not because I hesitated to tell you what I thought but because I really did not feel competent. In two or three years I shall understand the subject but I don't yet. I know that all the acting of verse that I have seen up to this has been wrong, and I can see that you and your brother have struck out a method which would be right for verse, but, till I have seen that method applied by many different people, I will only be able to criticise acting very vaguely. George Moore has precise ideas because he likes the 'natural school,' and has therefore many examples to judge by. Two years ago I was in the same state about scenery that I now am in about acting. I knew the right principles but I did not know the right practice because I had never seen it. I have now however learnt a great deal from Gordon Craig. Now as to the future of the National Theatre Company. I read your letters to a wealthy friend,[3] who said something like this 'Work on as best you can for a year, let us say, you should be able to persuade people during that time that you are something of a dramatist and Mr. Fay should be able to have got a little practice for his company. At the year's end do what Wagner did and write a "Letter to my Friends" asking for the capital to carry out your idea.' Now I could not get from this friend of mine whether he himself would give any large sum, but I imagine that

[1] Dictated.
[2] Yeats had written an article, 'The Acting at St. Teresa's Hall,' in the *United Irishman*, April 12, and contributed a second, a rejoinder to Edward Martyn, on April 26.
[3] Probably Miss Horniman, a devout Wagnerian.

he would do something. I think we must work in some such way, getting all the good plays we can from Cousins and Russell and anybody else, but carrying out our theories of the stage as rigorously as possible. The friend I have quoted is interested in me but Russell has his own following, and I think it likely that we will ultimately get a certain amount of money. I will do my best to do a great deal of strong dramatic work in the immediate future. I should not talk about what my friend said to me. It is all too vague, but I quote it to you to show how the wind may blow. Yours sincerely,

W B YEATS

[*In Yeats's handwriting*]

The Egyptian plays [1] were chiefly interesting for being in something like your method and for adopting decorative scenery. The scenery, which was supposed to represent Egyptian temple walls, was made by simply turning ordinary scenery wrong way front. Against this grey mass very charmingly dressed people posed looking really very like Egyptian wall paintings. The acting except for Miss Farr was much behind the acting in Dublin. Miss Young and Miss Farr are playing in the better of the two plays tomorrow and I am going to see Miss Young. The plays are fairly well written.

TO ARNOLD DOLMETSCH [2]

June 3rd, 1902   18 *Woburn Buildings*

Dear Mr. Dolmetsch, I shall have to get a chairman for my lecture on June 10th and I would sooner have you than anybody else. You are the only one, I suppose, in the world now, who knows anything about the old music that was half speech, and I need hardly say, that neither Miss Farr nor myself could have done anything in this matter of speaking to notes, without your help. Please let me know, as if you cannot be my chairman, I shall have to look round for some irrelevant man of letters. And besides, I suppose I had better send round a paragraph. I have written a reply to Symons' note

---

[1] *The Beloved of Hathor* and *The Shrine of the Golden Hawk* by Florence Farr and Olivia Shakespear. The plays were printed for sale in the theatre, but do not seem to have been published. Yeats wrote an account of their performance, at the Bijou Theatre, Bayswater, in the *Star*, January 23, 1902.

[2] Dictated. In Miss Horniman's handwriting.

in the *Academy*,[1] my reply should appear next Saturday. I hear too that some singing-teacher is writing a rejoinder from the point of view of the modern musician to my essay in the *Monthly Review*. I am writing a 'Prayer to the Seven Archangels to bless the Seven Notes.' This prayer is to be spoken first by two voices and then by one voice, then the other voice, and then two voices again. Yours sincerely
                                                                          W B YEATS

TO THE EDITOR OF THE *ACADEMY*

[*Published June* 7, 1902]

Sir, Mr. Arthur Symons has said, in his friendly account of my theories about the speaking of poetry to musical notes, that the fixing of the pitch by a notation makes 'any personal interpretation good or bad impossible.' The notation of a song is much more elaborate than any notation for speech made by Mr. Dolmetsch or Miss Farr, and yet the singer finds room for 'personal interpretation.' Indeed, I am persuaded that the fixing of the pitch gives more delicacy and beauty to the 'personal interpretation,' for it leaves the speaker free to preoccupy himself with the subtlest modulations. Before we recorded pitch we made many experiments in rhythmical speech, and I found that Miss Farr would speak a poem with admirable expression and then speak it quite ineffectively time after time. She found it impossible to recall her moment of inspiration; but now, though she varies, she does so within a far narrower range. Her best inspirations are at least as good as they were, while her failures never sink into disorder.

If Mr. Symons will borrow one of my psalteries and speak one of his own poems to a notation of his own, he will find—for I think his ear is good enough to speak to the notes without giving them too much attention—that he will light on all kinds of beautiful or dramatic modulations which would never have occurred to him had not the cruder effects been fixed by the notation. He will discover,

[1] Arthur Symons, at this time dramatic critic for the *Academy*, devoted the greater part of an article to a discussion of Yeats's essay 'Speaking to the Psaltery' and of a private demonstration of method given by Florence Farr. His essay is reprinted in the first edition of *Plays, Acting and Music*, London: Duckworth, 1903. Yeats's reply is given here.

too, that the right changes of pitch can seldom be got at once, and that once got they will seem so important that even the best recitation without fixed notes will generally show itself for mere disorder. Everything in any art that can be recorded and taught should be recorded and taught, for by doing so we take a burden from the imagination, which climbs higher in light armour than in heavy. If Mr. Symons will then make an extremely simple tune, like the very simplest folk-music, and record it and speak his poem to this tune, he will find, I think, that this new art is also an extremely old one, and that it is probable that we should sometimes speak an old folk song instead of singing it, as we understand singing. I have heard Irish country-women, whose singing is called 'traditional Irish singing,' speak their little songs precisely as Miss Farr does some of hers, only with rather less drama. The tune must be very simple, for if there are more than a few notes the one tune will not adapt itself to the emotions of different verses. Is it not possible that we have been mistaken in considering this kind of little tunes merely as undeveloped music? It might have been wiser to have sometimes thought of them as the art of regulated speech, already perhaps near its decadence. I imagine men spoke their verses first to a regulated pitch without a tune, and then, eager for variety, spoke to tunes which gradually became themselves the chief preoccupation until speech died out in music.

From time to time indeed musicians have tried to give speech some importance, but music has always been their chief preoccupation and their 'recitative' has got its variety from the accompaniment and not from the rhythm of the verse. If the speaker to musical notes will attend to the subtleties of rhythm as carefully as a singer attends to the musical inventions of the composer, his speech will not 'drift' into 'intoning.' It was said that 'the song of Rachel' degenerated into 'sing song' with the rest of her company, but that did not prove that her method of speaking verse was wrong. But after all, if I am right in claiming antiquity for this art of speaking to musical notes, discussion of its merits is idle. No art can pass away for ever, till the human nature it once delighted has passed away, and that can hardly be until Michael's trumpet. Yours truly,

W B YEATS

TO LADY GREGORY [1]

June 13th 1902   18 *Woburn Buildings*

My dear Lady Gregory, I propose to leave London on the evening of the 19th. I am waiting to see Maeterlinck's play *Monna Vanna* which is to be done by his French company.[2] I am less anxious to see the play than to see the method of the performance. My lecture was a great success. People were standing up and many could not get in. We sold £22 worth of tickets and if we had had the courage to take a big hall could have sold many more. We have spent the money on new psalteries and on charming dresses for our troubadours to speak in. Dolmetsch is now making little tunes for my 'Wandering Aengus' and some of my other things to be spoken to. I am taking two psalteries to Dublin and think of leaving one with Russell. I am also bringing my model theatre and have a plan of giving two lectures in the autumn. One on a simpler theatre, and one on the speaking of verse to notes. Perhaps I might get Mrs. Emery to come over for this lecture. I have been trying to let my rooms and will know to-day whether I have succeeded. I am letting them for very little to Sturge Moore's sister. Merely for my rent, and for enough over to pay wear and tear. She will be better pleased if she gets them till the end of November, so I think of remaining on after the play, which will be the last week of October, and of giving these two lectures to fill up the time. I have almost finished a first draft of that little play I told you of, *The Fool and the Wise Man*.[3] And I hope they will do it with *Kathleen ny Hoolihan* in October. Gordon Craig is greatly delighted with the scenario which I read him, he wants to show the play to Irving but my belief in the commercial theatre liking such a thing is but slight. What is more to the point is that he is very anxious to stage some of my things himself, and so far as I can make out there is a possibility of his mother taking part in the venture. But for divination I should believe that something will come of it. I shall stay a couple of days in Dublin and then would like to go on to Galway.

[1] Dictated.
[2] Maeterlinck's *Monna Vanna* had been refused a licence by the Lord Chamberlain. Lugné Poë brought his company to London and a private performance, sponsored by the Stage Society, was given at the Bijou Theatre, Bayswater, on June 20.
[3] Eventually named *The Hour-Glass*.

I am sorry to say I am desperately hard up. I have paid my rent and everything up to date, except typewriting, but unless Elkin Mathews to whom I have written owes me something I shall get away with difficulty. Yours ever W B YEATS

TO LADY GREGORY [1]

June 16th [Postmark 1902] 18 *Woburn Buildings*

My dear Lady Gregory, Many thanks. I am just up from Wilfrid Blunt's where I was from Saturday to Monday. It was a very pleasant party. The younger Lytton and his wife, Alfred Douglas and his wife, and Cockerell whom I have got to like very much. He is full of enthusiasm about you and your book, but these things can wait. Blunt is quite bent on the Cuchullin play and proposes to take 'the only jealousy of Emer' for his subject, which would fit into our plan very well. I shall have to find out in Dublin however whether the young men will let an Englishman write for them. I did not tell Blunt that I had any doubt on the matter but told him that I would write precise dates etc. in a couple of weeks. I enclose a copy of verses. They are a prayer for blessings upon the Psaltery, and were spoken at my lecture the other night. I don't think the last two or three lines are quite right yet. C/o George Russell will be my best address in Dublin. I shall have several little matters to look into. I have been suggested as one of three directors for the *U.I.* under new management. I have refused (all this is private) as I considered I could not make myself responsible for their attitude towards the Irish members. To my surprise my name was put forward as one that would be satisfactory to the extreme element. They would have found me anything but satisfactory but I am pleased at the compliment. As I am seeing you so shortly this letter is a mere piece of idleness. Yours ever W B YEATS

TO A. H. BULLEN

June 27 [1902] *Coole Park*

Dear Bullen, I send you a lot more of the book of essays,[2] everything indeed except two essays that are not yet finished—and the essay on

[1] Dictated. [2] *Ideas of Good and Evil.*

'The Happiest of the Poets'—the Editor of the *Fortnightly* will I have no doubt lend you my MS. of this, for I am sorry to say I have not a copy.

I have written to the *Speaker* to send you the copy containing 'The Way of Wisdom,' a short essay.[1] I daresay it will reach you at the same time with the copy I send. There are a few misprints which I will correct in proof.

I have had to borrow a copy of Horton's book, and of *Beltaine*, (2 numbers) from Lady Gregory containing essays, these I must beg you to return to her as soon as possible.

I gave you the Shelley essays I believe.

Please send my copies of *The Celtic Twilight* here, I am very impatient to see them. And will you send one copy with label I enclose. You might send a review copy to Arthur Symons, 134 Lauderdale Mansions, Lauderdale Road, Maida Vale.

As some of the longest essays in the book are about Blake's illustrations to Dante, what do you think of giving his Francesca and Paolo as a frontispiece? You could photograph my copy. Yours sincerely
W B YEATS

TO FRANK FAY [2]

Sept. 7th [1902]   *Coole Park*

My dear Fay, I want to alter the title of *The Beggarman*. Please change it to *A Pot of Broth* in any public announcement. I have a sufficient reason for this, which I have not time to explain now.

You have not sent back my MS. of *Kathleen ny Houlihan*, and I find it difficult without it to judge of some of the points you raise. One is obviously a misprint. 'I don't know is it here she's coming' is of course right. No doubt too there is a confusion between the names Peter and Patrick in the other passage you speak of. Certainly you may add the word 'tomorrow' to the word 'married' in that speech of Delia's. I have no doubt it dropped out of the typing.

---

[1] 'The Way of Wisdom,' which was mainly an account of the visit to Dublin of the Indian Mohini Chatterji, did not appear in the book. Yeats revised it drastically in 1908 and it appeared as 'The Pathway' in the eighth volume of the Shakespeare Head Press Edition of his writings. It has not been reprinted since.

[2] Dictated.

Lady Gregory is trying to get the air of 'There's broth in the Pot.' Your brother must get some common air for 'The Spouse of Naoise,' and sing it as much as possible as traditional singing. I adapted the words from 'Ben-Eirinn i' in Walsh's *Popular Songs*.

I will send sketches of costume for *The Hour Glass* and will have the skins in time. And we will get a few bits of crockery for cottage scenes.

I send you some Latin words which will do for the wise man's prayer, these are the Latin words, broken for the actor: 'Confiteor Deo omnipotenti—how does it go on?—Omnipotenti beatae Mariae—I cannot remember.'

I think it would be a mistake to have verses for the opening of the Theatre. Such things are never done well and give the air of a penny reading entertainment.

Digges should not make up too old. The wise man is a man in the full vigour of life. I hear from Mr. Quinn that he read the part very finely and you yourself I hear played very excellently. Quinn was very much struck. I should like, however, to hear how *The Pot of Broth* goes.

Let the fool's wig, if you can, be red and matted.

Hyde has done several new plays, including a most beautiful Nativity play, and will I think throw himself heartily into your work. Yours sincerely, W B YEATS

TO ELKIN MATHEWS [1]

Sept 20 [1902] *Coole Park*

Dear Elkin Mathews: I see by account sent me from A. P. Watt that you had only 98 copies of *The Wind Among the Reeds* last March. You must therefore have about exhausted the edition. I think it will be better in future to put the design in gold on a few vellum copies and to bind the ordinary copies in plain boards with a paper label. People will be all the more glad to buy the vellum copies if the design is not made common by printing it on all copies in some poorer way. Yours sincerely W B YEATS

[1] From a typewritten copy.

TO LADY GREGORY

[? *Sept.* 26 1902]   18 *Woburn Buildings*

Dear Friend, I have written to you little and badly of late I am afraid, for the truth is you have a rival in Nietzsche, that strong enchanter. I have read him so much that I have made my eyes bad again. They were getting well it had seemed. Nietzsche completes Blake and has the same roots—I have not read anything with so much excitement since I got to love Morris's stories which have the same curious astringent joy.

Paul [1] is at last finished, sermon and all, and is going to press. I have written in a good deal here and there—sermon gave me most trouble but it is right now. It is as simple as it was and no longer impersonal but altogether a personal dream and it has a Latin text. Edy Craig [2] is as enthusiastic as ever and would I think stage it finely doing great things with the monastery scene which is the most admired scene. There is to be a stone wall, a gallery wall in every outdoor scene as a kind of repeated *motif*. Craig thinks I ought to have given it to him and I may have played the fool in not doing so for I hear he is going into management with his mother. However he gave me no details and one does not take vague promises from a man of his kind. They are going to start with Ibsen's *Heroes of Heligoland* [*The Vikings at Helgeland*].

I have written Fay a very severe letter about Cousins' play *Sold* in U.I. They talk of doing it at once. I have made no objection to their doing it but I have told him that it is 'rubbish and vulgar rubbish.' I have wound up by saying that I did not mark the letter private—he might show it if he liked. Cousins is evidently hopeless and the sooner I have him as an enemy the better. I think Fay will see from my letter that, although I do not interfere with their freedom

---

[1] Paul Ruttledge, the leading character in the play *Where there is Nothing*. Yeats had, at one time, suggested that he and George Moore might collaborate in writing the play, but had later withdrawn it. Moore then said that he was writing a story on the theme and that he would injunct any attempt on Yeats's part to publish the play. It was, however, issued as a supplement to the *United Irishman*, November 1, 1902, and later appeared in book form.

[2] Edith Craig (1869–1947), Ellen Terry's daughter, was for a time on the stage, under Henry Irving and other managements, but devoted the greater part of her life to play production. She was a member of the Managing Committee of the Stage Society during its first five years, 1899–1903, and in 1911 founded the Pioneer Players, a Sunday play-producing society, for which she directed 150 plays.

to produce what they like, too much Cousins would make work in common out of the question. I have suggested that they play foreign masterpieces. I find I can get through Miss Horniman a translation of a fine play of the heroic age of Sudermann's. I have not spoken of this yet but have suggested the last act of *Faustus* to F. Fay. I have learned a great deal about the staging of plays from 'the nativity,' indeed I have learned more than Craig likes. His sister has helped me, bringing me to where I could see the way the lights were worked. He was indignant—there was quite an amusing scene. I have seen all the costumes too, and hope to get patterns. He costumed the whole play—30 or 40 people I should say—for £25.

... I have got £5 from Bullen and I have two coming for a poem from the *Pall Mall* so I am fairly well off for the moment. I have about an hour's work still to do on Spenser and then to dictate it to a typewriter—or some of it.

I shall see you soon now. I shall have so much to say and to hear, and to plan. Yours in all affection W B YEATS

TO LADY GREGORY

Saturday [*Oct.* 4, 1902] Nassau Hotel
South Frederick St.
Dublin

My dear Lady Gregory, All is arranged with the *United Irishman* and Moore has no suspicions. I have not told Russell my plans but have told him about things generally. He has seen Moore. Moore blustered and then Russell said 'Yeats will not lack money to fight it. His friends will give him any amount,' on which Moore got plaintive and after a little seemed inclined to give way. Russell sees him again to-night. There is too much to write. Moore has several quite new and circumstantial lies. He says for instance that when he consented to my writing [the] play he had an understanding that his name was to be on it also, 'second, only second—second on the title page.' This was half way to half profits. Miss Gonne was emphatic about our not telling Russell the plans about [the] play.

I saw rehearsals last night. All very good. Ryan's play is excellent. It is a really very astonishing piece of satire.¹ Am very busy. Yours always   W B YEATS

TO SYDNEY COCKERELL

Oct 17 [1902]   *Coole Park*

My dear Cockerell,² I have been a scandalously long time about writing to you, but my housekeeper in London didn't send your letter on for a couple of weeks. And when it came to me, I was caught in a strange sort of spider's web of George Moore's spinning, which I will explain to you when we meet. My plans were changing every day, and I found it impossible to say what I should publish next. I am not quite out of that web yet, but I know at any rate that I shall have a book to consult you about when I get to London.

Bullen has published a little play of mine, *Kathleen ni Hoolihan*, at the Caradoc Press—and though it is better than mechanical printing it is bad enough. I am sorry I agreed to it. It is not worth the price and I am ashamed to hear of anybody buying it. I shall get to London early in November. Many thanks for your letter and your promise of advice, which I am badly in need of. Yours sincerely   W B YEATS

TO GEORGE RUSSELL (AE)

Oct 18 [*Postmark* 1902]   *Coole Park*

My dear Russell: Many thanks for note about Moore.³ Of course I will publish play. Tell Moore to write his story and be hanged. Yours sincerely   W B YEATS

[1] Fred Ryan was secretary of the Irish National Theatre Society. His play 'The Laying of the Foundations' was produced at the Antient Concert Rooms, Dublin, on October 29, 1902.

[2] Sir Sydney Cockerell, M.A., Litt.D., born 1867, was secretary to William Morris and the Kelmscott Press, 1892–98, partner of Sir Emery Walker, 1900–1904, and Director of the Fitzwilliam Museum at Cambridge, 1908–1937. He remembers the Yeats family as children during their first sojourn in Bedford Park, 1876–1880, but Yeats seems to have met him first at William Morris's house, about 1888.

[3] See note 1, on p. 379.

TO LADY GREGORY[1]

Nov. 20th [1902]   18 *Woburn Buildings*

My dear Lady Gregory, I forgot in my letter to tell you that I went to Fisher Unwin on Monday about your book. He took both your address and the address of Hodges and Figgis, and will I understand write to either you or Hodges. He seemed anxious for the book but wants I imagine to get proofs from Hodges before deciding. All my Moore papers and also Quinn's letters about John Lane copyrights, etc. are now with A. P. Watt. He will keep them with my other papers. I dined with the Shorters last night. Shorter had got that Chancellor photograph of me. It was really very good, the first good photograph. He will put it in the *Sphere* when my next book comes out. Rhys and Mrs. Rhys were there and Shorter tells me they are now beginning to prosper. Mrs. Rhys' last book was a considerable success. The *Pall Mall Magazine* has taken my poem about the old men and the *Monthly Review* has sent me a proof sheet of 'Adam's Curse,' so that is probably taken too.[2] Courtney is going to use the article on William Morris in January. The book of Essays is to be kept back until then. I am going to add the essays I had sketched out in the rough and one or two new little essays. I have come to the conclusion, thinking over Bullen's objection to the sermon in *Where there is Nothing*, that it is too impersonal for Paul as we have now made him. I can easily make this change and the change will make the sermon more convincing and also give it a meaning for the individual soul. The extinguishing of every candle will as I think now associate itself with some precise principle of thought. Bullen complained that I had not written Paul's part in verse. He said an Elizabethan would have done so. Yours ever

                                              W B YEATS

TO LADY GREGORY[1]

November 27th 1902   18 *Woburn Buildings*

My dear Lady Gregory, I have had a message from the Stage Society; they want to play *Where there is Nothing* in January.[3] I am going

[1] Dictated.
[2] 'Adam's Curse' appeared in the *Monthly Review*, December 1902; 'The Old Men admiring themselves in the Water,' in the *Pall Mall Magazine*, January 1903.
[3] The play was eventually given by the Stage Society, though not in January 1903. Three performances took place on June 26, 27 and 28, 1904, at the Royal

down to A. P. Watt now to consult with him. I am inclined to think I ought to consent. Performance by the Stage Society is a slight drawback from the point of view of the ordinary Manager who likes to produce a play himself for the first time. On the other hand I have to decide at once about the Stage Society and if I consent it will be a very considerable advertisement. Shaw's plays were in the first instance performed either by the Stage Society or by the Independent Theatre or some similar body. One at any rate has been taken up by an ordinary theatrical management after a performance by the Stage Society, though not in London. However I shall be guided by A. P. Watt. It was Edith Craig, Ellen Terry's daughter, who introduced the play to them, she says it is the only play for the last fifteen years she has cared about. She wants to play Sabina Silver. Harry Irving, who is I understand good, will play Paul and possibly Welch who is a most accomplished comedian Charlie Ward. I hear there is a strange idea, doubtless started by Pixie Smith,[1] of getting Jack to play Paddy Cockfight. If they do it I shall be requested to change the Franciscans into some order with black habits as they can make black habits much more effective on the stage. I hear that there was a good deal of disputing at the Society about the play but Miss Craig wrote to Dublin and got twelve copies which she distributed. The opposition then came over to her side. I read the amended version last night to Binyon, Sturge Moore, Rhys and a lot of ladies. Everyone considered it greatly improved and the only hostile criticism was that the act in the Monastery was

---

Court Theatre. The direction was by H. Granville Barker and the part of Paul Ruttledge was played by Lyall Swete. Jack B. Yeats did not appear as Paddy Cockfight.

[1] Pamela Colman Smith, familiarly known as Pixie, an American girl who had been brought up in Jamaica, came to London about 1899, and called on the Yeats family in Bedford Park, as described by J. B. Yeats in a letter to his son, dated that year. She soon became a friend of all the family. An artist of considerable facility, with a better sense of colour than of line, she and Jack B. Yeats together provided the illustrations for *A Broad Sheet*, published monthly by Elkin Mathews in 1902–1903. She told Jamaican folk-stories very charmingly and, at one time, professionally, for children's parties, receptions, and the like. For a folder, printed to advertise her performances, appreciations were contributed by Yeats, Arthur Symons, J. M. Barrie, Maurice Hewlett, G. K. Chesterton and others. Yeats wrote: 'Miss Pamela Smith tells her little stories so naturally and simply that one cannot think she would have told them differently at the other side of the world, or a thousand years ago. Our father "time" and our mother "space" have said to her, as they say to none but excellent artists, "You are so good a child that we need not trouble about you. We are as contented as if you were a sod of grass." '

in a different key from the others. This is certainly the case, but whether it is a defect or not I don't quite know. I have after all practically left the sermon unchanged. The only difference is that the last candles put out symbolise hope, memory, thought, and the world, and that man is bid do this when drunk with the wine which comes from pitchers that are in Heaven. At the same time I will probably do a quite new sermon at my leisure but this one can remain for the present.

I am sorry you are putting that voice back at the end of the Raftery play. It is I am certain quite wrong. One of the impossible things. If you feel that it is necessary to make the fact of Raftery being a ghost quite unmistakeable I think you had better discover some other means. Why should not the young man go to the door to see what has happened to Raftery and see him vanish before his eyes? Perhaps into a little cloud of mist, or into a whirl of straw or shavings. After all those entrances and voices, another spoils the picture and the play. It takes away the completeness of the action in some way.

I do not think the Ride to Paradise changes the motive of the little Christ Play from what I suggested. Paradise is happiness, the abundance of earth, the natural life, every man's desire, or some such thing. Miss Owen spoke to the psaltery for me last week, but one felt always that she was a singer. She had learnt what I believe they call voice production, which seems to upset everybody's power of speaking in an impressive way. You felt that she had learnt to take words as musical notes, and not as things having a meaning. However she did very much better when I tried her with a lilt. There is a Mrs. Elliott who is working at it. She has a fine musical ear but has never learnt voice production, and she does it almost as well as Mrs. Emery. She makes her own little lilts and is extraordinarily impressive and poetical. She is a really beautiful person too and that helps things.

I have just failed to see Watt. He was out but on the way I have thought of a very fantastic opening—a comedy opening for Act 4 which will bring it into key with the rest. It is very wild.

I am reading at the allegories in the Museum every day, for Spenser. It is very interesting but there is so much to learn. Yours always   W B YEATS

I send 5/- worth of stamps received from Mrs. Coffey—one guarantor but who she does not say.

TO LADY GREGORY[1]

Dec. 4th 1902 18 *Woburn Buildings*

My dear Lady Gregory, I have had a letter from W. Fay. He makes no mention of the Dress Rehearsal, but speaks of starting with the Play in the middle of January. It seems that they want my Lecture by then and that their present performances are merely to keep the subscribers in good humour and themselves in practice. I have concluded therefore that he cannot get up that Dress Rehearsal. I am very sorry but under the circumstances I suppose I must give up that Dublin journey.

I have just been with A. P. Watt who has read *Where there is Nothing*. He is now of opinion that I should give it to the Stage Society. He praises the play very much but to use his own phrase 'thinks that it deals with too high things for the English theatre under existing circumstances.' He said he would show it to Forbes-Robertson if I liked, but spoke of the difficulty of getting an immediate answer from so busy a man. Delay might lose the chance of getting it performed at all. The performance by the Stage Society will not prevent it being taken up by somebody else. I have also been to see Bernard Shaw and found his wife, who was on the Committee of the theatre, very anxious for the play. In one matter I imagine little Pamela Smith went a little further in her enthusiasm than the facts quite warranted. She spoke of the Committee to me as unanimous. Mrs. Shaw, however, says there is a minority who are afraid of the expense of a play with so many scenes and think that it will be injured by not being played by Irish actors. I doubt if the matter has been definitely decided by vote yet. I think, however, that it is practically decided. Shaw asked me if our Irish Company could be got to come over and play it. However I imagine that this is impossible. Last Monday evening Pamela Smith brought round a big sketch book full of designs for the play made by herself and Edith Craig. They were particularly pleased

[1] Dictated.

because they know Gordon Craig's little stage dodges and are using them rather to his annoyance. He is rather disgusted at the chief part being offered to Harry Irving instead of himself. I thought the design for the Monastery scene extremely impressive. The design for Act I was a little humdrum. To some extent that was my own fault, for that croquet lawn and garden path has been the opening of so many plays. Suddenly while I was looking at it, it occurred to me that it could all be made fantastic by there being a number of bushes shaped Dutch fashion into cocks and hens, ducks, peacocks etc. Pamela began sketching them at once. It can be supposed that these fowl have been the occupation of Paul Ruttledge's ironical leisure for years past. I never did know before what he had been doing all that time.

The changes I am thinking of, the opening of the Monastery scene, in no way touched the vitals of the scene. They are all before the entrance of the Superior. I think that some comedy there will help the balance of the play. Every other act of the play has comedy. I wouldn't mind if one of the early acts was quite serious. They would balance then.

Yes, I have written to Quinn[1] and I have had Joyce with me for a day. He was unexpectedly amiable and did not knock at the gate with his old Ibsenite fury. I am trying to get him work on the *Academy* and *Speaker* and I have brought him to Arthur Symons. I have been twice to the *Speaker* about his affairs and have otherwise wasted a great deal of time. These last few days I have been working particularly hard on the history of Allegory. I had no sooner begun reading at the British Museum after my return when it flashed upon me that the Coming of Allegory coincided with the rise of the Middle Class. That it was the first effect on literature of the earnest spirit which afterwards created Puritanism. I have been hunting through all sorts of books to verify this and am now certain of it. I at last feel able to copy out and finish the Spenser essay. But my

---

[1] John Quinn, Irish-American attorney, had visited Galway in the summer of 1902 where he had met Yeats and Lady Gregory. From that time onward he did much to help their movement, producing small editions of plays by Yeats, Synge and Lady Gregory so as to secure their American copyright, arranging Yeats's first lecture tour in America in the winter of 1903–1904, and giving him hospitality in New York. After 1908, when J. B. Yeats settled in New York, Quinn looked after him as well as he could and often financed him when he was short of money, being repaid by the manuscripts which Yeats sent him for his collection.

work at the Museum has made my eyes very feverish again and I don't quite know what to do for the moment.

Bernard Shaw talks again of writlng a play for us.[1] Certainly it would be a great thing for our Company if he will do us an Irish play. I had the first proof sheets of my sister's print of the Poems,[2] they look very well indeed. I think I have arranged that they follow them up with a very witty and unknown story of Bernard Shaw's.[3] He offers to correct the proofs entirely for the purpose of making the print look nice. He says Morris never revised for any other reason. Yours always   W B YEATS

TO LADY GREGORY [4]

December 9th, 1902   18 *Woburn Buildings*

My dear Lady Gregory, I am on my way down to Edy Craig's to see some of the Stage Society people. I have been writing hard at Spenser and think it will be done in a few days. I am only using what I dictated to you as what Moore calls a smoky ceiling. It is full of suggestion and has fine passages I think but it is too incoherent. I am basing the whole thing on my conviction that England up to the time of the Parliamentary Wars was the Anglo-French nation and that the hitherto conquered Saxon elements rose into power with Cromwell. This idea certainly makes my essay very striking, it enables me to say all kinds of interesting things about that time.

Sturge Moore has done me some designs for *The Hour-Glass* working out Robert's sketch into practical detail.[5] He is emphatic, however, about the great difficulty of getting a green that will go

[1] The play Bernard Shaw wrote for the Irish players was *John Bull's Other Island*. It was considered then to be outside the company's range and was first played at the Court Theatre, London, as one of the earliest of the famous Vedrenne-Barker performances, on November 1, 1904. It was not given at the Abbey Theatre until September 1916.

[2] *In the Seven Woods*, the first book to be issued by the Dun Emer Press founded by Elizabeth C. Yeats. It appeared in August 1903.

[3] Bernard Shaw's story 'The Miraculous Revenge' had already been printed in the magazine *Time* in March 1885. Although announced by the Dun Emer Press it did not appear, but it was later printed in the *Shanachie*, Spring 1906. See the letter to Stephen Gwynn of June 13, 1906 (p. 473).

[4] Dictated.

[5] Lady Gregory's son. He designed some scenery for the Irish National Theatre Society and for the Abbey Theatre in its early days.

well with purple and wants me to have the curtains made of some undyed material. I have written to Fay for some patterns of the purple and to ask if there was to be any green in the costumes. I think the Moore design looks very impressive.

I have just been down to the *Academy* office to get them to take work from Joyce which they are ready to do. They showed me quite a long article there which some woman has sent about *Where there is Nothing*. Walkley's [1] comment on Bottomley's vague little play amused me very much. The insolence towards the present state of the stage which he found in poor Bottomley's stage direction is our wicked defiance and I am quite certain that it was Father Dineen's hare which has convinced him that all our stage directions are equally insolent.[2] I sent him a copy of *Samhain*. I send you an *Academy* though no doubt you will see it with Symons's letter and mine about the best books of the year.[3] This is a very scatter-brained letter, but I have been running about doing a lot of things and am in a great hurry to get down to Edy Craig's. If the Stage Society does the play it will be at the end of February. I had almost forgotten to tell you that Pamela Smith is bringing out a magazine to be called the *Hour-Glass* [4] after my play. I am to write the preface in

[1] Arthur Bingham Walkley (1855–1926) was a well-known dramatic critic, at first writing for the *Star* and the *Speaker*, and from 1900 to 1926 for *The Times*; he published several volumes of his collected criticisms.

[2] A review, unsigned but almost certainly by Walkley, in the *Times Literary Supplement*, December 5, 1902, of Gordon Bottomley's play *The Crier by Night*, said he was too much influenced by Yeats 'and his foolish friends,' and quoted the following stage-direction:

'In the cottage the sound of a heavily, unconsciously falling body is heard; after that nothing happens any more.

When the playhouse lights waken again, the curtain is found to have descended silently, unknown to the audience.'

The review commented: 'The point is not that these directions are impracticable in themselves, but that they are couched in a language which declares an attitude of completely stupid insolence towards the playhouse and its audience.'

[3] The *Academy* invited a number of well-known men and women to name the two books they had read with most interest and pleasure during the year. In 1901 Yeats mentioned Laurence Binyon's *Odes* and Sturge Moore's *Aphrodite against Artemis*; and in 1902 he wrote: 'But for a few works sent me by young authors I should have read no book published this year, so far as I can recollect, except Lady Gregory's *Cuchullain of Muirthemne*. I am entirely certain of the immortality of this book, and doubt if such noble and simple English has been written since the death of Morris.'

[4] Pamela Colman Smith did not bring out the projected magazine to be called the *Hour-Glass*, but in 1903 and 1904 she published thirteen numbers of the *Green Sheaf*, numbered but not dated except by year, with many hand-coloured illustrations by herself and other artists, and contributions by Yeats, J. M. Synge,

order to define the policy which I have got them to take up. The magazine is to be consecrated to what I called, to their delight, the Art of Happy Desire. It is to be quite unlike gloomy magazines like the *Yellow Book* and the *Savoy*. People are to draw pictures of places they would have liked to have lived in and to write stories and poems about a life they would have liked to have lived. Nothing is to be let in unless it tells of something that seems beautiful or charming or in some other way desirable. They are not to touch the accursed Norwegian cloud in any way, even though they may be all good Ibsenites, and they are not to traffic in Gorky. There is a fine mixture of metaphor. I tell you about it because I know they are going to ask you for some little stories out of your Finn book. Ricketts and Shannon are going to do them pictures and I think they will make quite a stir in the world for a little time at any rate.

I will write again to-morrow if I can. Yours always

W B YEATS

TO LADY GREGORY [1]

Dec. 12th, 1902   18 *Woburn Buildings*

My dear Lady Gregory, I have made the changes in *Where there is Nothing*. The new opening to Act IV. came quite easily. I have done a new opening to Act III also as the Act was rather short and I thought rather hurried at the outset. I have also done a new version of the Sermon and some slight changes at the outset of Act V. I find I manage the dialect pretty well, but will get you to go over it. It is possible that I shall be reading the revised play to Harry Irving on Sunday evening. He is rather hesitating over the part, I am sorry to say. He has begun to feel that it will be a very big undertaking. I am to read *The Hour-Glass* and *A Pot of Broth* to Edy Craig, Pamela and some other people on Monday night. I have had an enthusiastic letter from Maclagan about *Where there is Nothing* and a note from Grant Richards wanting to publish it.

Lady Gregory, John Masefield and others. A number of writers recounted dreams, Yeats describing a 'Dream of the World's End' in the second number. In the fourth number a reproduction of a pastel drawing by him of 'The Lake at Coole' was included as a supplement.
[1] Dictated.

No! I don't like that Sycamore poem, I think it perfectly detestable and always did and am going to write to Russell to say that the *Homestead* mustn't do this kind of thing any more.[1] I was furious last year when they revived some rambling old verses of mine but forgot about it. I wouldn't so much mind if they said they were early verses but they print them as if they were new work.

Fay writes to say that they had thin audiences in Dublin last week but that the profits were excellent. Brimley Johnson, who is becoming quite a large publisher (I mean a publisher of lots of books), writes to me 'What a lovely book Lady Gregory has given us. You didn't say a word too much for it.'

Have you read Gwynn in *Fortnightly* on our Theatre? Yours always   W B YEATS

P.S. I will shortly send you a new version of *The Travelling Man* to go over for me.[2] If I only had the plays done I might get some money out of Bullen for them. *The Travelling Man* will be wanted as *Kathleen* is not to go in I am sorry to say.

Could you send me that little bit about Finn killing the man of the children's Dana who burnt Tara to the sound of music. I want it for Spenser.

TO LADY GREGORY

Tuesday [*Dec.* 16, 1902]   18 *Woburn Buildings*

Dear Friend, Fay writes that they think of putting your play in rehearsal at once. They have also a three act comedy by Cousins. I have come to the conclusion that it will be better to publish *Where there is Nothing* by itself as Vol I of Plays for an Irish Theatre. Bullen does not want *Kathleen* reprinted for the present. Without it I thought the other two little plays would be overweighted and if I wanted to put in *The Travelling Man* I should have to wait until you came here before going to press. It would also keep me from

---

[1] See page 55.
[2] *The Travelling Man*, a one-act play, was apparently first written by Yeats, but he evidently handed it over to Lady Gregory. It was printed in her *Seven Short Plays*, Dublin: Maunsel & Co., 1909, with a note saying 'I owe the Rider's Song and some of the rest to W. B. Yeats.' It was first played at the Abbey Theatre on March 2, 1910.

getting them taken by a review in all likelihood. I can do another little play I have in my head and bring out all the little plays (including *Kathleen*) later on as Vol. 2. I can get some money at once out of Bullen on it as Paul is now ready (I have added a good deal here and there). What do you think of this plan?

Yes I like that new ending for the Raftery very well on thinking over it. I think it will make the play a good deal stronger. Do not forget to make the marriage guests show plenty of amazement at the dead man come to life. I have very near finished Spenser—it is quite a new essay though it contains many passages of the old. An hour's work will finish the critical part and then I have a day's work to do on the life. After that comes *Cuchullain* and this must be amended at once for my sister,[1] and then the wind up of this [book[2]] of which I have dictated some new little essays. I am getting along pretty well with my eyes except that I can no longer work at night at all, and have got to spare them a good deal always. How are your eyes? Have they got over their weariness? I need not tell you that I am always wishing for the time to pass swiftly until we are together again. Your always   W B YEATS

TO LADY GREGORY

[*Postmark Jan 3, 1903*]   18 *Woburn Buildings*

Dear Friend, Yesterday I sent off the Spenser essay to the publisher. It is a great relief to have got it done. I think you will find it very good. It is much saner than it was and yet quite as original. It is all founded now on a single idea—the contrast between Anglo-French England and Anglo-Saxon England. I hope in a couple more days to have got *Cuchullain* finally right and sent to my sisters. Then (I am afraid you will be sorry to hear) I propose to put certain parts of *The Hour-Glass* into verse—only the part with the Angel and the soliloquies. I have got to think this necessary to lift the 'Wise man's' part out of a slight element of platitude. The play will then go to enlarge my sister's book. I shall have a sub-title printed in red before the two plays 'Plays for an Irish Theatre' and

[1] This became *On Baile's Strand* and formed part of the first book published by Elizabeth C. Yeats from the Dun Emer Press, *In the Seven Woods*, August 1903.
[2] *Ideas of Good and Evil*, published in May 1903.

have same sub-title to *Where there is Nothing* and the other plays when they come. It is rather difficult to manage the issue of the little plays at the same time with the long one. *Kathleen* is a difficulty that I could get over, but if I put *The Hour-Glass* with the poems that is a worse difficulty. When you come we can do the little Christ play and that other one about the lawyer and make Bullen put *Kathleen*, *Pot of Broth*, Christ play and the new one together. I am planning a performance here of *The Hour-Glass*. The finding of a wonderful 'angel' has moved me to it.

I want you to write and ask Kuno Meyer (or send me his address that I may) to return the faery lore articles of mine that he borrowed a year ago.[1] I want them now. I am going to lecture in Cardiff on Feb. 19th on 'The Irish Faery Kingdom.' I am to be put up and to get £10. I am also going to lecture here on something or other and get £5. It looks as if lecturing was going to become profitable. Dolmetsch recommends it to me strongly.

I have just heard a ring and gone down to find that Mrs. Old has stolen a march on me. For some time I have talked vaguely of getting a gas oven in my inner room. It would cook my breakfast and warm the room while I was eating it—at present I catch colds constantly—especially if the fire refuses to light. It seems that Mrs. Old who wants the gas oven for her cooking went to the gas company without being told. It will cost me about £2 10s at the start. The gas man has just been and gone. Do you recommend me to have gas for lighting purposes or to keep it for cooking only? It will be a great comfort. I have a dressing gown (a Xmas present but by that hangs a tale) and I can slip down and light it and have the room warm for breakfast, which can be always set out in the inner room.

I have just heard from Shaw—he is afraid of our doing his 'Napoleon'[2] which has never been well acted enough.

A Madame Troncey is doing my portrait. She is a friend of Miss Horniman and is really a fine artist. It is the best yet. She is to give it me after sending it to the Salon. It is in black chalk. She is also to do a profile in colour which I am to have at once.

[1] Kuno Meyer, Ph.D. (1858–1919), philologist and Professor of Celtic Literature at the University of Berlin. He founded the School of Irish Learning, Dublin, 1903, and published many translations from the Gaelic.
[2] *The Man of Destiny*. It was eventually played at the Abbey Theatre, but not until March 1922.

You have not told me anything about your essays. Are they being printed yet and when are they to be published?

Yes it has been a good year with me too—a very good year. Yours always   W B YEATS

TO LADY GREGORY[1]

Jan. 6th, 1903   18 *Woburn Buildings*

My dear Friend, A great many thanks. I was just wondering what I was to do. After sending you that letter about the play I recollected how stupid I was. There was no reason in the world why including it in my sister's book should exclude it from the book of plays. However I will not include it in my sister's book if you still greatly object. My reasons for wishing to do so are these. They are going to charge ten shillings for the book and as an artistic press like theirs is forbidden to adopt the usual methods of padding out the poems, the Cuchullain play and all will come to about forty or fifty pages. This may be long enough. It will depend to some extent on the general look of the book. I do not agree with you that *The Hour-Glass* when I have put the verse into it would be out of tune with the rest. It repeats practically the Fool and the Blind Man of *The Hour-Glass*[2] and would have something the same proportion of verse and prose. I am rather glad on the whole that you have protested so strongly against the exclusion of any of the plays from the little book. Armed with this new reason I shall press my opinion on Bullen. I have not done so hitherto because although he always acknowledges my right to do what I like with *Cathleen* I have not liked to make his loss over that foolish little book greater than necessary. Through a very needless piece of good nature he seems to have greatly overpaid the printer. The result is that though I think I got too little I do not think he has got anything at all. It must be a lesson to me in the matter of vague agreements. Now however that you object to its

[1] Dictated.
[2] This is apparently a slip of the pen; the Fool and the Blind Man are characters in *On Baile's Strand*. Yeats did not complete his poetic version of *The Hour-Glass* until 1913 when it was published in Gordon Craig's magazine the *Mask* in April, and included in *Responsibilities* the following year. Both versions were printed in *Plays in Prose and Verse*, 1922, but only the poetic version in the *Collected Plays* of 1934.

exclusion I shall go to Bullen and say 'It's no use our wasting time while you are hoping to get back that lost money. We will both do very much better by bringing out the new plays soon, while the effect of the Stage Society performance of *Where there is Nothing* lasts. What is the soonest date at which you would agree to bring them out?'

I am not quite certain that it will be wise to publish them simultaneously with *Where there is Nothing*, as the publication a little later will mean double the amount of reviewing and double the amount of advertising therefore for both books. I am also inclined to think that if we published them together we should have to call them volume one and two and charge for them both together a sum much smaller than we would have to charge for them if they were published separately. However I will go and see Watt tomorrow about it. I have begun to have the greatest possible contempt for my dear Bullen's business capacity.

Sturge Moore was round with me last night and he made to Gordon Craig (through a friend of Craig's that was there) an offer on Ricketts's behalf. He proposed that Ricketts should raise nearly £600 which should be used by Craig to stage my *Countess Cathleen*. All the speaking of verse to be left entirely in the hands of Sturge Moore and of course the author. I need hardly say that this performance, which is evidently going to be a much bigger thing than I had foreseen, will enormously strengthen my position. It makes me a little anxious about the performance of *Where there is Nothing*. I have left the securing of the cast entirely to Miss Craig, and I have no way of judging whether she will be able to get good performers.

I have arranged for another lecture (or did I tell you about it?) which I am to give in London on March the 7th. I am to get £5. I believe that Mrs. Emery and myself are to get £20 between us for our lecture on the Psaltery in Manchester on Ash Wednesday. Mrs. Emery made me extremely cross last night. I had some people there whom I had a particular reason (they were friends of Craig's and Ellen Terry's) for wanting to hear her at her best, and out of sheer laziness she gave the worst performance on the Psaltery I have ever heard. There are times when she makes me despair of the whole thing. However Miss Owen is beginning to be a comfort. She has nothing like Mrs. Emery's gift but she is immensely painstaking.

If you still feel that *The Hour-Glass* will be out of place in my sister's book please write and tell me why you think so. Of course I shall not include it in the ordinary edition of the poems. My sister's book is merely a specially beautiful and expensive first edition of certain of my best things. I have been thinking of putting a note at the end explaining why I have called the book by the name of one of the shortest poems *In the Seven Woods*. Have you a copy of that poem which I wrote for three speakers—the one calling for a blessing on the Psalteries? I wrote to Mrs. Emery for a copy and she sent me what I am afraid is her only one and I am afraid I have lost it. I want to include it with the lyrics in my sister's book. I shall put the Cathleen na Hoolihan poem also amongst them. If you have the poem for the three voices please send it to me at once. Yours

W B YEATS

TO LADY GREGORY

[*Postmark* Jan 8, 1903]   18 *Woburn Buildings*

Dear Friend, I went to Bullen and arranged that the plays come out in two 3/6 volumes making vol 1 and vol 2 of 'Plays for an Irish Theatre.' *Kathleen* and *Hour-Glass* both will be in vol. 2. 3/6 a volume will enable Dublin people to buy them. I am in a great hurry as I have to get to Sturge Moore's. I am having an angry correspondence with Mrs. Emery about Monday's performance. Yours

W B YEATS

TO LADY GREGORY [1]

Jan 13*th* [1903]   18 *Woburn Buildings*

Dear Friend, Let me know as soon as you can when I am to expect you. I hear *Sold* has been given up, and that they are rehearsing Colum's *Saxon Shilling*. I am very glad of this as it will encourage him and be nothing against our dignity. Maud Gonne also wrote and protested against *Sold*. Bernard Shaw has given them leave to play either *Arms and the Man*, *Widowers' Houses* or *The Devil's Disciple*.

[1] Dictated.

Stephen Gwynn was dining with me last night and was full of the project of their coming to play in London. However I a little shrink, in spite of my curiosity, from seeing *Cathleen na Hoolihan* with either Miss Quinn or Miss Walker as the principal character. I have written to William Sharp asking your question about Fiona Macleod's book. At the same time I doubt if any book of hers will interfere with either you or me. She is quite certain to turn it all into her own sort of wild romance while both you and I give the foundations themselves. Neither does it follow that her book is really on the edge of publication for she has been announcing books for years which have never come out. I should not wonder at all if her plans were to completely change before my question reaches her.

I have heard from the Scottish publishers to whom I have sent the Spenser. They thank me for a 'particularly interesting essay and selection,' and send me £20 on account. At the same time they say that owing to the delay of several authors about sending in of MSS. they have had 'to reconsider' the series or the publication, I forget which, and that they cannot publish for some time. This makes me wonder whether the project may not be practically abandoned. I imagine therefore that I shall write and make an enquiry or two before accepting the cheque. Will you be able to find room for my Shrine when you come over? You can leave the picture which is at the Nassau until we go over for the play as you would find it rather a trouble. Yours always   W B YEATS

TO LADY GREGORY

[*Postmark Jan* 15, 1903]   18 *Woburn Buildings*

Dear Friend, I return the essay. It is admirable. I have pencilled one or two things which explain themselves. They are chiefly in one sentence that was not quite vocal. I am very glad that you have done it. I am very pleased to think that both you and I will have some books out together which will be fairly cheap and altogether for Irish readers. I am thinking of your essays and of my plays. I doubt if I could get 'the birds [?]' done, even if I could give it all my time, ready for my sisters when they got to that part of the book. I find that *Cuchullain* wants new passages here and there. You need not be troubled about my poetical faculty. I was never so full of new thoughts for verse, though all thoughts quite unlike the old ones. My work has got far more masculine. It has more salt in it. I have several poems in my head.

I believe that my gas stove is to be put to rights tomorrow. It will make a very substantial change for the better in my comfort....
Yours always   W B YEATS

TO SYDNEY COCKERELL

March 18 [1903] *Coole Park*

My dear Cockerell, I have two letters to thank you for. I am glad you liked the Morris article, which I think is one of the best things of the sort I have done. It is a part of my new book *Ideas of Good and Evil*.

By the bye, I want your advice about the binding of this book. I find that Bullen is rather petulant and I don't think always listens very carefully to one's directions—so I want to write him directions that cannot possibly be misunderstood.

I should like to have it bound in boards, grey or blue, a white back, bound round with real cords, like one of the examples you showed me.

Can you give me three or four sentences which Bullen can send to the binders? I don't know for instance how to describe the cords. I am telling him to bind the prose play in grey boards with unglazed holland back with a label on it. I suppose this is all right.

I had a play performed in Dublin last week, a morality play.[1] It was played with simplicity and beauty. It was a great success.
Yours sincerely   W B YEATS

TO SYDNEY COCKERELL

March 22 [1903] *Coole Park*

My dear Cockerell—I return proof of colophon,[2] for which many thanks. It is charming, but I rather agree with you that it would be

[1] *The Hour-Glass* was played by the Irish National Theatre Society at the Molesworth Hall, Dublin, on March 14.
[2] This was presumably the colophon for *In the Seven Woods*. Miss Yeats had received some advice and instruction as to the management of her hand press from Cockerell's partner, Emery Walker, the typographical adviser.

better somewhat larger. I don't quite know to what extent my sisters are in a hurry but Mr. Walker probably knows this. I only saw them amid a whirl of people in Dublin and shall not be able to go into details with them for another week or more when I shall be in Dublin again.

The book is a long way yet from the level of the printing but Mr. Walker will know perhaps when they mean to bring out a prospectus and whether the colophon is to be a part of it.

Many thanks for your information about the binding. I left the little lecture behind me unfortunately, but I remember the look of it. I will write at once and tell Bullen to bind in your hand-made paper with the glazed holland back and to send you a dummy. Yours sincerely   W B YEATS

TO LADY GREGORY

[*Late April* 1903]   18 *Woburn Buildings*

Dear Lady Gregory ... 'Paul' is bound now and I will get a copy sent you to-day. I wonder when it will be possible to publish it. The essays are to be published on May 7th and bound copies should be ready to-day or to-morrow.

I saw *Vikings* last night. I liked Ellen Terry in it and liked moments of the play altogether and it all interested me. Craig's scenery is amazing but rather distracts one's thoughts from the words. The poor verses I made for them are spoken with great energy but are quite inaudible.[1] There is a kind of lyre to which he is supposed to speak and out of that amazing lyre comes the whole orchestra, wind instruments and all, and every one of them makes the most of its naturally loud voice. I suggested that the fortunes of the theatre might be retrieved (house was half empty) by their imitating *The Times* and having a prize competition. So many hundreds for anybody who could hear three lines together, and £5 apiece for words heard anywhere. This amused Miss Craig who had tried to get the verses properly spoken. The play is not I think a

---

[1] Dr. Martin Shaw, who composed the music for Ellen Terry's production of *The Vikings*, says that he did not use the words supplied by Yeats but returned to William Archer's version of the song as being more like Ibsen; small wonder that Yeats could not distinguish his words during the performance.

really very great play. One constantly finds when one pierces beneath the stage tumult that the passions, or rather the motives, are conventional. There is a touch of melodrama in the characterization. These heroes alternate between impulses of very obvious Christian charity and more barbaric energies in the suddenest way. I felt that Ibsen had not really grasped and unified the old life. He had no clear thought or emotion about it. Of course however the play is better worth seeing than anything else that has been here this long while and for this reason it is failing. Ellen Terry, when I saw her for a moment after it was over, said 'Well it is a fine play to have made a failure with.' She added that everybody there had got a good living wage out of it and so it did not matter—everybody but she herself who would get nothing. She impresses me a good deal by her vitality and a kind of joyousness.

I saw Joyce in Dublin; he said his mother was still alive and it was uncertain whether she would die or not. He added 'but these things really don't matter.' I spoke to him about his behaviour at *Academy* office and other things of the kind rather sternly. He took it unexpectedly well. Yours ever   W B YEATS

[*On back of envelope, dated May 1st*] In one of Quinn's letters he spoke of misprints in 'Paul.' Please send me a list of misprints if you can find letter. I would want it at once.

TO LADY GREGORY

[*Postmark May 4, 1903*]   [*London*]

My dear Friend, Forgive this absurd paper—I have no other. The plays were a great success.[1] I never saw a more enthusiastic audience. I send you some papers, all that I have found notices in. When I remember the notices I have seen of literary adventures on the stage I think them better than we could have hoped. The *Daily News* one is by Philip Carr I think. The *Leader* is I imagine by Archer. I have

[1] Stephen Gwynn had arranged for the Irish National Theatre Society to pay a flying visit to London. They gave two performances at the Queen's Gate Hall on Saturday, May 2, 1903, playing *The Hour-Glass*, *Twenty-Five* by Lady Gregory, and *Kathleen ni Houlihan* at a matinée, and *The Pot of Broth*, *The Foundations* by Fred Ryan, and *Kathleen ni Houlihan* in the evening.

noticed that the young men, the men of my generation or younger, are the people who like us. It was a very distinguished audience. Blunt was there, but went after your play as he was just recovering from the influenza and seemed to be really ill. I thought your play went very well. Fay was charming as Christie. The game of cards is still the weak place, but with all defects the little play has a real charm. If we could amend the cards it would be a strong play too. Lady Aberdeen, Henry James, Michael Field, who has written me an enthuasiastic letter about the acting, Lord Aberdeen, Mrs. Wyndham, chief secretary Mathers, Lord Mounteagle, Mrs. Thackeray Ritchie, and I don't know how many other notables were there and all I think were moved. Lady Aberdeen has asked the Fay company to go to the St. Louis exhibition to play there for six months. She wants them to give another performance in London before the committee in summer and then if the committee like them all capital would be found. The company are so excited with their success that they are inclined to go. They may be more sober next week. I conclude they would have to give up their situations and become a regular company. It would be a year hence. Fay is very anxious for it, as he thinks it would start them with prestige and experience. My American tour would help them I dare say.

The evening audience was the more Irish of the two and *Cathleen* and *The Pot of Broth* got a great reception. *The Pot of Broth* was not gagged this time. Miss Laird is now the mother in *Cathleen* and is certainly much better than Miss Quinn was—indeed she seems to me as near perfect as possible. *The Foundations* went well, indeed everything went well. Yours always   W B YEATS

TO LADY GREGORY

[*Postmark May 9, 1903*]   [*London*]

Dear Friend: I lecture on Tuesday on Heroic and Folk poetry, Mrs. Emery to illustrate it on psaltery. Could you send me that story about the favourite music of the Fianna, and about Finn liking best 'what happens'? I would take great care of it and send it back safely. It would be a great help. I suppose if it went Sunday or first post Monday I would get it by Tuesday morning. The success of the

FLORENCE FARR

plays here will help the chanting and all the more practical side of my work immensely. What a beautiful notice Walkley has given us, in the *Times Supplement*. The only unhappy thing about the performance is that it was not 'the Irish Literary Society' people but a generally fashionable and artistic audience—that filled the Hall. In the evening there were a good many Irish people at the back but on the whole our own people did not support us (at least Gwynn says they did not). Those that were there however certainly made up for this by their enthusiasm.

I wish I was back in Ireland and at work again there, and with you near me. London is worse than it was I think. Yours

W B YEATS

TO FLORENCE FARR [1]

May 14th, 1903   18 *Woburn Buildings*

My dear Mrs. Emery, I hope that your illness is no worse than a day's discomfort and that you will be able to come after all to-morrow. Of course if you are ill there is no more to be said, but if you can come it will be of importance for it is much more important for that lecture to go well than for the Irish Literary Society evening to go well. I shall be quite content if you do one single poem to-morrow. I have had a letter from the editor of the *Daily News* asking permission to interview me on the Theatre and the New Art. Now to-morrow's lecture is got up by people connected with the *Speaker* and the *Daily News*. If the lecture goes well it will help towards other lectures. I have an invitation, for instance, from Edinburgh and if only we can get a little credit for this double performance of ours it may enable me to get the Edinburgh people to invite us both. In some ways the Theatre is a more taking subject than the New Art itself. I have much more to say about it and can group all our activities under this one title. A rich subject like this will enable me to tax you much less. You will always be able to speak to the Psaltery much or little as

[*The rest of this letter is lost*]

[1] Probably dictated. Text from *Florence Farr, Bernard Shaw and W. B. Yeats*, Cuala Press, 1941.

TO GEORGE RUSSELL (AE)[1]

May 14th, 1903   18 *Woburn Buildings*

My dear Russell, I send you *Ideas of Good and Evil*, a book which will I think have an interest. The only review that has been as yet is as enthusiastic as one could have wished. The book is only one half of the orange for I only got a grip on the other half very lately. I am no longer in much sympathy with an essay like 'The Autumn of the Body,' not that I think that essay untrue. But I think I mistook for a permanent phase of the world what was only a preparation. The close of the last century was full of a strange desire to get out of form, to get to some kind of disembodied beauty, and now it seems to me the contrary impulse has come. I feel about me and in me an impulse to create form, to carry the realization of beauty as far as possible. The Greeks said that the Dionysiac enthusiasm preceded the Apollonic and that the Dionysiac was sad and desirous, but that the Apollonic was joyful and self sufficient. Long ago I used to define to myself these two influences as the Transfiguration on the Mountain and the Incarnation, only the Transfiguration comes before [? after] the Incarnation in the natural order. I would like to know what you think of the book, and if you could make your Hermetists read it I have a notion that it would do them a world of good.

I have not yet been through your poems, for the truth is I had to ransack all my books to find your two published volumes, and now that I have got one at any rate and I think the two I am up to my ears in the preparation of lectures. I shall have leisure however after next Tuesday, when I return from Manchester, and will let you know at once then.[2] Yours ever   W B YEATS

TO JOHN QUINN[1]

May 15, 1903   18 *Woburn Buildings*

My dear Quinn, A great many thanks for your letter, which Lady Gregory has sent on to me. I sent you a corrected copy of *Where*

[1] Dictated.
[2] This suggests that Yeats was making the selection of AE's poems for *The Nuts of Knowledge* which the Dun Emer Press published in December 1903. The volume contained 32 poems, ten of which were reprinted from *Homeward: Songs by the Way* and ten from *The Earth Breath*.

there is Nothing that you might revise the American book. Tomorrow I shall send you my new book, *Ideas of Good and Evil*. I feel that much of it is out of my present mood; that it is true, but no longer true for me. I have been in a great deal better health lately, and that and certain other things have made me look upon the world, I think, with somewhat more defiant eyes. The book is too lyrical, too full of aspirations after remote things, too full of desires. Whatever I do from this out will, I think, be more creative. I will express myself, so far as I express myself in criticism at all, by that sort of thought that leads straight to action, straight to some sort of craft. I have always felt that the soul has two movements primarily: one to transcend forms, and the other to create forms. Nietzsche, to whom you have been the first to introduce me, calls these the Dionysiac and the Apollonic, respectively. I think I have to some extent got weary of that wild God Dionysus, and I am hoping that the Far-Darter will come in his place.

I am delighted with your New York Irish Literary Society and think it should do great service. Your proposed president, Charles Johnston, was a school-fellow of mine, as I daresay he has told you. He is a clever man, and why he has not done much more with his cleverness I do not know. I daresay he has some great work hidden away. I have not seen him for a good many years and so do not know what he is doing.

I think you had better choose for your actors *Cathleen ni Houlihan* and *The Pot of Broth*. They are in prose and that makes them easier. I do not know what to think about *The Land of Heart's Desire* as a play till we have done it in Dublin. It was played in London successfully enough about seven years ago, but certainly not well played or played with any right method. I wish I had seen the American performance of it. However, you had better stick to the prose for the present, more especially as there will be new verse plays of mine out shortly. These new plays, written with so much more knowledge of the stage, should act well. Besides, they will give you a larger range of selection and so make it easier for you to pick out what suits your players. I have not sent you the last play for the little book of short plays because I cannot make up my mind about it. I started it on one plan and re-wrote it on quite a different one, and I have got so confused about it that I shall not be able to judge it for a few weeks more, I suspect. Should I suddenly change my mind I will send it to you at once. I think it wants a few touches and that I had better forget it a little before I make them. There is a good lyric in it which Mrs. Emery speaks to the psaltery with great success. It reminds me that I must send you the musical setting for the verses in *Cathleen* and in *The Pot of Broth*.

I have left your letter at home and am dictating this at a typewriting office, so please excuse me if I have left any of your questions unanswered. I will write again presently if I have. I must finish now as I am off to St. James's Park, where I have to give a lecture on the Theatre. Mrs. Emery and another speaker to notes are to illustrate it. Yours ever

W B YEATS

TO SYDNEY COCKERELL

May 16th, 1903   18 *Woburn Buildings*

My dear Cockerell, I have behaved very badly in not writing to you, but I have expected each morning to get down to Clifford's Inn. However I have been heavy with a cold and working hard preparing for a lecture which came off yesterday afternoon, and so have not got down to you after all. I am very sorry that I cannot go to you tomorrow, but I am going down to Manchester with Mrs. Emery to give a lecture on Speaking to the Psaltery. We are getting £20 for it so the New Art is beginning to march. I think the proof of the colophon very delightful. When can my sister have the block to experiment with? I know she is anxious for it. I shall get back from Manchester on Tuesday, and Wednesday in all likelihood I shall look in on you and Walker. I want my sisters to bring out a Primer on the New Art. Dolmetsch is ready to write an Essay [1] and to go through Mrs. Emery's notations. To touch them up here and there and pick the best. I have been discussing with Dolmetsch the problem of music printing. As far as I can make out it will be impossible for my sisters to do this part of the work. What I want to know is, would it be out of the question to have the letter press printed by my sisters and the musical notations printed by the

[1] The book by Arnold Dolmetsch about Speaking to the Psaltery, though announced for publication by the Dun Emer Press, never appeared.

Chiswick Press (they have a charming musical type) and these notations made up into a little music book and put into a pocket made in the cover of the Primer? If this would be all wrong I must get Bullen to publish the Primer and to print the whole thing at the Chiswick Press.

Please tell Lady Margaret and her cousin that I am very sorry not to have been able to meet them at your place tomorrow. Yours ever   W B YEATS

TO A. B. WALKLEY [1]

June 20 [Postmark June 29, 1903]   *Coole Park*

Dear Mr. Walkley, I agree with you that *Where there is Nothing* is very loosely constructed; too loosely constructed I think; I have a plan for pulling it a little more together before it is acted. However it is not quite as ramshackle as you think it. Those children were not Paul's but his brother's, in fact the fools that he begot. If you look again at page 7 and page 16 you will find that the children are a part of the situation. I have tried to suggest, without saying it straight out, that Paul finds himself unnecessary in his own house, and therefore the more inclined to take to the roads. I think too that I could arrange the acting so that the end of Act I would not be an anti-climax. I see the perambulator on the middle of the stage, or rather I cannot see it, for everyone is standing round it, stooping over it with their backs to me. Is it not the conqueror of all the idealists? And are not all these magistrates but its courtiers and its servants?

I am writing these prose plays knowing well that they are rather a departure from my own proper work, which is plays in verse. I am doing them because prose plays are necessary to our little theatre, and also because one likes to try experiments. I am trying to learn my business and am very grateful for any criticism such as yours. I tried deliberately in *Where there is Nothing* to see how loose I could make construction without losing the actable quality. Perhaps I

[1] From a typewritten copy. At this time A. B. Walkley contributed a weekly article on drama, unsigned, to the *Times Literary Supplement*. His article on June 26, 1903, was devoted to a review of *Where there is Nothing*, then recently published.

405

have lost it, but when I tried at the outset to construct more tightly I found Paul losing his freedom and spontaneity. Other people's souls began to lay their burden upon him. I thought I would try if a play would keep its unity upon the stage with no other device than one always dominant person about whom the world was always drifting away. I am writing a play now in verse but it is in one act, and I am more confident in one act. I am dictating this letter, for I have to keep all my eyesight for my play. Yours sincerely

W B YEATS

TO JOHN QUINN

June 28, 1903 *Coole Park*

My dear Quinn, I should have written long ago to thank you for all you have done, but my eyes have been much worse than usual, and I was moving about. You must have had endless work, for I know what the production of a play is. The success of the plays has been a great pleasure and encouragement. I remember very well that when I first began to write plays I had hoped for just such an audience. One wants to write for one's own people, who come to the playhouse with a knowledge of one's subjects and with hearts ready to be moved. Almost the greatest difficulty before good work in the ordinary theatres is that the audience has no binding interest, no great passion or bias that the dramatist can awake. I suppose it was some thought of this kind that made Keats's lines telling how Homer left great verses to a little clan seem to my imagination when I was a boy a description of the happiest fate that could come to a poet. My work is, I am afraid, too full of a very personal comment on life, too full of the thoughts of the small sect you and I and all other cultivated people belong to, ever to have any great popularity. But certainly if Finvara, that ancient God, now King of Faery, whose sacred hill I passed the other day in the railway train, were to come into the room with all his hosts of the Sidhe behind him and offer me some gift, I know right well the gift I should ask. I would say 'Let my plays be acted, sometimes by professional actors if you will, but certainly a great many times by Irish societies in Ireland and throughout the world. Let the exiles, when they gather together to remember the country where they were born, sometimes have a play of mine acted to give wings to their thought.' I would say 'I do not ask even a fiftieth part of the popularity Burns has among his own people, but I should like to help the imaginations that are most keen and subtle to think of Ireland as a sacred land.'

Edward Martyn, excited, I suppose, by our success, has taken up another amateur company and is getting them to play his plays. He took a big theatre for them last week and paid them. George Moore did the stage-management, and the company played *The Heather Field* and *A Doll's House*. I wasn't able to get to Dublin to see it but Martyn seems satisfied with its success. I daresay this company may attract away a few of our actors, but I am not afraid of its rivalry and think it a good thing there should be two companies. Neither Martyn nor Moore would ever have been satisfied with our methods, and they have their own distinct work in training a company for the performance of the drama of social life. Our people have neither the accents nor the knowledge nor the desire to play typical modern drama. We will always be best in poetical drama or in extravagant comedy or in peasant plays. Lady Gregory has done us a new play which I think very good, and Bernard Shaw has just written to me to say he will do us an Irish play as soon as he has finished a book he has now in hand.... Yours ever   W B YEATS

TO MICHAEL FIELD [1]

July 27 [? 1903]   *Coole Park*

My dear Michael Field, I have read *Deirdre*, and I am afraid it would need a far bigger stage than we are likely to command for a long time to come. The company has just given up the idea of acting a play of Sudermann's for the same reason. I am inclined therefore, with your consent, not to offer them the play.

---

[1] Dictated. 'Michael Field,' the pseudonym of Katherine Bradley (1846–1914) and Edith Cooper (1862–1913), aunt and niece who collaborated to produce poems and a large number of plays in verse, none of which reached the stage. Fragments exist among Yeats's papers of a review he wrote, apparently in 1885, of three of their earliest plays, *The Father's Tragedy*, *William Rufus*, and *Loyalty or Love*, but its place of publication, if any, is unknown. He included nine poems by 'Michael Field' in *The Oxford Book of Modern Verse*.

To speak quite frankly I do not like it as well as your other work, and I should not like it to be the first of yours to be offered to them. Did you ever try your hand in a one act play? They are far easier to construct than a long play. I have myself as you know been writing one act plays in prose lately. I have done this chiefly as a discipline, because logic (and stage success is entirely a matter of logic) works itself out most obviously and simply in a short action with no change of scene. If anything goes wrong one discovers it at once and either puts it right or starts on a new theme, and no bones are broken. But I suppose every playwriter finds out the methods that suits him best. Yours sincerely W B YEATS

TO THE EDITOR OF THE *UNITED IRISHMAN*

[*Published August* 1, 1903]

Sir, I read in the English *Times* of July 25th this description of the room prepared for the King's reception at Maynooth:[1] 'The King's room afforded a very pleasant instance of the thoughtful courtesy of his hosts; for by a happy inspiration hardly to have been expected in such a quarter, the walls were draped in His Majesty's racing colours, and carried two admirable engravings of Ambush II and Diamond Jubilee. When the King and Queen had taken their places in the refectory Mgr Molloy read the following address,' etc.

Even a heretic like myself can admire the loyalty, so perfect that it becomes an enthusiasm, not only for the King in his public capacity, but for his private tastes. I can imagine that the narrow interests of the theological students needed enlarging, and I am glad to think that parishes in which race meetings are held will in future be the ones to be desired. Hitherto the priest has been almost the only man in Ireland who did not bet; all that is to be changed, so powerful are the smiles of Royalty. I expect to read in the sporting column of the *Irish Times* that Cardinal Logue has 'something on' Sceptre and that Archbishop Walsh has 'a little bit of all right' for the Chester Cup. Yours sincerely W B YEATS

[1] The National College of St. Patrick, Maynooth, Co. Kildare, founded in 1795 for theological training.

TO FRANK FAY[1]

August 8 [1903]   *Coole Park*

My dear Fay, I send back to you all but one of the articles which you lent me. I am keeping that one for a little time, as I think it may be useful to me in getting *Samhain* together. You mentioned having one on Antoine's theatre. I would very much like to see it if you could spare it for a little. I have written to Sturge Moore to send me back those letters of yours on the history of acting for possible use in *Samhain* also.

I am sending your brother Seanchan[2] to-day. (If you are reading it, pronounce 'Shanahan.') If I can get them done I shall send at the same time the maps of the more important positions. I think it will play about an hour and a half. It is quite a long elaborate play, and is constructed rather like a Greek play. I think it the best thing I have ever done, and with the beautiful costumes that are being made for it I should make something of a stir. I am afraid you will have an exhausting part in Seanchan, but you will find plenty to act and the best dramatic verse I have written to speak. Your brother told me that he meant to cast you as Seanchan, and I am very glad of it. I have long wanted to see you with some part which would give you the highest opportunities. Your playing of the Fool in *The Hour-Glass* was beautiful, wise and subtle, but such a part can never express anyone's whole nature. It has to be created more or less from without. Your performance of Seanchan will, I believe, establish all our fames. I wish very much you could send me the right measurements for a curtain, such a curtain as we can use when our fortunes have improved and our stage grown bigger. I want to get it embroidered if I can. I look upon it as part of the staging of Seanchan, for there is to be a prologue spoken by Mr. Russell in the Wise Man's dress.[3] I want the dark dress and the dark curtain to fix themselves on the minds of the audience before the almost white stage is disclosed. If I cannot get the measurements by Monday it may be too late, as the designer who is now here is going away.

[1] Dictated.
[2] Yeats's play *The King's Threshold*. It was produced, with Frank Fay as the poet, by the Irish National Theatre Society at the Molesworth Hall, Dublin, on October 8, 1903.
[3] The prologue was not used 'as, owing to the smallness of the company, nobody could be spared to speak it.'

Russell hears there were 'brilliant rows' last Monday, but he doesn't know what they were about. I suppose there is no secret; if not I should like to know. All theatrical companies make rows but ours seems to have more than the usual gift that way. Yours sincerely,
                     W B YEATS

TO STEPHEN GWYNN [1]

Sept 13 [1903]   *Coole Park*

My dear Gwynn, It is not yet settled whether I am going to America, but if I do go I shall leave London early in November.

I have left unanswered a letter from Barry O'Brien, asking what plays the National Theatre Society should perform. I think the programme should be arranged later, when we have had time to try our new plays. We have several plays that I think will be popular.[2] I have no doubt you are right about Christmas being the best time for the plays, but I shall probably miss them if I go to America. On the 24th, 25th and 26th of this month we are opening the season with *The King's Threshold*, a long one act verse play of mine; *In the Shadow of the Glen*, a comedy by Synge, and *Cathleen ny Houlihan*. I wish very much you could manage to come over. We have got new scenes and costumes for everything, and in any case *The King's Threshold* is the most ambitious thing we have attempted.

I think it is the best thing I have ever done in dramatic verse.

I am correcting to-day the proofs of *Samhain*, it will have a new play of Dr. Hyde's with translation by Lady Gregory and a new play by Synge. Yours ever   W B YEATS

[1] Dictated. Stephen Lucius Gwynn (1864–1950), M.P. for Galway City 1906–1918. He was a journalist and author of many books on literature, Ireland, travel and fishing.
[2] The National Theatre Society paid a second flying visit to London and gave two performances at the Royalty Theatre on March 26, 1904. The plays given were Synge's *In the Shadow of the Glen* and *Riders to the Sea* and Yeats's *The King's Threshold* at the matinée; Padraic Colum's *Broken Soil* and Yeats's *The Pot of Broth* and *The King's Threshold* in the evening.

TO A. H. BULLEN

[*Probably September* 1903] *Coole Park*

My dear Bullen: Send me the copies of new edition of *Ideas* here. I have sent your note to my sisters. I must have forgotten to give your name.

I will see you shortly in London about poems etc. I propose to keep back the narrative and lyrical part of my sister's book till I have finished a Masque I am working at and then to re-publish it with the new poem. This will make 3 volumes to be arranged for

A book of poems (containing contents of *Seven Woods* up to page 25 (will space out a good deal) and new poems.

The Hour-Glass etc, being volume II of plays for Irish Theatre (This contains 3 prose plays)

The King's Threshold etc, being vol III of same. (This contains new play in verse now rehearsing in Dublin and *On Baile's Strand* from my sister's book.)

These last two books are practically ready.

My play has been postponed to Oct 8th 9th and 10th. Yours ever

W B YEATS

TO JOHN O'LEARY[1]

Oct 25 [1903] 18 *Woburn Buildings*

My dear O'Leary, I go to America next week, and will be very much obliged for some introductions. You will remember that you kindly offered me them. I had a debate against Father Maloney last night at the Irish Literary Society. The subject was O'Connell. Father Maloney described O'Connell giving the laurel wreath to George IV, and said such a thing could never happen again now that Catholic and Gaelic Ireland had got the upper hand. I replied in my speech that it had happened again when Maynooth hung up the King's racing colours and the portrait of the King's racehorse which I called 'Ambush II out of Laurel Crown.' There was immense applause, and Father Maloney got very dark in the face and Mrs. Emery saw some priests groping for their hats to go home she

[1] Dictated.

supposes. However Barry O'Brien interrupted me, but it didn't matter, I had had my say.

I think Arthur Griffith has behaved handsomely in the U[*nited*] I[*rishman*]. Yours sincerely

W B YEATS

TO ALFRED NOYES [1]

Oct 25 [1903]   18 *Woburn Buildings*

Dear Mr. Noyes, I have never written to thank you for the book you sent me through Mrs. Emery.[2] It is full of beautiful things, some of which I have read again and again. I am dictating this, where I have not your book at hand, and cannot go into as much detail as I would like to, but I know I have read your 'imitation' from Théophile Gautier to quite a number of people, who have shared my liking for it. I believe I suggested it to Mrs. Emery for the psaltery, if I have not done so I will do so. I have only just come back from Ireland, and go to America next week or would hope to make your personal acquaintance, but that I hope is only deferred for a while. Yours sincerely

W B YEATS

TO LADY GREGORY

[*Postmark Nov* 16, 1903]   1 *West* 87*th St.*
New York

My dear Friend, I am now established at Quinn's. I came here from the hotel last night. Since I arrived I have been busy with a long stream of reporters. When I got out of the steamer I was beset by half a dozen at once and two of them had cameras. I give my first lecture at Yale on Monday, I then lecture at some Irish Literary Society in Newhaven, and then back to New York and off again on Thursday. I give about 4 lectures a week and I have already more

---

[1] Dictated.
[2] *The Loom of Dreams*. London: Grant Richards, 1902. The poem Yeats mentioned is called 'Art' and is imitated from 'Ars Victrix' by Théophile Gautier.

JOHN QUINN AND W. B. YEATS, 1904

than 30 to give to Universities. There will also if all goes well be big public lectures which will make much more money. But even with the lectures I have already certain I will make a good deal of money. Everybody is very kind but I am refusing all but the most important invitations as my chief anxiety is not to break down, for the work will be hard and dinner parties and the like would make it harder. I have found the reporters much more fatiguing than I have ever found lecturing. I had a long struggle with a woman reporter yesterday who wanted to print and probably will a number of indiscreet remarks of mine. Here is an example. 'What do you think of Kipling?' 'I shall say nothing whatever about Kipling if you please, I will say nothing about any living poet. If he would have the goodness to die I would have plenty to say. Good heavens have you written that down?'

'Yes, it is the one Irish remark you have made.'

'You will please rub it out again.'

Thereupon we had a struggle of ten minutes and in spite of her promises I expect to see printed in large black letters 'Yeats desires Kipling's death.' I have sent an urgent message demanding a proof. I had been painfully judicious for days, as the reporters had been Irish and asked about Ireland, but this woman asked about general literature and I was off my guard.

Burke Cocran has called and a certain Judge who found *Ideas of Good and Evil* in a hotel in a southern state and was pleased by what I had said of Morris. He is now starting on Morris. I lunch with him to-morrow, and Quinn is, I can see, full of his sense of the judge's importance, who is clearly a pillar in Quinn's house of labour. I also go to lunch with Cocran, or stay with him I forget which. I have also been sent visiting cards for three of the chief clubs. I hear too that I am to lecture to the Pauline Fathers who say they don't mind my heretical theology. I go to the Pacific Coast in January, a five days' journey, and lecture in Father Yorke's town and stay with his worst enemy.

Quinn's rooms are charming. Jack's pictures and Russell's and my father's portrait of me pretty well cover the walls and look very well. My father's portrait of me has a glass over it and seems to have been rubbed over with some kind of wax by the framer. It looks extremely well and has a richness of dark colour I never noticed in it before.

I have just heard a very painful rumour—Major MacBride is said to be drinking.[1] It is the last touch of tragedy if it is true. Mrs. MacBride said in one of her last letters that he has been ill all summer. Yours always

W B YEATS

TO LADY GREGORY

[*Postmark Dec.* 1903] *The Deanery*
Bryn Mawr
Pennsylvania

My dear Friend, You will see by the note-paper that I am on tour. This is the chief woman's college of America, the one to which the richer classes send their girls. I have just given my second lecture. I write to tell you of my success. At first I did not like my lectures at all. But last week I gave a lecture which was I thought the best I have ever given. It was on the 'intellectual movement.' Last night I lectured again on heroic poetry and there was not standing room in the hall. Not only the girls were there but a number of people from the neighbourhood. I could even see a few people standing out in the passage. One of the professors told me that I was the most 'vital influence' that had come near the college 'for 15 years.' What has pleased me so much is getting this big audience by my own effort. It has not meant much to me getting big audiences when I had never been heard—like the big Philadelphia one. They are getting all our books here now. Do you know I have not met a single woman here who puts 'tin tacks in the soup'? and I found that the woman that does is recognised as an English type. One teacher explained to me the difference in this way 'We prepare the girls to live their lives but in England they are making them all teachers.'

The head of this college has a passion for statistics and the head of a rival college declares that she once made a speech containing this sentence 'Fifty per cent of my girls get married and sixty per cent have children.' It is not known what she intended to say. She is a charming woman however and the college buildings made under her management are some of them really beautiful.

[1] Major John MacBride had married Maud Gonne earlier in this year. The marriage was not successful for long, and a separation was eventually arranged. MacBride took a prominent part in the 1916 Easter Rising and was executed on May 5, dying with great courage. Yeats recalls this in his poem 'Easter 1916.'

I have written to Miss Craig about *Where there is Nothing*, and given you authority. I doubt if I shall or can alter it till I get back. I wish you would get Mrs. Emery to write a note on the way to speak those poems in *Kathleen ni Hoolihan* and please revise her style —she won't mind. I wish too that Fay would send you the music Mrs. MacBride used for the lines 'They shall be remembered for ever.' That might go in too (as well as Mrs. Emery's)—it was a tune heard by clairvoyance. In fact all the music, even the unrhymed verse, would be a gain. There may be some delay with the poetical plays. I am trying to get *The King's Threshold* in the *North American Review* for January. If I can manage this both books can come out almost at once. If I cannot there will be delay.

I hear that somebody here is writing about *Cuchullain*. He told a friend of Quinn's that it was 'one of the great books of the world, a book like Homer.' I speak to-night at a club in Philadelphia on The Theatre. The ground is covered with snow and where the roads have not been beaten bare with horses' hoofs one is driven in sleighs with jingling bells.

I will stop now for I am trying to write a poem. Yours

W B YEATS

I find that I am keeping very well—a little nervous fatigue of the voice at times but very slight. At first I accepted invitations rather recklessly but now I am wiser and am keeping fresh.

[*On envelope*] If necessary you could, instead of getting Mrs. Emery to make a note, merely refer to the essay in *Ideas of Good and Evil*. I daresay Bullen is talking nonsense about the scores; he always talks some kind of petulant nonsense before one gets a book out.

TO GEORGE RUSSELL (AE)[1]

Dec 18, 1903
                                                        1 *West 87th Street*
New York

My dear Russell: Bryan has written to me as to selection from my poems in his proposed Irish Anthology.[2] He asks me whether I or

[1] Dictated.
[2] *Irish Literature*, an anthology in ten volumes. Philadelphia: J. D. Morris & Co., 1904.

you are to make the selection. Now I have a very great objection to making a selection from my own poems. I don't think an author should authoritatively take out certain poems and give them a sort of special imprimatur. Besides I have another objection. I don't want to be connected with the editorial side of Mr. Bryan's book; he is a more enthusiastic advertiser than I think becomes my dignity. So I think you had better make the selections as you are doing the introductory notice. At the same time, I think I must ask you to make it entirely from the last editions. I mean that I don't want any of the poems I have discarded to come into it. Rolleston did not please me over well by giving long extracts from what I think immature verse. With this reservation you can pick whatever you like from the garden.

I am constantly lecturing and I think doing fairly well. I am just on my way to Canada, and go to the Pacific Coast in January. I bring your work into the greater number of my lectures, and I notice from the number of people who ask me about you afterwards that you have a considerable following here. I am expecting every day a copy of your new book at the Dun Emer Press. I suppose it cannot be delayed much longer. When you write let me know how Colum's play has gone.[1] Faithfully yours W B YEATS

P.S. I don't want to be connected with the editorial side of Bryan's book because, as I have been lecturing here, Quinn thinks he would probably make some use of my name that might make me responsible for his scheme as a whole. I think of writing to *U.I.* challenging Griffith to a discussion—in the manner of Martyn and Redmond.

TO LILY YEATS[2]

December 25, 1903 1 *West 87th Street*

My dear Lilly: I have just seen *The Nuts of Knowledge*.[3] Tell Lolly I think it perfectly charming. It is better than *The Seven Woods* and

---

[1] *Broken Soil* by Patrick Colum was produced by the Irish National Theatre Society at the Molesworth Hall, Dublin, on December 3, 1903.
[2] Dictated.
[3] *The Nuts of Knowledge* by AE was the second book produced at the Dun Emer Press. It had been published on December 1.

should, I think, advance the fame of the press. But there are moments when I think that the winged sword is a little large as well as a little vague in design. I am very uncertain about this, but I think, on the whole, I would have liked it smaller; small, perhaps, as a penny piece, and up in the top right hand corner. Probably, though, if I saw it small I would think it ought to be big.

Please do not think I am responsible for those interviews about Drumcliff and the rest. The interviewer asks me a certain number of questions and then goes home and adds the rest from his imagination, and then another interviewer in another paper gets hold of what he has written and adds more imagination. I have been interviewed about places I have never seen and have talked copiously about them. However, on the whole, I think I have been fortunate, as really nothing has been put into my mouth that mattered. I am keeping in very good health and enjoying the novelty of the thing very much. Unhappily, the letter you forwarded me from Aunt Grace only reached me the day I arrived back here from Canada. I have not yet written to her, but will.

All you have told me about the theatre was very interesting. I heard, of course, also from Lady Gregory. Colum's success has overjoyed me. I was more nervous about that play than anything else, for my position would have been impossible if I had had to snuff out the work of young men belonging to the company. It would have always seemed that I did so from jealousy or some motive of that sort. Now, however, one can push on Colum and keep one's snuffers for the next. One man we did snuff out, Cousins, has been avenging himself on Colum in the *United Irishman*.

I have been sent a privately printed book by somebody here. It is not at all good. I think I will send it to Lolly as a bad example and tell her that I have seen the Roycroft books. These were the books that Russell said had coloured illustrations. They have, and nothing could be worse. The books are eccentric, restless and thoroughly decadent.

I have given about twenty lectures—rather more than twenty I think—and I have about twenty-four still to give. I speak in a big hall in New York on the 3rd of January and go to the Pacific Coast the day after, five days' journey in railway trains. There, I am told, I shall find a delightful climate. I get back from there some time about the beginning of February or end of January, and after one or two more lectures round about New York start for home, where I should arrive about the 20th of February.

I have seen a great deal that is very charming here—charming people and charming houses. The houses that cultivated people live in here seem to me the best things of the kind that I have seen. I was in a beautiful house belonging to a rich merchant a couple of days ago. He lives about an hour's journey from New York, on the side of a wooded hill, and his house, which is in what they call here their 'old colonial style,' would have been a delight to Morris. Everything very sober and stately, rather bare. Comfort, but only such comfort as an alert spirit can enjoy. Nothing to suggest a soft lounging life. The woman of the house is a very cultivated woman, and I suppose a great part of the taste is hers, but her husband has done his share, too, I think. He is constantly out in the woods and the mountains hunting moose and the like. There is something of his life in the decoration; something athletic, as it were. And I have seen a great many houses which have the same spirit though not in the same degree. Indeed, the thing that has surprised me in America has been the fine taste of the people, or, at any rate, of those I have met—and I have met a great number. I think the cultivated class is a good deal larger than it is in England. Certainly, it is more widely spread.

Well, I must stop now, for I am going to dictate a lecture. I have found that after giving a lecture seven or eight times, I begin to get tired of it, and I am going to try to make it vivid to myself again by dictating it and so getting it much more highly finished. After seven or eight times, one begins to remember sentences one used before, to speak by rote, and so one may as well finish highly. At first one has the joy of improvisation, and that gives one fire.

Yours affectionately W B YEATS

TO LILY YEATS [1]

January 2, 1904   1 *West* 87*th Street*

My dear Lilly: Your letter has just reached me. On Monday I go to St. Louis, a day and a half in the railway train, I think, and give a number of lectures there. I will be away three weeks before I get

[1] Dictated.

back again to New York. I lecture tonight in the neighbourhood of New York, and tomorrow I give the most important lecture of all in the big Carnegie Hall. A great place, which will be rather hard to speak in, if it is only partly filled, as is pretty certain. I could not get it at the time I wanted, and this is not a good time, for various reasons. Still, I expect to do fairly well. I have been down there practising, trying my eloquent passages in the big, empty hall. I got one compliment. I had just finished an elaborate passage, when I heard the clapping of hands in a dark corner. It was the Irish caretaker.

The Lord Dudley portrait is a great piece of luck for our father, but he will have some trouble to keep off politics, I expect. When you write again, if you do, you might tell me what the cottage scene Fay got made for Colum's play turned out like. Nobody has told me. What colour did they make it and had it a solid look? I asked Fay to have it all painted a dull smoke colour that it might tell as a tolerably flat homogeneous mass behind the figures of the players. When does Lolly expect to get through with Hyde's book?[1] I have got a certain number of people to write for copies. I want to have some idea, too, as to when the Red Hanrahan Tales are likely to be printed. I cannot write any more, for I have one or two more letters to do, and then my whole lecture to re-dictate. I cannot trust myself to extemporize before an immense audience. The larger an audience, the less conversational and the more formal, rhythmical, and oratorical must one's manner be. I trust, therefore, to the inspiration of the moment when speaking to a college, but I have to elaborate everything for a great audience. Yours affectionately

W B YEATS

TO LADY GREGORY[2]

January 2, 1904　　　　　　　　　　　　　　1 *West 87th Street*

My dear Lady Gregory... A great many thanks for your letter, which reached me this morning, and thanks, too, for the musical

[1] *The Love Songs of Connacht* collected and translated by Douglas Hyde with a preface by W. B. Yeats was the third book issued by the Dun Emer Press. It was finished in April and published in July 1904.
[2] Dictated.

notes. But I wish you could send me as soon as you get them a proof of your commentary upon them, for I shall want to put something of the kind into the American edition of the book.[1]

Do you know, I hope the company will not adopt Colum's suggestion and play the *Hippolytus*. It is altogether too soon for us to stray away from Irish subjects. Above all, it is too soon for us to put on any non-Irish work of such importance as the *Hippolytus*. It would be playing into the hands of our enemies. On the other hand, if we get through this season keeping our audiences with us and playing a considerable variety of good, new Irish work, we will be able to do as we like. If we are to play the *Hippolytus*, I want to be there before it comes on and to find out if I cannot get Ricketts, let us say, to stage it. Now that The Masquers has come to an end, I must see if I cannot get hold of that £170 Ricketts has for theatrical adventure. As soon as we feel strong enough to play non-Irish work, we should, I think, approach Ricketts and see if he will work for us. This is really important, so do try and restrain them over the *Hippolytus*, if you agree with me. If we had a big Irish play—a three-act play in verse, let us say, or a really important play in prose—we might then start with that and the *Hippolytus* and announce that we intend to carry out our full policy, Irish work and foreign masterpieces. I should like, however, to play Shaw first.

Yes, there are plenty of newspaper accounts, and I know Quinn is saving some for you. There have not been many actual reports of lectures, however. The accounts are, for the most part, interviews and descriptive paragraphs.

I spoke a couple of nights ago at the Authors' Club. You know the kind of people who make up authors' clubs in England—placid, rather Philistine writers, who have more practical capacity than anything else. They strike me as just the same here, only their practical capacity is rather more frank; and there is less pretence about their literature. However, a certain professor, who, I am told, is a person of great eminence here, made a very self-complacent speech, in which he said that writers ought not to think of posterity but merely write what it gave them pleasure to write and for their

---

[1] *The Hour-Glass and other plays* published in New York by the Macmillan Company did not contain the bars of music nor a 'Note on the Music' which appeared in the English edition published two months later.

own time. Of course, there is a half-truth in this, but he put it in such a way that it became a whole falsehood. I was asked to speak when he had finished and I took the other side altogether, and Quinn thinks got the better of him. He was the only man there I didn't like, for he was the only man there who pretended to literature, which it was quite obvious he had not got. I spoke of style and the painful labour that all style is, and so on.

I have just re-read your letter, and if there is any great trouble in sending a proof of your note about the music do not bother. I can make a good note out of what you say in the letter and add a few words about the method of delivery.

I have had difficulty in seeing Macmillan's man here. That is why there is so much delay. When I am here, he is away. When he wants to see me, I am away. I have just written to him and placed the matter in Quinn's hands, as I shall now not be able to attend to it. Quinn is very anxious for me to secure the copyright of the Red Hanrahan Tales by running them through the *Gael* before my sister brings them out. How do you feel about this? It should not be an injury to my sisters and if one does not do it Mosher may very likely pirate the book, for I have a notion that the Red Hanrahan Tales will be about the most popular thing I have done in prose. If you think well of this idea, I can arrange with the *Gael* and you can let them have a copy of the manuscript.

I am afraid it will be quite out of the question my getting to work on *Where there is Nothing* while I am here. I have hardly a moment, running from place to place and answering necessary letters. I am always, too, working at my lectures, changing them and bettering them, I hope. I find that if I do not keep making a continual effort I begin to get worse, for I lose the joy of improvisation and do not get finish to take its place. After all, I don't feel it would have been worth coming here unless I was to get full advantage out of the practice in speaking. And I can only get that advantage by working over and over my words. One does not want to speak as badly as a clergyman or a lawyer, and I have found to my surprise that, while they speak badly, they get too idle and easy. In a way, I think I spoke better years ago when I had to make more effort; and now I am making an effort again and hope to come back with a far better style.

Did I tell you my idea of challenging Griffith to debate with me in public our two policies—his that literature should be subordinate to nationalism, and mine that it must have its own ideal? I think that a challenge to him would be quite amusing, for his own party sent out so many that he would be a little embarrassed to refuse. I would offer to debate it with him or any other person appointed by his societies. He will refuse, of course, but the tactical advantage will be mine. I shall wait and choose my moment but will let him have the challenge before I get back. In any case, I am rather inclined to give a lecture as soon as I get to Dublin and to discuss very frankly the future of our movements.

No, the *North American* is not going to print *The King's Threshold*. It is too long for them to use in time not to delay Bullen even further.

I have so much work to do for this big lecture that I cannot write more now, but I will find time somewhere, in some railway train, probably, to write again and very soon.

[*Signed by Quinn for W. B. Y.*]

TO LADY GREGORY

[*Postmark January* 18, 1904]   *The Congress Hotel Company*
The Auditorium
Chicago

My dear Lady Gregory, I am on my way to a place called Indiana University and have just come from Notre Dame, a Catholic university, and before that I spoke here where I made a big success, and before that at an Engineering University where I spoke my best and made a big failure—scientific students attentive and polite but like wet sand until I got to my poetry which they liked. I have been entirely delighted by the big merry priests of Notre Dame—all Irish and proud as Lucifer of their success in getting Jews and Nonconformists to come to their college, and of the fact that they have no endowments. I did not succeed in my first lecture. I began of a sudden to think, while I was lecturing, that these Catholic students were so out of the world that my ideas must seem the thunder of a battle fought in some other star. The thought confused me and I spoke badly, so I asked if I might go to the literary classes and speak to the boys about poetry and read them some verses of my own. I did this both at Notre Dame and St. Mary's, the girls' college near, and delighted them all. I gave four lectures in one day and sat up late telling ghost stories with the Fathers at night. I said when I was going away 'I have made a great litter on the floor' and pointed to torn up papers, and one fat old priest said with a voice full of sincerity 'I wish you were making it there for a month.' I think they were delighted to talk about Ireland and the faery—one priest, or rather a teaching brother, told me that nothing could heal the touch of the fool except the touch of the queen, and that she always wanted something in return, sometimes a good looking young man to be her husband. He said the fool was ugly and deformed and always gave some deformity of body or mind. I think these big priests would be fine teachers, but I cannot think they would be more than that. They belong to an easy-going world that has passed away—more's the pity perhaps—but certainly I have been astonished at one thing, the general lack of religious prejudice I found on all sides here. I liked the woman's college much less. The nun I saw most of, the teacher of literature, showed me her course of instruction—no real grasp of ideas in it, and mere prettiness getting the foremost thought, it seemed to me—Mrs. Meynell's essays among the books taught and the like. But the radical defect was that the girls had obviously no real social life. I thought of the girls at the other colleges, with their abundant freedom, their pretty dressy look, and heard Sister Peta complain of their attention to such things. The boys too, though in a less degree, struck me as less masters in their life—but the priests were a delight—big children and all over six feet. A Sligo lad came to the train with us and was very sad at parting—he has, it seems, known my poetry since he was in Sligo and knew it for a neighbour's. I put a picture of the college in this letter. I go to San Francisco in a few days and am getting very tired of railway trains. Tomorrow I shall dine with Prof. Sampson—do you remember him? He is at Bloomington; and after that St. Paul's and more big priests.

No—I cannot do those changes in 'Paul.' I never have a moment. I find it hard enough to write a mere letter especially now that I am doing all in a rush, and I seem to have lost some of the desire to change it. They can do it as it is if they like, though I had sooner get home first and think it out in quiet, much sooner.

A Chicago woman asked if she might send Theatre 100 dollars and I gave her your address.

I will write again very soon. I am tired out—I have been up every morning very early and to-day I had a long journey. Yours

W B YEATS

TO FRANK FAY

[? 20 *January* 1904]   1 *West 87th Street*
New York

My dear Fay, I send the new *Cuchullain* dialogue.[1] I think it is all you will want. The repetition on Cuchullain's entrance will fix it on the mind. I write from Chicago though I give my New York address. I start for San Francisco in a couple of days and have just come from the Catholic College of Notre Dame where I gave four lectures—no, six but two were only little lectures on my own poetic doctrines to the literary classes at the college for men and the affiliated women's college. Tomorrow I speak at St. Paul's, another Catholic College—in Ireland neither Catholic nor Protestant college would let me among its students I suspect—here I find a really wonderful large tolerant spirit. One Catholic professor was told that I was a pagan and said 'There is a great deal that is very good about paganism' and now he has arranged for four lectures I believe, —and yet I think people are very pious here. Yet Catholics go without protest to the state schools in New England where the Protestant Bible is read every day, and there are a hundred Nonconformists and Jews in Notre Dame where all the teachers are priests. There are some intolerants but they seem to be fading out.

About Cuchullain. You have Lady Gregory's work I know. Remember however that epic and folk literature can ignore time as drama cannot—Helen never ages, Cuchullain never ages. I have to recognise that he does, for he has a son who is old enough to fight him. I have also to make the refusal of the son's affection tragic by

[1] Evidently for *On Baile's Strand* on which the Fays were then working. As the company at this period were nearly all amateurs, employed elsewhere during the daytime, rehearsals could be held only at night, and were conducted over a long period. The play was not finally produced until the opening of the Abbey Theatre on December 27.

suggesting in Cuchullain's character a shadow of something a little proud, barren and restless, as if out of sheer strength of heart or from accident he had put affection away. He lives among young men but has himself outlived the illusions of youth. He is probably about 40, not less than 35 or 36 and not more than 45 or 46, certainly not an old man, and one understands from his talk about women that he does not love like a young man. Probably his very strength of character made him put off illusions and dreams (that make young men a woman's servant) and made him become quite early in life a deliberate lover, a man of pleasure who can never really surrender himself. He is a little hard, and leaves the people about him a little repelled—perhaps this young man's affection is what he had most need of. Without this thought the play had not had any deep tragedy. I write of him with difficulty, for when one creates a character one does it out of instinct and may be wrong when one analyses the instinct afterwards. It is as though the character embodied itself. The less one reasons the more living the character. I felt for instance that his boasting was necessary, and yet I did not reason it out. The touch of something hard, repellent yet alluring, self assertive yet self immolating, is not all but it must be there. He is the fool—wandering passive, houseless and almost loveless. Concobhar is reason that is blind because it can only reason because it is cold. Are they not the cold moon and the hot sun?

Now about scenery. I think you will find that the persons in *Cuchullain* will stand out clearly against the plain sacking. It is not necessary to do this by contrasting colour always—light and dark will do it. *The Shadowy Waters* I thought an exception to rule and thought one should lose the persons in the general picture. I had a different feeling about [the] stage when I wrote it—I would not now do anything so remote, so impersonal. It is legitimate art however though a kind that may I should think by this time prove itself the worst sort possible for our theatre. The whole picture as it were moves together—sky and sea and cloud are as it were actors. It is almost religious, it is more a ritual than a human story. It is deliberately without human characters. *Cuchullain* or *The King's Threshold* are the other side of the halfpenny. I do not think the greys kept the people in the latter from standing out, though there were other defects—too many colours and so on. Miss Horniman has to learn her work however and must have freedom to experiment. I think her *Baile's Strand* will prove much better. I had told her that old stages permitted elaborate dress though not elaborate scenes, and this combined with [the] fact of its being a Court misled her into overdoing colour and the like in certain parts. Surely the people of heroic age wore trews? I have heard that the bare legs and kilts of the highlanders come from the Romans, that the Celts had both kinds. Anyway Miss Horniman has Joyce's *Social Ireland* and was deep in it when I saw her. Yours

W B YEATS

TO LADY GREGORY [1]

January 21st, 1904   *St. Paul, Minnesota*

My dear Lady Gregory, I am dictating this in St. Paul where I am to lecture at a Catholic College; Archbishop Ireland is partly responsible for arranging the lecture for me. The stenographer I am dictating this to is in the office of an Irishman who has had something to do with my lecture. I find myself here (between lunch and lying down to rest a bit before lecturing) and snatch at a few minutes to write this to you.

    I got rather a heavy cold a couple of days ago and have got it clinging about me, and that is the only inconvenience I think that has come to me in all this travelling. To-morrow I go to San Francisco, then New York, then Toronto, then home. I am awaiting the news of the plays in Dublin with great impatience. It will reach me at San Francisco a good many days late.

    It does not matter a bit, Mrs. Emery's note not going in that book of plays; indeed the note has disappointed me; it is too meagre to mean anything; but I thought her notation was to go in as well as the Dublin notations. I suppose Bullen objected, but it is a great mistake to humour him by giving in to him. However, it does not matter. I have sent off the proof sheets of *The King's Threshold* to Quinn and if he can't arrange an immediate edition with Macmillan, who seems to be travelling about, we will bring it out ourselves in the way he did with *Where there is Nothing*, so that Bullen will not have any further delay.

[1] Dictated.

I am full of curiosity to know what your *King Brian* will be like. Remember that a play, even if it is in three acts, has to seem only one action—at any rate it is the better for seeming only one action. Your danger will be that having thought of Act I first your other acts will be episodes by themselves. When you write to me next let me know, if you know yourself, when the performances come on in London. I want to try to keep that as a fixed date in my head; that and the performance in Dublin. I hope to leave here about February 10th, but I may be delayed four or five days longer.

I have written a long letter to Fay as to the character of Cuchullain and I have sent him the new lines he wanted, the bits about Cuchullain being a small dark man. He is anxious about the scenery and I have written to Miss Horniman suggesting as delicately as I could that there ought not to be gorgeousness of costume.

I have had a letter from Paris that rather irritates me. It speaks of my once having thought that our literature should be national but having given up that conviction. I replied on the first day of my cold and was somewhat vehement, and am now sorry that I was. One doesn't mind the misunderstandings of the indifferent world but one is hurt by the misunderstandings of friends.

This isn't much of a letter but the chance arose of dictating it in a hurry and I did not like to lose it.

By the bye I sent that poem to the Duchess of Sutherland.[1] I would let you have a copy but the copy is in New York and I am some hundreds of miles away from it. I think it was a very good poem. I made it when shut up in a railway train coming from Canada. I think a railroad train a good place to write when the journey is long enough. One will exhaust the scenery in the first two or three hours and the newspaper in the second two or three hours (even an American newspaper), and towards the end of the day one can hardly help oneself, but one has begun to write. Indeed I think that if some benevolent government would only shut one up in the smoking car of a railway train and send one across the world one would really write two or three dozen lyrics in the year. Yours always   W B YEATS

[1] *Wayfarer's Love*, 1904, an anthology of poems, was edited by the Duchess of Sutherland and sold in aid of a charity. Yeats's contribution was the poem 'Old Memory,' which doubtless reflects his distress at Maud Gonne's recent marriage; from 1906 onwards it was included in the collection *In the Seven Woods* in his various books of verse.

I have just heard from Quinn. Alas, more lectures. I lecture in Canada on Feb. 13th. That does not look like getting back as soon as I thought. I am very homesick, so you may be certain I will hurry all I can. In spite of my cold and some hoarseness my lecture last night was a great success—a great audience too—300 turned away. Most of the audience clerical students. Archbishop entertained me at dinner before lecture. The owner of the office where I dictated this is the son of a Galway landlord—Dillon O'Brien who lived near the town (or near Athlone which sounds vague but it is what they told me) and had a house called 'Fairview.' He sold out long ago.

TO LADY GREGORY

[*Postmark possibly Jan. 28, 1904*]　　　　　　　　*San Francisco*

Dear Lady Gregory, Yesterday Quinn wired asking me if I could accept an engagement for March 6th in New York to address Irish Societies on Emmet. They offer very good terms—about £40. I wired that I could not stay so long, play coming on in Dublin. I have just had another wire, urging again. I am about to answer—'subject difficult to me, outside my work, dislike political speaking, will accept if you think very desirable, leave decision to you, sooner spend few days with you in quiet.' I wish I need not decide in a hurry. It means more than £40, for Quinn talks of 2 or 3 other lectures and I am not sure that I should refuse but I hate the delay here. I am getting tired out, not bodily, but am getting bored and homesick. The only thing to be said for this new lecture is that with Toronto on 14th and an inevitable few days with Quinn I could hardly get away before end of month. I shall be at least £70 the richer—but the boredom of another month here, my heart at home all the while—and I have so much to tell you. I left St. Paul last Friday, amid ice and snow—14 degrees below zero and the first thing I saw in the railway station when I got here was a notice to say that for 11 dollars return people could take their children to see 'real ice and snow.' Here there are palm trees and pepper trees and one walks about without a coat. The bay is beautiful, all is beautiful. I gave my first lecture here, at a university amidst great trees, great evergreens, in a huge gymnasium to some 2000 people. I spoke on the theatre and did not do well because I was hoarse and a little deaf with a cold, and I gave my second to about 2000 people, Irish mostly, last night, and did well I think. I hope Moore does not see the interview I send; I lunched with the interviewer and so told about the Shelbourne. O the weariness of another month here, it would be a little less weary if it were here in this tropical place, but ice and snow and cold and wet and the weariness of ever new faces —but I am tired out to-day. You will I suspect have to be my eyes at *Baile's Strand.* Yours W B YEATS

TO LADY GREGORY

[*Postmark Jan 29, 1904*] *San Francisco*

Dear Lady Gregory, Have just written to Quinn to cancel Emmet lecture—I was perfectly miserable when I agreed—for I knew he would accept for me. The depression I should have endured during coming weeks would not have been worth £70 and besides I have made several hundreds and what's £70 now that I am feeling so rich? I am just setting out to a lecture and must stop; keep paper I send. Yours W B YEATS

I shall spend a few days with Quinn after 14th and then start home. He may want to go to sea shore for a few days with me.

TO LADY GREGORY

[*Postmark Jan 31, 1904*] *San Francisco*

My dear Lady Gregory, I have had an urgent letter from Quinn. The Irish Societies offer 250 dollars (£50) if I will give Emmet address and will change date to Feb. 28th. I have accepted this, not wanting to disappoint Quinn. As I had made up my mind to spend a week with him after I got back from Canada on the 15th or 16th this will cause but little delay. I shall have to speak I suppose some 15 minutes or so on Emmet and then 3 quarters of an hour on general doctrine. It will be bad to speak so long on a more or less political theme, but I shall try and serve the good cause—Hyde in chief. I send you Father Yorke's paper, he is a great Moran-ite [1] and as he is also an enemy of my host, a San Francisco rich man and ex-Mayor, I had rather expected attack. He is supposed to attack everyone. It is very hot here—I have sat all afternoon without coat or waistcoat with the window wide open. Yesterday I spoke at two colleges among palm trees and there was an orange tree by the hotel where I slept. Next week I shall be in Chicago, with the barometer [sic] below zero and then in Canada—colder still.

Do not let them give *Baile's Strand* till I return. I shall leave by the first boat after the 28th. Yours ever   W B YEATS

I get immense audiences here.

I hear that the O'Donovan, Father Finlay, Anderson lecture tour was a failure and that Finlay at a dinner, where there were some 14 or 15 people or so, made a violent attack on me. I was neither dramatist, poet, or orator and so on. Finlay is a *Leader* sympathizer I believe.

TO LADY GREGORY

[*Postmark Feb 8, 1904*]   *Chicago*

My dear Lady Gregory, I received the enclosed from my sister Lilly to-day. It is a worry. I have replied very shortly saying that I have asked your advice, and that I do not know if I can do anything, and must be back in Ireland first. I have said also that the printing looks like a good investment, but that if I were a rich man I would require the opinion of some authority like Ricketts or Image or Whall [2] as to the quality of the embroidery design.[3] I hope my letter

---

[1] D. P. Moran, an Irish journalist who founded a weekly paper, the *Leader*, in 1899. He quarrelled with the advanced nationalists in 1902 over the Queen's visit to Ireland, and eventually developed a sort of Catholic loyalty, attacking everybody who did not accept his view. In 1901 Lady Gregory included his essay 'The Battle of Two Civilizations' in *Ideals in Ireland*, a book to which AE, George Moore, Douglas Hyde, Standish O'Grady and Yeats also contributed.

[2] Christopher Whall, a designer, especially of stained glass, and an active member of the Art Workers' Guild.

[3] Lily Yeats had apparently written suggesting that Yeats should finance the project which ultimately became the Cuala Industries, combining the printing under Elizabeth Yeats's direction and the embroidery work done by girls taught and employed by herself.

was not too cold but I have written it again and again. I enclose a copy. I have foreseen this moment all the while but it is annoying. If I give much it will go without effect (for it will not be enough) and if I give little I shall be blamed always. I don't know whether it is selfish of me, but my sisters have for so many years written me so many complaints (I have had two letters of the usual kind since I came here—money that was coming from Sligo but coming too slowly and too much to do with it) that I feel a little cross. Lolly is businesslike within certain limits and a strong soul but my father is a heavy weight—Lilly would probably take advice but for him. I can think of nothing but going to George Pollexfen and having everything looked into, in a spirit of sound business, if he will consent to invest. I could then give whatever you thought right. I am feeling rather tired and cross—the lecturing has tired me a little at last and I am longing to be back and I confess I do not like the thought that the first money I ever earned beyond the need of the moment will be expected to go to Dun Emer, for I suppose that is what is expected, and do no good there. If Lolly were by herself how gladly I would give it. I feel loyalty to an idea very keenly and could sacrifice a great deal for a cause, but family duties—just perhaps because they are rather thrust upon one—leave me colder than they should. I feel too that the family difficulty has got into a mess that needs stronger hands than mine—of course the whole Dun Emer venture should have been thought out carefully at the start. I suppose I had best go to Sligo after the plays in London and do what I can with George. My sister would be content I have no doubt with a few pounds at once and then chaos, but that seems to me hopeless. There is one possibility that Miss Gleeson's 'panic' may pass and that the letter only means—like others I have had—the depression of the moment.

I wrote you a letter in the train from California but cannot remember if I posted it. I plan to start back at end of month and to go direct to London. If you write at once on getting this I will get letter before starting. Quinn wants me to wait for 2 more lectures on 6th and 8th but I will not.

I have just got three letters of yours all together—sent on from New York—California is too far off and so they waited. Yours always   W B YEATS

TO LADY GREGORY [1]

Feb. 26, 1904   1 *West* 87*th Street*
                                               New York

My dear Lady Gregory, I am dictating this letter, as it is my only possible way of writing this week. I am dreadfully busy over my Emmet lecture, which is a frightful nuisance. It is indeed, as you say, a sword dance and I must give to it every moment. I had no idea until I started on it how completely I have thought myself out of the whole stream of traditional Irish feeling on such subjects. I am just as strenuous a Nationalist as ever, but I have got to express these things all differently. I feel as if I wanted at least a fortnight to make the speech, and I shall have to speak for an hour. When I accepted I thought I should be able to make it a plea for Irish Ireland, but Quinn seems to think that I must touch all that rather lightly. He is so anxious for my glory that he has set me I am afraid an impossible task.

I shall leave here by the *Oceanic* on the 9th and should be in London by the 18th. I will wire on the 9th when actually starting. Robert has my keys, so I suppose somebody will have to meet me at the station. I am staying the extra week instead of going back on the 2nd because I have been so busy that I have not been to see anybody socially here in New York and I have been promised to a few people. I have also two lectures between the 2nd and the 9th.

Emmet lecture going better, the *Clan na Gael* ask for Irish Ireland thoughts rather than politics.

A note from my sister. The panic has quite died out and they say all is well. Yours   W B YEATS

TO EDWARD GARNETT [2]

April 12*th*, 1904   *Nassau Hotel*
                                                 Dublin

My dear Garnett, I hear that you are literary editor of the *Speaker*. Do you feel inclined to do a good deed? I daresay that you will remember that we performed a play called *Broken Soil* a couple of

---

[1] Dictated.   [2] Dictated. In the handwriting of Miss Horniman.

weeks ago at the Royalty. It was an immature play but most of the critics found it interesting and all I think found it original. It was by a young man called Patrick Colum, he is twenty-three and very young for his age but very simple and charming ... He has read a great deal, especially of dramatic literature and is I think, though of course one can never be certain about such things, a man of genius in the first dark gropings of his thought. Some here think he will become our strongest dramatic talent over here, though his work is little more at present than full of promise. I have seen some very good reviews by him in which there was always thought and sometimes beautiful sentences. I want to get him some reviewing. ... At the same time I think that it is probable that he ought to be in benevolent editorial hands for a little. Could you send him one or two books to review, Irish books if possible? If you let him sign I think that his name would be interesting to a few people. His address is—[*space left blank*]

I am sorry that I have not seen more of you in these recent years, but I get more and more absorbed in the work here and seem to be less and less in London. Yours sincerely W B YEATS

TO GEORGE RUSSELL (AE)

[? *April* 1904] *Nassau Hotel*

My dear Russell ... I was foolish enough to quote a phrase of Lady Gregory's which must have annoyed you, but when you think of it remember that she, like myself, puts your best poetry above any spiritual poetry written in our time and your best prose among the loftiest in the world. I myself sometimes give unbridled expression to my dislikes, moved perhaps by my knowledge of the strength of my likings and my loyalty to them. I am nothing but an artist and my life is in written words and they get the most of my loves and hates, and so too I am reckless in mere speech that is not written. You are the other side of the penny, for you are admirably careful in speech, having set life before art, too much before it as I think for one who is, in spite of himself perhaps, an artist. It is the careless printed word that remains after one's death to mar many people it may be, while the careless spoken word troubles an ear or two at the most. That is I think the root of all our differences.

I have just been reading some reviews of the *New Songs*.[1] Miss Gore-Booth's little poem about the roads is charming and delights my conscience, and I like the poem about the wise dead under grass and the strong gone over sea, but it leaves my conscience hungry. Some of the poems I will probably underrate (though I am certain I would recognize a masterpiece come out of any temperament) because the dominant mood in many of them is one I have fought in myself and put down. In my *Land of Heart's Desire*, and in some of my lyric verse of that time, there is an exaggeration of sentiment and sentimental beauty which I have come to think unmanly. The popularity of *The Land of Heart's Desire* seems to me to come not from its merits but because of this weakness. I have been fighting the prevailing decadence for years, and have just got it under foot in my own heart—it is sentiment and sentimental sadness, a womanish introspection. My own early subjectiveness rises at rare moments and yours nearly always rises above sentiment to a union with a pure energy of the spirit, but between this energy of the spirit and the energy of the will out of which epic and dramatic poetry comes there is a region of brooding emotions full of fleshly waters and vapours which kill the spirit and the will, ecstasy and joy equally. Yet this region of shadows is full of false images of the spirit and of the body. I have come to feel towards it as O'Grady feels towards it sometimes, and even a little as some of my own stupidest critics feel. As so often happens with a thing one has been tempted by and is still a little tempted by, I am roused by it to a kind of frenzied hatred which is quite out of my control. Beardsley exasperated some people in this way but he has never the form of decadence that tempted me and so I am not unjust to him, but I cannot probably be quite just to any poetry that speaks to me with the sweet insinuating feminine voice of the dwellers in that country of shadows and hollow images. I have dwelt there too long not to dread all that comes out of it. We possess nothing but the will and we must never let the children of vague desires breathe upon it nor

---

[1] *New Songs*. A Lyric selection made by AE from Poems by Padraic Colum, Eva Gore-Booth, Thomas Keohler, Alice Milligan, Susan Mitchell, Seumas O'Sullivan, George Roberts and Ella Young, with a frontispiece by Jack B. Yeats, was published by O'Donoghue & Co. in Dublin and A. H. Bullen in London in April 1904.

the waters of sentiment rust the terrible mirror of its blade. I fled from some of this new verse you have gathered as from much verse of our day, knowing that I fled that water and that breath. Yours ever
                                                                W B YEATS

P.S. When the spirit sinks back weary from its flight towards the final whiteness it sinks into the dim shadowy region more often than less aspiring spirits. I am angry when I see it, whether it is my spirit or your spirit, as in *Deirdre*, or the spirit of some of these young poets of yours. Some day you will become aware as I have become of an uncontrollable shrinking from the shadows, for as I believe a mysterious command has gone out against them in the invisible world of [?] inner energies. Let us have no emotions, however abstract, in which there is not an athletic joy.

TO LADY GREGORY

Express letter.   18 *Woburn Buildings*
   Postmark Ju ? 2 [1904]

My dear Lady Gregory . . . Let us meet at the box office of the Lyric Theatre about 2.40 or 2.45.[1] Do not take a ticket as I will try and change my 7/6 ticket for two 5/– seats.

George Moore was at Symons' last night. He refused to shake hands and walked out of the room without a word. He had no time to think and was left to his natural impulses which are bad. Symons went to the door with him and thought that he seemed undecided. Mrs. Symons was furious.

I am off to see Granville Barker about cast. Yours
                                                                W B YEATS

I find I left ticket for play at George St. Please look for it and bring it with you. I hope it is not lost.

[1] It seems probable that the matinée at the Lyric Theatre to which this note refers was the last of four performances of Euripides' *Hippolytus*, produced by the New Century Theatre and directed by Granville Barker, who also played the part of the Messenger, while the chorus was led by Florence Farr. Barker also directed the Stage Society performances of *Where there is Nothing* at the Court Theatre on June 26 and the two following days.

TO CHARLES RICKETTS [1]

26 July 1904 *Coole Park*

My dear Ricketts, I have been a long time in writing to thank you for having sent me such admirable designs for the Black Jester.[2] I showed them to Frank Fay in Dublin, and he was delighted with them. As soon as I can make some little progress with the poems I have in my mind for recitation, I will have the costume made. The Black Jester is one of the characters in a play I am now writing, and for that too the design will serve. I should have written to you before, but my eyes have been unusually bad, even a very few lines have been enough to set them aching. Lady Gregory has just read me a letter from Shannon, which has given her much pleasure. Those strange tales, with that curious wildness of theirs which is their compensation for lacking classic measure, and their sense of fine life, of a life that was lifted everywhere into beauty, are the energies, I think, behind all our movement here. I notice that when anybody here writes a play it always works out, whatever the ideas of the writer, into a cry for a more abundant and a more intense life. Synge and AE the poet are staying here, and though they have come to their task from the opposite sides of the heavens they are both stirring the same pot—something of a witches' cauldron, I think. Yours sincerely   W B YEATS

TO OLIVIA SHAKESPEAR

Friday [? July or August 1904] *Coole Park*

My dear Mrs. Shakespear: The novel [3] is a delight. I am only about two thirds through—I have got to Tony's discovery of his mother's drug taking—I cannot go quicker for my eyes are very bad indeed. It is much the best thing you have done. I know all the people intimately and I find all true and not the less charming and that is a rare thing. The meeting with the young man in the train is a very

[1] Text from *Self-Portrait taken from the Letters and Journals of Charles Ricketts, R.A.* London, 1939.
[2] No trace of any play or poem referring to the Black Jester has been found among Yeats's manuscripts.
[3] *The Devotees.* London: Heinemann, 1904.

fine invention, very dramatic and yet convincing. At first I thought the Russian prince a little unreal and then I remembered that he was an image in the mind of a child, that he is a child's 'bad man' and he became excellent. I wonder at the skill with which you make one feel the passage of Time and at the same time make the change gradual like time itself. Tony grows up under our eyes—you do not seem to skip a year. You must have been a young man and gone to school in Babylon or Alexandria. Perhaps you played with a pegtop somewhere in the hanging gardens.

I will write when I have finished the book but that will be some days hence. I have got rather run down with a series of colds and can hardly use my eyes at all. It is a passing inconvenience but annoying enough. Please write. Yours W B YEATS

TO LADY GREGORY [1]

Aug 4, 1904   *Nassau Hotel*

My dear Lady Gregory, Final decision is postponed until Monday but the battle is won to all intents and purposes. There appears to be no difficulty about our getting a patent for the plays of the Society. The difficulty comes in from the proposal to let the Theatre to other players when it is not being used by the Society. The Solicitor General has referred the matter back to our Counsel to draft in consultation with the opposing Counsel—some limitation of patent which will prevent Miss Horniman from letting to commercial travelling Companies of the ordinary kind. It looks as if it will be very difficult to find a definition. We have another consultation with Counsel tomorrow. I send you a paper with the report of proceeding. Miss Horniman gave her evidence first and was entirely admirable. She was complimented by the Solicitor General and is as proud as punch. Excitement always seems to give her the simplicity which she sometimes lacks. She was really most impressive. Plunkett and Commissioner Bailey did well for us, but I must say I was rather amused at their anxiety to show that they supported us—not out of love for the Arts but because of our use as antiemigration agents and the like. I think I was a bad witness. Counsel

[1] Dictated.

did not examine me but asked me to make a statement. The result was, having expected questions and feeling myself left to wander through an immense subject, I said very little. I was disappointed at being hardly cross-examined at all—by that time I got excited and was thirsting for everybody's blood. One Barrister in cross-examining T. P. Gill, who came after me, tried to prove that Ibsen and Maeterlinck were immoral writers. He asked was it not true that a play by Maeterlinck called *The Intruder* had raised an immense outcry in London because of its immorality. Quite involuntarily I cried out 'My God' and Edward Martyn burst into a loud fit of laughter. I suppose he must have meant *Monna Vanna*. He also asked if the Irish National Theatre Society had not produced a play which was an attack on the institution of marriage. Somebody asked him what was the name of the play. He said it didn't matter and dropped the subject. He had evidently heard some vague rumours about *The Shadow of the Glen*. The immense ignorance of these eminent Barristers was really rather surprising.

I have just been down to see the work on the Abbey Theatre. It is all going on very quickly and the Company should be able to rehearse there in a month. The other day while digging up some old rubbish in the morgue which is being used for dressing rooms, they found human bones. The workmen thought they [had] lit on a murder at least but the caretaker said, 'Oh I remember we lost a body about 7 years ago. When the time for the inquest came it couldn't be found.'

I forgot to say that Wm. Fay gave his evidence very well, as one would expect. He had the worst task of us all, for O'Shaughnessy—a brow beating cross-examiner of the usual kind—fastened on to him. Fay however had his answer for everything. I suppose I will have to wait for Monday. I have a good many odds and ends of news.

I hear that some man of a fairly respectable class was taken up with a lot of tinkers somewhere in Munster, and that the Magistrate compared him to 'Paul Ruttledge.' The next night one of the tinkers seems to have said something to the others about their being in a book. The others resented this in some way and there was a fight which brought them all into Court again. I am trying to get the papers. Yours   W B YEATS

TO OLIVIA SHAKESPEAR

Monday [*August* 8, 1904] *Nassau Hotel*
[*Postmark of receipt* 10 *Aug,* 1904]

My dear Mrs. Shakespear: I am up in Dublin on theatrical business but shall be back in Galway by Wednesday. My eyes have been very bad or I had written before—(I have to get new glasses I find) —to tell you again how the novel has delighted me. The end is entirely right, much better than the end I suggested. The book has a very curious charm—one has an affection for the people that keeps them long in the memory. Your Marie is a creation—her gambling is a very fine invention. In a wonderful way it makes one feel there are depths of feeling in her that life has hardly touched —it gives her the mysteriousness of all reality. It is always bad when a writer makes you feel that he knows all that is in any of his people—we can only salute the soul and let it pass by, we cannot understand it. If we could understand too much it flies away in terror. The whole book has a beautiful wisdom and sanity and gentleness.

We have practically got our theatre's patent now—we have been opposed by the Theatres with the most absurd arguments. We have the first endowed theatre in Great Britain, and I am glad to say no lack of plays, but it will be hard work. I am tired out with the excitement of the work of hunting out witnesses, dictating statements for them and so on. Tomorrow at 3.30 in the afternoon I shall be fishing for pike and perch on Coole lake.

I shall await your reading me the new book with expectation now that you are so fine a master. Yours W B YEATS

TO FRANK FAY[1]

August 28 [1904] *Coole Park*

My dear Fay, I send you Archer's letter. You will see by it that you can't make very much out of that point in stage management. You

[1] Dictated. The references in this letter are to André Antoine (1858–1943), the founder, in 1887, of the Théâtre Libre in Paris for the production of modern realistic plays. Inspired by his example J. T. Grein founded the Independent Theatre in London, in the work of which George Moore had taken a considerable and active interest. Antoine was director of the Odéon Theatre in Paris from 1906 to 1916.

can of course say that as Ibsen, who always gave the stage directions when he was certain, did not direct the actor to stand up, the stage management is free. I rather suggest however that you go very little into details of this kind, for your audience will be interested in general principles, they will not care three straws about Moore's competence. If I were you I would make your article an attack on realistic stage management. The position of attack is far stronger than the position of defence. Put Moore on the defensive and you will win. Be just to Antoine's genius, but show the defects of his movement. Art is art because it is not nature, and he tried to make it nature. A realist, he cared nothing for poetry, which is founded on convention. He despised it and did something to drive it from the stage. He broke up convention, we have to re-create it. It would be quite easy for us to get a superficial finish by choosing for our stage manager somebody who understood the perfected though temporary art of Antoine and his school. To do this would be to become barren. We must grope our way towards a new yet ancient perfection. We can learn from nobody to recreate tradition and convention except from those who have preserved it. We have learned with devout humility from the players of *Phèdre*, and though our problem is not quite theirs it is like theirs but unlike Antoine's. We desire an extravagant, if you will unreal, rhetorical romantic art, allied in literature to the art on the one hand of Racine and [on] the other hand of Cervantes. We can no more learn from Antoine than a writer of verse or a writer of extravagant comedy could learn from a realistic novelist. Moore once said to an interviewer 'nobody will ever write a realistic novel again. We are all gone now, Zola is dead, Huysmans is in a monastery, and I am in Dublin.' Moore knows that his kind of novel is obsolete, but because he is an amateur in plays and stage management, he does not understand that his kind of play and his kind of stage management is equally obsolete. Our movements are clumsy for we are children, but we are a devil of a long way farther from our coffins. If you care for this scheme, and I know of course that nobody can do more than suggest to another something that can awake that other's imagination, you will know how to carry it out, filling it with little bits of learning from your knowledge of the history of the stage, making my vague principles definite knowledge. Moore says for instance that the effect of words depends upon the place they are spoken on from the stage. There is the whole business in a thimble. There is the stage management that came to its perfection with Antoine. It is the art of a theatre which knows nothing of style, which knows nothing of magnificent words, nothing of the music of speech. Racine and Shakespeare wrote for a little stage where very little could be done with movement, but they were as we know careful to get a great range of expression out of the voice. Our art, like theirs, without despising movement, must restore the voice to its importance, for all our playwrights, Synge just as much as myself, get their finest effects out of style, out of the expressiveness of speech itself. Then too all Moore's ideas of stage management and the ideas of stage management of the people he believes in, De Lange for instance, (I cannot judge of Antoine in this matter) seem to me to aim at keeping the stage in a state of quite superficial excitement. Drama for them consists in a tension of wills excited by commonplace impulses, especially by those impulses that are the driving force of rather common natures. This is a very difficult thing to put, partly because I have not the necessary technical knowledge. Your brother understands for instance that in the first act of *The Well of the Saints* there must be long quiet periods, a suggestion of dreams, of indolence. The same is true of *Cathleen ni Houlihan*. Moore wanted Cathleen to walk up and down all the time in front of the footlights. When I explained that this would not be true to the play, that she was as it were wandering in a dream, made restless as it were by the coming rebellion, but with no more fixed intention than a dreamer has, he wanted me to re-write the play. Such emotions were impossible in drama; she must be Ireland calling up her friends, marshalling them to battle. The commonplace will, that is, the will of a successful business man, the business will, is the root of the whole thing. Indeed when I see the realistic play of our time, even Ibsen and Sudermann, much more when I see the plays of their imitators, I find that blessed business will keeping the stage most of the time. What would such writers or their stage managers do with the mockery king of snow? Or with Lear upon his heath? They would succeed with them just insofar as they forgot all that had given them their fame, and groped for fragments of a tradition they had done their best to destroy. But why do we want their stage managers? The commercial theatre is full of them, and we have founded our own theatre because we, and certain people who agree with us, dislike it. The little fame we have won has come to us because we have had the courage to do this.

I don't suppose there is anything in this letter that will be of help to you, but make any use of it you like. If you take any of the ideas you may either put them into your own words, or leave them in my words, and so make them part of your article, or you may quote them as from a letter written to you by one of the company. You may as well keep this letter, as I have taken some trouble to collect my ideas and express them clearly.

Lady Gregory I know has sent you *Kincora*; the chief amendment is in the part of King Brian. It is now I think a very fine part, perfectly coherent, and with great dignity. At first Gormleith seemed to run away with the play, but now the balance is struck even. Yours sincerely
W B YEATS

TO LADY GREGORY [1]

7th November, 1904   18 *Woburn Buildings*

My dear Lady Gregory, Jack is to design scenery for Synge's play, some tree wings, a cottage and two big chairs. I went out to Ricketts on Friday evening and he offered to do scenery for a play, we must think what we must set him at. I will discuss this with you when we meet. He said when we wanted him we should say how much money we could spend and so forth. He is full of fine ideas. If Robert wants advice about *Kincora* he will give it him. Robert came out on Friday evening, we met him there; he came on from Miss Horniman's.

I have seen Shaw's play; it acts very much better than one could have foreseen, but is immensely long.[2] It begins at 2.30 and ends at 6. I don't really like it. It is fundamentally ugly and shapeless, but certainly keeps everybody amused. O'Donovan and Quinn and Mrs. Emery are dining with me to-night. I have also asked Symons and Mrs. Symons to dine on Tuesday or Wednesday to meet Quinn.

[1] Dictated.
[2] *John Bull's Other Island*, first produced at the Court Theatre, London, on the afternoon of November 1, with Louis Calvert as Broadbent, John L. Shine as Larry Doyle, Granville Barker as Peter Keegan and Ellen O'Malley as Nora Reilly. King Edward VII commanded a special performance of the play on March 11, 1905, and this inaugurated the success of the Vedrenne-Barker performances.

I haven't been able to do much for O'Donovan, as Masefield is in Manchester and Nevinson on his way up the Congo to study the slave trade. I brought Quinn out to Mrs. Emery on Sunday to hear her speak to the Psaltery. Quinn wants to get a photograph of George Meredith and Hollyer won't sell it to him without permission from the family. Quinn wants you to send him a note of introduction to young Meredith. He is staying at the Carlton Hotel and would like to have the note, if you could send it, by Wednesday morning. I went to a performance at His Majesty's. Tree has turned *The Tempest* into a very common and vulgar pantomime, the verse is very badly spoken too. The whole thing is the worst that even Tree has done. Yours W B YEATS

P.S. I shall go back very soon—as soon probably as Quinn goes. There is nothing to do here and nothing coming that I care [to] wait for.

TO FRANK FAY [1]

November 13th 1904 18 *Woburn Buildings*

My dear Fay, I don't understand the point about Cuchulain's exclamation, I don't remember where he sinks on the bench, but I'll be over in Dublin in the middle of the week and we can discuss it then. I can't get your proofs I'm sorry to say, for there is no new edition coming for the present. I can however get you bound copies of the play to cut up if you like.

I should have thought that everyone knew by this time that Moore's return to the theatre is out of the question. If there were not other reasons, and there are very sufficient ones, it is enough that he represents a rival tradition of the stage and would upset your brother's plans at every turn. He is very jealous of the success of the theatre and has been laying pipe to get into it, for months past. He made [it] up with me the other day. I also had my object, (keep it to yourself) I want to get *Dermot & Grania* into my hands and think I see my way to an arrangement which will leave him free to do what he likes with it in England for a certain time; I to reshape it for you—it would make a fine verse play.

Lift the horn if it is effective, God knows what the old Irish did. Yours sincerely, W B YEATS

[1] In Miss Horniman's handwriting.

TO LADY GREGORY

24th Nov. 1904   *Abbey Theatre*

My dear Lady Gregory, I am afraid the postponement is inevitable. I have had a letter from Miss Horniman who seems to think that the delay is to suit your convenience. It is not, but we could modify the new date by a day or two. The delay is caused by the fact that the stage will hardly be finished in time to let us have sufficient dress rehearsals. Also Sarah Purser says she can't have the stained glass window ready for the first week in December. They were to have been finished by her contract in the middle of this month. I daresay we could be ready for the middle of December, though I am not even sure about this, but we are afraid to perform in Advent.[1] I cannot give an opinion about dates as it depends on local knowledge.

I asked Synge last night to make a cut in Jack's Smith's speech that we might find out how much he could speak while struggling in the hands of the crowd. He can hardly speak more than about 3 or 4 lines. I am afraid that you will have to cut altogether that speech beginning 'Isn't Bartley Fallon the boastful man.' It checks the speed of the play; we will try it again however to see if the shortening of the other speech makes it possible. Let us have your shortening up of Jack Smith's speech as soon as possible.

On Baile's Strand is the best play I have written. It goes magnificently, and the end is particularly impressive. When I got here I found that Frank Fay seemed to have a curious incapacity to understand the part. He could do nothing with it and was in despair. It now promises to be his finest part. I think I shall be able to arrange the scenery for *Spreading the News* all right. I am waiting on Jack's designs for Synge's play, as it may be possible to use some bits of scenery which will afterwards come in useful for Synge. They should come to-day or to-morrow. Failing this I shall get Pixie Smith, who alone seems to understand what I want, to make a design. I am extremely anxious now that I am here, and for the moment at any rate master of the situation, to get designs of a decorative kind, which will set a standard and come in serviceable for different sorts of plays.

Don't be in any anxiety about the wings for your play. I shall

---

[1] The Abbey Theatre was eventually opened on December 27, 1904, the plays being Yeats's *On Baile's Strand* and *Spreading the News* by Lady Gregory.

get everything made under my own eyes, but the moment I am gone the old business will begin again. Robert's wing will be very good for a remote play like *The Shadowy Waters* but it is too far from realism to go with comedy or with any ordinary play. I am very glad to have it. I have found out that the exact thing I want is the sort of tree one finds in Japanese prints. If Robert could find time to look up some prints and to make me a wing of this sort in the next three or four days I would be very glad. I may probably use it in your play, certainly, in fact, if suitable, if not it will come in for something else. We are in great need of different types of design. The wings are 16 ft. high and 6 ft. wide at their greatest width. They must never be very narrow. *Spreading the News* is going magnificently.

There is great and ever growing indignation over the 6d seats. I hear from Mrs. MacBride that the Clubs say I am lost in [? to] Nationalism. They had all got to look upon the Hall as their property. Yours   W B YEATS

TO LADY GREGORY

Undated   *Nassau Hotel*

My dear Lady Gregory, In writing to you to-day I forgot to enclose Miss Monsell's letter which I now do. I went round to Moore's on Saturday and he told me that he had asked Mrs. Craigie if she would object to my being arbitrator in the dispute between them. From quarrelling with him over *Where there is Nothing* to arbitrating in his quarrel with somebody else is an unexpected leap. He has also lent me his play and asked me to tell him whether it is good enough to go on fighting on.[1] If his version is not good, he thinks he had better give in. I am at present hoping that I shall like the second act. In the first act George Moore, who has joined the literary movement in Malvern and is trying to write in dialect instead of Irish, reads out his love letters with all details as to who the lady is, and where she lives, to a large audience after a dinner party. I went

[1] This appears to refer to a play in which George Moore and Mrs. Craigie ('John Oliver Hobbes') were collaborating. It was at one time named *Peacock's Feathers*, but was eventually produced by the Stage Society as *Elizabeth Cooper*, under Moore's name only, at the Haymarket Theatre on June 22, 1913. Moore afterwards entirely rewrote it and renamed it *The Coming of Gabrielle*.

round to remonstrate, and I find by a curious coincidence that Mrs. Craigie had also objected to this incident. I found a way out for him and he is very grateful, or says he is.

Please tell me how Robert is going on. Yours   W B YEATS

TO MRS. WILLIAM ALLINGHAM [1]

Dec. 7, 1904   *Nassau Hotel*

Dear Madam, I would very much like, if you would give me permission, to make a small selection from your husband's poetry for publication by the Dun Emer Press.[2] These books, which are printed by my sister in a very beautiful old type, have had considerable success. The edition is of course very small, 250 or 300 copies, but we could pay you a small royalty. It would be quite a small book, let us say 25 poems, and could not in any case interfere with the sale of the ordinary editions. Books by AE, by Lionel Johnson, by Douglas Hyde and by myself have already been printed and a book by Lady Gregory will follow the selection from your husband's poems should you give me permission. We are anxious to bring out in this series representative Irish books. I have the greatest possible admiration for Mr. Allingham's poetry. I am sometimes inclined to believe that he was my own master in Irish verse, starting me in the way I have gone whether for good or evil. I believe that I shall be able to make a little volume of his work which will be a great joy to a great many people. Yours sincerely

W B YEATS

TO JOHN QUINN

15 February 1905   *Nassau Hotel*

My dear Quinn, I send you a copy of Synge's play.[3] Moore has written to the *Irish Times* saying that it is a great play, more remark-

[1] Dictated.
[2] *Sixteen Poems* by William Allingham, selected by W. B. Yeats, was published by the Dun Emer Press in November 1905.
[3] *The Well of the Saints* by J. M. Synge was first published in Dublin by Maunsel & Co., as Volume I of the Abbey Theatre Series, in February of this year. Yeats wrote an introduction to the play when it appeared later in the English edition issued by A. H. Bullen as Volume IV of 'Plays for an Irish Theatre.'

able than any original play produced in England during his time. I wonder what has converted him, for he abused the play when he saw an act of it in rehearsal some months ago. He has also praised the acting in the same strenuous way. I imagine that his dislike of our work was artificial and that he has gradually come to feel that he would make himself absurd. He is now unbounded in his enthusiasm, both in public and private, which makes Miss Horniman perfectly furious. She threatens us with all kinds of pains and penalties should we accept any help from him. That quarrel is just now the only little annoyance in a very promising state of things. We had rather thin audiences for Synge's play, but they were always sufficient to play to and make expenses and a little more. Our first production this year, *On Baile's Strand*, etc., left us £90 after we had paid expenses. Synge's play left us £30. In the case of the first production, however, our expenses were heavier as we gave the actresses something, so the disparity between the two plays was greater than appears in the figures. Fay did not feel entitled to give anything to the actresses this time as he is most anxious to put as much as possible into the fund which is to be used to pay enough of the players to go on tour with. It will take us a little time amassing enough money but with reasonable luck we should be able to do it.

I count *The Well of the Saints*, in spite of the thin audiences, as a success. It was, I think, the finest piece of acting as a whole the company has done. Nobody was really bad. It ranked with a good professional performance; and of course ranked above any possible professional presentation of Irish peasant character. You will have judged the play for yourself. The audiences always seemed friendly, but the general atmosphere has for all that been one of intense hostility. Irish national literature, though it has produced many fine ballads and many novels written in the objective spirit of a ballad, has never produced an artistic personality in the modern sense of the word. Tom Moore was merely an incarnate social ambition. And Clarence Mangan differed merely from the impersonal ballad writers about him in being miserable. He was not a personality as Edgar Poe was. He had not thought out or felt out a way of looking at the world peculiar to himself. We will have a hard fight in Ireland before we get the right for every man to see the world in his own way admitted. Synge is invaluable to us because he has that kind of intense narrow personality which necessarily raises the whole issue. It will be very curious to notice the effect of his new play. He will start next time with many enemies but with many admirers. It will be a fight like that over the first realistic plays of Ibsen. I have done a preface for the more expensive edition of his play but it is not out yet.

I daresay you've seen my squabble with Arthur Griffith. I could not avoid it, as the story that Synge had taken a plot from Petronius and pretended that it was Irish was calculated to do a deal of mischief.

Lady Gregory has greatly improved *Kincora* since that version went out to you. She has added a new scene at the beginning, and heightened and ennobled the second and third acts a good deal. The scenery is now being made. It will be a fine spectacle, I think, with its rich, harmonious colour, which reminds me that our decorative scenery for Synge's play has been generally liked. It was scrambled through in a great hurry and cost, I think, about £5, and yet was, I am certain, though often mistaken in execution, obviously right in principle. We were in despair over it for a while.

Miss Horniman has undertaken to make the arrangements for our London expedition this year. We expect to bring there *Baile's Strand* (re-written since performance), *Spreading the News*, *Cathleen ni Houlihan*, and *The Well of the Saints*. Synge is pretty sure of a big success in London. We are to follow *Kincora* with a revival of *The King's Threshold* (partly re-written), and a new play by Boyle. We shall probably follow these a month later with Colum's three-act play. He read me an act last Sunday; really very good; simple and coherent, and with a curious dialect. Unlike Synge's and Lady Gregory's, his is the dialect of a non-Irish-speaking district. In addition to a certain number of phrases containing Gaelic construction there are quantities of phrases out of the school reading books and out of newspapers. It gives a very curious sense of reality, though rather a horrid one. There is a certain amount, too, of the pompous English of the hedge-schoolmaster days. It is unbeautiful Ireland, and he will contrast finely with our Western dialect-makers. He writes of his own Longford of course. I think he is really going to come off as a writer, but it will be as a harsh realist, rather of the German kind. Yours ever   W B YEATS

TO LADY GREGORY[1]

May 30th 1905   18 *Woburn Buildings*

My dear Lady Gregory, When do you go to Dublin? Will you wait till the very end or go up for a few days before the opening? I shall go there I suppose Tuesday or Wednesday of next week. It will take me, I should think, three or four days' solid struggle to get that new stool for *The Hour-Glass* out of William Fay. I have just completed the revision of *Shadowy Waters* but have a few lines more to do on *The King's Threshold*. Did I tell you that I have arranged with Bullen for him to bring out in the early autumn a volume containing all my poems since the Unwin book? I will call it *Poems, a new Series, 1899–1905*. The three verse-plays will be in it in their revised form. We are to put off the expensive collected edition until next year. I think this new book should sell very well for it will be the first big mass of verse that I have published for years, and will get a constant advertisement from the plays at the Abbey Theatre. Bullen is to publish enough copies to last him until 1907 when the Unwin copyright returns to me. He can then issue a complete edition of the Poems. I have heard nothing more about Hone. Bullen liked him very much and would have liked him still better if he could have got that thousand pounds for his own business. I found Bullen a very charming person to stay with. He is really a great scholar, probably the greatest Elizabethan scholar now. He seems to have lost all desire to write. He was very cross with Sidney Lee, an old friend of his, because he had not mentioned the Stratford Shakespeare in some speech, and would have attacked him for some theory about Shakespeare's sonnets, through desire of vengeance, if I had not dissuaded him. It was very beautiful at Stratford, and Marie Corelli pressed her gondola upon me but I did not want to be paragraphed as going about in her gondola, or rather Bullen's womenkind, who look upon me as one of the assets of the firm, did not want me to. She asked after you. The heat here is beyond words, indeed but for the heat I should be writing this and not dictating it. I came out to dictate letters in desperation of keeping sufficiently upright in a chair to hold a pen, with the forty volumes of Balzac which I have bought from Bullen calling me to the armchair. I did some lines, not very many, of the new *King's*

[1] Dictated.

Threshold and then came out. Philip Carr wants to bring out a play simultaneously with our production of it in Dublin. It might be well to let him have *Deirdre* or perhaps one of yours. I daresay they would think all the better of us in Dublin for having a theatre here producing us so promptly. Carr has not been doing very well [1] and will stop until the autumn when he makes another attempt. I saw *The Palace of Truth* at his Theatre, and thought it rather a bad play though written round an idea full of dramatic possibilities. There was no detailed life, no sense of character, and of course no speech, nothing but the central idea; the difference after the Elizabethan comedy was startling. In the Elizabethan comedy, *The Silent Woman* for instance, the details were full of invention and vitality, and the language was like a torrent. Yours always

W B YEATS

TO FLORENCE FARR

[*June* 1905]　　　　　　　　　　　　　　　　　*Nassau Hotel*

This damned beautiful weather is keeping our audiences very thin—however we have enough money now to pay half a dozen of our people who are to go on tour. I sent you the play-book. I could not send it as soon as I said for somebody stole out of the Green Room the copy I had bought for the purpose. General meeting has been put off till Sunday. I shall therefore start home on Monday morning on time for my usual 'Monday.' You might come and dine that day if you have nothing else to do and keep Tuesday evening free for me. You can dine with me after the rehearsal. I may have nobody on Monday but most likely somebody will turn up. I was very glad to get your letter—a dip into the river of life changes even an old handwriting and gives it a new and meaning face.

I have not a moment [to] write in. I am expecting an unknown caller who was described to me by the hotel messenger boy as 'a gentleman with a shaking mouth called by a name something like

[1] Philip Carr had founded the Mermaid Repertory Theatre which courageously revived early English classic plays, at that time almost entirely neglected. Yeats's name appears as a member of the Honorary Committee but it is unlikely that he took any active part in the venture. A short season at the Great Queen Street Theatre in 1905 had given performances of Ben Jonson's *The Silent Woman* on May 8, and W. S. Gilbert's *The Palace of Truth* on May 23, each for a week's run.

Holmes.' Examination of the boy reduced 'a shaking mouth' to a stutter. I met Roberts a while ago—he has been to an Irish printer to arrange for the new publishing house's first book.[1] He said 'How much for a novel of 80,000 words?' The printer said 'Are they long words or short?' The path of a patriot is—well it is described by a popular phrase that has become common since my play, 'The Thorny path of Kathleen-ni-Houlihan.' *The Hour-Glass* is beautiful now—Miss Walker a delight and Fay as Wise Man very varied and powerful.

The caller has come so—Yours ever,   W B YEATS

TO JOHN QUINN

June 29, 1905   18 *Woburn Buildings*

My dear Quinn, I have been meaning for some days to write and thank you for your large share in the gift of the Chaucer.[2] The book is a very great pleasure, coming as it does just when I am setting out to read Chaucer. I have always thought it the most beautiful of all printed books. The pictures have already raised images of stage scenery, and one of them has made an important change in the setting of the Deirdre play. I am busy rehearsing *The Shadowy Waters* for a performance under Mrs. Emery's direction at the Court Theatre.[3] The theosophists are paying the piper as it is to be one of the entertainments at their annual convention. Of course, this does not identify me with them in any way. They get the play from me as might any other manager. Mrs. Emery is to be Dectora, and will play it very beautifully. The Forgael is Farquharson who made a success as Herod in Wilde's *Salome* . . . He is over-emphatic and shoots his voice up and down the scale in a perfectly accidental way. I long to get him by himself and make him speak on a note day after day till he has got rid of accidental variety, but I cannot do that as

[1] The new publishing house, Maunsel & Co. Ltd., started in 1905. George Roberts, who had taken part in first performances of *The King's Threshold* and *On Baile's Strand* and contributed four poems to AE's anthology *New Songs*, was Managing Director of the company.
[2] Lady Gregory had invited a number of Yeats's friends to subscribe towards giving him a copy of the Kelmscott Chaucer as a present on his fortieth birthday.
[3] The first version of *The Shadowy Waters* was performed at the Court Theatre, London, for a Theosophical convention on July 8.

he is playing for nothing, or for the advertisement's sake, and would think he knew as much about it as I do. I have consented to the performance not because I think it a play I would like to be judged by, or because I think it can be well played, but because it gives me a chance of making a lot of changes and testing them. I missed the rehearsals of the play or most of them when it was done at first, through being in America, and besides I did not know as much then as I do now. I want to get it right for Brett's edition[1] and for an edition here which I am trying to arrange. I got your telegram and for that, too, thanks; but I got it in Ireland, where I had gone for the performances of *The Land*.[2] I imagine I wrote to you about that play and told you how beautifully played it was. The heroine's character is very unsatisfactory and that mars the play a good deal, for its construction develops from her character. Colum thinks he is getting that right now, but I doubt if he knows enough about the mind of women to do that for some years to come. The play has been well liked and better praised, though this largely for non-artistic reasons, than anything we have done except *Kincora*. The people are not yet sufficiently deep in their new artistic education to understand what temperament is. The very elements in Synge, let us say, which make him a man of genius repel them, and they like Colum for what is his defect. He has not yet much temperament. He does not pass the people through his imagination, and creates the main elements of his art more out of the critical capacity than out of the emotional or imaginative. I felt rather the same about a good deal in Lady Gregory's *Kincora*. You felt that it was a wonderful *tour de force*, a wonderful achievement of dramatic logic, considering the stubborn historical incidents that had to be brought together. You did not feel as one did about her *Spreading the News*, or as one feels about a play she is writing now—that only one mind could have made it and that everything has a colour and form and sound of that mind... Yours ever W B YEATS

[1] George Brett was the head of the Macmillan Company in America which was bringing out the first collected edition of Yeats's poetry: *The Poetical Works of William B. Yeats*. I. Lyrical Poems, 1906; II. Dramatical Poems, 1907.
[2] *The Land* by Padraic Colum was produced at the Abbey Theatre on June 9.

TO FLORENCE FARR

July 15 [1905]   *Coole Park*

My dear Mrs. Emery: I meant to write yesterday, for I have been afraid that I did not seem sympathetic enough about your accident. I had hoped to have some talk with you on Monday evening, or to get out to you on Tuesday and so learn how you were, but both became impossible. Please write and tell me, for it must have been a great shock and I have been afraid that you may have been more shaken than you thought. I brought the book of Johnson's poems with me that I might send it to you. Shall I send it while you are away from home or wait till you get there again? One of the covers has got a little soiled, on the journey as I think, but I shall get a vellum cover put on it when I get to London again. I am at work on *Shadowy Waters*, changing it greatly, getting rid of needless symbols, making the people answer each other, and making the groundwork simple and intelligible. I find I am enriching the poetry and the character of Forgael greatly in the process. I shall make it as strong a play as *The King's Threshold* and perhaps put it in rehearsal in Dublin again. I am surprised at the badness of a great deal of it in its present form. The performance has enabled me to see the play with a fresh eye. It has been like looking at a picture reversed as in a looking glass. When you went, Maclagan, after another thrust at Narcissus (who 'spoke the lines about holding a woman in his arms as if he were murmuring of his experiences in Piccadilly'), said 'it was worth while having the play done, well worth while, because Mrs. Emery was a delight. It was a great joy to hear her.' Or some such words, even stronger words I think, which I cannot remember. There is a good notice of the play—very well written—in *To-Day* where Synge and myself and Shaw are enumerated with Ibsen and Maeterlinck as great dramatists. You are commended for 'fine imaginative power,' and after you, Jules Shaw is praised with evident enthusiasm for his Aibric. Lady Cromarty was I think really delighted with the Psaltery and when she comes here, which she does in August, I shall find if she could arrange for the Duchess of Sutherland to hear you. Yours ever   [*Signature torn off*]

TO FLORENCE FARR

Wednesday [? July 1905] *Coole Park*

My dear Mrs. Emery: I am glad you are so much better—you spoke to the Psaltery very well but I was afraid—not because you did not hide it—that you were worse than [you] pretended to me. I am changing *The Shadowy Waters* on almost every page and hope you will be able to play the new version—I think if you investigated however you would find that 'the beautiful poetry' was whenever you spoke and 'the irrelevant drama' whenever Farquarson did. I am making Forgael's part perfectly clear and straightforward. The play is now upon one single idea—which is in these new lines—

> 'When the world ends
> The mind is made unchanging for it finds
> Miracle, ecstasy, the impossible joy,
> The flagstone under all, the fire of fires,
> The root of the world.'

There are no symbols except Aengus and Aedane and the birds—and I have into the bargain heightened all the moments of dramatic crisis—sharpened every knife edge. The play as it was came into existence after years of strained emotion, of living upon tip-toe, and is only right in its highest moments—the logic and circumstances are all wrong. I am going to make some fine sleep verses for Forgael when he enchants Dectora and I have done a good bit where he sees her shadow and finds that she is mortal. I have got into my routine here—always my place of industry. After breakfast Chaucer—garden for 20 minutes—then work from 11 till 2, then lunch, then I fish from 3 till 5, then I read and then work again at lighter tasks till dinner—after dinner walk. To this I have added Sandow exercises twice daily. Today I break the routine sufficiently to bicycle over to Edward Martyn's and dine there—I have therefore given up my fishing hour to writing. Mrs. Ladenburg—the American who heard you on Monday week—recited some of Browning's 'Saul' after you left to show it would do for you. She thinks you should try it. You might do it something like the Homer. It would be a change, with its resounding masculine music.

I have sent the Johnson. Yours always   W B YEATS

TO FLORENCE FARR

Friday night [*? July* 1905]   *Coole Park*

My dear Mrs. Emery: I was about to write to you to-day, when I was sent off to catch perch for some Catholics who are to dine here to-night—a fast day. Is not that a medieval way of getting a meal? I stayed out till I had caught six fish, enough for a dinner—and now the mail has gone. I am very sorry about your hurts—I am afraid you must have suffered a great deal and I think it was heroic of you to play the Psaltery that night. I am making a new play of *The Shadowy Waters*. It is strong simple drama now, and has actually more poetical passages. Aibric is jealous of Forgael's absorption in his dream at the outset and ends by being jealous of Dectora. Instead of the sailors coming back drunk at the end, Aibric comes to appeal to Forgael to go back to his own land, but on finding that he is taken up with Dectora bursts out in jealousy. Forgael bids Dectora chose whether she will go back to her own land or not, and she chooses to go on with him—then Aibric cuts the rope and leaves them. This gives me a strong scene at the end. I wish you could get a good verse speaker who is a man. I wish I could persuade you that you are mistaken over Farquharson. I have been taken in in the same way more than once myself. When a young man has even a slight vulgar element—and it is not slight in Farquharson—one thinks it will leave him as he grows older. I thought that about Le Gallienne—who had what seemed like genius. It never leaves them, but when the enthusiasm of youth is over it gets much stronger till finally all else has left them. I have never known an exception. Apart from all else Farquharson is a man who always requires to be explained. Mrs. Shakespear for instance thought his manner was personally very offensive to you off the stage. He is really impossible as an artist. I had to use the greatest self control over myself all through those rehearsals. Only my fear of making things difficult for you kept me quiet.

I want you to try and get me Paget's model for the *Shadowy Waters* scene. I will probably work out a scene for Dublin, which could be used by you if necessary. Our stage is nearly as big as the Court. I can probably get that harp made too—we have carpenters and so on of our own now. We are in all likelihood to have a large scene dock next door this winter and will be able to work things out very perfectly. You must come over some time and see our scenery, when the show comes off. You will I think prefer it to Craig. It is more noble and simple.

Saturday

I have an idea for a bicycle trip when I get back. I have my imagination full of Chaucer and would like to hire a bicycle and go the journey of the Canterbury pilgrims from Southwark and Greenwich to Canterbury through Rochester. I do not see why we should not go with some harmless person to keep up appearances.

Tell me if you try 'Saul' and if you try 'The Daughters of Jerusalem.' I doubt of the long grave poems like 'Dark Angel'[1] having enough internal movement for the Psaltery. One wants changes of voice—even different speakers at times—and choral bits for singing. The danger of the Psaltery is monotony. A thing the ancients were more alive to in all arts than we are—Chaucer for instance follows his noble 'Knight's Tale' with an unspeakable tale told by a drunken miller. If Morris had done the like—everyone would have read his *Earthly Paradise* for ever. By the by Chaucer in that same unspeakable tale calls a certain young wife 'white and small as a weasel.' Does it not bring the physical type clearly to the minds-eye? I think one wants that sort of vivid irresistible phrase in all verse to be spoken aloud—it rests the imagination as upon the green ground.

I have had a cold for some days and that is why my writing is so bad and my spelling. Yours ever   W B YEATS

Write soon. Lady Cromarty and Lady Margaret Sackville arrive next week. I will find out what can be done for the psaltery.

TO A. H. BULLEN [2]

July 28 [1905]   *Coole Park*

My dear Bullen, I won't do the Shakespeare article for you.[3] My mind is not on Shakespeare at present, and I might very possibly

[1] A poem by Lionel Johnson.   [2] Dictated.
[3] Bullen was at this time printing his fine ten-volume Stratford Town Shakespeare, in the last volume of which he included a number of essays by Shakespearean scholars. It would appear that he had asked Yeats to be a contributor.

have to upset all my habits to get it there. A chance such as seeing the historical series of plays which Carr is going to bring out might set me thinking of Shakespeare, but one can't count on such things. I imagine I'll be reading nothing but Chaucer for some time to come.

By the bye I don't think I ever thanked you for your share in giving me a big Kelmscott book. I like it all, it is a delight, even 'The picture of the Wife of Bath,' which by the bye is not the Wife of Bath at all but a person in her story, 'the loathly damsel' of the folk-lorists and very good at that. Yours sincerely   W B YEATS

TO A. H. BULLEN [1]

August 3 [1905]   *Coole Park*

My dear Bullen, Certainly I never meant those words 'I won't do the Shakespeare essay' to be rude. I wrote as if I was talking to you, forgetting that what is a friendly petulance when spoken becomes when the tone of the voice isn't there mere brusqueness. I dictated at great speed walking up and down the room and forgot that you weren't there listening to me. I should like to have done it for you, but I have *Samhain* notes ahead of me and some other things, and my imagination is getting so deep in Chaucer that I cannot get it down into any other well for the present ... Yours always
                                       W B YEATS

TO FLORENCE FARR

[*August* 1905]   *Coole Park*

My dear Florence Emery: Get the harp mended and I will pay the amount. I shall leave the harp with you for the present at any rate but I may want it in Dublin some time. If on the other hand you would prefer to have it altogether, then do as you suggest—I will give it you with pleasure—but I think you had better let it be mine and have the use of it. I have dreamed of you several times lately. Last night you had a friend who, as you phrased it, 'meddled a little

[1] Dictated.

with crime.' His name was 'Jehovah Cutthroat.' I distinctly remember being jealous and thinking it just like you. Lady Cromarty and Lady Margaret Sackville are here, and this has made life much more hurried [?] as it means various entertainments. It leaves me little time after my work is over but *Shadowy Waters* is getting gradually finished—doubled in beauty. Lady Cromarty is as simple as a child and as innocent. She remembers a past life and her present is utterly over-shadowed by it. She remembers people so beautiful looking that the people now seem ugly and trivial. This past is intensely vivid and has appeared to her since she was a child—long before she knew of incarnations. She was at Tara and describes curious details of that old life. She is less clever but has more nature than Lady Margaret. There has been a tea party, that the county may have a glimpse of these birds of paradise, and I am tired out after two hours' strained conversation. One lady, who is boycotted so that nobody is allowed to work in her garden but the village idiot, was my share of the festival. She had a little intelligence, the others were as dull and as healthy as cabbages. I have been waiting to answer your letters until I could send you a long passage out of *Shadowy Waters*—the first meeting of Forgael and Dectora, but Lady Gregory is too tired with entertaining for me to dictate it for the present. Write again soon. Yours ever   W B YEATS

I think the Paris affair is going all right but it goes very slowly.

TO ARTHUR SYMONS

August 3, 1905   *Coole Park*

My dear Symons, I have been awaiting with a great deal of expectancy your Wagner Essay,[1] and would be very much obliged for the proofs if you still have them. I have asked Heinemann to send you a little volume of translations from Petrarch by a Miss Tobin that I met in San Francisco.[2] I think them very delicate, very beauti-

[1] 'The Ideas of Richard Wagner,' a long essay by Arthur Symons, appeared in the *Quarterly Review* in July 1905, and was reprinted in his *Studies in Seven Arts*.
[2] Writing of San Francisco in his unreprinted essay 'America and the Arts,' in the *Metropolitan Magazine*, April 1905, Yeats said 'Perhaps it was only the enchantment of a still sea, of a winter that endured the violets, and of a lovely book of verses from Petrarch, sent me by a young writer, that made me fancy

ful, with a curious poignant ecstasy, and would have written about them but for my ignorance of Italian. One feels a sort of pathetic interest in books of good poetry, as if they were waifs in the street with tragic stories. One wishes to send them to some benevolent home where they will get a little encouragement. Miss Tobin did another book from Petrarch a year ago, and that too was beautiful. Of course there are bad lines, one may read through a whole poem and find very little now and then, but there is nearly always a line or a half line with the true ecstasy.

I am rewriting *The Shadowy Waters*, every word of it. I let them play it in London (and an execrable performance it was except for Mrs. Emery, and another,) that I might find out what was wrong. Farquharson who seemed good in Herod was unendurable as Forgael....

I believe I am making a really strong play out of *The Shadowy Waters* and am certainly losing no poetry. It is the worst thing I ever did dramatically and partly because it was written when I knew very little of the stage and because there were so many old passages written or planned before I knew anything, that the little I did know could not pull it into shape. We are going to have a fine season at our theatre here. Lady Gregory has done a very original play, at once merry and beautiful, and Synge is finishing a long and elaborate work. Yours always   W B YEATS

Remembrance to Mrs. Symons.

TO ARTHUR SYMONS

Sept 10 [1905]   *Coole Park*

My dear Symons, The Wagnerian essay touches my own theories at several points, and enlarges them at one or two, but that must wait

---

that I found there a little of that pleasure in the Arts, which brings creative art and not scholarship, because it is delight in life itself.' When Agnes Tobin came to England Yeats recommended her translations from Petrarch to Edmund Gosse and to Arthur Symons. Symons reviewed her 'On the Death of Madonna Laura' in the *Saturday Review*, July 28, 1906. In his *Confessions* he describes Agnes Tobin as 'bright, warm-hearted, very talkative, very amusing ... She had a passion for meeting famous writers.' Joseph Conrad dedicated his *Under Western Eyes* 'To Agnes Tobin who brought to our door her genius for friendship from the uttermost shore of the West.'

till we meet. I have spent the entire summer rewriting *Shadowy Waters*. There are not more than about thirty lines of the old left—just the few moments of lyric verse where the smoky flame burnt pure. I have made I think a strong play of it, and have got dramatic suspense throughout. In one way finding it so bad has been a comfort, for it shows me how much I have learned by watching rehearsals in Dublin and by altering my plays and other people's for the stage. In one place your Wagner essay helped me. A certain passage had always seemed wrong to me, and after I had rewritten it several times it was still wrong. I then came on that paragraph where Wagner insists that a play must not appeal to the intelligence, but by being, if I remember rightly, a piece of self consistent life directly to the emotions. It was just one of those passages which seemed to have no very precise meaning till one brings actual experience to their understanding. Your essay is a substitute for more volumes than anything of the kind I have seen, and has I believe greatly pleased Ashton Ellis.[1] At any rate I know it has Miss Horniman who I think speaks as his voice.

I am getting ready the one volume edition of all my poems since '95, and if you have in your memory any misdoings of mine, please tell me of them that I may put them right. You will hardly recognise not only *The Shadowy Waters* but *Baile's Strand* and a good deal of *The King's Threshold*. They have all been rewritten after rehearsal or actual performance, and *The King's Threshold* has been changed and rehearsed and then changed again and so on, till I have got it as I believe a perfectly articulate stage play. I have learned a great deal about poetry generally in the process, and one thing I am now quite sure of is that all the finest poetry comes logically out of the fundamental action, and that the error of late periods like this is to believe that some things are inherently poetical, and to try and pull them on to the scene at every moment. It is just these seeming inherently poetical things that wear out. My *Shadowy Waters* was full of them, and the fundamental thinking was nothing, and that gave the whole poem an impression of weakness. There was no internal life pressing for expression through the characters.

We hope to bring the plays over in November, and I believe we are going to Oxford as well as London.

---

[1] W. Ashton Ellis (d. 1919), the translator of Wagner's Prose Works, 8 volumes, 1892–1899, and of several volumes of his letters.

I see by an old post card that you asked me for Joyce's address. I don't know it, but care of Oliver Gogarty, 5 Rutland Square Dublin, might reach him. Yours ever   W B YEATS

TO JOHN QUINN

September 16, 1905   *Coole Park*

My dear Quinn, Many thanks for the magazines, which have just come. Fiona's articles I had not seen, which probably accounts for my having had a rather cantankerous letter from William Sharp. He had probably expected some gratitude. The articles are curiously bad, so bad that it is hard to understand how any practised writer can have escaped getting a little simplicity by this time. They are well meant, however, and I must write some thanks to that phantom Fiona.

The little books that you have copyrighted look fine. Synge's play is showing itself worthy of your care, for he writes that it has been accepted for immediate performance by what his translator calls the principal German theatre. *The Shadow of the Glen* has been put into Czech by somebody connected with the National Theatre there, but nothing definite has been arranged as to its performance. Synge's foreign success is worth more to us than would be the like success of any other of our people, for he has been the occasion of all the attacks upon us. I said in a speech some time ago that he would have a European reputation in five years, but his enemies have mocked the prophecy. I think we have seen the end of the democracy in the Theatre, which was Russell's doing, for I go to Dublin at the end of the week to preside at a meeting summoned to abolish it. If all goes well, Synge and Lady Gregory and I will have everything in our hands; indeed, the only practical limitation to our authority will be caused by the necessity of some sort of a permanent business committee in Dublin. We are too often away to do that part of the work, or at any rate Russell, who is urging on the changes, thinks so. It has been a long fight, but the change could not be made until the old method had discredited itself and until three or four people had got some sort of natural leadership. We are not out of the wood yet, but I think we are practically so. We start the autumn by playing the revivals that we are bringing to London in November, and on our return from London we start our new work with Lady Gregory's *White Cockade*, a very fine thing. Then we shall have new plays by Boyle [1] and Synge, and I hope Colum's new version of *Broken Soil*. He has made it altogether anew and put good common speech upon it, which will be a great sorrow to those admirers of his who thought that his little confusions and muddinesses were a profound knowledge of human nature. Gatty came to *The Land* and was very melancholy over it; a great falling off from *Broken Soil* he thought it—a symptom doubtless of the communications of heretical minds.

I have altogether re-written my *Shadowy Waters*. There is hardly a page of the old. The very temper of the thing is different. It is full of homely phrases and of the idiom of daily speech. I have made the sailors rough, as sailors should be, characterized all the people more or less, and yet not lost any of my lyrical moments. It has become a simple passionate play, or at any rate it has a simple passionate story for the common sightseer, though it keep back something for instructed eyes. I am now correcting the last few lines, and have very joyfully got 'creaking shoes' and 'liquorice-root' into what had been a very abstract passage. I believe more strongly every day that the element of strength in poetic language is common idiom, just as the element of strength in poetic construction is common passion.

I am beginning to be afraid you are not coming over this year. It will be a disappointment to the Company, too, who have planned a special show for you. You are to choose what you like out of the repertory. Yours ever   W B YEATS

TO FLORENCE FARR [2]

6th Oct 1905   *Nassau Hotel*

My dear Florence Emery, I am dictating this because I have had an influenza cold for the last week and anything of that kind always

---

[1] William Boyle, author of *The Building Fund, The Eloquent Dempsey*, and *The Mineral Workers*, produced in the early days of the Abbey Theatre. His plays were very popular but he withdrew them as a protest against the production of Synge's *Playboy of the Western World* in 1907. Later he returned to the Abbey which produced his *Family Failing* in 1912.   [2] Dictated.

affects my eyes and makes writing a much greater labour. I imagine I shall be over in London in a week or so but cannot say for certain. I have been kept all this while and am still kept by the affairs of the Theatre Society. We are turning it into a private Limited Liability Co. in order to get control into a few hands. If all goes well Lady Gregory, Synge and myself will be the Directors in a few days and will appoint all Committees and have more votes between us than all the other Shareholders. I have foreseen that something of this kind was inevitable from the first, but it has come rather sooner than I hope[d] for. I am pretty confident that we have the majority of the members with us in the change. It has been a very slow business winning their confidence, but I think we have it now. We have all the really competent people with us certainly. Hitherto the democratic arrangements have made it impossible to look ahead and settle dates and all that kind of thing. There were always too many people to consult. We started on our Autumn Session last Monday and are holding our audiences very well. This gets rid of my last anxiety, for I had been sometimes afraid that our last year's people came from curiosity and would fall off. I am now entirely certain that we will make a great Theatre and get an audience for it.

Did I tell you that *The Well of the Saints* has been accepted by a principal theatre in Berlin? It is a great triumph for us here as I foretold European reputation for Synge at the Catholic College and have been mocked for the prophecy. All the incompetentness united in making little of that play, and now its German acceptance comes just in time to prepare for the production of his new play, an even wilder business. He is a great man and I wish you could get a chance of playing him. I am still in the abyss over *Shadowy Waters*, it is not yet finished and my perplexity is as nothing to Fay's over that shining harp. He and the stage carpenter are at this moment working away boring holes in the half of an old wooden bicycle wheel which is to play a mysterious part in the instrument. There are to be wonderful effects prepared for months beforehand, burning jewels on the harp and twinkling stars in the sky, but I imagine that both stars and jewels will slowly dwindle and fade as the night of performance gets near. Fay has just given me a good deal of pleasure by telling me that the players discussed last night in the Green Room whose plays drew the best and decided that mine did. I should not begrudge it to anyone if his plays drew more than mine, but it gives one more than a personal pleasure to find that anything so difficult as poetry can, under modern conditions, even hold its own against comedy in prose. Of course a good deal of this popularity comes from the fact that my name is better known than that of the others, but it does mean that I have a small genuine following as a dramatist. I think myself that in the long run Boyle and Lady Gregory will be our most popular playwrights. Her new play *The White Cockade* is a beautiful, laughing joyful, extravagant and yet altogether true, phantasy. I have noticed by the by that the writers in this country who come from the mass of the people,— or no, I should say who come from Catholic Ireland, have more reason than fantasy. It is the other way with those who come from the leisured classes. They stand above their subject and play with it, and their writing is, as it were, a victory as well as a creation. The others—Colum and Edward Martyn for instance—are dominated by their subject, with the result that their work as a whole lacks beauty of shape, the organic quality. They are never really gay though they can sometimes write about people who are. I wonder if this is true everywhere of the man of the people as contrasted with the man of traditional leisure. Of course Edward Martyn, on the father's side, is of one of the oldest families in Ireland, but he always seems to have more of his mother's temper, and besides he has taken the habit of his mind from the mass of the people. But philosophic generalisations are bad things to set out on at five minutes to six with the typewriting office about to close.

Write to me, but I daresay I shall write again in a day or two, for I am not quite certain that a typewritten letter is a letter at all. Yours ever   W B YEATS

TO A. H. BULLEN [1]

Nov. 2nd, 1905   18 *Woburn Buildings*

Dear Mr. Bullen, After seeing Mathews [2] to-day I thought over the whole matter again. I have come to the conclusion that it would be

[1] Dictated.
[2] Elkin Mathews, who had published *The Wind Among the Reeds* in 1899. His contract was to expire in 1907, but was apparently renewed, for he printed an edition of the book in 1911. Bullen, however, was able to include the poems from it in the Collected Edition of 1908 and in the volume *Poems: Second Series*, published in 1910.

unwise to accept his proposal. If we agree to make the book 8/6, and not less than 7/6 for five years after 1907, we tie our hands very seriously when the time comes for you to have all my books. It would make any kind of a popular edition impossible. It would be better I think either to buy out Mathews, which I daresay you won't think worth while, or to publish the present book without the lyrics from the *Wind among the Reeds* volume at say 5/-. It would be practically a volume of new work, none of the *Seven Woods* lyrics or longer poems have been published in England before and the three plays have all been greatly re-written. *The Shadowy Waters* is entirely new. Nothing remains of the old except a few stray passages embedded in new writing. The first half of *Baile's Strand* is entirely new. Five shillings is a much better price than 8/6. And it will be a great matter to have an entirely free hand in 1907. Yours
W B YEATS

TO FRANK FAY[1]

Nov 4th, 1905   18 *Woburn Buildings*

My dear Fay, I have asked the lady who is typing this to look after that typewriter. She will hear by Monday as to whether it is still unsold and if it is will get an expert to look at it. If this falls through she knows of another place where they can be got. We should get one quite cheaply for it is, she says, an old machine now.

I went to *The Merchant of Venice* the other night and disliked the stage management even more than I expected.[2] I found that as usual for a Shakespeare play nothing moved me except the scenes of prolonged crisis. The Trial scene was moving, but owing to the stage management the rest was broken up. Shakespeare had certainly intended those short scenes of his to be played one after the other as quickly as possible and there is no reason that they should not, if played in this way, keep the sense of crisis almost as living as in the long scenes. The stage management, however, never lost an opportunity of increasing the breaking up caused by changes of scene by bringing in gondolas, crowds, masqueraders etc. One kept

[1] Dictated.
[2] Arthur Bourchier's revival of *The Merchant of Venice* was given at the Garrick Theatre, London, on October 11, 1905.

asking oneself 'What has brought me to this childish peepshow?' That wonderful succession of passages beginning 'On such a night as this' was cut out. It is almost the most beautiful thing in the whole play but they cut it out because there was nothing in it for the eye, no peepshow. I think the whole of our literature as well as our drama has grown effeminate through the over development of the picture-making faculty. The great thing in literature, above all in drama, is rhythm and movement. The picture belongs to another art. I thought Bourchier good in the quiet parts but merely an Old Father Christmas in a rage when he came to passion. One thought of Irving at every moment. Yours sincerely

W B YEATS

TO GEORGE RUSSELL (AE)

[*Postmark Jan* 8, 1906]   18 *Woburn Buildings*

My dear Russell . . . I desire the love of a very few people, my equals or my superiors. The love of the rest would be a bond and an intrusion. These others will in time come to know that I am a fairly strong and capable man and that I have gathered the strong and capable about me, and all who love work better than idle talk will support me. It is a long fight but that is the sport of it. The antagonism, which is sometimes between you and me, comes from the fact that though you are strong and capable yourself you gather the weak and not very capable about you, and that I feel they are a danger to all good work. It is I think because you desire love. Besides you have the religious genius to which all souls are equal. In all work except that of salvation that spirit is a hindrance.

I know quite well—I knew when Synge wrote his first play—I will never have the support of the clubs. I am trying for the general public—the only question with me (and it is one I have argued with Synge and Lady Gregory) is whether I should attack the clubs openly. Our small public at the theatre is, I am glad to say, almost entirely general public. I have no objection to a rival theatre by the by, nor can the old society give me any serious annoyance—if it observes its obligations to Miss Horniman, which it will do I have no doubt. Yours   W B YEATS

TO SYDNEY COCKERELL

Jan 22nd, 1906   *Abbey Theatre*

My dear Cockerell, Thank you ever so much for the promise of that book,[1] which I am most curious about. I have heard about it from Lady Gregory; but I have not seen it. I should very much like to have it while I am here, as I have very little to read. I have always felt that Byron was one of the great problems, the great mysteries— a first-rate man, who was somehow not first-rate when he wrote. And yet the very fascination of him grows from the same root with his faults. One feels that he is a man of action made writer by accident, and that, in an age when great style was the habit of his class, he might have been one of the greatest of all writers. His disaster was that he lived in an age when great style could only be bought by the giving up of everything else. Yours ever

W B YEATS

TO FLORENCE FARR

[*January* 1906]   *Nassau Hotel*

My dear Florence Emery: Thank you for your hint about the theatre —I will never mention it again. There is by the by a pretty scandal about—but I forgot I am not to speak of it. I want to see *Lady Inger* at [the] Stage Society [2] but though I should see it at any cost I have not enough resolution to go over as I must return at once. If you can give me Tuesday morning, afternoon or evening, or at worst Wednesday morning or afternoon or both, I will come over on Monday see the play and return after having had a little of your company. I have to be here for a week or so after that as—but I forgot I have sworn. I have written to the Leeds man (from whom I heard) again asking for a date for us both in March and to know how much we can expect. I shall also write to Edinburgh where I go for two more lectures in March—or rather one there, one at St.

---

[1] *Astarte* by the Earl of Lovelace, which was at first issued privately in an edition of 220 copies printed at the Chiswick Press, in December 1905.

[2] Performances of Ibsen's early play *Lady Inger of Östråt* were given by the Stage Society at the Scala Theatre, London, on January 28 and 29. This letter appears to have been written shortly before then.

Andrews—and see if you can come. I want to see you very much now and it will always be a great pleasure to be with you. I have such a fine book to show you, Lord Lovelace's privately printed book about Byron and Mrs. Leigh, his half sister, a very vivid powerful book and not to be bought. I have been sent a copy and will bring it over. You cannot think what a pleasure it is to be fond of somebody to whom one can talk—as a rule any sort of affection annihilates conversation, strikes one with a silence like that of Adam before he had even named the beasts. To be moved and talkative, unrestrained, one's own self, and to be this not because one has created some absurd delusion that it all is wisdom, as Adam may have in the beast's head, but not in Eve, but because one has found an equal, that is the best of life. All this means that I am looking forward to seeing you—that my spirits rise at the thought of it.

Synge—but I forget he is a part of what I have sworn off—well I cannot help it. His play was done in Germany in association with a play in one act by Wilde called I think *Florentine Nights*.[1] I don't think it has been even published in England. Why not get it and play it at your new theatre?

Do help me to get over to the play. I won't go if you are not kind. Yours ever   W B YEATS

TO FLORENCE FARR

Tuesday [? Feb. 1906]   [*Nassau Hotel*]

My dear Florence Emery: I have sent *Ideas of Good and Evil* to Mrs. King, so I hope I shall be forgiven, by you too, my too great preoccupation with yourself. Mrs. Patrick Campbell, on whose tail I have not succeeded in dropping salt, should receive a copy of the new *Shadowy Waters* with a devout letter, but not yet. I myself— though I am still at Nassau Hotel—leave for Coole to-day to spend a couple of weeks of most unwilling industry—so great is your power. I think you may take the Leeds lecture as settled—but I have had to delay about Edinburgh until I get some other dates right. We shall have to make our own way in lecturing—one

---

[1] Evidently *A Florentine Tragedy*. It was produced, together with Wilde's *Salome*, with decoration by Charles Ricketts, by the Literary Theatre Society at the King's Theatre (National Sporting Club), Covent Garden, on June 10, 1906.

lecture will lead to another—we have not the advantage of the sort of popular subject which advertises a lecture by itself—our reputations are too esoteric for the general public outside certain university towns. We shall make our way by our faculty, not by our subjects or fame. This was what happened in my own case—I was refused by the agencies and then made hundreds of pounds. The second week in April would suit me for Oxford or Cambridge lectures.

I have been speaking here lately—I at least find that I can move people by power not merely—as the phrase is—by 'charm' or 'speaking beautifully'—a thing I always resented. I feel this change in all my work and that it has brought a change into the personal relations of life—even things seemingly beyond control answer strangely to what is within—I once cared only for images about whose necks I could cast various 'chains of office' as it were. They were so many aldermen of the ideal, whom I wished to master the city of the soul. Now I do not want images at all, or chains of office, being content with the unruly soul. I think you have changed too—is it that those eastern meditations have freed you—made you free of all but holy church—now alas steering its malignant way, I suppose, through the Indian Ocean—a sort of diabolical Aengus carrying not a glass house for Etain—as did the Irish one—but a whole convent, altar lights, vegetarian kitchen and all?

I have myself by the by begun eastern meditations—of your sort, but with the object of trying to lay hands upon some dynamic and substantialising force as distinguished from the eastern quiescent and supersensualizing state of the soul—a movement downwards upon life, not upwards out of life. Yours ever   W B YEATS

TO A. H. BULLEN [1]

Feb 13 [? 1906]   *Coole Park*

My dear Bullen, You must have thought it very bad of me leaving that *Baile's Strand* so long unrighted, but I have had the devil of a time with it.[2] I have had two or three times to go to London and

[1] Dictated.
[2] This letter seems to refer to the revised version of *On Baile's Strand* which first appeared in the volume *Poems, 1899–1905*, issued in 1906.

back: I have been in Scotland lecturing, and I have had some odds and ends of the influenza, with the result that though I worked pretty constantly at the play I could not get it done. As soon as I got a few passages right I had to go away, and so the mood was broken, and some considerable scenes written which had no proper coherence. At last I asked Lady Gregory to let me come down here; and now having been for a week out of all distractions I have almost finished. Nothing remains but a little work on the prose opening and a few words here and there to knit the old to the new. The big scene is done, including thirty lines of a lyric chorus. I shall go to Dublin next Saturday and by that time all shall be done. I shall give Sidgwick the completed MS. and proofs in the middle of next week.

What I write to you about is this: would it be worth while making another attempt to get *The Wind among the Reeds* out of Mathews? I don't think it is any use Sidgwick[1] going, for he has a quarrel on with Sidgwick about some book of I think Bliss Carman's. I am disinclined to go again, as the failure of my last negociation was [*sic*] rather spoils my chances, but we could try him with A. P. Watt. Some months have now passed since I saw Mathews with Sidgwick, and Mathews's term with the book is so much nearer its end. It occurs to me that we might offer him whatever sum he is accustomed to make in a year of it and something more. This sum to be calculated on the average of the last three years, like the Income Tax people. I suppose he would be content to estimate his own profits as the same amount I get out of the book. The sum isn't very considerable and we could let him go on selling the book. If you think well of it I will see A. P. Watt when I get to London. I think Mathews is striking at his own interest to some extent out of spite over the Bliss Carman book and because he is cross at my book passing out of his hands at all. A letter from A. P. Watt might persuade him to look at the matter from a business point of view alone.

My book with Unwin is now bringing me about thirty-five pounds a year, and if we got the same proportion of lyrical work into this new book it ought to sell at least as well. At first when I wrote to you about it I was inclined to think that *The Wind among the Reeds* poems were in a mood so different from these later poems that they would be no great help, but so many people have asked me will

[1] Frank Sidgwick was at this time a partner with Bullen at the Shakespeare Head Press.

it contain those lyrics that I suppose I was wrong. I don't want to press the point but I would like your opinion upon it.

Lady Gregory has asked me to get her some copies—a dozen—of the old edition of *Shadowy Waters*, she wants them to give to friends who have stayed here among the Seven Woods. What are you selling the old edition at?

I was dining with Symons when I was in London, and Mrs. Symons said you are the most delightful man she ever met. Yours

W B YEATS

TO FLORENCE FARR

Friday [? February 16, 1906]   *Coole Park*

My dear Florence Emery: I enclose a letter from Leeds and have written to say that you will write direct about posters etc. Don't you think that we should get some more of those hand bills or circulars about the 'chanting' printed? I will now try and arrange for Liverpool and Edinburgh but had better wait till I get exact dates in Dublin where I go tomorrow. I have done magnificent work here. I have a sketch of a strange little play about the capture of a blind Unicorn, and I have written a choral ode about witches which contains these lines—suggested in some vague way by your letter, only suggested I mean, in phantasmal exaggeration of some sentence.

> Or, they hurl a spell at him
> That he follow with desire
> Bodies that can never tire
> Or grow kind, for they anoint
> All their bodies joint by joint
> With a miracle working juice,
> That is made out of the grease
> Of the ungoverned unicorn;
> But the man is thrice forlorn
> Emptied, ruined, wracked and lost
> That *they* follow, for at most
> They will give him kiss for kiss
> While they murmur 'After this

> Hatred may be sweet in the taste.'
> Those wild hands that have embraced
> All his body can but shove
> At the burning wheel of love
> Till the side of hate comes up.[1]

The hero had been praising an indomitable kind of woman and the chorus sing of her evil shadow. The unicorn in the little play is a type of masterful and beautiful life, but I shall not trouble to make the meaning clear—a clear vivid story of a strange sort is enough. The meaning may be different with everyone.

I shall get you to teach me meditation. My difficulty is that I get partly hypnotized at once and that a sleepy calm makes it very difficult to get the mood of fiery understanding which must represent the spirit which is, according to the old definition, 'that which moves itself.' I have never got this mood except in absolute trance at night.

Yours always, shall I say affectionately or would that arouse too much scorn?   W B YEATS

I shall be back in London next week.

TO SYDNEY COCKERELL

March 28th, 1906   18 *Woburn Buildings*

My dear Cockerell, I have been in a dream, rewriting a play and have awoken out of it to find that it was last Sunday I should have gone to you to see *Lancelot du Lac*. I am very sorry. May I come out a little later on, after my return from Dublin where I go in a few days? If you were in town on Monday I wish that you would come in, in the evening. I have asked Sturge Moore, but don't know whether he is coming.

Astarte is a fine book, a vehement confident book and that is a rare thing today, when Science has robbed us of our courage. It has a quality of personal exaltation about it, coming from I don't know what. It is I suppose the meditations of a lifetime. What a subject

[1] These lines form part of the revised version of *On Baile's Strand*, and were first published in the *Shanachie*, Spring number, 1906.

for a play the whole story is, but no English audience would endure it.

Lady Gregory brought me to see Lord Lovelace, but he was very unlike the man I had expected. How did that little short stumpy man ever get that hidalgo air that he puts on when he writes? I think that both as a man and as a writer (for I had some talk with him) he underrates Byron's imaginative power, certainly he underrates his letters. He has come to see in Byron the grandfather and not the poet. Yours sincerely W B YEATS

TO STEPHEN GWYNN[1]

June 13th 1906　　　　　　　　　　18 *Woburn Buildings*

My dear Gwynn, Many thanks for the cheque which is all right. What happened about that magazine [2] is this—Roberts saw me about it and told me that you seemed doubtful about its success— he seemed anxious for it himself. I talked over the matter with Lady Gregory and she objected to doing anything for it on the grounds that it would be merely another *Celtic Xmas,* and that amateurish things of that kind were injurious to the whole movement and that so long as they didn't pay they were bound to be amateurish. I then asked Roberts if contributors to it were to be paid and he said they were—I also talked out with him certain schemes as to the contents of the magazine, and gave him that story of Shaw's. I told him that Shaw had given it to me for the Dun Emer press. Roberts of course knows that we pay for everything that my sisters print. Indeed we pay a very decent price—about 15 per cent I think. Shaw does not care about money and whatever he would get for a little story like this, and it a reprint, would I daresay not seem worth having to him—but I rather think that my argument to him about this little story, for I think it was I who wrote, was that he would be encouraging the first Irish publication of its kind to pay

[1] Dictated. Stephen Gwynn was at first a director of the firm of Maunsel & Co., but resigned on being elected Member of Parliament in 1906.

[2] Yeats here alludes to the *Shanachie*, a quarterly magazine, six numbers of which were published by Maunsel & Co. during 1906–7. Bernard Shaw's story 'The Miraculous Revenge,' published in the first number, had already been printed in *Time*, March 1885. See note 3 on p. 387. The magazine was edited by Joseph Hone.

contributors. I certainly drafted a letter of this sort and I believe I sent it. It is possible therefore that you may have to pay Shaw—the whole thing is a mess owing to Roberts' vagueness of mind. When I saw Hone in Dublin he was under the impression that Roberts had got the various contributions I had to do with for nothing. I don't so much blame Roberts for the magazine itself being unlike the original scheme, or rather I don't blame him at all, for such things change under the hand and I put no definite question and made no condition on the point. I think it better however to say to you that I think it too scrappy . . . I do not find in the editing of this magazine any one selective mind or any one principle of selection . . . I don't believe it is possible to make a good magazine without making up your mind who it is for whom you are making it and keeping to that idea throughout. I suspect that you and Roberts and Hone have all done this thing and because you are all in it have felt no individual responsibility. Indeed Hone admitted something of the kind to me—but damn all *Celtic Christmases* now and for ever—what Dublin wants is some man who knows his own mind and has an intolerable tongue and a delight in enemies and I wish I could see you setting out upon that man's journal [? journey]. Yours ever   W B YEATS

TO J. B. YEATS [1]

July 21 [1906]   *Coole Park*

My dear Father, Thank you so much for your letters about Swinburne. I have seen nothing of his criticism, except one rather absurd sentence quoted I think by the *Sketch*. I did not get the *Athenaeum* as I did not intend to reply. The passage about him in the Blake book was by Ellis, and was entirely just and civil. I am not at all surprised at Swinburne's attitude, for one practically never converts anyone of a generation older than one's own. One's readers are one's contemporaries, or the generation that comes after them. Andrew Lang was hardly civil when I sent him my first book, and was very uncivil indeed when he reviewed the Rhymers' book.

[1] Dictated.

Two years later he wrote a very generous article of apology. He excused himself by saying that new work was very difficult to him, and that when he first read Verlaine's poetry he thought it no better than one finds in the poet's corner of a country newspaper. Swinburne is a delight. Ellis said he didn't understand 'the doctrine of the four Zoas,' a most intricate thing that we had spent four years working out; and fourteen or fifteen years after that criticism and because he thinks I wrote it, Swinburne is still so excited that he denies both reason and imagination to Ireland.

Mrs. Patrick Campbell has asked for my *Deirdre*, which she has seen though in somewhat incomplete form. She wants to produce it in the autumn and to take it on tour in America. I am not quite sure however whether I can let her have it, as my own theatre has first claims. And besides there is a new actress, a Miss Darragh, who may want it for England, and I am inclined to think that Miss Darragh has more intellectual tragedy in her. She is an Irishwoman, and played Leah in *The Walls of Jericho*.[1] She gave a magnificent performance of Salome the other day. I am inclined to think, though I have not seen enough of her yet to be quite certain, that she is the finest tragedian on the English stage. I feel that a change is taking place in the nature of acting; Mrs. Campbell and her generation were trained in plays like *Mrs. Tanqueray*, where everything is done by a kind of magnificent hysteria (one understands that when one hears her hunting her monkey and her servant with an impartial fury about the house). This school reduces everything to an emotional least common denominator. It finds the scullion in the queen, because there are scullions in the audience but no queens. It gives the scullion grace and beauty, but it must be the grace and beauty that the scullion dreams of. A new school of acting is now growing up under the influence of the various attempts to create an intellectual drama, and of changes deeper than that. The new school seizes upon what is distinguished, solitary, proud even. One always got a little of this in Mrs. Emery when she was good, and one gets a great deal of it in Miss Darragh. Both miss their climaxes as yet, for they are the reaction, and the old school missed everything else, at

[1] Miss Darragh, whose real name was Letitia Marion Dallas, did not remain at the Abbey Theatre for long. She afterwards formed her own company with which she toured the English provinces. She died in 1917.
The Walls of Jericho, a very successful play by Alfred Sutro, had been produced by Arthur Bourchier at the Garrick Theatre, London, on October 31, 1904.

least in tragedy. Besides they are interested, the best of them anyway, in building up character bit by bit. I feel these things rather vaguely, as one feels new things; the problem with me just now is whether, as I am rather inclined to, to leap at the advertisement of a performance by Mrs. Pat, or to keep to my own people and my own generation till they have brought their art to perfection. Yours

W B YEATS

TO KATHARINE TYNAN [1]

[? Autumn 1906]

... I am working very hard at my play *Deirdre*. Mrs. C[ampbell] saw my prose version and asked for the play but, after a struggle with temptation, I decided to keep it for my own people. I think it is my best play. I remember you were the first person who ever urged me to write a play about Ireland. I had shown you some wild thing I had called Spanish. After I have done a couple of little plays, written to complete the cycle of plays on Cuchullan which I have planned, I shall go back to lyric and narrative poetry for a bit. This dramatic work has been a great joy. Small as our audiences are, they are Irish and well pleased. We had an audience at Longford that would have stirred your imagination—shopkeepers and lads of the town, who smoked and were delighted, I think. I wonder if I had the dream of an Irish theatre when at Whitehall—I had it very soon after, I know—in 1892 certainly. I am doing my *Deirdre* side by side with a curious impressionist book on the work here—almost a spiritual diary. ...

TO KATHARINE TYNAN [2]

[? September 1906]   *[Coole Park]*

I should like very much to have a talk with you about our young writers and I hope I may do so some day. It is not easy to write fully about their work, but I will tell you roughly what I think of it.

The best thing about them is that they show some increase of

---

[1] Text from Katharine Tynan's *The Middle Years*, 1916.
[2] Text from the *Yale Review*, Winter, 1940.

culture in the country, and nearly all their faults rise out of the newness of that culture. They are vague, self-conscious, literary; the reverse of the young poets of our young days who were not literary at all—I remember getting into trouble for calling them electioneering rhymers. It is no longer possible to say that. They have not however yet learnt how to work at a poem. They play with words and have no organic structure. Colum has written a couple of little poems—'The Ploughman' and 'The Poor Scholar'—which are charming [1] ... The *Rushlight* man [2] knows better than the others what a poem is, though not a very interesting sort of poem, but he has not written it yet. I once hoped a great deal from George Russell's influence ... but he has the religious genius, and it is the essence of the religious genius, I mean the genius of the religious teacher, to look upon all souls as equal. They are never equal in the eyes of any craft, but Russell cannot bear anything that sets one man above another. He encourages everyone to write poetry because he thinks it good for their souls, and he doesn't care a rush whether it is good or bad. When we started on the theatre he actually avowed this about plays, and tried to persuade Lady Gregory and myself to keep it a small amateur theatre, that various interesting souls might be given the opportunity of dramatic expression for the soul's health ... He is just the same in painting, he urged upon a friend of mine last year the getting up of an annual exhibition of painters, the point of which was that nobody was to be bothered about drawing. The trouble is that Russell himself is absolutely charming and all the more charming because he suffers fools gladly ... His very mischief is a logical expression of his genius.

P.S. I have plans for improving our new poets myself. I want to get them to write songs to be sung between the acts. Herbert Hughes will set them and we have a fine singer in Sara Allgood. I hope to begin with two groups of songs—one selected from the *Rushlight* man, Colum, and so on, and one chosen from Johnson, you and myself. I will get them sung so as to make the words as expressive as possible. I am not quite sure that the time has come yet but I shall get one or two things set as a start.[3] One has to go

---

[1] Padraic Colum's two poems had appeared in *New Songs*, 1904.
[2] Joseph Campbell (1879–1944) published *Rushlight* in 1906.
[3] The plan for having programmes of Irish songs sung at the Abbey Theatre was carried out very much later, in 1937.

slowly, perfecting first one thing and then another. We have got our peasant work very good now and are starting on our verse work, and getting things like 'make-up' right. By the way, have you read Lady Gregory's books? She has a beautiful book *Saints and Wonders*, coming out with my sisters in a few days.[1]

TO A. H. BULLEN[2]

Sept 21 [1906]   *Coole Park*

My dear Bullen, I am groaning over the task of copying the next instalment of 'Thoughts and Second Thoughts',[3] and you shall have it by Monday, no, by Tuesday. The first instalment which reached me to-day sent on from Woburn Buildings looked very well. I wish you would let me know without crying 'Wolf' at me what is the real day for sending in. I didn't know that you were a middle month magazine till I found myself late last time. I also wish you would tell me when the poems are really coming out. I keep telling people that they are just coming, and the Bohemian Stage Manager not getting his copy thinks, I hear, that I have forgotten him altogether. If they are not coming for another month, let us say, I would like to know it. Besides I should stir up Masefield and one or two others to get it for review. This is the first number of the *Gentleman's Magazine* that I have seen, and you have kept the old fashioned leisurely air very well.

    I am deep in Ben Jonson, and have tried to buy your Marston in vain. I have a great desire upon me to read the *Satiromastix* of Dekker, and got the *Mermaid* Dekker, but it is not in that. Can you tell me where I can get it, or can you lend it me? I am thinking of writing something on Ben Jonson, or more likely perhaps upon the ideal of life that flitted before the imagination of Jonson and the

---

[1] *A Book of Saints and Wonders* by Lady Gregory was published by the Dun Emer Press on September 10, 1906.
[2] Dictated.
[3] 'My Thoughts and my Second Thoughts,' a series of short essays by Yeats, appeared, unsigned, in the September, October and November numbers of the *Gentleman's Magazine* of which Bullen had recently taken up the editorship. The essays were reprinted as *Discoveries*, Dun Emer Press, December 1907, and afterwards included in *The Cutting of an Agate*, Macmillan, New York, 1912; London, 1919.

others when they thought of the Court. The thought grows out of my Spenser essay which is just out. I would send it to you but they have only given me one copy (being Scotch). It is published by Jacks.

Is there any possibility that Jonson meant Shakespeare not Chapman by the character of Virgil in *The Poetaster*? I find it hard to believe that the few not too lively plays written by Chapman before that date could have made Jonson say as he does that whatever event of life came upon one, one could find appropriate words for it in the writings of 'Virgil.' I haven't read the Elizabethans for fifteen years, except Shakespeare and Spenser, and find myself drifting about a good deal.

Is there any book that would tell me about the various people the plays are dedicated to, and the various ladies one lights upon in Ben Jonson's Masques? I have been dipping into Clarendon. Yours

W B YEATS

TO FLORENCE FARR

Sunday Sept. 30 [1906] *Coole Park*

My dear Florence Emery: As a correspondent you are prompt but meagre—your last was anyway—four lines I think. I have been meaning to reply these two weeks past, but have been absorbed in *Deirdre*. What I wanted to do was to suggest your sending circulars of lectures to 'Hon. Sec. Philosophical and Literary Society, Cork.' I was also going to give you the name of the sec. of an Aberdeen society which has invited me, but on looking up his letters I find he has written from a French hotel and that I have neither the name of the society or the address. I shall have to find out these from a professor I know in Aberdeen. I have had a bad time with Miss Horniman, whose moon is always at the full of late, but hope a letter yesterday has quieted her. Miss Darragh is trying to play her for the chances it may lead to: but Fay is doing quite the reverse, for he has just encountered an enemy and they have fought with fists and with a result about which each is confused, for each seems to mix up what he did with what he had hoped to do. In other words each claims that he has licked the other and Fay's enemy says he will attack him next time 'before the public on the stage.' Fay meanwhile writes that the enemy 'will be sorry before he (Fay) has done with him.' I think after careful investigation that Fay had slightly the better for he was dragged off while imploring to be let finish. It is all about a young woman. Do not talk about it just now as I don't want it to get round to Miss Horniman's ears that people know about it. I have not tried to interfere but I think, for certain reasons, they will have to fight it out. No signs of my book yet and only an advance copy of my *Spenser*[1] but you will have both in good time. Miss Tobin is back in London—she is a charming talker—gave Synge and the principal players a dinner and was delightful—but well, if I should cross to London in the next month it would not be for her sake. I am getting restless—as the swallows do at this time of the year—but *Deirdre* has me tied to the table leg. I enclose some lines I wrote this morning. They are Deirdre's words spoken to the Musician in expectation of death.

I have just been sent an absurd book—very expensively got up—called *Osrac*[2] and largely an account in bad verse of Oscar Wilde. At the end are several poems by the author in his own person—one to Robert Ross, very emotional, and one to a negro boy whose 'lips like cupid's bow' are celebrated. There is an illustration of the author with a benign smile pointing to the negro boy, who is quite hideous, and looking much like a young missionary with his first convert. Yours ever   W B YEATS

DEIRDRE

There's nothing here for tears—a king and queen
Who've been true lovers are about to die.
And what is that? What is't but putting off
What all true lovers have cried out upon—
The too soon wearying body, barriers
That are not broken when lip touches lip,
And all those changes that the moon stirs up,
Or some worse star, for parting lip from lip
A whole day long. I'd have you laugh with me.

---

[1] Yeats's own book to which he refers is probably *Poems 1899–1905*; that and the edition of *Poems of Spenser* which he edited both appeared in October 1906.
[2] *Osrac, the Self-Sufficient* by J. M. Stuart-Young, published in 1905.

I am no more afraid of losing love
Through growing old, for temporal change is finished
And what I have I keep from this day out.[1]

TO FLORENCE FARR

Sunday [*October* 1906]   *Nassau Hotel*

My dear Friend: It is a long time since I heard from you. Isn't the debt on your side?—I think I sent you my book—I am a little anxious (I have become so since so long has passed without my hearing). You spoke of being 'seriously' out of sorts and then of being all right 'in a week.' I assume that it was only a passing upset. Do write and tell me how you are. I have been overwhelmingly busy and thoroughly overworked. The theatre is now a success, if it goes on as it is now we are through all our troubles. Last night for instance was a revival of *Doctor in Spite of Himself*,[2] *Hyacinth Halvey*, *Riders to the Sea* and the house was full. People standing up both in gallery and pit. The audiences have been steadily going up and this is the best yet. At this rate with our present expenditure we are making a profit—but of course we must raise salaries.

Since I wrote the above sentence Fay and Mrs. Fay (they eloped and got married a week ago)[3] have been in and Fay 'I have come round to crow.' Both Lady Gregory and I have been building castles in the air with you for one of their inhabitants. We mean to get you over to play for us presently. Miss Darragh is I notice not popular with the company. She says such things as 'Why do you not get that castor screwed on to the table leg?' instead of making enquiries and finding out that that castor cannot be screwed on because the woman who washes the floors and the stage carpenter have quarrelled about it—and the stage carpenter would sooner die than screw it on. She is considered to lack tact and the finer feelings. At any rate she has got them into the right state to welcome you. I think she will be very useful to us in a number of parts, but there

[1] These lines written for *Deirdre* do not appear in the published play.
[2] Lady Gregory's translation into Kiltartan dialect of Molière's *Médecin Malgré Lui* had been first performed at the Abbey Theatre on April 16, 1906.
[3] William Fay was married to Bridget O'Dempsey in October 1906.

are a number of others that neither she or our own people can touch. I do believe I have made a great play out of *Deirdre*—'the authors are in eternity' etc.—most powerful and even sensational. I will get a copy made and send it to you I think, as it may be some time before it is printed. The first musician was written for you—I always saw your face as I wrote, very curiously your face even more than your voice, and built the character out of that. I am a prisoner here until Dec. 15 but shall go over then and see you before you go to America. Yours ever   W B YEATS

We very nearly wired to you to come over and play 'first musician.' Lady Gregory went so far as to put it to Fay—but our players woke up then. I don't think you would have liked to come but we would have been very urgent.

TO KATHARINE TYNAN [1]

[*Late* 1906 *or early* 1907]

... I would have written to you before, but I have had a desperate three months of it, working for the theatre and doing its business. We are beginning to get audiences. Last winter we played to almost empty houses, a sprinkling of people in pit and stalls. Now we have big Saturday audiences. Last Saturday we turned away people from all parts of the house. My play *Deirdre*, after leaving me doubtful for a little, is now certainly a success.[2] It is my best play and the last half of it holds the audience in as strong a grip as does *Kathleen ni Houlihan*, which is prose and therefore a far easier thing to write. The difficulties of holding an audience with verse are ten times greater than with the prose play. Modern audience has lost the habit of careful listening. I think it is certainly my best dramatic poetry and for the first time a verse play of mine is well played all round. I think the Irish accent in blank verse is rather a shock to whatever ordinary theatregoers find their way to us, but they will get used to it. Miss Darragh, an Irish star on the English stage, who is playing for us, says our pit is a wonder; she never knew a pit to listen to tragedy

[1] Text from Katharine Tynan's *The Middle Years*, 1916.
[2] Yeats's *Deirdre* was produced at the Abbey Theatre on November 24, 1906, with Miss Darragh as Deirdre.

with such silent attention. I think we are gradually working down through the noisy and hypercritical, semi-political groups to a genuine public opinion, which is sympathetic...

I have been reading your old letter and I agree with what you say about Nora Chesson, and the way our Irish fairyland came to spoil her work, but there is one exception. There are a couple of lovely verses inspired by it in 'The King of Ireland's Son.'....[1]

TO A. H. BULLEN [2]

July 4 [? 1907]   *Coole Park*

My dear Bullen, I don't want to have anything to do with giving leave to people about translation rights. I have no way of finding out whether they are competent, and I suppose the matter is technically your concern as well as mine, or is it? Anyway it's much easier for you to be a curmudgeon than for me to be so, for that's your business as publisher, whereas it's a poet's business to be amiable. I only met that Russian woman once in my life, and that was for a moment during the performance of the plays in London. She wrote to me about two years ago asking me if I could go and see her about the question of translation. I answered that I would, and heard no more until I met her the other day. Now you have her address, for I sent it to you, and I have it not. Do you think you could write to her and ask her to write to A. P. Watt? I don't want to be bothered.

I have no objection to your selling fifty sets of the collected edition to Elkin Mathews, but if there is to be a slight extension to which I see no rooted objection, I should like that before it is finally ratified to come before A. P. Watt. I don't want anything done with

---

[1] Nora Chesson before her marriage wrote as Nora Hopper (see note 2, p. 244). In a short essay, prefacing a selection of her poems in Stopford Brooke and T. W. Rolleston's *Treasury of Irish Poetry*, 1900, Yeats quoted her lines

> All the way to Tir na n'Og are many roads that run,
> But the darkest road is trodden by the King of Ireland's son.
> The world wears on to sundown, and love is lost and won,
> But he recks not of loss or gain, the King of Ireland's son.
> He follows on for ever, when all your chase is done,
> He follows after shadows—the King of Ireland's son.

saying 'when once I remember them, they run in my head for hours.'

[2] Dictated.

either Mathews or Unwin which will make it impossible for you to arrange for popular editions of my books if they are found desirable when we are through the collected edition. I suppose when you have arranged with Unwin that you will communicate my part of the matter to Watt. I want him to have the threads of my affairs. Now Elkin Mathews is telling lies about that agreement, but he won't tell those lies to Watt. There is no document drawn up in a set form as there is with Unwin, but there is a letter written by Mathews three or four years ago to Watt, and stating the term of years for which he has the book, the amount of royalties &c. Acting upon this agreement which was considered by counsel to cover any arrangement made by Mathews with Lane, the Society of Authors got my book out of Lane's hands in America. Mathews may have written that letter because he wanted to hit Lane, but what's good of the dry tree is certainly good of the green. I tell you this not because I am likely to object or that Watt is likely to object to any arrangement you make, but because there is no reason why Elkin Mathews, drunk or sober, should bully you into giving him better terms than you want to give by pretending there is no agreement. You can write to A. P. Watt and tell him that I have no objection to two years' extension on the understanding that Mathews 'takes fifty sets of the collected edition at half price' if he (Watt) has no objection.

Where there is Nothing is going on quickly, I am all but through a very full scenario.[1] You will find the new version very much more to your mind than the old. Yours   W B YEATS

TO A. H. BULLEN[2]

July 5 [1907]   *Coole Park*

My dear Bullen,[3] I return proof which is not exactly what I wanted. I knew you could get the poem correct because you had the printed

[1] *Where there is Nothing* was now under revision for the Collected Edition. Eventually it became a three-act play *The Unicorn from the Stars*, mainly written by Lady Gregory.   [2] Dictated.

[3] This letter, with a number of letters which follow, written either to Bullen or to Miss E. M. Lister, a relation of Bullen's who helped him with the work of the Shakespeare Head Press at Stratford-on-Avon, deals with the preparation of the handsome Collected Edition, which eventually filled eight volumes and was published in the autumn of 1908.

copy in the book of poems. What I wanted was a proof sheet of poem and prose together; I want to be quite certain that the prose breaks the poem properly. You had better send me this proof sheet even now.

You needn't have any anxiety about my text being ready for you, provided you always give me proper notice. I should know three weeks, let us say, beforehand when a new book is wanted. I should also know when you start a book how long you calculate the printing will take. It is no use your going ahead with the poems till you have a list of the proper order of them from me. I don't propose to follow the order in the American book. I am not arranging any of these books on a chronological system. I had a special reason for arranging the American book in that way. I shall send you the proper order of the poems tomorrow. I conclude you will not want the preface until you are near the end of the printing. I will also look through *The Wind Among the Reeds* notes and see if they are worth reprinting. Don't give me vague dates or predate things in order to make me hurry, for if you do I'll find it out and won't believe a word. I shall want to know how long the printing of the poems will take that I may have another volume ready to follow them. I think it is probable that I will have the volume of prose plays ready by that time. I think the proof sheet I have returned explains itself, but I will summarise what I have done and want done. I have taken out, as you see, the chorus the second time it occurs, to give a more accidental look to the poem. The prose paragraph comes after the 'starry brink' and is followed by 'The little fox he murmured.' Yours   W B YEATS

TO A. H. BULLEN [1]

July 6 [1907]   *Coole Park*

My dear Bullen, Your letter has amazed me. It is the most extraordinary letter from a publisher I have ever seen. If this Library Edition is not to be carried through on the ordinary conditions I prefer that it should come to an end immediately. I will not have one word printed that I have not seen and passed. Furthermore I

[1] Dictated

now see that the whole arrangement must be made in detail by A. P. Watt, and I will think myself bound by nothing that is not put in those arrangements. Whether you go on printing now or wait till the arrangements are completed is your own matter. I told you that I would not require to see proofs but after your letter I withdraw that. I must see final proofs of everything, and other proofs if I ask for them. This will be my final text for many years, and I refuse to have any portion of that text settled by any person but myself. It seems to be perfectly outrageous that you should take a text which I have never authorized you to use and begin printing from that without consulting me. I enclose a list of poems in the order in which they are to be printed, and I require to see a revised proof of the proof of 'Hanrahan' which I sent you yesterday, a proof sheet which I sent back by return of post. Furthermore I object to your going to Miss Horniman and telling her you don't want coloured illustrations in the book of dramatic criticism . . . I insist on those illustrations which were part of our original bargain. On knowing on what day you require the material for the different books I shall do my best never to keep your Press waiting. But I shall not bind myself to anything that is not in the agreement with A. P. Watt. If you had seen A. P. Watt some time ago as I asked you, this confusion between the rights of author and publisher would never have arisen.

I am sending copies of our correspondence to A. P. Watt. Yours sincerely   W B YEATS

TO A. H. BULLEN[1]

July 8, 1907   *Coole Park*

My dear Bullen, At last I understand the situation. We have been at cross purposes, and the situation that has arisen is serious enough.

You were too hasty and I was too vague, or at any rate I did not succeed in making myself understood by you, or in understanding you. It is another warning that one must never start on serious undertakings without a very careful written business understanding. The first misunderstanding was this. You said that you

[1] Dictated.

hoped to be through with the whole matter in about thirteen months. I then gave *Discoveries*, part of one of the volumes, to my sister, and it will be issued by her in the autumn, and as I calculated would have run through its natural sales before you are ready to publish in the spring or the early summer of next year. I withdrew from active work in the Abbey Theatre with the purpose of devoting myself for a year to making a final text of all my books. But for this I would never have consented to a collected edition at this moment, as I believe that an edition containing so much that is immature or inexperienced as there is in my already published books would do me a very great injury. Now I find that instead of printing at the rate of between six and eight weeks a volume, you are printing at the rate of about three weeks a volume. When I talked to you of the volume to follow *The Celtic Twilight* it was in the belief that whichever volume you had it would not be required till autumn. I am accustomed to my sister's slow printing, and apart from that your words seemed unmistakeable. When 'Hanrahan' was taken out of *The Secret Rose*, it became very desirable to add something in its place, for two or three of the

[*The rest of this letter is missing*]

TO A. H. BULLEN [1]

July 10 [1907]   *Coole Park*

My dear Bullen, I am greatly obliged to you about what you say of putting the Press to something else for a short time. I have practically complete the notes for the present book and will send them to you to-morrow if I can. It is a question of getting them typed. I do not think I will write any preface unless you are particularly anxious for one. I have written so much direct or indirect criticism of my own work for the essays that I hardly think it is necessary. I have re-written that poem about Maid Quiet and hope it is not too late for you to put it in instead of the present version. I have changed it as you suggest. It is on the enclosed sheet. I forgot when sending you the list of poems that the 'chorus for a play' in *In the Seven Woods* is in the play of *Deirdre*. I shall be obliged therefore if

[1] Dictated.

you will leave it out and put instead of it the poem about the ragged hollow wood which I have taken out of *Red Hanrahan*. That won't be enough, so please put the enclosed with it. I quite recognise that I may be too late but I hope not. I shall always do my best to let you have the work in time, now that it is possible for you to give me reasonable notice and not to go too fast. Yours W B YEATS

TO A. H. BULLEN [1]

July 12 [1907] *Coole Park*

My dear Bullen, I shall write to A. P. Watt tomorrow about the arrangements I want made. I need hardly say that I am as anxious as you are to get everything settled with the least possible inconvenience to everybody concerned. What I want is a chance to finish the unfinished parts of the different books. I can work the entire summer from this on to early October at getting through. I had meant to give myself a longer time still, but I cannot do the necessary things in less than this time. When you have printed *Poems*, the first volume that is to say, you will have finished everything that has required practically no further work from me, at least unless I accept your proposed first volume of plays. Here are the remaining volumes as I see them.

A. A volume containing *Countess Cathleen, Land of Heart's Desire, Shadowy Waters* (possibly all three versions), *King's Threshold*, the Cuchulain cycle of plays (two of these still to be written), *Deirdre*.

B. *Where there is Nothing, Cathleen ny Houlihan, Pot of Broth, Hour-Glass*. (This volume to be called *Prose Plays*.)

C. *The Secret Rose, John Sherman, Dhoya*. (Very careful verbal revision necessary and two new stories desirable.)

D. *Discoveries* (this is to be a book of essays, very largely theatrical but containing the Spenser). I have a few more pages to write for this, but a good deal of work to do in the way of arrangement.

The objection to your suggested volume of plays is that it will make the apportioning of plays between the two volumes purely arbitrary.

[1] Dictated.

Another arrangement besides the one I have suggested has occurred to me, which is to divide them into legendary and philosophical, but this would put *Baile's Strand* and the two unwritten plays into the *Countess Cathleen* volume. Even if I were to agree to your proposed first volume of plays, that would only postpone the difficulty, as you would be through it before I was through my summer and had got a decent chance of doing the other plays.

The only thing I can suggest to you is that you interpolate some other piece of printing when you are finished with the poems, and the longer it takes the better. I don't see any way to promise to supply the printer with a volume every three weeks on the average.

If you have any other suggestion to make you might write to me about it. Remember that my original calculation was thirteen months. I enclose the notes to *Wind among the Reeds*, and will try and send the proofs before post, no, I have just remembered Sunday is so near, so tomorrow will do as well, and the same applies to the Notes. I will keep them back for afterthoughts. The text I sent you is correct, for the new titles correspond to the Notes as they are at present.

I am working very hard, and mean to work hard, but it is impossible to say how fast I can get on, that is why I was so glad to think that I had, as it originally seemed, ample time.

[*In Yeats's handwriting*]. Remember I must have proofs of the book of poems. Yours　　　　　　　　　　　　　　W B YEATS

TO A. H. BULLEN [1]

July 28 [1907]　　　　　　　　　　　　　　　　　　*Coole Park*

My dear Bullen, I return the proof sheets. I have modified a word in one poem in obedience to a suggestion of your own, and have changed one little poem, but as this practically, I think, brings you very near the end of the lyrics without any other change, you will not be greatly alarmed. I enclose the correct version of the poem which I call 'The Hollow Wood,' and I want you to substitute it for 'I heard under a ragged Hollow Wood.' I think you will admit

---

[1] Dictated.

the improvement. The old poem was always spoiled by the poverty of rhyme. This is practically only a change of four lines. Yours ever

W B YEATS

[*In Yeats's handwriting*] I have not yet had the section called 'The Rose.' I suppose that comes next.

TO FLORENCE FARR

[*? July* 1907]   *Coole Park*

My dear Florence Emery: Here is the music—your old *Shadowy Waters* among the rest. I don't know if you have a version of the Stage Version (but you might leave that over for a little as I am hoping for copies of the American edition which contains it).[1] Keep the music safe for me. I don't find here that music you did for the woman's song in *On Baile's Strand* and I must write for it again.

Miss Horniman is starting in Manchester on I think September 25 with that play of cockney life by McEvoy the Stage Society brought out a while back.[2] I don't know what else she has but she claims to have lots of plays—they must be pretty bad if she has. I hear that Shaw advised Payne to have nothing to do with her as she fights with everybody, but Payne thinks he can manage. Lady Gregory says that Miss Horniman is like a shilling in a tub of electrified water—everybody tries to get the shilling out. Lady Gregory is now quite definitely added to Miss Horniman's list of truly wicked people. I am looking forward to the moment when Manchester will begin to add names. The strange thing is that any old hatred years after you think it dead will suddenly awake. They are like the stops of an organ.

I am reading North's Plutarch and I find a beautiful thing. Alcibiades refused to learn the flute because he thought it ill became a gentleman either to put his cheeks out of shape or to make music he could not speak to. He had so much influence that ever after the flute was despised. This might help you with your lectures—you will find it in the account of Alcibiades. Alcibiades said the flute

[1] The second volume of the American edition of Yeats's Collected Poems, which contained the acting version of *The Shadowy Waters*, was published in July 1907; this letter is probably of about that date.
[2] *David Ballard* by Charles McEvoy was produced by the Stage Society at the Imperial Theatre, London, on June 9, 1907.

should be left to Thebans that did not know how to speak. He also claimed that the patrons [of] Athens, Pallas and Apollo, objected to the flute and that Apollo skinned a man for playing on it. Yours ever,
W B YEATS

TO A. H. BULLEN [1]

August 26 [1907]   *Coole Park*

My dear Bullen, Would you mind looking through the *Samhains* that you have, and noting as you suggested what seems to you most suitable for the book of essays, and sending them to me? I will be glad if you will do this as soon as possible. Please also send me the *John Sherman and Dhoya* if you can get one. I am anxious to get all the scrappy work done that I may go on to original work. I intend that you shall have four volumes to go on with before I leave this. That will give me time to try a couple of plays which are to go in the final volume before you come to it. But go to A. P. Watt. I have no agreement yet about *Poems '99* nor about *Deirdre*. There is a good deal of music ready to go to print for the plays, but it wants to be written out legibly. You had somebody in the office I understand who did that for Mrs. Emery when you brought out *Cathleen ni Houlihan*. Have you got that man with you still? Some of the music is Irish folk music, some is by Arthur Darley, but a good deal is by Mrs. Emery. This music is essential to the completeness of my record, even apart from its own merits it is necessary to show how I want the things set. I mean the degree of attention to the speaking voice. I don't want therefore to leave them to the last moment, especially as Mrs. Emery goes to America in November. Yours
W B YEATS

TO MISS E. M. LISTER [1]

Sept 14 [1907]   *Coole Park*

Dear Miss Lister, I heard from a friend in London that Bullen is very much against the inclusion of the three versions of *Shadowy Waters*. If this is so I don't want to press the point as the acting

[1] Dictated.

version is in my American edition appendix. I can merely put a note mentioning the edition published at sixpence for sale in the theatre. It is in no way a vital matter with me, though I would sooner have it in. If the plays are to go into two volumes I think there is a better order than you have chosen. But first let me say that there will be one new play, not two, about Cuchulain. This play is in prose and about as long as *Cathleen ny Houlihan*. The new *Where there is Nothing* is not at all so long as the old, being three acts instead of five. If it does not matter having one volume bigger than its companion volumes it might be well to put *Baile's Strand* and *Deirdre* into the volume you have marked Vol. II. and the prose plays into volume three (but I am at the present moment rather inclined to drop *Pot of Broth*). If this arrangement is adopted we will begin the volume of verse plays with *Deirdre* and *King's Threshold*, in fact with my most mature work, and begin the prose plays with the new *Where there is Nothing*.

If on the other hand the two volumes have to be of equal size, and not to include verse work, I think it will be best to print the plays in chronological order, *Deirdre*, and the new *Where there is Nothing* coming last, *Hour-Glass* and *Cathleen ny Houlihan* after *Land of Heart's Desire*.

Only I should like to know fairly soon as it will make a difference as to what I put into the appendix. In either case the second volume of the two will have to be delayed a considerable time, the prose stories &c coming first. I have to put the new work into rehearsal to test it.

I have written to Mrs. Emery about the music. You will probably find yourself out of sympathy with this music but it gets its meaning from the method of speaking and is a necessary record of that method. It is important to me that people whom I cannot personally teach and who may produce my work shall know my intentions. I will write a short appendix to go with the music. Yours

W B YEATS

TO FLORENCE FARR

[*September* 25, 1907]　　　　　　　　　　　　*Coole Park*

My dear Florence Emery: Augustus John has just left and I have time for letters. He has done numberless portraits of me to work up into an etching—all powerful ugly gypsy things. He behaved very well here, did the most wonderful acrobatic things on the floor and climbed to the top of the highest tree in the garden and did not talk much about his two wives and his seven children. Lady Gregory was always afraid some caller would say 'How many children?' 'Seven' 'You must have married very young' 'About four years' 'Twins I suppose' 'Oh no but—' and then all out. He wears hair down to his shoulders and an early victorian coat with a green velvet collar. Robert watches him with ever visible admiration and discipleship. To day Miss Horniman opens her Manchester theatre and for the next few months lives under the following secondary directions (nearly all from fifth house—house of theatres)

☽ sep for ☌ ♃ ℞	Sept and Oct
☽ ☐ ☽ ℞	about Oct and Nov
☽ ☌ ♀ ℞	about Jan
☽ ☐ ☉ P	about March
☽ ☌ ♂ P	abt July
☽ ☌ ♄ ℞	Nov and Dec

If this (and the transits are nearly as spirited) does not make hay with her Manchester theatre, Ananias was an astrologer and a planet and a star.

Many thanks about the music. The first five volumes are to come out almost at once. I think Miss Lister wrote as she did about Sidgwick because he and Bullen are I think in slightly strained relations. I have just glanced at your horoscope (but will work it out carefully). I note that ☽ is going to ☌ ♅, △ ☿ ℞, △ ♃ P, which should give you success in America (♃ ☌ ☿). Yours ever

W B YEATS

TO MISS E. M. LISTER [1]

Sept 26 [1907] *Coole Park*

Dear Miss Lister, Would you mind telling me exactly how much of my collected edition has been printed? I have had a letter from Mr. Bullen which I cannot understand. He writes among other things

[1] Dictated.

'I have not got an unlimited quantity of type . . . I have a whole volume in type . . . which I can't release.' This can only mean that there is some volume which he cannot print off, owing to having received incomplete copy. I am puzzled. He has had complete copy of four volumes. (a) *Celtic Twilight* and *Red Hanrahan*. (b) *Ideas of Good and Evil*. (c) *Poems*. (d) Verse Plays. The copy for the remaining three volumes is all in my hands. There has evidently been some mistake, it is very important to have this cleared up, as I am most anxious not to keep the Press waiting. Since I arranged with Mr. Bullen some time ago that I should get a reasonable time for my revisions, there has been no reason whatever for any hitch. Mr. Bullen also speaks of beginning the Verse Play volume with *Baile's Strand*. I had written asking him whether he thought it better to begin with *Deirdre* or *King's Threshold* and then saying that I thought it had better be *Deirdre*. I have an impression that I wrote to you from London, suggesting an order with *King's Threshold* first. If you have my letter would you please look it up. When I wrote these letters I did not know that the Press was at work on anything but *Countess Cathleen*. I had received two lots of proofs of *Countess Cathleen* and as the proofs left off at I think the second act I concluded that the Press had been put to something else. If I know what the Press is doing, and when things are wanted, I shall be able to let you know exactly what I want done and send copy punctually. But I must always know. It is also necessary that I should know when the next volume is wanted. I have done all my own work but it is necessary that I get the text of my revisions typed. Mr. Bullen asked me some time ago for five volumes which he could put upon the market without waiting for the last two.

However I think it very unwise going on as we are without definite agreements. I am sorry that A. P. Watt wasn't there to meet him the other day, but I imagine that he has all but retired, in which case the sooner his sons get the grip of my affairs the better. I shall write to A. P. Watt on hearing from you.

I haven't sent you the music I spoke of, as Bullen seems anxious to have the appendix which will contain it at the end of the Prose Plays, and this will enable me to look through a drawer I have of various musical odds and ends in London. The only thing absolutely necessary as a record is Miss Farr's music, and some fragments of folk music for the prose plays, as I don't want to burden the book

with too much I may as well wait till I look through the mass.
Yours sincerely   W B YEATS

TO JOHN QUINN

4th October 1907   *Nassau Hotel*

My dear Quinn, Very many thanks for your long letter which I was very glad indeed to get. I have just come up from Coole for the production of a new play called *The Country Dressmaker*. It is by a new writer called Fitzmaurice.[1] A harsh, strong, ugly comedy. It really gives a much worse view of the people than *The Playboy*. Even I rather dislike it, though I admire its sincerity, and yet it was received with enthusiasm. The truth is that the objection to Synge is not mainly that he makes the country people unpleasant or immoral, but that he has got a standard of morals and intellect. They never minded Boyle, whose people are a sordid lot, because they knew what he was at. They understood his obvious moral, and they don't mind Fitzmaurice because they don't think he is at anything, but they shrink from Synge's harsh, independent, heroical, clean, wind-swept view of things. They want their clerical conservatory where the air is warm and damp. Of course, we may not get through to-morrow night, but the row won't be very bad. Nothing is ever persecuted but the intellect, though it is never persecuted under its own name. I don't think it would be wise for me to write a reply to that absurd article by McManus. As I never now write about politics people would think I was paying him off or his party off for *The Playboy*. I argued that question at the meeting not because I thought I would convince anybody but because the one thing that seemed possible was that all should show, players and playwrights, that we weren't afraid. The result has been that we have doubled the enthusiasm of our own following. The principal actors are now applauded at their entrances with a heartiness unknown before, and both Lady Gregory and myself received several times last spring what newspaper writers call 'an ovation.' We have lost a great

[1] *The Country Dressmaker* by George Fitzmaurice was first produced at the Abbey Theatre on October 3, 1907; it is still played there from time to time. The Abbey also produced his plays *The Magic Glasses* on April 24, 1913 and *'Twixt the Giltenans and the Carmodys* on March 8, 1923.

many but the minority know that we are in earnest, and if only our finances hold out we will get the rest . . .

We have had another performance of *The Country Dressmaker* since I wrote, and the success was greater than before. The dear *Freeman*, or rather its evening issue which is called by another name, has congratulated us on having got a play at last 'to which nobody can take the slightest exception' or some such words, and yet Fitzmaurice, who wrote it, wrote it with the special object of showing up the sordid side of country life. He thinks himself a follower of Synge, which he is not. I have now no doubt that there will be enthusiasm to-night, and that the author, who has been thirsting for the crown of martyrdom, will be called before the curtain for the third night running. We are putting the play on again next week owing to its success.

Synge has just had an operation on his throat and has come through it all right. I am to see him to-day for the first time. When he woke out of the ether sleep his first words, to the great delight of the doctor, who knows his plays, were: 'May God damn the English, they can't even swear without vulgarity.' This tale delights the Company, who shudder at the bad language they have to speak in his plays. I don't think he has done much this summer owing to bad health but he will probably set to work now . . .

Augustus John has been staying at Coole. He came there to do an etching of me for the collected edition. Shannon was busy when I was in London and the collected edition was being pushed on so quickly that I found I couldn't wait for him. I don't know what John will make of me. He made a lot of sketches with the brush and the pencil to work the etching from when he went home. I felt rather a martyr going to him. The students consider him the greatest living draughtsman, the only modern who can draw like an old master . . . He exaggerates every little hill and hollow of the face till one looks like a gypsy, grown old in wickedness and hardship. If one looked like any of his pictures the country women would take the clean clothes off the hedges when one passed, as they do at the sight of a tinker. He is himself a delight, the most innocent-wicked man I have ever met. He wears earrings, his hair down over his shoulders, a green velvet collar . . . He climbed to the top of the highest tree in Coole garden and carved a symbol there. Nobody else has been able to get up there to know what it is; even Robert stuck half way.

He is a magnificent looking person, and looks the wild creature he is. His best work is etching. He is certainly a great etcher, with a savage imagination. Yours ever   W B YEATS

TO A. H. BULLEN [1]

4th Oct, 1907   *Nassau Hotel*

My dear Bullen, Sidgwick has written apologetically, and has sent me £10. I have just arrived here in Dublin, where we produced a new play last night. By the by don't forget that you have all my *Samhains*; you offered to look through them and make suggestions as to what extracts I should put into the book of essays. I wish you would do so as there is no reason why you should not, if there is enough material, which I am pretty confident there is, print the volume of criticism immediately after the volume of stories. I have a certain amount of difficulty in giving you a date for its publication as a part of it, *Discoveries*, is coming out with my sister at Christmas. You will remember that I arranged this when I thought that you would be thirteen months getting through the edition. This however need not prevent you from going to press. It is possible that by the time the critical volume and the stories are printed I shall have the volume of prose plays ready, but I cannot promise this. It all depends on how soon I get *The Unicorn from the Stars* on to the stage, and whether it wants much working on afterwards. I hope to get it on next month, and that a couple of weeks at latest after that date it would be ready to print. It may happen however that I cannot get it on until early January. I think you may however calculate upon the end of January being the latest possible date for its reaching you. You will have two books to get through before that. But the sooner you send me these *Samhains* again with your suggestions the better. I suppose you will be seeing Watt in a few days. In your negotiations with him keep in mind that we mustn't do anything in facilitating that collected edition which will prevent my having all my ordinary editions in one publisher's hands within a reasonable time. This edition ought to prepare the way for an ordinary edition at a moderate price, though not necessarily at once. I intend my next book after the collected edition to be a volume of

[1] Dictated.

lyrics and narrative poems. I don't see why it should not have a very tolerable success. Why I have been so insistent upon my revisions etc. in this expensive edition is that I know I must get my general personality and the total weight of my work into people's minds, as a preliminary to new work. I know that I have just reached a time when I can give up constant revisions but not till the old is right. I used to revise my lyrics as I now do the plays.

Saturday

I have just got your last letter sent on from Coole. I am very much amused at that exorbitant demand. I particularly admire the additional sixpence. When Watt jun. wrote to me saying that it was to be the same terms as *Ideas of Good and Evil*, I asked him what those terms were. I noticed in his reply that the sum you named was paid in advance, but it did not occur to me that he would consider that fact an integral part of the agreement. I have of course written to put the matter right. It was a sum paid by you that I might live while writing a novel that was never finished. You very generously considered it as advanced upon the later book. Of course, A. P. Watt's son has no recollection of the facts and merely looked up a pigeon-hole when you proposed the same terms as on *Ideas of Good and Evil*. Let the agreement be for the usual six years. I say that partly because if my books are going well you will be able to give me at the end of that period the same terms that Unwin gives me for *Poems*, which are slightly more, I think, than you are giving. *Poems* however is a very well selling book.

I am a little anxious about your arrangements with Mathews and with Unwin, and about the ordinary editions as distinguished from this expensive collected edition. I have written about this to Watt. And I hope that he and you will be able to come to some definite arrangement covering the whole ground. Yours

W B YEATS

TO FLORENCE FARR [1]

Oct. 7th, 1907   *Nassau Hotel*

My dear Florence Farr, I think Bullen is going to put all the music with all my other appendixes at the end of the volume of prose plays

[1] Dictated, except for the last paragraph.

as he wants to enlarge that volume. I came up to Dublin last Thursday. We produced a play called *The Country Dressmaker*, a rough but amusing piece of work which is showing signs of being popular. I have got to a typewriter as you see and feel I can tell the news at last. I have got so out of the habit of writing letters with my fingers that even apart from my sight I make them very short. I cannot recollect whether I told you or not about Allen Bennett. The day I left London I was at the dentist's and he began telling me about a friend of his, a man of science, who was interested in Buddhism. He had gone out to Burma and there he met an Englishman who was a Buddhist monk. This Englishman has converted him and now he and the monk were members of a Buddhist missionary Society. The Englishman was Allen Bennett.[1] He showed me a photographic group of the Committee of the Society with Bennett in the middle, evidently the most important person. He also told me that Bennett was now working on experimental science. The friend and a native Burmese widow and a third person paying the expenses. If any profit resulted from Bennett's researches the bulk of the profit is to go to the Missionary Society, but a certain percentage to those who have supplied the capital. The researches are concerned with N Rays. Bennett goes out every morning with his begging bowl as a monk, but always gives the contents of his bowl to some less well-provided-for brother. His own meals are sent in every day to the workshop. I think I told you something of all this but not the details. I don't know when I shall be able to get over. I am desperately hard up owing to the difficulty of getting A. P. Watt and my publisher to meet. They have been playing some sort of fantastic game for months. I got them together with much urgency last week, with the only result that Bullen took offence because it was Watt junior who received him, and so went back to Stratford. In any case a man with Saturn entering his second house by transit has to look out for bad times. Astrology grows more and more wonderful every day. I have some astonishing irrefutable things to show you. I imagine that the stars are beginning to tell on Miss Horniman, as since her first

[1] Allen Bennett (187?–1923), an analytical chemist and a student of theosophy, was at one time a member of the Golden Dawn, his name in the order being Iehi Aour, and an associate of Aleister Crowley. He became a Buddhist, emigrated to Ceylon, and went later to Burma. Author of *The Wisdom of the Aryas*, London: Kegan Paul, 1923.

elated letter written the day after the start at Manchester I have not heard a word of how they are doing, though she has written about something else. I put the date of some great disturbance concerning her to April, May or June. I am trying to work at primary directions, but my head reels with all the queer mathematical terms. I am hoping to find in the aspects a basis of evocation, which is really what interests me.

Did you see Bernard Shaw's letter in *The Times* a couple of days ago—logical, audacious and convincing, a really wonderful letter, at once violent and persuasive.[1] He knew his opponent's case as well as his own, and that is just what men of his kind usually do not know. I saw *Caesar and Cleopatra* with Forbes-Robertson in it twice this week and have been really delighted and what I never thought [to] be with work of his, moved. There is vulgarity, plenty of it, but such gay heroic delight in the serviceable man. Ah if he had but style, distinction, and was not such a barbarian of the barricades. I am quite convinced by the by that the whole play is chaff of you in your Egyptian period, and that you were the Cleopatra who offered that libation of wine to the table-rapping sphinx. Yours ever

W B YEATS

TO MISS A. E. F. HORNIMAN[2]

Tuesday [? early 1908]   18 *Woburn Buildings*

My dear Miss Horniman: I have thought carefully over your proposal of yesterday and have decided that it is impossible so far as I am concerned. I am not young enough to change my nationality —it would really amount to that. Though I wish for a universal audience, in play-writing there is always an immediate audience also. If I am to try and find the immediate audience in England I would fail through lack of understanding on my part, perhaps through lack

[1] Bernard Shaw contributed a long letter on Kulin Polygamy to *The Times*, October 5, 1907.
[2] From a draft in Yeats's handwriting, in the possession of Mrs. Yeats. It seems probable from the contents of this letter that Miss Horniman had made Yeats some proposal of a scheme by which she should acquire the right to present his plays in England. Miss Horniman opened her Manchester Repertory Theatre in September 1907; Yeats appears to have been in Dublin during the autumn of that year; I have, therefore, tentatively dated this letter early 1908.

of sympathy. I understand my own race and in all my work, lyric or dramatic, I have thought of it. If the theatre fails I may or may not write plays—but I shall write for my own people—whether in love or hate of them matters little—probably I shall not know which it is. Nor can I make any permanent allocation of my plays while the Irish theatre may at any moment need my help. At any moment I may have to ask friends for funds with the whole mass of plays for a bait. *[Unsigned]*

TO WILLIAM ROTHENSTEIN [1]

7th January 1908   18 *Woburn Buildings*

Dear Rothenstein, Will you be in town any day this week, except Saturday, when I shall be back in Dublin? Lane [2] has asked me to try and get some people to write up the opening of his gallery, which is at 4 o'clock on January the 20th, and I would like your advice. I shall be desperately busy, or I would go out to you on the chance. I hear it takes three quarters of an hour getting out. I don't want to bring you in specially, but if you were coming in about something else, would like to see you. It is very important to get enough notice taken of the opening of this gallery to make the corporation believe in Lane, for if they do, they will leave him free, and if they don't, they will sooner or later annoy him in the interest of some bad patriotic painter. He has so many enemies in Dublin that all the help we can get from outside is necessary. He ought to be over

[1] Text from *Men and Memories 1900–1922*, London, Faber & Faber, 1932.
[2] Hugh Lane (1875–1915) was the son of the Rev. J. W. Lane and a nephew of Lady Gregory. At the age of about 18 he was employed by Martin Colnaghi, and proved to be the possessor of an extraordinary flair for the appreciation of pictures, both old and modern. He soon became a dealer on his own account, and formed a fine collection of the works of the French impressionist painters which he intended should become the property of Ireland. In 1908 these were exhibited in a temporary gallery in Harcourt Street, Dublin; it was Lane's desire that a gallery should be built for them on a bridge over the Liffey, to be designed by Edwin Lutyens. The Dublin Corporation, however, did not fall in with his views and he removed the pictures to London, where they were lent to the National Gallery. Lane was knighted in 1909, and in 1914 became Director of the Irish National Gallery. Having to visit America during the first World War, he lost his life on his return journey when the *Lusitania* was torpedoed in 1915. By his will he left the French pictures to the English National Gallery, but a codicil, written just before he went to America, and signed but not witnessed, revoked this bequest and left the pictures, on certain conditions, to Dublin. On this subject see the letters from Yeats to the *Irish Times*, March 18, 1913 (p. 579), and to the *Observer*, January 21, 1917 (p. 616).

here himself, but cannot come as he is busy hanging the pictures. I wish there were any chance of you yourself going over. I would like to show you Augustus John's portrait of me. A beautiful etching, and I understand what he means in it, and admire the meaning, but it is useless for my special purpose. Robert Gregory agrees in this, and has recommended me to show it to you. If you are not likely to be in town, please let me know and I will try and get out to you. Yours, W B YEATS

TO JOHN QUINN

7th January 1908   18 *Woburn Buildings*

Dear Quinn ... I have arranged about the Shannon portrait and for the price you said. I am giving the first sitting tomorrow, and will ask you to let me have the right to publish a reproduction of the portrait in some book of mine. He has just done a drawing of me which is very charming, but by an unlucky accident most damnably like Keats. If I publish it by itself everybody will think it an affectation of mine. I have had adventures in trying to get a suitable portrait. My father always sees me through a mist of domestic emotion, or so I think; and Mancini, who filled me with joy, has turned me into a sort of Italian bandit, or half bandit half café king, certainly a joyous Latin, impudent, immoral, and reckless. Augustus John, who has made a very fine thing of me, has made me a sheer tinker, drunken, unpleasant and disreputable, but full of wisdom— a melancholy English Bohemian, capable of everything except living joyously on the surface.

I am going to put the lot one after the other: my father's emaciated portrait that was the frontispiece for *The Tables of the Law* beside Mancini's brazen image, and Augustus John's tinker to pluck the nose of Shannon's idealist. Nobody will believe they are the same man. And I shall write an essay upon them and describe them as all the different personages that I have dreamt of being but have never had the time for. I shall head it with what Wordsworth said about some marble bust of himself: 'No, that is not Mr. Wordsworth, the poet, that is Mr. Wordsworth, the Chancellor of the Exchequer.' ... Yours ever   W B YEATS

TO A. H. BULLEN[1]

12th February 1908   *Nassau Hotel*

My dear Bullen... No, I can't have *Where there is Nothing* in the edition.[2] Though *The Unicorn* is almost altogether Lady Gregory's writing it has far more of my spirit in it than *Where there is Nothing* which she and I and Douglas Hyde wrote in a fortnight to keep George Moore from stealing the plot. Hyde forbade me to mention his name for fear of consequences, and you must not mention it even now, and for the same reason I did not mention Lady Gregory except in that old Preface which you know. There is certainly much more of my own actual writing in *Where there is Nothing*, but I feel that this new play belongs to my world and that it does not. You couldn't leave it out, for you would not have enough to fill the volumes, and besides, there are sufficient precedents, Stevenson and Lloyd Osbourne for instance, for the inclusion of work done in collaboration in a collected edition of one of the two writers. I planned out *The Unicorn* to carry to a more complete realization the central idea of the stories in *The Secret Rose* and I believe it has more natural affinities with those stories than has *Where there is Nothing*...
Yours   W B YEATS

TO A. H. BULLEN[1]

4 March 1908   *Nassau Hotel*

My dear Bullen, The general opinion was bound to want a portrait in the first volume because general opinion has always seen a portrait there, only the portrait cannot be by Langfier because Thank God there is no such man. It is bad enough to have a man called Lafayette, who is quite well known for a great many glossy portraits of Royalties and Actresses. He understands the public perfectly, and is therefore celebrated in his world, but Coburn,[3] who

---

[1] Dictated.

[2] *Where there is Nothing* was superseded in the Collected Edition by the three-act play *The Unicorn from the Stars* written on a similar theme but very largely the work of Lady Gregory. Bullen, who disliked her, was very reluctant to include this and indeed considered it a blot on the edition.

[3] Alvin Langdon Coburn, the well-known American photographer, came to England in 1904 and has since made it his home. His work includes a number

503

understands photography, is celebrated in our world. I have written to him to find out when I can see his work. Of course if it is a great hurry we may have to use the drawing Shannon made of me instead of waiting for a reproduction of the oil painting, but I can get over the moment my play has been produced, which will be the week after next. I don't think it would do to put even the finest photograph into what is supposed to be the place of honour, and portraits by famous artists into what would seem by contrast a sort of appendix. I believe that these portraits will prove commercially of great value.... Yours ever   W B YEATS

TO A. H. BULLEN

[*March* 1908]   *Nassau Hotel*

My dear Bullen: I am desperately busy; please don't start new plans upon me. We decided to have all the portraits together and we would both get on quicker if we stuck to what we had decided. They can go in the first volume. (1) Coburn photo (2) Mancini's portrait (3) my father's (4) Augustus John (5) Shannon's.

I am writing to John and to the photographers of the Mancini to send you a photograph of that picture. You can write to Coburn yourself. I enclose his letter. I will see the photographs but you can take my word for it [it] is free. The Mancini, if you had enough knowledge of painting to see it, is a great chance. It costs nothing and it is a master work of one of the greatest living painters. I object to Miss Horniman being consulted. I have known her many years and she respects me because I follow my own opinions not hers in questions of this kind.

The Augustus John is a wonderful etching but fanciful as portrait. But remember that all fine artistic work is received with an outcry, with hatred even. Suspect all work that is not.

The one thing I will not have is sentimental representations of

of illustrated volumes devoted to London, New York, and elsewhere, the 'portraits of places' which form the frontispieces to the fine New York edition of Henry James's Novels and Tales (1907–1908), and a long series of photographs of 'Men of Mark,' two volumes of which were published in 1913 and 1922. Mr. Coburn records that he photographed Yeats in Dublin on January 24, 1908. The portrait intended for Yeats's Collected Edition did not appear there, but was used later as frontispiece to his *Poems: Second Series*, 1909 (1910).

myself alone. I will not have Lytton, or his like, and I will not have my father's alone, or alone in Vol. I, because he has always sentimentalized me. I have spent my life with pictures and was a painter for three years and I really think I might be trusted in this matter. I need hardly say Heinemann's opinion is worthless in a matter of art—stick to our point and he will give way.

If you had asked Shannon for 'a sketch of W. B. Yeats' he would have understood you. He has made no 'sketch for a portrait,' a very different thing. I shall go to London the week after next and sit to him for the portrait and we can use it if it is in time—there is always Rothenstein, but that would cost something for copyright. The Shannon 'sketch of W. B. Yeats' is not very good, the portrait will probably be very fine. Yours W B YEATS

I have looked through the *Samhains* and sent them but could you print in galley, as I think I shall interpolate a couple of controversial letters.

I am at my wit's end about *Helmet*.[1] My only copy, the prompt copy, has it seems been stolen from the theatre—at any rate it is lost. The actors will have to dictate the whole thing. Some photos were stolen about [the] same time, which makes me suspicious.

TO MISS E. M. LISTER

Wed [*March* 18, 1908] *Nassau Hotel*

My dear Miss Lister: I am sorry I wrote so harshly to Mr. Bullen. But his own letter to me was provocative enough. He arranges things with me (as he did the length of time the printing was to take)—we get everything quite precise—and then he writes to me accusing me, who am simply doing what was agreed upon, of springing something upon him, or of breaking some arrangement. He forgets things and I see now that when he and I make any plan

[1] *The Golden Helmet*, a prose version of the play about Cuchulain which later became the verse play *The Green Helmet*. It was played at the Abbey Theatre on March 19, 1908, so was evidently in rehearsal at this date. Bullen would have been requiring the text for the Collected Edition then in preparation. It was printed there in Volume IV.

we must get it down in writing. This time I had made all my arrangements (even to arranging the programme of the theatre to enable me to go to London and sit for Shannon to have his portrait as soon as possible) and written to various people, when he wrote to me that the plan we had decided on in London of putting all the portraits together was impossible, that I had sprung it upon him and he said this in an angry letter. I am so busy now, with every moment of my time marked out, that a little thing, even a small change of plan, puts all astray. I want those portraits together because it is the logical thing—they do not belong to one part of a book more than another, or to one volume more than another; because if one puts portraits all together it is obviously for comparison and completeness and not because one wants one's picture in every possible place. I also want Augustus John's emphasis to be balanced by emphasis in other directions. I have always in my life disliked the illogical scattering of pictures and portraits through books in obedience to book-sellers' prejudice. I shall try to send the photograph to-day if I can find somebody who knows how to do up a photograph for the post. You must send it back safe as I shall probably get no others.

I return the proof of note on music, but please cross out the new end sentence should Miss Farr *not* do the music to *Shadowy Waters*.

Tomorrow we play *Golden Helmet* and that over I will send you the note on performance and the notes on performance of *Kathleen ni Houlihan* and *Hour-Glass*. I think when I send you these and the 'Spenser' I shall have

[*The rest of this letter is missing*]

TO MISS E. M. LISTER [1]

March 27, 1908   *Nassau Hotel*

Dear Miss Lister, There has been a mix up in the *Samhain* proofs. First of all Mr. Bullen writes to me for the preface, which I sent you when I sent the copy. Secondly, an article of George Moore's has been printed as part of the text. I don't understand this, for I believe that I tore out from the *Samhains* my part of them, and sent that to

[1] Dictated.

you. Mr. Bullen may have copied my corrections into some other text, in which case please look up my original copy, and see if you can find the preface, which I don't now remember. I think something must have gone astray for I suggested for this section the title *Friends and Enemies*. If Mr. Bullen prefers, he can call it *The Irish Dramatic Movement*, or *Samhain*, however. The preface was quite short, and can go at the back of the page which contains the title, as Mr. Bullen suggests.

You can leave aside the matter of the portraits, as I am sitting to Sargent next week, as well as to Shannon. This will cost Mr. Bullen nothing. The only thing he will have to pay for portraits will I think be the £18 for the Augustus John. If the Sargent turns out well I may put it in the place of the John. I am sorry to hear that Mr. Bullen is so ill. Yours   W B YEATS

TO FLORENCE FARR

April [1908]   18 *Woburn Buildings*

My dear Florence Emery; When do you return? Have you lost all yet?

I have been sitting to Sargent for a charcoal drawing[1] and he has done a fine thing which is to go in the collected edition. I sit to Shannon every day or two and his portrait, certainly not flattering, is one of his grave distinguished old masterish things. Miss Bruce is to begin on Monday to do a bronze mask of me,[2] and that too I may have reproduced in the edition. By the by Ricketts says that Farquharson says that Granville Barker is Shaw's son.[3] I shall begin searching everywhere for the mother I suppose—I shall discover here his nose and there his earnest gaze.

I am just off to Stratford-on-Avon to see Bullen where I stay until Monday.

I have a poem in my head which will have a principal singer, a

[1] Sargent's drawing of Yeats, reproduced in the Collected Edition, is dated 1908.
[2] The bronze mask by Kathleen Bruce (Lady Kennet) is now in the National Portrait Gallery, London.
[3] The myth that Bernard Shaw was Granville Barker's father probably evolved because Barker, playing John Tanner in *Man and Superman*, made himself up to resemble Shaw. It soon died a natural death.

woman, and a chorus of younger women who will dance as they sing their answers to the principal. It is a duologue on love, from the woman's point of view and from the girls'. The girls dream and think they love the man who dreams [?] and the woman mocks them.[1] It was put into my head by a lot of children I saw dancing Morris dances. We should take up all those old things and make them subtle and modern. Yours　　　　　　　　　　W B YEATS

TO FLORENCE FARR

April 21, 1908　　　　　　　　　　　　18 *Woburn Buildings*

My dear Florence Emery: I send The M [*word indecipherable*]. I called at the office and as it was shut up for the holidays bribed a sort of office boy to get a copy sent to you. I then got a copy myself after going to four bookstalls which had none left.

I am just off to Stratford-on-Avon where Sara Allgood plays Isabella—we have lent her to Poel—in *Measure for Measure*. She has made a great success in the part at Manchester. Mrs. Campbell has announced that she will do Miss Tobin's *Phèdre* in London. You must be got to play in that. The second heroine is a very fine part and would suit you in some ways well.

When do you return? There is a slight chance of my going to Paris at once for a week though I don't think it likely. I wonder will you be there on your way. Let me know your plans at any rate. London is unendurable when you are not in it. I have no real friends—I have been too long away—and wander about without a soul to whom I can talk as if to myself. I go to bad plays or blind myself with reading by candle light out of boredom.

Here is Conder's account given to Sargent of how he came to enjoy music first. 'I never understood it until one day I thought it was like pink satin. I was going home one night in Paris. There was a decadent poet with me. He had a revolver. He fired it through keyholes. He shot off several bolts. Then a policeman took him away. His mistress was with us and I said "Come with me and sleep on the sofa." She slept on the sofa and I went to my room. In the middle of the night I heard a sound of broken glass. She had climbed through the skylight and was calling for the police

[1] This poem does not seem to have been written.

to protect her from me. A friend said nobody can help you now but the archbishop of Paris and when he came next day to the prison the archbishop was dressed in pink satin. That is how I came to understand music.' Yours ever   W B YEATS

TO JOHN QUINN

April 27, 1908   18 *Woburn Buildings*

My dear Quinn . . . The Shannon portrait is now finished and is, I believe, exceedingly fine. Shannon is himself delighted with it, and Miss Bruce, a sculptor, told me to-day that she thinks it one of the finest he has done and extraordinarily like. I am having it reproduced in the collected edition, as I warned you. I know you will not mind that. Shannon wants to exhibit it and asked me to find out if you would mind his keeping it for an exhibition of portraits which is being held here in the autumn. I have done nothing now, it seems to me, for about three weeks but sit for my portrait. The Sargent is to go in volume I and is a charming, aerial sort of thing, very flattering as I think. It will be in the first volume and the Shannon in the second. This collected edition is going to be a beautiful thing. I have seen the first specimen volume and am well content with my share of it and with Bullen's. I think I am better in the mass than in fragments.

Sargent is good company, not so much like an artist as like some wise, wealthy man of business who has lived with artists. He looks on at the enthusiasts with an ironical tolerance which is very engaging . . .

Moore is in Paris. Howard de Walden went to see him and asked for him at his hotel. He was in but they made a mystery about where he was. Howard de Walden insisted and was brought down to the kitchen, where he found Moore sitting in front of a mousehole with a loaded gun levelled at the hole and waiting for the mouse. There are moments when I think that Moore is really going off his head as well as Conder, though I must say mice are not the game his impulse drives him after usually. Miss Bruce has a beautiful story. He was paying attention to a friend of hers who belongs to Sickart, how does he spell his name? this is not right anyway. She didn't feel any interest in Moore and did like Sickart and was quite content.

Finally she became so emphatic as to send Moore away. Moore became plaintive and remonstrated with 'But Sickart and I always share.' Moore has just gone back to Dublin, where he has only two friends left, George Russell and John Eglinton, the two most virtuous members of the community, who are always faithful to him and turn up at his house Saturday after Saturday. I am avoiding him till he gets the next volume of his memoirs out, for I understand he is going to put the real conversations of his friends in over their names. He calls it a novel with real people in it. I hear it is going to be very dull, that it was quite lively but has grown dull as Eglinton and Russell pointed out all the different libels. He looks very gloomy and is, I imagine, feeling at last the weight of his years. He begins to look more and more like a sick chaffinch or starling, I don't quite know which, for a starling isn't right in the colour and a chaffinch has not the perfect droop of the head. I can imagine he took to shooting mice out of sheer boredom. I have no doubt he found himself forgotten in Paris and too old to make new friends.

Synge has taken charge of the Theatre in my place and is rehearsing the people now, and so on. It has probably interrupted his *Deirdre*, which is going to be very fine. He has written it in slight dialect so far as the king and queen are concerned, a little more dialect than there is in Lady Gregory's books, but he has given the minor characters a great deal of peasant idiom. The result is that the play, while seeming perfectly natural, has much the same atmosphere so far as the speech goes as his other plays. There is, however, nothing grotesque in it, and an astonishing amount of sheer lyrical beauty. It is much more beautiful than, though not in its present stage anything like so dramatic as, his other work. I think it would be impossible to any company except ours. I can't imagine anybody getting his peculiar rhythm without being personally instructed in it. He is at present rehearsing *The Well of the Saints*, which is being revived, with scenery by Charles Ricketts. We are producing new plays at a great rate but drawing as bad houses as usual. However, everybody is cheerful . . . I have a new play in my head and when that is written shall go back to lyric work. Indeed, for months now I have had lyrics wandering about in the air, waiting the moment of leisure to get them into words . . .

Will you be in Ireland this summer? Yours ever

                 W B YEATS

May 1. Since I wrote the above I have heard that poor Synge is ill again and has had to go into hospital for another operation—a lump in his side to be operated on. I go to Dublin at once to take his place.

TO FLORENCE FARR

[*? September* 1908]　　　　　　　　　　　　　　*Coole Park*

My dear Florence Emery: The result of your sending me those lines —alas—to put into chantable English is that I have never written to you. I have been ashamed to write and not send them and I have always had so much to do. I am in the worst stage of a new play [1]— the dreadful opening work on the scenario—working badly because one hates the work. I shall have no leisure or pleasure in life until I begin the verse writing and when that comes life will be worth living again and I shall have moments for my friends. As it is I sit down at 11, idle for an hour perhaps and then work an hour and then half idle half work and so till tea and five o'clock comes round and my heart and my conscience both are aching. I was only one day in London on my way from Paris driven on by this work. Have you seen Mrs. Campbell? Do you know what she plans to do? Is she really going to come here? I have put *Deirdre* into rehearsal but I have never really believed she would play in it. [2]

I have a fine tale of Althea Gyles. She brought a prosperous love-affair to an end by reading Browning to the poor man in the middle of the night. She collects the necessities of life from her friends and spends her own money on flowers.

I should think you will have your copy of the collected edition in about three weeks. I have written to them to put in the Augustus John after all.

My father is still in America. He gave orders that no windows were ever to be opened. A window was opened by the housemaid, and a mosquito got in. His letters are full of the mosquito. He makes after-dinner speeches and is evidently in great content.

[1] *The Player Queen*, on which Yeats worked for many years.
[2] Mrs. Patrick Campbell played in *Deirdre* with the Abbey Theatre company in Dublin on November 9 and the following days.

I have heard nothing of you this long time so please write and tell me about Mrs. Campbell. I know she has been thinking of altering her dates. Yours ever W B YEATS

TO JOHN QUINN

[*October*] 1908 *Nassau Hotel*

My dear Quinn . . . I have finished the prose version of what is to be a new verse play, *The Player Queen*, and Mrs. Patrick Campbell talks of producing it. I am trying to get the prose version typed that I may go through it with her. She wants me to write, as she phrases it, with her at my elbow. I am rather inclined to try the experiment for once as I believe that I shall be inspired rather than thwarted by trying to give her as many opportunities as possible. At the worst we can but quarrel. She plays my *Deirdre* at the Abbey Theatre on November 9th and the rehearsals begin on Monday; that is to say, the rehearsals with her, for our own people have been rehearsing for some time. The Abbey has been doing very well lately; for the last three months or so it has even been paying, and if it can keep on like this, which I doubt, we'll be able to do without a subsidy. The curious thing is that in spite of all the attacks upon us we have nothing but a pit and that is always full now. The stalls won't come near us, except when some titled person or other comes and brings guests. All the praise we have had from the most intellectual critics cannot bring the Irish educated classes, and all the abuse we have had from the least intellectual cannot keep the less educated classes away. I suppose the cause of it all is that, as a drunken medical student used to say, 'Pitt decapitated Ireland.'

November 15th
I thought I had posted this. I have just found it under my papers. *Deirdre* has been played with triumphant success—great audiences and great enthusiasm; and Mrs. Campbell has bought the English and American rights for five years (we keep the Irish rights). She has taken a London theatre and produces it there on November 27th. There has not been one hostile voice here and I am now accepted as a dramatist in Dublin. Mrs. Campbell was magnificent. Yours ever W B YEATS

TO J. B. YEATS

Sunday [*December* 27, 1908]   *Hotel de Passy*
Rue de Passy
Paris

My dear Father: I have been here for a month working at *The Player Queen* for Mrs. Campbell. She did very fairly well in London [1] with *Deirdre* and *Electra* and both drew good houses and were well received by the 'advanced' critics and abused by the old, which means in practice well received by the 1d papers and badly by the ½d, the usual reception of intellectual drama in London. In Dublin for the first time in my life there was no division of opinion. Here every morning I dictate and every afternoon I go to a French class at the other end of Paris. I am reading Balzac—but in English, for I prefer to read more concentrated French—and I go to the places in Paris he speaks of. In my usual way I shall read him all. I am at about the 12th or 13th of the 40 volumes and some of the remainder I read years ago. His philosophy interests me almost more than his drama. I go to London on Tuesday and shall be in Dublin on Monday (4th of January) producing Molière at the Abbey—*The Miser* put into Irish dialect by Lady Gregory. I hope Lady Gregory sent you your stories. I find that the woman come back from the dead sticks in my memory. I believe it is good as well as strange. It is not well constructed and that will go against its success in America where the short story is a national form.

No, I do not understand your dramatic ideas any more than you understand the ideas of my generation, or than I shall understand in a few years' time the generation now at school. Even Shaw, as I know, begins to find the young unintelligible. Here and there I already meet a young man who represents something which I recognize as new, and which is not of my time—he is very often a sort of Catholic by the by.

I am going to Maud Gonne's to lunch and must stop.

I wish you would ask Quinn if he ever got the Sargent portrait—he will not answer me—and what he wants done about the Shannon.
Yours   W B YEATS

[1] Soon after her performances at the Abbey Theatre Mrs. Patrick Campbell gave a series of matinées at the New Theatre in London, beginning on November 27. Her programme consisted of a double bill containing Yeats's *Deirdre*, and *Electra*, a tragedy in one act by Hugo von Hofmannsthal, translated into English blank verse by Arthur Symons.

PART FOUR

1909—1917

INTRODUCTION TO PART FOUR

SINCE the opening of the Abbey Theatre Yeats had written hardly any lyrics; such writing as he found time for was devoted to the stage. In the early part of 1909 he was busy turning a prose play on Cuchulain into ballad metre, and this appeared the following year as *The Green Helmet*; he was still struggling with *The Player Queen* for Mrs. Patrick Campbell. A letter to Florence Farr in March speaks of a recent breakdown. This month saw the death of Synge, who had been ill for some time. Yeats had begun to keep a diary, and two selections from this, called respectively *Estrangement* and *The Death of Synge*, were published in after years at the Cuala Press. Synge had asked Yeats to look after his unpublished works, and a little volume of his *Poems and Translations* appeared in July.

A new manager had been appointed for the Abbey, the Irish novelist and playwright Conal O'Riordan ('Norreys Connell'), and in June the Abbey company played a three weeks' season in London at the Court Theatre, Mrs. Patrick Campbell joining them for some more performances of *Deirdre*. Yeats went over to Paris soon after this, and then to Coole for his usual summer visit.

Bernard Shaw had written a long one-act play for Beerbohm Tree, *The Showing-Up of Blanco Posnet*, but the Lord Chamberlain considered some passages in it to be blasphemous and refused a licence. Shaw offered it to the Abbey, since the Irish stage did not lie within the Lord Chamberlain's jurisdiction. In the face of strong pressure from Dublin Castle the play was produced in August during Horse Show Week with immense success, and this defiance of English officialdom helped to restore to the theatre the popularity it had lost by the performance of *The Playboy of the Western World*.

Synge's death had reduced the Abbey Directors to two and this meant more responsibility than ever for Yeats. He was in charge during the early part of 1910 when the theatre produced Synge's posthumous *Deirdre of the Sorrows* as well as his own *Green Helmet*; both plays were among those given when the company appeared again in London that summer.

By this time Yeats was recognized as one of the leading men of letters. In April Edmund Gosse invited him to become a member of the Academic Committee of the Royal Society of Literature, then about to be constituted. There was also a possibility that he might be asked to succeed Edward Dowden as Professor of English Literature at Trinity College, Dublin; he was tempted by the thought of rooms in College but decided that his eyesight was too bad to allow him to undertake the amount of concentrated reading the appointment would have involved.

In May he visited Maud Gonne, now living at Colleville-sur-mer in Normandy, and in August he received notice that he had been awarded a Civil List pension of £150. He accepted this on the understanding that he was to remain perfectly free to undertake any political activities in Ireland he might wish.

The death in September of his uncle and old friend George Pollexfen was a great grief to him. He went from Coole to Sligo for the funeral, the ceremonial of which, Pollexfen having been a leading Freemason, much impressed him; he recorded it in a poem, 'In Memory,' seven years later.

In the autumn there was a lecture tour in the English provinces. The Abbey Theatre had now been taken over from Miss Horniman, and Yeats delivered a series of lectures in London to provide funds for its continuance. He had begun to write lyrics again, and in December his sister published a small collection of his latest poems, the book also including *The Green Helmet*. These poems show the beginning of his 'second manner,' a more colloquial style, the result, it can hardly be doubted, of his continuous work in the theatre. In the autumn he also finished a long memorial essay on Synge.

The early months of 1911 were spent in London, and in May he visited Paris in company with Lady Gregory. July brought the Abbey players again to London, and arrangements were made for them to go on tour in America later in the year.

Yeats had long been an admirer of the stage work of Gordon Craig and had lately been experimenting at the Abbey with the Craig invention of movable screens, which allowed an infinite amount of variation in the setting. A dinner in Craig's honour had been organized at the Café Royal in London at which Yeats was to be chairman. Discovering at the last moment that he would be expected to propose the King's health, he had to resign the chairmanship to Will Rothenstein, but made a magnificent speech when his turn came. That winter Bullen published a collected volume of *Plays for an Irish Theatre* illustrated with some Craig designs.

Yeats crossed to America with the Abbey company, and lectured at Harvard on 'The Theatre of Beauty,' but returned almost at once to take charge of the Abbey where a second company had been formed to carry on, leaving Lady Gregory to accompany the players on their American tour. *The Playboy* caused more riots, and in Philadelphia the entire company were arrested. John Quinn came valiantly to the rescue, and they were released and enabled to continue their tour.

Yeats had now turned to the revision of his earlier plays, and new versions of *The Land of Heart's Desire* and *The Countess Cathleen* were played in 1911 and 1912 respectively. He also put together a new volume of essays *The Cutting of an Agate*, at first published only in America, the English edition being delayed until 1919. When the company returned from the States Lennox Robinson, who had become one of their chief playwrights, took over the management of the theatre, and from this time onward Yeats had a certain amount of freedom from routine work there, though he still retained responsibility.

In June 1912 he met, through Rothenstein, the Indian poet Rabindranath Tagore, and helped to bring out the very successful selection of his poems in translation, *Gitanjali*, for which he wrote an enthusiastic introduction. With his friend Olivia Shakespear he made visits to various country houses in England, and again met Miss Hyde-Lees, whom he had known since 1911 and who afterwards became his wife. Her mother had married, as her second husband, Mrs. Shakespear's brother, H. T. Tucker. In August he went again to Normandy, and in the autumn a young American poet, Ezra Pound, who had come to England in 1908, and who first met Yeats the following year, became a frequent visitor at Woburn Buildings, and made himself useful by reading aloud to Yeats in the evenings to spare his eyesight; he also taught Yeats to fence.

The earlier part of 1913 was mainly spent in London. Controversy was still acute in Dublin over the choice of a site for the gallery to house Hugh Lane's pictures, and Yeats was eloquent both in verse and prose in Lane's support. When the Lutyens proposal was rejected, Lane withdrew in dudgeon and Yeats printed *Poems written in Dejection* in a small Cuala Press pamphlet for private circulation.

Bullen's affairs were not prosperous and he was trying to get his printing press at Stratford-on-Avon, where he had done much fine work, endowed as a Shakespeare memorial. A proposal to refurbish the Yeats Collected Edition and replace some of the contents by revised versions came to nothing. This summer there was no visit to Coole, and in the autumn Yeats took rooms in Sussex with Ezra Pound as companion and secretary.

At the end of January 1914 he sailed for America on another lecture tour and was away for three months. On his return he was for some time in London, and after the Abbey Theatre company had played their usual summer season there he went to Paris and on to Mirebeau, near Poitiers, in company with Maud Gonne and Everard Feilding, to investigate a miracle said to have taken place there. He wrote, but did not publish, an account of the investigation.

When the war broke out he was in England but went to Coole for the late summer. The autumn was devoted to writing the first section of his autobiography, published after some delay as *Reveries over Childhood and Youth*. He wintered again in Sussex; Ezra Pound had married Mrs. Shakespear's daughter Dorothy, and again accompanied him bringing his wife.

In May 1915 Hugh Lane went down on the *Lusitania*, and there began the controversy regarding the rightful ownership of his pictures which has continued ever since and is still unresolved. In July and August Yeats was instrumental, through Edmund Gosse, in securing for James Joyce a much needed grant from the Royal Literary Fund. At the end of the year he was informed, indirectly, that a knighthood was to be offered him; he made his refusal of the honour as gracious as he could.

Pound was now a considerable influence. He had been preparing translations left in manuscript by Ernest Fenollosa of some Japanese Noh plays. Inspired by these Yeats began to write *At the Hawk's Well*, another play of his Cuchulain cycle, to be acted by masked players against the bare wall of a room, needing neither stage nor curtain. 'I have invented a form of drama,' he wrote, 'distinguished, indirect, and symbolic, and having no need of mob or press to pay its way—an aristocratic form.' With the help of Edmund Dulac, who designed masks and costumes, and a clever Japanese dancer Michio Ito, discovered by Pound, two performances of the play were given in London; and for many years thereafter Yeats wrote his plays in this form or in a modification of it.

He was staying in the country in England when the Easter 1916 rising took place in Dublin. The executions which followed distressed him greatly; many of those executed he had known well. Among them was John MacBride, Maud Gonne's husband, and as soon as he could get a passport Yeats crossed to France to see her. He felt now that he should live in Ireland, and in the autumn, while at Coole, he bought from the Congested Districts Board the old tower at Ballylee (about which he had written many years before) and a ruined cottage at its foot. This he proposed to restore and use as a summer residence.

The Lane picture controversy was now at its height and Yeats wrote a number of letters to the English press in support of Ireland's claim. He had for years been unable to finish *The Player Queen* to his liking; it had been planned as a verse tragedy, but now, at Ezra Pound's suggestion, he turned it into a fantastic prose comedy, exemplifying his theory of the Mask, of the Self and the Anti-self. He was at work, too, on a prose exposition of the theory, first called *An Alphabet* but published in 1918 under the title *Per Amica Silentia Lunae*. He spent the early part of the summer of 1917 at Coole, and in August went to Colleville and while there proposed to Maud Gonne's daughter, Iseult, with whom he had fallen in love. She was very many years his junior and though she felt much affection for him refused to marry him. He brought her and Maud Gonne back to England, but, as a wartime security measure, they were forbidden to enter Ireland.

Yeats was unhappy. He was over fifty, and felt it was time he married; already, in a poem to his ancestors dated January 1914, he had lamented that

> Although I have come close on forty-nine,
> I have no child, I have nothing but a book,
> Nothing but that to prove your blood and mine.

He turned to Miss Hyde-Lees, whom he had now known for some years and who had shown him great sympathy and understanding, and they were married in the autumn of 1917.

The honeymoon was spent at Forest Row in Sussex. To distract his thoughts, for he seemed still to be worrying, Mrs. Yeats attempted automatic writing; messages which thus reached him excited Yeats enormously, and presently he began to construct a system of mystical philosophy, founded on these revelations, which was to occupy his mind almost continuously for many years, and to form the foundation for much of his poetry.

After a short time in Woburn Buildings, being unable to go, as they had wished, to the West of Ireland because of food difficulties, they found rooms which they liked in Oxford, and Yeats was able to work at the Bodleian. Of Mrs. Yeats he wrote to Lady Gregory: 'She has made my life serene and full of order.' He was happy at last, and began again to write verse.

1909-1917

TO LADY GREGORY

Monday Jan 4 [Postmark 1909]　　　　　45 *Ackers Street*
Manchester

My dear Lady Gregory . . . I went to see Symons, a very painful experience. Miss Tobin goes almost every day. He is sane when you speak of books but in a moment wanders away into his madness. He is writing a play about 'Teig the Fool'—a mad rigmarole—and wants to go to Galway to see Teig who is, he says, God. Yours

W B YEATS

TO ALLAN WADE

Thursday [Postmark Jan 15, 1909]　　　　　*Nassau Hotel*

My dear Wade: I am amazed at your bibliography.[1] You have old letters to the papers there, the date of which must have cost you endless trouble. The thing is of great value to myself and now you have made it possible I shall re-read endless old things I had thought never to see again.

Henderson our secretary was anxious for a week at Oxford but I am afraid it would be very dangerous. I should think Oxford is a three day town.

[1] I began to make a bibliography of Yeats's writings about the year 1898 or 1899. When A. H. Bullen was preparing the Collected Edition of 1908 he asked to be allowed to include this in the last volume, and in addition to doing so he printed a small separate edition of sixty copies, giving me twenty of them as remuneration. I believe the remaining forty copies were divided equally between England and America. Recently I have been enabled to bring the work up to date; a revised and much enlarged *Bibliography of the Writings of W. B. Yeats* was published in 1951 by Rupert Hart-Davis.

I would have gone to see you on passing through London but Lady Gregory's letter with your address there did not reach me in time. Yours

W B YEATS

TO J. B. YEATS

Sunday [*January* 17, 1909]   *Nassau Hotel*

My dear Father: I am working very hard now, trying to carry on the theatre and write for Mrs. Campbell at the same time. I dictate the prose structure of the new play every morning and then go to the theatre and rehearse Molière. We produce *The Miser* next Thursday. I find that my talent as a stage manager is in the invention of comic business, in fact I am coming to the conclusion that I am really essentially a writer of comedy, but very personal comedy. Wilde wrote in his last book 'I have made drama as personal as a lyric,' and I think, whether he has done so or not, that it is the only possible task now.

Lilly dined here last night and made out, in a book Lady Gregory has given me, a fine family tree. She is to keep the book by her and write in all she discovers. It is very ingenious and [a] sort of tree of knowledge in which all the apples of pride arrange themselves in the most beautiful order, an American invention. I thought her in great spirits and I foretold for her by the stars a very prosperous time in the next few years.

Somebody asked me the other day, in all seriousness, if it was true, as he had been told, that my father 'had married in America and settled there,' and Bullen writes to me that your portrait of me in the collected edition is the best. By the by your set of volumes is being sent to Dundrum which is, I conclude, as you would wish. I told Lilly to open it. The last volume contains, I believe, my best prose.

I met Hughes[1] when I was in Paris and paid him some com-

---

[1] John Hughes, Franco-Irish sculptor, was a fellow-student at the Art School with Yeats and George Russell. His statue of Queen Victoria was intended to stand on a pillar in Phoenix Park, Dublin, but owing to some difficulty about the site it was placed, on a much lower base, in the courtyard of Leinster House facing Kildare Street. More recently it has been removed from its position there and consigned to storage. Hughes spent his later life in Paris and is believed to have died there.

pliment on his statue of Queen Victoria, but he would none of my compliments. 'No,' he said, 'she was a horrid woman.'

I hear the statue called the hippopotamus but prefer Jack's description, 'I like it because she looks so old, and so dull, and so brave.'

I am working at French and a French teacher comes every day for an hour and talk[s] French with me. Yours   W B YEATS

TO LADY GREGORY

Sunday [March 8, 1909]   *Nassau Hotel*

My dear Lady Gregory . . . I did a good morning's work on *Player Queen* and then copied out, changing here and there, the rhyming *Golden Helmet*—it reads well. To-morrow I shall have to waste the best of the morning on Sinclair's ill doings.[1] However my discontents enlarge my diary. I have written a number of notes lately. I wound up my notes this morning with the sentence 'culture is the sanctity of the intellect.' I was thinking of men like Griffith and how they can renounce external things without it but not envy, revenge, jealousy and so on. I wrote a note a couple of days ago in which I compared Griffith and his like to the Eunuchs in Ricketts's picture watching Don Juan riding through Hell.[2] Yours with love
                                                            W B YEATS

TO FLORENCE FARR

Wednesday [? March 1909]   *Coole Park*

My dear Florence Emery: Neither Lady Gregory nor I would object to your playing *Shadow of the Glen* in the small hall you speak of in your letter but I am afraid you must do nothing for the present.

[1] Arthur Sinclair, a member of the Abbey Theatre company, a fine comedian. It is impossible to say what Yeats is here referring to; quarrels and insubordination were very frequent in the company at the time, and much of Yeats's correspondence with Lady Gregory is occupied with details of the difficulties of management.

[2] The note shortly became the epigram in verse *On those who Disliked the Playboy*. Yeats repeated a version of it to me during a lunch together in June or July 1909.

Synge is very ill in hospital and cannot be asked about matters of business. He is perhaps dying [1]—nothing is known with any certainty as the doctors don't know the nature of the growth or whether it is the coming again of that growth that has made him ill. He was very weak and pale when I saw him a week ago. He is not allowed to see any one except Molly Allgood [2] who sees him for a few minutes every second day. I cannot see him now for he finds any conversation about literature too exciting. His vitality is so low that he cannot read anything but the lightest literature and does not leave his bed.

I find in Patmore's book of Odes an appendix in which he states our theory of music and speech very clearly. In the 3/6 edition (*Poetical Works* Vol II) you will find a long passage starting on page 232 which will interest you and at any rate give you the support of a great authority. I am grateful for your dedication and expect to find your book very valuable.[3]

I came down here for a few days to write in peace, but not at *Player Queen*. My breakdown has left me with so much to do. I am afraid I must put *Player Queen* off for a time, as to do work of this kind amid all these distractions is a great strain and I don't do it well. If I can get all the fundamental thinking through before the summer I can finish the verse here in summer. Meanwhile I must do work that will bring in a little money, for Mrs. Campbell has sent me no agreement and when *Player Queen* is finished I may get nothing. She was to have paid me something on finishing the MS. I have a large MS book in which I write stray notes on all kinds of things. These will make up into essays. They will amuse you very much. They are quite frank and the part that cannot be printed while I am alive is the amusing part.

I go back to Dublin on Friday. I may be in London for a few days the first week in April. Yours ever   W B YEATS

[1] Synge died on March 24, 1909. This letter seems to have been written shortly before that date.
[2] The actress Maire O'Neill, a sister of Sara Allgood. See note 5 opposite.
[3] *The Music of Speech* by Florence Farr. London: Elkin Mathews, 1909. She wrote 'I dedicate this book to W. B. Yeats, who suggested to me the notation of speech; also to Arnold Dolmetsch, who invented for me a musical instrument sympathetic to the speaking voice, calling it a psaltery.'

TO LADY GREGORY

Monday [April 5, 1909]   *Nassau Hotel*

My dear Lady Gregory: I go to London to-morrow. I have been delayed by the finishing of the Synge preface [1]—I shall see Horniman and Bullen and return to Dublin to go through the *Deirdre* MSS [2] with you next week when you come up for *Heather Field*.[3] Miss O'Neill has written saying that we want it. Connell [4] is working very hard at the Abbey, six hours a day 11 to 2 and 8 to 11, at *Heather Field*. His play was well received by the audience. It was the papers that were stupid. At the same time it is Robinson who has roused the enthusiasm. I doubt if we have produced anything which has excited people quite so much. The young man told my sisters that it was *Kathleen-na-Houlihan* that changed his politics and also set him writing, so I should share the enthusiasm but I don't. At the same time he is far beyond Boyle or Casey in force. He is a serious intellect and may grow to be a great dramatist. He is only 22. I have spent the day returning plays—writing letters where there was reason for it.

Molly [5] has told me of a series of prophetic dreams and vision she had of Synge's death. The first years ago when she had no thought of such a thing. Curiously enough quite lately she had dreamed of him going away in a ship and waving good-bye.

There is a long letter about Synge in the *Nation*. I have written a short note contradicting the statement that he was ever under the influence of French decadents. Yours affectionately   W B YEATS

TO THE EDITOR OF THE *NATION*

April 6th, 1909   *Abbey Theatre*

Sir, There is an interesting, sympathetic letter in your issue of April 3rd on 'The Art of J. M. Synge,' which contains an error too slight

---

[1] The preface to *Poems and Translations* by John M. Synge, dated April 4, 1909, and published by the Cuala Press on July 5.
[2] Synge's last play *Deirdre of the Sorrows*.
[3] *The Heather Field* by Edward Martyn was revived at the Abbey Theatre on April 15, 1909.
[4] Conal O'Riordan, who was at this time in charge of the Abbey Theatre. He had written his earlier books under the pseudonym Norreys Connell. His play *Time* and Lennox Robinson's *The Cross Roads* had been produced on April 1.
[5] Molly Allgood (Maire O'Neill) who had been engaged to marry Synge. Yeats mentions these dreams in his reprinted diary *The Death of Synge*, section xxv, afterwards included in *Dramatis Personae*.

to notice were it not that it may strengthen some fool in his folly. Your correspondent quotes me correctly as having said that Mr. Synge's work before he went to Aran was too literary, too full of 'images reflected from mirror to mirror,' but he is wrong in supposing that it was 'the morbid remote poetry' that 'Englishmen and Frenchmen were writing at that time,' or that it showed the influence of 'poets of Montmartre.' He has been reading some Irish journalist (generally a mistake when literature is the subject) who believes, or pretends to believe, that the author of *The Playboy of the Western World* borrowed something of his genius from 'French decadents.' If there are 'decadents' in Montmartre, or elsewhere, Mr. Synge knew nothing of them. When I met him in Paris I found him reading Racine, and because he wished to make a little money by criticism of French literature, I urged him vainly to read the writers of his own time. He read throughout his life the great classics and these alone, and even in those early imitative poems and essays there was no other influence. Yours, etc. W B YEATS

TO J. B. YEATS

[*April* 29, 1909] *Dunsany Castle*
Co. Meath

My dear Father, I have left you long without writing but Synge's death brought with it troubles and journeys of various kinds. I had to go to Galway and then to London about the choosing of someone to take his place. We have appointed Norreys Connell, who is an experienced stage-manager, and he is to manage for the larger part of the working year at a salary. This sets me free until November or December next to finish my play for Mrs. Campbell. Then troubles over the Synge MSS began after endless delays caused (Heaven knows why) by the business man of the family, Synge's brother-in-law, Stephens. We have only just got the MS of *Deirdre*. On the back of a page we have found a direction in Synge's handwriting that it was to be sent to me. Stephens must I should think have seen this. We think Stephens must have got it into his head we wanted to make a profit out of Synge in some way, or have been offended because Synge had made his son and not himself executor. He would not answer letters and kept putting off the giving of the MS until it was too late to rehearse it for London. *Deirdre of the Sorrows* would have been a masterpiece if Synge had lived long enough to do about a month more work. He put into it all his hatred of death as well as his own acceptance of it. There is wonderful writing.

I am staying with Lord Dunsany but return to Dublin to-night to work at the Synge MSS and on Monday night I go to London. So write next to Woburn Buildings. Dunsany is a man of genius I think. We are doing a little play of his [1] about a burglar who when he gets to the next world burgles the door of Heaven and finds within 'nothing but blooming great stars,' and a burglar whose doom is to open beer bottles for ever and to find them empty and be too thirsty to stop opening them. Dunsany has a very fine style, which he shows in wild little fantastic tales. He is a handsome young man with a beautiful house full of pictures. I want to get him into 'the movement.' Yours affectionately   W B YEATS

TO LADY GREGORY

Sunday [*May* 23, 1909]   18 *Woburn Buildings*

My dear Lady Gregory: Venice has been a temptation—I think a *temptation*—I have two or three engagements so that I would not have started at once and it would have been such an expensive journey for seven or eight days. I want to be able to arrange for my affairs so as not to be quite penniless when I start the autumn. I did however very nearly set out but I am getting well here and I have just discovered that I can get a boat in Regent's Park. Last week I was ill again and so did nothing but I shall work now . . .

I am going this afternoon to see Symons. He is quite happy and the other day wrote these lines about himself:

> 'I am undone, my course shall swiftly run,
> Yet I am wrapt in an enchanted swoon.
> I die of rapture yet I see that soon
> The fatal sisters shall my web have spun.'

He is full of affection and overflowing thought. I saw him on Wednesday.[2] Yours   W B YEATS

[1] *The Glittering Gate* by Lord Dunsany was produced at the Abbey Theatre on April 29.
[2] After his mental breakdown in the autumn of 1908 Arthur Symons was confined for a while in an asylum in Clapton, London, E., which had once housed

TO LADY GREGORY

Thursday, 27 *May* [1909]   18 *Woburn Buildings*

My dear Lady Gregory . . . Maud Gonne has struck up the most surprising friendship with Miss Tobin. They met at Arthur Symons's on Sunday (Symons had asked to see Maud Gonne) and Maud Gonne said afterwards 'she is so good—it flows from her' and Miss Tobin wrote 'she is the most glorious of human creatures'—I think that was the phrase—and sent her a string of pearls. They spent Tuesday morning in Westminster Abbey. Maud Gonne leaves to-day.

I am now very well and working at *Golden Helmet*, but I notice that strain or fatigue bring on my headaches—I had a very bad week last week and very nearly started for Venice—I think I would have but for the expense. I want to get my affairs into order now that freedom has made it possible and do not like to begin by a big expense. My mind is getting fit again and I feel I shall write well. I had a great many people here on Monday, Lord Dunsany among the rest. He was very much excited I think at meeting Mabel Beardsley. Yours   W B YEATS

TO WILLIAM ARCHER

June 3 [1909]   18 *Woburn Buildings*

My dear Archer: I had hoped to get to you this evening but find it is impossible. This last week I have for the first time read through the report by the Executive Committee adopted on March 23.[1] The proposed governing body seems to me so arranged as to give authority to all the elements in English life which create in the arts timid and conventional work. The thought of it fills me with fury. How can any artist agree to give power to his already powerful enemies? If the Committee intends to do work for the arts let it give

---

Mary Lamb. Later he made a considerable, though not absolutely complete, recovery and was able to live at home and to continue writing.

[1] Archer had apparently asked Yeats to allow his name to appear as a supporter of the National Theatre scheme. Unfortunately the earlier minute-books of the National Theatre Committee are not available, having been lost or destroyed during the bombing of London. The report of the Committee was reviewed by Max Beerbohm in the *Saturday Review*, April 10, 1909, under the heading 'A Touching Document.' This is reprinted in *Around Theatres*, London, Rupert Hart-Davis, 1953.

control to the arts, and before it approaches the County Council or anybody else elect some artist as despot for a term of years—Barker or Carr or Craig could create something—or some distinguished German, with knowledge of what a national theatre is, might do better still. Surely the sense of fact which Englishmen are said to possess, as distinguished from my countrymen, should recommend this last proposal above all. The Germans have a theatre, England has not—they have also the knowledge of different kinds of dramatic production which Barker would lack.

So I will have nothing to do with this attempt to set society, college dons, the *Spectator* newspaper, Mayors and Lord Mayors, the Royal Academy, Colonial Governors, Members of Parliament, and some sort of a schoolmaster on the back of the wild horse.

I am sorry not to do what you want, but it would contradict all I have ever done or thought. Our age does not lack talent but the generosity that gives it power—it is the presence or absence of that generosity that makes ages great or small. That network of representative men would let nothing through but mediocrity. They would recognise in a great man their mortal enemy and would be right. Yours   W B YEATS

I am sorry I was out when you called.

TO STELLA CAMPBELL[1]

July 5 [? 1909]   *Coole Park*

Dear Miss Campbell: I began to cast your horoscope just now and found I had only day and year Sept 27. 1886, but neither place nor hour. I want these for a true judgement so please write and tell them to me. I can only judge very vaguely from what I have. You have a most emotional artistic temperament and I think I would have known from the stars that you have acting power. You will (unless the precise hour gives me some unexpected fact) have good luck in life but will be subject more than others to sudden changes, transformation by events. You have just *gone* through or are now

---

[1] Stella Campbell, now Mrs. Mervyn Beech, daughter of Mrs. Patrick Campbell.

going through one—not very happy, of this kind—probably it is over. You will be excellent in idealization of passion in your art —a kind of lyric feeling—and I think you will have a gift of high sentiment.

It is the horoscope of an artist certainly but I must know the hour to say if a great one. Your marriage will be strange in some way. The stars insist however that you are a charming person. Yours sincerely W B YEATS

TO J. B. YEATS

July 17 [? 1909] *Burren*
Co. Clare

My dear Father, We have come down to a desolate, windy spot on the coast of Clare, where Robert Gregory is sketching, and his wife getting health. There is a wood in a hollow of the hills where one can get in out of the wind, and feel very much as if one had pulled a blanket over one's head to keep the night air out. I don't know if one ever delights in trees and in the sea with equal intensity, and I am of the tree party.

I am working every day on *The Player Queen*, but will not for a long time yet get at the verse writing. It is still all scenario, I think it is my most stirring thing. There will be a certain number of lyrics put into the mouth of one of the characters, as in *Deirdre*.

I went to Paris for a few days before I came here, and met Sarah Purser at Maud Gonne's. She was characteristic as ever, as like herself as a John drawing. Maud Gonne had a cage full of canaries and the birds were all singing. Sarah Purser began lunch by saying 'What a noise! I'd like to have my lunch in the kitchen!' . . .

I think the only Galway news is that I dined with Edward Martyn the other day and that he told me he has left the Sinn Fein organization, retired from politics altogether. He did not say, but I suspect the collecting of shares for a proposed Sinn Fein daily paper had something to do with it. Some time ago, ardent Sinn Feiners were called upon to refuse to pay Income Tax. He, poor man, and one other being the only members of the party who paid any. He is busy writing as ever, is very amiable when one sees him, but never goes to see anybody so far as I can make out. Moore is his only friend, and as he thinks Moore is damned, he has no responsibility about him.

I wrote to George [Pollexfen] and suggested myself as a visitor while Lady Gregory is here, but George has Alfred staying with him. I laugh every time I think of it. The Rosses Point house is the draughtiest I was ever in, and at Merville Alfred used to have a little cloth flap over his keyhole to keep out the draught. George doesn't mind, as he often explained to me while I was suffering, as he is never in the house except at night, and then he walks between supper and bedtime. I am better here and am working well, and have done a new lyric and a good one. Side by side with my play I am writing a second series of *Discoveries*. I find that my philosophical tendency spoils my playwriting if I have not a separate channel for it. There is a dramatic contrast of character in the play which can be philosophically stated. I am putting the philosophic statement into a stream of rambling thoughts suggested by impressionist pictures and a certain Italian book, and Lane's gallery in general, and the pictures I pass on the stairs at Coole. Lady Gregory had a letter from Quinn the other day full of fiery energy. I have read all your lectures and like them immensely, and so you know does Lady Gregory. She has put me out of the job of writing her epitaph and put you into it. Your son   W B YEATS

TO J. B. YEATS

August 7 [? 1909]   *Coole Park*

My dear Father: I have here for about two weeks now—at first we were at Burren, a seaside place in Clare. There has been so much theatre correspondence of late that I have kept putting off writing to you. It always takes me some time before I get a manageable system of work. My ideal is, I work at my play from 11 till 2, and then do letters, criticism and so forth from 3 to 5. Then I go to fish or walk. I have at last begun the putting of my play for Mrs. Campbell into verse. Up to this I have been constructing it in prose, a most weary business. I have finished an essay on 'tragic drama' which is to be the introduction to a new edition of my plays. Craig is doing stage designs for the edition. I have written half an elaborate essay on Synge, an analysis of Irish public opinion and the reason why his work is so much hated in Ireland. It is in practice a summary of the last fifty years in Ireland. But of course nearly all my thoughts are on my long play, of which a great deal will be in rhyme. My theme is that the world being illusion, one must be deluded in some way if one is to triumph in it. One of the characters says

> 'Queens that have laughed to set the world at ease,
> Kings that have cried "I am great Alexander
> Or Caesar come again" but stir our wonder
> That they may stir their own and grow at length
> Almost alike to that unlikely strength.
> And those that will not make deliberate choice
> Are nothing, or become some passion's voice,
> Doing its will, believing what it choose.'

Your friend Brooks came to see me and I liked him very much. I also asked another American under the impression he was your man and did not like him at all. I had also made much of him at the theatre under this delusion. His aim in life was to persuade poets to give up saying 'the firm earth,' the 'unmoving earth,' etc because as it goes round the sun it should be 'moving' and 'infirm.'

I was delighted with your letter insisting on 'intimacy' as the mark of fine literature. The contrary thing to this intimacy, which is another name for experience, life, is I believe 'generalization.' And generalization creates rhetoric, wins immediate popularity, organizes the mass, gives political success, Kipling's poetry, Macaulay's essays and so on. Life is never the same twice and so cannot be generalized. When you go from an Irish country district, where there are good manners, old songs, old stories and good talk, the folk mind, to an Irish country town, generalization meets one in music-hall songs with their mechanical rhythm, or in thoughts taken from the newspapers.

There is a chance of the Abbey players going to New York, and if they do I may have to go too though I hope not. We are now waiting the final decision of the New York manager. Yours

W B YEATS

TO J. B. YEATS

Oct 10, 1909   *Coole Park*

My dear Father, There is an unfinished letter to you on Lady Gregory's typewriter—I was dictating it, but she went to Dublin a week ago to start rehearsing her new play and to put down a quarrel between two of our players, a lovers' quarrel. Each one said that he or she would leave the company if the other did not stop his or her insults during rehearsals. It is always the way with the members of the company—when they are out, they are very much out. I have intended to write for a long while, though I think it is you who owe me a letter, but I have been in a dream trying to get my new play finished for Mrs. Campbell on Nov 1st. I have now abolished all my work on it for four months and started quite afresh and am as a result in the highest spirits, a scheme before it is carried out always seems so delightful. To-morrow I shall start on the new plan and to-day I have more leisure than I have had for weeks.

We had a great victory over the Viceroy.[1] Birrell [2] when he heard it I am told used violent language and said the whole Government had been made ridiculous. The real offender was the King, who is trying to make England moral and as a means is supporting the censor, calling actors before him and getting them to speak at the Royal Commission in favour of the censorship—or rather he was doing these things at the time—he was in communication with Aberdeen. He told them to stop *Blanco*. Bailey, the Land Commissioner, asked some man at the Castle what they thought of *Blanco* now and was told that 'no one at the Castle spoke to any other on that subject,' it was too painful. The theatre made a good deal of money and is supported now even by Sinn Fein. We are trying to get enough capital to buy out Miss Horniman and go on after 1910.

I think you may have thought I was not interested in your letter, because I did not reply to some criticism in it. The criticism interested me very greatly. It is just the sort of letter I delight in getting

---

[1] Much pressure had been brought to bear on the management of the Abbey Theatre by Dublin Castle to induce them to abandon the production of Shaw's *The Showing-Up of Blanco Posnet*, but they did not give way and the play was presented, with much success, on August 25, 1909. The full story may be read in Lady Gregory's *Our Irish Theatre*, 1913 (1914).

[2] The Rt. Hon. Augustine Birrell, K.C. (1850–1937), was Chief Secretary for Ireland from 1907 to 1916.

from you. How did the pastel of the girl whose sisters are married to French noblemen get on? I do not remember any pastels of yours. I agree with what you wrote about Russell. I think he has set his ideal in so vague and remote a heaven that he takes the thoughts of his followers off the technique of life, or leaves only their poorer thoughts for it. No one has ever come to anything under his influence. The poets he gathers begin with a little fire but grow worse and worse. I am still reading Balzac. I have only four or five of the forty volumes left to read. How he hates a vague man—there is a certain poet in one of his books, Canalis by name, who is Russell, without Russell's honest heart.

I shall go to Dublin in a few days and get to London in November when I shall give some lectures for the money's sake. I will then return to Dublin and take charge of the theatre, as this is its time of crisis. All depends on our getting the capital.

I met an American woman in London who said to me: 'Your father, we think, is the best talker in New York.'

I have found your two stories—they were among papers of Lady Gregory's. I must have lent them to her and asked her to read them. I send them to you. The one without a name is much the best, I think. Yours affectionately   W B YEATS

TO H. J. C. GRIERSON

Oct 12 [1909]   *Coole Park*

Dear Grierson: I enclose 5/– for Mrs. Taylor's book.[1] I wish I could have subscribed for more copies but my work on a play for Mrs. Campbell, which will not be paid for till it is finished, has left me very hard up.

I was greatly obliged to you for that long letter. You decided me not to try for the Professorship at all. It was a temptation but for me a wicked one. I work with so much difficulty, and can work so little once I am tired, that it would have stopped my writing, and I am only just beginning to feel I can express myself. The enthusiasm

[1] Probably *Rose and Vine* by Rachel Annand Taylor, published by Elkin Mathews in 1909.

of some young men was pushing me on, and without good reason I did not like to refuse.

We had an exciting week in Dublin with *Blanco Posnet* and our fight with the Castle and it has ended our quarrel with the extreme party over *Playboy* which started while I was with you. We are going to produce *Oedipus the King* early in the New Year with Murray Carson in chief part, as a further precedent of our freedom from the Lord Chamberlain who has forbidden the play.[1] Yours

W B YEATS

[1] Although it was planned to produce *Oedipus the King* about this time the play was not actually given at the Abbey Theatre until 1926. At the end of Yeats's last lecture tour in America the *New York Times* of January 15, 1933, published this note, to which he gave the title 'Plain Man's *Oedipus*.'

'When I first lectured in America thirty years ago, I heard at the University of Notre Dame that they had played *Oedipus the King*. That play was forbidden by the English censorship on the ground of its immorality; Oedipus commits incest; but if a Catholic university could perform it in America my own theatre could perform it in Ireland. Ireland had no censorship, and a successful performance might make her proud of her freedom, say even, perhaps, "I have an old historical religion moulded to the body of man like an old suit of clothes, and am therefore free."

'A friend of mine used to say that it was all a toss-up whether she seemed good or bad, for a decision firmly made before breakfast lasted three months. When I got back to Dublin I found a young Greek scholar who, unlike myself, had not forgotten his Greek, took out of a pigeonhole at the theatre a manuscript translation of *Oedipus* too complicated in its syntax for the stage, bought Jebb's translation and a translation published at a few pence for dishonest schoolboys. Whenever I could not understand the precise thoughts behind the translators' half Latin, half Victorian dignity, I got a bald translation from my Greek scholar. I spoke out every sentence, very often from the stage, with one sole object, that the words should sound natural and fall in their natural order, that every sentence should be a spoken, not a written sentence. Then when I had finished the dialogue in the rough and was still shrinking at the greater labour of the choruses, the English censor withdrew his ban and I lost interest.

'About five years ago my wife found the manuscript and set me to work again, and when the dialogue was revised and the choruses written, Lady Gregory and I went through it all, altering every sentence that might not be intelligible on the Blasket Islands. Have I made a plain man's *Oedipus*? The pit and gallery of the Abbey Theatre think so. When I say intelligible on the Blasket Islands I mean that, being an ignorant man, I may not have gone to Greece through a Latin mist. Greek literature, like old Irish literature, was founded upon belief, not like Latin literature upon documents. No man has ever prayed to or dreaded one of Vergil's nymphs, but when Oedipus at Colonus went into the Wood of the Furies he felt the same creeping in his flesh that an Irish countryman feels in certain haunted woods in Galway and in Sligo. At the Abbey Theatre we play both *Oedipus the King* and *Oedipus at Colonus*, and they seem at home there.'

TO LADY GREGORY

Friday [*Nov.* 26, 1909]   18 *Woburn Buildings*

My dear Lady Gregory: I saw first act of *Tinker's Wedding* [1] yesterday but could not stand any more—a most disgraceful performance, every poetical and literary quality sacrificed to continuous emphasis and restlessness—a meretricious stage moonlight scene and Mona Limerick (for whom we get some of the discredit or credit it seems) with a cockney pronunciation and a chocolate box make up. As I was going out in a rage I met a member of our Abbey audience and found him even angrier than I was. He had been denouncing it to the people round him. One interesting thing I did notice—the continual emphasis and change of note made the speeches inaudible, as they are in verse plays treated in the same way. This emphatic delivery and movement—which is the essence of the English idea of romantic acting—evidently fits nothing but plays written in short sentences without music or suggestion. I tried to analyse the general impression of vulgarity—and found it came either from this emphasis, from the necessary separation from life of players who had never seen the life they had to copy, or from a conventional standard of handsomeness—the thing they tied the tin can in was a spotless white sheet. I have not had such a sensation of blind fury in a theatre for fifteen years. Before the end of the opening dialogue, which Synge meant to be quiet, with the heaviness of roads in it, the feet of the tinkers must have trodden out some such measure as this.

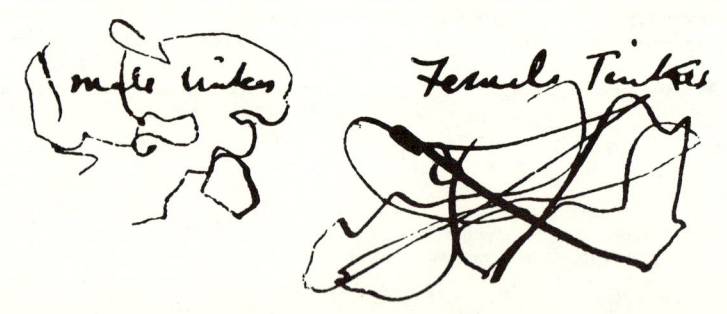

I am going to Cambridge on Wednesday next to see the performance of *The Wasps* with a view to *Oedipus*. I have gone through

[1] Some matinée performances of Synge's *The Tinker's Wedding* were given at His Majesty's Theatre, London, by the 'Afternoon Theatre' organization, beginning on November 11.

translations and find Jebb's much the best. I ordered it some days ago. It should have come by this. I ordered an edition used in a performance at Oxford, a performance in Greek I think—2/-. I will write about Mrs. Campbell later on. Yours   W B YEATS

I have just written to Mrs. Campbell refusing to consider Tree in writing my play. I have described his ideal of beauty as thrice vomited flesh.

TO J. B. YEATS[1]

November 29th 1909   18 *Woburn Buildings*

My dear Father: I'm here again in London, for the time. I came over to read my play to Mrs. Campbell. She wrote to me to come at 1.15, lunch and read it afterwards (this was yesterday week). I went and word was sent down with apologies she wasn't yet ready. On towards two she and lunch appeared. After lunch she listened, much interrupted by the parrot, to Act I with great enthusiasm. I was just starting Act II when a musician arrived, to play some incidental music she was to speak through in some forthcoming performance. She said: 'This won't delay me long, not more than ten minutes,' and then began an immense interminable quarrel with the musician about his music. After an hour and a half of this I said 'I think I had better go and put off an invitation to dinner I had for to-night.' She begged me to do so—full of apologies. I went away and returned at 6.30 just as the musician left. I then started Act II. A deaf man sat there whose mission was, it seemed, to say irrelevant enthusiastic things to Mrs. Campbell. I got through Act II well. Mrs. Campbell still enthusiastic. Then there came in telephone messages and I was asked to stay to dinner and read it afterwards. At dinner there was young Campbell and his wife and two other relations of hers, probably poor ones. After dinner arrived Mrs. Campbell's dressmaker, this would also take only a few minutes. Presently there was a mighty stir upstairs and somebody sent down in an excited way, like a messenger in a Greek Tragedy, to say that the dress was 6 inches too short in front. At half past ten there was a consultation in the

[1] Dictated.

drawing room as to whether somebody shouldn't go up and knock at Mrs. Campbell's door. It was decided that somebody should but everybody refused to be the one. I wanted to go home but I was told on no account must I do that. At half past 11 Mrs. Campbell came down, full of apologies, it would only be a few minutes longer. At twelve young Campbell's wife, who is an American heiress, and therefore independent, announced that she was going home and did, taking her husband. I sat on with the relations, whose business it seems was to entertain me. We sighed together at the amount it would cost us in taxi cabs to get home. At half past twelve Mrs. Campbell came in so tired that she had to lean on her daughter to get into the room. I said: 'This is absurd! You must go to your bed, and I must go home.' She said: 'No, I must hear the end of a play the same day as I hear the beginning.' I began to read. She did not know one word I was saying. She started to quarrel with me, because she supposed I had given a long speech which she wanted to a minor character and because of certain remarks which I applied to my heroine which she thought applied to her. She said at intervals, in an exasperated sleepy voice: 'No, I am not a slut and I do not like fools.' Finally I went home and I'm trying to find a halcyon day on which to read her the play again. I've even had to assure her by letter that it was not she but my heroine who liked fools.

I am dining out a great deal. I sat next the Prime Minister at a men's dinner party given by Edmund Gosse the other night. I started off rather badly, for Edmund Gosse whispered to me in the few minutes before dinner: 'Mind, no politics.' And then introduced me to Lord Cromer and Lord Cromer's first sentence was: 'We had a very interesting debate in the House of Lords this afternoon.' I being still wax under Gosse's finger replied: 'Oh I look on at English politics as a child does at a race course, taking sides by the colour of the jockeys' coats. And I often change sides in the middle of a race.' This rather chilled the conversation and somebody said to me presently: 'Lord Cromer is interested in nothing but politics.' I got on better with Asquith. I found him an exceedingly well read man, especially, curiously enough, in poetry. Not a man of really fine culture, I think, but exceedingly charming and well read. We talked a good deal about Ireland and the new University and education. I told him how I had met a girl of 12 in a railway carriage who had never heard of Gladstone or Parnell, and he said that comes from bad education. Presently he said: 'I see you've had a lively time over Shaw's play and that the state of things is so perfect in Dublin that we need not bring it under the censorship.' He meant this as a compliment, for we had, of course, to fight the censorship, and the report of the Commission, so far as it touches on Ireland, supports us in having done so. Then he began asking about anti-clericalism in Dublin.

I've also been meeting lately General Ian Hamilton, a man of the really finest culture, as fine as that of anybody I've ever met. A very gentle person, and his friends say of him that he is the greatest soldier in the English army.

Next Sunday the Abbey Company does *Blanco* for the Stage Society. I think it will be a fine performance and it will help our reputation. Yours   W B YEATS

TO LADY GREGORY

Thursday [*December* 9, 1909]   18 *Woburn Buildings*

My dear Lady Gregory: I have got my MS back from Scotland Yard. I was getting anxious—I thought Mrs. Campbell was off it but I saw her last night at *The Blue Bird*, and she seemed as eager as ever. *Blanco* was a really great success, and everybody commends the acting.[1] On Tuesday I forgot about the papers until evening and so only saw the evening ones, which were all one could wish. I have had a letter of thanks from the Stage Society sec who encloses programmes (I send some).

Last night Mrs. Meeking and Miss Tobin took me to the first night of *The Blue Bird*. I thought it very bad, but that it might have a popular success in the wake of *Peter Pan*. There were great things, an excellent cat and dog who quarrelled always and a delightful personification of sugar but my chief impression was of a rather meretricious pantomime. The audience was delighted for they had expected a masterpiece and boredom. I have not read the play and so do not know if it is as poor as it seemed, a mere libretto for the

[1] The Abbey Theatre company had given two performances of Bernard Shaw's *The Showing-Up of Blanco Posnet* for the Stage Society on December 5 and 6, 1909. The play was, at that time, still unlicensed by the Lord Chamberlain for public performance in England.

scene painter with here and there a pretentious piece of traditional poetry. It is probably another of the gasping things Maeterlinck, struggling well beyond his nature, does to please his wife, who was there last night, in a red turban, looking like Messalina. I amused somebody by saying that Maeterlinck was like a little boy who has jumped up behind a taxi cab and can't get off.

I am gradually getting my clothes in order but only just in time. When I got home last night my dress trousers had gone all over like the dog cart in some poem of Wendell Holmes's [1] that was so well made that it lasted many years and then fell to powder—all parts had been equally strong. Bullen promises if he gets through his troubles —it was, as I thought, the binders not being paid had refused to work—to let me have a £100 for sales and on account. This will leave me £30 after paying Miss H[orniman]. He showed me a letter from Whibley saying that Harmsworth has no doubt of getting the money to buy him for the nation—meanwhile Budget stops all.[2]

Miss Tobin told me the other day that Gosse has asked her to sound me as to my getting a government pension. He has said very generously 'We cannot neglect our greatest poet.' Miss Tobin told him that she knew I felt it impossible to accept anything from government owing to Irish conditions.

My days are full of all sorts of nothing—visits to Scotland Yard about MS., to shops, to friends and till Sunday to rehearsals, but now that the MS is back I shall go to work.

How about Coole? Is it let? I wish you were coming to London.
Yours
                                                                W B YEATS

TO LADY GREGORY

Friday [*December* 10, 1909]   18 *Woburn Buildings*

My dear Lady Gregory: I did not realize that you were alone at Coole —it is gloomy weather to be alone anywhere even in London . . .

I will write to-day to [Murray] Carson and try to get things

---

[1] 'The Deacon's Masterpiece: or, The Wonderful "One-Hoss Shay."'
[2] Bullen was hoping to get the Shakespeare Head Press at Stratford-on-Avon endowed as a permanent Shakespeare memorial and expected help from Lord Northcliffe, but after many delays his scheme had to be given up. The Press was eventually acquired by Messrs. B. H. Blackwell of Oxford.

settled. I have been trying for more copies of the Jebb but do not yet know if I can get them—1/- copies. There is a metrical version of the choruses given, and the notes state that Stanford has done music, but I suppose we had better stick to O'Brien. If we do, it makes it desirable that he should justify himself by making it as good speech as he can or he will hardly beat Stanford as a musician. Which reminds me that this queer creature Ezra Pound, who has become really a great authority on the troubadours, has I think got closer to the right sort of music for poetry than Mrs. Emery—it is more definitely music with strongly marked time and yet it is effective speech. However he can't sing as he has no voice. It is like something on a very bad phonograph. A German or Hungarian theatrical agent is reading my plays—Shaw recommends him with a view to taking them for the German and Hungarian markets—but he wants a press-cutting for each of the plays. I have recommended to him (1) *Deirdre* (2) *King's Threshold* (3) *Kathleen ni Houlihan* (4) *Hour-Glass*. Have you the books? I am sorry to give you this job but I have only the books with opinion on my non-dramatic work. There was an article in *Pall Mall* or *Westminster* (last June) that said *Deirdre* 'kept one breathless' or some such phrase. And Archer wrote in a word about *King's Threshold*.

Did I leave a trouser stretcher in my room at Coole—in the cupboard I think? Could I have it sent? I have gone to a cheap place I used to go to long ago (though to the Stores for the dress ones) and got several pairs and it will keep them in order.

I have just got a letter (from some American schoolgirls inviting me to Masque in U.S.A.) addressed 'Mr. Yeats, Ireland,' re-addressed 'Opera House Cork,' re-addressed from there 'Dublin Theater (note spelling) Dublin' and sent here from the Abbey. I have not been able to call at the Birchs'.[1] I shall do so next Monday and arrange about lectures if I can. I have been rather afraid of critical eyes with my clothes but now I am safe. I have just got an invitation from Gosse to lunch with him next Thursday at the House of Lords. I wonder what he is at? I hear he was very pleased with me at his dinner party—says I kept things going.

[1] Una Birch, daughter of Sir Arthur Birch. She married Major-General L. H. R. Pope-Hennessy in 1910. She was the author of various works including lives of Walter Scott, Edgar Allan Poe, Charles Dickens and Charles Kingsley. She was created D.B.E. in 1920, and died in 1949.

I saw an ordinary sort of melodrama last night called *The House Opposite*.[1] I liked it much better than *The Blue Bird* which I hate even more in memory than at the time.

I saw Miss H[orniman] yesterday, she was very cross because we had not submitted to her our second statement. I thought her unusually mad.

I did not say I think that I saw Mrs. Campbell in [? at] *Blue Bird*—I must say she seemed as eager as ever about the play. I had thought she was off it. Yours   W B YEATS

TO LADY GREGORY

Monday [*December* 13, 1909]   18 *Woburn Buildings*

My dear Lady Gregory . . . Yesterday I had a serious talk with Miss Tobin about the Civil List pension, which would it seems be £150. I imagine I am to speak of it to Gosse on Thursday. I think he has asked me for the purpose, perhaps even that it was with some such kind purpose he got me to meet the Prime Minister. I said to Miss Tobin again that I don't want to be wilfully poor but that no Irishman in my position could accept anything from the government which limited his political freedom, no matter how little he wished to use that freedom. Gosse it seems says it would not, but Miss Tobin I think shares my doubts as to its being possible. I am afraid it comes from the King's privy purse but I do not know for certain. It is difficult for me to speak of the Nobel prize but I may see a chance of doing so. Yours   W B YEATS

TO LADY GREGORY

26 *Dec* [1909]   18 *Woburn Buildings*

My dear Lady Gregory: I dined last night with Gosse—Sickert the painter was there. I managed to say to Gosse 'I want to have a talk.' He said 'I know but let it be later on—nothing can be done during the present political excitement.' Miss Tobin told me some days ago that she thought it could certainly be got if I would take it but

[1] By Perceval Landon, produced at the Queen's Theatre, London, on November 20.

Gosse said we must mention it to nobody as a newspaper paragraph would ruin all. I have come to think I would like it without inconsistency if Gosse repeats to me what he said to her about one's being bound in nothing. Justin McCarthy had it—but I confess I still have some moments of doubt and I am glad the thing is put off. I will send *The Land of Heart's Desire* (enough copies) when the typist's over again. *Golden Helmet* is finished and I am copying it out...

I find a lot of little things to alter, to copy out *Golden Helmet*. I am working well again—I hope you are free of headache.

I have just had a letter from my father wanting to borrow five pounds to help pay the rent of his studio in Dublin, Jack to give another five.[1] He says it would be such a triumph for Sir Thomas Drew if he was evicted. I have not yet answered but can't see where I am to get the £5. Yours

W B YEATS

TO LADY GREGORY

Wednesday [*Postmark Jan* 5, 1910]   18 *Woburn Buildings*

My dear Lady Gregory: I have had a bad cold—it started Sunday morning, and I am only just getting my brain to work again. That is why I have not written. However I will come to Ireland next week and take my share of the burden. I also want to show you *Golden Helmet* and see if it is good enough to publish somewhere...

I enclose a letter of Craig's which explains itself. He is to dine here on Friday to meet Binyon. He wants to get the Print Room to take a series of designs (not plans but drawings and effects) of the new 'invention' as a record. I have not asked Ricketts (whom I can see he suspects of stealing his thunder) and Binyon does not know what he is in for. If we are to get this design I may be anxious to put off *King's Threshold* till we can use it but I will try and get a date from Craig. He may prefer to wait too long—say until our future is secure. I am inclined to get his advice on all our scenic difficulties —perhaps to come to Dublin for the purpose. It would be a fine

[1] J. B. Yeats had gone to America on a visit in the previous year. Evidently he had still at this time an intention to return to Dublin, but as time went on, although his family often pressed him to come back, he grew more and more attached to his life in New York, and eventually died there in 1922 without revisiting Ireland.

new start for us and put a new force in much that we do. It would not prevent Robert designing but would give us all the mechanism —a mountain to put our mountain on.

I am still stupid with the cold. Yours　　　　　W B YEATS

TO LADY GREGORY

Saturday [*Postmark January* 8, 1910]　　　18 *Woburn Buildings*

My dear Lady Gregory: Yes, I shall arrive on Tuesday night and look you up at the Nassau or Theatre by 11 next day. I am still heavy with influenza but getting better, as I know from having improved a lyric in *Golden Helmet* this morning. Emer's song which is now quite good.

Craig dined with me last night and after Binyon had gone made drawings etc and explained further his 'place' or whatever one should call his invention. I am to see his model on Monday at 5—I think I shall, if it seems right, order one for us (this will cost he says about £2 for material and about £4 for the man's time). I asked if we would get his scene in time for *Oedipus* but he wants us to play about with his model first and master its effects. If we accept the invention I must agree, he says, to use it for all my poetical work in the future. I would gladly agree. I now think from what he told me that a certain modification will give us an entirely adequate open air scene. That we shall have a means of staging everything that is not naturalistic, and that out of his invention may grow a completely new method even for our naturalistic plays. I think we could get rid of side scenes even for naturalistic plays. I am writing in the British Museum where I have been trying to read Swinburne. Even the things that once excited me beyond measure seem to me mere rhetoric, but I know I must be deceived—I suppose that one tires of all abundant things.

I think you will like *Golden Helmet* now. It has got some passion in it at last. I have not touched the long play but will come to it fresh from being so long off it. Yours　　　　　W B YEATS

TO LADY GREGORY[1]

January 24th, 1910 *Abbey Theatre*

My dear Lady Gregory . . . Last night George Moore read out to me the chapter in his Autobiography about the dinner at the Shelbourne,[2] it was amusing, *very* bitter about T. P. Gill, quite amiable though inaccurate about myself and enthusiastic about Russell. It was very journalistic in style but if the book is what he describes, it will probably help us rather than otherwise. There was a very amusing description of Professor Tyrrell's conversation at dinner which was it seems all about 'mutton cutlets, whiskey and Guiness's stout;' he turns him into a kind of worldly chorus. He does not name him, in fact I doubt his committing many indiscretions except about Edward Martyn and his brother with whom he quarrels in the book perpetually about Catholicism. He wants to write a play founded on *Esther Waters* but the scene to be laid in Ireland. He is in a state of triumphant delight because he has discovered that his family were Protestants until his grandfather turned Catholic in order to trade in Spain, the book is to wind up with a violent repudiation of Sir Thomas More from whom the family are supposed to be descended. Yours W B YEATS

TO J. B. YEATS[1]

February 16th, 1910 *Fairfield*
 Glasnevin

My dear Father, I got your letter just after I had taken charge of the Abbey again and as I was setting out on a very busy period, that is why I have not answered you before. I thought your letter most wonderful, it came at a moment when I was busy with an almost similar problem and it clarified my thought a great deal, in fact I may read some of it—I conclude you will not mind—at the end of a lecture I am to give in a private drawing-room in London next

[1] Dictated.
[2] George Moore's account of this dinner, given after the first productions of the Irish Literary Theatre in 1899, appears in Chapter IV of *Ave*, the first volume of the trilogy *Hail and Farewell*. The passage about 'mutton cutlets, whiskey and Guiness's stout' does not appear in the printed version.

month. The lecture is on Contemporary Poetry, a vague name chosen before I knew what the lecture was going to be about. I am describing the group of poets that met at the Rhymers' Club, more especially Ernest Dowson. The doctrine of the group, or rather of the majority of it, was that lyric poetry should be personal. That a man should express his life and do this without shame or fear. Ernest Dowson did this and became a most extraordinary poet, one feels the pressure of his life behind every line as if he were a character in a play of Shakespeare's. Johnson had no theories of any sort but came to do much the same through the example of Dowson and others and because his life grew gradually so tragic that it filled his thoughts. His theory was rather impersonality so far as he had any, I should say. In poetry the antithesis to personality is not so much will as an ever growing burden of noble attitudes and literary words. The noble attitudes are imposed upon the poet by papers like the *Spectator* and any

[*The rest of this letter is missing.*]

TO J. B. YEATS [1]

February 23rd, 1910   *Abbey Theatre*

My dear Father, I have just finished dictating a first sketch of my lecture in London, it is on the dialect drama with Synge as the principal figure. All three lectures have worked themselves out as a plea for uniting literature once more to personality, the personality of the writer in lyric poetry or with imaginative personalities in drama. The only ground on which I differ from you is that I look upon character and personality as different things or perhaps different forms of the same thing. Juliet has personality, her Nurse has character. I look upon personality as the individual form of our passions (Dowson's in his poetry or Byron in *Manfred* or Forbes-Robertson in a romantic part have all personality but we do not necessarily know much about their characters). Character belongs I think to Comedy, but all that's rather a long story and is connected with a whole mass of definitions.

[1] Dictated.

I probably get the distinction from the stage, where we say a man is a 'character actor' meaning that he builds up a part out of observation, or we say that he is 'an emotional actor' meaning that he builds it up out of himself, and in this last case—we always add, if he is not commonplace—that he has personality. Of course Shakespeare has both because he is always a tragic comedian.

In the process of writing my third lecture I found it led up to the thought of your letter which I am going to quote at the end. It has made me realize with some surprise how fully my philosophy of life has been inherited from you in all but its details and applications. What I want you to tell me

[*The rest of this letter is missing.*]

TO EDMUND GOSSE

April 12 [*in pencil* 1910] 18 *Woburn Buildings*

My dear Gosse: Of course I accept and am flattered at being asked to do so. An English Academy [1] would save us, perhaps, from the journalists, who wish to be men of letters, and the men of letters who have become journalists. I shall have to be in Manchester on Sunday, I think, or I would have called on you to hear some details, but my players are at Manchester and want me. This is the first generation in which the spirit of literature has been conquered by the spirit of the press, of hurry, of immediate interests, and Bernard Shaw is the Joseph whose prosperity has brought his bretheren into captivity. Yours W B YEATS

[1] Evan Charteris, in his Life of Gosse, quotes at length a letter from Gosse to Thomas Hardy, dated February 13, 1910, in which he outlines the constitution of the proposed English Academy of Letters. There were to be 30 original members, who would co-opt colleagues, leisurely, up to the number of 40; the system was to follow that of the Académie Française; history, philosophy, poetry, literary history, the novel and the drama were to be represented as proportionately as possible; and the only objects paramount were to be the preservation of the purity of the language and a high standard of style. The original members were Alfred Austin, Laurence Binyon, A. C. Bradley, Robert Bridges, S. H. Butcher, Joseph Conrad, W. J. Courthope, Austin Dobson, J. G. Frazer, Edmund Gosse, R. B. Haldane, Thomas Hardy, Henry James, W. P. Ker, Andrew Lang, Sir Alfred Lyall, J. W. Mackail, Viscount Morley, Gilbert Murray, Henry Newbolt, E. H. Pember, Sir Arthur Pinero, George W. Prothero, Walter Raleigh, George M. Trevelyan, A. W. Verrall and W. B. Yeats.

TO A. H. BULLEN

Thursday [? 1910]   18 *Woburn Buildings*

Dear Bullen: I like the thought of the book of selections [1] very much but it should not come out until after October that my new book may be among things selected from.

    Can you send me by return to Jury's Hotel Dublin 2 copies of my bibliography by Wade? They may be useful in this professorship affair.[2] I shall be in Dublin only one day but may see a couple of supporters. Yours   W B YEATS

TO EDMUND GOSSE

[Aug 10, 1910—not dated by Yeats]   *Coole Park*

My dear Gosse: I have just received a letter from the Prime Minister's sec sent on from my London address. I have been granted a pension [of] £150. I thank you for what will set me free from a continual anxiety and permit me to do only the work I am most fitted for. But for you I would never have even thought of such a thing, for since a project of the kind some ten years ago, I had put it altogether from my mind. You have taken much trouble and given much thought for my freedom and my wellbeing and I am grateful and always shall be. I cannot write more for the servant has come for the letters. I should have written earlier in the day but I have celebrated the event by a day's fishing, the first holiday for a long time. Yours   W B YEATS

TO SYDNEY COCKERELL

Sept 22nd, 1910   *Abbey Theatre*

Dear Cockerell, I did not send you the enclosed manuscript because I did not like to do so till the essay was in print. I was afraid I might

---

[1] The suggested book of selections did not appear. The new book mentioned must have been *The Green Helmet and other Poems*, printed by the Cuala Press in September 1910, though not actually issued until December.

[2] There had been a suggestion that Yeats should succeed Edward Dowden in the Chair of English Literature at Trinity College, Dublin.

have to refer to it. I had put some manuscript aside for you in London but of course that is out of my reach at present. Please do not try to read this essay on tragic drama. I could not even do that myself for my writing gets illegible to me in about a fortnight after I have written it.

Many thanks for the enquiries you made for me about the Professorship of Poetry. I am beginning to think I had better keep to my wandering life. I long for a life without dates and without any settled abode. If I could find that I could write lyrics again. Yours ever   W B YEATS

TO LILY YEATS

Sunday [*Postmark Sept* 25, 1910]   *Coole Park*

My dear Lilly: I returned here yesterday and found your very tragic letters.[1] I had heard that there was no hope from Lolly when I was in Dublin, and to-day Lolly sends on to me your letter written on Friday. I wish he had had a better life. He has a strongly religious nature and that must give him courage and peace. Mary Battle's death must have made his last two or three years very lonely.

It must be a heavy strain upon you.

It is a curious thing that George, who complained so much when well, has always been brave and calm before real calamity. It was just the same when he was ill in London that time. He was always cheerful and dignified and uncomplaining. Lady Gregory who used to go and see him remembers that and spoke of it to-day. Yours affectionately   W B YEATS

TO LILY YEATS

Monday [*Postmark Sept* 26, 1910]   *Coole Park*

My dear Lilly: That I feel George's death very much I need not say to you—I knew his mind so well and for long had so many activities in common with him.

[1] This letter and the next refer to the last illness and death of Yeats's uncle George Pollexfen to whom he was greatly devoted.

I shall go to Sligo tomorrow—I think there is a train about 12 but do not yet know for certain. I shall go to the Imperial Hotel for the night.

I am glad the Banshee cried—it seems a fitting thing. He had one of those instinctive natures that are close to the supernatural. Yours affectionately   W B YEATS

TO LADY GREGORY

Wednesday [Sept. 28, 1910]   *Imperial Hotel*
                                                                                          Sligo

My dear Lady Gregory: I write while I am waiting to start for the funeral—I think there is much real sorrow. My sister told me last night that all day the workmen and pilots were coming. They all used the same phrase—they had come to see 'Master George'—(their imagination going back to the time when his father lived) then they would say 'I have been thirty years' or 'I have been forty years' or whatever it was 'in the firm.' On the way here my uncle's man met me and walked beside me. He called me 'Mr Willy' and repeated his lamentation over and over: 'I have been thirty years in the firm—I have lost my poor friend. Rich or poor it was all the same to him. I thought he would be there always and now he has gone away I have lost my poor friend.'

Jack is here. He has just been telling me that it will be a harder rule now—Belfast rule. That George knew every man in his employ and had the gift of getting discipline without ever being harsh. That men would be let back, after a time, if they had done wrong and so on. That he would, as it were, degrade a carter to the ranks. He would take his whip from him and hang it on his wall—and then when the man was penitent give it back and the workmen understood this way and liked it. Every case decided as an individual case and with sympathy. Now if a man goes he will go forever.

Arthur Jackson told last night how he tried for a long time in vain to get George to come up from Rosses Point in the motor instead of the public car, but that presently he found that George liked talking to the old women on the car and helping them up and down.

Lily heard the Banshee as well as the nurse. He died the night after at the same hour the Banshee had cried at. Yours

W B YEATS

TO LADY GREGORY

Thursday [*Sept.* 29, 1910]   *Nassau Hotel*

My dear Lady Gregory: I have just got to Dublin and am tired out with the strain. I found it hard to see George's house again, every detail as it was when I stayed with him and worked at Astrology. The funeral was very touching—the church full of the working people, Catholics who had never been in a Protestant church before, and the man next me crying all the time. I thought of Synge's funeral—none at that, after some two or three, but enemies [1] or conventional images of gloom. The Masons (there were 80 of them) had their own service and one by one threw acacia leaves into the grave with the traditional Masonic goodbye 'Alas my brother so mote it be.' Then there came two who threw each a white rose, and that was because they and he were 'Priori Masons,' a high degree of Masonry. It was as George would have wished it for he loved form and ceremony. Last night when I was coming away Arthur Jackson took me aside and told me that he did not know the contents of the will but that he had been made executor and that there was enough money 'for all to have something.' He then told me how, when I first stayed with George,—at least I think that was the date he said—George was worried at the thought that he had nothing. He had lost all his money except [£]10,000 which was in the firm. Jackson saw this and refused to take anything for himself till George was able to take out his [£]10,000 and invest it. He thought this would restore to George the feeling of security. He was anxious that I should know that he had always spared George in every way and left him free for other things than business. George has left £50,000 now. Jackson said George was very much surprised lately when he told him he had so much. It is I believe almost the exact sum he had lost. Jackson

---

[1] Yeats had noted in his diary the names of those people attending Synge's funeral who had been inimical to him during his lifetime. The passage is printed in *The Death of Synge*, section XIV, the names being concealed under letters of the alphabet, and is included in *Dramatis Personae*, 1936.

talked as if he believed we had been left money but evidently knew nothing. I imagine that the money will be divided among many, something for all who had even a distant claim. I do not think Jack was right in what he said to me about the harsh rule that would come now. Jackson impressed me with his force and his kindness —what he will lack is George's patient tolerance of human nature and so he will not be loved as he was loved . . . Yours

W B YEATS

TO LADY GREGORY

Friday [*Postmark October* 21, 1910]   18 *Woburn Buildings*

My dear Lady Gregory: What did Robert think of the designs? I am going to show them to Ricketts to-night. We were right about the pupils as you see. I am very much excited by the thought of putting the fool into a mask and rather amused at the idea of an angel in a golden domino. I should have to write some words into the play. 'They fear to meet the eyes of men being too pure for mortal gaze' or the like. Craig evidently wants to keep what is supernatural from being inhuman. If the masks work right I would put the fool and the blind man in *Baile's Strand* into masks. It would give a wildness and extravagance that would be fine. I should also like the Abbey to be the first modern theatre to use the mask.

I have been to two plays, *Speckled Band*[1] by Conan Doyle and *Grace*[2] by Somerset Maugham, both very bad, and am working well. I have written each morning and, as if I were at Coole, begun at 11. Yours

W B YEATS

TO J. B. YEATS

Nov 24 [1910]   *Nassau Hotel*

My dear Father: I have just finished a lecture tour—Manchester, Leeds, Liverpool, Harrogate—and at Liverpool Oliver Elton was in the audience and said to me afterwards 'I heard the voice of

---
[1] Produced at the Adelphi Theatre, London, June 4.
[2] Produced at the Duke of York's Theatre, London, October 15.

J. B. Y.' I had spoken of the old writers as busy with their own sins and of the new writers as busy with other people's. I had put Shakespeare among the old writers and Milton with the new. I have had great audiences. Part of my object was to help the theatre to audiences when it goes on tour. I am now in Dublin working at the Craig scenery and seeing the lawyers etc with Lady Gregory in connection with the new patent. The Craig scenery will give us a very strange and beautiful stage. He has designed all the costumes and scene for a new production of *The Hour-Glass*. Given one of the characters a mask in the old Italian way. I shall get all my plays into the Craig scene and a new one of Lady Gregory's which is a symbolical play ostensibly about Moses really about Parnell.[1]

Yesterday our patent application was heard by the Solicitor General. The Theatre of Ireland appeared by counsel and asked that a clause be put into our patent directing us to let the Abbey to them at 40 per cent less than anybody else because they had similar aims. The Solicitor General said they were attempting to get something they had not paid for! Meanwhile Miss Walker has returned to the Abbey and had a success in a play called *The Shuiler's Child*.[2] We are getting good audiences and are even fashionable. My own new play goes on very slowly, interrupted by lectures and business—and indeed you can see by this letter that I have not another thought than business in my head. To-morrow Lady Gregory and I dine with Prof. Tyrrell. There is a question of my some day taking Dowden's place but I know little yet of what the work would be and have my sight as well as my own creative work to think of. The chief matter however is that I feel bound in honour to give the authorities full information about my eyesight, which compels me to dictate and be read to as much as possible. If I am offered the post I shall have to ask assistance and this they may not be able to give. I have been talking things over with Oliver Elton. I am not very anxious one way or the other but would I think like the work and I know I would like rooms in College. Do not speak of the matter, for the whole thing, as Dowden's health may improve, is hypothetical. Yours affectionately   W B YEATS

[1] *The Deliverer* by Lady Gregory, produced at the Abbey Theatre, January 12, 1911.
[2] By Seumas O'Kelly, produced at the Abbey Theatre, November 24, 1910.

TO EDMUND GOSSE

Jan 17 [1911] 18 *Woburn Buildings*

My dear Gosse: Sturge Moore published a story in the *English Review* in January [1] and the Vigilance Society is threatening a prosecution. Harrison [2] says he may have to go to prison and Moore has written to me and asked me to see you about it. He in fact appeals to the Academic Committee. I have not yet seen the story, but will to-day, so I know nothing yet of the rights of the case. Will you be in on Sunday so that I may see you if it seems a matter for private or official action? The worst of the matter is that I have a possible big theatrical dispute on my hands and may have to go to Manchester on Monday or Tuesday. Yours W B YEATS

TO EDMUND GOSSE

Thursday [*Jan.* 19, 1911] 18 *Woburn Buildings*
[*Postmark Jan* 20, 1911]

Dear Gosse: I have got from the office of the *English Review* a copy with the passage attacked marked. It is an attack on the most ordinary freedom of language, on the right to use the natural word. I cannot imagine any question more entirely the business of our committee. Thomas Hardy has I hear offered help. My only fear is that the Vigilance Committee will not dare to go on.[3] Yours
W B YEATS

TO SYDNEY COCKERELL

March 6th, 1911 18 *Woburn Buildings*

Dear Cockerell, My article on the Tragic Theatre appeared in the last number but one of the *Mask*. I shall reprint it, or part of it, as

[1] 'A Platonic Marriage' by T. Sturge Moore was published in the *English Review*, January 1911. It is difficult to discover what even the most prurient-minded could have found objectionable in this delicate fantasy.
[2] Austin Harrison, editor of the *English Review*.
[3] Nothing more happened. See Yeats's letter to Sturge Moore, January 24, 1911 in *W. B. Yeats and Sturge Moore: their Correspondence* and the editor's note thereon.

the introduction to a new edition of my Plays. If you want the *Mask* you will have to write to the Publisher of the *Mask*, Arena Goldoni, Florence.

I thank you very much for your good offices in the matter of that Professorship. They are still running me for Dowden's place in Dublin. I went to see Mahaffy to tell him that the state of my sight kept me from using my eyes for more than say a couple of hours in the day for a good part of the year, and that I had therefore to be read out to. I think I was needlessly despondent about my sight, but it was very bad just then and I thought it honest to tell him. His answer amused me very much. He said: 'It has been of great value to this University having Professor Dowden associated with it, because he has a reputation as a scholar; but he has been teaching here for thirty years and hasn't done a pennyworth of good to anybody. Literature is not a subject for tuition!' From which I gather that the less work I did the better pleased everybody would be. It seemed to me a very ideal state of things. I had always heard that the Fellows were jealous of Dowden—I do not know if that has anything to do with it. My great objection to taking it is having to live in Dublin during so much of the year, for after all, even if it were but for conscience' sake, I should have to do the work.

Are you ever in London? I believe I shall be in every Monday now for some time. Up to this I have been continually flitting to Dublin. Yours ever   W B YEATS

TO EDMUND GOSSE

Monday [? March 27, 1911]   18 *Woburn Buildings*

Dear Gosse: I have just read Mrs. Ward (I sent for *The Times* on getting your note).[1] I think we should leave her alone for the moment at any rate. It may be another matter if she starts a controversy and others join in. The attack is chiefly on the Society of Authors. I should think that her motive is quite plain enough to keep her from influencing anybody, nor can I imagine anybody wanting an Academy elected of the two organizations. We must be

[1] A letter from Mrs. Humphry Ward attacking the management of the Society of Authors was printed in *The Times*, March 27.

judged by the authority inherent in us, because we are ourselves, not because of them that picked us. Had we been picked by George Vth or by the Independent Labour Party we had been no more and no less. Another reason for silence is that it is rather hard to defend the exclusion of women without saying ungracious things. Haldane's speech will show that we are not abashed. Yours W B YEATS

I go to Ireland on Wednesday for a few days.

TO J. B. YEATS [1]

May 9th, 1911   18 *Woburn Buildings*

My dear Father, I got your letter in Paris but could not write then for Lady Gregory was there and friends of hers, and we were very busy. I got rather out of sorts, and went there for a rest as I knew so few people in Paris I would not find it distracting. Finding myself unfitted for verse, which is always a strain, I started with Lady Gregory putting into final shape the big book on Fairy Belief that we have been doing for years.[2] My part is to show that what we call Fairy Belief is exactly the same thing as English and American spiritism except that Fairy Belief is very much more charming. Now I am quite well again and back in London writing verse. I thought your letter beautiful and profound. I read it out to Lady Gregory and the friends who were with her, that is to say Pope-Hennessy and his wife, Una Birch that was. I think it interested Pope-Hennessy. He is in what they call the Staff College and will probably have high command in the Army for he is very able. He was in France studying the Campaign of 1870. He is a great hater of German methods and admirer of French. The French, he says, will win the next war. He says that the Germans aim at

[*The rest of this letter is missing.*]

[1] Dictated.
[2] *Visions and Beliefs in the West of Ireland*, a collection of folklore which grew out of the essays Yeats had contributed to several English reviews between 1897 and 1901, finally appeared in Lady Gregory's name only, with notes and two essays by Yeats; the book was not actually published until 1920.

TO J. B. YEATS[1]

July 17, 1911   18 *Woburn Buildings*

My dear Father, I am not quite sure whether I answered your last letter or not. The last six weeks have been full of business with the players here and an American tour being arranged. All that is now finished and on Wednesday I go to Dublin in time for Ruth's [2] wedding and then to Galway to do some work, for I must soon start for America. The Company are expected to open, either in Boston or New York, about September 25th. I go out before them. Arrive about a fortnight before they do and probably stay for their first week. We have got fairly good terms, a guarantee of all expenses and 35 per cent of the profits. Slightly better terms for next year, and after that if we have had a success we can make terms where we please, I mean that we are free of the agents, who are now taking us out. The Company has been making money even for the last few months, though of course Lady Gregory and I take none of it.

I have just come from lunching with Mrs. Asquith. Her house in Downing Street is an interesting old house, full of uninteresting copies of famous pictures. I was next Mrs. Asquith, who asked me a lot of questions about Lady Gregory. She said to me 'I am told that she is quite simple and yet always such a great personage.' I didn't think Mrs. Asquith herself had much capacity, but she was interested in everything. I had also some talk with Sir Edward Grey. Every afternoon I go to Hugh Lane's, he has a wonderful old house in Chelsea, full, of course, of pictures. Lady Gregory is staying there, and we do there our theatre business. We are planning a second Company to take the place of the first when it is away.

You tell me in your last letter that you are introducing to me two ladies who want to study the theatre in Ireland, but you don't tell me who they are, probably I shall be in New York before they are in Ireland. Neither have I received *Blossoming Bough* [3] with your portrait of the author. I wonder will I write to the author when

---

[1] Dictated.
[2] Ruth Pollexfen. She was a cousin, and Yeats was best man at her wedding to Charles Lane-Poole of St. Columba's College, Rathfarnham, County Dublin.
[3] The title of this book was *The Blossomy Bough*. Poems by Shaemus O Sheel. It was published by the author through the Franklin Press, New York, in 1911. The ordinary edition had no portrait, but there was a special edition of 100 signed and numbered copies on vellum paper, having as frontispiece a small reproduction of a pencil portrait of the author signed J. B. Yeats 1910.

I do get it? I think a man who tried to commit suicide 'because some girls had proved unworthy of his esteem' must have delightful capacity for abstract affection. It is like dying on a barricade for humanity.

We gave a public dinner to Gordon Craig last night with Rothenstein in the chair. I was to have been the chairman and was on all the tickets, but at the last moment they sent me a toast list by which I discovered that I should have to propose the King's health and that was impossible, as Lady Gregory and I have only held our movement together by insisting that nobody in England ever thinks of proposing such a toast at a gathering which has an exclusively artistic object.[1] At last we have got all parties to accept this and Unionist and Nationalist are quite peaceful with each other, and various viceroys have very good-humouredly accepted the fact there was no God Save the King at the Abbey. We both, for Lady Gregory was even more urgent about it than I was, felt that it would be impossible to go back to Ireland having admitted the contrary. If the fact gets into the papers I am quite certain to have no chance for the Trinity professorship, but I am not sure that I want it.

Send me anything you write. I want very much to see your essay on the American woman. I am sorry to hear what you tell me about Edwin Ellis. I have heard nothing about him for years. Some twelve years ago, I went to see him in Paris and realized with a shock how intolerable his wife was. Sometimes, when one has not seen a person for years, one goes back to them and realises that there is some burden there which one can never take up again, though it did not seem too heavy once. I think he felt my hostility to her.

—— —— has not been a success in comedy with us. Her body has lost all mobility. It never had very much, but what it had is gone. We are not taking her to America, and I think this is a great disappointment to her. We want somebody who can take Miss O'Neill's or Miss Allgood's place when they are ill, and that she cannot do. We will, however, use her in Dublin in some poetical production during the absence of the main Company. Yours

W B YEATS

[1] Although he was not in the chair at the dinner given to Gordon Craig at the Café Royal, London, on July 16, Yeats made a brilliant speech in defence of artists.

TO MISS E. M. LISTER

July 28 [1911] *Coole Park*

Dear Miss Lister: There has been so much to do in connection with this American tour that I have neglected your letter. I will try and send you new note for *Green Helmet* so that you will get it on Monday. I thought you had it. There is no need to print the whole story of 'The Priest's Soul.' If Mr. Bullen will put a sentence in about the source of the story and send it with proof of note on staging that may save trouble.

I enclose a note from 'Boy Scouts' organization which explains itself. Do what you think best. Imagine 'Innisfree' as a marching song—poor island.[1]

I enclose a note just received from Unwin. The arrangement with him has had to be that he makes the business arrangements and sends you half the fee, for musical rights as distinguished from the right to print the words. It is all the state of the law enables me to get out of him.

Have you any waste sheets of 'Literature and Tradition' in Vol 8 of collected edition? If Mr. Bullen does not think it would injure the collected edition I would get out *in America* while the company are there a volume of essays containing (1) *J. M. Synge and the Ireland of his Time* (just published by my sister) (2) *Discoveries* (3) *Literature and Tradition* (4) Essay from the *Mask* (5) *Edmund Spenser*. Let me [know] at once about this. I think it might have a large sale as the players would be there. Yours   W B YEATS

TO MISS E. M. LISTER

August 15 [1911] *Coole Park*

Dear Miss Lister: I am very much distressed to hear that Mr. Bullen is so ill. I had hoped that he was better and that things generally were going better.

I must explain about *Shadowy Waters*. I am most anxious that this book, which I hope will go about among people who have a

---

[1] At this period Miss Lister acted as agent for Yeats in dealing with musicians who wanted to set his poems to music.

technical interest in the stage, should show that I understand my trade as a practical dramatist. It will injure me if it contains a play which is evidently unfit for the stage as it stands. I should not have minded if *Shadowy Waters* had been left out altogether. Indeed I had intended to leave it out, when I arranged the contents of *Poems: Second Series*, but now that it is in I must ask for stage version in Appendix or elsewhere. I had told this to Mr. Bullen but I don't wonder that he has forgotten it with so much to worry him. We are calling the book *Plays for an Irish Theatre* and that means actable plays or nothing.

You have also 6d and 1/– copies of all or nearly all the other plays. These copies are for sale when the plays are performed. They will sell just in so far as I get on to the stage. Yours   W B YEATS

TO RENÉ FRANCIS[1]

September 5th, 1911 *Abbey Theatre*

Dear Mr. Francis, I haven't been able to write to you about your *Temptation of St. Anthony* because by a curious accident the book only reached me a month or six weeks ago.[2] It is a long story which I don't myself quite understand but it took South Africa on the road. I have been reading it regularly since it came, a little of it most days, but got parted from it a week ago. I shall finish it when it and I meet again a few weeks hence. I have however read three fourths and do not like to delay longer. I think you have made a beautiful translation of a beautiful book, when I get to London I will compare it with the more generally known text, but I have the impression of greater drama in your version. It has been an exciting thing to me reading it, for it is many years since I have read Flaubert. How much of what is most typical in our generation, Wilde's *Salome* for instance and much elsewhere in his work, has come out of it. Flaubert has made enough fabulous beasts to make the wilderness of romance terrible for another hundred years. I have to go to America with my players but when I return and have compared the two versions

[1] Dictated.
[2] René Francis had translated an early version of Flaubert's *Tentation de Saint Antoine*, and had evidently sent Yeats a copy.

I may write to you again. I think you have done your work very finely. Yours W B YEATS

TO EDMUND GOSSE

Tuesday [? September 12, 1911] *Coole Park*

Dear Mr. Gosse: I have just got your letter and am very glad of your news. I hardly like to say it, but I see only one man considerable enough by energy and imagination to be given that prize [1]—John Masefield. I would give it to him for his *Pompey the Great* and for *Nan*. You told me once that he had criticized you in a very unfair way. I spoke to him about it and he said 'impossible. I have the most profound respect for Gosse. He is the last man I would attack.' The next day he wrote to me to say that he had written an article, he found on going to some scrap-book, that may have given you pain. He did not show it to me. I know nothing of its contents but when I was thirty and less I wrote articles I sometimes remember now with a start. I was so clumsy that I could not say what I really thought and through fear of insincerity was sometimes particularly harsh to those for whom I had much respect. If I disliked anything they did I felt bound to set it down without disguise or qualification. It may have been so with him.

One might crown Hudson but he is not a coming force and so worthy of the less honour. We cannot give it to ourselves of course. Yours sincerely W B YEATS

I start for America tomorrow. I shall be back I hope by Oct 15 or 16 but not if *Playboy* fight grows violent. *Irish World* (Patrick Ford) is already attacking.

[1] This most probably refers to the Edmund de Polignac Prize founded in 1910 by the Princess Edmund de Polignac in memory of her husband, and for the encouragement of literature. A sum of £100 was to be awarded annually for five years, the award to be made by the Academic Committee of Literature. A reading committee of six members, on which Yeats and Gosse evidently served, was appointed to make recommendations. In 1911 the Prize was awarded to Walter de la Mare for *The Return*, in 1912 to John Masefield for *The Everlasting Mercy*, in 1913 to James Stephens for *The Crock of Gold*, and in 1914 to Ralph Hodgson for 'The Bull' and 'A Song of Honour.' No award seems to have been made in 1915.

TO LADY GREGORY[1]

October 28th, 1911   *Nassau Hotel*

Dear Lady Gregory . . . George Moore's *Hail and Farewell* is out,[2] I got it yesterday and have read a good deal of it. It is not at all malicious. Of course there isn't the smallest recognition of the difference between public and private life, except that the consciousness of sin in the matter may have made him unusually careful. It is the first book for ten years where he has not been petulant. It is curiously honest, very inaccurate and I think, for anyone not in the book itself, rather dull. Of course he has lots of unfavourable things to say about everybody but they are balanced by favourable things too and he treats himself in the same way. There is a description of his first visit to Coole and of your conversation and so on. There are things which would seem undignified and spiteful if taken by themselves, but the total impression is more than usually sincere. He certainly does not see either you or I as we are seen by a sympathetic friend. It is a slightly humorous, slightly satirical but favourable impression. A stranger's impression. I shall get the book sent to you next mail c/o of the Plymouth Theatre as I suppose Wright will forward it. The book is important for it is just the sort of book that gets in biography . . . Yours sincerely   W B YEATS

TO LADY GREGORY[1]

January 18th, 1912   *Abbey Theatre*

My dear Lady Gregory . . . I saw Shaw in London and he was very pleased with the number of papers that had quoted his interview.[3] He turned up at the last Academic Committee and proposed you. I don't think we will get you in however, too many old men don't know what's going on. Austin Dobson was half asleep; he woke up suddenly and murmured into my ear 'What's that? Is he proposing Lady Grove?' When he found it wasn't Lady Grove—whom I have no doubt he very properly hates—he sank back into sleepiness again.

[1] Dictated.
[2] Only the first volume, *Ave*, of George Moore's trilogy was published in 1911.
[3] This was presumably an interview with Shaw which he sent to the *New York Sun* where it appeared on some date in December 1911.

It was a mere general discussion as to possible people in view of an election some time hence; you would have a better chance if I wasn't there. I am a little too obviously your advocate. Our new elections will I'm afraid result in Masefield, Arnold Bennett and Galsworthy. I think I will not try to put forward your name till we have got Masefield in. Masefield and Shaw might manage it, it would give a proposer and seconder apart from me. Fortunately it doesn't matter. It will be 10 or 20 years before the Academic Committee matters so far as anyone's public position is concerned, the one advantage of it is that one gets to know writers and to find out one's friends and enemies. I never look at old Prothero for 5 minutes without a desire to cut his throat, he frequently takes the chair and is a very bad chairman. We are getting up a Browning celebration, he will probable deliver the oration. In the middle of his last Maurice Hewlett said to Henry James (it was Sir Alfred Lyall's memorial meeting) 'This is dull' to which Henry James sternly replied 'Hewlett, we are not here to enjoy ourselves.' Yours   W B YEATS

TO EDMUND GOSSE [1]

February [*25th in pencil*] 1912   *Abbey Theatre*

Dear Mr. Gosse, I think the Academic Committee should send a deputation to the Home Secretary with yourself at its head to explain the attitude of Men of Letters to this new Censorship. The Government are preparing a Bill, or so one is given to understand, and the evidence they have before them is that of Strachey's deputation.[2] If the Bill makes us all captive we shall have nobody but ourselves to blame if we don't put our point of view on record, and the only body in a position to do that is the Academic Committee. If we can't agree on a simple matter of that kind we can never agree upon anything of importance. I do not believe it possible for the Government to ignore anything so authoritative as our deputation. I suggest that the Academic Committee should be called together to consider the matter, it is very difficult for me to get away from this for the

[1] Dictated.
[2] John St. Loe Strachey, editor of the *Spectator*, had introduced to the Home Secretary a deputation asking for a Bill, and calling for more vigilance from the Home Office, in suppression of what was described as 'demoralizing literature.' The text of his speech was published in the *Spectator*, January 27, 1912.

next three weeks. To get away I should have to stop all rehearsals here, as I shall be in sole charge till about the 14th March, but after that I will go over to a meeting. I suppose as we have not acted immediately after Strachey's deputation it might be better to wait a few weeks. You will probably know what stage the Bill is in. I am anxious for this deputation, apart altogether from the practical effect on the Bill. To some extent I am in a better position to judge the mischief Strachey is doing than anybody who lives in London. Here, there has been a violent agitation to prevent the sale of English Sunday newspapers. The pretended object is to prevent the people being demoralised by reports of divorce cases, the real object is to keep out socialistic papers, Reynolds' newspapers, for instance, and all opinions disagreeable to the parish priest and, what is worse, disagreeable to the bigoted little weekly papers which are edited and printed in Dublin. Strachey's deputation is constantly quoted as if it represented all worthy English opinion. An attempt is now being made—though not yet very authoritatively—to make the agitation apply to novels which contain what are called 'anarchic opinions.' A number of bishops have shown the tendency of the whole thing by their speeches. If this agitation does not succeed, one says, 'Catholicism will be dead in Ireland in fifty years.' It is an attack on opinion pretending to be an attack on morals. A Deputation from our Committee would help throughout the country all the people who are fighting this censorship here in Ireland and be the true work of an Academy. I write to you first before talking to anybody else on the Committee because you have done more against the book-censorship than anyone else. I think you as Leader of the Deputation would be much better than Shaw, whose opinion would be a foregone conclusion. I wish I was not so busy here. I could go over this week but from to-morrow week I shall be tied down for at least a fortnight and perhaps longer. You can show this to anybody you like. Yours
                                                                W B YEATS

P.S. The aim of the Catholic Press and the Catholic organisations here in Ireland is to 'boycott' every newsagent who sells the English Sunday newspapers. Recent articles have been calling out quite openly for mob violence to enforce the boycott; once extend this to books and the small Irish country town will be plunged a little deeper in ignorance even than it is.

TO J. B. YEATS [1]

March 5th 1912 *Abbey Theatre*

My dear Father, I've been very busy since I came back working at the Abbey Theatre School, we advertised for pupils last autumn, and got more than 60, out of these we have finally extracted, at the end of a long season of playing and being taught, a most excellent company of 17, plus a good many pupils we have not taken into it, some of whom promised to be good in time. We have produced a great number of plays and so kept the theatre open and we have now so many understudies that I think even Sara Allgood—if she comes back from America, as Jack says she will, 'like Boadicea,' will be much milder than ever before. The new people are better in tragic work of my sort than the old. Some we will bring to America next tour, and some we will leave here in Dublin as B Company to keep the theatre open and gradually, as we hope, to make a career for themselves as the old people have done. It is a moment of transition with us here. Nugent Monck—who has been the teacher of the School—has gone, and I am in charge until the Company arrives, which should be next week. I have done nothing but theatre for months now, and have hardly seen anyone outside it. When I have got away to London it has been for a very few days and I have seen nobody but very intimate friends. I have therefore no news except theatre news and news of my own work which has almost entirely been the re-writing of old work, *The Countess Cathleen* and *The Land of Heart's Desire* and *The Hour-Glass*, to get them as effective on the stage as possible. Even the coal strike seems very far off. I wrote to Edmund Gosse a few days ago asking him to do something about a certain literary matter in which a Government bill is involved. In his reply he mentioned having seen various Cabinet Ministers and wound up 'In the sixty-two years of my life the political outlook has never been so black. The star of literature may be obscured and we may be all fighting for our lives against Socialist anarchy.' From which I imagine that they are all in a panic over there, for though I don't think the panic would grow thin near Gosse, who has I think the timidity of the sedentary man, he would not invent it.

I have been lecturing on the Other World and am now writing

[1] Dictated.

the lecture as an introduction to Lady Gregory's big book of Fairy Belief. I think I have made the first philosophic generalization that has been made from the facts of spiritism and the facts of folk-lore in combination. I have got nearly all the thought down now on paper, but I shall have to spend a long time making it vivid to the senses and making it emotionally sincere. It is always such a long research getting down to one's exact impression, one's exact ignorance and knowledge. I remember your once writing to me, that all good art is good just in so far as it is intimate. It always seems to me that that intimacy comes only from personal sincerity. The hardest thing of all to get rid of is the affectation of knowledge which is contained in certain forms of words. If you write on a subject it is usual to assume that you know all the facts that are known and have all the necessary faculties to interpret them. Yet this assumption is never really true. I shall probably spend a good deal of time the next two or three months trying to give my readers an exact measure in these things.

I haven't done anything for a couple of months at my big play for Mrs. Campbell. I did not feel capable of doing it till I had got all the other plays into final order, they were always there like an untidy litter in the corner of the room. When the attack was made upon our plays in New York it re-acted powerfully here, and the papers began attacking us, but Philadelphia seems to have helped us. The arrest of the players—who are as popular in Dublin as the Protestant and Pagan authors are unpopular—was the thing 'too much' that made everybody ashamed.

I see Lilly and Lolly only very occasionally and Jack still more seldom. I have no free evenings, for rehearsals begin at 6.30 always. However they come to the theatre and I see them there. We have a number of new plays, Robinson's is very fine, a man who went to prison in '93 for killing an informer comes out in the present epoch to find everything changed.[1] It was begun and much of it written a year ago but it will play like an answer to the Clan-na-Gael attack. I am told we are to go to the Western States next time in America, but I shall know nothing definite till I see Lady Gregory next week. I must now stop, for my rehearsals begin rather earlier than usual to-day (5.30). I hope all is going well with you, when you have time write to me. Yours affectionately   W B YEATS

[1] *Patriots* by Lennox Robinson, produced at the Abbey Theatre on April 11.

TO FLORENCE FARR

June 27 [1912]   18 *Woburn Buildings*

Dear Mrs. Emery: I do not think I can get to you this afternoon. The usual theatre distractions draw me to Lindsay House at 5, and at 7.30 I dine with Rothenstein to meet Tagore the Hindu poet. I am engaged to-morrow afternoon (Friday). Can I come Saturday at 5.30 or six? We could dine somewhere and go on to the theatre where there will be a new play by Boyle.[1]

I had a seance last night with Mrs. Thompson, Myers' medium, very interesting though nothing exactly evidential. The control Nelly came—it was curious to watch the sudden change in the midst of a lively conversation. Nelly spoke of being in the medium's stomach (her mother's stomach she said) and complained that there was still some medium left in the head. She distinguished between what she got from spirits and what [she] saw in our stomachs. I was introduced as Mr. Smith. Nelly said my stomach was hard to read (her phrase was 'not clear' or 'clean') and that I should wear a black beard and a white robe and be a Yogi priest and that she was uncomfortable because my hypnotism 'screwed out Mother's stomach' instead of Mother's 'screwing out' mine as it should be. She told me that in her own home she understood things, that there she got into a state which she called 'chrysalis,' a state it seems of partial unconsciousness though she felt people in it but they had no 'bodies' or 'feet or boots' and then she got at mother's stomach and could see nothing but what mother saw, and felt like 'a wet chicken.' If she could only come straight without being a chrysalis she could tell a lot. Yours   W B YEATS

TO WILLIAM ROTHENSTEIN[2]

Sept 7 [1912]   *Coole Park*

My dear Rothenstein, Your letter of August 24 only reached me to-day—sent on from London. I sent the text and book[3] to Tagore

[1] The Irish players were giving a season in London at the Court Theatre in June–July 1912. William Boyle's new play was called *Family Failing*.
[2] From a typewritten copy.
[3] *Gitanjali*, which was first issued in a limited edition by the India Society

yesterday, and I expect my essay back from my typist on Monday. I think I had better send it to you. You will, I think, find it emphatic enough. If you like it you can say so when you send it on to Tagore. In the first little chapter I have given what Indians have said to me about Tagore—their praise of him and their description of his life. That I am anxious about—some fact may be given wrongly, and yet I don't want anything crossed out by Tagore's modesty. I think it might be well if somebody compiled a sort of *Who's Who* paragraph on Tagore, and put after the Introduction a string of dates, saying when he was born, when his chief works were published. My essay is an impression, I give no facts except those in the quoted conversation. Yours W B YEATS

TO H. J. C. GRIERSON

Nov 14 [1912] *Coole Park*

Dear Prof Grierson: I write to thank you for your edition of Donne. It was very generous of you to send it to me. I have been using it constantly and find that at last I can understand Donne. Your notes tell me exactly what I want to know. Poems that I could not understand or could but understand are now clear and I notice that the more precise and learned the thought the greater the beauty, the passion; the intricacy and subtleties of his imagination are the length and depths of the furrow made by his passion. His pedantry and his obscenity—the rock and the loam of his Eden—but make me the more certain that one who is but a man like us all has seen God.

I would have written before but I have been ill—a combination of rheumatism and nervous indigestion—and am indeed still rather weak. I do not like however to delay longer about thanking you for work that has given me and shall give me I think more pleasure than any other book I can imagine. I came here a couple of days ago to get well in the quiet of the country. I shall fish for pike and plan out poems. Yours W B YEATS

---

in 1912. A public edition was issued by Macmillan & Co. the following year. The selection published in the book was made by Yeats out of an immense mass of material, but he made hardly any alterations in the English of the translations, which were by Tagore himself.

I find it difficult to believe from the evidence you give that Donne was not the lover of Lady Bedford. You I notice still doubt it but as George Moore would say 'I hope for the best.' The poem written on the supposition of her death, if it indeed refers to her, seems to me conclusive. No courtly compliment could go so far, no courtly beauty accept such compliments—and then he thinks her dead and so may well speak out.

TO J. B. YEATS

November 21*st*, 1912   18 *Woburn Buildings*

My dear Father, I have a great project, would you like to write your autobiography? My plan is to go to a publisher and to arrange that you should be paid chapter by chapter on the receipt of the MS. at the rate of £1 per 1,000 words up to say £50. This £50 to be a first charge on the book. I shall try and arrange so that you will keep the serial rights. You will probably get very decent terms for some of the chapters in America. You could go on as you please, quick or slow, and say what you pleased. I suggest—but this is only to start your imagination working—that in your first chapter or chapters you describe old relations and your childhood. You have often told us most interesting things, pictures of old Ireland that should not be lost. Then, you could describe your school life and then weave a chapter round Sandymount. Isaac Butt would come into this. Later on, your memories of Potter and Nettleship and Wilson would have real historical importance. When you came to the later period, you could use once more what you have already written about York Powell, then, if you liked, you could talk about Synge and about America. I will get the publisher to illustrate the book. There are your own pictures to choose from, the portrait of Isaac Butt, of course, and pictures in the Tate Gallery by Potter and at Aberdeen by Wilson, and Mrs. Nettleship has still those early designs of Nettleship's and would probably be glad to have them published and him praised. You might do a wonderful book. You could say anything about anything, for after all, you yourself would be the theme, there would be no need to be afraid of egotism, for as Oscar Wilde said, that is charming in a book because we can close it whenever we like, and open it again when the mood comes. I think you might really do a wonderful book, and I think a profitable one. It would tell people about those things that are not old enough to be in the histories or new enough to be in the reader's mind, and these things are always the things that are least known. If you agree, the book can be done, for even if the publisher lacked faith, I know I could get the money. The point is, can you write it for £1 a thousand words in the first instance? You wouldn't have to hurry, and I think that in the long run it might produce a very considerable sum for you. I would do all the bargaining and make the publisher collect the pictures for illustrations. Probably, a good deal that you have written recently would fit in somewhere. The first chapter or two might be difficult, but after that, I know by experience of my own books that your thought would go on branching and blossoming in all directions; in the end, it might grow to longer than 50,000 words, but I do not say it might not be shorter. The great thing is to do it in some form, long or short. An ordinary 6/- book is expected to be about 60,000 words, but if the pictures turn out well, though no longer, it might be a guinea book and very profitable indeed, for there would be nothing to pay for copyrights of pictures. If it were much less than 60,000 words, one could still—with the pictures to help—charge 6/-. Let me know as soon as you can and I will arrange the whole thing at once. Yours W B YEATS

TO EDMUND GOSSE

[*Nov 25, 1912—not dated by Yeats*]   *Coole Park*

Dear Mr. Gosse: I have asked the India Society to send you a copy of Tagore's poems. Will you please read it, and think over a suggestion I now make. I think it would be an imaginative and notable thing for us to elect him to our Committee. He is the great poet of Bengal though eligible for election because of his English translation of his work alone. I think from the English point of view too it would be a fine thing to do, a piece of wise Imperialism, for he is worshipped as no poet of Europe is. I will not tell you what page to turn to for though he is unequal and there are dull pages, you will not read far without coming to great beauty. I believe that if we pay him honour, it will be understood that we honour India also for he is its most famous man to-day.¹

I came here from London a little while ago having got knocked up. I am writing poetry and doing as much general work as my eyes permit; and getting well. I shall be in London early in December I think. Yours sincerely
W B YEATS

TO HUGH LANE²

Jan 1 [1913]   18 *Woburn Buildings*

My dear Lane, Here is the poem.³ If it is not politic tell me so frankly. If you think it is politic I will try and see Hone to see if fitting publication and comment could be made in the *Irish Times*. I have tried to meet the argument in Lady Ardilaun's letter to somebody, her objection to giving because of Home Rule and Lloyd George, and still more to meet the general argument of people like Ardilaun that they should not give unless there is a public demand. I shall quite understand if you think it would be unwise to draw attention to the possible slightness of 'Paudeen's' (little Patrick) desire for any kind of art. I left Dublin nearly a month ago and have no idea how the fund is or what has occurred. I kept the poem longer than I intended, to make some slight changes. Yours ever
W B YEATS

The 'correspondent' to whom the poem is addressed is of course an imaginary person.

TO LADY GREGORY

Jan 8 [*Postmark* 1913]   18 *Woburn Buildings*

My dear Lady Gregory . . . I dined with Lane on Sunday. He is very pleased with the poem which Hone has now. Hone was excited

---

¹ It does not appear that Rabindranath Tagore was elected to the Academic Committee.
² From a typed copy.
³ Published in the *Irish Times* of January 8, 1913, under the title 'The Gift.' It was later renamed 'To a Wealthy Man who promised a second subscription to the Dublin Municipal Gallery if it were proved the people wanted pictures,' and was included in *Responsibilities*, 1914.

with doing a leader elaborating the thought of the poem. I am not very hopeful. The Corporation has voted about £2000 a year and I told Lane I thought he should consider that as the country's support and not make the action of half a dozen people—who alone have money enough to subscribe £20,000—the deciding thing. He replied that he hated Dublin. I said so do we. He then said that unless the gallery were built at once it would be a long time before he would have the pleasure of hanging the pictures. I urged him to buy the site himself, if need [be] by selling some of the pictures for the purpose. He said he could buy it without selling any of the pictures but thought it a mistake to do so unless £20,000 was subscribed, so we were back again at the half dozen people. He took all I said in good part and has asked me to invite myself to dinner when I liked . . .

Strange that just after writing those lines on the Rhymers who 'unrepenting faced their ends'[1] I should be at the bedside of the dying sister of Beardsley,[2] who was practically one of us. She had had a week of great pain but on Sunday was I think free from it. She was propped up on pillows with her cheeks I think a little rouged and looking very beautiful. Beside her a Xmas tree with little toys containing sweets, which she gave us. Mr. Davis— Ricketts' patron—had brought it—I daresay it was Ricketts' idea. I will keep the little toy she gave me and I daresay she knew this. On a table near were four dolls dressed like people out of her brother's drawings. Women with loose trousers and boys that looked like women. Ricketts had made them, modelling the faces and sewing the clothes. They must have taken him days. She had all her great lady airs and asked after my work and my health as if they were the most important things in the world to her. 'A palmist told me,' she said, 'that when I was forty-two my life would take a turn for the better and now I shall spend my forty-second year in heaven' and then emphatically 'O yes I shall go to heaven. Papists do.' When I told her where Mrs. Emery was she said 'How fine of her, but a girls' school! why she used to make even me blush!' Then she began telling improper stories and inciting us (there were two

---

[1] Yeats refers to the lines addressed to his fellow members of the Rhymers' Club in his poem 'The Grey Rock,' included in the volume *Responsibilities*, 1914.

[2] Mabel Beardsley, Aubrey Beardsley's sister, was married to George Bealby Wright, a brilliant but unappreciated actor, and had herself been on the stage for some years. She was an occasional guest at Yeats's Monday evenings in Woburn Buildings.

men besides myself) to do the like. At moments she shook with laughter. Just before I was going her mother came and saw me to the door. As we were standing at it she said 'I do not think she wishes to live—how could she after such agony? She is all I have left now.' I lay awake most of the night with a poem in my head.[1] I cannot over-state her strange charm—the pathetic gaiety. It was her brother but her brother was not I think loveable, only astounding and intrepid. She has been ill since June last . . .

I have finished all my Tauchnitz proofs and should get copies in a week or so . . . Yours   W B YEATS

TO LADY GREGORY

Feb 11 [*Postmark* 1913]   18 *Woburn Buildings*

My dear Lady Gregory . . . Mabel Beardsley said to me on Sunday 'I wonder who will introduce me in heaven. It should be my brother but then they might not appreciate the introduction. They might not have good taste.' She said of her brother 'He hated the people who denied the existence of evil, and so being young he filled his pictures with evil. He had a passion for reality.' She has the same passion and puts aside any attempt to suggest recovery and yet I have never seen her in low spirits. She talked of a play she wanted to see. 'If I could only send my head and my legs,' she said, 'for they are quite well.' Till one questions her she tries to make one forget that she is ill. I always see her alone now. She keeps Sunday afternoon for me. I will send you the little series of poems when they are finished. One or two are I think very good.

I have many letters so good bye. Yours   W B YEATS

TO A. H. BULLEN[2]

22nd Feb, 1913   18 *Woburn Buildings*

My dear Bullen, Before finally deciding what we are to do with the 'Collected Edition' I wish you would tell me if it really is more

---

[1] One of the seven poems which form the series 'Upon a Dying Lady.' Mabel Beardsley died in 1916; the poems were published in the *Little Review* and in the *New Statesman* in August 1917, and first appeared in book form in *The Wild Swans at Coole, other Verses and a Play,* Cuala Press, November 1917.

[2] Dictated.

expensive to substitute than to add. And if so, why? The place where substitution is most required is in the case of *Deirdre*. The alterations are small and continuous. Nothing of value is left out, and there is no reason, on literary grounds, for the old version remaining. I should prefer substitution throughout in the case of all the changes, but if there are solid reasons against this, most changes can be done by addition. I am convinced however that, if it can be avoided, it is a great practical mistake except in the case of *The Hour-Glass*, which is practically a different work of art. It changes the volumes from being a collection precisely [of] those things I wish to be my permanent self, into a collection of odds and ends, including some that should not have been published. However, give me an opportunity of judging by telling me your reasons against substitution. The one thing I do vehemently object to is substitution in smaller print. To consent to that would be to avow the inferiority of my final version. If you let me know at once, I won't keep you waiting. My idea is, that you should bring your edition sufficiently up to date to drive out of the market the remainder of copies, which you can describe by saying that those copies which were already bound up are being sold off. It is obvious that no mere additional volume gives you the opportunity of saying this. The difficulty remains of your own 24 bound copies—I think that's the number—. We have to face that. It would be a mistake, however, to spoil a large number of unbound copies for the sake of so few.

I wonder if you would some time let me bring out with my sister a selection from my Love Poems. I think that a limited edition, sold at a high price, could not injure your sales, and might even be helpful. I would put in three or four from the Unwin book, but not more. So far as I have any object of my own in it, apart from feeding my sister's hungry press, a task of growing difficulty, I want to draw attention to my later work. Accident has given the work written before I was thirty all the public attention I get. For many years Unwin's volume has brought me in between £30 and £40 a year, and the sale's always slightly increasing. My sister's book would go for review. Now that I am writing a number of lyrics and shall probably do so for another eight or nine months, I rather want to think out the wisest method of publication. The last few days I have been thinking that it might be wiser to delay the book my sister proposes to publish in May, and substitute some other book for it in the press—say this volume of Love Poems. To make up for you a ninth volume without the new poems, if you felt that it would not do to delay your ninth volume till the Autumn, and then in the Autumn to publish a large volume of lyrical poems with my sister, and follow it immediately (my sister's volume will sell out before publication) with an ordinary edition of same poems. I know from the experience of Robert Bridges, that it is unwise to allow the public to get the idea that they can only buy one's poems in expensive editions from a hand-press. If I did this, the volume of Selections might be published in May or June, sent rather widely for review, and a new volume would follow in the early Autumn. Let me know quite candidly what you think. The truth is that the sickness of a friend has caused me to spend some weeks writing poems which cannot be published for the present, and I am feeling that the volume of new poems, if brought out in May, will be a little meagre so far as lyrics go.

Have you succeeded in extracting money from your Trustee? I have just had your account from A. P. Watt. Yours   W B YEATS

TO LADY GREGORY

[*Postmark March 5, 1913*]   18 *Woburn Buildings*

My dear Lady Gregory: I have finished a new poem 'The Three Hermits,' my first poem which is comedy or tragi-comedy. I will send it to you when I get to the typist. I have as a result taken several days at letter writing etc. before I start another. Craig is in London and there is a possibility of a big scheme of poetic drama emerging with myself as literary adviser. Craig has got all the money he wants for his school from Lord Howard de Walden and starts for Florence in a few days and will be followed by a troop of some 15 young men his pupils. In Florence they are to master every detail of the craft of the theatre and to undertake productions, sending designs and if wanted scenery etc. to all who employ them. They must accept a course of three years. Craig, in addition to the Arena Goldoni which he has, is to hire in Florence a large theatre for experiment and teaching. He claims that he can get for almost nothing what in London would cost £5000 a year. Craig came here on Sunday and at once discovered Robert's designs—he was enthusiastic and began considering how one could get on the stage the cold light. He thought a few candles could get it.

There is to be a refurbished edition of my collected edition, all pages I have re-written replaced, and illustrations.[1] I am anxious to get into it some of Robert's designs. The Nativity for one thing as I think it would not lose too much, losing colour. I talked to Bullen about this last week and now I have Craig's opinion to reinforce mine. Bullen admired the design I have but hesitates on other grounds. The books will be rearranged, all the *Samhains* and theatre essays in general making up one volume, and it is into this volume I would like to get Robert's work. I may pay some of the money myself out of what Bullen owes—to get a free hand. There will also be two new designs of Craig's.

Do what you think right about my father. I have that £160 legacy instalment and I leave you quite free within this limit—I would prefer not to pay more than £50 but I trust you entirely in the matter. I think my digestion is getting better—I shall know in about a month—and unless the big Craig project develops more quickly than I hope I can go to America to lecture and arrange as soon as I have had a few weeks' good digestion—I have been quite well the last week for the first time. I have not seen the doctor again yet—he is evidently leaving the regimen time to do its work. Much to my satisfaction I am thin, and have had to be re-measured by the tailor.

If I had a good press over *Cathleen* [2]—a thing I have never had before—I should like to see it. Yours always   W B YEATS

Have finished 30 French lessons and have just paid for 50 more.

TO A. H. BULLEN [3]

March 16th, 1913   *Abbey Theatre*

Dear Bullen, I have come to the conclusion that you had better start a new issue of the Collected Works with the volume of dramatic

---
[1] This refurbished edition did not appear.
[2] The rewritten version of *The Countess Cathleen* had been produced at the Abbey Theatre on September 26, 1912. Yeats is perhaps enquiring about a more recent revival.   [3] Dictated.

criticism; you can, if you like, publish the volume of Lyric poetry at the same time. The volume of dramatic criticism should, I think, contain two of Gregory's designs. The reason why I suggest it coming first is that it contains matter which has never been reviewed and never been accessible in a volume by itself. Coming at this moment when people have in their memories the Reinhardt productions, the scenery and costumes of the Russian Ballet, the Barker productions of Shakespeare—all examples of the new decorative method—it would probably get considerable attention. It would contain the only serious criticism of the new craft of the Theatre. It is the exact moment for it. I think it now probable that my sister will postpone the new book of verse till the autumn. You might find it well to delay the volume of the uniform edition containing the lyrics till you have first brought out the new poems in a separate volume. The uniform volume might then include these poems also . . . Yours

W B YEATS

TO THE EDITOR OF THE *IRISH TIMES*

March 17th, 1913 *Abbey Theatre*

Sir, I am convinced that the Mansion House Committee for the provision of a permanent Municipal Art Gallery in Dublin has done well in deciding upon a bridge for the site of the new building. Since I first saw the list of possible sites, I have liked but two—that in Earlsfort Terrace, which would have put the pictures into the midst of the students of the new University, and the bridge site which would put them into the busiest part of Dublin. For two years I copied from the antique in our National Gallery (so unfortunate in its site), and I know how few visitors find their way there, and what a good portion of these are children and seemingly poor people, who must have come from a distance. The other day an old man who was painting a friend's bathroom spoke about Mancini's painting—how you had to stand some distance away, and how fine it was when you did stand so. The pictures once set up upon their bridge will be near to many men and women of his sort, and close to the doors of many business men and women. I give up the thought of students wandering the Gallery between lectures with regret, but they will be young enough, and—when they care at all to become really educated men and women—enthusiastic enough for the twenty minutes' walk. The bridge will give to Sir Hugh Lane an opportunity for a building that will become—partly from the strangeness of its position, partly, as I believe, from its beauty—one of the most famous characteristics of the town. The emigrant will recall it in his memory side by side with the old Parliament House and the College; and to-day, as I looked up the river from O'Connell Bridge, and pictured the scene so changed, I felt certain that the whole scene would be the better for it. It is a fine scene, especially when a little disguised by evening light; but it lacks the look of being cared for, the look of being valued; it lacks somewhere some touch of ornament, of conscious pleasure and affection. We have in Sir Hugh Lane a great *connoisseur*, and let us, while we still have him—for great *connoisseurs* are as rare as any other kind of creator—use him to the full, knowing that, if we do, our children's children will love their town the better, and have a better chance of that intellectual happiness which sets the soul free from the vicissitudes of fortune. Yours, etc., W B YEATS

TO ROBERT BRIDGES

April 25 [1913]   18 *Woburn Buildings*

My dear Mr. Bridges, You are quite right about that fraction [1] and if I should ever reprint the essay (the popular edition is out) I will change it. I am grateful for your praise, no other man's could have the same worth for me. I had a short illness six months ago and the first sign of returning health was the excitement of finding that I could read poetry again and the poem that brought on this excitement was your poem on the dead child. In my weak state it produced an almost unendurable emotion.

I will write and invite myself to come and see you a little later. My players to whom I am always a little tied, though seldom now

---

[1] Writing to Yeats on April 20, 1913, Bridges had expressed great admiration for the introduction to Rabindranath Tagore's *Gitanjali*—'there is no one but you who could write so'—but suggested that he should alter the phrase 'Four-fifths of our energy is spent in the quarrel with bad taste' when the popular edition was published.

stage manage or the like, return from America next week, and for a week or two after that I shall be busy over financial details and so on. I thank you for asking me. Yours always   W B YEATS

TO KATHARINE TYNAN [1]

[*June* 19, 1913]   18 *Woburn Buildings*

... I thank you very much for your charming book[2] which has been beside me on my writing table since it came that I might open it from time to time amid this hubbub of theatre work. I like among the best 'The Train that goes to Ireland.' I think you are at your best when you write as a mother and when you remember your old home and the Dublin mountains. The first of the two poems should be in all the little ballad books, if there will be any more little ballad books —alas—now that we—you and I chiefly—have made a change and brought into fashion in Ireland a less artless music. Yet I hope the ballad books will not go out with the pipers. But there are other moving little poems beside these two—'The Mother' I have been reading this morning—and I thank you for the book. I am very glad indeed to have it.

The Irish players are drawing great houses—Robinson's political play has been a great success here—the theatre makes a good profit now which is divided between the players and the working capital. We hope to put on *The Countess Cathleen* of which I send you my latest version. I think I have made a good play of it. ...

TO LADY GREGORY [3]

22nd July, 1913   18 *Woburn Buildings*

Dear Lady Gregory, I have carried the identification of John Mirehouse further. I have now found by considerable research that his family come, as the spirit claimed, from Miresike. The will at Somerset House described him as belonging to a place in Pembrokeshire. The spirit gave the family motto as Qualis ab incepto—this is correct. I have no doubt I shall find that his wife's name was also

[1] Text from the *Yale Review*, Winter 1940.
[2] The title of her book was *Irish Poems*, 1913.   [3] Dictated.

given correctly as Elizabeth Fisher. Her name was not given in the will but the daughter's name was Elizabeth. This case is I think perfectly conclusive, for no theory of sub-conscious action could account for the bringing together of all these scattered facts. I have no doubt I shall trace the wife's name. I am going to ask Marsh, Churchill's secretary, to find out at the Home Office if there was a policeman called Thomas Emerson who committed suicide in April, 1850 at Richmond Bridge. He came together with Mirehouse—they had died in the same year, the policeman two months after. One wonders what bonds kept them together in the other world, the policeman and the Old Bailey magistrate. I've no doubt I should have found Sister Mary Ellis, the *Freeman* of the time must give the names of the Sisters who went with Florence Nightingale, but the British Museum stores all the Irish newspapers at Hendon. I cannot get it for a week. She may not have belonged to Gort Convent but she probably did. I expect you'll write and tell me that Sister Aloysius is very recently dead. The other who went before her has evidently been waiting impatiently and is in great unhappiness at not finding her. It is evident that a blind impulse brought her to me. She knew that I knew Galway and Gort and was so blind with trouble that she thought a living man could help her, indeed indirectly I have helped her, if the spirit in charge brings them together as he said he would.

I brought a script to the Museum this morning which contained Catalan and Coptic. I imagine that I am deeply stirring the soul of the British Museum—the Assyrian authority, shortly after I had brought him some strange Assyrian information, saw a ghost in the Assyrian department. I am hoping to be able to date the Greek by the unusual form given to the letter pi. My sight gave out over a photograph of a Greek manuscript just now (Robert will probably laugh at my Greek scholarship) so I had to postpone the search until to-morrow. The form of pi used in [the] script is not now used and was used in the Fifth Century. That's as far as I've got. The most astonishing speculative problems are opening up before me. I had a long conversation with one of the spirits and put to him my difficulties. He answered in a very detailed way. I cannot do any more for the present, for the medium, who knows nothing of the importance of her work, is bored by it. She asked me what the word antithesis meant the other day, and it must be a bore to get twelve tongues she does not understand. One spirit just managed to get out 'My Lord' in Turco-Arabic when he was driven away by the control. He had evidently meant to be very polite.[1]

I am dictating this to Miss Jacob who went to Somerset House for me. Yours W B YEATS

TO J. B. YEATS

August 5, 1913 18 *Woburn Buildings*

My dear Father: I thought your letter about 'portraiture' being 'pain' most beautiful and profound. All our art is but the putting our faith and the evidence of our faith into words or forms and our faith is in ecstasy. Of recent years instead of 'vision', meaning by vision the intense realization of a state of ecstatic emotion symbolized in a definite imagined region, I have tried for more self portraiture. I have tried to make my work convincing with a speech so natural and dramatic that the hearer would feel the presence of a man thinking and feeling. There are always two types of poetry—Keats the type of vision, Burns a very obvious type of the other, too obvious indeed. It is in dramatic expression that English poetry is most lacking as compared with French poetry. Villon always and Ronsard at times create a marvellous drama out of their own lives.

I wonder if I may put together for Cuala a volume of criticism and philosophy extracted from your letters and lectures? It would help Cuala and be a most beautiful book.[2] Are you writing the autobiography now that a magazine has asked for it? I think you would write it better in the way I said, for you would be free of the editorial criticism, but I am grateful for anything that sets you to the doing of it.

I have had wonderful 'psychic' evidence of late. A charming girl I know, very simple and pious, a girl of good family, has developed automatic writing of the most astounding type. She only knows English and a little French but writes, in her mediumistic state, Greek, Latin, Italian, Chinese, Provençal, Hebrew, Italian and other

[1] For explanation of the contents of this letter see the letter to J. B. Yeats which follows it.
[2] *Passages from the Letters of John Butler Yeats*, selected by Ezra Pound with an introduction by W. B. Yeats, was published by the Cuala Press on May Eve 1917. *Further Letters of John Butler Yeats*, selected by Lennox Robinson, was also published by the Cuala Press, in March 1920.

languages; she answers mental questions in Greek. The case cannot be published but I am examining it carefully with the help of British Museum language experts and writing a report as elaborate as if for publication. Various spirits have also written through her hand and given their names and the dates of their deaths, etc. I have in every case been able to verify their statements, though sometimes only after long research. In no case had I ever heard of their existence. I know all the rationalist theories, fraud, unconscious fraud, unconscious action of the mind, forgotten memories, and so on and have after long analysis shown that none can account for this case; and I have just had a certificate of caution from a well-known American medium who has turned me out of her seances because she says 'nothing ever satisfies' me. I am now elaborating a curious theory of spirit action which may I believe make philosophic study of mediums possible. I am really absorbed in this for the moment.

I cannot write more now, I have a huge pile of letters—a daily plague—to deal with. Next winter I am taking a secretary [1] though I shrink from the expense, believing that I shall be able to bear the expense because I shall be able to write. When my sec comes at the end of October you will find me a better correspondent as he will answer the business letters. Yours affectionately   W B YEATS

TO THE EDITOR OF *POETRY* [2]

[*? November* 1913]

... When I got the very unexpected letter with the prize of £50,[3] my first emotion was how much it would have meant to me even ten years ago; and then I thought surely there must be some young American writer today to whom it would mean a great deal, not only in practical help, but in encouragement. I want you therefore not to think that I am in any way ungrateful to you, or in any way anxious to put myself into a different category to your other contributors because I send back to you £40. I will keep £10, and with

[1] Ezra Pound.
[2] Text from *A Poet's Life Seventy Years in a Changing World* by Harriet Monroe. New York, 1938.
[3] The magazine *Poetry* had offered a prize of $250 for the best poem appearing in its pages during its first year, and had awarded this to Yeats for 'The Grey Rock.' The award was announced in the issue for November 1913.

that I will get Mr. Sturge Moore to make me a book-plate, and so shall have a permanent memory of your generous magazine. I vacillated a good deal until I thought of this solution, for it seemed to me so ungracious to refuse; but if I had accepted I should have been bothered by the image of some unknown needy young man in a garret. Yours sincerely   W B YEATS

TO THE EDITOR OF POETRY[1]

[? *December* 1913]

... I want to make a suggestion which you need not follow in any way. Why not give the £40 to Ezra Pound? I suggest him to you because, although I do not really like with my whole soul the metrical experiments he has made for you, I think those experiments show a vigorous creative mind. He is certainly a creative personality of some sort, though it is too soon yet to say of what sort. His experiments are perhaps errors, I am not certain; but I would always sooner give the laurel to vigorous errors than to any orthodoxy not inspired.

I would like to say, however, that I have liked other work in your magazine; I remember finding one number particularly charming. But I think one is always safest if one selects a personality. Of course there may be other men equally creative, but then you see I am in ignorance, and that is precisely why I feel I can only suggest to you a little timidly; not to put my judgment before yours but because I may help you out of a difficulty. ...

TO KATHARINE TYNAN[2]

[*December* 12, 1913]   [*Stone Cottage*]
                                                   [*Coleman's Hatch*]
                                                   [*Sussex*]

... I find my sight practically useless after artificial light begins ... No, you were not very indiscreet, though you were a little.[3]

---

[1] Fragment. Text from *A Poet's Life Seventy Years in a Changing World* by Harriet Monroe. New York, 1938.
[2] Text from the *Yale Review*, Winter 1940.
[3] In her volume of reminiscences *Twenty-Five Years* (1913) Katharine Tynan had quoted long passages from a number of Yeats's early letters to her, without first asking his permission.

There was a sentence about X that I would have crossed out but nothing that really mattered. However if you are going to publish any more letters of mine, please let me see them first. I may even, in defiance of all right conduct, improve them. I liked your book very much and not merely because it brought back so many memories. You have the gift to describe many people with sympathy and even with admiration, and yet to leave them their distinct characters. Most people have to choose between caricature and insipidity. I was especially interested in all that period before I knew you. You called up the romance of a forgotten phase of politics and gave it dignity. —Your next volume will I am afraid give you much more trouble, with nothing but the squalid years of the split for a background . . . I have often felt that the influence of our movement on the generation immediately following us will very largely depend upon the way in which the personal history is written. It has always been so in Ireland. Our interest in the Young Irelanders was largely a personal interest and I doubt if we would have cared for them half as much but for Gavan Duffy's books. Even the Dark Rosaleen was only part of a drama explained to us by Duffy.

I am glad, too, that George Moore's disfiguring glass will not be the only glass. . . .

TO J. B. YEATS[1]

[*January* 1914] *Stone Cottage*

My dear Father, I am going to America by the *Mauretania* and she starts on the 31st, arrives on fifth or sixth. I give my first lecture on the ninth. You will find that I use many of your ideas. I have delivered the lecture twice in London in order to get it into shape. The last time to a huge audience, a good deal more than a thousand, in a hall associated with the City Temple, Campbell's church.

Your last letter came just in time to give me a most essential passage. The way in which you contrast pleasure which is personal and joy which is impersonal brought into my memory an essay of mine in *The Cutting of an Agate*. I have forgotten the name of the essay, but it's the one about Lionel Johnson. I discover there two

[1] Dictated.

elements in style, one impersonal and generally in great poetry sorrowful, and the other personal and pleasurable. I show them existing side by side in all great poetry. The pleasurable element is the element of style, the conscious choice of words. It is, I suppose, all that remains of the ego. The curious thing is that this thought, which I feel quite certain of, has always, until I got your letter, refused to relate itself to the general facts of life. If you have the book, you might look up the essay and tell me if you agree. I shall not be able to use the word joy in my lecture for it would confuse things, I shall have to use the word 'ecstasy.' Ecstasy includes emotions like those of Synge's Deirdre after her lover's death which are the worst of sorrows to the ego . . . Yours W B YEATS

TO CHARLES RICKETTS [1]

11th June, 1914 *Royal Societies Club*
[London]

My dear Ricketts, When I got to the theatre this morning I found you had not been asked to the rehearsal. Lady Gregory had thought I had asked you, and I had thought she had. We are both very sorry, yet I do not think you could have bettered anything.

I think the costumes the best stage costumes I have ever seen. They are full of dramatic invention, and yet nothing starts out, or seems eccentric. The Company never did the play so well, and such is the effect of costume that whole scenes got a new intensity, and passages or actions that had seemed commonplace became powerful and moving.[2]

The play is to-morrow night and Saturday afternoon and evening, and there are of course seats for you whenever you come. You have done a great deal for us, and I am very grateful. Yours ever
W B YEATS

[1] Text from *Self-Portrait taken from the Letters and Journals of Charles Ricketts, R.A.*, London, 1939.
[2] Ricketts had designed new costumes for *The King's Threshold*, revived during the Abbey Theatre Company's 1914 London season at the Court Theatre.

TO J. B. YEATS

Sept 12 [1914] *Coole Park*

My dear Father: I have sent your letters to my London typist, not so much because your handwriting is difficult in itself as that all handwriting rather tires my eyes. The typewritten essay I have of course read. I think with you that the poet seeks truth, not abstract truth, but a kind of vision of reality which satisfies the whole being. It will not be true for one thing unless it satisfies his desires, his most profound desires. Henry More, the seventeenth century platonist whom I have been reading all summer, argues from the goodness and omnipotence of God that all our deep desires must be satisfied, and that we should reject a philosophy that does not satisfy them. I think the poet reveals truth by revealing those desires.

I hear that Ian Hamilton has written home that his men are heroic but can achieve nothing because all the officers are incompetent. At least that is what people say he has written. At the start of the war one heard that the Guards were a failure because they did not know their officers, who had been too busy with games and society to learn their work. These young officers died with useless heroism when the moment came. England is paying the price for having despised intellect. The war will end I suppose in a draw and everybody too poor to fight for another hundred years, though not too poor to spend what is left of their substance preparing for it. Gregory who is in London writes describing the Zeppelin raid. The mob cheered every bomb that fell and every shot from an anti-aircraft gun. High up a Zeppelin shone white under a cloud.

I return to London on Oct 2 when Lady Gregory starts for America. I shall have almost finished my new play, to be called perhaps *The Woman born to be Queen*.[1] It is a wild comedy, almost a farce, with a tragic background—a study of a fantastic woman. What you say is true about abstract ideas. They are one's curse and one has sometimes to work for months before they are eliminated, or till the map has become a country. Yet, in some curious way, they are connected with poetry or rather with passion, one half its life and yet its enemy. Yours affectionately   W B YEATS

[1] Yeats finally reverted to the original title *The Player Queen*. The play, begun as a tragedy and intended to have been written in verse, became, in the end, a fantastic comedy in prose.

TO J. B. YEATS

Dec. 26, 1914   *Coole Park*

My dear Father, When I get the last batch of the old letters typed from my typist—there are still a few to come (one typist gave up the job)—I will be able to send her the new ones as they come and so comment on them before your thought has gone on to something else. They always interest me deeply. Yesterday I finished my memoirs;[1] I have brought them down to our return to London in 1886 or 1887. After that there would be too many living people to consider and they would have besides to be written in a different way. While I was immature I was a different person and I can stand apart and judge. Later on, I should always, I feel, write of other people. I dare say I shall return to the subject but only in fragments. Some one to whom I read the book said to me the other day: 'If Gosse had not taken the title you could call it *Father and Son*.' I am not going to ask your leave for the bits of your conversation I quote. It is about 17,000 words, which is just the right size for Lolly's press and will prepare for my quotations from your letters. There is a great deal about my grandfather in Sligo and I have grouped round Aunt Mickie some passages about our ancestors. Later on I speak of Wilson and Potter (I would be glad if you could write me your memory of his death. I have given an account as I remember the story. Farrar came and told us). Then Dowden and O'Leary and J. F. Taylor give me short chapters. The book is however less an objective history than a reverie over such things as the first effect upon me of Bedford Park and all it meant in decoration. Everybody to whom I have shown the work has praised it and foretold a great success for it. You need not fear that I am not amiable. I shall illustrate it with a photograph of Jack's *Memory Harbour* at any rate.

I came over here two days ago to see Lady Gregory about the theatre before she starts for America. Thanks for your recent letters, Lady Gregory has read some of them to me but I must read them again and so must get them typed. The week after next I go to the Sussex Cottage and Ezra Pound will be my secretary again for a couple of weeks. He brings his wife with him this time. She is very pretty (Mrs. Shakespear's daughter) and had a few years ago seven

[1] The first instalment, published by the Cuala Press in 1915 under the title *Reveries over Childhood and Youth*, and later included in *Autobiographies*, 1926.

generals in her family all living at once and all with the same name—
Johnson, relations of Lionel Johnson. Yours ever   W B YEATS

TO J. B. YEATS [1]

Jan. 18, 1915   *Stone Cottage*

My dear Father, I am down here in Sussex, as you see. Ezra Pound and his wife are staying with me, we have four rooms of a cottage on the edge of a heath and our back is to the woods. I was amused by your description of Crowley.[2] Crowley is not a man I appreciate. I am amused to find that he now praises Mrs. Macgregor, he slandered her in a very cruel way in one of his books but I suppose Bergson's sister is now worth considering. I am sorry Quinn has taken up with Crowley.

I have just started to read through the whole seven vols of Wordsworth in Dowden's edition. I have finished *The Excursion* and begun *The Prelude*. I want to get through all the heavy part that I may properly understand the famous things. At the same time I am not finding the long poems really heavy. Have you any impressions of him? He strikes me as always destroying his poetic experience, which was of course of incomparable value, by his reflective power. His intellect was commonplace, and unfortunately he has been taught to respect nothing else. He thinks of his poetical experience not as incomparable in itself but as an engine that may be yoked to his intellect. He is full of a sort of utilitarianism and that is perhaps the reason why in later life he is continually looking back upon a lost vision, a lost happiness.

I have just got your last letters back from the typist, as always they interest me very much. I am thinking out a long poem, a conversation upon philosophical subjects between a duellist and a gambler.[3] There will be a wild comedy setting, but some of the thoughts will be those you discussed in letters to me a year ago. I take the duellist and the gambler as two contrary principles of life,

[1] Dictated.
[2] For Yeats's experience of Aleister Crowley see his letters to Lady Gregory, April 25 and 28, 1900, pp. 339–342.
[3] Mrs. Yeats has been unable to find any poem answering this description; possibly it was never written.

and my gambler is your American woman. I wonder will you have seen Lady Gregory, or is she somewhere a thousand miles from New York? She hadn't her list of lectures before she left. I saw Lily the other day and read her the greater portion of my memoirs but Lolly is not to know this, as it would make her jealous. Lily approved the memoirs, and so you may judge from that I have not been too indiscreet. Yours affectionately W B YEATS

TO ERNEST BOYD [1]

Jan. 20, 1915   18 *Woburn Buildings*

Dear Mr. Boyd: I quite approve of the idea of your plan but it is only an idea so far. Everything depends on the form of action into which you throw your thought. You have to express the thought by action, of course. The subject would, I think, raise a great deal of Irish interest. The difference between the Dublin *talkers* and any real workers is that the *talkers* value anything which they call a principle more than any possible achievement. All achievements are won by compromise and these men, wherever they find themselves, expel from their own minds—by their minds' rigidity—the flowing and existing world.

The Sinn Fein party in order to affirm the abstract principle that an Irish building should have an Irish architect supported Dr. Murphy in defeating Hugh Lane's municipal gallery project.

He offered £70,000 worth of pictures, and a man believed by many to be the greatest of living architects—but they preferred their abstract principle. It was nothing to them that we have no Irish architect whom anybody suspects of remarkable talent. They preferred their mouthful of east wind.

This rigidity of the 'intellectual' helps the dishonest time-servers for it enables them to claim that they are the only practical people.

The Hermetic Society was founded by Chas. Johnston and myself. It was not Theosophical (in the present sense of that word) at

[1] From a typewritten copy. Dictated. Ernest Boyd (1887–1946), Irish author and journalist, served in the British Consular Service until 1919. In 1920 he settled in New York where he spent the rest of his life. His work includes *Ireland's Literary Renaissance*, 1916, and many other books and translations.

the start, but was for general mystical study. It had no connection with the later society. George Russell was not a member. He was then very young. Yours W B YEATS

TO ERNEST BOYD[1]

[*Feb.* 1915] 18 *Woburn Buildings*

Dear Mr. Boyd: In answer to your first question, who did I know in London. I knew, besides Johnson, Dowson, Symons and the other Rhymers' Club members (but I notice you say 'Irish.)' I knew Nora Hopper slightly and Moira O'Neill not at all. I think Moira O'Neill stands apart from the movement I belong to. The only Irish poet of this period I knew intimately was George Russell (AE). I think I influenced him at the start. I was a little older.

(2). No—my early poems as far as I know had nothing to do with the Hermetic Society. The original body in Dublin was not the Theosophical but an earlier Hermetic Society founded by myself and a few friends in 1884 or thereabouts. Then came a theosophical society and then the later Hermetic Society. My interest in mystic symbolism did not come from Arthur Symons or any other contemporary writer. I have been a student of the medieval mystics since 1887 and found in such authors as Valentin Andrea authority for my use of the rose.[2]

Stone Cottage

My chief mystical authorities have been Boehme, Blake and Swedenborg.

Of the French symbolists I have never had any detailed or accurate knowledge.

As to No. 3 question. I am afraid I do not know how to answer it. I do not remember any development with that precision. I have

---

[1] From a typewritten copy.
[2] Johannes Valentine Andreae or Andreas (1586–1654), a German theologian and mystic. As his books were written either in German or Latin it seems unlikely that Yeats studied them extensively. He is perhaps referring to a book ascribed to Andreas, *The Hermetic Romance or the Chymical Wedding*, written in High Dutch by C[hristian] R[osenkreuz], translated by E. Foxcroft. London, 1690. This was reprinted in *The Real History of the Rosicrucians* by A. E. Waite, 1887.

never consciously abandoned the wish to write out of the scenery of my own country.

4th question. I am afraid I could only answer your fourth question by a criticism of Irish poetry, which, to be of any value, would have to be more detailed than I could make it at present. I admire many things in contemporary poetry very much; and would, I dare say, have been glad to have foreseen it in 'The Eighties.'

I find I have forgotten part of your first question.

I knew Nora Hopper slightly. Her work shows certain obvious influences which cannot have escaped you. Moira O'Neill I have never known, nor was she, I believe, known to any of my friends. Her development was, I should imagine, quite distinct, and her associations were probably with an older generation of writers.

I am afraid my answer has been somewhat delayed, but I brought half your letter to Ireland, and after I had finished the first part of this letter, discovered my mistake. Sincerely yours   W B YEATS

TO JOSEPH HONE

April 13 [1915]   18 *Woburn Buildings*

My dear Hone, I write to thank you for your most generous article in the *New Statesman*. You quote what I myself care most for and saw what I have tried to do. One great pleasure is that whereas I used to feel that the articles people wrote in praise of my early work were, with some few exceptions, vague and a little sentimental, the very few who praise the later work (and you have been the most subtle) have praised it in words full of intellect and force. That convinces me, that and my own emotion when I write, that I am doing better and plunging deeper. Yours   W B YEATS

TO ROBERT BRIDGES

June 23 [1915]   18 *Woburn Buildings*

Dear Mr. Bridges: I send you Ezra Pound's *Cathay,* his book of Chinese translations.

I have just read once more all through your daughter's book.[1] It is certainly the best poetry done by any woman in our time.

I thank you and Mrs. Bridges for a visit that has given me great pleasure. Yours   W B YEATS

TO JOHN QUINN

24 *June*, 1915   18 *Woburn Buildings*

My dear Quinn, I don't know whether I owe you a letter or not. I sent you the manuscript and typed copy of the Memoirs about three weeks ago, but I cannot remember if I wrote with it. I may not have done so for I was very busy with the players. We had much business to think of and I was rehearsing *Baile's Strand*, of which we gave a good performance—Ricketts doing the costumes. The war has hit us hard. We came to London expecting a loss and lost more than we expected. We had to come for the sake of the advertisement. A music-hall tour has come of it, and another music-hall tour in America is probable, and after that a tour to Australia for the whole company is possible. If all these good things happen we may survive the war unscattered, but if they do not we shall have to close, while there is still enough money to keep the building in our hands, waiting another attempt when the Irish Parliament opens. Lane's death has been a great upset to many plans. For various reasons, Lady Gregory is still keeping private the facts about his will. However, I know she will not mind my telling you, and indeed she may have told you herself already. The only properly signed and witnessed will found was made some years ago and at a time when he was angry with the Dublin Corporation. It made a few private bequests, amounting in all to very little. He left pictures that had been offered to Dublin towards the foundation of a modern gallery in London, and all the rest of his property to the Dublin National Gallery. From various things Lane had said to various people Lady Gregory believed there was a later will, and a search started by her resulted in the discovery of an unwitnessed codicil leaving back the modern pictures to the Dublin Municipal Gallery on certain conditions: they were to make

[1] *Charitessi*, published anonymously by Bowes & Bowes, Cambridge, in 1911. The authorship of the book was acknowledged later by Bridges's daughter, Mrs. Elizabeth Daryush.

a fitting building and put it in a fitting place, and of place and building Lady Gregory was to be the sole judge. We are now trying to get a competent successor to Lane appointed by the Governors of the Irish National Gallery. I daresay we shall fail and have to submit to some local job, for with exceptions they are local nobodies. To-day I saw Laurence Binyon and suggested his going in for it, but I doubt if he will. For a time we hoped for the appointment of Robert Ross but I am afraid the opposition is too strong. It is wonderful the amount of toil and intrigue one goes through to accomplish anything in Ireland. Intelligence has no organization whilst stupidity always has. I suppose because it is the world itself. I have often thought that all ages are the equal of one another in talent, and that we call an age great merely because it knew how to employ talent.

Theatre affairs keep me here in London but I am trying to get away, for the performance of *Baile's Strand* has restored my confidence in myself. The audience was manifestly pleased, and even I was pleased. By a beneficent accident there was no press to tell me I am a fool for my pains. The result is that I am full of new poems—dramatic and lyrical. All my mythological people have come alive again and I want to complete my heroic cycle. I have also nearly finished my Notes for Lady Gregory's book, and that has laid the ghosts for me. I am free at last from the obsession of the supernatural, having got my thoughts in order and ranged on paper. Here in London I have nothing to keep me except my Monday evenings when various poets come to discuss literature, and Friday evenings when I am very constantly at Charles Ricketts' to discuss painting. The last important event has been, I think, the discovery of the genius of Cole.[1] He is a thorn in the Futurist and Cubist flesh for he draws incomparably in the style of Michael Angelo. If his sculpture, which no one seems to have seen, is as fine as his drawings, it will be

---

[1] Ernest Albert Cole was born in 1890, and was therefore a very young student when, at the Goldsmiths' School of Art at New Cross, London, he produced some remarkable drawings in the style of Michael Angelo, which attracted the attention of the painters Charles Ricketts and Charles Shannon, who, later on, managed to arrange that he should visit Italy. Soon after his return he was commissioned to do some of the sculptures on County Hall, Westminster; and he was then employed for a couple of years or so as Professor of Sculpture at the Royal College of Art, with Mr. Henry Moore as his assistant. He is said to have married an American lady and to have retired to the country. Details concerning his later life and work are lacking.

like the publication of *Paradise Lost* in the very year when Dryden announced the final disappearance of blank verse. Personally, I am as much moved by Gregory's work as by anything else. He has a fine picture in the New English, a decorative landscape suggested by Coole Lake, full of airy distinction.

I have just come from staying with Robert Bridges, and the chief event there was the discovery that certain lofty, impassioned verses which have delighted me since their publication three years ago are his daughter's work. If she can add to their number she will be the most considerable poetess since Christina Rossetti. Yours sincerely

W B YEATS

TO ROBERT BRIDGES

June 30 [? 1915] 18 *Woburn Buildings*

Dear Mr. Bridges: I send you a copy, a hateful American copy decorated in my despite, of *The Green Helmet* and also Lady Gregory's two books which you need not return. I think these two books of hers very beautiful, *Gods and Fighting Men* especially is full of fine lyric passages. In the other book read especially the lamentation of Deirdre at the end of her story, and the Emer lamentation at the end of the book.

I have been reading your daughter's work to a number of people who admire it as much as I do. I have done some poems not yet published and I will try to let you have copies when I can get them typed. Yours ever W B YEATS

TO EDMUND GOSSE

Tuesday [in pencil July 6th, 1915] 18 *Woburn Buildings*

My dear Gosse: I write from the country so please excuse paper. I have only this block. I have just heard that James Joyce, an Irish poet and novelist of whose fine talent I can easily satisfy you, is in probably great penury through the war. He was at Trieste teaching English and has now arrived at Zürich. He has children and a wife. If things are as I believe, would it be possible for him to be given a

18 Woburn Buildings
W.C.

Tuesday
July 6th 15

My dear Gosse: I write from the country so please excuse paper. I have only this block. I have just heard that James Joyce, an Irish poet & novelist of whom from Talent I can easily satisfy you [...] to me unknown, [...] has [...] 15 [...]. He was at Trieste teaching English & has now arrived in Zurich. He has children & a wife. If there are all [...], as I believe, would it be possible for him to be given a grant from the Royal Literary Fund? what form should the application take? I am sorry to give you [...] trouble but I know in a case of hardship you [...] do not think anything a trouble.

I would like to show you some of Joyce's work.

Yrs W B Yeats

grant from the Royal Literary Fund? What form should the application take? I am sorry to trouble you but I know in a case of hardship you do not think anything is trouble. Yours sincerely W B YEATS

I would like to show you some of Joyce's work.

TO EDMUND GOSSE

Thursday [*in pencil July* 8, 1915]   18 *Woburn Buildings*

Dear Gosse: I am trying to get at the facts. Joyce has written a book of verse *Chamber Music* and a most remarkable book of stories called *Dubliners* which I thought of for our Academic Committee prize. I would be inclined however to base his claim on a most lovely poem in Katharine Tynan Hinkson's Irish Anthology *The Wild Harp*. It is to the end of that book. I will try and find my copy. Yours

W B YEATS

TO EDMUND GOSSE

Saturday [*in pencil July* 24, 1915]   18 *Woburn Buildings*

My dear Gosse: I enclose letters and statements about James Joyce of whose need I told you. I suggested that he was worthy of help from the Royal Literary Fund. I believe him to be a man of genius. Had you not pointed out to me, what I already vaguely felt, that we could not give our annual prize to another Irishman just now I would have proposed him for it this year. He has written *Dubliners* a book of satiric stories of great subtlety, a little like Russian work, and *Chamber Music* a book of verse, a little of it very beautiful and all of it very perfect technically. I will try to find these books and send them to you. I would think it a great kindness if you would do something for this man whose life has always been hard, but who was emerging into luckier circumstances when the war came. Yours

W B YEATS

The typed passages I send are all from an intimate friend of Joyce. You must not attribute to me that remark about publishers.

TO ROBERT BRIDGES

Tuesday [? July 1915]   18 *Woburn Buildings*

Dear Bridges, I have not written because I have mislaid your last letter but one and have been hoping to find it again. I chiefly remember you asked me about my stops and commas. Do what you will. I do not understand stops. I write my work so completely for the ear that I feel helpless when I have to measure pauses by stops and commas.

I have been looking through Sturge Moore for poems to draw your attention to. Read 'Kindness' in *Poems* (Duckworth 1906) and the 'Dying Swan' and 'Semele' in *The Sea is Kind* (Grant Richards 1914). There are other beautiful things but much that is too loose and easy.

If you wish it I could call on you Friday or meet you anywhere; but I expect you will not have time. Yours   W B YEATS

I heard from Binyon a week ago that Rothenstein had told him of the difficulty with Tagore about your book.[1] —— is the mischief maker. I have written Rothenstein an urgent letter and suggested his sending it to Tagore but have not heard from Rothenstein.

I wish I could see more of your daughter's work. I have read out the best of what I have to a number of people.

TO THE SECRETARY OF THE ROYAL LITERARY FUND

July 29 [1915]   *Coole Park*

Dear Sir: I have only to-day received your letter. I believe that Joyce is in immediate need of help. I sent to Mr. Gosse a statement of Mr. James Joyce's present circumstances so far as they are known to me, if more particulars are needed you could perhaps get them from Mr. Ezra Pound, 5 Holland Place Chambers, Kensington, who has been in fairly constant correspondence with Mr. Joyce and arranged for the publication of his last book. I think that Mr. Joyce has a most beautiful gift. There is a poem on the last page of his

[1] Robert Bridges wished to include some extracts from Tagore's *Gitanjali* in his anthology *The Spirit of Man*, but Tagore at first objected to a slight re-wording of the translation which Bridges wanted to make. Eventually, however, he consented.

Chamber Music which will, I believe, live. It is a technical and emotional masterpiece. I think that his book of short stories *Dubliners* has the promise of a great novelist and a great novelist of a new kind. There is not enough foreground, it is all atmosphere perhaps, but I look upon that as a sign of an original study of life. I have read in a paper called *The Egoist* certain chapters of a new novel, a disguised autobiography, which increases my conviction that he is the most remarkable new talent in Ireland to-day.[1] Yours sincerely
W B YEATS

TO ROBERT BRIDGES

August 1 [1915]   *Coole Park*

My dear Mr. Bridges, I have written to Tagore; I wrote a couple of days ago and hope we have prevailed.

'O hurry where by waters among trees' is a late re-writing of a poem published by Bullen. I imagine you should write to him. The amended poem is only in Tauchnitz, so for this you need no leave but mine.

Tell your daughter that the other day Lady Gregory, who was dining with me, took up while waiting for me—I had gone out to post a letter—your daughter's poems. I had not told her of them and she found them herself and read them with admiration. I have made Sturge Moore very enthusiastic about them.

I shall be here till September I imagine. It is my one chance of finishing a new play. Yours
W B YEATS

TO HENRY JAMES

August 20 [1915]   *Coole Park*

Dear Mr. Henry James: I have sent your friend these verses

'A reason for keeping silent.' [2]
'I think it better that at times like these
We poets keep our mouths shut; for in truth

[1] *A Portrait of the Artist as a Young Man* was serialized in the *Egoist* (London). Twenty-five instalments appeared between February 2, 1914 and September 1, 1915.

[2] This poem Yeats contributed to *The Book of the Homeless*, which was edited

> We have no gift to set a statesman right;
> He's had enough of meddling who can please
> A young girl in the indolence of her youth
> Or an old man upon a winter's night.'

It is the only thing I have written of the war or will write, so I hope it may not seem unfitting. I shall keep the neighbourhood of the seven sleepers of Ephesus, hoping to catch their comfortable snores till bloody frivolity is over. Yours sincerely   W B YEATS

TO EDMUND GOSSE

August 21 [1915]   *Coole Park*

My dear Gosse, I have sent all the information I have about Joyce but could of course get more if I knew what was wanted. Joyce would answer questions. In a letter of thanks he says 'I am trying to arrange here about the typing of my play *Exiles* and I shall send it then to Mr. Pringle,' an agent I believe. 'I think I can arrange to have it typed in exchange for a certain number of lessons.' He speaks also of hoping for 'badly needed relief' from your fund. I shall try and get a sight of his play but our players have had to go to the music halls to keep in existence till the war is over, so I can do nothing for him there. I believe him to be a man of genius, that he and James Stephens are the most promising people we have in Ireland. I thank you very much for the trouble you are taking. Yours   W B YEATS

TO EDMUND GOSSE

August 28 [1915]   *Coole Park*

My dear Gosse: I thank you very much for what you have done;[1] but it never occurred to me that it was necessary to express sympathy

---

by Edith Wharton and published in March 1916. A version with the second line altered appeared under the title 'On being asked for a War Poem' in *The Wild Swans at Coole*, 1917.

[1] By the courtesy of the Committee and Secretary of the Royal Literary Fund in relaxing their rule regarding secrecy as to the awards made by the Fund, I am able to state that the sum granted to James Joyce was £75.

at Coole Park
August 20   Gort
                   Co Galway

Dear Mrs Henry James: I have
sent you five new verses
  'A reason for keeping silent.
"I think it better that in times like these
We poets keep our mouths shut; for in truth
We have no gift to set a statesman right;
He's had enough of meddling who can please
A young girl in the indolence of her youth
Or an old man upon a winter's night."
It is the only thing, I have written of the
war or will write my critics so I hope it may
not seem unfelt,. I shall keep the
neighbourhood of the seven sleepers
of Ephesus, hoping to catch their
comfortable snore, till bloody frivolity
is over.
                     Yrs ever
                     WB Yeats

'frank' or otherwise with the 'cause of the Allies.' I should have thought myself wasting the time of the committee. I certainly wish them victory, and as I have never known Joyce to agree with his neighbours I [*a line missing where the paper has been torn and mended*] in Austria has probably made his sympathy as frank as you could wish. I never asked him about it in any of the few notes I have sent him. He had never anything to do with Irish politics, extreme or otherwise, and I think disliked politics. He always seemed to me to have only literary and philosophic sympathies. To such men the Irish atmosphere brings isolation, not anti-English feeling. He is probably trying at this moment to become absorbed in some piece of work till the evil hour is passed. I again thank you for what you have done for this man of genius. Yours   W B YEATS

TO ERNEST BOYD

Sept 26 [1915]   *Coole Park*

Dear Mr. Boyd: Forgive my not having written but I have been wrapped up in a new play. Now here is the trouble about those proofs. A hand press prints very slowly and I have had to put off publication until Xmas and the proofs will not be all corrected until the end of November, and it is the later part that would be of help to you. I revise in proof a great deal and hate, even if I had a spare copy of the script, which I have not, to let anybody see it before it has come to its final form.

    Yes, the Abbey has been hard hit but hopes to survive. We have had to send some of our people to music halls with our short pieces and to allow others to go on tour in the English provinces or in Africa with other companies. The anxiety of the war and the many deaths reduced our audience both in Dublin (where we could play only the more popular pieces and those at a loss) and in England till we were losing heavily. If however we can hold on at music halls we will restore our fortunes and be able to open soon again. In any case however we will start again after the war. Yours sincerely
W B YEATS

TO J. B. YEATS [1]

[circa *November–December* 1915]

[*The first two pages of this letter are missing.*]

I also used another sentence of yours that when two Irishmen meet in a railway train they are not happy until they get to terms of equality, and that when two Englishmen meet they are not happy till they know who is master and who is man. Indeed it was that sentence started the discussion about English manners. There was a disagreeable young man whose name I did not catch who, oblivious of the fact that he would have been a very unpopular crossing-sweeper, tried to explain that the students of Oxford and Cambridge disliked anybody who came among them from a superior class. I thought his presence gave great point to our discussion.

I think the real object of this letter is to announce that you may receive at any moment a copy of my 'Memoirs.' Lolly may send you an advance copy, or she may wait till publication, which has been delayed to suit the American publisher. I would have sent you one out of my six but I have used up mine as gifts to people who helped at my lecture, one for instance goes to the Aga Khan, the head of the Mohomedan community, who to my great surprise sent £30. I had said to him 'I am going to send you a little book' and he said 'If it is your poems I already know them by heart.' I had meant to send my poems but after that I had to substitute the Memoirs. If Lolly does send you a copy before the date of publication be very careful to keep it from the journalists, as Macmillan will be bringing out an American edition.

I am rather nervous about what you think. I am afraid you will very much dislike my chapter on Dowden, it is the only chapter which is a little harsh, not, I think, really so, but as compared to the rest, which is very amiable, and what is worse I have used, as I warned you I would, conversations of yours. I don't think the chapter good, there have been too many things I could not say because of the living, the truth is that it is the one chapter in the biography which would have been the better if I had written it for my own eye alone and delayed publication many years. I couldn't leave Dowden out, for, in a subconscious way, the book is a history

[1] Dictated.

of the revolt, which perhaps unconsciously you taught me, against certain Victorian ideals. Dowden is the image of those ideals and has to stand for the whole structure in Dublin, Lord Chancellors and all the rest. They were ungracious realities and he was a gracious one and I do not think I have robbed him of the saving adjective. The chapter, I should tell you, gives particular satisfaction to Lady Gregory who felt in Dowden a certain consciousness of success which makes it amusing to her that I have quoted from you a very kind analysis of the reasons of his failure. If you feel inclined to be angry with me, remember the long life of a book. If it is sincere it has always a difficult birth and can not help disturbing the house a little. Amiable as I have been, I wonder if Mrs. Smith, Dowden's daughter, whom I like . . . will invite me to any more seances at her house. I am going on with the book but the rest shall be for my own eye alone, and perhaps I may re-do that Dowden chapter, the first Mrs. Dowden, her sister, the young family, all set out in order this time, and leave it to be substituted for the other chapter some day. I think you will like the early part, and I would like from you any reveries or suggestions that occur to you. You wrote to Lilly once that you began writing a letter to me about your early years but gave that up and began your memoirs instead. I suppose you have abandoned them, as I have not heard, but may I not see what you have done? I hope you do not object to a typewritten letter, but my writing is less legible than yours. Your letters are always a delight, one recent one I thought very fine, and I read it out to a number of people upon a Monday evening. It was the letter about Wordsworth. I am continually telling myself to comment upon your letters, but there are so many letters which I have to do about practical matters, that I never seem to have time. Your son

W B YEATS

TO LILY YEATS

Friday [10 *December* 1915]　　　　　18 *Woburn Buildings*

My dear Lilly: I saw your show at the Irish Literary yesterday and brought Mrs. Shakespear who bought some small things. The woman who was in charge for you said Sturge Moore had been in in the morning and that she had told him that her buyers wanted stronger colours and liked anything distinctive—Celtic design for instance. Sturge Moore, she says, declared that he would have made the same criticism. Her comment to me was that owing to the scenery of the Russian Ballet and the designs for it by Bakst (I am not certain of the spelling of his name) the sense of design has changed. I told her of the Van Arnem design and she said she knew his work and that [though] she might not have sold it, people are so impoverished or cautious because of the war, its being there would have helped. She confirmed my own impression. Now I want to give Mrs. Shakespear a present of a table centre and I have asked Sturge Moore to design it. He is doing a design full of beauty to illustrate my line 'The infinite fold.' I shall pay you for working it, but if it is good I shall want you to make a second version for selling purposes. Sturge Moore thinks the design would also do for a quilt. My plan is if I can afford it, and I am not quite sure till I have transferred my works to Unwin, to spend quite a largish sum of money but in any case to spend some money on getting you designs, which will be suited to the change of taste. Sturge Moore wants us to go slowly because owing to the war it is hard to get good colours, but I would like to keep your own needle reasonably busy.

Here is a piece of very private information for you. I have just refused a knighthood. Lady Cunard had already sounded the authorities and asked me about it to-day. Please keep it to yourself as it would be very ungracious of me to let it get talked about in Dublin. It was very kindly meant. I said 'As I grow old I become more conservative and do not know whether that is because my thoughts are deeper or my blood more chill, but I do not wish anyone to say of me "only for a ribbon he left us." ' Lady Cunard then said 'Well you can have it whenever you like.'

By the by it was Ruth who first told me of your need for new designs. I liked best yesterday, as always, your own little bunches of flowers. I do not like the large tulips. I thought that they were a form of design spoilt for us by Liberty's shop. Sturge Moore went in hope of seeing your child's quilt but it was not there. I would like you presently to have a show in London of only the best work. I think I could get some rich people to go to see it, but that must wait. I am half inclined to think that Lolly

[*The rest of this letter is missing.*]

TO JOSEPH HONE[1]

Jan 2, 1916   *Stone Cottage*

Dear Hone, I would have written to thank you for your book [2] before, but when I came down here from London I left my copy behind me. I have now got it and am turning over the pages to remind myself of what occurred to me when I first read it. You have done me great service in putting into this book exactly what I would have wished some young men in Dublin to know. I know that my work has been done in every detail with a deliberate Irish aim, but it is hard for those who know it in fragments to know that, especially if the most that they know of me is about some contest with Irish opinion. You have put together the main outline of my work as it most concerns Ireland and have had the self-abnegation to interpret rather than to criticize. Your difficulties have come from my house being still unfinished, there are so many rooms and corridors that I am still building upon foundations laid long ago. In some ways it is a pity that you had not the new book my sister is bringing out in your hands so that you could have quoted it instead of merely for your own reading, and yet perhaps not. It has left you freer to tell things in your own way. I am particularly glad of the book just now for I am making some alterations in my publishing scheme and hope to make my work as a whole accessible. Up to this no young Irishman as poor as I was when I was twenty could afford to read me.

    I think I have been as lucky in my biographer as 'AE' has been unlucky. Figgis [3] showed himself an efficient man of action in that gun-running business, but he is the most chuckle-headed, tongue-clotted of writers. I am waiting for Ervine's *Carson*, which should be more interesting than the *AE*. Yours sincerely   W B YEATS

TO J. B. YEATS

[? early 1916]   *Stone Cottage*

My dear Father, This will probably be a very short letter for I have a number of letters to dictate to-day. I write because you have begun

---

[1] Dictated.
[2] *William Butler Yeats. The Poet in Contemporary Ireland* by Joseph Hone. Dublin and London: Maunsel & Co., 1916.
[3] Hone's volume was one of a series 'Irishmen of To-Day.' Others in the series were *AE* by Darrell Figgis, and *Edward Carson* by St. John Ervine.

addressing yours to Woburn *Place* instead of Woburn *Buildings*. You addressed a letter right on the 18th of January, but went wrong on the nineteenth and I am afraid that letters may go astray. I value the letters very much. I send them to be typed the moment they come. If you don't object I think I shall start in a week or two making a collection of thoughts from them for Lolly's press, quite a little book as a beginning, and not perhaps for publication till, let us say, the end of the year. I am trying to let her have a number of books together, so that she can make her plans of work for some time ahead.

I don't think you will very much object to what I have said of Dowden, it is not hostile, it is merely a little unsympathetic. It is difficult for me to write of him otherwise; at the start of my movement in Dublin he was its most serious opponent, and fought it in ways that seemed to me unfair. He was always charming in private but what he said in private had no effect upon his public word. I make no allusion to these things but of course they affect my attitude; he was helpful and friendly when I first began to write and I give him credit for it. But in my account of Dublin I had to picture him as a little unreal, set up for contrast beside the real image of O'Leary. Probably the book will reach you a few days after this letter, and I want you when you read it to keep in mind how the balance lies between Dowden and myself. I often wish I could comment upon your letters but there is never time. There are always so many practical letters to write. To some extent you must take the book of Memoirs as a comment. When I was writing it I thought constantly that you would write me, after it [*word torn*] letters about it. For that reason I am pleased to think that you must find there things to correct. Yours   W B YEATS

TO J. B. YEATS

March 5, 1916   18 *Woburn Buildings*

Dear Father, I cannot reply to your last letter, the one with the amusing picture of Wilson, favourite of heaven, for I have sent it to the typist to be copied. I am handing the letters over to Ezra Pound, who is to make a first small volume of selections for Lollie's press, I thought he would make the selection better than I should.

I am almost too familiar with the thought, and also that his approval, representing as he does the most aggressive contemporary school of the young, would be of greater value than my approval, which would seem perhaps but family feeling. It will also enable me to have a new book for Lollie sooner than if I did the work myself, as I shall be busy writing at something else and my sight makes my work slow. In the last letter but one, you spoke of all art as imitation, meaning, I conclude, imitation of something in the outer world. To me it seems that it often uses the outer world as a symbolism to express subjective moods. The greater the subjectivity, the less the imitation. Though perhaps there is always some imitation. You say that music suggests now the roar of the sea, now the song of the bird, and yet it seems to me that the song of the bird itself is perhaps subjective, an expression of feeling alone. The element of pattern in every art is, I think, the part that is not imitative, for in the last analysis there will always be somewhere an intensity of pattern that we have never seen with our eyes. In fact, imitation seems to me to create a language in which we say things which are not imitation.

At the present moment, after a long period during which the arts had put aside almost everything but imitation, there is a tendency to over-emphasise pattern, and a too great anxiety to see that those patterns themselves have novelty. I write all this not because I think it particularly striking or because I think you have no answer to it, but to suggest to you some new thoughts which will come to you from meeting it.

I return to London to-morrow, mainly to get rehearsed and to get ready for rehearsal a little play in which the principal characters wear masks designed by the painter, Dulac, it is an experiment and is to be played in Lady Cunard's drawing room.[1]

We have had all kinds of copyright difficulties, the usual ones accentuated by wartime, over the autobiography. You have probably, therefore, not yet received your copy. I saw Lady Gregory a couple of weeks ago on her return, and looking very vigorous; she

---

[1] The play was *At the Hawk's Well*, the first to be written in Yeats's new dramatic form founded on the Japanese 'Noh.' The cast was Cuchulain, Henry Ainley; Old Man, Allan Wade; The Guardian of the Well, Michio Ito; the costumes and masks were designed and made by Edmund Dulac. The first performance, which was in the nature of a *répétition generale*, was given in Lady Cunard's drawing-room in Cavendish Square on the afternoon of Sunday, April 2, 1916, before a small audience of invited guests.

is now in the West of Ireland again, correcting the proofs of the big book on fairy belief, which I have annotated copiously. Yours ever

W B YEATS

TO J. B. YEATS

March 14 [? 1916]   18 *Woburn Buildings*

My dear Father: The typist has just sent me a letter of yours dated Feb 12. I had not noticed when it came that you asked me a question. You ask for examples of 'imitation' in poetry. I suggest that the corresponding things are drama and the pictorial element and that in poetry those who lack these are rhetoricians. I feel in Wyndham Lewis's Cubist pictures an element corresponding to rhetoric arising from his confusion of the abstract with the rhythmical. Rhythm implies a living body, a breast to rise and fall, or limbs that dance, while the abstract is incompatible with life. The Cubist is abstract. At the same time you must not leave out rhythm and this rhythm is not imitation. Impressionism by leaving it out brought all this rhetoric of the abstract upon us. I have just been turning over a book of Japanese paintings. Everywhere there is delight in form, repeated yet varied, in curious patterns of lines, but these lines are all an ordering of natural objects though they are certainly not imitation. In every case the artist one feels has had to *consciously* and deliberately arrange his subject. It was the impressionists' belief that this arrangement should be only unconscious and instinctive that brought this violent reaction. They are right in believing that this should be conscious, but wrong in substituting abstract scientific thought for conscious feeling. If I delight in rhythm I love nature though she is not rhythmical. I express my love in rhythm. The more I express it the less can I forget her.

I think Keats perhaps greater than Shelley and beyond words greater than Swinburne because he makes pictures one cannot forget and sees them as full of rhythm as a Chinese painting. Swinburne's poetry, all but some early poems, is as abstract as a cubist picture. Carlyle is abstract—ideas, never things or only their common worn out images taken up from some preacher, and to-day he is as dead as Macpherson's *Ossian*. Insincere and theatrical, he saw nothing.

His moral zeal cast before his mind perpetually 'God,' 'Eternity,' 'Work,' and these ideas corresponding to no exact pictures have their analogy in all art which is without imitation. I doubt if I have made myself plain. I separate the rhythmical and the abstract. They are brothers but one is Abel and one is Cain. In poetry they are not confused for we know that poetry is rhythm, but in music-hall verses we find an abstract cadence, which is vulgar because it is apart from imitation. This cadence is a mechanism, it never suggests a voice shaken with joy or sorrow as poetical rhythm does. It is but the noise of a machine and not the coming and going of the breath.

It is midnight and I must stop. Yours   W B YEATS

I am back again in London.

TO LADY GREGORY

March 26 [1916]   18 *Woburn Buildings*

My dear Lady Gregory ... I have just done a feeble thing of a similar kind. A man has issued, by mistake he says, by design I suspect, a pirated edition of some of my recent poems.[1] He had proposed to make technical publication as his magazine *Form* was delayed and the poems were coming out in America. I got in a rage and limited him to 50 copies. He wrote this would ruin him and that he had not enough to eat. I did [not] believe and told Watt who was acting for me to be firm. Then Ricketts said he would pay any loss the man was under. I gave way at once, not wishing to have Ricketts pay, and now Ricketts says he misunderstood the situation. I feel I have rather injured Cuala, which should have all my first editions, and myself because the pirated edition is pretentious and has a vulgar drawing (which Ricketts had not seen).

The play goes on well except for Ainley, who waves his arms like a drowning kitten, and the musician, who is in a constant rage. She says 'in the big London theatres the action is stopped from time to time to give the musician his turn.' I am going this afternoon to Dulac's to go on working out gestures for Ainley. They are then to

[1] *Eight Poems* by W. B. Yeats, transcribed by Edward Pay, published by *Form*. 200 copies were issued in April 1916.

be all drawn by Dulac. I believe I have at last found a dramatic form that suits me ... Yours

W B YEATS

TO JOHN QUINN

April 2, 1916 18 *Woburn Buildings*

My dear Quinn, I believe that I sent you the typed script of *Reveries* at the moment when I wrote. Till I got your letter I had no doubt on the subject. I wonder if it went down on some torpedoed ship? However, here is another typed script. I send you also a pirated publication which may interest you as a collector. I got sorry for the young man, who said he had not enough to eat and was ruined if I wasted the edition, and so I gave way. He had my poems free for his magazine, and then when 'a technical publication' was made necessary by his own delays and he and Watt had arranged for such publication, brought out 200 copies of this disgusting pamphlet.

I hope I am not incoherent but I am tired out with the excitement of rehearsing my new play—*The Hawk's Well* in which masks are being used for the first time in serious drama in the modern world. Ainley, who is the hero, wears a mask like an archaic Greek statue. I enclose a paragraph from the *Observer*. The play can be played in the middle of a room. It is quite short—30 or 40 minutes. I am not satisfied with the production and shall withdraw it after Tuesday and start afresh. I hope to create a form of drama which may delight the best minds of my time, and all the more because it can pay its expenses without the others. If when the play is perfectly performed (musicians are the devil) Balfour and Sargent and Ricketts and Sturge Moore and John and the Prime Minister and a few pretty ladies will come to see it, I shall have a success that would have pleased Sophocles. No press, no photographs in the papers, no crowd. I shall be happier than Sophocles. I shall be as lucky as a Japanese dramatic poet at the Court of the Shogun.

My dress rehearsal, or really first performance, is given at Lady Cunard's to-day at 3-40, and I am to be there at 3. I shall go to lunch and then lie down for a little and after that I may be able to face the musicians. One of them insists on a guitar, and the scene of the play is laid in Ireland in the heroic age! His instrument is to

appear to-day disguised by Dulac in cardboard, but the musician will struggle for the familiar shape. Beecham is coming to support me.
Yours ever
                                                                  W B YEATS

TO LADY GREGORY

[*The earlier part of this letter appears to be missing.*]

March 28 [1916]   18 *Woburn Buildings*

The play goes well but the musicians give more and more trouble and will have to be eliminated when we are through our first performances. The masks have the most wonderful effect. They keep their power when you are quite close.

Monday [*Postmark* 10 *April* 1916]

I think *At the Hawk's Well* was a real success though a charity audience is a bad one.[1] We refused to admit the press as we considered it an experiment and in any case have no need of press in work intended for a few. We shall not do it again until June in order to get rid of Ainley and the musicians. The music Beecham says is good but one cannot discuss anything with a feud between Dulac and a stupid musician at every rehearsal. It seems better to get very simple music that can be kept under control. I may even repeat the lyrics myself and have no singing and no music but gong and drum played by Dulac and perhaps a dulcimer or flute. The form is a discovery and the dancing and masks wonderful. Nobody seemed to know who was masked and who was not on Tuesday. Those who were not masked were made up to look as if they were. It was all very strange. Two press people got in, a wretched woman who came to describe the clothes of the fine ladies, and an American who paid a guinea for his ticket and who wants pictures from Dulac of masks and costumes for some American magazine. We turned a most obstinate photographer out of the dressing rooms. Coburn is to photograph us. It amuses me defying the press.

Now that it is over I find myself overwhelmed with work—

[1] A public performance of *At the Hawk's Well* (described on the programme as *The Hawk's Well, or the Waters of Immortality*) was given in aid of the Social Institute Union at 8, Chesterfield Gardens, London, W., on Tuesday, April 4. It was preceded by a concert arranged and conducted by Sir Thomas Beecham.

introduction to book of Japanese [plays] for my sisters ¹—two books of verse by Tagore to revise for Macmillan who has no notion of the job it is, and revision of a book of my own verse for Macmillan, so I hope I may delay another week with your proofs.

    There is a chance of Ricketts, Dulac and I running a season at the Aldwych Theatre next year with Beecham. We have been asked and have sent in statement of conditions—absolute control. I am keeping my responsibility as slight as possible. It may mean a fine performance of *Player Queen* and use of properties in Dublin. Meanwhile would you send me a copy of your *Golden Apple* to show to Dulac and if he approves put on the list. My chief object will be to get performances of Irish plays to impress Dublin. If it comes off there will be no compromise—romance, fine scenery, the whole *Hamlet*, *Volpone* and some Molière plays staged strangely and beautifully. Yours
                                                  W B YEATS

    PS. I want to follow *The Hawk's Well* with a play on *The Only Jealousy of Emer* but I cannot think who should be the changeling put in Cuchulain's place when he is taken to the other world. There would be two masks, changed upon the stage. Who should it be— Cuchulain's grandfather, or some god or devil or woman? Yours
                                                  W B YEATS

TO LADY GREGORY

Thursday [11 *May*, 1916]   *Royal Societies Club*
                                          St James's Street. S.W.

My dear Lady Gregory, The Dublin tragedy has been a great sorrow and anxiety.² Cosgrave, who I saw a few months ago in connection with the Municipal Gallery project and found our best supporter, has got many years' imprisonment and to-day I see that an old friend Henry Dixon—unless there are two of the name—who began with me the whole work of the literary movement has been shot in a

   ¹ *Certain Noble Plays of Japan* chosen from the manuscripts of Ernest Fenollosa by Ezra Pound, with an introduction by W. B. Yeats, was published by the Cuala Press on September 16, 1916.
   ² The Rising in Dublin and Proclamation of the Irish Republic took place on Easter Monday, April 24, and between May 3 and 9 Patrick Pearse, Thomas McDonagh, Joseph Plunkett, John MacBride and others of the leaders were executed.

barrack yard without trial of any kind.[1] I have little doubt there have been many miscarriages of justice. The wife of a Belgian Minister of War told me a few days ago that three British officers had told her that the command of the British army in France should be made over to the French generals, and that French generals have told her that they await with great anxiety the result of the coming German attack on the English lines because of the incompetence of the English Higher Command as a whole. Haig however they believed in—he was recommended by the French for the post. I see therefore no reason to believe that the delicate instrument of Justice is being worked with precision in Dublin. I am trying to write a poem on the men executed—'terrible beauty has been born again.'[2] If the English Conservative party had made a declaration that they did not intend to rescind the Home Rule Bill there would have been no Rebellion. I had no idea that any public event could so deeply move me—and I am very despondent about the future. At the moment I feel that all the work of years has been overturned, all the bringing together of classes, all the freeing of Irish literature and criticism from politics. Maud Gonne reminds me that she saw the ruined houses about O'Connell Street and the wounded and dying lying about the streets, in the first few days of the war. I perfectly remember the vision and my making light of it and saying that if a true vision at all it could only have a symbolised meaning. This is the only letter I have had from her since she knew of the Rebellion. I have sent her the papers every day. I do not yet know what she feels about her husband's death. Her letter was written before she heard of it. Her main thought seems to be 'tragic dignity has returned to Ireland.' She had been told by two members of the Irish Party that 'Home Rule was betrayed.' She thinks now that the sacrifice has made it safe. She is coming to London if she can get a passport, but I doubt her getting one. Indeed I shall be glad if she does not come yet—it is better for her to go on nursing the French wounded till the trials are over. How strange that old Count Plunkett and his wife and his three sons should all be drawn into the net.

[1] This was a journalist named Thomas Dickson, who was not even a sympathiser with Sinn Fein. Henry Dixon, a solicitor, who was in the Rising, was arrested, but set free in the general release of June 1917.
[2] Yeats's famous poem 'Easter 1916,' with its refrain 'A terrible beauty is born,' is dated September 25, 1916.

I sent on to you yesterday the proof sheets I had finished and fastened up at the start of the Rebellion. I sent a letter with them giving an explanation of what I want you to do. I have been able to do little work lately and that chiefly on *Player Queen* which always needs new touches in its one bad place—first half of second act.
Yours   W B YEATS

TO JOHN QUINN

May 23, 1916   18 *Woburn Buildings*

My dear Quinn . . . This Irish business has been a great grief. We have lost the ablest and most fine-natured of our young men. A world seems to have been swept away. I keep going over the past in my mind and wondering if I could have done anything to turn those young men in some other direction.

At the moment I feel as if I shall return to Dublin to live, to begin building again. I look sadly about my rooms for I have just taken in and furnished the floor below my old rooms and so have practically the whole house. I am pleased with the look of things and shall be sad to shift. Yet perhaps tomorrow I may be in another mood and not sad at the thought or have given the thought up. I chiefly dread the temptation to controversy one finds in Dublin. I knew several of the executed men, and others were familiar figures . . . Yours ever   W B YEATS

TO ROBERT BRIDGES

June 13 [1916]   18 *Woburn Buildings*

Dear Bridges: Please forgive me for not having answered your letter of May 12. All my habits of thought and work are upset by this tragic Irish rebellion which has swept away friends and fellow workers. I have just returned from Dublin where of course one talks of nothing else, and now, if I can get a passport, I must go to a friend in Normandy who has been greatly troubled by it all. But for this I would have gone to you and had indeed, before you wrote, intended to suggest myself as a visitor. I thank you very much.
Yours   W B YEATS

TO OLIVIA SHAKESPEAR

Nov 8 [*probably* 1916]   *Stephen's Green Club*
Dublin

My dear Olivia: Yes I had a bad passage—the worst I have had for 20 years. I went next morning to the theatre and came away from it with Donovan. A stranger (a newly engaged actor I found) came up to us with the pleased gravity of those who have really bad news and announced 'The mail boat went down last night and Mr. Yeats was on board.' I think in future I shall not despise the weather but will choose windless days. So far I have prided myself on my indifference to storms.

I hear there is quite a sound cottage at the foot of my castle, so I may be there even before the castle is roofed.[1] I shall probably go to Coole to go over the castle, on Saturday. If I get it I shall plant fruit trees as soon as possible—apple trees for the sake of the blossoms and because it will make me popular with the little boys who will eat my apples in the early mornings.

I am very busy, reading plays, seeing plays at the Abbey, seeing numerous people about business. This is the first day on which I have been enough at leisure to get a fire lit in my own room and to write there—a little at the new play but mostly at letters. Yours affectionately   W B Y

TO LADY GREGORY

[*Postmark Nov* 13, ? 1916]   *Stephen's Green Club*

My dear Lady Gregory . . . Here is a queer story. Last night a rather drunken man got into my carriage coming from Greystones. I was in a first to escape the crowd. He began by asking a series of questions such as why third class carriages on that line were so bad —he himself always went first class with a third class ticket 'on principle,' and then 'why are so many men dead that should be alive and so many men alive that should be dead?' He then said there was

---

[1] First mention of the castle in Galway, which Yeats afterwards named Thoor Ballylee, and which he bought from the Congested Districts Board for £35 and made into a summer residence for himself and his family.

a strange thing he could not understand. He was in Tipperary during the rising and he heard a lot of plainly false news. The guard of the train brought it and the Police Sergeant spread it. He thought it would be a good joke to spread his own false news so he said to the Sergeant 'Sheehy Skeffington has been shot' and he saw the Sergeant spreading it and the people coming out of the shops to listen. And 'shot he was that very morning and not a soul knew it—now is not that a queer thing?' A man in the club tells me that when he was at school he invented, as he thought, a story of Lord Frederick Cavendish being killed, and when later in the day the news of the assassination came in he thought it was only his own story coming back to him and would not believe. Probably this is how news spreads in India. People get the thought by telepathy and think they are inventing. Yours always W B YEATS

TO THE EDITOR OF THE *OBSERVER*[1]

[*Published January* 21, 1917]

I.

It is important from the outset to weigh the moral weight of the will of 1913, leaving Sir Hugh Lane's French pictures to the National Gallery of London. I will show that so far as we can ever know another man's mind, we know he made it in 'momentary irritation' and when he was deceived about essential facts, and that Mr. Mac-Coll is wrong in supposing that he ever abandoned his Dublin work. For some years before 1913 a project had been discussed between him and his friends for a temporary exhibition of the French pictures in the London National Gallery. On July 27, 1913, he wrote to Sir Charles Holroyd: 'These pictures are complementary to the collection I have already given them (the Dublin Corporation) and the other pictures given and subscribed for by others. . . . I think if they were hung in the National Gallery or the Tate Gallery it might

[1] Yeats contributed a number of letters to the controversy which took place in 1916–1917, in the *Observer, The Times* and other papers, regarding Sir Hugh Lane's will and its codicil, and his intentions as to the ultimate destination of his collection of French paintings. It has seemed that to reprint these out of their context would be unnecessary, since Yeats resumed all his arguments in this long essay-letter in the *Observer*.

encourage the Corporation to fulfil my conditions.' A little later, when it had become probable that the Dublin Corporation would refuse the building upon a bridge over the Liffey that he had asked for, he got a letter from one of the London Trustees asking if there was any chance of the National Gallery receiving a gift of the pictures, 'or would the loan, if accepted, be a loan in reality for the aid of Dublin.' A gift of the pictures to London would have implied the foundation of some kind of international gallery to contain them, for neither the National Gallery nor the Tate can, by their constitution, permanently exhibit modern Continental works of art.

It must have been about this date (I have no means of fixing the exact date) that Lord Curzon proposed to him the foundation of such a gallery. There was always someone at his elbow in moments of despondency to suggest that he should give to England so rich in pictures what he had promised to Ireland in her poverty. He replied on August 8: 'As I still hope that my work in Dublin will not prove a failure, I cannot think of giving them to any other gallery at present, but the gallery that, not having such, refused the loan of them for one or two years would appear to be quite unworthy of them as a gift. I confess to being quite out of sympathy with the English National Gallery.' On August 12 the secretary of the National Gallery replied, unconditionally accepting loan of the pictures. A few days later came the Dublin refusal, and this refusal was aggravated by a disgraceful Press attack. In a cautious interview in the *Manchester Guardian* he spoke of a possible international gallery. He took his French pictures from Dublin, sent them to the National Gallery, where they are still in the cellars, and changed his will. He had left everything he possessed to the Dublin Municipal Gallery, but now, with the exception of these pictures left to London, he gave all to the Dublin National Gallery. Dublin was still, it is plain, his chief interest.

Yet in letters to Lady Gregory, who always pleaded for Ireland and the work there, he spoke of Ireland with great bitterness. We were all very angry, less, indeed, with the Corporation than the newspapers, and some of us thought that only the sale of the pictures in the open market would prove their value. I myself printed, as a pamphlet, *Poems Written in Discouragement, 1912–1913*, and certainly these poems are as bitter as the letters Mr. MacColl has quoted. That is the manner of our intemperate Irish nature (and I think the

Elizabethan English were as volatile); we are quick to speak against our countrymen, but slow to give up our work. I once said to John Synge, 'Do you write out of love or hate for Ireland?' and he replied, 'I have often asked myself that question;' and yet no success outside Ireland seemed of interest to him. Sir Hugh Lane wrote and felt bitterly, and yet when the feeling was at its height, while the Dublin slanders were sounding in his ears, he made a will leaving all he possessed, except the French pictures, to a Dublin gallery. A few days after writing that Ireland had so completely 'disillusioned' him that he could not even bear 'to hear of his early happy days in Galway,' he had bequeathed to Dublin an incomparable treasure. I think Mr. MacColl by quoting these intimate letters has but proved how profound and how stable the subconscious purpose was.

II.

Dr. Haydn Brown has given evidence to prove the will no final decision. Mr. MacColl would put this evidence aside, because the consultations were before the Dublin decision. Well, I offer him a document he cannot put aside. I saw Sir Hugh Lane at Lady Gregory's request on November 4—that is to say, a few days after the writing of the will—and I have before me a careful record of our conversation posted to Lady Gregory the following day. I asked him to offer the pictures to Ireland once more, perhaps after the establishment of the Home Rule Government that seemed coming so quickly, and pointed out that the disgraceful attack upon his pictures and himself had come from ignorant men in accidental power. Generous and irascible beyond any man I have known, he seemed without bitterness, and [I] will now quote the words of my letter.

'All should be allowed to rest for the present;' he wanted 'time to recover his enthusiasms . . . but you may be very sure,' he said, 'I have no desire to leave the present Dublin collection to represent me.'

Lady Gregory was to write privately to her subscribers, who had given her many thousands (all returned on the Dublin refusal for the building of the Dublin gallery), that we hoped to carry through our Dublin plan, 'though we have been defeated for the moment through passing conditions of economic strife.'

III.

Now a wonderful thing happened which certainly did not incline his mind to London. The Trustees, after they had accepted his loan unconditionally, after they had hung his pictures, after he had announced in Dublin (he was still thinking of Dublin) the day when they were to be first shown to the public, decided to make conditions. They would only hang a small collection chosen by themselves; fifteen pictures which they considered 'well worthy of temporary exhibition in the national collection,' and they would not hang even these fifteen, unless he promised to bequeath them to the Gallery in his will. The selection was capricious or careless; it rejected, for instance, Daumier's 'Don Quixote,' according to the mind of some of us a master work surpassing all the rest in beauty. Sir Hugh Lane, though his new will was only some three months old, refused both conditions.

It became exceedingly difficult to get any reparation made to him for the Dublin Press attack; all his enemies were heartened. The rumour ran: 'The National Gallery in London has refused the Lane pictures because they are not good enough.' He considered himself abominably treated, and remained, so far as I know, of this mind to the end. On November 12, 1914, he wrote to an official of the National Gallery: 'I will leave the pictures at the National Gallery as you wish. I understand that my distinguished friends who are responsible for their being at the National Gallery are hoping to arrange to exhibit them at the Tate Gallery. It was this suggestion that induced me to refrain from publishing the particulars of the annoying affair. . . . I cannot even return the pictures to Dublin without removing the slur that has been cast upon them.'

IV.

From early in 1914 his London friends tried once more to secure the pictures for London and certainly at first they had heavy work, for the Trustees had not been ingratiating; he was once more 'quite out of sympathy with the English National Gallery.' Mrs. Shine remembers a conversation on March 3 or 4 when he flatly refused. Mr. Witt, Mr. MacColl, and Mr. Aitken do, however, claim that they did get in the end a conditional promise, but they have not claimed and cannot claim that the condition was fulfilled. 'He was prepared,' says Mr. Aitken in the *Morning Post*, 'to give at any rate his French pictures to whichever city seemed first ready to show some appreciation.' And Mr. MacColl says that on March 5, 1914, he promised 'to wait and see what appreciation of them was shown, the test being the foundation of a gallery.'

These sentences are vague. There was clearly nothing in the nature of a compact. It was plain that he reserved for his own judgment what constituted 'some appreciation.' The only document cited by Mr. MacColl in support of these memories is a letter written in February to an official of the National Gallery saying that if his pictures could lead to the establishment of an international gallery in London—'a crying want'—he would 'be greatly tempted to give them,' but added 'I refuse to give any definite promise, as I do not intend to act hastily.' I will assume that he was ready, or at the moment ready or half ready to give his French pictures to an international gallery, but I do not believe that this man, whom I know to have been even more tenacious than excitable, would have given a single picture but that he believed he could buy as good or better for the gallery that was created from his fancy as his lasting monument.

The matter is one of merely biographical and psychological interest now. Mr. Witt and his friends may believe that if he had lived, he would have liked their present plan and have endowed it, but Parliament will only concern itself, I believe, with his intentions while he lived. 'He told me,' said Mr. Aitken, 'that he intended altering his will in favour of Dublin if his French pictures were not to be exhibited in London;' and they were not exhibited.

V.

His interest in Dublin was returning; he had become Director of the National Gallery there. Dublin became as little distasteful to him as any place can be to a man whose nerves are kept upon edge by bad health and the desire to achieve more than the public opinion of his time permits of. He took a keener interest in his Municipal Gallery, and began to give it gifts once more, adding to it, for instance, a fine bust by Rodin. After all, Dublin had founded a gallery for him, and exhibited his French pictures for years, and that gallery was well attended, and among the rest by working people. His most vehement years had been expended in its service; it could but remain his chief work, his monument to future generations, and lacking important pictures that he had gathered for it, that noble monument would lack a limb. Was it not more natural to wish to leave behind him a small perfect thing with the pattern of his own mind than to be half remembered for a bequest soon lost in the growing richness of a London gallery? More than all the rest, he was Irish and of a family that had already in their passion and in their thought given great gifts to the people.

VI.

In January, 1915, he told his sister that he was about to make a new will; and in February, 1915, he wrote the codicil, leaving the French pictures once more to the Municipal Gallery in Harcourt Street. He wrote it so carefully that his sister is convinced that he must have made several drafts. It was well written, and he was accustomed to write even a letter with difficulty. He had always a prejudice against lawyers, and had dictated his two previous wills to his sister, and it was to her now that he addressed the envelope in which the codicil was sealed. It was signed but it was not witnessed, and she has testified that neither of his previous wills, neither that which left all he possessed to the Municipal Gallery, nor that leaving the French pictures to London, would have been witnessed but for her persistency. When he made the second will, he had forgotten all that she had said at the making of the first. He was a man of no business habits in the ordinary sense of the word, and though he never forgot any detail about a picture that once interested him, nothing else seemed to stay in his mind. If he remembered anything she had told him about the need of a witness, he perhaps thought that a postscript to an already witnessed will needed no new formality. Being signed and in his own handwriting, even as it is, it would be legal in Scotland or the trenches. If he had not gone down in the *Lusitania*, he would have spoken about it to someone and have learnt his mistake, and I cannot believe that a great English institution would wish to benefit by a German act of war. When he wrote, he expected to start for America, not in seven or eight weeks as he did, but in three or four, and he felt the danger of the journey so acutely that at first he had refused to go unless those who invited him would insure his life for £50,000 to clear his estate of certain liabilities in case of death. For what purpose could that codicil have been written if he did not believe it to be legal, and certainly it was written with the thought of death in his mind?

VII.

Mr. Aitken says that he told Sir Hugh Lane shortly before he left for America that there was at last some real likelihood of the international gallery, and that Sir Hugh Lane said that he would decide the ultimate destination of the pictures, as Mr. MacColl puts it, 'according to the action of the authorities in London and Dublin respectively.' A vague sentence that committed him to nothing even if he lived (especially as he was about to withdraw his claim for the bridge site, his one serious difficulty with the Corporation), and the codicil was a provision for his death. Mr. Witt thinks that by leaving it unwitnessed he meant to keep 'the question of a change of destination' for the French pictures in suspense. We can put aside all such speculation. The day before he left Dublin and two days before he left England (for he spent but a day in London, I believe) he told Mrs. Duncan, Curator of the Dublin Municipal Gallery, that he was about to take the French pictures from London, where 'they were not even seen,' and rehang them in Dublin, and that he was content if the Corporation gave him a gallery on a site of their own choice. He had not decided merely, as he might well have done, that because if he died now he would have no chance of endowing both galleries, his own gallery must have all he had collected for it. It was plain that even if he lived he would wait no longer, negotiate no more. He was very delicate and had already explained, in conversation with a Dublin alderman, the impatience which had caused some of his Dublin troubles by saying that he wanted to see his gallery finished as he would not live long. He told his friend, Mr. Martin, who travelled with him to Liverpool, that he was giving the pictures to Dublin. He had found waiting him in London as a last exasperation a bill of some pounds for mending his picture frames, damaged on their journey from Dublin to the cellars in Trafalgar Square, and his language was sufficiently definite.

Just before the *Lusitania* sailed from America he told Mr. John Quinn, a well-known lawyer and one of the governing body of the Metropolitan Museum of New York, that 'if they would make some provision for a gallery . . . not necessarily the bridge site, he would give them (the pictures), as he always meant them to go there.'

VIII.

The clause in the will of 1913 leaving the French pictures to London was founded upon a misunderstanding of the intentions of the London Trustees and in 'momentary irritation,' and has no moral weight. The codicil has as much moral weight as any such document ever had or could have, and I believe that Parliament will give it the effect of law. Dublin is prepared to build for the pictures a suitable gallery. Even on Mr. Aitken's own test Dublin has shown 'some appreciation' first. I gave evidence some twelve months ago before what I believe to be the Finance Committee of the Dublin Corporation, and the Lord Mayor, at my request, renewed the promise, already upon the books of the Corporation, of a suitable building. The Lord Mayor and the Corporation and representatives of all the principal learned and educational societies in Dublin and such distinguished men as Mr. William Orpen, Sir Horace Plunkett, Mr. George Russell, and Mr. George Bernard Shaw have asked the Trustees for an act of generosity and of justice, and we shall ask Parliament to make that act possible. W B YEATS

P.S. Lady Gregory has asked me to say that she regrets that Mr. MacColl, carried away by the excitement of discussion, should have published certain intimate letters of Sir Hugh Lane which she gave him 'after much hesitation for biographical purposes alone.' They were written 'in a dark transitory mood' and cannot be understood apart from the life and letters in their entirety. She adds, 'Of course I do not imagine that Mr. MacColl did this with the knowledge or consent of the National Gallery Trustees. It was certainly done without mine.' Mr. MacColl points out that in a letter, published in *The Times*, certain letters were wrongly dated. I had found out the error immediately and written to withdraw the letter and to substitute another which I enclosed. *The Times* promised to make the substitution, but the political crisis was at its height, and after a considerable delay the original uncorrected letter was published.

There is a misunderstanding in Mr. Konody's sympathetic letter. The pictures given by him and others to the Dublin Municipal Gallery are still there. They are not involved in the present dispute.[1]

[1] From this time onwards Lady Gregory, with some help from Yeats, carried on an untiring agitation for the return of the Lane pictures to Ireland. In July 1924 the English Parliament appointed a commission to consider the question. In its report, dated January 28, 1925, the commission found that 'in

TO J. B. YEATS

May 12, 1917   *Coole Park*

My dear Father, I think I must have had all your letters. You speak of anxiety on the subject in a letter to Lady Gregory. I have had them all typed and they are on my shelves in little packets all in order and dated. I think I shall be able to run a new series of extracts, through a review Ezra Pound edits,[1] and this should bring you a little money, though I doubt if Ezra can pay much. I am delighted that you tell me you have written so much of the biography. Do not attempt to send MSS. till after the war. Apart from submarines, there are all kinds of restrictions, and I think MSS, as apart from letters, can only be sent through publishers. I will offer it to Macmillan and it can be illustrated with reproductions of designs by Nettleship, and pictures by Potter (now a great reputation) and Wilson and your own pictures. At least that is what I will try for. I keep hearing praises of the little book of your *Letters*,[2] but as yet have seen no reviews. I came here to take over my Tower, Ballylee Castle. I shall make it habitable at no great expense and store there so many of my possessions that I shall be able to have less rooms in London. The Castle will be an economy, counting the capital I spend so much a year, and it is certainly a beautiful place. There are trout in the river under the window. Jack can come there when he wants Connaught people to paint. I have finished a little philosophical book—60 pages in print perhaps—*An Alphabet*.[3] It is

---

signing the codicil of the 3rd February 1915 [Lane] thought he was making a legal disposition.' They advised the Government, however, against giving legal effect to the codicil, partly on the ground that Lane would have approved of the new gallery at the Tate, Millbank, and would have destroyed the codicil.

Although the question of returning the pictures to Ireland has been raised in Parliament from time to time, the pictures still remain in England, while the Municipal Gallery at Charlemont House, Dublin, keeps a room always empty, awaiting their return.

Hugh Lane and his Pictures by Thomas Bodkin, published in 1932 by the Pegasus Press for the Government of the Irish Free State, contains a short life and appreciation of Lane, a full statement of Ireland's claim, and fine collotype reproductions of the pictures.

[1] Probably the *Little Review*, edited in New York by Margaret Anderson. Ezra Pound acted as Foreign Editor.

[2] *Passages from the Letters of John Butler Yeats* selected by Ezra Pound, Cuala Press, May Eve, 1917.

[3] *An Alphabet* was later given the Virgilian title *Per Amica Silentia Lunae*. It was published by Macmillan in January 1918; the new book of verse, *The Wild Swans at Coole*, was published earlier, by the Cuala Press, in November 1917.

in two parts: *Anima Hominis* and *Anima Mundi* and is a kind of prose backing to my poetry. I shall publish it and a new book of verse side by side, I think. Reviewers find it easier to write if they have ideas to write about—ideas or a narrative like that in my *Reveries*. I have just made a revision of my *Player Queen*, a prose comedy, and Mrs. Campbell talks of playing [it] for the Stage Society. It is very wild, and I think, amusing.

I wonder would you be easier in your mind about your letters if you kept a record of the dates and sent them to me. I would then let you know if they reach me. Or you might number the letters. Yours ever   W B YEATS

I am told one should sign in full for censor.
WILLIAM BUTLER YEATS

TO OLIVIA SHAKESPEAR

May 15 [1917]   *Coole Park*

My dear Olivia: I have been here for some weeks looking after my castle chiefly. I go to London on Saturday but only for a few days as I do lectures at Edinburgh and Birmingham. I shall probably return here. The castle is to be handed over to me tomorrow. The architect has been down and I know what I am going to do. The little cottage is to be repaired and extended so as to put in a quite comfortable and modern part—kitchen, bathroom, sitting room, three bedrooms. I am then to go on to the castle at my leisure. The cottage on the island will be arranged so as to give me privacy shutting me off from the road thus. [*Here follows a rough plan.*]
The cottage will make a kind of cloister and will be thatched. [*Here follows a rough sketch, marked* 'very bad drawing.']
This will give me a little garden shut in by these and by the river. The cottage will cost I believe £200. The old outhouses to supply the stonework. My idea is to keep the contrast between the mediaeval castle and the peasant's cottage. As I shall have the necessities in the cottage I can devote the castle to a couple of great rooms and for very little money.

I shall never be in good health but in the country. I have been better since I came here than I have been for months. I have never been here in Spring before. The woods full of crabtrees in flower and here and there double cherries in flower. The fruit trees in the garden too a mass of flowers. I have finished the elaborate philosophical essay and revised *Player Queen* again and started another play in the manner of *The Hawk's Well*. I do not mean to be in any town for more than a few days till September or October when I hope and almost believe the war will be over. I am not in the best of spirits but when the day is fine life is endurable.

Robert Gregory wrote a week ago to say things at the front are going better than people at home seem to think. Yours always

W B YEATS

TO LADY GREGORY

June 11 [*Postmark June* 12, 1917] 18 *Woburn Buildings*

My dear Lady Gregory . . . I saw *L'Annonce faite à Marie* of Claudel played in English last night. It was except for the last scene the most moving play I have seen for many years. I noticed that everybody near me was either overwhelmed with emotion or untouched and making jokes. The last scene was not, as I expected, a bore—it held the house but it was absurd. The old man who is so serene after all the tragedy is fine when one reads it but a fool when one sees it. If the play ended at his entrance it would be most powerful.

I have almost finished my Dervorgilla play,[1] I think the best play I have written for years. It has grown greatly since you saw it and is I am afraid only too powerful politically. I have nothing now to write but the lyrics and must leave London for that. Yours

W B YEATS

TO J. B. YEATS

June 14 [1917] 18 *Woburn Buildings*

My dear Father . . . Your letters are as interesting as ever—those of last November were I think especially good. Much of your

[1] *The Dreaming of the Bones*; it was included in *Two Plays for Dancers*, Cuala Press, January 1919, but was not played at the Abbey Theatre until December 1931.

thought resembles mine in *An Alphabet* but mine is part of a religious system more or less logically worked out, a system which will I hope interest you as a form of poetry. I find the setting it all in order has helped my verse, has given me a new framework and new patterns. One goes on year after year gradually getting the disorder of one's mind in order and this is the real impulse to create. Till one has expressed a thing it is like an untidy, unswept, undusted corner of a room. When it is expressed one feels cleaner, and more elegant, as it were, but less profound so I suppose something is lost in expression.

I shall be back in Ireland before you get this and later I hope to go to Normandy and I am to give some lectures in Paris and probably in Milan—my old subjects—and shall earn enough to roof the castle. Yours affectionately W B YEATS

TO OLIVIA SHAKESPEAR

July 10 [*Postmark* 1917]　　　　　　　　　　*Coole Park*

My dear Olivia: I got here this morning after spending some days in Dublin, where a young man called Power made an admirable bust of me. It is to be bronze and mounted on a rough block of green marble. I look rather humorous and intellectual than poetical.[1] I have come here to work at my French lectures. Did I tell you I am going to Paris to lecture according to some government scheme and one lecture is to be 'Modern Ireland'? I go there next month but will not lecture till September. While here I shall start the builders at the castle and walk over a mountain side where I have laid the scene of a new play. I saw my architect in Dublin and he wants to begin at once on the castle and leave the cottage until later.

I stayed in Dublin with Gogarty the witty doctor—who is a friend of John's and Orpen's. It is he who has ordered the bust. After his death and mine it is to be put in a public garden. Stevens [? Stephens] and Russell and Hyde all called to see me and some less known people and I lived in a whirl of excellent talk. I am glad to be out of London where I was disconsolate and mostly tired. I have

[1] I have been unable to discover where this bust is now. After Yeats's death Albert Power made a second bust of him.

got to the last state of a man when only work is of interest. Here I find the people, without any reason to give, are expecting peace. One man said that Belfast merchants had received some hint and so on—rumours one cannot build on. I hear (through a letter to a friend from the mother of an airman who did not return) that an attempt has been made by England and France to raid Berlin but it was a failure. Out of 42 machines only 28 returned. I suppose the great distance made the defence too strong. No, I have done no more about the *Windsor Mag* prophecies. They were identified by Bessie's brother—the one who was killed—and it may be too late to find the date of their composition. A certain William Chapel a rifleman has been identified. He was killed in the war. I wish you had taken on hay-making. I wonder if you are sun-burned. Yours affectionately W B YEATS

Did I tell you of Mrs. Emery's death in Ceylon?

TO LADY GREGORY

August 12 [1917]　　　　　　　　　　*c/o Madame Gonne*
　　　　　　　　　　　　　　　　　　Colleville S. Mer
　　　　　　　　　　　　　　　　　　　　Calvados

My dear Lady Gregory: I have been here since last Tuesday. Iseult [1] and I are on our old intimate terms but I don't think she will accept. She 'has not the impulse.' However I will think the matter undecided till we part. They talk of returning to Paris at the end of the month and of going to London in middle of September. They hope to be allowed back to Ireland but do not yet know. At present there is refusal. I must stay on in Paris for my lectures. Whatever happens there will be no immediate need of money, so please see that Raftery goes to work at Ballylee. I told him to put 'shop shutters' on cottage but now I do not want him to put any kind of shutter without Scott's directions.[2] When you need another £50 from me let

---

[1] Maud Gonne's daughter, whom Yeats, at that time, thought of marrying.
[2] William A. Scott (1871–1918) was Professor of Architecture at the National University of Ireland from 1911. He was the designer of many churches and public buildings in Ireland.

me know. I have finished my play. I think of calling it *The Dreaming of the Bones*. I have greatly improved it since you saw it—improving and adding to the lyrics and strengthening the atmosphere. Here they say it is my best play. It has evidently some popular quality. Rummel has consented to write the music and that was Dulac's wish. I read him the play in Paris where I was delayed one day by passport difficulties. It is very pleasant here. Maud Gonne is no longer bitter and she and Iseult are on good terms now and life goes on smoothly. Iseult herself seems to have grown into more self mastery after months of illness from cigarettes. She has only had one outbreak so far and that was only one cigarette and a half and was secret. Yours always
                                                            W B YEATS

(I hear one should sign in full for Censor so I add William Butler Yeats)

TO LADY GREGORY

August 15 [*Postmark Aug* 18, 1917]   *Colleville S. Mer*

My dear Lady Gregory: I return *Andy Doyle*,[1] which I agree with you in thinking should be accepted. I think it will play fairly well and fill a gap. It is very much of course an imitation of Murray.[2] I have no particular news—our household has the usual number of cage birds, a parrot, a monkey, a goat, two dogs, a cat and seven rabbits. The parrot has one accomplishment, a scream of laughter, and if anyone laughs in its hearing the scream comes at once. As I write the monkey is on the window outside scratching at the glass to draw my attention. Two days ago a neighbour called, a young widow, and she and the parrot became hysterical with laughter—each setting the other off. I have just driven the monkey off the window sill.

Iseult and I take long walks, and are as we were last year

---

[1] No play of this title appears in the Abbey Theatre record of productions. It may possibly have appeared under another title.

[2] T. C. Murray (b. 1873), one of the Abbey Theatre dramatists. His fine tragedies *Birthright* (1910) and *Maurice Harte* (1912) were at first unpopular, but he continued to write for the theatre until 1939. *Autumn Fire* (1924) is generally considered his masterpiece.

affectionate and intimate and she shows many little signs of affection, but otherwise things are as I wrote. I have done nothing since I finished the play but read for my lectures. I am working at Blake who has been substituted to my relief for the Irish lecture. Yours
W B YEATS

TO LADY GREGORY

August 21 [*1917*]   *c/o Madame Gonne*
17 *Rue de l'Annonciation*
Passy

My dear Lady Gregory: I give the Paris address for though we shall be at Colleville for another eight days we shall be in Paris before a letter can reach me. I shall be at some Hotel there but Madame Gonne's is the only address I can give.

Thanks for Raftery's estimate which is much what I thought it would be. I think it possible that Scott may think it better not to wall up that door—I want him to decide. I have also asked him to advise about doors etc. If Raftery has got to wait he will have plenty to do on roof, walls etc, so Scott's advice will not be late. (Prof. Scott, 45 Mountjoy Square is his address.)

No change here. This morning the monkey tried to pluck the parrot. Iseult has been ill and came down this morning after two days in bed, full of affection owing to a dream she had had in which I had sympathised with her in some nightmare circumstances. Yet I don't think she will change her mind. The little boy is now quite tall and is going to be very clever and to my amusement has begun to criticize his mother's politics. He has a confident analytical mind and is more like a boy of 17 than 13. Life goes smoothly after one outbreak from Maud Gonne, the result of my suggesting that London was a better place for Iseult than Dublin. They go to London in the middle of September to try and get the government refusal to allow Maud Gonne to go to Ireland withdrawn. It has just been repeated however—so everything is very uncertain.

I think that a resolution from that conference would settle the picture question but I doubt if their terms of reference will admit of it. Yours   W B YEATS

I am doing nothing but read Blake for my lecture—working at his philosophy again.

TO LADY GREGORY

Sept 8 [*Postmark Sept* 10, 1917]   *Hôtel Gavarni*
                                                                                                                           Rue Gavarni
                                                                                                                           Passy

My dear Lady Gregory: I return to London on Sept 14. My only doubt about your dragon play is who, Robert being away, is to stage it. I cannot think of anybody in Dublin who could. If one had the designs it might be managed—perhaps we may find somebody but till that is done I doubt putting it on list. I expect [to] carry back to London with me part at least of the music to my Noh play *The Dreaming of the Bones.* Sooner or later I shall want to get it up in Dublin but not yet. I am really getting ready a mass of work to start in Dublin and London if I can make some settlement in my life. I am just now too restless. Iseult has always been something like a daughter to me and so I am less upset than I might have been—I am chiefly unhappy about her general prospects. Just at the moment she is in one of her alarming moods—deep melancholy and apathy, the result of having left the country—and is always accusing herself of sins—sins of omission not of commission—She has a horoscope that makes me dread melancholia. Only in the country is she amused and free of this mood for long. Maud Gonne on the other hand is in a joyous and self forgetting condition of political hate the like of which I have not yet encountered. As soon as I reach London I shall be in the midst of another crisis of my affairs, (about which I need not write for the possible eye of the censor,) so you must not expect to get much good of me for a while. I return here for my lectures in December. I have made a fine Blake lecture which I shall hope to deliver in Dublin. I will not fix a date for I am very tired of moving about. Yours always   W B YEATS

TO LADY GREGORY

[Sept. 18. Postmark Sep. 19 1917]   *Arts Club*
                                       40 *Dover Street, W.*1

> I am at this Club till the Savile re-
> opens next week. It is being cleaned.

My dear Lady Gregory: I got back yesterday . . . I don't think I can come to Coole just now. Mrs. Tucker has asked me down to where she and her daughter are.[1] I am however in rather a whirlpool. Maud Gonne and the harmless Iseult have been served with a notice under the defence of the realm forbidding their landing in Ireland. Their getting back to Paris is also doubtful. We had a difficult time at Southampton. They were searched as possible spies by the order of polite and plainly shamefaced officials who kept the train waiting for us. I am just going to see them. Poor Iseult was very depressed on the journey and at Havre went off by herself and cried. Because she was so ashamed 'at being so selfish' 'in not wanting me to marry and so break her friendship with me.' I need hardly say she had said nothing to me of 'not wanting.' Meanwhile she has not faltered in her refusal of me but as you can imagine life is a good deal at white heat. I think of going to Mrs. Tucker's on Monday but may not as I am feeling rather remorseful especially now that this last business of the defence of the realm act has come. I wrote to Mrs. Tucker from France thinking that Iseult was going to Dublin and that I would not see her for months. I feel that Iseult has [? will] badly need my friendship and watch over her interests in the next few weeks. Maud Gonne will certainly do something wild. I would be glad of a letter of counsel. Yours   W B YEATS

TO LADY GREGORY

Sept 19 [*Postmark* 1917]   *Arts Club*

My dear Lady Gregory: I wrote you a very disturbed letter yesterday. Since writing I have decided to be what some Indian calls 'true of

[1] Mrs. Tucker, formerly Mrs. Hyde-Lees, had married H. T. Tucker who was a brother of Olivia Shakespear. Mrs. Tucker's daughter by her first marriage became Mrs. W. B. Yeats in September 1917. Hereafter, in the letters, she appears as Georgie or, more frequently, George.

voice.' I am going to Mrs. Tucker's in the country on Saturday or Monday at latest and I will ask her daughter to marry me. Perhaps she is tired of the idea. I shall however make it clear that I will still be friend and guardian to Iseult.

... I have seen Iseult to-day and am doing as she wishes. All last night the darkness was full of writing, now on stone, now on paper, now on parchment, but I could not read it. Were spirits trying to communicate? I prayed a great deal and believe I am doing right. Yours ever
W B YEATS

TO LADY GREGORY

Oct 29 [Postmark 1917]   *Ashdown Forest Hotel*
Forest Row

My dear Lady Gregory: The last two days Georgie and I have been very happy. Yesterday we walked to a distant inn on the edge of the Forest and had tea. There has been something very like a miraculous intervention. Two days ago I was in great gloom, (of which I hope, and believe, George knew nothing). I was saying to myself 'I have betrayed three people;' then I thought 'I have lived all through this before.' Then George spoke of the sensation of having lived through something before (she knew nothing of my thought). Then she said she felt that something was to be written through her. She got a piece of paper, and talking to me all the while so that her thoughts would not affect what she wrote, wrote these words (which she did not understand) 'with the bird' (Iseult) 'all is well at heart. Your action was right for both but in London you mistook its meaning.' I had begun to believe just before my marriage that I had acted, not as I thought more for Iseult's sake than for my own, but because my mind was unhinged by strain. The strange thing was that within half an hour after writing of this message my rheumatic pains and my neuralgia and my fatigue had gone and I was very happy. From being more miserable than I ever remember being since Maud Gonne's marriage I became extremely happy. That sense of happiness has lasted ever since. The misery produced two poems [1] which

---

[1] The two poems, 'The Lover Speaks' and 'The Heart Replies,' were not published till 1924 when they appeared in the American *Dial* and in *The Cat and the Moon and certain Poems*, Cuala Press, July. They were later included in *The Tower*, 1928, under the single title 'Owen Ahern and his Dancers.'

I will send you presently to hide away for me—they are among the best I have done.

I enclose a letter of congratulation from Helen Bayly (now Mrs. Lawless) you will remember her at Florence. I send it as it shows you how well George is liked—I have had other like testimonies. I think Georgie has your own moral genius. She says by the by that you are the only friend of mine she has never feared. Should have said that after Georgie had written that sentence I asked mentally 'when shall I have peace of mind' and her hand wrote 'you will neither regret nor repine' and I think certainly that I never shall again.

Is Raftery at work on Ballylee?—if he is I will write to Gogarty and ask him to stir up Scott.

I enclose a note from the Chiswick Press. Yours   W B YEATS

TO LADY GREGORY

Dec 16 [*Postmark* 1917]   18 *Woburn Buildings*

My dear Lady Gregory, We shall I think not be with you until end of the first week of January or thereabouts. We were going to Dulac's for Xmas but have decided to go there after Xmas as George has formed the kind idea of our taking Iseult to Stone Cottage for Xmas that she may be a few days in the country. She and Iseult are becoming great friends—Iseult stayed here last night as she seemed too tired to go home and they have spent the morning talking dress. And now I find that George is giving Iseult a dress as a Xmas present. They made friends first for my sake but now it is for each other's, and as both according to the new fashion for young girls are full of serious studies (both work at Sanskrit) it should ripen. My wife is a perfect wife, kind, wise, and unselfish. I think you were such another young girl once. She has made my life serene and full of order. I wish you could see Woburn Buildings now—nothing changed in plan but little touches here and there, and my own bedroom (the old bathroom) with furniture of unpainted unpolished wood such as for years I have wished for. Then there is a dinner service of great purple plates for meat and various earthenware bowls for other purposes. Then too all is very clean yet Mrs. Old is not unhappy. She comes in the evening for better pay and someone else does the rough work in the mornings.

I have stopped work on my philosophic dialogue for the moment as it was keeping me awake at night and am writing verse again. I have just all but finished another rebellion poem. I shall now finish my play and then return to the dialogue.

George is reading your *Gods and Fighting Men* and is about half way through. She prefers it to the Eddas which she had been reading just before. Yours W B YEATS

Robinson has just sent me a very fine play—the supposed return of Parnell—your old subject—nearly a great play but not quite.[1] I shall suggest one or two changes before I send it you. I got Gogarty to strengthen his last act.

[1] *The Lost Leader* by Lennox Robinson, produced at the Abbey Theatre, February 9, 1918.

PART FIVE

1918—1928

INTRODUCTION TO PART FIVE

AT Oxford Yeats worked well and completed another Cuchulain play, *The Only Jealousy of Emer*. The revelations which continued to come to him through Mrs. Yeats's automatic writing filled him with excitement and he began a dialogue between two of his fictional characters, Michael Robartes and Aherne, which ultimately became his book *A Vision*. Robert Gregory had been killed in the war while flying in Italy, and Yeats wrote the first of his memorial poems on him, the pastoral 'Shepherd and Goatherd.' He and Mrs. Yeats went to Ireland in March, visited Coole Park in May, and then lived for several months in Ballinamantane House, Gort, which Lady Gregory lent them in order that they might oversee the building operations at Ballylee. In the autumn they were in Dublin, where Maud Gonne gave them the use of her house in Stephen's Green, and in February of 1919 their daughter was born in Dublin and was christened Anne Butler. That summer they were at last able to move into Ballylee. An invitation came from Japan to go there and lecture for a year or possibly two, but after consideration this was refused. Early in 1920 Yeats sailed for America on a third lecture tour, Mrs. Yeats going with him, and they remained in the States for several months. In the autumn they returned to Oxford where they had taken a house at 4 Broad Street, and presently Yeats crossed to Dublin to have his tonsils removed by his friend Dr. Oliver Gogarty.

He had now begun work on the next instalment of his autobiography which he called *Four Years*, and he read much history and philosophy. In April 1921 they let the Broad Street house and stayed in a cottage at Shillingford in Berkshire. While there Yeats received an offer of £500 from the publisher Werner Laurie for the right to print a limited edition of the later autobiographical chapters, and these were issued to subscribers in October 1922 under the title

The Trembling of the Veil. In August they moved to Thame in Oxfordshire, where on the 22nd of the month their son was born and was christened William Michael. In the autumn they returned to Oxford.

In February 1922 J. B. Yeats died in New York; he had lived there since 1908. Both Yeats and Mrs. Yeats, who had met and liked him in America, felt his loss much; but his death relieved Yeats of considerable financial responsibility. Conditions in Ireland were now very threatening and he began to feel that he ought to be living there, so Mrs. Yeats went to Dublin and found a suitable large house, 82 Merrion Square. The family crossed to Ireland but went for the summer to Ballylee. On May 21 Michael Collins and Mr. De Valéra had made peace; the Free State Constitution was issued in June and a verdict in favour of the Treaty given at the General Election. By the end of the month the Civil War had begun. Cut off from any definite news, but otherwise undisturbed, Yeats finished the first section of his memoirs, *Reveries over Childhood and Youth,* that summer and wrote the series of poems called 'Meditations in Time of Civil War.' He was busy also correcting the proofs of the first two volumes of a new collected edition of his works which Macmillan began to issue in the late autumn. At the end of September the move to Merrion Square was made; and he began to find that a poet, at least, was not without honour in his own country. He was invited to become a member of the Senate, membership of which carried an income of £360 a year, and in December a D.Litt. was conferred on him by Trinity College. As Senator he was given an armed guard at his house. He was now working hard on 'the system' as he called his book *A Vision*; Werner Laurie was anxious to publish it.

The year 1923 was divided between Dublin and Ballylee, and in November the Nobel Prize was conferred on him. Accompanied by Mrs. Yeats he journeyed to Stockholm to receive the prize in person, and on his return wrote an essay 'The Bounty of Sweden' to express his thanks. He was assiduous in his attendance at the Senate, and spoke occasionally though at first not often at any great length. Work on *A Vision* was continued throughout 1924. In November Mrs. Yeats took him to Sicily, and on the way back he visited Capri and Rome.

In 1925—a year for which there are hardly any letters—he remained in Dublin, and in June delivered a long and eloquent speech in the Senate on the subject of divorce. In the autumn of this year he went to Switzerland to lecture and then to Milan. The first version of *A Vision* was at last finished, and copies were issued to subscribers in January 1926.

The Abbey Theatre, which, after some years of depression, had begun to prosper owing to the production of Sean O'Casey's first two plays, ran into a further gale of rioting at the production of *The Plough and the Stars*; as usual the directors held firm, the theatre played to full houses, and the play was soon given a revival; it is still one of the most popular plays in the repertory. Yeats had now undertaken a translation of Sophocles' *Oedipus Rex*—the revival of an old project of 1914—and was reading much philosophy. In May he retired to Ballylee and found, as always, that he could write poetry there more easily than in a city; the work done there included the two series of lyrics 'A Man Young and Old' and 'A Woman Young and Old.' His version of *Oedipus* was produced at the Abbey in December 1926, and he at once started a translation of *Oedipus at Colonus*. A committee was formed to advise on a new coinage for the Free State and Yeats accepted the chairmanship; meetings continued over the next two years.

March 1927 produced another important speech in the Senate on the subject of a suggested copyright bill. Ballylee was visited in the summer, and in the autumn both *Oedipus* plays were given with much success. In October a bad cold brought on congestion of the lungs. When he was sufficiently recovered Mrs. Yeats took him to Spain, first to Algeciras and then to Seville, but as his lung was not yet healed they moved to Cannes. Here he had an attack of influenza which led to a general breakdown in health. Asking the doctor who attended him what had caused his illness, he was told it was the result of 'the overwork of years.' Complete rest was prescribed and he was allowed to read only the lightest kind of literature. In February 1928 they moved along the coast to Rapallo, beyond Genoa. Yeats was now convalescent but had to be careful; by April he was well enough to go to Switzerland where his son Michael was at school, and so home via Cherbourg and Queenstown. In Dublin he was examined by doctors; his ill health had been diagnosed as due to lungs, high blood-pressure, and nervous breakdown; he was persuaded to stay in bed and work there until lunch time. In May the house in Merrion Square was sold, and a flat found soon afterwards at 42 Fitzwilliam Square; while it was being made ready Yeats stayed at Howth. His term of office as Senator had come to an end; he was asked to stand for re-election but did not do so, knowing that his strength would be insufficient for anything but his own work. After a short visit to London in October he went back to Rapallo where a large sunny flat had been found which they were able to furnish with their own furniture and books. Ezra Pound and his wife were also living at Rapallo and Yeats was glad of their companionship. He had been working at a much revised text of *A Vision* ever since its first publication, and now began a small book giving a true account of the book's origin which he had hitherto disguised in fiction; he called it *A Packet for Ezra Pound*.

1918-1928

TO LADY GREGORY

Jan 4 [Postmark Jan 7, 1918]   45 *Broad Street*
                                                                                                     Oxford

My dear Lady Gregory: George wired to say we could not go to Ireland at present. I had an attack of influenza, and now Gogarty writes about food difficulty at his Galway house. He had to leave because of the difficulty. Our plans are therefore to stay here until near Easter when you said you could have us. We would go to Dublin a couple of weeks before you were ready for us, and I could give two lectures and produce *Baile's Strand* if you approved. Meanwhile there are various things Raftery can do at Ballylee (George is in correspondence with him) and when we go to see it the daffodils may be in flower. These are charming old rooms near the Bodleian. I have plans (if we like Oxford) of living here when not in Ireland and making this a centre for my Noh plays which have to be worked out with Dulac.

    I am sending you on Monday (when it can be registered) a very fine play, as I think, by Robinson. I think it might be put in rehearsal at once and before Gogarty's T.C.D. play which may I suspect be finished any day.[1] Robinson's play should have a great success. He made one or two changes at my suggestion. If you have any play for me to read send it here where we shall be I hope until we go to Ireland.

    A very profound, very exciting mystical philosophy—which seems the fulfilment of many dreams and prophecies—is coming in strange ways to George and myself. It began of a sudden when things were at their worst with me, and just when it started came this curious message from Bessie Radcliffe, 'They departed with the

---

[1] Dr. Oliver Gogarty's play does not seem to have been given.

rewards of divination in their hands.' It is coming into my work a great deal and makes me feel that for the first time I understand human life. I am writing it all out in a series of dialogues about a supposed medieval book, the *Speculum Angelorum et Hominum* by Giraldus, and a sect of Arabs called the Judwalis (diagrammatists).[1] Ross [2] has helped me with the Arabic. I live with a strange sense of revelation and never know what the day will bring. You will be astonished at the change in my work, at its intricate passion. Yours affectionately   W B YEATS

TO LADY GREGORY

Jan 12 [Postmark Jan 13, 1918]   45 *Broad Street*

My dear Lady Gregory . . . I think of staying a couple of weeks or so in Dublin before going on to you for Easter, and lecturing in Dublin (2 lectures, one on Blake) and producing a play, probably *Baile's Strand*, at least if there seems a company for such work.

Here I have so far only seen Walter Raleigh and Bridges. We are asking people for week ends—Iseult next week, then Bessie Radcliffe, and Mrs. Aldington, a scholar and poet.[3] My work goes on well, and before long I will send you the new Cuchullain play.[4] I have written two good lyrics for it. I then think of a narrative poem. I want to publish together the Macmillan edition of *Swans at Coole* and my four or five Noh plays. I mean two distinct books, and to follow in the autumn by *The Discoveries of Michael Robartes*.[5] So you see I am full of plans. I am in better health now than I have been for a long while. Yours always   W B YEATS

[1] This is the earliest mention of the book which eventually appeared as *A Vision* in 1925, and again, very largely revised and rewritten, in 1937.
[2] Sir Edward Denison Ross (1871–1940), a great authority on oriental languages and traveller in the Middle East and in Russia, was Director of the School of Oriental Studies in London University from 1916 to 1937, and Counsellor to the British Embassy at Istanbul from 1938.
[3] Mrs. Aldington was the imagist poet who wrote under the initials H. D.
[4] *The Only Jealousy of Emer*, one of the 'plays for dancers'.
[5] *The Discoveries of Michael Robartes* did not appear. It was probably a projected early version of *A Vision*.

TO LADY GREGORY[1]

January 14, 1918   45 *Broad Street*

Dear Lady Gregory . . . To-day I finished my new Cuchulain play and am hesitating on a new one, where a Sinn Feiner will have a conversation with Judas in the streets of Dublin. Judas is looking for somebody to whom he may betray Christ in order that Christ may proclaim himself King of the Jews. The Sinn Feiner has just been persuading a young sculptor to leave his studio and shoulder a rifle.

Judas is a ghost, perhaps he is mistaken for the ghost of an old rag-picker by the neighbourhood. I will not know whether the idea is too theoretical and opinionated (?) till I have made prose draft.[2] Before that I shall write a couple of lyrics . . . Yours sincerely

W B YEATS

TO JOHN QUINN[1]

February 8, 1918   45 *Broad Street*

Dear Quinn, I am dictating this to my wife, as you see. I have written four plays in the style of the 'Noh,' including *The Hawk's Well*, and have the plan of the fifth. I would like to publish them this season, or in the early autumn, but I want to make the edition interesting to people who are interested in the stage technically. Rummel has written very fine music for one of the plays (a play about a Sinn Feiner and a ghost), and I also want to include reproductions of Dulac's designs . . .

We are living at Oxford, instead of Stone Cottage, Coleman's Hatch, where I generally go for the winters, to be near the Bodleian. My wife never knows which to be most surprised at, the hats or the minds of the dons' wives, and is convinced that if we live here every winter, which is possible, she will be given to great extravagance out of the desire for contrast.

News will have reached you before this of Robert Gregory's death in action. I feel it very much for his own sake, still more for

---

[1] Dictated.   [2] This play was not written.

his mother's. I think he had genius. Certainly no contemporary landscape moved me as much as two or three of his, except perhaps a certain landscape by Innes,[1] from whom he had learnt a great deal. His paintings had majesty and austerity, and at the same time sweetness. He was the most accomplished man I have ever known; I mean that he could do more things well than any other. He had proved himself a most daring airman, having been particularly successful in single combat with German planes. What brought him to his end is not known. He seems to have fainted while flying at a great height, on his return from a scouting expedition. They judge this from his not having stopped his machine as a man does when he is wounded. Lady Gregory writes me grief-stricken but courageous letters. We are going there at Easter, and may possibly take a small house near Coole till our own house is ready for us. Yours ever

W B YEATS

TO LADY GREGORY

Feb 22 [1918]   *45 Broad Street*

My dear Lady Gregory: I am trying to write something in verse about Robert but do not know what will come. I am trying a poem in manner like one that Spenser wrote for Sir Philip Sidney. It may come to nothing. We have found a house here that may suit us and may be vacant next September. Very big, old beams in the ceilings; and very close to the Bodleian. At the Bodleian one can leave one's book on one's table and read there at odd moments. My table there is covered with such things as the etchings and woodcuts of Palmer and Calvert. If you ever do any work that needs a library you must come and stay with us here for it is well understood that the Bodleian is the most comfortable and friendly library in the world and I suppose the most beautiful. I wonder if you have the heart to complete the book of Gaelic selections? My sister can only keep her press busy at odds and ends three or four weeks more, and if you are not ready I do not know where to get a book.

[1] James Dickson Innes (1887–1914) was born at Llanelly, Wales, of Scottish parentage. He won a scholarship at the Slade School in 1905, but at first made slow progress. His painting life was short, his best work being done between 1910 and 1914, in which year he died of consumption.

We shall be with you at Easter as you are so kind [as] still to wish it. Raftery gets on slowly but fairly steadily with his work at Ballylee, and has just written that the rats are eating the thatch. Scott has asked for dimensions of fire-places so evidently will send designs and the Castle has been cleaned out. It looks as if this Spring may see the roof on but I don't want my wife to spend more money till she has seen the place. We have heard of a shop in Dublin that could hire us furniture for Ballinamantane should we go there, and perhaps Mount Vernon might be available for a while. We shall be houseless until the autumn but can if need be fill up a little time at small hotels by some inland water. I noticed the hotels were good along the Shannon. As we are both students we can entertain ourselves and each other. Ballinamantane is our main thought but we are very vague and know nothing yet of the expense of hiring furniture.

I went to London for one day this week and came away wishing that I might never go there again. It was a great delight to walk on my return through these quiet and stately streets.

. . . I hope you thought my little essay on Robert was right.[1] I tried to imagine to myself those who knew his pictures a little and what they thought and to write so as to settle and define their admiration. I think a little later there should be some essay on his work with reproductions of some of his pictures, but what form it should take, or by whom it were best done I do not know . . . Yours affectionately   W B YEATS

TO LADY GREGORY[2]

March 19, 1918   *Royal Hotel*
                                                              Glendalough
                                                               Co. Wicklow

I have to-day finished my poem about Robert, a pastoral, modelled on what Virgil wrote for some friend of his and on what

---

[1] Yeats wrote a short memorial essay on Robert Gregory in the *Observer*, February 17. It has never been reprinted in any of his books.
[2] This is a postscript written in Yeats's hand to a dictated letter concerning his future movements.

Spenser wrote of Sidney.[1] My wife thinks it good. A goatherd and a shepherd are talking in some vague place, perhaps the Burren Hills, in some remote period of the world. It is a new form for me and I think for modern poetry. I hope it may please Margaret also.[2]

TO CLEMENT SHORTER

[? *May* 1918]   *Coole Park*

My dear Shorter, I am giving a lecture in Dublin shortly on recent poetry including war poetry. May I quote from your wife's privately printed rebellion poems? I wonder if you would be so kind as to send me a wire. I shall lecture to a popular audience at the Abbey and shall also quote Rupert Brooke and the English war poems and perhaps some French and Italian. Yours   W B YEATS

TO CLEMENT SHORTER

May 17 [1918]   *Ballinamantane House*
                                                                                   Gort
                                                                                Co Galway

Dear Shorter: I thank you very much for leave to quote these poems, and for the new book. It is strange but your wife, like all the rest of us, is most powerful and most simple and touching when she writes of Ireland or of herself, whereas an Englishman is dramatic when at his best, and as a rule at his worst when he speaks of himself or of England. When he writes well of England it is (—there are of course exceptions,)—when he writes as a moralist and calls up old England to vex or encourage the new. You will remember that Swinburne

[1] In all, Yeats wrote four poems on the subject of Robert Gregory's death: 'The Sad Shepherd' (now named 'Shepherd and Goatherd'), 'In Memory of Major Robert Gregory,' 'An Irish Airman foresees his Death,' all of which appeared in *The Wild Swans at Coole*, Macmillan, 1919; and a fourth, 'Reprisals,' which was not published at the time because Yeats feared that Lady Gregory might feel distressed at the suggestion that her son's death had been in vain. It was printed in *Rann*, an Ulster Quarterly of Poetry, in the autumn of 1948, but has not yet found a place in the Collected Poems.
[2] Mrs. Robert Gregory.

said that personal utterance was contrary to the English genius in literature (his personal poems had the sincerity of a *Times* Leader).

I have had to postpone my lecture. Your wife's poems would have been my chief effect; and times are too dangerous for me to encourage men to risks I am not prepared to share or approve. If the Government go on with conscription there may be soon disastrous outbreaks—I doubt the priests and the leaders being able to keep the wild bloods to passive resistance. I have seen a good many people here in the West and I cannot imagine a more dangerous condition of things, the old historical passion is at its greatest intensity. I hear of an old cabinet maker saying two years ago 'There will be more wild work. The young men are mad jealous of their leaders for being shot.' Yours   W B YEATS

TO J. B. YEATS

June 14, 1918   *Ballinamantane House*

My dear Father, I have never written to you about your play.[1] You chose a very difficult subject and the most difficult of all forms, and as was to be foreseen, it is the least good of all your writings. I have been reading plays for the Abbey Theatre for years now, and so know the matter practically. A play looks easy, but is full of problems, which are almost a part of Mathematics.—French Dramatists display this structure and 17th century English Dramatists disguise it, but it is always there. In some strange way, which I have never understood, a play does not ever read well if it has not this mathematics. You are a most accomplished critic—and I believe your autobiography will be very good, and this is enough for one man. It takes a lifetime to master dramatic form. I am full of curiosity about the memoirs, but of course I cannot see them until the war is over.

This is a very old house of the usual eighteenth century or early nineteenth century sort with its own fields about it, which the Gregorys have lent us till Ballylee Castle is ready. George is, at this

[1] There are several earlier references to his play, in letters from J. B. Yeats during 1916 and 1917, but he never mentions its title. He described it as a 'psychological comedy,' on the authority of Percy Mackaye, the American playwright. It is not known if the manuscript has survived.

moment, at the Castle, where she has a man digging in front of the cottage that she may plant flowers as we expect to be there in a month. She has just come back and says all has gone well and that her workman is doing his work. (He had hated the prospect of so much digging!) Last week, we had a fine dish of trout, grey trout and salmon trout, caught, though not by us, in the Ballylee river. The best place is almost under the Castle walls.

I do nothing but write verse, and have just finished a long poem in memory of Robert Gregory, which is among my best works. Yours affectionately W B YEATS

TO J. B. YEATS

June 24 [1918]   *Ballinamantane House*

My dear Father: Why do you call Bunyan a mystic? It is not possible to make a definition of mysticism to include him. The two great mystics of that epoch are Spinoza and Pascal. Nearly all our popular mysticism derives indirectly from the first, or from a movement he was first to explain. I remember hearing Madame Blavatsky explain the identity of predestination and freedom exactly as he explains the identity of the self determination and the freedom of the self (in him God and self are one). Beside the intellect of Spinoza I do not think you will place the more merely professional intellect of the Victorians, even that of Mill. I only know Pascal slightly but I do know that his influence has been as great on orthodox mysticism as that of Spinoza on heterodox and that his intellect is sufficient. You should not conclude that if a man does not give his reasons he has none. Remember Zarathustra's 'Am I a barrel of memories that I can give you my reasons?' All the great mystics have been great in intellect. In that they differ from great pietists like Bunyan as certainly all the great mystics [do] except some few (mainly Catholics) whose natures have been overmasteringly moral—St. Francis perhaps—and perhaps we should call these pietists or visionaries not mystics.

We hope to be in Ballylee by the end of July but building is slow now and there is no certainty. Yours affectionately   W B YEATS

TO JOHN QUINN

July 23, 1918   *Ballylee Castle*
                                                      Gort, Co. Galway

My dear Quinn, This heading is written in hope, that is to say, I hope it will be true a day or two after this letter reaches you, at the latest. We are surrounded with plans. This morning designs arrived from the drunken man of genius, Scott, for two beds. The war is improving the work for, being unable to import anything, we have bought the whole contents of an old mill—great beams and three-inch planks, and old paving stones; and the local carpenter and mason and blacksmith are at work for us. On a great stone beside the front door will be inscribed these lines:

> I, the poet, William Yeats,
> With common sedge and broken slates
> And smithy work from the Gort forge,
> Restored this tower for my wife George;
> And on my heirs I lay a curse
> If they should alter for the worse,
> From fashion or an empty mind,
> What Raftery built and Scott designed.[1]

Raftery is the local builder . . .

I am making a setting for my old age, a place to influence lawless youth, with its severity and antiquity. If I had had this tower when Joyce began I might have been of use, have got him to meet those who might have helped him. His new story in the *Little Review* [2] looks like becoming the best work he has done. It is an entirely new thing—neither what the eye sees nor the ear hears, but what the rambling mind thinks and imagines from moment to moment. He has certainly surpassed in intensity any novelist of our time . . .

I have finished another 'Noh' play, and if you saw the New York performance of my *Hawk's Well* I would be glad for some news of it.

---

[1] A revised version of this poem, reduced to six lines, and headed 'To be Carved on a Stone at Ballylee,' was printed in *Michael Robartes and the Dancer*, Cuala Press, 1920 (1921).
    The Tower and its cottage still belong to the Yeats family but have not been inhabited for many years; the roof of the cottage has fallen in 'and all is ruin once again.'

[2] James Joyce's *Ulysses* was appearing as a serial in the American *Little Review*; the magazine suffered suppression several times on that account.

Fate has been against me. I meant these 'Noh' plays never to be played in a theatre, and now one has been done without leave; and circumstances have arisen which would make it ungracious to forbid Ito to play *The Hawk* as he will. I had thought to escape the press, and people digesting their dinners, and to write for my friends. However, Ito and his Japanese players should be interesting. Yours ever   W B YEATS
(William Butler Yeats)

TO CLEMENT SHORTER

Sept [1918]   *Ballinamantane House*

My dear Shorter: I enclose 9 poems.[1] If you can publish during October that will be near enough to American serial publication [*word illegible*] to save my copyright. I shall probably publish in volume form in December.

I find it hard to judge of my own work but some I think are good.

I hope K.T. book has reached you by this. I could not send it till I got to London, where I was for less than a week.

We are hoping every day to get into our castle where we are, or it is, constantly looking after carpenters and the like. We shall live on the road like a country man, our white walled cottage with its border of flowers like any country cottage and then the gaunt castle.

[*Here follows a sketch.*]

All work—furniture and all—is being done by local labour. We have plenty of timber as we bought the hundred year old floors and beams of a mill. Yours   W B YEATS

TO J. B. YEATS

Oct. 17 [1918]   73 *Stephen's Green*
                                                                                  Dublin

My dear Father, I have often pointed out to George that you and I are in telepathic communication. For instance, your letter about

[1] Clement Shorter issued *Nine Poems* in a privately printed edition of twenty-five copies in October. Seven of the poems were published simultaneously in the *Little Review*, and all were included later in *The Wild Swans at Coole*, Macmillan, 1919.

Keats and Shelley came when I had been writing about Keats and Shelley, and except that you put things better once or twice had exactly the same thought. The only difference is that I look on them as two distinct types of men, who could not exchange methods. Each had to perpetuate his own method and neither lived long enough to do so. If you accept metempsychosis, Keats was moving to greater subjectivity of being, and to unity of that being, and Shelley to greater objectivity and to consequent break-up of unity of being.

Your last letter, however, shows the most curious of all this telepathic exchange. When it came, I said to George (without letting her see the date of your letter), 'When did I write my poem of the Hare?'[1] She said 'about Sept. 20th.' Your letter is dated Sept. 22. My memory is that I was full of my subject for some days before Sept. 20th. I send you the two poems. One line,—'The horn's sweet note, and the tooth of the hound,' may have reached you, or the hare's cry—which is to you a symbol of exultation at death. 'The horn's sweet note' might well mean that. Your poem has a fine idea, but I cannot make out whether the symbolizing the joy at death by the scream of the hare is, or is not, too strained an idea.

Do nothing about 'The Memoirs' without consulting me.[2] I think it should be published here by Macmillan & Co (quite a distinct firm from the Macmillan Company New York) and the most reputable English firm, with reproductions of work by you and by Nettleship etc. I think Cuala should publish in the spring a new volume of letters and Macmillan issue both volumes of letters together. Yours   W B YEATS

TO STEPHEN GWYNN

Oct. 18 [1918]   73 *Stephen's Green*

My dear Gwynn: Do you think *Everyman* would publish enclosed play[3] if I can arrange serial publication in America (Pound's *Little*

[1] One of the 'Two Songs of a Fool' published in *The Wild Swans at Coole*, 1919.
[2] *Early Memories; some chapters of Autobiography* by J. B. Yeats was published by the Cuala Press in September 1923.
[3] Evidently *The Dreaming of the Bones*. It did not appear in *Everyman*, a weekly periodical, but was published in *Two Plays for Dancers*, Cuala Press, January 1919.

Review perhaps) so as to secure my copyright there? 'Cuala' will not, or at least need not, publish till February.

It is one of my best things but may be thought dangerous by your editor because of its relation to rising of 1916. My own thought is that it might be published with editorial note either repudiating its apparent point of view or stressing the point of view. England once, the point of view is, treated Ireland as Germany treated Belgium. I doubt if a long poem or verse play is worth anything to a popular paper unless they make a feature of it and relate it to current interests. Yours   W B YEATS

TO W. S. KENNEDY [1]

Jan. 21, 1919   96 *Stephen's Green*

Dear Mr. Kennedy, Mrs. Campbell has wired to me that she sees no 'present' likelihood of a performance at a London theatre such as she wants of my play, and that she cannot play it for you.[2] I still don't know what she means by that word present; perhaps she thinks that I should leave her the play, and will think that I am treating her ungraciously if I take it from her. However I don't know what I can do except consent to your performance. If I could go to London now I would go and talk it over with her, but I can't. If she had any desire to keep the play I would leave it with her, but it is impossible to find that out. I cannot go to London till May 15 at the earliest and I must be there for the rehearsals; so I am afraid March is an impossible date. Don't commit yourself to Miss O'Neill about the part till we have had time to think. She may be the best possible, but I have been much out of London in recent years, and in any case I don't know what London actresses you can get. Miss O'Neill is an exquisite actress in dialect. I have never yet seen her equally good out of it. In dialect she is the one poetical actress our move-

[1] Dictated. W. S. Kennedy was at this time Honorary Treasurer, and for many years afterwards Chairman of the Council, of the Incorporated Stage Society.
[2] *The Player Queen*, which received its first production by the Stage Society in London. Two performances were given at the King's Hall, Covent Garden, on May 25 and 27, 1919; the part of Decima was played by Maire O'Neill, Nona by Edith Evans and Septimus by Nicholas Hannen. The play was revived at the Abbey Theatre on December 9, 1919.

ment has produced. Of course if I had produced the play here there was no one else possible for heroine, and she may be the best one can get. Everything depends upon the actress. It wants a dominating personality with very varied powers, a woman full of animal force. It might be better to put the play off till your next season. We might persuade Mrs. Campbell to play it; at least if she saw her way to playing it occasionally on some tour afterwards. Yours

W B YEATS

TO J. B. YEATS

Feb. 4, 1919   *96 Stephen's Green*

My dear Father, I hope you will come back as soon as you can. You will be very comfortable with Lily and you can devote yourself to finishing your autobiography, and if we put you up for the University Club you will not lack conversation. Lily has for a long time been most anxious for your return, and Dublin is I think a more amusing place than it used to be. But perhaps you will have set out before this reaches you and will read my words—sent back to Ireland—at Gurteen Dhas.[1] Yours affectionately   W B YEATS

TO GEORGE RUSSELL (AE)

Tuesday [? April 1919]   *Stephen's Green Club*

My dear Russell, Many thanks but it was not Maud Gonne who quoted you but Iseult. She likes Russian Communism no more than I do; and she said 'But Mr. Russell tells me that he has information from a source which can be relied on—or some such phrase—that they have only executed 400 people,' that is why I sent you certain Russian comments on the figure, as well as on the figure of 13,000 which was published some time ago as coming from the Russian government itself. There are financial reasons why American comment is just now sometimes biassed. Thomas said in the House of Commons a couple of weeks ago 'Every responsible representative

---

[1] The house in Churchtown, Dundrum, near Dublin, where the Yeats sisters lived for many years. The name means 'the nice little field.'

of English Labour is convinced, owing to information come into its possession, that the present Russian government is worse than that of the Autocracy.'

What I want is that Ireland be kept from giving itself (under the influence of its lunatic faculty of going against everything which it believes England to affirm) to Marxian revolution or Marxian definitions of value in any form.. I consider the Marxian criterion of values as in this age the spear-head of materialism and leading to inevitable murder. From that criterion follows the well-known phrase 'Can the bourgeois be innocent?' Yours ever   W B YEATS

Do you ever remember a European question on which Ireland did not at once take the opposite side to England?—well, that kills all thought and encourages the most miserable kind of mob rhetoric.

TO BRINSLEY MACNAMARA[1]

June 22 [1919]   *Ballylee Castle*

Dear Mr. Macnamara: I have unfortunately while leaving London allowed the typed copy of your play to get packed up among my things and sent to Oxford where we have our winter house. I hope this will not greatly inconvenience you. I shall be there in September.

I did not think your play would act. I have no objection to the subject but the characters do not express themselves enough. I find it rather hard to define what is wrong. I think I shall be clearer if I say that I have noticed in successful plays that no one, on the stage, is quite normal after the first twenty minutes or so of exposition. By that time they should have acted on one another. One should be angry, one distressed, one merely excited, one gay, one astonished and so on. Now your people remain too normal emotionally and on the stage this would give the impression of too much talk. As I have let your play go I cannot prove what I mean from its details. I do not mean that the growing emotional stress should be

[1] Irish novelist and playwright. He has contributed many plays to the repertory of the Abbey Theatre and has written both novels and short stories. In 1949 he compiled a most valuable list of *Abbey Plays 1899–1948*, published in Dublin.

acute to the point of melodrama but that it must be felt increasing to the end of the play. I think the trouble is that you have now the habit of narrative and the habit is standing in your way. In the play we did of yours and which I admired very much,[1] you spoke too much of the provincial nature of the people. Think of *Magda* where the provincial attitude is shown, and shown by people all under emotional strain, though at the end theatrically and insincerely, if I remember the play rightly after twenty years. We should not as a rule have to say things for their own sake in a play but for the sake of emotion. The idea should be inherent in the fable.

I think you have a real dramatic gift apart from this defect—a real gift for construction and characterization. Yours sincerely

W B YEATS

TO BRINSLEY MACNAMARA

June 29, 1919　　　　　　　　　　　　　　*Ballylee Castle*

Dear Mr. Macnamara: I am sorry to hear that it was a MS I read— I had thought it was typed script—I should have said heard, not read, for I get plays read out to me. I was considering it just before all my things were packed up for Oxford and am afraid it is out of reach until I get there in September. I am very sorry. If I see a chance I will get it for you.

I think *The Rebellion of Ballycullen* is worth rehandling. You might consult Robinson and ask if he thinks we can revive it in the winter. It failed partly or mainly because of bad casting. It was performed when we were in chaos. I wanted, by the by, to see you at the time to talk over something and forgot. Did not you re-write Act II after I had read it and before performance? My memory was that your hero joined the popular party, not from conviction, but to help his parents; but when I saw it certain passages which seemed new—a quotation from myself among the rest—made his action seem the result very largely of personal conviction. This seemed to me to weaken the character motive and make the act too much an act of talk for the sake of the opinions. As I came away from the play a very clever girl said to me 'Mr. Macnamara should have put

[1] *The Rebellion in Ballycullen*, produced at the Abbey Theatre in March 1919.

into action the provincial nature of the people, and into talk those ideas only which are in themselves interesting talk. The provincial characters of the people would have been very interesting in action, as an idea it is not striking enough for talk.' I quote you this which struck me as a valuable general principle, but do not think that I undervalue your play as it stands. If cut in the first half of the second act and strongly played it should succeed.

I still think you could get the subject matter of *Broken Fences* into a more dramatic form. A play of mine, performed the other day in London, had given me great trouble in the start of its second act. It was a scene when a Prime Minister has to find fault with a troop of players. I wrote and re-wrote and it was nothing but talk. Then one day I made the Prime Minister get into a real rage; when it was played the curtain went up on a man, pacing to and fro half inarticulate with rage. I hardly recognized my own work the scene had gained so in being acted. After all a play is merely a bundle of acting parts. There must be always something for the actors to do. I have on occasion made a character mad, that there might be something to act. However I am not a successful dramatist and so my example cannot carry weight except for the sake of the theory it illustrates. [*Unsigned*]

TO JOHN QUINN

July 11, 1919   *Dublin*

My dear Quinn, I have now sent you two MSS.: (1) *The Wild Swans at Coole* (Macmillan edition); (2) *Per Amica Silentia Lunae*. I posted them to-day, registered and insured (parcel post). I have other MSS but I want to know if these arrive safely, if you like them, and if you want the others or not. I did not send them before for I have no liking for the —— post-office and so waited till I was in Dublin. The —— post-office is a happy, inattentive place where one never knows what unexpected thing may happen. Besides, the mail was robbed a month ago and the parcel office robbed twice a little later. We are reeling back into the middle ages, without growing more picturesque.

George has gone back to Ballylee where she is, I hope, catching trout, and I follow in a few days. I have just been invited to lecture for two years in Japan at a university there but have not had time to decide anything. It looks as if I may have a spirited old age. It would be pleasant to go away until the tumult of war had died down, and perhaps Home Rule established, and even the price of coal settled on. But would one ever come back?—would one find some grass-grown city, scarce inhabited since the tenth century, where one seemed surpassing rich on a few hundred a year? And would I mind if Sinn Fein took possession of my old tower here to store arms in, or the young scholars from the school broke all the new windows? I think my chief difficulty in accepting will be my tower, which needs another year's work under our own eyes before it is a fitting monument and symbol, and my garden, which will need several years if it is to be green and shady during my lifetime. Ballylee is a good house for a child to grow up in—a place full of history and romance, with plenty to do every day.

I hear my father is really coming back. I have a couple of letters from him which I am waiting to read when my eyes recover from a strain I have put them to in the last few days. I shall, I hope, read them to-morrow morning. Yours ever   W B YEATS

TO A. H. BULLEN

Nov. 15 [1919]   4 *Broad Street*
Oxford

My dear Bullen: I have had several letters from Watt asking what we were to do about certain moneys which you owe on Collected Edition. I said no doubt you could not pay, for if you could you would, and proposed that we ask you to pay in kind. Perhaps you could spare a set or two of the Stratford Shakespeare (Watt would like a copy for his share and I notice signs of coming marriage in the deportment of my brother-in-law and Shakespeare might mitigate certain theological asperities). And then there is Aphra Behn which my daughter having a ♂ ♀ conjunction in her horoscope may some day appreciate.

As you have remaindered the collected edition you cannot mind if I use again the Sargent, Shannon and other portraits, so you would not mind giving the plates also in payment. I don't know what is due, Watt says a little over thirty pounds, and if that is all what I say might rather more than cover it, but I think there must have been sales since that account was furnished. If you agree with what I suggest you might write to Watt who will arrange the matter.

I go to America on Jan 6 and may after lecturing go on to Japan where I have been offered some lectures at Tokyo University and be away a little over a year.

Remember me to your household. I shall hope to bring my wife to see you someday. Yours   W B YEATS

This is my permanent address. I plan to make this charming old house my winter home while keeping the old castle at Ballylee for the summer. We let our house here when away and so pay but little.

TO W. LYON PHELPS [1]

February 12, 1920   *Hotel Algonquin*
New York

Dear Mr. Phelps, I accept your invitation to dine after the lecture with pleasure and to stay the night. The lecture has not been printed before or delivered before. I never write a lecture but speak from a few notes. They come gradually into shape as I speak them. If you can get it taken down by a stenographer I would have to re-write it carefully, in fact greatly modify it. What speaks well, doesn't read well. If you like I will re-write it, but I don't suppose I shall be able to do so until I am home again. I could then let you have it for the University to print but I should have to reserve the right to include it in a book of my own and I would arrange for simultaneous publication in England or Ireland so as to preserve the copyright. However I can discuss this all when I see you. Yours sincerely   W B YEATS

[1] William Lyon Phelps (1865–1943), university professor and author. He was Professor of English Literature at Harvard, 1896–1901, and Lampson Professor at Yale, 1901–1933. He published many books on English and other literatures, especially on fiction and the drama.

TO OLIVIA SHAKESPEAR

March 14 [Postmark 1920]   *Hotel Utah*
Salt Lake City

My dear Olivia: You see we are in the Mormon city and on Sunday the streets all very quiet, for the Mormons are great keepers of the Sunday, which however they combine with a great passion for the theatre and music—music and speech are taught as religious duties. I lectured yesterday to a Mormon university in a wonderful little town among quiet mountains—like a little Greek town. On Monday I lecture at a University that is Mormon in all but name. Tomorrow I am to meet some of the officials of their Church. I hope to ask questions about their doctrine of continuous inspiration. They claim that the miraculous has never ceased among them. They have great wealth, number about 750,000 and now alas pride themselves on never having more than one wife. They claim that their once generous plurality was a temporary measure after a great war—so at least an enthusiast for the faith has been explaining to me. I told him that America and Germany had both made the same mistake, the mistake of standardizing life, the one in interest of monarchy the other in interest of democracy, but both for the ultimate gain of a sterile devil. That once both America and Germany had been infinitely abundant in variation from type and now all was type.

Tell Ezra to come to America and found a paper devoted to the turning of the U.S.A. into a monarchy to balance Germany. Yours always   W B YEATS

TO EDMUND DULAC[1]

March 22, 1920   *50 East 42nd Street*
New York

My dear Dulac, I will be greatly obliged if you will write *at once* to Birnbaum[2] and ask him to—no—better write to *me* and empower

[1] From a typewritten copy.
[2] Martin Birnbaum, at that time a partner in the firm of Scott and Fowler, art dealers in New York, had arranged an exhibition of Edmund Dulac's work at the firm's gallery, and also organized a performance of *At the Hawk's Well* at the Greenwich Village theatre, in which he played the Chorus. The masks made by Dulac are now in the possession of Mrs. Yeats.

me to get the Masks from Birnbaum. He told someone he would give them if he had this authority. If I don't find an answer from you when I get back to N. York at end of April I will *wire* for your authority.

A rather wonderful thing happened the day before yesterday. A very distinguished looking Japanese came to see us. He had read my poetry when in Japan and had now just heard me lecture. He had something in his hand wrapped up in embroidered silk. He said it was a present for me. He untied the silk cord that bound it and brought out a sword which had been for 500 years in his family. It had been made 550 years ago and he showed me the maker's name upon the hilt. I was greatly embarrassed at the thought of such a gift and went to fetch George, thinking that we might find some way of refusing it. When she came I said 'But surely this ought always to remain in your family?' He answered 'My family have many swords.' But later he brought back my embarrassment by speaking of having given me 'his sword.' I had to accept it but I have written him a letter saying that I 'put him under a vow' to write and tell me when his first child is born—he is not yet married—that I may leave the sword back to his family in my will.

We are not going to Japan. At least not for the present. The offer from there grew vaguer and the expense of living is immense. We should be bankrupt before we reached Tokyo. We are starting tonight for San Francisco. We shall be two nights in the train and we have just come from Salt Lake City where I have lectured to two Mormon Universities. Yours   W B YEATS

TO ELIZABETH C. YEATS

[? *autumn* 1920]   *Coole Park*

My dear Lolly: I now send you the Solomon correction. I do not think it will upset [the] page.

I forgot to tell you about *Unicorn from the Stars*. You must just tell your correspondents that it is the name of a play of mine and refer them to me and when they write to me I will forget to answer. The truth is that it is a private symbol belonging to my mystical order and nobody knows what it comes from. It is the soul. Yours   W B YEATS

TO JOHN QUINN[1]

October 30, 1920   4 *Broad Street*
                                             Oxford

My dear Quinn, When your letter arrived some weeks ago it awaited us at breakfast. Before I opened it George told me of a dream she had had that morning. I had two spots in my throat and she and I were disputing whether I should have them taken out in Dublin or in London. She thought I would be better cared for in Dublin but I was for London. When I read your letter I saw that her dream expressed it in allegory. This dream proves (like much else) that people explain by telepathy what telepathy has nothing to do with. No telepathy could have told George that your letter was about to arrive.

Some time afterwards I went to London, having made an appointment with a surgeon there. But when I rang at his door the servant maid, who was in a wild hurry, explained that he was no longer there. She gave me a new address and when I went to it he wasn't there either; she had given me a wrong address. I went to the telephone book, but couldn't find it, through a muddle of my own. He had a hyphenated name and I looked him up under the second half. I went back to Oxford and, being a superstitious man, began to think the finger of providence was in it. George consulted the stars and they said quite plainly that if I went to the London operator I would die, probably of hemorrhage. Then later we did another figure to know should I go to the Dublin operator. Then the stars were as favourable as possible—Venus, with all her ribbons floating, poised upon the mid-heaven! We went to Dublin. Gogarty, with his usual exuberant gaiety, removed my tonsils. As long as I retained consciousness he discussed literature, and continued the discussion when I awoke. He would probably have continued it most of the afternoon (he came 6 times) but I had a hemorrhage and was preoccupied with my possible end. I was looking, secretly, of course, for a dying speech. I rejected Christian resignation as too easy, seeing that I no longer cared whether I lived or died. I looked about for a good model (I have always contended that a model is necessary to style), but could think of nothing save a certain old statesman who, hearing a duck quack, murmured 'Those young

[1] Dictated.

ducks must be ready for the table,' and added to that 'Ruling passion strong in death.' Then I wondered if I could give the nurses a shock by plucking at the bedclothes.

The day after I came out of the home we went on shipboard to be ready for the morning start and returned to Oxford, taking three days upon the road. We had to hurry because a railway strike was supposed inevitable and it might have lasted weeks. I am now almost well again. But it is too soon to say how much I have benefitted. My rheumatism seems already better. There is no fear that the operation has not been done thoroughly, for as Gogarty looked at me over the end of the bed as I was meditating on the ducks he said, 'I have been *too* thorough.' I am bored by convalescence, not having yet my full powers of work. And when I am dressing in the morning I look out of the window at Anne strapped into her perambulator in the garden.[1] I watch her twisting about trying to get into the bottom of the perambulator, with her heels up, and I say to myself, 'Which is the greater bore, convalescence or infancy?'

I have been arranging the portraits in my study. Swift wrote to Stella once, 'I am bringing back with me portraits of all my friends;' meaning by that, doubtless, mezzotints. I have lithographs, photogravures, pencil drawings, photographs from pictures. There is only one absent—John Quinn. Will you send me a photograph of Augustus John's drawing of you? My sister has one, but I don't like to beg it of her . . . Yours ever   W B YEATS

I don't write about politics, for obvious reasons. Censorship is exceedingly severe, if capricious.

TO MISS FREDMAN [2]

Feb 8 [1921]   4 *Broad Street*

Dear Miss Fredman, How much do I owe you for my orchestral stall for *Volpone*? I hope I may be able to see the other Ben Jonson

[1] Anne Yeats, his daughter, had been born on February 24, 1919.
[2] The secretary of The Phoenix, which had invited Yeats to witness a production I made of Ben Jonson's *Volpone*. The impression made on him by the two young people in the play remained in his mind and reappeared many years later in *On the Boiler*, published in 1939.

when you do it. I am very sorry you have given up the fine Dryden for a much poorer play by Congreve. I well understand 'those many requests.' Whenever one undertakes any fine unusual work one receives 'many requests' to drop it, and do some usual work instead and Congreve is now usual.

Volpone was even finer than I expected. I could think of nothing else for hours after I left the theatre. The great surprise to me was the pathos of the two young people, united not in love but in innocence, and going in the end their separate way. The pathos was so much greater because their suffering was an accident, neither sought nor noticed by the impersonal greed that caused it. Yours
W B YEATS

TO GEORGE RUSSELL (AE)

March 14 [1921]   4 *Broad Street*

My dear Russell, Yes, I think you must be right. It is certainly a very interesting suggestion. I think by the way that the line is

'Dust has closed Helen's eye'

not 'Eyes.' At least I have always quoted it as 'eye.' I cannot look it up for I have no edition of Nash who I think wrote it.

I hope you will do that essay on Unity and Culture. I will send you the final chapter of my *Four Years* on the subject. Your essay need not be finished for months and need not be long. My sister will know when it should be done and how long it should be. I will let you know. If we can present this one idea from many sides we might affect the future of Ireland! In my essay I would go more into detail than I can in the last chapter. You could start off by referring to your essay in the *Express* and so assert the independence of your thought. In my *Four Years* it comes after the chapters on Madame Blavatsky, Morris, Macgregor, Henley and so on and will come as a logical deduction. The idea is much more obvious a deduction from all the past work of intellectual Ireland. The idea has been forced again into my mind, after a long interval of apparent individualism, by my present philosophy. I find something of the kind is stirring among the young here,—an Indian called Mallik is having great influence—and here philosophy is now the one great

intellectual influence, politics being dead. I do not yet understand the Oxford thought on the subject except that it is more metaphysical than ours. Mallik I have met but I have not met him enough. I hear also of an American who has left I know some similar thought. Macdougal was I think the first source. 'Now,' one undergraduate said to me, 'every conversation that is not merely practical, ends in philosophy.' Henry Adams is being read. We should be the first to express the idea of unity in a practical form.
Yours
W B YEATS

P.S. I have read all Adams and find an exact agreement even to dates with my own 'law of history.'

TO GEORGE RUSSELL (AE)

March 29th [1921]   *4 Broad Street*

My dear Russell, I admired your letter in yesterday's *Times* very much.[1] In many ways a great state kills all under its shadow like a horse chestnut. I have little hope: something we will get but not enough to set things right. I have little hope of the future anywhere. I think all the old systematic idealisms are dead and are forced to death by sheer mathematics. The world is like the schools of painting which exhaust any technical method in a few years. We have to discover a new force and till it is discovered mere hungers and futilities will reign.

I agree with all you said in your letter to me about 'True National Culture.' You know too that a period of 2000 years was also given to me for the complete circle, but one must of course not insist too literally on the figure. It has only an ideal existence and ends in one country sooner than another. One gets an average date. All this however is too remote to help us in our Irish Crisis.

I wish you would do that essay—it won't be wanted for some months—laying down a cultural economic political policy of national unity. Not so much as a fragment of any philosophical system but as a practical advice in simple words given to some young man. Had some young Greek found Shelley's 'Ahasuerus' in that shell strewn

[1] A long letter from Russell on the subject of Irish Finance appeared in *The Times*, March 28, 1921.

cavern, the sage would not have talked mathematics or even 'those strong and secret thoughts . . . which others fear and know not' but given I think very simple advice, not indeed fitted to any momentary crisis but fitted perhaps for the next fifty years.

This conception of unity and culture has become a cardinal principle in all exposition of the future in my system. My friends who are not with me at the moment insist upon it constantly. I am most anxious not to appropriate the idea or seem to do so. If I only express it it will seem but a deduction from one man's unpopular system. They will say 'O that is Yeats' and pass it by. You spoke it all long ago and I would like to hear you speak it again—not indirectly only as in dialogue but directly so that men can act upon it, and not only as culture but as economics. We writers are not politicians, the present is not in our charge but some part of the future is. Our speech will not make it very happy, but it will be even less happy than it might be perhaps if we are silent on vital points. Yours   W B YEATS

TO OLIVIA SHAKESPEAR

April 9 [Postmark 1921]   *Minchen's Cottage*
Shillingford
Berks

My dear Olivia: We are in a little road-side cottage and have the comfort, in our slight discomfort, of knowing that we are making a pot of money out of Broad St. We are nerving ourselves however to go to Ireland (do not tell Mrs. Tucker) at the first sign of lull in the storm there [1] as George pines for Ballylee. I begin to think she would be in better health there with even an occasional murder in the district than in this place or any other spot. We cannot move, if we do move, till Anne stops whooping, and whooping cough seems a long business. I remember nothing of it except a moment of

[1] In January 1919 the Dail had met and proclaimed the Irish Republic. It was allowed to function, against increasing repression, until September 1919 when it was suppressed, and then went underground. A resistance movement had begun, at first sporadically, and an attack on armed police had been made by a group of Tipperary Volunteers in January 1919. The movement spread to other areas and was then co-ordinated by Michael Collins, and developed into a guerilla war. Riots, burnings, strikes and unrest generally prevailed, and life in the country was by no means safe.

surpassing pride when I whooped in the middle of a large class room at the age of twelve, drew all eyes and was sent home. George and the nurse watch Anne by turns at night and at the moment George is sleeping off the effects of her last watch. I am reading a book that I find very exciting, *Apotheosis and After Life* by Mrs. Strong. It is a work on Greek and Roman religion mainly as displayed on tombs. One finds the Greeks and Romans were very religious and that their religion was full of all those images you and I have found in vision. The things wild people, half scholars and rhapsodical persons wrote about, when you and I were young, and were scorned by whole scholars for writing, seem now proved. It is a well written book and you should get it from the library. I read many books of this kind now, searching out signs of the whirling gyres of the historical cone as we see it and hoping that by this study I may see deeper into what is to come.

I am writing a series of poems ('thoughts suggested by the present state of the world' or some such name).[1] I have written two and there may be many more. They are not philosophical but simple and passionate, a lamentation over lost peace and lost hope. My own philosophy does not make brighter the prospect, so far as any future we shall live to see is concerned, except that it flouts all socialistic hope if that is a brightening.

The tea has just come in and George will be coming down and after tea we shall walk so I must end. Yours affectionately

W B YEATS

TO LADY GREGORY

April 10 [*Postmark* 1921]   *Shillingford*

My dear Lady Gregory ... I am writing a series of poems on the state of things in Ireland and am now in the middle of the third. I do not know what degree of merit they have or whether I have now enough emotion for personal poetry. I begin to feel a difficulty in finding themes. I had this about twelve years ago and it passed over. I may have to start another Noh play and get caught up into

---

[1] 'Thoughts upon the Present State of the World,' published in the *Dial*, September 1921, included in *Seven Poems and a Fragment*, 1922, and, under the title 'Nineteen Hundred and Nineteen,' in *The Tower*, 1928.

it if these poems turn out badly. The first poem is rather in the mood of the Anne poem but the rest are wilder. Newspapers and letters alike [*word indecipherable*] now till my work is finished: 'bring out weight and measure in a time of dearth' Blake wrote. Yours ever

W B YEATS

TO OLIVIA SHAKESPEAR

May 27 [1921] *Shillingford*

My dear Olivia: How much do I owe you for the nest? I forgot to ask you. The hen-bird is now sitting on two eggs and there is peace. The cock-bird brings her food and only chirps reproaches when she leaves the nest for a moment. He never pecks her and indeed I am inclined to think that he was never a sadist but that they had quarrelled because she insisted on 'marriage lines.' 'Marriage lines' are plainly in the canary language a nest. They used to roost at opposite ends of their perch but now the cock-bird goes to sleep as close to the nest as he can. He sings more than ever.

I was in London for a few hours on Tuesday last on my way to Lincoln to lecture but had to spend them between Lady Gregory, my tailor and the New Oxford music hall where I spent 19/- to see a woman dance in masks in imitation of Ito. She danced beautifully and looked very beautiful masked, though when she showed her own head it was plain and tousled. The rest of the performance, or what I saw of it, was dull and mechanical. I knew that a grotesque mask was enormously effective, but was not sure of the effectiveness of a beautiful one till I saw her.

We have got about £530 for the Abbey by our lectures and I am to give one more lecture, this time at Eva Fowler's. Yours

W B YEATS

TO LADY GREGORY

June 10 [*Postmark* 1921] *Shillingford*

My dear Lady Gregory . . . Laurie, the publisher, has written to me and offered me £500 for the right to issue the Memoirs I am publishing in the *Mercury* in the same form in which he issues Moore's new books.¹ I am afraid the Cuala book will knock this out. Have you been reading me? I get a good deal of commendation. I shall carry them down to the start of the theatre probably.

I am reading *Barchester Towers* and have just finished *The Warden*. They have gained with time, and not from any merit of their own, like Frith's 'Derby Day' and 'The Railway Station' of which an engraving hangs in our house at Thame. I think Frith was the better observer. I feel always how much better Miss Austen was. Yours

W B YEATS

TO GEORGE RUSSELL (AE)

July 1 [1921]   *at Cuttlebrook House*
Thame
Oxon

My dear Russell, Why not do a small selection of your new work first, a complete section say for Cuala? You could speak of it as a first book in the preface or put that in the sub-title; or leave it as a distinct book, a statement of difference and put off the reconciliation until later. A statement of apparently irreconcilable difference would affect the imagination as drama does and excite an expectation for your later book. I am publishing in this way 20,000 words in the *Mercury* and in the *Dial*, and later at Cuala, of what will be a 60,000 word book, and doubt if I would have faced the whole book with a good heart, but for starting with the lesser task.

I shall insert a study of the Ely Place group, and of your ascendency there, but I will submit to you whatever I write about yourself and publish nothing that you dislike. I wish to be able to say in my preface that wherever I have included a living man I have submitted my words for his correction. This is especially important as Werner Laurie (Moore's publishers) have bought the right to publish a special edition for 3 years. I want to show that though I am being published by Moore's publishers I do not accept Moore's practice,

¹ This section of Yeats's autobiography appeared as *The Trembling of the Veil* in 1922 and was issued, in an edition of 1000 signed copies, in the series of privately printed editions which Werner Laurie had inaugurated with George Moore's *A Story Teller's Holiday* in 1918 and continued with his *Avowals* and *Héloise and Abélard*.

which would be very out of drawing as part of my picture. I may call the book *The Trembling of the Veil* (Mallarmé said 'The whole age is full of the trembling of the veil of the temple') but some better title may occur. You may perhaps have seen what the *London Mercury* has published. I shall insert fresh chapters in that and lead up to the later part and my object will be to suggest, indirectly, things descriptive of characters and events in the main, and only here and there to directly state certain simple philosophical ideas about Ireland, and about human nature in general.

I agree about Shaw—he is haunted by the mystery he flouts. He is an atheist who trembles in the haunted corridor. Yours

W B YEATS

TO ALLAN WADE

July 10 [1921]   *4 Broad St*

My dear Wade: By a strange mischance your letter to me got under a heap of papers and I found it there unopened many days after the performance had been given. I was very sorry to have missed it; would have journeyed many miles at any time to have seen that play.[1] I had always wanted especially to know how the puppet scenes would work out.

I thank you very much. Yours sincerely   W B YEATS

Bartholomew Fair was one of the things that influenced Synge.

TO OLIVIA SHAKESPEAR

August 1 [1921]   *Thame*

My dear Olivia: I owe you a letter for a long time but there is so much to do that one procrastinates. Today I have just finished a long description of Lionel,[2] comparing his head to the head of a Greek athlete you showed me at the British Museum. I am extending

---

[1] I had invited Yeats to see the production of Ben Jonson's *Bartholomew Fair* which I made for The Phoenix, the first production of the play since 1731.

[2] Lionel Johnson, Mrs. Shakespear's cousin.

my Memoirs, a publisher having offered me £500 for a special edition. I am mired in my propaganda in Ireland 1891-2-3-4, the years just before you and I met, and it is difficult as so much that is essential has to be left out. I am characterizing Hyde, AE, O'Grady, Lionel; and characterizing, without naming, my especial enemies, the Tower and wolf-dog, harp and shamrock, verdigris-green sectaries who wrecked my movement for the time. Then I shall take up London again, Wilde's collapse, *Savoy* etc, and pray that some imp of abundance brings all without strain up to the needed 60,000 words (20,000 have appeared in the *London Mercury*—though part a little cut down and despoiled of my best Blavatsky tale). I find this memoir writing makes me feel clean, as if I had bathed and put on clean linen. It rids me of something and I shall return to poetry with a renewed simplicity. Have you been reading me in the *Mercury*? I am afraid Ezra will not forgive me for publishing there: he had recommended the *English Review* but I have just as fierce a quarrel with that periodical as he has with the *Mercury*, so what could I do?

Our canaries are now feeding four strapping but very ugly chicks —their third attempt—and I had hoped that young canaries would be as engaging as kittens. Meanwhile Anne is as energetic as possible. The other day she asked me to put on her shoes (which she had pulled off). I got on one but could not get on the second. Then I found that she had screwed up her toes to prevent me. It was sheer coquetry and she has never been known to ask a woman to put her shoes on. In fact she cannot bear shoes. Next day when I went into the garden she pointed to the shoes, which were lying on the grass where she had thrown them, but I was not to be snared a second time. George expects her great event in ten days or so.

I had almost forgotten to tell you, what is the real occasion of my letter. I said to George 'None of us are really happy with our parents or approve of our bringing up.' 'Oh yes,' she answered, 'some do. Dorothy [1] said to me once, that if she could live her life again she would not alter anything in her early years—school and all was as it should be. There had been one matter, in which she had thought it wrong (some governess I think. W B Y) but afterwards she came to the conclusion that also was right.' I told George I would tell you. Yours   W B YEATS

[1] Mrs. Shakespear's daughter, now Mrs. Ezra Pound.

TO JOHN QUINN

August 25, 1921   *Thame*

My dear Quinn, George had a son on August 22nd (as I hope J.B.Y. told you), and we want you to be godfather. The other godfather will, I hope, be Lennox Robinson, who has already been godfather to two Czech-Slav children whose names he has forgotten and could never pronounce (they were born on the boat that carried him and the Abbey players to Boston). I tell you this that you may not shrink from the responsibility. It is George's idea. She is very set on your taking the post.

Both George and the child are well, and the doctor says that he has 'a beautiful head.' All I can say is that he is better looking than a new-born canary (I had four hatch out in my bedroom a little while ago) and nothing like as good looking as the same bird when it gets its first feathers.

I have decided to leave the completion of my philosophy to him and to Anne. Anne needs something to sober her, as she is already a coquette interested by every little boy that passes and bored by little girls. She even flirts with her father, calling him to put on her shoes, which she has pulled off, and then twisting up her toes so that he cannot do so; owing to her flighty heart she wants as much attention as possible. The philosophy is very complicated and difficult, so that will be just what is wanted. I shall lay the foundations, that is all. Yours ever   W B YEATS

I owe you a letter, I know, and this is none. I shall write later.

TO ELIZABETH C. YEATS

August 29 [1921]   *Thame*

My dear Lolly, Write to Whitehead that your authors are always free to do as they like with their books after your edition is exhausted, or after a certain time has passed; that you 'believe' that the Laurie edition will not be published till the end of 1922 at earliest. If you use the word 'believe' it will not bind you too precisely. I am bound to deposit the MS by June 1922 and they must then publish within six months. I may possibly send in the MS by (say) March (as I am paid half the sum when I do and I shall want money for J.B.Y.'s clearance from U.S.A. and his arrival home). If I had thought of it I would have asked Laurie to delay his appeal for subscribers till you were out, but it is too late now. Whitehead has no case. Your book is the first edition and Laurie will be much more expensive, £2.2.0 at least. Yours W B YEATS

[*On envelope*] I have just seen Anne's cradle, quite charming. You should go in for painted furniture. W B Y

TO ALLAN WADE

Oct 18 [1921] *4 Broad Street*

My dear Wade, Yes you may do *Land of Heart's Desire*.[1] Franco Leoni has turned it [into] an opera so you could do it in that form possibly if you had a mind to. He had, he claims, a success with it in Milan but not to the point of royalties, owing to the pitching of certain bombs by heated politicians at certain other politicians in some Milan theatre.

Have you looked lately at my *Green Helmet*?—that might suit your turn better. It is easier to do and Patric Colum says it is my 'most effective play.' However pick anything you like, but arrange terms with Watt. *Green Helmet* gives an animated gay objective stage not too far from the mood of the world and could be made a very phantastic picture.

Leoni was in England some months ago to arrange for his opera founded on my *Countess Cathleen*. I think that is probably my 'most effective' play and as a play it acts about an hour. *The King's Threshold* and *Deirdre* and *Baile's Strand* want each one player of genius and that is out of reach probably henceforth for ever. *Deirdre* was once only played and that was by Mrs. Pat Campbell. Yours W B YEATS

Let me know if you ever come to this city. I am often sorry that

[1] *The Land of Heart's Desire* was revived at the Kingsway Theatre, London, on November 14, in a programme otherwise consisting of ballet. It ran for about three weeks.

I do not see more of you. I am so greatly your debtor for the work you did in my collected edition and I have no way of showing gratitude.

You will of course use the current version of *Land of Heart's Desire* (published I think in 1912).

TO OLIVIA SHAKESPEAR

Dec 22 [1921]   4 *Broad Street*

My dear Olivia, I send *Four Years* which is the first third of the complete memoirs. As they go on they will grow less personal, or at least less adequate as personal representation, for the most vehement part of youth must be left out, the only part that one well remembers and lives over again in memory when one is in old age, the paramount part. I think this will give all the more sense of inadequateness from the fact that I study every man I meet at some moment of crisis—I alone have no crisis.

I am in a deep gloom about Ireland for though I expect ratification of the treaty from a plebiscite I see no hope of escape from bitterness, and the extreme party may carry the country. When men are very bitter, death and ruin draw them on as a rabbit is supposed to be drawn on by the dancing of the fox.

In the last week I have been planning to live in Dublin—George very urgent for this—but I feel now that all may be blood and misery. If that comes we may abandon Ballylee to the owls and the rats, and England too (where passions will rise and I shall find myself with no answer), and live in some far land. Should England and Ireland be divided beyond all hope of remedy, what else could one do for the children's sake, or one's own work? I could not bring them to Ireland where they would inherit bitterness, nor leave them in England where, being Irish by tradition, and by family and fame, they would be in an unnatural condition of mind and grow, as so many Irishmen who live here do, sour and argumentative.

[*The rest of the sheet is torn off.*]

TO LILY YEATS[1]

February 3, 1922　　　　　　　　　　　　*4 Broad Street*

My dear Lily, It is possible that things have happened in the best way, for he has had no growing infirmities, no long illness. He wrote to me but a little while ago, saying that he felt in such good health, and his mind had lost nothing of its vigour. I had a letter two or three weeks ago that was among the best he ever wrote. If he had come home he would have lived longer but he might have grown infirm, grown to feel himself a useless old man. He has died as the Antarctic explorers died, in the midst of his work and the middle of his thought, convinced that he was about to paint as never before. And in all probability he has died in sleep after an illness that was almost all sleep, and so without any consciousness of death. Several times lately (the last, two or 3 months ago) he wrote of dreaming of our mother and of seeing her in his illness of 1919 and also last summer. I was turning over an old note-book the other day and I find that she came to me at a London séance and told me that from that on she would be much with me. I think in spite of his misfortunes that his life has been happy, especially of recent years; for more than any man I have ever known he could live in the happiness of the passing moment. I think we did all for him that could be done and that there is nothing to regret.

We have been expecting to see you after the Cadbury's but if you care to come before you [go] we shall be very glad to see you, and Anne will be glad to see you too. Yours affectionately　W B YEATS

TO ALLAN WADE[2]

13th February, 1922　　　　　　　　　　*4 Broad Street*

My dear Wade, You wrote to me on Nov. 25th and asked me a question about Michael Robartes which I forgot to answer. I have brought him back to life. My new story is that he is very indignant because I used his real name in describing a number of fictitious

---
[1] Dictated. The letter which Yeats wrote, on the same date, to his younger sister, Elizabeth C. Yeats, concerning their father's death, has been printed by Joseph Hone in *J. B. Yeats: Letters to his Son*, London, 1944; New York, 1946
[2] Dictated.

adventures, and that because I called my fictitious hero by his name, many people have supposed him to be dead. He lived for years in Mesopotamia, but when the war came there returned to England for a short time. In England he got into communication with a certain John Aherne, and through him got into correspondence with me, and finally conveyed to me, without quite forgiving me, the task of editing and publishing the philosophy which he has discovered among certain Arabian tribes. That philosophy now fills a very large tin box upon which my eyes at this moment are fixed. I am giving it to the world in fragments, poems, notes, and a Cuala volume.

My wife is in Dublin, trying to get a house there. Having finally revolted against dons' wives, their hats being their principal offence. Yours   W B YEATS

TO OLIVIA SHAKESPEAR

Feb 17 [*Postmark Feb* 18, 1922]   4 *Broad Street*

My dear Olivia: I thank you very much for your letter. My father was taken ill on a Wednesday evening, shortness of breath and pains in chest—he had over exerted himself [by] some long walk and got a chill—then after an injection of some kind got apparently ease and content. He died in his sleep and his last words were—to a Mrs. Foster who was sitting at his bedside—'Remember you have promised me a sitting in the morning.' A good death I think.

George is in Dublin. She has taken a large house in Merrion Square which is brought within our means by letting its stables, and perhaps its top floor. She has indeed already let the top floor to two young men of our acquaintance for six months. She says the house is beautiful with fine mantelpieces and that there is a view of the mountain. The rooms are very large and stately. I feel very grand especially as I remember a street ballad about the Duke of Wellington

'In Merrion Square
This noble hero first drew breath
Amid a nation's cheers.'

George returns on Monday and brings my sister with her. My sister has been ill and my father's death has made things worse.

I find it hard to realise my father's death, he has so long been a mind to me, that mind seems to me still thinking and writing. George is arranging his letters for publication and I shall arrange his autobiographical chapters for Cuala. I got him to write his memories of his early days. I wish he could have lived to see us in Dublin. He was fond of George.

We shall go to Ballylee in April, return here in August and September and then flit. I am not much disturbed about the state of Ireland—it will come right in three or four months I think. Dublin house rents are rising, so many Americans are taking houses. Yours affectionately   W B YEATS

I think my father's death has upset George a good deal.

TO OLIVIA SHAKESPEAR

March 1 [1922]   4 *Broad Street*

My dear Olivia: About two weeks [ago] George announced that she could stand Oxford no longer and was going at once to Dublin to get a house. My Saturn suggested delay but her Mars carried it and she went. By a most strange stroke of luck she bought for a very small sum a great house in Merrion Square (which is to Dublin what Berkeley Square is to London) and within three days could have re-sold at a profit of £600. She went on to Galway and found two castle rooms almost ready at Ballylee. We start for Ireland on March 22, having let our house here for 4 months, and in August shift our furniture to Dublin. We shall have a pleasant energetic life, if the Treaty is accepted at the general election, and turmoil if it is rejected. (Lady Gregory is anxious. It is the young men, who have not yet fought, who are strongest for rejection she says.) It is right for us to go, though I left all for George to decide, for I have much to fight for—an Irish Academy being founded and perhaps a government theatre. Our carpets will look like postage stamps in the great eighteenth century Dublin rooms but at any rate we shall have a comfortable room for a friend. Have you read the correspondence of Granville Leveson Gower? I am deep in the endless vivid letters from his mistress in early years, Lady Bessborough. They go on till he is fifty and she sixty, and touch me very much. Asquith I hear says they are the best ever written but I think that too great praise. They are perhaps the best of their kind, their kind being letters with an agreed subject matter and that subject matter an eighteenth century absorption in gossip of politics and of politicians' lives.

Matt-Matt [1] would have delighted in them. Sheridan is the villain of the play and a very strange villain, a worse George Moore. Yours affectionately   W B YEATS

TO OLIVIA SHAKESPEAR

March 8 [1922]   *4 Broad Street*

My dear Olivia: Can you come to us next week? Any day you like. March 20 I go to Ireland and we may not meet for so long.

I am reading the new Joyce [2]—I hate it when I dip here and there but when I read it in the right order I am much impressed. However I have but read some thirty pages in that order. It has our Irish cruelty and also our kind of strength and the Martello Tower pages are full of beauty. A cruel playful mind like a great soft tiger cat— I hear, as I read, the report of the rebel sergeant in '98: 'O he was a fine fellow, a fine fellow. It was a pleasure to shoot him.'

Tell me when you have the Leveson Gower letters and I will tell you something of their still unpublished scandals, collected from Lady Ottoline and from David Cecil. Yours   W B YEATS

No I am not alarmed about Ireland nor are my correspondents there though I expect a few months' more trouble. The disturbances are in two or three places and sound worse when reported in the papers, the quiet districts showing nothing to interest the press. De Valera is losing. Yours   W B Y

[1] Arthur Galton, a clergyman and friend of Mrs. Shakespear's. Matt-Matt was a nickname.
[2] *Ulysses*, which had been published in Paris by Shakespeare & Co. on February 2, 1922.

TO OLIVIA SHAKESPEAR

[? *April* 1922] *Thoor Ballylee*

My dear Olivia: We are settled here now and our tower much near[er] finishing so that we have a large bed-room with a fine wooden ceiling, but it will be another year, so little labour is there to be got even if our money permitted, before we shall be complete. George is very happy to be back here and declares that the children have at once increased in weight. As I have not seen a paper for days I do not know how far we have plunged into civil war but it will hardly disturb us here. Even through the terror nothing happened here, except a mysterious visit from some persons, who broke all locks and some windows (and then mended the windows) but stole nothing; nor has anything in the house or outside been stolen during the two years and a half of our absence except our garden syringe. All we can see from our windows is beautiful and quiet and has been so; yet two miles off near Coole, which is close to a main-road, the Black and Tans flogged young men and then tied them to their lorries by the heels and dragged them along the road till their bodies were torn in pieces. I wonder will literature be much changed by that most momentous of events, the return of evil. The one sign of disturbance I notice is that everybody speaks with caution as no one knows who will be master to-morrow. In Dublin I found people gay and anxious and no one, not even Gogarty (who sees Arthur Griffith constantly), with any knowledge of what is planned, so well are all secrets kept. I write my memoirs daily and find I write better for all the uncertainty just as I am better in body for having left Oxford for this stormbeaten place, but I am glad to be out of Dublin where men talk themselves bitter. I was at Coole for two or three days and while I was there the I.R.A. arrived, having arrested two young men for a theft from the harness room, and, though Lady Gregory tried to beg the two thieves off, carried them away to Galway Gaol where the Free State reigns, while the long barracks over the way from it is in the hands of De Valera's party.

What do you think of our address—Thoor Ballylee? Thoor is Irish for tower and it will keep people from suspecting us of modern gothic and a deer park. I think the harsh sound of 'Thoor' amends the softness of the rest.

Will you help my canaries who are nest making but with sheeps' wool and green moss which they dislike? Can you get me at the bird-shop a bundle of nesting material? The shops all sell it. Yours affectionately   W B YEATS

TO OLIVIA SHAKESPEAR

May [1922]   *Thoor Ballylee*

My dear Olivia: I never thanked you for your nesting material—there are now four nests, two with eggs. I have no doubt that in a few weeks' time we shall be the embarrassed owners of 20 new born canaries. I have suggested a pie but George won't hear of it. There is also a nest of stares in a hole over my bed-room window, no end of jackdaws in the chimneys, so George must be satisfied. I have just reminded her that when we came here first she asked me if I thought anybody would give us a couple of crows, and if I thought the crows, if they did, could be got to build in the big tree. Apart from the jackdaws all is quiet in this part of the country except that two weeks ago the commander of the Gort irregulars robbed the neighbouring post-office of the dog tax, that he might pay his men, was hunted by the Gort regulars who shot at him and made him swim a river. He got off with the money and he and the regulars are now the best of friends. The Post Mistress says that he was so nice mannered that when she found that the dog tax did not amount to quite £20 she made it up to that amount with her own money. I am not alarmed at anything but the murders of protestants in Cork and at that perhaps because I have been expecting it for weeks—I knew that when there were so many fire-arms in wild hands an attempt to reply in that way to Belfast must come. I think it has been stopped but one cannot be quite certain for Cork is inflammable. The whole situation in Ireland interests me. We have here popular leaders representing a minority but a considerable one, who mock at an appeal to the vote and may for a time be able to prevent it. One saw the same thing in Russia when the communists dissolved the constitutive assembly. On the other hand I hear that the Free State party will bring in a constitution especially arranged to give power to the heads of departments as distinguished from the politicians, and with a second chamber so arranged as to put power into the hands of able men who could not expect election in the ordinary way. It may be changed at the last moment, for Ireland is too turbulent to be settled even in plan, but when I was in Dublin that was the expectation. In other words out of all this murder and rapine will come not a demagogic but an authoritative government. I admit that the present scene is not pleasing to the mind and must last for some months. I am a timid man and I was not cheered, as I walked along one side of Stephen's Green the other night, to hear twenty revolver shots on the other side, but the drunken men took very little notice for they zigzagged on singing 'He's a jolly good fellow.'

Our house is getting into order and George is painting the bedroom ceiling in blue and black and gold, and is planting flowers and vegetables in great abundance in our acre of land.

I read *Ulysses* and Trollope's Barchester novels alternately.

I think I hear dinner. Yours affectionately   W B YEATS

TO JOHN QUINN[1]

June 5, 1922   *Thoor Ballylee*

My dear Quinn, I have finished and dispatched to the publisher my book of memoirs, *The Trembling of the Veil*, and dedicated it to you. If you object cable, for Laurie is in a devil of a hurry. I thought I should be receiving proof-sheets for the next four months, but though the manuscript was dispatched only a week ago he writes that I am to get all the proof-sheets in a bunch in another month.

We have been in Ballylee now for the last two months and shall be for another three, when we move to Dublin. Our bedroom is upstairs in the Castle and is a delight to us, and the third floor which is to be my study is almost ready. Our dining room on the ground floor was finished three years ago. This is the first year in which we have been able to sleep in the Castle itself. We have added an extra cottage, which is ultimately to be a garage, though not for anything nobler than a Ford and not even that till next year at the earliest. This country is still so disturbed that even Ford cars don't stay with their owners. None of these improvements has cost much. The stone for the cottage was dug out of our garden and the slates were bought two years ago for the Castle, which has to be concreted over

[1] Dictated.

instead, for our builder declares that no slate would withstand the storms. I went on my last American tour for Ballylee and that money is not all gone yet.

It is a great pleasure to live in a place where George makes at every moment a fourteenth century picture. And out of doors, with the hawthorn all in blossom all along the river banks, everything is so beautiful that to go elsewhere is to leave beauty behind.

It is no use writing you politics, except perhaps that I have information from Dublin that the De Valera-Collins pact was caused by the fear of revolution.[1] There is great disorder, as the newspapers will have told you, and even a little of it reaches us and reaches Coole, but so far nothing serious. There was what seemed a raid at Coole; men came and shouted at night and demanded to be let in, and then went away either because the moon came out or because they only meant to threaten. This last was seemingly the explanation. Two men who were being prosecuted for theft thought that if they created alarm the case might be withdrawn. Lady Gregory asked me to come and stay there, as some protection. I went, but I got the Free State Garrison at Gort to send two young soldiers, very nice, simple, young country lads, to sleep in the house for the first two or three days and after that to patrol the woods. We were hoping for better order from the pact, but in this locality it has not come. Lands have been seized at Lough Cutra, and 50 Free State troops are there now to protect it. Here nothing worse has happened than a threatening letter sent to an old man who works for us. Another old man wants the job, and so the first old man receives a letter winding up: 'Prepare to meet your doom. Red Hand never fails.' I gave the threatening letter to a Free State Lieutenant, who called upon the second old man, who was overheard by George next day saying to a crony, 'Queer sort o' cattle, those Free Staters.'

I have had to interrupt this dictation to George to find out why

---

[1] The pact was made as an endeavour to prevent civil war. It provided that the parties should not oppose each other in the constituencies but remain content with the seats they held at the dissolution of the Dail. Mr. De Valera's followers interpreted this in their speeches as an agreement more or less to shelve the Treaty, and said there would never be a vote on the Treaty. Collins then announced that there was no bar to the nomination of Independents; as a result, his party lost eight seats and Mr. De Valera's party lost twenty-two. Seventeen Labour members were elected, seven Farmers, and six Independents; and there were four Unionists (Trinity College). All of these were pro-Treaty. But before the Dail met the Civil War had broken out.

our collie puppy should start barking at eleven o'clock at night. George has just returned to say that he is barking at the cuckoo. It is only ten o'clock by the true time of the sun so not too dark for the cuckoo, but the Free State earned its first unpopularity here by continuing English 'summer time.'

The children are well, and your godson has eight teeth, and nothing ails Anne but her theology. When she says the Lord's Prayer she makes such interjections as 'Father not in heaven—father in the study,' or 'Dada gone to Coole.' Then again, finding Kingdom difficult to pronounce, she has been accustomed to say 'Thine is the Kitten, the Power, and the Glory.' But owing to the growth of her intelligence has lately noticed that my cat Pangur is not a kitten, so the last form has been, 'Thine is the Cat, the Power, and the Glory.'

Lady Gregory is writing her memoirs and has read me about half. I have criticized a good deal the old political friends of her youth—Sir Alfred Lyall's bad poetry, and the like—and she is interjecting my criticisms into the text, like a Greek chorus. It will be a rich book, with some chapters of historical importance, but all objective, extracts from old letters, diaries and the like; one chapter bringing back vividly to the imagination the dinner talk of the London season during the first Home Rule Bill debates. The reverse of my memoirs in every way, for I could not have quoted a letter or a diary without spoiling my effect.

This very day Lolly has sent me the first proof sheets of my father's memoirs; not quite all that he wrote but all that he finished. I have always been convinced that memoirs were of great importance to our movement here. When I was 20 years old we all read Gavan Duffy's *Young Ireland*, and then read the Young Ireland poets it had introduced to us. Hyde, Russell, Lady Gregory, my father, myself, will all be vivid to young Irish students a generation hence because of the memoirs we are writing now. Yours ever   W B YEATS

TO OLIVIA SHAKESPEAR

June 7 [1922]   *Thoor Ballylee*

My dear Olivia: You owe me a letter unless, as is very likely, my last letter to you has gone astray. The post is not secure and several of our letters never seem to have reached their destination. The country is getting more settled however since the Collins-De Valera pact. I have had a letter from a Dublin friend who sees both Collins and Griffith, saying that the pact was caused (1) by fear of social revolution (2) by the belief in a secret agreement among army chiefs in Ulster to provoke war with a view to 'the reconquest of Ireland.' I think that we will have a settled condition of things very soon now if the constitution goes through. How dull and topical I am but you must forgive me. Ten days ago I finished *The Trembling of the Veil* and posted it to Watt. Then I got ill—headache, exhaustion—and am not right yet. I have great masses of unanswered letters but just now I said 'I will not go on postponing my friends to mere business any longer.'

Do not judge my account of Lionel by the short passage in last *Mercury*. I think when I have finished you will see that I have shown him as the noble tragic figure that he was, and that those who follow me are likely to take their key from what I have written. The *Mercury* has had to shorten everything, to leave out everything mystical or startling to their readers for they have only space for 16,000 words of the 30,000 I sent them, so do not judge the memoirs as a whole till you get the book. It needs the wild mystical part to lift it out of gossip, and that mystical part will not be as clear as it should be for lack of diagrams and the like. Lady Gregory is in great enthusiasm over the book and it has already brought in much money.

Macmillan has in the press a book with all my lyrical poems (except those Unwin has) and another with all my plays (except those in Unwin's book). They are to be in a cover, which is to be that of all my forthcoming books, and that cover will be I hope by Ricketts. These books have meant a great deal of work, and I am tired and in a rage at being old. I am all I ever was and much more but an enemy has bound me and twisted me so I can plan and think as I never could, but no longer achieve all I plan and think . . .

I interrupt my letter at intervals and watch my canaries in their big cage where there are two nests; one, which disturbs George, is the nest of a half caste, a bird that looks half sparrow and it threatens to abound in young. It is the American negro question and all the more because George's English mind has conceived a project of selling canaries through the newspapers. Who will want half castes? Will even our friends accept them as presents? The other nest however is above reproach. There is a wire partition between the two nests and the cocks hang on to the wires and peck each other through them. The trouble is that each bird sings by preference to the hen at the other side of the wires, not to his own hen.

The castle, which we call *Thoor* (Tower) and escape from associations of modern gothic, is a joy to us both and the country all white with the may flower full of plenty. Stone stairs to my surprise are the most silent of all stairs and sitting as I am now upstairs in the Tower I have a sense of solitude and silence. As yet we have no stranger's room, mainly because there is so little labour to be had. It will be the room above this, a beautiful room high in the tower. It is ready but for furniture and door. We have made a garage meaning to get a Ford car next year or the year after if the coarse broom of political violence leaves anybody to call on except Lady Gregory and Martyn who are in walking distance. For the moment at any rate other houses of the gentry stand empty, sometimes protected by I.R.A. sometimes occupied by irregulars. Yours affectionately

W B YEATS

TO H. J. C. GRIERSON [1]

June 7, 1922 *Thoor Ballylee*

Dear Professor Grierson; I am most grateful to you for your splendid gift. It was most generous of you, and you have given me what I had already greatly wished for but known to be beyond my means. I have spent some time over the book [2] and shall spend much more, and hope to write to you again when I have made up my mind what pages I like the best. Here in the country I have no way of comparing it with the published illustrations to Young's *Night Thoughts* but I have the impression that it is more like some of the unpublished ones. I have not however seen them for many years. When I was working at Blake they were in the possession of Bain of the Haymarket, and he used to show them to students in a room facing the street but above the shop. They were in colour, or some of them were, and I seem to remember a fanciful spirit as of the Cat and the Goldfish illustrations, the fading light of Blake's boyish art...

---

[1] Dictated.   [2] Blake's designs for Gray's Poems.

I am writing in my bedroom which is also, for the most part, my study; it is on the first floor of the Tower, there is an open fire of turf, and a great elm-wood bed made with great skill by a neighbouring carpenter, but designed by that late drunken genius Scott; and over my head is a wooden ceiling made according to his design. Some day it will be painted in brilliant colours. And the window is full of canaries, they and their nests, in a huge cage. We are, however, much troubled by the colour question, for a mother bird, who looks half sparrow, has just started a new nest, though the offspring of the first nest, plain mulatto, have hardly begun to peck. From my window I can see river banks fringed now with elm, now with whitethorn, and beyond that rocks and whitethorn everywhere.

I wonder if I shall ever see Edinburgh again.[1] I have left England, and when I leave this house in August or September, we go to a house in Dublin. We have bought a house there, 82 Merrion Square, a place with large rooms and plenty of them, got at a fortunate moment, for very little money. If you ever come to Dublin we shall be very glad to put you up.

82 Merrion Square will always find us. Yours ever

W B YEATS

TO OLIVIA SHAKESPEAR

July 27 [1922]   *Coole Park*

My dear Olivia, Please send on enclosed to Ezra. Read it first as it will give you some general news of things here, and of George. All is I think going well and the principal result of all this turmoil will be love of order in the people and a stability in the government not otherwise obtainable. At another moment I would have many amusing or picturesque things to tell you but do not yet put my trust in the post.

Did you ever read George Sand's *Consuelo* and its sequel? Lady Gregory has read them out to me—a chapter at a time—during the summer. They fill one with reverie—secret societies of the eighteenth century, all turmoil of an imagined wisdom from which came

[1] Sir Herbert Grierson was Professor of Rhetoric and English Literature at Edinburgh University, 1915–1935, and Rector of the University, 1936–1939.

the barricades. George Sand is a child when she tries to philosophise, but seems to know everything while she unrolls images before us as we see things in the fire. I am writing verse, a long poem (long for me) about Ballylee. Four parts of (say) two dozen lines each. I have written three of the parts and have also written a lyric about the civil war. It has been rather a comfort to be without letters or newspapers. We have often sat all day in our garden, George gardening—I writing and Michael under a tree asleep. After dinner George has read out Cellini's Memoirs; and is to bring back from the London Library some big book on his art. My own Memoirs are most damnably cut down by *London Mercury* so do not judge till you get the whole. Yours affectionately   W B YEATS

TO HERBERT EDWARD PALMER

August 9th [1922] *Thoor Ballylee*

Dear Mr. Palmer, Forgive my long silence. Two or three days, if I remember rightly, after your poems came, Civil War broke out in this country and for weeks we had neither railways, newspapers, nor posts here in Galway. We have all now, though not always, and so far as posts are concerned not often. I have a great admiration for some of your poems, especially for 'The Wolf Knight' [1] and for passages in 'A Trinity of Song' [2] and for 'Wonder Horses.' [2] These things, especially the first, seem to me different in kind from all the rest, more imaginative, more passionate, as if they came from a different part of the mind or from beyond the mind. I can well believe that you had some strange experience when you wrote 'The Wolf Knight' and I would be greatly interested could you tell me of it. It is full of the most astonishing metaphors and has an effect of great intensity—'A bird's claw scratches my brain,' 'jagged eternity,' 'her metal heart chained'—and so on. I recognize a symbolic vision of our past age as lunar, ambitious, metallic, and of a change, which you symbolise as sun-rise and in which you, more clearly than I, have been able to discover joy and health. I do not question—your vision of joy is something which I believe in but

[1] Published in *Two Minstrels*, 1921.
[2] Published in *Two Foemen*, 1920. In H. E. Palmer's *Collected Poems* (1932) the title 'A Trinity of Song' was changed to 'England, Germany and Europe.'

cannot see or feel. Much as I am interested in this poem—and I read it with much emotion—I am perhaps more interested still in thoughts which I divine beyond it. I think you have genuine symbolic vision, but do not allow the sensitiveness that so often goes with it to lead you into anger.

You send me an automatic script published in a newspaper which clearly resembles, in certain ways, your 'Trinity of Song,' but this does not surprise me in an automatic script, which is often affected by 'telepathic influence' as I could prove to you if necessary (I have mislaid your letter at the moment, but when I find it I will return the newspaper cutting).

Examine your style, word for word, 'study the dictionary,' study the most concentrated masters till writing grows very arduous and you will attain to a greater general height of accomplishment, to a steadier light, and yet not lose your flashes of lightning. Yours sincerely W B YEATS

I would ask you to call and see me but I live in a mediaeval Tower in the West of Ireland, beside a bridge that may be blown up any night; and it may be a long time before I am in London.

TO OLIVIA SHAKESPEAR

Oct 9 [1922] 82 *Merrion Square*

My dear Olivia: We have been in Dublin now for a couple of weeks and our house is getting into order. There is a great drawing room with a beautiful mantelpiece and George has made it look very fine. Someday, when Ireland gets quiet, you will come and stay with us. We have seen no shot fired, or come in for any trouble, though most nights one hears a few shots. Some are perhaps fired out of high spirits or by accident. A friend of mine was talking to the porter at the Shelbourne Hotel when a shot came between them and smashed a glass-door. 'O,' said the porter, 'that's the young man who is instructing us,' pointing to the sentry at the door.

Anne and Michael and George are all well and Anne very lively. She demands sweets every time she sees me.

I spent the summer correcting proofs and writing a series of poems called 'Meditations in time of civil war' which I shall send to the *Mercury*. Now I am busy writing out the system—getting a 'Book A' written that can be typed and shown to interested persons and talked over. I also find various things to do in connection with the Lane pictures and the like. I go to England to lecture in middle of November and I dare say we shall meet.

The situation here is very curious—a revolt against democracy by a small section. Under the direction of an Englishman Childers they burn houses that they may force the majority to say 'It is too expensive to remain Free State, let us turn republican.' At any rate that is believed to be the policy. I have met some of the ministers who more and more seem too sober to meet the wildness of these enemies; and everywhere one notices a drift towards Conservatism, perhaps towards Autocracy. I always knew that it would come, but not that it would come in this tragic way. One wonders what prominent man will live through it. One meets a minister at dinner, passing his armed guard on the doorstep, and one feels no certainty that one will meet him again. We are entering on the final and most dreadful stage. Perhaps there is nothing so dangerous to a modern state, when politics take the place of theology, as a bunch of martyrs. A bunch of martyrs (1916) were the bomb and we are living in the explosion.

Have you news of Ezra and Dorothy? We hope to be in Rome next April. Yours affectionately   W B YEATS

TO H. J. C. GRIERSON

Oct 21 [1922]   82 *Merrion Square*

Dear Grierson: I am sending you my *Trembling of the Veil* as I promised though it is but a poor return for your magnificent gift. I think what I say of Ireland, at least, may interest you. I think things are coming right slowly though very slowly; we have had years now of murder and arson in which both nations have shared impartially. In my own neighbourhood the Black and Tans dragged two young men tied alive to a lorry by their heels, till their bodies were rent in pieces. 'There was nothing for the mother but the head' said a countryman and the head he spoke of was found on the road side. The one enlivening Truth that starts out of it all is that we may learn charity after mutual contempt. There is no longer a virtuous nation and the best of us live by candle light.

You have just possibly read certain of the chapters of my work in the *London Mercury* but they appeared there in a condensed form. Squire left out all passages that might shock, or that were too philosophical for his readers, and in fact reduced what I sent him by about one half. I consented to this and even advised it, yet my book is a whole, one part depending upon another and all on its speculative foundation. It was mainly written for this country and will be read anywhere'rather than here.

I am working at present at the project of getting the Abbey Theatre adopted as the Irish State Theatre and I think I may succeed.

Remember me to your family. Yours   W B YEATS

TO CHARLES RICKETTS

Nov 5 [1922]   82 *Merrion Square*

My dear Ricketts: Yesterday my wife brought the books up to my study, and not being able to restrain her excitement I heard her cry out before she reached the door 'You have perfect books at last.'[1] Perfect they are—serviceable and perfect. The little design of the unicorn is a masterpiece in that difficult kind. You have given my work a decoration of which one will never tire and all I have done will gradually be put into this form. It is a pleasure to me to think that many young men here and elsewhere will never know my work except in this form. My own memory proves to me that at 17 there is an identity between an author's imagination and paper and book-cover one does not find in later life. I still do not quite separate Shelley from the green covers, or Blake from the blue covers and brown reproductions of pictures, of the books in which I first read them. I do not separate Rossetti at all from his covers.

Life here is pleasant but disturbed. Last night I was entertained at dinner by an Arts Club and decided to use the occasion to speak

---

[1] The first two volumes of Macmillan's green-cloth collected edition of Yeats's writings, *Later Poems* and *Plays in Prose and Verse*, for which Ricketts had designed the binding and a decoration showing a unicorn and fountain for the end-papers, had been published on November 3.

very seriously about the state of the country. We began at 7.30 and the tide of frivolous speech and parody ran so fast and high that I was in despair—not seeing how I should interest such an audience. At 10.15 (and I was to speak at 10.30) somebody threw a bomb outside in the street and the parodist, who was in the middle of a parody of my 'Innisfree,' did not pause nor did his voice hesitate. However there was a slight increase of solemnity of which I took advantage. Only last Monday evening at 9.30 there was a terrific explosion at the other side of the square, which cracked our kitchen windows, and very thoroughly broke the drawing room windows of the next house. When it was all over my wife and I and Lennox Robinson and a rather nervous guest went out and questioned the sentry at the corner. He answered our questions in a gentle, depressed and rather educated voice and then said 'I think this is a dangerous place for you as they may start shooting at me any moment.' We hurried home but felt rather heartless.

We left Gort about five weeks ago and the day we left had two feet of water on our kitchen floor as the blowing up of our bridge had dammed the river. The neighbourhood is now I hear quite peaceful as there are no bridges left. Yet I don't find one ever gets quite used to explosions, one is always a little scared. I imagine one has to take them young. Our children will I think have excellent nerves. They will not find a new devilishness in the slamming of the kitchen door. However, though too old for the business, I am in excellent spirits.

Lady Gregory was very well and very busy and has suffered no inconveniences of any kind. She is writing as usual. My wife and I had hoped to stay with her next week as we were going down to superintend the finishing of another room in the Tower which will be necessary to us next spring, as we shall be liable in wet weather to a few hours' flood on the ground floor—perhaps twice in six months or so. However we are not going as somebody has shot our builder and he is in hospital.

We have a stately house here built in 1740 and though it has great rooms, a drawing room with three windows and a most lovely marble mantelpiece, we bought it for very little money. We hope to be of some use now that order is the conspiracy of a few.

Remember me to Shannon and believe that I am very grateful to you for a very considerable service. Yours ever   W B YEATS

TO H. J. C. GRIERSON

Nov 6 [1922]　　　　　　　　　　　　　　82 *Merrion Square*

Dear Prof. Grierson, Has *The Trembling of the Veil* reached you? Our post is subject to such vicissitudes that I am a little anxious. Your *Metaphysical Poets* has not yet come; and yesterday morning our wild men blew up the sorting office. We are preparing here, behind our screen of bombs and smoke, a return to conservative politics as elsewhere in Europe, or at least to a substitution of the historical sense for logic. The return will be painful and perhaps violent, but many educated men talk of it and must soon work for it and perhaps riot for it.

A curious sign is that AE who was the most popular of men is now suffering some slight eclipse because of old democratic speeches —things of years ago. I on the other hand get hearers where I did not get them because I have been of the opposite party. AE has still however his great popularity in co-operative Ireland. The Ireland that reacts from the present disorder is turning its eyes towards individualist Italy. Yours ever　　　　W B YEATS

TO EDMUND DULAC[1]

Dec. 1st [1922]　　　　　　　　　　　　　82 *Merrion Square*

My dear Dulac, When you send the Chinese pictures you will have, I think, to make a declaration as to contents of parcel—but the post office or parcel post office will explain—and you had better register and insure and send in the bill for the amount of this.

Those last two nights when I dined with you I was very tired and overflowed, as almost always when tired, in phantastical scandalous patter, a patter made all the worse from having lunched with a woman friend brought up like myself under the shadow of England's first emancipation in 1890 or so. It is my refuge from logic, and passion, and the love of God and charity to my neighbours and other exhausting things. Tell your friend to read *The Player Queen* and my note on it and she will understand.

I am on the Irish Senate and a probable income as senator, of

[1] From a typewritten copy.

which I knew nothing when I accepted, will compensate me somewhat for the chance of being shot or my house burned or bombed. We are a fairly distinguished body, much more so than the lower house, and should get much government into our hands. I have only spoken a few sentences in the house but cherish various projects.

Relations of whom I have seen nothing call on me and are kind, and old acquaintances press my hand.

I am working every morning on the philosophy which Werner Laurie is ready to accept with effusion.[1] He would sign an agreement at once, if I would let him, but I am insisting on his reading a hundred pages or so first. He may cry off when he does. The Senate does not meet till after lunch and so but gets my weariness.

How long our war is to last nobody knows. Some expect its end this Xmas and some equally well informed expect another three years. However the nights are quieter than they have been since the start. I have heard neither bombs nor shot since my return. They burn houses in the suburbs instead. Yours sincerely

W B YEATS

TO OLIVIA SHAKESPEAR

Dec 18 [1922] 82 *Merrion Square*

My dear Olivia: George has written to you about the shoes, which fill her with satisfaction, and I write to remind you to send me the bill.

My work on the Senate interests me, a new technique which I am learning in silence—I have only spoken once and then but six sentences and shall not speak again perhaps till I am (if I shall ever be) at ease with it. To-night I hear rumours of peace, but it may come to nothing or never have been anything. At the Senate house I have for near neighbours two senators, one of whom has had his house bombed for being senator, and one is under sentence of death because he owns the *Freeman's Journal*. For all that we are a dull (and as President Cosgrave has pointed out with evident content) well-dressed crowd. I shall speak very little but probably intrigue a great deal to get some old projects into action. On

---

[1] *A Vision*, issued by Werner Laurie in 1925 (1926), in an edition of 600 signed copies, uniform with *The Trembling of the Veil*.

Wednesday next I get a D.Litt. from Trinity College, and feel that I have become a personage. The Senate when it meets meets in the afternoon; and in the morning I work at the system, which Werner Laurie wants to publish and would sign an agreement for at once, if I did not insist on his first reading a little of it. If Laurie does not repent, a year from now should see the first half published. It will need another volume to finish it.

Not a shot by night or day! You cannot imagine what a sense of quiet that gives after the constant firing and bombing. People say is it the negociations or is it really ominous, the silence before some great outbreak? Yours sincerely   W B YEATS

Dec. 19. An official's house—a charming beautifully furnished place belonging to friends of ours—was burned last night and this morning I hear firing so I suppose the peace move has failed—I shall hear tomorrow at the Senate. George has just come in to say more executions. Somebody said last night 'In Ireland Catholicism has walked the plank.' I said 'Yes, but in England it treads the boards'—I alluded to its theatrical nature in England.

Dec. 21. Peace negociations still going on. I have just heard that when Mrs. Campbell's house was burnt—the house I speak of on last page—she appealed to the irregulars not to turn her children out in the night. The irregulars cried but said they could not help themselves, the new orders. Presently one of them went up stairs with Mrs. Campbell to fetch down—the house was I think already burning—the children's Xmas toys. Strange tragedy of thought that creates for such men such crimes but I don't suppose that these men were mere conscripted rebels. Democracy is dead and force claims its ancient right, and these men, having force, believe that they have [the] right to rule. With democracy has died too the old political generalizations. Men do not know what is, or is not, legitimate war. Yours affectionately   W B YEATS

TO ROBERT BRIDGES

Jan 4 [1923]   82 *Merrion Square*

My dear Bridges: I have just found a letter of yours dated Dec 2 stuffed into the hollow place between the arm and the cushions of a leather arm-chair. I wonder if I ever answered—to the best of my belief it only reached me here after my return from England. I have in fact been looking in vain through my letters because of an uncertain idea that I had some unanswered letter from you. If it was really unanswered please forgive me. When I got back here I found myself a senator and the Senate, though it does not break in upon my morning hours when I write verse etc, took away a large part of those afternoon hours when I write letters. I wish very much I could have gone to you and heaven knows when I shall be in England—probably not till peace has been made. Life here is interesting, but restless and unsafe—I have two bullet holes through my windows—as it must always be when the sheep endeavour to control the goats who are by nature so much the more enterprising race.

Yes I know the young American by letters I think. He has the American passion for ideas, combined, I judge, with the American intellectual indolence and physical energy. He will probably reach me sooner or later—in one letter he threatened to come to Co. Galway. His mother, when with child with him, probably listened to fifteen lectures a week, two a day including Sundays, which is quite moderate in New York. Yours W B YEATS

TO OLIVIA SHAKESPEAR

Jan 5 [1923]   82 *Merrion Square*

My dear Olivia: I think Anne is going on quite well, yesterday was the seventh day and after that the doctor said she should mend. We are not confident though the nurse here is, it may have been something else, however we are certainly a house of sickness. Now about Enoch & Sons. George sent the cheques to Watt as, I have no doubt, they have heard by this time.

I think we shall soon have peace here—the irregulars are evidently breaking up and only fighting to get a little better terms. They know they are beaten but may drag it on for a few more weeks. I have two bullet holes in my windows but one gets used to anything and there has been no fighting in our Square for a couple of weeks. I find that everybody is very polite to a senator, and if there are any that want his money or his life—which is probable

—they do not show by daylight. At my club people come and turn up the electric light for me if I forget to do so myself; and quite a number of persons with very slight conversational powers come and talk to me in public places.

I cannot write any more as I have just learned that Maud Gonne has been arrested and I must write to Iseult and offer to help with the authorities in the matter of warm blankets. The day before her arrest she wrote to say that if I did not denounce the Government she renounced my society for ever. I am afraid my help in the matter of blankets, instead of her release (where I could do nothing), will not make her less resentful. She had to choose (perhaps all women must) between broomstick and distaff and she has chosen the broomstick—I mean the witches' hats. Yours affectionately   W B YEATS

TO OLIVIA SHAKESPEAR

March 22 *[Postmark* 1923*]*   82 *Merrion Square*

My dear Olivia: I think things are mending here—my own projects in that matter postponed but not abandoned—the war seems fading out. In spite of all that has happened, I find constant evidence of ability or intensity which makes one hopeful. I was on a committee of the Senate the other day, which is considering legislation based on a series of blue books, with elaborate maps of coalfields etc, issued by the revolutionary government at the start of its war with England. It spent many thousands upon collecting evidence and over publication. Then again when the news came in of Michael Collins' death, one of the Ministers recited to the Cabinet—or to seven Ministers—the entire *Adonais* of Shelley. One strange thing is the absence of personal bitterness. Senators whose houses have been burnt (one man has lost archives going back to, I think, the 16th century) speak as if it were some impersonal tragedy, some event caused by storm or earthquake. Our debates are without emotion, dull, businesslike and well attended. We have just legalized, after detailed discussion, and approved, changes in local government, and in the poor laws, made in the very midst of the revolutionary war, changes that have meant considerable economy and better treatment of the poor.

My armed guard very much on the alert just now (many republicans are I think in town for a conference) and I was challenged last night on the stairs. I was in my stocking feet so as not to wake the children. I give my guard detective stories to train them in the highest tradition of their profession. Last week the theatres were ordered to close by the republicans and all closed except the Abbey (which I thought would go up in flames and so removed my father's portraits from the vestibule) but next day all theatres were open again at the command of the government.

George is almost well again—not quit of quarantine—but able to go out for short walks, and to be gay and cheerful. Pound sends me a postcard from S. Marino addressed to me at the Senate and heads it 'from the last republic.'

Yes I would greatly like Binyon's *Blake* which I saw at Ricketts' and admired.[1] Yours affectionately W B YEATS

My plans are still government policy but are postponed till peace has come by other means. They will be used not to bring peace but to lay War's ghost. At least so I am told officially. Unofficially I hear that the War party carried the day (this all very private). Certainly peace seems coming. Only isolated shots now at night; but one is sure of nothing.

TO OLIVIA SHAKESPEAR

June 28 [Postmark June 29, 1923]   82 *Merrion Square*

My dear Olivia: George heard in London that you are still very anxious about Hope.[2] If this is true I can only give you all my sympathy.

George brings back much news of Dorothy and a little of Ezra and under her incitement I have asked Joyce to come and stay for a few days. If he comes I shall have to use the utmost ingenuity to hide the fact that I have never finished *Ulysses*. I shall have to hide him from the politicians, who are scarce ready for his doctrine, while collecting what we have in the way of men of letters. Here one works at the slow exciting work of creating the institutions of a new

[1] *The Drawings and Engravings of William Blake*, 1922.
[2] Mrs. Shakespear's husband.

nation—all coral insects but with some design in our heads of the ultimate island. Meanwhile the country is full of arms and explosives ready for any violent hand to use. Perhaps all our slow-growing coral may be shattered but I think not—not unless Europe takes to war again, and starts new telepathic streams of violence and cruelty. You remember I told you I was anxious about my health. I seem to have got quite well again—thanks to meditation and perhaps a little to the passing away of the strain of civil war. That has passed completely though Ministers tell me not to get my pictures back yet. Have you read *Gods, Beasts and Men* by a Russian?[1] It is a strange vivid book, with much supernatural incident, by a Russian traveller. I commend it to people here for it describes a half-German half-Russian Baron, who tries to organize Asia under the rule of China to fight 'the depravity of Revolution' in the world. One reads it with delight but wondering if incidents are not a little heightened as in *Lavengro*.

I am in the middle of my new play and as usual under such circumstances wanting to do half a dozen other things instead. Yours affectionately
W B YEATS

TO EDMUND DULAC[2]

Oct. 14 [1923]   82 *Merrion Square*

My dear Dulac, The portrait of Giraldus is admirable. I enclose the sketch for the diagram.[3] The pencilled words all have to be in Latin and I will get the Latin I hope tomorrow. The man I count on for it was out yesterday. You can use any symbolism you like for the elements—nymphs, salamanders, air spirits, or Roman gods or more natural objects.

I think perhaps the name 'Giraldus' might as you suggest go under his portrait in contemporary handwriting. I think the two pictures are all that is really necessary.

The book will be finished in I hope another month—it contains

---
[1] *Beasts, Men and Gods* by Ferdynand Ossendowski. London: Edward Arnold, 1924.
[2] From a typewritten copy.
[3] Edmund Dulac designed the portrait of Giraldus and a diagram of 'The Great Wheel' for *A Vision*. These were included in the book anonymously and were supposed to be old woodcuts.

only a little of my system but the rest can follow. Werner Laurie is to publish it uniform with *The Trembling of the Veil*. That introduction I sent you has been greatly re-written and is much more authentic looking. It keeps the 'modesty of nature' in mind now, and the canary is gone.[1] I don't know when I shall get to London and at the moment can think of nothing but writing out the system. The MS. sent off, I shall give myself three months' more writing and perhaps produce here a Noh play if Civil War does not start again with the long nights.

The round objects in the enclosed diagram are of course the lunar phases 1. 8. 16. 22. making new moon, half moon, full moon and half moon respectively. They will be nasty things to draw but your Kracow artist would not have drawn them very carefully. I can give the *speculum* what date you please.

The Chinese pictures hang now in my study and are the great ornaments of the room.

Tea has just come so I must stop. I am most grateful to you.
Yours   W B YEATS

I doubt if Laurie would have taken the book but for the amusing deceit that your designs make possible. It saves it from seeming a book for specialists only and gives it a new imaginative existence.

As I look at all the blots on this I envy your neat hands.

---

[1] In an Introduction to the first version of *A Vision*, written supposedly by the fictitious character Owen Aherne and dated December 1922, which Yeats discarded before publication, the following passage occurred:

'He [Robartes] called upon me the next day, made some kind of an apology, and said that I must come to see Mr. Yeats and that he had made an appointment for us. At Woburn Buildings he told of his Arabian discoveries and spread out upon the table his diagrams, his notes, my written commentary without even explaining that it was mine; and after a couple of hours' exposition, and answering many questions, asked Mr. Yeats to undertake the editorship.

'Mr. Yeats opened a larged gilded Moorish wedding chest, took out a number of copy-books full of notes and diagrams; showed that our diagrams and his were almost exactly the same; that our notes only differed from his because our examples were Arabian whereas his were drawn from European history and literature.

' "You can only have found that all out," said Robartes, who was pale and excited, "through the inspiration of God."

' "Is not that a rather obsolete term?" said Mr. Yeats. "It came in the first instance quite suddenly. I was looking at my canary, which was darting about the cage in rather brilliant light, when I found myself in a strangely still and silent state and in that state I saw with the mind's eye symbols streaming before me. That still and silent state always recurs in some degree when I fix my mind upon the canary." '

TO EDMUND GOSSE

Nov 23 [1923]   82 *Merrion Square*

My dear Gosse: I am grateful for the honour and grateful for the money.[1] A sister of mine developed consumption five months ago and has been in a nursing home near London ever since. She has worried at the thought of so much expense falling upon me but now she need not worry—I feel a tower of strength. I am grateful too because I have a better chance of being listened to here in Dublin than ever before.

Of course I know quite well that this honour is not given to me as an individual but as a representative of a literary movement and of a nation and I am glad to have it so. People are grateful to me for having won them this recognition and life is pleasant. Yours

W B YEATS

TO LADY GREGORY

Jan 13 [Postmark 1924]   82 *Merrion Square*

My dear Lady Gregory: Are you coming up for the Carnegie meeting on Jan 16? Your room is ready and we shall [be] delighted to have you here.

Since I came back from Stockholm [2] I have been overwhelmed with letters and work—letters [*word indecipherable*] me from all parts of the world, and I have been writing out Stockholm impressions to be a sort of 'bread and butter letter' to Sweden, and at last a part of my autobiography.[3] I long to be back at my philosophy and then back at my poetry.

I have invested £6,000 of the money, and kept £500 to go to pay off the debt on this house, or pay Lilly's expenses as the case may be. There was almost £400 which we have largely spent on our trip to Sweden and on completing the furnishing of this house—my bookcases, stair carpets, plates, dishes, knives and forks and something I

---

[1] This letter evidently refers to the recent award to Yeats of the Nobel Prize.
[2] Where he had been to receive the Nobel Prize in person.
[3] *The Bounty of Sweden*, published in the *London Mercury* and in the *Dial*, September 1924, and then as a volume by the Cuala Press in 1925, was eventually included in *Dramatis Personae*, Macmillan, 1936, and, in America, in *The Autobiography of William Butler Yeats*, The Macmillan Co., 1938.

have always longed for, a sufficient reference library—*Encyclo[pae]dia Britannica, Cambridge Medieval, Ancient* and *Modern History* and a good edition of Gibbon and some art books. As I look at the long rows of substantial backs I am conscious of growing learned minute by minute.

    I shall ask you when you come up to let me see a copy of 'The old Woman remembers.'[1] I would like, if Jack can be got to do it, [to] see it turned into a new Broadside for Cuala. If Jack will [not] one might find some other artist. Yours   W B YEATS

TO EDMUND DULAC[2]

January 28, 1924   82 *Merrion Square*

Dear Dulac, I have been a long time without writing, and now only dictate, I hope you won't mind a dictated letter, but my handwriting is a dreadful thing to inflict upon anyone. I am still struggling with letters that have reached me from all parts of the world, and so a secretary comes to me for some time most days. I remember after the '*Playboy* row' in Dublin it was much the same. It would be very kind of you, if, when the railway strike is over, you would get some picture packer at, of course, my expense, to pack up the masks, etc. and make the necessary Customs declaration, and send them to me here. I want to begin arranging performances. The psychological moment has come, for Dublin is reviving after the Civil War, and self-government is creating a little stir of excitement. People are trying to found a new society. Politicians want to be artistic, and artistic people to meet politicians, and so on. It seems to be the very moment for a form of drama to be played in a drawing-room. It is quite amusing trying to create a society without hostesses, and without wealth. If you know a hostess of genius and great wealth, you might tell her that here is an opportunity worth living for, especially if she will search her ancestors till she finds an Irish one. And after all if you go far enough back, everybody is descended from everybody.

    [1] A monologue, written by Lady Gregory. The actress reciting it lights one candle for each hundred years; there are seven candles. It was first produced at the Abbey Theatre on December 31, 1923, and was spoken by Sara Allgood.
    [2] Dictated.

If anything brings you to a sale of Chinese pictures do not forget me. There is a space of 46 inches wide between two bookcases, and I want a Chinese picture for that space. I don't imagine any Chinese picture is as wide as that. The two pictures you sent me are about 36 inches, margin and all, and that will do excellently. I shall have to get it framed, as far as I can remember the way yours are framed. I won't specify what kind of a picture, except that you can pay a reasonable price for it. I wouldn't mind £20 for another 'Henry VIII.' I feel this is giving you a horrible amount of trouble, especially considering all that you have done for me already, and don't do it unless it amuses you to go to an auction.

I am just returning to work on *A Vision*, having finished my Essay on Stockholm, which I felt I had to do, as a kind of 'bread and butter' letter to Sweden. I am still very far from finished, so there is no hurry about your design. I work for days and then find I have muddled something, and have to do it all again, especially whenever I have to break new ground. Yours   W B YEATS

TO JOHN QUINN

January 29, 1924   82 *Merrion Square*

My dear Quinn, I haven't written to you because Stockholm has brought with it an immense correspondence. People have written from all over the world, not only strangers but people whom I knew many years ago. I sometimes dictate seventeen or eighteen letters in an afternoon, and I am only just beginning to get through the flood. You needn't fear that we shall spend any of that money on Ballylee. I put aside the proceeds of my last 'lecturing tour' for that purpose and I have still a substantial sum left, intended in part for the concrete roof, for we still live, when there, protected not very perfectly by stone floors alone. We are not in a mood to spend much on it at present for, with Cuala and the Senate, neither of us can be long away from Dublin. Its chief use for some time to come will be to house the children, my wife and I going down for but a few days at a time.

Yes, this as you say has been a lucky year for me.

I am glad indeed to have my father's portrait, though I have not yet found the right place to hang it, for the best light for that purpose is in our dining-room, and the dining-room is in the possession of Cuala for the present. I will, of course, correct the errors in the account of my father's when we come to reprint it in the ordinary publishing trade. I was very glad to have your notes upon him. They will help me very much when that moment comes . . .

I am overwhelmed with work, for Stockholm meant my doing nothing for some time, and I have to finish for Werner Laurie my philosophical book, as well as revise the various volumes of my new uniform edition for Macmillan, London.

Politics are amusing and don't take much of my time. I am pressing upon the Government the appointment of an Advisory Committee of Artists, and have got Orpen, Shannon and Lavery to promise to act upon that Committee. I think I shall succeed. I am also trying to get the designs of Irish lace improved, but do not yet know what success I shall have. In the Senate I speak as little upon politics as is possible, reserving myself for the things I understand. Dublin's social life is becoming interesting, various classes wanting to meet each other, and not knowing how. Last night, however, I was at a very melancholy attempt of this sort, a club ostensibly for conversation where the guests were selected for the worth of their characters or for their near relationship to this person or that other. Carrying on conversation was like shaking a sack of wet sand. I breakfasted in bed this morning to recover. Yours
W B YEATS

TO OLIVIA SHAKESPEAR

May 26 [1924]   82 *Merrion Square*

My dear Olivia, I have sent you *Essays* in which however you will find but one new essay 'Art and Ideas'—new to you, I mean, for it is old enough—but I want you to have my work in its best dress. Did I send you *Plays and Controversies?* I meant to, but my correspondence was recovering slowly from the deluge before and after Stockholm— a deluge that seems to have cut me off from all my friends, it so broke down the frail dykes of my letter-writing industry. However both you and I are too old to really enjoy my writings—especially those in prose. I write for boys and girls of twenty but I am always thinking of myself at that age—the age I was when my father painted me as King Goll, tearing the strings out [of] a harp, being insane with youth, but looking very desirable—alas no woman noticed it at the time—with dreamy eyes and a great mass of black hair. It hangs in our drawing room now—a pathetic memory of a really dreadful time.

Why did you not come that time when George wrote to you? Will you come some time this year when George feels recovered enough to ask people to dinner? Our ministers and their wives would interest you—the two or three we sometimes see. They are able and courageous but as yet—I admit—without play of mind. Honest modern-minded men swimming still in seas of conspiracy of others' making when no one's letters are safe and no one's telephone wires. (This for your own ear.)

I have just heard from Ezra from Rome. 500 copies of *Ulysses* confiscated in the English customs, and he would like to import into this country. I have promised enquiries but no one dare wake an ecclesiastic terrier, which is at present only hunting in its dreams. George Russell and I and the head of the Education Board are accused, by the by, of being in a conspiracy to destroy the Catholic faith through free education. At least I am told so, but I never see the popular Catholic press. The Head of the Board tells me that objection is made to 'The Lady of Shalott' because 'Tennyson is a poet of Revolt.' It must not be permitted in the school books. But *Ulysses*—that would wake the terrier in earnest.

I must return to my day's work—codifying fragments of the philosophy. Yours   W B YEATS

TO OLIVIA SHAKESPEAR

June 21 [*Postmark June* 22, 1924]   82 *Merrion Square*

My dear Olivia: I am in high spirits this morning, seeing my way to a most admirable row. I heard that a group of Dublin poets, a man called Higgins and the Stuarts and another, whose name I do not know, were about to publish a review. I said to one of them 'Why not found yourselves on the doctrine of the immortality of the soul, most bishops and all bad writers being obviously atheists.' I heard no more till last night when I received a kind of deputation. They had adopted my suggestion and were suppressed by the printers for blasphemy. I got a bottle of Sparkling Moselle, which I hope youthful ignorance mistook for champagne, and we swore alliance. They are to put the offending parts into Latin and see if the printers will stand that; and begin an agitation. I saw a proof sheet marked by the printer 'with no mention meant or made of the Blessed Virgin' —the good lady as we all know being confined to church. My dream is a wild paper of the young which will make enemies everywhere and suffer suppression, I hope a number of times, with the logical assertion, with all fitting deductions, of the immortality of the soul.

By the by I wonder if I told you of a remark of Lady Gregory's the other day. She hates all clergy though she never misses church and is a great reader of her bible and, as she believes, very orthodox —furthermore she is a great prude so far as what others say to her is concerned. She suddenly astounded me by saying—apropos of nothing—a couple of weeks ago—and with an air of gratified malice —'That Russell case [1] shed a new light on the immaculate conception'—she evidently felt that a doctrine which belonged in an especial sense to the clergy had been hit—a perplexity with simple laity abated.

If I had said such a thing to her I would have been in disgrace for the afternoon. She spoke from depths of meditation. As she grows older she grows very strong and obstinate.

All those of us here who are in the secret are laughing over a government enquiry which has just been held about the state of our army. One man has [been] 'convicted of manslaughter and condemned to be very severely reprimanded.'

If you were an active member of society I would not dare write this to you for fear Lady Lavery would report me to the President. The whole enquiry is a comment on democracy which may have historical effects, if the facts get out. Yours affectionately

W B YEATS

[1] A much publicised divorce case of the time.

TO OLIVIA SHAKESPEAR

July 26 [1924]   82 *Merrion Square*

My dear Olivia, Here is the circular I told you of.[1] Please subscribe and help a first beginning of new political thought where we need it above all things—Municipal workers and hotel employees are about to strike on the edge of the Tailteann festival [2]—and besides you will probably agree with it.

I am sending you this post my new book.[3] I think that it contains some of my best work but it is very slim—the philosophy absorbs me. But that once finished I think I shall do deeper and more passionate work than ever before. My head is full of things I want to write.

This is not a letter for I have to go out on Tailteann work before lunch. George is busy repainting. Yours   W B YEATS

TO SIEGFRIED SASSOON[4]

October 7, 1924

Dear Sassoon, I enclose a subscription for Mr. Bridges' clavichord. I am very glad indeed to do so as I have always so greatly admired his work. It has an emotional purity and rhythmical delicacy no living man can equal. Yours sincerely   W B YEATS

TO RICHARD ASHE KING

October 26, 1924   82 *Merrion Square*

Dear Ashe King, Will you permit me to print the enclosed letter of dedication in my new book *Early Poems and Stories*?

---

[1] The circular, presumably, for *To-Morrow*, the weekly paper mentioned in his previous letter. The first number appeared in August 1924 and contained a manifesto, signed by the editors but actually written by Yeats. After two numbers had appeared the paper was suppressed for publishing a story by Lennox Robinson.

[2] A revival of ancient Irish games.

[3] *The Cat and the Moon and certain Poems*, Cuala Press, published in July.

[4] Dictated.

I have long looked for some opportunity of showing you that a certain clumsy sentence in *The Trembling of the Veil* was not intended to mean what you thought. I will of course change the sentence in the next edition, but I had meant by it that you were 'typical of nothing' in the Dublin of those days, meaning that you were typical of no thing that I was satirising, that you stood apart from all the little groups and cliques. You were not to blame for putting that construction upon the sentence as I found out when I showed it to other people and tried to explain my meaning. Yours

W B YEATS

TO OLIVIA SHAKESPEAR

Monday April 27 [1925]   82 *Merrion Square*

My dear Olivia: I go to London tonight to try and see politicians in preparation for a question about Lane pictures a certain Howard Bury asks in the House on Monday week. I shall be at the Savile so let me know your plans. I shall probably wire on my first free moment. I shall be only a few days in London as I have to speak in the Senate on May 3. However I shall return to London after that. This first visit will—unless I fail to see the people I want which is probable—be all business. Lady Gregory has asked me to go over —I should have been sent a week ago, now I shall have to try and get hold of Birkenhead and others, whom I do not even know, at a day's notice.

I enclose a set of proofs of my new Cuala book—keep them for me. As I want to send them to Sturge Moore later on.

I am not quite certain that George has not conspired with Lady Gregory—she was at Coole on Friday—to send me on this wild-goose chase for the good of my health. I have been doing too much philosophy and writing too much verse. Yours   W B YEATS

TO L. A. G. STRONG[1]

June 25*th*, 1925   82 *Merrion Square*

My dear Strong, Thanks very much for your letter and for all the friendly things you say in it. I will go much more deeply into the

[1] Dictated.

problem in the new book—*A Vision*—but it will be horribly expensive, so don't think of getting it, but wait until you can see it at the Bodleian Library. It mightn't be of any value to you, for a great deal of it is exceedingly technical, a form of science for the study of human nature, as we see it in others, and so, less personal than the little book you speak of.

I noticed in your dream that I 'differed in appearance from' myself. That is always so. No concrete dream image is ever, according to my experience, taken from the conscious memory. Our dreams select for their purpose images that may go extraordinarily close to those of memory, but never coincide with them.

Certainly you may use my 'Leda.' If you will, write to Watt or get your publisher to write and make the usual arrangement, but I don't want you to use it in the form it had in *To-Morrow*. I have re-written it since. The worst of it is, I don't [know] where my new version is at the moment. I shall, however, receive it very shortly in the proof sheets of *A Vision*. I open a section with it. In fact there are 40 pages of commentary, for I look upon it as a classic enunciation. If I can find my manuscript I will send you a copy in a few days and if I cannot, you had better tell me how long you can wait.

[*The rest in Yeats's handwriting*]

Yours sincerely   W B YEATS

P.S. Proofs of *A Vision* has just come—I enclose it but ask you to return proof when you have copied the poem. It would be no use my doing so, considering what my writing is, and there is no typist here I would ask to copy it—one a few days ago wept because put to type a speech in favour of divorce I was to deliver in the Senate. My wife is not very well so I cannot ask her.

TO H. J. C. GRIERSON

February 21 [1926]   82 *Merrion Square*

My dear Prof Grierson: I have long put off writing to thank you for *The Background of English Literature* but my procrastination has not meant any lack of liking. I have had your book at my bed side for weeks and have read it very constantly. I am particularly indebted to you for your essay on Byron. My own verse has more and more adopted—seemingly without any will of mine—the syntax and vocabulary of common personal speech. The passages you quote —that beginning 'our life is a false nature' down to almost the end of the quotation where it becomes too elaborate with 'couch the mind' [1] and a great part of the long passage about Haidée [2]—I got a queer sort of half dream prevision of the passage the day before your book came with a reiteration of the words 'broad moon'—are perfect personal speech. The over childish or over pretty or feminine element in some good Wordsworth and in much poetry up to our date comes from the lack of natural momentum in the syntax. This momentum underlies almost every Elizabethan and Jacobean lyric and is far more important than simplicity of vocabulary. If Wordsworth had found it he could have carried any amount of elaborate English. Byron, unlike the Elizabethans though he always tries for it, constantly allows it to die out in some mind-created construction, but is I think the one great English poet—though one can hardly call him great except in purpose and manhood—who sought it constantly. Blunt, though mostly an infuriating amateur, has it here and there in some Elizabethan sounding sonnet and is then very great. Perhaps in our world only an amateur can seek it at all— unless he keep to the surface like Kipling—or somebody like myself who seeks it with an intense unnatural labour that reduces composition to four or five lines a day. In a less artificial age it would come with our baby talk. The amateur has the necessary ease of soul but only succeeds a few times in his life.

I have been reading your Donne again—I have just spelt him 'done,' that is because I have been writing the material version of a chorus for a version of *Oedipus* intended for the stage and my faculties have gone to the deuce—especially that intoxicating 'St. Lucies Day' which I consider always an expression of passion and proof that he was the Countess of Bedford's lover. I have used the arrangement of the rhymes in the stanzas for a poem of my own, just finished. I have the Blake illustration to Gray open on a little table which makes a kind of lectern between two book shelves. My

---

[1] *Childe Harold's Pilgrimage*, canto IV, Stanzas 126–127. The words 'couch the mind' should be 'couch the blind.' The word is misprinted in *The Background of English Literature*.
[2] *Don Juan*, canto II, Stanzas 177, 181, 183–185, 188.

large picture books take their turn there and yours has been there for the last month. The pictures grow in beauty with familiarity.

You may have noticed that we have had riots in the theatre again. I was with you when word reached me of the *Playboy* row. This time [1] we had a packed theatre, and had a packed theatre every day while the play was running, indeed numbers could not get in. The riot was soon over and displayed one curious effect of fine acting. When the Republicans rushed the stage a man caught up a girl, who had been playing a consumptive invalid, and folded her in a cloak as a preliminary to carrying her from the stage—she was not the actress in his eyes but the consumptive girl.

The theatre has now a great following. Indeed all things of the kind are going well with us—minds have been suddenly liberated from hereditary political passion and are looking for other interests. I feel constantly if I were but twenty years old and not over sixty all I ever wanted to do could be done easily. One never tires of life and at the last must die of thirst with the cup at one's lip. Yours ever

W B YEATS

TO OLIVIA SHAKESPEAR

March 4 [*On envelope:* 'I forgot to post this. So sorry. March 12.']
[*Postmark Mar* 13, 1926]
82 *Merrion Square*

My dear Olivia, I am so sorry about your teeth—I suppose you will get this in the nursing home—however the worst trial will be over. I know that one of the things I dread most is gas—'laughing gas' is I believe its lying name and that liar Southey called it 'a brave gas.'

I do not think Carmichael or any other spirit spends his thought on such things as the preference for a tub rather than a tin or a fixed bath. When they come to us they take up old thoughts and interests. I had once to stay silent for some minutes as the spirit was listening to the hoot of an owl. 'Those sounds,' he said, 'give us intense pleasure.' When you are well again I want you to read the part of my book called 'The Gates of Pluto' [2]—it is overloaded with

---

[1] The riots this time were caused by the production of *The Plough and the Stars* by Sean O'Casey, at the Abbey Theatre on February 8, 1926.

[2] Book IV of *A Vision*, 1925. It does not appear in the revised version of 1937.

detail and not as bold in thought as it should have been but does I think reconcile spiritual fact with credible philosophy.

Why not send the embarrassing book to Harry Tucker anonymously? He would be charmed to get it and at once attribute the gift to some old friend—you cannot tell how deeply touched he would be. He would hide it away and read it like his prayer book.

A Vision reminds me of the stones I used to drop as a child into a certain very deep well. The splash is very far off and very faint. Not a review except one by AE—either the publisher has sold the review copies or the editors have—and no response of any kind except from a very learned doctor in the North of England[1] who sends me profound and curious extracts from ancient philosophies on the subject of gyres. A few men here are reading me, so I may found an Irish heresy. Yours affectionately   W B YEATS

TO OLIVIA SHAKESPEAR

April 15 *[Postmark April 16, 1926]*   82 *Merrion Square*

My dear Olivia: I have not written for a long time—life has been too eventful. As I have grown older I have increased always the intensity of my morning Swedish drill, struggling with my figure; and then I discovered that I had ruptured myself—not badly but enough for general annoyance with life, and then I took to my bed with what I suspect was the ignoble complaint of measels—how do you spell it?—which has now transferred itself to Anne. Have you got out of your trouble with the dentist—do please tell me. I am enjoying convalescence, which means that I stay in bed for breakfast and read modern philosophy. I have found a very difficult but profound person Whitehead, who seems to have reached my own conclusions about ultimate things. He has written down the game of chess and I, like some Italian Prince, have made the pages and the court ladies have it out on the lawn. Not that he would recognise his abstract triumph in my gay rabble.

[1] Dr. Frank Pearce Sturm (? -1942) who practised at Southport, Lancashire. He published three small books of poems, *An Hour of Reverie* in 1905, *Umbrae Silentes* in 1918, and *Eternal Helen* in 1921; Yeats included one poem by him in *The Oxford Book of Modern Verse*. I have not been able to discover if Yeats's letters to him still exist.

I very nearly wrote to you and asked you to put me up, as I thought Lady Gregory might want me for her final struggle over the Lane pictures, but in the end she preferred to work alone. However that was for the best, as when I do come I want to be in good health and spirits; you yourself are probably off somewhere for change and recovery.

At present I am suffering from a play. A certain Irish dramatist a year ago sent us a rather vulgar but highly skilful play,[1] which we Directors and the whole theatre hated. We put it off and off. Then at last the evil moment had to come and last Monday it was played and now as we feared every seat is taken and at night the streets before the Theatre packed with motors. I sat it out in misery and had two furious interviews with the author by telephone. Every country likes good art till it produces its own form of vulgarity and after that will have nothing else. The theme is young women throwing themselves at the heads of horrible old men for marriage' sake. I phoned to the author 'We did your play that you might judge it for yourself. Do you think the degradation of youth a theme for comedy—the comedy of the newspapers? To me it is a theme for satire or tragedy.' I have given orders that all the young women are to tousle their heads that we may not mistake them for whole women, but know them for cattle. Yours in affection and memory

W B YEATS

TO OLIVIA SHAKESPEAR

April 22 [*Postmark* 1926]   82 *Merrion Square*

My dear Olivia: I had no idea you had been so ill. I am very sorry indeed. I should not have let so long pass without writing,—that is why I did not know.

The work of Whitehead's I have read is *Science in the Modern World* and I have ordered his *Concept of Nature* and another book of his. He thinks that nothing exists but 'organisms,' or minds—the 'cones' of my book—and that there is no such thing as an object 'localized in space,' except the minds, and that which we call physical

---

[1] *Look at the Heffernans!* by Brinsley Macnamara, produced at the Abbey Theatre on April 12.

objects of all kinds are 'aspects' or 'vistas' of other 'organisms'—in my book the 'Body of Fate' of one's being is but the 'Creative mind' of another. What we call an object is a limit of perception. We create each other's universe, and are influenced by even the most remote 'organisms.' It is as though we stood in the midst of space and saw upon all sides—above, below, right and left—the rays of stars—but that we suppose, through a limit placed upon our perceptions, that some stars were at our elbow, or even between our hands. He also uses the 'Quantum Theory' when speaking of minute organisms—molecules—in a way that suggests 'antithetical' and 'primary,' or rather if he applies it to the organisms we can compare with ourselves it would become that theory.

I partly delight in him because of something aristocratic in his mind. His packed logic, his way of saying just enough and no more, his difficult scornful lucidity seem to me the intellectual equivalent of my own imaginative richness of suggestion—certainly I am nothing if I have not this. (He is all 'Spirit' whereas I am all 'Passionate Body.') He is the opposite of Bertrand Russell who fills me with fury, by his plebeian loquacity.

I must get to work on an *Oedipus* chorus—we are to do the play at the Abbey. Yours affectionately   W B YEATS

P.S. and Private

I have had a hint from an important republican that the anti-Casey republicans are going to blow up the Abbey the week after next when we revive *The Plough and the Stars*. We shall of course be well guarded but I shall not tell the company. Lennox knows and is seeing to the fire extinguishing apparatus. Nothing will happen but it shows the state of feeling. If we had not been warned we might no doubt have been blown up as were certain Cinemas a couple of years ago. The man who has warned me is certainly not a friend—rather the reverse.

TO OLIVIA SHAKESPEAR

May 25 [Postmark 1926]   *Thoor Ballylee*

My dear Olivia: We are at our Tower and I am writing poetry as I always do here, and as always happens, no matter how I begin, it becomes love poetry before I am finished with it. I have lots of subjects in my head including a play about Christ meeting the worshippers of Dionysus on the mountain side—no doubt that will somehow become love poetry too. I have brought but two books, Baudelaire and MacKenna's *Plotinus*. Plotinus is a most ardent and wonderful person. I am also writing answers to a long series of questions sent me by a reader of *A Vision*, and Plotinus helps me there. Do you remember the story of Buddha who gave a flower to some one, who in his turn gave another a silent gift and so from man to man for centuries passed on the doctrine of the Zen school? One feels at moments as if one could with a touch convey a vision—that the mystic way and sexual love use the same means—opposed yet parallel existences (I cannot spell and there is no dictionary in the house).

An old beggar has just called I knew here twenty years ago as wandering piper but now he is paralysed and cannot play. He was lamenting the great houses burned or empty—'The gentry have kept the shoes on my feet, and the coat on my back and the shilling in my pocket—never once in all the forty and five years that I have been upon the road have I asked a penny of a farmer.' I gave him five shillings and he started off in the rain for the nearest town—five miles—I rather fancy to drink it.

The last I gave to was at Coole and he opened the conversation by saying to Lady Gregory—'My lady you are in the winter of your age'—they are all full of contemplation and elaborate of speech and have their regular track.

My moods fill me with surprise and some alarm. The other day I found at Coole a reproduction of a drawing of two charming young persons in the full stream of their Saphoistic enthusiasm, and it got into my dreams at night and made a great racket there, and yet I feel spiritual things are very near me. I think I shall be able to feel [*word indecipherable*] for those more remote parts of the System that are hardly touched in *A Vision*. I suppose to grow old is to grow impersonal, to need nothing and to seek nothing for oneself —at least it may be thus.

As you see I have no news, for nothing happens in this blessed place, but a stray beggar or a heron. Yours affectionately

W B YEATS

TO OLIVIA SHAKESPEAR

July 2 [1926 G. Y.] *Ballylee*

My dear Olivia: I am up in Dublin but returning to Galway to-day. Some time ago you asked me for some love poems I had written. I did not send them because they want revision. They are part of a series. I have written the wild regrets, for youth and love, of an old man, and the poems you asked for are part of a series in which a woman speaks, first in youth and then in age. I enclose one of those spoken when she is old which I greatly like.[1] Keep the MS as yet there is no other correct copy—it is just finished. Do you think it would be less shocking if I put a capital to 'he' in the last stanza?

I am in better health than I was and I do really believe that I owe it to Plotinus as much as to the Tower. By the way do get Spengler's *Decline of the West* and compare his general scheme with mine in 'Dove or Swan.' While his first volume was going through the press in 1918 I was getting the outline—and I think all the main diagrams of mine. There is exact correspondence in date after date. He was not translated till after my book was published. Had he been I could not have written. Yours affectionately   W B YEATS

TO THE PRESIDENT, ROYAL IRISH ACADEMY[2]

July 27, 1926 *82 Merrion Square*

Dear Sir, We are anxious to see added to the Academy an autonomous committee of men of letters who would give it the character of the French Institute. Our suggestion is that you limit the number of this committee to, say, twelve members and that once the committee, or a nucleus of it, has been formed it should nominate for membership persons eminent in Irish literature. It may be impossible to give this proposed committee the power of actually electing its own members, but this need not be any obstacle, its nominations would come before the General Council which, follow-

---

[1] Note by Mrs. Yeats: The poem referred to in this letter is 'The Friends of his Youth,' Section VII of 'A Man Young and Old.'
[2] Typewritten.

ing the analogy of the Council of the Royal Society of Literature which accepts nominations in this way from what is called the Academic Committee of that Society, would no doubt elect persons so nominated. What would be essential is that some modification in the rules of the Academy should be made to permit of the election, during the next year or two, of at any rate the majority of the ten members. All the other acts of this committee of literature could if necessary be re-enacted by the General Council, it would not, therefore, be necessary to change the constitution. I am assuming that the men of letters so nominated and so elected would pay the ordinary annual subscription to the Society. Their principal function would probably be at first to crown certain books, say, every three years. For this purpose it would be necessary for us to raise a small sum of money; we should require a medal designed and cast for the purpose. The names we have in mind are George Bernard Shaw, Mr. James Stephens, Mr. George Russell, Mr. Lennox Robinson, W. B. Yeats, Mr. Stephen MacKenna (the translator of Plotinus), Mr. Sean O'Casey, and in consideration of his Gaelic plays and poems, Dr. Hyde, and let us say, Mr. St. John Ervine or Mr. Forrest Reid. That would be enough for a start. Any names after this would be nominated by the committee itself. We should be very much obliged if you would bring this idea before the Council of the Academy and if they think it desirable and practicable Mr. Yeats will see Mr. Bernard Shaw when in London in September and try to get his acceptance. We feel pretty confident of the others—except Mr. Stephen MacKenna, who should be asked, however, as a matter of duty. Once such a body were established it would have no difficulty in finding out duties for itself, our feeling is that at the beginning of a new State, where conditions are unsettled, it is important to have an authorative body, not merely in matters of learning but in creative literature. The only scholar who is upon our list is Mr. Stephen MacKenna, and we have put him there not because of his scholarship but because that scholarship is united to great beauty of style; we are assuming that a great scholar or man of learning would be already a member of the Academy.

Geo. W. Russell.
W. B. Yeats.
Lennox Robinson.

TO OLIVIA SHAKESPEAR

Sept 5 [*Postmark Sept* 6, 1926]   82 *Merrion Square*

My dear Olivia: I hear that you are to be a grandmother and that the event is taking place in the usual secrecy. You are probably furious, but will find a grandchild a pleasing distraction in the end. It is an ideal relationship, for your business will be unmixed indulgence. I congratulate you upon it. Dorothy being doubtless still more furious will make an excellent mother. Motherly 'O God fill my quivers' mothers have made the world the disagreeable place it is. Your [grand-]child—I am as you know a prophet—will grow up intelligent and revere your memory.

Is it true you go to Paris in October? I shall be in London the first half of that month if I can bring myself to stay, for with George busy with her mother and you away I shall have little reason to. I had hoped you could put me up when Nelly [1] returned to Sidmouth. I feel that my aged habits have been upset by an earthquake.

I have not written for the absurd reason that some time ago I finished three series of poems—from which I sent you one—and have been hoping every week to get the final typed version, to send you a copy. I got it typed once but started re-writing. There have been constant interruptions—the last time I wrote a poem about Byzantium to recover my spirits. Now I am deep in revising and seeing through the press a new Lane Picture Pamphlet of Lady Gregory.[2]

I send you a little book of mine, *Estrangement*, some of the thoughts of which—but only a few—are in my other books. Yours affectionately   W B YEATS

TO OLIVIA SHAKESPEAR

Sept 24 [*Postmark* 1926]   *Thoor Ballylee*

My dear Olivia: I divine that you have already adopted the grandchild. When do you and he arrive in London? George and I shall

---

[1] Mrs. Yeats's mother.
[2] *Case for the Return of Sir Hugh Lane's Pictures to Dublin*. By Lady Gregory. Dublin: Talbot Press, 1926. The pamphlet contained no original contribution from Yeats but reprinted in an appendix part of a speech he had made on the subject in the Senate.

get there on Oct 4, or rather I shall, for George gets there the day before. I have to give a lecture in Liverpool on Sunday Oct 3. (It will pay for my railway tickets etc.) We are going to stay at Orchard's Hotel, Portman St., George and Nelly and I—pray that there may be no rats in the rafters—and for how long I do not know. I have to be back early in November to vote a man into a position in a hospital —I am a governor—but how much of the time before that I can spend out of Ireland I do not know.

I read Croce and write verse and as a result have nothing to say. Here is a fragment of my last curse upon old age. It means that even the greatest men are owls, scarecrows, by the time their fame has come. Aristotle, remember, was Alexander's tutor, hence the taws (form of birch)

> Plato imagined all existence plays
> Among the ghostly images of things;
> Solider Aristotle played the taws
> Upon the bottom of the King of Kings;
> World famous, golden thighed Pythagoras
> Fingered upon a fiddle stick, or strings,
> What the star sang and careless Muses heard.—
> Old coats upon old sticks to scare a bird.[1]

Pythagoras made some measurement of the intervals between notes on a stretched string. It is a poem of seven or eight similar verses. I am also gradually enlarging my woman series and one of the poems which you have not seen is among the best I have written. I read Croce and his like that I may at last make the conception of the [?] Daimon—Croce because it is the opposite of his thought in many ways—clear and so find a positive ageless energy or perception. Yours affectionately W B YEATS

TO OLIVIA SHAKESPEAR

Dec 7 [Postmark Dec 8, 1926]   82 *Merrion Square*

My dear Olivia: I have not written as life has been rather broken since I returned—writing a couple of poems or so in a dream,

[1] These lines, somewhat revised, appear as Section VI of the poem 'Among School Children' in *The Tower*, 1928.

entertaining a great Swedish architect,[1] giving up my study to a Cuala sale. Now I have got back to system as far as this is compatible with a new poem. I told you and showed you part of two series of poems in which a man and woman in old or later life remember love. I am writing for each series contrasting poems of youth

> 'I laid a hand upon that head
> of blossom tinted stone
> And can neither work nor play
> Since the deed was done:
> O but hands are lunatic
> That travel on the moon.' [2]

I think it likely that there will be yet another series upon the old man and his soul as he slowly comes to understand that the mountains are not solid, that all he sees is a mathematical line drawn between hope and memory. Whatever I do, poetry will remain a torture.

My version of *Oedipus* comes on to-night. I think my shaping of the speech will prove powerful on the stage, for I have made it bare, hard and natural like a saga, and that it will be well, though not greatly, acted—it is all too new to our people. I am more anxious about the audience, who will have to sustain an hour and a half of tension. The actor who plays Oedipus[3] felt the strain at dress rehearsal so much that he could hardly act in the last great moments —a good audience will give him life, but how will the Catholics take it? In rehearsal I had but one overwhelming emotion, a sense as of the actual presence in a terrible sacrament of the god. But I have got that always, though never before so strongly, from Greek Drama.
Yours   W B YEATS

[*On the envelope*] *Oedipus* great success.[4] Critics and audience enthusiastic.

[1] Ragnar Östberg, the architect of the Stockholm Stadshus.
[2] These lines, much revised, form the second verse of the poem 'First Love' in the group 'A Man Young and Old,' included in *The Tower*, 1928.
[3] F. J. McCormick, a prominent and very talented member of the Abbey Theatre company.
[4] *King Oedipus* was produced at the Abbey Theatre on December 6, 1926; Yeats was at work on his version of *Oedipus at Colonus* at this time.

TO OLIVIA SHAKESPEAR

Dec 6 [1926]   82 *Merrion Square*

My dear Olivia, I won't send you *Oedipus* yet, I have only one complete copy—beside the prompt copy—and that I keep by me to alter in odd moments. My work on *Oedipus at Colonus* has made me bolder and when I look at *King Oedipus* I am shocked at my moderation. I want to be less literal and more idiomatic and modern. I shall finish tonight all the dialogue for *Oedipus at Colonus* and then will come six weeks' work at the lyrical choruses, two of which are very famous. I shall be in England before I have finished. They are playing my *Baile's Strand* at Cambridge from Jan 31 to Feb 5. The fool and blind man masked, and elaborate dancing of the witches and strange lighting. Perhaps I shall insist on your coming to Cambridge with me or meeting me there. In any case I shall be in London after, I think, though not for more than a few days. Some time in the middle of February all designs for our coinage will be in Dublin for our verdict.

I came upon two early photographs of you yesterday, while going through my file—one that from *Literary Year Book*. Who ever had a like profile?—a profile from a Sicilian coin. One looks back to one's youth as to [a] cup that a mad man dying of thirst left half tasted. I wonder if you feel like that.

This work on *Oedipus*—unless I break off in the middle as I may for change['s] sake—puts off my new Autobiography. I had hoped to bring you chapters not for present publication and hear similar chapters out of yours. My new Autobiography—1900 to 1926—may be the final test of my intellect, my last great effort, and I keep putting it off. Yours affectionately   W B YEATS

                                            82 *Merrion Square*

> A madman found a cup of wine
> And half dead of thirst
> Hardly dared to wet his mouth,
> Imagining, moon accurst,
> That another mouthful
> And his beating heart would burst.
>
> But my discovery of the change
> For it cannot be denied

> That all is ancient metal now
> The four winds have dried—
> Has kept me waking half the night
> And made me hollow-eyed.[1]

W B Y
Dec 7

[*On back flap of envelope*]

The Cambridge show will probably be a bore—I think I shall have to go and see and perhaps acquire the masks—but do not leave your gas-fire for it.   W B Y

TO OLIVIA SHAKESPEAR

March 13 [*Postmark* 1927]   82 *Merrion Square*

My dear Olivia, I have been taken up with a political crisis of sorts. The printers have tried to get inserted in our new copyright Bill a section only giving Irish copyright to Free State citizens, who printed in Ireland. It would have been very ruinous but I got the Senate last Friday to drop the thing. I made a long impassioned speech and have now a wonderful sense of repose, and am back at *Oedipus at Colonus*. The strength behind the printers was the dislike of the more ignorant sort of Catholic for our school. Which reminds me—have you read O'Flaherty's *Informer* or his *Mr. Gilhooley*? I think they are great novels and too full of abounding natural life to be terrible despite their subjects. They are full of that tragic farce we have invented. I imagine that part of the desire for a censorship here is the desire to keep him out. He joyously *imagines* where Moore *constructs* and yet is more real than Moore.

You speak of the long speech in *Oedipus the King* as being unactable. It is so on our stage but I cut all of it out but a few lines. I am in quite good spirits, impersonal, active, enjoying public admiration etc etc and so I cannot write a good letter. Presently somebody will call me names, I will remember that I am old, that 'we go no more a-roaming by the light of the moon' and then I will

---

[1] This poem, much rewritten, became 'The Empty Cup,' the fifth poem of the group 'A Man Young and Old,' included in *The Tower*, 1928.

OLIVIA SHAKESPEAR

write you beautiful letters. However as a consolation for this hateful cheerfulness here are two stanzas from a Sophocles chorus

Down the long echoing street the laughing dancers throng;
The Bride is carried to the Bridegroom's chamber through torch-
    light and tumultuous song;
I celebrate that silent kiss that ends short life or long.

Not to have lived is best, the ancient writers say,
Not to have drunk the breath of life at all, nor looked into the eye
    of day,
The second best's a gay 'good-night' and quickly turn away.[1]

The last line is very bad Grecian but very good Elizabethan and so it must stay. Yours affectionately   W B YEATS

TO OLIVIA SHAKESPEAR

March 24 [Postmark March 28, 1927]   *82 Merrion Square*

My dear Olivia: I enclose a cutting from the *Sunday Times* which will tell you adequately but inaccurately—I made a long dullish speech —about the copyright question.

For some months I have been perplexed by certain strange philosophical judgements in the *Times Literary Supplement*. Somebody told me that they came from the papistical wife of the editor but I now find that your friend Wyndham Lewis's effect upon a contributor, or contributors, has done the trick. I have been dipping into his essay in the *Enemy* and find his proof that the popularity of Charlie Chaplin has been caused by the spread of Bergson's philosophy the most stirring thought I have met this long time.[2] But what will Ezra do? Will he 'pass by in silent dignity' as we were told to do in childhood or will he fill his pockets with all the necessary missiles and rush to the defence of Joyce, Picasso, Miss Stein and all the gods? The *Catholic Bulletin* agrees with Lewis about Einstein—it has just described him as a 'mutual aesthetic booster'—he had protested

---

[1] These lines, revised, form part of 'From Oedipus at Colonus,' eleventh poem in the group 'A Man Young and Old,' included in *The Tower*, 1928.
[2] *The Enemy*, Vol. I, January 1927. This passage was later reprinted as 'The Revolutionary Simpleton' in Wyndham Lewis's *Time and Western Man*, 1927.

against the pirating of *Ulysses* in America. I shall never finish the essay. Englishmen are babes in philosophy and so prefer faction-fighting to the labour of its unfamiliar thought. I have finished a profound book by Angelo Crespi on *Contemporary thought of Italy*. He attacks what Lewis attacks but is so obsessed by courtesy that he not only explains his opponent's thought more fully than his own, but expounds it with great eloquence.

I am slowly revising my *Oedipus at Colonus* and reading Plato—Lewis would find the problem he discusses in *The Theaetetus*—here is the opening of another chorus and rather a famous one

> Come praise Colonus' horses and come praise
> The wine-dark of the wood's intricacies,
> A nightingale that deafens daylight there,
> If daylight ever visit where,
> Unvisited by tempest or the sun,
> Immortal ladies tread the ground
> Dizzy with harmonious sound,
> Semele's lad a gay companion.[1]

Yours affectionately   W B YEATS

Lewis has some profound judgements—when he analyses public opinion or some definite work of art—and often a vivid phrase.

TO MAY MORRIS [2]

April 2, 1927   82 *Merrion Square*

Dear Miss Morris, To begin with, forgive me for dictating this to my wife: for many years now I have had to avoid using my eyes by artificial light, and to be careful of them in all lights. Of course you may have my name, and I am exceedingly glad to be connected again, however slightly, with one who is still my chief of men. The little drawing of the hall looks charming, just such a hall as Morris would have liked.[3]

[1] The first verse of the chorus published as 'Colonus' Praise' in *The Tower*.
[2] Dictated.
[3] Yeats had obviously been asked to give his support to a fund which was being raised for the Morris Memorial Hall at Kelmscott in Oxfordshire. The hall was not completed till 1934, when it was formally opened by Bernard Shaw.

My wife and I continually talked when we were at Oxford of how we should find some means of introducing ourselves to you, in fact shortly before we left we had arranged with Lady Ottoline that she should bring us to see you.[1] But we left quite suddenly. It seemed necessary that I should come to Ireland, for I had heard that our new Government had appointed as Curator of the Municipal Gallery a man who had been very useful to them in identifying exhumed revolutionary corpses.

Next Cambridge term I shall go there to see a performance of a play of mine at the Festival Theatre there, and my plan is to go from there to Oxford to see the Morrells and one or two other friends. May I call upon you then? Yours   W B YEATS

TO OLIVIA SHAKESPEAR

[on paper headed] 82 *Merrion Square*
June 23 [Postmark Gort 1927]

My dear Olivia: We have been here for some days [2]—in perfect tranquility—no children, no telephone, no callers. No companion but a large white dog which has a face like the Prince Consort, or a mid-Victorian statue—capable of error but not of sin. I write verse and read Hegel and the more I read I am but the more convinced that those invisible persons knew all. Here is an innocent little song —one of the first [of] my woman series to balance that of 'The Young and Old Countryman,' and after that one not so innocent.

A first confession.[3]

I declare that briar
Entangled in my hair
No injury to me;
My blenches and trembling
Nothing but dissembling,
Nothing but coquetry.

[1] Lady Ottoline Morrell, daughter of the 6th Duke of Portland, and her husband Mr. Philip Morrell entertained largely at the Manor House, Garsington, near Oxford.
[2] This letter, although on Merrion Square notepaper, is obviously written from Thoor Ballylee.
[3] 'A First Confession' was included, with some revision, as third in the series of poems 'A Woman Young and Old' in *The Winding Stair*, 1929.

I long for truth and yet
I cannot stay from that
My better self disowns;
For a man's attention
Turns to satisfaction
The craving in my bones.

Brightness I have pulled back
From the zodiac.
Why those questioning eyes
That are fixed upon me?
What can they do but shun me
If empty Night replies?

  [*Consolation.*]
[O *but there is wisdom*
In what the sages said;] [1]
But stretch that body for a while
And lay down that head
Till I have told the sages
Where man is comforted

How could passion run so deep
Had it never thought
That the crime of being born
Had blackened all our lot;
But where the crime's committed
The crime can be forgot.

    Yours affectionately W B YEATS

TO OLIVIA SHAKESPEAR

Undated [*July or August* 1927]   *Thoor Ballylee*

My dear Olivia: You were right about our peace not lasting. The murder of O'Higgins was no mere public event to us.[2] He was our

[1] Half a page was torn away. I have restored in brackets the missing title and first two lines of the published poem 'Consolation,' fifth in the series 'A Woman Young and Old,' included, after revision, in *The Winding Stair*, 1929.
[2] Kevin O'Higgins, Vice-President and Minister for Justice, was shot on

personal friend, as well as the one strong intellect in Irish public life and then too his pretty young wife was our friend. We got the news just when we reached the Gresham Hotel where we were to dine and we left without dining and walked about the streets till bed-time. The night before George had suddenly called the dog out of the way of what she thought was a motor car—there was no car—and a moment after when inside our own door we both heard two bursts of music, voices singing together. At the funeral at the Mass for the dead I recognized the music as that of the choir which—just before the elevation of the host—sang in just such short burst of song. You will remember the part the motor car had in the murder. Had we seen more he might have been saved, for recent evidence seems to show that those things are fate unless foreseen by clairvoyance and so brought within the range of free-will. A French man of science thinks that we all—including murderers and victims—will and so create the future. I would bring in the dead. Are we, that foreknow, the actual or potential traitors of the race-process? Do we, as it were, forbid the banns when the event is struggling to be born? Is this why—even if what we foresee is not some trivial thing—we foresee too little to understand?

I have finished those love poems—19 in all—and am now at a new Tower series, partly driven to it by this murder. Next week I must go to Dublin to help vote the more stringent police laws the government think necessary. I hear with anxiety that they will increase the number of crimes punishable by death, and with satisfaction that they will take certain crimes out of the hands of jurors. But I know nothing except what I find in the papers.

I am expecting a visit from my Italian translator—perhaps if we have lived good lives we may be reborn in some peaceful eastern village and have sweethearts with beautiful golden brown skins. Yours affectionately   W B YEATS

July 10 at Booterstown, Co. Dublin, while on his way to Mass, and died some hours later. During the Civil War the Government had taken powers to execute anybody captured with arms in his hands, and under this ordinance 77 Irregulars, including Erskine Childers, had been executed. It was believed that the assassination of O'Higgins was an act of revenge for the uncompromising attitude he had adopted over these executions, but though the identity of his murderers was suspected nothing could be proved against them.

TO OLIVIA SHAKESPEAR

Sept 7 [*Postmark* 1927]   82 *Merrion Square*

My dear Olivia: We are back from Ballylee for *Oedipus*—the *King* this week and *Colonus* next. Yes 'The Tower' seems a success, people have written.[1] Curious but I have suddenly awakened out of despondency. I found myself praying between sleeping and waking and then saw a 'key' and after that a long white walled road, and from that, though not particularly well, have had all my cheerfulness back again. I constantly notice that change comes from some formula of words used quite lightly. I suppose the words are but the finger on the trigger and that the gun has been long loaded.

. . . This is a poor letter, my dear, and I wrote more when I sent the book but I have a mass of letters mainly to Japanese to write. I will write again in a few days. Yours   W B YEATS

TO JOSEPH HONE

Sept 24 *Saturday* [? 1927]   82 *Merrion Square*

Dear Hone, Can you tell me Miss Burnand's address? She gave it me but I forget all except that it is Ely Place.

Apropos of much. I think that much of the confusion of modern philosophy, perhaps the whole realism versus idealism quarrel, comes from our renouncing the ancient hierarchy of beings from man up to the One. What I do not see but may see or have seen, is perceived by another being. In other words is part of the fabric of another being. I remember what he forgets, he remembers what I forget. We are in the midst of life and there is nothing but life. Yours   W B YEATS

TO OLIVIA SHAKESPEAR

Oct. 2 (*or* 4) [*Postmark* 1927]   82 *Merrion Square*

My dear Olivia: I owe you a letter but I have been writing verse. Two or three weeks ago an American with a private press offered

---

[1] This must refer to the appearance of the poem 'The Tower' either in the *Criterion*, June 1927, or in the volume *October Blast*, Cuala Press, August 1927. Yeats's book *The Tower* was not published till the following year.

me £300 for six months' use of sixteen or so pages of verse.[1] I had about half the amount. I agreed and undertook to write a hundred and fifty lines in two months. I have already written 50 or 60 lines, and he has already paid £150. I am giving him 'The Woman Young and Old,' a poem called 'Blood and the Moon' (a Tower poem) which was written weeks ago; and I am writing a new tower poem 'Sword and Tower,'[2] which is a choice of rebirth rather than deliverance from birth. I make my Japanese sword and its silk covering my symbol of life . . .

We all, with George added, are now turning Lennox's greenhouse into a cage of canaries. We had a noisy and cantankerous dinner at a restaurant last night. Tom [McGreevy] brought us favourable news of you and Omar. To him you are always a symbol of elegance, a kind of gold and ivory image, and I approve.

Oedipus is haunted. Two typed copies sent to the publisher have [gone] astray in the post and that has held up publication for months. Then a couple of weeks ago Mrs. Phillimore (author of *Paul*) invited a woman to meet George who asked for the introduction because at the first performance of *The King* a year ago she had seen George, she said, first take me by the shoulders and shake me and then kiss me. I said nothing of the kind had happened but she insisted. Then George came into the room; upon which she said 'But that was not the woman.'

Then there is a phantom dog. During *Colonus* George and I were infuriated by the loud barking of a dog apparently in the gallery. We were surprised that nobody laughed. I went out after the play to find who had brought the dog. Person after person said they had heard no dog, then I met two people who had, but each heard it in a different place. It had barked, I heard, in the middle of a performance of *The King*, a week before. One chorus appeals to Cerberus not to disturb Oedipus with its barking. The company think it is a dog that starved to death in the theatre once, when it was closed for the summer. Poems seem to disturb the spirits—once at Gogarty's when I was reading out my *Calvary* and came to the description of the entrance of Lazarus, the door burst open as if by the blast of

[1] This was *The Winding Stair*, of which 642 copies were printed and 600 numbered copies, signed by the author, were for sale. Printed by William Edwin Rudge and issued by the Fountain Press, New York, in October 1929.
[2] This poem appeared in *The Winding Stair*, 1929, under the title 'A Dialogue of Self and Soul.'

wind where there could be no wind, and the family ghost had a night of great activity. From all which you will see that I am still of opinion that only two topics can be of the least interest to a serious and studious mind—sex and the dead.

These new poems interrupted my rewriting of *A Vision*; perhaps were that finished I might find some third interest . . . Yours affectionately   W B YEATS

TO OLIVIA SHAKESPEAR

Oct 27 [1927]   82 *Merrion Square*

My dear Olivia, I have had such an exhausting cold—I have but just recovered, but warmth will dominate every other consideration about my London domicile. I shall try to get to the Orchard [1] as before with a shilling in the slot gas fire and hope to arrive there on Nov 6 (may I dine with you Sunday evening or better still will you dine with me and we can go back to Abingdon Court after?). Nelly would not have mattered, I would not have ventured it when she was in London. She would or might have got it into her head that instead of the arrangement of her own planning—she, I and George —I preferred to go to you. As it was George and I were perpetually on the watch that she might not think when we made some arrangement for ourselves that we were avoiding her. She is overflowing with kindness (wanted to come to London again and look after me in November) but she is always on the watch for the wolf with 'privy paw.' George and I have been alternately wolf.

I send you a couple of Ballylee pictures—one my bed and one of the Tower from the river side.

When I went to London I had just finished a poem in which I appeal to the saints in 'the holy fire' to send death on their ecstasy. In London I went to a medium called Cooper and on the way called to my people for their especial wisdom. The medium gave me 'a book test'—Third book from R bottom shelf—study—Page 48 or 84. I have only this morning looked it up. The book was the complete Dante designs of Blake. It is not numbered by pages but by plates. Plate 84 is Dante entering the Holy Fire (Purgatorio—Canto

[1] The Orchard Hotel, Portman Street, London, W.1.

27). Plate 48 is 'The serpent attacking Vanni Fucci.' When I looked this up in Dante I found that at the serpent's sting Vanni Fucci is burnt to ashes and then recreated from the ashes and that this symbolizes 'the temporal Fire.' The medium is the most stupid I know and certainly the knowledge was not in my head. After this and all that has gone before I must capitulate if the dark mind lets me. Certainly we suck always at the eternal dugs. How well too it puts my own mood between spiritual excitement, and the sexual torture and the knowledge that they are somehow inseparable! It is the eyes of the Earthly Beatrice—she has not yet put on her divinity —that makes Dante risk the fire 'like a child that is offered an apple.' Immediately after comes the Earthly Paradise and the Heavenly Beatrice. Yesterday, as if my soul already foresaw today's discovery, I rewrote a poor threadbare poem of my youth called 'The Dream of a Blessed Spirit' and named it 'The Countess Cathleen in Paradise.' It now runs thus and is almost a poem for children—

> All the heavy days are over;
> Lay the bodies coloured pride
> Underneath the grass and clover
> With the feet laid side by side.
>   (This stanza is unchanged)
>
> Bathed in flaming founts of duty
> She'll not ask a haughty dress;
> Carry all that mournful beauty
> To the scented oaken press.
>
> Did the keen of Mother Mary
> Put that music in her face?
> Yet she goes with footstep wary
> Full of earth's old timid grace.
>
> 'Mong the feet of angels seven
> What a dancer glimmering!
> All the heavens bow down to heaven
> Flame on flame and wing on wing.

I like the last verse, the dancer Cathleen has become heaven itself. Is there jealousy in such dancers or did Dante find them as little so as colour is of colour? Yet could that come at once. I forget what my own *Vision* says.

I rewrote this poem while correcting a new edition of Unwin's book of my poems.[1] Yours affectionately   W B YEATS

P.S.
I speak at the Irish Literary Society on Monday. Would it bore you if I get you an invitation? Shall make a short speech and probably not a good one, as it is a speech of compliment to Ashe King and must be so in the main. Only come if the alternative is worse.

TO THE SECRETARY, ROYAL IRISH ACADEMY

November 27th, 1927   *Hôtel St. George*
            Cannes

Dear Sir, Some two years ago I wrote to the Secretary and Council of the Academy, after consultation with certain of its members, suggesting a means by which the Academy might act as an Academy of Letters for Ireland. I was told that the matter was under consideration but have had no other communication.

I can only conclude that the Academy does not care to consider the matter further, and as I only joined that body for the sake of my proposal, I must ask you to accept my resignation. Yours faithfully,
            W B YEATS

TO OLIVIA SHAKESPEAR

Nov 29 [Postmark Dec 1, 1927]   *Château St. George*

My dear Olivia: When I wrote to you—being staggered by my first nervous illness—I hardly expected to recover but now I do expect to. George is planning already winters abroad and various contraptions, which will make it possible for me to give up everything

[1] This poem was first included in the play *The Countess Kathleen*, 1892, but was removed and printed separately as 'A Dream of a Blessed Spirit' in *Poems*, 1895, and in many later editions. This new version appeared in the edition of 1929, and in the *Collected Poems*, 1933.

I really don't like and keep everything that I like. I did not know how tired I was till this last blessed illness began, and now I dream of doing nothing but mystical philosophy and poetry.

I am reading *Time and the Western Man* [1] with ever growing admiration and envy—what energy!—and I am driven back to my reed-pipe. I want you to ask Lewis to meet me—we are in *fundamental* agreement. I shall not get to London until the middle of January I think. George goes back to fetch the children out here for Xmas so that my lung may have time to mend. Three days ago I spat a little red and that roused me to defy George and begin to work and now though I am better again I write verse a little every morning—I want to finish that book for the American before some doctor gets at me—and I am going to allow myself when I am in the mood to write a little in the afternoon. How strange is the subconscious gaiety that leaps up before danger or difficulty. I have not had a moment's depression—that gaiety is outside one's control, a something given by nature—yet I did hate leaving the last word to George Moore.

Please write and say where you will be in the middle of January. I need not say that George is all goodness and kindness. Yours always   W B YEATS

TO OLIVIA SHAKESPEAR

Dec [*Postmark Dec* 12, 1927]   *Hôtel St. George*

My dear Olivia: George arrives tomorrow. I feel perfectly well—no symptoms, no blood now—my mind alert. Yet when the doctor came yesterday he said 'I am not at [all] satisfied. You must live between the bed and the couch, and down stairs to lunch is effort enough. If you must go out go but a few hundred yards.'—then he went down stairs and wired George—the hall porter says—that I was reading too much. Heaven knows how long it will last, and I would not so much care but I have read all the good detective stories— there is not one left.

Tell Wyndham Lewis (I suppose the doctor's telegram will cut

[1] *Time and Western Man* by P. Wyndham Lewis. London: Chatto and Windus, 1927.

off his books) that I am in all essentials his most humble and admiring disciple. I like some people he dislikes but I accept all the dogma of the faith.

George and Anne arrive tomorrow, Michael the day after, and I 'must not allow their arrival to excite me.' I am probably taking the cure that should have come years [ago] but remain quite cheerful.

Write to me and write again without waiting for an answer. I am hungry for news of my friends. You spoke in your last letter of *The Kingdom of God*[1]—we played it in Dublin a year ago—a lovely thing. Yours affectionately

W B YEATS

TO OLIVIA SHAKESPEAR

Jan 12 [*Postmark Jan* 18, 1928]   *Hôtel Château St. George*

My dear Olivia, Last night George read me extracts from André Maurois' *Disraeli*, amongst them one about a Wyndham Lewis who was member of parliament in 1840 or so and whose widow married Disraeli. Do find out if he is any relation to the artist. It seems unlikely that there should be two Wyndham Lewises in London to-day and another there in our grandfathers' day if they are not connected together. The member of parliament was hardly eminent enough to have unrelated babies named after him. You will see from this that *Time and Western Man* still fills my imagination. I have a curiously personal feeling of gratitude. He has found an expression for my hatred —a hatred that being half dumb has half poisoned me. I read the last chapter again and again. He reminds me of a Father of the Church —of Origen, the only one of them I have read or rather dipped into. He has some of the same virtues and faults, the same disordered energy. He will have an immense effect—but alas he is so clear the fools will think they understand him and hiss or bray what they have found. He should have remembered that even the least of the nine hierarchies choses to remain invisible—afraid perhaps of those Academy painters.

Jan 15

Yesterday the doctor gave me a shock. I said 'Why am I so exhausted?' He replied 'The overwork of years.' I said 'When can

[1] A translation of *The Kingdom of God* by G. Martinez Sierra was produced at the Abbey Theatre on November 3, 1924.

I work again?' He replied 'I will not hold out false hopes. Your recovery will be very slow but in three or four months you may be able to work a little. If you want to do anything before that, go to the Casino and gamble; live like an animal.' I had thought to begin work next week, and the blow was so obviously heavy that George made me spend the whole day in bed. After a day and night of gloom I am a little proud. I have always found it very hard to work and now at last I can permit myself a good conscience. I know that I have of late years, at any rate, done all I could.

We have had the revolutionary temperament here. A man and his wife and daughter, the man Russian and the wife French, arrived some weeks ago from 'the Russian Embassy, Paris.' They shouted to one another across the passages, quarrelled with one another, banged doors in the middle of the night and complained of the food. Then the wife selected a victim. There was a charming young German countess, who always dined at the same table with an equally charming young German Prince who was, the management said, her brother. But the wife said he was not her brother and 'if she was an honest woman she would not have the next bedroom to the prince.' She said it so loud that the countess heard and she and the Prince departed to Switzerland. They had been the glory of the management, had the most expensive rooms, and their prestige was all the greater because they never spoke to anybody. The communistic lady then pitched upon me, though I was not to know anything about it for some ten days. I had consumption and was a danger to everybody. She tried to persuade various guests to go and finally she and her husband went to the manager and said that if I did not go they would. The manager suggested that they should go on Saturday which was 3 days off. Then the communistic lady wept all over the house; and George, who knew nothing of what had happened, met her sobbing loudly on the sea shore, her husband trying to pacify her. At last on Saturday morning we heard what was happening and went to the manager and asked if he would like us to go, as such rumour might injure his hotel. But he would not hear of it and assured us that the Russians were leaving that day. There is an old French lady who prides herself upon 'knowing everything about everybody for the good of the hotel'—as she has money in it, and her comment to George was 'if in the old days they had said "we are from the Russian Embassy" one would have understood at once—the Ambassador's concierge and family; but now how can one know anything? May be it is the Ambassador, his wife and daughter.' Meanwhile our allowance of clean sheets and of baths has been increased; and the communists are doubtless trying somewhere else to create the revolutionary situation.

This is the longest letter I have written for months. Yours affectionately   W B YEATS

P.S.

Can you choose for me a translation of one of Proust's novels; and also get me a book called *The Idea of the Holy* by some German Theologian?[1] I will remit when I know how much. I want something to read a little more solid than detectives.

TO OLIVIA SHAKESPEAR

Feb 23 [1928]   *Albergo Rapallo*
                                                                                                         Rapallo
                                                                                                         Italy

My dear Olivia: I enclose 7/6 which is I think what I owe you for *The Idea of the Holy*—I will not start on Proust as I have now enough books to last me till I get to London and Dublin next month. George has this very moment started for Switzerland with Michael who is to be left there at school. She returns on Friday week. I remain here in Dorothy's and Ezra's charge. We have made great changes of plan and intend now to take a flat here and move over some of our furniture, and let all but one floor of 82 Merrion Square. We can then spend say from August to April here and the rest of the year in Dublin, with passing visits to London. Doctors tell us the Dublin climate will no more suit Michael than his father, so we think to keep both children at a Swiss school and fetch them here for summer and winter holidays (hence August is included in our time here). George is longing for the freedom of flats and a daily help and all heavy meals out. We have the refusal—George decides on her return from Switzerland—of a large flat—9 or 10 rooms—with balconies and the most lovely view imaginable. Better not tell Nelly of all this as George may want to do so at her own time. We shall

---

[1] By Rudolf Otto, translated by John W. Harvey. London: Milford, 1923.

live much more cheaply, and this change of plan and climate at my time of life is a great adventure one longed for many a time. Once out of the Senate—my time is up in September—and, in obedience to the doctors, out of all public work, there is no reason for more than 3 months of Dublin—where the Abbey is the one work I cannot wholly abandon. Once out of Irish bitterness I can find some measure of sweetness and of light, as befits old age—already new poems are floating in my head, bird songs of an old man, joy in the passing moment, emotion without the bitterness of memory.

At last I am really convalescent—all the exhaustion gone. I think I could do a day's work again, but under doctor's orders shall idle out this month, walking in the mornings by this brimming sea, in bed in the afternoon, and from 7 till 9 or 10 with Dorothy or Ezra, or alone with George. Then from 10 to 11 or 11.30 base fiction in bed, any sort of swift adventure that can break the stream of thought. Part of my cure, by the by, is to walk slowly, even turn my head slowly, that my thoughts from sympathy with my movements may slacken. If it does not I may become my own funeral pyre.

Ezra and Dorothy seem happy and content, pleased with their way of life, and Dorothy and George compare their experience of infancy and its strange behaviour—George instructing Dorothy out of her greater store. If we carry out our plans and settle here they will renew all their old friendship and to George at any rate that will be a great happiness. Yours affectionately   W B YEATS

TO LADY GREGORY

[*Postmark Feb 24, 1928*]   *Albergo Rapallo*

My dear Lady Gregory . . . We hope to let all Merrion Square house except the top floor which George and I can use, or if we sell the Merrion Square house we shall get a small flat elsewhere. We can, we calculate, have our two flats for less than Merrion Square costs us. Of course all this is a mere first idea. One thing is I think certain, that we shall be at Ballylee this summer with the children. We shall do some planting there and visit it occasionally, for if George and I go alone it will not be expensive. If we get our flat here we shall have room for guests and perhaps you will come to see us, perhaps we can take the place of Lady Layard. Do not think of me as uncomfortably ill or even as tired. I am merely incapable of any prolonged effort, but the results while the effort lasts are as good as ever, and they are growing longer though they may never again belong. It is merely an exaggeration of something I have always suffered from.

The Tower is out with a fine picture of Ballylee on the cover by Sturge Moore. I am asking Macmillan to send you a copy which I will sign when we meet. I am also sending you the new edition of *Red Hanrahan* with the archaic illustrations.[1] I lent the artist a lot of Byzantine mosaic photographs and photographs of old Irish crucifixes and asked her to re-create such an art as might have been familiar to the first makers of the tales. The result is I think amusing and vivid.

Michael and George have departed for Switzerland (George returns next week). Michael was looking much more vigorous. George and I will return to Ireland at the end of April.

Ezra Pound has been helping me to punctuate my new poems, and thinks the best of all is a little song I wrote at Cannes just before I was ordered to stop work, so you must not think of me as out of the saga.

This is an indescribably lovely place—some little Greek town one imagines—there is a passage in Keats describing just such a town. Here I shall put off the bitterness of Irish quarrels, and write my most amiable verses. They are already, though I dare not write, crowding my head. *The Tower* astonishes me by its bitterness. Yours affectionately

W B YEATS

TO LADY GREGORY

April 1 [*Postmark* 1928]   *Hôtel Victoria*
                                Villars-sur-Bex
                                Switzerland

My dear Lady Gregory: We got here a couple of days ago and in another eight days return to Dublin—long sea from Cherbourg to

[1] *Stories of Red Hanrahan and The Secret Rose*, illustrated and decorated by Norah McGuinness. London: Macmillan, 1927.

Queenstown. We are here to see Michael, who looks more vigorous and self reliant and has—choice being offered—decided to stay here. We asked him if he would like to lunch with us on Easter day, and he said he was not sure as he did not yet know what the school would have for lunch but would find out. He has however consented to come for tea. We think now of sending Anne to the same school till Xmas and then sending her to a well known Swiss school where only French is talked. I am delighted to get the children out of Dublin which I always dreaded for them. They will learn French and German thoroughly and with the impulse that should come from their parents should have enough intellectual curiosity to create minds for themselves.

For the moment I am very well but have gusts of fatigue and George doubts if I shall be well enough for the walk between Ballylee and Coole. My own belief is that I shall be—but the doubt remains. I recover my powers of work—I work now every second day—rather more quickly than power of standing, which is grotesque. I am at work on the final version of *A Vision*, and on an essay, which takes a poem of Guido Cavalcanti's for text and discusses the latest movements in contemporary literature.[1] Have you read Wyndham Lewis? He attacked Ezra Pound and Joyce in *Time and Western Man*, and is on my side of things philosophically. My essay takes up the controversy and explains Ezra Pound sufficiently to keep him as a friendly neighbour, for I foresee that in the winter he must take Russell's place of a Monday evening. He has most of Maud Gonne's opinions (political and economic) about the world in general, being what Lewis calls 'the revolutionary simpleton.' The chief difference is that he hates Palgrave's *Golden Treasury* as she does the Free State Government, and thinks even worse of its editor than she does of President Cosgrave. He has even her passion for cats and large numbers wait him every night at a certain street corner knowing that his pocket is full of meat bones or chicken bones. They belong to the oppressed races.

I suppose you suggested to the Commission that they could follow Italian precedent by building at first the merely utilitarian part. This ought to bring the price of the Gallery far below the

[1] This essay was intended to form part of the volume *A Packet for Ezra Pound*. Yeats wrote it and then destroyed it, finding it, he said, difficult to make clear or even readable.

sum you name. I think that we artists should demand merely what is necessary to house the pictures safely and show them adequately and leave the rest to national pride. The more practical we are the greater will our influence be. Of course the building should be such as can afterwards be made handsome. It should be a matter of honour to the commissioners to carry out an original pledge and house the pictures properly. If there was a pledge (such as I seem to remember) it should be rubbed in.

Tower is receiving great favour. Perhaps the reviewers know that [I] am ill, and think that I am so ill that I can be commended without future inconvenience. I gather that I am the last Victorian (with George Moore as a kind of last but one). Even the Catholic press is enthusiastic. Yours always   W B YEATS

We shall be in Dublin on the 14 of April. That is a Saturday. By Monday 16 we shall be ready for you if [you] care to come and stay. Stay as long as you like and keep your eye on the Abbey.

TO SEAN O'CASEY[1]

April 20, 1928   82 *Merrion Square*

My dear Casey . . . I had looked forward with great hope and excitement to reading your play,[2] and not merely because of my admiration for your work, for I bore in mind that the Abbey owed its recent prosperity to you. If you had not brought us your plays just at that moment I doubt if it would now exist. I read the first act with admiration, I thought it was the best first act you had written, and told a friend that you had surpassed yourself. The next night I read the second and third acts, and to-night I have read the fourth. I am sad and discouraged; you have no subject. You were interested in the Irish Civil War, and at every moment of those plays wrote out of your own amusement with life or your sense of its tragedy; you were excited, and we all caught your excitement; you

[1] Dictated.
[2] *The Silver Tassie.* The letter was communicated by Mr. O'Casey to the *Observer*, which published it, together with some portion of Mr. O'Casey's reply, in its issue of June 3. The play was first produced in London at the Apollo Theatre on October 11, 1929; it was revived at the Abbey Theatre on August 12, 1935.

were exasperated almost beyond endurance by what you had seen or heard, as a man is by what happens under his window, and you moved us as Swift moved his contemporaries.

But you are not interested in the great war; you never stood on its battlefields or walked its hospitals, and so write out of your opinions. You illustrate those opinions by a series of almost unrelated scenes, as you might in a leading article; there is no dominating character, no dominating action, neither psychological unity nor unity of action; and your great power of the past has been the creation of some unique character who dominated all about him and was himself a main impulse in some action that filled the play from beginning to end.

The mere greatness of the world war has thwarted you; it has refused to become mere background, and obtrudes itself upon the stage as so much dead wood that will not burn with the dramatic fire. Dramatic action is a fire that must burn up everything but itself; there should be no room in a play for anything that does not belong to it; the whole history of the world must be reduced to wallpaper in front of which the characters must pose and speak.

Among the things that dramatic action must burn up are the author's opinions; while he is writing he has no business to know anything that is not a portion of that action. Do you suppose for one moment that Shakespeare educated Hamlet and King Lear by telling them what he thought and believed? As I see it, Hamlet and Lear educated Shakespeare, and I have no doubt that in the process of that education he found out that he was an altogether different man to what he thought himself, and had altogether different beliefs. A dramatist can help his characters to educate him by thinking and studying everything that gives them the language they are groping for through his hands and eyes, but the control must be theirs, and that is why the ancient philosophers thought a poet or dramatist Daimon-possessed.

This is a hateful letter to write, or rather to dictate—I am dictating to my wife—and all the more so, because I cannot advise you to amend the play. It is all too abstract, after the first act; the second act is an interesting technical experiment, but it is too long for the material; and after that there is nothing. I can imagine how you have toiled over this play. A good scenario writes itself, it puts words into the mouths of all its characters while we sleep, but a bad scenario exacts the most miserable toil. I see nothing for it but a new theme, something you have found and no newspaper writer has ever found. What business have we with anything but the unique?

Put the dogmatism of this letter down to splenetic age and forgive it.   W B Y

TO OLIVIA SHAKESPEAR[1]

April 25 1928   82 *Merrion Square*

My dear Olivia, For once I am dictating a letter. We got back a week ago, and there has been so much to do that I am tired. Two Dublin doctors have sat upon me; the Cannes man said 'Lungs and nervous breakdown can be neglected, nothing matters but blood pressure' and gave me a white pill. The Monte Carlo man said 'Blood pressure and lungs can be neglected, nothing matters but nervous breakdown,' and gave me a brown pill. The Dublin men say 'Blood pressure and nervous breakdown can be neglected, nothing matters but lungs,' and have given me a black pill, and as a sort of postscript I am to have a vaccine injection once a week for the next three months. However I shall cut out one week in order to spend ten days in London in June. We came direct from Cherbourg to Queenstown so I have seen nobody.

The Tower is a great success, two thousand copies in the first month, much the largest sale I have ever had. I do nothing at present but potter over a new edition of *A Vision* which should be ready some time next year. When I get back to Rapallo I hope to write verse again but no more bitter passion I think. Re-reading *The Tower* I was astonished at its bitterness, and long to live out of Ireland that I may find some new vintage. Yet that bitterness gave the book its power and it is the best book I have written. Perhaps if I was in better health I should be content to be bitter.

Is Dorothy with you? Tell her that steak and onions are a disappointment. It was our first meal. She is forgiven. But I still sigh for badger's flesh. She will understand.

Will you be in London in June? I want to see you, and George is

[1] Dictated.

bringing Michael through London on his way to Ireland for the holidays. Omar is still at the happy age.[1] We are struggling with Anne's desire to debauch her intellect with various forms of infantile literature presented by servants etc. Yours always   W B YEATS

TO OLIVIA SHAKESPEAR

May 22 [Postmark May 28, 1928]   *82 Merrion Square*

My dear Olivia: Since I came back I have been writing all morning in bed and getting up for lunch and this has meant a continuous putting off of letters. I write all morning in a big MS book, and my note paper is all downstairs. After lunch I have said each day I will write a letter but at first I was tired and now that I am much better Lady Gregory has been here and so on. At the moment my head is all frozen hard because of a morning of mystic geometry, and I am trying to melt it.

       Half hour later.

I have read a chapter in a detective story and that has melted my head.

We have sold this house to a Professor of Architecture who is attracted by its beauty, and we must be out by August 1, unless he will hire to us, as we have reason to hope, the upper part as a flat. I say goodbye sadly to this beautiful room, but I shall have the mountains of Rapallo in exchange. It will be a delight to get there for quiet winters—here all is storm. Perhaps I say that because we have refused Casey's new play [2]—a sort of secret a good many people know because he has told, but you are the first I have told and theoretically I should not. He has written furious letters and has threatened to publish our opinion of the play. However in the end I think we have avoided a quarrel. He will get a London performance I am afraid and injure his fame. The play is all anti-war propaganda to the exclusion of plot and character ... Of course if we had played his play, his fame is so great that we would have had full house for a time, but we hoped to turn him into a different path.

[1] Omar Pound, Mrs. Shakespear's grandson, was at this time aged about eighteen months.
[2] *The Silver Tassie.* See letter to Sean O'Casey of April 20, 1928, on p. 740.

Do not be surprized if you read in your morning newspaper extracts from a Casey preface quoting my opinion and denouncing it.

My blood-pressure was normal three weeks ago and though Casey and late hours have sent it up a bit I am really very well. Next month I shall be in London. George on her way to Switzerland to fetch Michael will drop me there and pick me up again. Yours always

W B YEATS

TO OLIVIA SHAKESPEAR

July 9 [*Postmark July* 11, 1928]   82 *Merrion Square*

My dear Olivia, I was very tired after London and after the journey back, but after a couple of days in bed have got better. Then came a psychic event. I was struggling with fatigue and this made me afraid again that I might not be able to finish the *Vision* and because of that I was working too much. That has always happened when I think I am permanently ill. I did not tell anybody. Now Dolly Travers Smith was staying here—her mother is Hester Dowden the medium—George had to go downstairs on some household job and said to keep me occupied 'Dolly had better do automatic writing.' Dolly did so and wrote 'Have no fear. You have time,' repeated this several times and then signed 'Thomas of Odessa.' Thomas of Odessa was the first spirit who came to George and myself ten years ago. He stayed so short a time that I had almost forgotten his existence. This message has cheered me greatly—so much so that to-day being tired I have been content to do nothing.

I began this to say I was posting *Oedipus the King* but I cannot because it is in a locked cupboard and I have just learned that the key is lost. Yours affectionately   W B YEATS

TO LADY GREGORY

July 30 [*Postmark* 1928]   *Brook-lawn*
        Howth

My dear Lady Gregory. I have not written for a long time but life has been hurried and bothered—first London and then Dublin, change of houses, ill health and so on. I have snatched every moment to finish *A Vision* and put off till to-morrow everything else. When I have routine (here at Howth for instance) I am very well and work steadily but shifting about knocks me up. Probably I have made my last Senate appearance. A little speech, three sentences, was followed by a minute of great pain, and that comforts me for I feel I could have been re-elected and that would have been £360 a year for nine years and I hate taking all that money from my family. Personally I gain greatly by the change. I have arranged two interviews and other things to fight the censorship so I am still in public life and shall be till I get to Rapallo. Glenavy stopped me coming out of the Senate the other day to say 'The Senate will re-elect you whenever you like.' He meant they would co-opt me if I wished when there was a vacancy. I doubt it, but am pleased that he should think so.

George has made our flat at 42 Fitzwilliam Square charming, my study is about as big as the old and looks out over the square—blue walls and ceiling and gold-coloured curtains. Her dining room I have not yet seen, but Lennox saw it and was loud in its praise—he spent a night here to keep me in talk while George was in Dublin . . . Yours always W B YEATS

TO OLIVIA SHAKESPEAR

August 12 [*Postmark* 1928] 42 *Fitzwilliam Square*
  Dublin

My dear Olivia: I have sent a letter to Wyndham Lewis care of you. He sent me his book and I have mislaid his letter. I am delighted with the first 100 pages of *Childermass*, interested and a little bored by the next. But those 100 pages are a masterpiece. I wish by the by you could tell me at what moment of p. 53 or 54 did Pulley and Slatters depart from innocence. It is the most obscure piece of writing known to me.

The Baily is of course my Hunchback—phase 28—though Lewis does not know that, and those 100 pages are the first region of the dead as the ghosts everywhere describe it.

I go to Coole to-morrow for a couple of weeks in pursuit of

tranquility not obtainable here—Dublin is always like an electric eel—and have my notes upon the new coinage [1] to write and my notes on Ezra for Cuala.[2] I have my last inoculation—there have been twelve and latterly they have meant a day in bed with a temperature—and now I have a chance of getting well. I am constantly being urged to go on in the Senate, which pleases me as it shows I have not failed there, but of course I will not. It is suggested that I should go up for election and be absent for 2 years or so. I am tired, I want nothing but the sea-shore and the palms and Ezra to quarrel with, and the Rapallo cats to feed after nightfall. Yours affectionately

W B YEATS

This is not a letter. I will write later—this is a mere explanation and apology for writing to Lewis care of you.

TO OLIVIA SHAKESPEAR

[*Postmark Sept* 15, 1928]   42 *Fitzwilliam Square*

My dear Olivia: We go to London on October 15 and stay in London a couple of weeks, George at a hotel and I at the Savile. Then leave for Rapallo. I hope your visits 'early in October' will be over. It is always a delight to see you for as you have grown older you have grown into the essence of yourself.

I am much better—the ending of my weekly inoculations seems to have set me right. I may, I imagine, mount up in blood pressure for I find that my power of enduring bores, never great, is now negligible, and besides I am in the throes of a violent conflict here. Holy Church—no, the commercial tourist agency that conducts the annual Lourdes pilgrimage, and the Catholic Truth Society, and The Society of Angelic Welfare have pressed on the Government a bill which will enable Holy Church to put us all down at any moment.

---

[1] Yeats was chairman of a committee of six members appointed by the Irish Government to select designs for a new coinage. His notes, 'What we did or tried to do,' are included in a volume *Coinage of Saorstát Éireann*, published by the Stationery Office in Dublin, 1928.

[2] 'To Ezra Pound,' an essay included in the Cuala Press volume *A Packet for Ezra Pound*, 1929, and afterwards in the revised edition of *A Vision*, 1937.

I know from the anonymous letters that the Catholic press is calling me all the names it can think of. I am in the highest spirits.

George has gone to Switzerland to take Anne to school. Left this morning and returns next Wednesday—once upon a time you and I had a like energy. Yours affectionately W B YEATS

TO OLIVIA SHAKESPEAR

Oct 11 [*Postmark* 1928] 42 *Fitzwilliam Square*

My dear Olivia: I go to London on Oct 17 and shall be at the Savile. Where shall we meet and when? George stays till a week later to see Lennox's play [1] which has been put off until Oct 22 and finish packing. I was to do the same but I have come to hate this weather and by going to London on Oct 17 I shall get the sooner to Rapallo. On Tuesday Oct 23 I must meet George at Stafford for a two days' visit to friends near there—people we met at Algeciras and on the boat out. The address of the Savile is 69 Brook St and its telephone is Mayfair 5143 (or 5144).

I am longing to get away. Here we are at the start of anticlericalism which the ecclesiastics with the familiar folly of their sort are inviting. I have said what had to be said and can do no more. For the moment the situation is ignorance organized under its priests, and unorganized and largely terrified intelligence looking on helpless and angry. Catholicism uses all sorts of naive methods and Mrs. Kevin O'Higgins told me that a few years ago she was at a Retreat and on the day she left she and the others were addressed by the Mother Superior. They were told that there were two men 'they must never know, must not even bow to in the streets'—Lennox Robinson and W. B. Yeats. I wonder [what] the Mother Superior is saying now. Yours W B YEATS

[1] *The Far-Off Hills* by Lennox Robinson, produced at the Abbey Theatre on October 22, 1928.

TO OLIVIA SHAKESPEAR

Nov 23 [1928]   *Via Americhe* 12–8
                                                                                 Rapallo

My dear Olivia, Here is often bright sun, sometimes so hot that I am driven in from my balcony, but to-day it is cold, not cold enough to make a fire necessary, but enough to make me light my paraffin lamp. The furniture arrived this morning and George is at the flat settling things in order. We move in next Tuesday and have tried to persuade the Pounds to join us in a vigorous house-warming but Dorothy seems to classify champagne with steak and onions and badger's flesh, and other forms of the tinsel of this world. I write each morning and am well, much better than I ever am at home and am already sunburnt. I am finishing a little book for Cuala to be called either *A Packet* or *A Packet for Ezra Pound*. It contains first a covering letter to Ezra saying that I offer him the contents, urging him not to be elected to the Senate of his country and telling him why. Then comes a long essay already finished, the introduction to the new edition of *A Vision* and telling all about its origin, and then I shall wind up with a description of Ezra feeding the cats ('some of them are so ungrateful' T. S. Eliot says), of Rapallo and Ezra's poetry—some of which I greatly admire, indeed his collected edition is a great excitement to me. He constantly comes round to talk of Guido who absorbs his attention.

We bought some furniture in Genoa, but when we explained to the maker of it that it must be without his favourite curves and complications he said he once made such plain furniture for an English family but it was 'brutto.' However he has been obedient and the results are excellent. The flat is our great excitement, it will be full of electric gadgets, but if you do not come to Rapallo who shall we have to describe them to? Indeed I see no reason in the world why you and Omar should not presently settle here or in the next little town which would give us all exercise walking the mile and a half between.

If one had not to take exercise life would be perfect, but 3.30 when I must go out for mine has just come—at 4.30 it will be the chill of evening. Yours affectionately   **W B YEATS**

TO THOMAS BODKIN[1]

Dec 20 [1928]   *Via Americhe* 12-8

My dear Bodkin: I have read that full, lucid and gracious lecture of yours and thank you for sending it. I see an occasional Irish newspaper and noticed some letter or speech which said we were all under the influence of the Freemasons who wanted to drive out of Ireland all traces of the Christian Religion. I wish they would tell us what coinage seems to them most charged with piety. The Governor General and his wife are here and have shown me a set. Foreign coins cannot be sent into Italy through the post so my own set could not come. They are full of admiration, and that so far as I can judge is the general attitude among all above the level of mechanical scurrility. I have not heard of anything in music, art or literature that has better treatment in Ireland, and we should be more than content. 'The bust outlives' . . . who was it? . . . 'the coin Tiberius.'[2]
Yours ever   W B YEATS

I have ceased to be a Senator.

[1] From a typed copy. When the new Irish coinage was first issued, Professor Bodkin, at that time Director of the Irish National Gallery, delivered a lecture at the request of the Government and a typescript of this was sent to Yeats.

[2] The quotation which Yeats's memory could not supply comes from Austin Dobson's poem *Ars Victrix*, imitated from Théophile Gautier:

> All passes. Art alone
> Enduring stays to us;
> The Bust outlasts the throne—
> The Coin, Tiberius.

PART SIX
1929—1939

INTRODUCTION TO PART SIX

AT Rapallo Yeats felt well and happy. He found himself able to write lyrics with more facility than he had ever known. 'All praise of joyous life,' he wrote of them to Mrs. Shakespear, and delighted to think of his future with 'no more opinions, no more politics, no more practical tasks.' These poems were a part of the series 'Words for Music Perhaps' published in 1932. In April 1929 he spent a fortnight in London and then went on to Fitzwilliam Square. That summer Ballylee was visited for the last time; it was too damp for him now, and had other inconveniences. An offer of a professorship in Japan tempted him greatly, and he was much disappointed at having to refuse it. In August he went to Dublin for a performance of the dance-play *Fighting the Waves* which he had dictated at Cannes; with Ninette de Valois dancing, this was a great success. By September he was able to report himself as 'back to something like normal health.' But during a short stay in London on the way back to Rapallo he caught cold; in Italy he began to develop a high temperature at nights, and on December 21 collapsed completely. He was found to be suffering from Maltese fever.

He was gravely ill for some months, but by March 1930 was able to move up to Portofino Vetta where the high mountain air did him much good. After a fortnight in the hills he went back to the flat and stayed in Rapallo till July, bathing and browning himself in the sun. On returning to Ireland he visited Coole once more and while there wrote *The Words upon the Window-Pane,* his play on spiritualism and Jonathan Swift. It was acted in Dublin that autumn. Feeling that he was now strong enough to winter in Ireland he decided not to go back to Rapallo.

In the spring of 1931 a furnished house at Killiney was taken for four months, and in May Yeats visited Oxford to receive a Doctor of Letters degree. Lady Gregory's health was now failing; he went to Coole in August and at her family's request stayed on there, going up to Dublin occasionally on Abbey Theatre business, and in December to see a performance of his play *The Dreaming of the Bones*, which had been written as far back as 1918. On his return he was laid up with a bad cold and exhaustion.

In May 1932 Lady Gregory died; the long association with Coole had come to an end. With his family now beginning to grow up and because his health was always better away from towns, search was made for a country home not too far from Dublin, and presently a suitable house with a garden was found at Rathfarnham. The Fitzwilliam Square flat was given up in July, and after a short stay at Glendalough Yeats moved in to Riversdale, his last home in Ireland. For some time he had been laying plans for the establishment of an Irish Academy of Letters; now in September invitations to proposed members were sent out and a public meeting held. At the end of October he sailed for America on his last lecture tour.

He was back in London at the end of January 1933, and after a short stay there returned to Riversdale. He was much occupied with plans for the Academy, for which he had made a substantial sum of money by lectures in America. In May a degree was conferred on him at Cambridge.

Irish politics now began once more to interest him: he had some hopes of General O'Duffy and his 'blue shirts' movement, but they faded before long; he wrote them three marching songs, but presently rewrote them 'so that nobody could sing them.' In November Macmillan brought out a collected one-volume edition of all his lyrical and narrative poems, and he began work on a new dance-play *The King of the Great Clock Tower*.

After Lady Gregory's death he decided to continue his memoirs; *Dramatis Personae* deals with their first meeting and their work for the Irish Literary Theatre, with vivid portraits of George Moore, Edward Martyn and other associates of that period. Some time during this spring he underwent the Steinach rejuvenation operation, and found it beneficial in lowering his blood-pressure. In May 1934 he and Mrs. Yeats went out to Rapallo to bring back the furniture they had left there. *The King of the Great Clock Tower* was performed at the Abbey in July, together with an earlier play *Resurrection*. More poetry was written, the 'Supernatural Songs' published the following year. October took him to Rome to the Fourth Congress of the Alessandro Volta Foundation. He was asked to take the chair at the Congress, and delivered a lecture on the Irish National Theatre. A small volume of plays with introductions, *Wheels and Butterflies*, appeared in November. He stayed in London on his way back, and on reaching Riversdale in January 1935 developed congestion of the lungs; he was kept in bed and forbidden work. By March he was well again, and received a commission from the Clarendon Press to compile an *Oxford Book of Modern Verse*. In June his seventieth birthday was celebrated with gifts and a banquet in his honour.

In this year he had made the acquaintance of Dorothy Wellesley, whose poetry he had already much admired. He paid a visit to her Sussex home, Penns in the Rocks, in August, the first of many visits, and from this time onward they corresponded frequently; he was again at Penns in October after seeing at the Little Theatre in London a performance of his *Player Queen* in which a young actress-poet, Margot Ruddock, in whose work he was interested, took a part. Soon after his return to Riversdale in November he finished his work on the Oxford anthology, and a small volume containing lyrics and two plays, *A Full Moon in March*, was published.

A warmer climate was felt to be necessary for the winter, and it was arranged that Yeats should go to Majorca in company with the Indian Swami, Shri Purohit, whose work he had known for some years and whom he was now to help in a translation of the *Upanishads*. They stayed at first in a hotel at Palma and he began a new play *The Herne's Egg*. At the beginning of 1936 he was taken ill, suffering much from breathlessness, the beginning of that dropsical condition which finally brought his life to an end. Work was forbidden him and Mrs. Yeats was sent for. By April he was better again and they had moved into a villa, the Casa Pastor. When they were on the point of leaving for home Margot Ruddock arrived unexpectedly, without money or luggage, and soon afterwards temporarily lost her reason in Barcelona; Yeats and Mrs. Yeats had to assume responsibility for her. Eventually they were able to return to England; Yeats went to Penns for a short time and then back to Ireland in June. Here he began to compile ballads for a second series of *Broadsides* (a first had been issued during 1935) and prepared a lecture on Modern Poetry which he delivered for the B.B.C. in October. Next month *The Oxford Book of Modern Verse* was published and in spite of some adverse criticism regarding poems included and excluded it had an immense sale.

Yeats's old interest in the problem of writing words to music had revived strongly, and with the encouragement of the poets F. R. Higgins and Frank O'Connor, who knew many Irish traditional airs, he began a series of ballads to be sung; two of these, one on Parnell and one on Roger Casement, the latter published in a leading Dublin newspaper, won great popularity. A programme of songs, given at the Abbey Theatre, was broadcast from Athlone, and during 1937 the B.B.C. induced Yeats to arrange and take part in four programmes of poetry, recited or sung: two contained poems by a variety of authors and two were devoted to Yeats's work alone. Edmund Dulac, who had composed music for many of Yeats's poems, had introduced him to Miss Edith Shackleton Heald and her sister, and he stayed with them at their home, the Chantrey House, Steyning, Sussex, dividing his time in England between that and Penns in the Rocks.

A committee of admirers in America had arranged a testimonial to Yeats which guaranteed him a sum of money each year so that his life should be free from all financial anxiety; the intention was that this should be a private matter, but Yeats would only accept on condition that it should be made public; he announced it at a Banquet given in August by the Irish Academy of Letters. In the autumn of 1937 he was once more in London and at Steyning; the revised version of *A Vision* was published in October, and a small volume of essays and prefaces to books, *Essays 1931–1936*, in December.

It was now evident that the winter months would have to be spent in a mild climate. Early in 1938 he went out to the South of France, staying first at the Hôtel Carlton in Menton and then moving to the Hôtel Idéal Séjour on Cap Martin. He was busy with a new project, a little periodical to be published at irregular intervals in which he could express his opinions; he called it *On the Boiler*. When he returned to Riversdale in May he was taken ill again but recovered, and crossing to England stayed at the Chantrey House, beginning there a new play. *Purgatory*. This was produced at the Abbey Theatre in August, and Yeats made a brief speech from the stage, his last public appearance. In October his friend Mrs. Shakespear died, the last link with his early days. After some visits in England he went out again to Cap Martin; although his strength was failing he was still hard at work, writing poetry and his last play *The Death of Cuchulain*, and planning a book on speech and music. Friends who were staying near by called to see him and found him in good spirits. But he became gravely ill on Thursday January 26th, 1939, and on the following Saturday he died.

1929-1939

TO OLIVIA SHAKESPEAR

March 2 [1929]   *Via Americhe* 12–8
                                                  Rapallo

My dear Olivia, It is long since I have written—partly cold which has made the corner of the room where my desk and note-paper are look very unpleasant, and partly certain days in bed with rheumatism. No matter how bad the weather I can make myself write verse—if I have it in my head—but little else. Now we are thawing. I am writing *Twelve poems for music*—have done three of them (and two other poems)—no[t] so much that they may be sung as that I may define their kind of emotion to myself. I want them to be all emotion and all impersonal. One of the three I have written is my best lyric for some years I think. They are the opposite of my recent work and all praise of joyous life, though in the best of them it is a dry bone on the shore that sings the praise. Last night I saw in a dream strange ragged excited people singing in a crowd. The most visible were a man and woman who were I think dancing. The man was swinging round his head a weight at the end of a rope or leather thong, and I knew that he did not know whether he would strike her dead or not, and both had their eyes fixed on each other, and both sang their love for one another. I suppose it was Blake's old thought 'sexual love is founded upon spiritual hate'—I will probably find I have written it in a poem in a few days—though my remembering my dream may prevent that—by making my criticism work upon it. (At least there is evidence to that effect.)

    To-night we dine with Ezra—the first dinner-coated meal since I got here—to meet Hauptmann who does not know a word of English but is fine to look at—after the fashion of William Morris. Auntille—how do you spell him? [1]—and his lady will be there and

---

[1] George Antheil, who wrote music for Yeats's play *Fighting the Waves*. It is published with the play in the volume *Wheels and Butterflies*.

probably a certain Basil Bunting, one of Ezra's more savage disciples. He got into jail as a pacificist and then for assaulting the police and carrying concealed weapons and he is now writing up Antille's music. George and I keep him at a distance and yet I have no doubt that just such as he surrounded Shakespeare's theatre, when it was denounced by the first puritans.

I have turned from Browning—to me a dangerous influence—to Morris and read through his *Defence of Guenevere* and some unfinished prose fragments with great wonder. I have come to fear the world's last great poetic period is over

> Though the great song return no more
> There's keen delight in what we have—
> A rattle of pebbles on the shore
> Under the receeding wave.[1]

The young do not feel like that—George does not, nor Ezra—but men far off feel it—in Japan for instance. Yours affectionately

W B YEATS

I knew nothing of your illness until it was over. I hope all is very well now. I shall be in London on May 1 and stay perhaps a fortnight, so keep some hours for me.

TO LADY GREGORY

March 9 [1929] *Via Americhe* 12–8

My dear Lady Gregory, Beautiful summer weather these last two or three days and a settled look about it. George and I are recovering from our winter ailments accordingly. Sam Brown (who is here as I think you know) goes down to the sea shore every morning and George sees him from her window always on the same seat. On his way back to his hotel he leaves me his *Irish Times* and I read with satisfaction of the frozen pond in St. Stephen's Green.

I have written seven poems—16 or 18 lines each—since Feb 6 and never wrote with greater ease. The poems are two 'meditations' for *A Packet for Ezra Pound* which Lolly is printing and the first

---

[1] With the alteration of one word this was included in *Words for Music Perhaps and other poems*, 1932, under the title 'The Nineteenth Century and After.'

five of *Twelve Poems for Music*. The getting away from all distractions has enriched my imagination. I wish I had done it years ago. Antheil is here and has started on a musical setting for a trilogy consisting of *The Hawk's Well, On Baile's Strand* and the new version of *The Only Jealousy* which I call *Fighting the Waves*. If he persists, and he is at present enthusiastic, it means a performance in Vienna in the autumn. He has a great name there since his setting of *Oedipus* a few months ago. He is a revolutionary musician—there was a riot of almost Abbey intensity over some music of his in America. There will be masks and all singing within the range of the speaking voice —for my old theories are dogmas it seems of the new school. His setting of *Fighting the Waves* should be ready for Miss de Valois to do in Dublin in May. He is about 28 and looks 18 and has a face of indescribable innocence. His wife, a first violinist from somewhere or other, looks equally young and innocent. Both are persons of impulse and he may or he may not get through his month of toil upon the three plays. He promises to keep the instruments required for *The Fighting of the Waves* within the range of the Abbey. During the fight in *Oedipus at Colonus* (he did both plays) there were twelve pianos played at once. Yours always   W B YEATS

TO OLIVIA SHAKESPEAR

March 29 [1929] *Via Americhe* 12–8

My dear Olivia: Dorothy tells me you are better, and told George that Omar was cross because he could not see you, and that is all my news of you. George is in Switzerland with Anne and Michael and I am filling up my time by sitting in the sun when not reading or writing. I have written eleven lyrics in the last two months—nine of them *Words for Music*, these last unlike my past work—wilder and perhaps slighter. Here is a *Lullaby* that I like.[1] A mother sings to her child

> Beloved may your sleep be sound
> That have found it where you fed;
> What were all the world's alarms

---

[1] *Lullaby*, in a revised version, appears as one of the series 'Words for Music Perhaps' in *The Winding Stair*, 1933.

　　　　To that great Paris when he found
　　　　Sleep upon a golden bed
　　　　That first dawn in Helen's arms?

　　　　　　　　II
　　　　Sleep beloved such a sleep
　　　　As did that wild Tristram know
　　　　When, the potion's work being done,
　　　　Stags could run and hares could leap,
　　　　The beech-bough sway by the oak-bough
　　　　And the world begin again.

　　　　　　　　III
　　　　Beloved such a sleep as fell
　　　　Upon Eurota's grassy bank
　　　　When the holy bird, that there
　　　　Accomplished his predestined will,
　　　　From the limbs of Leda sank
　　　　But not from her protecting care.

I have done two or three others that seem to me lucky and that does not often happen. Yet I am full of doubt. I am writing more easily than I ever wrote and I am happy, whereas I have always been unhappy when I wrote and worked with great difficulty. I feel like one of those Japanese who in the middle ages retired from the world at 50 or so—not like an Indian of that age to live in jungle but to devote himself 'to art and letters' which was considered sacred. If this new work do not seem as good as the old to my friends then I can take to some lesser task and live very contentedly. The happiness of finding idleness a duty. No more opinions, no more politics, no more practical tasks　　　　　　　　　　　　　　[*Unsigned*]

　　　　　　　TO LADY GREGORY

April 10 [1929]　　　　　　　　*Via Americhe* 12–8

My dear Lady Gregory . . . I heard some of George Antheil's music for *The Only Jealousy* the other day and it seemed to me the only dramatic music I ever heard—a very strong beat, something heroic and barbaric and strange. I have written a couple more lyrics since I wrote and am now resting for a couple of days but hope before I leave to do at least two more. Since I came here I have written 14 besides some little scraps of satirical verse on —— and other people. This has all been in three months I think—for at first I wrote prose. Having thrown off all my burdens I am quite happy and am a little anxious to know how this is affecting my verse. I write it rapidly for the first time in my life.

We leave here on April 26 I think, George to go straight to Ireland, I to spend a couple of weeks in London first. Yours

W B YEATS

TO P. WYNDHAM LEWIS[1]

[Possibly April 1929]   *Rapallo*

Dear Wyndham Lewis, This is a belated letter of thanks but I am a slow and capricious reader. I read nothing as a rule but poetry and philosophy (and of course detective stories) and when *Tarr* came I laid it aside, till I had finished a course of these I had set out upon. Then about a month ago I took up *Tarr*. It does not excite me as *Childermass* did yet is sincere and wonderful work, and its curious, almost unconscious, presentation of sex through mechanical images and images of food—there also its mechanism unites itself in my mind with so much in contemporary painting and sculpture. There is the feeling, almost Buddhist, that we are caught in a kind of steel trap. My only objection to your book is that you have isolated an element for study, as if in a laboratory, which cannot be isolated unless we take this element out of the actual world as in romantic art (or as in *Childermass*). This is not a defect of treatment, but of the contemporary form you have chosen. How interested Balzac would have been in Anastasya's business dealings with Soltyk—in her character as a whole—the art politics of all these people! Is it not the prerogative of science to isolate its deductions? If sex and their love life is a steel trap, then I want to set up against it the realization of Buddha, and so restore the unity of my thought—of Buddha or, let us say, *Seraphita*.[2]

[1] From a typed copy belonging to Mrs. Yeats.
[2] Balzac's Swedenborgian novel, written between December 1833 and November 1835.

I shall be in London at the Savile from Tuesday next for ten days or so and hope to see you. Yours   W B YEATS

TO OLIVIA SHAKESPEAR

April 26 [1929]   *Via Americhe* 12–8

My dear Olivia, I shall get to London at 5 PM on Monday—can I come and see you any time on Tuesday? I am probably engaged on Wed, Thursday and Friday evening but otherwise have no plans. Wednesday evening I shall go to my 'Ghosts Club' [1] and on Friday to Ricketts—at least I think so.

I am well and more cheerful than I have been for years—have written 19 lyrics for the numbers keep on mounting. I want to read some to you. Yours   W B YEATS

I shall be at The Savile Club, 69 Brook St W.1

TO OLIVIA SHAKESPEAR

May 4 [*Postmark May* 6, 1929?]   *Savile Club*

My dear Olivia, Tuesday 7.30 will suit me perfectly—many thanks.

Have just had tea with Wyndham Lewis. Both of us too cautious, with too much sympathy for one another not to fear we might discover some fundamental difference. We played with all topics and said as little as possible. Yours affectionately   W B YEATS

TO LADY GREGORY

Sunday May 19 [*Postmark* 1929]   42 *Fitzwilliam Square*

My dear Lady Gregory, After the general meeting at the Abbey I want you to come here to lunch. You can rest here till you want to return to the Vice-regal Lodge.

[1] The Ghosts Club used to meet once a month at Pagani's Restaurant in Great Portland Street.

I spent a fortnight in London—usual round of friends, Sturge Moore, Ricketts, Lady Ottoline and so on. I got back here three days ago. I find life sufficiently tranquil and that it may continue so I shall keep away from politicians.

I went out to Jack's this afternoon and saw there much of his new work—very strange and beautiful in a wild way. Joyce says that he and Jack have the same method. He bought two of Jack's pictures of the Liffey.

In London I went to the Round Pond to see what sort of boat I should buy for Michael. I had a talk on the subject with a regular Round Pond old tar—a man of seventy. He had a little cutter yacht which he described as old fashioned. Yours   W B YEATS

TO OLIVIA SHAKESPEAR

July 2 [Postmark 1929]   42 *Fitzwilliam Square*

My dear Olivia: At last after more than a month I have tidied my study, my big table and my desk are no longer covered with a disorder of books and loose papers. It is possible to think of my friends again and find the envelopes. I am now full of virtue.

I am still putting the philosophy in order but once that is done, and this summer must finish, I believe I shall have a poetical rebirth for as I write about my cones and gyres all kinds of images come before me. In a few days I go to Coole and escape charming Americans with introductory letters.

Get Lord Alfred Douglas's *Autobiography*. I took it up at the Kildare St. Club and spent an evening over it. Twenty years ago he published a kind of life [1] and then he was an innocent man full of moral indignation. But times have changed. Now he is no longer innocent—has repented however and is a Catholic. There is an amazing account of an affair with 'the divorced wife of a peer' at Monte Carlo. His tutor knocked on her bedroom door in the middle of the night and demanded his pupil. The pupil was handed over dressed in one of the lady's 'be-ribboned nightgowns' (feminine to the last). When the tutor told her that she was corrupting innocence the pupil protested that he was not innocent and apparently never

[1] *Oscar Wilde and Myself*, 1914.

had been. There are some friendly paragraphs about Lionel and his distress at the result of his introduction of Douglas and Wilde. Douglas is an unpleasant person—an hysterical woman essentially and one feels that his persecution of Ross is a woman's jealousy—Ross was Wilde's executor and so a successful rival. I met Douglas once—before the Ransome life,[1] the avowed cause of the enmity—and he hated Ross then and tried to make out that Ross had been Wilde's lover after Wilde came out of jail—he himself was at the time posing, or about to pose, as a persecuted and pious innocent. According to Douglas, Wilde—at the very time when he was about to write the indictment in the unpublished *De Profundis*—was begging Douglas to wait for him, to be faithful and so on. Douglas was the pretty woman who had ruined him and so loved and hated. Yours always
W B YEATS

TO OLIVIA SHAKESPEAR

August 31 [*wrong date—perhaps July* 31. *Postmark* 1929]   42 *Fitzwilliam Square*

My dear Olivia: I write from Coole but return to Dublin on Monday to meet George who has gone to Switzerland for the children. I have just finished my last bout of hard work at the philosophy and have taken a day for rest and letters. In Dublin they are rehearsing my *Fighting the Waves* with Antheil's music and the Dutch sculptor's masks.[2] The birth of a new art—if one does not make these announcements one looks so old fashioned.

I have just had an offer of a professorship in Japan for a year—8 hours a week work, £1000 a year, a residence and travelling expenses. Do not tell anybody for I am a little tempted—George does not know yet. If my health is good enough it would be new life. 3 months, while Formosa (where the University is) is too hot for a European, wandering about Japanese temples among the hills—

---

[1] *Oscar Wilde: A Critical Study* by Arthur Ransome was published by Martin Secker in 1912. Lord Alfred Douglas brought an action for libel against the author in the King's Bench Division in April 1913, but judgement was given in the author's favour, and the book was reissued in May 1913 by Methuen & Co. though with the references to Douglas omitted.

[2] Hildo Van Krop who made the masks for *Fighting the Waves*, and to whom Yeats dedicated the play when it was included in *Wheels and Butterflies*, 1934.

all the best Chinese art is in Japan. What an adventure for old age —probably some new impulse to put in verse. However, George will make up my mind for me in five minutes, being in her decisive youth.

One of my Dublin friends, Starkie, a professor of Trinity College Dublin, is now somewhere in Central Europe with a tribe [of] Gypsies. He has brought no money and lives by playing his guitar. He will return to his students with an undisturbed Academic face. Another of my friends, a neighbour here in Galway, has just had 17 rifle and revolver shots fired through his window in the dead of night and he does not know why. And you, and I, and Dorothy and Omar vegetate. Yours affectionately W B YEATS

TO OLIVIA SHAKESPEAR

August 8 [Postmark Aug 9, 1929]   42 *Fitzwilliam Square*

My dear Olivia, No—we are not going to Japan. George has been quite firm—Michael's health would not stand it and of course she is right. I am relieved and disappointed.

I am convinced that were God in His heaven as is alleged you and Dorothy and Omar would come to Dublin for my play next Tuesday, but as it is Omar's phlegmatic temperament will overpower your natural enterprise.

This is but to tell you about Japan—besides you owe me two letters. Yours ever   W B YEATS

TO SEAN O'FAOLAIN [1]

August 15 [? 1929]   42 *Fitzwilliam Square*

Dear Mr. O'Faolain, If you will give me an undertaking to reprint nothing of mine, prose or verse, which is not in my collected edition (Macmillan) I will give you what help I can. I certainly do not want to see verse or prose, which I have never reprinted, reprinted by

---

[1] Mr. O'Faolain believes that this letter refers to a review of Yeats's *Selected Poems Lyrical and Narrative*, 1929, which he was then preparing, and which was published in the *Criterion*, April 1930. The review reprinted some early poems, and Yeats was annoyed.

somebody else. Of course you can ask my permission in some special case, but you must not expect permission except under circumstances not likely to arise. The origins of a poet are not in that which he has cast off because it is not himself, but in his own mind and in the past of literature. Yours　　　　　　　[*Unsigned*]

TO LADY GREGORY

August 21 [*Postmark* 1929]　　　　　42 *Fitzwilliam Square*

My dear Lady Gregory ... The *Irish Times* to day has a leader on the production of *Fighting the Waves* and *The Apple Cart* as both 'produced amid such stir of attention as seldom gratified the most notable of dramatists,' which is of course nonsense so far as my play is concerned but friendly. However they abate the compliment by thinking the first but 'an interesting experiment' and the second as 'no more than a skit.' I saw the chief English papers yesterday at the club. Shaw has had an exclusively party reception—the Conservative papers, especially the *Morning Post*, enthusiastic and the Labour papers abusive. All agree that the play was enthusiastically received. I imagine that Shaw has made the sensation of his life, and can join Snowden in the Carlton Club. Yours　　W B YEATS

TO OLIVIA SHAKESPEAR

August 24 [*Postmark* 1929]　　　　　42 *Fitzwilliam Square*

My dear Olivia: I send you *A Packet for Ezra Pound*—heaven knows what will happen when it reaches Mrs. Tucker [1] so I send it to you in London. I want to send a copy to Ezra, so please tell me where he is. Even if he is at Rapallo please tell me his address. I am going to Sligo and George and the children to Coole and I will send the book from there. George's memory not at hand—and I shall get a letter from you the sooner.

　My *Fighting the Waves* has been my greatest success on the stage since *Kathleen-ni-Houlihan*, and its production was a great event here,

[1] Mrs. Yeats's mother.

the politician[s] and the governor general and the American minister present—the masks by the Dutchman Krop magnificent and Antheil's music. Everyone here is as convinced as I am that I have discovered a new form by this combination of dance, speech and music. The dancing of the goddess in her abstract almost non-representative mask was extraordinarily exciting. The play begins with a dance which represents Cuchullan fighting the waves, then after some singing by the chorus comes the play which has for its central incident the dance of the goddess and of the ghost of Cuchullan, and then after more singing is the dance of the goddess mourning among the waves. The waves are of course dancers. I felt that the sea was eternity and that they were all upon its edge. The theatre was packed night after night, so the play will be revived.

I regretted, as I often do when we are more than usually spirited at the Abbey, that [you] could not be here. One writes and works for one's friends, and those who read, or at any rate those who listen, are people about whom one cares nothing—that seems the general rule at any rate. Yours affectionately   W B YEATS

TO OLIVIA SHAKESPEAR

Sept 13 [*Postmark* 1929]   42 *Fitzwilliam Square*

My dear Olivia, I shall be in London for the first two weeks of November. George wants to go later this year and stay later so as to get the benefit of the Italian May; and my *King Oedipus* is being revived on Oct 10.

The essay in the *Packet* will be the introduction of a new edition of the *Vision* under the name of 'The Great Wheel.' But this new edition will be a new book, all I hope clear and as simple as the subject permits. Four or five years' reading has given me some knowledge of metaphysics and time to clear up endless errors in my understanding of the script. My conviction of the truth of it all has grown also and that makes one clear. I am taking to Rapallo what will be I hope a clear typed script of the whole book. I will work at it here and there free at last, now that all is constructive, to sharpen definitions and enrich descriptions. I should go to press with it next spring. I shall begin also I hope the new version of the Robartes stories. Having proved, by undescribed process, the immortality of the soul to a little group of typical followers, he will discuss the deductions with an energy and a dogmatism and a cruelty I am not capable of in my own person. I have a very amusing setting thought out. I shall also finish the book of thirty poems for music I am more than half through. 'For Music' is only a name, nobody will sing them.

I wish I could be in London more, though mainly to see you and perhaps Dulac—for there is no one else; perhaps I may next year. I have only just this last two months got back to something like normal health. Henceforth a journey should not mean fatigue and noise won't wear me out. I think I shall 'live on.' When Lady Gregory goes, and she is now very frail, I too shall have but one old friend left. (M[aud] G[onne] has been estranged by politics this long while.) Yours affectionately W B YEATS

TO LADY GREGORY

Monday [*Sept* 30. *Postmark Oct* 1, 1929] 42 *Fitzwilliam Square*

My dear Lady Gregory, I have not written because I had hoped to send you that poem—however though it has taken a new leap into life to-day it is not finished—and now I must not delay longer . . .

It was very pleasant at Coole but I am too dazed with my day's verse writing to add more now. Here are two lines that may or may not remain in the poem

'She taught me that straight line that sets a man
Above the crooked journey of the sun.' [1]

Yours

W B YEATS

[1] These lines do not now appear in the poem 'Coole Park, 1929.' The third stanza of the poem ends:

The intellectual sweetness of those lines
That cut through time or cross it withershins.

TO OLIVIA SHAKESPEAR

Oct 13 [*Postmark Oct* 14, 1929]   42 *Fitzwilliam Square*

My dear Olivia, I go to London on Oct 23 and, with the possible exception of two days to the west of England to look up a little groups of Kabalists, will stay three weeks. I am eager to see you—let me know your plans. I have formed none except that I must meet an old Kabalist in London and must accept his date for lunch or dinner—a sign that the great work is almost finished and that I want to give it to the right people. In private life he [is], I think, an Hegelian professor—how surprised his pupils would be. What shall you and I do? Shall we go to the Zoo or to Richmond?—no, the weather is too bad—I feel that I want a celebration.

Lennox's play is a very great success, house packed night after night.[1] It [is] a satire on American lectures. Life grows generally crowded and I long for Rapallo.

George comes to London on Nov 4. Yours affectionately

W B YEATS

TO LADY GREGORY[2]

Nov 16, 1929   *Knightsbridge Hotel*
London

Dear Lady Gregory, I wrote to you yesterday and asked on the back of the envelope if there was anything I could do. I could see somebody on Tuesday or Wednesday for you. I have left these two days completely free. I can't at present do a very great deal; I overtired myself yesterday—a lunch with Mrs. Hall and tea with Gerald Heard —and to-day I have coughed up blood again. That's why I am dictating, for I am in bed.

I am looking forward very much to the quiet of Rapallo and I long for the sight of a table with my papers arranged upon it and a prospect of so much writing per day. I shall finish the philosophy for I cannot face verse just yet, though I have no lack of themes.

I caught the cold that undid me at *The Apple Cart* and perhaps it was the cold coming on, but I hated the play. The second act was theatrical in the worst sense of the word in writing and in acting,

---

[1] *Ever the Twain* by Lennox Robinson was produced at the Abbey Theatre on October 8.   [2] Dictated.

and the theme was just rich enough to show up the superficiality of the treatment. It was the Shaw who writes letters to the papers and gives interviews, not the man who creates. That's the only play I have seen.

We leave for Rapallo on the morning of the 21st and go to the Grosvenor on the 19th—we have a dinner party that night, the Dulacs and other friends. So if you are writing on Monday, write to the *Grosvenor Hotel, Victoria.* Yours   W B YEATS

TO OLIVIA SHAKESPEAR [1]

Dec 12, 1929   *Via Americhe* 12–8

My dear Olivia, I am dictating this because I still find letter-writing very fatiguing. Dorothy will have told you that I have been unwell, some sort of nervous collapse and a temperature that rises to greet the setting sun. However the last three or four days have brought a great change, and I shall write to you with my own hand in two or three days.

Hauptmann has returned. He also has had blood-pressure. He ventured uncautiously to the doctor, enticed there by his son though feeling 'perfectly well.' The doctor said 'Blood-pressure, produced by the strain of walking upright, you must become a quadruped once more,' and put him to bed for a month, depriving him of meat dinners and champagne. 'But why should anybody say I drink too much champagne? I only drink two or three bottles a day, and there are men who drink four.' Now he is out of bed and cannot make out why he feels so extraordinarily vigorous but is quite certain that the doctor is a great genius, especially as he is now allowed to eat and drink as much as he likes. (It would have been no use telling him not to.) Yours   W B YEATS

TO OLIVIA SHAKESPEAR

Dec 16 [*Postmark Dec* 18, 1929]   *Via Americhe* 12–8

My dear Olivia: To-day I write my first letters—hitherto I have dictated. I write to you and to Lady Gregory who hates my dictated

[1] Dictated.

letters—old complaint of hers for I used to dictate letters on Abbey business. I am now physically well—my temperature has ceased to go up at nightfall, but consecutive thought still soon wearies me. I think however I shall be normal again in a few days. When I first got here I was fairly vigorous though shaky, and wrote this little poem of which I showed you the prose draft. Here it is

> Speech after long silence; it is right—
> All other lovers being estranged or dead,
> Unfriendly lamp-light hid under its shade
> The curtains drawn upon unfriendly night,—
> That we descant and yet again descant
> Upon the supreme theme of art and song:
> Bodily decrepitude is wisdom; young
> We loved each other and were ignorant.[1]

My volume of *Selections* is passing into its second edition and is out little over a month. Until quite lately the only reviews were in papers like the *East Anglian News or Echo*, and the *Blackpool Eagle* and the like. George insisted from the beginning that such papers were more important than the London press, for only rustics read. Did Theocritus write of shepherds from a similar discovery? Yours affectionately
W B YEATS

TO OLIVIA SHAKESPEAR

March 4 [Postmark Mar 8, 1930]   *Via Americhe* 12–8

My dear Olivia, This is the first letter I have written with my own hand since I became ill. Last week I dictated two or three to George —one for Lady Gregory and the others business and that is all since I got this fever nine weeks ago. I go out every day or two for an hour but have discovered that I must spend the rest of each day in bed and there read nothing but story-books. Having exhausted the detective literature of the world I have just started upon the Wild West and shall probably, if my illness last long enough, descend to Buffalo Bill. To-day I met Ezra for the first time—you know his dread of infections—seeing me in the open air and the sea air, he sat

[1] This poem appeared, with no verbal revision, under the title 'After Long Silence' in *The Winding Stair*, 1933.

beside me in front of the café and admired my beard, and declared I should be sent by the Free State as Minister to Austria, that Austria would alone perfectly appreciate my beard. Certainly I need a new career for I cannot recognise myself in the mirror—if Pirandello is right, my friends, taking their impulse from my appearance, which they see so much more steadily than I can, will connect me with something reckless and dashing.

Write—though indeed till very lately you have [been] very good about letters—I must not write more than a few words ... consecutive thought, though even in a letter, tires me and now I am tired. Yours affectionately W B YEATS

TO LADY GREGORY[1]

April 7, 1930   *Via Americhe* 12–8

Dear Lady Gregory, I had meant to write this with my own hand, but I have begun to work again and that uses up all my writing energy for the day. I begin in bed immediately after breakfast and work for about an hour.

We are on a mountain top about five miles from Rapallo in a hotel with large woody grounds about it and views over miles of mountain and sea; a most lovely place. I will never say again that I do not believe in climate, for after two or three days here I found myself almost normal again. We are staying another week and have been here a week. Just outside the gate of the hotel grounds there is a small restaurant and hotel which was once the lodging, or rather tenement house, where Nietzsche lived for some months and boasted to his friends of having found a place where there were eight walks. When we are not lost in mountain clouds it is brilliant sunlight and blue sea which melts imperceptibly into the sky. When I am not reading detective stories I am reading Swift, the *Diary to Stella*, and his correspondence with Pope and Bolingbroke; these men fascinate me, in Bolingbroke the last pose and in Swift the last passion of the Renaissance, in Pope, whom I dislike, an imitation both of pose and passion.

Masefield and his family, Siegfried Sassoon and a friend, arrive

[1] Dictated.

in Rapallo in a few days, and I am hoping the mountain will not deter them. Ezra Pound arrived the other day, his first visit since I got ill—fear of infection—and being warned by his wife tried to be very peaceable but couldn't help being very litigious about Confucius who I consider should have worn an Eighteenth Century wig and preached in St. Paul's, and he thinks the perfect man. Yours affectionately   W B YEATS

TO GEORGE RUSSELL (AE)

April 13 [*Postmark Apr* 14, 1930]   *Via Americhe* 12–8

My dear AE, I have to-day your farewell [1]—I knew from Brown that was coming—and regret it on all public grounds—it leaves us 'sheep without a shepherd when the snow shuts out the day' [2]—but not on private for you can now write books. I thought your summing up of things done or attempted full of dignity and grace.

I am well again thanks to the clear air of a mountain top where I spent a fortnight to descend yesterday. I have been at work most mornings but dare not yet attempt verse, or anything that would follow me when I laid down the pen. I have been ill for five months, and now blink at the world as if fresh from the cloisters. My wife tells me that the little wrinkles are gone out of my face. All days or nights of discomfort or delirium have been blotted from my memory and I recall nothing but peace. Yours affectionately   W B YEATS

TO MRS. ROBERT BRIDGES

May 7 [1930]   *Via Americhe* 12–8

Dear Mrs. Bridges, May I, despite the slightness of our acquaintance, tell how much I feel your great loss.[3] I think I remember your husband most clearly as I saw him at some great house near you

---

[1] This refers to the cessation on April 12, 1930, of the *Irish Statesman*, a weekly paper which AE had edited continuously since September 15, 1923.

[2] The line which Yeats quotes here is from Thomas Davis's 'Lament for Owen Roe O'Neill.' He had included the poem in *A Book of Irish Verse*, 1895.

[3] Robert Bridges, the Poet Laureate, had died on April 21.

where there were some Servian delegates. He came through the undistinguished crowd, an image of mental and physical perfection, and one of the Servians turned to me in obvious excitement to ask his name. He has always seemed the only poet, whose influence has always heightened and purified the art of others, and all who write with deliberation are his debtors.

My wife joins with me in sending you our sympathy. Yours
W B YEATS

TO OLIVIA SHAKESPEAR

June 1 [*Postmark June* 3, 1930]   *Via Americhe* 12–8

My dear Olivia: The children are here and are—now that Dorothy and Ezra are gone—our only event. Anne has achieved her first act of independence. At lunch she was not to be found and Michael said, with a voice full of disgust, 'Anne has run away.' Meanwhile a friend of George's and mine had met her on a country road 'talking to herself and trying to walk like a queen in a faery tale' and asked her to lunch. Anne accepted but insisted on eating her own food and unpacked a knapsack. She brought out (wrapped up in separate pieces of newspaper), biscuits, a bottle of lemonade, a looking-glass, a comb, a brush, and a piece of soap. She said she would go home 'after dark' but was persuaded to do so at the end of lunch by the suggestion that George and Michael were probably making ices. Anne and Michael have been given their first chess-board and taught the moves. An hour later there came yells and bangs from the nursery. All the chairs were upset, and Michael had his two hands in Anne's hair, and Anne was pounding Michael. The point was —had Michael check-mated Anne? What a lot Dorothy is missing by leaving Omar in London!

If nothing happens to change our plans we shall stay here till well on in July. Gogarty says John wants 'to paint a serious portrait' of me, and should this turn out true we may have to leave rather sooner. I hope not for I am writing verse again, and pleased with what I am doing. I enjoy my life when it is not interrupted by too many days of fatigue, but those days come more seldom. I am trying to avoid them by working three days and then resting three days. We sit in the sun—George and the children on the sea-shore after a bathe—I on my balcony, as naked as usage permits—and then oil ourselves. We colour like old meerschaum pipes.

I read Swift constantly and George reads out Morris's *Well at the World's End*. I read to the children at six every evening. O how intolerable *The Lay of the Last Minstrel* is, and yet the magic book in Melrose made them put their faces up side by side at the edge of my bed. I generally go to bed before dinner for a while. I have read them *The Ancient Mariner, The Lays of Ancient Rome, How the Good News* and *The Pied Piper*. Yours affectionately W B YEATS

TO P. WYNDHAM LEWIS [1]

[? September 1930] 42 *Fitzwilliam Square*

Dear Wyndham Lewis . . . I have heard that you attack individuals, but that drove me neither to detraction nor admiration for I knew nothing of it; I recognised nobody—I spend one week in London every year. Your work, like that of Pirandello, who alone of living dramatists has unexhausted, important material, portrays the transition from individualism to universal plasticity, though your theme is not, like his, plasticity itself but the attempted substitution for it of ghastly homunculi in bottles. Somebody tells me that you have satirised Edith Sitwell. If that is so, visionary excitement has in part benumbed your senses. When I read her *Gold Coast Customs* a year ago, I felt, as on first reading *The Apes of God*, that something absent from all literature for a generation was back again, and in a form rare in the literature of all generations, passion enobled by intensity, by endurance, by wisdom. We had it in one man once. He lies in St. Patrick's now under the greatest epitaph in history. Yours very sincerely, W B YEATS

TO OLIVIA SHAKESPEAR

Oct 23 [*Postmark Oct* 25, 1930] 42 *Fitzwilliam Square*

My dear Olivia, Yes, Nov 2: I can be certain of that date. I think now of going to London about Nov 1, going to Masefield on Nov 3

[1] Fragment. Text from *Satire and Fiction* by Wyndham Lewis [1930]. This letter refers to *The Apes of God* by Wyndham Lewis, first issued in a limited edition in June 1930.

and then getting back to London after a day or two and spending a week in London. I had meant to spend the week in London before going to Masefield but a young man has turned up to whom I can dictate. I am trying to dictate some of the final version of the system. It has been all in manuscript for some months but it is very hard to get a possible typist. If I dictate to George it would almost certainly put her nerves all wrong. I don't want any more mediumship. I am well and enjoy life; the doctor came the other day to decide on my fitness for the London journey. He said 'Your wife says you are still working.' 'Yes' says I. 'How much?' said he. 'Just finished a play on Jonathan Swift'[1] says I. 'Do you find those stairs very tiring?' says he. 'No' says I. 'Go up very slowly?' says he. 'No' says I. 'You are a wonderful man,' says he, 'but blood-pressure is up.' 'What am I to eat?' says I. 'Well now,' says he, 'I will tell you something that would ruin me if my patients knew it. We took ten people with blood-pressure the other day and clapped them into ten beds in the hospital and we gave five everything that should have been bad for them, and the other five everything that should have been good, and at the end of it there was not a pin's difference. I think it wouldn't do you any harm if you soused.' Yours affectionately W B YEATS

Here is a dream I had about a certain Betty Duncan who has just run off for the third time, and her father Jim Duncan. Betty Duncan kept shooting off rockets and whenever a rocket exploded Jim Duncan picked up the stick and baptised it out of a soap dish. He is devoted to his grandchildren.

TO LADY GREGORY

Oct 29 [*Postmark* 1930]   [*On printed Rapallo notepaper but obviously written from Dublin.*]

My dear Lady Gregory: I should have written long ago, but I have been dictating in the morning and tired and procrastinating the rest of the time. Yesterday George decided that I was not fit for town life, and when I get back from England (where I go on Friday) I

[1] *The Words upon the Window-Pane*, produced at the Abbey Theatre on November 17, 1930, and published by the Cuala Press in April 1934.

shall probably find that we have shifted to a furnished house in some place like Dalkey. I think George's decision was hurried by the state of irritation into which I was thrown by *King Lear*,[1] which I thought but half visual and badly acted by everybody. I was too tired to stay beyond the middle but will see the second half to-night. McCormick used all his power in the first act and had nothing left to work up to later on. An elaborate verse play is beyond our people. If I dared I would put *King Lear* into modern English and play it in full light throughout—leaving the words to suggest the storm—and invite an audience of Connaught farmers, or sailors before the mast. However the moment it became intelligible it would be put on the list of censored books.

There is an absurd little man called —— who walked to Holyhead from London to see me, and is now walking from Dublin to Gort to see you. I told him that he should not on any account inflict himself on you for more than an hour, and I wish I had said half an hour. He came here in a black velveteen coat with an immense black bow tie and a white waistcoat. I found out after long questioning that he bought the costume when he persuaded a German society to let him lecture instead of an English bishop who did not turn up. He said 'I thought I should be respectively [*sic*] dressed as I had to take the bishop's place.' If he does not wear that costume he will wear an embroidered Russian blouse.

George hates him; I find him harmless. We both did our best to keep him out of Galway.

I wish I were back with you at Coole—nothing is good for me now but utter quiet. Yours affectionately   W B YEATS

Swift is in rehearsal—I shall dedicate it to you.

The Athenaeum Club wants to make me a member under a rule which authorises the election of a limited number of distinguished persons, without the usual formalities, and Rothenstein writes that 'it is a greater honour than a knighthood and less expensive than a peerage' but I gather that entrance fee and subscription will make it more expensive than it would be worth for a man so little in London as I.

---

[1] *King Lear* was first produced at the Abbey Theatre on November 26, 1928. Yeats had evidently seen a revival.

TO JOSEPH HONE

Nov 20 [? *1930*]   42 *Fitzwilliam Square*

My dear Hone, Lady Gregory has just read your book and is delighted with it—I imagine she skipped the philosophy.[1] You have set Berkeley in his Irish world, and made him amusing, animated and intelligible. He is of the utmost importance to the Ireland that is coming into existence, as I hope to show in my introduction. I want Protestant Ireland to base some vital part of its culture upon Burke, Swift and Berkeley. Rossi's help is of course of the first importance. Gentile and other Italian philosophers found themselves on Berkeley, and Rossi has the further advantage of being an authority on Berkeley's immediate predecessors and contemporaries. You and I are absorbed in Ireland but he sees Berkeley's European position.
Yours
                                                                W B YEATS

TO OLIVIA SHAKESPEAR

Tuesday [*Dec.* 2. *Postmark Dec* 4, *1930*] 42 *Fitzwilliam Square*

My dear Olivia: Forgive my not writing, but I have been excited and busy—first my play which has been a much greater success than I ever hoped and beautifully acted, and then the writing an introduction for it, a series of comments on various statements about Swift contained in it. I want to bring out a book of four plays called *My Wheels and Butterflies*—the wheels are the four introductions. Dublin is said to be full of little societies meeting in cellars and garrets so I shall put this rhyme on a fly-leaf

>   To cellar and garret
>   A wheel I send
>   But every butterfly
>   To a friend.

The 'wheels' are addressed to Ireland mainly—a scheme of intellectual nationalisms. Every morning I have said 'I will write to Olivia' and then having worked my two hours or so I am tired.

[1] *Bishop Berkeley, his Life, Writings and Philosophy* by J. M. Hone and M. M. Rossi, with an introduction by W. B. Yeats. London: Faber & Faber, 1931.

779

The children are back from Switzerland since Saturday. Anne has I am told perfect French. She is growing very pretty and remain[s] very much of a flirt. On Saturday night she was roused up to see Lennox and put her arms round his neck. Next morning she revealed that owing to her sleepiness she had not known who it was. 'But,' said George, 'you put your arm round his neck.' Upon which Anne said without the slightest sense of shame 'Oh I could see it was a man.' I suppose she will presently be smitten with shyness.

James Stephens's three best books are *The Demigods*—it came out at the same time as Anatole France's book about the angels and has the same theme—I prefer it, *The Crock of Gold* and *The Land of Youth*, both of which I have loved. He is in the telephone book—Colindale 6126. Yours affectionately   W B YEATS

TO OLIVIA SHAKESPEAR

Dec 27 [Postmark Dec 28, 1930]   42 *Fitzwilliam Square*

My dear Olivia: I think you owe me a letter but I am not sure. I know that I have not heard for a long time. I am working very hard but have rested these last two days. Macmillan are going to bring out an Edition de Luxe of all my work published and unpublished. The unpublished to include *A Vision* (rewritten of course), my *Wheels and Butterflies* (a book of plays and essays almost finished) and *Byzantium* (the new book of verse). The new stories of Hanrahan and those Cuala diaries and the Sophocles versions. I am to be ready next autumn at latest. Months of re-writing. What happiness! At the moment I am putting the last touches to a play called *The Resurrection*—young men talking, the apostles in the next room overwhelmed by the crucifixion. Christ newly arisen passes silently through. I wrote a chaotic dialogue on this theme some years ago. But now I have dramatic tension throughout.

Anne and Michael have a French governess every morning and are plainly very fluent. I wish I could send Michael to a school at Cambridge where Greek and Latin are learned in the same way and spoken, but we must keep him under our eyes for a couple of years yet, and by that time I shall have submitted to the local influences or he will be too old to pick up languages without knowing it.

I have a great sense of abundance—more than I have had for years. George's ghosts have educated me. Yours affectionately

W B YEATS

TO OLIVIA SHAKESPEAR

Feb [*Postmark Feb 9, 1931*]   42 *Fitzwilliam Square*

My dear Olivia, I am convinced that those authorised persons helped to punctuate the Lord's Prayer 'which art (stop) in heaven (stop) . . . thy kingdom come (STOP).' Placing the last stop right required of course the grace of God.

I have really finished *A Vision*—I turn over the pages and find nothing to add. I am still at Coole but go to Dublin to-morrow to dictate *A Vision* from my MSS to a certain young man, a friend of McGreevy's, who has come from Paris for the purpose. I write very much for young men between twenty and thirty, as at that age, and younger, I wanted to feel that any poet I cared for—Shelley let us say—saw more than he told of, had in some sense seen into the mystery. I read more into certain poems than they contained, to satisfy my interest. The young men I write for may not read my *Vision*—they may care too much for poetry—but they will be pleased that it exists. Even my simplest poems will be the better for it. I think I have done one good deed in clearing out of the state from death to birth all the infinities and eternities, and picturing a state as 'phenomenal' as that from birth to death. I have constructed a myth, but then one can believe in a myth—one only assents to philosophy. Heaven is an improvement of sense—one listens to music, one does not read Hegel's logic. An oriental sage would understand even that very abstruse allusion to the Lord's Prayer. Apart from these young men—who will only glance at *A Vision*—I shall have a few very devoted readers like a certain doctor in the North of England who sits every night for one half hour in front of a Buddha lit with many candles—his sole escape from a life of toil. He has already found some proof, which he has not explained, that it is all 'very ancient.' Perhaps if I recover my health and am not too poor I may travel to meet such men. When I was young—but ah my dear, old men must be content with philosophies. Yours ever   W B YEATS

TO OLIVIA SHAKESPEAR

August 2 [1931] *Coole Park*

My dear Olivia: I have not written through procrastination. When I got to Dublin, Berkeley and an Italian philosopher who came to work on Hone's book absorbed my vitality. The Italian spoke English copiously, never hesitated for a word but had never heard a word of English spoken till he came to Ireland. You can imagine my toil. I go to Dublin in a couple of days, and bring him down here then for a few days. Then he goes back to Italy with I hope a faultless Irish accent. I finished my own work on Berkeley two or three weeks ago and since then I have been writing poetry—that poem I told you of in London among the rest and to be sent to you presently—I write in bed in the morning and in the afternoon think of writing to my friends but procrastinate. When I stop verse and take up some lighter work for a time my letters will I hope be more abundant; for the present I beg for letters even if I do not answer.

I am reading the *Savage Messiah* [1] a most moving book but one wonders how much is from Miss Brzeska['s] diary and if she was not after all a great novelist. The letters where he speaks of art and literature are Ezra articulate. It is the generation of Bergson. I am full of admiration and respect, but I hate the Jewish element in Bergson, the deification of the moment, that for minds less hard and masculine than Gaudier's turned the world into fruit-salad.

I began a letter to you weeks ago—it lies unfinished on my desk in Dublin, and there I said that later philosophy has in general agreed with your dislike of Berkeley['s] deism. You asked for some book of Croce's but may have meant *The Mind as Pure Art* by Gentile, for that founds itself on Berkeley. It is a dry difficult beautiful book. Croce's *Aesthetics* is much easier and perhaps a better preparation for philosophy.

Though I have not written I am full of affection and remain always yours W B YEATS

[1] *Savage Messiah* by H. S. Ede. London: Heinemann, 1931.

TO OLIVIA SHAKESPEAR

August 30 [1931]   *Coole Park*

My dear Olivia: I too wondered if the diary is genuine. It may exist, that kind of woman probably would keep a diary, and yet serve as a mere excuse for Ede's own reconstruction. He never quotes it and the story ends at Gaudier's death, as though his material ended when he could not draw upon the memories of Gaudier's friends. If the diary were his authority would he not have spent a few pages on Sophie's collapse? If she kept a diary of any psychological quality she would not have ended when her own tragedy began. On the other hand the letters must be genuine, and their extreme freedom of speech—I am thinking among others of that letter in which he describes his greater pleasure in the act when the woman's body is muscular and dry—is strange though not impossible in letters addressed to a woman, with whom he lived platonically, but would be impossible if addressed to a woman who had not sexual experience. I think she must have had experience, have thought herself wronged perhaps and developed an hysterical dread of experience, and that he must have desired her. I cannot think the letters which express that desire forgeries—nobody would dare such a thing. An hysterical woman has sometimes a strong fascination, she is a whirlpool—such a problem to herself that everybody within reach is drawn in. She rouses an ungovernable pity and pity soon touches the senses.

I shall be here for some time ... Meanwhile Lady Gregory is really very ill, constantly without sleep through pain and dreads my going

                   [The rest of this letter is missing.]

TO MARIO M. ROSSI

Oct 5 [1931]   *Coole Park*

Dear Rossi: I thank you very much for your long and valuable quotations from Nicolas of Cusa, which I hope to understand better in a few days. I have got a just published translation of Ludwig Fischer's book *Die Natürliche Ordnung unseres Denkers* made by Mr.

Johnson, the editor of *The Common Place Book*. It deals with the problem of the universe as 'an opposition in unity' and has a long historical section which gives a page or so to Nicolas of Cusa, speaks of him as of great importance.

In some ways I find it easier to understand your exposition of him, but then I have not got deep enough into Ludwig Fischer's thought, which I find hard and salutary, the kind of exact analysis that drives me back to poetry with my vigour renewed. I should have written before but I have been waiting for the Magazine with my notes on Swift [1] which you asked me to send you. I now send it. They are notes to a still unpublished play and some of the paragraphs begin with quotations from the play. The comparison between Swift and Vico may interest you. Vico is known to me through Croce's book which has been translated. I hear the Berkeley is to be out on Oct 15. I may write again when I read it.

Your visit gave great pleasure to Lady Gregory. She continually speaks of it. Yours sincerely   W B YEATS

TO MARIO M. ROSSI[2]

... I have written to you twice and torn up each letter, stamps and all. The truth is that you have pulled me out of my depth. I understand that reality is timeless, and the past and present constitute the most obvious of the antinomies. But I cannot follow your further analyses. There is 'the straight line' in every novelty and there is the circle joined, or the absolute return or finish. There is no spiral, no curve. We have only those two absolutes and all partial returns are constructions of the mind. Is that your thought? Yet every old man has lived differently through Shakespeare's seven ages and there is an annual return of spring or a partly novel spring. Do you mean that in reality it is always the same spring? That we are like a man running round a pillar, who thinks the uneven bit of the floor whenever he comes to it is a new uneven bit and that he has been running in a straight line? Or rather that line and circle are no antinomy? ...

[1] 'The Words upon the Window Pane: a Commentary' was first published in the *Dublin Magazine*, October–December 1931 and January–March 1932.
[2] Fragment.

TO OLIVIA SHAKESPEAR

November. Last Sunday [but one].   *Coole Park*
[Postmark Nov 23, 1931]

My dear Olivia: You ask how long I shall be here. I do not know. I think the family want me to be here while the days are so short, unless Lady Gregory should have to go to a nursing home. My only fixed plan is [to] be in London in Spring. I am trying to get some broadcasting, and do this through Gerald Heard. Negociations have only reached the point however that I should call on them when in London. I was to arrange one broadcast which I can do on arrival.

I go to Dublin for December when my *Dreaming of the Bones* is to be acted, as part of what we are going to call 'Mainly ballet: the Abbey Directors' Sunday entertainments.' These entertainments are to keep our audiences together till the company returns from America. I shall be just long enough in Dublin to see a rehearsal as well as the performance. I was there some days ago to start the rehearsals—it will be admirably played, sung and danced, but we have had to abandon the Rummel music as too difficult.

The night before letters [?] came I went for a walk after dark and there among some great trees became absorbed in the most lofty philosophical conception I have found while writing *A Vision*. I suddenly seemed to understand at last and then I smelt roses. I now realized the nature of the timeless spirit. Then I began to walk and with my excitement came—how shall I say?—that old glow so beautiful with its autumnal tint. The longing to touch it was almost unendurable. The next night I was walking in the same path and now the two excitements came together. The autumnal image, remote, incredibly spiritual, erect, delicate featured, and mixed with it the violent physical image, the black mass of Eden. Yesterday I put my thoughts into a poem which I enclose, but it seems to me a poor shadow of the intensity of the experience.[1] Crazy Jane is more or less

---

[1] 'Crazy Jane and Jack the Journeyman,' included in *Words for Music Perhaps*. The last stanza, in the version sent to Mrs. Shakespear, read:

> But should I lie alone there
> In an empty bed,
> The skein so bound us ghost to ghost,
> When you turned your head
> Passing on the road that night,
> They shall walk when dead.

founded upon an old woman who lives in a little cottage near Gort. She loves her flower-garden—she has just sent Lady Gregory some flowers in spite of the season—and [has] an amazing power of audacious speech. One of her great performances is a description of how the meanness of a Gort shopkeeper's wife over the price of a glass of porter made her so despair of the human race that she got drunk. The incidents of that drunkenness are of an epic magnificence. She is the local satirist and a really terrible one. Yours affectionately

W B YEATS

If you think of any poems of mine that would do for broadcasting tell me. I cannot use again the Belfast poems.[1] I cannot think of more than perhaps two groups—six poems each. I wish I could think of anything else besides poems.

P.S.

Would you write the name of the Chinese book—golden flowers or whatever it is [2]—on the enclosed postcard and post it.

I have no English stamp.

TO JOSEPH HONE

Nov 27 [? 1931] *Coole Park*

My dear Hone, Forgive my delay in thanking you for the Berkeley. The *Sunday Times*, though MacCarthy had plainly neither read your book nor any other works of philosophy, must have sold some copies. I have only seen that review and those in *The Times* and *Times Supplement*. Your book is the kind that produces its effect slowly but always does produce it. You are fortunate that my 'introduction' is so obscure, for it saves you from being reviewed out of the 'introduction' merely because it comes first. My *Poems* when first published by Unwin was always reviewed out of *The Wanderings of Usheen* until I got in a rage and put that poem last.

[1] Yeats had taken part in an Irish Programme broadcast from Belfast on September 8, 1931. The poems he then read were 'The Lake Isle of Innisfree,' 'The Fiddler of Dooney,' 'The Song of Wandering Aengus,' 'Running to Paradise' and 'In Memory of Eva Gore-Booth and Con Markiewicz.'

[2] Possibly *The Secret of the Golden Flower*, an ancient Chinese classic, translated by Richard Wilhelm, with introduction by Professor Jung.

Rossi writes that he sent you an essay on Swift, so that work is I conclude on its way. Yours   W B YEATS

TO L. A. G. STRONG[1]

December 4 [1931]   42 *Fitzwilliam Square*

My dear Strong, Fable and rumour were I believe goddesses and some of the charming stories you tell about me are doubtless their handiwork. As I do not remember anything about it I cannot refute them even if I would. Sometimes when they are in an evil humour they spread very different stories and I am content to take their good gifts as a compensation for their bad. I shall take an early opportunity of making some of those telling retorts my own in very deed. I thank you very much for your essay.[2] My wife reminds me—I am dictating this to her—that I said to her when I came downstairs after reading it 'You must treat me with great reverence to-night,' I was seeing myself as your essay sees me.

Now about your letter of October 21st; I am staying at Coole Park at present, I have been asked to stay with Lady Gregory who is now very old and infirm (private); the family has asked me to be there as much as I can at present. I come up to Dublin only for Abbey business and never stay more than two or three days, and my wife looks through my correspondence and puts such letters as I must attend to myself on my table. I overlooked your book and letter. I have only this moment found them and read the letter. I begin by saying that I hope your child is born and that it is of whichever sex you most desired, and that your wife is well. Now about the Berkeley; I am delighted that you have got it for the *New Statesman*. The only reviews that I have seen up to this are *The Times*, the *Times Supplement*, and the *Sunday Times*. I did not mean my allusion to 'right and left' as a criticism of Dunne. I was merely suggesting an extension of his experiment. By 'before and after' I meant past and future, and these Dunne had investigated with his experiments, and by 'right and left' I meant the relationship in space, not in time, which I am most anxious that he or somebody else should investigate. I won't go into the question now of the infinite observer, for

[1] Dictated.
[2] *A Letter to W. B. Yeats* by L. A. G. Strong. London: Hogarth Press, 1932.

I should have to look up Dunne again. I may perhaps write to you later about it. It happens to touch on a very difficult problem, one I have been a good deal bothered by. If I could know all the past and all the future and see it as a single instant I would still be conditioned, limited, by the form of that past and the form of that future, I would not be infinite. Perhaps you will tell me I misunderstood Dunne, for I am nothing of a mathematician. I came up from Coole yesterday on Abbey business and am returning there on Monday and taking your book with me.

Greetings from both to both. Yours   W B YEATS

TO OLIVIA SHAKESPEAR

Dec 15 [1931]   *Coole Park*

My dear Olivia: Probably you wrote me a charming letter the moment you got mine (enclosing that lyric which should take its place with 'Innisfree' in the popular anthologies), probably you even undertook to celebrate your seventieth birthday the moment I get to London, but if you did your letter has gone astray. I know mine did not because the invaluable Chinese book has come. Now that I write, you will write at the same moment and our letters will cross again and we will never know who owes the other a letter.

I have begun a longish poem called 'Wisdom' in the attempt to shake off 'Crazy Jane' and I begin to think I shall take to religion unless you save me from it. That Chinese book has given me something I have long wanted, a study of meditation that has not come out of the jungle. I distrust the jungle.

After I wrote you I went to Dublin to rehearse my play and when I got there found that I had mistaken the day of the month. I had been dating all my letters wrong and was a week too soon. I came back here and went to Dublin a week later. The play (*Dreaming of the Bones*) as put on the stage with its ceremonial movements (half round the stage meant a mountain climbed) seemed to me very beautiful. It was enthusiastically received. Then I came back here with George, to whom I dictated from my illegible MSS all the corrections and additions to *A Vision*. Two days ago she went back to Dublin taking it with her. I asked her to take it that I might return to verse.

Some time at the end of March the Irish Literary Society celebrates what they are good enough to call my foundation of it forty years ago and I must be there—unless something untoward keeps me here. Probably unless I think it will be all a great bore I will ask you to come to it. I am trying to persuade the government to let me announce at it the formation of an Irish Academy of Letters. If I may do so the dinner will be a great event. But I have just remembered that I once took you to a very boring dinner of the same society, so I am certain that nothing will bring you there again. Yours affectionately   W B YEATS

TO OLIVIA SHAKESPEAR

Jan 3, 1932   *Coole Park*

My dear Olivia: I have been laid up—very bad cold, consequent exhaustion, waking at night and sleeping by day. Yesterday was the first day when I was well enough to think and I spent it in writing verse. I think the Irish Literary Society have picked March 27 for their dinner so I shall be in London from a little before that date. I am arranging with the B.B.C. to broadcast twice when in London and cannot know my dates accurately until this is arranged.

You will be too great a bore if I get religion.[1] I meant to write to you this morning (it is now 3.15) but thought of that sentence of yours, and then wrote a poem, which puts clearly an argument that has gone on in my head for years. When I have finished the poem I began yesterday I will take up the theme in greater fullness. Here is the poem. Heart and soul are speaking: [2]—

    Soul
Search out reality; leave things that seem.
    Heart
What be a singer born and lack a theme?

[1] In his letter of December 15, 1931, Yeats wrote: 'I begin to think I shall take to religion unless you save me from it.' Mrs. Shakespear's reply has not survived, but it would appear that she wrote: 'You will be too great a bore if you get religion,' and it is evidently this sentence which Yeats quotes—or, rather, misquotes—in this letter. In existing letters Mrs. Shakespear declares herself an agnostic, so there could be no question that she would 'get religion.'

[2] This poem, much rewritten, appears as Section VII of 'Vacillation,' in *The Winding Stair*, 1933.

> *Soul*
> Ezekiel's coal and speed leaps out anew.
> *Heart*
> Can there be living speech in heaven's blue?
> *Soul*
> Knock on the door, salvation waits within.
> *Heart*
> And what sang Homer but original sin.

I feel that this is the choice of the saint (St Theresa's ecstasy, Gandhi's smiling face): comedy; and the heroic choice: Tragedy (Dante, Don Quixote). Live Tragically but be not deceived (not the fool's Tragedy). Yet I accept all the miracles. Why should not the old embalmers come back as ghosts and bestow upon the saint all the care once bestowed upon Rameses? Why should I doubt the tale that when St Theresa's tomb was opened in the middle of the nineteenth century the still undecayed body dripped with fragrant oil? I shall be a sinful man to the end, and think upon my death-bed of all the nights I wasted in my youth.

I cannot write more now—I must walk before dark and it is clouding over.

Lady Gregory is much as usual, except that to-day she is unusually hopeful, having had her first night without pain. Yours affectionately

W B YEATS

[*On back of envelope*]
Leave the 'And' out of last line of poem. Have vacillated all day. Not 'And what sang' but 'What sang.'

W B Y

TO JOSEPH HONE

Feb 3 [1932] *Coole Park*

My dear Hone: What is happening? Are you going on with the Swift? An article in to-day's *Irish Press* has put you into my head. De Blacam speaks of the attempt now being made by certain 'Anglo-Irish Leaders' to bring back the Irish Eighteenth Century; he names you, me, AE (this I think a mistake) and Lennox Robinson (his *Brian Cooper*). I did not do more than glance at the rest of the article, which is the usual sort of thing—only the Gael or the Catholic is Irish . . . However he is not discourteous . . .

The Berkeley seems now the established authority, but the full effect will take place slowly for it will be on individuals. You were ignored by the Dublin press because there are only two men in Dublin capable of reviewing such a book—Macran who thinks of nothing but Hegel, and Creed Meredith, who at the moment could probably think of nothing but sweepstakes.

De Blacam's passing mention is valuable as it conveys an idea that something is happening, and that may get it [into] some undergraduate's head. Yours W B YEATS

TO JOSEPH HONE

Feb 14 [1932] *Coole Park*

My dear Hone, I go to Dublin to-morrow (Monday) as I must vote. I shall be there at any rate until Tuesday Feb 23.

I return Swift. It is sometimes profound, sometimes beautiful, sometimes obscure through over concentration (first paragraph), sometimes mixes metaphors (he 'ferrets' in a 'corpse'). The *Criterion* would refuse it because too obviously an introduction to a book. It is less an introduction than a first setting down of what the author intends to prove, and much of it would be transferred to various parts of the book itself. I am not sure if it would commend the book to a publisher who is looking for something easily read. I feel a barrier of language between myself and Rossi, something therefore that seems inexpert.

It is not my Swift though it is part of the truth and may well be the beginning of a more profound Swift criticism. There was something not himself that Swift served. He called it 'freedom' but never defined it and thus has passion. Passion is to me the essential. I was educated upon Balzac and Shakespeare and cannot go beyond them. That passion is his charm. Yours W B YEATS

TO JAMES S. STARKEY (SEUMAS O'SULLIVAN)

Feb 20 [*Postmark* 1932]   42 *Fitzwilliam Square*

My dear O'Sullivan: I wish I could do what you ask but Macmillan blocks the way. I have leave for nothing but the Cuala Press. Owing to the fact that he is about to publish 'an edition de luxe' of my work, when the depression has moved off, he insisted on buying up a limited American edition of my *Oedipus at Colonus* of which I had passed the last proof. I on my side had to return a quite substantial sum of money I had received in advance on the edition. I cannot start on any more such adventures if for no other reason that they are too racking for the nerves. Yours   W B YEATS

TO JOSEPH HONE

March 5 [1932]   *Coole Park*

My dear Hone: Yes I think you might let Starkey have the Swift.[1] We want some organ, and one that pays us nothing is better than no organ at all.

I think your method of translation is a mistake in this essay. An English or Irish reader has a faint prejudice against an Italian because he thinks him given to 'high falutin.' Your translation gives the impression that you are struggling with an over eloquent original, which our language cannot do justice to. This comes from your use of words which English poetry has abandoned for many years. I suggest that when you translate Rossi 'sea' should never become 'ocean' or 'main' or its 'blue' become 'azure' or a 'wave' a 'billow.' If you were a poet not a prose writer you would not use these words because you would feel very acutely that we are in a frenzy of reaction against all the old conventions. I should have warned you that Eliot, who is himself the most typical figure of the reaction, would refuse the essay on that account. Think of his bare poetry. His position would be compromised by its inclusion in the *Criterion*. Your syntax also in translating Rossi should be as simple as possible, but that it probably is—I have not the essay for

[1] 'Essay on the Character of Swift' by M. M. Rossi, translated by Joseph Hone, was printed in *Life and Letters*, September 1932.

comparison. I have been blaming myself for not writing all this before, but unlike most of my countrymen I am timid in finding fault. Yours   W B YEATS

My letter was so long in reaching you because I forgot to post it.

TO OLIVIA SHAKESPEAR

Wednesday [*March* 9. *Postmark Mar* 10, 1932]   *Coole Park*

My dear Olivia, I got your letter last night. On Saturday last I was called to Dublin on Abbey business and have had an amusing time. On Saturday evening a man called and read me a play. He is at present wanted by the police and probably my arrival was reported to him by some railway porter for he is the head of the most extreme of all Irish organizations and of course my bitter opponent politically. His play was impossible as a play but full of the most beautiful humorous dialogue and talk of West of Ireland fishermen. He is by temperament vague and gentle and so always sees himself as a terrible gunman. He told me that when he escaped from prison in an officer's cap and cape he was so 'keyed up' that he would have been furious at the insult if anybody had said he was not an officer. He will always act according to the second nature. For the present, it makes him a very dangerous man. He told me of a man he hates, who sometimes writes articles in the English press against Ireland because as he claims, and half believes, they give him so much suffering that they are the only penance acceptable in the sight of God. That journalist is the sub-editor of an Irish republican newspaper. This same man, if a story I heard is true, lately hit a man in the face, had an instantaneous crisis of the conscience, held his own hands down and said 'Now hit me in the face.' Pirandello and St John of the Cross are strangely mixed up here. One of my Saturday evening visitor's associates is, I have been told, a man with a passion for suffering, he seeks opportunities of being persecuted. But I have told you enough of the Irish political underworld, the strange gallery I and mine play our part before, the 'dying chatelaine' and all the rest of it.

Lady G. is confined to one floor now and has at last consented to take some pain-killing drugs which I have brought her from Dublin, but guaranteed not to contain morphia or to affect the mind. I am not at my best; I cannot spell, thanks to another of those [*word illegible*] and I have a long manuscript by an Indian saint to read—the wonderful thing I told you of: the reality of which the theosophists have dreamed.[1] How they will hate its homely precisions! Yours affectionately   W B YEATS

TO OLIVIA SHAKESPEAR

April 22 [Postmark 1932]   42 *Fitzwilliam Square*

My dear Olivia, When you see the Swami I want you to get him to sing and to tell me what you think of it. He sings little poems in his native tongue, poems of his own, that he sang in India when taken in for the night. I may speak of these songs in my introduction and want to know whether he sings well and what sort of voice he has and what the music (his own) sounds like to a musician. I asked him to sing to you but you must ask him.

This morning I spent house-hunting but so far without result. We must move next month and want an old detached house with a garden. The Shaw-Yeats letter inviting Academicians has been typed out by George for the printer and an appointment with a lawyer and other steps taken.[2]

Ireland I hear feels nothing of the disturbance about the oath they feel in England, is in fact bored. Yours affectionately.

W B YEATS

TO OLIVIA SHAKESPEAR

May 9 [Postmark 1932]   *Coole Park*

My dear Olivia . . . I go to Dublin on Wednesday as Lennox Robinson returns that day from America and I have a lot of Abbey business to do. We have been hit by the bad times and I do not even know whether the new government will continue our sub-

[1] *An Indian Monk* by Shri Purohit Swami, with introduction by W. B. Yeats, published by Macmillan & Co. in September 1932.
[2] The text of this letter of invitation, as finally printed and issued, appears on pp. 801–2.

sidy. For once we have no lack of new plays. Our play-writing, which has been coarse and superficial for four or five years, shows signs of deepening knowledge—at least in two writers. An Irish poet Austin Clarke has just sent me a romance called *The Bright Temptation* which you should get from a library. It is published by George Allen. It is like one of William Morris's romances—12th Century—on the surface, but turns out when you read it to be a charming and humorous defiance of the censorship and its ideals. It is the falling into temptation of a clerical student and all set in a fantastic extravagant world. Read it and tell me should I make him an Academician. I find it very difficult to see, with impartial eyes, these Irish writers who are as it were part of my propaganda. What you wrote me about the Swami is most valuable.

Goodbye for the present. Yours ever   W B YEATS

TO OLIVIA SHAKESPEAR

May 31 [1932]   42 *Fitzwilliam Square*

My dear Olivia: You will have known why I have not written, for you will have seen Lady Gregory['s] death in the papers.[1] I had come to Dublin for a few days to see about Abbey business. On Sunday night at 11.30 I had a telephone message from her solicitor who had been trying to find me all day. I took the first train in the morning but she had died in the night. She was her indomitable self to the last but of that I will not write, or not now.

We have taken a little house at Rathfarnham just outside Dublin. It has the most beautiful gardens I have seen round a small house, and all well stocked. I shall step out from my study into the front garden—but as I write the words I know that I am heartbroken for Coole and its great woods. A queer Dublin sculptor dressed like a workman and in filthy clothes, a man who lives in a kind of slum and has slum children, came the day after Lady Gregory's death 'to pay his respects.' He walked from room to room and then stood where hang the mezzotints and engravings of those under or with whom (I cannot spell to-night—that word looks wrong) the Gregorys have served, Fox, Burke and so on, and after standing silent said

[1] Lady Gregory died on May 22.

'All the nobility of earth.' I felt he did not mean it for that room alone but for lost tradition. How much of my own verse has not been but the repetition of those words. Yours   W B YEATS

TO MARIO M. ROSSI

June 6 [1932]   42 *Fitzwilliam Square*

Dear Rossi: It was kind of you to write. I have lost one who has been to me for nearly forty years my strength and my conscience. I had come away for a few days to do some necessary business arising out of the return of the Irish Players from America, and on Sunday night at 11.30 the Gregory family solicitor 'phoned to me that Lady Gregory was dying. He had been trying to find me for several hours (I had been dining at a friend's). I took the earliest possible train, but Lady Gregory had died in the night. She had been indomitable to the last, seeing to all her household duties and weekly charities—there were many. On the Wednesday though every movement gave her pain and she had long lived between two rooms on the same floor—the room that you had, I think, and a room which I used as a study when you were at Coole—she got herself helped downstairs that she might visit all the chief rooms—'saying good bye' the servants thought.

Your visit to Coole gave her great pleasure. She several times spoke of you as 'dear Rossi' and I wish she had lived to read your beautiful description of Coole lake—it [was] published, as you no doubt know, in one of the Dublin newspapers a couple of days after her death.

When she died the great house died too. The heirlooms and pictures go to Celbridge—Vanessa's House.[1] Yours ever

W B YEATS

TO H. J. C. GRIERSON

June 9 [1932]   42 *Fitzwilliam Square*

Dear Grierson: Your letter was sent on from my old house in Merrion Square, and I have no doubt your book will be sent on

[1] Esther Vanhomrigh, Swift's 'Vanessa,' settled at Marlay Abbey, Celbridge, on the river Liffey, about 1714.

too. (The Abbey Theatre is my safest address—I am leaving here for a new house in a month [1] and go to America with the players in the Autumn.) I look forward to your book for you are one of the few scholars with whose work I never quarrel. Which reminds me that your daughter delighted me. She had charm and she had character so well blended that one did not know which was which. I would like to have her address, though indeed, seeing that I am more and more fixed here apart from this American tour, it seems unlikely that we should meet.

My summer will be spent over proof sheets: my own new collected edition [2]—limited to 300 copies—and the autobiography of an Indian monk which I persuaded him to write for its own sake and for the sake of a light it throws on discoveries that Lady Gregory and I made thirty years ago in the Irish cottages. It contains what Christianity, as priests have shaped it, took out of our legends. Lady Gregory read the typed copy a little before she died. I may also have work to do on Lady Gregory's unpublished memoirs and that she left in my charge. Yours ever   W B YEATS

Up till three months ago I had for a year or more written nothing but verse, then my imagination stopped and has showed no sign of moving since.

TO OLIVIA SHAKESPEAR

June 30 [*Postmark* 1932]   42 *Fitzwilliam Square*

My dear Olivia, Two weeks ago I wrote you a long letter, but I wrote in such an excited condition of gloom that I tore it up, stamped envelope and all. Now I am normal and cheerful, though at the moment weary. I have had a long directors' meeting at the theatre, and then had my sister to lunch and then a discussion as to designs. I have had that rarest of things a success in my own family. You remember those stations of the cross. I got three examples designed

---

[1] The move to Riversdale, Rathfarnham, was made in July 1932.
[2] Plans had been made for a limited edition of Yeats's Collected Works to be completed in eleven volumes. A prospectus of this, which was to be called the Coole Edition, was issued in 1939, after Yeats's death, but the second world war involved delays, and eventually only two volumes, the Definitive Edition of the Poems, limited to 375 copies, appeared in 1949.

and worked in preparation for Eucharistic Week. The whole set has been sold and my sister has profitable work till next May. My next scheme will be much more ambitious and much more charming —at least it will if I can come to terms with a certain designer. The last designs were all St Peter's at Rome and a bore, the furthest the average Catholic mind can go back. Now Byzantium, the ages of faith and modern perversion. The house at Westminster used by Wilde and his friends had a really noble crucifix, and —— will end at Lourdes. I have found the perfect designer. St Peter's is so salubrious.

This is the last letter you will get from this house. George is at our new house, painting walls and doors and generally moving in. I shall go to a hotel in a few days, probably at Glendalough in Co. Wicklow, and then to our new house 'Riversdale, Willbrook, Rathfarnham.' There apple trees, cherry trees, roses, smooth lawns and no long climb upstairs. I shall be there three months, then after two weeks in London I start for America and lecture but will return in time for your seventieth birthday. I spend my days correcting proofs. I have just finished the first volume, all my lyric poetry, and am greatly astonished at myself. As it is all speech rather than writing, I keep saying what man is this who in the course of two or three weeks—the improvisation suggests the tune—says the same thing in so many different ways. My first denunciation of old age I made in *The Wanderings of Usheen* (end of part 1) before I was twenty and the same denunciation comes in the last pages of the book. The swordsman throughout repudiates the saint, but not without vacillation. Is that perhaps the sole theme—Usheen and Patrick—'so get you gone Von Hügel though with blessings on your head'? Yours affectionately   W B YEATS

TO OLIVIA SHAKESPEAR

July 8 [1932]   *Royal Hotel*
                                                  Glendalough

My dear Olivia: Yesterday I left Fitzwilliam Square that George might pack the contents of my study. I shall be here for I think eight days and then go to our new house Riversdale, Willbrook,

Rathfarnham. I hope I shall there re-create in some measure the routine that was my life at Coole, the only place where I have ever had unbroken health. I am just too far from Dublin to go there without good reason and too far, I hope, for most interviewers and the less determined travelling bores. I shall have a big old fruit garden all to myself—the study opens into it and it is shut off from the flower garden and the croquet and tennis lawns and from the bowling-green. George is painting my walls lemon yellow and the doors green and black. We have a lease for but thirteen years but that will see me out of life. George will probably try to renew the lease but there is some building project that may defeat her. At any rate the home will be there while the children are being educated and making friends.

I have brought with me to this hotel only two books, Virginia Woolf's *Orlando* which I shall probably find faint of pulse and dislike and *The Saint and Mary Kate* by Frank O'Connor, one of my Academicians to be. I recommend it to you—a beautiful strange book. Yours affectionately   W B YEATS

TO OLIVIA SHAKESPEAR

July 25 [1932]   *Riversdale*
                                                    Willbrook
                                                  Rathfarnham

My dear Olivia, I am writing in my new study—sometimes I go out of the glass-door into the fruit garden to share the gooseberries with the bullfinches. I can hear the workmen putting in the electric bells; through the window to my left I can see pergolas covered with roses. At first I was unhappy, for everything made me remember the great rooms and the great trees of Coole, my home for nearly forty years, but now that the pictures are up I feel more content. This little creeper-covered farm-house might be in a Calvert woodcut, and what could be more suitable for one's last decade? George's fine taste has made the inside almost as beautiful as the garden which has some fame among gardeners.

Read *The Coloured Dome* by Francis Stuart. It is strange and exciting in theme and perhaps more personally and beautifully written than any book of our generation; it makes you understand the strange Ireland that is rising up here. What an inexplicable thing sexual selection is. Iseult picked this young man, by what seemed half chance, half a mere desire to escape from an impossible life, and when he seemed almost imbecile to his own relations. Now he is her very self made active and visible, her nobility walking and singing. If luck comes to his aid he will be our great writer. Read also *The Saint and Mary Kate* by Frank O'Connor. The same theme but from outside by a realist. When you read these unpolitical books I will write to you about politics.

Last night a new play by Lennox Robinson [1]—a packed house, great enthusiasm and excellent acting—the theme a mother's jealousy of her daughter . . . Yours affectionately   W B YEATS

TO JAMES JOYCE [2]

September 2, 1932   *Riversdale*

My dear Joyce, Bernard Shaw and I are busy founding an Academy of Irish Letters, we are nominating the first members, twenty-five, who have done creative work with Ireland as the subject matter, and ten who have given adequate grounds for their election but do not fall within this definition. The creators Academicians, the others Associates. When we began talking over members we found we had to make this division or we should have been over-run with people from England or Scotland with a little Irish blood and a great desire to acquire a national character.

Of course the first name that seemed essential both to Shaw and myself was your own, indeed you might say of yourself as Dante said 'If I stay who goes, if I go who stays?' Which means that if you go out of our list it is an empty sack indeed. By the end of next week I shall have the signed form of nomination and I will send it to you with a copy of the rules. I would however think it a great thing if you would trust us so far as to give your assent when this letter reaches you. It will have to be sent on from your London

[1] *All's Over Then* by Lennox Robinson was produced at the Abbey Theatre on July 25. It is probable that Yeats is a day out in dating this letter.
[2] Dictated.

solicitor's and I am alarmed lest your name does not reach me in time. There will be no subscription, the little money wanted, apart from fifty pounds Shaw has given us, will be raised by lectures. The Academy will be a vigorous body capable of defending our interests, negotiating with Government, and I hope preventing the worst forms of censorship. All the writers here who are likely to form our Council are students of your work.[1] Yours W B YEATS

TO PROSPECTIVE ACADEMICIANS

THE IRISH ACADEMY OF LETTERS

Dear Sir, We have at present in Ireland no organisation representing *Belles Lettres*, and consequently no means whereby we Irish authors can make known our views, nor any instrument by which action can be taken on our behalf.

There is in Ireland an official censorship possessing, and actively exercising, powers of suppression which may at any moment confine an Irish author to the British and American market, and thereby make it impossible for him to live by distinctive Irish literature.

As our votes are counted by dozens instead of thousands and are therefore negligible, and as no election can ever turn on our grievances, our sole defence lies in the authority of our utterance. This, at least, is by no means negligible, for in Ireland there is still a deep respect for intellectual and poetic quality. In so far as we represent that quality we can count on a consideration beyond all proportion to our numbers, but we cannot exercise our influence unless we have an organ through which we can address the public, or appeal collectively and unanimously to the Government.

[1] Joyce did not accept membership of the Irish Academy of Letters. Writing from Nice, he replied gratefully to this letter and sent his thanks also to Bernard Shaw, whom he had never met. He said that his situation was unlikely to change, and that he did not feel he had the least right to accept nomination. In saying this he probably referred to his voluntary exile from Ireland.

The following were the original members of the Irish Academy of Letters: *Founder Members:* George Bernard Shaw, William Butler Yeats, George W. Russell (AE), Miss E. OE. Somerville, Padraic Colum, Lennox Robinson, Seumas O'Sullivan, T. C. Murray, St. John Ervine, Liam O'Flaherty, Forrest Reid, Brinsley Macnamara, Austin Clarke, F. R. Higgins, Oliver St. John Gogarty, Frank O'Connor, Peadar O'Donnell, Francis Stuart, Sean O'Faolain. *Associate Members:* Eugene O'Neill, Helen Waddell, Walter Starkie, J. M. Hone, Stephen Gwynn, T. E. Shaw (Lawrence), L. A. G. Strong, John Eglinton.

We must therefore found an Academy of *Belles Lettres*. Will you give us your name as one of the founder members?

In making this claim upon you we have no authority or mandate beyond the fact that the initiative has to be taken by somebody, and our age and the publicity which attaches to our names makes it easier for us than for younger writers.

Please send your reply to the Provisional Hon. Secretary, George Russell, Esq., 17 Rathgar Avenue, Dublin. Yours faithfully,

G BERNARD SHAW
W B YEATS

TO OLIVIA SHAKESPEAR

Oct 1 [*Postmark Oct* 2, 1932] *Riversdale*

My dear Olivia, I shall be in London on about Oct 8 at the Savile Club, 69 Brook St. What are you doing on Sunday (9th)? I go to America on Oct. 21.

I enclose picture of this house and myself from the *Dublin Evening Mail*. They have transferred the word 'beautiful,' which belongs to the gardens, to the little plain eighteenth-century house. If I were a young man I would dream of the day when I would be rich enough to take out the plate-glass. The downstairs right-hand window is that of my study (there is a glass door behind the conservatory from study to garden and a window into the conservatory). It is a long room, walls and ceiling all lemon yellow. It is full of pictures. The room upstairs is my bedroom and there too there is another window (not shown) where the meat bone hangs for the tomtits. The great flowers in the portrait of myself are poker flowers. We are surrounded by trees. I have no time for a real letter. Yours affectionately

W B YEATS

I was at a séance near here last week. The medium, a Mrs. Duncan. The child control got reminiscent and described having seen Hannen Swaffer in pyjamas 'without a bum' and washing his face with a napkin dipped in a tumbler. He seems to have admitted her accuracy.

TO OLIVIA SHAKESPEAR

[*Postmark Jan 1, 1933*]   *The Waldorf-Astoria*
New York

My dear Olivia: My tour is ending. I leave this day week. I have earned or shall have earned about £600 for myself, and collected almost exactly the same amount for the Irish Academy of Letters.[1] My mind is like an hotel lobby—endless movement seemingly nowhither. I have read *Assault at Arms* and thought little of it, *Women in Love*, *The Rainbow* and *Sons and Lovers* with excitement, and have

---

[1] When Yeats returned from his last American lecture tour, he left the following memorandum with his friend Judge Richard Campbell, a New York jurist, who had been active in raising funds in America for the Irish Academy of Letters:

> The money which I have received in New York for the Irish Academy of Letters I propose to keep as far as possible intact until a minimum of £1200 has been obtained. I hope to be able to put, say, £1000 to capital. This will enable a prize to be given for the best Irish book (not manuscript) of the year (or since the last award) by an author under 35, or to the best first book (not manuscript)—members of the Academy to be eligible. The moment when a prize of, say, £50 may be of the utmost importance to a writer is when he has given up his position in office or workshop, and is trying to make a living as a professional writer. Very few writers, even of those who attain a vast popularity, escape from a hard struggle during their first ten years of authorship.
>
> In addition to this £1000 I want a sum of about £200 to get a bronze medal designed by some famous artist—possibly Milles—to be awarded at rare intervals to the best Irish book of the year, irrespective of the author's age.
>
> It is probable, as Mr. Russell considers his appointment as secretary as but temporary, that I shall want a sum of about £25 a year to pay some young man for the loss of time involved in the secretaryship of the Academy of Letters. It may be necessary in the near future to pay an instalment of this salary out of capital.   W B YEATS

The Academy gave three Awards: The Harmsworth Award, bestowed by the Harmsworth family, of one hundred pounds annually for a work of 'imaginative prose.' This has since lapsed.

The Casement award, bestowed by Marquis MacDonald (U.S.A.), of fifty pounds annually, alternating between drama and poetry. This was named after Roger Casement, and was first awarded in August 1933. This also has lapsed.

The O'Growney Award, bestowed by Dr. McCartan, of fifty pounds per annum for three years, beginning in April 1934. It was for Gaelic, and was named after O'Growney, the Gaelic scholar.

There is also the Gregory Medal, bestowed every three years, and so named in memory of Lady Gregory. This comes from the money collected in America by Yeats and Judge Campbell. The medal was designed by Maurice Lambert and fifteen items were struck. Three 'foundation' awards were made in 1935, to Bernard Shaw, W. B. Yeats, and AE. Later awards of the Medal were made to Douglas Hyde, Somerville & Ross, Eoin McNeill, Stephen Gwynn and Padraic Colum.

had a convincing séance with Mrs. Crandon of Boston. I stay with her Wednesday and Thursday for more séances. I am in as near perfect health as I can recall ever having been and I have nothing to say—this hotel lobby on my shoulders is a dumb beast. I can but write Yours affectionately W B YEATS

TO OLIVIA SHAKESPEAR

Jan 29 [1933] *Riversdale*

My dear Olivia: I arrived here last night. I had reached London the day before (Friday) and spent Friday night in the Euston Hotel. I wavered between wiring to you on the chance that you might be in on Friday evening, and looking up the Swami. I rejected you, my dear, and chose the Swami. I had Alan Duncan with me. Mrs. Foden had written to me to see an American lecture-agent on his behalf. I had seen two and wanted to tell him so, and still more to persuade him not to go to America at all. This I succeeded in doing. After I have done my work here I will return to London to see my friends. I have been successful. I have brought George about £700 and the Academy all the money it wants. It can now give an annual prize of £50 to a young Irish writer or a bi-annual prize of £100; a bronze medal, designed by some famous sculptor, irrespective of age. I had meant to lecture with these objects in London but that is now unnecessary.

George has just told me of your brother's horrible illness. You have, I need not say, my sympathy. How strange this violence, come to one [who] was always so gentle! Yours affectionately

W B YEATS

I will [write] again in a few days.

TO OLIVIA SHAKESPEAR

Feb 2 (perhaps) [*Postmark Feb* 3, 1933] *Riversdale*

My dear Olivia: I send you my new book.[1] It was published while I was in America and I saw it yesterday for the first time. George

[1] *Words for Music Perhaps*. It had been published by the Cuala Press on November 14, 1932.

says that letters have come from Masefield, Bottomley and others full of praise, and among the rest an offer of an honorary degree at Cambridge. I am gratified. Here I am, I suppose, about to be involved in a four years' conflict with the ignorant. (An Irish government need not go to the country for five years.) While I was away free articles were sent to country newspapers from Dublin— from some Jesuit, anti-Catholic friends declare—attacking the Irish Academy of Letters. I got all the money I want for the Academy in America. If I were a young man I would welcome four years of conflict, for it creates unity among the educated classes, and force De Valera's Ministers, in all probability, to repudiate the ignorance that has in part put them into power. Yours affectionately

W B YEATS

TO OLIVIA SHAKESPEAR

Feb 21 [1933]   *Riversdale*

My dear Olivia, No—I am not coming over for your birthday. I do not think your invitation has been pressing enough—besides I have just had the influenza and do not get up till midday. I got it two days after my arrival and spent a considerable time in bed. This is my first letter. I lectured on Friday last (and got through it with toil and difficulty) an arrangement made months ago—a great audience. All part of the fight over the Academy, against which the Jesuits and the Catholic Press have been and are active. Fortunately, even in this country, they can merely make a row in the kitchen.

Have you read *Louis Lambert* of recent years?—I have just re-read it and think of making 'Michael Robartes' write an annotation or even of doing it myself.[1] Perhaps *Faust*, *Louis Lambert*, *Seraphita* and *Axel* are our sacred books, man self-sufficing and eternal, though *Axel* is but a spectacle, an echo of the others, as *Louis Lambert* might have been of that saying of Swedenborg's that the sexual intercourse of the angels is a conflagration of the whole being.

I was very glad to get your letter about my poems, and above all to know that you like the poems that you name—by 'Coole

[1] Yeats wrote an essay on Balzac's *Louis Lambert* which was printed in the *London Mercury*, July 1934, and included in *Essays 1931 to 1936* issued by the Cuala Press in 1937.

Park' I conclude you mean both the poems under the name. I prefer the second I think. I have I think of late come to a coherent grasping of reality and whether that will make me write or cease to write I do not know. I have learnt a good deal from the Swami, who suddenly makes all wisdom if you ask him the right questions. I do not think his book has 'fallen flat.' Mrs. Foden says that Macmillan is satisfied with the sales, an American edition is coming out and may, I should think, be almost a best seller there, where there is no anti-Indian prejudice. At any rate it should do well.

Do not think of me as living here amid disturbances—everything is peaceful, but you are right in comparing De Valera to Mussolini or Hitler. All three have exactly the same aim so far as I can judge. Meanwhile living is cheap, the trouble is yet to come I suppose. I shall go to London later but not until I have got the Academy well started. Yours affectionately W B YEATS

When is your birthday by the by?

TO OLIVIA SHAKESPEAR

March 9 [Postmark 1933] *Riversdale*

My dear Olivia, I shall be in London on April 10. I had meant to go rather sooner as my gardener says I should not miss the garden in April. You can apply much of the Swami thought to our life if you translate it. 'Act and remain apart from action.'

During the last few days I have been in conflict with certain people in the government about the Abbey. I had to risk its future: only yesterday did I get the decision I wished. I watch myself with interest. I found that once I had a clear idea, and knew I was not acting from temper, I did not seem to be personally involved. I looked on as if some stranger was doing it all. I had an hour's interview with De Valera. I had never met him before and I was impressed by his simplicity and honesty though we differed throughout. It was a curious experience, each recognised the other's point of view so completely. I had gone there full of suspicion but my suspicion vanished at once. You must not believe what you read in the English papers. They decide moral questions in the interest of their parties and express their decisions with a complacency that rouses other nations to fury. Here I think we are generally troubled about right and wrong, we don't decide easily. The hungry man is nearer to the Saint than the full man. 'A hair divides the false and true'—one should never be satisfied in any controversy until one has found the hair—one is liable to think it must look like a ship's cable.

I wish I could put the Swami's lectures into the Cuala series but I cannot. My sister's books are like an old family magazine. A few hundred people buy them all and expect a common theme. Only once did I put a book into the series that was not Irish—Ezra's Noh plays—and I had to write a long introduction to annex Japan to Ireland.

I have finished my essay on *Louis Lambert*. How one loves Balzac's audience—great ladies, diplomatists, everybody who goes to grand opera, and ourselves. Then think of Tolstoy's—all the bores, not a poor sinner amongst them.

At the club the other day I spent an hour reading Comte de Tilly but when I went back for another read it had gone. I like the love affairs but I would [like] more detail, they are too abstract. That affair in the carriage which was so unsatisfactory. One feels that neither the Persian nor the pedantic Indian amorist should have omitted from his work, travelling by carriage.

The Comte de Tilly should have been able to refer to precedents, or to create one, to find perhaps a new rhythm.

Joyce and D. H. Lawrence have however almost restored to us the Eastern simplicity. Neither perfectly, for D. H. Lawrence romanticises his material, with such words as 'essential fire,' 'darkness' etc, and Joyce never escapes from his Catholic sense of sin. Rabelais seems to escape from it by his vast energy. Yet why not take Swedenborg literally and think we attain, in a partial contact, what the spirits know throughout their being. He somewhere describes two spirits meeting, and as they touch they become a single conflagration. His vision may be true, Newton's cannot be. When I saw at Mrs. Crandon's objects moved and words spoken from some aerial centre, where there was nothing human, I rejected England and France and accepted Europe. Europe belongs to Dante and the witches' sabbath, not to Newton. Yours affectionately

W B YEATS

TO OLIVIA SHAKESPEAR

March 14 [*Postmark March* 16, 1933]   *Riversdale*

My dear Olivia: In looking through some recent letters of yours I find that you asked me what the work was that kept me from London for the present. I shall be there on April 10th; but I could not get away much sooner because of the Irish Academy. All Irish institutions tend to fly apart in their early months, but if they survive those months are immortal. The Irish Academy has all the usual tendencies.

Can we or can we not accept a hundred a year from 'a corrupt Sunday Newspaper' (*Sunday* ——)? I say 'yes' but I am not through the wood yet. Then I cannot leave before the Budget because a Government Director has to be chosen for the Abbey. I have already fought off a man, who would have brought us under complete clerical domination. I have finished my essay on *Louis Lambert* and some Irish historical notes. To-morrow I begin a longish poem which should last me until I start for London. Yours affectionately

W B YEATS

I am in correspondence with American backers about an Academy medal by Paul Manship the greatest American sculptor.

TO OLIVIA SHAKESPEAR

April [*Postmark* 1933]   *Riversdale*

My dear Olivia: Will it be all right if I come to London on April 19? Will you have returned from your Easter holidays? or Easter distraction?

I have been in a dream finishing a poem, the first I have done for perhaps a year. I have written nothing in verse since Lady Gregory's death. American lectures and so on filled up my time. I have endless occupation always, which in some way feeds my verse when the moment comes. At the moment I am trying in association with [an] ex-cabinet minister, an eminent lawyer, and a philosopher, to work out a social theory which can be used against Communism in Ireland—what looks like emerging is Fascism modified by religion.

This country is exciting. I am told that De Valera has said in private that within three years he will be torn in pieces. It reminds me of a saying by O'Higgins to his wife 'Nobody can expect to live who has done what I have.' No sooner does a politician get into power than he begins to seek unpopularity. It is the cult of sacrifice planted in the nation by the executions of 1916. Read O'Flaherty's novel *The Martyr*, a book forbidden by our censor, and very mad in the end, but powerful and curious as an attack upon the cult. I asked a high government officer once if he could describe the head of the I.R.A. He began 'That is so and so who has [the] cult of suffering and is always putting himself in positions where he will be persecuted.'

Michael is back for the Easter holidays and there is much croquet. George is always busy with her flowers. Yours affectionately

W B YEATS

Not a real letter but I have so many letters to write now the poem is done.

TO DEREK VERSCHOYLE[1]

May 21, 1933   *Riversdale*

Dear Mr. Verschoyle, I send you that review and it is the last I shall ever write.[2] I haven't that gift, my writings have to germinate out of each other. I spent about ten days on the thing and it's not worth the trouble. It is something else altogether, dressed out to look like a review. Yours   W B YEATS

TO OLIVIA SHAKESPEAR

May 22 [Postmark 1933]   *Riversdale*

My dear Olivia: I shall reach London on June 9 (I get my degree on June 8). I have refused an invitation to Cambridge (to read my verse to English Club) as I would have had to go there before June 15

---

[1] Dictated.
[2] Yeats's short review of *Twenty Years a-Growing* by Maurice O'Sullivan appeared in the *Spectator*, June 2, 1933.

and so missing you. You are leaving London on I think June 15 or thereabouts. Please let me know your plans, as I rather forget them.

My two sensations at the moment are Hulme's *Speculations* and *Lady Chatterley's Lover*. The first in an essay called *Modern Art* relates such opposites as *The Apes of God* and *Lady Chatterley*. Get somebody to lend you the last if you have not read it. Frank Harris's *Memoirs* are vulgar and immoral—the sexual passages were like holes burnt with a match in a piece of old newspaper; their appeal to physical sensation was hateful; but *Lady Chatterley* is noble. Its description of the sexual act is more detailed than in Harris, the language is sometimes that of cabmen and yet the book is all fire. Those two lovers, the gamekeeper and his employer's wife, each separated from their class by their love, and by fate, are poignant in their loneliness, and the coarse language of the one, accepted by both, becomes a forlorn poetry uniting their solitudes, something ancient, humble and terrible. Yours affectionately   W B YEATS

I write no more that I may catch the post.

TO OLIVIA SHAKESPEAR

May 25 [Postmark May 27, 33]   *Riversdale*

My dear Olivia, I have changed my plans. I go to London on Friday June 2, so please keep some portion of Saturday and Sunday for me. On Monday I go to Oxford where I spend the night at the Eights' Club and then go to Cambridge for my degree and will be back in London on June 9.

Of course Lawrence is an emphasis directed against modern abstraction. I find the whole book interesting and not merely the sexual parts. They are something that he sets up as against the abstraction of an age that he thinks dead from the waist downward. Of course happiness is not where he seems to place it. We are happy when for everything inside us there is an equivalent something outside us. I think it was Goethe said this. One should add the converse. It is terrible to desire and not possess, and terrible to possess and not desire. Because of this we long for an age which has the unity which Plato somewhere defined as sorrowing and rejoicing over the same things. How else escape the Bank Holiday crowd?

I have bought a suit of rough blue serge. Yours W B YEATS

Read *Twenty Years a-Growing* or some of it. I once told you that you would be happy if you had twelve children and lived on limpets. There are limpets on the Great Blasket.

TO BARON ERIC PALMSTIERNA

June 3 [1933] *Savile Club*

Dear Baron Palmstierna, I am in England for a few days as they are conferring an Honorary Degree upon me at Cambridge next week. I am giving a dinner party at the Savile Club on my birthday, June 13, at 8 o'clock. Would you do me the honour of dining with me? Kant said the guests at dinner should be not less than the number of the Graces and not more than the number of the Muses. I shall hope for some number between these extremes. Black ties I imagine. Yours W B YEATS

TO OLIVIA SHAKESPEAR

July 13 [1933] *Riversdale*

My dear Olivia, Heaven knows where you are but I suppose this will find you. The garden is full of roses and there are lilies in the lily pond and the croquet goes on from day to day and I can still beat my family. All is well, what more is to be said? I am revising a one-volume edition of my poems and doing odds and ends. I am to write my memory of Coole and Lady Gregory for Macmillan and have made peace with —— ——, who has suddenly and inexplicably turned amiable.

Politics are growing heroic. De Valera has forced political thought to face the most fundamental issues. A Fascist opposition is forming behind the scenes to be ready should some tragic situation develop. I find myself constantly urging the despotic rule of the educated classes as the only end to our troubles. (Let all this sleep in your ear.) I know half a dozen men any one of whom may be Caesar—or Cataline. It is amusing to live in a country where men will always act. Where nobody is satisfied with thought. There is so little in our stocking that we are ready at any moment to turn it inside out, and how can we not feel emulous when we see Hitler juggling with his sausage of stocking. Our chosen colour is blue, and blue shirts are marching about all over the country, and their organiser tells me that it was my suggestion—a suggestion I have entirely forgotten—that made them select for their flag a red St Patrick's cross on a blue ground—all I can remember is that I have always denounced green and commended blue (the colour of my early book covers). The chance of being shot is raising everybody's spirits enormously. There is some politics for you of which your newspapers know nothing (I can write it because my letters are not being opened).

History is very simple—the rule of the many, then the rule of the few, day and night, night and day for ever, while in small disturbed nations day and night race. Yours affectionately

W B YEATS

Tell me always where you are and what you are doing.

TO OLIVIA SHAKESPEAR

July 23 [*Postmark July* 25, 1933]   *Riversdale*

My dear Olivia: I have a lot of dull letters to write, and to make myself sit down on this hot day I have bribed myself by saying that I would begin by writing to you. Yet do I write to you as to my own past.

The great secret is out—a convention of blue-shirts—'National Guards'—have received their new leader with the Fascist salute and the new leader announces reform of Parliament as his business.

When I wrote to you, the Fascist organiser of the blue shirts had told me that he was about to bring to see me the man he had selected for leader that I might talk my anti-democratic philosophy. I was ready, for I had just re-written for the seventh time the part of *A Vision* that deals with the future. The leader turned out to be

Gen[eral] O'Duffy, head of the Irish police for twelve years, and a famous organiser. The man who brought him was one of the two men who came to me when we were threatened with a mutiny in the army. He is an old friend of mine, served in India, is crippled with wounds . . . and therefore dreams an heroic dream. 'We shall be assassinated,' he said, 'but others have been chosen to take our place' —his dream perhaps but possibly not. Italy, Poland, Germany, then perhaps Ireland. Doubtless I shall hate it (though not so much as I hate Irish democracy) but it is September and we must not behave like the gay young sparks of May or June. Swinburne called September 'the month of the long decline of roses.' The *Observer*, the *Sunday Times*, the only English papers I see, have noticed nothing though Cosgrave's ablest ministers are with O'Duffy. O'Duffy himself is autocratic, directing the movement from above down as if it were an army. I did not think him a great man though a pleasant one, but one never knows, his face and mind may harden or clarify.

I have done nothing but revise proofs and finish *A Vision*. But shall this week begin my work for the Swami or so I hope. Yours affectionately   W B YEATS

We are about to exhaust our last Utopia, the State. An Irish leader once said 'The future of mankind will be much like its past, pretty mean.'

TO OLIVIA SHAKESPEAR

August 17 [*Postmark Aug* 18, 1933]   *Riversdale*

My dear Olivia, That was an excellent photograph of the Swami. In the photograph of the Swami and Omar they are, no doubt, one as stout as the other. We are all Asiatic in our youth according to the Hegelian philosophy. If you see the Swami tell him that I have now finished my study of various authorities and am about to start my essay upon his master's journey in Tibet.[1] In fact I am answering letters to-day that I may begin the essay to-morrow with a free mind.

The papers will have told you of the 'blue shirt' excitement here. The government is in a panic and has surrounded itself with armed men and armoured cars. The blue shirts are starting up all over

[1] *The Holy Mountain* by Bhagwan Shri Hamsi, London: Faber & Faber, 1934.

the country. The shirts themselves are made in batches of 600 and cannot be made fast enough. The organization is for an independent Ireland within the commonwealth. Whether it succeeds or not in abolishing parliamentary government as we know it to-day, it will certainly bring into discussion all the things I care for. Three months ago there seemed not a trace of such a movement and when it did come into existence it had little apparent importance until that romantic dreamer I have described to you pitched on Gen[eral] O'Duffy for a leader. About him the newspapers have probably told you enough. He seemed to me a plastic man but I could not judge whether he would prove plastic to the opinions of others, obvious political current, or to his own will ('Unity of being'). The man plastic to his own will is always powerful. The opposite kind of man is like a mechanical toy, lift him from the floor and he can but buzz.

I have corrected the proofs of my new book *The Winding Stair* (not the little book published in America but all work I have written since *The Tower*). 'Crazy Jane' poems (the origin of some of these you know) and the little group of love poems that follow are, I think, exciting and strange. Sexual abstinence fed their fire—I was ill and yet full of desire. They sometimes came out of the greatest mental excitement I am capable of. Now for a year I have written some twenty or thirty lines in all—result of recovered health, this crowded Dublin life which always incites me to prose, and the turn given to my mind by a lecture tour. When my essay on the Swami is finished I think of interpolating a little dance play in between the essay and my book about Lady Gregory. It does not matter whether I do or not, one's life is a whole and my account of Coole will add to the solidity of what I have already written. Yours affectionately

W B YEATS

TO OLIVIA SHAKESPEAR

Sept 20 [*Postmark Sept* 21, 1933]   *Riversdale*

My dear Olivia, My new book [1] goes to you this post I hope—it depends on George, brown paper and string.

[1] *The Winding Stair*, Macmillan & Co. It had been published the day before, and included the poems from *The Winding Stair*, New York, 1929, and from *Words for Music Perhaps*, Cuala Press, 1932.

I wonder if the English newspapers have given you any idea of our political comedy. Act I. Capt Macmanus, the ex-British officer I spoke of, his head full of vague Fascism, got probably from me, decided that Gen[eral] O'Duffy should be made leader of a body of young men formed to keep meetings from being broken up. He put into O'Duffy's head—he describes him as 'a simple peasant'—Fascist ideas and started him off to organise that body of young men. Act II. Some journalist announced that 30,000 of these young men were going to march through Dublin on a certain day (the correct number was 3,000). Government panic. Would not O'Duffy, who had once been head of the army, and more recently head of the police, march on the Government with 30,000, plus army and police? Result, martial law—in its Irish form—armoured cars in the streets, and new police force drawn from the I.R.A. to guard the government, and O'Duffy's organization proclaimed. Act III. O'Duffy is made thereby so important that Cosgrave surrenders the leadership of his party to O'Duffy and all the opposition united under him. Two months ago he was unknown politically . . . Yours affectionately   W B YEATS

You will know the poems in my book, and have written me of them before when they came out at Cuala or another press, yet write again. Say what you think of Crazy Jane (I approve of her) and of the poems on pages 76, 77, 78.[1]

TO OLIVIA SHAKESPEAR

Oct 24 [1933]   *Riversdale*

My dear Olivia, I think that George and I will be in London for a few days in about three weeks, George to see her mother and I to go through my essay on the Tibetan travels of his Master with the Swami. This essay—seven or eight thousand words—has taken me two months at least, has grown to have great importance in my scheme of things. George, by the by, wants you to arrange for her to meet the Swami and I had better not be there.

Thank you for your praise of my book. The next book you will

---

[1] 'Three Things,' 'Lullaby,' and 'After Long Silence'

get from me will be my *Collected Poems* (all my lyrical poems in one volume) in the middle of November. I think I have finished with self-expression and if I write more verse it will be impersonal, perhaps even going back to my early self. I have a longing for remote beauty. I have been reading Morris' *Sigurd* to Anne and last night when I came to the description of the birth of Sigurd and that wonderful first nursing of the child, I could hardly read for my tears. Then when Anne had gone to bed I tried to read it to George and it was just the same.

Study the little angels on the new Irish postage stamps. The artist brought the design, much larger of course than the stamp, to the proper officials. The officials said the expression of the angels' eyes must be changed. He said they would be all right when reduced in size. Officials would not believe and he went home in a rage. He kept the design for two weeks and sent it back unaltered. The officials thought it was changed and sent it to the printer. When the artist got the proof, being still in a rage, [he] said that it was all wrong and must be altered, though there was nothing wrong, and altered it was. He considers that the cost of this alteration was necessary punishment. I don't think much of his stamp but he is a competent person, a designer of stained-glass in the best studio here.[1]

A number of the reviews of my book have quoted that poem ending

> Young
> We loved each other and were ignorant.

I wonder if you remember those autumn evenings when I was on my way to Rapallo. Yours affectionately   W B YEATS

TO OLIVIA SHAKESPEAR

Nov 11 [Postmark Nov 13, 1933]   *Riversdale*

My dear Olivia: I think our letters crossed so that we both owe each other letters. I had thought to be in London by this but Michael got sore feet at school, was laid up, had to have special boots made and George would not stir. Now George will not go until after

---

[1] The artist was Mr. Richard J. King; he worked in Mr. Harry Clarke's studio.

Xmas but I hope to be in London in a couple of weeks. At any rate I must get there before the rush of Xmas. I want first to finish a mass of dictation and get for the Swami the corrected copy of my already dictated essay on his Master's travels. London is horribly expensive so I shall not stay for more than a very few days. I wish I knew some benevolent hostess or cheap lodging, for I long for conversation on something else but politics. I am writing a dance play and have just finished the verses for the opening of the curtain. Here they are—the chiming bells is part of the play.

> First musician (singing)
> I wait until the tower gives forth the chime;
> And dream of ghosts that have the speech of birds;
> Because they have no thoughts they have no words;
> No thought because no past or future; Time
> Comes from the torture of our flesh, and these,
> Cast out by death and tethered there by love,
> Touch nerve to nerve throughout the sacred grove
> And seem a single creature when they please.
> Second musician (singing)
> I call to mind the iron of the bell
> And get from that my harsher imagery,
> All love is shackled to mortality,
> Love's image is a man-at-arms in steel;
> Love's image is a woman made of stone;
> It dreams of the unborn; all else is nought;
> To-morrow and to-morrow fills its thought;
> All tenderness reserves for that alone.[1]

The inner ideas in these lines are taken up later. One might say the love of the beloved seeks eternity, that of the child seeks time.

Did I tell you that my apparition came a seventh time? As I awoke I saw a child's hand and arm and head—faintly self-luminous —holding above—I was lying on my back—a five of diamonds or hearts I was [not] sure which. It was held as if the child was standing at the head of the bed. Is the meaning some fortune teller's meaning attached to the card or does it promise me five months or five years?

[1] These lines were intended for the opening of the play *The King of the Great Clock Tower*. By the time the play came to be published they had been completely rewritten.

Five years would be about long enough to finish my autobiography and bring out *A Vision*. I have just had a letter from Finland from a man who has read my old version twice and is writing a book on me and it. I think I shall have to dictate what is undictated of the new version and send him a copy. There is also a Frenchman at the same task.

That portrait was painted in 1907 at Coole by Augustus John. I am using it as a frontispiece for my collected volume of lyrics which you get in a day or two. Yours affectionately   W B YEATS

TO OLIVIA SHAKESPEAR

Nov 30 [*Postmark* 1933]   *Riversdale*

My dear Olivia, May I lunch Tuesday at 1 but not go to the lecture? I would like to go to the lecture but I dare not. Please tell the Swami that to get through the evening I shall have to lie down, probably to get right into bed at the Savile for a part of the afternoon. I am sorry.

The book has not reached you because my copies only came on Monday. I decided to bring you your copy out of sheer laziness.

I am slightly suffering from blood pressure and an attempt to write a new national song—three versions to the tune of O'Donnell Abu to be sung at the Abbey Theatre. Yours   W B YEATS

TO MARIO M. ROSSI [1]

[*In the last months of* 1933]

... In your Berkeley chapters you described the history of his ideas, in Swift you are surely [? merely] concerned with the history of a manner or limitation of perception. Swift's absorption in the useful, (the contemporary decline of common sense), all that made him write *The Tale of a Tub*, compelled his nature to become coarse. The man who ignores the poetry of sex, let us say, finds the bare facts written up on the walls of a privy, or himself is compelled to write

[1] Fragment.

them there. But all this seems to me of his time, his mere inheritance. When a [man] of Swift's sort is born into such dryness, is he not in the Catholic sense of the word its *victim*? A French Catholic priest once told me of certain holy women. One was victim for a whole country, another for such and such a village. Is not Swift the human soul in that dryness, is not that his tragedy and his genius? Perhaps every historical phase may have its victims—its poisoned rat in a hole. . . .

TO OLIVIA SHAKESPEAR

Jan 27 [1934] *Riversdale*

My dear Olivia . . . George and I go to Rapallo in June and fetch back books, pictures and furniture. Some of our furniture we shall continue to lend to the old Pounds. I suppose we shall return by sea from Genoa. The Swami's translation of his Master's book has been taken by Faber & Faber. They say it will not have a large sale but will continue to sell for a long time.

When I came back here I had my cold clinging to me for a long time. I have been working in bed in the morning, at first finishing that dance play. There are four lyrics including the one I sent you though altogether re-written.

I made up the play that I might write lyrics out of dramatic experience, all my personal experience having in some strange way come to an end. They are good lyrics a little in my early manner. Then I have worked on *The Vision*, having faced at last and finish[ed] the prophecy of the next hundred years. Now George's work begins —to draw the diagrams—and the book is done. My letters to Lady Gregory have come. Did I tell you that when that apparition appeared to me for the tenth time I saw, in broad daylight, an arm waving goodby at the edge of a screen beside my door? It has not appeared since.

Tell me what you are doing. Your life is too tranquil, mine too exciting. My rest from excitement is to meet people. This week for two days I had to sit in my chair reading nothing, probably because I had been too excited—the dance play, *The Vision*. Yours affectionately W B YEATS

TO OLIVIA SHAKESPEAR

Feb 27 [Postmark Feb 28, 1934] *Riversdale*

My dear Olivia: I come out of my reveries to write to you. I do nothing all day long but think of the drama I am building up in my *Lady Gregory*.[1] I have drawn Martyn and his house, Lady Gregory and hers, have brought George Moore upon the scene, finished a long analysis of him, which pictures for the first time this preposterous person. These first chapters are sensations and exciting and will bring George much household money when she sends them out to English and American magazines. I am just beginning on Woburn Buildings, building up the scene there—alas the most significant image of those years must be left out.[2] This first part will probably be made up of extracts from letters to Lady Gregory and my comments. My first fifty pages—probably to be published before the rest—will bring me to about 1900. They begin where my old autobiography ends. It is curious how one's life falls into definite sections—in 1897 a new scene was set, new actors appeared.

I do not find anything the matter [with] the Swami['s] book, it is his master's book that is incredible. I have so many wonders that I have gone completely to the miracle workers. Did you see old Budge's[3] interview in the *Daily Express* of, I think, Jan 14? Egyptian magicians had, he said, 'materialized' in his presence the souls of men who were excavating for him twenty-four miles away. He had given orders to the 'materialized' forms that the men miles away had carried [out]. He says he has now mastered from certain inscriptions the whole method of Egyptian magic and is putting the knowledge into the hands of men sworn never to publish it.

Here is our most recent event. Next door is a large farm-house in considerable grounds. People called —— live there, 'blue shirts' of local importance, and until one day two weeks ago they had many dogs. 'Blue shirts' are upholding law, incarnations of public spirit, rioters in the cause of peace, and George hates 'Blue shirts.' She was delighted when she caught their collie-dog in our hen-house

[1] The continuation of his autobiography, eventually published as *Dramatis Personae* in 1935 by the Cuala Press.
[2] An allusion to the early days of his friendship with Mrs. Shakespear.
[3] Sir Ernest A. Wallis Budge (1847-1934) the famous Egyptologist. The interview with him was headed 'This Man knows the Forbidden Secrets of the East,' and appeared in the *Daily Express*, January 17, 1934.

and missed a white hen. I was going into town and she said as I started 'I will write to complain. If they do nothing I will go to the police.' When I returned in the evening she was plunged in gloom. Her letter sent by our gardener had been replied to at once in these words: 'Sorry, have done away with collie-dog'—note the Hitler touch—a little later came the gardener. In his presence, Mrs. —— had drowned four dogs. A fifth had revived, when taken out of the water, and as it was not her own dog but a stray she had hunted it down the road with a can tied to its tail. There was a sixth dog, she said, but as it had been with her for some time she would take time to think whether to send it to the dogs' home or drown it. I tried to console George—after all she was only responsible for the death of the collie and so on. But there was something wrong. At last it came. The white hen had returned. Was she to write and say so? I said 'No; you feel a multi-murderess and if you write, Mrs. —— will feel she is.' 'But she will see the hen.' 'Put it in the pot.' 'It is my best layer.' However I insisted and the white hen went into the pot. Yours affectionately   W B YEATS

TO ERNEST RHYS[1]

May 3 [1934]   *Riversdale*

My dear Rhys, I have wondered where you were and so am glad to get a letter with a letter heading so attractive. 'The Bell House,' there is antiquity in that name. I too have a garden, the small house and the big garden somebody prayed for.[2] I play croquet and am still able to beat my family; my domestic authority is therefore unshaken. My daughter is fifteen and has just discovered Shakespeare and at her own suggestion is writing an essay upon Hamlet. Her sole education is languages, the Academy Act school and my conversation. My son aged $12\frac{1}{2}$ toils through the ordinary curriculum and will go to St. Columba's in a year or so and then to College. Yours ever   W B YEATS

[1] Text from *Letters from Limbo* by Ernest Rhys. London, 1936.
[2] Yeats is here evidently thinking of Abraham Cowley's poem *The Wish*:

>   Ah, yet, ere I descend to the grave
>   May I a small house and large garden have.

TO SEAN O'FAOLAIN

[Possibly 1934] *Riversdale*

Dear O'Faolain, H. Lane got me into the P.E.N. by a curious accident. He wrote 'Lady Gregory says she will join if you will.' I could not make out why Lady Gregory did something so out of character, but, as I supposed it would please her, joined. Then came a letter from Lady Gregory asking why I had done something so out of character. To get out of joining without offending Hugh Lane she had said she would not join as I had not, and now she had to send him a flat refusal.

How the devil I became president I don't know. I never consented, never knew anything about it, never went to a meeting. Consider me as resigned. I am sorry but, as I told the London Secretary, with every year of life I hate more intensely the heterogeneous. Yours   W B YEATS

TO OLIVIA SHAKESPEAR

Wednesday [Postmark May 10, 34] *Riversdale*

My dear Olivia, I have been working in bed in the mornings almost since my return but this is the first day in which I have had enough concentration, my work finished, to write a letter. I am out in the garden at a little green-baize-covered table the gardener has carried out for me. It is too soon to know whether I have benefited by the operation [1] but I feel as if my blood pressure was down—I am not irritable and that is a new event. I am still busy writing about George Moore, and in reading him that I may write. I find him amusing and tragic, given over to his incredible violence except when moved by some objective scene.

We delay our journey to Italy till May 20 as George wants me to be quite recovered before we start, and will hardly be in London until the middle of June if George carries out her intention to go from Cork to Cherbourg and from there to Italy ... Yours affectionately   W B YEATS

[1] Yeats had recently undergone the Steinach operation for rejuvenation.

TO OLIVIA SHAKESPEAR

[*Postmark June* 1, 1934]   *Riversdale*

My dear Olivia, Explain to the Swami that all my working life I have said to Irish patriots who wanted me for President, Vice-President, Patron or the like, 'I have never and will never accept an official position in a society unless I can take an active part in the work of that society.' I have given the Swami the support of my name already, my taking official rank in his society would add nothing.

We go to Italy on June 6, we go from Cork to some port in France and then by train. We shall be in London by the end of June, George passing through to Sidmouth, I to see you and one or two others. If you write at once write here—I want the letters you did not write—if not c/o Dorothy or Ezra. I am still marvellously strong, with the sense of a future, in some ways better than I was at Woburn Buildings, at least towards the end. This is not a letter. I have got to get into town to do some dictation.

I have just sent back the final proofs of *The Holy Mountain* and have just read it all through. It seems to me one of those rare books that are fundamental. For generations writers will refer to it as they will to *An Indian Monk*. The Swami will fulfill the prophecy of his astrologers 'Preach to the whole world,' though not as did Vivekānanda, whose eloquence bores me. Of course 'all the world' is a vague phrase like 'The World and his Wife.' Two such books will shift for those, who move others, the foundation of their thought, but it will take years.

I cannot write—the truth is I want to talk to you. I have so much quaint information. Yours   W B YEATS

TO OLIVIA SHAKESPEAR

July 24 [*Postmark July* 25, 34]   *Riversdale*

My dear Olivia, This magnificent note-paper is from Rapallo and out of a packet labelled 'Dante.' Yes that book is important. Notice this symbolism

Waters under the earth ⎫
The Earth   ⎬   The bowels etc.   *Instinct*

The Water	= The blood and the sex organ.	*Passion*
The Air	= The lungs, logical thought	*Thought*
The Fire	=	*Soul*

They are my four quarters. The Earth before 8, the Waters before 15, the Air before 22, the Fire before 1. (See *A Vision*, page 86.) Note that on page 85 of *A Vision* [1] the conflict on which we now enter is 'against the Soul,' as in the quarter we have just left it was 'against the intellect.' The conflict is to restore the body.

Here are two verses out of a poem I have just written [2]

'Natural and supernatural with the self-same ring are wed;
As man, as beast, as an ephemeral fly begets, God-head begets God-head,
For things below are copies the great Smaragdine Tablet said.

Yet must all copy copies, all increase their kind,
When the conflagration of their passion sinks, damped by the body or the mind
That juggling Nature mounts, her coil in their embraces twined;

The mirror scaled serpent is multiplicity'

and so on. The point of the poem is that we beget and bear because of the incompleteness of our love.

I have another poem in my head where a monk reads his breviary at midnight upon the tomb of long-dead lovers on the anniversary of their death, for on that night they are united above the tomb, their embrace being not partial but a conflagration of the entire body and so shedding the light he reads by.[3]

Strange that I should write these things in my old age, when if

---

[1] Yeats here gives a wrong reference to a page in *A Vision*, the edition of 1925. This he corrects in his next letter of the following day.

[2] These lines form part of the poem first called 'Ribh Prefers an Older Theology' and afterwards 'Ribh Denounces Patrick,' the second of the Supernatural Songs in *The King of the Great Clock Tower*, Cuala Press, 1934, and in *A Full Moon in March*, Macmillan, 1935.

[3] 'Ribh at the Tomb of Baile and Aillinn,' first published in the *London Mercury* and in *Poetry*, December 1934, and included as the first of 'Supernatural Songs' in *The King of the Great Clock Tower*, 1934, and in *A Full Moon in March*, 1935.

I were to offer myself for new love I could only expect to be accepted by the very young wearied by the passive embraces of the bolster. That is why when I saw you last I named myself an uncle.

> The Earth = Every early nature-dominated civilization
> The Water = An armed sexual age, chivalry, Froissart's chronicles
> The Air = From the Renaissance to the end of the 19th Century.
> The Fire = The purging away of our civilization by our hatred.
> (on these two I have a poem)

Adah Menken [1] was given £5 a week by Prinsep and others to seduce Swinburne. She said at the end of a couple of weeks that she had always been an honest woman and could not accept the money. 'We have been constantly together for two weeks and nothing has happened except that he has bitten me twice.' She had some talent, wrote a sort of free verse (the American vice). I do not know the book you speak of. I must stop now, I have many letters to do. I have been so busy writing verse that I have written no letters this long time. To-day I am fresh. I finished my poem and last night slept eleven hours. Yours affectionately   W B YEATS

TO OLIVIA SHAKESPEAR

July 25 [1934]   *Riversdale*

My dear Olivia, I muddled the explanation and the quotation from my own book. It is from page 35 (not 85) and it is there written that in the last quarter of a civilization (the quarter we have just entered,) the fight is against body and body should win. You can define soul as 'that which has value in itself,' or you can say of it 'it [is] that which we can only know through analogies.'

I have now to put another large sum to my sisters' industry, but henceforth I shall take part in the management. I have often failed

---

[1] Adah Isaacs Menken (1835 ?–1868), actress, was born probably in New Orleans. She came to England in 1864 and made a sensational appearance in *Mazeppa* at Astley's Circus. Her book of poems *Infelicia*, edited by Swinburne's secretary John Thomson and dedicated to Dickens, was published in 1868. She died in Paris.

as a poet but not yet as a businessman and am feeling quite cheerful. It means however a lot of work keeping them supplied with books.

Yesterday rehearsals of my new dance play [1] and on Monday performances of that and of *Resurrection*. Yours W B YEATS

TO OLIVIA SHAKESPEAR

August 7 [*Postmark Aug* 9, 34] *Riversdale*

My dear Olivia: After writing much verse I have taken a day off. Yesterday I put into rhyme what I wrote in my last letter.

> The Four Ages [2]
> He with body waged a fight;
> Body won and walks upright.
>
> Then he struggled with the Heart;
> Innocence and peace depart.
>
> Then he struggled with the Mind;
> His proud Heart he left behind.
>
> Now his wars with God begin;
> At stroke of midnight God shall win.

They are the four ages of individual man, but they are also the four ages of civilization. You will find them in that book you have been reading. First age, *earth*, vegetative functions. Second age, *water*, blood, sex. Third age, *air*, breath, intellect. Fourth age, *fire*, soul etc. In the first two the moon comes to the full—resurrection of Christ and Dionysus. Man becomes rational, no longer driven from below or above. My two plays, of which I send you the *Sunday Times* notices, both deal with that moment—the slain god, the risen god. I think I read you and Dorothy *The King of the Great Clock Tower*. It has proved most effective—it was magnificently acted and danced. It is more original than I thought it, for when I looked up

[1] *The King of the Great Clock Tower*, produced at the Abbey Theatre on July 30.
[2] 'The Four Ages,' slightly revised, appeared as 'The Four Ages of Man' in 'Supernatural Songs,' in *The King of the Great Clock Tower*, 1934 and in *A Full Moon in March*, 1935.

Salome I found that Wilde's dancer never danced with the head in her hands—her dance came before the decapitation of the saint and is a mere uncovering of nakedness. My dance is a long expression of horror and fascination. She first bows before the head (it is on a seat,) then in her dance lays it on the ground and dances before it, then holds it in her hands. Send the enclosed cutting to Dorothy to show to Ezra that I may confound him. He may have been right to condemn it as poetry but he condemned it as drama. It has turned out the most popular of my dance plays.

The poem in this letter is one of a group of philosophical poems I am writing for the new Cuala book. Yours affectionately

W B YEATS

I write on Rapallo note-paper.

[*On back of envelope*]

I have a copy of *The Bounty of Sweden* (Cuala) with your name in it. Did I never send it? (I may have sent another copy.) Please let me know. W B Y

TO OLIVIA SHAKESPEAR

August 25 [*Postmark Aug* 28, 1934] *Riversdale*

My dear Olivia, I send *The Bounty of Sweden* that you should have had years ago—I wonder if you ever read it. I had a Swedish compliment the other day, that has pleased me better than [any] I have ever had. Some Swede said to my wife 'Our Royal Family liked your husband better than any other Nobel prize winner. They said he has the manners of a Courtier.' I would like to think this true but I doubt—my kind of critical mind creates harshness and roughness. Which somehow reminds me, have you read *Hadrian the Seventh* by Lionel's friend or acquaintance 'Baron Corvo'?—it is quite cheap and nearly a great book, my sort of book, the love of the ruling mind, the ruling race. An imaginary Pope is the theme, with enough evil to be a great man. I hate the pale victims of modern fiction—that suffer that they may have minds like photographic plates. I want to give you some more rhymes. I was told, you may remember, that my two children would be Mars conjunctive Venus, Saturn conjunctive Jupiter respectively; and so they were—Anne the Mars-Venus personality. Then I was told that they would develop so that I could study in them the alternating dispensations, the Christian or objective, then the Antithetical or subjective. The Christian is the Mars-Venus—it is democratic. The Jupiter-Saturn civilization is born free among the most cultivated, out of tradition, out of rule.

> Should Jupiter and Saturn meet,
> What a crop of mummy wheat!
>
> The sword's a cross; thereon He died:
> On breast of Mars the goddess sighed.[1]

I wrote those lines some days ago. George said it is very strange but whereas Michael is always thinking about life Anne always thinks of death. Then I remembered that the children were the two dispensations. Anne collects skeletons. She buries little birds and beasts and then digs them up when worms and insects have eaten their flesh. She has a shelf of very white little skeletons. She has asked leave to go to the geological museum to draw skeletons. Then she loves tragedies, has read all Shakespeare's, and a couple of weeks ago was searching reference books to learn all about the poison that killed Hamlet's father. When she grows up she will either have some passionate love affair or have some close friend that has—the old association of love and death.

I have written a lot of poetry of a personal metaphysical sort. Here is one on the soul—the last written

> As the moon sidles up,
> She has sidled up,
> As trips the crazed moon
> Away must she trip
> 'His light had struck me blind·
> Dared I stop'
>
> As sings the moon she sings
> 'I am I am I,
> The greater grows my light

---

[1] The two poems in this letter both appear in the Supernatural Songs, the first as 'Conjunctions,' the second as 'He and She.' In the latter poem 'the crazed moon' becomes 'the scared moon' and this has been mistakenly printed as 'the sacred moon' in the *Collected Poems*, both the English and American editions.

>   The further I fly'
>   All creation shivers
>   With that sweet cry.

It is of course my centric myth. Yours affectionately

W B YEATS

When George spoke of Michael's preoccupation with Life as Anne's with death she may have subconsciously remembered that her spirits once spoke of the centric movement of phase 1 as the kiss of Life and the centric movement of phase 15 (full moon) as the kiss of Death.

TO OLIVIA SHAKESPEAR

Sept 17 [*Postmark Sept* 19, 34] *Riversdale*

My dear Olivia, When you say that my 'introduction' gives my 'attitude fairly clearly' and 'amazes you a great deal'—I wish you would explain. I feel that I have been too discursive and shied from my subject as a horse shies. I did not dare expound the vision of the lake, nor examine its reality. I had not knowledge to do the first, and had I done the second nobody would have had knowledge to understand me. There are moments when I long to escape from this practical life—Academy, theatre etc—that I might go to see the one or two people who understand such things and begin again my old spiritual adventures. The main reason I think why *The Holy Mountain* is being so well received is that the Swami's own book has gone before. Perhaps too all the dull 'saying what everything costs' helps, it makes the reader trust the travellers. The Swami's own book is much more exciting.

Here are some episodes that amuse me. I have a friend who looks like 'the Duke' in an old *Punch* drawing. He has a horror of having his conversation heard. Two days ago I lunched with him and another friend of his in a private room at the Shelbourne Hotel. In the middle of lunch I noticed that the door was not shut and said in a low voice 'I think you will find the waiter behind that door.' My host walked to the door on his toes, flung the door open and there was the waiter. The waiter fled and when we rang later on a waitress came instead. Probably a press-spy. Five shillings for a paragraph . . .

George and I will pass through London early in October on our way to Rome. We go there as guests of the Royal Academy of Italy. I am to speak at a dramatic conference. We shall be in London, or I shall, again at the end of month. Yours affectionately

W B YEATS

TO EDMUND DULAC[1]

Monday [? December 10, 1934] *Savile Club*

My dear Dulac, Margot and I will dine with you to-morrow Tuesday as you so kindly suggested.

You may be right about *The Full Moon in March* but I am not sure. I thought you would say what you have said, for I have been working at something opposed to the clear, bright dry air of your genius. I do not understand why this blood symbolism laid hold upon me but I must work it out. If I had a volume of my poems I could show you when it began about six years ago. Such things come from beyond the will, they exhaust themselves and the mind turns to some opposite.

I will discuss your suggested programme with Margot. I imagine that Ninette will want to substitute *The Clock Tower* but I don't like *The Clock Tower* which is theatrically coherent, spiritually incoherent. Yours

W B YEATS

TO OLIVIA SHAKESPEAR

Feb 5 [Postmark Feb 6, 1935] *Riversdale*

My dear Olivia: In London I had as you know 'a crowded hour,' but no sooner did I get here than I caught, or developed, congestion of the lungs. I was getting better, then a week ago I had a relapse caused by a long visit from a solicitor, old family sort, sort that 'on

[1] From a typewritten copy.

W. B. YEATS IN OLD AGE

sweet reserve and modesty grow fat'. . . . I was holding my own until I collapsed, spitting blood, panting, shivering, too exhausted to stay still for a moment. Now I am once more recovered, but am not allowed to leave my bed or see a soul, and do a stroke of work. I am always in the midst of a spider's web of my own spinning and every day I expect to learn that all the threads are tangled or broken, through lack of attention. 'Summer is a coming in—God damn.' Probably they will let me up in a few days and for a few more I shall wobble on my legs. When I shall be less weak I don't know but hoping to be in London in (say) the second week in March.

I cannot write a longer letter till I mend. Yours affectionately

W B YEATS

Certain societies are preparing for my next birthday. The alarmed sec of one called on George. 'O Mrs. Yeats,' he said, 'don't let him slip away before June.'

TO ETHEL MANNIN

March 4 [? 1935] *Riversdale*

My dear, I have not written because, being somewhat better, I have used each day's brief energy on work—proof sheets and Abbey Theatre—but now I am much better. I was out in the garden to-day and played croquet with my daughter.

I have had a friendly letter from O'Casey, about my illness. He must have written it the day after he read your letter in the *New Statesman*. He is very emotional, and your attack, perhaps, made him lonely. Since we quarrelled with him years ago he has refused to speak to anybody belonging to the Abbey Theatre. Only two years ago he refused an invitation to lunch because he heard I was to be there. Though your defence of propaganda has had this admirable result do not let it come too much into your life. I have lived in the midst of it, I have been always a propagandist though I have kept it out of my poems and it will embitter your soul with hatred as it has mine. You are doubly a woman, first because of yourself and secondly because of the muses, whereas I am but once a woman. Bitterness is more fatal to us than it is to lawyers and journalists who have nothing to do with the feminine muses. Our traditions only permit us to bless, for the arts are an extension of the beatitudes. Blessed be heroic death (Shakespeare's tragedies), blessed be heroic life (Cervantes), blessed be the wise (Balzac). Then there is a still more convincing reason why we should not admit propaganda into our lives. I shall write it out in the style of *The Arabian Nights* (which I am reading daily). There are three very important persons (1) a man playing the flute (2) a man carving a statue (3) a man in a woman's arms. Goethe said we must renounce, and I think propaganda—I wish I had thought of this when I was young—is among the things they thus renounce.

When do you get back to London if ever? Yours always

W B YEATS

I have found a quotation in the Powys Mathers translation of *The Arabian Nights* which would serve for a motto to such a book on the education of children as you may have written. Sherazada tells her king that she is about to tell three anecdotes which she thinks moral but others think profligate. The king suggests that they send away her little sister who is playing among the cushions. 'No,' says Sherazada, 'it is not shameful to talk of the things that lie beneath our belts.'

TO OLIVIA SHAKESPEAR

28/11/5 [1] *Riversdale*

My dear Olivia: I am convalescent but, as my attack was brought on by a too great mental effort and the doctor allows but little activity, I sit in a little library next to my bedroom for a few hours each day, for an hour correct proof-sheets or the typed MSS for the printers. Then I read Balzac or *The Arabian Nights*, for an hour or so, then George comes and says 'That's enough serious literature' and puts 'a wild-west' into my hands. 'Wild west' is the only form of popular literature I can endure. Like the old writers its writers live with the

[1] This dating cannot be satisfactorily explained. The letter was obviously written shortly after that of March 4 to Ethel Mannin. Yeats never himself dated letters thus; it is possible he may have taken up a sheet of paper already dated by somebody else.

visible and so help rather than injure my own literary sense. I feel that a poet lives always with sight and sound, and that makes modern life a snare he has somehow to evade.

I shall probably be in London towards the end of March—I have work to do there—but it will be April I am told [before] I can be my old self.

The proof sheets and typescripts I am correcting are for the Cuala edition of *Dramatis Personae*, as I call the coming instalment of autobiography. After that will come the proof-sheets of *A Vision* and then my work as editor of *The Cambridge* [sic] *Book of Modern Verse*. I can never do any kind of work (apart from verse) unless I have a clear problem to solve. My problem this time will be: 'How far do I like the Ezra, Eliot, Auden school and if I do not, why not?' Then this further problem 'Why do the younger generation like it so much? What do they see or hope?' I am to write a long introduction. But for months to come I shall have no serious writing to do.

O'Casey has written me a friendly letter about my illness, and this—the first sign of amity since our quarrel—has given me great pleasure. He has attacked propagandist plays in the *New Statesman* and that may have made him friendly to me. I have just written to someone, tempted to propaganda (writing more or less in *The Arabian Nights* manner) 'We must keep propaganda out of our blood because three important persons know nothing of it—a man modelling a statue, a man playing the flute, a man in a woman's arms.'

I meant to write more but I cannot. Yours affectionately

W B YEATS

TO ETHEL MANNIN

April 2 [1935] *Savile Club*

My friend, I am here but shall have to return to Dublin in all likelihood before this reaches Monte Carlo. I came over in a hurry to settle some business affairs and they are now settled. I have seen nobody, apart from this business, for I have been stuck in one room with a violent cold. My great sensation of recent weeks has been Toller's *Seven Plays*. *Hoopla* and *The Blind Goddess* are magnificent in their passion for justice. *Mrs. Eddy* I am trying to get acted in Dublin soon after Easter. It is not Toller at his best, but can one get an audience interested in anything they have not read of in a newspaper? Later on we can do one or more of the other plays.

When I read a play that satisfies me, I am dumb—I have nothing to say; but when I read a play like *Mrs. Eddy* I see at once another play on the same theme. I want to right the balance, and complete the statement. 'A masterpiece is a portion of the conscience of mankind.' *Hoopla* and *The Blind Goddess* prove that Toller has taken up drama as it came from Ibsen and transposed it as completely (turning towards the crowds) as Pirandello (turning towards the individual). But he is a greater technical inventor than Pirandello. That night when you brought him to see me I could not explain myself because I had a completely false picture of the man in my mind, founded upon a very bad performance of an early play of his. I had no notion of his intellectual power. If the new Directorate of the Abbey which I have just appointed support me I will incorporate him in our repertory.

I am not at the club but in my bedroom in Seymour Street and so have not had my letters. Perhaps there is one from you. But why should you write? If I were by the Mediterranean, a friend at my side, I would not. Yours affectionately   W B YEATS

I hope when I return to London, as I shall in a few weeks, to see something of Toller.

TO WILLIAM ROTHENSTEIN [1]

[*Postmark May* 7, 193?—*probably* 1935]   *Riversdale*

My dear Rothenstein, Damn Tagore. We got out three good books, Sturge Moore and I, and then, because he thought it more important to see and know English than to be a great poet, he brought out sentimental rubbish and wrecked his reputation. Tagore does not know English, no Indian knows English. Nobody can write with music and style in a language not learned in childhood and ever since the language of his thought. I shall return to the question of Tagore but not yet—I shall return to it because he has published, in

[1] From a typewritten copy.

recent [? years], and in English, prose books of great beauty, and these books have been ignored because of the eclipse of his reputation as a poet. Yours

W B YEATS

TO OLIVIA SHAKESPEAR

June 16 [Postmark June 17, 1935]   *Riversdale*

My dear Olivia: I send you an Irish paper with articles etc about myself. I have had many telegrams, and 129 signatures on vellum, and have been generally praised and petted.[1] I am writing letters, correcting proofs of *A Vision* and reading poetry for *Oxford Book of Modern Verse*. I cannot climb stairs without panting but otherwise am well. My life and work are settled for some months which pleases me. I shall be in London in August and you will doubtless be away. Ashley Dukes says he will do *The Player Queen* in September but I don't believe him—'false, fleeting perjured Ashley.' We were to have opened in March last . . .

O my dear I have so many letters to write. Yours affectionately

W B YEATS

TO ETHEL MANNIN

June 24 [Postmark 1935]   *Riversdale*

My dear Ethel, It was so good of you to send me the telegram of congratulation signed 'Ethel.' I have put off answering from day to day. I have had endless letters and telegrams to answer and it is always the friend who will not misunderstand who is put off to tomorrow. Then too I have been correcting the proofs of my book of philosophy and reading poets for my *Oxford Book of Modern Verse*. Each poet is a week's reading and I am forbidden all exercise, and all work that is a strain—congestion of the lungs has left me an enlarged heart . . .

I have had to make an important decision. Have I written all the good poetry I can expect to write? Should I turn my measure of fame into money for the sake of my family? It was brought to a head by an offer from Harvard of a thousand pounds and above a

---

[1] The occasion was his seventieth birthday, on June 13.

hundred pounds travelling expenses for six lectures on poetry and some weeks' residence in the university. I hesitated for days and then with my wife's approval refused. I am about to cut myself adrift, as far as I can, from all external circumstance (the Abbey Theatre will soon be able to go its own road). I want to plunge myself into impersonal poetry, to get rid of the bitterness, irritation and hatred my work in Ireland has brought into my soul. I want to make a last song, sweet and exultant, a sort of Europen *geeta*, or rather my *geeta*, not doctrine but song. Yours affectionately   W B YEATS

I feel very well, full of energy and life but am soon made breathless if I am not careful. I was worse before the operation.

TO DOROTHY WELLESLEY[1]

July 6, 1935　　　　　　　　　　　　　　　　　　　　*Riversdale*

Dear Lady Gerald, Do you know the works of Elinor Wylie? Since I found your work I have had as sole excitement her 'Eagle and Mole', a lovely heroic song. My wife tells me that Elinor Wylie had a tragic love affair; where she learnt the fact I do not know. I have written for all her work but I doubt if there will be anything else as good. I think that the true poetic movement of our time is towards some heroic discipline. People much occupied with morality always lose heroic ecstasy. Those who have it most often are those Dowson has described (I cannot find the poem but the lines run like this or something like this)

> Wine and women and song,
> To us they belong
> To us the bitter and gay.[2]

---

[1] The text of this, and of all following letters to Dorothy Wellesley, is taken from *Letters on Poetry from W. B. Yeats to Dorothy Wellesley*, Oxford University Press, 1940.

[2] From Ernest Dowson's *Villanelle of the Poet's Road:*

> 'Wine and woman and song,
> 　Three things garnish our way:
> Yet is day over long.
> . . . .
> Unto us they belong,
> 　Us the bitter and gay,
> Wine and woman and song.'

'Bitter and gay,' that is the heroic mood. When there is despair, public or private, when settled order seems lost, people look for strength within or without. Auden, Spender, all that seem the new movement, *look* for strength in Marxian Socialism, or in Major Douglas; they want marching feet. The lasting expression of our time is not this obvious choice but in a sense of something steel-like and cold within the will, something passionate and cold. I went from Elinor Wylie to —— and except one rather clumsy poem with a fine last line, found her all what my wife calls 'hot lobster.'

In the last few days I have re-read all Edith Sitwell and found her very hard to select from, poem is so dependant upon poem. It is like cutting a piece out of a tapestry. If you have strong preferences among her poems please tell me. I have made my choice but feel very uncertain. I take back what I said of your friend Sackville-West, having found 'The Greater Cats,' that has the irrational element rhetoric never has. It is very moving.

I notice that you have much lapis lazuli; someone has sent me a present of a great piece carved by some Chinese sculptor into the semblance of a mountain with temple, trees, paths and an ascetic and pupil about to climb the mountain. Ascetic, pupil, hard stone, eternal theme of the sensual east. The heroic cry in the midst of despair. But no, I am wrong, the east has its solutions always and therefore knows nothing of tragedy. It is we, not the east, that must raise the heroic cry.

I am a poor letter writer because I have so many letters to write —this is the 16th letter to-day and the only one it was a pleasure to write. Yours ever   W B YEATS

TO H. J. C. GRIERSON

July 7 [1935]   *Riversdale*

Dear Grierson, I thank you for the generous gifts, from you and others, brought by Masefield.

The Rossetti delights me because of its beauty and because of its subject. Lucretia Borgia has always filled me with wonder. The woman of infamous reputation described by Bayard as his ideal woman. Yours   W B YEATS

TO DOROTHY WELLESLEY

July 26 [1935]   *Riversdale*

Dear Lady Dorothy, My daughter and I—she is talented, gay and timid—will reach you on August 14. My wife cannot come for she will be engaged with my son's birthday and other matters. My daughter will go on to Stratford or to Masefield's but I doubt if I shall. I shall after a few days in London return here. I am still an invalid dreading fatigue, though thank heaven my friends will not notice it for my mind is lively. I am suffering at present from AE's funeral. I had to use all my powers of intrigue and self-assertion to prevent a fanatical woman from making it a political demonstration by draping the coffin with the tricolour. I shall recover my strength after a winter in Majorca out of reach of the telephone. All is well with AE. His ghost will not walk. He had no passionate human relationships to draw him back. My wife said the other night 'AE was the nearest to a saint you or I will ever meet. You are a better poet but no saint. I suppose one has to choose.' When the mail-boat arrived it was met by a small fleet of aeroplanes, rising and dipping in salute—Lady X and her pupils: the devotion of the sinner to the poet even when the poet is a saint. AE was my oldest friend—we began our work together. I constantly quarrelled with him but he never bore malice and in his last letter, a month before his death, he said that generally when he differed from me it was that he feared to be absorbed by my personality. He had no passions, but as a young man had to struggle against his senses. He gave up writing poetry for a time because it stirred his senses. He wanted always to be free.

Your praise of the poem by Edna St Vincent Millay—I have only known her so far in Anthologies and have liked one or two things—has made me order all her books.

I wish you would let me read some of your new poems. As you go on writing and thinking your ideas will arrange themselves. They will arrange themselves as sand strewn upon stretched parchment does—as I have read somewhere—in response to a musical note. To me the supreme aim is an act of faith and reason to make one rejoice in the midst of tragedy. An impossible aim; yet I think it true that nothing can injure us.

Yes, Synge was a supreme writer. His *Deirdre of the Sorrows* is an unfinished sketch, but the last act is supreme in pathos and majesty. He had simple and profound passions. Yours ever,

W B YEATS

Would you send me one of your new poems or must I wait until I see you?

TO DOROTHY WELLESLEY

August 11 [1935] *Riversdale*

Dear Lady Dorothy, My daughter and I plan to arrive some time on August 14th. My wife goes into Dublin to-morrow to find out about trains and I will wire you when I know. I have delayed to see the first performance in Dublin of *The Silver Tassie* on Monday night. I shall go to London Tuesday.

I read your poem last night to F. R. Higgins, a man with more poetical genius than his verse has shown as yet. He agrees with my admiration. It has been an excitement reading and selecting modern poets. I have found most excitement in your work, in that of Elinor Wylie, in that of Richard Hughes. Richard Hughes has something of your modernity and intensity of style, but his subject matter like that of Elinor Wylie is not rich. When I get to Penns in the Rocks I would like to go over your last poem, word for word, perhaps read it out. There may be one or two absurdities in the syntax—I am not sure. You will grow into a great poet.

I began this volume of selections, just as I planned to spend the winter with the Indian monk, Purohit Swami, working on the *Upanishads*, that I might be reborn in imagination. I did [not] foresee that the work would bring me your friendship, and for that you have my gratitude. Yours ever, W B YEATS

TO DOROTHY WELLESLEY

Sept. 3 [1935] *Riversdale*

Dear Lady Dorothy . . . The sea was calm (I had neither to 'like' or dislike the elements) but not my work here. The day before I left I had a wire asking me not to delay. When I arrived **priests**, mainly country priests, were denouncing the Abbey for blasphemy, calling on the Government to withdraw our subsidy and institute a censorship of the stage. Our offence was producing O'Casey's *Silver Tassie*. Meanwhile Dublin was crowding the theatre. *The Silver Tassie* was over, but all our plays are crowded, last Saturday we could have filled the theatre twice over and there are priests in the audience. On Sunday night at a lecture on T. S. Eliot's *Murder in the Cathedral* an old white-haired priest asked to be introduced to me. On Saturday I had been denounced in the *Standard*, the chief clerical newspaper. The educated Catholics, clerics or laymen, know we are fighting ignorance. They cannot openly support us . . . I spent a gloomy evening, wondering whether I am, as my wife sometimes says, 'ruthless' . . . Forgive all this—it is my reason for not having written before.

Better leave the poems in the order we put them in; an arrangement by subject looks mechanical, especially in a small book.

I will write again when my head is less full of controversy.

My children return to-morrow, probably having quarrelled all the way. They have reached that embarrassing moment in their lives when it is no longer possible to settle things with the fists. Yours always   W B YEATS

TO MAURICE WOLLMAN[1]

September 23, 1935   *Riversdale*

Dear Sir, Forgive me for having left your letter unanswered for so long, it slipped my memory. Your anthology[2] is of course exceedingly well known, I have found poems there I did not otherwise know of. Your note on 'targetted' is quite correct.

I don't want to interpret *The Death of the Hare*. I can help you to write a note, if that note is to be over your own name, but you must not give me as your authority. If an author interprets a poem of his own he limits its suggestibility. You can say that the poem

---

[1] Dictated.
[2] *Modern Poetry 1922–1934* edited by Maurice Wollman, London: Heinemann, 1935.

means that the lover may, while loving, feel sympathy with his beloved's dread of captivity. I don't know how else to put it. Yours

W B YEATS

TO DOROTHY WELLESLEY

Sept. 25 [1935] *Riversdale*

Dear Lady Dorothy, The date of my play is Sunday, Oct. 27, at the Little Theatre.

You said I might stay with you for a few days in October. Is that still possible? Could I go to you Oct. 18 or 19?

I may ask you to help a great project of mine by asking W. J. Turner down for the night. But that depends on how he views my project. I shall get him in London. Here the poet F. R. Higgins and I (his head is full of folk tunes) are publishing at the Cuala Press a series of handpainted broadsides (2/6 each, edition limited to 350), in each a poem by a living Irish poet and a traditional ballad and the music for each and a picture for each. We want to get new or queer verse into circulation, and we shall succeed. The work of Irish poets, quite deliberately put into circulation with its music thirty and more years ago, is now all over the country. The Free State Army march to a tune called 'Down by the Salley Gardens' without knowing that the march was first published with words of mine, words that are now folklore. Now my plan is to start a new set of 12 next Spring with poems by English as well as Irish poets. I want to get one of Turner's strange philosophical poems set, let us say, for the bamboo flute (now taught in English schools) and I want Turner (who is a musical critic) to choose other poems and tunes. I have various ways of getting poems sung here. I want to make another attempt to unite literature and music.

We are accepting into our friendship (but not our theatre) the man we put out. Higgins said to my wife 'I cannot quarrel with the man. I like the way he looks at a glass of porter. He gives it a long look, a delicate look, as though he noticed its colour and the light on it.' Yours always, W B YEATS

TO DOROTHY WELLESLEY

15 Nov. [1935] *Riversdale*

Dear Lady Dorothy, My wife and I looked at your horoscope the other night. When I am through with my book I will send you some kind of judgment. It has greatly surprised me, your profile gives a false impression, it suggests cumulative energy, masculinity. You are not sensual, but emotional, greatly wishing to please and to be pleased; fundamental common sense but too impatient for good judgment until deliberation calls up this common sense; deeply imaginative but the star that gives this makes drugs attractive.[1] (I knew a woman with this star (ψ) placed as in your horoscope and I threw her bottle of chloroform into the Thames—she had soaked her pocket handkerchief in it and clapped it over my mouth to see what would happen. At the same time, so far as I knew, she did herself no harm.) You have a Roman mask and from its eyes looks out an exceedingly feminine nature. I think, starting now and for several months, you will create, because (ψ) or Neptune is passing over parts of your horoscope.

Yes, I am deep in my work, writing in bed every day from 9.30 till 12; after that I can read, or I can write letters but do no more creative work. I am counting every moment until Nov. 29 when my boat sails. The very fact that I am going with a man whose mind I touch on only one point, means peace. I can live in my own mind and write poetry; can go into a dream and stay there.

When I had added a paragraph to my account of Turner, objecting to what he said about Lady Ottoline Morrell, I forgave him. He was no more malicious than a butterfly-hunter, before the day of collectors' poison-bottles, putting a pin through a peacock butterfly or a red admiral. I was upset and therefore a dull man when you saw me.

I have finished my account of you—it is longer than I thought it would [be]—here is the present calculation of number of pages. T. S. Eliot 14½ pages, Turner 17 pages, Lady Dorothy 17½ pages, Edith Sitwell 19 pages, but nobody will count. Yours always

W B YEATS

[1] Dorothy Wellesley writes 'Fortunately I have been able to resist this temptation, of which I am unaware.'

TO DOROTHY WELLESLEY

Nov 28 [1935] *Riversdale*

Dear Lady Dorothy, I have heard from Harold Macmillan. I heard on Saturday on his return from election work. He wants you to send the copy to him. But for his election I could have sent it weeks ago and argued the matter out.

I return Introduction corrected.[1]

I await Friday with longing, on that day a curtain blots out all my public life, theatre, Academy, Cuala. My work on the anthology is finished—the rest, the business arrangements, are my wife's task. I have a three-act tragi-comedy in my head to write in Majorca, not in blank verse but in short line[s] like 'Fire' [2] but a larger number of four-stress lines—as wild a play as *Player Queen*, as amusing but more tragedy and philosophic depth.[3] But first I must rest a week or two—too much has happened of late.

I am planning a new life, four months in every year in some distant spot and nothing to do but poetry—the rest of the year mainly in Dublin and work for my family. Why do you not own a coral island? My public life I will pare down to almost nothing. My imagination is on fire again.

I have asked Macmillan to send you my new book.[4] I don't like it—it is a fragment of the past I had to get rid of. The swift rhythm of 'Fire,' and the study of rhythm my work for the anthology entailed, have opened my door. I shall get through if for the next four months there are no events except in my mind and perhaps an occasional motor drive. Once I am through the door I can face the storm.

I told my wife that I would reply to your letter. She comes with me to Liverpool to see me start. Yours always, W B YEATS

I will write from Majorca and send you my address there. It is not yet decided upon.

[1] His Introduction to *Selections from the Poems of Dorothy Wellesley*, published by Macmillan & Co. in June 1936.
[2] A poem by Dorothy Wellesley. Yeats included it in *The Oxford Book of Modern Verse*, 1936.
[3] This play became *The Herne's Egg*; it was in six scenes.
[4] *A Full Moon in March*, published by Macmillan & Co. on November 22.

TO DOROTHY WELLESLEY

Dec. 16 [1935] *Hotel Terramar*
Palma de Mallorca

Dear Lady Dorothy, I have been here for the last three days, after a brief stay in town. I work in my bed till noon at a verse play, though as yet it is but prose scenario—very wild but I think well constructed. I think of writing for the first time in sprung verse (four stresses) with a certain amount of rhyme, part may be in the verse of your 'Fire.' Shri Purohit Swami is with me, and the play is his philosophy in a fable, or mine confirmed by him. Every afternoon I go through his translation of the *Upanishads*. It is 2.45 and he comes to my room at 3 with his MSS. We have both drunk very strong coffee to keep ourselves awake, having formed the habit of afternoon sleep after our sea voyage, which was the stormiest I have ever known and left us worn out. I hear his step.

Dec. 17

My days are as full now of creative impulse as they were, when in Dublin, of distractions, but there is nothing to record—always the same bright white walls and blue sea, the same struggle to keep Shri Swami from treating me as an invalid; if I would let him I should be helped up and down stairs, because the holding on and balancing, during four days of storm, upset my heart a little.

Write to me and tell me about Macmillan—I waited till Nov. 18 when I knew he returned from electioneering before writing him.

I sent the corrected introduction to my wife some days ago, and the anthology is now, I have no doubt, with the publishers. Yours ever
W B YEATS

Robert Graves wrote the other day to two people who sent him a letter of introduction 'If you are the couple I saw on the beach yesterday afternoon, I don't want to know you.'

TO ETHEL MANNIN

Dec 19 [1935] *Hotel Terramar*

My dear Ethel, I have asked my publisher to send you my new book *A Full Moon in March*. Not much in it—illness interfered. A few weeks after I wrote to you I became well enough for work and pleasure. Haire examined me (I told you I would go to him) and approved my state. I went back to Ireland and after some time decided that I must escape the telephone, committees and the like; and attempt before it was too late a masterpiece; so I asked the Swami, who suffered from the London climate, to come here, promising help with his translation of the *Upanishads* . . . I am taken immense care of, if I go up or down stairs the Swami, very wide and impassable in his pink robes, walks in front that I may not walk too fast (I have still something of a heart, though apart from accidents I know nothing of it).

To-morrow morning I shall finish the long detailed scenario of a play, the strangest wildest thing I have ever written. Indeed for some three months now I have had more vigour of style than I have had for years.

Write and tell me what you think of my book. Tell me if you like any particular poem. That is always what interests me most. Yours   W B YEATS

PS. I have just finished *The Book of Modern English Verse* for the Clarendon Press, an anthology with a 30 page introduction.

TO DOROTHY WELLESLEY

Dec 21 [1935]   *Hotel Terramar*

Dear Lady Dorothy, I did not bring your poems, I put a copy out to bring and forgot—I wish now I had it and could follow your emendations. Force yourself to write, even if you write badly at first. The first verse after long inaction is, in my case, almost always artificial, and then it branches out. The prose version of *The King of the Great Clock Tower* was written to force myself to write lyrics. Yesterday I finished the scenario of my new play and to-day began the verse. It has begun well, but much of it will, I am certain, be artificial till I re-write and re-write. I am writing in short lines, but think that I shall not use 'sprung verse'—now that I am close to it I dislike the constant uncertainty as to where the accent falls; it seems to make the verse vague and weak. I like a strong driving force. If there should be a subtle hesitating rhythm I can make it. I do not want it as part of the metrical scheme. I shall write 'sprung verse' only if I find it comes spontaneously—if a foot of four syllables seems natural I shall know I am in for it. My play will, I think, be a full evening's entertainment, if it is ever played—my first full length play. One of the characters is a donkey, represented by a toy donkey with wheels, but life size. I am trusting to this play to give me a new mass of thought and feeling, overflowing into lyrics (these are now in play).

I am delighted with my life here. I breakfast at 7.30, and write in bed until 11 or 11.30. From 3 to 4 I help Purohit Swami to translate the *Upanishads*. It is amusing to see his delighted astonishment when he discovers that he can call a goddess 'this handsome girl,' or even 'a pretty girl,' instead of a 'maiden of surpassing loveliness.' I say to him 'think like a wise man but express yourself like the common people,' and the result is that he will make the first great translation of the *Upanishads* . . .

You have the best language among us because you most completely follow Aristotle's advice and write 'like the common people.' You have the animation of spoken words and spoken syntax. The worst language is Eliot's in all his early poems—a level flatness of rhythm. I have said of you in my essay that you have 'lucky eyes and a full sail,' or some such words. Some day I shall say much more of you than I can say now. If I said much now, seeing that you have not —— ——'s disarming appearance, I would only defeat my own purpose. —— ——'s appearance has great privileges.

Turner wrote an admirable review of the *Broadsides* in the *New Statesman* of Dec. 17. Read if you chance on it; he is to some extent fighting all our battles.

Shri Swami has just come in with his *Upanishads*. Yours always
W B YEATS

TO ETHEL MANNIN

Jan 6 [Postmark 1936]   *Hotel Terramar*

My dear Ethel, I am staying [at a] very new white hotel fifty yards nearer Palma than your 'Fonda' which is still dirty and still frequented by muleteers. My window is wide open and the sun streams and lights up the white walls. I am writing verse and helping the Swami to translate the *Upanishads* (it will come out in both names) . . . When I leave this in early April I shall have to go to Dublin for a time, bringing there a new book of verse.

I got your letter with the Symons quotation but evidently never noticed the question about the Warlock curlew music. I do not know where the music is to be got. Years ago he and I fell out because of his rudeness to a harmless, well-bred woman who acted as a kind of musical agent for me. I hardly knew her but felt I had to protect her. The result was that very regretfully, for I knew his music was good, I forbade him to use my words in future and he was of course enraged. He threatened to pirate my words and I called in the Society of Authors. One thing led to another. I rather think he left unpublished music to words of mine which I would of course gladly see published—one's quarrels stop at the grave. Yours affectionately
W B YEATS

TO DOROTHY WELLESLEY

[*Jan.* 19*th or* 20*th*, 1936]　　　　　　　　　　　*Hotel Terramar*

Dear Lady Dorothy, I have had an unexpected attack, breathing became difficult and painful. I sent for a very able Spanish doctor, who stopped all writing and cured me by more or less drastic treatment. He says that the enlargement of my heart is very slight, but that my heart misses a beat, and that this has come about through the overwork of years and should not be incurable. It seems I turn my food to poison, or, as the Swami put it before I ever saw the doctor, 'Give grass to a cow and the cow turns it into milk; give milk to a serpent and the serpent turns it into poison. Give an ageing man food and he turns it into poison.' The Swami is always profound and unexpected.

This, with the exception of a letter to my wife, is the first letter I have written since my illness. I have been too unwell to go through your corrections on the poems. This is the first morning on which I have felt well. I shall write again about the poems.

The Swami is a constant instruction and delight. He puts sugar in his soup, in his salad, in his vegetables, and then unexpectedly puts salt on stewed pears. Sometimes he mixes salt, sugar and pepper merely, I think, because his eyes light upon them. He says 'I like all the six flavours but prefer sugar.'

Our translation of the *Upanishads* is going to be the classic translation, you especially perhaps will find it exciting. Yours,

W B YEATS

TO DOROTHY WELLESLEY

[*April 6, 1936*]   *Casa Pastor*
                                 San Agustin
                                Palma-de-Mallorca

Dear Lady Dorothy, I am convalescent; in a pleasant hill-side villa; from a wide balcony I look out over a great stretch of very blue sea. Little remains of my illness except weakness; the doctor assures me that in a little while I shall be better than I have been for a long time. My heart is normal. The drawback is that I shall have a long list of things I must not eat. I imagine myself unrolling at a restaurant something like a ballad singer's sheet at a fair. There was a consultation, and one doctor was a monarchist, the other a socialist, and it needed the energy of the British consul to make them meet (my wife had selected the socialist on expert London advice), and they disagreed as to the cause of my illness, and both theories are allowed for in the list of forbidden foods.

Rothenstein has sent a photograph of the new portrait; it is more like you, except that it gives you a slightly acid look, though combined with much sensitiveness. The old portrait was the more impressive, but this is more personal and more intimate—though I incline for the old portrait. I wish however I had a photograph of the other to put beside it, to judge of the effect of reducing the coloured chalk to black and white. At present I feel that I would sooner put a reproduction of the old portrait over my mantelpiece —it has a stronger public appeal.

In my introduction to the translation of the *Upanishads* Purohit Swami and I are working at, I think I shall take up once more the theme of the sudden return of philosophy into English literature round about 1925. I will speak again of you and Turner, adding Huxley's *Barren Leaves*, which has the pessimism of modern philosophy. I read it a couple of weeks ago—it has historical significance but is not I think a lasting work. Its style belongs to the previous movement—it has precision but no rhythms—there is not a single sentence anybody will ever murmur to himself.

Can you recommend me some novels of the first intensity written in the last few years? I want to study the prose as I have studied the verse of contemporary writers—now that I have much time on my hands is a good moment. I want especially the names of any books that are philosophies, as *Barren Leaves* is. *The Edwardians*, which I have just read, of course is not; it is the social satire of the previous movement. Behind Huxley's satire is a satire which has for theme the whole of life. Miss Sackville-West sees only the futility of her own class—and all that is admirable; but O those radical critics—O that Augustus John model who loves the duke but refuses to be a duchess or to receive a thousand a year, out of Bohemian frenzy; O that Arctic explorer who carries through two voyages to the South Pole 'a derisive expression.' Fundamentally I hate the book, the hero is passive, and the assumption throughout is that everybody is passive. It is not true that it is easier to live a profound life in an arctic hut than at Knole, unless the arctic hut means the ascetic's contemplation. Do you remember that phrase in one of Dante's letters 'Cannot I anywhere look upon the stars and think the sweet thoughts of philosophy'? Some few of us, you, Turner, I, have in the very core of our being the certainty that man's soul is active. I find this dialogue in the *Upanishad*: 'I want to think.' 'You cannot think without faith.' 'How can I get faith?' 'You cannot get faith without action.' 'How learn to act?' 'Be happy.' (I have a little condensed it but not much.)

I said I hate the book, yet I admire it immensely. I am getting another of her novels from the local library.

Remember me to Miss Matheson if she is still with you.[1] The B.B.C. must have given her great powers of command; tell her to

---

[1] Hilda Matheson (1888–1940) served as a V.A.D. in the first world war and was afterwards engaged in intelligence work at the War Office. In 1926 she joined the B.B.C. and shortly became the first director of talks. She resigned from the B.B.C. in 1932, but later rejoined it and was, at the time of her death, Director of the Joint Broadcasting Committee responsible for foreign broadcasts on gramophone records. She was made an O.B.E. in 1939.

set you to work every day at 11 A.M. and never let you rise from your writing-table until you have written at least one line. But you are ill, or have been, and perhaps I am heartless to suggest even one line. Yours affectionately   W B YEATS

I have just read through your letters. In one you speak of having written some new verses and say that you would send them. They have not come. I think you alone of our present poets are 'natural.' I may point out to you one or two places where, in my selections from your work, the thought is good, but the words are not in their natural order—'the natural words in the natural order' is the formula. I would never alter a fine passage to conform to formula, but one gets careless in connecting passages and then formula helps.

TO ETHEL MANNIN

[*Postmark April 8, 1936*]   *Casa Pastor*

My dear, I am now convalescent—all unpleasant symptoms gone and all organs sound—but still weak. This letter which I am writing in bed may if it tires me be my day's work. Yesterday for the first time for months I put on my ordinary clothes. Only twice for months, some days ago and then last night, have I known that I was a man full of desire—is there not something in Wordsworth about a bird sitting among solitary seas?—perhaps I have only imagined it.[1] This villa is a charming but melodramatic house—tall marble pillars, white walls ornamented with stucco panels, a wide balcony going all the way round, the summer villa of a Palma stockbroker suggesting a film. I spend much of each day in an arm-chair on the balcony looking out over miles of coast and sea, away to the right I see the house you stayed in. My family have come out to look after me, my son and daughter are still asleep having spent yesterday exploring.

Do not try to make a politician of me, even in Ireland I shall

---

[1] Yeats was perhaps recalling the lines from 'The Solitary Reaper,'
> 'A voice so thrilling ne'er was heard
> In spring-time from the Cuckoo-bird,
> Breaking the silence of the seas
> Among the farthest Hebrides.'

never I think be that again—as my sense of reality deepens, and I think it does with age, my horror at the cruelty of governments grows greater, and if I did what you want, I would seem to hold one form of government more responsible than any other, and that would betray my convictions. Communist, Fascist, nationalist, clerical, anti-clerical, are all responsible according to the number of their victims. I have not been silent; I have used the only vehicle I possess—verse. If you have my poems by you, look up a poem called *The Second Coming*. It was written some sixteen or seventeen years ago and foretold what is happening. I have written of the same thing again and again since. This will seem little to you with your strong practical sense, for it takes fifty years for a poet's weapons to influence the issue.

If the Nobel Society did what you want, it would seem to the majority of the German people that the Society hated their Government for its politics, not because it was inhuman—that is the way their newspapers would explain it.[1] What victims of the Russian Government had been given the peace prize and so on? If Germans are like my own countrymen the antagonism so roused would doom the prisoner you want to help, either to death or to long imprisonment.

Forgive me my dear and do not cast me out of your affection. I am not callous, every nerve trembles with horror at what is happening in Europe, 'the ceremony of innocence is drowned.' Yours always W B YEATS

TO OLIVIA SHAKESPEAR

April 10 [1936]   *Casa Pastor*

My dear Olivia, This is a pleasant house on a hill, a balcony goes all round the house, from the balcony one sees miles of wooded coast. I am well except that my strength comes back somewhat slowly. From 8 to 1 I am as well as ever, then I grow watchful of my vitality.

[1] The German poet Ossietsky was in a concentration camp and very ill with tuberculosis. Ernst Toller, the dramatist, had thought that a recommendation for the Nobel Prize might induce the Nazis to release him. Such recommendation has to come from a Nobel Prize winner, and Ethel Mannin had taken Toller with her to ask Yeats to make it. Yeats, however, refused; this letter gives his reasons.

I can do little but every morning I work on the *Upanishads*—my work there almost finished. We shall be here until the end of May or early June. Swami stays while we stay—he is at a house near—and then goes to India. I shall see the *Upanishads* through the press, and perhaps a commentary on Patanjali which he is writing. I am glad he does not return to London but goes now that his work is complete . . .

Early June we shall be in England. According to the doctors I must be very firmly looked after for six months, but George means to look after me for the rest of my life—'You must never go away without Anne or me'—and that will suit me not at all. I trust to the strong constitutions of my family to restore my strength, it will probably be more difficult to restore my bank account. And O my dear, as age increases my chains, my need for freedom grows. I have no consciousness of age, no sense of declining energy, no conscious need of rest. I am unbroken. I repent of nothing but sickness. I ask myself perpetually what acts of my youth have weakened me—I think of the sick people in Butler's *Erewhon* with admiring understanding.

I am reading Aldous Huxley and Miss Sackville-West. I admire Huxley immensely and Miss Sackville-West a little and dislike both. Huxley seems unaware how badly his people are behaving. I sympathise however with his sadistic hatred of life. I want the reply and have half found it. Yours affectionately   W B YEATS

TO DOROTHY WELLESLEY

Sunday (no way here of finding out day and   Casa Pastor
month) [Postmark April 20, 1936]

Dear Lady Dorothy (I began my last letter 'Dear Dorothy,' believing that I had your permission; then came to the conclusion that my belief might be a delusion of my illness, and crossed out those words —yet I would like to begin 'Dear or My dear Dorothy'), You are right about Laura Riding. I had rejected her work in some moment of stupidity, but when you praised her I re-read her in *The Faber Book of Modern Verse* and delighted in her intricate intensity. I have written to her to apologise for my error and to ask leave to quote 'Lucrece and Nara,' 'The Wind Suffers,' 'The Flowering Urn.' She will refuse, as Graves has, but as a matter of honour I must ask. This difficult work, which is being written everywhere now (a professor from Barcelona tells me they have it there), has the substance of philosophy and is a delight to the poet with his professional pattern; but it is not your road or mine, and ours is the main road, the road of naturalness and swiftness, and we have thirty centuries upon our side. We alone can 'think like a wise man, yet express ourselves like the common people.' These new men are goldsmiths, working with a glass screwed into one eye, whereas we stride ahead of the crowd, its swordsmen, its jugglers, looking to right and left. 'To right and left'—by which I mean that we need, like Milton, Shakespeare, Shelley, vast sentiments, generalizations supported by tradition. (Hence your allusions to Heraclitus and his contemporaries, my toil at the *Upanishads*—just finished by the way—my use of legend.) We can learn from poets like —— ——, they purify diction, though they contort it, and see what we in our swift movement forget. Let us even imitate them, precisely because we cannot do so, swiftness and the lilt of songs in our blood. Being the crowd-scorned creatures we always murmur in the end

> 'Let us sit upon the ground
> And tell sad stories of the death of kings.'

Do you not feel there the wide-open eyes?

Thank you for the list of books (I have two in Dublin, *Waves* and *Orlando*, but have only read *Waves*). I will not ask you to send any of the others because parcel post is very slow and the books might not reach me before May 26 when we leave. The posts are incredible except air-mail and that is only for letters. Post or no post, they could not reach me in time for my introduction to the *Upanishads* which I begin to-morrow. I have to hurry with it because when we leave for England the Swami returns to India. You will find in the *Upanishads* wonderful things, now that they are for the first time translated as poetry.

My doctor said to me yesterday 'Your body is now normal.' I have still some detriments, I am weak from a long illness, and have drugs to take, but I feel better than I have felt for years. I have a slip-shod Spanish doctor who says 'I am not a mechanical doctor, I work by faith.' He said to me the other day 'I am a bad doctor

but I have done you more good than the good doctors did'; he has very little English, so heaven knows if he meant to say that, but the last part is true. He is an amusing man; I could always tell by his face when he thought I was going to die. I have no sense of age, no desire for rest, but then perhaps the French saying is true: 'It is not a tragedy to grow old, the tragedy is not to grow old.'
Yours always   W B YEATS

TO OLIVIA SHAKESPEAR

April 26 [1936]   *Casa Pastor*

My dear Olivia, We hope to leave here by sea on May 26, which should get us to London on June 2. The Swami, as near that date as he can, takes a boat for India. He says there are only three people he regrets not seeing again—Mrs. Shakespear, Omar, and Margot Collis. The *Upanishads* are finished, though there are typescripts to revise, and we are at work on a translation of the *Aphorisms of Patanjali*. I am also at work upon my play.[1] I work five mornings in the week and rest or write letters upon two. I am comparatively thin and elegant and on my present diet may keep so. Will you be in London in early June? Yours   W B YEATS

TO DOROTHY WELLESLEY

May 3 [1936]   *Casa Pastor*

My dear Dorothy: Yes, begin your letter 'My dear Yeats,' I have a detestable Christian name.

I have made a few changes in your 'Songs for Street Corners,' and with these changes they are, I think, delightful things. I read them out amid delighted laughter to an artist and her husband (she is doing my bust), and hated to part with them. My changes in No. 2 are mainly because 'innocent' seems dragged in, and because lines 5 and 6 belong to a different kind of writing, they are 'literary,' and the writer of ballads must resemble Homer, not Vergil. His metaphors must be such things as come to mind in the midst of

[1] *The Herne's Egg*, published by Macmillan in January 1938.

speech (the pen confounds us with its sluggish deliberation). I altered two lines in No. 4. In line 3 I put 'bussed' instead of 'loved to avoid the complicated profile involved by any discovery on her part that a mule lacks that cudgel which a Roman author describes the gardener as taking from the garden god that he might beat some boys who were stealing apples. I have altered line 7 because 'did' in 'Suetonius did say' is impossible. Our words must seem to be inevitable. Apuleius describes a woman and donkey having connection in a crowded circus. I wish I knew what Suetonius wrote, but I love your wayward verses. Keep the one general name and put numbers only to the sections—a name pins the butterfly.

I shall arrive about June 2 (I go by sea). I shall spend (say) a week in London to be examined by doctors. Then it would be a great joy if I could go to you. Could you have me for ten days or a fortnight? Is that too long? I shall be in Dublin for months, I suppose, being looked after, which I shall not like. Yesterday the doctor released me from all restrictions of diet except a general preference for little meat. (He has a way of saying of any diet he objects to, 'it is not convenient.' He uses this word for everything. He surprised a woman patient by saying 'It will be convenient if you sleep with me for a couple of nights;' he meant go to his Nursing Home.) He has told me to walk up hills, beginning with low hills and going slowly at first. He thinks I have been kept on the flat. I am full of mental activity and taking great joy in my play. I have delayed writing because Friday and Sunday are my letter-writing days—this being part of my cure. I shall probably keep up the habit—it has restored to me my friends, and is a great rest. I long for quiet; long ago I used to find it at Coole. It was part of the genius of that house. Lady Gregory never rebelled like other Irish women I have known, who consumed themselves and their friends; in spite of Scripture she put the new wine into the old bottles. Perhaps it was the New Testament that started the bad habit of breaking them. Till we went there Asia had all its old bottles—we should copy it and say with Henry Airbubble 'I am a member of the Church of England but not a Christian.'[1] Yours affectionately,

W B YEATS

[1] Henry Airbubble was the leading character in two novels by W. J. Turner, *Blow for Balloons* (1933), and *Henry Airbubble in search of a circumference to his breath* (1936).

TO OLIVIA SHAKESPEAR

May 22 [1936]   *Casa Pastor*

My dear Olivia: The girl [1] who is quite a beautiful person came here seven or eight days ago. She walked in at 6.30, her luggage in her hand and, when she had been given breakfast, said she had come to find out if her verse was any good. I had known her for some years and had told her to stop writing as her technique was getting worse. I was amazed by the tragic magnificence of some fragments and said so. She went out in pouring rain, thought, as she said afterwards, that if she killed herself her verse would live instead of her. Went to the shore to jump in, then thought that she loved life and began to dance. She went to the lodging house where Shri Purohit Swami was, to sleep. She was wet through, so Swami gave her some of his clothes; she had no money, he gave her some. Next day she went to Barcelona and there went mad, climbing out of a window, falling through a baker's roof, breaking a kneecap, hiding in a ship's hold, singing her own poems most of the time. The British consul in Barcelona appealed to me, so George and I went there, found her with recovered sanity sitting up in bed at a clinic writing an account of her madness. It was impossible to get adequate money out of her family, so I accepted financial responsibility and she was despatched to England and now I won't be able to afford new clothes for a year. When her husband wrote it had not been to send money, but to congratulate her on the magnificent publicity. The paragraph you saw is certainly his work. Will she stay sane? it is impossible to know.

When I am in London I shall probably hide because the husband may send me journalists and because I want to keep at a distance from a tragedy where I can be no further help. I am going to Lady Gerald Wellesley's, and shall go as soon as possible.

I should be in London about June 2 and will phone or wire at once. I shall be at the Savile but help me to remain there in obscurity.

The Swami left for India a few days ago. The *Upanishads* are finished ... Yours   W B YEATS

[1] Margot Collis, a young actress and poet; her stage name was Margot Ruddock. Yeats wrote an introduction to her small volume of verse *The Lemon Tree*, London: Dent, 1937, in which she gives her own recollection of this adventure. In 1937 she took part in some broadcast recitals of poetry arranged by Yeats.

TO DOROTHY WELLESLEY

May 22 [1936]   *Casa Pastor*

My dear Dorothy, I shall probably go to you as soon as you will have me, and my doctor has finished his examinations (if my wife still insists on these).

No, I do not want other people unless you do. I want to see you and I am tired and we have much to talk over and to plan. You seem to underrate those 'street-corner' rhymes—I wrote to-day to Laura Riding, with whom I carry on a slight correspondence, that her school was too thoughtful, reasonable and truthful, that poets were good liars who never forgot that the Muses were women who liked the embrace of gay warty lads. I wonder if she knows that warts are considered by the Irish peasantry a sign of sexual power? Those little poems of yours are nonchalant, and nonchalance is declared by Castiglione essential to all true courtiers—so it is to warty lads and poets. After this wild week—not without its fineness—I long for your intellect and sanity. Hitherto I have never found these anywhere but at Coole.

I have asked Macmillan to send you my *Dramatis Personae*. Read the two series of extracts from my diaries; you will find that I wrote in 1909 all that I have said to you about Knole and its like. Living in a disordered nation, social order has become a passion, it is the country against the town. Why should we who, like most students of literature ('all,' a publisher once said to me), are country people, be intimidated by the critics who travel daily by tube and look at the electric signs? We want, not a new technique, but the old passion felt as new. Yours affectionately,   W B YEATS

My spelling and writing are worse than usual—fatigue, results of Barcelona. I enclose photographs of a fine bust of me by a local sculptor, Mary Klauder (Mrs. Jones, in actual life),[1] and of myself and Purohit Swami. We were waiting for the steamer to take him back to India.

---

[1] A bronze of this bust is now in Mrs. Yeats's possession. It was sent to Ireland from Barcelona after the sculptress and her family had been taken from Majorca in an American warship at the beginning of the Spanish Civil War.

TO DOROTHY WELLESLEY

June 30 [1936]   *Riversdale*

My dear Dorothy, On my arrival I was met by the various persons in the *Irish Times* photograph—some of the faces (Gogarty's, Higgins') may interest you, as I have much of their work in 'The Anthology.' Dr. Hayes is the government director on the Abbey board. The fat man is Dr. Starkie, who most years spends a couple of months among gypsies in Spain, Austria, etc., playing his fiddle and escaping among the gypsy women, according to one of his reviewers, with great difficulty, 'a fate worse than death.' He was appointed by the previous Government to conduct himself as Dr. Hayes does.

Last Sunday at 4.30 I was about to start from the Savile to see the Chinese Collection at 'South Kensington' when the porter told me that the museum closed at 5 on Sunday. I wondered if I could reach the Park, decided that I could not. A stalwart oldish man, who was standing by the gate into Grosvenor Square, saw the desire in my eyes, and said, 'Mr. Yeats, would you like to go in?' He brought me in. He was Clifford Bax, whom I last saw thirty years ago when he was a thin pale youth . . . He and I and some friends of his sat under the trees for an hour.

My sister the embroideress has a pleasant memory of Chesterton. She was staying there. He got very drunk one night. Next morning he did not appear at breakfast. Presently a servant came in to say 'Mr. Chesterton asks for a Bible and a tumbler of milk.' Mrs. Chesterton, in unbroken gloom, told the servant where the Bible could be found . . .

I have seen nobody since I came back, except for that meeting on Kingstown pier—all yesterday I was hot, sleepy and lonely; sat in the garden; my daughter beat me at croquet. The mallet seemed very heavy. My daughter strayed away with a magnifying glass, looking for a slater to count its legs—this because she is at present in love with an entomologist. To-day I am content with life again —my work has gone well, and if the rain would leave off I am certain that the mallet would be light and that I could beat my daughter.

To-morrow I shall finish the play, then I write the ballad of lovers, the lady and the servant. Yours with love and affection,

                                                                         W B YEATS

TO DOROTHY WELLESLEY

July 26, 1936 *Riversdale*

Dear Lady Dorothy, I did not write because I have been busy, mainly writing poetry. I get up every morning about 4, work at proof sheets until about 5.30, then go to bed again, breakfast at 7.30, and then write poetry, with interruption for rest, till 12. The rest of the day I try to do this or that, but generally cannot. I remain sunk in indolence. Yesterday I finished my longer poem 'Lapis Lazuli,' and so to-day have come down full of energy, having done nothing but my proof sheets in the small hours. Higgins came in last night and I showed him your poem, which he likes as much as I do. Turner has sent three poems of his own, set by himself, which my wife will send you in a couple of days, together with a song by York Powell which I delight in. Would you care to go through the poems of Davies, and see if there is anything that you think suitable?

The poem 'Lapis Lazuli' is almost the best I have made of recent years, I will send it when I can get it typed. To-morrow I write a story to be added to the Michael Robartes series, (a prelude to *A Vision* which I am now revising in proof). It is almost an exact transcript from fact. I have for years been creating a group of strange disorderly people on whom Michael Robartes confers the wisdom of the east.

I have not put anything in place of 'The Thorn Tree.' I did my best, I went through your *Selections*, and your *Poems of Ten Years*, but found myself vacillating. I have an idea that I left out the nature poems because I wanted your poems to give an impression of rapidity. Rapidity is returning, it is no longer left to the popular poetry. I try to arrange the selections from each poet so that they will have unity of effect. I had great trouble with —— who wanted a more 'representative' selection, even wrote to the publishers. I have changed my selection from Turner to increase its unity.

Can I come to you in October? They have fixed my broadcast for Oct. 11. If I cannot come then I will do it from Belfast. But Oh my dear, my dear. Yours affectionately, W B YEATS

P.S. Have *Selections* been reviewed?

TO OLIVIA SHAKESPEAR

August 1 [*Postmark* 1936]   *Riversdale*

My dear Olivia, I am writing much and sleeping little—if I could sleep upright all would be well—writing better and more than I have done for years. I have proclaimed myself an invalid and got rid of bores, business and exercise. Every day I get into a wheeled chair and am driven along some country road for an hour—O why did I not think of this life years ago? Everybody is charming to me and those that I want come to see me.

I hope that you and Omar [are] as happy as I am on the whole. Synge used to delight in an old French comedy about a man who having given away his last possession, his wooden leg—said 'Now I am ready to enjoy life.' Yours affectionately   W B YEATS

TO DOROTHY WELLESLEY

Thursday, August 13 [1936]   *Riversdale*

My dear Dorothy, You should not bother about the *Irish Times* review; we have no critical press in this country. We have only hacks and amateurs. (One wrote to me a few weeks ago 'For months I have done the sports articles and now am being given a little literary work'—he wanted an interview.) The amateurs review without payment, for the sake of the books, which they sell. Latterly these amateurs have been what —— called 'racketeers'—that is to say, disciples of various radical schools—Auden, Day Lewis, etc. Here they are of no importance. But, my dear, you must be prepared for silly reviews until you are so old that you are beyond caring, and then they will only take another form of silliness. For twenty years I never sent a book for review in Ireland, knowing that any review here would be an attack. The more alive one is the more one is attacked.

I am in the middle of a commotion (partly press).

Write verse, my dear, go on writing, that is the only thing that matters. Beardsley said to me 'I make a blot and shove it about till something comes.' It is six in the morning. I have been at work for the last hour and a half, and must now sleep.

This is not the letter I meant to write, but this new excitement put everything but it only out of my head. Yours   W B YEATS

TO OLIVIA SHAKESPEAR

What is the date?   *Riversdale*
[*Outside envelope*] *August* 26
[*Postmark* 1936]

My dear Olivia, I now live entirely on milk, peaches and grapes—all from my own garden. George is anxious but admits that I look much healthier. I think the performance of my *Deirdre* has come and gone since I wrote to you last. Great crowds and enthusiasm but a bad performance which has put the board and myself into a rage. The producer is a fool and Miss ——, who took the chief part, no hand at such work. She is charming, pretty, and seemingly very shy. After she had left however the stage manager . . . reported to a member of the board 'One night I could not find Deirdre's crown so I went to Miss ——'s dressing room. I knocked and she said 'Who is there?' I said 'Stage-manager' she said 'Come in.' I went in, there she was without a stitch on her. I turned my head away and there she was facing me in the mirror. I went out and she said 'What do you want? I said 'Deirdre's crown' and she gave it me stretching out her long bare arm. I don't mind seeing —— in her knickers but nothing like this was ever seen in the Abbey before. At first I was not going to tell you—I did not want to insult your mind with such a story!' He was told it was not a matter for the board. She could not have felt the slightest amorous interest in our stage-manager, I can but suppose that she wanted to see the effect, that it appealed to her sense of humour . . .

I have finished the play I read [you] some part of and I have written many lyrics.

Remember me to Dorothy. Yours   W B YEATS

Faber & Faber have taken the *Upanishads* subject to Swami giving up the Indian rights which he wants to reserve that he may get the book issued very cheaply in India.

TO DOROTHY WELLESLEY

8th September 1936   *Riversdale*

My dear Dorothy, I am convalescent. The dire effects of a plate of duck made me take the law into my own hands. I refused everything but milk and fruit. Immediate improvement. Doctor had been sent for, prescribed digitalis (foxglove). Some days ago he congratulated me on my recovery. I said 'Diet.' He said 'Digitalis.' I said 'Diet.' He said 'O that helped.' Now I breathe like anybody else, sleep like anybody else, and walk about for the short time allowed like anybody else. My wife said 'I know what caused your relapse.' I said 'What?' She said 'The row at the Abbey.' I said 'Liver.' The question is, will this pleasant state continue now that digitalis is stopped, and I have been persuaded that the diet of the golden age may be kept in reserve to allow slight additions to my diet . . . I was really ill up to about three weeks ago. My young incautious doctor had made it plain that I might expect to be henceforth an invalid, living between bed and chair. Now he talks of complete recovery. He had all but forbid[den] me to go to England or anywhere else. There is nothing wrong with me now but that I tire easily, that I am weak (No, my dear, I will do my best not to upset your nerves), that I suppose I must go up and down stairs at a snail's pace and rather drive than walk. I mean that I no longer feel, look, or seem ill.

That ballad sent by Rothenstein does not come within our scope. All our poets are contemporary poets, and all except York Powell are living. Turner's poems do. I do not want *Broadsides* to be archaic. They contain such poems for unaccompanied singers which we want to hear sung. I plan quite deliberately that about one fourth should reflect the modern mind where most subtle, but I do not want a larger portion than one fourth. I send you a ballad of mine which I propose to put with Turner's 'Men fade like rocks.' It has an interesting history; about three weeks or a month ago a man, Henry Harrison, an old decrepit man, came to see me. As a young Oxford undergraduate fifty years ago he had joined Parnell's party, and now had written a book to defend Parnell's memory. Mrs. O'Shea was a free woman when she met Parnell, O'Shea had been paid to leave her free, and if Parnell had been able to raise £20,000 would have let himself be divorced instead of Parnell.

The Irish Catholic press had ignored his book.[1] It preferred to think that the Protestant had deceived the Catholic husband. He begged me to write something in verse or prose to convince all Parnellites that Parnell had nothing to be ashamed of in her love. The result is the enclosed poem, and an historical footnote which I reserve for my next book of essays. You will understand the first verse better if you remember that Parnell's most impassioned followers are now very old men.

I will write to you later about the music you offer to send. I want to see if I cannot suggest a tune for your chambermaid ballad. Though I have never ceased working, I had not until this recovery enough energy. Yours affectionately, W B YEATS

TO ETHEL MANNIN

Oct 26 [1936]
Penns in the Rocks
Withyham
Sussex

My dear Ethel, After I saw you I came here, except for one night in London to broadcast, stayed two weeks. I went back to London, my head full of your *Samarkand*. I wanted to see you but was confined to my room with cold for days. I came back here to rest and to recover my power of sleeping; and now I must return home. I hope however to be in London again before long. I have been unlucky my dear.

Samarkand delights me. I urged Hilda Matheson, a most active person in the Royal Institute of International Affairs, to seek your help. 'You people,' I said, 'measure maps, she walks upon the soil!' I love your maternal justice, that rich, sweet earthly justice.

Perhaps it is better that our meeting is put off until my *Vision* and the version of the *Upanishads*, of which I am part author, comes out. I think we have been working towards the same position, we have the same hatred of the built and mechanical, a hatred that sees no expression in action, perhaps the most we can discover is what we must not do.

[1] *Parnell Vindicated* by Henry Harrison. London: Constable, 1931. Yeats published his own historical footnote, 'Parnell,' in *Essays 1931 to 1936*, Cuala Press, 1937.

Because I want to live without automatic love and hate, I find that I must play my part in life as if in a charade. Yours affectionately

W B YEATS

TO DOROTHY WELLESLEY

Thursday [*October* 29, 1936]   *Savile Club*

Dear Lady Dorothy, I return Tuesday next—Sunday evening go with the Dulacs to Macneice's translation of the *Agamemnon*.

O my dear, I thank you for that spectacle of personified sunlight. I can never while I live forget your movement across the room just before I left, the movement made to draw attention to the boy in yourself. Also [? Alas] that so long must pass before we meet—at last an intimate understanding is possible.

I am busy at all kinds of things and am tired. I am very well. I have put off my return to Dublin because my wife thought Friday a bad day—an excursion—and Saturday seems little better, and if I have to dress for the *Agamemnon* I should hate to pack on Sunday night.

I am enjoying my last idleness for a long time to come. The proofs of *Upanishads* and *A Vision* await me in Dublin, and an edition of all my work, with new preface and an introduction for America, and of course the *Broadsides*. Yours affectionately

W B YEATS

TO ETHEL MANNIN

[*Postmark* Nov 2, 1936]   *Savile Club*

My dear Ethel, Alas I must return to Dublin on Tuesday morning, and until then have odds and ends to do. Perhaps it is just as well—when I last saw you I was in the shadow of my illness, and now there is still a little shadow. I feel I have a great mass of thought to arrange, before I can say some of the things I want to say to you. Some of your criticism of Russian imposition of mechanical society in Asia had touched and disturbed my convictions. The proof-sheets of the

Upanishads, as well as those of my own book of mainly social philosophy, await me in Dublin—I feel as if I cannot face my friends till those proof-sheets are finished and despatched. I am tired and so good bye for a little my dear. Yours   W B YEATS

Dulac spoke of your work last night, using the word I use—'honesty'—its great honesty.

TO DOROTHY WELLESLEY

Nov. 8 [1936]   *Riversdale*

My dear Dorothy: I am writing in bed, the coverlet strewn with proof-sheets of the *Upanishads*, on which I have spent the morning. In front of me, over the mantelpiece, is a large lithograph by Shannon, boys bathing, the most conspicuous boy drawn with voluptuous pleasure in back and flank, as always with Shannon. Under it a charcoal study by Burne Jones of sirens luring a ship to its doom, the sirens tall, unvoluptuous, faint, vague forms flitting here and there. On the other wall are drawings, paintings or photographs of friends and relatives, and three reproductions of pictures, Botticelli's 'Spring,' Gustave Moreau's 'Women and Unicorns,' Fragonard's 'Cup of Life,' a beautiful young man and girl running with eager lips towards a cup held towards them by a winged form. The first and last sense, and the second mystery—the mystery that touches the genitals, a blurred touch through a curtain. To right and left are windows, one opening on to a walled garden full of fruit, one on a flower garden, a field and trees. When I came home I got the two shocks I always get—the smallness of my house, the bigness of my Persian cat. I have a longing to tell these things because our last talk has created a greater intimacy.

There is no news—every afternoon since I returned has been spent answering letters, a month's accumulation, some from publishers requiring much thought. At this moment my wife is opening and arranging on my desk twenty-one believed to be about my broadcast.

Gogarty has come and gone, shedding behind him an admirable 'limerick.' Higgins, who gave a vote I object to at an Academy meeting, is I am told afraid to come. I shall invite him to dinner and make peace. The wind is howling in the trees and my windows tight shut against the draught.

Tell me if, after serious thought, you still want the Majorca bust of me, and I will write to the sculptor and find what she wants for it.

Your friend, who feels so much more than friend, W B YEATS

Over my dressing table is a mirror in a slanting light where every morning I discover how old I am. 'O my dear, O my dear.'

TO OLIVIA SHAKESPEAR

Nov 12 [*Postmark Nov* 15, 1936]　　　　　　　　　*Riversdale*

My dear Olivia, I saw Street's death in some newspaper some days ago.[1] You knew [him] once so well, he was so much a part of the past, of your youth, that you must have felt his death.

I am busy correcting proofs of the *Upanishads*, a long exciting task; that finished, as it will be in a few days, I go back to proofs of *A Vision*. The Anthology has been delayed (trouble about some omitted acknowledgements to publishers has made an errata slip necessary) but I hear that the first edition has been already subscribed for twice over. You will get your copy in due time.

My Broadcast [2] has brought me two letters about Lionel, one from Arabella Johnson denouncing me for 'meanness' in publishing the fact that Lionel drank, the other from a mad woman roused to fury by his line 'the old saints prevail' from 'The Church of a Dream' which I read. She says that 'old saints are the worst,' that the only hope is from the young and that the world is cursed by the lies of the Church and the poets. I have only just got her letter which was sent to Coole Park by mistake.

I am in excellent health, still mainly live on milk and fruit and am doing much work. With love, my dear　　　　　　W B YEATS

[1] George Smythe Street (1867–1936), author of the very amusing *Autobiography of a Boy*, 1894, and also an essayist of wit and distinction. In later life he was official Reader of Plays for the Lord Chamberlain's Office.
[2] *Modern Poetry*, the eighteenth of the Broadcast National Lectures, delivered on October 11, 1936.

TO ETHEL MANNIN

Nov 15 [*Postmark* 1936]   *Riversdale*

My dear Ethel, I have asked the Oxford University Press to send you a copy of my anthology of modern verse which comes out next Thursday. I hear that the first edition has been subscribed twice over so it will not be a copy of the first edition, but probably you are like me and care but little what edition you read. I will write your name in it when we meet. The introduction may interest you—a little of my favourite thoughts are there. I broadcasted on modern poetry a month ago and have already a crop of enemies because I have left men out or praised their enemies. Even my favourite crony here (Higgins) is cold and if the chill remains he will be a loss. We poets would die of loneliness but for women, and we choose our men friends that we may have somebody to talk about women with; and Higgins is full of fine discourse about the lovers of Connaught women and Dublin typists. I don't think women choose their women friends to talk of men—I don't know.

Here is a scrap of verse that came into my head some days ago

> Bird sighs for the air,
> Thought for I know not where,
> For the womb the seed sighs.
> Now comes the same rest
> On the mind, on the nest,
> On the straining thighs.[1]

I am in a rage. I have just got a book published by the Talbot Press called *The Forged Casement Diaries*. It is by a Dr. Maloney I knew in New York and he has spent years collecting evidence. He has proved that the diaries, supposed to prove Casement 'a Degenerate' and successfully used to prevent an agitation for his reprieve, were forged. Casement was not a very able man but he was gallant and unselfish, and had surely his right to leave what he would have considered an unsullied name. I long to break my rule against politics and call these men criminals but I must not. Perhaps a verse may come to me, now or a year hence. I have lately written a song in defence of Parnell (about love and marriage less foul lies were

[1] This poem, slightly revised, appeared as 'The Lover's Song' in *New Poems*, Cuala Press, 1938.

circulated), a drinking song to a popular tune and will have it sung from the Abbey stage at Xmas. All my life it has been hard to keep from action, as I wrote when a boy,—'to be not of the things I dream.'

I have been busy, *Upanishad* proofs, *Vision* proofs, letters (multitudes of letters about my B.B.C. broadcast that went to a wrong address and descended upon me here that needed answers and are not all answered yet).

Mother goddess, I put your hand to my lips.   W B YEATS

TO DOROTHY WELLESLEY

Nov. 28 [1936]   *Riversdale*

My dear Dorothy: Yesterday was a most eventful day. I finished my last proof sheet (*Vision* and *Upanishads* galleys both done); my daughter came in, have learned that she is to be paid a pound a week for six months and then get a rise; the Abbey announce that they will play *The Herne's Egg* in early spring—there will be uproar; and I sent off a ferocious ballad written to a popular tune, to a newspaper. It is on 'The Forged Diaries of Roger Casement,' a book published here, and denounces by name —— and —— for their share in abetting the forgeries. I shall not be happy until I hear that it is sung by Irish undergraduates at Oxford. I wrote to the editor saying I had not hitherto sent him a poem because almost [all] my poems were unsuitable because they came out of rage or lust. I heard my ballad sung last night. It is a stirring thing . . .

My dear, my dear—when you crossed the room with that boyish movement, it was no man who looked at you, it was the woman in me. It seems that I can make a woman express herself as never before. I have looked out of her eyes. I have shared her desire.

The Anthology, which is being hurriedly reprinted, is having an immense sale.

Now that I am free from proof sheets I shall take the bus to town and begin my usual life. I shall begin by going round the picture galleries—there is a new Gainsborough in one. Yours with love and affection,   W B YEATS

You will not find the four-line stanza 'too easy' if you struggle to make your spirit at once natural and imaginative. My 'Casement' is better written than my 'Parnell' because I passed things when I had to find three rhymes and did not pass when I had to find two.

TO ETHEL MANNIN

Sunday, November 30, 1936   *Riversdale*

My dear Ethel, Here is my Casement poem—the daily press will have it in a day or two—it is now with the editor of the *Irish Times* and if he funks it will go to the *Irish Press*. If my rage lasts I may go on in still more savage mood. The editor of the *Irish Times* had been pressing me for poetry. I told him that as all my poetry came out of rage and lust little of it was fitted for such as he.

Some day you will understand what I see in the Irish National movement and why I can be no other sort of revolutionist—as a young man I belonged to the I.R.B. and was in many things O'Leary's pupil. Besides, why should I trouble about communism, fascism, liberalism, radicalism, when all, though some bow first and some stern first but all at the same pace, all are going down stream with the artificial unity which ends every civilization? Only dead sticks can be tied into convenient bundles. My rage and that of others like me seems more important—though we may but be the first of the final destroying horde. I remember old O'Leary saying 'No gentleman can be a socialist though he might be an anarchist.'

I have [? written] much curious love poetry of late which I would send you if I had a typist. There is a long ballad about a chaste lady who wishing to keep her lover sent her chambermaid to take her place in the dark. Besides the ballad, which I shall publish in my new *Broadsides* with music, and [sic] there are lyrics for the characters in it. Here are two for the chambermaid

I

Whence came this ranger
Now sunk into rest,
Stranger with stranger
On my cold breast?

　　　　May God's love hide him
　　　　　Out of all harm
　　　　When pleasure has made him
　　　　　Dull as a worm.

　　　　　　　　II
　　　The summing up, after his death

　　　　From pleasure of the bed
　　　　　Dull as a worm,
　　　　His rod and its butting head
　　　　　Limp as a worm;
　　　　A shadow among the dead
　　　　　Thin as a worm,
　　　　His spirit that has fled
　　　　　Bare as a worm.[1]

You are right about my letters. They were unreal because I was afraid we might quarrel about politics. And my dear, though bold in public speech and public writing, I am a timid man. Yours affectionately　　　　　　　　　　　　　　　　　　　W B YEATS

TO DOROTHY WELLESLEY

Dec. 4 [1936]　　　　　　　　　　　　　　　　　　　　*Riversdale*

My dear Dorothy, I could not stop that ballad if I would, people have copies, and I don't want to . . .

But the Casement evidence was not true as we know—it was one of a number of acts of forgery committed at that time. I can only repeat words spoken to me by the old head of the Fenians years ago. 'There are things a man must not do even to save a nation.'

By the by, my ballad should begin

　　　　'I say that Roger Casement
　　　　　Did what he had to do
　　　　But died upon the scaffold,
　　　　　But that is nothing new.'

[1] Revised versions of these poems appeared as 'The Chambermaid's First Song' and 'The Chambermaid's Second Song' in *New Poems*, Cuala Press, 1938.

I feel that one's verse must be as direct and natural as spoken words. The opening I sent you was not quite natural.

No, I shall not get the ballad sung in Oxford: that was but a 'passing' thought, because I happen to know a certain wild student who would have been made quite happy by the task—the idea amused me.

We will have no great popular literature until we get rid of the moral sycophants. Montaigne says that a prince must sometimes commit a crime to save his people, but if he does so he must mourn all his life. I only hate the men who do not mourn.

Forgive all this my dear, but I have told you that my poetry all comes from rage or lust. Yours affectionately W B YEATS

TO DOROTHY WELLESLEY

Dec. 9 [1936] *Riversdale*

My dear Dorothy . . . The Abbey Theatre has decided not to do my new play.[1] I am greatly relieved. I am no longer fit for riots, and I thought a bad riot almost certain. The situation here is affected by the Civil War in Spain. A movement called the Christian Front is gathering all the bigots together. We have all been threatened with what can only mean mob violence by a Catholic preacher. 'Those responsible,' ran one sentence, 'for the outraging of nuns in Spain are all the intellectuals since the Renaissance who have opposed the supernatural,' and then came sentences which are supposed to refer to the Irish Academy of Letters and to myself. We were told we were watched, and that the Catholics of Ireland would not be always patient. Sóme of the results of the frenzy are exhilarating . . . It almost competes as a topic with an outbreak among the young in favour of the King, which has astonished everybody. For the first time in the history of Ireland they are loyal. I wonder if anything of the kind is happening elsewhere. I imagine that the old anti-English feeling has now concentrated on Baldwin.

The Oxford University Press has congratulated me on my 'courage' in stirring up 'such a hornet's nest' and offers me a further

[1] *The Herne's Egg.*

advance on royalties. Most of my critics are very vindictive, a sure sign that I have somewhere got down to reality.

O my dear, O my dear, do write. I feel I am in such disgrace. Do burn that letter about ——. Yours   W B YEATS

TO ETHEL MANNIN

Dec 11 [*Postmark* 1936]   *Riversdale*

My dear: Of course I don't hate the people of England, considering all I owe to Shakespeare, Blake, Morris—they are the one people I cannot hate. I remember old John O'Leary, the Fenian leader, saying 'I think the English have finer native characters than we have, but we cannot become English.' I hate certain characteristics of modern England, characteristics that come because of government in the interests of a financial policy the people so little understand, or like, that they have to be tricked into supporting it. If an angel were to stand before me and say the policy is right and only through tricking the people can it be carried through, I would say 'Because you are an angel I must believe what you say. But what am I to do? Certain things drive me mad and I lose control of my tongue.'

> You think it horrible that Lust and Rage
> Should dance attendance upon my old age;
> They were not such a plague when I was young;
> What else have I to spur me into song? [1]

All through the Abyssinian war my sympathy was with the Abyssinians, but those feelings were chilled by my knowledge that the English Government was using those feelings to help an Imperial policy I distrusted. To the wife of a Cabinet Minister who had discoursed to him on England's noble attitude, the monk Shree Purohit Swami said 'There cannot be two swords in one scabbard' and said no more.

Yes, I have a pension not given for poverty, though I was poor enough, but for 'intellectual services' or some such phrase. It was given at a time when Ireland was represented in parliament and voted out of the taxes of both countries. It is not voted annually, my surrender of it would not leave a vacancy for anybody else.

[1] With the alteration of 'attendance' to 'attention,' this poem appeared as 'The Spur' in *New Poems*, Cuala Press, 1938.

When it was offered first I refused it (though my income was less than £200 a year). The second time it was offered it was explained to me that it implied no political bargain. I said 'Am I free to join an Irish insurrection?' The answer was 'Yes, perfectly.' I consider that I have earned that pension by services done to the people, not to government, and I accept it from the people. It has helped to set me free from the one thing I have always dreaded, that some day I might have to think of the prejudices or convictions of others before I wrote my own.

I am alarmed at the growing moral cowardice of the world, as the old security disappears—people run in packs that they may get courage from one another and even sit at home and shiver. You and I, my dear, were as it were put naked into the midst of armed men and women and we have both found arms and kept our independence. Dr. McCartan (Irish revolutionary agent to America during the Irish-English war, travelling to and fro as a sailor before the mast) invited members of the Executive Council and other notables to dinner here the other day, and spoke in his speech of 'the attack on Mr. Yeats which has lasted for fifty years.' For twenty years I never even sent my books for review in to the Irish newspapers, an ignorant form of Catholicism is my enemy. At this moment as a reflection from civil war in Spain this Catholicism is more inflamed than ever before—but that is another story. Forgive me, I cannot recall ever having written so much in self-defence. Yours affectionately
                                                                    W B YEATS

   As a young man I used to repeat to myself Blake's lines
         'And he his seventy disciples sent
         Against religion and government'
I hate more than you do, for my hatred can have no expression in action. I am a forerunner of that horde that will some day come down the mountains.

             TO DOROTHY WELLESLEY

Dec. 21 [1936]   *Riversdale*

My dear Dorothy: My wife has heard from the maker of the bust. She is in New York (expropriated from Majorca) and asks leave to exhibit it there in February. We have asked her after that to send it to London. We should do that in any case, as it will need negociation with the Irish Government to escape a heavy duty. It can be sent to you for inspection. But all that can wait.

Gogarty once described the wit and phantasy of a friend of his called Tancred (who was, he declared, a descendant of the Crusader of that name). I knew him once, he had just been received into the Catholic Church. The ceremony over, some priest asked what had led him to the truth, and Tancred said 'I was in the Brompton Oratory and I saw on a tablet "Pray for the soul of Elinor de Vaux," and I thought the name so beautiful that I wanted to gain the privilege of praying for her.'

Turner writes to me 'They will some day be grateful for your discovery of Lady Dorothy.' A very strange man would have liked to do so ten years ago. Did you see in the papers about two years ago that a writer wrote a book which he meant 'as a serious work of art,' but which was alleged to contain obscene passages. He sent it to a publisher—the publisher reported him to the police, and he got six months. He had no talent but his case made some stir, and there was much indignation against the publisher. That man, I have just heard, had a cult of royalty—and had selected you—whom he imagined probably as somewhere near the throne—for boundless admiration. I cannot remember his name.

I thought the ex-King's broadcast moving, restrained and dignified, and from what I hear, the Archbishop's was the reverse.

My Anthology continues to sell, and the critics get more and more angry. When I excluded Wilfred Owen, whom I consider unworthy of the poets' corner of a country newspaper, I did not know I was excluding a revered sandwich-board man of the revolution, and that somebody has put his worst and most famous poem in a glass-case in the British Museum—however, if I had known it, I would have excluded him just the same. He is all blood, dirt and sucked sugar-stick (look at the selection in *Faber's Anthology*—he calls poets 'bards,' a girl a 'maid,' and talks about 'Titanic wars'). There is every excuse for him, but none for those who like him.

I had a black fortnight, the result of nervous strain writing the Casement poem you have seen, and another that you have not—beating the paste-board men—and some other odds and ends. I got sleepy and tired, and spent my day in bed and thought of my soul.

Then I noticed that every time I thought of my soul I used some second-hand phrase, and knew by that that I was thinking of my soul from ambition and vanity. I said to myself 'Your job is to avoid deep places and to die blaspheming,' and I got well at once, went to the theatre at night, and by day took the bus to Dublin.

The B.B.C. have asked me to rehearse one of the programmes I suggest early in March. Will I find you then?

What makes your work so good is the masculine element allied to much feminine charm—your lines have the magnificent swing of your boyish body. I wish I could be a girl of nineteen for certain hours that I might feel it even more acutely. But, O my dear, do force yourself to write, it should become as natural to you as the movement of your limbs. When I cannot do anything else I take up some old fragment and try to add to it and perfect it—there are always so many fragments—I have just turned out a thing of joy, just such a fragment. Once more I am starting on another. Yours with all affection, W B YEATS

Have you noticed that the Greek androgynous statue is always the woman in man, never the man in woman? It was made for men who loved men first.

TO DOROTHY WELLESLEY

Dec. 23 [1936] *Riversdale*

My dear Dorothy, Do not reply to ——. There is a saying 'Never reply to a reviewer unless to correct an error of fact.' If you reply you choose a jury that is packed against you, and the editor will cut down your letters, or stop them altogether if you seem likely to score off his paper. And very seldom correct even a matter of fact. The paper in which ——'s articles appear is Communist. You have no friends there. ——'s article is illbred and dishonest. He is not himself illbred, but men of his kind, when they take to proletarian politics, copy the worst manners of the mob. I return the article and suggest that you read the poem of Wilfred Owen's, which he quotes with so much admiration. I cannot imagine anything more clumsy, more discordant. One reason why these propagandists hate us is that we have ease and power. Your tum-ta-ti-tum is merely the dance music of the ages. They crawl and roll and wallow. You say that we must not hate. You are right, but we may, and sometimes must, be indignant and speak it. Hate is a kind of 'passive suffering,' but indignation is a kind of joy. 'When I am told that somebody is my brother Protestant,' said Swift, 'I remember that the rat is a fellow creature;' that seems to me a joyous saying. We that are joyous need not be afraid to denounce. A Dutch mystic has said 'I must rejoice, I must rejoice without ceasing, though the whole world shudder at my joy.' Joy is the salvation of the soul. You say we must love, yes but love is not pity. It does not desire to change its object. It is a form of the eternal contemplation of what is. When I take a woman in my arms I do not want to change her. If I saw her in rags I would get her better clothes that I might resume my contemplation. But these Communists put their heads in the rags and smother.

I will send that ballad but will not be able to do so for a few days. My last typed copies went off to America on Monday, and it is always difficult to get a typist here who can read my writing or take my dictation. Then you may as well have the two Casement ballads together, they are meant to support each other. I am fighting in those ballads for what I have been fighting all my life, it is our Irish fight though it has nothing to do with this or that country. Bernard Shaw fights with the same object. When somebody talks of justice who knows that justice is accompanied by secret forgery, when an archbishop wants a man to go to the communion table when that man says he is not spiritually fit, then we remember our age-old quarrel against gold braid and ermine, and that our ancestor Swift has gone where 'fierce indignation can lacerate his heart no more,' and we go stark, staring mad.

I said when I started my movement in my 25th or 26th year 'I am going to stiffen the backbone.' Bernard Shaw may have said the same in his youth; it has been stiffened in Ireland with results. I am an old man now, and month by month my capacity and energy must slip away, so what is the use of saying that both in England and Ireland I want to stiffen the backbone of the high-hearted and high-minded, and the sweet-hearted and sweet-minded, so that they may no longer shrink and hedge, when they face rag-merchants like ———. Indeed before all I want to strengthen myself. It is not our business to reply to this and that, but to set up our love and indignation against their pity and hate—but how I run on—Forgive me. Yours always, W B YEATS

I do not know what Clifford Bax meant by saying that I had not made the anthology myself. You chose those two Kipling poems, my wife made the selections from my own work. All the rest I did.

TO L. A. G. STRONG

Jan 12 [1937] *Riversdale*

Dear Strong, Of course I am delighted and honoured that you should dedicate your Tom Moore to me.

There are two poems of Moore's that I immensely admire.[1]

Forgive my delay but I have been writing endless ballads to music and forget everything in my excitement. Yours W B YEATS

TO EAMONN DE VALERA[2]

January 15, 1937 *Riversdale*

Dear Mr. de Valera, I read in the newspapers that you are in negotiation with the British Government on vital matters of politics. I write to draw your attention to a matter all Irish writers and artists have very greatly at heart—'The Lane Pictures.' Over a series of years Lady Gregory or I saw leading English statesmen upon this question. I came away from every interview with the certainty that it only required a determined demand from the Irish Government to bring those pictures back to Dublin. Mr. Blythe told me once that he realized too late that they had been offered to him during financial negotiations some years ago. You will find the whole question argued in Lady Gregory's life of Sir Hugh Lane, and in Thomas Bodkin's *Hugh Lane and his Pictures*, published under the auspices of

---

[1] Yeats probably had in mind the two poems by Thomas Moore which he had included, years before, in his anthology *A Book of Irish Verse*: 'The Light of Other Days' and 'At the Mid Hour of Night.' L. A. G. Strong's book *The Minstrel Boy: Portrait of Tom Moore* was published in 1937.

[2] From a typewritten copy. Mr. de Valera was, at this time, President of the Executive Council.

the Irish Government. You yourself were so kind as to send me a copy of this book.

You will no doubt remember that a Royal Commission found that Sir Hugh Lane had intended the signed but unwitnessed codicil to have the authority of a legal document, but that, had he lived and seen the beautiful gallery his enemy Duveen had built in London, he would have preferred to hang his pictures there instead of [in] his own gallery in Dublin. W B YEATS

TO GEORGE BARNES[1]

Jan 27 [1937] *Riversdale*

Dear Mr. Barnes, I got a telegram from you yesterday, too late to answer before Monday morning, and to make matters worse I have lost it.

You want to know now the date of the Broadcast from Athlone. The date will be either Feb 1 (8.15 to 8.30) or Feb 9 (8.15 to.8.30). The decision between these dates will be made by the Abbey Board on Wednesday next. (I will let you know.) They will then decide whether to prolong the run of the current play or not. If it is prolonged the date will be Feb 9.

I have no doubt I can arrange for the record you ask for. The last item is unsuited for the B.B.C., being political. It may be best to send you a record of the whole thing.

My plans are now fairly clear. I will put on a second programme at the Abbey at end of February. The first part of this will be the same as the first part of my programme for you, but as we will not broadcast our second programme, this will not I think matter to you. I will learn from this if it will be best to do *In the Poet's Garden* in Dublin and telephone it over. If it is done from Dublin I would help rehearse *In the Village Ale-house* (I forget our exact title) in March and come back here for final rehearsals of *In the Poet's Garden* which could be ready for April. It is just possible that my second Dublin programme would do for London (with some slight changes)

[1] Dictated. Mr. George Barnes had charge of the arrangements for Yeats's broadcast programmes of songs and poems from the B.B.C. These were four, all in this year: 'In the Poet's Pub' on April 2, 'In the Poet's Parlour' on April 22, 'My Own Poetry' on July 3, and 'My Own Poetry Again' on October 29.

but I cannot say yet. I think you are right that short rolls of the drum are better for the wireless than taps. We are using the bamboo flute in my second Dublin programme. But in my first programme using the violin. I think the great thing is to make everybody understand that we don't want professionally trained singers but the sort of people who sing when they are drunk or in love. I think professional musicians have a corpse-factory, mankind melted down and poured out of a bottle.

My first programme here will be a rough singing of rough songs; the second programme will be the best. I shall not have so many people and silent fun, as the Abbey Company will be on tour, but if I put confidence into a certain timid young woman I shall get on all right.

I like working here because I am not afraid of anybody and most people are afraid of me. It is the reverse in London. Yours

W B YEATS

TO GEORGE BARNES[1]

Feb 2 [1937] *Riversdale*

Dear Mr. Barnes, Broadcast a fiasco. Every human sound turned into the groans, roars, bellows of a wild [beast]. I recognise that I am a fool and there will be no more broadcasts of verse from the Abbey stage if I can prevent it. Songs were at the Abbey itself a success—through curtains and so on.

I shall attend what rehearsals you ask me to, but it is quite plain that all I can do is choose the poems and make certain general suggestions. You must take responsibility. Possibly all that I think noble and poignant in speech is impossible. Perhaps my old bundle of poet's tricks is useless. I got Stephenson while singing 'Come all old Parnellites' to clap his hands in time to the music after every verse and Higgins added people in the wings clapping their hands. It was very stirring—on the wireless it was a schoolboy knocking with the end of a pen-knife or a spoon.

I am an humbled man—when you get those 'records' you will know all about it. Yours   W B YEATS

[1] From a typewritten copy.

TO DOROTHY WELLESLEY

Feb. 8 [1937] *Riversdale*

My dear Dorothy, I too was delighted with the Cuala *Broadsheet*. My brother has got to perfection the old fashioned highly ornamented Dublin hotel or tavern where such men would gather after a Parnell Commemoration. The pictures on the wall are right; and the old Dublin waiter holding the bottle on to the salver. My poem too is, as it should be, an old street ballad and it sings well. On Feb. 2 my wife went to Dublin shopping and was surprised at the deference everybody showed her in buses and shops. Then she found what it was—the Casement poem was in the morning paper. Next day I was publicly thanked by the Vice-President of the Executive Council, by De Valera's political secretary, by our chief antiquarian and an old revolutionist, Count Plunkett, who called my poem 'a ballad the people much needed.' De Valera's newspaper gave me a long leader, saying that for generations to come my poem will pour scorn on the forgers and their backers. The only English comment is in the *Evening Standard,* which points out my bad rhymes and says that after so many years it is impossible to discuss the authenticity of the diaries. (The British Government has hidden them for years.)

Politics, as the game is played to-day, are so much foul lying. Last night, being no longer infectious, I had Macmanus in. He is the gunman I have told you of. He is a good deal in England where he has a brother. He says that in England the educated classes are politics-mad, but that the mass of the people have free minds, whereas it is the opposite with us. Certainly I never meet anybody who seems to care which side wins in Spain or anywhere else. Yet we are not ignorant; Macmanus knows more about military conditions in Spain than anybody I have met. I suppose we have had too much politics in the past to care about them now. Even as to Irish politics there is complete indifference.

A dull letter—forgive. I have been working hard, having had my first good night—no drug, sound sleep, though in a chair.

The Anthology continues to be a best seller. I cannot find out that 'The Racketeers' have had the least effect.

I am most anxious to see your new poems—all that you need, I think, to perfect your style is to watch yourself to prevent any departure from the formula 'Music, the natural words in the natural order.' Through that formula we go back to the people. Music will keep out contemporary ideas, for music is the nation's clothing of what is ancient and deathless. I do not mean, of course, what musicians call the music of words—that is all corpse factory, humanity melted down and poured out of a bottle. Yours

W B YEATS

TO ETHEL MANNIN

Feb 11 [*Postmark* 1937] *Riversdale*

My dear Ethel, An Irish revolutionist told me a couple of days ago that English educated persons were mad with politics whereas the uneducated were indifferent—he added 'It is the reverse here.' That man's name is Macmanus, he fought in the great war and then though crippled with wounds became one of Michael Collins's men, after this during the civil war he was the Free State general in command of Limerick. I know no man who in the service of his convictions has lived a life of such danger. I see him almost every week—we constantly discuss the war in Spain, in which he is deeply learned because all war interests him. The last time I met him I suddenly remembered that I did not know on which side were his sympathies and he did not know on which side mine were, except that neither of us wanted to see General O'Duffy back in Ireland with enhanced fame helping 'the Catholic front.' I don't know on which side a single friend of mine is, probably none of us are on any side. I am an old Fenian and I think the old Fenian in me would rejoice if a Fascist nation or government controlled Spain, because that would weaken the British empire, force England to be civil to Indians, perhaps to set them free and loosen the hand of English finance in the far East of which I hear occasionally. But this is mere instinct. A thing I would never act on. Then I have a horror of modern politics —I see nothing but the manipulation of popular enthusiasm by false news—a horror that has been deepened in these last weeks by the Casement business. My ballad on that subject has had success . . . I shall return to the matter again, in a new ballad. These ballads of mine though not supremely good are not ephemeral, the young will sing them now and after I am dead. In them I defend a noble-natured man, I do the old work of the poets but I will defend no cause. Get out of the thing, look on with sardonic laughter. All Germany on [one] side and kept there by rhetoric and manipulated news; all England on the other side and kept there by rhetoric and manipulated news. When the rivers are poisoned, take to the mountain well; or go with Dante into exile—'Cannot I everywhere look upon the stars and think the sweet thoughts of philosophy?'

I must return to the day's business—correcting the final proofs of Shree Purohit Swami's and my translation of the *Upanishads*. Yours affectionately   W B YEATS

By 'manipulated news' I mean more than the manipulation of the news of the day. I mean something that goes deeper, which I come up against in all my thoughts whenever modern interests are concerned. One toils every day to keep one's well pure.

TO THE EDITOR OF THE *IRISH PRESS*[1]

[*Published February* 13, 1937]

Dear Sir, I accept Mr. Alfred Noyes' explanation and I thank him for his noble letter. I, too, think that the British Government should lay the diaries before some tribunal acceptable to Ireland and to England. He suggests that Dr. G. P. Gooch, a great expert in such matters, and I should be 'associated with such an enquiry.' I have neither legal training nor training in the examination of documents, nor have I the trust of the people. But I thank him for his courtesy in suggesting my name.

I add a new version of my song. Mr. Noyes' name is left out: but I repeat my accusation that a slander based on forged diaries was spread through the world and that, whatever the compulsion, 'Spring-Rice had to whisper it.' He was an honourable, able man in the ordinary affairs of life; why then did he not ask whether the evidence had been submitted to the accused? The British Government would have been compelled to answer.

I was dining with the wife of a Belgian Cabinet Minister after

[1] When Yeats's ballad 'Roger Casement' was first published in the *Irish Press* on February 2, 1937, the last verse but one contained a reference to Mr. Alfred Noyes. Mr. Noyes thereupon wrote a disclaimer to the paper, and Yeats's letter in rejoinder was accompanied by a revised version of the ballad.

Casement's condemnation, perhaps after his execution, somebody connected with *The Times* was there; he said they had been asked to draw attention to the diaries. I said it was infamous to blacken Casement's name with evidence that had neither been submitted to him nor examined at his trial. Presently Roger Fry, the famous art critic, came in, and the journalist repeated his statement, and Roger Fry commented with unmeasured fury. I do not remember whether *The Times* spoke of the diaries or not.

Had Spring-Rice been a free man he would have shared my indignation and that of Roger Fry. Yours faithfully   W B YEATS

TO DOROTHY WELLESLEY

Feb. 18 [1937] *Riversdale*

My dear Dorothy: I do not know whether I owe you a letter or not but I feel a desire to gossip—and you are the only person outside my own house with whom I am intimate enough to gossip. Life is suspended for the moment—my recovery from influenza was checked a few days ago, and now I am sitting up in bed completely recovering again. This letter is my first activity. I have just been pleasantly reminded that my friends must not regard me as normal for the present. Yesterday I received (through a New York friend) an invitation from an American Millionaire I have never met to stay with him in Florida, my expenses paid out and back, as he had heard I was in need of change of scene and rest. Clearly an alarum bell is sounding above my head (Gogarty is probably pulling the string). I have cabled my refusal and my gratitude. Florida is a place where the chief entertainment is, I understand, fishing for fish so large that it must be like fly-fishing for cows. To-day comes a letter saying that (through Rothenstein's grace) I have been elected to the Athenaeum Club under Rule 2 (which means no entrance fee); it is, I fear, too expensive for me, but as election under that rule is looked on as a great honour I join for a year at any rate. That means I shall have somewhere to entertain you, for they have a woman's annexe in Carlton Gardens. I have always had a childish desire to walk up those steps and under that classical facade—it seems to belong to folklore, like 'London Bridge,' and that is my subject. I told you that my Casement ballad came out in De Valera's paper some three weeks ago—it has stirred up no end of a commotion. Shaw has written a long, rambling, vegetarian, sexless letter, disturbed by my causing 'bad blood' between the nations; and strange to say Alfred Noyes has done what I asked him in the ballad—spoken 'his bit in public' in a noble letter—I have called it that in my reply—various ferocious Irish patriots have picked off some of the nobility but not all. Public opinion is excited and there is a demand for a production of the documents and their submission to some impartial tribunal. It would be a great relief to me if they were so submitted and proved genuine. If Casement were a homosexual, what matter? But if the British Government can with impunity forge evidence to prove him so, no unpopular man with a cause will ever be safe. Henceforth he will be denied his last refuge—Martyrdom. Hilda Matheson has asked me about Edith Sitwell's name which is in the Broadside advertisement. Do you remember our going through her works, looking in vain for a poem about a Queen of China's daughter, which you remembered? You wanted something of hers. I found that poem in *Faber & Faber's Anthology*—she had left it out of her *Collected Poems*. It is very simple and very charming. I was writing to her—about something else—and asked for it, forgetting that I should have first consulted you. Please forgive me.

No, my dear, this is not a letter—it is gossip. It does not count and if I owe you a letter, I still owe it. Yours affectionately,

W B YEATS

[*On envelope*] I send two or three newspapers with letter of Noyes and my ballad, etc.

TO ETHEL MANNIN

Feb 20 [1937]   *Riversdale*

My dear Ethel, Here is an anonymous subscription for your labour poor-box—not for politics—I am finished with that for ever. It was sent me by the *Irish Press* as payment for my Casement ballad and I do not want to take money for that poem.

Good luck my dear.   W B YEATS

TO ETHEL MANNIN

Monday March 1 [1937]   *Riversdale*

My dear Ethel, Give it to your gardener—that is the best possible use for it. The signature is that of De Valera's son—at least my wife says so. I forgot to look at the Christian name. De Valera is a director of the paper, so it may be his.

The political situation here is unexpected and threatening. De Valera introduced his bill to stop volunteers—the opposition promised support and then in twenty-four hours everything changed. Cosgrave went to bed, the opposition turned against the bill and demanded the recognition of Franco. Cosgrave stayed in bed. De Valera carried his bill against the most violent opposition, his own party doubtful. The reason was that it was suddenly realized that vast numbers of the people believe that Franco is a Catholic fighting against paganism. I have it on good authority that he has been alarmed for months past at the growth of what is called the 'Catholic Front.' I have noticed an ever increasing bigotry in the little pious or semi-literary reviews. I am convinced that if the Spanish war goes on, or if [it] ceases and O'Duffy's volunteers return heroes, my 'pagan' institutions, the Theatre, the Academy, will be fighting for their lives against combined Catholic and Gaelic bigotry. A friar or monk has already threatened us with mob violence.

I go to London in a few days. I shall be at the Athenaeum which has just elected me under Rule 2 which is an honour and frees me from an entrance fee. There is an annex where I can give you lunch. Yours with affection   W B YEATS

TO MRS. LLEWELYN DAVIES[1]

March 19 [1937]   *The Athenaeum*

... Though I do not mention Sassoon in my broadcast—he did not come into the story I was telling—I have put him in the *Oxford*

[1] From a typewritten copy. Moya Llewelyn Davies, daughter of an Irish Nationalist M.P., was married to an English Civil Servant. During the troubles she took a house in Dublin, where she sheltered Michael Collins from the Black and Tans. She collaborated with Professor George Thomson in the translation of *Twenty Years a-Growing* from the Irish of Maurice O'Sullivan. London: Chatto & Windus, 1933.

Book *of* Modern [*Verse.*] I will send you a copy. In spite of universal denunciation from both right and left, fifteen thousand have been sold in three months. I admire Auden more than I said in the Anthology. (His best work has not been published.) The young Cambridge poets write out of their intellectual beliefs and that is all wrong. (Am I a barrel of memories that I should give you my reasons? said Zarathrustra.) My poetry is generally written out of despair—I have just come out of a particularly black attack. I have no such pleasant world as they seem to do. Like Balzac, I see decreasing ability and energy and increasing commonness, and like Balzac I know no one who shares the premises from which I work. What can I do but cry out, lately in simple peasant songs that hide me from the curious?

'What are the things I find as far and wide I go—
Nothing but Cromwell's House and Cromwell's murderous crew! [1]

I had meant to return on April 8 but the B.B.C. may keep me a few days longer. I shall know by Monday night.

I am asking Bumpus to send you the Anthology.

I will write in it when we meet . . .

TO DOROTHY WELLESLEY

May 4th, 1937   *Riversdale*

My dear Dorothy, Only yesterday did I finish the proof sheets of *A Vision*, and I had put off all letter-writing until that finish. I hear that you are still unwell . . . In a sense I am glad, for illness, if not too great, will get you rest, and I doubt if anything else could.

A Vision off my hands, I am getting to other things, and will write to you in a few days about the Broadsides. I may want you to get music for certain poems.

Nothing is happening here of importance, except this: the roses you gave my wife are planted round our front door and are flourishing. The gardener after all repented of his rigour and shovelled mud into the lily pond, and the arum lilies are tall and white, and there are small sprouts on the water lilies.

[1] These two lines differ slightly from the opening of Yeats's ballad 'The Curse of Cromwell,' published in *New Poems*, Cuala Press, 1938.

My next B.B.C. is fixed for July 3rd. I shall be in London at end of June for rehearsals and hope you will have me for a time.

Ottoline has not acknowledged my *Upanishads*. However I shall walk in on her some Thursday.

My daughter has suddenly grown up, spends considerable time on her face with admirable results.

I am reading Roger Fry's translation of Mallarmé. He gives the originals and a commentary by a French critic. I find it exciting, as it shows me the road I and others of my time went for certain furlongs. It is not the way I go now, but one of the legitimate roads. He escapes from history; you and I are in history, the history of the mind. Your 'Fire' has a date or dates, so has my 'Wild Old Wicked Man.'

I begin to see things double—doubled in history, world history, personal history. At this moment all the specialists are about to run together in our new Alexandria, thought is about to be unified as its own free act, and the shadow in Germany and elsewhere is an attempted unity by force. In my own life I never felt so acutely the presence of a spiritual virtue, and that is accompanied by intensified desire. Perhaps there is a theme for poetry in this 'double swan [? sun] and shadow.' You must feel plunged, as I do, into the madness of vision, into a sense of the relation between separated things that you cannot explain, and that deeply disturbs emotion. Perhaps it makes every poet's life poignant, certainly every poet who has 'swallowed the formulas.'

Goodbye for a little. I am your affectionate   W B YEATS

TO EDITH SHACKLETON HEALD [1]

May 4 [1937]   *Riversdale*

Dear Miss Shackleton, A few days before I left London I was in a taxi, held up among a lot of other taxis, near midnight. An art student, whose name I do not know, ran out among the taxis and thrust a bad picture by himself through the window. It was a tribute. I send you a lecture of mine. You need not read it. It is a tribute—that is all. Yours   W B YEATS

[1] From a typewritten copy.

TO THE EDITOR OF THE *IRISH TIMES*

May 13th, 1937   *Rathfarnham*

Sir, I would go into mourning but the suit I kept for funerals is worn out. Our tom fools have blown up the equestrian statue of George II in St. Stephen's Green, the only Dublin statue that has delighted me by beauty and elegance. Had they blown up any other statue in St. Stephen's Green I would have rejoiced. Yours etc,

W B YEATS

TO EDITH SHACKLETON HEALD

May 18 [1937]   *Riversdale*

My dear Edith Shackleton, I hope to be in London in about a month ... I am kept here by my work. I am selecting the poems by living poets which go into my sister's *Broadsides*. In each of the twelve numbers there are two poems with music (no accompaniment); generally it is folk music, and the poet F. R. Higgins whose head is full of tunes sings me the proposed poem and its music. Then I must arrange for the singing of these songs, to put them into circulation. At a banquet of the Irish Academy of Letters at the end of the month Frank O'Connor and Higgins will sing their own songs and an Abbey actor will sing mine. Later some of the songs, or others, will be sung from the Abbey stage. I am, from the musician's point of view, without music. I can only understand it in association with words. I will send you a *Broadside* or two when I can get to my sister's press. Some of the contents, though published now for those who can afford 2/6, will become popular songs in the next generation.

On July 3 I broadcast some of my own poems in London, so I must go there and rehearse beforehand. I am trying to get Dulac to compose the music.

My other work is writing introductions for a new American collected edition of my work, and correcting proofs of a work called *A Vision* (not to be confused with its first edition published years ago). This book is the skeleton in my cupboard. I do not know whether I want my friends to see it or not to see it. I think 'Will

so-and-so think me a crazed fanatic?' but one goes on in blind faith. The public does not matter—only one's friends matter. Friends die, are estranged, or turn out but a dream in the mind, and we are poisoned by the ungiven friendship that we hide in our bones. Yours,
                 W B YEATS

TO ETHEL MANNIN

May 24 [*Postmark* ?1937]   *Riversdale*

My dear: Nothing has changed in my feeling for you. I have nothing but gratitude, and kindness because of your kindness. I have not written to you because I have procrastinated from day to day. I have been busy and bothered. I am writing a general introduction and short prefaces for an expensive American collected edition of my works [1] and I hate writing prose. The only kind of prose I can write is a great toil.

 I say to myself 'I feel' this is [? or] that—I 'hate' something or 'like' something. I thus analyse my feeling, relate one feeling to other and so on until I say 'Yes, I must always have believed that' or 'known that.' AE says in one of his books that by similar analysis he traced his experience back to a pre-natal condition and was filled with terror as if about to approach some act nature desired to keep hidden. No reasoning forward ever gives me a conviction. My analysis has a result the opposite of AE's, mine dissolves terror. Two days ago while trying to analyse my periodical outbursts of political hatred—I remembered how I had deliberately exasperated a friendly audience. I found it was from fear of a theme they were thinking of; now I have got rid of this fear by finding its root in my general conception of life I shall keep my temper better. If one is afraid of looking into a face one hits the face ... Yours
                 W B YEATS

[1] Proposals for an expensive American collected edition of Yeats's writings were made in November 1935. The edition, however, never appeared.

TO EDMUND DULAC[1]

May 27 [1937]   *Riversdale*

My dear Dulac, I shall go to London on June 8. I wrote some days ago to Turner about service flats but have not yet heard from him. As time is getting on I suppose I had better take rooms at the Club for a few days. Is London still full?

On Wednesday night at our Academy Dinner I heard 'The Three Bushes' sung to your music. I never saw an audience more moved, a good many joined in the chorus but softly and with evident feeling. Gogarty was in the chair and made a speech about it—'We are at a great historic moment, a moment as important as that which saw the birth of Elizabethan lyric and its music.' . . . I have had a letter from Starkie this morning praising the method of your music which unites 'poetry and music in the true original way' and is the start of 'a new movement' and 'an art of infinite subtlety of rhythms with music faintly pencilling in the rhythms of the verse.'

Here is the broadcast I propose for the B.B.C.

(*The Three Bushes* is too long and would make unity of theme impossible and would be barred out on moral grounds.)
September 1913 (spoken) or *A Political Prisoner* (spoken)
The Rose Tree
The Curse of Cromwell (sung—two voices)
The Irish Airman
Running to Paradise
The Happy Townland (spoken and sung)
The Song of Wandering Aengus (spoken)

These poems give me the opportunity I want for comment, and in the first four poems I have the great advantage of a public theme. The first four are the tragic real Ireland, the final three the dream. I would like you to set 'The Curse of Cromwell', remembering that it may be sung by two voices, the woman (Margot) singing the chorus. In 'The Happy Townland', though I would be delighted if you set the whole, all you have to do is to set the 'little red fox' lines. I suggest that the poems be knit together by flute music, selected and arranged by you and on such a flute as you approve. If you like, we could publish something of it all, of course we publish your music.

[1] From a typewritten copy.

'The Curse of Cromwell' (of which I send a copy) was sung at the dinner to an Irish folk tune, but its setting was so infinitely inferior to your setting of 'The Three Bushes' that I long for a setting by you. If necessary it could be sung by one voice, man or woman. Yours
W B YEATS

B.B.C. want contents of Broadcast by June 7

If the fact that I cannot undertake to close on any particular note would not put out the flutist I would speak several of the poems myself. If I could speak all except what is sung, I would let Margot sing 'The Curse of Cromwell.'

TO OLIVER ST. JOHN GOGARTY

[*Postmark June 22, 1937*]   *The Athenaeum*

My dear Gogarty, I think I have found

> Mary Kilpatrick—very young
> Ugly face and pleasant tongue [1]

1778 (was that the date?) If so my discovery is certain. She was the sister of the Earl of Ossory and married the second Lord Holland and died of consumption beloved by everybody in 1778. See her portrait by Gainsborough in *The Homes of the Hollands* by the Earl of Ilchester.

I am worried about McCartan. I have just heard from Mrs. He wrote from Cork and expects to be in Dublin in something more than a week from then. I broadcast on July 3rd, a Saturday, and will return to Dublin on Monday, July 5th. I did not expect him till July 1st. I cannot get out of my broadcast as this would break faith not only with the B.B.C. but the performers I am rehearsing. The Academy is to give him a banquet.[2] Stir them up—I must not. He has just sent me £600. Yours   W B YEATS

[1] In 1910 Yeats lived for a time in a house named Fairfield, then belonging to Dr. Gogarty. In one of the three bedrooms which looked on the garden was a window, on a pane of which the words which Yeats here quotes were cut with a diamond. This fact gave rise, many years later, to his play *The Words upon the Window-Pane*.

[2] A Testimonial Committee for W. B. Yeats had been formed in America, the Executive Committee being James A. Farrell, Chairman, George Mac-Donald, Vice-Chairman, Eugene F. Kinkead, Treasurer, William P. Maloney,

If McCartan is returning at once to U.S.A. let me know. I must go over even if only for a day, though it may leave me a wreck. He wired ten days ago but my wife forgot to send me the wire or thought it might worry me and so kept it back.

[*Written at head of letter*] My wife wires that McCartan is thought to be staying several weeks—a great relief.

TO EDMUND DULAC[1]

July 15, 1937   *The Chantry House*
Steyning
Sussex

My dear Dulac, I am most grateful for your typed notes. They are most valuable. I have never accused you of writing 'organised music' or questioned your music in any way. I have questioned a method of singing it. When in Dublin we have played *The Hawk's Well*, the songs of the chorus have been sung by O'Neill, a Cathedral singer. He was accustomed to sing folk songs and the words were fairly intelligible. I was not satisfied because I wanted, and could not get, a singer trained in a theatre. I have now that singer, a man called Stephenson, and when he sang 'The Three Bushes' there was not a word, not a cadence I would or could have changed.

You say that poetry cannot be changed but all my life I have tried to change it. Goethe said that all our modern poetry is wrong because subjective; and in the part in *The Battle of the Books* connected with the fable of the bee and the spider Swift has said the same. All my life I have tried to get rid of modern subjectivity by insisting on construction and contemporary words and syntax. It was to force myself to this that I used to insist that all poems should be spoken (hence my plays) or sung. Unfortunately it was only about a year ago that I discovered that for sung poetry (though not for poetry chanted as Florence Farr chanted) a certain type

---

Secretary, Joseph S. Cullinan, James A. Healy, Cornelius F. Kelley, Dr. Patrick McCartan, Thomas J. O'Neill, James Reeves and Edward F. Tilyou. The object was to provide a fund to ensure that Yeats should have no financial anxieties for the rest of his life. Yeats accepted on condition that he should be allowed to make the matter public; this he did at an Academy Banquet in Dublin on August 17, 1937.
[1] From a typewritten copy.

of 'stress' was essential. (I would like to discuss this with you.) It was by mastering this 'stress' that I have written my more recent poems which have I think, for me, a new poignancy.

I want to get back to simplicity and can best do it—I believe—by writing for our Irish unaccompanied singing. Every change I make to help the singer seems to improve the poems. A man of my ignorance learns from action. Yours W B YEATS

My 'manifesto' [1] says some of the things you say in your notes.

TO EDMUND DULAC [2]

Thursday [*?July* 1937] *Penns in the Rocks*
Withyham
Sussex

My dear Dulac, I mean nothing by 'go over' except that George would like somebody to sing it for her. George's dislike of the singer surprised me even more than her approval of Margot. I have no doubt I shall like your new music as much as I have liked your old when I have heard it sung. It has not yet been sung, because one half the ancient art of song concerns the words. Your (or should I say Barnes') modern young woman had never heard of the English language. Yours W B YEATS

I am a violent man and I am sure that I said and did much that I should not and for that pardon. W B Y

I had told my wife that I disliked the songs—but her letter filled me with astonishment, for on the subject of music we have never been in agreement. She has, I think, generally disliked 'folk' settings. I had indeed awaited her letter with alarm. Of one thing you may be quite certain—she means exactly what she says.

Why not choose for the theme of our public discussion—modern

[1] Presumably the essay 'Music and Poetry' which was included in the bound volume of *Broadsides* issued from the Cuala Press in 1937. The essay was signed by W. B. Yeats and Dorothy Wellesley.
[2] From a typewritten copy.

music and singing?[1] There we have a real difference and in this will rouse much interest and passion.

TO EDITH SHACKLETON HEALD[2]

[*Postmark Aug* 2, 1937]   *Riversdale*

My dear Edith, This is my first perfect day—good health again and all work finished. Since I came home I have worked every morning (6 poems finished, a new poem written, an essay finished, proof sheets of my new play *The Herne's Egg* corrected and so on) and then I was tired out and wrote only three letters though I dictated some. Now I have the delight of health again. Yesterday my sister came with a half finished embroidery, the design the work of Diana Murphy, and it promises to be a beautiful thing. Henceforth she is to do only what I direct. This gives me great pleasure because I think I shall be able to keep her from being wasted. I have the same pleasure that I felt when I turned a great waste room full of cobwebs and dust at the Abbey Theatre into a beautiful little experimental theatre called The Peacock. I shall get more work from Diana Murphy and have suggested that she chooses for her next theme 'Sailing to Byzantium,' or 'Byzantium' or 'The Sleeping [Happy] Townland' or 'The [Song of] Wandering Aengus.' She has done already an 'Innisfree' but I have postponed it as it is an amusing symbolic with no resemblance to the object, and mocking comment might disconcert my sister.

F. R. Higgins and I are, I think, to edit for Macmillan a book of a hundred Irish songs old and new—a good many are already in the *Broadsides*.[3] Our musician will, I think, be a Dublin man who knows music, especially Chinese. The diatonic scale will not be used. As in the case of the *Broadsides* many of the traditional songs will be worked over by Higgins and myself. You can imagine what an improvement it is when all 'steeds' become 'horses' and all 'maids' 'girls.' I find it amusing and easy work and that it incites me to write my own poetry. The work will contain many

[1] Yeats had proposed a broadcast discussion between Edmund Dulac and himself, but had to return to Dublin before it could take place. It was never given.
[2] From a typewritten copy.   [3] This book never appeared.

songs by Higgins and myself. It will be the first Irish song book made by poets and will be intended for 'national singers' only.

The Irish Academy of Letters Banquet to the deputation from my American benefaction will be next week, songs by Higgins and myself. Higgins sings his own, and mine are to be sung by an Abbey actor. The Committee has selected my 'Curse of Cromwell' (to Dulac's music), a melancholy biographical poem you do not know with the burden 'Sang Plato's ghost "What then?"' and my gay poem about the pilgrimage to Lough Derg.

The deputation consists of Pat McCartan, ex-revolutionary, and Farrell, a steel magnate. For the sake of the last a great effort will be made to keep the Academy respectable for one evening. The presence of women has no longer a restraining influence—they recognise no limit except when they recognise little else—I speak of Dublin. Yours affectionately,   W B YEATS

TO EDITH SHACKLETON HEALD[1]

August 6 [1937]   *Riversdale*

My dear Edith . . . I have seen the delegates—two pleasant men here for the Horse Show. P. Farrell, head of the American Steel Trust, a big old man in perfect health, and Pat McCartan, ex-revolutionary agent, now doctor for the Steel Trust. (How does a doctor look after 4000 clerks and 60,000 factory hands?) I dined with them the night before last, with Higgins, and Higgins and the old man's secretary spent the evening singing songs in Gaelic and English—all sung as 'disreputable' people sing. You ask what people here think of Dulac's music. I have met nobody who did not like it, and nobody who liked his singers. The only criticism I have heard was from Higgins, who said 'Good, but too complete in itself—its completeness drew attention from the words.' I am setting out on a great task, a hundred Irish songs, new and old, for Macmillans . . . The Irish race—our scattered 20 millions—is held together by songs, but we must get the young men who go to the American universities as well as those in factories and farms. That is what I say to Irish Americans in justification of all my work, and

[1] From a typewritten copy.

to our own Government and politicians generally. But in reality I am more anarchic than a sparrow . . .

Yes, I am living like a butterfly, and writing poetry. My only healthy life.

I understand what you feel about those Indian books. The teaching of English in India is the worst imaginable. Sturge Moore and I cut out of the *Indian Monk*, and I cut out of *The Holy Mountain*, 'Dear Readers' and like phrases without end. Yet, in spite of all, I find in both works an experience not described elsewhere and occupied with things of the first importance. I feel that I must get that experience recorded without interference from me or from my time. Every writer should say to himself every morning 'Who am I that I should not seem a fool?' Certainly no European, and no Indian living in Europe, should attempt to live by an Indian ethic. Every civilisation must create its own ethic. Yours affectionately　　W B YEATS

TO EDITH SHACKLETON HEALD[1]

August 10, 1937　　　　　　　　　　　　　　*Riversdale*

. . . When you read this last poem of mine,[2] be careful to get the scansion of the third line of the second stanza right. There must be an accent on 'from'—'Túrn from drúdgery'—You will notice how bothered I am when I get to prosody—because it is the most certain of my instincts, it is the subject of which I am most ignorant. I do not even know if I should write the mark of accent or stress thus ́ or thus ̀ . . .

. . . Did I tell you that Macmillan has accepted the book of a hundred and one songs edited by Higgins and myself? The old Irish scales to be used throughout. I doubt if anybody outside Ireland (except, of course, 'unmusical people') will like our work. Certain words lose their literary vitality if the voice keeps on the centre of the note.

I have just finished a long ballad—seven eight-line stanzas—on a Galway story.[3] It has a curious pathos which I cannot define. I

---

[1] From a typewritten copy.
[2] 'Those Images.' In *Last Poems* the line now reads 'Renounce that drudgery.'
[3] 'Colonel Martin.' In *Last Poems* the poem has eight stanzas.

have known from the start what I wanted to do, and yet the idea seemed to lie below the threshold of consciousness—and still lies. There is a chorus almost without meaning, followed by concertina and whistle.

I am back on my old diet—milk, fruit, salad—this time urged by my wife. The fate of all successful revolutions is to become the next orthodoxy. I am encouraged by Frank O'Connor, who came in two evenings ago and told that he followed my example a year ago and now never touches flesh, fowl or fish. . . .

TO DOROTHY WELLESLEY

September 5th, 1937   *Riversdale*

My dear Dorothy, I hear you have been working over old scraps of verse and I am eager to see the result. I have just finished a poem which for the moment I like exceedingly. It is on the Municipal Gallery and is the poem I promised in my speech.[1] It is very much what my speech foreshadowed—perhaps the best poem I have written for some years, unless the 'Curse of Cromwell' is. After I had left the Academy Banquet somebody called for the 'Curse of Cromwell,' and when it was sung a good many voices joined in.

I have no very clear plans except to be back in Ireland during November and December (where I have to keep an eye on the Abbey), and then get to a warm climate with friends and dig myself in to some inexpensive spot until spring. Then I hope to get back to Dublin and face the great problem of my life, put off from year to year, and now to be put off no more; and that is to put the Cuala Press into such shape that it can go on after my death, or incapacity through old age, without being a charge on my wife. Then I can fold my hands and be a wise old man and gay. Yours affectionately,

                                                                          W B YEATS

[1] At the Banquet given by the Irish Academy of Letters to Dr. Patrick McCartan on August 17, Yeats referred to the gift to himself from the American Testimonial Committee, and said: 'I think, though I cannot yet be sure, that a good poem is forming in my head—a poem that I can send them. A poem about the Ireland we have all served, and the movement of which I have been a part.' In the following December he had a small pamphlet privately printed, *A Speech and Two Poems*, for presentation to the subscribers to the Fund. The poems were 'Dedication' and 'The Municipal Gallery Re-Visited.' The first of these has not been printed elsewhere; the second appeared in *New Poems*, Cuala Press, 1938.

TO EDITH SHACKLETON HEALD[1]

Sept. 5 [1937] *Riversdale*

My dear Edith, I go to London Saturday, Sept. 11, to the Athenaeum. If you are back I can go to you two or three days later, but do not hurry your return. I had a telegram from Dorothy a few days ago asking when I could go there and answered Sept. 21. My idea was that I could spend a few days with you and then go to her for a few days and return to you. But if you want to remain on in the South of France my first visit can be to her—but let me know as soon as you can. You know that I am eager to see you, but do not spoil your holiday.

I have not written for some time because about ten days ago I began work on that poem on my visit to the Municipal Gallery I promised in my speech. I had first to make the prose notes and then write the verses at a little over a verse a day. It is finished now— seven verses of eight lines each—one of my best poems. I wrote also a short poem to go with it. My speech and these two poems must now be printed in a pamphlet for the subscribers—there are fifty subscribers and I will limit the edition to sixty. I will bring these and other poems. I often want to send them to you but I have no typist here . . . I have now been writing verse for six weeks and that is as long as I think wise. I now wish to finish off letters, business, etc. and then idle with my friends and read for a short time before I begin the introduction to the Aphorisms of Patanjali, an important book of Swami's. By that time the *Vision* should be out, and the disgust and bewilderment of my friends should start me at verse again . . . Yours affectionately   W B YEATS

TO JAMES A. HEALY[1]

Sept. 7 [1937] *Riversdale*

Dear Mr. Healy, At the Banquet given by The Irish Academy of Letters to Dr. McCartan I thanked him for the gift which gave my declining years 'dignity and ease.' I said that I would thank the other subscribers later.

[1] From a typewritten copy.

I spoke of my renewed visits to the Municipal Gallery where my friends' portraits were—visits made possible, or at any rate easy, now that I could go by taxi. I spoke of my emotion in the Gallery where Modern Ireland is pictured, and said I had a poem on this subject in my head I would send to the subscribers. I am now having that speech, a poem of thanks, and that poem on the Municipal Gallery printed in a pamphlet, of which there will be some sixty copies only.

Please ask your Secretary to send me the names of the fifty subscribers that I may send them copies. I shall of course sign each copy. Yours   W B YEATS

TO DOROTHY WELLESLEY

September 27th, 1937   *The Athenaeum*

My dear Dorothy, You very kindly said that you would introduce the Broadsides to Lady Colefax for her shop, if you had some advertisement leaflets. I enclose three or four. Yours ever,

W B YEATS

I have no news except that I went to *Richard II* last night, as fine a performance [as] possible, considering that the rhythm of all the great passages is abolished. The modern actor can speak to another actor, but he is incapable of reverie. On the advice of Bloomsbury he has packed his soul in a bag and left it with the bar-attendant. Did Shakespeare in *Richard II* discover poetic reverie?

TO ETHEL MANNIN

Oct 18 [Postmark 1937]   *The Chantry House*

My dear Ethel, I have asked Macmillan to send you a copy of my book *A Vision*, which is just out. Please read the first 50 pages and perhaps 'Dove or Swan.' I think they will amuse you and tell you why I am no proletarian. The rest is not for you or for anybody but a doctor in the North of England with whom I have corresponded for years.

Begin to read at page 32. Yours affectionately   W B YEATS

I will send you a suitably inscribed label from Dublin. It was designed for me by Sturge Moore. You can stick it [in]. I will try and remember to gum the back.

TO DOROTHY WELLESLEY

November 11th, 1937 *Riversdale*

My dear Dorothy . . . At Christmas or a little later I go to Monte Carlo or near by, and my wife comes and stays for a few weeks. If you and Hilda hate your fellow travellers on that cruise (and you will), come and join me. I shall be busy writing a *Fors Clavigera* of sorts—my advice to the youthful mind on all manner of things, and poems.[1] After going into accounts I find that I can make Cuala prosperous if I write this periodical and publish it bi-annually. It will be an amusing thing to do—I shall curse my enemies and bless my friends. My enemies will hit back, and that will give me the joy of answering them. I have finished my book of lyric poems, and a new poem which is the start of a new book. I will not send it you until I have done the poem that follows and explains. For five weeks I could not write a line, and then the poem came and a new mass of themes.

I hope that health and happiness are coming back to you. Yours,
W B YEATS

TO EDITH SHACKLETON HEALD[2]

28th November [1937] *Riversdale*

My dear Edith, It is 3.45 and I am downstairs in the study but not sitting idle and motionless, unable to sleep or read, but feeling as

---

[1] This was given the title *On the Boiler* because a mad ship's carpenter named McCoy used occasionally to make speeches from the top of an old boiler on Sligo Quay. Only one number was published, in 1939, after Yeats's death. He was preparing a second but did not live to complete it. *Fors Clavigera* was the title of a miscellany which John Ruskin issued at irregular intervals between 1871 and 1884, in which he vented his opinions on a wide variety of subjects. The papers were eventually collected into eight volumes.

[2] From a typewritten copy.

well as I ever did and this has come all of a sudden. I have had a poor time since I returned, convinced, as my doctor (no cheerful man) was, or seemed, that the rest of my life would be a daily struggle with fatigue. I have worked every morning for a short time and after that was useless. My wife thought it might be climate and wanted to take me to the South of France and stay until you arrived, but I would not have that for certain practical reasons (one being I shall need my library for the next three weeks). Here is the outline of my study which I may never be able to show you.

[*Rough plan of study*]

All round the study walls are book-cases but some stop half way up and over them are pictures by my brother, my father, by Robert Gregory. On each side of the window into flower garden are two great Chinese pictures (Dulac's gift) and in the window into the greenhouse hangs a most lovely Burne-Jones window (Ricketts's gift). Through the glass door into the flower garden I see the bare boughs of apple trees and a few last flowers . . .

My head is full of my first *Fors*. I propose to write out a policy for young Ireland. Yours with love, W B YEATS

I have shaken off depression as a dog shakes off water.

TO EDITH SHACKLETON HEALD[1]

December 10*th* [1937] *Riversdale*

My dear Edith . . . I was particularly glad to get Charles Williams's review of *A Vision*. It was generous of him, for he is a poet I left out of the Anthology and was my first correspondent at the Oxford University [Press,] and greatly shocked at my leaving out certain poets. I imagine it was this that made the firm choose somebody else to continue the correspondence. He is the only reviewer who has seen what he calls 'the greatness and terror of the diagram.' . . . Yours, W B YEATS

[1] From a typewritten copy.

TO DOROTHY WELLESLEY

December 17th, 1937   *Riversdale*

My dear Dorothy, I send you a little book about your favourite poem as a substitute for the old-fashioned Christmas card. The Phoenix was, it seems, the Duchess of Bedford, and if you look up Donne's poem 'St. Lucy's Day,' a poem of great passion, I think you will be convinced, as I am, that to console herself, perhaps for the faithlessness of the Turtle, she had an affair with Donne . . .

I am writing my *Fors Clavigera*; for the first time in my life I am saying what are my political beliefs. You will not quarrel with them, but I shall lose friends if I am able to get on to paper the passion that is in my head. I shall go on to poetry and the arts, and shall not be less inimical to contemporary taste.

I shall be in London but two or three days, long enough to go and see you, and then I go to Monte Carlo. If I stay long in London I shall wear myself out. Yours always,   W B YEATS

TO ETHEL MANNIN

Dec 17 [Postmark 1937]   *Riversdale*

My dear Ethel, I have not written because I have not been out of the house for weeks, and since Higgins and the principal part of the Abbey Company has gone touring in U.S.A. no well-informed person has come into it—at least until two days ago. Two days ago Frank O'Connor came. I said 'Where is O'Faolain?' 'Moving into his new house.' I said 'Ethel Mannin wrote to him but has had no answer.' 'O, he has been talking about that, and says he owes her a letter. He will doubtless write in a few days.' You must remember the undisciplined character of the young Irish man; I never learned to reply to a letter under two or three months until I was about fifty.

I shall be at Monte Carlo early in January. Edith Shackleton takes me out and stays there a month until my son goes back to school, then my wife comes out and takes charge. I shall stay there, or thereabouts, until April. While there I shall do an abominable thing. I have never discussed with you my political opinions—I always dreaded some fundamental difference—indeed I have never

discussed them with anybody. The other day I discovered that I must increase the income of the Cuala Press by about £150 a year and decided to issue a kind of *Fors Clavigera*. I must in the first number discuss social politics in so far as they affect Ireland. I must lay aside the pleasant paths I have built up for years and seek the brutality, the ill breeding, the barbarism of truth. Pray for me, my dear, I want an atheist's prayers, no Christian can do me any good. Yours affectionately
W B YEATS

TO DOROTHY WELLESLEY

December 21st, 1937　　　　　　　　　　　　　　　　　*Riversdale*

My dear Dorothy, I have just wired 'Date not fixed writing.' I could not wire yesterday because the telegraph boy went off without waiting for an answer and I did not like to send the gardener to the village in the wet and rain . . .

My sister came on Sunday to see and approve a new design. A priest had called to see her, and told her that when he confessed a convent of nuns he felt as if he had been eaten alive by ducks. Think of all those blunt bills.

Post goes in a few minutes. Here is a rhyme that has come into my head.

> Unlike that soul of fire
> Sir John ——
> I but raise your finger tip
> To my lip:

and remain your affectionate
W B YEATS

TO DOROTHY WELLESLEY

26th Jan, 1938　　　　　　　　　　　　　　　　　　*Hôtel Carlton*
　　　　　　　　　　　　　　　　　　　　　　　　　　　　Menton

My dear Dorothy, Here I am in a very pleasant and cheap hotel, my window looking out on to a still and smooth sea. I was ill for a few days, and am now well and likely to remain so, for this laborious meditative [life], uninterrupted, perfectly suits me. I have corrected the proofs of *New Poems*, my poems of the last few years, that for the moment please me better than anything I have done. I have got the town out of my verse. It is all nonchalant verse—or it seems to me—like the opening of your 'Horses.'

I shall in all likelihood be here a couple of months. I am finishing my belated pamphlet and will watch with amusement the emergence of the philosophy of my own poetry, the unconscious becoming conscious. It seems to increase the force of my poetry.

Tell me of yourself. Do not try to write verse. You are young, as poets count age, and will be better for meditation and rest. Rest is a great instructor, for it brings the soul back to itself. We sink down into our own soil and take root again. Yours, W B YEATS

TO ETHEL MANNIN

Feb 17 [1938]   *Hôtel Carlton*

My dear Ethel, When you wrote to me from Hyères you said one could live well in the South of France for 10/- a day. If you paid this at Hyères, did it include taxes, tips etc? I pay about 10/- a day here, but taxes, tips etc run it up quite a lot. My wife is with me here and our expenses (this includes milk and mineral water for me) are about £11 a week for the two of us. The service tax is 15 per cent.

It would be very kind of you if you would give me information, as I may have to come here every winter, and I don't know whether to take a villa or not. If a villa is essential I must take it soon.

I have decided that you will not dislike my pamphlet.[1] It has meant a long exploration of my convictions, or instincts, and at first I had black moods of depression, thinking you and one or two other friends would turn against me. Certainly no party will be helped by what I say, and no class. You will find me amusing and I have begun writing poetry from this new subject matter.

I am sending you a copy of my very Rabelasian play *The Herne's Egg*, but do not ask me what it means. It disturbed the Abbey board

[1] *On the Boiler.*

until I withdrew it. An admiring member had decided that the seven ravishers of the heroine are the seven sacraments.

I send my respects to your friend. Yours affectionately.

W B YEATS

TO EDITH SHACKLETON HEALD[1]

Feb 21 [1938] *Hôtel Carlton*

My dear Edith . . . I am often bored, I would like to talk to those people about me who have interesting heads, but I do not know their tongues, but the life is good for my mind and body. I am writing poetry and I had come to think I never would, and the big essay is finished. My life is fixed henceforth—the winters here or near here.

Four days ago came some document for my wife to sign, and her signature had to be witnessed by somebody with an English address. I spoke to a woman who looked as if she had such address. I said 'May I ask you a question?' She met me with stone silence, thinking I was trying to pick her up. Then my wife tried [it] on an old white haired man—he turned out to be the most complete cockney, not an h, but he had no fixed address, lived entirely in hotels. He had just come from Nice. There was an Englishman there, rich, about fifty years of age, quite sane, no friends, a gentleman. This Englishman led about a wooden dog on wheels and addressed all his conversation to the dog. Sometimes he took a photograph, then he would explain to the dog why it must stand in the foreground. My wife had to go to the British Consul to witness her signature. She had not wanted to go, because the Consul at Cannes, soon after the Treaty, became very rude when he saw her Irish passport—however, this one was a pleasant man.

The *Irish Church Gazette* has given *A Vision* a long eloquent enthusiastic review, which makes up for the stupidities of men who attribute to me some thought of their own and reply to that thought. They all think I was bound to explain myself to them. It is just that explaining which makes many English books empty. A Frenchman thinks of his friend and his friend's mistress, with whom he dines at some café, an Englishman of the chance woman he brings

[1] From a typewritten copy.

down to dinner. I have always deliberately left out this explaining. Intensity is all. I want to be some queer man's companion.

We went the other day to Miss Le Gallienne's picture show. Found ourselves at the door, read notice and went in—it was the first day, show just opened—pictures charming and humorous exaggerations of Victorian life—much that was delightful, and Miss Le Gallienne herself . . . with one of those quite natural faces which in a moment you seem to have known all your life—no mask, a kind of cousinly goodwill . . . Yours W B YEATS

TO EDITH SHACKLETON HEALD[1]

March 12 [1938] *Hôtel Idéal Séjour*
Cap Martin

My dear Edith, I have not written because I have been in active letter and telegraphic communication with Dorothy. On March 30 she goes off with Hilda on a tour to Greece and then somewhere for the summer. She wants me to go to Penns in the Rocks first and I cannot refuse under the circumstances. She is writing poetry and is vehement. I shall go there on either the 24th or 26th and then by motor to Steyning on Monday (March 28). I am expecting a telegram which will fix these dates. We are leaving earlier than I thought. We arrive in London on Wednesday (March 23). Can you dine with me at the Grosvenor Hotel that evening? Say eight o'clock. I assume you will be in London.

My revival of *The Poet's Pub* is April 8. I wonder if I could stay at Steyning until I go up for that. I should probably go up on April 6 and get a rehearsal. I have refused to do the Yeats-Starkie broadcast and wish I could get out of the other too. Since this long quiet, with its daily meditation on strange and remote things, I have developed a hatred of crowds. Except for *The Poet's Pub* I had not meant to be in London at all . . . I wonder how much of me you can stand. There is the Guest House. I am in better health than you have ever known me but I am as shy as a mouse. I must peep out from the wainscoting a few times before returning to Dublin at the end of the month, for I will have much business there . . . Yours affectionately, W B YEATS

[1] From a typewritten copy.

TO EDITH SHACKLETON HEALD[1]

March 15th [1938]   *Hôtel Idéal Séjour*

My dear Edith, Dorothy has just wired to fix my final dates to come to her on March 24th and to Steyning on 28th (Monday). I am writing in bed—very well, but I incautiously admitted a bad night . . .

When I wrote to you last I was under the influence of long dream-like absorption in my work. I could not bear the thought of dealing with other men . . .

I knew nobody that I thought of with pleasure outside Chantry House and Penns in the Rocks. But now that I have created nothing for a good many days and have ceased to read my brother and Milton I begin to feel that I can face my fellow men again. I have a one-act play in my head,[2] a scene of tragic intensity, but I doubt if I will begin it until I get to Steyning, or perhaps not till I get to Ireland. I am so afraid of that dream. My recent work has greater strangeness and I think greater intensity than anything I have done. I never remember the dream so deep.

This is a most lovely place. 'If only Laegha were here,' as the mediaeval Irish song to Spring says. Yours affectionately,

                                                 W B YEATS

TO VERNON WATKINS[3]

March 19, 1938   On *Riversdale* notepaper.
                                       [*Hôtel Idéal Séjour*]

Dear Mr. Watkins, I am writing from the S. of France, and will have no fixed address until the end of April when I expect to be back in Dublin. If you should happen to be in Ireland at any date after that I shall be delighted to see you, but please telephone or write beforehand; the servant will always say I am 'out' unless there is some previous arrangement.

I am grateful to you for sending *Wales*.[4] I find your poem 'Yeats'

---

[1] From a typewritten copy.
[2] *Purgatory*. Yeats did begin to write it while staying at the Chantry House.
[3] Dictated.
[4] A small magazine, published irregularly over twelve years. The third number, Autumn 1937, contained Mr. Watkins's poem 'Yeats' Tower.' The last line of all six stanzas read 'O under grass, O under grass, the secret.' The

Tower' rich, strange and moving, and the repetition of that line at the end of every stanza is not only right but essential to the whole. It is a strange, beautiful line. I am not quite certain that I always get your meaning, but I always find beauty. There is another poem in the collection which interests me: 'William Morris,' by Idris Davies. If I were a millionaire I would pay somebody to set it to music and whenever I was visited by any person who knew Morris I would pay somebody to sing it to us.

I thank you very much for the photograph of Ballylee. Yours
W B YEATS

TO MARTIN E. BROWN

May 23 [possibly 1938]   *Riversdale*

Dear Sir, I named the characters in my play [1] Harts and Bruins to the best of my memory because those names were common in the village of Rosses at Rosses Point, Sligo. There were pilots and innkeepers of the name of Bruin and probably also of the name Hart, though in the case of the Harts my memory is more vague. Yours
W B YEATS

My memory is that about half the village were called Bruin. I lived there a good deal when a child.

TO DOROTHY WELLESLEY

May 24th, 1938   *Riversdale*

My dear Dorothy, There has been an article upon my work in the *Yale Review*, which is the only article on the subject which has not bored me for years.[2] It commends me above other modern poets because my language is 'public.' That word, which I had not thought

---

poem is reprinted in *The Ballad of The Mari Lwyd and other poems*, London: Faber & Faber, 1941. Mr. Watkins visited Yeats in Ireland in 1938, and has recorded much of his conversation in a poem 'Yeats in Dublin,' published in *Life and Letters Today*, April 1939, and included in *The Lamp and the Veil*, London, Faber & Faber, 1945. Idris Davies, author of the poem 'William Morris' which Yeats liked, died in 1953, aged 48.

[1] *The Land of Heart's Desire*.
[2] 'Public Speech and Private Speech in Poetry' by Archibald MacLeish. The *Yale Review*, Spring, 1938.

of myself, is a word I want. Your language in 'Fire' is 'public,' so is that of every good ballad. (I may send you the article because the criticism is important to us all.) It goes on to say that, owing to my age and my relation to Ireland, I was unable to use this 'public' language on what is evidently considered the right public material, politics. The enclosed little poem is my reply. It is not a real incident, but a moment of meditation.

I am recovering from a wet dirty sky (always bad for my heart), a bad crossing and a too benevolent existence, but I write daily. Yours affectionately, W B YEATS

P.S. In part my poem is a comment on ———'s panic-stricken conversation.

No artesian well of the intellect can find the poetic theme.

POLITICS [1]

'In our time the destiny of man presents its meaning in political terms.'
(Thomas Mann)

> Beside that window stands a girl;
> I cannot fix my mind
> On their analysis of things
> That benumb mankind.
> Yet one has travelled and may know
> What he talks about;
> And one's a politician
> That has read and thought.
> Maybe what they say is true
> Of war and war's alarms;
> But O that I were young again
> And held her in my arms.

TO MAUD GONNE MACBRIDE [2]

June 16 [1938]   *The Chantry House*

My dear Maud, Yes of course you can say what you like about me.[3] I do not however think that I would have said 'hopeless struggle.'

---

[1] A revised version of this poem appeared in *Last Poems*, 1939.
[2] From a typewritten copy.
[3] In her autobiographical book *A Servant of the Queen*, London: Gollancz, 1938.

I never felt the Irish struggle 'hopeless.' Let it be 'exhausting struggle' or 'tragic struggle' or some such phrase. I wanted the struggle to go on but in a different way.

You can of course quote those poems of mine, but if you do not want my curse do not misprint them. People constantly misprint quotations.

I do not know if Agnes Tobin is living . . . She is probably dead. A week ago I was talking to Mrs. Moody, the great tennis player, about the Tobin family. She lives in San Francisco and knows them well, but she had never heard of Agnes Tobin.

When I came back from the south of France in, I think, April I was ill for a time. When I got better I thought of asking you to dine with me, then I put it off till *On the Boiler* is out. *On the Boiler* is an occasional publication like my old *Samhain* which I am about to bring out. The first number will be published in about a month. Perhaps you will hate me for it. For the first time I am saying what I believe about Irish and European politics. I wonder how many friends I will have left. Some of it may amuse you.

I am staying now with an old friend Miss Shackleton Heald, once the best paid woman journalist in the world. She found she had no leisure and so gave up most of it. On Tuesday I go to Penns in the Rocks, Withyham, also in Sussex, and stay with Lady Gerald Wellesley, another good friend, then back here and then to Ireland for the first performance of my one-act play *Purgatory*.

God be with you,   W B YEATS

TO DOROTHY WELLESLEY

June 22nd, 1938   *Riversdale*

My dear Dorothy . . . I had meant to go to England in July or early August, but am held here by reconstruction at the Abbey and at Cuala.

I am out of sorts and will be, while this weather lasts. Yesterday I reminded myself that an Eastern sage had promised me a quiet death, and hoped that it would come before I had to face *On the Boiler No. 2*. To-day I am full of life and not too disturbed by the enemies I must make. This is the proposition on which I write:

'There is now overwhelming evidence that man stands between two eternities, that of his family and that of his soul.' I apply those beliefs to literature and politics, and show the change they must make. Lord Acton said once that he believed in a personal devil, but as there is nothing about it in the Cambridge Universal History which he planned, he was a liar. My belief must go into what I write, even if I estrange friends; some when they see my meaning set out in plain print will hate me for poems which they have thought meant nothing. I will not forget to send you that poem about the Greek statues, but I have not yet had it re-typed. Yours affectionately, W B YEATS

TO EDITH SHACKLETON HEALD[1]

June 28th [1938] *Riversdale*

My dear Edith, May I come almost at once? I think I could come towards the end of next week. In the next day or two my sister will get my Cuala proposal and if she accepts it I can get away a few weeks.

I hope you can have me. Dorothy will no doubt take me for a time or I can put [in] a few days in London. I could return here in August, not only for Cuala but for my new play [2] and certain other plays of mine at the Abbey, all staged by my daughter. My plan is to spend most of July and part of August in England, return here and then go back to England at the end of September and stay there until November when I go to France with my wife . . .

I am writing to Gort to find out if there is a photographer there who could photograph Coole. There used to be an old man but he must be dead. I thank you for all you have done in the matter . . .

I enclose the poem you asked for.[3] In reading the third stanza remember the influence on modern sculpture and on the great seated Buddha of the sculptors who followed Alexander. Cuchulain is in the last stanza because Pearse and some of his followers had a cult of him. The Government has put a statue of Cuchulain in the rebuilt post office to commemorate this. Yours affectionately, W B YEATS

Please wire if you can have me.

[1] From a typewritten copy.   [2] *Purgatory.*
[3] 'The Statues.' The poem was not published until after Yeats's death; it appeared in the *London Mercury*, March 1939, and in *Last Poems.*

TO DOROTHY WELLESLEY

13th July, 1938 *Steyning*

My dear Dorothy . . . Before I left Dublin I gave *On the Boiler* to Higgins, who is to send it to the printer. He has been away eight months and so was quite unprepared. His comment was, 'I expected an old man's oracular serene remarks—death holding the ledger—and I got this. The boiler is going to be very hot.'

I am writing a new 'Crazy Jane' poem—a wild affair. Yours affectionately, W B YEATS

TO EDITH SHACKLETON HEALD[1]

July 21 [1938] *Penns in the Rocks*

My dear Edith, Life is pleasant and uneventful. That day when I left the telephone I left because Dorothy had got out the plans of the Folly—besides, a telephone makes me timid and scared. The Folly itself is showing one white pillar among the rocks and trees . . .

Hilda[2] came down but went back this morning and now Dorothy is out on the lawn reading *On the Boiler*, for which I thank you. On Friday Turner[3] comes. I am in the midst of a new poem. That is all my budget—No, I have just found the new Agatha Christie in my room. I shall begin it at once. Yours affectionately, W B YEATS

Cornish[4] told Dorothy that she gave me too much to eat, so all is well. Agatha Christie has opened well. I have just thought of a chorus for a ballad. A strong farmer is mourning over the shortness of life and changing times, and every stanza ends 'What shall I do for pretty girls now my old bawd is dead?'[5] I think it might do for a new *Broadside*.

[1] From a typewritten copy.
[2] Hilda Matheson.
[3] W. J. Turner, the poet and music critic.
[4] The butler at Penns in the Rocks.
[5] The ballad became 'John Kinsella's Lament for Mrs. Mary Moore.' It was published in *Last Poems*.

TO DOROTHY WELLESLEY

August 15th, 1938   *Riversdale*

My dear Dorothy, I enclose an account of the production of my play.[1] My speech is misreported. I said: 'I have put nothing into the play because it seemed picturesque; I have put there my own conviction about this world and the next.' A Boston Jesuit has tried to stir up trouble, but has, I think, failed. The mass of the people do not like the Jesuits. They are supposed to have given information to the Government in 1867. This story, which may be quite untrue, has made the Franciscans the chief religious influence in Dublin. The chief character in my play was magnificently played by a player who could probably go to the Barn.[2] The other character was played by a fine actor too old for the part. There was a fine performance of my *Baile's Strand*. 'Cuchulain' seemed to me a heroic figure because he was creative joy separated from fear.

I have found a book of essays about Rilke waiting me; one on Rilke's ideas about death annoyed me. I wrote on the margin:

> Draw rein; draw breath.
> Cast a cold eye
> On life, on death.
> Horseman pass by.

Yours affectionately   W B YEATS

TO EDITH SHACKLETON HEALD[3]

August 15, 1938   *Riversdale*

... My play has been a sensational success so far as the audience went. I have never seen a more excited house. (I enclose cutting.) But I have had this before. The trouble is outside. The press or the clerics get to work—the tribal dance and the drums. This time the

---

[1] *Purgatory*, which was produced at the Abbey Theatre on August 10. The part of the Old Man was played by Michael J. Dolan, that of the Boy by Liam Redmond. The setting of the play was by Anne Yeats.

[2] Dorothy Wellesley and Yeats were planning a programme for the Barn Theatre at Smallhythe, Tenterden, Kent, established by Edith Craig as a memorial to her mother, Ellen Terry.

[3] From a typewritten copy.

trouble is theological. As always I have to remain silent and see my work travestied because I will not use up my fragile energies on impermanent writing. The night after *Purgatory* my *Baile's Strand* was revived with a magnificent Cuchulain. I have not seen it for years and it seemed to me exactly right—ornate, elaborate, like a Crivelli painting. My daughter's designs for it and *Purgatory*—especially for this—were greatly admired. *Purgatory* perfectly acted. House crowded ... Yours affectionately   W B YEATS

TO ETHEL MANNIN

August 22 [*Postmark* 1938]   *Riversdale*

My dear Ethel, Will you and your friend [1] dine with me at the Shelbourne Hotel on Sunday evening at 8 p.m.? (Sunday is I think the 28th.)

I have not written to you because I was waiting for *On the Boiler*. Half my friends may never speak to me when it comes out. However I had just decided that it was better to see them while I was sure that they would see me. You I have long wanted to see. There are things I want to ask. Strange to say, at certain points our political thought is the same. Yours affectionately   W B YEATS

I am arranging my burial place. It will be in a little remote country churchyard in Sligo, where my great grandfather was the clergyman a hundred years ago. Just my name and dates and these lines

> Cast a cold eye
> On life, on death;
> Horseman pass by.

On Monday night next Abbey plays *Plough and the Stars* by O'Casey, almost our best play.

[1] The friend mentioned in this letter, as in that of February 17, 1938, is Mr. Reginald Reynolds, whom Miss Mannin married in 1938.

TO EDITH SHACKLETON HEALD[1]

September 4th [1938]   *Riversdale*

My dear Edith, Welcome. Tomorrow you get home.[2] You have seemed so far off. I have done nothing but write and occasionally intervene in Abbey affairs. There, by a curious coincidence, a crisis germane to my thought is forming ... Ireland is getting a proletariat which in Dublin is pushing aside the old peasant basis of the nation. We talk of getting players from the country but don't know how to do it.

The religious controversy over *Purgatory* died down. Most people seem to be on our side and the daily newspapers had leaders in our support. The Festival drew great crowds but our performances were not as good as they should have been ... I am talking by hearsay for I went only twice. Some of the acting in my two plays—the two I saw—was magnificent. I have written a long poem called [*illegible*] which you will like[3] ...

I am much better. All my old clothes fit again but I have to keep my legs up—dammit—and take no exercise, and I had begun to take delight in my twenty minutes up and down your garden.

When we meet at the end of this month or thereabouts I shall have much poetry to read to you. *On the Boiler* has at last gone to the press ... Yours affectionately   W B YEATS

TO EDITH SHACKLETON HEALD[1]

[? *September* 1938]   *Riversdale*

My dear Edith ... I told my sister, the embroideress, that I had described my own burial and tombstone in a poem. She said 'This is a break with tradition. There has not been a tombstone in the Yeats family since the eighteenth century. The family has always been very gay.' It seems that we let the grass grow over the dead and speak of them no more. Yet we are pious and affectionate. Yours affectionately   W B YEATS

[1] From a typewritten copy.
[2] Miss Shackleton Heald had been staying at Ramatuelle, Var.
[3] This poem was finally called 'Under Ben Bulben.' It was published after Yeats's death in the *Irish Times*, February 3, 1939, and in *Last Poems*.

TO DOROTHY WELLESLEY

October 8th, 1938 *Riversdale*

My dear Dorothy, I have been arranging my Cuala business and at last have made it almost certain that I could reach you by October 15th at latest, and now am confined to my room with lumbago. I have no choice but to ask if I may postpone my visit. Forgive me.

Yesterday morning I had tragic news. Olivia Shakespear has died suddenly. For more than forty years she has been the centre of my life in London and during all that time we have never had a quarrel, sadness sometimes but never a difference. When I first met her she was in her late twenties but in looks a lovely young girl. When she died she was a lovely old woman. You would have approved her. She came of a long line of soldiers and during the last war thought it her duty to stay in London through all the air raids. She was not more lovely than distinguished—no matter what happened she never lost her solitude. She was Lionel Johnson's cousin and felt and thought as he did. For the moment I cannot bear the thought of London. I will find her memory everywhere. Yours affectionately, W B YEATS

TO ETHEL MANNIN

Oct 9 [? 1938] *Riversdale*

My dear Ethel, I have read your novel [1] with very deep interest. All reading is slow with me because my eyes tire. I read a few pages and then sit idle for many minutes. I vexed George Moore by taking six weeks over his *Esther Waters*, a book I greatly admired. When I had finished your book I re-read an essay on 'the idea of death' in the poetry of Rilke and compared your thought with Rilke's and with the same thought as it is in what I call my 'private philosophy' (The *Vision* is my 'public philosophy'). My 'private philosophy' is the material dealing with individual mind which came to me with that on which the mainly historical *Vision* is based. I have not published it because I only half understand it. Your admirable and vivid book is the first book in England on the subject and is a very great stimu-

[1] *Darkness my Bride.*

lant to understanding. According to Rilke a man's death is born with him and if his life is successful and he escapes mere 'mass death' his nature is completed by his final union with it. Rilke gives Hamlet's death as an example. In my own philosophy the sensuous image is changed from time to time at predestined moments called *Initiationary Moments* (your hero takes ship for Bordeaux, he goes to the Fair, he goes to Russia and so on). One sensuous image leads to another because they are never analysed. At *The Critical Moment* they are dissolved by analysis and we enter by free will pure unified experience. When all the sensuous images are dissolved we meet true death. Franz will follow the idea of liberty through a series of *initiationary* movements—(1) Spain, and then somewhere else, but will never I think analyse the meaning of 'liberty' nor the particular sensuous image that seems to express it, and so will never meet true death. This idea of death suggests to me Blake's design (among those he did for Blair's *Grave* I think) of the soul and body embracing. All men with subjective natures move towards a possible ecstasy, all with objective natures towards a possible wisdom. A German philosopher has said that men in Italian portraits seem to wait an accidental death from the blow of a dagger, whereas the men painted by Rembrandt have death already in their faces. Painters of the Zen school of Japanese Buddhism have the idea of the concordance of achievement and death, and connect both with what they call 'poverty.' To explain poverty they point to those paintings where they have suggested peace and loneliness by some single object or by a few strokes of the brush.

Is all this too abstract for your dear concrete soul? Yours affectionately   W B YEATS

TO ETHEL MANNIN

Oct 20 [Postmark 1938]   *Riversdale*

My dear Ethel, Goethe said the poet needs all philosophy but must keep it out of his work. I am writing a play on the death of Cuchulain, an episode or two from the old epic. My 'private philosophy' is there but there must be no sign of it; all must be like an old faery tale. It guides me to certain conclusions and gives me precision but

I do not write it. To me all things are made of the conflict of two states of consciousness, beings or persons which die each other's life, live each other's death. That is true of life and death themselves. Two cones (or whirls), the apex of each in the other's base.

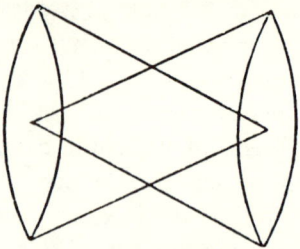

I am trying to get off to England but have been delayed again and again—this time by a dentist. Yours   W B YEATS

TO DOROTHY WELLESLEY

Dec. 1st, 1938   *Hôtel Idéal Séjour*

My dear Dorothy, I am back at my old Cap Martin hotel. The other was impossible, motor horns, trains, children, wireless. An affable landlady, in return for an audience, forgave us leaving in an hour . . .

This hotel is perfect as ever. We are the only guests; all the other hotels are empty too; the strike scared people away. The climate is perfect and it is so warm that on a couple of nights I have slept with nothing over me but a sheet and the window wide open. I am in the garden for a large part of each day. Lots of villas to let, including one with the most lovely garden in the world; it was once the garden of the Empress Eugénie; so if you tire of your present villa you can come here.

I do nothing but write verse. Yours,   W B YEATS

TO EDITH SHACKLETON HEALD[1]

Wed. Dec. 8th [1938]   [*Hôtel Idéal Séjour*]

My dear Edith, The night before last I hardly slept at all, and yesterday, because my mind was full, did a wonderful day's work and had

[1] From a typewritten copy.

a letter in my head I wanted to write to you but was brought away to see my doctor. Last night I was given a sedative, slept for many hours and cannot do any work and the letter has faded. Indeed I am still half asleep.

It is very warm here—sometimes too warm in the sun and at night...

On Monday night *Purgatory* was probably revived in Dublin but I have no news. May hear tomorrow. I know nothing except that the theatre is making money and has been for weeks. I envy the players who can never idle because the task is always there and the day's rehearsal. They have nothing to disturb their conscience except an occasional fit of intoxication and a little daily spite—I mean the old players whom I have known always. Yours affectionately,

W B YEATS

TO V. C. CLINTON-BADDELEY[1]

December 13, 1938   *Hôtel Idéal-Séjour*

Dear Clinton-Baddeley, Have you got those essays, I think there were three, which you spoke to the B.B.C.? I read them at Penns in the Rocks, and though I differed somewhat, thought them excellent. I would like to go through them with Higgins. I have not yet discussed it with him, but I think it possible that we might be able to arrange a small book for the Cuala Press; these essays or some part of them, some work by Higgins and by myself, and some by an Abbey expert on verse-speaking. What I am hoping for is a small book dealing with the relations between speech and song.

You might let me know to this address, where I shall be for some weeks to come. Yours   W B YEATS

TO EDITH SHACKLETON HEALD[2]

Dec. 22 [1938]   *Hôtel Idéal Séjour*

My dear Edith, My son is expected. He should have been here at 2 p.m., then it was to be at 4. Now it is to be 12 p.m. at the earliest.

[1] Dictated.   [2] From a typewritten copy.

The hotel proprietor, who is always in bed by 10, is keeping himself awake in the hall. It is now 10.30. The mischief is all caused by the weather. Here it has been cold but I was able to sit out after lunch as usual. Yesterday Dorothy and Hilda came, finding their villa cold, I think, and glad to find somebody to talk to. Hilda incredibly gay at the sudden variety. I had not known they were in France. Their telephone sounded in the morning. They had been here a week, arriving on the edge of our only bad weather.

My wife says you may fix any date in January you like to arrive on. She has much to arrange with my sister about Cuala. When, or if, we go to Dorothy I do not know. Dorothy seemed overwhelmed by the cold of her villa and the warmth of our hotel. The villa was a childish memory of Dorothy's.

Nothing seems going on in Dublin, or if it is I am being told nothing. Higgins has dropped in a gulph. Owes me four letters—damn.

All friendly here except the cats which look at one as if they expect to be eaten—perhaps they do. The Rapallo cats did not seem to mind—not in the same personal way. Yours affectionately

W B YEATS

I am getting much better.

TO ETHEL MANNIN

Dec 23 [1938] *Hôtel Idéal Séjour*

My dear Ethel, Do not ask me to say anything. I should have to think of such a lot of things. Did I say this or do that? or did so and so? I don't want to think except when I must. Besides, I may want some day to write a book of etiquette and it might be an embarrassment. Did I go to sleep? I don't think so but it does not matter. I always get Dulac to arrange the wine and the food for I [he] knows more about it. It is a pleasant tale and in this atheistic age nobody believes anything, so why should I bother? [1]

Damn Toller, but you should know that no nationalist of the

[1] This letter was written after reading the proofs of Miss Mannin's book *Privileged Spectator*. The 'half-Russian novel' mentioned is *Darkness my Bride*.

school of John O'Leary has ever touched international politics. But no need to correct—this atheistic age protects us all.

This is the bother about *The Boiler*. Went to the printer seven months ago—small Longford printer selected in pure eccentricity by the poet Higgins—not yet out.

Am I a mystic?—no, I am a practical man. I have seen the raising of Lazarus and the loaves and fishes and have made the usual measurements, plummet line, spirit-level and have taken the temperature by pure mathematic. But on the other hand the author of the last chapters of the half-Russian novel is not a 'materialist.' I greet the lamb.

I am in better health than usual and writing *Boiler No. 2.* Yours
W B YEATS

I return typed copy. I have just found your typed envelope. You're neat—you always are.

TO EDITH SHACKLETON HEALD[1]

Saturday [? December 1938]   *Hôtel Idéal Séjour*

My dear Edith, Dec. 27 [2] will be quite suitable.

For two days I have been tired—that is my one impediment. I have tired myself finishing the play [3] and writing a lyric [4] that has risen out of it, and also talking. Last night I dined at the villa, and the two days before Hilda (Dorothy had a dentist) and Turner and his wife—they are staying at the villa—came over. Dorothy goes home early in February and you and I will be alone here, and I, despite all this pleasant excitement which gives me subjects for poems, will be glad of it. Indeed that quiet will be a necessity for me. My whole mind has changed, it is more sensitive, more emotional. I can only hope that you will not find this quiet dull. The car will be a great pleasure. Yours affectionately, W B YEATS

[1] From a typewritten copy.
[2] A slip for January 27, the proposed date of Miss Shackleton Heald's arrival.
[3] *The Death of Cuchulain.*
[4] 'Cuchulain Comforted.' It appeared in *Last Poems*.

TO EDITH SHACKLETON HEALD[1]

January 1st [1939]   *Hôtel Idéal Séjour*

My dear Edith, Too many journeys between Dorothy's villa and here, too much excitement at finishing my play and reading it out, too much conversation, villa and here, too much chess in which I am always beaten by my son, and so on and so on. Result—have been tired and lazy and out of the mood for letters. But now I am all right again.

Are your plans settled yet? Have you found anybody who can help bring the car? Hilda has hired one in Nice but is not a very confident driver and the villa is some way off. Dorothy, I imagine, pays for the car. It is much more expensive than bringing one's own car . . .

I think my play is strange and the most moving I have written for some years. I am making a prose sketch for a poem—a kind of sequel—strange too, something new. Yours   W B YEATS

TO LADY ELIZABETH PELHAM[2]

January 4, 1939   *Hôtel Idéal Séjour*

. . . I know for certain that my time will not be long. I have put away everything that can be put away that I may speak what I have to speak, and I find 'expression' is a part of 'study.' In two or three weeks—I am now idle that I may rest after writing much verse—I will begin to write my most fundamental thoughts and the arrangement of thought which I am convinced will complete my studies. I am happy, and I think full of an energy, of an energy I had despaired of. It seems to me that I have found what I wanted. When I try to put all into a phrase I say, 'Man can embody truth but he cannot know it.' I must embody it in the completion of my life. The abstract is not life and everywhere draws out its contradictions. You can refute Hegel but not the Saint or the Song of Sixpence. . . .

[1] From a typewritten copy.
[2] Fragment. Text from Joseph Hone's *W. B. Yeats 1865-1939*.

EPILOGUE

YEATS died on January 28, 1939. He had expressed his wish to be buried at Drumcliffe in Sligo, but had said that if he should die in France he might be buried there. His burial took place in the cemetery of Roquebrune, which lies high above the village, looking out to the sea. This was intended to be only a temporary resting-place; a plain stone with inscription W. B. YEATS, 1865–1939 marked the spot. After her return to Ireland and consultation with the family, Mrs. Yeats decided that his body should be brought home; the French Government offered the services of a destroyer, but the outbreak of the war that autumn brought all plans to a standstill.

A plot of ground had been secured in Drumcliffe churchyard, and in September 1948, nine years after his death, the body of the great poet was brought back to his own countryside. After lying in state in the Town Square of Roquebrune, where a poet from Menton delivered his tribute, the coffin went by road to Nice and was there taken aboard the Irish corvette *Macha*, reaching Ireland eleven days later. As it was feared that the channel at Sligo might be too narrow for a safe landing, the boat entered Galway Bay. Mrs. Yeats, her children, and Jack Yeats, the poet's brother, went aboard and the coffin was piped ashore. From Galway the funeral procession made its way by road to Sligo where a military guard of honour waited. The Government was represented by Mr. Sean MacBride, Maud Gonne's son, Minister for External Affairs; the Mayor and Corporation of Sligo attended, and friends and admirers of the poet gathered in the churchyard of Drumcliffe; the last resting-place was reached. A stone, inscribed as he had directed, now stands there, 'under bare Ben Bulben's head.'

   No marble, no conventional phrase;
   On limestone quarried near the spot
   By his command these words are cut:

    Cast a cold eye
    On life, on death.
    Horseman, pass by!

INDEX

Abbey Theatre, The, 210, 237, 262, 287, 387, 390, 392, 424, 437, 438, 439, 444, 449, 452, 462, 463, 477, 481, 482, 487, 495, 505, 511, 512, 527, 534, 535, 537, 538, 541, 543, 547, 554, 555, 559, 567, 568, 578, 601, 615, 626, 629, 635, 648, 649, 654, 656, 657, 669, 673, 691, 698, 702, 711, 713, 714, 720, 734, 737, 740, 747, 760, 763, 768, 770, 772, 777, 778, 785, 787, 788, 793, 794, 795, 797, 800, 806, 808, 818, 826, 829, 831, 834, 836, 840, 843, 862, 868, 871, 878, 879, 885, 888, 894, 897, 900, 904, 910, 913, 914, 915, 916, 919
Academic Committee of the Royal Society of Literature, The, 549n, 556, 557, 563, 564, 565, 566, 572
Academy, The, 35, 45, 49, 101, 102, 105, 112, 120, 163, 169, 173, 174, 228, 373, 386, 388, 399
Acton, Lord, 911
Adam, Villiers de L'Isle, 240, 325
Adams, Henry, 666
AE. *See* Russell, George W.
Aga Khan, The, 602
Ainley, Henry, 607, 609, 610, 611
Aitken, Charles, 619, 620, 622, 623
Aldington, Mrs. (H. D.), 644n
Allgood, Sara, 477, 508, 560, 567, 702
Allingham, William, 73, 85, 92, 116, 176, 179, 187, 206, 247, 250, 253, 446
Antheil, George, 758, 759, 760, 761, 765, 768
Antoine, André, 409, 439n, 440, 441
Apes of God, The, 776
Apple Cart, The, 767, 770
Arabian Nights, The, 832, 833
Aran Islands, The, 266, 268, 278, 280, 528
Archer, William, 308, 310, 398, 399, 439, 530, 543
Ardilaun, Lady, 573
Armstrong, Laura, 117n
Armstrong, G. F. Savage-, 211n, 300, 301
Armstrong, Sir Walter, 333
Arnold, Matthew, 135
Art Review, The, 150, 154
Asquith, The Rt. Hon. H. H. (afterwards Lord Oxford), 540, 610, 679
Asquith, Mrs. (afterwards Lady Oxford), 559

Athenaeum, The, 114, 296, 474
Auden, W. H., 833, 837, 860, 886
Axel, 805

Balfour, Rt. Hon. Arthur James, 610
Balfour, Lady Betty, 306
Balfour, Gerald, 306
Balzac, Honoré de, 233, 357, 449, 513, 536, 762, 791, 805, 807, 832, 886
Banim, Michael and John, 127n, 128, 129, 134, 136, 143, 144, 146, 188, 247, 248
Barker, H. Granville, 383, 435, 442, 507, 531, 579
Barlow, Jane, 239, 248
Barry, Dr. William, 300, 316, 332
Battle, Mary, 305, 551
Baudelaire, Charles, 325, 715
Bax, Clifford, 259, 858, 877
Beardsley, Aubrey, 237, 264, 298, 434, 574, 575, 860
Beardsley, Mabel, 530, 574n, 575
Beecham, Sir Thomas, 611, 612
Beerbohm, Sir Max, 264, 530
Bell, The, 267
Bending of the Bough, The, 327, 334, 356
Bennett, Allen, 499n
Benson, F. R., 342, 349, 355
Bergson, Henri, 723, 782
Berkeley, Bishop, 779, 782, 784, 786, 787, 791, 818
Besant, Mrs. Annie, 137, 150, 236
Binyon, Laurence, 383, 388, 545, 546, 549, 595, 598, 698
Birch, Una, 543n, 558
Birrell, Rt. Hon. Augustine, 535
Björnson, Björnstjerne, 360
Blake, Dr. Carter, 113
Blake, William, 112, 118, 125, 133, 145, 150, 152, 153, 154, 158, 169, 170, 199, 227, 262, 263, 264, 265, 324, 347, 360, 377, 379, 592, 630, 631, 644, 669, 686, 691, 698, 710, 730, 758, 872, 873, 917
Blavatsky, Helena Petrovna, 40, 56n, 57, 58, 59, 86, 88, 90, 91, 97, 123, 125, 126, 137, 145, 162, 236, 650, 665, 672
Blunt, Wilfrid Scawen, 376, 400, 710
Bodkin, Thomas, 624, 749, 877
Boehme, Jacob, 234, 262, 592

925

Bookman, The, 59, 208, 211, 214, 218, 220, 221, 229, 233, 254, 257, 258, 267, 279, 281, 285, 286, 322
Boston Pilot, The, 38, 42, 63, 91, 96, 102, 141, 142, 144, 152, 153, 155, 165, 167, 170, 171, 172, 188, 221
Botticelli, 65, 865
Bottomley, Gordon, 388, 805
Boucicault, Dion, 143
Bourchier, Arthur, 465, 466, 475
Bourget, Paul, 267
Boyd, Ernest, 591n
Boyle, William, 448, 462n, 464, 495, 527, 569
Brandes, Georg, 268
Brett, George, 452
Bridges, Robert, 549, 577, 580, 596, 598, 644, 707, 774
Briggs, Miss, 264, 265
Broadcasts, 786, 789, 859, 863, 866, 867, 868, 875, 878n, 879, 886, 887, 888, 891, 906
Brooke, Rupert, 648
Brooke, Stopford A., 62, 188, 200, 251, 483
Brown, Dr. Haydn, 618
Browning, Robert, 46, 55, 170, 266, 454, 511, 565, 759, 776
Bruce, Kathleen (afterwards Lady Kennet), 507, 509
Budge, Sir Ernest A. Wallis, 820n
Bullen, A. H., 350, 352, 361, 362, 380, 381, 382, 390, 391, 392, 393, 394, 395, 397, 398, 405, 415, 422, 426, 434, 446, 449, 456, 469, 470, 478, 484, 491, 495, 494, 498, 499, 503, 505, 506, 507, 509, 523, 524, 527, 542, 561, 562, 578, 599
Bulloch, P. W., 283, 340
Bunyan, John, 650
Burke, Edmund, 779, 795
Burne-Jones, Sir Edward, 35, 865, 901
Burns, Robert, 67, 246, 407, 583
Butler, H. Montague, 123n
Butler, Samuel, 852
Butt, Isaac, Q.C., 124n, 571
Byron, Lord, 467, 468, 473, 548, 710

Calvert, Edward, 646, 799
Campbell, J. G., 136, 359
Campbell, Joseph, 477
Campbell, Mrs. Patrick, 360, 468, 475, 476, 508, 511, 512, 513, 524, 526, 528, 533, 535, 536, 539, 540, 541, 544, 568, 625, 654, 655, 674
Campbell, Stella (Mrs. Mervyn Beech), 531, 540
Carleton, William, 75, 78, 79, 121, 124, 126, 127, 128, 129, 130, 136, 142, 143, 144, 147, 247, 248, 350
Carlyle, Thomas, 608
Carr, Philip, 399, 450n, 457, 531
Carson, Murray, 537, 542
Casement, Sir Roger, 803, 867, 868, 869, 870, 874, 876, 880, 881, 882, 883, 884

Casey, W. F., 527
Celtic Christmas, A, 53, 473, 474
Cervantes, 440, 790, 832
Chamber Music, 597, 599
Chapman, George, 479
Chatterji, Mohini J., 57, 377
Chattopâdhyây, Sarojini, 293
Chaucer, 451, 454, 456, 457
Chesterton, G. K., 383, 858
Chicago Citizen, The, 221
Childermass, The, 745, 762
Childers, Erskine, 690, 727
Civil List Pension, 542, 544, 550
Clan na Gael, The, 131, 432, 568
Clarke, Austin, 795, 801
Claudel, Paul, 626
Coburn, Alvin Langdon, 503n, 504, 611
Cockerell, Sir Sydney, 376, 381n
Coffey, George, 63n, 84, 115, 123, 124, 128, 145, 168, 200, 202, 203, 306, 315, 316, 365
Coffey, Mrs. George, 118, 123, 145, 203, 332, 365, 385
Cole, Ernest Albert, 595n
Collins, John Churton, 82
Collins, Mabel (Mrs. Keningale Cook), 123n, 125
Collins, Michael, 667n, 683, 685, 697, 881, 885
Colum, Padraic, 395, 410, 416, 417, 419, 420, 433, 434, 448, 452, 462, 464, 477, 674, 801, 803
Commonweal, The, 41, 42, 67, 73, 102, 106, 108
Conder, Charles, 508, 509
Congreve, William, 665
'Connell, Norreys'. *See* O'Riordan, Conal
Conrad, Joseph, 459, 549
Contemporary Review, The, 323
Corelli, Marie, 449
'Corvo, Baron,' 827
Cosgrave, William Thomas, 612, 694, 739, 813, 815, 885
Cosmopolis, 292
Courtney, W. L., 346, 382
Cousins, James H., 370n, 372, 379, 380, 390, 417
Craig, Edith, 379n, 380, 383, 385, 387, 388, 389, 394, 398, 415, 913
Craig, Edward Gordon, 366, 371, 375, 379, 380, 386, 393, 394, 398, 456, 531, 534, 545, 546, 554, 555, 560, 577, 578
Crandon, Mrs., 804, 807
Cremers, Alicia, 123, 125
Crespi, Angelo, 724
Criterion, The, 728, 766, 791, 792
Croce, Benedetto, 719, 782, 784
Croker, T. C., 45, 50, 75, 78, 79
Cromarty, Lady, 453, 456, 458
Cromer, Lord, 540
Crone, Dr. J. S., 33
Cronin, Dr., 131n
Crook, W. M., 94, 115

Crowe, Catherine, 79
Crowley, Aleister, 209, 340, 342, 343, 344, 346, 499, 590
Cuala, Press, The, 527, 550, 575, 583, 589, 601, 609, 624, 626, 633, 651, 653, 654, 670, 677, 678, 701, 702, 703, 704, 707, 708, 720, 728, 746, 748, 777, 792, 804, 805, 807, 814, 820, 824, 827, 833, 841, 843, 867, 870, 872, 879, 886, 893, 897, 903, 910, 911, 916, 919, 920
Cunard, Lady, 604, 607, 610
Cunninghame Graham, Mrs., 64
Curtin, Jeremiah, 249
Curzon, Lord, 617

Daily Chronicle, The, 308, 311, 335
Daily Express, The (Dublin), 94, 102, 211, 217, 251, 252, 254, 258, 304, 312, 314, 315, 318, 329, 337, 338, 665
Daily Express, The (London), 820
Daily News, The, 399, 401
Dante, 83, 128, 235, 377, 730, 731, 790, 800, 807, 849, 882
Darragh, Miss, 457n, 479, 481, 482
Davidson, John, 173, 181
Davies, W. H., 859
Davis, Thomas, 74n, 201, 204, 206, 213, 250, 351, 774
Davitt, Michael, 83
Davray, Henry D., 265n, 314
Day Lewis, C., 860
de Crémonte, Conte, 282
Deirdre (by AE), 365, 367, 368, 369, 370, 435
Dekker, Thomas, 478
De Valera, Eamonn, 679, 680, 683, 685, 805, 806, 809, 811, 877, 880, 884, 885
de Valois, Ninette, 760, 830
de Vere, Aubrey, 33, 49, 72, 97, 106, 232n, 250, 253, 257
de Walden, Lord Howard, 509, 577
Dial, The, 633, 668, 670, 701
Dickens, Charles, 143, 543, 825
Digges, Dudley, 378
Dillon, John B., 35, 83, 180, 300, 303, 337
Dobson, Austin, 549, 564, 749
Dolmetsch, Arnold, 354, 359, 362, 373, 375, 392, 404, 526
Dome, The, 313, 328n, 329, 334, 337, 341
Donne, John, 570, 571, 710, 902
Douglas, Lord Alfred, 376, 764, 765
Dowden, Edward, 78, 103, 105, 106, 107, 108, 180, 245, 246, 251, 252, 267, 281, 289, 349, 350, 352, 550, 555, 557, 589, 590, 602, 603, 606
Downey, Edmund, 34
Dowson, Ernest, 181, 232, 335, 548, 592, 836
Dublin Evening Mail, The, 802
Dublin Figaro, The, 253, 339
Dublin Magazine, The, 306, 326, 784
Dublin University Review, The, 32, 48, 53, 54, 57, 112
Dubliners, 597, 599

Duffy, Sir Charles Gavan, 36, 62, 72, 74, 146, 147, 151n, 188, 200, 207, 208, 211, 212, 215, 216, 217, 222, 223, 224, 225, 226, 227, 233, 250, 586, 684
Dukes, Ashley, 835
Dulac, Edmund, 607, 609, 610, 611, 612, 629, 634, 643, 645, 661, 699, 769, 771, 864, 865, 888, 894, 895, 901, 920
Duncan, Mrs. Ellen, 622
Dun Emer Press, The, 387, 391, 402, 404, 416, 419, 431, 446, 473, 478
Dunne, J. W., 787, 788
Dunsany, Lord, 529, 530

East and West, 132, 136, 139, 140, 141, 146
Edgeworth, Maria, 143n, 247
Edwards, Osman, 293
'Eglinton, John'. *See* Magee, W. K.
Eliot, George, 31, 76, 241
Eliot, T. S., 748, 784, 792, 833, 840, 842, 846
Ellis, Edwin John, 59n, 60, 70, 71, 93, 106, 107, 128, 129, 136, 141, 145, 150, 154, 157, 159, 160, 161, 162, 163, 164, 167, 170, 173, 181, 182, 187, 202, 208, 209, 223, 265, 474, 475, 560
Ellis, W. Ashton, 71, 460
Elton, Oliver, 172n, 554, 555
Emerson, Ralph Waldo, 241
Emery, Mrs. Edward. *See* Florence Farr
Emmet, Robert, 428, 429, 432
English Illustrated Magazine, The, 69, 161
English Review, The, 556, 672
Ermitage, L', 265
Ervine, St. John, 605, 717, 801
Esther Waters, 547, 916
Evening Herald, The, 188
Evening Mail, The, 109, 114
Evening Standard, The, 880
Exiles, 600

Fahy, Francis A., 64n
Farquharson, Robert, 451, 454, 455, 459, 507
Farr, Florence (Mrs. Edward Emery), 121, 151, 170, 230, 234, 236, 237, 259, 262, 283, 292, 293, 312, 315, 318, 332, 340, 354, 359, 363, 372, 373, 374, 375, 384, 394, 395, 400, 404, 411, 412, 415, 426, 435, 442, 443, 451, 453, 459, 475, 491, 492, 494, 506, 526, 543, 574, 628, 892
Farrell, James A., 891, 895
Faust, 805
Fay, Frank, 355n, 380, 409, 427, 436, 444, 451
Fay, William G., 365, 367, 369, 370, 371, 379, 385, 388, 390, 400, 415, 419, 438, 447, 449, 463, 479, 480, 481, 482
Ferguson, Sir Samuel, 35, 58, 61, 69, 206, 213, 232, 245, 247, 248, 253
'Field, Michael,' 39, 40, 400, 407n
Fingal, Lady, 305, 306
Finlay, Father Peter, 212, 213, 316, 350, 430

927

Fitzmaurice, George, 495, 496
Flaubert, Gustave, 562
Forbes-Robertson, Johnston, 385, 500, 548
Fortnightly Review, The, 180, 237, 297, 304, 323, 346, 377, 390
Fragonard, 865
France, Anatole, 780
Freeman's Journal, The, 39, 88, 94, 98, 109, 111, 113, 149, 150, 168, 180, 251, 259, 496, 582, 694
French, Cyril, 347
Fry, Roger, 883, 887

Gael, The (Dublin), 33n, 34, 36, 37, 39, 41, 46, 47, 48, 49, 55, 56
Gael, The (New York), 328, 421
Gardner, F. L., 282n
Garnett, Edward, 155, 157n, 165, 167, 171, 181, 198, 199, 201, 214, 216, 217, 221, 241
Gautier, Théophile, 412, 749
Gentili, Giovanni, 779, 782
Gilchrist, Alexander, 112
Gill, T. P., 68, 115, 288, 291, 315, 316, 318, 329, 438, 547
Girl's Own Paper, The, 122
Gladstone, W. E., 78, 540
Gleeson, Evelyn, 431
Glenavy, Lord, 745
Goethe, 344, 810, 832, 892, 917
Gogarty, Oliver St. John, 461, 627, 634, 635, 643, 663, 664, 680, 729, 775, 801, 858, 865, 874, 883, 890, 891
Gogarty, Pat, 63n, 133, 134
Golden Dawn, The Order of the, 182n, 183, 259, 260, 261, 262, 264, 282, 283, 339n, 365, 499
Gonne, Iseult (afterwards Mrs. Francis Stuart), 628, 629, 630, 631, 632, 633, 634, 644, 655, 697, 705, 800
Gonne, Maud, 77, 106n, 108, 110, 116, 118, 139, 168, 181, 182, 183, 184, 185, 186, 200, 202, 203, 208, 209, 211, 213, 217, 220, 282, 287, 288, 289, 295, 296, 297, 298, 299, 300, 303, 304, 306, 311, 312, 313, 314, 317, 327, 329, 337, 338, 365, 367, 368, 369, 380, 395, 414, 415, 427, 445, 513, 530, 532, 613, 628, 629, 630, 631, 632, 633, 655, 697, 739, 769, 909
Gore, Miss, 239, 243
Gore-Booth, Eva, 239, 252, 256, 434
Gorky, Maxim, 389
Gosse, Edmund, 82, 296, 332, 459, 540, 542, 543, 544, 545, 549, 563, 567, 589, 598
Grace, Valentine, 291n, 306, 350
Graphic, The, 35, 41, 44, 63
Graves, A. P., 341
Graves, Robert, 844, 853
Green Sheaf, The, 388n
Greene, G. A., 181, 232n
Gregg, Frederick J., 31n, 42
Gregory, Lady, 38, 53, 267, 284, 287n,
289, 296, 302, 315, 316, 321, 323, 326, 328, 352, 353, 354, 377, 378, 387, 388, 389, 390, 399, 402, 407, 410, 417, 424, 430, 433, 436, 442, 444, 446, 448, 452, 458, 459, 461, 462, 463, 464, 466, 467, 470, 471, 473, 477, 478, 481, 482, 490, 493, 495, 501, 503, 510, 513, 524, 525, 526, 533, 535, 536, 537, 551, 555, 558, 559, 560, 568, 587, 588, 589, 591, 594, 595, 596, 599, 603, 607, 617, 618, 623, 624, 646, 648, 649, 669, 678, 680, 683, 684, 685, 686, 687, 692, 702, 706, 708, 713, 715, 718, 743, 769, 771, 772, 779, 783, 784, 785, 786, 787, 790, 793, 795, 796, 797, 803, 808, 811, 814, 819, 820, 822, 855, 877
Gregory, Robert, 287, 347, 365, 387, 432, 442, 445, 446, 493, 496, 502, 532, 546, 554, 578, 579, 582, 588, 596, 626, 631, 645, 646, 647, 648, 650, 901
Grierson, Sir Herbert, 687n
Griffin, Gerald, 136, 143n, 148, 188, 247
Griffin, Montague, 60, 105, 106, 107, 111, 120
Griffith, Arthur, 351, 352n, 355, 412, 416, 421, 448, 525, 680, 685
Guiney, Louise Imogen, 154n
Gwynn, Stephen, 370, 387, 390, 396, 399, 401, 410n, 473n, 801, 803
Gyles, Althea, 313n, 328, 330, 332, 347, 511

Hail and Farewell, 291, 304, 315, 547, 564
Hall, Mrs. S. C., 79
Hamilton, General Ian, 541, 588
Hamlet, 612, 741, 821, 828, 917
Hardy, Thomas, 235, 549, 556
Harris, Frank, 810
Harrison, Austin, 556
Harrison, Henry, 862, 863
Hauptmann, Gerhart, 758, 771
Hayes, Dr. R. J., 858
Healy, T. M., 35, 163, 180, 300
Heald, Edith Shackleton, 902, 910, 915, 921
Heard, Gerald, 770, 785
Heather Field, The, 210, 304, 308, 314, 316, 318, 407, 527
Hefernan, Liam, 96
Hegel, G. W. F., 725, 770, 781, 791, 813, 922
Heinemann, William, 165, 259, 458, 505
Henley, William Ernest, 83, 86, 89, 93, 96, 101, 112, 113, 115, 116, 126, 157, 159, 163, 167, 169, 170, 184, 185, 187, 665
Hewlett, Maurice, 383, 565
Hickey, Emily, 129n, 245
Higgins, F. R., 705, 801, 839, 841, 858, 859, 865, 867, 879, 888, 894, 895, 896, 902, 912, 919, 920, 921
Hillier, A. C., 181, 232n
Hinkson, Henry A., 33, 175n, 238
Hippolytus, The, 420, 435
Hitler, Adolf, 806, 812, 821
Hollyer, Frederick, 157, 239, 443

928

Homer, 347, 406, 415, 454, 854
Homestead, The, 290, 292, 390
Hone, J. M., 267, 449, 473, 474, 573, 605, 676, 779, 782, 801, 922
Hope, Anthony, 244
Hopkins, Gerard Manley, 281
Hopper, Nora (Mrs. W. H. Chesson), 244n, 247, 254, 483n, 592, 593
Horne, Herbert Percy, 65n, 67, 115, 181
Horniman, Annie E. F., 230, 262n, 282, 283, 371, 372, 380, 392, 425, 426, 427, 437, 442, 444, 447, 448, 460, 466, 479, 480, 486, 490, 493, 499, 500, 504, 527, 535, 542, 544
Horton, W. T., 260n, 325, 377
Hueffer, Ford Madox, 290
Hughes, John, 112, 524n
Hughes, Richard, 839
Hugo, Victor, 71, 93
Hulme, T. E., 810
Hunter, Dorothea, 264n, 293, 340
Hurlbert, William Henry, 84
Huxley, Aldous, 849, 852
Huysmans, Joris Karl, 440
Hyde, Douglas, 33, 38n, 39, 45, 46, 47, 56, 70, 73, 85, 88, 91, 94, 136, 138, 142, 164, 166, 167, 177, 186, 200, 201, 202, 204, 211, 212, 215, 217, 222, 223, 224, 225, 226, 227, 238, 239, 247, 248, 249, 250, 252, 302, 355, 364, 365, 370, 378, 410, 419, 430, 446, 503, 627, 672, 684, 717, 803

Ibsen, Henrik, 131, 162, 290, 291, 331, 370, 379, 386, 389, 398, 399, 438, 439, 441, 448, 453, 467, 834
Image, Selwyn, 65, 181, 244, 430
In the Shadow of the Glen, 410, 438, 461, 525
Innes, J. D., 646n
Irish Academy of Letters, The, 716, 732, 789, 794, 800, 801n, 802, 803n, 805, 806, 808, 829, 843, 865, 871, 885, 888, 890, 891, 892, 895, 897, 898
Irish Book Lover, The, 91
Irish Fireside, The, 32, 34, 39, 42, 44, 45, 50
Irish Literary Society (London), 188, 198, 199, 200n, 221, 222, 224, 225, 226, 227, 238, 245, 251, 252, 265, 300, 341, 370, 401, 411, 603, 732, 789
Irish Literary Theatre, The, 210, 288, 290, 291, 304, 313, 315, 318, 320, 321, 326, 327, 328, 333, 334, 342, 353, 355, 356, 364, 547
Irish Monthly, The, 31, 36, 39, 53, 55, 61, 71, 76, 83, 84, 88, 104, 108, 111, 114, 116, 126, 128, 129, 136, 142, 144, 153, 172, 173, 174, 182
Irish National Literary Society (Dublin), 207, 209, 212, 213, 215, 221, 223, 224, 225, 227, 233, 251, 316
Irish National Theatre Society, The, 237, 262, 370, 371, 381, 387, 397, 399, 409, 410, 416, 438
Irish Press, The, 790, 869, 882, 884

Irish Times, The, 94, 102, 109, 245, 408, 446, 501, 573, 759, 767, 858, 860, 869, 915
Irving, Henry, 107, 375, 379, 466
Irving, H. B., 383, 386, 389
Ito, Michio, 607, 652, 669

Jackson, Arthur, 552, 553, 554
James, Henry, 68, 400, 504, 549, 565
John, Augustus, 492, 493, 496, 502, 504, 506, 507, 511, 610, 627, 664, 775, 818, 849
John Bull's Other Island, 335, 387, 407, 442n
Johnson, Lionel, 65, 181, 200, 201, 228, 232, 235, 237, 244, 250, 256, 257, 296, 318, 446, 453, 454, 456, 477, 548, 586, 590, 592, 671, 672, 685, 765, 827, 866, 916
Johnston, Miss A. I., 76, 137, 151, 160, 183, 184
Johnston, Charles, 40n, 88, 90, 91, 159, 162, 168, 171, 175, 176, 177, 403, 591
Jonson, Ben, 450, 478, 479, 664, 671
Joubainville, D'Arbois, 247, 249
Joyce, James, 386, 388, 399, 461, 596, 597, 598, 599, 600, 601, 651, 679, 698, 723, 739, 764, 801, 807
Joyce, Patrick Weston, 96, 100, 102, 112, 247, 250, 426
Judge, William Q., 236n, 237, 345

Kalidasa, 109
Kavanagh, Rose, 36, 42n, 47, 80, 94, 95, 98, 165, 174
Keats, John, 334, 406, 502, 583, 608, 653, 738
Keegan, John, 146, 151, 152
Keeling, Elsa D'Esterre, 141n
Kennedy, Patrick, 75, 78, 81, 249
Kickham, Charles, 49, 127, 128, 130, 132, 143n, 146, 232
King Lear, 441, 741, 778
King, Richard Ashe, 45n, 89, 168, 182, 184, 185, 212, 223, 246, 732
Kingsford, Mrs. Anna, 97n
Kipling, Rudyard, 253, 413, 534, 710, 877
Klauder, Mary (Mrs. Jones), 857, 873

Lambert, Maurice, 803
Lane, Sir Hugh, 501n, 533, 559, 573, 574, 580, 591, 594, 595, 616, 617, 618, 619, 622, 623, 624, 690, 708, 713, 718, 822, 877, 878
Lane, John, 181, 382, 484
Lane-Poole, Ruth (formerly Ruth Pollexfen), 559, 604
Lang, Andrew, 120, 132, 237, 474, 549
Larminie, William, 211n, 249, 304
Laurie, T. Werner, 669, 670, 673, 674, 682, 694, 695, 700, 704
Lavery, Sir John, 704
Lawless, Hon. Emily, 238, 239, 247, 248, 254
Lawrence, D. H., 803, 807, 810

929

Leader, B. W., 309
Leamy, Edmund, 177n, 214, 238
Lecky, W. H., 318, 338
Lee, Sir Sidney, 449
Lefanu, J. Sheridan, 146
Le Gallienne, Gwen, 906
Le Gallienne, Richard, 138, 170, 181, 232, 455
Legge, James, 36, 39, 115
Leisure Hour, The, 39, 43, 45, 48, 70, 110, 113, 120, 122, 140
Lever, Charles, 247
Lewis, P. Wyndham, 608, 723, 724, 733, 734, 739, 745, 746, 763, 776
Linnels, The, 145, 153
Lippman, Friedrich, 118n, 149
Lister, Miss E. M., 484n, 493
Little, Grace, 129, 131, 157, 160
Little Review, The, 575, 624, 651, 652, 653
Logue, Cardinal, 319, 408
London Mercury, The, 669, 670, 671, 672, 685, 688, 690, 691, 701, 805, 824, 911
Louis Lambert, 805, 807, 808
Lovelace, The Earl of, 467, 468, 473
Lover, Samuel, 79, 136, 206, 247
Luby, T. C., 143
Lucifer, 71, 75, 76, 91, 113, 119, 160, 162
Ludwig, William (Ledwidge), 209n, 210
Lutyens, Sir Edwin, 501, 591
Lynch, Arthur, 172n, 181
Lytton, Hon. Neville, 376, 505

Macaulay, T. B., 534, 776
MacBride, Major John, 338, 414n, 612, 613
MacColl, D. S., 616, 617, 618, 619, 620, 622, 623
MacGregor. *See* Mathers, S. L.
MacKenna, Stephen, 328, 715, 717
'Macleod, Fiona,' 43, 266n, 267, 298, 301, 321, 358, 396, 461
MacManus, Captain Dermot, 813, 814, 815, 880, 881
Macmillan and Co., 342, 570, 612, 624, 644, 653, 685, 691, 704, 738, 766, 780, 792, 806, 811, 843, 857, 894, 895, 896, 899
Macmillan, Rt. Hon. Harold, 843, 844
Macnamara, Brinsley, 656n, 657, 713, 801
Macneice, Louis, 864
Maeterlinck, Maurice, 255, 375, 438, 453, 542
Magazine of Poetry, The, 33, 137, 140
Magee, W. K. ('John Eglinton'), 289, 304n, 510, 801
Mahaffy, Professor, 245, 353, 557
Maitland, Edward, 97
Mallarmé, Stephane, 230, 265, 671, 887
Maloney, Dr. William P., 867, 891
Manchester Chronicle, The, 105, 106
Manchester Courier, The, 121, 122
Manchester Guardian, The, 105, 106, 107, 108, 617
Manchester Repertory Theatre, The, 262, 490, 493, 500

Mancini, Antonio, 502, 504, 579
Mangan, James Clarence, 74, 96, 146, 147, 151, 152, 178, 206, 213, 250, 253, 447
Mannin, Ethel, 832, 851, 902, 914, 920
Marston, John, 478
Marston, Philip Bourke, 49
Martin, Sir Alec, 622
Martyn, Edward, 210, 287, 290n, 292, 300, 304, 308, 311, 312, 314, 315, 316, 317, 318, 327, 329, 330, 331, 332, 333, 334, 337, 357, 363, 364, 365, 370, 371, 407, 416, 438, 454, 464, 527, 532, 547, 686, 820
Marzials, F. T., 93
Masefield, John, 363, 365, 389, 442, 478, 563, 565, 773, 776, 777, 805, 837, 838
Mask, The, 393, 556, 557
Mason, Miss, 95
Mathers, S. L. (MacGregor), 208n, 209, 210, 230, 259, 282, 297, 298, 339, 340, 343, 344, 346, 665
Mathers, Mrs. S. L., 183n, 184, 262, 297, 590
Matheson, Hilda, 849n, 863, 884, 900, 906, 912, 920, 921, 922
Mathews, Elkin, 138n, 151, 181, 187, 235, 237, 238, 244, 335, 362, 376, 464, 465, 470, 483, 484, 498, 526, 536
McAnally, D. R., Jr., 78, 79, 101
McCall, P. J., 41, 238
McCartan, Dr. Patrick, 803, 873, 891, 892, 895, 897, 898
McCarthy, Justin, 62, 70, 545
McDonagh, Thomas, 612
McGrath, John, 238n, 264
McGreevy, Thomas, 729, 781
McNeill, Eoin, 803
Menken, Adah Isaacs, 825n
Merchant of Venice, The, 465, 466
Mercure de France, Le, 265, 314
Meredith, George, 86, 93, 443
Merrill, Stuart, 265n
Meyer, Kuno, 285, 392n
Meynell, Wilfrid and Alice, 126, 136, 166, 423
Miles, Alfred H., 174, 175, 176, 179
Mill, John Stuart, 650
Millay, Edna St. Vincent, 838
Milton, John, 235, 555, 853, 907
Mitchel, John, 39, 67, 93, 202, 336
Mitchell, Susan, 323, 434
Molière, 481, 513, 524, 612
Molloy, Dr., 315, 316, 408
Montaigne, 871
Monthly Review, The, 363, 369, 373, 382
Moore, George, 68, 264, 291, 301, 304, 308, 311, 312, 314, 315, 316, 317, 326, 327, 329, 330, 331, 332, 334, 335, 336, 337, 338, 339, 344, 345, 348, 350, 351, 353, 355, 356, 357, 359, 367, 368, 369, 371, 379, 380, 381, 382, 387, 407, 429, 430, 435, 440, 441, 443, 445, 446, 503, 506, 509, 510, 533, 547, 564, 571, 586,

669, 670, 679, 722, 733, 740, 820, 822, 916
Moore, T. Sturge, 366, 375, 383, 387, 388, 394, 395, 409, 472, 556, 585, 598, 599, 603, 604, 610, 708, 738, 764, 896, 900
Moore, Thomas, 48, 133, 206, 250, 447, 877
Moran, D. P., 350, 430n
More, Henry, 588
Moreau, Gustave, 865
Morning Post, The, 619, 767
Morrell, Lady Ottoline, 679, 725n, 764, 842, 887
Morris, Lewis, 220n
Morris, May, 41, 44, 77, 95, 101, 118
Morris, William, 41, 42, 44, 46, 48, 59, 67, 70, 77, 94, 95, 99, 101, 102, 103, 106, 108, 145, 149, 151, 170, 218, 219, 379, 381, 382, 387, 388, 397, 413, 418, 456, 665, 724, 758, 759, 776, 795, 816, 872, 908
Moulton, C. W., 101
Mulholland, Rosa, 121, 128, 142n, 143, 144, 166
Murray, T. C., 629n, 801

Nation, The (Dublin), 74, 89, 90, 99, 101, 113, 119, 147, 148, 151, 163
Nation, The (London), 527
National Observer, The, 100, 159, 162, 163, 164, 167, 169, 173, 179, 184, 187, 189, 206, 221
Nettleship, J. T., 59, 121, 129n, 130, 150, 154, 170, 571, 624, 653
New Ireland Review, The, 251
New Irish Library, The, 45, 198, 200n, 233, 247, 250
New Review, The, 290
New Statesman, The, 575, 593, 787, 831, 833, 846
Newton, Sir Isaac, 807
Nicoll, W. Robertson, 322n
Nietzsche, Friedrich, 379, 403, 773
Nineteenth Century, The, 289, 297
'98 Celebrations, 287, 293, 295, 296, 302, 303, 314
Nobel Prize, The, 544, 701, 703, 827, 851
North American Review, The, 237, 318, 323, 332, 415, 422
Noyes, Alfred, 882, 884
Nutt, David, 81, 83, 85, 132, 133, 134, 136, 285

O'Brien, R. Barry, 199n, 201, 209, 211, 217, 226, 251, 292, 410, 412
O'Brien, William, 83n, 96
Observer, The, 335, 501, 610, 616, 647, 740, 813
O'Casey, Sean, 711, 714, 717, 740, 743, 744, 831, 833, 840, 914
O'Connor, Frank, 799, 800, 801, 888, 897, 902
O'Donnell, Frank Hugh, 318
O'Donnell, Peadar, 801

O'Donoghue, D. J., 37, 47, 56, 73n, 107, 113, 134, 162, 237, 267
O'Duffy, General, 813, 814, 815, 881, 885
O'Faolain, Sean, 766, 801, 902
O'Flaherty, Liam, 722, 801, 809
O'Grady, Standish, 199, 200, 201, 217, 221, 238, 239, 246, 247, 249, 250, 254, 279, 292, 307, 321, 369, 430, 434, 672
O'Grady, Standish Hayes, 247
O'Hegarty, P. S., 64, 306
O'Higgins, Kevin, 726n, 809
Olcott, Colonel H. S., 56, 125n, 236
Oldham, C. H., 163, 181, 251
Oldmeadow, E. J., 328n, 350, 351
O'Leary, Ellen, 33, 34, 35, 36, 37n, 38, 39, 42, 44, 45, 48, 51, 53, 56, 71, 81, 89, 92, 95, 106, 108, 120, 126, 127, 128, 134, 138, 139, 140, 141, 162, 163, 165, 167, 169, 175, 176
O'Leary, John, 33, 36, 37n, 39, 42, 51, 55, 57, 61, 62, 65, 66, 76, 95, 100, 101, 102, 106, 109, 126, 133, 135, 137, 139, 143, 150, 151, 157, 158, 159, 166, 167, 172, 174, 212, 216, 218, 221, 222, 223, 224, 225, 267, 289, 336, 589, 606, 869, 872, 921
O'Neill, Eugene, 801
O'Neill, Maire (Molly Allgood), 526, 527n, 560, 654
O'Neill, Moira, 592, 593
O'Reilly, John Boyle, 38n, 47, 60, 141
O'Riordan, Conal ('Norreys Connell'), 527n, 528
Orpen, Sir William, 623, 627, 704
Osbourne, Walter, 307, 359
O'Sullivan, Seumas. *See* Starkey, Dr. J. S.
Outlook, The, 297, 298
Owen, Wilfred, 874, 875

Paget, Dorothy, 236, 318
Paget, H. M., 121, 151, 455
Paget, Walter, 121
Palace of Truth, The, 450
Pall Mall, Gazette, The, 75, 86, 102, 138, 153, 172, 174, 233, 543
Pall Mall Magazine, The, 380, 382
Palmer, Herbert E., 688
Palmer, Samuel, 646
Parnell, Charles Stewart, 83, 112, 113, 163, 177, 179, 185, 199, 333, 540, 555, 635, 862, 863, 867, 869, 880
Pascal, Blaise, 650
Pater, Walter, 68, 237
Patmore, Coventry, 526
Paul, Kegan, 61, 62, 63, 65, 66, 67, 68, 69, 73, 82, 85, 91, 92, 100, 102, 107, 108, 109, 111, 133, 157, 159, 198, 499
Pearse, Patrick, 612, 911
Phelps, William Lyon, 660n
Phillips, Stephen, 296
Piatt, John James, 54, 233
Pigott, Richard, 112, 113n, 115
Pirandello, Luigi, 773, 776, 793, 834

Plarr, Victor G., 181, 232n
Plato, 719, 724, 811
Playboy of the Western World, The, 459, 462, 495, 528, 537, 563, 702, 711
Plotinus, 715, 716, 717
Plough and the Stars, The, 711, 714, 914
Plunkett, Count, 79, 212, 215, 217, 222, 226, 227, 613, 880
Plunkett, Sir Horace, 289, 290, 291, 292, 316, 317, 437, 623
Poe, Edgar Allan, 325, 447, 543
Pollexfen, Alfred, 533
Pollexfen, George, 87, 236, 240, 245, 246, 252, 304, 305, 323, 326, 341, 351, 431, 533, 551, 552, 553, 554
Pound, Ezra, 543, 583, 584, 585, 589, 590, 593, 598, 606, 612, 624, 653, 661, 672, 687, 690, 698, 705, 723, 736, 737, 738, 739, 746, 748, 758, 759, 767, 772, 774, 775, 782, 807, 823, 827, 833
Pound, Mrs. Ezra, 589, 590, 672, 690, 698, 718, 736, 737, 742, 748, 760, 766, 771, 775, 823, 826, 827, 861
Pound, Omar, 729, 743, 748, 760, 766, 775, 813, 854, 860
Powell, Frederick York, 70n, 80, 85, 93, 120, 124, 126, 127, 130, 131, 132, 134, 155, 172, 200, 201, 230, 235, 244, 339, 571, 859, 862
Power, Albert, 627
Probyn, Miss, 72
Proust, Marcel, 736
Providence Sunday Journal, The, 38, 63, 73, 78, 85, 92, 101, 113, 140, 141, 169, 170, 178, 184
Punch, 335, 829
Purser, Sarah, 77n, 80, 131, 299, 307, 444, 532
'Pyne, Evelyn' (Miss Noble), 71, 72, 75, 76

Quaritch, Bernard, 145, 156, 157, 167
Quinn, John, 210, 359, 378, 382, 386n, 399, 412, 413, 415, 416, 420, 421, 426, 428, 429, 431, 432, 442, 443, 513, 533, 590, 622, 664
Quinn, Dr. J. P., 210n, 214, 220

Rabelais, 807
Racine, 440, 441, 528
Radcliffe, Bessie, 643, 644
Radford, Dollie, 171
Radford, Ernest, 171, 181
Raftery (Builder), 628, 630, 634, 643, 647, 651
Raleigh, Professor Walter, 549, 644
Ranking, Montgomery, 35n, 40, 41, 42, 44, 49, 63, 72, 73 85, 90, 94
Rann, 648
Ransome, Arthur, 765n
Redmond, John, 289, 300, 303, 333, 336, 416
Reid, Forrest, 717, 801
Renan, Ernest, 85

Review of Poetry, The, 101
Reynolds, Horace, 38
Rhymers' Club, The, 35, 65, 167, 170, 172, 181n, 185, 187, 188, 203, 204, 206, 232, 474, 548, 574, 592
Rhys, Ernest, 36, 39, 40, 41, 44, 50, 57, 58, 61, 92, 93, 102, 103, 114, 118, 136, 146, 157, 160, 166, 178, 181, 184, 188, 382, 383, 821
Rhys, John, 92n
Richard II, 899
Ricketts, Charles, 389, 394, 420, 430, 442, 468, 507, 510, 525, 545, 554, 574, 587, 594, 595, 609, 610, 612, 685, 691, 698, 763, 764, 901
Riding, Laura, 852, 857
Rilke, Rainer Maria, 913, 916, 917
Roberts, George, 434, 451, 473, 474
Robinson, Frances Mabel, 68n
Robinson, Lennox, 527, 568, 581, 583, 635, 643, 657, 673, 692, 707, 714, 717, 729, 745, 747, 770, 780, 790, 794, 800, 801
Rolleston, Thomas William, 33, 35n, 44, 45, 49, 57, 71, 73, 75, 102, 145, 149, 150, 168, 173, 181, 186, 188, 198, 199, 200, 201, 203, 212, 213, 215, 216, 217, 221, 222, 223, 224, 226, 227, 232, 246, 250, 306, 314, 326, 339, 343, 416, 483
Ronsard, Pierre de, 583
Rooney, William, 351n
Ross, Sir Denison, 644n
Ross, Robert, 480, 595, 765
Rossetti, Christina, 38, 67, 253, 596
Rossetti, Dante Gabriel, 42, 46, 145, 175, 266, 287, 691, 837
Rossetti, W. M., 241
Rossi, Mario M., 779, 782, 787, 791, 792, 796
Rothenstein, Will, 505, 560, 569, 598, 778, 848, 862, 883
Rousseau, J. J., 182
Ruddock, Margot (Margot Collis), 830, 854, 856N, 890, 891, 893
Rummel, Walter, 629, 645, 785
Runciman, J. F., 348, 365
Ruskin, John, 241, 900n
Russell, A. G. B., 347n
Russell, Bertrand, 714
Russell, Sir Charles, 113, 340
Russell, George W. (AE), 40n, 53, 76, 80, 91, 118, 175, 179, 231, 250, 254, 287, 289, 290, 291, 292, 296, 298, 299, 300, 302, 303, 304, 306, 307, 312, 317, 318, 324, 329, 344, 350, 364, 365, 367, 368, 370, 372, 375, 376, 380, 390, 402, 409, 410, 413, 416, 417, 430, 434, 436, 446, 451, 461, 477, 510, 524, 536, 547, 592, 605, 623, 627, 655, 666, 672, 684, 693, 705, 712, 717, 739, 774, 790, 801, 802, 803, 838, 889
Russell, Father Matthew, 36, 38, 39, 49, 60, 61n, 76, 103, 104, 105, 106, 111, 116, 120, 144, 147

Russell, Theodore, 86n, 90
Ryan, Fred, 380, 381n, 399
Ryan, Margaret, 144
Ryan, W. P., 200

Sackville, Lady Margaret, 456, 458
Sackville-West, V., 837, 849, 852
St. James Budget, The, 112
St. Martin, Tristram, 206, 207
St. Theresa, 790
Salome, 451, 468, 475, 562, 827
Sand, George, 687, 688
Sargent, John Singer, 507, 508, 509, 513, 610, 659
Sassoon, Siegfried, 773, 885
Saturday Review, The, 67, 87, 89, 116, 119, 120, 174, 245, 348, 365, 459
Savage Messiah, 782, 783
Savoy, The, 233, 260, 264, 265, 266, 280, 389, 672
Scots Observer, The, 113, 115, 116, 119, 120, 121, 122, 126, 129, 148, 150, 153, 155, 158, 161, 164
Scott, Sir Walter, 246, 543, 776
Scott, Professor William A., 627, 628n, 630, 634, 647, 651, 687
Senate, The Irish, 693, 694, 695, 696, 697, 703, 704, 709, 718, 737, 745, 746
Seraphita, 762, 805
Shakespear, Olivia, 233, 244, 372, 455, 589, 603, 604, 632, 698, 785, 789, 820, 854, 916
Shakespeare, 349, 352, 366, 441, 449, 456, 457, 465, 479, 548, 549, 555, 579, 659, 741, 759, 784, 791, 821, 828, 832, 853, 872, 899
Shanachie, The, 387, 472, 473n
Shannon, Charles Hazelwood, 389, 436, 496, 502, 504, 505, 506, 507, 509, 513, 595, 659, 692, 704, 865
Sharp, William, 43n, 49, 151, 266, 280, 396, 461
Shaw, George Bernard, 59, 67, 231, 233, 335, 383, 385, 387, 392, 395, 407, 420, 442, 453, 473, 474, 490, 500, 507, 513, 535, 541, 543, 549, 564, 565, 566, 623, 671, 717, 724, 767, 771, 794, 800, 801, 802, 803, 876, 884
Shaw, T. E. (T. E. Lawrence), 801
Shelley, P. B., 211, 266, 323, 361, 377, 608, 653, 667, 691, 697, 781, 853
Shine, Mrs. Ruth, 619, 621
Shorter, Clement K., 42, 320n, 322, 348, 382, 652
Showing-Up of Blanco Posnet, The, 535n, 537, 541
Shri Purohit Swami, 794, 795, 804, 806, 807, 813, 814, 815, 817, 818, 819, 820, 823, 829, 839, 844, 845, 846, 847, 848, 852, 853, 854, 856, 857, 861, 872, 882, 898
Sickert, Walter, 509, 510, 544
Sidgwick, Frank, 470, 493, 497
Sigerson Dora (afterwards Mrs. C. K. Shorter), 42, 82, 83, 233, 320, 321, 348, 648, 649
Sigerson, Mrs. Hester, 42, 43, 82
Sigerson, Dr. George, 42n, 71, 74, 77, 82, 102, 178, 186, 201, 204, 212, 213, 226, 263, 284, 320
Silent Woman, The, 450
Silver Tassie, The, 740, 743, 839, 840
Sinclair, Arthur, 525n
Sinnett, A. P., 260n, 261
Sitwell, Dr. Edith, 776, 837, 842, 884
Skeffington, Sheehy, 616
Sketch, The, 295, 320, 474
Sladen, Douglas, 89
Smith, Pamela Colman, 383n, 385, 386, 388, 389, 444
Smithers, Leonard, 237, 264n, 268, 325, 330, 332
Somerville, E. OE., 801, 803
Sparling, Herbert Halliday, 41n, 44, 52, 56, 58, 64, 66, 70, 73, 74, 92, 118
Speaker, The, 172, 199, 209, 228, 230, 233, 285, 346, 350, 362, 377, 386, 388, 401, 432
Spectator, The, 163, 314, 326, 531, 548, 565, 809
Spender, Stephen, 837
Spengler, 716
Spenser, Edmund, 219, 365, 380, 384, 386, 387, 390, 391, 396, 479, 480, 488, 506, 561, 646, 648
Spinoza, 650
Stage Society, The, 375, 379, 382, 383, 385, 387, 388, 394, 435, 445, 467, 490, 541, 625, 654
Star, The, 172, 174, 372, 388
Starkey, Dr. J. S. (Seumas O'Sullivan), 183, 434, 792, 801
Starkie, Walter, 766, 801, 858, 890, 906
Stephens, James, 563, 600, 627, 717, 780
Stephenson, 879, 892
Stevenson, Robert Louis, 96, 169, 244, 246, 503
Street, G. S., 866n
Strong, L. A. G., 787, 801, 877
Stuart, Francis, 705, 799, 801
Sturm, Dr. F. P., 712n, 781, 900
Sudermann, Hermann, 380, 407, 441
Sullivan, Mrs. Alexander, 131
Sullivan, T. D., 60, 163n
Sunday Times, The, 723, 786, 787, 813, 826
Sutherland, Duchess of, 427, 453
Swaffer, Hannen, 802
Swami, The. *See* Shri Purohit Swami
Swedenborg, 592, 805, 807
Swift, Jonathan, 664, 741, 773, 776, 777, 779, 784, 787, 790, 791, 792, 796, 818, 819, 876, 892
Swinburne, Algernon Charles, 46, 71, 112, 218, 219, 220, 474, 475, 546, 608, 648, 813, 825
Symons, Arthur, 167, 170, 181, 230, 260, 266, 267, 293, 296, 298, 304, 314, 328, 329, 330, 332, 337, 339, 345, 348, 372,

933

373, 374, 377, 383, 386, 388, 435, 442, 458, 459, 471, 513, 523, 529n, 530, 592, 847
Synge, John Millington, 314, 341, 386, 388, 410, 436, 441, 442, 444, 446, 447, 448, 452, 453, 459, 461, 462, 463, 466, 468, 480, 495, 496, 510, 511, 523, 526, 527, 528, 529, 534, 538, 548, 553, 571, 587, 618, 671, 838, 860

Tadema, Laurence Alma, 293
Tagore, Rabindranath, 569, 570, 572, 573, 580, 598, 599, 612, 834
Tale of a Town, The, 327n, 329, 331, 332, 357
Tarr, 762
Taylor, John F., 76n, 77, 176, 185, 186, 251, 589
Tealing, Macarthy, 282
Tennyson, Alfred Lord, 46, 105, 109, 218, 219, 221, 705
Terry, Ellen, 106, 379, 383, 394, 398, 399, 913
Thompson, Francis, 181
Thoor Ballylee, 615, 624, 625, 628, 634, 643, 647, 649, 650, 651, 652, 658, 659, 660, 667, 675, 678, 679, 680, 682, 683, 686, 687, 688, 689, 692, 703, 714, 716, 728, 730, 737, 738, 739, 908
Time and Western Man, 723, 733, 734, 739
Times, The, 112, 279, 335, 388, 398, 408, 500, 557, 616, 623, 649, 666, 786, 787, 883
Times Literary Supplement, The, 388, 401, 405, 723, 786, 787
Tinker's Wedding, The, 538
Tobin, Agnes, 458n, 459, 480, 508, 523, 530, 541, 542, 544, 910
Todhunter, John, 33n, 36, 38, 41, 42, 43, 44, 45, 48, 49, 59, 61, 62, 63, 64, 65, 66, 67, 69, 70, 71, 74, 75, 78, 85, 88, 90, 92, 94, 95, 101, 102, 105, 106, 109, 112, 113, 119, 120, 126, 138, 151, 153, 154, 162, 163, 168, 169, 170, 173, 181, 188, 200, 202, 230, 231, 232, 250
Todhunter, Mrs. John, 68, 123
Toller, Ernst, 833, 834, 851, 920
Tolstoi, Leo, 93, 807
To-morrow, 707, 709
Tone, Wolfe, 199, 212, 295
Travelling Man, The, 390
Tree, H. Beerbohm, 309, 443, 539
Trollope, Anthony, 670, 682
Tucker, Mrs. H. T., 632n, 633, 667, 718, 719, 730, 736, 767, 815
Turgenev, Ivan, 93
Turner, W. J., 841, 842, 846, 849, 855, 859, 862, 874, 890, 912, 921
Twenty Years a-Growing, 809, 811, 885
Tynan, Katharine, afterwards Hinkson, 33n, 35, 37, 38, 45, 48, 56, 74, 91, 103, 108, 109, 112, 128, 129, 136, 138, 141, 142, 151, 176, 180, 244, 245, 248, 250, 585, 597

Tyrrell, R. Yelverton, 321, 547, 555

Ulysses, 651, 679, 682, 698, 705, 724
United Ireland, 39, 60, 63, 65, 66, 76, 83, 111, 152, 155, 177, 178, 179, 181, 182, 185, 186, 188, 198, 207, 211, 221, 257, 258
United Irishman, The, 304, 341, 351, 352, 355, 370, 371, 376, 379, 380, 412, 416, 417
Unwin, T. Fisher, 156, 157, 158, 165, 167, 168, 173, 177, 179, 184, 185, 186, 198, 199, 200, 201, 202, 203, 207, 211, 215, 216, 217, 220, 222, 223, 224, 225, 226, 228, 231, 237, 239, 243, 252, 258, 313, 320, 351, 382, 449, 470, 484, 498, 561, 576, 604, 685, 732, 786

Van Krop, Hildo, 765, 768
Varian, Ralph, 42, 232
Vegetarian, The, 67, 68, 75, 99
Verlaine, Paul, 230, 240, 255, 475
Vers et Prose, 265
Villon, François, 583
Volpone, 612, 664, 665

Wachtmeister, Countess, 59
Waddell, Helen, 801
Wade, Allan, 550, 607
Wagner, Richard, 371, 458, 459, 460
Walker, Sir Emery, 381, 397, 398, 404
Walkley, A. B., 388n, 401, 405
Walsh, Edward, 47, 204, 206, 250, 378
Ward, Mrs. Humphry, 557
'Warlock, Peter,' 847
Watkins, Vernon, 907
Watson, William, 40, 181
Watt, A. P., 351, 352, 359, 361, 362, 364, 378, 382, 383, 384, 385, 394, 470, 483, 484, 486, 488, 491, 494, 497, 498, 499, 577, 609, 610, 659, 660, 674, 685, 696, 709
Webster, Ben, 330, 331
Weekly Register, The, 43, 158
Weekly Review, The, 159n, 160
Welch, James, 383
Well of the Saints, The, 441, 446, 447, 448, 463, 510
Wellesley, Dorothy, 836, 842, 843, 856, 874, 893, 898, 906, 907, 910, 911, 912, 913, 920, 921, 922
Westminster Gazette, The, 228, 233, 236, 543
White, Elizabeth, 103n, 105, 107
White, H. O., 103
Whitehead, Alfred North, 712, 713
Whitman, Walt, 32, 40, 58, 61, 238, 241
Wilde, Lady, 75, 79, 80, 97, 123, 140, 150, 188, 212, 249
Wilde, Oscar, 102, 114, 146, 151, 170, 347, 451, 468, 480, 524, 562, 571, 672, 764, 765, 798, 827
Wilde, Sir William, 80
Williams, Charles, 901

Wilson, George, 59, 571, 589, 606, 624
Witt, Robert C., 619, 620, 622
Wollman, Maurice, 840
Woman's World, The, 102, 103, 107
Woolf, Virginia, 799, 853
Wordsworth, William, 219, 502, 590, 603, 710, 850
Wylie, Elinor, 836, 837, 839
Wynne, Frances, 120, 162, 171, 174, 176

Yeats, Anne Butler, 659, 664, 667, 668, 672, 673, 674, 684, 689, 696, 712, 734, 739, 743, 747, 760, 775, 780, 816, 821, 828, 829, 831, 838, 839, 852, 858, 868, 887, 911, 913, 914
Yeats, Elizabeth Corbet (Lolly), 55, 57, 58, 60, 86, 99, 106, 115, 118, 120, 121, 123, 126, 134, 140, 145, 146, 150, 154, 156, 165, 243, 306, 312, 387, 391, 397, 416, 417, 419, 430, 431, 487, 497, 551, 568, 577, 589, 591, 602, 604, 605, 606, 607, 676, 684, 759, 807, 911, 920
Yeats, Jack B., 34, 51, 55, 58, 60, 67, 68, 75, 80, 99, 124, 126, 134, 138, 140, 146, 154, 156, 173, 178, 180, 199, 243, 252, 292, 302, 312, 361, 364, 383, 413, 434, 442, 444, 525, 545, 552, 554, 567, 568, 589, 624, 702, 764, 880, 901, 907
Yeats, John Butler, 34, 39, 48, 55, 57, 58, 59, 60, 70, 71, 72, 73, 76, 85, 93, 94, 98, 106, 115, 121, 124, 126, 130, 134, 138, 150, 159, 163, 166, 172, 173, 177, 252, 267, 302, 312, 329, 339, 352, 359, 364, 383, 386, 413, 419, 431, 502, 504, 505, 511, 545, 555, 559, 578, 583, 649, 659, 674, 676, 677, 684, 703, 704, 705, 901
Yeats, Rev. John, 104, 124
Yeats, Susan (Mrs. John B. Yeats), 52, 55, 58, 64, 67, 107, 115, 154, 187, 676
Yeats, Susan Mary (Lily), 52, 54, 58, 64, 67, 68, 77, 86, 95, 99, 101, 115, 118, 130, 134, 137, 145, 146, 149, 151, 154, 156, 177, 178, 260, 430, 431, 524, 552, 553, 568, 591, 603, 655, 677, 701, 797, 798, 858, 894, 903, 915

Yeats, W. B. Books by:
Alphabet, An (Per Amica Silentia Lunae), 624, 627
Autobiographies, 76, 589
Bounty of Sweden, The, 701, 703, 827
Cat and the Moon and certain Poems, The, 633, 707
Celtic Twilight, The, 164, 173, 214, 229, 230, 265, 266, 286, 324, 361, 362, 363, 364, 365, 377, 487, 494
Collected Edition: Shakespeare Head Press, 1908, 377, 449, 464, 484, 485, 486, 487, 488, 489, 491, 492, 494, 496, 497, 498, 502, 503, 504, 505, 506, 507, 509, 511, 523, 524, 575, 578, 659
Collected Plays, The, 393
Collected Poems, The, 53, 732, 816, 818, 828
Countess Kathleen and Various Legends and Lyrics, The, 100, 148, 158, 173,

Yeats, W. B. Books by (*cont.*):
185, 186, 188, 189, 199, 203, 205, 208, 213, 220, 242, 253, 255, 278
Cutting of an Agate, The, 478, 561, 586
Death of Synge, The, 527, 553
Discoveries, 478, 487, 488, 497, 533, 561
Dramatis Personae, 315, 527, 553, 701, 721, 820, 833, 857
Early Poems and Stories, 40, 707
Eight Poems, 609, 610
Essays, 704
Essays 1931 to 1936, 805, 836, 863
Estrangement, 718
Four Years, 665, 675
Ideas of Good and Evil, 170, 267, 281, 337, 350, 363, 369, 376, 382, 391, 397, 398, 402, 403, 411, 413, 415, 468, 494, 498
In the Seven Woods, 387, 391, 395, 397, 411, 416, 465, 487
Irish Adventurers, 154, 155, 156, 158, 171, 173, 214, 221, 223, 227
John Sherman and Dhoya, 55, 167, 168, 169, 170, 173, 174, 179, 180, 181, 182, 184, 185, 186, 491
Last Poems, 896, 909, 911, 912, 915, 921
Later Poems, 691
Letters to the New Island, 38, 85, 96, 121
Michael Robartes and the Dancer, 651
Modern Poetry, 866, 887
Mosada, 32, 63, 88, 101, 362
New Poems, 867, 870, 872, 886, 897, 904
Nine Poems, 320, 652
October Blast, 728
On the Boiler, 664, 900, 901, 902, 903, 904, 910, 912, 914, 915, 921
Packet for Ezra Pound, A, 739, 746, 748, 759, 767, 768
Per Amica Silentia Lunae, 624, 658
Plays and Controversies, 704
Plays for an Irish Theatre, 390, 391, 395, 411, 562
Plays in Prose and Verse, 393, 691
Poems, 1895, 50, 59, 205, 237, 243, 253, 254, 255, 258, 260, 279, 732, 786
Poems, 1899 and later editions, 205, 313, 320, 498
Poems, 1899-1905, 237, 449, 460, 469, 478, 480, 491
Poems: Second Series, 464, 504, 562
Poems Written in Discouragement, 1912-1913, 617
Responsibilities, 393, 573, 574
Reveries over Childhood and Youth, 364, 589, 591, 594, 598, 599, 602, 605, 606, 610, 625
Secret Rose, The, 260, 266, 268, 280, 282, 284, 285, 286, 313, 350, 361, 364, 487, 488, 503
Selected Poems, 766, 772
Seven Poems and a Fragment, 668
Speckled Bird, The, 267n, 278, 280, 301, 342, 345
Speech and Two Poems, A, 897, 898, 899
Stories of Michael Robartes, 768

Yeats, W. B. Books by (*cont.*):
Synge and the Ireland of his Time, J. M., 534, 561
Tower, The, 633, 668, 719, 720, 722, 723, 724, 728, 738, 740, 742, 814
Trembling of the Veil, The, 365, 669, 670, 671, 672, 673, 674, 682, 685, 690, 693, 694, 700, 708
Two Plays for Dancers, 653
Under the Moon, 243n
Vision, A, 644, 690, 694, 695, 699, 703, 704, 709, 711, 712, 713, 715, 730, 732, 739, 742, 744, 745, 746, 748, 764, 768, 780, 781, 785, 788, 812, 813, 818, 819, 824, 825, 833, 835, 859, 863, 864, 866, 868, 886, 888, 898, 899, 901, 905, 916
Wanderings of Oisin and other poems, The, 32, 50, 53, 57, 62, 84, 87, 99, 102, 111, 112, 113, 118, 119, 138, 158, 174, 198, 202, 204, 253, 362
Wheels and Butterflies, 758, 765, 779, 780
Wild Swans at Coole, The, 575, 600, 624, 644, 648, 652, 653, 658
Wind Among the Reeds, The, 313, 353, 378, 464, 465, 470, 485, 489
Winding Stair, The, 725, 726, 729, 760, 772, 789, 814
Words for Music Perhaps, 758, 759, 760, 769, 785, 804, 814

Yeats, W. B. Books and periodicals edited by and books containing contributions from:
Beltaine, 318, 333n, 334, 350, 351, 352, 377
Blake, The Works of William, 59, 133, 136, 138, 145, 149, 153, 155, 156, 157, 159, 161, 162, 163, 164, 165, 166, 167, 168, 169, 170, 171, 173, 181, 182, 183, 184, 185, 186, 188, 198, 199, 202, 204, 211, 223, 227, 228, 265, 474
Book of Images, A, 260, 377
Book of Irish Verse, A, 173, 232, 244, 250, 251, 252, 253, 254, 774, 877
Broadsides, 702, 841, 846, 862, 864, 869, 880, 884, 886, 888, 893, 894, 899, 912
Certain Noble Plays of Japan, 612
Coinage of Saorstát Éireann, 746, 749
Deirdre of the Sorrows, 510, 527, 528, 529, 838
Early Memories, by J. B. Yeats, 124, 571, 653, 678, 684
Fairy and Folk Tales of the Irish Peasantry, 78, 80, 85, 88, 90, 91, 92, 93, 94, 102, 103, 114, 119, 130, 174, 182, 247, 346
Holy Mountain, The, 813n, 815, 819, 823, 829, 896
Ideals in Ireland, 430
Indian Monk, An, 794, 797, 823, 829, 896
Irish Fairy Tales, 173, 176, 177, 189, 199
Irish Minstrelsy, 41, 52, 56, 58
Letters of J. B. Yeats, 124
Literary Ideals in Ireland, 211, 304
Oxford Book of Modern Verse, The, 70,

Yeats, W. B. Books edited by (*cont.*):
407, 712, 833, 835, 843, 845, 866, 867, 868, 874, 880, 885, 886
Patanjali, Aphorisms of, 852, 854, 898
Poems and Ballads of Young Ireland, 31, 37n, 41, 42, 47, 61, 70, 73, 76, 87, 115, 118, 119, 120, 137, 139, 142, 153, 204
Representative Irish Tales, 63, 127, 132, 136, 142, 143, 146, 149, 150, 151, 152, 154, 156, 160, 165, 166, 167, 168, 170, 174
Samhain, 326, 333, 364, 388, 409, 410, 457, 491, 497, 505, 506, 507, 578, 910
Selections from the Poems of Dorothy Wellesley, 843, 859
Stories from Carleton, 124, 128, 130, 136, 144, 147, 174
Treasury of Irish Poetry, A, 244, 313
Upanishads, The, 839, 844, 845, 846, 847, 848, 849, 852, 853, 854, 856, 861, 863, 864, 865, 866, 868, 882, 887
Visions and Beliefs in the West of Ireland, 305, 558, 568, 595, 608

Yeats, W. B. Essays by:
'Academic Class and the Agrarian Revolution, The,' 315
'Acting at St. Teresa's Hall, The,' 371
'America and the Arts,' 458
'At Stratford-on-Avon,' 349, 350, 352
'Celtic Movement in Literature, The,' 292, 296
'De-Anglicising of Ireland, The,' 221
'Happiest of the Poets, The,' 377, 382, 397
'Hopes and Fears for Irish Literature,' 221
'Irish Dramatic Movement, The,' 507
'Irish Rakes and Duellists,' 155
'Irish Witch Doctors,' 346
'Literary Movement in Ireland, The,' 318
'Magic,' 363
'Music and Poetry,' 893
'Noble and Ignoble Loyalties,' 341
'Plain Man's *Oedipus*,' 537n
'Popular Ballad Poetry of Ireland,' 48
'Prisoners of the Gods, The,' 289
'Queen and the Fool, The,' 324
Return of Ulysses, The, 281, 294
'Speaking to the Psaltery,' 369, 373
'Symbolic Artist and the Coming of Symbolic Art, A,' 313
'Symbolism of Poetry, The,' 337, 339
'Tribes of Danu, The,' 290
'Way of Wisdom, The,' 377n

Yeats, W. B. Plays by:
At the Hawk's Well, 607n, 610, 611, 612, 626, 645, 651, 652, 661, 760, 892
Calvary, 729
Cathleen ni Houlihan (also *Kathleen ni Hoolihan*), 351, 365, 367, 368, 369, 370, 375, 377, 381, 390, 391, 392, 393, 395, 396, 399, 400, 403, 404, 410,

Yeats, W. B. Plays by (*cont.*):
415, 441, 448, 482, 488, 491, 492, 506, 527, 543, 578, 767
Countess Kathleen, The (also *Cathleen*), 108, 114, 117, 119, 122, 125, 126, 129, 132, 135, 165, 173, 178, 179, 180, 181, 184, 204, 210, 211, 237, 243, 245, 252, 257, 291, 306, 308, 315, 316, 318, 319, 346, 347, 350, 356, 394, 488, 489, 494, 567, 578, 581, 674, 732
Death of Cuchulain, The (1939), 921, 922
Deirdre, 450, 451, 475, 476, 479, 480, 481, 482, 487, 488, 491, 492, 494, 511, 512, 513, 532, 543, 576, 674, 861
Diarmuid and Grania, 326n, 327, 347, 355, 356, 359, 368, 443
Dreaming of the Bones, The, 626, 627, 629, 631, 653, 785, 788
Fighting the Waves, 758, 760, 765, 767
Full Moon in March, A, 824, 826, 830, 843, 844
Golden Helmet, The, 505, 506, 525, 530, 545, 546
Green Helmet, The (formerly *The Golden Helmet*), 505, 525, 530, 545, 546, 561, 596, 674
Herne's Egg, The, 843, 845, 854, 868, 871, 894, 904
Hour-Glass, The, 375, 378, 387, 388, 389, 391, 392, 393, 395, 397, 399, 409, 411, 420, 449, 451, 488, 492, 506, 543, 555, 567, 576
King Oedipus. See *Oedipus the King*
King of the Great Clock Tower, The, 817, 819, 824, 826, 830, 845
King's Threshold, The, 59, 409, 410, 411, 415, 422, 425, 426, 448, 449, 451, 453, 460, 488, 492, 494, 543, 545, 587, 647
Land of Heart's Desire, The, 229, 231, 236, 237, 253, 280, 320, 352, 355, 403, 434, 488, 492, 545, 567, 674, 675, 908
Oedipus at Colonus, 537, 720, 721, 722, 724, 728, 729, 760, 792
Oedipus the King (also *King Oedipus*), 537n, 538, 546, 710, 714, 720, 721, 722, 728, 729, 744, 760, 768
On Baile's Strand, 353, 363, 364, 365, 369, 391, 393, 396, 411, 424, 425, 426, 429, 430, 444, 447, 448, 451, 460, 465, 469, 472, 489, 490, 492, 494, 554, 594, 595, 643, 644, 647, 674, 721, 760, 913, 914
Only Jealousy of Emer, The, 612, 644, 645, 760, 761
Player Queen, The, 511, 512, 513, 525, 526, 528, 532, 533, 535, 568, 588, 612, 614, 625, 626, 654, 658, 693, 835, 843
Pot of Broth, The, 377, 378, 389, 392, 399, 400, 403, 404, 410, 488, 492
Purgatory, 907, 910, 911, 913, 914, 915, 919
Resurrection, The, 780, 826

Yeats, W. B. Plays by (*cont.*):
Shadowy Waters, The, 236, 237n, 245, 268, 279, 280, 320, 322, 323, 324, 327, 331, 332, 337, 342, 350, 425, 445, 449, 451, 453, 454, 455, 458, 459, 460, 462, 463, 465, 468, 471, 488, 490, 491, 506, 561, 562
Unicorn from the Stars, The, 484, 492, 497, 503, 662
Where there is Nothing, 379n, 382, 385, 388, 389, 390, 392, 394, 398, 399, 402, 403, 405, 415, 421, 423, 426, 435, 438, 445, 484, 488, 492, 503
Words upon the Window Pane, The, 777, 778, 779, 784, 891

Yeats, W. B. Poems by:
'A double moon or more ago,' 117n
'A flower has blossomed, the world heart core,' 30
'Adam's Curse,' 382
'After Long Silence,' 772, 815, 816
'All Souls' Night,' 260
'Among School Children,' 719
'Baile and Aillinn,' 353
'Ballad of Father Gilligan, The,' 206
'Ballad of Moll Magee, The,' 93
'Ballad of the Old Foxhunter, The,' 140, 141
'Blessed, The,' 281
'Chambermaid's First Song, The,' 869
'Chambermaid's Second Song, The,' 870
'Colonel Martin,' 896
'Conjunctions,' 828
'Coole Park, 1929,' 769, 805
'Countess Cathleen in Paradise, The,' 731
'Cradle Song, A,' 148, 155
'Crazy Jane and Jack the Journeyman,' 785
'Cuchulain Comforted,' 921, 922
'Curse of Cromwell, The,' 886, 890, 891, 895, 897
'Dawn Song, A,' 32
'Death of Cuchullin, The,' (1892), 207
'Death of the Hare, The,' 840
'Dedication,' 897
'Down by the Salley Gardens,' 86, 841
'Easter 1916,' 320, 414, 613
'Epitaph, An,' 189
'Fairy Doctor, The,' 50
'Fairy Song, A,' 204
'Fergus and the Druid,' 278
'Four Ages of Man, The,' 826
'Grey Rock, The,' 574, 584
'He and She,' 828
'Hollow Wood, The,' 489
'How Ferencz Renyi Kept Silence,' 66
'In Church,' 122
'In the Firelight,' 110
'Indian Song, An,' 53
'Island of Statues, The,' 87, 88, 102, 106, 112, 116, 118
'John Kinsella's Lament for Mrs. Mary Moore,' 912

937

Yeats, W. B. Poems by (*cont.*):
'Kanva on God,' 116
'King Goll,' 42, 44, 45, 48, 49, 70, 116, 705
'Lake Isle of Innisfree, The,' 100, 159, 257, 353, 561, 692, 788
'Lament of the Old Pensioner, The,' 158
'Lapis Lazuli,' 859
'Leda,' 709
'Legend, A,' 99
'Love Song, from the Gaelic,' 47n
'Lover's Song, The,' 867
'Lug na Gall,' 42, 45
'Lullaby,' 760, 815
'Man who dreamed of Fairy Land, A,' 167, 245
'Man Young and Old, A,' 716, 720, 722, 723
'Meditation of the Old Fisherman, The,' 53, 116
'Meditations in Time of Civil War,' 688, 690
'Municipal Gallery Re-Visited, The,' 897, 898, 899
'Nineteen Hundred and Nineteen,' 668
'Nineteenth Century and After, The,' 759
'Old Memory,' 427
'Old Men admiring themselves in the Water, The,' 382
'Old Song Resung, An,' 204
'On Mr. Nettleship's Picture at the Royal Hibernian Academy,' 32
'On those who Disliked the Playboy,' 525
'Owen Ahern and his Dancers,' 633
'Phantom Ship, The,' 63, 85
'Politics,' 909
'Priest of Coloony, The' ('Father John O'Hart'), 41, 58, 65
'Reason for Keeping Silent, A,' 599
'Ribh at the Tomb of Baile and Aillinn,' 824
'Ribh Denounces Patrick,' 824
'Rosa Mundi,' 189
'Rose in my Heart, The,' 221
'Sad Shepherd, The,' 265
'Second Coming, The,' 851
'Seeker, The,' 66, 88
'She who dwelt among the Sycamores,' 53, 110, 390
'Song of the last Arcadian,' 116
'Sorrow of Love, The,' 353
'Spur, The,' 872
'Statues, The,' 911
'Stolen Child, The,' 53, 63, 84
'Summer Evening, A,' 122
'Supernatural Songs,' 824, 826, 828
'Those Images,' 896
'Thoughts upon the Present State of the World,' 668
'Three Bushes, The,' 890, 891, 892

Yeats, W. B. Poems by (*cont.*):
'Three Hermits, The,' 577
'Three Things,' 815
'Time and the Witch Vivien,' 88, 103, 118, 120
'To an Isle in the Water,' 86, 204
'To a Wealthy Man . . .,' 573
'To be Carved on a Stone at Ballylee,' 651
'To the Rose upon the Rood of Time,' 261
'Two Songs of a Fool,' 653
'Two Trees, The,' 256, 257
'Under Ben Bulben,' 915
'Vacillation,' 789
'Wanderings of Oisin, The' (also Usheen), 41, 51, 52, 54, 55, 58, 59, 60, 69, 82, 85, 87, 88, 101, 102, 103, 105, 106, 108, 111, 116, 120, 132, 243, 244, 252, 257, 786, 798
'When you are Old,' 205
'When you are Sad,' 205
'Wild Old Wicked Man, The,' 887
'Woman Young and Old, A,' 725, 726, 729

Yeats, W. B. Stories by:
'Adoration of the Magi, The,' 280
'Crucifixion of the Outcast, The,' 285
'Devil's Book, The,' 221
'Dhoya,' 55, 56, 169, 184, 185, 187, 488
'John Sherman,' 66, 72, 92, 94, 95, 157, 165, 187, 188, 346, 488
'Michael Clancy, the Great Dhoul and Death,' 307
'Rosa Alchemica,' 264, 265, 266
'Stories of Red Hanrahan,' 361, 419, 421, 485, 486, 487, 488, 494, 738
'Tables of the Law, The,' 280, 502

Yeats, Mrs. W. B., 259, 283, 315, 316, 317, 347, 537, 590, 632, 633, 634, 635, 643, 648, 649, 651, 652, 653, 658, 661, 662, 663, 667, 668, 672, 673, 675, 677, 678, 680, 681, 682, 683, 684, 685, 687, 688, 689, 694, 695, 696, 698, 705, 707, 708, 709, 716, 718, 719, 725, 727, 729, 730, 732, 733, 734, 735, 736, 737, 738, 739, 742, 744, 745, 746, 747, 748, 759, 760, 761, 762, 765, 766, 767, 768, 770, 772, 775, 776, 777, 778, 780, 781, 787, 788, 794, 798, 799, 804, 809, 814, 815, 816, 819, 820, 821, 822, 823, 828, 829, 830, 831, 832, 836, 838, 839, 842, 843, 844, 847, 852, 856, 857, 859, 861, 862, 865, 873, 877, 880, 893, 900, 901, 902, 905, 911, 920

Yeats, William Michael, 673, 684, 688, 689, 734, 736, 738, 739, 743, 744, 760, 764, 766, 775, 780, 809, 816, 821, 828, 829, 838, 839, 902, 919, 922

Yellow Book, The, 281, 389

Zola, Emile, 440